Holinshed's Chronicles of England, Scotland, and Ireland ..

Raphael Holinshed, William Harrison, Richard Stanyhurst, John Hooker, Francis Thynne, Abraham Fleming, John Stow, Henry Ellis

HOLINSHED'S

CHRONICLES

OF

ENGLAND, SCOTLAND,

AND

IRELAND.

IN SIX VOLUMES.

VOL VI.

IRELAND

LONDON

PRINTED FOR J. JOHNSON, F C. AND J RIVINGTON; T PAYNE, WILKIE AND ROBINSON, LONGMAN, HURST, REES, AND ORME; CADELL AND DAVIES, AND J. MAWMAN

1808

Printed by T. DAVISON,
Whitefriars.

[*Original Title.*]

THE

SECOND VOLUME OF

CHRONICLES:

CONTEINING THE

DESCRIPTION, CONQUEST, INHABITATION, AND TROBLESOME ESTATE OF

IRELAND;

FIRST COLLECTED BY

RAPHAELL HOLINSHED,

AND NOW NEWLIE RECOGNISED, AUGMENTED, AND CONTINUED FROM THE DEATH OF KING HENRIE THE EIGHT VNTILL THIS PRESENT TIME OF SIR IOHN PEROT KNIGHT, LORD DEPUTIE AS APPEARETH BY THE SUPPLIE BEGINNING IN PAG 109, &c

BY IOHN HOOKER ALIAS VOWELL GENT.

WHEREVNTO IS ANNEXED

THE DESCRIPTION AND HISTORIE OF SCOTLAND,

FIRST PUBLISHED BY THE SAID R H AND NOW NEWLIE REUISED, INLARGED, AND CONTINUED TO THIS PRESENT YEARE, AS APPEARETH IN PAG 405 &c

By F. T

WITH TWO TABLES SERUING BOTH COUNTRIES ADDED IN THE END OF THIS VOLUME

HISTORIÆ PLACEANT NOSTRATES AC PEREGRINÆ

1586.

TO THE

RIGHT HONORABLE

Sir HENRIE SIDNEIE Knight,

LORD DEPUTIE GENERALL OF IRELAND, LORD PRESIDENT OF WALES, KNIGHT OF THE MOST NOBLE ORDER OF THE GARTER, AND ONE OF HIR MAIESTIES PRIUIE COUNCELL WITHIN HIR REALME OF ENGLAND

TAKING in hand (right honorable) to gather the particular histories of diuerse countries and nations, to ioine with a cosmographie, which one Reginald Wolfe late printer to the queenes maiestie meant to publish in our English toong: when I came to consider of the histories of Ireland, I found my self so vnprouided of helps, to set downe anie particular discourse therof, that I was in despaire to enterprise to write anie thing at all concerning that realme, otherwise than incidentlie as fell to purpose to touch the same in the historie of England. At length yet as maister Wolfes vse was, to impart to me all such helps as he might at anie hand procure for my furtherance, in the collections of the other histories, wherewith I speciallie dealt, his hap was to light also vpon a copie of two bookes of the Irish histories, compiled by one Edmund Campion, fellow sometime of S. Iohn Baptists college in Oxford, verie well penned certeinlie, but so breefe, as it were to be wished, that occasion had serued him to haue vsed more leasure, and thereby to haue deliuered to vs a larger discourse of the same histories: for as he himselfe confesseth, he had not past ten weekes space to gather his matter: a verie short time doubtlesse for such a peece of worke. But how breefe so euer I found him, at the persuasion of maister Wolfe, vpon the hauing of that copie, I resolued to make shift to frame a speciall historie of Ireland, in like maner as I had doone of other regions, following Campions order, and setting downe his owne words, except in places where I had matter to inlarge that (out of other authors) which he had written in breefe. And this I haue thought good to signifie, the rather for that I esteeme it good dealing in no wise to defraud him of his due deserued praise

But now after I had continued the historie, and inlarged it out of Giraldus Cambrensis, Flatsburie, Henrie of Marleburgh, and other, till the yeare 1509, in which that famous prince Henrie the eight began his reigne, some of those that were to bestow the charges of the impression, procured a learned gentleman maister Richard Stanihurst, to continue it from thense forward as he saw occasion, being furnished with matter to inlarge the worke, whereof for those latter times I found my selfe vtterlie void, more than that which Campion had deliuered. What I haue doone heerein, your honors discretion shall easilie conceiue. For the imperfection sith it is the first that hath beene set foorth in print, I craue most humble pardon of your good lordship, beseeching you rather to respect my good will than the perfectnesse of the worke, which (the wants considered) for the orderlie furnishing thereof, is not to be looked for in the skilfull, much lesse in me the meanest of all, and least able to performe it. Hauing presented the right honourable the earle of Leicester with the historie of Scotland, to whom (as I haue heard) Campion made dedication of his booke, I could not remember me to whome I might more conuenientlie offer this my trauell in this historie of Ireland, than to your lordship, being hir maiesties lieutenant in that realme. And therefore in most humble wise I exhibit the booke to your honour, beseeching the same to beare with my bold attempt therein, and to receiue it in good part from him that wished to haue more amplie satisfied your good lordships expectation, if abilitie might haue answered good will. Thus I beseech the Lord to guide your heart in his holie waies, & to furnish you with politike prudence and skilfull knowledge to gouerne in your estate and office, so as your doings may redound to his glorie, the suertie of hir maiesties dominion there, your owne aduancement in honour, and consequentlie to the sure support and peaceable quietnesse of the true and loiall subiects of that realme.

Your honours most humble to command,

Raphael Holinshed.

THE

CONTENTS OF THE CHAPTERS

FOLLOWING IN

THE DESCRIPTION OF IRELAND.

1 *The names of Ireland, with the compasse of the same, also what shires or counties it conteineth, the diuision or partition of the land, and of the language of the people.* Chap 1

2 *Of the nature of the soile and other incidents* Chap 2.

3 *The names of the cities, boroughs, and hauen towns in Ireland* Chap 3

4 *Of the strange and woonderfull places in Ireland.* Chap 4

5 *Of the lords spirituall of Ireland, their names and dignities* Chap. 5.

6 *The lords temporall, as well English as Irish, which inhabit the countrie of Ireland.* Chap. 6.

7 *The names or surnames of the learned men and authors of Ireland, and what bookes they wrote.* Chap 7.

8 *The disposition and maners of the meere Irish, commonlie called the wild Irish.* Chap. 8

THE AUTHORS

OUT OF WHOM THIS

HISTORIE OF IRELAND

HATH BEENE GATHERED.

Giraldus Cambrensis.
Flatsburie.
Henricus Marleburgensis.
Saxo Grammaticus.
Albertus Crantz.
Rogerus Houeden.
Guilielm. Paruus Nouoburgensis.
Polychronicon, siue Ranulfus Higeden.
Iohannes Bale.
Edmund Campion.
Records and rolles diuers.

TO THE

RIGHT HONORABLE

Sir HENRIE SIDNEIE Knight,

LORD DEPUTIE GENERALL OF IRELAND, LORD PRESIDENT OF WALES, KNIGHT OF THE MOST NOBLE ORDER OF THE GARTER, AND ONE OF HIR MAIESTIES PRIUIE COUNCELL WITHIN HIR REALME OF ENGLAND

MY verie good Lord, there haue beene diuerse of late, that with no small toile, and great commendation, haue throughlie imploied themselues, in culling and packing togither the scrapings and fragments of the historie of Ireland. Among which crue, my fast friend, and inward companion, maister Edmund Campion did so learnedlie bequite himselfe, in the penning of certeine breefe notes, concerning that countrie, as certes it was greatlie to be lamented, that either his theame had not beene shorter, or else his leasure had not beene longer. For if Alexander were so rauisht with Homer his historie, that notwithstanding Thersites were a crabbed and a rugged dwarfe, being in outward feature so deformed, and in inward conditions so crooked, as he seemed to stand to no better steed, than to lead apes in hell: yet the valiant capteine, weighing how liuelie the golden poet hath set forth the ouglie dandeprat in his colours, did sooner wish to be Homer his Thersites, than to be the Alexander of that doltish rithmour, which vndertooke with his woodden verses to blase his famous and martiall exploits: how much more ought Ireland (being in sundrie ages seized of diuerse good and couragious Alexanders) sore to long and thirst after so rare a clarke, as maister Campion, who was so vpright in conscience, so deepe in iudgement, so ripe in eloquence, as the countrie might haue beene well assured to haue had their historie trulie reported, pithilie handled, and brauelie polished.

Howbeit,

Howbeit, although the glose of his fine abbridgement, being matcht with other mens dooings, bare a surpassing kind of excellencie: yet it was so hudled vp in hast, as in respect of a Campion his absolute perfection, it seemed rather to be a woorke roughlie hewed, than smoothlie planed. Vpon which ground the gentleman being willing that his so tender a suckling, hauing as yet but greene bones, should haue beene swadled and rockt in a cradle till in tract of time the ioints thereof were knit, and growen stronger: yet notwithstanding he was so crost in the nicke of this determination, that his historie in mitching wise wandred through sundrie hands, and being therewithall in certeine places somewhat tickle toonged (for maister Campion did leaue it to speake) and in other places ouer spare, it twitled more tales out of schoole, and drowned weightier matters in silence, than the author (vpon better view and longer search) would haue permitted. Thus much being by the sager sort pondered, and the perfection of the historie earnestlie desired: I, as one of the most that could doo least, was fullie resolued to enrich maister Campion his chronicle, with further additions. But weighing on the other side, that my course packthred could not haue beene sutablie knit with his fine silke, and what a disgrace it were, bunglerlie to botch vp a rich garment, by clouting it with patches of sundrie colours, I was forthwith reclamed from my former resolution, reckoning it for better, that my pen should walke in such wise in that craggie and balkish waie, as the truth of the matter being forprised, I would neither openlie borrow, nor priuilie imbezell ought to anie great purpose from his historie. But as I was hammering that worke by stealths on the anuill, I was giuen to vnderstand by some of mine acquaintance, that others had brought our raw historie to that ripenesse, as my paine therein would seeme but needlesse. Whervpon being willing to be eased of the burden, and loath also in lurching wise to forstall anie man his trauell, I was contented to leaue them thumping in the forge, and quietlie to repaire to mine vsuall and pristinat studies, taking it not to stand with good maners, like a flittering flie to fall in an other man his dish. Howbeit the little paine I tooke therein was not so secretlie mewed within my closet, but it slipt out at one chinke or other, and romed so farre abroad, as it was whispered in their eares, who before were in the historie busied. The gentlemen conceiuing a greater opinion of me, than I was well able to vphold, dealt verie effectuallie with me, that as well at their instance, as for the affection I bare my natiue countrie, I would put mine helping hand to the

building

building and perfecting of so commendable a worke. Hauing breathed for a few daies on this motion, albeit I knew that my worke was plumed with downe, and at that time was not sufficientlie feathered to flie, yet I was by them weied not to beare my selfe coy, by giuing my entier friends in so reasonable a request a squeemish repulse. Wherefore, my singular good lord, here is laid downe to your lordship his view a briefe discourse, with a ragged historie of a ragged wealepublike. Yet as naked as at the first blush it seemeth, if it shall stand with your honor his pleasure (whom I take to be an expert lapidarie) at vacant houres to insearch it, you shall find therein stones of such estimation, as are worth to be coucht in rich and pretious collars. And in especiall your lordship, aboue all others, in that you haue the charge of that countrie, maie here be schooled, by a right line to leuell your gouernement. For in perusing this historie, you shall find vice punished, vertue rewarded, rebellion suppressed, loialtie exalted, haughtinesse disliked, courtesie beloued, briberie detested, iustice imbraced, polling officers to their perpetuall shame reprooued, and vpright gouernours to their eternall fame extolled. And trulie to my thinking, such magistrats as meane to haue a vigilant eie to their charge, can not bestow their time better, than when they sequester themselues from the affaires of the wealepublike, to recreat and quicken their spirits by reading the chronicles that decipher the gouernement of a wealepublike. For as it is no small commendation for one to beare the doings of manie, so it breedeth great admiration, generallie to haue all those qualities in one man harboured, for which particularlie diuerse are eternised. And who so will be addicted to the reading of histories, shall readilie find diuerse euents worthie to be remembred, and sundrie sound examples dailie to be followed. Vpon which ground the learned haue, not without cause, adiudged an historie to be the marrow of reason, the creame of experience, the sap of wisdome, the pith of iudgement, the librarie of knowledge, the kernell of policie, the vnfoldresse of treacherie, the kalendar of time, the lanterne of truth, the life of memorie, the doctresse of behauiour, the register of antiquitie, the trumpet of chiualrie. And that our Irish historie being diligentlie heeded, yeeldeth all these commodities, I trust the indifferent reader, vpon the vntwining thereof, will not denie. But if anie man his stomach shall be found so tenderlie minced, or so deintilie spiced, as that he maie not, forsooth, digest the grosse draffe of so base a countrie, I doubt not, but your lordship, who is thoroughlie acquainted with the

woorthinesse

woorthinesse of the Iland, will be soone persuaded to leaue such quaint and licorous repastours, to feed on their costlie and delicate woodcocks, & willinglie to accept the louing present of your heartie welwiller. The gift is small, the giuer his good will is great, I stand in good hope, that the greatnesse of the one will counterpoise the smalnesse of the other. Where-fore that I maie the sooner vnbroid the pelfish trash that is wrapt within this treatise, I shall craue your lordship to lend me either your eares in hearing, or your eies in reading the tenor of the discourse following.

RICHARD STANIHURST.

A TREATISE

CONTEINING

A PLAINE AND PERFECT

DESCRIPTION OF IRELAND,

With an Introduction to the better Vnderstanding of the Histories apperteining to that Iland.

COMPILED BY RICHARD STANIHURST.

THE NAMES OF IRELAND, WITH THE COMPASSE OF THE SAME, ALSO WHAT SHIRES OR COUNTIES IT CONTEINETH, THE DIUISION OR PARTITION OF THE LAND, AND OF THE LANGUAGE OF THE PEOPLE

CHAPTER I

THE more part aswel of Cosmographers, as Chronographers, do with one accorde affirme, that the nation of Ireland (the vttermost westerne Ile known) is halfe as big as Britannia. Which I take to be true, if the word Britannia so farre displaie the signification, that it comprise England, Wales, and Scotland. To which opinion Giraldus Cambrensis leaneth, saieng, that Britannia conteineth in length eight hundred miles, and two hundred in breadth. Ireland he taketh to be in length from the mounteins called Torrach (the author of Polychronicon termeth them Brendane his hilles) to saint Columbe his Iland eight daies iourneie, rating of long Irish miles fortie miles to the daie: and in breadth from Dublin to saint Patrike his hilles and the sea of Connaght foure daies iorneie, according to the former rate. So as by Cambrensis his surueie, who was a curious insearcher therof, Ireland is thrée hundred & twentie miles long of Irish miles, and one hundred and three score miles broad. And accounting thrée hundred and twentie Irish miles to amount to foure hundred English miles, which may well be reckoned according to their iudgements that haue trauelled in the Irish territories, Ireland will be found halfe as big as Britannia: which Girald Cambrensis auoucheth, saieng, that Ireland is as big as Wales and Scotland. Ireland hath on the east, England, within one daies sailing, on the southeast it hath France, Hispaine on the south, distant thrée daies sailing, on the west the maine ocean sea.

The length and breadth of Ireland. Girald. Cambrens. lib. 1. topog. dist. 1. lib. 2. Polych. lib. 1. cap. 32.

Touching the name Hibernia, historiographers are not yet agreed from whense it is deducted. Some write it Hibernia corruptlie, and suppose that the strangers finding it in an od end of the world, forstie and moistie, tooke it at the first for a verie cold countrie, and thereof named it Hibernia, as to saie, the Winter land. But this error being vpon short experience reformed, it could not be that the name should haue liued long, especiallie the first impositors suruiuing the triall, and able

The name Hibernia whense it proceedeth.

to alter the first nomination. Others bring a ghesse, that it should be named of Irlamale. But because I read nothing of them in anie probable historie, I purpose not to build vpon that coniecture.

Most credible it is holden, that the Hispaniards (the founders of the Irish) for deuotion towards Hispaine, called then Iberia of Iberus the sonne of Iuball, and the rather, for that themselues had dwelled beside the famous riuer Iberus, named the land Iberia (for so Leland and manie forren chroniclers write it) or Iberrnia, adding the letter (n) for difference sake. And from Ibernia procéedeth Iberland, or Iuerland, from Iuerland, by contraction Ireland: forsomuch as in corruption of common talke we find that (u) with his vocale is easilie lost and suppressed, so we saie ere for euer, nere for neuer, shoole for shouell, ore for ouer, ene for euen, dile for diuell. At the same time it was also named Scotia, in reuerence of Scotach the wife of Gathelus, ancient capteine of those Iberians that flitted from Hispaine into Ireland: & the said Scotach was old grandame to Hiberus and Hermon after the Scotish chronicles, who in anie wise will haue their countriemen deriued from the Irish, and not from the Britons. The name Scotia is of late yeares so vsuallie taken for that part of Britaine that compriseth Scotland, that diuerse ancient Irish authors are holden to be borne in Scotland, whereas in verie déed their natiue soile is Ireland. As the famous schooleman Iohannes Duns Scotus, otherwise named Doctor subtilis, for his subtill quiddities in scholasticall controuersies, was an Irish man borne, and yet is taken for a Scot.

Some hold opinion that he was borne in Thathmon, a market towne fiue miles distant from Weiseford. Others auouch, and that more trulie, that he was borne in Downe, an old ancient citie in the north of Ireland, and thereof they ghesse him to be named Dunensis, and by contraction Duns, which tearme is so triuiall and common in all schools, that whoso surpasseth others either in cauilling sophistrie, or subtill philosophie, is forthwith nickenamed a Duns. Wherefore as Scotland is named Scotia minor, so Ireland is tearmed Scotia maior, as the head from whense the name of Scotia minor tooke his ofspring. The Irish also were named of the foresaid Gathelus, or Gaudelus, Gaudeli. In their Irish rithmes, they tearme Ireland verie often Banno. I cannot diuine what reason should lead their makers therto, vnlesse it be the riuer in the countie of Weiseford, named the Banne, where the Britons vpon the conquest first arriued. The place otherwise is called Bagganbun, according to the old ancient rithme:

At the creeke of Bagganbun,
Ireland was lost and wun.

For the remembrance of which riuer so notoriouslie famosed, it carieth great likelihood, that the name should be to the whole realme generallie ascribed. Sundrie Latine authors write Ireland Inuerna, others Iuerna, diuerse Ierna. Claudius nameth it Iberia. The diuersitie of which names grew, for that in their time the true and certeine name was not knowne, so that they were contented to take it as they found it: which matter is handled by Hermolaus Barbarus.

Iuerna Ioan Camers in cap 35 Solini

Hermol Barb in 16 nino Plin castig

There are some of the ruder sort so quaint in seuering the name Irish and Ireland, as that they would be named Ireland men, but in no wise Irishmen. But certes, in my fantasie such curious distinctors may be verie aptlie resembled to the foolish butcher, that offred to haue sold his mutton for fiftéene grots, and yet would not take a crowne. Who so will grate vpon such nice diuersities, in respect that he is ashamed of his countrie, trulie (in mine opinion) his countrie maie be ashamed of him. Ireland is diuided into foure regions, Leinster, east: Connaght, west: Vlster, north: Mounster, south: and into a fift plot, defalked from euerie fourth part, and yet meating on each part, called thereof Media, Méeth, comprising as well east Meeth, as west Méeth. Leinster butteth vpon England, Vlster vpon the Scotish

1 Lagenia 2 Connacia 3 Hultenia 4 Monionia 5 Media V vs West 6 Eas Mee h

Margin notes: Scotia. Scotach. Gathelus. — Iohannes Duns Scotus borne in Ireland. — Why schoolemen are called Dunses. — Scotia maior. Scotia minor. — Gaudeli. — Banno. — The riuer Banne. — Bagganbun. — Inuerna. — Hermol. Barb. — The name Irish and Ireland curiouslie seuered. — 1 Lagenia 2 Connacia 3 Hultonia 4 Momonia 5 Media.

Scotish Islands: which face with Hebriades scattered betweene both the realms, wherin at this daie the Irish Scot, successor of the elder Scithian, Pict, or Redshanke dwelleth. Ech of these fiue, where they are tramable to ciuilitie, & answer the writs of the princes courts, be sundried into shires or counties in this manner. In Leinster lieth the counties of Dublin, Kildare, Weisford, or Guesford, Catherlach, Kilkennie, the counties of Leise & Ophalie, called the kings and quéenes counties: these two latelie so named by parlement, in the reignes of Philip and Marie hauing shire townes accordant, Philips towne, and Marie burgh. Connaght hath the countie Clare. Vlster the counties of Louth, Doune, Antrim, one moitie of the towne of Droghedagh (for the rest is in Méeth) and Carregfergus. In Mounster lie the counties of Waterford, Limerike, Corke, the countie palantine of Tipperarie, Kerie, & the crosse of Tipperarie. Mounster was of old time diuided into east Mounster, Ormond, west Mounster, Desmond, south Mounster, Toonmound. The occasion why Ireland was parted into these fiue principall regions grew of this. There arriued in Ireland fiue brethren, that were valiant & martiall gentlemen, to wit, Gandius, Genandius, Sagandus, otherwise named Gangandus, Rutheragus or Rutheranus, & Slanius. These fiue perceiuing that the countrie was not sufficientlie peopled, were agreed (as it were) to cast lots, and to share the whole realme betwéene themselues. The foure elder brethren seuering the countrie into foure parts, and being loth to vse their yoongest brother like an outcast or stepsonne, condescended that each of them foure should of their owne portion allot to Slanius a parting or parcell of their inheritance. Which being as heartilie receiued of Slanius, as it was bountifullie granted by them, he setled himselfe therein, and of that partition it tooke the appellation of Media, Méeth. The foure parts méet at a certeine stone at Méeth, néere the castell of Kilaire, as an indifferent meare to seuer the foure regions.

But although Slanius in the beginning had the least parcell, yet in short space he stood so well to his tacklings, and incroched so far vpon his neighbors, that he obteined the whole monarchie of Ireland. At which time he did not suppresse in obliuion his inheritance of Meeth, but did inlarge it, and decréed it should be a countrie appendant to the monarch his diet or table. And albeit the confines thereof were by Slanius stretched, yet it conteineth not so much land as anie of the other foure parts comprehendeth, but rather by indifferent surueie the halfe deale, whereof also it is not vnlikelie named Méeth. For whereas in the time of Slanius, each of the foure parts compriseth two and thirtie cantreds, Meeth conteineth but sixteene cantreds. A cantred is named so much land as conteineth an hundred towneships. This Slanius is intoomed at an hill in Méeth, which of him is named Slane. There hath béene in ancient time one Galfride Geneuile lord of the libertie of Meeth. This noble man became a frier preacher, and deceased in the yeare of our Lord 1314, the twentith of October, and was intoomed in the abbeie of the Black friers at Trim.

There is also another diuision of Ireland, into the English pale, and Irishrie. For when Ireland was subdued by the English, diuerse of the conquerors planted themselues néere to Dublin, and the confines thereto adioining, and so as it were inclosing and impaling themselues within certeine lists and territories, they feazed awaie the Irish: insomuch as that countrie became méere English, and thereof it was termed the English pale: which in ancient time stretched from Dundalke to Catherlagh or Kilkennie. But now what for the slacknesse of marchours, and incroching of the Irish enimie, the scope of the English pale is greatlie impaired, & is cramperned and coucht into an od corner of the countrie named Fingall, with a parcell of the king his land, Méeth, the counties of Kildare and Louth, which parts are applied chieflie with good husbandrie, and taken for the richest and

Hebriades.

The shires and counties of Ireland.

Of the fiue gentlemen brethren.

Meeth wherof it is named.

Meeth appointed for the king his table.

Cantred.

Slane.

Galfride Geneuile.

The English pale.

 ciuilest

Fingall excellent in husbandrie.

Collonnes of Fingall Clowne.

fruitfullest soiles in Ireland. But Fingall especiallie from time to time hath bin so addicted to all the points of husbandrie, as that they are nickenamed by their neighbours, for their continuall drudgerie, Collonnes, of the Latine word Coloni, wherevnto the clipt English word clowne seemeth to be answerable.

Fingall, why so named.

The word Fingall counteruaileth in English the race or sept of the English or estrangers, for that they were solie seized of that part of the Iland, gripping with their talants so firmelie that warme nest, that from the conquest to this daie the Irish enimie could neuer rouse them from thense. The inhabitants of the English pale haue béene in old time so much addicted to their ciuilitie, and so farre sequestered from barbarous sauagenesse, as their onelie mother toong was English. And trulie, so long as these impaled dwellers did sunder themselues as well in land as in language from the Irish, rudenesse was daie by daie in the countrie supplanted, ciuilitie ingraffed, good lawes established, loialtie obserued, rebellion suppressed, and in fine the coine of a yoong England was like to shoot in Ireland. But when their posteritie became not altogither so warie in kéeping, as their ancestors were valiant in conquering, the Irish language was frée denizized in the English pale: this canker tooke such déepe root, as the bodie that before was whole and sound, was by little and little festered, and in manner wholie putrified. And not onlie this parcell of Ireland grew to that ciuilitie, but also Vlster and the greater part of Mounster, as by the sequele of the Irish historie shall plainlie appéere. But of all other places, Weisford with the territorie baied and perclosed within the riuer called the Pill, was so quite estranged from Irishrie, as if a trauellor of the Irish, (which was rare in those daies) had pitcht his foot within the Pill and spoken Irish, the Weisfordians would command him foorthwith to turne the other end of his toong and speake English, or els bring his trouchman with him. But in our daies they haue so acquainted themselues with the Irish, as they haue made a mingle mangle or gallimaufreie of both the languages, and haue in such medleie or checkerwise so crabbedlie iumbled them both togither, as commonlie the inhabitants of the meaner sort speake neither good English nor good Irish.

The ciuilitie of Ireland in ancient time.

Weisford wholie English. The Pill.

The saieng of a noble man touching the English of Weisford.

There was of late daies one of the péeres of England sent to Weisford as commissioner, to decide the controuersies of that countrie, and hearing in affable wise the rude complaints of the countrie clowns, he conceiued here & there some time a word, other whiles a sentence. The noble man being verie glad, that vpon his first comming to Ireland, he vnderstood so manie words, told one of his familiar friends, that he stood in verie great hope to become shortlie a well spoken man in the Irish, supposing that the blunt people had pratled Irish, all the while they iangled English. Howbeit to this daie, the dregs of the old ancient Chaucer English are kept as well there as in Fingall, as they terme a spider, an attercop, a wisp, a wad, a lumpe of bread, a pocket, or a pucket, a sillibucke, a copprous, a faggot, a blease, or a blaze, for the short burning of it (as I iudge) a physician, a leach, a gap, a shard, a base court or quadrangle, a bawen or rather (as I doo suppose) a barton, the houshold or folks, meanie, sharpe, kéene, estrange, vncouth, easie, éeth or éete, a dunghill, a mizen. As for the word bater, that in English purporteth a lane, bearing to an high waie, I take it for a méere Irish word that crept vnwares into the English, through the dailie intercourse of the English and Irish inhabitants. And whereas commonlie in all countries the women speake most neatlie and pertlie, which Tullie in his third booke *De oratore*, speaking in the person of Crassus séemed to haue obserued: yet notwithstanding in Ireland it falleth out contrarie. For the women haue in their English toong an harsh & brode kind of pronuntiation, with vttering their words so péeuishlie and faintlie, as though they were halfe sicke, and readie to call for a posset. And most commonlie in words of two syllables they giue the last the accent: as they saie, markeat, baskeat, gossoupe, pussoat, Robart, Niclase,

Old English in Weisford and Fingall.

Bater.

The pronuntiation of the Irish women.

Niclase, &c: which doubtles dooth disbeautifie their English aboue measure. And if they could be weaned from that corrupt custome, there is none that could dislike of their English.

Here percase some snappish carper will take me at rebound, and snuffinglie snib me for debasing the Irish language: but trulie whosoeuer shall be found so ouerthwartlie bent, he takes the matter farre awrie. For as my skill is verie simple therein, so I would be loth to disueile my rashnes, in giuing light verdict in anie thing to me vnknowen: but onelie my short discourse tendeth to this drift, that it is not expedient that the Irish toong should be so vniuersallie gagled in the English pale: because that by proofe and experience we sée, that the pale was neuer in more florishing estate than when it was wholie English, and neuer in woorsse plight than since it hath infranchised the Irish. But some will saie, that I shew my selfe herein as friuolous as some loosing gamsters séeme superstitious, when they plaie themselues drie: they gogle with their eies hither and thither, and if they can prie out anie one that giueth them the gaze, they stand lumping and lowring, fretting and fuming, for that they imagine that all their euill lucke procéeded of him: and yet if the stander by depart, the looser may be found as drie shauen as he was before. And euen so it fareth with you, because you sée all things run to ruine in the English pale, by reason of great enormities in the countrie either openlie practised, or couertlie winked at, you glanse your eie on that which standeth next you, & by beating Jacke for Gill, you impute the fault to that which perhaps would little further the weale publike if it were exiled. Now trulie you shoot verie néere the marke. But if I may craue your patience till time you sée me shoot my bolt, I hope you will not denie, but that as néere the pricke as you are, and as verie an hagler as I am, yet the scantling shall be mine. First therefore take this with you, that a conquest draweth, or at the leastwise ought to draw to it thrée things, to wit, law, apparell, and language. For where the countrie is subdued, there the inhabitants ought to be ruled by the same law that the conqueror is gouerned, to weare the same fashion of attire wherewith the victor is vested, and speake the same language that the vanquisher parleth. And if anie of these thrée lacke, doubtlesse the conquest limpeth. Now whereas Ireland hath bin by lawfull conquest brought vnder the subiection of England, not onelie in king Henrie the second his reigne, but also as well before as after (as by the discourse of the Irish historie shall euidentlie be deciphered) and the conquest hath beene so absolute and perfect, that all Leinster, Meth, Vlster, the more part of Connagh and Mounster, all the cities and burroughs in Ireland haue beene wholie Englished, and with English conquerors inhabited, is it decent (thinke you) that their owne ancient natiue toong shall be shrowded in obliuion, and suffer the enimies language, as it were a tettar or ringwoorme, to harbor it selfe within the iawes of English conquerors? No trulie.

The superstition of gamsters.

A conquest implieth three things.

And now that I haue fallen vnawares into this discourse, it will not be farre amisse to stand somewhat roundlie vpon this point. It is knowen, and by the historie you may in part perceiue, how brauelie Vlster whilom florished. The English families were there implanted, the Irish either vtterlie expelled or wholie subdued, the laws dulie executed, the reuenue great, and onelie English spoken. But what brought it to this present ruine and decaie? I doubt not but you gesse before I tell you. They were inuironed and compassed with euill neighbours. Neighbourhood bred acquaintance, acquaintance wafted in the Irish toong, the Irish hooked with it attire, attire haled rudenesse, rudenesse ingendered ignorance, ignorance brought contempt of lawes, the contempt of lawes bred rebellion, rebellion raked thereto warres, and so consequentlie the vtter decaie and desolation of that worthie countrie. If these chinks, when first they began to chap, had beene

diligentlie

diligentlie by the dwellers stopped, his maiestie at this daie, to his great charges, should not haue béene occasioned to dam vp with manie thousand pounds, yea and with the worthie carcases of valiant souldiors, the gaps of that rebellious northerne countrie.

Now put the case that the Irish toong were as sacred as the Hebrue, as learned as the Gréeke, as fluent as the Latine, as amarous as the Italian, as courteous as the Spanish, as courtlike as the French, yet trulie (I know not which waie it falleth out) I sée not but it may be verie well spared in the English pale. And if reason will not lead you to thinke it, trulie experience must force you to grant it.

Cic. lib. 2 de orat.

In old time, when the Romans were first acquainted with the Greeke toong, as it is commonlie the nature of man to be delighted with newfangle wares: so he was accounted no gallant among the Romans, that could not prattle and chat Gréeke. Marcus Cicero father to Tullie, being at that time stept in yeares, perceiuing his countrimen to become changelings, in being bilwise and polmad, and to sucke with the Gréeke the conditions of the Grecians, as to be in words talkatiue, in behauiour light, in conditions quaint, in manners hautie, in promises vnstedfast, in oths rash, in bargains wauering (which were reckoned for Gréekish properties in those daies) the old gentleman not so much respecting the neatnesse of the language, as the naughtie fruit it brought with it, said, that his countrimen the Romans resembled the bondslaues of Siria, for the more perfect they were in the Greeke, the worse they were in their manners and life. If this gentleman had béene now liuing, and had séene what alteration hath happened in Ireland, through the intercourse of languages, he would (I dare saie) breake patience, and would demand whie the English pale is more giuen to learne the Irish, than the Irishman is willing to learne English: we must imbrace their language, and they detest ours. One demanded merilie whie Oneile that last was would not frame himselfe to speake English? What (quoth the other) in a rage, thinkest thou that it standeth with Oneile his honor to writh his mouth in clattering English? and yet forsooth we must gag our iawes in gibbrishing Irish? But I dwell too long in so apparent a matter. As all the cities & towns in Ireland, with Fingall, the king his land, Meth, the countie of Kildare, Louth, Weisford, speake to this daie English (whereby the simplicitie of some is to be derided, that iudge the inhabitants of the English pale, vpon their first repaire into England, to learne their English in thrée or foure daies, as though they had bought at Chester a grotes worth of English, and so packt vp the rest to be carried after them to London) euen so in all other places their natiue language is Irish.

Oneile whie he would not learne English.

Camb. lib. 1. dist. 3. rub. 8. The founder of the Irish language.

I find it solemnlie auouched, aswell in some of the Irish pamphlets as in Girald. Camb. that Gathelus or Gaedelus, & after him Simon Brecke, deuised the Irish language out of all other toongs then extant in the world. And thereof (saith Cambrensis) it is called Gaidelach, partlie of Gaedelus the first founder, and partlie for that it is compounded of all languages. But considering the course of interchanging and blending of speeches togither, not by inuention of art, but by vse of talke, I am rather led to beléeue (séeing Ireland was inhabited within one yeare after the diuision of toongs) that Bastolenus a branch of Japhet who first seized vpon Ireland, brought thither the same kind of spéech, some of the 72 that to this familie befell at the desolation of Babell. Vnto whom succeeded the Scithians, Grecians, Egyptians, Spaniards, Danes, of all which the toong must néeds haue borowed part, but especiallie reteining the steps of Spanish then spoken in Granado, as from their mightiest ancestors. Since then to Henrie Fitzempresse the conqueror no such inuasion happened them, as whereby they might be driuen to infect their natiue language, vntouched in maner for the space of seuenteene hundred yeares after the arriuall of Iberius. It seemeth to borow of the Spanish the common phrase,

Bastolenus.

Epiphan. cont. her. lib. 1. tom. 1.

phrase, Commestato, that is, How doo you? or how fareth it with you? It fetcheth sundrie words from the Latine, as arget of *Argentum*, monie: salle of *sal*, salt; cappoulle of *Caballus*, a plough horsse, or (according vnto the old English terme) a caball or caple. bireat of the old motheaten Latine word *Birretum*, a bonnet. The toong is sharpe and sententious, & offereth great occasion to quicke apophthegms and proper allusions. Wherefore their common iesters and rimers, whom they terme Bards, are said to delight passinglie these that conceiue the grace and propertie of the toong. But the true Irish indéed differeth so much from that they commonlie speake, that scarse one in fiue hundred can either read, write, or vnderstand it. Therefore it is preserued among certeine of their poets and antiquaries. And in verie deed the language carrieth such difficultie with it, what for the strangenesse of the phrase, and the curious featnes of the pronuntiation, that a verie few of the countrie can atteine to the perfection thereof, and much lesse a forreiner or stranger.

Bards

The obscuritie of the true Irish

The difficultie

A gentleman of mine acquaintance reported, that he did see a woman in Rome, which was possessed with a babling spirit, that could haue chatted anie language sauing the Irish: and that it was so difficult, as the verie diuell was grauelled therewith. A gentleman that stood by answered, that he tooke the speech to be so sacred and holie, that no damned féend had the power to speake it, no more than they are able to saie (as the report goeth) the verse of saint John the euangelist, "Et verbum caro factum est." Naie by God his mercie man (quoth the other) I stand in doubt (I tell you) whether the apostles in their copious mart of languages at Jerusalem could haue spoken Irish, if they were apposed: whereat the companie heartilie laughed. As fluent as the Irish toong is, yet it lacketh diuerse words, and borroweth them verbatim of the English. As there is no vulgar Irish word (vnlesse there be some od terme that lurketh in anie obscure shrowds or other of their storehouse) for a cote, a gowne, a dublet, an hat, a drinking cup: but onelie they vse the same words with a little inflexion. They vse also the contracted English phrase, God morrow: that is to saie, God giue you a good morning.

John 1 ... 14.

The want of the Irish

I haue apposed sundrie times the expertest men that could be had in the countrie, and all they could neuer find out an equiualent Irish word for knaue. The Grecians (according to Tullie his iudgement) were in the same predicament as touching the terme *Ineptus*: his words are these. "Ego mehercule ex omnibus Latinis verbis, huius verbi vim vel maximam semper putaui. Quem enim nos ineptum vocamus, is mihi videtur ab hoc nomen habere ductum, quòd non sit aptus, idque in sermonis nostri consuetudine perlatè patet. Nam qui aut tempus, quo quid postulet, non videt, aut plura loquitur, aut se ostentat, aut eorum, quibuscum est, vel dignitatis vel commodi rationem non habet, aut denique in aliquo genere aut inconcinnus aut multus est, is ineptus esse dicitur. Hoc vitio cumulata est eruditissima illa Græcorum natio. Itaque qui vim huius mali Græci non viderent, ne nomen quidem ei vitio imposuerunt. Vt enim quæras omnia, quomodo Græci ineptum appellent, non reperies."

No Irish word for knaue

Lib. 2 de orat. Ineptus

Certes I haue béene of opinion (saith Tullie) that amongest the whole crue of Latine terms the word *Ineptus* hath béene of greatest importance or weight. For he, whom we name *Ineptus*, seemeth to me to haue the etymologie or ofspring of his name here hense deriued, that he is not apt, which stretcheth far and wide in the vsuall custome of our dailie spéech or communication. For he that dooth not perceiue what is fitting or decent for euerie season, or gableth more than he hath commission to doo, or that in bragging, bosting, or pecockwise setteth himselfe foorth to the gaze, by making more of the broth, than the flesh is worth, or he that regardeth not the vocation and affaires of them, with whome he intermedleth, or in fine, who so is stale without grace, or ouer tedious in anie matter, he is

tearmed

learned *Ineptus*, which is asmuch in English, in my phantasie, as saucie, or malapert. The famous & learned Gréeke nation is generallie dusked with this fault. Saluines [illegible] And for that the Grecians could not spie the enormitie thereof, they haue not so much as framed a terme thereto. For if you should ransacke the whole Gréeke language, you shall not find a word to counteruaile *Ineptus*. Thus far Tullie. Yet Budæus would not séeme to acknowledge this barrennesse, but that the Gréeke word ἀπειρόκαλος is equiposlent to *Ineptus*: but that I referre to the iudgement of the learned, being verie willing to find out some other Budæus, that could fashion an *Bud. lib. 2. de Asse & part.* [illegible] Irish word for knaue, whereof this discourse of *Ineptus* grew. As the whole realme of Ireland is sundried into foure principall parts, as before is said, so each parcell differeth verie much in the Irish toong, euerie countrie hauing his dialect, or peculiar maner in speaking the language: therefore commonlie in Ireland they ascribe a propertie to each of the foure countries in this sort. Vlster hath the right Irish phrase, but not the true pronunciation, Munster hath the true pronunciation, but not the phrase, Leinster is deuoid of the right phrase, and true pronunciation; Connaght hath both the right phrase and true pronunciation. There is a cholerike or disdainfull interiection vsed in the Irish language called Boagh, which is Irish boagh. as much in English as twish. The Irish both in ancient time and to this daie commonlie vse it, and therefore the English conquerors called them Irish poghes, or pogh Morrice. Which tawnting terme is at this daie verie wrongfullie ascribed to Fough. them of the English pale. The English interiection, Fough, which is vsed in lothing a ranke or strong sauour, seemeth to be sib to the other.

OF THE NATURE OF THE SOILE, AND OTHER INCIDENTS.

THE SECOND CHAPTER.

THE soile is low and waterish, including diuerse little Ilands, inuironed with lakes & marrish. Highest hils haue standing pooles in their tops. Inhabitants especiallie new come, are subiect to distillations, rheumes and fluxes. For remedie whereof, they vse an ordinarie drinke of *Aqua vitæ*, being so qualified in the making, that it drieth more, and also inflameth lesse than other hot confections doo. One Aqua vitæ. Theoricus wrote a proper treatise of *Aqua vitæ*, wherein he praiseth it vnto the ninth *Theoric. Epis. Hermenensis in Pomanda iuxta be [illegible]* degrée. He distinguisheth thrée sorts thereof, *Simplex, Composita* and *Perfectissima*. He declareth the simples and ingrediences thereto belonging. He wisheth it to be taken as well before meat as after. It drieth up the breaking out of hands, The commodities of Aqua vitæ. and killeth the flesh wormes, if you wash your hands therewith. It scowreth all scurfe & scalds from the head, being therewith dailie washt before meales. Being moderatlie taken (saith he) it sloweth age, it strengthneth youth, it helpeth digestion, it cutteth flegme, it abandoneth melancholie, it relisheth the heart, it lighteneth the mind, it quickeneth the spirits, it cureth the hydropsie, it healeth the strangurie, it pounceth the stone, it expelleth grauell, it puffeth awaie all ventositie, it kéepeth and preserueth the head from whirling, the eies from dazeling, the toong from lisping, the mouth from maffling, the teeth from chattering, and the throte from ratling: it kéepeth the weasin from stifling, the stomach from wambling, and the heart from swelling, the bellie from wirtching, the guts from rumbling, the hands from shiuering, & the sinewes from shrinking, the veines from crumpling, *[illegible] philosophiæ [illegible] nat. cap. 11.* the bones from aking, & the marrow from soaking. Vlstadius also ascribeth thereto a singular praise, and would haue it to burne being kindled, which he taketh to be a token to know the goodnesse thereof. And trulie it is a soueraigne liquor, if it be orderlie taken.

The

The aire is verie holesome, not generallie so cleare and subtill as that of England. The weather is more temperat, being not so warme in summer, nor cold in winter, as it is in England and Flanders. The countrie is stored with bees, contrarie to the opinion of some writers, who both in this and other errors, touching this countrie, may easilie be excused, as those that wrote by hearesaie. No vineyards, yet grapes grow there as in England. They doo lacke the Robucke, as Polychronicon writeth. *Pol. lib. 1 cap. 32.* They also lacke the bird called the pie. Howbeit in the English pale to this daie, they vse to tearme a slie coosener, a wilie pie. *Wilie pie.* Giraldus Cambrensis in his time complaineth, that Ireland had excesse of wood, & verie little champaine ground: *Camb. part. 1 dist. 3.* but now the English pale is too naked: turffe is their most fewell and seacole. No venemous creeping beast is brought forth, or nourished or can liue in Ireland, *No venemous wormes in Ireland.* being brought or sent. And therefore the spider of Ireland is well knowne not to be venemous, onelie because a frog was found liuing in the medowes of Waterford *Camb. part. 1. dist. 1.* somewhat before the conquest, they construed it to import their ouerthrow.

Bede writeth, that serpents conueied into Ireland did presentlie die, being touched *Bed. lib. 1 Angl. Hist. cap. 1.* with the smell of the land, that whatsoeuer came from Ireland was then of soueraigne vertue against poison. He exemplifieth in certeine men stung of adders, who dranke in water the scrapings of bookes that had beene of Ireland, and were cured. Generallie it is obserued, the further west, the lesse annoiance of pestilent creatures. The want whereof is to Ireland so peculiar, that whereas it laie long in question, to whether realme, Britaine or Ireland, the Ile of Man should apperteine, *The controuersie of the Ile of Man decided.* the said controuersie was decided, that forsomuch as venemous beasts were knowen to bréed therein, it could not be a naturall part of Ireland. And contrariwise, the *Orchades appendant to Ireland.* Orchades are adiudged to be appendant to Ireland, because those Ilands, neither bréed nor foster anie venemous worme, as Hector Boetius auoucheth. *Hector Boet. in Scot. reg. descrip. pag. 9 sect. 30.* Giraldus Cambrensis writeth that he heard certeine merchants affirme, that when they had vnladen their ships in Ireland they found by hap some toads vnder their balast. *Camb. topo. lib. 1 dist. 1 rub. 29.* And they had no sooner cast them on the shore, than they would puffe and swell vnmeasurablie, & shortlie after turning vp their bellies, they would burst in sunder. And not onelie the earth and dust of Ireland, but also the verie thongs of Irish leather haue the verie same force and vertue. I haue séene it, saith Cambrensis, *Cam. ibid. rub. 30. 31.* experimented, that a toad being incompassed with a thong of Irish leather, and créeping thitherward, indeuoring to haue skipt ouer it, suddenlie reculed backe, as *Irish leather expelleth venemous wormes.* though it had béene rapt in the head: wherevpon it began to sprall to the other side. But at length perceiuing that the thong did embare it of all parts, it began to thrile, and as it were to dig the earth, where finding an hole, it slunke awaie in the presence of sundrie persons.

It happened also in my time, saith Giraldus Cambrensis, that in the north of *Cambr. ir. cod. lo. c.* England a knot of yonkers tooke a nap in the fields: as one of them laie snorting with his mouth gaping, as though he would haue caught flies, it happened that a snake or adder slipt into his mouth, and glided downe into his bellie, where harboring it selfe, it began to roame vp and downe, and to féede on the yoong man his entrals. The patient being sore distracted and aboue measure tormented with the biting pangs of this gréedie ghest, incessantlie praied to God, that if it stood with his gratious will, either wholie to bereaue him of his life, or else of his vnspeakeable mercie to ease him of his paine. The worme would neuer ceasse from gnawing the patient his carcasse, but when he had taken his repast, and his meat was no sooner digested, than it would giue a fresh onset in boring his guts. Diuerse remedies were sought, and medicins, pilgrimages to saints, but all could not preuaile. Being at length schooled by the graue aduise of some sage and expert father, that willed him to make his spéedie repaire to Ireland, would tract no time, but busked himselfe ouer sea, and arriued in Ireland. He did no sooner drinke of the water of that

Iland, and taken of the vittels of Ireland, but forthwith he kild the snake, auoided it downeward, and so being lustie and liuelie he returned into England. Thus far Giraldus Cambrensis.

Whether venemous wormes were expelled Ireland through the praiers of saint Patrike.

There be some that moue question, whether the want of venemous wormes be to be imputed to the propertie of the soile, or to be ascribed to the praiers of saint Patrike, who conuerted that Iland. The greater part father it on saint Patrike, especiallie such as write his life aswell apart, as in the legend of Irish saints. Giraldus Cambrensis disafhrmeth flatlie that opinion, and taketh it to be a secret or hidden propertie naturallie vnited to the soile, from whom Polychronicon dooth not swarue. (*Polychr lib 1. cap. 32*) For my part as I am wedded to neither of both the opinions, so I would haue béene easilie persuaded, being neither hot nor cold in the matter, to rest as a lukewarme neuter, in omitting the one and the other vnskand, were it not that one maister Alan Cope, or some other that masketh vnder his visours, more slanderouslie than pithilie had busied himselfe therein. Wherefore, sith I may with better warrant defend my natiue countrie, than he or his betters may reprooue it, especiallie where his slanderous reports are vnderpropt with flim flam surmises. I purpose vnder maister Cope his correction to cope and buckle with him herein: and before he beare the ball to the goale, to trip him if I may in the way. And because (gentle reader) I mind to make thée an indifferent vmpier in this controuersie, for the better vnderstanding of the matter, I will laie downe maister Cope his words, in such wise as they are imprinted in his booke. First therefore thou must vnderstand, that his booke is made in dialog wise, a kind of writing as it is vsed, so commended of the learned. In these dialogs Irenæus an Englishman and Critobulus a Germane plaie the parts. Irenæus entreth into the stage, and in this wise beginneth.

Alan Copus dialog 2. cap 28

"Incipiam à sancto Paulo. nosti in Melita (quam hodie Maltam appellant) Paulum viperam à manu pendentem in ignem excussisse. In ea insula scorpiones, qui alibi eunt lætales, Pauli, vt creditur, munere sunt innoxij.

"*Critobulus.* Fortasse hoc habet à natura.

"*Irenæus.* Falleris. nam insulani, vt Lucas refert, clamabant, delatum eò parricidam, cui cùm mare pepercisset, nati dij serpentes, qui eum tollerent, immisissent: nec quicquam magis quàm præsentem eius mortem expectabant. A qua cùm ille tantùm abesset, vt nihil omnino damni aut doloris inde sentiret, in admirationem acti, dixerunt, eum longè supra hominem esse, & deum sub humana specie.

"*Critobulus.* Sic est, vt dicis.

"*Irenæus.* Cætera itaque audi. E specu, ad quem diuertisse dicitur, colliguntur lapides in tota fermè Europa salutares. Adhæc, quos nasci octauo calendas Februarij contingit (qui dies conuersionis eius memoriæ dicatus est) quæcunque eos orbis pars in lucem proferat, non horrent nec formidant angues, imò, quod magis est, sola saliua horum morsibus medentur. Id quod homo doctissimus & diligentissimus Thomas Fazellus nuper prodidit, vsu ipso rerum, & certis, ni fallor, exemplis ab eo obseruatum. (*Thomas Fazellus*)

"*Critobulus.* Ista quidem digna sunt obseruatione. & iam recordor, me legisse ac sæpiùs audisse, precibus beati Patricij Hiberniæ apostoli, ei regioni simile beneficium indultum, ne ea insula aliquid lætale pariat. Dici fortassè inde à nonnullis solet, nihil esse in Hibernia venenati præter ipsos homines, quod propter feros & agrestes eorum mores dictum à plerisque accipitur.

"*Irenæus.* Eam regionem nihil pestiferum aut venenatum alere, tum ex multorum sermonibus, tum ex Beda intelligo: (*Bed lib 1 Ang hist c 1*) adèo vt terra illius regionis exportata, pestifera ac venenata animalia extinguat. Verùm id quicquid est, non Patricio, sed naturæ regionis tribuo, propterea quòd longè antè Patricium natum constet, eam fuisse eius regionis dotem, quam non est difficile alibi reperiri." (*Sententia definitiua Solin cap. 35*)

"I will

"I will begin (saith Irenæus) with saint Paule. You know that in Melita (which at this daie is called Malta) saint Paule flung into the fire a viper that stucke or did cleaue to his hand. In that Iland scorpions which are elsewhere deadlie or venemous, are become through the gift of saint Paule (as it is supposed) harmelesse.

"Tush (quoth Critobulus) that may be percase incident to the nature of the soile.

"Naie then (replieth Irenæus) you are in a wrong box. For the Ilanders (as saint Luke mentioneth) showted, that a parentquellor was brought thither, and because he was not swallowed in the gulfes of the sea, the gods being in their fustian fumes, sent serpents to slaie him. And they looked for nothing sooner than to see him euen at a twinkling to perish. But when they perceiued him to be so farre distant from death, as that he susteined no harme, ne felt anie paine, the people therewith amazed, said he far surpassed mans estate, & that he was a god inuested in man his shape.

"You haue reason (answereth Critobulus) you haue hit the naile on the head.

"Yea but I praie you clip not my tale (saith Irenæus) but take me with you. Stones are culled in the caue or den wherein saint Paule is said to haue baited or soiorned, which stones in maner in all Europe are soueraigne medicines to cure the bitings and stinges of scorpions and serpents. Furthermore, they that are borne the fiue and twentith of Januarie (which daie is named the conuersion of S. Paule) in what part soeuer of the world they are borne, they feare not or grudge not at snakes: yea, that which is more to be admired, the stingings of poisoned worms are healed by the verie spittle of this Januarie blood. Which thing hath béene of late published by a well lettered man Thomas Fazellus, to haue béene curiouslie noted of him, as well by proofe and experience, as by sure and substantiall examples, if I take not the matter amisse.

"Then commeth in Critobulus, whome maister Cope maketh (I will not saie the vice or iestcorner) but the plesant conceipted gentleman of this enterlude, and fetcheth a long leape (for I am sure he could not iumpe so farre) from Malta to Ireland, and frameth his tale in this sort. By the faith of my bodie sir, here is stuffe woorth the noting. And now I call to mind, that I haue read and often heard, that the like benefit hath béene imparted to Ireland, through the praiers of saint Patrike the apostle of the said Iland, that is to saie, that Ireland breedeth no venemous worme. And therevpon percase some are accustomed to saie, that there is no poisoned or venemous thing in Ireland, but onelie the people, which is taken to haue beene said of most men for their brutish and sauage maners.

"To this (saith Irenæus) I am doone to vnderstand by the report of diuerse, and also by Bede, that no poisoned or venemous thing is bred in that realme: in somuch that the verie earth of that countrie being brought into other realmes, killeth all venemous and poisoned wormes." But let the matter fall out which waie Judgement.
it will, I ascribe that propertie not to saint Patrike, but to the nature of the soile, because it hath béen knowen long before saint Patrike was borne, that Ireland was indued with that propertie, which is elsewhere easie to be found. Hitherto Maister Cope.

In this discourse (gentle reader) thou seest that Maister Cope handleth two principall points, the propertie of Malta, and the nature of Ireland in destroieng venemous worms, the one he ascribeth to the blessed apostle saint Paule, the other he will not in anie wise impute to saint Patrike. Touching the first, as I have no occasion to intermeddle therein, so I purpose not for the quarell I haue to the person, to disproove his opinion so farre as it standeth with truth. Wherefore that God that of his bountifull goodnesse gaue the grace to Moses, to turne Aarons rod into a Exod. c. 7
serpent, to turne the riuer into blood, and to worke diuerse other effects that are verse 10 (a) Josue c. 10
mentioned in the scripture, to (a) Josue, to staie the sun, to (b) Elias to raise verse 13. (b) 3. Reg. 17
the

v rse 22, and
Eccles 48 vers
50
(c) Act 3 ver 7
(d) A t 9 ver
34
(e) Act 9 vers
7
(f) A t 5 vers
15
(g) A t 14 vers
10
(h) A t 20 v rse
10 & 11
(i) A t 27 verse
25
A • 9 v rs 40
Act 28 v rse 0

the dead child , to *(c)* Peter to make the lame go , to heale *(d)* Eneas ; to reuiue *(e)* Tabitha , yea with his verie *(f)* shadow to cure the sicke , and the God that gaue to that Paule, of whome maister Cope speaketh, his gratious gift to make the *(g)* lame go, to *(h)* quicken and raise the deceased, and for his sake to *(i)* salue his fellow passengers it is not to be denied, but that God would impart his goodnes to anie region, euen the sooner that any of his blessed seruants would harborough there And as I doubt not but Simon the tanners house was nothing the woorse for lodging so happie a ghest as Peter so I am sure Malta was farre the better for harboring so blessed a traueller or passenger as Paule Which S Luke letteth not to tell, declaring that all they which were sicke in the Iland, flocked to Paule, and were cured and also the patient that was father to Publius, in whose house they were thrée daies, verie courteouslie intertemed, was by S Paule healed Which cure as well of that patient, as of the residue of the Ilanders, did not onlie extend to their bodies, but chéeflie & especiallie to their soules, according to the opinion of the learned diuines For as our sauior Iesus Christ was neuer thought to cure

Augu tract 50
n Iohan Th
p 3 q 42 a 3 ad
3 m

anie ones bodie, but he would also heale his soule so it must be thought of his apostles, in whose steps both in life and miracles they traced. And therfore the learned hold opinion, that S Paule being in Malta expelled from diuerse of their soules the

Gen. 3 vers 13.

old serpent that deceiued our progenitors Adam and Eue , for which God is to be magnified and glorified Thus much I thought good here to insert, as a clause not wholie swaruing from that we treat of, and also that I would be found prest and readie, as farre as my simple skill stretcheth, to vnderstand anie opinion that tendeth to the honor and glorie of God

How beit forsomuch as M. Cope hath so strictlie dealt with Ireland, as with a countrie nothing apperteining to this matter, I trust he will pardon me, to be somewhat bold with him, touching the historie of Malta, that as his negligence shall be in the one disshowed, so his slanderous iudgement maie be in the other reuersed First therfore where he writeth, that the inhabitants of Malta *Clamabant,* that is,

Act 28 vers 4

cried, or showted, it was not so The Giéeke text runneth, ἔλεγον πρὸς ἀλλήλας, *Dicebant ad inuicem,* that is to saie, they muttered one to an other And saint Luke paraphraseth his meaning after For when they perceiued that the viper did not annoie Paule, then saith saint Luke, *Conuertentes se, dicebant eum esse deum ,* They turning the one towards the other, whispered or muttered that Paule was a god

Saint Paule
heard not the
inhabitants of
Malta

Now put the case they cried, as M Cope saith, is it like that Paule was so busie in making of a fire, or that his eares did wander so farre off, as that he could not heare them ? And if he heard them, thinke you that he would haue béene whist, in hearing God so faire blasphemed, as that he would suffer himselfe to be defied ? No trulie. He would haue taken on, as he and Barnabas did at Listris,

Act 14. vers 11,
12, 13, 14

where the inhabitants named them gods, Barnabas to be Iupiter, and Paule, for that he was well spoken, to be Mercurie. For when the apostles heard of their idolatrie, renting their clothes, they rusht into the throng, crieng and speaking, that they were mortall men, &c In which place S Luke putteth an expresse difference as it were of set purpose, betwéene both the words, *Clamantes & dicentes.* M Cope addeth further, *Delatum eò parricidam,* and yet the Giéeke hath πάντας φονεὺς, *Omninò interfector,* or as the vulgar text is, *Vtique homicida est homo hic* So that they tooke him to be but a manquellor, yet M Cope maketh him a parricide, which is woorse For although euerie parricide be a manquellor, yet *E conuerso,* euerie manquellor is not a parricide

M Cope procéedeth further, " *Irati dij, serpentes, qui eum tollerent, immisissent .* The gods being angrie sent serpents to dispatch Paule " And yet forsooth, all these serpents were but one viper, as is plainelie exprest in the text, vnlesse M Cope would teach saint Luke to tell his tale after the finest fashion, least the apostle should

haue

haue béene thought to haue fitoned. As the parson that preached to his parishoners of the gospell, wherein mention is made of them that Christ fed in the desert, or wildernesse. O (quoth the parson) what a Christ was that, that with fiue barlie loaues, and fiue fishes fed fiue hundred persons. The clerke hearing his master to grate ouerlong on that point, for he did often iterate that sentence, stole up to the pulpit, and plucking the parson by his gowne, whispered in his eare that Christ fed fiue thousand. Hold thee contented thou foolish fellow (quoth the parson) if I should tell mine hearers of so great a number, I should but discredit the gospeller, and they would not beléeue me. So it fareth with M. Cope. Belike he mistrusted, that if he had said, that one viper could haue slaine Paule, the reader would haue suspected the vntruth of the matter: bicause it carrieth great likelihood with it, that one man could withstand one viper: and therefore to saue saint Luke his credit, he increaseth the number by putting the plurall for the singular. Whereas therefore it standeth with M. Cope his pleasure, to florish in his rhetoricall figure named, *Veritatis superlatio*, in terming muttering, showting, a manquellor, a paricide, one viper, serpents: he must be borne withall, if in the heat of his figure he step a little awrie in the remnant of his discourse. For thus he saith.

A parson his sermon.

M. Cope his rhetorike.

And therevpon it is reported percase by some men, that there is nothing venemous or poisoned in Ireland, but the men and women. Which is taken to haue béene spoken by most men for their brutish and sauage maners. Here (good reader) thou must vnderstand that M. Cope putteth the text downe and the glose. The text is, There is nothing in Ireland venemous but the inhabitants. The glose is, This is said to haue béen spoken for their brutish and sauage conditions. Now well harpt by saint Lankfield. Here is a glose, I vndertake you, sutable to the text. But let vs sée, how cunninglie M. Cope becquiteth himselfe. First he obserueth not *Decorum personæ*, secondlie he followeth not *Decorum dialogi*, thirdlie he sheweth herein little diuinitie. Touching the first point, who knoweth not, that these iapes and gibes are onelie fit for ruffians, vices, swashbucklers & tospots. And trulie they beeset a diuine as well, as for an asse to twang quipassa on a harpe or gitterne, or for an ape to friske trenchmoore in a paire of buskins and a doublet. The heathen misliked in an orator scurrilitie, what should be thought then of a diuine, whome saint Paule would haue to be sober, modest, graue, and wise? Vnlesse M. Cope leaning to the letter of saint Paule his words would beare vs in hand, that saint Paule would haue modestie to rest onelie in bishops. We are commanded in the old and new testament, to loue our neighbors as our selues. Which dooth implie, that we ought not to slander our neighbours.

Cic. lib. 2. de orat.

Tit. 3. vers. 2. & 3.

And shall a diuine then speake vncharitablie, not onelie of one, but of an whole realme, and not onelie speake but also write, yea and that in the language that is vniuersallie spoken, thorooughout the greater part of the world, vpon no sure ground, but onelie vpon hearesaie, weieng not what the prophet writeth, *Perdes omnes qui loquuntur mendaciũ*. Thou shalt destroie all them that speake vntruths? And were it that anie such flim flam flirts were soothed by anie person of credit, yet (as me seemeth) it would stand more with the grauitie of a diuine, than such childish quips, and scornefull tawnts should sooner by his meanes charitablie be whisted, than thorough his procurement carpinglie published. I will stand no longer on this point, but onelie craue M. Cope to resort to the fift of Matthew, and there peruse Christ his verdict touching slanderous toongs. To come to the second part, in which he obserueth not *Decorum dialogi*, thou shalt vnderstand (good reader) that Critabulus, or Critobulus, whome M. Cope maketh his bagpipe to belch out his rancour, is a Germane borne, as M. Cope saith, who séemeth to be Critabulus his godfather. Now let anie one, that is acquainted with the maners of Germans, iudge, if it be decent, that one of them should scoffe and scorne the conditions and fashions

Psal. 5. vers. 7.

Sap. cap. 1.

Vide August. in eundem Psal.

Mark 3. vers. 22.

fashions of other countries I will not speake by heare saie, as M. Cope dooth, but by eiesight. I could neuer espie nor probablie haue I heard it reported, no not of the méere sauage Irish, such quaffing, such swilling, such bolling, such gulling, such brutish drunkennesse, such surfetting, such vomitting, as I haue seene some Germans doo. In good sooth it is knowne, and for my part I haue seene it being beyond the seas, that in their carowsing and cup friendship, they threaten such kindnesse on their companions, that least their felowes should mistrust them with double dealing, they will not sticke to shew them the bottome of their stomachs, & to the end they should take the better view thereof, they will place it now and then in their neighbors bosome.

The Germans freendship

Thus when they haue cast their gorges, they clap on their thrumd hats, and run like bedlem barretors into the stréets with their naked flatchets, and there they keepe such a stinking stirre with hacking of stones, with hewing of blocks, with thwitting of stocks, with striking of stalles, with thumping at doores, that it would make a horsse breake his halter, to see so drunken a pageant. In fine, this qualitie is so naturallie ingraffed in the greater part of them, that a famous diuine did not sticke of late to saie openlie in his lecture, that drunkennesse in that countrie man, was either *Peccatum originale* or *Accidens inseparabile*. I write not this (I take God to record) to the reproch or slander of that countrie (being loth to commit the selfe same fault that I reprehend in anie other) but onelie my meaning is to settle before the reader his eies the absurditie of M. Cope, in framing poore Critabolus to flout Ireland, considering that if he cast his eie homeward, he shall find as filthie puddle in his owne countrie, as in other realms. And therefore this quip sat as vnseemlie in his mouth, as for an whoore to reprehend bitcherie, or for an vsurer to condemne simonie. For as there is nothing lesse to be tollerated, than for anie one to haue an other to account for his life, that can yeeld no account of his owne: so there is nothing that ought to moozzell vp anie one from rebuking other nations, than to see the misdemeanor of his owne natiue countrie. I would wish M. Critabolus or M. Cope, if it shall please him to make vp the muster, with indifferencie to weie the estate of Ireland, and so without parcialitie to frame his iudgement.

Ireland how it maie be reformed

Ireland, and especiallie the ruder part is not stored with such learned men as Germanie is. If they had sound preachers, and sincere liuers, that by the imbalming of their carren soules with the swéet and sacred flowers of holie writ, would instruct them in the feare of God, in obeieng their prince, in obseruing the lawes, in vnderpropping in ech man his vocation the weale publike, I doubt not, but within two or thrée ages M. Critabolus his heires should heare so good a report run of the reformation of Ireland, as it would be reckoned as ciuill as the best part of Germanie. Let the soile be as fertile and betle as anie would wish, yet if the husbandman will not manure it, sometime plow and eare it, sometime harrow it, sometime till it, sometime marle it, sometime delue it, sometime dig it, and sow it with good and sound corne, it will bring foorth wéeds, bindcorne, cockle, darnell, brambles, briers, and sundrie wild shoots. So it fareth with the rude inhabitants of Ireland, they lacke vniuersities, they want instructors, they are destitute of teachers, they are without preachers, they are denoid of all such necessaries as apperteine to the training vp of youth: and notwithstanding all these wants, if anie would be so frowardlie set, as to require them, to vse such ciuilitie, as other regions, that are sufficientlie furnished with the like helps; he might be accounted as vnreasonable, as he that would force a créeple that lacketh both his legs to run, or one to pipe or whistle a galiard that wanteth his vpper lip.

But such is the corrupt nature of vs worldlings, and me thinketh such vaine humors are not vtterlie dried vp in our sage and mortified diuines. We are most commonlie giuen rather to taunt that which is amisse, than to praise that which is good,

good; and rather we follow the spider in soking the poison, than in imitating the bée by sucking the honie Now that it appeareth, that it was not fitting for the author being a diuine, to write so vncharitablie, nor for M Citabolus being a Germane to carpe other countries so snappishlie let vs see what wholesome diuinitie hath beene here vttered, and how well the sinewes of M Critabolus his argument shall be found to hang togither, when the anatomie therof by peecemeale shall be examined I call to mind (quoth M Citabolus) that I have read and often heard, that the like benefit hath béene granted to Ireland through the praiers of S Patrike. M. Critabolus read & heard that by the praiers of S Patrike, Ireland hath no venemous worme· *Ergo* some hold opinion, that the poison resteth onlie in the people Truly this argument hangeth togither by verie strange gimbols And I dare say, M Cope neuer learned this kind of reasoning in the famous college of Magdalene in Oxford, whatsoeuer M Critabulus did in Germanie But let vs put the logike apart, & scan the singular point of diuinitie I would gladlie lerne in what part of scripture or in what ancient father M Critabulus read or heard (for most of his learning hath beene, as it seemeth, purchased by heare-saie) that anie holie prelat, that came of meere charitie to conuert a countrie from night to light, from rudenesse to knowledge, from infidelitie to christianitie, from vice to vertue, from the diuell to God (which dooth implie an especiall zeale in sauing their soules) would purge the soile of all venemous wormes, & leaue the soules that haue more néed to be wéeded, wholie infected with the contagion of vice and sinne. Wherby insueth that the place is better than the inhabitants, and so consequentlie the saieng of the Machabées must be falsified: *Non propter locum gentem, sed propter gentem locum Deus elegit* God did not choose the people for the place, but he elected the place in respect of the people. Our sauiour Iesus Christ dipossessing the patient of the legion of diuels, permitted them to enter into an heard of hogs Citabulus would haue Christs saints doo the contrarie, to dispossesse the hogs, and to leaue the men possessed with diuels. For so he reporteth saint Patrike to haue doone, by ridding the land of all poisoned wormes, & leauing the rancour to lurke in the people. Trulie if the matter stood so farre out of ioint, I doubt not, but the Ilanders might haue come as lawfullie to him, as the Gergesens came ingratefullie to Christ, requiring him to depart their countrie For such a scoffing prelat, his roome had béene better than his companie, sith his abode would tend rather to the peruerting, than the conuerting of their Iland

2 Mac 5 ver. 19

Luc 8 ver 32.

Luc 2 ver 37.

Hitherto thou hast heard (gentle reader) how gallanthe Citabulus hath plaied his part now shall I desire thée to view how sagelie Ireneus claspeth up all the whole controuersie He saith it is the nature of the soile, not to breed anie venemous worme, and that was incident thereto before saint Patrike was borne How prooue you that sir? Pleaseth you to skew your eie towards the margent, and there shall you find the fiue and thirtith chapter of Solinus solemnlie quoted. Touching this matter, there is nothing in Solinus but this, *Illic anguis nullus, auis rara,* In Ireland is no snake, and seldome a bird, & yet birds are as commonlie there as in anie other countrie. But I would gladlie vnderstand how this authoritie of Solinus furthereth M Ireneus his opinion Ireland bred no snake before saint Patrike was borne. *Ergo* it ingendred no toad, no adder, no frog, nor anie other virulent worme As if a man would reason thus. Before saint Patrike his time there was no horssemill in Ireland. *Ergo* before his time there was no millhorsse Certes he that would wind vp his conclusion so fondlie, might be thought to haue as much wit as a rosted horse. This authoritie of Solinus is so far from vpholding Ireneus his assertion, as that it plainelie séemeth quite to ouerthrow it, & as it were in his owne turne, it giueth him a fall

For the cause whie saint Patrike was mooued to expell all the venemous wormes out

out of Ireland, might probablie haue béene coniectured, to haue procéeded of this, that he perceiuing the land to bréed no snakes, thereof was occasioned, for the furthering of christian faith, to expell other kind of wormes that lurked there before

Obiection.

his comming, as toades, adders, blindwormes, frogs &c. Héere perchase M. Cope may blench me, in replieng that *Anguis* may be construed generallie for all kind of vermine, and so I might be taken tardie in building my discourse vpon a misconstruction.

Answer.

In good sooth to omit what strange and absurd signification *Anguis* should beare, by notifieng a poisoned spider and such like, and in mine opinion further from the purpose, than the father that dissuading his sonne from plaieng on sundaie, fortified his reason with the old said saw, *Non est bonum ludere cum sanctis*, It is not good, quoth he, to plaie on sundaies or holie daies. Is it (thinke you) fellonie or treason, to bring the credit of Solinus in question, for mistaking *Anguis* aswell as *Auis*? For as he was groslie deceiued in the one, in writing that birds were rare in Ireland, so might he haue straied as likelie in the other, by disburdening Ireland of all venemous wormes, bicause the Iland wanted in his time but one or two kinds, as a snake

Rumor catcheth fethers.

and a toad. Where a man buildeth vpon euerie twatling and pratling rumor, and his eie is not his iudge, he may be sure, that such flieng tales will catch manie feathers before they come at him that is as far distant from their nests, as Solinus was from Ireland when he wrote his pamphlet. The proofe whereof as it is dailie tried, so not manie yeares past hath béene verie prettilie verefied. There was a gentleman of mine acquaintance that met his enimie in the fields, where they both vpon a trifling quarell fought so fréendlie, as they had more néed to haue beene grapled togither with cables, than parted by indifferent stickiers. Howbeit, bicause the gentleman was neuer before flesht, and yet nothing at all that daie, for each of their blowes did commonlie light on the medow where they fought, a friend of his reported well of him to an other, saieng, that he was like in time to prooue a proper man of his hands, for the well handling of his weapon in his late combat. Whereupon soon after, the other doubling the gentleman his praise, gaue notice to an other, that such a gentleman (naming him) fought valiantlie such a daie in such a place. Immediatlie vpon this in a shire or two off, it was noised that the partie praised, fought with two at once in such a place, naming the medow. At length it was bruted, that he fought foure seuerall daies, and I am well assured that was the first fraie that euer he made, and I thinke it will be the last, vnlesse he be forced maugre his heart to the contrarie.

Not long after it happened, that a gentleman and I trauelled abroad the countrie of set purpose to disport our selues, and so to returne afresh to our books, where entering in communication with a blunt countrie lob (yet such an one as tooke his halfepenie to be good siluer) that knew the foresaid champion. My companion and I made wise, as though we were not acquainted with him, or euer heard of the

A freendlie commendation.

combat. Now in good faith gentleman (quoth he) you would doo verie well to enter in acquaintance with him, for ouer this, that he is a gentleman abundantlie endued with singular good qualities, he is become of late so valiant a cutter, as he maketh blading his dailie breakefast. By saint Marie, quoth my companion, that is verie cold roste, and if his breakefasts be no better than a péece of cold yron, I little weigh how seldome I take a repast in his companie at anie such ordinarie. Naie, my meaning is (quoth the other) that he vseth to fight fresh and fasting euerie morning, in so much that of late, I dare bide by it, he fought eight daies in one weeke. At which words I for my part could not refraine from laughing, séeing how demurelie the fellow kept his countenance, and how that he spake *Bona fide*. Whereupon I shaped him an answer and said, that I neuer heard of anie that fought eight daies in one weeke, but onelie in old time, when fiue quarters made vp the yeare.

The

The fellow perceiuing that he ouershot himselfe, replied Sir, you take me verie short, as long and as verie a lowbie as you imagine to make me my meaning is, that he fought eight seuerall times in one weeke Eight times (quoth my companion) then belike he fought once aboue commons For you told vs right now, that he made his fraie his morning breakefast, and whereas there are but seauen daies in the wéeke, & he fought (as you report) eight times, and you know that eight maketh one aboue seauen, and seauen maketh six and one vnder eight, either you must confesse that he fought out his breakfast, dinner, beuer or supper, or else you must grant that there be eight daies in one wéeke, or at the least two breakefasts in one daie and that I am sure you will confesse to be as great an absurditie as the other Naie (quoth the clowne) and you intrap me with such sophistrie, you shall dine, sup and breake your fast alone for me, and therewithall departed Whereby may be gathered, that if he had bin soothed vp, & his toong let run at libertie vncontrold, like a bowle that runneth in a smooth allie without anie rub, he would haue brought himselfe to that bare, as he would not sticke to saie that his fréend had fought eight daies in one houre Wherefore as this pudding his pricke grew at length by report to an huge post, so the want of one venemous worme in Ireland, being bruited in forren realmes, might haue beene so thwitted and mangled in the cariage before it came to Solinus his eares, as he might haue beene informed, that the countrie was deuoid of all venemous woormes, whereas indéed there lacked but one kind.

Like as God of his iustice punisheth a countrie that is hardhearted, with outward wormes so of his mercie they are remooued from a realme that is pliant to follow his lawes and precepts As when Pharao would not listen to God his threats denounced him by the preachers of God, Moses and Aaron, Egypt was punished with frogs and diuerse kind of flies, as is exprest at full in holie writ and againe vpon Pharao his feined promises (the secrets of whose hollow heart God perfectlie knew) at the instance of Moses, these plagues were appeased, and the vermine quite extinguished. so I praie you, is it so absurd a position to hold, that saint Patrike finding the Irish priest to embrace the gospell, as he did in verie deed, might stand so highlie in God his fauor, as though his earnest petition made to God, the poisoned woormes should be abandoned ? This is not so rare a thing vpon the implanting of christian faith in anie region, but rather a propertie incident thereto, according to Christ his promise "Signa autem eos, qui crediderint, hæc sequentur, In nomine meo dæmonia eijcient linguis loquentur nouis serpentes tollent: & si mortiferum quid biberint, non eis nocebit super ægros manus imponent, & bene habebunt" And these tokens shall follow them that beléeue, In my name shall they cast out diuels, they shall speake with new toongs, they shall driue awaie serpents, and if they drinke anie deadlie thing it shall not hurt them they shall laie hands on the sicke, and they shall be cured. Wherefore, sith it is so euidentlie warranted by scripture, that in the name of Iesus, serpents may be driuen awaie, if Ireland be found through anie such means to be deuoid of poisoned woormes, we are to ascribe the glorie hereof to God, according to the saieng of the prophet, "A domino factum est istud, & est mirabile in oculis nostris," That hath béene doone by God, and it séemeth woonderfull in our eies

Thus farre (gentle reader) incroching vpon thy patience, I haue implored my trauell in defending my natiue countrie against such as labour to distaine it with their slanderous scoffes Touching the principall question, whether S Patrike did expell poisoned woormes out of Ireland, or whether it be the nature of the soile as I said in the entrie of this discourse, so I saie againe, that I weigh not two chips which waie the wind bloweth, bicause I sée no inconuenience that may insue either of the affirmatiue or negatiue opinion. And therefore if M Cope had dealt as

Exod 8 vers 7, 17, & 24.
Vide Apoc 9 verse 3, at 2 Reg 8 verse 37.

Grego hom 29, in euang

Mar 16 v 17

Psalm 117, vers 12

modestlie as Cambrensis, the author of Polychronicon or others, that stood to the deniall, haue doone, he should haue gone scottice with his complices, and haue made in mountebankwise the most he could of his wares. But for that he would needs sée further in a milstone than others, and not onelie slenderlie disprooue the triuiall opinion, but scornefullie slander an whole realme, wherein he shall find his superiors in honour, his betters in parentage, his peeres in learning, his mates in wisdome, his equals in courtesie, his matches in honestie: I must craue him to beare it patientlie if by erring him quittance, I serued him with a dish of his owne cookerie. And if for this my streict dealing with him (whereunto I was the sooner led, for that as it is courtesie to mollifie wild speaches with mild answers, so I reckon it for good policie now and then to cleaue knurd knobs with crabbed wedges) he will séeme to take pepper in the nose, for anie recompense he is like to haue at mine hands, he may wipe his nose on his sléeue. And if it shall stand with his pleasure, to replie either in English or in Latine (the occasion of which is rather of him growne than by me giuen) he shall find me willing, if God spare me health, to reioine with him in so good a quarrell, either in the one language or the other: and when both tales are heard, I beshrow him, for my part, that shall be driuen to the wall.

The barnacle. Cambrensis reporteth of his owne knowledge, and I heare it auowed by credible persons, that barnacles thousands at once are noted along the shores in Ireland to hang by the beakes about the edges of putrified timber, as ships, oares, masts, anchor holds, and such like, which in processe taking liuelie heat of the sunne, become waterfoules, and at their time of ripenesse either fall into the sea, or flie abroad into the aire. The same doo neuer couple in the act of generation, but are from time to time multiplied, as before is exprest.

Sabel part 3. Ene 10 lib 5 Cam lib topog dist 1 rub 15 Thom p 3 q 51 ar 4 corp. Æneas Syluius writeth himselfe to haue pursued the like experiment in Scotland, where he learned the truth hereof to be found in the Ilands Orchades. Giraldus Cambrensis gathereth hereof a pretie conclusion against the Iewes in this wise following: "Respice infœlex Iudæe, respice, vel serò, primam hominis generationem ex limo sine mare & fœmina. Secundámque ex mare sine fœmina, ob legis venerationem, diffiteri non audes. Tertiam solam ex mare scilicet & fœmina, quia vsualis est, dura ceruice approbas & affirmas. Quartam verò, in qua sola salus est ex fœmina scilicet sine mare obstinata malitia in propriam perniciem detestaris. Erubesce miser, erubesce, & saltem ad naturam recurre, quæ ad argumenta fidei, ad instructionem nostram noua quotidie animalia sine omni mare vel fœmina procreat & producit. Prima ergo generatio ex limo, & hæc vltima ex ligno. Illa quidem quoniam à Domino naturæ tantùm semel, ideò semper obstupenda processit. Istam verò non minùs admirabilem, minus tamen admirandam (quia sæpè fit) imitatrix natura administrat. Sic enim composita est humana natura, vt nihil, præter inusitatum & raró contingens vel pretiosum ducat vel admirandum. Solis ortum & occasum, quo nihil in mundo pulchrius, nihil stupore dignius, quia quotidie videmus, sine omni admiratione prætermittimus. Eclipsin verò solis quia rarius accidit, totus orbis obstupescit. Ad idem etiam facere videtur, flatu solo, & occulta quadam inspiratione citra omnem mixturam apum ex fauo procreatio."

"Marke thou wretched Iew, saith Cambrensis, marke yet at length the first creation (that is of Adam) of earth without male or female. As for the second, of a man without a woman (that is to saie Eue) for that thou hast the old law in reuerence, thou darest not denie. As for the third, both of man and woman, bicause it is dailie vsed as stiffeneckt as thou art, thou doost acknowledge and confesse. But the fourth procreation, in which consisteth our onelie iustification (he meaneth the incarnation of Christ) of a woman without man, with sturdie and obstinat rancor to thine vtter destruction thou doost detest. Blush therefore thou

vnhappie

vnhappie Iew, be ashamed of this thy follie, and at the least wise haue recourse to nature, and settle hir works before thine eies, that for the increase of faith, and to the lessoning of vs, dailie bréedeth & ingendreth new liuing creatures, without the coupling of mascle or female. Adam was created of earth, the barnacles are ingendred of wood, bicause Adam was once created by him, who is Lord of nature, therefore it is continuallie admired. But for that dame nature the counterfeitresse of the celestiall workeman, eftsoones bréedeth barnacles, therefore their brood is accompted more maruellous than to be maruelled, more woonderfull than woondered. For such is the framing of man his nature, as he deemeth nothing pretious or woonderfull, but such things as seldome happen. What may be thought more beautifull than the course of the sunne? And yet bicause we sée it dailie rise and set, we let it ouerslip vs as an vsuall custome, without anie staring or gazing. Yet we are amazed and astonied at the eclipse, bicause it happeneth verie seldome." The bées that are ingendred of the honie combe, onlie by a puffe or secret breathing without anie coupling, séeme to vphold this procreation of barnacles. Hitherto Cambrensis, with whom concerning the ingendring of bées Iohannes de sancto Geminiano accordeth.

Be'es how they are ingendered.
Iohan de S Gem in lib de exempl & simili. rerum li 4 c 3

The inhabitants of Ireland are accustomed to moue question, whether barnacles be fish or flesh, & as yet they are not fullie resolued, but most vsuallie the religious of streictest abstinence doo eat them on fish daies. Giraldus Cambrensis, and after him Polichronicon suppose, that the Irish cleargie in this point straie. For they hold of certeintie that barnacles are flesh. And if a man saie they had eaten a collop of Adam his leg, he had eaten flesh. And yet Adam was not ingendred of mascle or female, but onelie created of claie, as the barnacles of wood & rotten timber. But the Irish clergie did not so farre straie in their opinion, as Cambrensis & Polichronicon, in their disproofe. For the framing of Adam and Eue was supernaturall onelie doone by God, & not by the helpe of angels or anie other creature. For like as it surpasseth natures course to raise the dead, to lighten or insight the blind, so it stood not with the vsuall & common linage of nature, but onlie with the supereminent power of God, to frame a man of claie, and a woman of a mans rib. But the ingendring of barnacles is naturall, & not so woonderfull as Cambrensis maketh it. And therefore the examples are not like.

Whether the barnacle be fish or flesh.
Camb. lib 1. topog dis 1 r b 15
Poly. lib 1 c 32.
Adam & Eue onelie created by God
August super Genes ad lit lib 9 c 18.

Now it should séeme that in Cambrensis his time, the Irish clergie builded their reason vpon this plot. What soeuer is flesh, is naturallie begotten or ingendred of flesh, barnacles are not naturallie ingendred of flesh, but onelie of timber and wood, barnacles therfore are not flesh, vnlesse you would haue them to be wooden flesh. And if the reason be so knit it may not be disiointed by Cambrensis his example. As if a man should argue thus. She that is begotten of anie man, must be of force daughter to that man, Melcha was begotten of Aran, *Ergo* Melcha was Arans daughter. This argument is of all parts so fortified, as it séemeth of all sides to be impregnable. Yet a busie braine sophister cauilling on the terme (begotten) might saie, that Eue was begotten of Adam, and yet she is not Adams daughter. True it is that Adam was not Eues father, no more than Eue was Adams mother, neither by that ingendring was there anie degree of consanguinitie sprong betwéene them. But bicause the word (begotten) is taken in the argument for the naturall ingendring of man and woman, the instance giuen of Eue dooth not disproue the Maior. And yet for the better vnderstanding of the question, it is to be noted that the philosophers distinguish *Animalia sensitiua*, that is, sensible liuing things, in two sorts, perfect and vnperfect. The perfect are they that are ingendred of seed, the vnperfect without seed. Those that are naturallie ingendred with séed, can neuer be naturallie ingendred without séed. albeit Auicenna verie erroniouslie holdeth the contrarie: as for example.

Genes 11 v 29.
Adam & Eue of no kin
Thom p 1 q 92. art 2 ad 3. m
Thom p 1 q 91 art 2 ad 2 m
Liuing things are of two sorts.
Thom p 1 q 71 1 a. 1 m
Auicenna

Because man is naturallie ingendred of man and woman, no man may naturallie be ingendred without the copulation of man and woman: yet supernaturallie it may be. As Adam was made without man and woman, Eue framed without woman: our sauiour Christ begotten without man. And therefore the diuell could not haue atteinted him of originall sinne. Contrariwise, the vnperfect may be ingendred without séed by mire, mud, doong, carren, rotten timber, or anie other thing, and chieflie by the secret influence and instillation of the celestiall planets, as the sunne and such other. As if you put the haire of an horsse taile in mire, puddle, or in a doonghill for a certeine space, it will turne to a little thin spralling worme, which I haue often séene & experimented. And they are termed vnperfect, not in respect of their owne nature, in which they are perfect, but in comparison of other sorts of liuing things. Among this crue must barnacles be setled. But here some will saie, Let them be perfect or vnperfect, what then? I would faine know, whether Cambrensis be in an errour, or the Irish clergie. For hitherto I sée nothing, but Cambrensis his reason disprooued. And it is often séene that a sound opinion may be weakened by a feeble reason, as we sée manie fine garments marred in the making. It is true: and if anie be desirous to know my mind herein, I suppose, according to my simple iudgement, vnder the correction of both parties, that the barnacle is neither fish nor flesh, but rather a meane betwéene both. As put the case it were enacted by parlement, that it were high treason to eat flesh on fridaie, and fish on sundaie. Trulie I thinke that he that eateth barnacles both these daies, should not be within the compasse of the estatute: yet I would not wish my friend to hazard it, least the barnacle should be found in law fish or flesh, yea and perhaps fish and flesh. As when the lion king of beasts made proclamation, that all horned beasts should auoid his court, one beast hauing but a bunch of flesh in his forehead departed with the rest, least it had béene found in law that his bunch were an horne.

Ge. 2. vers. 7.
Gen. 2. ver. 21.
Mat. 1. ver. 10.
Luc. 1. vers. 34.

Vid. Arist. lib. 1. Meteor. ca. 5. 6. 7.

The barnacle neither fish nor flesh.

But some will peraduenture maruell, that there should be anie liuing thing, that were not fish nor flesh. But they haue no such cause at all. Nits, fleshwormes, bees, butterflies, caterpillers, snailes, grassehoppers, beetels, earewikes, reremise, frogs, toads, adders, snakes, & such other, are liuing things, and yet they are neither fish nor flesh, nor yet red herring: as they that are trained in scholasticall points may easilie iudge. And so I thinke, that if anie were so sharpe set (the estatute aboue rehearsed, presupposed) as to eat fried flies, butterd bees, stued snailes, either on fridaie or sundaie, he could not be therefore indicted of haulte treason, albeit I would not be his ghest, vnlesse I tooke his table to be furnisht with more wholesome and licorous viands. The like question may be mooued of the sell: and if it were well canuassed, it would be found at the leastwise a moot case. But thus farre of barnacles.

The sell whether it be fish or flesh. Thom. p. 1. q. 71. a. 1. q. 3. o.

Ireland is stored of cowes, of excellent horsses, of hawkes, of fish and of foule. They are not without woolues & greihounds to hunt them, bigger of bone and lim than a colt. Their cowes, as also the rest of their cattell, and commonlie what else soeuer the countrie ingendreth (except man) is much lesse in quantitie than those of England, or of other realms. Shéepe few, and those bearing course fleeces, whereof they spin notable rug. Their shéepe haue short and curt tailes. They shéere their shéepe twise yearlie, and if they be left vnshorne, they are therewith rather pained than otherwise. The countrie is verie fruitfull both of corne and grasse. The grasse (for default of good husbandrie) suffered vncut, groweth so ranke in the north parts, that oftentimes it rotteth their cattell. Egles are well knowen to bréed in Ireland, but neither so big, nor so manie as bookes tell. The horsses are of pase easie, in running woonderfull swift, in gallop both false and full indifferent. The nag or the hackenie is verie good for trauelling, albeit others report the contrarie. And if he be broken accordinglie, you shall haue a little tit that

Shéepe.

Egle.

The Irish hobbie.
The nag.

that will trauell a whole daie without anie bait. Their horsses of seruice are called chiefe horsses, being well broken they are of an excellent courage. They reine passinglie, and champe vpon their bridels brauelie, commonlie they amble not but gallop and run. And these horsses are but for skirmishes, not for trauelling, for their stomachs are such, as they disdaine to be hackned. Thereof the report grew, that the Irish hobbie will not hold out in trauelling. You shall haue of the third sort a bastard or mongrell hobbie, néere as tall as the horsse of seruice, strong in trauelling, easie in ambling, and verie swift in running. Of the horsse of seruice they make great store, as wherin at times of néed they repose a great péece of safetie. This brood Volaterane writeth to haue come from Asturea, the countrie of Hispaine, betwéene Gallicia and Portugall, whereof they were named Asturcones, a name now properlie applied to the Hispanish genet.

The chiefe horsse

The mongrell hobbie

Volat. lib. 3 Geog.

Asturcones.

THE NAMES OF THE CIUITIES, BOROUGHS AND HAUEN TOWNES IN IRELAND.

THE THIRD CHAPTER.

DUBLIN the beautie and eie of Ireland, hath béene named by Ptolome, in ancient time, Eblana. Some terme it Dublina, others Dublinia, manie write it Dublinum, authors of better skill name it Dublinium. The Irish call it, Ballée er Cleagh, that is, a towne planted vpon hurdels. For the common opinion is, that the plot vpon which the citie is builded hath béene a marish ground, and for that by the art or inuention of the first founder, the water could not be voided, he was forced to fasten the quakemire with hurdels, and vpon them to build the citie. I heard of some that came of building of houses to this foundation: and other hold opinion that if a cart or waine run with a round and maine pase through a stréet called the high stréet, the houses on ech side shall be perceiued to shake. This citie was builded, or rather the buildings thereof inlarged, about the yeare of our Lord 155. For about this time there arriued in Ireland thrée noble Easterlings that were brethren, Auellanus, Sitaracus, and Yuorus. Auellanus being the eldest brother builded Dublin, Sitaracus Waterford, and Yuorus Limerike. Of the founder Auellanus, Dublin was named Auellana, and after by corruption of speach Eblana. This citie, as it is not in antiquitie inferiour to anie citie in Ireland, so in pleasant situation, in gorgious buildings, in the multitude of people, in martiall chiualrie, in obedience and loialtie, in the abundance of wealth, in largenesse of hospitalitie, in maners and ciuilitie it is superiour to all other cities and townes in that realme. And therefore it is commonlie called the Irish or yoong London. The seat of this citie is of all sides pleasant, comfortable, and wholesome. If you would trauerse hils, they are not far off. If champion ground, it lieth of all parts. If you be delited with fresh water, the famous riuer called the Liffie, named of Ptolome Lybnium, runneth fast by. If you will take the view of the sea, it is at hand. The onlie fault of this citie is, that it is lesse frequented of merchant estrangers, bicause of the bare hauen. Their charter is large. King Henrie the fourth gaue this citie the sword, in the yeare of our Lord 1409, and was ruled by a maior and two bailiffes, which were changed into shiriffes by a charter granted by Edward the sixt, in the yeare of our Lord 1547. In which yeare Iohn Rians and Robert Ians, two worshipfull gentlemen, were collegues in that office, & thereof they are named the last bailiffes & first shiriffes that haue béene in Dublin. It appéereth by the ancient seale of this citie, called *Signum præpositura*, that this citie hath béene in old time gouerned by a prouost.

Dublinum.

Dublin builded.

Auellanus the founder of Dublin

Auellana Eblana.

Dublin the Irish London

The situation of Dublin

The Liffie.

The sword giuen to Dublin

Shiriffes of Dublin 1547

Dublin gouerned by a prouost

The hospitalitie of the maior and the shiriffes for the yeare being, is so large and bountifull, that soothlie (London forepriced) verie few such officers vnder the

The hospitalitie of the maior and shiriffes.

crowne

crowne of England kéepe so great a port, none I am sure greater. The maior, ouer the number of officers that take their dailie repast at his table, keepeth for his yeare in maner open house. And albeit in tearme time his house is frequented as well of the nobilitie as of other potentats of great calling: yet his ordinarie is so good, that a verie few set feasts are prouided for them. They that spend least in their maioraltie (as those of credit, yea and such as bare the office haue informed me) make an ordinarie account of fiue hundred pounds for their viand and diet that yeare: which is no small summe to be bestowed in houskéeping, namelie where vittels are so good cheape, and the presents of friends diuerse and sundrie.

1551. There hath beene of late yeares a worshipfull gentleman, named Patrike Scarsefield, that bare the office of the maioraltie in Dublin, who kept so great port in this yeare, as his hospitalitie to his fame and renowme resteth as yet in fresh memorie. One of his especiall and entire friends entring in communication with the gentleman, his yeare being well neere expired, mooued question, to what he thought his expenses all that yeare amounted? Trulie James (so his friend was named) quoth maister Scarsefield, I take betwéene me and God, when I entered into mine office, the last saint Hierome his daie (which is the morrow of Michaelmasse, on which daie the maior taketh his oth before the chiefe baron, at the excheker within the castell of Dublin) I had thrée barnes well stored and thwackt with corne, and I assured my selfe, that anie one of these thrée had bene sufficient to haue stored mine house with bread, ale, and béere for this yeare. And now God and good companie be thanked, I stand in doubt, whether I shall rub out my maioraltie with my third barne, which is well nigh with my yeare ended. And yet nothing smiteth me so much at the heart, as that the knot of good fellowes that you sée here (he ment the sergeants and officers) are readie to flit from me, and make their next yeares abode with the next maior.

Patrike Scarsefield his hospitalitie.

The maior of Dublin when he is sworne.

And certes I am so much wedded to good fellowship, as if I could mainteine mine house to my contentation, with defraieng of fiue hundred pounds yearelie, I would make humble sute to the citizens, to be their officer these thrée yeares to come. Ouer this, he did at the same time protest with oth, that he spent that yeare in housekéeping twentie tuns of claret wine, ouer and aboue white wine, sacke, malmeseie, muscadell, &c. And in verie deed it was not to be maruelled: for during his maioraltie, his house was so open, as commonly from fiue of the clocke in the morning, to ten at night, his butterie and cellars were with one crew or other frequented. To the haunting of which, ghests were the sooner allured, for that you should neuer marke him or his bedfellow (such was their buxomnesse) once frowne or wrinkle their foreheads, or bend their browes, or glowme their countenances, or make a sowre face at anie ghest, were he neuer so meane. But their interteinment was so notable, as they would sauce their bountifull & deintie fare with heartie and amiable chéere. His porter or anie other officer durst not for both his eares giue the simplest man that resorted to his house Tom drum his interteinment, which is, to hale a man in by the head, and thrust him out by both the shoulders. For he was fullie resolued, that his worship and reputation could not be more distained, than by the currish interteinment of anie ghest. To be briefe (according to the golden verses of the ancient and famous English poet Geffreie Chaucer.)

Tom drum his interteinment,

Chaucer in the prolog of his Canturburie tales

"An housholder, and that a great, was hee,
Saint Iulian he was in his countrie.
His bread, his ale, was alwaie after one,
A better viended man was no where none.
Without bakte meat was neuer his house,
Of fish and flesh, and that so plenteouse.

It

It snewed in his house of meat and drinke,
Of all deinties that men could thinke.
After the sundrie seasons of the yere,
So changed he his meat and his suppere.
Full manie a fat partrich had he in mew,
And manie a breme, and manie a luce in stew."

Some of his friends, that were snudging penniefathers, would take him vp verie roughlie for his lauishing & his outragious expenses, as they tearme it. Tush my maisters (would he saie) take not the matter so hot: who so commeth to my table, and hath no néed of my meat, I know he commeth for the good will he beareth me, and therefore I am beholding to thanke him for his companie: if he resort for néed, how maie I bestow my goods better, than in reléeving the poore? If you had perceiued me so far behind hand, as that I had bene like to haue brought haddocke to paddocke, I would patientlie permit you, both largelie to controll me, and friendlie to reproue me. But so long as I cut so large thongs of mine owne leather, as that I am not yet come to my buckle, and during the time I kéepe my selfe so farre aflote, as that I haue as much water as my ship draweth. I praie pardon me to be liberall in spending, sith God of his goodnesse is gratious in sending.

And in déed so it fell out: for at the end of his maioraltie he owght no man a dotkin. What he dispended was his owne: and euer after during his life, he kept so woorthie a standing house, as that hée séemed to surrender the princes sword to other maiors, and reserued the port & hospitalitie to himselfe. Not long before him was Nicholas Stanihurst then maior, who was so great and good an housholder, that during his maioraltie, the lord chancellor of the realme was his dailie and ordinarie ghest. There hath béene of late worshipfull ports kept by maister Fian, who was twise maior, maister Sedgraue, Thomas Fitz Simons, Robert Cusacke, Walter Cusacke, Nicholas Fitz Simons, Iames Bedlow, Christopher Fagan, and diuerse others. And not onelie their officers so farre excell in hospitalitie, but also the greater part of the citie is generallie addicted to such ordinarie and standing houses, as it would make a man muse which waie they are able to beare it out, but onelie by the goodnesse of God, which is the vpholder and furtherer of hospitalitie. What should I heere speake of their charitable almes, dailie and hourelie extended to the néedie? The poore prisoners both of the Newgate and the castell, with thrée or foure hospitals, are chieflie, if not onelie, relieued by the citizens.

Nicholas Stanihurst

The hospitalitie of Dublin

Furthermore, there are so manie other extraordinarie beggers that dailie swarme there, so charitablie succored, as that they make the whole citie in effect their hospitall. The great expenses of the citizens maie probablie be gathered by the woorthie and fairelike markets, weeklie on wednesdaie and fridaie kept in Dublin. Their shambles is so well stored with meat, and their market with corne, as not onelie in Ireland, but also in other countries you shall not sée anie one shambles, or anie one market better furnished with the one or the other, than Dublin is. The citizens haue from time to time in sundrie conflicts so galled the Irish, that euen to this daie, the Irish feare a ragged and tagged blacke standard that the citizens haue, almost through tract of time worne to the hard stumps. This standard they carrie with them in hostings, being neuer displaied but when they are readie to enter into battell, and come to the shocke. The sight of which danteth the Irish aboue measure.

The shambles and markets at Dublin

The blacke standard.

And for the better training of their youth in martiall exploits, the citizens vse to muster foure times by the yeare: on Blacke mondaie which is the morrow of Easter daie, on Maie daie, saint Iohn Baptist his eeue, and saint Peter his eeue. Whereof two are ascribed to the maior & shiriffes: the other two, to wit, the musters on Maie daie and saint Peter his eeue, are assigned to the maior and shiriffes of the Bull ring. The maior

The musters of Dublin

The maior of the Bull ring

maior of the Bull ring is an office elected by the citizens, to be as it were capteine or gardian of the batchelers and the vnwedded youth of the ciuitie. And for the yeare he hath authoritie to chastise and punish such as frequent brothelhouses, and the like vnchast places. He is tearmed the maior of the Bull ring, of an iron ring that sticketh in the cornemarket, to which the bulles that are yearelie bated be vsuallie tied: which ring is had by him and his companie in so great price, as if anie citizen batcheler hap to marrie, the maior of the Bull ring and his ciuic conduct the bridegroome vpon his returne from church, to the market place, and there with a solemne kisse for his *Vltimum vale*, he dooth homage vnto the Bull ring.

The blacke mondaie

Dublin inhabited by the Bristollians. This was about the yeare of our Lord 1209.

The Blacke mondaie muster sprong of this occasion. Soone after Ireland was conquered by the Britons, and the greater part of Leinster pacified, diuerse townesmen of Bristow flitted from thense to Dublin, and in short space the ciuitie was by them so well inhabited, as it grew to bée verie populous. Whereupon the citizens hauing ouer great affiance in the multitude of the people, and so consequentlie being somewhat retchlesse in héeding the mounteine enimie that lurked vnder their noses, were woont to rome and roile in clusters, sometime thrée or foure miles from the towne. The Irish enimie spieng that the citizens were accustomed to fetch such od vagaries, especiallie on the holie daies, & hauing an inkling withall by some false clatterfeit or other, that a companie of them would haue ranged abrode, on mondaie in the Easter weeke towards the wood of Cullen, which is distant two miles from Dublin, they laie in stale verie well appointed, and laid in sundrie places for their comming. The citizens rather minding the pleasure they should presentlie inioy, than forecasting the hurt that might insue, flockt vnarmed out of the ciuitie to the wood, where being intercepted by them that laie hoouing in ambush, they were to the number of fiue hundred miserablie slaine. Wherevpon the remnant of the citizens deeming that vnluckie time to be a crosse or a dismall daie, gaue it the appellation of Black mondaie.

The citie soone after being peopled by a fresh supplie of Bristollians, to dare the Irish enimie, agréed to banket yearelie in that place, which to this daie is obserued. For the maior and the shiriffs with the citizens repaire to the wood of Cullen, in which place the maior bestoweth a costlie dinner within a mote or a rundell, and both the shiriffs within another: where they are so well garded with the youth of the ciuitie, as the mounteine enimie dareth not attempt to snatch as much as a pastie crust from thense. Dublin hath at this daie within the citie and in the suburbs these churches that insue, of which the greater number are paroch churches, onelie Christs church with a few oratories and chappels excepted. Christs church, otherwise named *Ecclesia sanctæ trinitatis*, a cathedrall church, the ancientest that I can find recorded of all the churches now standing in Dublin. I take it to haue beene builded, if not in Auellanus his time, yet soone after by the Danes. The building of which was both repaired & inlarged by Citrius prince of Dublin, at the earnest request of Donat the bishop, and soone after the conquest it hath béene much beautified by Robert Fitz Stephans and Strangbow the erle of Penbroke, who with his sonne is in the bodie of the church intoomed. The chappell that standeth in the choire, commonlie called the new chappell, was builded by Gerald Fitz Thomas earle of Kildare, in the yeare of our Lord 1510, where he is intoomed.

The churches of Dublin

Christs church

Saint Patrikes church, a cathedrall church, indued with notable liuings, and diuerse fat benefices. It hath a chappell at the north doore which is called the paroch church. This church was founded by the famous and woorthie prelate Iohn Commin, about the yeare of our Lord 1197. This foundation was greatlie aduanced by the liberalitie of king Iohn. There hath risen a great contention betwixt this church and Christes church for antiquitie, wherein doubtlesse S. Patrike his church ought to giue place, vnlesse they haue further matter to shew, and

The controuersie betwéene Christ church and saint Patriks church and better reasons to build vpon than their foundations, in which this church by manie yeares is inferior to the other. Saint Nicholas, Saint Michaell, Saint Verberosse, or Saint Warburgh, so called of a Chesshire virgine. The citizens of Chester founded this church, with two chappels thereto annexed, the one called our ladies chappell, the other S. Martins chappell. Hir feast is kept the third of Februarie. This church with a great part of the citie was burned in the yeare 1301, but againe by the parochians reedified. Saint Iohn the euangelist, Saint Audeon, which is corruptlie called Saint Ouen, or Owen. His feast is solemnized the fourtéenth of August. The paroch of this church is accounted the best in Dublin, for that the greater number of the aldermen and the worships of the citie are demurrant within that paroch.

Saint Tullocke now prophaned. In this church in old time, the familie of the Fitz Simons was for the more part buried. The paroch was meared from the Crane castell, to the fish shambles, called the Cockhill, with Preston his innes, & the lane thereto adioining, which scope is now vnited to Saint Iohn his paroch. S. Katharine, S. Michan or Mighan, Saint Iames, his feast is celebrated the fiue and twentith of Iulie, on which date in ancient time was there a woorthie faire kept at Dublin, continuing six daies, vnto which resorted diuers merchants, as well from England, as from France and Flanders. And they affoorded their wares so dog-cheape, in respect of the citie merchants, that the countrie was yeare by yeare sufficientlie stored by strangers: and the citie merchants not vttering their wares, but to such as had not readie chinkes, and therevpon forced to run on the score, were verie much impouerished. Wherefore partlie thorough the canuasing of the towne merchants, and partlie by the winking of the rest of the citizens, being woon vpon manie faire glosed promises, by placing bopéepe to beare themselues ouerlie in the matter, that famous mart was supprest, and all forren saile wholie abandoned. Yet for a memoriall of this notable faire, a few cottages, booths, and alepoles are pitched at Saint Iames his gate. Saint Michaell of Poules, *alias* Paules, Saint Brigide, Saint Keuin, Saint Peter *Demonte*, or vpon the hill, appendant to Saint Patrikes church. Saint Stephan, this was erected for an hospitall for poore, lame, and impotent lazers, where they abide to this date, although not in such chast and sincere wise, as the founders will was vpon the erection thereof. The maior with his brethren on Saint Stephan his date (which is one of their station daies) repaireth thither, and there dooth offer. Saint Andrew now prophaned.

Fitz Simons.

S. Iames his faire.

Both the gates neere the White friers, Saint Keuen his gate, Hogs gate, Dammes gate, Poule gate, *alias* Paules gate, Newgate, a goale or prison, Wine tauerne gate, Saint Audeon his gate, hard by the church going downe towards the Cockestréet. The reason why this gate, and the Wine tauerne gate were builded, procéeded of this. In the yeare 1315, Edward Bruse a Scot, & brother to Robert Bruse king of Scots arriued in the north of Ireland. From whence he marched on forwards with his armie, vntill he came as far as Castleknocke. The citizens of Dublin being sore amazed at the sudden and Scarborough approch of so puissant an enimie, burned all the houses in Saint Thomas his stréet, least he should vpon his repaire to Dublin haue anie succour in the suburbs. The maior (named Robert Notingham) and communaltie being in this distresse, razed downe an abbeie of the frier preachers, called Saint Sauiour his monasterie, and brought the stones thereof to these places, where the gates now stand, and all along that waie did cast a wall for the better fortifieng of the citie, mistrusting that the wals that went along both the keies, should not haue béene of sufficient force to outhold the enimie. The Scots hauing intelligence of the fortifieng of Dublin, and reckoning it a follie to laie siege to so impregnable a citie, marched toward a place not far from Dublin, called the

The names of the gates of the citie and suburbs of Dublin.

Salmon

Salmon leape, where pitching their tents for foure daies, they remooued towards the Naas. That when the citie was past this danger, king Edward the second gaue strict commandement to the citizens to build the abbeie they razed, saieng, that although lawes were squatted in warre, yet notwithstanding they ought to be reuiued in peace. Gurmund his gate, hard by the Cucall, or Coockolds post. Some suppose, that one Gurmundus builded this gate, and thereof to take the name. Others iudge, that the Irish assaulting the citie, were discomfited by the earle of Ormond, then by good hap soiourning at Dublin. And because he issued out at that gate, to the end the valiant exploit and famous conquest of so woorthie a potentate should be ingrailed in perpetuall memorie, the gate bare the name of Ormond his gate. The bridge gate, Saint Nicholas his gate, Saint Patrike his gate, Bungan his gate, the Newstréet gate, Saint Thomas his gate, Saint Iames his gate.

The names of the streets, bridges, lanes, and other notorious places in Dublin. The Dammes stréet, the Castle stréet, stretching to the pillorie, Saint Verberosses stréet, Saint Iohn his stréet, *alias* fish shamble street, Skinners rew reaching from the pillorie to the tolehall, or to the high crosse. The high stréet bearing to the high pipe. This pipe was builded in the yeare 1308, by a woorthie citizen

John Decer. named Iohn Decer, being then maior of Dublin. He builded not long before that time the bridge hard by Saint Woolstans that reacheth ouer the Liffie. The Newgate stréet, from the Newgate to Saint Audoen his church. Saint Nicholas his street, the Wine tauerne street, the Cooke street, the Bridge stréet. This stréet with the greater part of the keie was burnt in the yeare 1304. The Woodkeie, the Merchant keie, Osmontowne, so called of certeine Easterlings or Nor-

Ostmanni. mans, properlie the Danes that were called Ostmanni. They planted themselues hard by the water side neere Dublin, and discomfited at Clontarfe in a skirmish diuerse of the Irish. The names of the Irish capteins slaine were Brian Borrough,

1050. Magh macke Bren, Tadie Okellie, Dolin Abertegan, Gille Barramede. These were Irish potentates, and before their discomfiture they ruled the rost. They were interred at Kilmainanne ouer against the great crosse. There arriued a fresh sup-

1095. plie of Easterlings at Dublin in the yeare 1095, and setled themselues on the other side of the citie, which of them to this daie is called Ostmantowne, that is, the

Ostmantowne why so called. towne of the Ostmannes, whereof there ariseth great likelihood to haue béene a separat towne from the citie, being parted from Dublin by the Liffie, as Southworke is seuered from London by Thames. Saint Thomas his street; this street was burnt by mishap in the yeare 1343. The New buildings, the New stréet, Saint Francis his stréet, the Kowme, Saint Patrike his street, the backeside of Saint Sepulchres, Saint Keuen his street, the Poule, or Paulmilstréet, Saint Brigids stréet, the Shéepe street, *alias* the Ship stréet. For diuerse are of opinion, that the sea had passage that waie, and thereof to be called the Ship stréet.

This as it séemeth not wholie impossible, considering that the sea floweth and ebbeth hard by it: so it carieth a more colour of truth with it, because there haue béene found there certeine iron rings fastned to the towne wall, to hold and grapple botes withall. Saint Verberosses lane, vp to Saint Nicholas his stréet, now inclosed,

The lanes. Saint Michaell his lane, beginning at Saint Michaell his pipe, Christchurch lane, Saint Iohn his lane, Ram lane, *alias* the Schoolehouse lane, Saint Audoen his lane, Kesers lane. This lane is stéepe and slipperie, in which otherwhiles, they that make more hast, than good spéed, clinke their bums to the stones. And therefore the ruder sort, whether it be through corruption of spéech, or for that they giue it a nickename, commonlie terme it, not so homelie, as trulie, Kisse arsse lane. Rochell lane, *alias* Backelane, on the southside of the flesh shambles, the Cookestréet lane, Frapper lane, Giglottes hill, Marie lane, Saint Tullocke his lane, Scarlet lane, *alias* Isouds lane, Saint Pulchers lane, Saint Keuin his lane, the White

Whitefriers lane, Saint Stephan his lane, Hogs lane, the Sea lane, Saint George his lane, where in old time were builded diuerse old and ancient monuments. And as an insearcher of antiquities may (by the view thereto be taken) coniecture, the better part of the suburbs of Dublin should séeme to haue stretched that waie. But the inhabitants being dailie and hourelie molested and preied by their prolling mounteine neighbors, were forced to suffer their buildings fall in decaie, and embaied themselues within the citie wals.

The old Escheker

Among other monuments, there is a place in that lane called now Collets innes, which in old time was the Escaxar or Excheker. Which should implie that the princes court would not haue béene kept there, unlesse the place had béene taken to be cocksure. But in fine it fell out contrarie. For the baron sitting there solemnlie, and as it seemed retchlesse, the Irish espieng the oportunitie, rushed into the court in plumps, where surprising the vnweaponed multitude, they committed horrible slaughters by sparing none that came vnder their dint: and withall as far as their Scarborough leasure could serue them, they ransacke the prince his threasure, vpon which mishap the excheker was from thence remooued. There hath béene also in that lane a chappell dedicated to saint George, likelie to haue béene founded by some worthie knight of the garter. The maior with his brethren was accustomed with great triumphs and pageants yéerelie on saint George his feast to repaire to that chappell, and there to offer. This chappell hath béene of late razed, and the stones thereof by consent of the assemblie turned to a common ouen, conuerting the ancient monument of a doutie, aduenturous, and holie knight, to the colerake swéeping of a puffloafe baker. The great bridge going to Ostmantowne, saint Nicholas his bridge, the Poule gate bridge, repaired by Nicholas Stanihurst about the yeere one thousand fiue hundred forty & foure, the Castell bridge, S. Iames his bridge.

S. George his chappell

The bridges

1554

The castell

The castell of Dublin was builded by Henrie Loundres (sometime archbishop of Dublin, and lord iustice of Ireland) about the yéere of our Lord one thousand two hundred and twentie. This castell hath beside the gate house foure goodlie and substantiall towers, of which one of them is named Bermingham his tower, whether it were that one of the Berminghams did inlarge the building thereof, or else that he was long in duresse in that tower. This castell hath béene of late much beautified with sundrie and gorgious buildings in the time of sir Henrie Sidneie, sometimes lord deputie of Ireland. In the commendation of which buildings an especiall welwiller of his lordships penned these verses.

1220

Bermingham his tower

1566

"Gesta libri referunt multorum clara virorum,
Laudis & in chartis stigmata fixa manent.
Verùm Sidnæi laudes hæc saxa loquuntur,
Nec iacet in solis gloria tanta libris.
Si libri pereant, homines remanere valebunt,
Si pereant homines, ligna manere queunt.
Lignáque si pereant, non ergò saxa peribunt,
Saxaque si pereant tempore, tempus erit.
Si pereat tempus, minimè consumitur æuum,
Quod cum principio, sed sine fine manet.
Dum libri florent, homines dum viuere possunt,
Dum quoque cum lignis saxa manere valent,
Dum remanet tempus, dum denique permanet æuum,
Laus tua, Sidnæi, digna perire nequit."

Isonds tower.

There standeth neere the castell ouer against a void roome called Preston his innes, a tower named Isonds tower. It tooke the name of la Beale Isoud, daughter to Anguish king of Ireland. It séemeth to haue béene a castle of pleasure for the

E 2 kings

kings to recreat themselues therein. Which was not vnlike, considering that a meaner towne might serue such single soule kings as were at those daies in Ireland. Chappell Isoud. There is a village hard by Dublin, called of the said la Beale, chappell Isoud.

Saint Pulchers. Saint Pulchers, the archbishop of Dublin his house, as well pleasantlie sited as gorgeouslie builded. Some hold opinion, that the beautifuller part of this house was of set purpose fired by an archbishop, to the end the gouernors (which for the more part laie there) should not haue so goodliking to the house: not far disagréeing from the policie that I heard a noble man tell he used: who hauing a surpassing good horsse, and such a one as ouer ran in a set race other chosen horsses, did bobtaile him vpon his returne to the stable, least anie of his fréends casting a fantasie to the beast, should craue him. The noble man being so bountifullie giuen, as that of liberalitie he could not, & of discretion he would séeme to giue his fréend the repulse in a more weightie request than that were.

The names of the fields adioining to Dublin. Saint Stephans gréene, Hogging gréene, the Steine, Ostmantowne gréene. In the further end of this field is there a hole commonlie termed Scald brothers hole, a labyrinth reaching two large miles vnder the earth. Scaldbrother. This hole was in old time frequented by a notorious théefe named Scaldbrother, wherein he would hide all the bag and baggage that he could pilfer. The varlet was so swift on foot, as he hath eftsoones outrun the swiftest and lustiest yoong men in all Ostmantowne, maugre their heads, bearing a pot or a pan of theirs on his shoulders to his den. And now and then, in derision of such as pursued him, he would take his course vnder the gallows, which standeth verie nigh his caue (a fit signe for such an inne) and so being shrowded within his lodge, he reckoned himselfe cocksure, none being found at that time so hardie as would aduenture to intangle himselfe within so intricat a maze. But as the pitcher that goeth often to the water, commeth at length home broken: so this lustie youth would not surcease from open catching, forcible snatching, and priuie prolling, till time he was by certeine gaping groomes that laie in wait for him, intercepted, fléeing toward his couch, hauing vpon his Scaldbrother executed. apprehension no more wrong doone him, than that he was not sooner hanged on that gallowes, through which in his youth and iolitie he was woont to run. Little Iohn. There standeth in Ostmantowne gréene an hillocke, named little Iohn his shot. The occasion proceeded of this.

1180 Robert Hood. In the yéere one thousand one hundred foure score and nine, there ranged thrée robbers and outlaws in England, among which Robert Hood and little Iohn were chéefeteins, of all théeues doubtlesse the most courteous. Robert Hood being betraied at a nunrie in Scotland called Bricklies, the remnant of the crue was scattered, and euerie man forced to shift for himselfe. Wherevpon little Iohn was faine to flée the realme by sailing into Ireland, where he soiorned for a few daies at Dublin. The citizens being doone to vnderstand the wandering outcast to be an excellent archer, requested him hartilie to trie how far he could shoot at randon: who yéelding to their behest, stood on the bridge of Dublin, and shot to that mole hill, leauing behind him a monument, rather by his posteritie to be woondered, than possiblie by anie man liuing to be counterscored. But as the repaire of so notorious a champion to anie countrie would soone be published, so his abode could not be long concealed: and therefore to eschew the danger of lawes, he fled into Scotland, Little Iohn deceased. where he died at a towne or village called Morauie. Gerardus Mercator in his cosmographie affirmeth, that in the same towne the bones of an huge and mightie man are kept, which was called little Iohn, among which bones, the hucklebone or hipbone was of such largenesse, as witnesseth Hector Boetius, that he thrust his arme through the hole thereof. And the same bone being suted to the other parts of his bodie, did argue the man to haue béene fourtéene foot long, which was a prettie length for a little Iohn. Whereby appéereth that he was called little

Iohn

Iohn nonicallie, like as we terme him an honest man whom we take for a knaue in graine.

Neere to the citie of Dublin are the foure ancient manors annexed to the crowne, which are named to this daie, the Kings land, to wit, Newcastell, Missaggard, Eschire, and Crumlin. The manor of Crumlin paieth a great chéefe rent to the prince than anie of the other thrée, which procéeded of this. The seneschall being offended with the tenants for their misdemeanor, tooke them vp verie sharplie in the court, and with rough and minatorie spéeches began to menace them. The lobbish and desperat clobberiousnesse, taking the matter in dudgeon, made no more words, but knockt their seneschall on the costard, and left him there spralling on the ground for dead. For which detestable murther their rent was inhansed, and they paie at this daie nine pence an acre, which is double to anie of the other thrée manors. The Kings land. Crumlin.

Waterford was founded by Sitaracus (as is aforesaid) in the yeere one hundred fiftie and fiue. Ptolome nameth it Manapia, but whie he appropriateth that name to this citie, neither dooth he declare nor I ghesse. This city is properlie builded, and verie well compact, somewhat close by reason of their thicke buildings and narrow stréets. The hauen is passing good, by which the citizens through the intercourse of forren traffike in short space atteine to abundance of wealth. The soile about it is not all of the best, by reason of which the aire is not verie subtill, yea nathelesse the sharpnesse of their wittes séemeth to be nothing rebated or dulled by reason of the grossenesse of the aire. For in good sooth the townesmen, and namelie students are pregnant in conceiuing, quicke in taking, and sure in kéeping. The citizens are verie héedie and warie in all their publike affaires, slow in the determining of matters of weight, louing to looke yer they leape. In choosing their magistrate, they respect not onlie his riches, but also they weigh his experience. And therefore they elect for their maior neither a rich man that is yoong, nor an old man that is poore. They are chéerefull in the interteinment of strangers, hartie one to another, nothing giuen to factions. They loue no idle benchwhistlers, nor luskish faitors: for yoong and old are wholie addicted to thriuing, the men commonlie to traffike, the women to spinning and carding. As they distill the best *Aqua vitæ*, so they spin the choisest rug in Ireland. A friend of mine being of late demurrant in London, and the weather by reason of an hard hoare frost being somwhat nipping, repaired to Paris garden, clad in one of these Waterford rugs. The mastiffs had no sooner espied him, but déeming he had béene a beare, would faine haue baited him. And were it not that the dogs were partlie muzzled, and partlie chained, he doubted not, but that he should haue béene well tugd in this Irish rug, wherevpon he solemnlie vowed neuer to see beare baiting in anie such wéed. The citie of Waterford hath continued to the crowne of England so loiall, that it is not found registred since the conquest to haue béene distained with the smallest spot, or dusked with the least freckle of treason, notwithstanding the sundrie assaults of traitorous attempts: and therefore the cities armes are deckt with this golden word, *Intacta manet*: a posie as well to be hartilie followed, as greatlie admired of all true and loiall townes. Waterford. Manapia. The posie of Waterford.

Limerike called in Latine *Limericum* was builded by Yuorus, as is before mentioned, about the yéere one hundred fiftie and fiue. This citie coasteth on the sea hard vpon the riuer Sennan, whereby are most notablie seuered Mounster and Connaght: the Irish name this citie Loumneagh, and thereof in English it is named Limerike. The towne is planted in an Iland, which plot in old time, before the building of the citie was stored with grasse. During which time it happened, that one of the Irish potentates, raising warre against another of his peers, incamped in that Ile, hauing so great a troope of horssemen, as the horsses eate vp the grasse Limerike. Sennan the riuer of Limerike. Limerike why so called.

iii

in foure and twentie houres. Wherevpon for the notorious number of horsses, the place is called Loum ne augh, that is, the horsse bare, or a place made bare or eaten vp by horsses. The verie maine sea is thrée score miles distant from the towne, and yet the riuer is so nauigable, as a ship of two hundred tuns may saile to the kere of the citie. The riuer is termed in Irish Shaune amne, that is, the old riuer: for shaune is old, & amne is a riuer deducted of the Latine word *Amnis*. The building of Limerike is sumptuous and substantiall.

Corke

Corke, in Latine *Coracium* or *Corracium*, the fourth citie of Ireland happilie planted on the sea. Their hauen is an hauen roiall. On the land side they are incombred with euill neighbors the Irish outlaws, that they are faine to watch their gates hourlie, to kéepe them shut at seruice times, at meales from sun to sun, nor suffer anie stranger to enter the citie with his weapon, but the same to leaue at a lodge appointed. They walke out at seasons for recreation with power of men furnished. They trust not the countrie adioining, but match in wedlocke among themselues onelie, so that the whole citie is welnigh linked one to the other in affinitie.

Drogheda

Drogheda, accounted the best towne in Ireland, and trulie not far behind some of their cities. The one moitie of this towne is in Meth, the other planted on the further side of the water lieth in Ulster. There runneth a blind prophesie on this towne, that Rosse was, Dublin is, Drogheda shall be the best of the thrée.

Rosse

Rosse, an hauen towne in Mounster not far from Waterford, which séemeth to haue béene in ancient time a towne of great port. Whereof sundrie & probable coniectures are giuen, as well by the old ditches that are now a mile distant from the wals of Rosse, betweene which wals and ditches the reliks of the ancient wals, gates, and towers, placed betweene both are yet to be seene. The towne is builded in a barren soile, and planted among a crue of naughtie and prolling neighbours. And in old time when it florished, albeit the towne were sufficientlie peopled, yet as long as it was not compassed with wals, they were formed with watch & ward, to keepe it from the gréedie snatching of the Irish enimies. With whome as they were generallie molested, so the priuat cousening of one pezzant on a sudden, incensed them to enuiron their towne with strong and substantiall wals. There repaired one of the Irish to this towne on horssebacke, and espieng a peece of cloth on a merchants stall, tooke hold thereof, and bet the cloth to the lowest price he could. As the merchant and he stood dodging one with the other in cheaping the ware, the horsseman considering that he was well mounted, and that the merchant and he had growne to a price, made wise as though he would haue drawne to his purse, to haue defraied the monie. The cloth in the meane while being tucked vp and placed before him, he gaue the spur to his horsse and ran awaie with the cloth, being not imbard from his posting pase, by reason the towne was not perclosed either with ditch or wall. The townesmen being pinched at the heart, that one rascal in such scornefull wise should giue them the slampaine, not so much weieng the slendernesse of the losse, as the shamefulnesse of the foile, they put their heads togither, consulting how to preuent either the sudden rushing, or the posthast fliens of anie such aduenturous rakehell hereafter.

Rose of Rosse

In which consultation a famous Dido, a chast widow, a politike dame, a bountifull gentlewoman, called Rose, who representing in sinceritie of life the swéetnesse of that hearbe whose name she bare, vnfolded the deuise, how anie such future mischance should be preuented, and withall opened hir coffers liberallie, to haue it furthered: two good properties in a councellor. Hir deuise was, that the towne should incontinentlie be inclosed with wals, & therewithall promised to discharge the charges, so that they would not sticke to find out labourers. The deuise of this worthie matrone being wise, and the offer liberall, the townesmen agreed

to

to follow the one, and to put their helping hands to the atchiuing of the other. The worke was begun, which thorough the multitude of hands séemed light. For the whole towne was assembled, tag and rag, cut and long taile, none exempted, but such as were bedred and impotent. Some were tasked to delue, others appointed with mattocks to dig, diuerse allotted to the vnheaping of rubbish, manie bestowed to the carriage of stones, sundrie occupied in tempering of morter, the better sort busied in ouerseeing the workmen, ech one according to his vocation imploied, as though the ciuitie of Carthage were afresh in building, as it is feathe versified by the golden poet Virgil, and neathe Englished by master doctor Phaer.

The Moores with courage went to worke,
some vnder burdens grones.
Some at the wals and towrs with hands
were tumbling vp the stones.
Some measurd out a place to build
their mansion house within.
Some lawes and officers to make
in parlment did begin.
An other had an hauen cast,
and deepe they trench the ground,
Some other for the games and plaies
a statelie place had found.
And pillers great they cut for kings,
to garnish foorth their wals.
And like as bees among the flours,
when fresh the summer fals,
In shine of sunne applie their worke,
when growne is vp their yoong:
Or when their hiues they gin to stop,
and home sweet is sproong,
That all their caues and cellars close
with dulcet liquor fils,
Some doo outlade, some other bring
the stuffe with readie wils.
Sometime they rome, and all at once
doo from their mangers fet
The slothfull drones, that would consume,
and nought would doo to get.
The worke it heats, the home smels,
of flours and thime ywet.

But to returne from Dido of Carthage, to Rose of Rosse, and hir worke. The labourers were so manie, the worke, by reason of round and exchekeř paiment, so well applied, the quarrie of faire marble so néere at hand (for they affirme, that out of the trenches and ditches hard by their rampiers, the stones were had: and all that plot is so stonie, that the foundation is an hard rocke) that these wals with diuerse braue turrets were suddenlie mounted, and in manner sooner finished, than to the Irish enimies notified: which I wisse was no small corsie to them. These wals in circuit are equall to London wals. It hath thre gorgeous gates, Bishop his gate, on the east side: Algate, on the east southeast side: and Southgate, on the south part. This towne was no more famoused for the [illegible], than it was for a notable wooden bridge that stretched from the towne vnto the other side of the water, which must haue béene by reasonable surmise at the [illegible], if not more

[illegible]

Diuerse of the poales, logs, and stakes, with which the bridge was vnderpropt, sticke to this daie in the water. A man would here suppose, that so flourishing a towne, so firmelie builded, so substantiallie walled, so well peopled, so plentiouslie with thriftie artificers stored, would not haue fallen to anie sudden decaie.

Rosse decaie.

But as the secret and déepe iudgements of God are veiled within the couerture of his diuine maiestie, so it standeth not with the dulnesse of man his wit, to beat his braines in the curious insearching of hidden mysteries. Wherefore I, as an historian vndertaking in this treatise, rather plainelie to declare what was doone, than rashlie to inquire why it should be doone, purpose, by God his assistance, to accomplish, as néere as I can, my dutie in the one, leauing the other to the friuolous deciding of busie heads. This Rose, who was the foundresse of these former rehearsed walls, had issue thrée sonnes (howbeit some hold opinion, that they were but hir nephues) who being bolstered out thorough the wealth of their moother, and supported by their traffike, made diuerse prosperous voiages into forren countries. But as one of the thrée chapmen was imploied in his traffike abroad, so the prettie poplet his wife began to be a fresh occupieng giglot at home, and by report fell so farre acquainted with a religious cloisterer of the towne, as that he gat within the lining of hir smocke. Both the parties wallowing ouerlong in the stinking puddle of adulterie, suspicion began to créepe in some townesmens braines, and to be briefe, it came so farre, thorough the iust iudgement of God, to light, whether it were that she was with child in hir husband his absence, or that hir louer vsed hir fondlie in open presence, as the presumption was not onelie vehement, but also the fact too apparent. Hir vnfortunat husband had no sooner notice giuen him vpon his returne of these sorowfull newes, than his fingers began to nibble, his teeth to grin, his eies to trickle, his eares to dindle, his head to dazell, insomuch as his heart being seared with gelousie, and his wits installed thorough phrensie, he became as mad as a March hare.

The pangs of gelousie.

But how heauilie soeuer hir husband tooke it, dame Rose and all hir friends (which were in effect all the townesmen, for that she was their common benefactresse) were grilled at their hearts, as well to heare of the enormious adulterie, as to sée the bedlem pangs of brainsicke gelousie. Wherevpon diuerse of the townesmen grunting and grudging at the matter, said that the fact was horrible, and that it were a deed of charitie vtterlie to grub awaie such wild shrubs from the towne, and if this were in anie dispunishable wise raked vp in the ashes, they should no sooner trauerse the seas, than some other would inkindle the like fire afresh, and so consequentlie dishonest their wiues, and make their husbands to become changelings, as being turned from sober mood to be hornewood, because rutting wiues make often rammish husbands, as our prouerb dooth inferre. Others soothing their fellowes in these mutinies turned the priuat iniurie vnto a publike quarell, and a number of the townesmen conspiring togither flocked in the dead of the night, well appointed, to the abbeie, wherein the frier was cloistered (the monument of which abbeie is yet to be séene at Rosse on the south side) where vnderspairing the gates, and bearing vp the dormitorie doore, they stabbed the adulterer with the rest of the couent thorough with their weapons. Where they left them goaring in their bloud, roaring in their cabbins, and gasping vp their flitting ghosts in their couches.

The vprore was great, and they to whome the slaughter before hand was not imparted, were wonderfullie thereat astonied. But in especiall the remnant of the cleargie bare verie hollow hearts to the townesmen, and how fréendlie their outward countenances were, yet they would not with inward thought forget nor forgiue so horrible a murther, but were fullie resolued, whensoeuer oportunitie serued them, to sit in their skirts, by making them soulfe as sorowfull a kyrie. These three thrée brethren not long after this bloudie exploit, sped them into some outlandish countrie to continue their trade. The religious men being doone to vnderstand, as it seemed, by some of their neighbors, which forsailed them homeward, that these thrée brethren were readie to be imbarked, slunkt priuilie out of the towne, and resorted to the mouth of the hauen, néere a castell, named Hulke tower, Hulke tower which is a notable marke for pilots, in directing them which ware to steine their ships, and to eschew the danger of the craggie rocks there on euerie side of the shore peking. Some iudge that the said Rose was foundresse of this tower, and of purpose did build it for the safetie of hir children, but at length it turned to their bane. For these reuengers nightlie did not misse to hare a lanterne on the top of the rocks, that were on the other side of the water. Which practise was not long by them continued, when these thrée passengers being saile with a lustie gale of wind, made right vpon the lanterne, not doubting, but it had beene the Hulke tower. But they tooke their marke so farre amisse, as they were not ware, till time their ship was dasht and pasht against the rocks, and all the passengers ouerwhirled in the sea.

This heauie hap was not so sorowfull vnto the townesmen, as it was gladsome to the religious, thinking that they had in part cried them acquittance, the more that they, which were drowned, were the archbrochers of their brethrens bloud. Howbeit they would not crie hoa here, but sent in post some of their couent to Rome, where they inhansed the slaughter of the fraternitie so heinouslie, and concealed their owne prankes so couertlie, as the pope excommenged the towne, the towne accursed the friers: so that there was such cursing and banning of all hands, and such dissentious hurlie burlie raised betwéene themselues, as the estate of that flourishing towne was turned arsie versie, topside the otherwaie, and from abundance of prosperitie quite exchanged to extreame penurie.

The wals stand to this daie, a few stréets and houses in the towne, no small parcell thereof is turned to orchards and gardens. The greater part of the towne is stéepe and steaming vpward. Their church is called Christs church, in the north side whereof is placed a monument called the king of Denmarke his toome, whereby coniecture may rise, that the Danes were founders of that church. This Rosse is called Rosse *Noua*, or Rosse *Ponti*, by reason of their bridge. That which they call old Rosse, beareth east thrée miles from this Rosse, into the countrie of Weisford, an ancient manour of the earle of Kildares. There is the third Rosse on the other side of the water, called Rosse Ibarcan, so named, for that it standeth in the countrie of Kilkennie, which is diuided into thrée parts, into Ibercan, Ida, & Idouth. Weisford a hauen towne not far from Rosse, I find no great matters thereof recorded, but onelie that it is to be had in great price of all the English posteritie, planted in Ireland, as a towne that was the first fortresse and harboresse of the English conquerors.

The present estate of Rosse.

New Rosse, old Rosse.

Rosse Ibarcan.

Weisford.

Kilkennie, the best vplandish towne, or (as they terme it) the properest drie towne in Ireland, it is parted into the high towne, and the Irish towne. The Irish towne claimeth a corporation apart from the high towne, whereby great factions grow dailie betwéene the inhabitants. True it is, that the Irish towne is the ancienter, and was called the old Kilkennie, being vnder the bishop his becke, as they are or ought to be at this present. The high towne was builded by the English after the conquest, and had a parcell of the Irish towne thereto vnited, by the bishop his grant, made vnto the founders vpon their earnest request. In the yeare 1400, Robert Talbot a worthie gentleman, inclosed with wals the better part of this towne, by which it was greatlie fortified. This gentleman deceased in the yeare 1415. In this towne in the choire of the frier preachers, William Marshall earle marshall and earle of Penbroke was buried, who departed this life in the yeare 1231.

Kilkennie.

1400

Robert Talbot.

William Marshall.

1231 Richard brother to William, to whome the inheritance descended, within thrée yeares after deceased at Kilkennie, being wounded to death in a field giuen
1234 in the heath of Kildare, in the yeare 1234, the twelfe of Aprill, and was intoomed with his brother, according to the old epitaph héere mentioned

"Hic comes est positus Richardus vulnere fossus,
Cuius sub fossa Kilkenia continet ossa."

The churches of Kilkennie.

This towne hath thrée churches, saint Kennies church, our ladies church, *alias* S. Maries church, and S. Patrikes church with the abbeie of S. John. S. Kennies church is their chéefe and cathedrall church, a worthie foundation as well for gorgeous buildings, as for notable liuings. In the west end of the churchyard of late haue béene founded a grammar schoole by the right honorable Peirce or Peter Butler erle of Ormond and Ossorie, and by his wife the countesse of Ormond, the ladie Margaret fitz Gerald, sister to Girald fitz Girald the earle of Kildare that last was. Out of which schoole haue sprouted such proper impes, through the painefull diligence, and the laboursome industrie of a famous lettered man M. Peter White (sometime fellow of Oriall college in Oxford, and schoolemaister in Kilkennie) as generallie the whole weale publike of Ireland, and especiallie the southerne parts of that Iland are greatlie thereby furthered. This gentlemans method in training vp youth was rare and singular, framing the education according to the scholers veine. If he found him frée, he would bridle him like a wise Isocrates from his booke; if he perceiued him to be dull, he would spur him forward; if he vnderstood that he were the woorse for beating, he would win him with rewards: finallie, by interlasing studie with recreation, sorrow with mirth, paine with pleasure, sowernesse with sweetnesse, roughnesse with mildnesse, he had so good successe in schooling his pupils, as in good sooth I may boldlie bide by it, that in the realme of Ireland was no grammar schoole so good, in England I am well assured none better. And bicause it was my happie hap (God and my parents be thanked) to haue béene one of his crue, I take it to stand with my dutie, sith I may not stretch mine abilitie in requiting his good turnes, yet to manifest my good will in remembring his paines. And certes, I acknowledge my selfe so much bound and beholding to him and his, as for his sake I reuerence the meanest stone cemented in the wals of that famous schoole. This towne is named Kilkennie, of an holie and learned abbat called Kanicus, borne in the countie of Kilkennie, or (as it is in some bookes recorded) in Connaght. This prelat being in his suckling yeres fostered, through the prouidence of God, with the milke of a cow, and baptized and bishoped by one Luracus, thereto by Gods especiall appointment deputed, grew in tract of time to such deuotion and learning, as he was reputed of all men to be as well a mirrour of the one, as a paragon of the other: whereof he gaue sufficient coniecture in his minoritie. For being turned to the kéeping of sheepe, and his fellow shéepheards, wholie yéelding themselues like luskish vagabunds to slouth and sluggishnesse, yet would he still find himselfe occupied in framing with osiars and twigs, little wodden churches, and in fashioning the furnitures thereto appertenning. Being stept further in yeares, he made his repaire into England, where cloistering himselfe in an abbeie, whereof one named Doctus was abbat, he was wholie wedded to his booke, and to deuotion: wherein he continued so painefull and diligent, as being on a certeine time penning a serious matter, and hauing not fullie drawne the fourth vocall, the abbeie bell tingd to assemble the couent to some spirituall exercise. To which he so hastened, as he left the letter in semicirclewise vnfinished, vntill he returned backe to his booke. Soone after being promoted to ecclesiasticall orders, he trauelled by the consent of his fellow moonks to Rome, and in Italie he gaue such manifest proofe of his pietie, as to this daie in some parts thereof he is highlie renowmed.

The grammar schoole. Pierce Butler. Margaret fitz-gerald.

Peter White.

Kilkennie whie so called. The life of Kanicus.

Thomas

Thomas towne, a proper towne builded in the countie of Kilkennie, by one Thomas Fitzantonie an Englishman. The Irish thereof name it Ballie mac Andan, that is, the towne of Fitzantonie. This gentleman had issue two daughters, the one of them was espoused to Denne, the other married to Archdeacon, or Mackodo, whose heires haue at this daie the towne betwéene them in coparcenarie. But bicause the reader may sée in what part of the countrie the cities and cheefe townes stand, I take it not far amisse to place them in order as insueth.

Thomas towne. Thomas Fitzantonie.

Drogheda, Carregfergus, Downe, Armagh, Arglash, Cloagher, Muneghan, Doonnegaule, Karreg mac Rosse, Newrie, Carlingford, Ardie, Doondalke, Louth. Dublin, Bulrudrie, Luske, Swords, Tashaggard. Lions, Newcastle, Rathcoule, Oughter arde, Naas, Clane, Mainooth, Kilcocke, Rathaimgan, Kildare, Luranne, Castletowne, Philips towne, Marlborough, Kilcullen, Castle Marten, Thistledermot, Kilca, Athie, Catherlaugh, Leighelen, Garranne, Thomas towne, Enestiocke, Cashelle, Callanne, Kilkennie, Knocktofer, Rosse, Clonmelle, Weiseford, Fernes, Fiddeid, Enescortie, Tathmon, Wickloa, Ackloa. Waterford, Lismore, Doongaruan, Yoghill, Corke, Limerike, Kilmallocke. Aloane, Galuoie, Arrie, Louaghriagh, Claie, Toame, Sligagh, Rossecomman, Arctlowne. Trimme, Doonshaghlenne, Rathlouth, Nauanne, Abooie, Scrine, Taraugh, Kemles, Doonboine, Gréenocke, Duléeke. Molingare, Fowre, Loughseude, Kilkenwest, Morlagagh, Delumne.

The names of the chéefe townes in Vlster. The names of the chéefe townes in Leinster. Chéefe towns in Mounster. Chéefe towns in Connaght. Chéefe towns in Méeth. Chéefe towns in Westméeth.

In the foure and thirtith yeare of the reigne of king Henrie the eight, it was enacted in a parlement holden at Dubline before sir Anthonie Sentleger knight, lord deputie of Ireland, that Méeth should be diuided, and made two shires, one of them to be called the countie of Meeth, the other to be called the countie of Westméeth, and that there should be two shiriffes and officers conuenient within the same shires, as is more exprest in the act.

1542

Loughfoile, the Banne, Wolderfrith, Crarcgfergus, Strangford, Ardglas, Lougheuen, Carlingford, Kilkeale, Dundalke, Kilclogher, Dunane, Drogheda, Houlepatrike, Narie, Baltraie, Brimore, Balbriggen, Roggers towne, Skerrish, Rush, Malahide, Banledoorle, Houth, Dublin, Dalkée, Wickincloa, Arckloa, Weisford, Bagganbun, the Passage, Waterford, Dungaruan, Rosse noua, Youghille, Corke mabegge, Corke, Kinsale, Kierie, Rosse Ilbere, Dorrie, Baltimmoie, Downenere, Downeshead, Downelounge, Attannanne, Craghanne, Downenebwine, Balineskilliedge, Daugine Ichouse, Tralie, Seninne, Cassanne, Kilnewine, Limerike, Innis kartée, Belalenne, Armenewine, Glanemaugh, Balliweiham, Binwarre, Dowris, Woran, Roskam, Galwaie, Killinillie, Innesbosinne, Owran, Moare, Kilcolken, Burske, Belleclare, Rathesilbene, Bierweisowre, Buraueis hare, Ardne makow, Rosbare, Kilgolmne, Wallalele, Rabranne, Strone, Burweis now, Zaltia, Kalbalie, Ardnocke, Adrowse, Sligaghe, Innes Bowsenne.

The names of the chiefe hauen towns in Ireland.

Cambrensis obserued in his time, that when the sea dooth eb at Dublin, it ebbeth also at Bristow, and floweth at Milford and Weisford. At Wickloa the sea ebbeth when in all other parts it commonlie floweth. Furthermore this he noted, that the riuer which runneth by Wickloa vpon a low eb is salt, but in Arckloa the next hauen towne, the riuer is fresh when the sea is at full. He writeth also, that not far from Arckloa standeth a rocke, and when the sea ebbeth in one side thereof, it floweth in the other side as fast. Cambrensis insearcheth diuerse philosophicall reasons in finding out the cause, by obseruing the course of the moone, who is the empresse of moisture. But those subtilties I leaue for the schoolestréets.

Camb. lib. 1. top. dist. 2. rub. 3. & 4.

OF THE STRANGE AND WOONDERFULL PLACES IN IRELAND.

THE FOURTH CHAPTER.

S. Patrike his purgatorie

I THINKE it good to begin with S. Patrike his purgatorie, partlie bicause it is most notoriouslie knowne, & partlie the more, that some writers, as the author of Polychronicon and others that were miscaried by him, séeme to make great doubt where they néed not. For they ascribe the finding out of the place not to Patrike that conuerted the countrie, but an other Patrike an abbat, whom likewise they affirme to haue béene imploied in conuerting the Iland from heathenrie to christianitie.

But the author that broacheth this opinion, is not found to carie anie such credit with him, as that a man may certeinlie affirme it, or probablie coniecture it, vnlesse we relie to the old withered worme eaten legend, loded with as manie lowd lies, as lewd lines. The better and the more certeine opinion is, that the other Patrike

Camb. lib. 1. topog. dist. 2. rub. 6.

found it out, in such wise as Cambrensis reporteth. There is a poole or lake, saith he, in the parts of Vlster, that inuironneth an Iland, in the one part whereof there standeth a church much lightned with the brightsome recourse of angels: the other part is oughlie and gastlie, as it were a bedlem allotted to the visible assemblies of horrible and grislie bugs. This part of the Iland conteineth nine caues. And if anie dare be so hardie, as to take one night his lodging in anie of these ins, which hath béene experimented by some rash & harebraine aduenturers, streight these spirits claw him by the backe, and tug him so ruggedlie, and tosse him so crabbedlie, that now and then they make him more franke of his bum than of his toong; a paiment correspondent to his interteinement. This place is called S. Patrike his purgatorie of the inhabitors. For when S. Patrike laboured the conuersion of the people of Vlster, by setting before their eies in great heat of spirit, the creation of the world, the fall of our progenitors, the redemption of man by the blessed and pretious bloud of our sauiour Iesus Christ, the certeintie of death, the immortalitie of the soule, the generall resurrection, our latter doome, the ioies of heauen, the paines of hell, how that at length euerie man, small and great, yoong and old, rich and poore, king and keaser, potentate and pezzant must either through God his gratious mercie be exalted to the one, to floorish in perpetuall felicitie, or through his vnsearchable iustice tumble downe to the other, to be tormented in eternall miserie. These and the like graue and weightie sentences, wherewith he was abundantlie stored, so far sunke into their harts, as they seemed verie flexible in condescending to his behest: so that some proofe of his estrange preaching could haue béene verefied. Wherevpon, without further delaie, they spake to the prelat in this wise.

"Sir, as we like of your preaching, so we dislike not of our libertie. You tell vs of manie gugawes and estrange dreames. You would haue vs to abandon infidelitie, to cage vp our libertie, to bridle our pleasure: for which you promise vs for our toile and labour a place to vs as vnknowen, so as yet vncerteine. You sermon to vs of a dungeon appointed for offendors and miscredents. In deed if we could find that to be true, we would the sooner be weaned from the sweet napple of our libertie, and frame our selues pliant to the will of that God, that you reueale vnto vs." S. Patrike considering, that these sealie soules were (as all dulcarnanes for the more part are) more to be terrified from infidelitie through the paines of hell, than allured to christianitie by the ioies of heauen, most hartilie besought God, so it stood with his gratious pleasure, for the honour and glorie of his diuine name, to giue out some euident or glimsing token of the matter they importunatlie required.

Finallie

Finallie by the especiall direction of God, he found in the north edge of Vlster a desolate corner hemmed in round, and in the middle thereof a pit, where he reared a church, called Reglis or Reglasse. At the east end of the churchyard a doore leadeth into a closet of stone like a long ouen, which they call S. Patrike his purgatorie, for that the people resort thither euen at this daie for penance, and haue reported at their returne estrange visions of paine and blisse appearing vnto them. Reglasse.

The author of Polychronicon writeth that in the reigne of king Stephan, a knight named Owen pilgrimaged to this purgatorie, being so appalled at the strange visions that there he saw, as that vpon his returne from thense he was wholie mortified, and sequestring himselfe from the world, he spent the remnant of his life in an abbeie of Ludensis. Also Dyonisius a chaterhouse moonke recordeth a vision seene in that place by one Agneius, Egneius, whereof who so is inquisitiue, may resort to his treatise written *De quatuor nouissimis*. Iohannes Camertes holdeth opinion, which he surmiseth vpon the gesse of other, that Claudius writeth of this purgatorie. Which if it be true, the place must haue béene extant before saint Patrike, but not so famouslie knowen. The poet his verses are these following. Polychr lib 1 c 36. 1138 Dyon Cart in lib de quatu nouiss art 48. Iob Camert in l b. Solini cap 35.

"Est locus, extremum pandit qua Gallia littus,
Oceani prætentus aquis, quo fertur Vlysses
Sanguine libato populum mouisse silentum,
Flebilis auditur questus, simulachra colont
Pallida, defunctásque vident migrare figuras."

Claud lib 1 in Ruffin

"There is a place toward the ocean sea from brim of Gallish shore,
Wherein Vlysses pilgrim strange with offred bloud ygore,
The people there did mooue, a skritching shrill from dungeon lug
The dwellers all appall with gastlie galpe of grislie bug.
There onelie shapes are seene to stare with visage wan and sad,
From nouke to nouke, from place to place, in eluish skips to gad."

They that repaire to this place for deuotion his sake vse to continue therein foure & twentie houres, which dooing otherwhile with ghostlie meditations, and otherwhile a dread for the conscience of their deserts, they saie they see a plaine resemblance of their owne faults and vertues, with the horror and comfort therevnto belonging, the one so terrible, the other so ioious, that they verelie déeme themselues for the time to haue sight of hell and heauen. The reuelations of men that went thither (S. Patrike yet liuing) are kept written within the abbeie there adioining. When anie person is disposed to enter (for the doore is euer sparid) he repaireth first for deuise to the archbishop, who casteth all perilles, and dissuadeth the pilgrime from the attempt, bicause it is knowen that diuerse entering into that caue, neuer were seene to turne backe againe. But if the partie be fullie resolued, he recommendeth him to the prior, who in like maner fauourablie exhorteth him to choose some other kind of penance, and not to hazard such a danger. If notwithstanding he find the partie fullie bent, he conducteth him to the church, inioineth him to begin with praier and fast of fiftéene daies, so long togither as in discretion can be indured. This time expired, if yet he perseuere in his former purpose, the whole conuent accompanieth him with solemne procession & benediction to the mouth of the caue, where they let him in, and so bar vp the doore vntill the next morning. And then with like ceremonies they await his returne and reduce him to the church. If he be séene no more, they fast and praie fiftéene daies after. Touching the credit of these matters, I sée no cause, but a christian being persuaded that there is both hell and heauen, may without vanitie vpon sufficient information be resolued, that it might please God, at sometime, for considerations to his wisdome knowen, to reueale by miracle the vision of ioies and paines eternall. But that altogither in such sort, The ceremonies vsed in entring S. Patrike his purgatorie.

and

and by such maner, and so ordinarilie, and to such persons, as the common fame dooth vtter, I neither beléeue nor wish to be regarded. I haue conferred with diuerse that had gone this pilgrimage, who affirmed the order of the premisses to be true, but that they saw no sight, saue onelie fearefull dreams when they chanced to nod, and those they said were excéeding horrible. Further they added, that the fast is rated more or lesse, according to the qualitie of the penitent.

Camb. lib. 1. topog. dutinc. 2. rub. 5.

Cambrensis affirmeth, that in the north of Mounster there be two Ilands, the greater and the lesse. In the greater there neuer entereth woman or anie liuing female, but forthwith it dieth. This hath béene often prooued by bitches and cats, which were brought thither to trie this conclusion, and presentlie they died. In this Iland the cocke or mascle birds are seene to chirpe, and pearch vp and downe the twigs, but the hen or female by instinct of nature abandoneth it, as a place vtterlie poisoned. This Iland were a place alone for one that were vexed with a shrewd wife. The lesse Iland is called *Insula viuentium*, bicause none died there, ne maie die by course of nature, as Giraldus Cambrensis saith. Howbeit the dwellers when they are sore frusht with sicknesse, or so farre withered with age as there is no hope of life, they request to be conueied by boate to the greater Iland, where they are no sooner inshored, than they yéeld vp their ghosts. For my part, I haue béene verie inquisitiue of this Iland, but I could neuer find this estrange propertie soothed by anie man of credit in the whole countrie. Neither trulie would I wish anie to be so light, as to lend his credit to anie such feined gloses, as are neither verefied by experience, nor warranted by anie colourable reason. Wherfore I see not why it should be termed *Insula viuentium*, vnlesse it be that none dieth there, as long as he liueth.

Insula viuentium.

Cambren. in eodem loco.

Cambrensis telleth further, that there is a churchyard in Vlster, which no female kind maie enter. If the cocke be there, the hen dareth not follow. There is also in the west part of Connaght an Iland, placed in the sea, called Aren, to which saint Brendan had often recourse. The dead bodies need not in that Iland to be grauelled. For the aire is so pure, that the contagion of anie carrien maie not infect it. There, as Cambrensis saith, maie the sonne sée his father, his grandfather, his great grandfather, &c. This Iland is enimie to mice. For none is brought thither, but either it leapeth into the sea, or else being staied it dieth presentlie. There was in Kildare an ancient monument named the Firehouse, wherein Cambrensis saith, was there continuall fire kept day and night, and yet the ashes neuer increased. I trauelled of set purpose to the towne of Kildare to sée this place, where I did sée such a monument like a vault, which to this daie they call the Firehouse.

Aren.

The Firehouse of Kildare.

Touching the heath of Kildare Cambrensis writeth that it maie not be tild: and of a certeintie within this few yeares it was tried, and found, that the corne which was sowed did not prooue. In this plaine (saith Cambrensis) stood the stones that now stand in Salisburie plaine, which were conueied from thense by the sleight of Merlin the Welsh prophet, at the request of Aurelius Ambrosius king of the Britons.

The heath of Kildare.

The stones of Salisburie plaine.

There is also in the countie of Kildare a goodlie field called Moolleaghmast, betwéene the Norrough and Kilka. Diuers blind prophesies run of this place, that there shall be a bloudie field fought there, betwéene the English inhabitants of Ireland and the Irish, and so bloudie forsooth it shall be, that a mill in a vale hard by it shall run foure and twentie houres with the streame of bloud that shall powre downe from the hill. The Irish doubtlesse repose a great affiance in this balducktum dreame. In the top of this height stand motes or rundles verie formalie fashioned, where the strength of the English armie (as they say) shall be incamped.

Moolleaghmast.

The Earle of Sussex being lord lieutenant of Ireland, was accustomed to wish, that if anie such prophesie were to be fulfilled, it should happen in his gouernement, to the end he might be generall of the field. Not farre from Moolleaghmast, within a mile

The earle of Sussex.

a mile of Castledermot, or Thistledermot, is there a place marked with two hillocks, which is named the Geraldine his throw or cast The length of which in verie déed is woonderfull The occasion procéeded of this. One of the Geraldins, who was ancestor to those that now are lords of Lackath, preded an enimie of his. The earle of Kildare hauing intelligence therof, suppressing affection of kinred, and mooued by zeale of iustice, pursued him with a great troope of horssemen, as the other was bringing of the prede homeward The Geraldine hauing notice giuen him, that the earle was in hot pursute, and therefore being warned by the messenger to hie him with all speed possible the gentleman being nettled, that his kinsman would séeme to rescue the prede of his deadlie fo, and as he was in such fretting wise frieng in his grease, he brake out in these cholerike words, "And dooth my cousine Kildare pursue me in déed? Now in good faith, whereas he séemeth to be a suppresser of his kindred, and an vpholder of my mortall enimie, I would wish him no more harme, than that this dart were as far in his bodie as it shall sticke foorthwith in the ground" and therewithall giuing the spurres to his horsse, he hurled his dart so farre, as he abashed with the length thereof aswell his companie as his posteritie

The Geraldine throw 1470

The Geraldines wish.

The Geraldine was not verie farre from thense, when the earle with his band made hot foot after, and dogging still the tracke of the predours, he came to the place where the dart was hurled, where one pickthanke or other let the earle to vnderstand of the Geraldine his wild spéeches there deliuered And to inhanse the heinousnesse of the offense, he shewed how farre he hurled his dart, when he wished it to be pitched in his lordship his bodie. The erle astonied at the length thereof, said "Now in good sooth, my cousine in behauing himselfe so couragiouslie, is woorthie to haue the prede shot free. And for my part I purpose not so much to stomach his cholerike wish, as to imbrace his valiant prowesse" And therewithall commanded the retreat to be blowne and reculed backe. There is in Meeth an hill called the hill of Taragh, wherein is a plaine twelue score long, which was named the Kempe his hall there the countrie had then méetings and folkemotes, as a place that was accounted the high palace of the monarch The Irish historians hammer manie fables in this forge of Fin mac Coile and his champions, as the French historie dooth of king Arthur and the knights of the round table. But doubtlesse the place séemeth to beare the shew of an ancient and famous monument

The earle of Kildares answer

The hill of Taragh

There is in Castleknocke a village not far from Dublin, a window not glazed nor latized, but open, and let the weather be stormie, the wind bluster boisterouslie on euerie side of the house, yet place a candle there, and it will burne as quietlie as if no puffe of wind blew This maie be tried at this daie, who so shall be willing to put it in practise Touching the strange wels that be in Ireland, I purpose to speake litle more than that which I find in Cambrensis, whose words I will English, as they are Latined in his booke There is (saith he) a well in Mounster, with the water of which if anie be washed, he becōmeth foorthwith hoare. I haue séene a man that had one halfe of his beard, being died with that water hoare, the other halfe vnwashed was browne, remaining still in his naturall colour Contrariwise, there is a fountaine in the further edge of Vlster, and if one be bathed therewith, he shall not become hoare in which well such as loath greie heares are accustomed to diue There is in Connaght a well that springeth on the top of an hill farre and distant from anie sea, ebbing and flowing in foure and twentie houres, as the sea dooth; and yet the place is vplandish, and the water fresh There is another spring in the same countrie, the water of which is verie wholsome to men and women, but poison to beasts and if a man but put the grauell of this well into his mouth, it quencheth presentlie his thirst.

Castleknocke. The strange welles

Camb. in lib 1. topog dist 1 rub. 8 & 10

There

There is in Vlster a standing poole thirtie thousand pases long, and fiftéene thousand pases brode, out of which springeth the noble northerne riuer, called the Banne. The fishers complaine more often for bursting of their nets with the ouer great take of fish, than for anie want. In our time vpon the conquest a fish swam from this poole to the shore, in shape resembling a salmon, but in quantitie so huge, that it could not be drawne or carried whole togither, but the fishmongers were forced to hacke it in gobbets, and so to carrie it in péecemeale throughout the countrie, making thereof a generall dole. And if the report be true, the beginning of this poole was strange. There were in old time where the poole now standeth, vicious and beastlie inhabitants. At which time was there an old said saw in euerie man his mouth, that as soone as a well there springing (which for the superstitious reuerence they bare it, was continuallie couered and signed) were left open and vnsigned, so soone would so much water gush out of that well, as would foorthwith ouerwhelme the whole territorie. It happened at length, that an old trót came thither to fetch water, and hearing hir child whine, she ran with might and maine to dandle hir babie, forgetting the obseruance of the superstitious order tofore vsed. But as she was returning backe to haue couered the spring, the land was so farre ouerflowne, as that it past hir helpe. and shortlie after she, hir suckling, & all those that were within the whole territorie were drowned. And this séemeth to carie more likelihood with it, bicause the fishers in a cleare sunnie daie see the stéeples and other piles plainlie and distinctlie in the water. And here would be noted, that the riuer of the Banne flowed from this head spring before this floud, but farre in lesse quantitie than it dooth in our time. Hitherto Giraldus Cambrensis.

Hector Boet. in Scot. reg. descript. pag. 4. Sect. 50

Boettus telleth a rare propertie of a poole in Ireland, & for that he maketh himselfe an eiewitnesse of the matter, he shall tell his owne tale. "Ac quoniam Hiberniæ incidit mentio, præter infinita in ea rerum miracula, haud importunum fore existimem, si vnum, quod ob portentuosam nouitatem fidem omnium excedere videatur, nos tamen verum experti sumus, adiunxerimus. Lacus in ea est, circa quem amplissimo circumquaque spatio nec herba nec arbor vlla nascitur, &c. in quem si lignum infigas anni circiter vnius curriculo, id quod in terra fixum erit, in lapidem conuertetur, quod demceps aquâ operietur, in ferrum: reliquum aquâ exstans ligni formam naturámque seruabit. Ita coniuncta, lapis, ferrum & lignum eodem in stipite inaudita nouitate conspectantur." But for that mention is made of Ireland, ouer and aboue the infinite number of woonders in that land, it will not be wholie beside the purpose, to insert one maruellous thing, which although it may seeme to some to haue no colour of truth: yet because it hath beene by vs experimented, and found out to be true, we maie the better auouch it. There is a standing poole in that Iland, neere which of all sides groweth neither herbe, shrub, nor bush. If you sticke a rod or péece of timber in this poole, that which sticketh in the earth within the space of one yeare turneth to a stone, as much as is dipt in the water, is conuerted to iron, all that is aboue the water remaineth still in the pristinat and former woodden shape. So that you may sée that which is strange, in one stocke or sticke, stone, iron and wood linkt and knit togither. Thus much Hector Boetius.

Melashee

In the countrie of Kilkennie and in the borders thereto confining, they vsed a solemne triall by a water they call Melashée. The propertie of this water is, as they say, that if a periured person drinke thereof, the water will gush out at his bellie, as though the drinker his nauill were bord with an auger. The riuer that runneth

The Liffe

by Dublin named the Liffie hath this propertie for certeine, and I haue obserued it at sundrie times. As long as it reigneth, yea if it stood powring six daies, you shall find diuerse shallow brookes, and the riuer will be nothing thereby increased: but within foure and twentie houres after the showres are ceast, you shall perceiue such

such a sudden spring flow, as if the former raine were great, a verie few places or none at all will be found pasable. Cambrensis writeth, that in the south part of Mounster, betwéene the maine sea coasting on Hispaine and saint Brendan his hills, there is an Iland of the one side incompassed with a riuer abundantlie stored with fish, & on the other part inclosed with a little brooke. In which place saint Brendan was verie much resiant. This plot is taken to be such a sanctuarie for beasts, as if anie hare, fox, stag, or other wild beast be chased néere that Iland by dogs, it maketh straight vpon the brooke, and assoone as it passeth the streame, it is so cockesure, as the hunter may perceiue the beast resting on the one banke, & the dogs questing on the other brim, being as it were by some inuisible railes imbard from dipping their féet in the shallow foord, to pursue the beast chased. On the other side of this Iland there runneth a riuer stored aboue measure with fresh water fish, and in especiallie with salmon. Which abundance, as Cambrensis writeth, procéeded of God, to mainteine the great hospitalitie that was kept there. And because the dwellers thereabout shall not like pinching corsticels make anie sale of the fish, let it be poudered as artificiallie as may be, yet it will not kéepe (as though it were manna) aboue the first night or daie that it be taken. So that you must eate it within that short compasse, otherwise it putrifieth and standeth to no stéed. Cambr. lib. 1 dist. 2 rub. 41

This riuer ouerfloweth a great rocke, vsuallie called the Salmon leape: for as it is commonlie the propertie of all fish to swim against the tide, as for birds to flitter against the wind, so it is naturallie giuen to the salmon to struggle against the streme, and when it approcheth neere this high rocke, it bendeth his taile to his head, and sometime taketh it in his mouth, and therewithall beareth it selfe ouer the water, and suddenlie it fetcheth such a round whiske, that at a trice it skippeth to the top of the rocke. The like salmon leape is néere Leislip, but not so high as this. There be also, as witnesseth Cambrensis, in the further part of Vlster, certeine hils néere to saint Bean his church, where cranes yearelie bréed. And when they haue laid their egs, if anie purpose to ransacke their nests, let him but attempt to touch the egs, they will shew like yoong scralling pullets without feather or downe, as though they were new hatched, and presentlie brought out of their shels. But if the partie plucke his hand from the nest, forthwith they shew (whether it be by anie metamorphosis, or some iugling legier de maine by dazeling the eies) as though they were transformed into egs. And further, saith Cambrensis, let two at one instance be at the nest, and let the one of them onelie giue the gaze, and the other attempt to take awaie the egs, they will séeme to the looker on as egs, and to the taker as yoong red little cranets, being as bare as a bird his arsse. The Salmon leape

The towne of Armagh is said to be enimie to rats, and if anie be brought thither, presentlie it dieth. Which the inhabitants impute to the praiers of saint Patrike. But to omit the strange places, that either by false reports are surmised, or by proofe and experience dailie verefied: there are in this Iland such notable quarries of greie marble and touch, such store of pearle and other rich stones, such abundance of cole, such plentie of lead, iron, latin and tin, so manie rich mines furnished with all kind of metals, as nature séemed to haue framed this countrie for the storehouse or iewelhouse of hir chiefest thesaurie. Howbeit she hath not shewed hir selfe so bountifull a mother in powring foorth such riches, as she prooueth hir selfe an enuious stepdame, in that she instilleth in the inhabitants a drousie lithernesse to withdraw them from the insearching of hir hourded and hidden iewels. Wherein she fareth like one, that to purchase the name of a sumptuous frankelen or a good viander, would bid diuerse ghests to a costlie and deintie dinner, and withall for sauing of his meat with some secret inchantment would benum them of their lims, or with some hidden lothsomnesse would dull their Armagh Ireland the storehouse of nature

stomachs,

stomachs, as his ghests by reason of the one are not able, or for the other not
willing, by taking their repast to refresh themselues, in so much as in my phantasie
it is hard to decide whether estate is the better either for a diligent laborer to be
planted in a barren or stonie soile, or for a luskish loiterer to be setled in a fertill
ground because the one will, and may not, the other may and will not through
his painefull trauell reape the fruit and commoditie that the earth yéeldeth.

OF THE LORDS SPIRITUALL OF IRELAND, THEIR NAMES AND DIGNITIES.

THE FIFT CHAPTER

THE spirituall iurisdiction is ordered into foure prouinces, whereof the primasie
was euer giuen (in reuerence of saint Patrike that conuerted the countrie) to the
archbishoprike of Armagh, who is called *Primas totius Hiberniæ*, and the archbishop
of Dublin, *Primas Hiberniæ* This custome was since confirmd by Eugenius the
third, 1148, or 1152 who sent withall three other palles of archbishops to be
placed, one at Dublin one at Cashill, & the last at Twene To these are suffragans
in right nine and twentie, and they all to the *Primas* of Armagh, vnder whose
prouince are the bishops of Meeth and Deren, Ardach, Kilmore, Cloghei,
Donne Coner, Clonknos, Raboo, Dromoore Vnder Dublin, whereunto Innocentius the third vnited Glandelagh, the bishop of Elphine, Kildare, Fernes, Ossorie
and Leighlin Vnder Cashill, the bishop of Waterford, to whome Lismore is
vnited, Corke and Clone, Rosse, Ardigh Limenke, Emelie Killalooe, and Ardfert.
Vnder Twene, Kilmaco, Olfine, Auaghdoune, Clonfert, Moroo In this recount
some difference hapneth by reason of personall and reall vnion of the sees, and for
other alterations I haue obserued in perusing of old bookes the names of certeine
bishops and archbishops of Dublin and albeit I could not find a iust register or
catalog of them, yet I tooke it to be better to place such as I could find, than to
omit the whole ¶Cormachus was one of the first bishops that I haue read of, but
I am well assured that there were diuerse others before his time. He flourished
about the yeare 893, of this bishop Hector Boetius maketh mention ¶Dunanus
was bishop of Dublin long after Cormachus for Dunanus died in the yeare 1074
He was buried in Christs church in Dublin, in the vpper part of the chancell on the
right hand
¶Patricius was consecrated bishop of Dublin in Paule his church at London by
the archbishop of Canturburie Lanfranus or Lanfrancus The reason of this consecration was, for that as yet the metropolitans of Ireland receiued not then pall A
pall is an indowment appropriated to archbishops, made of white silke the breadth
of a stole, but it is of another fashion And where you shall espie the armes of anie
archbishop blazed, there you may perceiue the pall set out in white, with a great
manie blacke crosses vpon it An archbishop within three moneths after his consecration or confirmation ought to demand his pall, otherwise he may be remooued,
neither ought he to name himselfe archbishop before the receit, neither may he
before summon or call a councell, make chrisme, dedicate churches, giue orders, or
consecrat bishops He may not weare his pall without the church, neither in other
prouinces, albeit in another prouince he may be in his pontificalibus, so that pon-
tificalia differeth from the pall Furthermore, an archbishop may not lend his pall
vnto another, but it ought to be interred with him. But to returne to Patricius,
his time was but short, for soone after as he was crossing the seas to Dublin ward,
he was drowned with his felow passengers the same yere that he was consecrated,
the ninth of October.

¶Donatus,

Armagh.

Dublin

Cashill.

Twene

In 10 Scot
Hist fol 212
· 1 &)

1074.

Pall what it is

c quoniam c dis

c quod sicut de
lect penul
De priuil &
exces priuil cap
Archie & in
glor
c ex tuarum, &
c adhic de auct
'§§ vsu pal.

¶Donatus, of some called Bangus succéeded Patricius, and likewise consecrated by Lanfrancus archbishop of Canturburie, at the instance of Terdilnacus king of Ireland, the bishops of Ireland, the clergie and the citizens of Dublin he deceassed in the yéere one thousand ninetie and fiue Samuell succéeded Donatus, and died in the yéere one thousand one hundred two and twentie Gregorius did not succéed immediatlie after Samuell, for there be thirtie yéeres betweene them both This Gregorius was the first metropolitan of Dublin, and was consecrated archbishop in the yéere one thousand one hundred fiftie and two, and died in the yéere one thousand one hundred thrée score and two 1075 1095 1152 1162.

S Laurentius Othothille This prelat was first abbat of S Keuins in Glindelagh, and after he was solemnlie consecrated and installed in Christ church at Dublin by Gelacius the primat of Armagh, and not by Canturburie, as the bishops of Dublin were before the pall giuen them He died in Normandie, and was buried in our ladie church of Angie in the yeare one thousand one hundred and foure score, the fourtéenth of Nouember

Iohan Cummin an Englishman succéeded Laurence This famous prelat being cloistered vp in the abbeie of Eusham in Worcestershire was highlie renowmed of all men, as well for his déepe learning, as for the integritie of his life The clergie of Dublin being giuen to vnderstand of so woorthie a clerke, became humble petitioners to the king his maiestie Henrie the second, that through his means such an vnvaluable iewell should be installed in Laurence his dignitie The king bowing to their earnest sute agréed he should be consecrated their archbishop, which was an happie houre for that countrie For besides the great trauell he indured in edifieng his flocke in Christian religion, he was founder of S Patrike his church in Dublin, as is before specified He deceassed in the yéere one thousand two hundred and twelue, and was intoomed in the quéere of Christs church 1180.

Henrie Londres succéeded Cummin This man was nicknamed Scorchbill, or Scorchvillein thorough this occasion Being setled in his sée, he gaue commandement to all his tenants to make their appeerance before him at a daie appointed · and for that he was raw as yet in his reuenues, he tooke it to stand best with their ease and quietnes, and his commoditie, that ech of them should shew their euidences, whereby he might learne, by what tenure they held of him His tenants mistrusting no sluttish dealing, but construing all to be meant for the best, deliuered their euidences to their landlord, who did scantlie well peruse them when he floong them all in the fire The poore tenants espieng this subtill pranke to be verie vnfitting for a bishop, could not bridle their toongs, but brake out on a sudden Thou an archbishop? Naie, thou art a scorchvillein But it could not be gessed to what end this fact of his tended, for notwithstanding this, the tenants inioied their lands, vnlesse he did it because they should be tenants at will, and so to stand to his deuotion This prelat doubtlesse was politike, and well lettered, and for his wisedome and learning he was elected lord iustice of Ireland. He was the founder of the castell of Dublin, as is before mentioned He deceassed in the yeare one thousand two hundred twentie & fiue, and lieth buried in Christs church Whereby appéereth that Matthæus Parisiensis did ouershoot himselfe, in writing one Hu or Hugo to be archbishop of Dublin in the yeare one thousand two hundred and thirtéene, whereas Londres at that time was in the sée, as from his consecration to his death may be gathered, being the space of thirtéene yeares Scorchvillein *Matth. Paris in vita Ioan, pag* 311

Iohan Stamford succéeded Londres, but not immediatlie, and was consecrated in the yeare one thousand two hundred foure score and fiue This man, vpon the death of Stephan Fulborne archbishop of Tune, was made lord iustice of Ireland in the yeare one thousand two hundred foure score and seauen And soone after being in England he was sent from Edward the first as ambassador to the French king, and 1285. 1294.

vpon his returne he deceassed in England, & soone after was buried in saint Patrike
his church at Dublin.
Wilhelmo Hothom is placed by some antiquaries to be archbishop of Dublin
1207 *Ioan Caius de antiqu Cant Academ lib 1* much about this time, but whether the man haue béene installed in this see at all
or no, I am not able to affirme, nor to denie but certeine it is that the date is
mistaken, for vpon Iohan Stamford his death, Richard Ferings was consecrated
Edmund Butler archbishop of Dublin, betwéene whome and the lord Edmund Butler there arose
1032 a great controuersie in law, touching the manner of Holliwood with the appur-
Holliwood in Fingall tenances Which manor the lord Butler recouered by an arbitrement or composition taken betwéene them in the king his bench at Dublin This prelat departed
1306 this life in the yere one thousand thrée hundred and six
Richard de Hauerings was successor vnto Ferings, who after that he had continued welnéere the space of fiue yeares in the see, was sore appalled, by reason of
an estrange and woonderfull dreame For on a certeine night he imagined that he
had séene an vglie monster standing on his breast, who to his thinking was more
weightie than the whole world, in so much as being as he thought in manner squised
or prest to death with the heft of this huge monster, he would haue departed with
the whole substance of the world, if he were thereof possessed, to be disburdened
of so heauie a load Upon which wish he suddenlie awooke. And as he beat his
Hauerings dreame braines in deuining what this dreame should import, he bethought himselfe of the
flocke committed to his charge, how that he gathered their fléeces yearelie, by receiuing the reuenues and perquisits of the bishoprike, and yet suffered his flocke to
starue for lacke of preaching and teaching Wherefore being for his former slacknesse sore wounded in conscience, he trauelled with all spéed to Rome, where he
resigned vp his bishoprike, a burthen too heauie for his weake shoulders, and being
vpon his resignation competentlie beneficed, he bestowed the remnant of his life
wholie in deuotion
1311 Iohan Lech nephue to Hauerings, vpon the resignation was consecrated archbishop This prelat was at contention with the primat of Armagh, for their iurisdictions insomuch as he did imbarre the primat from hauing his crosse borne before
De priui & excest pri c Archiep him within the prouince of Leinster, which was contrarie to the canon law, that
admitteth the crosier to beare the crosse before his archbishop in an other
prouince This man deceassed in the yeare one thousand thrée hundred and thirtéene
1313 Alexander Bigenor was next Lech consecrated archbishop with the whole consent aswell of the chapter of Christs church as of S Patriks Howbeit vpon the
death of Lech there arose a schisme & diuision betwéene Walter Thorneburie lord
chancellour of Ireland and Bigenor then treasuror of the same countrie The
cancellor to further his election determined to haue posted to Rome, but in the
waie he was drowned with the number of 156 passengers Bigenor staieng in Ireland, with lesse aduenture and better spéed, with the consent of both the chapters
was elected archbishop And in the yeare 1317 there came buls from Rome to
confirme the former election At which time the archbishop and the earle of Vlster
1318 were in England This prelat soone after returned lord iustice of Ireland, and
soone after he had landed at Yoghill, he went to Dublin, where as well for his spirituall iurisdiction, as his temporall promotion he was receiued with procession and
1320 great solemnitie In this man his time was there an vniuersitie founded in Dublin,
whereof maister William Rodiard was chancellor, a well learned man and one that
procéeded doctor of the canon law in this vniuersitie. Bigenor deceased in the
1349 yéere 1349.
Iohn de saint Paule was consecrated archbishop vpon Bigenor his death He
1363 deceassed in the yeare one thousand thrée hundred sixtie and two Thomas Minot
succéeded

succéeded Iohn, and died in the yeare one thousand thrée hundred seuentie & six. 1375
Robert Wikeford succéeded Thomas, and died in the yeare one thousand thrée hundred and nintie. Robert Waldebie succéeded Wikeford, this prelat was first an 1390
Augustine frier, and a great preacher, and accounted a vertuous and sincere liuer.
He deceassed in the yeare one thousand thrée hundred ninetie and seauen. Richard 1397
Northalis was remooued from an other sée and chosen archbishop of Dublin, who
likewise deceassed the same yeare he was elected. Thomas Craulie an Englishman
succéeded him the same yeare, and came into Ireland in the companie of the duke
of Surreie. This archbishop was chosen lord iustice of Ireland in the yeare one
thousand foure hundred and thirtéene. In whose gouernement the English did 1413
skirmish with the Irish in the countie of Kildare néere Kilka, where the English The skirmish of Kilka
vanquished the enimie, slue an hundred of the Irish. During which time the archbishop being lord iustice, went in procession with the whole clergie in Tristeldermot, or Castledermot, a towne adioining to Kilka, praieng for the prosperous successe of the subiects that went to skirmish with the enimie. This prelat was of
stature tall, well featured, and of a sanguine complexion, decking his outward
comelinesse with inward qualities. For he was so liberall to the rich, so charitable
to the poore, so déepe a clerke, so profound a doctor, so sound a preacher, so vertuous a liuer, and so great a builder, as he was not without good cause accounted
the phenix of his time. In dailie talke as he was short, so he was swéet. Hard
in promising, bountifull in performing. In the yeare one thousand foure hundred
and seuenteene, he sailed into England, and ended his life at Faringdon, and was
buried in New college at Oxford. In the yeare one thousand foure hundred thirtie 1439
& nine, there hath béene one Richard archbishop of Dublin, and lord iustice of
Ireland, before whome a parlement was holden at Dublin, in the eightéenth yéere
of the reigne of king Henrie the sixt. In the yeare one thousand foure hundred
and sixtie, Walter was archbishop of Dublin, & deputie to Iasper duke of Bed- 1460
ford, lieutenant of Ireland. I found in an ancient register the names of certeine The bishops of Kildare
bishops of Kildare, that were in that sée since the time of saint Brigid, the names
of whome I thought here to insert. Lome was bishop in saint Bridgids time, which
was about the yeare of our Lord foure hundred fortie and eight, the rest doo heere 418
follow.

2	Inor.	14	Robert
3	Conlie	15	Bonifacius.
4	Donatus	16	Madogge
5	Dauid	17	William.
6	Magnus.	18	Galfride.
7	Richard.	19	Richard.
8	Iohn	20	Iames.
9	Simon.	21	Wale
10	Nicholas.	22	Baret
11	Walter	23	Edmund Lane, who florished in the yeare 1518.
12	Richard		
13	Thomas.		

There hath béene a worthie prelat, canon in the cathedrall church of Kildare, Maurice Iake
named Maurice Iake, who among the rest of his charitable déeds, builded the 1310
bridge of Kilcoollen, and the next yeare following he builded in like maner the The bridge of Kilcoollen, and
bridge of Leighlin, to the great and dailie commoditie of all such as are occa- Leighlin
sioned to trauell in those quarters.

THE LORDS TEMPORALL, AS WELL ENGLISH AS IRISH, WHICH INHABIT THE COUNTRIE OF IRELAND.

THE SIXT CHAPTER.

GERALD Fitzgerald, earle of Kildare This house was of the nobilitie of Florence, came from thense into Normandie, and so with the ancient earle Strangbow his kinsman, whose armes he giueth, into Wales, néere of bloud to Rice ap Griffin, prince of Wales by Nesta the moother of Maurice Fitzgerald & Robert Fitzstephans, with the said earle Maurice Fitzgerald remooued into Ireland, in the yeare one
1169 thousand one hundred sixtie and nine The familie is verie properlie toucht in a sonnet of Surreies, made vpon the earle of Kildares sister, now countesse of Lincolne.

From Tuscane came my ladies worthie race,
Faire Florence was sometime hir ancient seat
The westerne Ile whose pleasant shore doth face
Wild Cambers cliffes, did giue hir liuelie heat,
Fostred she was with milke of Irish brest,
Hir sire an earle, hir dame of princes bloud,
From tender yeares in Britaine she dooth rest
With kings child, where she tasts costlie food
Hunsdon did first present hir to mine eine,
Bright is hir hew, and Geraldine she hight,
Hampton me taught to wish hir first for mine
And Windsor, alas, dooth chase me from hir sight,
Hir beautie of kind, hir vertues from aboue,
Happie is he, that can obteine hir loue.

The corrupt orthographie that diuerse vse in writing this name, dooth incorporat it to houses thereto linked in no kinred, and consequentlie blemisheth diuerse worthie exploits atchiued as well in England and Ireland, as in forren countries and dominions Some write Gerold, sundrie Gerald, diuerse verie corruptlie Gerrot, others Gerard But the true orthographie is Girald, as maie appeare both by Giraldus Cambrensis, and the Italian authors that make mention of the familie. As for Gerrot it differeth flat from Girald yet there be some in Ireland, that name and write themselues Gerrots, notwithstanding they be Giraldins, whereof diuerse gentlemen are in Meeth But there is a sept of the Gerrots in Ireland, and they séeme forsooth by threatning kindnesse and kindred of the true Giraldins, to fetch their petit degrees from their ancestors, but they are so néere of bloud one to the other, that two bushels of beanes would scantlie count their degrées. An other reason why diuerse estrange houses haue béene shuffled in among this familie, was, for that sundrie gentlemen at the christening of their children, would haue them named Giralds, and yet their surnames were of other houses, and if after it happened that Girald had issue Thomas, Iohn, Robert, or such like, then would they beare the surname of Girald, as Thomas Fitzgirald and thus taking the name of their ancestors for their surname, within two or thrée descents they shooue themselues among the kindred of the Giraldins. This is a generall fault in Ireland and Wales, and a great confusion and extinguishment of houses

Matth. Paris in vita Ioh. pag. 310. vers. 40 This noble and ancient familie of the Giraldins, haue in sundrie ages florished in the most renowmed countries of Europe. Warring Fitzgirald was one in great credit

credit with King Iohn. I find an other Giraldine *Archiepiscopus Burdegalensis*, who 1231
flourished in king Henrie the third his time. There was an other Giraldine patriarch of Ierusalem, in the yéere one thousand two hundred twentie and nine, as witnesseth Matthæus Parisiensis. There was one Girald of Bernell an excellent *Pag. 180.*
poet in the Italian toong: an other named Baptist Girald, was a famous citizen of Ferrara, an expert physician, and an exquisit philosopher, being publike professor of philosophie in the said citie, during the space of ten yeares. I haue seene a worke of one *Gregorius Giraldus Ferrariensis de dijs gentium*, dedicated to Hercules duke of Ferrara, a pithie booke and verie well penned. Also Syluester Giraldus Cambrensis hath béene one of this familie, néere of kin to sir Maurice *Giraldus Cambrensis.*
Fitzgirald. This gentleman was borne in Wales, and thereof he is named Cambrensis, of the word *Cambria*, that in old time was adapted to that part of *Britannia*. He was verie inward with Henrie the second, conqueror of Ireland, being at that time the kings secretarie. And for that speciall affiance king Henrie reposed in him, he was appointed to accompanie prince Iohn the kings sonne into Ireland, as one of his chiefest and discréetest councellors.

This gentleman was verie well learned, a tolerable diuine, a commendable philosopher, not rude in physike, skilfull in cosmographie, a singular good antiquarie, an orator, in indeuor comparable to the best, in his stile not in those daies taken for the woorst, rather eschewing the name of a rude writer, than purchasing the fame of an eloquent chronicler. Among other his works, he wrote one booke of the description of Ireland, other two of the conquest thereof. Iohn the abbat of *Ioannes de loco frumenti part. prima granarij.*
saint Albons saith, that this clerke was somewhat spare in words, and liberall in sentences. What he meaneth by this verdict I know not, vnlesse he taketh the man to be ouerlauish of his pen in trumping of his aduersaries with quipping tawnts, which (as I gesse) flowed rather from a flanting ostentation of a roisting kind of rhetorike, than from anie great malice he bare anie one. Howbeit, I maie not gainesaie, but as he was kind where he tooke, so he was somewhat biting where he disliked. But what his iudgement is of the Giraldins maie plainlie appeare in his chronicle, out of which I haue culled this praiseworthie sentence insuing.

"Hoc est huius generis omen & hæc conditio. Semper in armata militia chari, semper primi, semper rebus in Martijs ausu nobili præstantissimi. Cessante verò necessitatis articulo, statim exosi, statim vltimi, statim ad ima liuore depressi. Veruntamen *Cambrensis lib. 2. conqu. Hib. rub. 17.*
tantæ generositatis syluam liuor ad plenum extirpare non potuit. Vnde & vsque in hodiernum gens hæc nouis plantularum succrementis vires in insula non modicas habet. Qui sunt, qui penetrant hostium penitralia? Giraldidæ. Qui sunt, qui patriam conseruant? Giraldidæ. Qui sunt, quos hostes formidant? Giraldidæ. Qui sunt, quos liuor detractat? Giraldidæ. Si principem tantæ strenuitatis merita dignè pensantem reperissent, quàm tranquillum, quàm pacificum olim Hiberniæ statum reddidissent? Sed horum sine causa semper est suspecta strenuitas." This hath béen continuallie, saith Cambrensis, a destinie or fatall propertie annexed to this house. In warre and martiall broiles they are dandaled, they are colled, they are lulled, who but they? They rule the rost. But when these martiall garboiles are appeased, they are either through false informations wrongfullie behated, or else by enuious carpers sinisterlie suspected. Howbeit, enuie with all hir malicious drifts, could neuer wholie supplant the fertill groue of this couragious & noble progenie. And maugre the beads of all malicious promoters, this sept, yea euen at this daie beareth, with the few slips there ingraffed, no small stroke in Ireland. Who are they that scale the enimies fort? The Giraldines; Who are they that defend their countrie? the Giraldines. Who are they that make the enimie quake in his skin? The Giraldines. And who are they whome enuie backbiteth? The Giraldines. If it had stood with

the

the good fortune of the Giraldines, that the king with equall balance would poise their valure, long yer this had all Ireland beene put in quiet and peaceable state. But their valiantnesse and power hath beene from time to time without sufficient cause suspected. Hitherto Cambrensis.

And soothlie, as often as I call to mind the saieng of this historiographer, I may not but muse how rumpe he hitteth the naile on the head. And who so will conferre their continuall successe from the penning of this sentence (which was written aboue 400 yeares and vpward) with this age of ours, shall soone perceiue, that these words were rather prophesies of future mishap, than complaints of former iniuries. At this daie let them behaue themselues valiantlie in warre, and loiallie in peace, yet notwithstanding, such slanders are raised, such rumors noised, such tales bruted, such fables twitled, such vntrue reports twatled, such malicious inuentions forged, that such as are in authoritie cannot but of force suspect them, vnlesse they were able, like gods, to prie in the bottome of each mans conscience. But who so wisheth anie goodnesse to that miserable countrie, and noble progenie, let him with all the veines of his heart beséech God, first that the higher powers be slowe in beléeuing the despitefull reports of enuious backbiters. Secondlie, that the Giraldines beare themselues in all their affaires so dutifullie, that these curious searchers be not able to depaint their feigned gloses with anie probable colours. So shall suspicion be abandoned, so shall malicious slanders be squatted, so shall that noble house be trusted, and consequentlie the battered weale-publike of Ireland reedified. The familie is English, and it is well knowne that the Irish rather feare their force, than loue their persons. And reason good pardie. For the Irish bearing in mind, that the Giraldine being thereto deputed by the prince, hath in all ages conquered their lands, abated their courages, discomfited their men, vanquished their armies, daunted their power, suppressed their force, and made them become true and tributarie subiects to the crowne of England: they haue good cause to beare that sept but holow hearts, what shew so euer they make in outward appearance. Thus much generallie of the Giraldines, now I purpose particularlie to treat of the house of Kildare.

Maurice Fitzgerald, one of the earles progenitors, was lord iustice of Ireland in the yeare 1242, at which time he builded the castell of Sligagh. This Maurice
The castell of Sligagh. Tireconille. was lord of Tireconille, and being entirelie seized of the whole countrie, he gaue the one moitie thereof to Cormocke mac Dermot, mac Rorie. I read the Gi-
Baron of Ophalie. raldine baron of Ophalie, in the yeare 1270. I haue séene it registred, that there died a Giraldine the fourth earle of Kildare, in the yeare 1287. But I take that kalendar to beare a false date. Wherefore the truth & certeintie is, that Iohn
The first earle of Kildare. Fitzgerald, sonne to Thomas Fitzgerald, was the first earle of Kildare, and was created earle vpon this occasion.

1290 In the yeare 1290, and in the eighteenth yeare of Edward the first, William
Vescie lord iustice. Vescie was made lord iustice of Ireland. This man being either negligent or raw in the gouernment of the countrie, emboldened the Irish enimie to indamage the kings subiects more eftsoones than they were accustomed to doo. These enormities being for the space of foure yeares tolerated, the subiects misliking of the slacknesse of their gouernour, gaue out such sinister spéeches of the lord iustice, as he was glad to the hart root. Soone after, as the nobles in open assemblie were
Vescie accuseth the lord Fitzgerald. ripping vp by péecemele the seuerall harms their tenants suffered, the lord iustice willing to disburden himselfe of the crime, began with mistic kind of speaches to laie the whole fault on the lord Iohn Fitzgeralds shoulders, saieng in parable wise, that he was a great occasion of these disorders, in that he bare himselfe in priuat quarrels as fierce as a lion, but in these publike iniuries he was as méeke as a lambe.

The

The baron of Ophalie spelling and putting these syllables together, spake in this wise.

"My lord, I am hartilie sorie that among all this noble assemblie, you make me your onelie marke whereat to shoot your bolt. And trulie were my deserts so heinous as I suppose you would wish them to be, you would not labour to cloud your talke with such darke riddles, as at this present you haue doone, but with plaine & flat English, your lordship would not sticke to impeach of fellonie or treason. For as mine ancestors with spending of their bloud in their soueraignes quarell aspired to this type of honour, in which at this daie (God and my king be thanked) I stand: so your lordship taking the nigher waie to the wood, by charging me with treason, would gladlie trip so roundlie on my top, that by shedding of my bloud, and by catching my lands into your clouches, that butt so neere vpon your manors of Kildare and Rathimgan, as I dare saie they are an eie-sore vnto you, you might make my maister your sonne a proper gentleman." The lord Giralds answer.

"A gentleman?" quoth the lord iustice. "Thou bald baron, I tell thee the Vescies were gentlemen before the Giraldines were barons of Ophalie, yea and before that Welsh bankrupt thine ancestour (he meant sir Maurice Fitzgerald) fethered his nest in Leinster. And whereas thou takest the matter so farre in snuffe, I will teach thée thy lyripups after an other fashion than to be thus malapert in cocking and billing with me that am thy gouernour. Wherefore, albeit thy taunts are such as they might force the patientest philosopher that is, to be chokt with choler: yet I would haue thée ponder my spéeches, as though I deliuered them in my most sober and quiet mood. I saie to the face of thée, and I will auow what I saie vnto thée, that thou art a supporter of theeues, a bolsterer of the kings enimies, an vpholder of traitors, a murtherer of subiects, a firebrand of dissention, a ranke théefe, an arrant traitor: and before I eate these words, I will make thée eate a péece of my blade." The lord iustice replieth

The baron bridelling with might and maine his choler, bare himselfe as cold in countenance, as the lord iustice was hot in words, and replied in this wise. "My lord I am verie glad, that at length you vnwrapped your selfe out of that net, wherein all this while you masked. As for mine ancestor, whome you terme a bankerupt, how rich or how poore he was vpon his repaire to Ireland, I purpose not at this time to debate. Yet thus much I may boldlie saie, that he came hither as a buier, not as a begger. He bought the enimies land by spending his bloud: but you lurking like a spider in his copweb to intrap flies, endeuor to beg subiects liuings wrongfullie, by despoiling them of their innocent liues. And wheras you charge me with malepertnes, in that I presume to chop logike with you being gouernour, by answering your snappish *Quid*, with a knappish *Quo*: I wold wish you to vnderstand, now, that you put me in mind of the distinction, that I as a subiect honour your roiall authoritie, but as a noble man I despise your dunghill gentilitie. Lastlie, whereas you charge me with the odious termes of traitor, murtherer, and the like, and there withall you wish me to resolue my selfe that you rest vpon reason, not vpon rage: if these words procéed from your lordship, as from a magistrate, I am a subiect, to be tried by order of law, and am sorie that the gouernour, who ought by vertue of his publike authoritie to be my iudge, is by reason of priuat malice become mine accuser.

"But if you vtter these spéeches as a priuat person, then I Iohn Fitzgerald, baron of Ophalie, doo tell thee William Vescie, a single sole gentleman, that I am no traitor, no felon, and that thou art the onelie buttresse, by which the kings enimies are supported, the meane and instrument by which his maiesties subiects are dailie spoiled. Therefore I as a loiall subiect saie traitor to thy téeth, and that shalt thou well vnderstand when we both shall be brought to the rehersall of these matters before our betters. Howbeit, during the time you beare office, I am resolued to giue you the mastrie in words, and to suffer you like a brawling cur to barke, but when I sée my time I will be sure to bite."

The lord Gerald posteth into England.

These biting spéeches passing to and fro, great factions on both sides were raised, with high and mightie words, and deepe othes, till time either part appeased his owne. The baron of Ophalie not sleeping nor slacking his matter, spudded with all hast into England, where he was no sooner inshored, than Vescie, after he had substituted William Haie in his roome, was imbarked, making as hot foot after the baron as he could. The king and his councell vnderstanding the occasion of their sudden arriuals, to the end the truth should be brought to light, appointed a set daie for the deciding of their controuersie, and that each of them should speake for himselfe what he could. Wherevpon Vescie being commanded to begin, spake to this effect.

Vescie followeth.

Vescies oration.

"My dread soueraigne, as I must acknowledge my selfe somewhat agréeued, to be intangled in so intricate a matter, so I am as glad as hart can thinke that so weightie a controuersie is brought to the deciding of so vpright an vmpire. And whereas it stood with your maiesties pleasure, with the aduise of this your honourable councell, that I, as vnwoorthie, should haue the gouernment of your realme of Ireland; and during my time, your maiesties subiects, haue béene, I may not denie it, diuerslie annoied, for my discharge, as I said in Ireland, so I auow héere in England, that he kneeleth heere before your highnesse (pointing to the baron of Ophalie) that is the root and crop of all these enormities. For it is well knowne, that he beareth that stroke with the Irish, as if he once but frowne at them, they dare not be so hardie as once to peake out of their cabbins. And whereas his force dooth greatlie amaze them, thinke you but his countenance dooth woonderfullie incourage them? To the furtherance of which, it is apparantlie knowne, and it shall be prooued, that he hath not onelie in hucker mucker, by sundrie messages imboldened your maiesties enimies, to spoile your subiects, but also by his personall presence, in secret méetings, he gaue them such courage, as neither the roialtie of your highnesse, nor the authoritie of your deputie, neither the force of your lawes, nor the strength of your puissant armie, was able to quench the flame of these hurlie burlies, that through his traitorous drifts were inkindled. These and the like enormities through his priuie packing with rebels being dailie committed, to bring me your maiesties gouernour in the hatred of the people, his adherents both secretlie muttered, and openlie exclamed against me and my gouernment, as though the redresse of all these harmes had wholie lien in mine hands.

"Wherevpon being in conference with such as were the chiefteins of your realme of Ireland, albeit I tooke it to be expedient, to point with my finger to the verie sinke or headspring of all the treasons, that by secret conspiracies were pretended and practised against your maiestie and your subiects, yet notwithstanding hauing more regard to modestie, than to the deserts of the baron of Ophalie, I did but glanse at his packing in such secret sort, as none or a verie few of the companie could gesse, whome with my mistie speaches I did touch. And as commonlie the gald horsse dooth soonest kicke, so this gentelman being prickt, as it should seeme with the sting of his giltie conscience, brake out on a sudden, and forgetting his allegiance to your highnesse, and his dutie to me your deputie, he tooke me vp so roughlie, as though I had béene rather his vnderling than his gouernour. The summe of which despitefull speaches I refer to the testimonie of the honorable audience where they were deliuered. As for his manifold treasons, I am ashamed to rehearse such things as he did not sticke to commit. And if it shall stand with your maiesties pleasure, to adiourne the triall for a few daies, I will charge him with such apparent items, as were his face made of brasse, he shall not be able to denie

anie

anie one article that shall be booked against him." When Vescie had ended, the baron of Ophalie prest himselfe somewhat forward, and in this wise spake.

"Most puissant prince and my dread soueraigne, were maister Vescie his mouth of so iust a measure, as what he spake, should be holden for gospell, this had béene no fit place for so arrant a traitor, as he with his feigned glosing would gladlie proou me to be. But sith it pleased your maiestie, with so indifferent balance to ponder both our tales, I am throughlie persuaded, that my loiall innocencie shall be able, to ouerpoise his forged treacherie. Your maiestie hath heard manie words to small purpose. And as his complaint hitherto hath béene generallie hudled vp, so mine answer thereto may not particularlie be framed. Whereas therefore he termeth me a supporter of théeues, a packer with rebels, a conspirator with traitors, if I should but with a bare word denie the premisses, all his gaie glose of glitering speache, would suddenlie fade awaie. Yea, but he craueth respit for the booking of his articles. Trulie so he hath need. For loitering and lingring is the onlie waie he may deuise to cloke his feigning and forging. Wherin he sheweth himselfe as craftie, as the philosopher was accounted wise that promised a tyrant vpon menacing wordes, to schoole his asse in philosophie, so he had seuen yeares respit, bicause that in that space he was persuaded, that either the tyrant, the asse, or he would die. In likewise master Vescie, vpon respit granted him, would hang in hope, that either the life of your maiestie (which God forbid) should be shortened, or that I, in tract of time, would be disfauoured, or that he by one subtill pranke or other should be of this heauie load disburdened.

"But if I haue béene as manie yeares a malefactor as he adoucheth, how happeneth it, that his toong was tied before this late dissention begun? Whie did he not from time to time aduertise the councell of my treasons? Whereas now it may be probablie coniectured, that he was egd to this seruice rather for the hatred he beareth me, than for anie loue he oweth your loiall maiestie. Touching the words I spake in Ireland, I purpose not, for ought I heard as yet, to eat them in England. And when I shall be cald to testifie such speaches as I deliuered there, I will not be found so raw in my matter, as to lose my errant in the carriage, as master Vescie hath doone, or to craue further respit for the registring of his manifold treasons. As for my secret méetings with Irish rebels, where I persuaded master Vescie, that you were able to prooue them, I would be found willing to acknowledge them. For if my conscience were so deeplie stoong, as you pretend, I would take it for better policie, by acknowledging my trespasse, to appeale to my king his mercie, than by denieng my faults, to stand to the rigor of his iustice.

"And as for méetings, I had neuer so manie in woods with rebels, as you master Vescie, haue had in your chamber with cowes. For it hath béene manifestlie apparented, that when the baron of Ophalie, and the best of the nobilitie of Ireland haue béene imbard from entring your chamber, an Irish cow should haue at all times accesse vnto you. No, master Vescie, a cow, an horsse, an hauke, and a siluer cup haue béene the occasion of your slacknesse. When the subiects were preided, you would be content to winke at their miserie, so that your mouth were stopt with briberie. And when you had gathered your crums sufficientlie togither, you held it for a pretie policie (and yet it was but a bare shift) to charge the nobilitie with such packing, as you dailie did practise. But you must not thinke that we are babes, or that with anie such stale deuise, or grosse iuggling tricke, you may so easilie duske or dazell our eies. Can anie man that is but slenderlie witted, so far be carried, as to beleeue, that master Vescie, being the kings deputie in Ireland, hauing his maiesties treasure, hauing the nobilitie at his becke, the kings armie at his commandement, but that, if he were disposed to bestirre himselfe, he were able to ferret out such barebréech brats as swarme in the English pale? If he said

 he

he could not, we must smile at his simplicitie; if he could and would not, how may he colour his disloialtie?

"Yea, but I beare such stroke with the Irish, as that vpon anie priuat quarell I am able to annoie them. What then? Bicause the baron of Ophalie can reuenge his priuat iniuries without the assistance of the deputie, therefore the deputie may not vanquish weake and naked rebels without the furtherance of the baron of Ophalie: whereas the contrarie ought to be inferd, that if a priuat person can tame the Irish, what may then the publike magistrat doo, that hath the princes pare? But in déed it is hard to take hares with foxes. You must not thinke, master Vescie, that you were sent gouernour into Ireland to dandle your truls, to pen your selfe vp within a towne or citie to giue rebels the gaze, to pill the subiects, to animat traitors, to fill your coffers, to make your selfe by marring true men, to gather the birds whilest other beat the bushes, and after to impeach the nobilitie of such treasons, as you onelie haue committed.

"But for so much as our mutuall complaints stand vpon the one his yea, and the other his naie, and that you would be taken for a champion, & I am knowne to be no coward: let vs, in Gods name, leaue lieng for varlets, berding for ruffians, facing for crakers, chatting for twatlers, scolding for callets, booking for scriueners, pleading for lawyers, and let vs trie with the dint of sword, as become martiall men to doo, our mutuall quarels. Wherefore to iustifie that I am a true subiect, and that thou Vescie art an archtraitor to God & to my king, here in the presence of his highnesse, and in the hearing of this honorable assemblie, I chalenge the combat." Whereat all the auditorie shouted.

The combat chalenged.

Now in good faith, quoth Vescie, with a right good will. Wherevpon both the parties being dismist vntill the kings pleasure were further knowne, it was agréed at length by the councell, that the fittest triall should haue béene by battell. Wherefore the parties being as well thereof aduertised, as the daie by the king appointed, no small prouision was made for so eager a combat, as that was presupposed to haue beene. But when the prefixed daie approched néere, Vescie turning his great boast to small rost, began to crie creake, and secretlie sailed into France. King Edward thereof aduertised, bestowed Vescies lordships of Kildare and Rathimgan on the baron of Ophalie, saieng that albeit Vescie conueied his person into France, yet he left his lands behind him in Ireland.

Vescie fled into France. Kildare bestowed on the lord Girald.

The baron returned to Ireland with the gratulation of all his friends and was created earle of Kildare, in the ninth yeare of Edward the second his reigne, the fourteenth of Maie. He deceassed at Laraghbrine (a village néere to Mainooth) in the yeare 1316, and was buried at Kildare, so that he was earle but one yeare. The house of Kildare among diuerse gifts, wherewith God hath abundantlie indued it, is for one singular point greatlie to be admired, that notwithstanding the seuerall assaults of diuerse enimies in sundrie ages, yet this earle that now liueth is the tenth earle of Kildare, to whome from Iohn the first earle, there hath alwaies continued a lineall descent from father to son: which trulie in mine opinion is a great blessing of God. And for as much as this earle now liuing as his ancestors before him, haue beene shrewdlie shooued at by his euill willers, saieng that he is able, but not willing to profit his countrie: the posie that is framed for him, signifieng his mind, runneth in this wise.

The first earle of Kildare created 1315.

The number of the earles of Kildare.

"Quid possim, iactant: quid vellem, scire recusant:
Vtraque Reginæ sint, rogo, nota meæ."

Lord Gerald.

His eldest sonne is lord Girald, baron of Ophalie, for whom these two verses following are made.

"Te pulchrum natura fecit, fortuna potentem,
Te faciat Christi norma, Giralde, bonum."

Sir Thomas Butler earle of Ormond and Osserie. The Butlers were ancient English gentlemen, and worthie seruitors in all ages. Theobald Butler lord of Carrike and Iohn Cogan were lord iustices of Ireland. This Butler died in the castell of Arckelow, in the yeare 1285. This lord Theobald Butler the yoonger, and son to the elder Theobald, was sent for by Edward the first, to serue against the Scots. This noble man deceased at Turuie, and his bodie was conueighed to Weneie, a towne in the countie of Limerike. Sir Edmund Butler a wise and valiant noble man was dubbed knight at London by Edward the second. Earle of Ormond 1247 The Butlers (as I am informed) are found by ancient records to haue béene earles of the Carrike 1290 1309

This man being appointed lieutenant of Ireland, vpon the repaire of Iohn Wogan (who before was lord iustice) to England, besieged the Obirnes in Glindalone, and 1312
were it not that they submitted themselues to the king and the lieutenants mercie, they had not béene onelie for a season vanquished, but also vtterlie by him extirped. This noble man was in his gouernement such an incourager and furtherer of seruitors, as that he dubd on saint Michaell the archangels daie thirtie knights in 1314
the castell of Dublin. He was a scourge vnto the Scots that inuaded Ireland, when he was lieutenant. He discomfited Omough a notorious rebell, neare a towne 1315
named Balie lethan. After diuerse victorious exploits by him atchiued, he sailed into England, and so to Hispaine in pilgrimage to saint Iames. Vpon his returne 1316
to England, he deceased at London, and his bodie being conueied into Ireland was 1321
intoomed at Balligauran.

Iames Butler earle of Ormond was lord iustice of Ireland in the yeare 1359. The 1359
lord Butler and vicount Thurles was dubd knight by Henrie the sixt in England, in the yeare 1425, at which time sir Iames Butler, sir Iohn Butler, sir Rafe Butler 1425
were in like maner knighted. Iames Butler, who maried the earle of Herefords 1327
daughter, was preferred to the earledome of Ormond in the first yeare of Edward the third, which fell vpon the heirs generall lastlie vpon sir Thomas Butler earle of Wilshire, after whome it reuersed to Pierce Butler, whome a little before king Henrie the eight had created erle of Ossorie. I read Butler earle of Tipperarie in the yeare 1300. The Latine historie calleth him *Dominum de pincerna*, the English le Butler. Whereby it appeareth, he had some such honour about the prince. His verie name is Becket, who was aduanced by Henrie the seconds eldest sonne, lord Butler, in recompense of the death of Thomas of Canturburie their kinsman. His eldest sonne is the lord Butler and vicount Thurles. For the earle now liuing these two verses (in the remembrance of him) are made. The first earle of Ormond. Tipperarie

"Magnus auus, maiórq; pater, sed natus vtróq;
Corporis aut animi non bonitate minor."

Gerald fitz Gerald earle of Desmond. Maurice fitz Thomas a Geraldine, was created earle of Desmond the same yeare, soone after that Butler became erle of Ormond. His eldest sonne is lord fitz Gerald of Desmond. The erle now liuing, thus speaketh. Desmond.

"Quasi tandem, iactatus fluctibus alti,
Et precor in portu sit mea tuta ratis."

Sir Richard Bourke earle of Clenrickard, a branch of the English familie de Burgo. The Bourkes haue beene ancient noble men before their comming to Ireland, and in old time they haue beene earles of Vlster. His eldest sonne is lord Bourke baron of Enkelline. His verse is this. Clenrickard.

"Quam mihi maiorum fama bona gesta dederunt,
Hanc mihi natorum barbara facta negant."

Connogher Obren earle of Tomond, the name of earle giuen to Muriagh Obren for tearme of life, and after to Donogh Obren, in the fift yeare of the reigne of Edward the sixt, now confirmed to the heires males, his eldest sonne is baron of 1550
Ibracan. Vpon the erle now liuing this fantasie was deuised. Tomond.

"Non

"Non decet externos, sine causa, quærere reges,
Cùm liceat in tuta viuere pace domi."

Clencare Mac Cartie More earle of Clencare, created in the yeare 1565. Vicount Barrie.
Barrie Roch Vicount Roch. Preston Vicount of Gormanstowne: wherevnto is latelie annexed
Gormanstowne the baronie of Lawnedresse. One of their ancestors sir Robert Preston, then chiefe
baron of the exchecker, was dubbed knight in the field, by Lionell duke of Clarence.
This gentleman matched in wedlocke with Margaret Birmingham ladie of Carbrie,
1361 who deceassed in the yeare 1361. After whose death sir Robert Preston was seized
1367 of the said lordship in the right of his wife, and being molested by rebels, placed a
garison in the castell, whereby the subiects were greatlie eased, and the rebels
greatlie annoied.

1476 There hath béene another sir Robert Preston of this house, great grandfather to
the vicount now liuing. This gentleman was deputie to Richard, second son to
Edward the fourth, in the sixteenth yeare of the reigne of his father: and after
1492 likewise in the reigne of Henrie the seuenth, he was deputie to Iasper duke of
Bedford, erle of Penbroke, & lieutenant of Ireland: and at the same time was he
appointed by the king generall receiuer of his reuenue in Ireland. How wiselie this
noble man behaued himselfe in peace, and how valiantlie he bequit himselfe in
warre, sundrie of king Henrie the seuenth his letters to him being deputie, addressed,
doo manifestlie witnesse. There was a parlement holden before him at
1494 Drogheda, which was repealed in the tenth yeare of Henrie the seuenth. Sir
Christopher Preston was dubbed knight in the field by Edmund earle of March,
1397 lord deputie of Ireland. William Preston was lord iustice of Ireland in Henrie the
eight his reigne. The house is ancient, planted in Lancashire, and from thense
Preston came from Lancashire departed into Ireland, being to this daie seized of a manour in Lancashire, named
of the house Preston. The vicount now liuing speaketh in this wise, as it were
present in person, and saith:

"Si quantum vellem, tantum me posse putarem,
Nota esset patriæ mens mea firma meæ."

Baltinglasse. Eustace *alias* Powar, vicount of Baltinglasse, lord of Kilcullen to him and his
1542 heires males the foure and thirtith yeare of Henrie the eight. Their ancestor Robert
de Powar was sent into Ireland with commission, and his ofspring hath rested
1175 there since the yeare 1175. Powar *alias* Eustace is written baron of Domuile in the
yeare 1317. The vicounts poesie now liuing is this that followeth:

"Cùm bonus ipse manes, an non laus magna putatur,
Prudenter cunctis posse placere viro?"

Mountgarret 1550 Sir Richard Butler vicount Mountgarret to him and his heires males in the fift
Decce Athenrie yeare of Edward the sixt. Vicount Décee. Lord Bermingham baron of Athenrie,
now degenerate and become meere Irish, against whome his ancestors serued
valiantlie in the yeare 1300. Iohn Bermingham was lord of Athenrie Anno 1316.
Ardigh Iohn Bermingham baron of Ardigh, called in Latine de alrio Dei, in the yere 1318.
Kerie Courcie Mac Maurice, *alias* Fitzgerald, baron of Kerie. L. Courcie, not verie Irish, the
ancient descent of the Courcies planted in Ireland with the conquest. Fleming
Slane baron of Slane. Simon Fleming was baron of Slane, 1370. The L. now liuing
thus speaketh:

"Slanius inuictus princeps mihi nomen adaptat,
In bello clarum nomen & omen habens."

Killine Plunket baron of Killine, his familie came in with the Danes, whereof they haue
as yet speciall monuments. Sir Christopher Plunket lord of Killine, was lord lieutenant
of Ireland, which title is to be seene at this day in Killine, grauen on his
toome. The baron that now liueth, thus frameth his poesie:

"Ornant

"Ornant viuentem maiorum gesta meorum,
Talia me nequeunt viua cadente mori."

Nugent baron of Deluen, an ancient house. Sir Gilbert de Nogent, or Nugent, came into Ireland, with sir Hugh de Lacie, one of the first and valiant conquerors of the countrie. This Gilbert matched with Rosa de Lacie, sister to Hugh de Lacie. He had giuen him vpon the conquest the baronies of foure, and of Delume by the said sir Hugh, of whose brother Richard de Nogent, otherwise called Richardus de Capella, the house of Deluin is descended. In a conueiance past from sir Gilbert to his brother Richard, these words are inserted: "Dedi & concessi fratri meo Richardo de Capella totum conquestum meum in Hibernia, & terram quam dedit mihi dominus meus Hugo de Laci, qui vocatur Deluin, & totam terram meam in Anglia." The baron now liuing & louing his countrie thus speaketh: Deluin.

"In patria natus, patriæ prodesse laboro,
Viribus in castris, consilijsq. domi."

S. Laurence, baron of Howth, signifieng the disposition of his mind, he speaketh in this wise: Howth.

"Si redamas, redamo, si spernis, sperno. Quid ergo?
Non licet absq. tuis viuere posse bonis?"

Plunket baron of Dunsanie. Vpon the baron now liuing, this deuise was framed as you sée: Dunsan.

"Gratia quod dederat, si non fortuna negabit,
Dux tam præclaro stemmate dignus erit."

Barnewall baron of Trimlestowne. They came from litle Britain, where they are at this day a great surname. Vpon their first arriuall, they wan great possessions at Benhauen, where at length by conspiracie of the Irish they were all slaine, except one yoong man, who then studied the common lawes in England, who returning, dwelt at Drunnagh besides Dublin, where his heires to this date are setled. This house as well for antiquitie, as for the number of worshipfull gentlemen that be of the surname, beareth no small stroke in the English pale of Ireland: howbeit of late it hath béene greatlie maimed thorough the decease of thrée woorthie and famous Barnewals. The first was Robert Barnewall L. of Trimlestowne that last was, a rare noble man, and indued with sundrie good gifts, who hauing wholie wedded himselfe to the reformation of his miserable countrie, was resolued for the whetting of his wit, which nathelesse was pregnant and quicke, by a short trade and method he tooke in his studie, to haue sipt vp the verie sap of the common law, and vpon this determination sailing into England, sickened shortlie after at a worshipfull matrones house at Cornuberie, named Margaret Tiler, where he was to the great gréefe of all his countrie pearsed with death, when the weale publike had most néed of his life. The second Barnewall that deceased was M. Marcus Barnewall of Donbroa, whose credit and authoritie had it béene correspondent to his valure and abilitie, he would (I doubt not) haue béene accounted and knowne for as od a gentleman (none dispraised) as anie in the English pale of Ireland. Trimlestowne Drunnagh Robert Barnewall 1572 1574 Marcus Barnewall

The third of the surname that departed this life, was sir Christopher Barnwall knight, the lanterne and light as well of his house, as of that part of Ireland where he dwelt: who being sufficientlie furnisht as well with the knowlege of the Latine toong, as of the common lawes of England, was zealouslie bent to the reformation of his countrie. A déepe and a wise gentleman, spare of spéech, and therewithall pithie, wholie addicted to grauitie, being in anie pleasant conceipt rather giuen to simper than smile, verie vpright in dealing, measuring all his affaires with the safetie of conscience, as true as stéele, close and secret, fast to his friend, stout in a good quarell, a great housholder, sparing without pinching, spending without wasting, of nature mild, rather choosing to pleasure where he might harme, than willing Sir Christopher Barnwall knight.

willing to harme where he might pleasure. He sickened the thrée and twentith of
1175 Iulie of an hot burning ague, and ended his life at his house of Turuie the fift of
August, to the great losse as well of his friends as of his countrie, vpon whose death
a sonne in law of his framed this epitaph consisting of sixtéene verses.

"Læta tibi, sed mœsta tuis mors accidit ista,
Regna dat alta tibi, damna dat ampla tuis.
Lætus es in cœlis illo sine fine triumphans,
Mœstus at in terris diues inópsque iacet.
Nam sapiente caret diues, qui parta gubernet,
Nec, qui det misero munera, pauper habet.
Te gener ipse caret, viduæ, te rustica turba,
Atque vrbana cohors, te (socer alme) caret.
Non est digna viro talis respublica tanto,
Nam sanctos sedes non nisi sancta decet.
Mira loquor, sed vera loquor, non ficta reuoluo,
Si maiora loquar, nil nisi vera loquar.
Mortuus es? Nobis hoc crimina nostra dederunt.
Mortuus es? Virtus hoc tibi sacra dedit.
Viuus es in cœlo, dedit hoc tibi gratia Christi,
Viuus et in mundo sis, tibi fama dabit."

For the lord of Trimlestowne now liuing, desiring a name of fame after death, this was deuised.

"Quod mihi vita dedit, fratri Mors sæua negauit,
Quod dederat fratri, det mihi fama precor."

Dunboin 1541 Edward Butler baron of Donboin, giuen to Edmund Butler esquier, and his heires males, in the thrée and thirtith yeare of king Henrie the eight. For the baron now liuing, these verses are made.

"Dum sequitur natus summi vestigia patris,
Illius optato tramite cuncta geret."

Vpper Osserie 1541 Sir Barnabie Fitzpatrike baron of Vpper Osserie, giuen to Barnabie Mac Cullopatrike and his heires males, in the thrée and thirtith yeare of Henrie the eight. Donat Clonnagh Machgilpatrike was a péerelesse warriour in the yeare 1219. Sir
1558 Barnabie Fitzpatrike, now lord of vpper Osserie, was knighted by the duke of Norffolke at the siege of Leith in Scotland, in the beginning of Q. Elizabeths reigne, for whome these verses are made.

"Principis in gremio summi nutritus & altus,
Hausit ab illustri regia dona schola."

Louth 1541 Plunket, baron of Louth, to sir Christopher Plunket and his heires males, in the 33 yeare of K. Henrie the eight. This baronie was an erldome perteining to the Bermingham, in the yeare 1316, & sooner. For the baron now liuing, this was deuised:

"Nobilis, ingenuus, firmis quoque firmus amicis,
Nubila seu cœlum lúxue serena regat."

Dungannon Oneile baron of Dungannon, to whom the earledome of Tiron was intailed by
Curraghmore gift of king Henrie the eight. Powar, baron of Curraghmore. Mac Surtan, lord
Desert Desert, his ancestors were lords in the time of Lionell duke of Clarence, earle of
Insikoin Vlster, in the yeare 1360, now verie wild Irish. Murragh Obrene, baron of Insi-
1543 kome, to him and his heires males, in the fiue and thirtith yeare of king Henrie the eight. There are besides these noble men, certeine gentlemen of woorship com-
Baronets. monlie called baronets, whom the ruder sort dooth register among the nobilitie, by terming them corruptlie barons, whereas in verie déed they are to be named neither barons, nor baronets, but banrets. He is properlie called a banret, whose father was

no carpet knight, but dubbed in the field vnder the banner or ensigne. And bicause it is not vsuall for anie to be a knight by birth, the eldest sonne of such a knight with his heires, is named a banneret, or a barnet. Such are they that here insue: Sentleger, barnet of Flemarge, meere Irish. Den, barnet of Pormanstowne, waxing Irish. Fitzgirald, barnet of Burnechurch. Wellesle, barnet of Norragh. Husee, barnet of Galtrim. Saint Mighell, barnet of Scrine. And Nangle, barnet of the Nauan. English gentlemen of longest continuance in Ireland are those, which at this day either in great pouertie or perill doo keepe their proprieties of their ancestors lands in Vlster, being their companions to Courcie, the conqueror and earle of that part. These are the Sauages, Iordans, Fitz Simons, Chamberleins, Russels, Bensons, Audleies, Whites, Fitz Vrsulies, now degenerat and called in Irish Mac Mahon, the Beares sonne.

Banret what it is.

THE NAMES OR SURNAMES OF THE LEARNED MEN AND AUTHORS OF IRELAND, AND WHAT BOOKS THEY WROTE.

THE SEUENTH CHAPTER.

ARDERICUS, whome Marianus Scotus termeth Barbosus, because of his long beard, a learned man greatlie in old time renowmed in Ireland. But for as much as in his age the countrie was not stored with such as imploied their labors in gathering together the saiengs and doings of sage persons, the discontinuance of his fame is rather to be imputed to the ignorance of the time, than to the want of his deserts. He flourished in the yeare 1053. Alen, a learned physician. Iames Archer a student of diuinitie. Argobastus, the second bishop of Argentine, successor to the holie prelat saint Amand, borne in Ireland, a learned and deuout clerke: who leauing his countrie and liuing in heremit wise, in certeine solitarie places of France, instructed the people of that realme in the feare of God, and the knowledge of the scriptures. In his preaching he was noted to haue so singular a grace, and so prosperous successe, that such as were by anie worldlie misaduenture afflicted, vpon the hearing of his godlie sermons would suddenlie be comforted. The French king Dagobertus, aduertised of his lerning and vertue, caused him to be sent for, vsing him as his chiefe councellor in all his weightie affaires, and after aduanced him to be bishop of Argentine: he wrote a booke of homilies. He deceassed in the yeare 658. & was buried hard by a gibbet neere the citie, pitcht on the top of an hill called saint Michaels hill, which was doone by his owne appointment, in that he would follow the example of his maister Christ, who did vouchsafe to suffer without the citie of Ierusalem, where offendors and malefactors were executed. Barnwall. Bradie a preacher. Brendan an abbat borne in Connagh, in his youth trained vp vnder Hercus a bishop: and being further stept in yeres, he trauelled into England, where he became a protest moonke, vnder an abbat named Congellus, he flourished in the yeare 560, and wrote these bookes insuing: "Confessio christiana lib. 1. Charta cœlestis hæreditatis lib. 1. Monachorum regula lib. 1."

Ardericus. Alen. Archer. Argobastus. C46. Barnwall. Bradie. Brenuan.

Edmund Bernerden a frier, he procéeded doctor of diuinitie in Dublin, in the yeare 1320. Brigide the virgine, borne in Leinster, she flourished in the yeare 510: she wrote a booke of hir reuelations. Browne a ciuilian. Burnell. Butler a Waterfordian, sometime scholer to maister Peter White, he translated Maturinus Corderius his booke of phrases into English, in the yeare 1562. Iames Caddell, he wrote "Diuersa epigrammata." Carberie a profound ciuilian. Celsus archbishop of Armagh, borne in Ireland, and schooled in the vniuersitie of Oxford, he flourished

Bernerden. Brigide. Browne. Burnell. Butler. Caddell. Carberie. Celsus.

in the yeare 1128 he wrote these bookes following "Testamentum ad ecclesias lib. 1. Constitutiones quædam lib. 1. Ad Malachiam epistolas complures." Clere, borne in Kilkennie and procéeded maister of art in Oxford. Iohn Clin borne in Leinster, being profest a greie frier, he bestowed his time in preaching, chiefie in the towne of Kilkennie. This man was a good antiquarie, as appeared by a chronicle he wrote, beginning at the natiuitie of Christ, and stretching to the yeare 1350 in which yeare he flourished. He wrote these bookes following. "Annalium chronicon lib. 1. De regibus Anglorum lib. 1. De custodijs prouinciarum lib. 1. De Franciscanorum cœnobijs & eorum distinctionibus lib. 1."

Clere. Clin.

Henrie Cogie doctor of diuinitie, procéeded in the vniuersitie of Dublin, in the yeare 1320. Colme, a learned and an holie monke, he flourished in the yeare 670. he wrote a booke intituled "Pro socijs Quartadecimanis." Columbanus, borne in Vlster, and trained in learning and knowledge as well in England as in France, for his learning and vertue, was elected to be abbat. Hauing trauelled diuerse countries, at length he repaired to Italie, and there in an abbeie by him founded, called *Monasterium Bobiense*, he ended his life the twentith of Nouember.
598
He left to his posteritie these bookes "In psalterium commentarios lib. 1. Collationes ad monachos librum 1. De moribus monachorum metricè lib. 1. Monasteriorum methodos lib. 1. Epistolas ad commilitones lib. 1. Aduersus regem adulterum lib. 1." Conganus an Irish abbat, of whom saint Barnard maketh great account, he flourished in the yeare 1150 and wrote to saint Bernard "Gesta Malachiæ archiepiscopi lib. 1. Ad Bernardum Clareuallensem epist. plures." Connour. Walter Conton he wrote in the Latine toong diuerse epigrams and epitaphs. Simon Cornell a diuine. Cornelius Hibernus, otherwise named Historicus, by reason that he was taken in his time for an exquisit antiquarie, as may appeare by the Scotish historian Hector Boetius, by whom he acknowledgeth himselfe to be greatlie furthered. He flourished in the yeare 1230. and wrote "Multarum rerum Chronicon. lib. 1." Richard Creagh borne in Limerike, a diuine, he wrote "Epistolas complures. Responsiones ad casus conscientiæ. De vitis sanctorum Hiberniæ. Topographiam Hiberniæ," with diuerse other bookes.

Cogie. Colme. Columbanus. Conganus. Barnardus in vit. Malachiæ in præfat. Connour. Conton. Cornell. Cornelius. Hec. or Boet. in præfat. Scot. hist. Creagh.

Henrie Crumpe borne in Ireland, and brought vp in the vniuersitie of Oxford, where he grew by reason of his profound knowledge in diuinitie to no small credit. Hauing repaired to his natiue countrie, minding there to defraie the talent wherewith God had indued him, he was suddenlie apprehended by Simon bishop of Meth, and kept in duresse, by reson that he was suspected to be of no sound religion. He florished in the yeare one thousand thrée hundred ninetie and two, and wrote these bookes "Determinationes scholast. lib. 1. Contra religiosos mendicantes lib. 1. Responsiones ad obiecta lib. 1." Edmund Curren archdeacon of old Laghlin, there hath béene an Irish bishop of the name. Patrike Cusacke a gentleman borne, and a scholer of Oxford, sometime schoolemaister in Dublin, and one that with the learning that God did impart him, gaue great light to his countrie, he imploied his studies rather in the instructing of scholers, than in penning of books, he florished in the yeare one thousand fiue hundred thrée score and six, and wrote in Latine "Diuersa epigrammata."

Crumpe. Curren. Cusacke.

Dalie schooled in the vniuersitie of Paris, hauing a pretie insight in scholasticall diuinitie, he made "Diuersas conciones." Sir Willielme Darcie knight, a wise gentleman he wrote a booke intituled "The decaie of Ireland." Dauid Delahide, an exquisite and a profound clerke, sometime fellow of Merton college in Oxford, verie well séene in the Latine and Gréeke toongs, expert in the mathematicals, a proper antiquarie, and an exact diuine. Whereby I gather that his pen hath not béene lazie, but is dailie bréeding of such learned bookes as shall be auailable to his posteritie. I haue séene a proper oration of his in the praise of master Herwood being

Dalie. Darcie. Delahide.

being Christmasse lord in Merton college intituled, "De ligno & fœno," also "Schemata rhetorica in tabulam contracta." Deurox, there are two brethren of the name learned, the elder was sometimes schoolemaister in Weisford. Deurox

Peter Dillon a diuine, and Iohn Dillon likewise a student in diuinitie. Doudall, sometime primat of Armagh, a graue, a learned, and a politike prelat, verie zealouslie affected to the reformation of his countrie, he made "Diuersas conciones." Dormer a lawyer, borne in Rosse, scholer of Oxford, he wrote in ballat roiall, "The decaie of Rosse." Iohannes Duns Scotus an Irishman borne, as in the forefront of this treatise I haue declared. Howbeit Iohannes Maior a Scotish chronicler would faine prooue him to be a Scot. Leland on the other side saith he was borne in England. So that there shall as great contention rise of him, as in old time there rose of Homers countrie. For the Colophonians said that Homer was borne in their citie, the Chians claimed him to be theirs, the Salaminians auouched that he was their countriman: but the Smirnians were so stiffelie bent in prooning him to be borne in their territorie, as they would at no hand take no naie in the matter, & therevpon they did consecrat a church to the name of Homer. But what countriman soeuer this Scotus were, he was doubtlesse a subtill and profound clerke. The onelie fault wherewith he was dusked, was a litle spice of vaineglorie, being giuen to carpe and taunt his predecessor diuines, rather for blemishing the fame of his aduersaries than for aduancing the truth of the controuersies. Wherevpon great factions are growen in the schooles betwéene the Thomists and Scotists, Thomas being the ringleader of the one sect, and Scotus the belweadder of the other. He was fellow of Merton college in Oxford, and from thense he was sent for to Paris to be a professor of diuinitie. Finallie, he repaired vnto Cullen, where in an abbeie of greie friers (of which profession he was one) he ended his life. The books he wrote are these: "Commentarij Oxonienses lib. 4. Reportationes Parisienses lib. 4. Quodlibeta scholastica lib. 1. In Analytica posteriora lib. 2. In metaphysicam quæstiones lib. 12. De cognitione Dei lib. 1. De perfectione statuum lib. 1. Sermones de tempore lib. 1. Sermones de Sanctis lib. 1. Collationes Parisienses lib. 1. Lectura in Genesim lib. 1. De rerum principio lib. 1. Commentarij in euangelia lib. 4. In epistolas Pauli lib. plures. Quæstiones vniuersalium lib. 1. Quæstiones prædicamentorum lib. 1. In Aristotelis physica lib. 8. In categorias Aristotelis lib. 1. Tetragrammata quædam lib. 1. Commentariorum imperfectorum lib. 1."

Dillon Doudall

Dormer

Duns Iohannes Maior lib. 4 cap. 10

Cic. in orat. pro Arch. poeta

Thomistæ Scotistæ

1308

Eustace a doctor of diuinitie, a verie good schooleman, he florished in the yeare one thousand fiue hundred thirtie and six. Oliuer or Oliuer Eustace a student of the ciuill and canon law, a good humanician, and a proper philosopher. Nicholas Eustace a gentleman borne, surpassing both by learning, and learning by vertue. Maurice Eustace a student of diuinitie, one that notwithstanding he were borne to a faire liuing, yet did wholie sequester himselfe from the world. Fustace

Fagan a batchellor of art in Oxford, and a schoolemaister in Waterford. Daniell Ferraile, a diuine and a schoolemaister. Fergutius son to Ferquhardus king of Ireland, the first king of Scots, whome some affirme to be borne in Denmarke, the more part suppose him to haue béene an Irish man. He florished in the yeare of the world thrée thousand six hundred seuentie and eight, and before the incarnation two hundred ninetie and two, in the fiue and twentith yeare of his reigne. He was by misaduenture drowned néere a rocke in the north of Ireland that of him is called to this daie Carregfergus, vpon whose mishap these verses were made: Carregfergus

Fagan Ferraile Fergutius

> "Icarus Icareis vt nomina fecerat vndis,
> Fergusius petræ sic dedit apta suæ."

This Fergusius wrote a booke intituled, "Leges politicæ lib. 1." Finnanus scholer to one Nennius and Segenius, taken for a deepe diuine in his age, he florished in the yeare six hundred sixtie and one, he wrote "Pro veteri paschatis Finnanus.

Field situ lib. 1. Field a physician. Thomas Field a master of art. Iohn Fitzgirald, commonlie named Iohn Fitzedmund, a verie well lettered ciuilian, a wise gentleman, and a good housholder.

Fitzgirald Robert Fitzgirald *alias* Robert Fitzmaurice borne in the countie of Kildare. Dauid Fitzgirald, vsuallie called Dauid Duffe, borne in Kerie, a ciuilian, a maker in Irish, not ignorant of musike, skilfull in physike, a good & generall craftsman

Hippias much like to Hippias, surpassing all men in the multitude of crafts, who comming on a time to Pisa to the great triumph called Olympicum, ware nothing but such as was of his owne making, his shooes, his pattens, his cloke, his cote, the ring that he did weare, with a signet therin verie perfectlie wrought, were all made by him. He plaied excellentlie on all kind of instruments, and soong therto his owne verses, which no man could amend. In all parts of logike, rhetorike, and philosophie he vanquished all men, and was vanquished of none.

Fitzrafe Richard Fitzrafe, primat of Armagh, scholer in the vniuersitie of Oxford to Baconthorpe a good philosopher, & no ignorant diuine, an enimie to friers, namelie such as went begging from doore to doore: whereby he purchased the hatred of all religious persons. He was by Edward the third his means made archdeacon of Lichfield, after created primat of Armagh, being cited before pope Clement the

1360 sixt, for reproouing the begging friers. In the heat of the said contention he deceassed in Italie, whose bones were caried into Ireland, and buried at Dondalke, where he was borne. He wrote these bookes insuing: "De paupertate seruatoris lib. 7. Contra fratres mendicantes lib. 16. In extrauagantem Ioannis 23 lib. 1. Determinationes ad eundem lib. 1. Contra suum archidiaconum lib. 1. Propositiones ad papam lib. 1. Contra fratrum appellationem lib. 1. Sermones ad crucem Pauli lib. 1. Sermones coram pontifice lib. 1. De statu vniuersalis ecclesiæ lib. 1. Lectura sententiarum lib. 4. Quæstiones earundem lib. 1. Lectura theologica lib. 1. Sermones ad clerum lib. 1. Sermones de tempore lib. 1. Sermones de sanctis lib. 1. Mariæ laudes Auenion: lib. 1. Illustrationes euangeliorum lib. 4. De passione dominica lib. 1. De peccato ignorantiæ lib. 1. De Iure spirituali lib. 1. De vafricijs Iudæorum lib. 1. Propositionum suarum lib. 1. Epistolarum ad diuersos lib. 1. Dialogorum plurium librum vnum."

Fitzsimons Walter Fitzsimons, archbishop of Dublin, lord iustice and lord chancellor of Ireland at one time, a famous clerke, and exquisitelie learned both in philosophie and diuinitie: being in companie with king Henrie the seuenth, and hearing an oration that was made in his praise, the king demanded him, what fault he found most in the oration? Trulie (quoth he) if it like your highnesse, no fault, sauing onelie that the orator flattered your maiestie ouermuch. Now in good faith, our father of Dublin (quoth the king) we minded to find the same fault our selues. Thomas Fitzsimons, a verie proper diuine: he wrote in English a treatise of the church. Leonard Fitzsimons, a deepe and pithie clerke, well séene in the Greeke and Latine toong, sometime fellow of Trinitie college in Oxford, perfect in the mathematicals, and a painefull student in diuinitie: he hath a brother that was trained vp in learning in Cambridge now beneficed in Trim. Michaell Fitzsimons, schoolemaster in Dublin, a proper student, and a diligent man in his profession, he wrote "Orationem in aduentum comitis Essexiæ Dubliniam, Epitaphium in mortem Iacobi Stanihursti. Diuersa epigrammata."

Flattisburie Philip Flattisburie, a worthie gentleman, and a diligent antiquarie, he wrote in the Latine toong, at the request of the right honorable Girald Fitzgirald erle of Kildare, "Diuersas chronicas:" he flourished in the yeare one thousand fiue hundred and seauenteene, & deceassed at his towne named Iohnstowne néere the Naas.

Fleming Thomas Fleming: there is a Fleming now liuing, of whome I heare great report to

Foillanus be an absolute diuine, and a professor thereof. Foillanus a learned moonke, he trauelled

trauelled into France, where thorough the liberalitie of an holie virgine, named 655
Gertrude, he founded an abbeie called Monasterium Fossense, where at length he
suffered martyrdome. Fursæus peregrinus, so called, bicause he was borne in Furseus
Ireland, and did bestow his yeares as an estranger in France, where he founded an
abbeie named Cœnobium Latiniacense: he wrote certeine pamphlets, that by tract 657
of time are perished, he flourished in the yeare six hundred and sixtie, and was
buried in his owne monasterie.

Robert Garuie, fellow of Oriall college in Oxford, a student of both the lawes, Garuie
a man well spoken as well in the English as in the Latine. Robert Cogan a Cogan
preacher. William Hardit a doctor of diuinitie, proceeded in the vniuersitie of Hardit
Dublin, in the yeare one thousand thrée hundred and twentie. Hickie, physicians Hickie
the father and his sonne. Hugo de Hibernia, so called, bicause his surname is not Hugo
knowne, he was a greie frier, and a great trauellet, he flourished in the yeare one
thousand thrée hundred and sixtie, he wrote "Itinerarium quoddam lib. 1." Oliuer
Hussie, a professor of the arts in Dowaie. Derbie Hurlie, a ciuilian, and a com- Hussie Hurlie
mendable philosopher: he wrote "In Aristotelis physica." Robert Iorse, borne in Iorse
Kilkennie, a good humanician. Radulphus Kellie a moonke, brought vp in the Kellie
knowledge of the Latine toong in Kildare, in which he profited so well, that for his
eloquence and wisedome he was sent to Clement the sixt, as the speaker or prolocutor of all his order, and also was appointed the generall aduocat or deputie vnder
Petrus de Casa, master generall of the order. After he was aduanced to be archbishop of Cashill, in which honour he deceassed, hauing at vacant houres written 1342
"In iure canonico lib. 1. Epistolarum familiarium lib. 1." Thomas Kenedie, a Kenedie
ciuilian.

Kerme, he wrote in Irish "Catechismum, Translationem bibliæ." Cagher, a Kerme
nobleman borne, in his time called Mac Murrough, he descended of that Mac Keuenagh
Murrough that was sometime king of Leinster, he was a surpassing diuine, and
for his learning and vertue was created bishop of Leighlin and abbat of Grage: he
flourished in the yeare one thousand fiue hundred and fiftie, and was an hundred
yeares old when he deceassed. Iames King, borne in Dublin, and scholer to M. King
Patrike Cusacke, vnder whome being commendablie trained he repaired to the
vniuersitie of Cambridge, where he deceassed before he could atteine to that ripenesse of learning, whereto one of so pregnant a wit was like in time to aspire, he 1569
wrote "Carmina in laudem Henrici Sidnæi, Diuersa epigrammata." Leie, a learned Leie
and an expert physician. Leurouse a learned diuine, sometime bishop of Kildare, and Leurouse
deane of saint Patriks in Dublin. Aeneas Loghlen, or Mackleighlen, master of art, 1550 Loghlen
and a preacher. Thomas Long doctor of both the lawes, he procéeded at Paris, in Long
the yeare one thousand fiue hundred seuentie and six in August, he is a proper
philosopher, no stranger in scholasticall diuinitie, a pretie Latinist: he wrote "De
speciebus contra mendacem monachum, In Aristotelis physica, Theses ex præcipuis
iuris vtriusque partibus selectas Carolo Borbonio cardinali consecratas."

Peter Lombard borne in Waterford, scholer to master Peter White, hauing im- Lombard
ploied two yeares and a halfe in the studie of philosophie at Louaine, he was chosen
when he procéeded master of art, Primus vniuersitatis, by the vniforme consent of
the foure principals, which preferment did happen to none in such consenting wise,
in manie yeares before: he wrote "Carmen heroicum in doctoratum Nicholai Que-
merfordi." Dorbie Macchragh, a student in diuinitie. Macgrane, a schoolemaster Macchragh
in Dublin, he wrote carols and sundrie ballads. Malachias borne in Vlster, his Macgrane Malachias
life is exactlie written by saint Barnard, in whose abbeie he died in the yeare one
thousand one hundred fortie and eight, he wrote "Constitutionum communium
lib. 1. Legum cœlibatus lib. 1. Nouarum traditionum lib. 1. Ad D. Barnardum
epist. plures." Malachias, the minorit or greie frier, a student in the vniuersitie Malachias minorit
of

of Oxford, where he attened to that knowledge in diuinitie, as he was the onelie man in his time that was appointed to preach before the king and the nobilitie, a sharpe reproouer of vice, a zelous imbracer of vertue, enimie to flatterie, friend to simplicitie, he flourished in the yeare one thousand thrée hundred and ten, he wrote "De peccatis & remedijs, lib 1 Conciones plures, lib 1"

Mauricius *Ioannes Camert' in cap 35 Sol* Mauricius Hybernus, of him Iohannes Camertes, thus writeth "Annis ab his proximis excelluit, ex ea insula oriundus Mauricius, D. Francisci ordinis professus, in dialecticis, vtraque philosophia, metaphysicis, ac sacra theologia plurimum eruditus Vix insuper dici potest, qua humanitate, quáue morum sanctimonia præditus fuerit Is cum annis plurimis in Patauino gymnasio bonas artes docuisset, cum summa omnium gratia, ob eius singularem eruditionem, ac candidissimos mores, à Iulio secundo pontifice maximo in Tuanensem archiepiscopum creatus est Quo cùm relicta Italia bellis in ea sæuientibus proficisceretur, non multùm post, magna studiorum iactura, cùm nondum quinquagesimum ætatis suæ attigisset annum, mortem obijt Erant plurima suæ doctrinæ in manibus monumenta, sed ea ob immaturam eius mortem edere non licuit Quantum fuerit inter eum, dum viueret, & me necessitudinis vinculum, testantur sexcentæ epistolæ, quas plenas charitatis indicijs, varijs temporibus ad me dedit. Eis (quanta veræ amicitiæ vis) post amici obitum, relegens soleo assiduè recreari"

There did (saith Ioannes Camertes) of late yeares one Mauricius borne in Ireland excell, a greie frier profest, verie well séene in logike, deepelie grounded in philosophie, both morall & naturall, learned in the metaphysiks, in diuinitie péerelesse Scantlie maie I tell with how great courtesie & vertue he was indued When he had professed at Padua the liberall arts manie yeares with no small renowme, he was created by Iulius the second, not onelie for his profound knowledge, but also for the sinceritie of his life, archbishop of Tuen When he was trauelling thitherward, being departed frō Italie, by reason of the vproires that were there daily increasing, he ended his life to the great losse of learning, before he was full fiftie yeares old He had sundrie works in hand, which he could not haue finished by reason of his vntimelie death How déere and entier friends he and I were one to the other during his life, the letters he addressed me from time to time, to the number of six hundred, thwackt with loue and kindnesse, doo manifestlie declare. And by perusing of them after his death (such is the force of friendship) I am greatlie comforted Thus farre Camertes This Mauricius wrote "Commentarios super Scotum in prædicabilia, In magistrium sententiarum lib 4" Mauricius archbishop of Cashill, he flourished in king Iohns reigne Giraldus Cambrensis, vpon his comming into Ireland, and debasing the countrie in the hearing of this prelat, saieng that albeit the inhabitants were woont to brag of the number of their saints, yet they had no martyrs You saie verie well sir (quoth the archbishop) indéed as rude as this countrie is or hath béene, yet the dwellers had the saints in some reuerence But now that the gouernement of the countrie is come to your kings hands, we shall (I trust) shortlie be stored with martyrs

Iohn Magh a diuine, he wrote a treatise, "De possessionē monasteriorum" Moonie a ciuilian and a good Latinist Neilan, sometime fellow of Alsoules college in Oxford, a learned physician Patrike Nigran a diuine Philip Norris a scholer of Oxford and after deane of S Patriks in Dublin, he flourished in the yeare 1446, and wrote these workes "Declamationes quasdam lib. 1. Lecturas scripturarum lib. 1 Sermones ad populum lib. 1 Contra mendicitatem validam lib 1" Nugent, baron of Deluin, schooled in the vniuersitie of Cambridge William Nugent a proper gentleman, and of a singular good wit, he wrote in the English toong diuerse sonets

David Cbrge, borne in the towne of Kildare; for his learned lectures, and subtile

tile disputations openlie published in Oxford and Treuers in Germanie, he was taken for the gem and lanterne of his countrie. In his time Giraldus Bononiensis, being maister generall of the Carmelits, was at iar with William Lidlington, the prouinciall of all the English Carmelites. Whervpon tenne of the wisest and learnedest Carmelits that then were resiant in England, being fullie elected to resist their generall, Obuge was chosen to be the forman of all the said crew. Giraldus Bononiensis vnderstanding that he being an Irishman, was so hot in the controuersie, was egerly bent against Obuge, because he assured himselfe to haue had fauour at his hands, by reason Obuge was borne in that countrie where the Giraldines his kinsmen were planted, and therevpon he was banished Italie. This storme in processe of time being appeased, the outcast Carmelite was made the generall gardian of all his fraternitie in Ireland: which countrie by his continuall teaching and preaching was greatlie edified. Ouer this he was so politike a councellor, that the nobilitie and estates in causes of weight, would haue recourse to him as to an oracle. He was in philosophie an Aristotle, in eloquence a Tullie, in diuinitie an Augustine, in the ciuill law a Iustinian, in the canon a Panormitane, he flourished in the yeare 1320, he deceased at Kildare, leauing these learned workes insuing to posteritie: "Sermones ad Clerum lib. 1. Epistolæ 32 ad diuersos lib. 1. Propositiones disputatas lib. 1. Lectiones Treuerenses lib. 1. Regulæ Iuris lib. 1. Contra Giraldum Bononiensem." Giraldus Bononiensis.

Owen Odewhee, a preacher, and a maker in Irish. Thomas Oherunaine, deane of Corke, a learned diuine, he wrote in Latine "Ad Iacobum Stanihurstum epist. plures." Thomas Oherligh, bishop of Rosse, an exquisite diuine, brought vp in Italie. Pander, a man zelouslie addicted to the reformation of his countrie, whereof he wrote a politike booke in Latine, intituled "Salus populi." Patricius, who notwithstanding he be no Irishman borne, yet I may not ouerslip him in the catalog of Irish authors, for as much as his whole works tended to the conuersion and reformation of that countrie: he was surnamed Succetus or Magonius, an absolute diuine, adorning his deepe knowledge therein with sinceritie of life. Being sent into Ireland by the appointment of Celestinus the first, accompanied with Segetius a priest, he conuerted the Iland from idolatrie and paganisme to christianitie. He wrote these bookes following. "De antiquitate Aualonica lib. 1. Itinerarium confessionis lib. 1. Odoiporicon Hyberniæ lib. 1. Historia Hyberniæ ex Ruano lib. 1. De tribus habitaculis lib. 1. De futura electorum vita lib. 1. Abiectoria quædam 366 lib. 1. Ad Ceretic um tyrannum epist. 1. Sermones lib. 1. Ad Aualonicos incolas epist. 1. Ad Hybernicas ecclesias epist. plures. Ad Britannos epist. plures." He deceased, being one hundred, twentie, and two yeares old, in the yeare 458, or as some suppose 491, and lieth buried in an ancient citie, in the north of Ireland, named Downe, according to the old verse, which saith. Odewhee. Oherunaine. Oherligh. Pander. Patricius. 432.

"Hi tres in Duno tumulo tumulantur in vno,
Brigida, Patricius, átque Columba pius."

Patricius Abbas a learned man, and much giuen to the edifieng of his countriemen: he florished in the yeare 850, and deceased at Glasconburie. Some ascribe the finding of saint Patrikes purgatorie to this abbat, not to Patrike that conuerted the countrie, but that errour hath béene before sufficientlie reprooued. This abbat wrote "Homilias lib. 1. Ad Hybernos epist. plures." Petrus Hybernicus, professor of philosophie in Naples, at which time Thomas Aquinas that after became the lanterne of scholemen, both in philosophie and diuinitie, was his scholer, being therefore as highlie renowmed as Socrates is for being maister to Plato, or Plato is, for hauing Aristotle to his scholer. This Petrus flourished in the yeare 1230, he wrote "Quodlibeta theologica lib. 1." Plunket, baron of Dunsanie, scholer in Ratough, to M. Staghens, after sent by sir Christopher Barnewall knight, his freendlie father Patricius abbas. Petrus Hybernicus. Plunket.

father in law, to the vniuersitie of Oxford. Where, how well he profited in knowledge, as such as are of his acquaintance presentlie perceiue, so hereafter when his workes shall take the aire, that now by reason of bashfull modestie, or modest bashfulnesse are wrongfullie imprisoned, and in manner stiefled in shadowed couches, I doubt not, but by his fame and renowme in learning, shall be answerable to his desert and value in writing.

Poomrell. Poomrell, a batchelor of diuinitie, sometime chapleine in New college in Oxford, after returning to his countrie, he was beneficed in Drogheda, from thense flitted to Louaine, where through continuall hearing of lectures and disputations, more than by his priuat studie, he purchased a laudable knowledge in diuinitie. Whereby The force of exercise. he gaue manifest shew of the profit that riseth of exercise and conference. Vpon this occasion, one of his acquaintance was accustomed to tell him that he had all his diuinitie by hearesaie. He deceased at Louaine in the yere 1573. Nicholas Quemerford 1575. Quemerford, doctor of diuinitie, proceeded the thrée and twentith of October, he wrote in English a verie pithie and learned treatise, and therewithall exquisitelie pend, intituled, Answers to certeine questions propounded by the citizens of Waterford, Diuerse sermons. There liued latelie of the surname a graue prelat in Waterford, and properlie learned.

Rian. Rian, there liued two brethren of the surname, both scholers of Oxford, the Richard one a good ciuilian, the other verie well séene in the mathematicals. Richard archdeacon of saint Patriks, chancellor in the vniuersitie of Dublin, procéeded doctor of the canon law, in the yeare one thousand thrée hundred and twentie. Robert Rochford Rochford borne in the countrie of Weisford, a proper diuine, an exact philosopher, and a verie good antiquarie. There is another Rochford that is a student Rooth of philosophie. Rooth, batchelor of law, procéeded in the vniuersitie of Oxford. There hath béene another Rooth vicar of S. Iohns in Kilkennie pretilie learned. De sacrobosco Iohannes de sacro bosco, borne in Holiwood, and thereof surnamed De sacro bosco, Sedgraue he wrote an excellent introduction, "De Sphæra." Sedgraue, two brethren of the Shaghens name, both students in diuinitie. Shaghens fellow of Balioll college in Oxford, Sheine after schoolemaister in Ireland, a learned and a vertuous man. Sheine, scholer in Sheth Oxford and Paris, he wrote, "De Repub." Elias Sheth borne in Kilkennie, sometime scholer of Oxford, a gentleman of a passing good wit, a plesant conceited companion, full of mirth without gall, he wrote in English diuerse sonets. Michaell Sheth borne in Kilkennie, master of art. Skidmor Skidmor borne in Corke, and gardian of Yoghill.

Smith. Richard Smith borne in a towne named Rackmacknere, thrée miles distant from Weisford, surnamed Smith, of his father, who was by occupation a smith, being fourtéene yéeres of age he stole into England, and repaired to Oxford, where in tract of time he procéeded doctor of diuinitie, was elected doctor of the chaire, taken in those daies for a péerelesse pearle of all the diuines in Oxford, as well in scholasticall as in positiue diuinitie. Vpon the death of queene Marie he went to Louaine, where he read openlie the apocalypse of saint Iohn, with little admiration and lesse reprehension, he wrote in English against licentious fasting, or the libertie of fasting, "The assertion of the sacrament of altar, A defense of the sacrifice of the masse one booke, Of vnwritten verities one booke, Retractations one booke." In the Latin toong he wrote "De cœlibatu sacerdotum lib. 1. De votis monasticis lib. 1. De iustificatione hominis librum vnum."

Stanihurst. Nicholas Stanihurst, he wrote in Latine "Dietam medicorum lib. 1." he died in the yeare one thousand fiue hundred fiftie and foure. Iames Stanihurst, late recorder of Dublin, ouer his exact knowlege in the common lawes, he was a good orator, and a proper diuine. He wrote in English, being speaker in the parle-1557 ments, "An oration made in the beginning of a parlement holden at Dublin before the

the right honorable Thomas earle of Sussex, &c in the third and fourth yeares of Philip and Marie, An oration made in the beginning of the parlement holden at Dublin before the right honorable Thomas earle of Sussex, in the second yeare of 1560
the reigne of our soueraigne ladie quéene Elisabeth, An oration made in the beginning of a parlement holden at Dublin before the right honorable sir Henrie Sidneie knight, &c in the eleuenth yeere of the reigne of our soueraigne ladie quéene 1568
Elisabeth ' He wrote in Latine, " Pias orationes Ad Corcaciensem decanum epistolas plures ' he deceassed at Dublin the seuen and twentith of December, being 1578
one and fiftie yeares old Vpon whose death, I, as nature and dutie bound me, haue made this epitaph following

" Vita breuis, mors sancta fuit (pater optime) visa,
Vita timenda malis, mors redamanda bonis.
Vrbs est orba sopho, legum rectore tribunal,
Causidicóque cliens, atque parente puer
Plurima proferrem, sed me prohibere videtur,
Pingere vera dolor, fingere falsa pudor
Non opus est falsis, sed quæ sunt vera loquenda,
Non mea penna notet, buccina fama sonet
Hoc scripsisse satis, talem quandóque parentem
Est habuisse decus, sed caruisse dolor
Filius hæc dubitans, talem vix comperit vsquam,
Vllus in orbe patrem, nullus in vrbe parem
Mortuus ergo, pater, poteris bene viuus haberi,
Viuis enim mundo nomine, mente Deo "

Walter Stanihurst, sonne to Iames Stanihurst, he translated into English " Innocent de contemptu mundi " There flourished before anie of these a Stanihurst, Circa annum Dom 1506
that was a scholer of Oxford, brother to Gennet Stanihurst, a famous and an ancient matrone of Dublin, she lieth buried in saint Michaels church Sutton, one Sutton.
of that name is a verie good maker in English. Matthew Talbot schoolemaster, Talbot.
a student in Cambridge. William Talbot. Iohn Talbot sonne to William, a master of art, he wrote in Latine, " Orationem in laudem comitis Essexiæ, Diuersa epigrammata ' Edmund Tanner a profound diuine, he wrote " Lectiones in summam Tanner.
D Thomæ ' Tailer batchelor of art, procéeded in the vniuersitie of Oxford, he Tailer
wrote in Latine " Epigrammata diuersa "

Thomas Hybernus borne in Palmerstowne néere the Naas, he procéeded doctor Thomas Hybernus
of diuinitie in Paris, a déepe clerke and one that read much, as may easilie be gathered by his learned workes · he flourished in the yeare 1290, and wrote with diuerse other workes, these bookes insuing. " Flores bibliæ, Flores doctorum lib 2 De christiana religione lib 1 De illusionibus dæmonum lib. 1 De tentatione diaboli lib 1. De remedijs vitiorum lib 1 " Laurentius Toole archbishop of Dub- Toole
lin Trauerse doctor of diuinitie, he flourished in the reigne of Henrie the eight Trauerse
There hath beene after him a schoolemaister in Dublin of that name. Tundalus Tundalus
Magus a knight, after he became a Charterhouse moonke, much giuen to contemplation, wherein he is reported to haue seene diuerse visions of heauen and hell, and therevpon he wrote " Apparitionem suarum lib. 1." he flourished in the yeare 1149

Virgilius Soliuagus a noble man borne, being stept in yeares, he trauelled into Virgilius Soliuagus
Germanie, where being knowen for a vertuous and learned prelat, he was chosen by Odilon duke of Bauaria, to be then rector or gardian of an ancient abbeie, 754
named S Peters abbeie, placed in the citie of Salisburgh, after he was created Episcopus Iuuauiensis, and founded in the said towne of Salisburgh a church. In his time one Bonifacius an Englishman, being generall visitour in Bauaria, rebap-

tized certe ne, whome he suspected not to haue béene orderlie baptized. Virgilius detesting the fact, hauing consulted with Sidonius archbishop of Bauaria, withstood Bonifacius in his fond attempt. The controuersie being brought before pope Zacharias, he decréed that Bonifacius held an error, and that Virgilius and Sidonius published in that point sound doctrine, as who so will read Zacharias his epistle vnto Bonifacius shall plainelie see. *Tomo primo conciliorum* Virgilius deceassed 784, and lieth buried in his church at Salisburgh. he wrote "Ad Zachariam Rom. pont. epist. 1."

Virgil. Owen Vltagh a physician, his father procéeded doctor of physike in Paris. *Vltanus* Vltanus a lerned moonke fellow to Foillanus, with whome he trauelled into France, and with continuall preaching edified the inhabitants of that realme; he florished in the yeare 640. *Vigalius* Gilbertus Vigalius a profest Carmelite, and a student in Oxford, he florished in the yeare 1330, he wrote in two great tomes, "Summam quarundam legum, De rebus theologicis lib. 1." *Vsher* Vsher, or Vscher a student in Cambridge, and a preacher. *Wadding* Wadding a proper versifier he wrote in Latine vpon the burning of Paules stéeple, "Carmen heroicum, Diuersa epigrammata." *Walsh* Edward Walsh, he florished in the yeare 1550, and wrote in English "The dutie of such as fight for their countrie, The reformation of Ireland by the word of God." Iames Walsh, master of art, and student in diuinitie, he translated into English, "Giraldum Cambrensem," he wrote in Latine "Epigrammata diuersa."

Richard Walsh master of art and student in diuinitie. There is a learned man of the name beneficed in S. Patrikes church in Dublin, student in Cambridge, and now a preacher. Peter Walsh a proper youth, and one that would haue béene an ornament to his countrie, if God had spared him life, he died of a surfet at London, about the yeare 1571. There dwelleth in Waterford a lawyer of the surname, who writeth a verie proper Latine verse. *Wellesleie* Wellesleie deane of Kildare, there liueth an other learned man of the name, who is archdeacon of saint Patrikes. *White* Peter White borne in Waterford, fellow of Oriall college in Oxford, the luckie schoolemaster of Mounster, he bestowed his time rather in the making of scholers, than in the penning of bookes, and to the instruction of youth, he wrote "Epitom. in copiam Erasmi, Epitom. figurarum rhetoricar. Annotationes in orat. pro Archia poeta. Annotat. in orationem pro T. A. Milone. Epigrammata diuersa." Iohn White batcheler of diuinitie borne in Clonmell, he wrote in Latine "Diuersa pia epigrammata." Andrew White a good humanician, a pretie philosopher. *Wise* Wise, of this surname there florished sundrie learned gentlemen. There liueth one Wise in Waterford, that maketh verie well in the English. Andrew Wise a toward youth, and a good versifier. *William.* William an abbat, and (as it is thought) a soothsaier, he florished in the yeare 1298, and wrote "Prophetias rerum futurarum lib. 1." *Woulfe* Daniel Woolfe, a diuine.

Thus far (gentle reader) haue I indeuoured to heape vp togither a catalog of such learned Irishmen, as by diligent insearch could haue bin found. Howbeit, I am to request thée not to measure the ample number of the learned of that countrie by this briefe abstract: considering, that diuerse haue béene, yea and are yet liuing, of profound knowledge that to me are vnknowne, and therefore in this register not recorded.

THE DISPOSITION AND MANERS OF THE MEERE IRISH, COMMONLIE CALLED THE WILD IRISH.

THE EIGHT CHAPTER

BEFORE I attempt the vnfolding of the maners of the méere Irish, I thinke it expedient, to forewarne thée reader, not to impute anie barbarous custome that shall

shall be here laid downe, to the citizens, townesmen, and inhabitants of the English pale, in that they differ litle or nothing from the ancient customes and dispositions of their progenitors, the English and Welsh men, being therefore as mortallie behated of the Irish, as those that are borne in England. For the Irish man standeth so much vpon his gentilitie, that he termeth anie one of the English sept, and planted in Ireland, Bobdeagh Galteagh, that is, English churle: but if he be an Englishman borne, then he nameth him, Bobdeagh Saxonnegh, that is, a Saxon churle: so that both are churles, and he the onelie gentleman. And therevpon if the basest pezzant of them name himselfe with his superior, he will be sure to place himselfe first, as I and Oneile, I and you, I and he, I and my master, whereas the courtesie of the English language is cleane contrarie.

Irish gentilitie

The people are thus inclined, religious, franke, amorous, irefull, sufferable of infinit paines, verie glorious, manie sorcerers, excellent horssemen, delighted with wars, great almesgiuers, passing in hospitalitie. The lewder sort, both clearkes and laie men are sensuall and ouer loose in liuing. The same being vertuouslie bred vp or reformed, are such mirrors of holinesse and austeritie, that other nations reteine but a shadow of deuotion in comparison of them. As for abstinence and fasting, it is to them a familiar kind of chastisement. They follow the dead corpse to the graue with howling and barbarous outcries, pitifull in appearance: whereof grew, as I suppose, the prouerbe, To weepe Irish.

The inclination of the people

To weepe Irish

Gréedie of praise they be, & fearefull of dishonor, and to this end they estéeme their poets, who write Irish learnedlie, and pen their sonets heroicall, for the which they are bountifullie rewarded; if not, they send out libels in dispraise, whereof the lords and gentlemen stand in great awe. They loue tenderlie their foster children, and bequeath to them a childes portion, whereby they nourish sure friendship so beneficiall euerie waie, that commonlie fiue hundred cowes and better, are giuen in reward to win a noble mans child to foster, they loue & trust their foster brethren more than their owne. The men are cleane of skin and hew, of stature tall. The women are well fauoured, cleane coloured, faire handed, big & large, suffered from their infancie to grow at will, nothing curious of their feature and proportion of bodie.

Poets esteemed

Foster children.

The stature of the people

Their infants, they of meaner sort, are neither swadled nor lapped in linnen, but folded vp starke naked in a blanket till they can go. Proud they are of long crisped bushes of heare which they terme glibs, and the same they nourish with all their cunning, to crop the front thereof they take it for a notable péece of villanie. Water cresses, which they tearme shamrocks, roots and other herbs they féed vpon, otemeale and butter they cram togither, they drinke wheie, milke, and béefe-broth. Flesh they deuoure without bread, and that halfe raw: the rest boileth in their stomachs with *Aqua vitæ*, which they swill in after such a surfet by quarts and pottels: they let their cowes bloud, which growne to a gellie, they bake and ouerspread with butter, and so eate it in lumps. No meat they fansie so much as porke, and the fatter the better. One of Iohn Oneles houshold demanded of his fellow whether béefe were better than porke? That (quoth the other) is as intricat a question, as to aske whether thou art better than Onele.

Infants.

Glibs

Their diet

Porke

Their noble men, and noble mens tenants, now and then make a set feast, which they call coshering, wherto flocke all their reteiners, whom they name followers, their rithmours, their bards, their harpers that féed them with musike: and when the harper twangeth or singeth a song, all the companie must be whist, or else he chafeth like a cutpurse, by reason his harmonie is not had in better price. In their coshering they sit on straw, they are serued on straw, and lie vpon mattresses and pallets of straw. The antiquitie of this kind of feasting is set foorth by Virgil, where Dido intertaineth the Troian prince and his companie. They obserue di-

Coshering
Followers.

Lib. pri Aen. circa finem

uerse

diuerse degrées, according to which each man is regarded. The basest sort among them are little yoong wags, called Daltins, these are lackies, and are seruiceable to the groomes or horssebotes, who are a degrée aboue the Daltins. Of the third degrée is the kerne, who is an ordinarie souldior, vsing for weapon his sword and target, and sometimes his peece, being commonlie so good markemen as they will come within a score of a great castell. Kerne signifieth (as noble men of deepe iudgement informed me) a shower of hell, because they are taken for no better than for rakehels, or the diuels blacke gard, by reason of the stinking sturre they keepe, wheresoeuer they be.

Daltin. Groome. Kerne. Kagheren.

Galloglasse.

The fourth degrée is a galloglasse, vsing a kind of pollar for his weapon. These men are commonlie weieward rather by profession than by nature, grim of countenance, tall of stature, big of lim, burlie of bodie, well and stronglie timbered, chieflie feeding on béefe, porke & butter. The fift degrée is to be an horsseman, which is the chiefest next the lord and capteine. These horssemen, when they haue no staie of their owne, gad & range from house to house like arrant knights of the round table, and they neuer dismount vntill they ride into the hall, and as farre as the table. There is among them a brotherhood of karrowes, that proffer to plaie at cards all the yeare long, and make it their onelie occupation. They plaie awaie mantle and all to the bare skin, and then trusse themselues in straw or leaues, they wait for passengers in the high waie, inuite them to game vpon the gréene, and aske no more but companions to make them sport. For default of other stuffe, they pawne their glibs, the nailes of their fingers and toes, their dimissaries, which they léese or redéeme at the courtesie of the winner.

Horsseman. Karrow.

A taleteller. Latin spoken as a vulgar language.

One office in the house of noble men is a taleteller, who bringeth his lord asléepe with tales vaine and friuolous, whereunto the number giue sooth and credit. Without either precepts or obseruations of congruitie, they speake Latine like a vulgar language, learned in their common schooles of leachcraft and law, whereat they begin children, and hold on sixtéene or twentie yeares, conning by rote the aphorismes of Hippocrates, and the ciuill institutes, with a few other parings of those faculties. In their schooles they groouell vpon couches of straw, their bookes at their noses, themselues lie flat prostrate, and so they chant out with a loud voice their lessons by péecemeale, repeating two or thrée words thirtie or fortie times togither. Other lawyers they haue liable to certeine families, which after the custome of the countrie determine and iudge causes. These consider of wrongs offered and receiued among their neighbors: be it murther, felonie, or trespasse, all is remedied by composition (except the grudge of parties séeke reuenge) and the time they haue to spare from spoiling and preieng, they lightlie bestow in parling about such matters. The Breighon (so they call this kind of lawyers) sitteth on a banke, the lords and gentlemen at variance round about him, and then they proceed. To rob and spoile their enimies they déeme it none offense, nor seeke anie meanes to recouer their losse, but euen to watch them the like turne. But if neighbors & friends send their purueiors to purloine one another, such actions are iudged by the Breighons aforesaid. They honour and reuerence friers and pilgrims, by suffering them to passe quietlie, and by sparing their mansions, whatsoeuer outrage they shew to the countrie besides them. The like fauor doo they extend to their poets & rithmours.

Breighon. Religious fauoured.

Matrimonie abused.

In old time they much abused the honorable state of mariage, either in contracts vnlawfull, méeting the degrées of prohibition, or in diuorsements at pleasure, or in reteining concubines or harlots for wiues: yea euen at this daie, where the clergie is faint, they can be content to marie for a yeare and a daie of probation, and at the years end, or anie time after, to returne hir home with hir mariage goods, or as much in value, vpon light quarels, if the gentlewomans friends be vnable to to reuenge the iniurie. In like maner maie she forsake hir husband. In some corner of the land they vsed a damnable superstition, leauing the right armes of their infants vnchristened (as they tearme it) to the intent it might giue a more vngratious and deadlie blow. Others write that gentlemens children were baptised in milke, and the infants of poore folke in water, who had the better or rather the onelie choise. Diuerse other vaine and execrable superstitions they obserue, that for a complet recitall would require a seuerall volume. Whereto they are the more stiflie wedded, bicause such single preachers as they haue, reprooue not in their sermons the péeuishnesse and fondnesse of these friuolous dreamers. But these and the like enormities haue taken so déepe root in that people, as commonlie a preacher is sooner by their naughtie liues corrupted, than their naughtie liues by his preaching amended.

Superstition in baptisme

Iohn Cam. Cant. [illegible]

Ireland why superstitious.

Againe, the verie English of birth, conuersant with the sauage sort of that people become degenerat, and as though they had tasted of Circes poisoned cup, are quite altered. Such force hath education to make or mar. God with the beams of his grace clarifie the eies of that rude people, that at length they maie see their miserable estate: and also that such as are deputed to the gouernement thereof, bend their industrie with conscionable policie to reduce them from rudenes to knowledge, from rebellion to obedience, from trecherie to honestie, from sauagenesse to ciuilitie, from idlenesse to labour, from wickednesse to godlinesse, whereby they maie the sooner espie their blindnesse, acknowledge their loosenes, amend their liues, frame themselues pliable to the lawes and ordinances of hir maiestie, whome God with his gratious assistance preserue, aswell to the prosperous gouernment of hir realme of England, as to the happie reformation of hir realme of Ireland.

FINIS.

THE FIRST INHABITATION OF

IRELAND,

BY WHOME IT WAS INSTRUCTED IN THE FAITH, WITH THE SEUERALL INUASIONS OF THE SAME, &c.

THE AUTHORS PREFACE OR INTRODUCTION TO THE SEQUELE OF THE HISTORIE.

ALTHOUGH (vndoutedlie) the originall of all nations for the more part is so vncerteine, that who soeuer shall enter into the search thereof, further than he findeth in the holie scriptures, may seeme as it were rather to talke with men that dreame, than to gather authorities sufficient whervpon to ground anie warranted opinion: yet for as much as the authors (whom in this Irish historie we chieflie follow) haue set downe what they haue found in the Irish antiquities, concerning the first inhabitation of this countrie of Ireland, and because the reader also may be peraduenture desirous to vnderstand the same, we haue thought good to recite what they haue written thereof, leauing the credit vnto the due consideration of the circumspect reader; and where the errors are too grosse, giuing by the way some cautions, in like sort as our authors themselues haue doone. According therefore to the order of all other nations and people that seeke to aduance the glorie of their countries, in fetching their beginning with the furthest from some one of ancient antiquitie: so likewise the Irishmen haue registred in their chronicles, that their countrie was first inhabited by one of Noahs neeces, after the manner following.

THE
FIRST INHABITATION OF IRELAND, &c.

IN the yeare of the world, 1525 the patriarch Noah began to admonish the people of vengeance to followe for their wickednesse and detestable sins, to build his arke to forshew his kinsfolkes and friends of that vniuersall floud which was to come, wherewith the whole face of the earth should be couered with water, & that within few yeares, except they amended in time This did he before the generall floud, one hundred & fiue and twentie yeares But when euerie man séemed to neglect this wholesome admonition, one Cesara that was néece to Noah, (Cesara neece to Noah) hearing hir vncles prophesie, doubted least the same should come to passe, and therefore determined with certeine hir adherents to séeke aduentures in some forren region, persuading hir selfe, that if she might find a countrie neuer yet inhabited, and so with sin vnspotted, the generall sentence of Gods wrath should not there take effect Wherevpon rigging a nauie, she committed hir selfe to the seas, sailing foorth, till at length she arriued in Ireland onelie with three men, & fiftie women, hauing lost the residue of hir companie by misfortune of sundrie shipwracks made in that hir long & troublesome iourneie. The names of the men were these, Bith, Laigria, and Fintan The coast where she first set foot on land, and where also she lieth buried, is called *Nauiculare littus*, that is, the shipping rnage or shore The stones wherein the memorie hereof was preserued from violence of waters, (An mundi 1556) haue béene seene of some (as they themselues haue reported) but how trulie I haue not to say within fortie daies after hir comming on land there, the vniuersall floud came & ouerflowed all that coast as well as all other parts of the world But where as this tale bewraieth it selfe too manifestlie to be a meere vntruth, if the time and other circumstances be throughlie examined, I will not stand longer about the proofe or disproofe thereof, sauing that it is sufficient (as I thinke) to bring it out of credit, to consider, how that the art of sailing was vnknowne to the world before the vniuersall floud, and no part inhabited except the continent of Syria, and thereabouts. But to passe such a forged fable, with the record thereof grauen in a stone (*Pob Lyra in Gene 5*) (a deuice borowed from Iosephus, as some thinke) it shall be sufficient for the glorie of the Irish antiquitie to grant that Ireland was discouered and peopled by some of Noahs kinred, euen with the first Ilands of the world (if they will needs haue it so, as the likelihood is great) according to that which is set foorth in their (An mundi 1557) histories, when about thrée hundred yeares after the generall floud immediatlie (After the best authors make 300 yeares, and not 100 betweene Noahs floud and Babell) vpon the confusion of toongs, Iaphet & his posteritie imboldened by Noahs example, aduentured to commit themselues by ship to passe the seas, & to search out the vnknowne corners of the world, and so finding out diuerse Iles in these west parts of the world

There was (saie they) in that retinue one of the same progenie named Bartolenus (Bartolenus, or Bastoler) or Bastolenus, who incouraged with the late attempt and successe of Nimrod kinsman to Ninus (then newlie intruded vpon the monarchie of Assyria) searched so far (*Clem li Cambre*) west, intending to atteine to some gouernement, where he might rule without anie

 partner

partner in authoritie, till at length fortune brought him and his people vpon the coast of Ireland. Here he settled himselfe with his three sonnes Languina, Salamis, and Ruthurgus, right actiue and stout gentlemen, who searching the land from side to side, and from end to end, left remembrances of their names in certeine notable places named after them, as Languinie, Stragruus and mount Salanga,

Ruthurgus ag-nun

since named saint Dominiks hill, and Ruthurgus his poole. Little is remembred of Bartolenus, sauing that in short space with manie hands working at once, he rid and made plaine a great part of the countrie ouergrowen with woods and thickets.

Ireland first inhabited

Thus was Ireland inhabited by this people vnder the gouernment of those thrée sons of Bartolenus and their offspring, about the space of thrée hundred yeares. Togither with Bartolenus arriued Ireland certeine godles people of Nimrods stocke, woorthilie termed giants, as those that in bodilie shape excéeded the common pro-

Giants

portion of others, and vsed their strength to gaine soueraigntie, and to oppresse the

Bergon the sonne of Neptune and brother to Albion (as Iohn Bale hath) conquered Ireland and the Orkneis

Euill examples soone followed

weake with rapine and violence. That linage (Chams brood) did grow in short while to great numbers, and alwaie indeuored themselues where soeuer they came to beare the rule ouer others. One cause hereof was their bodilie strength, answerable to their hugenesse of stature, another, the examples of Cham or Zoroastres the magician, and Nimrod grandfather to Ninus. Which two persons in themselues and their progenies were renowmed through the world as victorious princes, ruling ouer two mightie kingdoms Egypt and Assyria. A third cause there was, as this they repined at the blessings bestowed vpon Sem and Iaphet, thinking it necessarie to withstand and preuent all lawfull rule and dominion, least the cursse of slauerie prophesied by Noah should light vpon them, as at length it did. Herevpon rebelliouslie withdrawing their due obedience from their lawfull gouernors

Rebellion against gouernors

here in Ireland, and taking head, set vp a king of their owne faction, and mainteining his estate to the oppression of the subiects, by bringing them into continuall bondage. The successe was variable on both sides betwixt the lawfull gouernors & these vsurpers, with dailie raises and skirmishes, so much to the griefe of them that coueted to liue in quiet vnder their rightfull princes, that they determined

A woorthie resolution

with the chance of one generall battell, either wholie to subdue those proud rebellious tyrants, or else to end their liues in fréedome, and so to be rid of further miserie. But first, where there had growen certeine debates and enimitie among themselues, whereby they had inféebled their owne forces, they thought good to make peace togither, before they put their whole state in hazard of one battell against the giants, concluding therefore an agréement, and ioining in league with promise to assist eeh other to subdue their common enimies, they assemble their power foorth of all parts of the land, and comming to ioine battell with the giants, after they had fought right fiercelie togither for the space of certeine houres, the victorie inclined to the rightfull part, so that the lawfull kings preuailing against the wicked tyrants, great slaughter was made on the whole brood of that mis-

Victorie too cruellie vsed

chéefous generation. For the kings meaning to deliuer themselues of all danger in time to come, vsed their happie victorie with great crueltie, which turned to their owne confusion: for where they neither spared man, woman, nor child that came in the waie for more despite, & fuller satisfieng of their whole reuenge, they

Anno mundi 2257

did not vouchsafe to burie the carcasses of their slaine enimies, but cast them out like a sort of dead dogs: whereof through stench of the same, such an infectiue pestilence insued in all places through corruption of aire, that few escaped with life, beside those that got them awaie by sea.

Ruanus how long he liued

And hereby lieth a vaine tale among the Irishmen, that one of the giants named Ruanus, chancing to be preserued from this mortalitie, liued forsooth two thousand and one and fortie yeares, which is more than twise the age of Methusalem. By this man (saie they) saint Patrike was informed of all the estate of the countrie:

and

and after that vpon request, he had receiued baptisme of the said Patrike, he deceassed in the yeare after the birth of our sauior foure hundred and thirtie, as in the Irish histories hath bin vnaduisedlie registred. But such foolish tales and vaine narrations may warne the aduised reader how to beware of yéelding credit vnto the like idle fantasies and forged tales, when they hap to light vpon such blind legends. For where some of the poets vsed for inuention sake to faine such dreaming fables for exercise of their stiles and wits: afterwards through error and lacke of knowledge, they haue béene taken with the ignorant for verie true and most assured histories. But now to the matter, as we find it recorded of an infinit number of giants slaine and made awaie in manner afore rehearsed, certeine there were that got them into some lurking dens or caues, and there kept them till lacke of vittels inforced them to come foorth, and make shift for sustenance, and perceiuing no resistance because the land was in manner left desolat, they waxed bolder, and when they vnderstood how things had passed, they settled themselues in the best part of the countrie, easilie subduing the poore séelie soules that remained, and so renuing their linage, they became lords of the whole Iland, kéeping the same in subiection for the space of thrée score yeares togither.

Forged tales and fables win credit in time, to passe among the vnskilfull people for true histories.

Among Iaphets sons we read in Genesis that Magog was one, who planted his people in Scythia neere Tanais, from whense about the yeare of the world two thousand thrée hundred & seuenteene Nemodus with his foure sonnes, Starius, Garbaneles, Annimus, Fergusius, capteins ouer a faire companie of people, were sent into Ireland, who passing by Grecia, and taking there such as were desirous to séeke aduentures with them, at length they landed in Ireland, inhabited the countrie, and multiplied therein, although not without continuall warre, which they held with the giants for the space of two hundred and sixteene yeares, in the end of which terme the giants preuailing chased them thense againe, so that they retired into Syria. This was about the yeare after the creation (as by their account it should seeme) two thousand fiue hundred thirtie and thrée, from which time the giants kept possession of the land without forren inuasion, till the yeare two thousand seauen hundred and fouretéene, but yet in all that space they were not able to frame a common-welth: for falling at variance among themselues, and measuring all things by might, seditiouslie they vexed ech other. Which thing comming to the knowledge of the Grecians mooued fiue brethren, sonnes to one Dela, being notable seamen and skilfull pilots to rig a nauie, and to attempt the conquest of this Iland. These were of the posteritie of Nemodus, and named Gandius, Genandius, Sagandus, Rutheranus, & Slanius. When all things were readie, and their companies assembled, they tooke the sea, and finallie arriuing here in Ireland, found the puissance of the giants sore weakened through their owne ciuill dissention, so that with more ease they atchiued their purpose, and wan the whole countrie, vtterlie destroieng and rooting out that wicked generation enimies to mankind, and after diuided the Iland into fiue parts, and in each of them they seuerallie reigned. Furthermore, to satisfie all sides, and auoid contention, they concluded to fix a mere-stone in the middle point of Ireland, to the which ech of their kingdoms should reach, so as they might be equallie partakers of the commodities found within that countrie soile.

Gen. 10.
Anno mundi 2317
Nemodus with his foure sonnes
Ireland eftsoones inhabited by the offspring of Iaphet
The giants preuaile.
2533
The sonnes of Dela a Grecian skilfull in the art of sailing
They passe into Ireland, and destroied the giants
They diuide the countrie into foure parts

These are also supposed to haue inuented the distribution of shires into cantreds, euerie cantred or baronie conteining one hundred townships. At length desire of soueraigntie set the fiue brethren at variance, & greatlie hindred their growing wealths. But Slanius getting the vpper hand, and bringing his foure brethren to a low eb, tooke on him as cheefe aboue his other brethren, incroching round about the midle stone for the space of certeine miles, which plot in time obteined the priuilege & name of one entier part, & now maketh vp the number of fiue parts

A cantred
Desire of soueraigntie cause of variance

 (into

(into the which Ireland is said to be diuided) and is called Meth, and in Latine *Media*, taking that name (as some haue gessed) for that in respect of the other, it conteined but the moitie of cantreds, that is, sixtéene (where ech of the other comprehended two and thirtie a péece) or else for that it lieth in the middest of the land. This part Slanius ioined as a surplusage ouer and aboue his inheritance, to the monarchie: which part notwithstanding grew to a seuerall kingdome. Thirtie yeares the monarchie yet continued in this order, but finallie Slanius departed this life, and was buried in a mounteine of Meth, that beareth hitherto (as they saie) the name after him. Then the princes subiect to him, began to stomach the matter, and denied their obeisance to his successor: wherevpon insued continuall warrs betwixt them, falling still at debat for the land of Meth, which strife of long time might neuer fullie be appeased. In the necke of these troubles also there arriued in Ireland a new armie of Scythians, who made claime to the land by a title of right which they pretended from their forefather Nemodus: and so taking & making parts, they set all in an vprore, that hauocke was made on each side with fire and sword in most miserable maner.

Slanius departed this life.

A new armie of Scythians land in Ireland. Partakings.

To be short, they spent themselues in pursuing one an other with such outrage, that now they cared not what nation or what souldier they receiued to their aid, to kéepe vp or beat downe a side. By which occasion the Britons also put in a foot among them, who procured Brennus the brother of Belinus to direct his course thither, with the same nauie which he had made readie to passe ouer into Gallia, now called France, to the aid of Segwin then king of the Allobroges that inhabited the countries called Sauoie and the Delphinat. But his enterprise into Ireland tooke small effect, though there were other kings of the Britons that gat dominion there, in so much that Gurguntius, or Gurgwintius, the sonne of Belinus, accompted Ireland among other his dominions to belong to him by lineall descent: notwithstanding the British princes neuer inioied the quiet possession thereof, longer than they held it by maine force, but were often repelled and put to the worsse with séeking after it, finding there small gaine other than stripes, whereof they bare awaie great plentie. But now to come to the Spaniards, that lastlie (vnder the conduct of foure capteins) passed into Ireland from Biscaie, and inhabited that Iland, it shall not be impertinent in following the order which our author kéepeth, to speake somewhat of their originall, that it may appéere from whense the Irish nation had their first beginning.

Brennus called into Ireland to aid one part of the factious people. Segwin. Allobroges.

2436 In the yeare of the world 2436, after the vniuersall floud 780, whilest the Israelits serued in Egypt, Gathelus the sonne of one Neale, a great lord in Grecia, was vpon disfauor exiled his countrie with a number of his factious adherents and friends. This noble gentleman being right wise, valiant, and well spoken, comming into Egypt, got honorable interteinment of Pharao surnamed Orus, as in the Scotish historie more plainelie appeereth. And afterwards departing that countrie, trauersed the seas, and landing first in Portingall, after some bickering with the inhabitants, at length yet he got by their consent a portion of the countrie, lieng by the banks of the riuer anciențlie called Munda, & now Mondego, where shortlie after he began to build a citie first named Brachara, but now Barsalo, as Hector Boetius hath. After this, when Gathelus his people began to increase in power, through persuasion of the Spaniards their neighbors, they remooued into Galicia, where they also builded a citie named Brigantium, which is now called Coruna. Finallie, when they grew into such an huge multitude, that Galicia was not able to susteine them, Gathelus with a certeine number of them passed ouer into Ireland, and there grew into such estimation with the barbarous people, that for his knowledge speciallie in all languages, he was highlie honored: for he not onelie inriched and beautified the Irish toong, but also taught them letters, sought vp their antiquities,

See more of this matter in the beginning of the Scotish historie.

The riuer of Munda, now Mondego. Brachara now Braga.

Brigantium. See more hereof in Scotland. Gathelus passeth into Ireland.

quities, practised their youth in warlike feats after the maner of the Greekes and Egyptians, from whense he descended.

To conclude, he was so acceptable to them, that to gratifie such a benefactor, they agreed to name the Iland after him Gathelia, and after his wife Scotia. This is one opinion but yet incredible, not onelie to Humfreie Lhuid, but also to other learned men, and diligent searchers of antiquities, by reason of the sundrie arguments of improbabilitie, aswell in the miscount of yeares as other vnlikelihoods found therein, when the circumstances come to be dulie examined, throughlie weied, and well considered. Yet certeine it is, that Ireland was ancientlie named Scotia, and the people Scots, as by diuerse old writers it may be sufficientlie prooued: albeit by what occasion it first tooke that name, or from whense they came, it is as yet doubted. But to proceed with the historie as we find it. The residue of Gathelus his people, which remained in Spaine, founded the citie of Baion in the confines of Gascoigne, and replenished the seacoasts of Spaine with store of inhabitants, and welnéere about two hundred yeares after their first arriuall there (when they were eftsoones pestered with multitude of people) they began to fansie a new voiage, but whether at that time they passed ouer into Ireland, or some whither else, it is vncerteine.

The names of Ireland, & whereof the same were deriued, as they hold opinion.

Notwithstanding sure it is, that in the daies of Gurguntius king of the Britons, the chiefe gouernour of Baion with foure brethren Spaniards, of the which two are said to be Hiberus and Hermion, not the sonnes (some thinke) of Gathelus (as Hector Boetius affirmeth) but some other perhaps that were descended from him, who vnderstanding that diuerse of the westerne Iles were emptie of inhabitants, assembling a great number of men, women, and children, imbarked with the same in thrée score great vessels, and directing their course westward, houered a long time in the sea about the Iles of Orkenere, vntill by good hap they met with Gurguntius then returning from the conquest of Denmarke (as in the British historie it appéereth) whom they besought in consideration of their want of vittels and other necessaries, being such as they were not able longer to abide the seas, incumbred with a sort of women and children, to direct and appoint them to some place where to inhabit, promising to hold the same of him, and to become liege people to him and his heires for euer.

Gurguntius.

Gurguntius aduising himselfe hereof, remembred with what trouble he held the Irish in subiection, and conceiuing hope that those strangers should either subdue or whole destroie that vnruhe generation, tooke the othes of those Spaniards with hostages, and furnishing them and their ships with all things néedfull, set them ouer into Ireland, where assisted with such Britons as Gurguntius had appointed to go with them for their guids, they made a conquest of the whole countrie, & setled themselues in the same. Some write, that Ireland was before that present void of all inhabitants: but yet they agrée that these Spaniards were guided thither by the Britons, & that vnder such conditions as before is recited. So that it appéereth the kings of this our Britaine had an elder right to the realme of Ireland, than by the conquest of Henrie the second, which title they euer maintemed, and sometimes preuailed in pursuing thereof, as in the daies of king Arthur, to whom the Irish (as in some histories is remembred) acknowledged their due subiection with paiement of their tribute, and making their appéerance at the citie called in the British toong Caer Lheon. Whereunto when their frée assent, the submission of the princes with lawfull conquest and prescription are adioined, an inuincible title must néeds be inforced.

Gurguntius appointeth the Spaniards seats in Ireland to liue vnder his subiection.

The arriuall of the Spaniards in Ireland.

Geffrei Mon.

The Irish were subiect to K. Arthur.

Westchester.

But now to our purpose. The Spaniards substantiallie aided by the Britons, setled themselues, and diuided their seats in quarters, the foure brethren reigning seuerallie apart in foure sundrie portions in good quiet and increase of welth, vntill their pride

Dissention betwixt the brethren.

Such are the fruits of ambition.

pride and ambition armed two of them against the other two, as Hiberus and one of his brethren against Hermion and the other brother. In this dissention Hermion slue his brother Hiberus. Of whom at the same time the countrie (as some hold) was named Hibernia, as in the description further appeareth: although some rather hold, that it tooke the name of iron, of the plentifull mines of that kind of mettall wherewith that land aboundeth: and so those ancient writers which name it Ierna, named it more aptlie after the spéech of the inhabitants than others, which name it Hibernia. But to procéed. Hermion herevpon to auoid the ill opinion of men, for that he had thus attеined to the soueraignetie by the vnnaturall slaughter of his brother, in that vnhappie ciuill warre, purged himselfe to his subiects, that neither maliciouslie nor contentiouslie, but for his necessarie defense and safetie he had borne armes against his brethren: and to witnesse how farre he was from all desire to rule alone, he appointed certeine capteins as kings, to rule vnder him seuerall countries, reseruing to himselfe but one fourth part, and the portion of Meth allotted to the monarchie for the better maintenance of his estate.

See more hereof in the description.

No crime so manifest or detestable that wanteth a colourable pretense to excuse it.

Ireland diuided into fiue kingdomes. One soueraigne ruler ouer the rest.

These parts appointed foorth in this wise at length grew to fiue kingdomes, Leinster, Connagh, Vlster, and Mounster diuided into two parts, and sometime to more, by vsurping or compounding among themselues: but euer one was chosen to be chiefe soueraigne monarch ouer them all. Thus it séemeth that certeinelie the Spaniards of the north parts of Spaine, inhabiting the countries about Biscaie and Galicia, came and peopled Ireland (as both their owne histories and the British doo wholie agrée) but from whense they came first to inhabit those countries of Spaine, verelie I haue not otherwise to auouch: for no other writers that I can remember, but (such as haue registred the Scotish chronicles) make mention of the comming thither of Gathelus with his wife Scota and their people, in maner as by the said chronicles is pretended. But now to our purpose. An hundred and thirtie chiefe kings are reckoned of this nation from Hermion to Laogirius, the sonne of Nealus Magnus, in whose time that holie estéemed man Patrike conuerted them to christianitie. But now in the meane time whilest the Irishmen liued in some tollerable order and rest vnder their seuerall kings, one Rodorike a Scithian prince with a small companie of men, being weather driuen round about the coasts of Britaine, was by chance cast vpon the shore of Ireland.

Picts arriue in Ireland.

These were Picts, and the first that had been heard of in these parties (as some authors haue recorded) a people from their verie cradle giuen to dissention, landleapers, mercilesse, fierce and hardie. They being brought and presented to the Irish king, craued interpretors, which granted, Rodorike their cheefeteine made this request for him and his, as followeth. Not as denegrate from the courage of our ancestours, but fashioning our selues to fortunes course, we are become to craue of Ireland, as humble supplicants that neuer before this present haue so embased our selues to anie other nation. Behold sir king, and regard vs well, no light occasion causeth these lustie valiant bodies to stoope. Scithians we are, & Picts of Scithia, no small portion of glorie resteth in these two names. What shall I speake of the ciuill warre that hath expelled vs from our natiue homes, or rip vp old histories to mooue strangers to bemone vs? Let our seruants and children discourse therof at leisure, if perhaps you will vouchsafe to grant vs some time of abode in your land, to the which effect and purpose our vrgent necessitie beséecheth your fauors, a king of a king and men of men are to craue assistance. Princes can well discerne and consider how néere it toucheth their honour and suertie, to vphold and releeue the state of a king, by treason decaied. And manifest it is to all men of reasonable consideration, that nothing more beseemeth the nature of man, than to be mooued with compassion, and as it were to féele themselues hurt, when they heare and vnderstand of other mens calamities. Admit (we beseech you) and

The oration of Rodorike king of the Picts king of Ireland.

receiue

receiue amongst you these few scattered remnants of Scithia if your roomes be narrow, we are not manie if the soile of your countrie be barren, we are borne and enured to hardnesse if you liue in peace, we are at commandement as subiects if you warre, we are readie to serue you as souldiours we demand no kingdome, no state, no pompous triumph in Ireland we are héere alone, and haue left such things behind vs with our enimies howsoeuer you estéeme of vs, we shall content our selues therewith, and learne to frame our liking to yours calling to mind not what we haue beene, but what we are

Great consultation was had about this request of these strangers, and manie things debated to and fro In conclusion, the Irish laid foorth for answer the opinions of their antiquaries, that is, such as were skilfull in old histories and sayengs of their elders, whereVnto they gaue credit, and therefore they gathered it could not be expedient to accept the Scithians into the land, for that mingling of nations in one realme bréedeth quarels, moreouer, that the multitude of the inhabitants was such, as roome in the whole Ile was vneth able to receiue them, and therefore those few new commers, being placed among so manie old inhabitants, might bréed quicklie some disturbance to bring all out of ioint But (said they) though we may not conuenientlie receiue you among vs, yet shall you find vs readie to further you to be our neighbours. Doubtfull consultation The answer of the Irish to the request of the Picts

Not far hense there lieth the great Ile of Britaine, in the north part whereof, being void of inhabitants, your manhoods and policies may purchase for you roomes to place your selues at ease we shall appoint you capteins to guide you thither, we shall assist to settle you with our forces in that countrie, make readie your ships that yée may passe thither with all conuenient spéed Incouraged with this persuasion, they tooke their course towards the north parts of Britaine now called Scotland, where contrarie to their expectation Marius king of Britaine was readie to await their comming, and with sharpe battell vanquishing them in field, slue Rodorike with a great number of his retinues Those that escaped with life, and sought to him for grace, he licenced to inhabit the vttermost end of Scotland. This Marius Humfrie Lhuid taketh to be the same, whome the Romane writers name Aruiragus, who reigned about the yere of our Lord seuentie, a prince of a noble courage and of no small estimation in his daies (as should séeme by that which is written of him) His right name (as the said Humfrere Lhuid auoucheth) was Meurig The Irish persuadeth the Picts to place themselues in Britaine Marius otherwise called Aruiragus king of Britons

But now concerning the Picts, whether that those that escaped with life, got seats by king Meurigs grant (as aboue is specified) or that getting to their ships, they withdrew into the Iles of Orkeneie, and there remained Wiues they wanted also to increase their issue and bicause the Britons thought scorne to match their daughters with such an vnknowne and new come nation, the Picts continued their first acquaintance with the Irish, and by intreatie obteined wiues from them, with condition, that if the crowne should hap to fall in contention, they should yéeld thus much to the prerogatiue of the woman, that the prince should be elected rather of the bloud roiall of the female kind than of the male Which order (saith Beda) the Picts were well known to képe vnto his time Picts marieng with the Irish doo couenant the succession of their king

But howsoeuer we shall giue credit to this historie of the first comming of Picts into this land, if we grant that to be true which Geffreie of Monmouth reporteth of this victorie obteined by Marius against the Picts yet haue I thought good to aduertise the reader, that the Britons of this Ile were disquieted by that nation long before the supposed time of the said king Marius For Mamertinus in his oration intituled "Panegyricus, Max Dictus" hath these words (speaking of the conquest which Iulius Cesar had héere against the Britons) But in that age (saith he) Britaine was neither furnished with anie ships of warre for battell on the sea, and the

the Romans after the warres of Affrike and Asia, were well practised with the late warres against the pirats, and after that against Mithridates, in which they were exercised as well by sea as land. Moreouer, the British nation was then vnskilfull, and not trained to feats of war, for the Britons then being onelie vsed to the Picts and Irish enimies, people halfe naked through lacke of skill, easilie gaue place to the Romans force, so that Cesar might onelie as it were glorie in this, to haue passed in that iournie ouer the ocean sea.

See *Diodorus Siculus lib. 5. cap. 5.* who saith they should inhabit a portion of Britaine.

Hec. Boetius.

Héereby it should séeme that the Picts and Irish did disquiet the Britons, before the comming of Iulius Cesar into this Ile of Britaine. But whether they inhabited at that time in some part of Ireland, or in some of the out Iles by Scotland, either in anie part of Germanie, or Scandinauia, or else whether they were alreadie setteled in the furthest parts of Scotland, as in Cathnesse, towards Dungesbie head we haue not to affirme, other than that which in Scotland we haue written, in following Hector Boetius, whose opinion how farre it is to be suspected in matters of antiquitie, I leaue to the consideration of others. But for the first comming as well of the Picts as Scots (whom he maketh inhabitants within this Ile so long before) either the name of the one nation or the other is remembred to haue had anie gouernement heere, by anie ancient or approoued writer. I cannot persuade my selfe, that either Scots or Picts had anie setteled seats within the bounds of this Ile of Britaine, till after the birth of our sauiour: but that rather the Scots, as yet inhabiting in Ireland, and in the westerne Iles called by the Romane writers Hebrides, and the Picts, in the Iles of Orkneie called in Latine *Orchades*, did vse to make often inuasions vpon the Britons, dwelling vpon the coasts that lie néere to the sea side ouer against those Iles.

See more heereof in England.

The Picts when they first inhabited Britaine.

The Scots in Britaine.

Ham. Lhuid.

From whense they comming ouer in such vessels or boats, as the fishermen doo yet vse, at length the Picts first about the yere of our Lord 290, as Humfreie Lhuid hath noted, entred generallie into Cathnesse, and other the north parts of Britaine, where they setteled themselues, and remooued the Britons that there inhabited before that time: and shortlie the Scots likewise came ouer and got seats in the west parts ouer against the north of Ireland, and in those westerne Iles, which Iles they first got into their possession. And in this sort those nations Picts and Scots came first to inhabit héere in this our Ile of Britaine, as the said Humfreie Lhuid, not without aduised coniectures grounded vpon good reason and sufficient authoritie to lead him so to estéeme, hath written in his short commentaries of the description of Britaine.

Gefferie Monmouth the translator not the author of the British historie.

The doubt of the time of the comming of Picts and Scots into Britaine.

Ferguse king of Scots.

The marble stone.

And verelie I thinke we may more safelie beléeue that which he auoucheth in this behalfe, than that which Hector Boetius setteth downe, sith for anie thing I can perceiue, his authorities bring no such warrant with them, but we may with good reason suspect them. But for the man himselfe, euen as he hath verie orderlie, and with no lesse cunning than eloquence set downe diuerse things incredible, and reported some other contrarie to the truth of the historie for the glorie of his nation, as we may take it: so in his excuse it may be alledged, that he was not the author of those matters, but wrote what he found in Cambell, Veremound, Cornelius Hiberniensis, and such other, in like case as Gefferie of Monmouth wrote what he found in old ancient British monuments, & was not the deuiser himselfe (as some haue suspected) of such things as in his booke are by him expressed. But now to returne to the Picts. It may be that they came at seuerall times in like manner as the Scots did out of Ireland, of whome the first is remembred to be Ferguse, the son of Ferquhard, a man right skilfull in blasoning of armorie, himselfe bare a lion gules in a field of gold. The marble stone wherof in the Scotish historie is mentioned, brought into Ireland by Simon Brechus, and kept till those daies as a precious iewell, this Ferguse obteined towards the prospering of his iournie: for that

that it was thought, who so had the same in possession, could not but obteine soueraigntie and rule ouer others as a king, namelie those of the Scotish nation. This stone Ferguse bringing into Scotland, left it there. But although that Ferguse be put in ranke among those Scotish kings that should reigne in Britaine, yet he bare small rule there, & was diuers times beaten backe into Ireland, where finallie he was drowned by misfortune in the créeke of Knockfergus. Knockfergus.

That he incountred with Coilus king of the Britons (as the Scots write) is not possible, as our author hath verie well noted, except they mistake the name of Coilus for Cailus, with whome the age of Ferguse might well méet: the rather, for that in the first yeare of Cailus reigne the Picts entered, Ferguse immediatlie after them, 330 yeares yer Christ was borne, where Coilus reigned in the yeare after the incarnation 124, about which time befell the second arriuall of the Picts in Britaine. 124 And thus it may be they mistake by errour of the name, Coilus for Cailus, and the second arriuall of the Picts for the first. But now to the course of the historie. Whilest the Picts were setled in the north of Britaine, and grew to a great multitude, the Irish made sundrie errands ouer to visit their daughters, nephues and kinsfolks, and by their often comming and going they were aware of certeine waste corners, and small Ilands void of inhabitants, as that which seemed rather neglected and suffered to lie waste.

Hereof they aduertised their princes, namelie Reuther or Reuda, who being descended of Ferguse, determined to inuest himselfe in certeine portions of land beside the Picts. Reuther or Reuda He therefore well appointed passed ouer, and partlie by composition, and partlie by force, got possession of those quarters which were desolate, & began to erect a kingdome there, by little and little increasing his limits. and finallie got betwixt the Picts and Britons, possessing that countrie which tooke the name of him called Reudersdahall, and now Riddesdale (as you would saie) Rheuda's part, for Dahall in the Scotish toong signifieth a part. In these quarters he could not setle himselfe, but that he was oftentimes assailed by the Britons that bordered next vnto him, and at length his chance was to be slaine, but the kingdome continued still in the hands of his successors: and the Picts and Scots grew in friendship togither, permitting ech other to liue in quiet. The amitie betwixt Scots and Picts.

The Scots nestled themselues in the Iles and coasts alongst the sea side. The Picts held the middle part. But shortlie after, the peace began to hang doubtfull betwixt them: for the diuersitie of people, place, custome and language, togither with the memorie of old grudges, mooued such gelousie and inward hate betwixt those nations, that it seemed they were readie to breake out into open dissention vpon the first occasion. Their falling out. And as in such cases there neuer wanteth one deuise or other to raise tumults: it chanced that certeine of the Scotish nobilitie had got out of Greece (as some write) a Molossian hound, which both in swiftnesse of foot, and pleasantnesse of mouth, was accounted peerlesse. This hound being stollen by a Pict, was cause of the breach of peace, so that cruell warre thereof insued, as in the Scotish historie more at large appéereth. Strife about a dog But where some write, that Eugenius should reigne ouer the Scots when this quarell fell out for stealing of this hound, Hector Boetius saith, it was in king Crathlinthis daies. Moreouer it should séeme by that which the same Boetius writeth, that the hound or greihound for the which this trouble rose, was not fetched so far as out of Grecia, but rather bred in Scotland. notwithstanding bicause the Latinists call such kind of dogs *Molossi*, for that the first generation of them, or the like, came from a citie of Grecia called Molosse, it may be, that some haue thought that this greihound came from thense, for that he was so called after the name of that place from whense the bréed of him first came. But to returne to the historie.

Carausius agréeth them
Anno Christi 288

After the Scots and Picts had tugged togither a while, at length one Carausius a Briton laboured a friendship betwixt them, and bringing his purpose to passe, persuaded them to lend him their helpe to expell the Romans out of Britaine, but his hap was shortlie after to be slaine by the Romane capteine Alectus. And so new sturs were in hand betwixt the Britons and Romans, the Scots & Picts for the most part taking part with the Britons, till at length Maximus the Romane lieutenant found means to set the Scots and Picts at variance, and ioining with the Picts in league, vsed their aid against the Scots, whome he so earnestlie pursued with all the power he might make, that in the end they were vtterlie expelled out of all the coasts of Britaine, so that they fled some into one part, some into another, but the most number got them ouer into Ireland, and the Iles, where they remained for the space of fourtie thrée yeares, and then at length returned thither, vnder the leading of their prince Ferguse, being the second of that name, as they account him. From thensefoorth the Scots kept such foot in Britaine, that they incroched vpon their neighbors, in such wise as they waxed stronger than the Picts, whome in the end they quite rooted forth, and nestled themselues in their seats, although now at their first returne they concluded a firme amitie with the same Picts, that ioining their forces togither, they might the better make head against both Romans and Britons, whome they reputed as common enimies to them both.

The Scots expelled
See more of this matter in Scotland
326

The Picts rooted foorth by the Scots.

Thus the Scots a liuelie, cruell, vnquiet, ancient and victorious people, got place within this Ile of Britaine, mixed first with Britons, secondlie with Picts, thirdlie and chieflie with the Irish, which after this time left their name of Scots vnto those in Britaine, and chose rather to be called Irish: and then came vp the distinction of the name, as *Scotia maior* for Ireland, *Scotia minor* for the countrie inhabited by the Scots within Britaine. But Cambrensis saith, that the Scots chieflie preuailed vnder the leading of six valiant gentlemen, sons to Muredus king of Vlster, who in the time of Neale, surnamed the great that inioied the monarchie of Ireland, passing ouer into Scotland to succour their countriemen there, at length tooke vp for themselues certeine parcels of ground, which their posteritie were owners of in the time that Cambrensis liued, to wit, about the yeare of our Lord 1200, who treateth hereof more largelie in his booke intituled "Topographia Britanniæ." Since which time they haue béene euer taken, reputed and named Scots, the Pictish nation being driuen into corners, albeit the mounteine parts and out Iles euen vnto this daie are inhabited with a wild kind of people called Redshanks, estéemed by some to be mingled of Scots and Picts.

Giraldus Cambrensis

Gregorie king of Scots subdueth Ireland
875

The Scots write, that their king Gregorie the sonne of Dongall, who began his reigne in the yeare of our Lord 875, pretending a title to Ireland, as belonging to him by right of lawfull succession, made a iourneie thither, and within a small time made a conquest of the countrie. This Gregorie lieth buried in one of the out Iles called Iona, or Colmekill, where they speake naturallie Irish: and therefore some of the Scots would séeme to make the conquest of Henrie the second in Ireland, a reuolting from the right inheritors: although they doo confesse they can not tell how they came from the possession of it, otherwise than by forging a tale that they willinglie forewent it, as reaping lesse by reteining it, than they laid foorth, and so not able to discharge that which was to be defraied about the kéeping of it they gaue it ouer, persuading themselues that the kings of England haue gained little or nothing by the hauing of Ireland. And yet in the time whilest sir Henrie Sidneie was gouernour there, when the countie of Vlster was auouched to belong vnto the crowne: it was prooued in open parlement, that the reuenues of that earledome, in the daies of Edward the third were reckoned, and found to amount vnto the summe of one and thirtie thousand marks yearelie, the same being

Sir Henrie Sidneie.

but

but a fift part of Ireland. so that if things were well looked vnto, and such improouement made as might be, Ireland would suffice to beare the necessarie charges, and yéeld no small surplusage vnto the princes coffers.

But now as it falleth foorth in the historie. We haue thought good here to shew in what sort Ireland came to receiue the christian faith. We find in deed that immediatlie after Christes time, saint Iames the apostle, & other trauelling into these west parts, did first instruct the Irish people, and teach them the glad tidings of the gospell, so that diuerse amongst them euen then were christened, and beléeued, but not in such numbers (as may be thought) whereby it should be said, that the countrie was generallie conuerted. Notwithstanding, the Scotish chronicles auouch, that in the daies of their king Fincomarke, who departed this life in the yeare of our redemption thrée hundred fiftie and eight, Ireland was conuerted to the faith by this meanes.

Ireland instructed in the faith by saint Iames the apostle.

A woman of the Pictish bloud chanced (saie they) to serue in those daies the queene of Ireland, which woman being a christian hir selfe, first instructed hir mistresse in the faith and true points of christianitie, and the quéene hir husband, who conuerted the whole Irish nation. Howbeit, by the report of the Irish writers themselues, this should not seeme altogither true: for they affirme, that their countrie was rather still estéemed as one of the vnchristened Iles, till about the yeare foure hundred twentie and six, whilest Celestine the first of that name gouerned the sée of Rome, who vpon conference had with his cleargie, touching the restoring of the christian faith in the west parts of the world, greatlie decaied there by the heresie of Pelagius, vnderstood that Ireland also by reason of distance from the hart of christendome, and rudenesse of the nation, had receiued little fruit at all of true religion, a thing much to be lamented.

Among other that then were assembled to treat of those matters was one Paladius archdeacon of Rome, who offered his charitable trauell towards the conuersion of anie of those lands whither it shuld please them to appoint him to go. Celestine knowing the sufficiencie of the man consecrated him bishop, authorised his iourneie by letters vnder his seale, furnished his wants, and associating to him such religious persons and others as were thought necessarie to assist him, deliuered to him the bible with great solemnitie, & other monuments in furtherance of his good spéed. At length he landed in the north of Ireland, from whense he escaped right hardlie with his life into the Iles adioining, where he preached the gospell, and conuerted no small number of Scots to the christian beliefe, and purged that part that was christened from the infection of the Pelagians, as in the Scotish historie more at large appéereth. He was required by the Scots that inhabited here in Britaine, to leaue the Iles and come ouer vnto them, there to instruct the people in the waie of true saluation, to the which with the popes licence he séemed willing enough: and the bishop of Rome the more readilie condescended thereto for that in the instant time, when Paladius was to depart, one Patrike attended at Rome suing for licence to be sent into Ireland.

Paladius offereth to go into Ireland

He is consecrated bishop.

Paladius landed in Ireland

The pope therefore granted that Paladius might passe ouer to the Scots in Britaine, and appointed Patrike to go with authoritie from him into Ireland, where, vpon his arriuall he found the people so well bent to heare his admonitions, contrarie to their accustomed frowardnesse, that a man would haue thought that had séene their readines, how that the land had béene reserued for him to conuert. And bicause it pleased God to bestow such an vniuersall benefit to this land by his meanes, we haue thought good in following our author herein, to touch some part of the course of his life. This Patrike in Latine called *Patricius*, was borne in the marches betwixt England and Scotland, in a towne by the sea side called Eiburne,

Patrike sent into Ireland

Paladius appointed to go into Scotland

The towardnesse of the Irishmen to heare Patrikes preaching.

Where saint Patrike was borne.

 whose

whose father hight Calphurnius, a deacon and sonne to a priest: his mother named Conches, was sister to saint Martine that famous bishop of Towers in France.

The life of saint Patrike in or e'e

Patrike of a child was brought vp in learning, and well instructed in the faith, and much giuen to deuotion. The Irishmen in those daies assisted with Scots and Picts were become archpirats, sore disquieting the seas about the coasts of Britaine, and vsed to sacke litle small villages that laie scattered along the shore, and would often lead awaie captiue the inhabitants home into their countrie. And as it chanced, Patrike being a lad of sixtéene yeares old, and a scholer then in secular learning, was taken among other, and became slaue to an Irish lord called Macbuaine, from whome after six yeares terme he redéemed himselfe with a peece of gold which he found in a clod of earth, that the swine had newlie turned vp as he followed them in that time of his captiuitie, being appointed by his maister to keepe them. And as affliction commonlie maketh men religious, the regard of his former education printed in him such remorse and humilitie, that being thensefoorth weaned from the world, he betooke himselfe to contemplation, euer lamenting the lacke of grace and truth in that land: and herewith not despairing, but that in continuance some good might be wrought vpon them, he learned their toong perfectlie. And alluring one of that nation to beare him companie for exercise sake, he departed from thense, and got him into France, euer hauing in his mind a desire to sée the conuersion of the Irish people, whose babes yet vnborne séemed to him in his dreames (from out of their mothers wombs) to call for christendome.

S. Patrike was take prisoner when he was yoong

Affliction maketh men religious

In this purpose he sought out his vncle Martine, by whose means he was placed with Germanus the bishop of Auxerre, continuing with him as scholer or disciple for the space of fortie yeares: all which time he bestowed in like studie of the holie scriptures, praiers, and such godlie exercises. Then at the age of thréescore and two yeares, being renowmed through the Latine church for his wisedome, vertue and skill, he came to Rome, bringing letters with him in his commendation from the French bishops vnto pope Celestine, to whom he vttered his full mind and secret vow, which long since he had conceiued touching Ireland. Celestine inuested him archbishop and primat of the whole Iland, set him forward with all fauour he could deuise: and brought him and his disciples onward to their countrie.

He passeth into France

Patrike is inuested archbishop of Ireland

In the thrée and twentith yeare therefore of the emperor Theodosius the yoonger, being the yeare of our Lord 430, Patrike landed in Ireland, & bicause he spake the toong perfectlie, and withall being a reuerend personage in the eies of all men, manie listened and gaue good eare to his preaching, the rather for that (as writers haue recorded) he confirmed his doctrine with diuerse miracles: but speciallie those regarded his words before all others, they had some tast of the christian faith aforehand, either by the comming into those parties of Paladius, and his disciple one Albius an Irish bishop, or otherwise by some other: for it is to be thought, that continuallie there remained some sparke of knowledge of christianitie euer since the first preaching of the gospell (which was shortlie after the ascension of our sauiour) by saint Iames (as before is mentioned.) In continuance of time Patrike wan the better part of that kingdome to the faith.

430

Albius an Irish bishop, disciple to Paladius

Laigerius sonne of Neale the great monarch, although he receiued not the gospell himselfe, yet permitted all that would to imbrace it. But sith he refused to be baptised, & applie to his doctrine, the bishop denounced against him a curse from God accordinglie, but tempered yet with mercie and iudgement, as thus: That during his life he should be victorious, but after him neither the kingdome should stand, nor his linage inherit. From thense he tooke his waie vnto Conill lord of Connagh, who honourablie receiued him, and was conuerted with all his people, and after sent him vnto his brother Logan king of Leinster, whome he likewise conuerted. In Mounster he found great friendship and fauour by means of an erle

Laigerius son to Neale the great monarch of Ireland, permitteth the Irishmen to become christians

Conill lord of Connagh

Logan king of Leinster.

there,

there, called the earle of Daris, who honoured him highlie, and gaue him a dwelling place in the east angle of Armagh called Sorta, where he erected manie celles and monasteries, both for religious men and women. He trauelled thirtie yeares in preaching through the land, planting in places conuenient bishops and priests, whose learning and vertuous conuersation by the speciall grace and fauor of God, established the faith in that rude nation. Other thirtie years he spent in his prouince of Armagh among his brethren placed in those houses of religion, which by his meanes were founded, and so he liued in the whole about one hundred twentie two yeares, and lieth buried in Downe.

The earle of Daris

Of saint Patrikes purgatorie ye shall find in the description of the countrie, and therefore we doo here omit it. But yet bicause we are entered to speake of the first foundation of churches and religious houses here in Ireland, in following our author in that behalfe, we will speake somewhat of such other holie men and women as are renowmed to haue liued in Ireland, as ornaments to that Ile, more glorious than all the triumphs & victories of the world, if their zeal had béene seasoned with true knowledge of the scriptures, as it maie well be that in some of them it was, howsoeuer mistaken by the iudgement and report of the simple, which hath raised not onelie of these persons, but also of the verie apostles themselues, certeine fantasticall tales, which with the learned are out of all credit. But this matter I will leaue to diuines to discusse, trusting that the reader will content himselfe to heare what we find recorded by old writers, which we shall set downe, and offer to their considerations to thinke thereof as reason maie best mooue them.

S Patrikes purgatorie

Religious houses & churches founded

Mens doings mistaken.

Giraldus Cambrensis telleth that in saint Patriks time florished saint Bride the virgine, and saint Colme, which two, with the same Patrike, were buried in Downe (as in the Scotish historie ye maie find) and (as the same Giraldus saith) their thrée bodies were found there shortlie after the conquest. Sir Iohn Conwere being president of Vlster, in viewing the sepulture, testified to haue séene thrée principall iewels, which were then translated, as honourable monuments woorthie to be preserued. Of saint Colme it is doubted in what age he liued. Briget, otherwise called Bride, was base daughter to one Dubtactius, a capteine in Leinster, who perceiuing the mother with child, sold hir secretlie (fearing the gealousie of his wife) to an Irish Peet, reseruing to himselfe the fruit of hir wombe. She was there deliuered of this Briget, whome the Péet trained vp in learning, and vertuous education, and at length brought hir home to hir father.

Giral Camb.

Sir Iohn Conwere president of Vlster

S Colme

Peet, that is, Magus in Latine, or (as we may say) a magician or soothsaier in English.

The damsell also was instructed in the faith by saint Patrike, that preached then in those quarters, wherevpon she became so religious and ripe in iudgement, that not onlie the multitude of people, but also a whole synod of bishops assembled néere to Dublin to heare hir aduise in weightie causes, such estimation they had of hir. One fact of hir being yet a child, made hir famous. The king of Leinster had giuen to hir father Dubtactius as a token of his good liking towards him for his valiant seruice, a rich swoord, the furniture whereof was garnished with manie costlie iewels. And as it chanced, the damsell visiting the sicke neighbours diuerslie distressed for want of necessarie reliefe (hir father being a sterne man, and his ladie a cruell shrew) she could deuise no other shift to helpe to reléeue the want of those poore and needie people, but to impart the same iewels of that idle swoord among them. This matter was heinouslie taken, and being brought to the kings eares, it chanced that shortlie after he came to a banket in hir fathers house, and calling the maid afore him that was not yet past nine yeres of age, he asked hir how she durst presume to deface the gift of a king in such wise as she had doon his? She answered that the same was bestowed vpon a better king than he was, whom (quoth she) finding in such extremitie, I would haue giuen all that my father hath, and all that you haue, yea your selues too & all, were yée in my power to giue, rather than

An. Dom. 409

The estimation wherein she was had

The king of Leinster

She professed virginitie.
An. Dom. 500. Briget departed this life.

than Christ should starue. She professed virginitie, and allured other noble yoong damsels vnto hir fellowship, with whome she continued in hir owne monasterie, where she was first professed, vntill the yeare of our Lord 500, and then departing this life, shee was buried in Downe in saint Patriks toome.

A concordance of the foure euangelists.
Cenanus first a man of war, and after a bishop.
Abbat Brendan.

Giraldus Cambrensis reporteth of his owne knowledge, that among other monuments of hirs, there was found a concordance of the foure euangelists, séeming to be written with no mortall hand, beautified with mysticall pictures in the margent, the colours and cunning workemanship wherof at the first blush appeared darke and nothing delectable, but in the héedfull view of the diligent beholder verie liuelie and woonderfull artificiall. Cenanus that was first a souldier, succéeded saint Patrike in the see of Armagh, after he had certeine yeares followed the warres. Brendan abbat at the age of ten yeares was of such incomparable holinesse (as they saie) and therwith so wise and learned, that his father and mother, thinking themselues to haue gained the most worthie fruit that might issue of their mariage, by mutuall consent professed continencie, and abandoned matrimoniall companie. He flourished in the daies of saint Briget, and liued in familiar societie with saint Arons the bishop, and Fintan the abbat.

Madoc.
Melingus.

Madoc *alias* Edan of noble parentage taken prisoner by the king of Temore, and kept in his court with diuerse yoong men his schoolefellowes, openlie admired the king to licence him and them to depart, that they might serue God as they were accustomed, the which being now kept in sunder and restreined of libertie, they were forced to discontinue. Herevpon immediatlie they were dismissed. He died bishop of Fernes, and laid the foundation of that burrow. His successor Melingus, although he was bishop, gaue himselfe yet to voluntarie labour, and with his owne hands deriued and brought a running spring to his monasterie, induring that trauell daily after praier and studie for the space of eight yeares togither.

Colme king of Leinster.
The answer of the archbishop of Cashill to Giraldus Cambrensis.
Malachias.

Fintan abbat was had in such reuerence, that whereas Colme king of Leinster kept Cormake the kings son of Tensill prisoner, he went boldlie with twelue of his disciples through the prease of all the souldiors, and in sight of the king was suffered to borow the yoong prince. For the Irish are not sterne against those of whom they haue conceiued an opinion of holinesse. I remember (saith our author) that Cambrensis writeth himselfe merilie to haue obiected to Morice then archbishop of Cashill, that Ireland in so manie hundred yeares had not brought foorth one martyr. The bishop answered pleasantlie (alluding to the late dispatching of Thomas archbishop of Canturburie) Our people (quoth he) notwithstanding their other enormities, yet haue spared euer the bloud of vertuous men. Marie now we are deliuered to such a nation that is well acquainted with making martyrs, so that from hensefoorth I trust no complaint shall néed for want of martyrs. Malachias was borne in Armagh of a noble progenie, brought vp in vertue by the example of his mother, and trained foorth in learning, profited greatlie in deuotion: so that being yet but a verie babe, he was espied diuerse times to steale awaie from his companions to praie in secret. He was so graue and modest, that of himselfe he chose the most graue and seuere schoolemaister, refusing an excellent clearke, because he saw him somewhat lightlie demeaning himselfe at game. In the beginning of his youthfull yeares, he became the disciple of Imarius an old recluse, whose austeritie of conuersation the whole towne had in great reuerence. There he became a deacon, and at fiue and twentie yeares a priest.

The monasterie of Banchor repared.

The archbishop, for the fame and the opinion of his woorthinesse, receiued him to be assistant to him in office, in the which he so behaued himselfe, that he reformed superstitions, and reuiued the force of religion, namelie in the vniformitie of their church seruice, wherin before time they varied. The famous monasterie of Banchor he reedified of the patrimonie and legacies by his vncle left him. The same

monasterie

monasterie was of old time gouerned by Congellus, and after him by Columbanus the father of manie religious houses in France. This abbeie being spoiled and nintie of his brethren murdered in one day by the prior, the possessions whereof being come to the hands of Malachias by his vncles assignement, he restored foorthwith, and aduanced the foundation. At the age of thirtie yeares he was by canonicall election forced to accept the bishoprike of Conereth, a people of all the Irish then most sauage and wild, whome with inestimable trauell he reclamed from their beastlie maners. In the meane while died Celsus bishop of Armagh, after whome succeeded Malachias, at the age of eight and thirtie yeares. But before this, neere hand the space of two hundred yeares togither, a custome had crept into the countrie, that the metropolitane sée was conferred vpon such bishops as were maried, and were of the bloud roiall, in maner by way of inheritance. Wherefore Nigellus or Neale the next of kinred, animated by the parcialitie of some princes, and getting into his custodie the bible and staffe, and other monuments of saint Patrike, wherevnto opinion of the common people tied the prelacie, came to his palace with a band of souldiors to haue slaine the bishop. When all the people wept and houled for his perill, he alone stepped into the bosome of his enimies, demanding what was their purpose? The bloudie souldiors letting fall their weapons, in stead of executing the pretensed murtherer, fell to reuerence him, and at length departed from him as friends.

Maried bishops held the see successiuelie and of one familie, neither would the Irish haue had anie other than of the house.

See saint Barnard *In vita Malachiæ. Bale, &c.*

The bible and staffe.

Thrée yeares he sat in the primasie rather to discontinue the horrible corruption before vsed, than with intent to settle himselfe there. After he had remoued the abuse, he procured Gelasius to succéed him in the archbishops sée, and he returned to his former see of Downe, to the which as then was annexed the bishoprike of Coner. But Malachias vnderstanding that in times past they were six seuerall sées, he diuided them againe, and ordeined an other to the bishoprike of Coner, desirous rather to lessen his cure than to inlarge the fruits by taking more charge vpon him. Malachias being demanded of his brethren the monkes of Benchor, where and when he would wish to die and to be buried, if it laie in his choise? He answered: If in Ireland, beside the bodie of saint Patrike: if beyond the seas, at Clareuale, where saint Barnard was then resiant, and in the feast of Alsoules. He purposed within few daies to sue to pope Eugenius for increase of the number of metropolitans, which request was shortlie after accomplished. And in this viage which he thus made, he staied at Clareuale, and there diuerse times openlie foreshewed, that the yeare of his departure foorth of this world was come, and accordinglie when he had taken leaue of saint Barnard and the brethren, he went downe from his chamber to the church and there did communicat. Which doone, he returned to his lodging, and there on Alsouls daie in the yeare of his age 54, he gaue vp the ghost, so mildlie and quietlie, that it seemed rather a sléepe than a death.

For lineall descent of bishops.

Malchus, though borne in Ireland, yet he spent the most part of his time in the monasterie of Winchester in England, and from thense was taken and admitted bishop of Lismore. Saint Barnard remembreth of him, by occasion he cured a lunatike child in confirming, else (as they termed it) in bishopping him. This miracle seene and confessed by manie hundreds of people, was blowen through the world. The same time happened discord betwixt the king of Mounster and his brother, and as the matter was handled, the king was ouermatched and fled into England, where he visited Malchus in his abbeie, and would by no meanes depart from him, but remaine there vnder his rule and gouernment, so long as it pleased God to denie him quiet returne into his countrie. He contented himselfe with a poore cell, vsed dailie to bath himselfe in cold water, to asswage the wanton motions of his flesh, and for his diet receiued none other delicats than bread, water, and salt, daie and night, sobbing and bewailing with great remorse of conscience his former misdemenors

Malchus.

Discord betwéene the king of Mounster and his brother.

menors

mened life. At length the other kings and people of Ireland began to repine at the vsurper, set vpon him with open war, vanquished him in a pitcht field, and called home the rightfull prince his brother againe, to resume his kingdome, who with manie earnest persuasions of Malchus and of Malachias could vneth be brought to forsake that trade of life and companie, the which he had with such delectation ioined himselfe vnto.

Thus far of the Irish saints. Of the which, as some of them are to be estéemed right vertuous and godlie men, so other of them are to be suspected as persons rather holie by the superstitious opinion of the people, than indeed with anie such knowledge of true godlinesse and sincere religion, as are woorthie to be registred in the number of those that of right ought to passe for saints, as by certeine late writers may appeare. But this we leaue to the iudgement of the aduised reader, Ex Bal. for that in such matters we mind not to preiudice anie mans opinion, but onelie wish the reader to take héed how he giueth credit to that which oftentimes is found written by authors touching feigned miracles, and other vaine superstitious dealings, wherethrough manie zealous persons haue often béene deceiued. Now therefore to leaue saints, and returne to other matters touching the Irish historie. In the yeare 586 the Norwegians had got dominion ouer the Islands in the northwest ocean called the Iles of Orkeneie, and scowred the seas, that none other nation durst vneth appeare in sight for dread of them. (586 The Norwegians scoure the seas, and inuade the Iles of Orkeneie) A people giuen greatlie to séeke the conquests of other realmes, as they that could not faile to find more warme and fruitfull places for to inhabit than their owne. These hot fellowes chanced to light into Ireland by this meanes. (They inuade Ireland.) Careticus the king of Britaine ran into such hatred of his people, that they raised warres against him. The Saxons that possessed now six seuerall kingdomes in the Ile of Britaine, reioised not a litle at this ciuill discord betwixt the Britaine king and his subiects.

Wherevpon meaning to make a full conquest of the Britains, & vtterlie to expell them foorth of all the Ile, he assembled their powers, & ioined to the same Gurmundus, a notable rouer of the Norwegians, who hauing at all times a nauie in a readinesse, and men to furnish it, holpe the Saxons to chase the Britains into the marches of Wales. (Gurmundus an archpirat of the nation of Norwaie.) For from thense (being retired into the mounteins and woods) they could not driue them. This Gurmound (as some thinke) builded at the same time the towne of Gurmondchester, and after being assisted by the Saxons, made a viage into Ireland, where he sped not greatlie to his desire, and therefore the Irish account not this for anie of their conquests, as some of their antiquaries informed our author. (Campion) Gurmound therefore finding but some successe, built a few slight castels and forts in the frontiers, and so left the land, and sailed from thence into France, where at length he was slaine. Our chronicles in déed name him king of Ireland. but the Irish affirme that before Turgesius, there was none of the easterne people that obteined dominion in their countrie. (Turgesius.)

Giraldus Cambrensis to make the matter whole (a Gods name) thinketh Turgesius to haue conquered the land, as lieutenant or deputie vnder Gurmundus. But this being granted, there ariseth a more manifest contradiction than the former: for he himselfe numbreth betwixt Laogirius king of Ireland that liued in the yéere foure hundred and thirtie, and Edlumding, whome Turgesius vanquished, 33 monarchs, whose reigns comprehended foure hundred yeares, so that Turgesius liued in the yeare after the incarnation eight hundred and thirtie. (Laogirius 430) Then it is too plaine that he could not haue anie doings with Gurmundus, who ioined with the Saxons against Careticus, in the yeare fiue hundred foure score and six. This knot (saith our author) might be vntwined with more facilitie thus. (The doubt resolued) Gurmundus made much of that little he got, and wrote himselfe king, which title our histories doo allow him, because he made the waie plaine, moied it a while, and set open the gate vnto

vnto his countrimen. Turgesius atchiued the whole exploit, and brought it to perfection, and in these respects either of them may be called king and conqueror of Ireland.

Turgesius therefore with his Norwegians the second time inuaded Ireland, sustemed diuerse losses and ouerthrowes: but in the end fortifieng himselfe by the sea coasts, & receiuing thereby his fréends at his pleasure, waxed so strong that he subdued the whole Ile, still erecting castels and fortresses as he wan ground, so to maister the Irish that with such manner of strengths of wals and rampires had not as yet beene acquainted: for till those daies they knew no defense but woods, bogs, or strokes. Turgesius so brideled the Irish kings, and kept them in awe, that without interruption he reigned like a conqueror thirtie yeares. He cried hauocke & spoile where anie rich preie was to be had: sparing neither those of the laitie nor of the clergie, neither church nor chappell, abusing his victorie verie insolentlie. Omalaghlilen king of Meth was in some trust with the tyrant. His onelie daughter Turgesius craued for his concubine. The father hauing a readie wit, and watching his time, began to breake with Turgesius in this wise. Sauing your fansie my lord (quoth he) there are diuerse ladies of bloud in this countrie méeter bedfellows for a king than that browne girstle: and therewith he began to reckon vp a number of his néeces and cousines, indowed (as he set them foorth) with such singular beautie, as they séemed rather angels than mortall creatures. The tyrant as it were rauished, and doting in loue of those péereles péeces before he saw them, by reason of such exceeding praises as he thus heard of them, doubted yet least Omalaghlilen extolled them to preserue his daughter out of his hands: and the subtill father cloked his drift with modest behauior, lingering time to inflame the leachers follie, as he that wished anie thing more to be suspected, than that which he meant most earnestlie to bring to passe.

Turgesius what he did.

He buildeth fortresses.

Turgesius reigned in Ireland thirtie yeares.

Omalaghlilen king of Meth.

The policie of Omalaghlilen.

At length, when Turgesius séemed to take his delaieng thus of time somewhat displeasantlie, he vsed this or the like speech. 'If I should saie (quoth he) that I gaue you my sole daughter with goodwill to be deflowred, your high wisdome would soone ghesse that I did but flatter you, and yet if ten daughters were déerer to me than your good pleasure and contentation, by whose bountifull goodnes both she, & I, and we all are supported, I were vnwoorthie that secret and neere fréendship wherein it liketh you to vse me. As for the wench, it will be in part honorable for hir to be required to the bed of such a prince, sith quéenes haue not sticked to come from farre, and yeeld the vse of their bodies to noble conquerors, in hope by them to haue issue. And howsoeuer it be taken, time will weare it out, and redéeme it: but such a fréend as you are to me and mine, neither I nor mine shall liue to see. And verelie I meane not to hazard your displeasure, if it were for a greater matter than the value of twentie maidenheads, séeing fathers haue not sticked to giue vp their owne wiues to quench the lusts of their sons. Therefore am I thus agréed, name the daie and place, separat your selfe from the view of your court, conferre with those that haue a deintie insight, & skilfull eies in discerning beauties, I will send you my daughter, & with hir the chois of twelue or sixteene gentlewomen, the meanest of the which may be an empresse in comparison. When they are before you, make your game as you like, and then if my child please your fantasie best, she is not too good to be at your commandement: onelie my request is, that if anie other shall presume vpon your leauings, your maiestie will remember whose child she is.'

This liberall proffer was of Turgesius accepted (whose desire was most insatiable) with manie good words, thanks, & faire promises. To be short, the same daie Omalaghlilen put his daughter in prince-like apparell, attired after the trimmest wise, and with hir sixteene proper yoong men beautifull and amiable to behold

The like was practised by

Alexander son to Amyntas king of Macedon against the Persian imbassadors. [illegible] [illegible]

and so being sent to the king were presented vnto him in his priuie chamber, hauing none about him but a few dissolute youthfull persons, wherevpon those disguised yoong striplings drew foorth from vnder their long womanish garments their skeins, and valiantlie bestirring themselues, first stabbed their weapons points through the bodie of the tyrant, and then serued all those youths that were about him with the like sawce, they making small or no resistance at all. The brute of this murther was quicklie blowne abrode through all Ireland: and the princes readie to catch hold on such aduantage rose in armes with one assent, in purpose to deliuer themselues from bondage, and recouer libertie.

The persuasion of Omalaghlen

All Meth and Leinster were speedilie got togither, resorting vnto Omalaghlilen the author of this practise, who lightlie leapt to horsse, and commending their forward rednesse in so naturall a quarell, said: "My lords and fréends, this case neither admitteth delaie, nor requireth policie, hart and hast is all in all. Whilest the matter is fresh and gréene, and that some of our enimies lie still and sléepe, some lament, some cursse, some are togither in councell, and all the whole number dismaied: let vs preuent their furie, dismember their force, cut off their flight, seize vpon their places of refuge and succour. It is no victorie to plucke their feathers, but to breake their necks, not to chase them in, but to rowse them out, to wéed them, not to rake them, not to tread them downe, but to root them vp. This lesson the tyrant himselfe did teach me. I once demanded of him as it were in a parable, by what good husbandrie the land might be rid of certeine rauening foules that annoied it. He aduised vs to watch where they bred, and to fire their nests about their eares. Go we then vpon these cormorants which shrowd themselues in our possessions, and let vs so destroie them, that neither nest nor root, neither séed nor stalke, neither branch nor stumpe shall remaine of this vngratious generation." Scarse had he ended his tale, but that with great showts and clamors they extolled the king, as defendor of their liues and liberties, assuring them both of their bold and hardie stomachs and speedfull expedition ioined with their confederats, and with a running camp swept euerie corner of the land, rased the castels to the ground, chased awaie the strangers, slue all that abode battell, ech man recouering his owne, with the state of gouernment.

Thus in effect haue the Irish writers reported of Turgesius a Norwegian, whether he did reigne before the supposed time of Gurmond, or whether that he came thither as lieutenant to him: which if it shuld be true, no doubt the same Gurmond was some king of the Danes, or Norwegians, and not of the Affricans (as some of our countrimen name him.) Which error is soone committed, in taking one heathenish nation for another, as those men haue doone that haue named the Hungarians (when they did inuade Gallia before they were christians) Saracens. And so likewise might that author (whosoeuer he was) whome Geffriee of Monmouth followeth, finding Gurmond written to be a king of the miscreants, mistake the Norwegians for Affricans, because both those nations were infidels: and therfore sith happilie the Affricans in the daies when that author liued, bare all the brute aboue other heathenish nations then, as the Turks doo now, he named them Affricans. Howsoeuer it was, certeine it is that the Danes or Norwegians made sundrie inuasions into Ireland, and that at seuerall times. But for Turgesius, whether he were an absolute king, or but a lieutenant of some armie, vnder some other king named Gurmound, or peraduenture Gormo, (as such names are soon corrupted) I cannot affirme, bicause that no certeine time is set downe in the chronicles which are written of those nations, whereby they may be so reconciled togither, as sufficeth to warrant anie likelie coniecture in this behalfe.

Gurmond

But if I should saie (with the readers licence) what I thinke, this Gurmound whatsoeuer he was, made no such conquest of Ireland, nor of this our Ile of Britaine

taine (as by some writers is supposed) but yet might he peraduenture land in Wales, and either in fauor of the Saxons then enimies to the Britons, or in hatred of the christian name persecute by cruell wars the British nation, and vse such crueltie as the heathenish nations then were accustomed to practise against the christians in all places where they came, and chanced to haue the vpper hand. The chiefest cause that mooueth me to doubt thereof, is for that I find not in anie of our approoued ancient English writers, as Beda, Malmesburie, Huntington, Houeden, or such like, anie plaine mention made of him, whereby I may be throughlie induced to credit that which I find in Geffrie Monmouth and others recorded of him, except his name be mistaken, and so thereby some error crept in, which I am not able to resolue.

But sith we are entred to speake thus farre of the Norwegians, here by the waie I haue thought it not impertinent to the purpose of this Irish historie, to write what we find recorded in the chronicles of those northernlie regions, Denmarke, Norweie, and Sweden, written by Saxo Grammaticus, Albertus Crantz and others, *Saxo Gram. Alber. Crantz.* concerning the sundrie inuasions made by the Danes, Norwegians, or Normans (whether we list to call them) into Ireland. Fridleie or Fridlenus king of Denmarke *Fridlenus.* that succeeded Dan the third of that name, surnamed the Swift, arriuing in Ireland, besieged the citie of Dublin, & perceiuing by the strength of the walles, *Dublin besieged.* that it would be an hard matter to win it by plaine force of hand without some cunning policie, he deuised to catch a sort of swallowes that had made their nests in the houses within the towne, tied wild fier to their wings, and therewith cast them vp, and suffered them to flie their waies, wherevpon they comming to their *Dublin set on* nests, set the houses on fier, which whiles the citizens went about to quench, the *fire, and won by the Danes.* Danes entred the citie and wan it.

Secondlie, Frotho king of Denmarke, the third of that name, after he had sub- *Frotho the third.* dued the Britons here in this Ile, made a voiage into Ireland also, where he landed with some danger: for the Irishmen had strawed all alongest the shore a great *Caltrops strawed by the Irish to anno e the* number of caltrops of iron, with sharpe pricks standing vp, to wound the Danes in *Danes.* the feet, as they should come foorth of their ships to follow them, for they meant to flee of a pretensed policie for that purpose. But Frotho perceiuing their deceitfull craft, followed them more aduisedlie than rashlie, and so put their capteine named Kerull to fight, and slue him in the field, whose brother remaining in life, *Kerull gouernour of Irishmen slaine.* & mistrusting his owne puissance, yéelded himselfe to Frotho, who diuiding the preie amongst his souldiers and men of warre, shewed thereby that he onelie sought for glorie and not for gaine, reseruing not a pennie of all the spoile to his owne vse. After this, in the daies of king Frotho the fourth of that name, which reigned ouer *Frotho the fourth.* the Danes, one Starcater a giant, in companie of Haco a Danish capteine, made a *Starcater a giant.* iournie likewise into Ireland, where in the same season, one Huglet reigned as *Huglet king of Ireland.* monarch ouer that Ile: who hauing plentie of treasure, was yet so giuen to couetousnesse, that by such vnprincelie parts as he plaid, to satisfie his greedie desire to fill his coffers, he became right odious, and farre out of all fauor with his subiects. Yet there were of his nobles, verie valiant and worthie men, namelie two, Gegathus *Gegathus & Suibdauus.* & Suibdauus: wherevpon, when it came to passe that he should ioine in battell with his enimies the Danes, the most part of all his people fled out of the field, so that Gegath and Suibdaue were in maner left alone. For they regarding their honors and dutie that apperteined to men of their calling, would not flie, but manfullie did what laie in their powers to beat backe the enimies: insomuch that Gegathus raught Haco such a wound, that the vpper part of his liuer appeared *Haco wounded.* bare. He also wounded Starcater in the head right sore, so that in all his life daies, *Starcater wounded.* he had not before that time receiued the like hurt: in the end yet Huglet the mo- *Huglet slaine.* narch of Ireland was slaine, and Starcater obteining the victorie, did make great slaughter of the Irish subiects, the which had followed their king to this battell, being men (thorough his corrupt example and slouthfull trade of life) degenerat from all warlike order and vse of manlike exercise.

Dublin woon

After this, the Danes went vnto Dublin, which towne they easilie tooke, and found such store of riches and treasure therein, that euerie man had so much as he could wish or desire, so as they needed not to fall out among themselues for the partition, sith there was so much for each mans share as he could conuenientlie carrie awaie. Thus hath Saxo Grammaticus written in effect of Starcaters comming into Ireland, of whome the Danish writers make such mention, both for his huge stature and great manhood. Some haue thought, that Starcater was the verie same man which the Scots name Finnaccole, of whome in the Scotish historie we haue made mention: but whereas the Scotish writers affirme that he was a Scotish man borne, the Danish writers report that he was borne in Eastland, among the people called Estones. Reignerus the sonne of Siwardus the second king of Denmarke, hauing atchiued sundrie victories in England and Scotland, and subdued the Iles of Orkneie, he passed likewise into Ireland, slue Melbricke king of that land, and tooke the citie of Dublin by siege, where he remained the whole tearme of twelue moneths before he departed from thense.

Reignerus

Melbricke king of Ireland slaine

Gurmo the third of that name king of Denmarke

He marrieth Thira daughter to Etheldred king of England

Canute and Harold

After this, Gurmo the third of that name king of Denmarke, although an infidell himselfe, and a cruell persecutor of the christian religion, yet tooke to wife a christian ladie named Thira, daughter to Etheldred king of England, who had issue by him two sonnes Knaught, or Canute, and Harold, prooouing men of high valiancie and notable prowesse, insomuch that after the atchiuing of diuerse worthie victories against the enimies néere home, they made a voiage into England, not sparing to inuade the dominions of their grandfather king Etheldred: who rather reioising, than séeming to be offended with those manlike enterprises of his cousins, proclamed them his heires to succéed after him in all his lands and dominions, although of right the same were to descend first vnto their moother Thira. The yoong men being incouraged with their grandfather his bountifull magnificence, attempted the inuasion of Ireland, where at the siege of Dublin, Canute or Knaught the elder brother was shot into the bodie with an arrow, and died of the wound: howbeit his death was kept close by his owne commandement giuen before he died, till his people had got the citie into their possession. But the game was small in respect of the losse, which was thought to redound vnto the whole Danish nation by the death of that noble yoong gentleman Canute, who for his high prowesse and valiancie was most tenderlie beloued of all men, but namelie of his father king Gormo, insomuch that he sware to kill him with his owne hands, whosoeuer should first tell him newes of his death.

They inuade Ireland

Canute is slaine

This Gormo was now a man far striken in age, and blind, hauing small ioie of anie worldlie pleasures, otherwise than to heare of the welfare and prosperous procéedings of his sonnes. When therefore his wife quéene Thira had perfect aduertisement of hir sonnes death, and that neither she nor anie other durst breake the matter vnto hir husband, she deuised a shift how to signifie that vnto him by outward signes, which by word of mouth she was afraid to expresse, as thus. She caused moorning apparell to be made for hir husband, & putting off his roiall robes, clad him therewith, and other things apperteining to moorners she also put about him, and prepared all such furniture and necessaries as were vsed for funerall exequies, witnessing the lamentable griefe conceiued for the losse of some friend, with that kind of moorning wéed and funerall ceremonies. Which when Gormo perceiued: Wo is me (saith he) you then signifie the death of my sonne Canute. Whereto she made answer, that he and not she did discouer the truth of that which was meant by those moorning garments, and with that spéech ministred cause of hir

The policie of Thira to signifie to hir husband the death of hir sonne Canute hir husbands death, whereby she became presentlie a widow, not openlie mourning for hir sonne, before she mourned likewise for hir husband: for he tooke such griefe for Canutes death, that immediatlie he died thorough sorow and dolor: so as Thira was thus driuen to lament, as well the death of hir sonne, as of hir husband both at once. But now to the purpose of the Irish historie.

Gormo dieth of sorow.

Ye haue thus partlie heard what the Danish writers doo record in their histories, touching the conquests which their people made in Ireland: but whether the same be meant of that which goeth before, or rather of that which followeth, touching the trade which the Norwegian merchants vsed thither, or whether the Irish writers haue passed these iournies ouer with silence which the Danish writers in forme (as before is touched) doo make mention of, I cannot affirme. But like it is that as the Danes, or Normans, whether you will call them, did inuade Ireland as well as England, France, and Scotland, in those daies according to the report of their writers, and that by waie of open warre as well to conquer the countrie, as to take preies, prisoners, and booties, and not for trade of merchandize onelie: albeit that they might peraduenture so get entrie at the first, as by the Irish histories it should seeme they did shortlie after the slaughter of Turgesius. And afterwards when they saw themselues setled, and perceiued that they began to grow to be enuied of their Irish neighbours, who therevpon would not sticke to molest them as occasions serued, they saw no better meane to assure themselues against their aduersaries, than to send vnto their countriemen, which in those daies roued abroad (as before I haue said) in euerie quarter of this our west ocean, waiting for opportunitie to aduance their conquests in each countrie where anie thing might be gotten. And so this maie agrée verie well with the Irish writers, whom as I doo not take vpon me to controll, but rather to report the storie as I find it by them written, I will procéed with the order which they follow. After the countrie was deliuered of the tyrannie wherewith it was oppressed by the same Turgesius & his people, Danes or Norwegians whether they were (for so Cambrensis estéemeth them) the Irish deliuered of seruile bondage, fell to their old woonted vomit, in persecuting each other: and hauing latelie defaced their fortified townes and castels, as receptacles and couerts for the enimie, all sides laie more open to receiue harme.

This being perceiued and thoroughlie considered, the princes that in the late rule of Turgesius had espied some towardnesse to wealth & ease, fell in hand to discourse the madnesse & follie of their ancestors, which saw not the vse of that which their enimies abused: they begun to loth their vnquiet trade of life, to wish either lesse discord, or more strength in each mans dominion, to cast the danger of naked countries, readie to call in the enimies: as the strength of forts & castels was a meane to preserue them from losse. Faine would they haue prouided remedie in this case, if they had knowne how. The former subiection, though it seemed intollerable, yet they felt therein procéeding steps towards peace. The gaine that rose of merchandize, rest and suertie to the whole estate of the countrie. For the difference was great betwixt the indeuours of the two nations, Norwegians and Irish. The first knew the waie to thriue, might they get some commodious seats and soile. The other had commodities plentie, and cared not for them.

While the princes and potentats staied vpon such a good consideration, certeine merchants of Norwaie, Denmarke, and of other those parties, called *Ostomanni*, or (as in our vulgar language we tearme them) Easterlings, bicause they lie East in respect of vs, although indeed they are by other named properlie Normans, and partlie Saxons, obteined licence safelie to arriue here in Ireland with their wares, and to vtter the same. Herevpon the Irish, thorough traffike & bartering with these Normans or Danes (for so they are called also in our English chronicle) by exchanging of wares and monie, finding them craftie and tractable: and delting also with

Eastorlings began to trade into Ireland

with

with gaie conceipts, brought into them by those merchants (such as till they saw them they neuer estéemed néedfull) they began to enter into a desire that a trade might be open betwixt them & the other nations, wherevpon to allure other they licenced these merchant strangers to build (if they thought good) hauen townes in places most commodious. This was no sooner granted, than begun, and with spéed finished.

They build townes on the sea coasts.

Waterford, Limerike, Dublin.

Amlanus founded Waterford, Sitaracus, Limerike, Iuorus, Dublin, and so by others diuerse other townes were built as leisure serued. Then by the helpe and counsell of these men, manie castles, forts, steeples, and churches, euerie where were repaired. And thus are the Irish mingled also with the bloud of the Danes, Norwegians, or Normans, who from thensefoorth continuallie flocked into Ireland, to the great commoditie of the inhabitants, liuing amongst them obedientlie, till wealth pricked and mooued them to raise rebellion: but they could not haue holden out, had not the conquest insuing determined both their quarrels. In the meane while they became lords of the hauens and burrow townes, planted men of warre in the same, and oftentimes skirmished with their aduersaries; but yet measured their fortune with indifferent games, and crept no higher than the same would giue them leaue. Onelie a memorie is left of their field in Clontars, where diuerse of the Irish nobilitie were slaine, that lie buried before the crosse of Kilmainam. These are by our author, not without good iudgement, reported to be Danes, which people then being pagans, sore afflicted England, and after that France, from whense they came againe into England with William Conqueror. So that those people called *Ostomanni*, Esterlings, Normans, Danes, Norwegians, & Suedenceis are in effect all one nation, borne in that huge region called Scandinauia, and as it appeareth by conference of times and chronicles, muchwhat about one season, vexed the Frenchmen, afflicted Scotland, subdued England, and multiplied in Ireland.

The merchant strangers mooue rebellion.

The field of Clontars.

The seuerall names of the strangers which in these daies afflicted France, England, Scotland and Ireland.

1095 But in the yeare of Christ 1095, perceiuing great cause to remaine and lurke in the distinction of the names Easterlings and Irish, that were altogither westerne, and the Easterlings not easterne indéed, but rather simplie northerne, in consideration whereof, and bicause they magnified themselues in the late conquest of their countriemen, who from Normandie comming ouer into England ruled there at their pleasure, these strangers in Ireland would algate now be also called and accompted Normans.

The Easterlings will be called Normans.

Long before this time (as yée haue heard) Ireland was bestowed into two principall kingdomes, and sometime into more, whereof one was euer elected and reputed to be cheefe, and as it were a monarch, whome in their histories they name *Maximum regem*, that is, the greatest king, or else without addition, *Regem Hiberniæ*, the king of Ireland: the other they name *Reguli* or *Reges*, that is to wit, small kings or else kings, by limiting the places whereof they were to be reputed kings, as of Leinster, Connagh, Vlster, Mounster, or Meth. To the monarch, besides his allowance of dominion, titles of honor, and other priuileges in iurisdiction, there was granted to him a negatiue in nomination of bishops, when they were vacant: for the cleargie and laitie of the diocesse commended one, whom they thought conuenient vnto their king, the king to the monarch, the monarch to the archbishop of Canturburie: for that as yet the metropolitans of Ireland had not receiued their palles.

Maximus Rex the great king or monarch of Ireland.

The power of the monarch in election of bishops.

In this sort was nominated to the bishoprike of Dubline then void, in the yeare of Christ 1074, at the petition of Godericus king of Leinster, by sufferance of the cleargie and people there, with the assent of Terdienatus the monarch, a learned prelat called Patricius, whome Lanfranke of Canturburie consecrated in Paules church at London, and sware him to obedience after the maner of his ancestors.

Godericus king of Leinster. Terdienatus the monarch. Patricius consecrated bishop of Dublin by Lanfranke.

1152 Christian bishop of Lismore, legat to Eugenius the third, summoned a prouinciall counsell

Christian bishop of Lismore.

councell in Ireland, wherein were authorised foure metropolitan seas, Armagh, Dublin, Cashill, and Tuen, of the which places were bishops at that present, Gelasius, Gregorius, Donatus, Edonius. For hitherto though they yéelded a primasie to the bishop of Armagh in reuerence of saint Patrike the first bishop there, yet the same was but of good will, and confirmed rather by custome than by sufficient decree, neither did that archbishop take vpon him to inuest other bishops, but sent them to Canturburie (as before is mentioned) which from hensefoorth they vsed not to doo, insomuch that the next bishop named Laurence, sometime archbishop of saint Keuins in Golandilagh, was ordered and installed at home by Gelasius primat of Armagh.

Foure metropolitan sees in Ireland

The bishop of Armagh.

Laurence archbishop of S. Keuins

1162

FINIS.

Not well vnderstanding what the writer of this part of the Irish historie ment to fall vpon so blunt a conclusion, but supposing it was vpon some reasonable inducement: we thought it conuenient to leaue it as we found it intending (without anie addition hereunto) to set downe the conquest of Ireland, as the same was left recorded by Girald of Cambria: whose prefaces and historie, right worthie the reading, doo immediatlie follow.

THE NAMES OF THE GOUERNORS, LIEUTENANTS, LORD IUSTICES, AND DEPUTIES OF IRELAND,

SINCE THE CONQUEST THEREOF BY KING HENRIE THE SECOND

The yeere of our Lord

1174 RICHARD Strangbow earle of Penbroke gouernor, hauing Reimond le Grace ioined in commission with him

1177 Reimond le Grace lieutenant by himselfe.

William Fitz Aldelme lieutenant, hauing Iohn de Curcie, Robert Fitz Stephans and Miles Cogan ioined in commission with him.

Hugh Lacie lieutenant

1182 Iohn Lacie constable of Chester and Richard de Peche } gouernors.

Hugh Lacie againe lieutenant

Hugh Lacie the yoonger, lord iustice

1227 Henrie Loundons archbishop of Dublin, lord iustice

1228 Maurice Fitzgirald lord iustice

1253 Iohn Fitzgeffreie knight, lord iustice

Alain de la Zouch lord iustice

1258 Stephan de Long Espe lord iustice

William Deane lord iustice.

1261 Sir Richard Rochell or Capell lord iustice

1267 Dauid Barrie lord iustice

1268 Robert Vfford lord iustice.

1269 Richard de Excester lord iustice

1270 Iames lord Audleie lord iustice

1272 Maurice Fitzmaurice lord iustice

Walter lord Genuille lord iustice

Robert Vfford againe lord iustice

1281 Fulborne bishop of Waterford lord iustice

Iohn Samford the archbishop of Dublin, lord iustice.

William Vescie lord iustice

1295 William Dodingsels lord iustice.

Thomas Fitzmaurice lord iustice

1298 Iohn Wogan lord iustice

1311 Theobald Verdon lord iustice

1315 Edmund Butler lord iustice

1317 Roger lord Mortimer lord iustice

Alexander Bignor archbishop of Dublin lord iustice

The yeares of our Lord

Roger lord Mortimer second time lord iustice 1319

Thomas Fitziohn earle of Kildare lord iustice 1320

Iohn Birmingham earle of Louth lord iustice 1321

Iohn lord Darcie lord iustice. 1323

Roger Outlaw prior of Kilmainan lord iustice 1327

Anthonie lord Lucie lord iustice

Iohn lord Darcie second time lord iustice 1332

Iohn lord Charleton lord iustice 1337

Thomas bishop of Hereford lord iustice 1338

Iohn lord Darcie ordeined lord iustice by patent during his life, by Edward the third 1339

Rafe Vfford lord iustice.

Robert Darcie lord iustice 1346

Iohn Fitzmaurice lord iustice

Walter lord Bermingham lord iustice, his deputies were Iohn Archer, prior of Kilmainan & Baron Carew, with sir Thomas Rokesbie

Maurice Fitzthomas earle of Desmond had the office of lord iustice for terme of his life, of king Edward the third his grant

Thomas Rokesbie knight lord iustice 1355

Almericke de saint Amand, Iohn Butler earle of Ormond, Maurice Fitzth. earle of Kild. } appointed L. I. by turnes. 1357

Lionell duke of Clarence lord iustice. 1361

Gerald Fitzmaurice earle of Desmond L. I. 1367

William lord Windsor the first lieutenant in Ireland 1369

Richard Ashton lord iustice 1372

Roger Mortimer, Philip Courtneie, Iames erle of Orm. } Iustices and lieutenants speciallie recorded in Richard the seconds daies 1381

Robert

The yeare of our Lord

Robert Vere earle of Oxford marques of Dublin created duke of Ireland.

1394 Roger Mortimer earle of March lieutenant

Roger Mortimer earle of March and Vlster lieutenant

Roger Greie lord iustice

Iohn Stanleie knight lord lieutenant.

1401 Thomas of Lancaster brother to king Henrie the fourth lord lieutenant, whose deputies at sundrie times were Alexander bishop of Meth, Stephan Scrope knight, and the prior of Kilmainan.

1403 Iames Butler earle of Ormond lord iustice

Girald earle of Kildare lord iustice

1407 Iames Butler earle of Ormond, sonne to the foresaid Iames, lord iustice

1413 Iohn Stanleie againe lord lieutenant

Thomas Crauleie archbishop of Dublin lord iustice

1414 Iohn lord Talbot of Shefield lieutenant.

1420 Iames Butler erle of Ormond the second time lieutenant

Lieutenants to king Henrie the sixt:

- Edmund earle of March, Iames earle of Ormond his deputie
- Iohn Sutton lord Dudleie, sir Thomas Strange knight his deputie.
- Sir Thomas Stanleie, sir Christopher Plunket his deputie
- Lion lord Welles, the earle of Ormond his deputie.
- Iames erle of Ormond by himselfe
- Iohn earle of Shrewesburie, the archbishop of Dublin in his absence lord iustice

Richard Plantagenet duke of Yorke, father to king Edward the fourth, had the office of lieutenant by king Henrie the sixt his letters patents for ten yeares. His deputies at sundrie times were, the baron of Deluin, Richard Fitzeustace knight, Iames earle of Ormond, and Thomas Fitzmoris earle of Kildare

Thomas Fitzmoris earle of Kildare, lord iustice in king Edward the fourth his daies, vntill the third yeare of his reigne. After which George duke of Clarence brother to the K. had the office of lieutenant during his life, & made his deputies by sundrie times these:

Deputies to the duke of Clarence (1470):

- Thomas earle of Desmond,
- Iohn Tiptoft erle of Worcester,
- Thomas erle of Kildare,
- Henrie lord Graie of Ruthine

Sir Rouland Eustace lord deputie

Richard duke of Yorke, yoonger sonne to king Edward the fourth, lieutenant

Edward sonne to Richard the third lieutenant, his deputie was Girald earle of Kildare

Iasper duke of Bedford and earle of Penbroke, lieutenant, his deputie was Walter archbishop of Dublin.

Edward Poinings knight, lord deputie 1494

Henrie duke of Yorke, after king by the name of Henrie the eight, lieutenant, his deputie Girald earle of Kildare 1501

Girald Fitzgirald earle of Kildare, lord deputie

Thomas Howard earle of Surreie, after duke of Norfolke, lieutenant 1520

Piers Butler earle of Ossorie, lord deputie 1523

Girald Fitzgirald earle of Kildare againe lord deputie

The baron of Deluin lord deputie

Piers Butler earle of Ossorie againe lord deputie 1529

William Skeffington knight, lord deputie

Girald Fitzgirald earle of Kildare, againe lord deputie.

William Skeffington againe lord deputie

Leonard lord Graie, lord deputie. 15[illegible]

Sir William Brereton knight, lord iustice 15[illegible]

Sir Anthonie Sentleger knight, lord deputie. 1541

THE NAMES OF ALL THE LORDS DEPUTIES AND IUSTICES IN IRELAND,

SINCE THE DEATH OF KING HENRIE THE EIGHT 1546, WHO DIED IN JANUARIE.

The yeare of our Lord	
1546	SIR Anthonie Sentleger knight by patent, dated 24 *Martij, Anno primo Edw.* 6.
1546 / 1547	Sir Edward Bellingham lord deputie, 22 *Aprilis, Anno eodem*
1548	Sir Francis Brian lord iustice.
1549	Sir William Brabeston lord iustice
1550	Sir Anthonie Sentleger lord deputie, 3. 4 *Augusti.*
1551	Sir Iames Crofts lord deputie, 29 *Aprilis*
1553	Sir Anthonie Sentleger lord deputie, 1 *Sept* 4
1555	Thomas lord Fitzwalter lord deputie, 27 *April*
1556	Sir Henrie Sidneie, Doctor Coren — Lords iustices.
1556	Sir Henrie Sidneie lord iustice alone, 18 *Ianuary*
1557	Thomas erle of Sussex L. lieutenant, 19 *Martij.*
1558	Sir William Fitzwilliams lord iustice

	The yeare of our Lord
Thomas earle of Sussex lord deputie, 6 *May*	1559
Sir Nicholas Arnold lord iustice.	1564
Sir Henrie Sidneie lord deputie.	1565
Doctor Weston lord chancellor, Sir William Fitzwilliams	1567
Sir Henrie Sidneie lord deputie	1568
Sir William Fitzwilliams lord iustice	1570
Sir William Fitzwilliams lord deputie, 11, *Decemb Anno* 14 *Elisab.*	1571
Sir Henrie Sidneie lord deputie 3. 5 *Augusti* 3.	1572
Sir William Drurie lord iustice, 14 *Septemb* by patent, 18 *May*	1579
Sir William Pelham lord iustice.	1580
The lord Arthur Graie.	1580
Adam archbishop of Dublin, Sir Henrie Wallop — Lord iustices.	1582
Sir Iohn Perot lord deputie.	1584

THE

IRISH HISTORIE

COMPOSED AND WRITTEN BY

GIRALDUS CAMBRENSIS,

AND TRANSLATED INTO ENGLISH (WITH SCHOLIES TO THE SAME)

BY IOHN HOOKER

OF THE CITIE OF EXCESTER GENTLEMAN,

TOGITHER WITH

THE SUPPLIE OF THE SAID HISTORIE, FROM THE DEATH OF KING HENRIE THE EIGHT, VNTO THIS PRESENT YEERE 1587,

DOONE ALSO BY THE SAID IOHN HOOKER:

AND DEDICATED TO

THE HONORABLE SIR WALTER RALEGH KNIGHT,

LORD WARDEN OF THE STANNARIE IN THE COUNTIES OF DEUON AND CORNWALL

---

1 Esdras 4. And king Artaxerxes commanded the chronicles to be searched whether it were true that had beene informed

---

Acts 17. And they dailie searched the scriptures whether the things taught were true or not

---

Historiæ placeant nostrates ac peregrina

O 2

TO THE

RIGHT WORTHIE AND HONORABLE GENTLEMAN

Sir WALTER RALEIGH Knight,

SENESCHALL OF THE DUCHIES OF CORNEWALL AND EXCESTER, AND LORD WARDEN OF THE STANNARIES IN DEUON AND CORNEWALL:

IOHN HOOKER

Wisheth a long, a happie, and a prosperous life, with the increase of honour.

AMONG all the infinit good blessings, right honorable, which the Lord God hath bestowed vpon vs, I thinke none more expedient and necessarie, than the vse and knowledge of histories and chronicles, which are the most assured registers of the innumerable benefits and commodities, which haue and dailie doo grow to the church of God, and to the ciuill gouernment through out all nations. The vse of them began and was receiued euen from the first beginning, and immediatlie vpon the dispersing of the sonnes of Adam through out the world for they were no sooner diuided into seuerall nations, but they did (as Cicero saith) make choise of some one man among themselues, who surpassed the rest in wisedome, knowledge and vnderstanding, *Ad quem confugiebant* These kind of men for the most part in those daies were preests and philosophers, and for their great knowledge, wisedome and credit, had the charge to commend to their posteritie such notable and good acts as were woorthie the memorie. And as all other nations had such men, so the remote Ilands in the great Ocean had the like For Britaine, now conteining England, Scotland and Wales, had then Druides and Bardos, and Ireland had then Odalies or Rimers, who being verie wise men & of great credit, did deliuer all their saiengs in meeter, and were therefore called Poets And these for the better alluring of the people to attention, and to frame them to the knowledge of vertue, did vse to sing with an instrument such lessons and instructions as they were woont to giue, whether it were concerning manners and common conuersation, or matters of policie and gouernment, or of prowesse and martiall affaires, or of the gests of their ancestors, or of anie other thing thought meet to be learned and woorthie the knowledge, by which meanes they made men the more apt, readie, and willing to applie themselues to vertue and to a commendable course of life, both concerning God how he was to be honored, the magistrate how he was to be obeied, & the common societie how it was to be conserued, and finallie how the whole course of mans life was to be ordered and directed These and manie other like commodities when Cicero had considered, did grow by these means which is the verie substance of an historie he described the same to be the witnesse of time, the light of truth, the life of memorie, and the mistresse of life

The first vse of histories

The first chronographers

The first chronographers in England and Ireland

Poets were the first chronographers in Britaine

The definition of an historie

Cicero de oratore

willing

willing and aduising euerie man at all times and in all matters to haue their recourse to the same, and to be well exercised in the knowledge thereof, bicause the thing past are set downe therin, and by them a man may learne what to doo in the life to
Ecclesiast 1 3 come For as the wise man saith, There is nothing new vnder the sunne for the thing which is now hath beene, and by the things past we are taught the things to
August de ciuit Di come. And so saith Augustine " Historia magis vel certe non minùs prænunciandis futuris, quàm enunciandis præteritis inuenitur intenta " Histories doo teach and aduertise vs as well of the things to come, as of the things past and the knowledge
Chronica Carionis Thucidides thereof is so no necessarie that Melancthon would haue no man to be vnlearned in histories, bicause " Sine qua nulla in re quispiam lucem habet " And Thucidides the old ancient historiographer of Grecia would that euerie man should haue about him a booke of histories, as a thing most necessarie for him in all matters whatsoeuer. and this did he draw and learne (as it should seeme) from Moses, who when he had faithfullie and diligentlie written and set downe the whole course of the world, the woonderfull works of God, and all the most necessarie precepts and rules for mans life, either concerning matters of religion or causes of ciuill policies, or of common societie then he and Iosua assembling all the people togither, did deliuer vnto
Deutero 5 Iosue 1 them the whole Pentatychon of Moses to be dailie read & taught, with a commandement that they should neuer haue that booke out of their hands, but to haue alwaies their continuall recourse to them as well for their life, as also for their direction in all their causes. Which thing they did most diligentlie obserue and keepe, and not onelie in matters of religion, but in all doubtfull matters, as to the most true oracles, they would make their recourse for their full resolutions As the enimies of Iehuda, when they saw the prosperous successe of the building of the temple in the times of Ezras and Nehemias, and they much maligning the
1 Esdras 4 Nehemias same, made sute to king Artaxerxes that he would reuoke the decree which king Cyrus had made vnto the Iewes, licencing them to build the temple, alledging manie great and sundrie matters against them Wherevpon the king commanded the chronicles to be searched, whether it were true that had beene informed against
Esther 6 them Likewise when Hamon had greeuouslie complained vnto king Ahasuerus against Mardocheus and the Iewes, charging them with sundrie hamous offenses worthie death, the king commanded the chronicles to be searched Also when
Acts 17 Paule and Sylas first preached the gospell at Thessalonica and Bærea, a doctrine then accompted strange and new, they searched and examined the books " Num hæc ita se haberent " For as they found things there recorded, so gaue they credit, and by the same they did proceed in the like For it was a common thing among the Romans, that not onelie they would make recourse in all doubtfull matters to their owne annales but what so euer they found in the like in anie other nation or commonwealth, which might further them in anie thing touching their owne affaires, they would draw the same into an example for themselues to follow, which was no small benefit to their commonwealth

Alexander Likewise Alexander the great, notwithstanding he were brought vp in all good letters vnder Aristotle, yet when he was to inlarge his empire, he gaue himselfe to the diligent reading of Homer, the most exact chronographer of the Troian wars and so he esteemed that booke, that in the daie time he caried it about him, and in the night time he laid it vnder his beds head, and at all times conuenient he would be reading of it, and in the end was so perfect therein, that he could verbatim repeat the whole without booke; the stratagems, the policies, and the manie deuises vsed in those warres he practised in his owne warres, which stood him in great
Iulius Cæsar steed Iulius Cæsar also in his wars searched the ancient bookes and histories of the citie of Rome and did not onelie thereby draw a paterne for his owne direction, both for his ciuill and his martiall affaires but also, he being then the greatest monarch

monarch of all the world, thought it not preiudiciall to his imperiall estate and maiestie, to commend vnder his owne hand writing vnto his posteritie, the historie of his owne age and doings. Manie like princes hath England bred, who haue bin verie carefull, that the memoriall of the good things doone in their times should be commended to their posteritie, to follow in the like. (*Mat Parisiensis in prefat*) And therefore euerie king for the course of sundrie hundreds of yeares, was woont to reteine and keepe some wise, learned, and faithfull scribes, who should collect and record the things doone in euerie their seuerall times, and all which as time and course of yeares did serue, were published; and what great good benefits haue growne thereby to this present age, and like to serue to the future time, all the world maie easilie see and iudge: for this I dare boldlie saie and affirme. No realme, no nation, no state, nor common wealth throughout all Europa, can yeeld more nor so manie profitable lawes, directions, rules, examples & discourses, either in matters of religion, or of ciuill gouernment, or of martiall affaires, than doo the histories of this little Isle of Britaine or England. I would to God I might or were able to saie the like, or the halfe like of Ireland, a countrie, the more barren of good things, the more replenished with actions of bloud, murther, and lothsome outrages, (Ireland yeeldeth small matter for an historie) which to anie good reader are greeuous & irkesome to be read & considered, much more for anie man to pen and set downe in writing, and to reduce into an historie. Which hath beene some cause whie I was alienated and vtterlie discouraged to intermedle therein: for being earnestlie requested, by reason of my some acquaintance with the maners and conditions of that nation during my short abode therein, to continue the historie of that land, from the death of king Henrie the eight vnto these presents, which hitherto hath not beene touched; I found no matter of an historie woorthie to be recorded, but rather a tragedie of cruelties to be abhorred, and no historie of good things to be followed: and therefore I gaue the matter ouer, and was fullie resolued not at all to haue intermedled therewith. Neuerthelesse, being againe verie earnestlie requested, and no excuse neither of my age, nor of my often sicknesse, nor of my calling in the seruice of the commonwelth, nor of my small learning and skill, sufficient to compas such a matter, could be accepted: then (but with an euill will) I entred into it, and the more I bethought my selfe of the matter, the more I began to consider, and at length to behold the too great and woonderous workes of God, both of his seuere iudgement against traitors, rebels, and disobedient, (The iustice of God against rebels) and of his mercie and louing kindnesse vpon the obedient and dutifull. Whereof, though there be infinite examples both in the sacred histories and humane chronicles: yet I find none more apparant and effectuall, nor more fit for vs, and for this our time and age, than the histories of our owne nation, which yeeld vnto vs most infinite examples, how yoong princes rebelling against the kings their fathers, (Hen 2 Edw 2) noble men against their soueraignes, and the commons against the kings and rulers: some by the mightie hand of God swallowed vp in the seas, some deuoured with the swoord, some by martiall and some by ciuill lawes executed to death: and few or none which haue escaped vnpunished. But of all others, none to be compared to this tragicall discourse of Ireland, and the most vnnaturall wars of the Desmonds against hir sacred maiestie. Whose disobedience the Lord hath in iustice so seuerelie punished and reuenged, as the like hath not in our age beene seene nor knowne: which albeit somewhat at large it be set downe in the historie, yet breefelie and in effect is as followeth.

The earle of Desmond, named Girald Fitzgirald, was descended of a yoonger house of the Giraldines of Kildare, and both of them descended from one and the same ancestor Girald of Windsor, a noble gentleman of Normandie, who after his arriuall into England, trauelled into Wales, and there maried the ladie Nesta daughter to the great Roesiues prince of south Wales, and by hir among others

had

had issue Moris Fitzgirald, ancestor to these the foresaid Giraldines; and he being assistant to Derman mac Morogh king of Leinster in Ireland, was one of the cheefest and most principall seruitors in the conquest, or rather one of the conquerors of that land vnder king Henrie the second. The issue and ofspring of this Moris as they were honourable in blood, so they were no lesse honorable in all their actions: they being verie famous for their good gifts of the mind, in wisedome and policie in their ciuill gouernment, and renowmed for their valiantnesse and prowesse in martiall affaires, in both which they had well tried themselues, and therefore manie times they had the cheefe gouernment of the whole realme, being sometime lord iustices, sometime lord lieutenants, and sometime lord Deputies of the whole land. And for their truth and fidelitie were aduanced to honor. For Thomas Fitzgirald being the elder house, was created earle of Kildare in the eighteenth yeare of king Edward the first, in the yeare one thousand two hundred foure score and nine. And in the beginning of king Edward the third his reigne, in the yeare one thousand three hundred twentie and seuen, Moris Fitzthomas a yoonger brother of that house was created earle of Desmond: and from thense as before, they continued verie honourable, dutifull & faithfull subiects, for the course of sundrie hundreds of yeares: vntill that this brainesicke and breakedanse Girald of Desmond, and his brethren, alies, and complices, forgetting the honour of his house, and forsaking their faith, dutie and alegiance, did breake into treasons, and shewed themselues open enimies, traitors and rebels, vsing all maner of hostilities and outrages, to the impeach of hir most sacred maiestie, and the destruction of the commonwelth: the price whereof in the end he paied with his and their own bloods, to the vtter destruction of themselues and that whole familie, there being verie few Giraldines in the prouince of Mounster left to bemone or bewaile their deaths. For first the earle himselfe, the cheefe of his familie, after his long repast in his traitorous follies, was driuen in the end to all extremities and penuries, and at the last taken in an old cotage, and his head was cut off and sent to London, and there set vpon London bridge, and his lands and inheritance confiscated and

Sir Iames of Desmond taken and hanged

discontinued from his house and name for euer. Sir Iames one of his yoonger brethren, in taking of a preie, was taken and made a preie, he was hanged as a theefe, quartered as a traitor, and his head and quarters dispersed and set vpon the gates

Sir Iohn of Desmond killed and hanged

and wals of the citie of Corke. Sir Iohn of Desmond, an other of his yoonger brethren, and next to himselfe the cheefe ringleader of this rebellion, was taken, his head cut off and set vpon the castell of Dublin, and his bodie hanged by the

The earles sonne a prisoner in the Tower of Londō.
The countesse of Desmond liueth a woful life.
D. Allen slaine.
D. Sanders dieth miserablie.

heeles at Corke. His onelie sonne and heire being wholie disinherited, is prisoner in the Tower of London. His ladie and wife destituted of all honour and liuings, liueth a dolefull and miserable life. His capteins, soldiers, and men of warre, put all for the most part to the swoord. The popes two prelats and nuncios, the one slaine in the field, and the other died most miserablie in the woods. The Italians and strangers few or none left aliue to returne to aduertise of their successe vnto their holie father. The common people such as escaped the swoord, all for

The land left altogether baren

the most part are perished with famine or fled the countrie. The land it selfe being verie fertile, is waxed baren, yeelding nor corne nor fruits, the pastures without cattell and the aire without fowles, and the whole prouince for the most part desolate and vnhabited, sauing townes and cities: and finallie, nothing there to be seene but miserie and desolation.

A notable and a rare example of Gods iust iudgement and seuere punishment, vpon all such as doo resist and rebell against the higher powers and his annointed: which is so greeuous an offense in his sight, that next to the capitall offenses against the first table, this is accounted the greatest and in the highest degree. For as it

Rom. 13.

is written, Who resisteth against the higher power, resisteth against Gods ordinances,

nances, and he shall receiue iudgement. And the Lord shall root him from out of the face of the earth that shall blaspheme his gods, and curseth the prince of the people. Euen as of the contrarie, when the people liue in all subiection, humblenesse, and obedience, the Lord defendeth and keepeth them, and with his manifold blessings prospereth them, as hir maiesties good subiects dwelling within the English pale, and inhabiting within hir cities and townes can witnesse. They sow and till the land, and doo reape the fruits. Their fields are full of sheepe, and they are clothed with the wooll. Their pastures are full of cattell, and they inioie them. Their cities and townes are well inhabited, and they liue in safetie. All things go well with them, and peace and plentie resteth in their houses. Two notable examples (I saie) and woorthie to be thoroughlie obserued, the one of Gods iust iudgement against the rebels and traitors, and the other of mercie and loue towards the obedient and dutifull subiect. Which examples the later they are, the more should they imprint in vs an inward affection and an vndoubted resolution, to yeeld to the superiours all dutie and obedience: and by the examples of the rebels, to shun as a pestilence all disobedience and rebellion, least in dooing the like, we doo receiue the like iust iudgements with them. Let therefore the examples of the elders be sufficient persuasions and instructions to the posteritie, to follow that which is good, and to eschew that which is euill. For albeit good counsell of our friends, and conferences with the good men, maie much preuaile with vs: yet none can so much preuaile nor be of such vertue and effect, as the examples of our ancestors, and the actions of our forefathers when they be laid before vs. "Magis enim exemplis potest persuaderi, quàm argumentis extorqueri." And therfore in times past, the surest course which our forefathers tooke, either in ciuill gouernment or in martiall affaires, was that which they drew from the examples of their ancestors before them. And for as much as such is the value and vertue of the footsteps of our forefathers, I trust it shall not be offensiue vnto you, that I doo a little digresse and speake somewhat of your selfe and of your ancestors, who the more honourable they were in their times, the greater cause haue you to looke into the same: that what in some of your later forefathers was consopited, maie not in you be consepulted, but rouzed and raised vnto his former and pristinat state. And for as much as I am somewhat acquainted in their descents, let me make bold with you to laie the same downe before you.

The prosperitie and quietnes in the English pale.

Patric. de instit. reip.

There were sundrie of your ancestors by the name of Raleigh, who were of great account & nobilitie, and allied as well to the Courtneis earls of Deuon, as to other houses of great honour & nobilitie, & in sundrie succeeding descents were honoured with the degree of knighthood. One of them being your ancestor in the directest line, was named sir Iohn de Raleigh, who then dwelled in the house of Fardell in Deuon, an ancient house of your ancestors, and of their ancient inheritance: and which at these presents is in the possession of your eldest brother. This knight maried the daughter and heire to sir Roger Dameror, or de Amerer, whome our English chronicles doo name lord de Amerete, who was a noble man and of great linage, and descended of the earls de Amerete in Britaine, and allied to the earls of Montfort in the same duchie and prouince. This man being come ouer into England, did serue in the court, and by the good pleasure of God and the good liking of the king he maried the ladie Elsabeth, the third sister and coheire to the noble Gilbert earle of Clare and of Glocester, who was slaine in the battell of Brokesborough in Scotland, in the time of king Edward the second. This earle died sans issue, he being the sonne and the said ladie Elsabeth the daughter to Gilbert de Clare earle of Glocester, by his wife the ladie Iane de Acres or Acon, daughter to king Edward the first. This Gilbert descended of Robert earle of Glocester, sonne to king Henrie the first, and of his wife the ladie Mawd, daughter and heire

The descent of the lord warden.

to

to Robert Fitzhamon, lord of Astrouill in Normandie, coosen to the Conqueror, knight of the priuie chamber to king William Rufus, and lord of the lordship of Glamorgan in Wales. So that your ancestor sir Iohn de Raleigh married the daughter of de Amerie, Damerere of Clare, Clare of Edward the first, and which Clare by his father descended of king Henrie the first. And in like maner by your mother you maie be deriued out of the same house. These all were men of great honour and nobilitie, and whose vertues are highlie recorded sparsim in the chronicles of England, some greatlie commended for their wisedomes and deepe iudgements in matters of counsell, some likewise much praised for their prowesse & valiantnesse in martiall affaires, and manie of them honored for both.

All things haue an end.

But yet as nothing is permanent in this life, and all things variable vnder the sunne, and time hath deuoured and consumed the greatest men and the mightiest monarchs, and most noble commonwealths in the world, according to the old countrie saieng, Be the daie neuer so long, yet at length it will ring at euensong: so this honorable race, though for so manie descents, and for the course of so manie yeares it continued in great honor, nobilitie, and reputation, yet in processe of time the honour became to be of worship (neuerthelesse allied alwaies and matched in houses of great honour and nobilitie) and so euer since possessed by knights of your owne name, vntill by little and little the honour and estimation of your noble and worthie ancestors seemed at length to be buried in obliuion, and as it were extinguished and to be vtterlie forgotten as though it had neuer beene. And now when all was past anie hope and vnremembred to the world, it hath pleased God to raise the same euen as it were from the dead, and to looke vpon you the yoongest sonne of manie, as he did vpon Ioseph, one of the yoongest sonnes of Iacob, and in you hath left a hope to restore the decaied house of your sept and familie. He hath brought you into the good fauour of your prince, who hath pleased to reward and honour in you the approoued faithfull seruice of your late ancestors and kindered deceassed, and inclined hir princelie hart, conceiuing a great hope of your owne sufficiencie and abilitie to restore you againe, being the last branch remaining of so manie noble and famous houses descended. And whereof commeth this, that the Lord hath thus blessed you, and so bountifullie hath dealt with you? but onelie (as the wise man saith) "Vt noscas in omni virtute omnibus prodesse," and that you should be beneficiall and profitable to all men. And

Cicero de offic.

therefore in all our actions, "Semper aliquid ad communem vtilitatem est afferendum." for we are not borne to our selues alone, but the prince, the countrie, the parents, freends, wiues, children and familie, euerie of them doo claime an interest in vs, and to euerie of them we must be beneficiall: otherwise we doo degenerate from that communitie and societie, which by such offices by vs is to be conserued, & doo

Cicero

become most vnprofitable. "Nam inutilis prorsus est, qui nullam vtilitatem reipublicæ ac communi societati possit afferre," and euerie such man, as a member vnprofitable is to be cut off. And as the bee is no longer suffered to haue a place in the hiue, than whiles he worketh, no more is that man to haue place in the publike weale than whiles he dooth some good therein, bicause through idlenesse they doo not

Cato.

Idlers ought not to haue place in the commonwealth.

onelie no good, but as Cato saith, they doo euill: "Nihil agendo homines malè agere discunt." Idlenesse therefore the mother of all wickednesse, and idlers the sonnes of so bad a mother, are vtterlie to be exiled and expelled out of all well gouerned commonweales, and they onelie to be fostered, nourished and cherished, who as they are borne to the countrie, so if they doo good and be beneficiall to the same.

And how great your care hath beene heerein, the course of your life hitherto dooth manifest it. For after that you had seasoned your primer yeares at Oxford in knowledge and learning, a good ground and a sure foundation to build thereupon all your good actions, you trauelled into France, and spent there a good part of of your youth in the warres and martiall sciences. And hauing some sufficient knowledge and experience therein, then after your returne from thense, to the end you might euerie waie be able to serue your prince and commonweale, you were desirous to be acquainted in maritimall affaires. Then you, togither with your brother sir Humfreie Gilbert, trauelled the seas, for the search of such countries, as which if they had beene then discouered, infinit commodities in sundrie respects would haue insued, and whereof there was no doubt, if the fleet then accompanieng you, had according to appointment followed you, or your selfe had escaped the dangerous sea fight, when manie of your companie were slaine, and your ships therewith also sore battered and disabled. And albeit this hard beginning (after which followed the death of the said woorthie knight your brother) was a matter sufficient to haue discouraged a man of a right good stomach and value from anie like seas attempts, yet you, more respecting the good ends, whereunto you leuelled your line for the good of your countrie, did not giue ouer, vntill you had recouered a land, and made a plantation of the people of your owne English nation in Virginia, the first English colonie that euer was there planted, to the no little derogation of the glorie of the Spaniards, & an impeach to their vaunts, who bicause with all cruell immanitie, contrarie to all naturall humanitie, they subdued a naked and a yeelding people, whom they sought for gaine and not for anie religion or plantation of a commonwelth, ouer whome to satisfie their most greedie and insatiable couetousnesse, did most cruellie tyrannize, and most tyrannicallie and against the course of all humane nature did scorch and rost them to death, as by their owne histories dooth appeare. These (I saie) doo brag and vaunt, that they onelie haue drawne strange nations and vnknowne people, to the obedience of their kings, to the knowledge of christianitie, and to the inriching of their countrie, and thereby doo claime the honor to be due to themselues onelie and alone. But if these your actions were well looked into, with such due consideration as apperteineth, it shall be found much more honorable in sundrie respects, for the aduancement of the name of God, the honour of the prince, and the benefit of the common wealth. For what can be more pleasant to God, than to gaine and reduce in all christianlike manner, a lost people to the knowledge of the gospell, and a true christian religion, than which cannot be a more pleasant and a sweet sacrifice, and a more acceptable seruice before God? And what can be more honorable to princes, than to inlarge the bounds of their kingdoms without iniurie, wrong, & bloudshed; and to frame them from a sauage life to a ciuill gouernment, neither of which the Spaniards in their conquests haue performed? And what can be more beneficiall to a common weale, than to haue a nation and a kingdome to transferre vnto the superfluous multitude of fruitelesse and idle people (heere at home dailie increasing) to trauell, conquer, and manure another land, which by the due intercourses to be deuised, may and will yeeld infinit commodities? And how well you doo deserue euerie waie in following so honourable a course, not we our selues onelie can witnesse, but strange nations also doo honour you for the same: as dooth appeare by the epistle of Bassimerus of France, to the historie of Florida: and by Iulius Cæsar a citizen of Rome in his epistle to his booke intituled "Cullombeados." It is well knowne, that it had beene no lesse easie for you, than for such as haue beene aduanced by kings, to haue builded great houses, purchased large circuits, and to haue vsed the fruits of princes fauours, as most men in all former and present ages haue doone; had you not preferred the generall honour and commoditie of your prince and countrie before all priuat gaine and commoditie, whereby you haue beene rather a seruant than a commander to your owne fortune. And no doubt the cause being so good, and the attempt so honorable, but that God will increase your talent, and blesse your doings, and euerie good man will commend and further the same. And albeit the more noble enterprises a man shall take in hand, the more aduersaries he shall haue to depraue and hinder the same; yet I am persuaded, as no good man shall haue iust cause, so there is none so much carried with a corrupt mind, nor so enuious of his countries honour, nor so bent against you, that he will derogate the praise and honour due to so worthie an enterprise, and that so much the sooner, because you haue indured so manie crosses, and haue through so much enuieings and misfortunes perseuered in your attempts: which no doubt shall at last by you be performed when it shall please him, who hath made you an instrument of so worthie a worke. And by how much the more God hath pleased thus to blesse you, so much the more are you bound to be thankefull vnto him, and to acknowledge the same to proceed from his grace and merce towards you. Giue me leaue therefore (I praie you) to be bold with you, not onelie to put you in mind hereof, but also to remember you, how it hath pleased God to bring you into the fauour of your prince and soueraigne: who besides hir great fauour towards you manie waies, she hath also laid vpon you the charge of a gouernement in your owne countrie, where you are to command manie people by your honourable office of the stannarie, and where you are both a iudge and chancellor, to rule in iustice and to iudge in equitie. Wherin you are so much the more to be circumspect and wise, because vpon your iudgement (and such as you shall appoint to be vnder you) the determinations of all their causes dooth rest and depend, knowing that a hard iudgement abideth for such as be in authoritie, if they iudge not vprightlie and doo not yeeld iustice to euerie man indifferentlie. But you therefore carefull in this respect, that you be well reported for your vpright dealings, both herein, & in euerie or all your other actions to all men. Be you a patterne of vertue, & an example of true nobilitie, which is grounded & hath hir

Paling. nus foundation vpon vertue, for as the poet saith, "Ex virtute nobilitas nascitur, non ex nobilitate virtus: virtus sola nobilitat, nō caro nec sanguis." And therfore saith

Demosthenes Demosthenes, If thou draw thy descent & pedegree euen from Iupiter himselfe, yet if thou be not vertuous, iust & good, *Ignobilis mihi videris*. In my opinion thou art no gentleman. It is a noble thing to be borne of noble ancestors (as Aristotle saith) but his nobilitie faileth, when his ancestors vertues in him faileth. "Hic enim verè nobilis est cēsendus, cui non aliena sed sua virtus ad gloriam opitulatur." Your ancestors were verie ancient, and men of great nobilitie, beneficiall to their princes and countrie manie & sundrie waies. And as in nature you are descended from them, so it hath pleased God to blesse you with knowledge in learning, with skill of warlike seruice, and in experience in maritimall causes, and besides hath placed you among the nobles, and in the good grace and fauour of your prince. Wherefore you are so much the more to be carefull to restore the house of your deceased forefathers to their ancient honor and nobilitie, which in this later age hath beene obscured, abiding the time by you to be restored to their first and primer state: which you are not onelie taught by their old and good examples, but also

Fusils, instruments of labours by the ensignes of their and your nobilitie. For the fusils, being an instrument of trauell and labour, doo aduertise you, that you are one of the sonnes of Adam, borne to walke in a vocation, and therein to be a profitable member in the church of God, and in maintenance of the common societie: which when you behold

Agathocles and looke vpon, you must so endeuour your selfe, euen as Agathocles king of Syracusa, whose cupbords though they were well furnished with great store and varietie of rich plate, yet he thought not the same sufficientlie fraughted, vnlesse he had also his earthen pitchers and stone cups, in which he vsed to drinke, to teach & remember him in the middle of his roialtie, to be mindfull of his origin estate and dutie.

White colour. The white colour or siluer mettall dooth teach vnto you vertue, sinceritie & godlinesse.

finesse. For as siluer is a most excellent mettall, and next vnto gold excelling all others, and with which for the excellencie thereof, the Lord God would haue his tabernacle and his temple to be adorned and beautified with vessels and ornaments thereof, and as the white colour, if it be spotted and foule, dooth lose his grace: euen so it teacheth you to be a man of an honest and of a godlie conuersation, to lead a life in all vprightnesse, without reproch and disgrace: and that you should be seruiceable to God and your countrie in all good actions, and therewith also (which by the gulie colour is meant) you be bold and valiant for the defense of your countrie and for the safetie thereof to spend both life and goods, that you should be beneficiall to all men, hurtfull and iniurious to no man. And such kind of men were your ancestors, who for the same were beloued and honoured, and their names for euer registred in immortall fame and memorie. And so shall it be with you, if you doo the like and follow their steps and examples, God shall blesse you, & you shall prosper & florish as did Ioseph, you shall be honored, as was Daniell, and you shall be in fauor before God & man, as were your ancestors, the whole people shall speake good of you, the honour of your house shall be restored, & your talent shall be augmented & increased, & all things shall go well with you. But to returne where we left. When I had waded as far as I could in the discourse of this historie, according to such instructions as partlie by my selfe, but more by other mens helps, I had collected and gathered, and thought to haue continued the same from the death of King Henrie the eight, vnto these presents: it came vnto my mind and I thought it verie expedient, to make a new review of that, which by others had beene doone in the interuall betweene Cambrensis and my doings, wherein I found great paines had beene taken, and that the authors had well deserued great praises and commendations. And yet in this they were much to be blamed, that all of them were beholding vnto Giraldus, and not one of them would yeeld that curtesie either to publish his historie, or vsing the same to acknowledge it. For some misliking both method and phrase, framed it into another forme, and penned it in a more loftie stile, and vnder that colour haue attributed vnto themselues the honour and fruits of another mans doings. In which, their discourtesie was the more, because they iniuried so noble and woorthie a personage. For Giraldus was a noble man by birth, he being the sonne vnto Mauricius, the sonne vnto Giraldus de Windsor, and to his wife the ladie Nesta, daughter to the great Roesius prince of south Wales. He was from his youth brought vp in learning, and prooued verie well learned in all good letters both diuine and likewise humane: and by profession he was a man of the clergie, and liued by the patrimonie of the church. He was chapleine to king Henrie the second, and to king Iohn his sonne, and both of them he attended in their iorneis into Ireland, and at the request and commandement of the king the father, he wrot the historie of this land according as what he saw and knew to be true. The more noble then that this man was by birth, the more reuerend in calling, the more painfull in trauels, and the better learned he was: euen so much the more is their fault, that will borrow of him and not acknowledge it, nor thinke themselues beholding vnto him. For as Plinie saith, "Ingenui pudoris est, fateri per quos profecerimus," It is the part of a good nature not to be ashamed to acknowledge and confesse by whom he is the better, and benefited. I know it hath beene an old vsage in all ages, and among all the ancient writers, both Græcians & Latinists, that they would borrow of other mens writings, and inlarge their owne therewith: as Plato did of Socrates and Pythagoras, Aristotle out of Plato, Cicero of them both, and so likewise others: and these men would not onelie confesse the same, which was accounted to be some part of recompense, but also they accounted their owne doings to be so much the better, as that they were confirmed by the authoritie of such wise, graue, and well learned

Gules

The ingratefulnesse vnto Cambrensis

The genealogie of Giraldus

learned men. The like reason might suffice to persuade such in this later age, as which be so curious that they will not haue anie father, doctor, or anie other writer to be named nor alleaged in sermons, readings, preachings, or writings, and yet they will not sticke to vse & recite verbatim, whole sentences, yea & whole pages out of other mens writings, and attribute the same to themselues, as of their owne inuention. A great fault and a point of ingratitude, not allowed among the gentiles: much lesse should it be so among christians, especiallie among them of the highest profession, "Non profiteri per quos profecerint."

But leauing euerie man to himselfe, for as much as all histories are to be doone with all sinceritie & truth, which in this cannot be so well doone, vnlesse the first writer and author of this historie of Ireland haue his place: I haue thought good to publish and set foorth Giraldus his owne workes as they are, which, leauing all other translations, I haue as faithfullie translated as the historie requireth, and in as fit an English phrase as is most meete and conuenient for the reader. And because the same so long hense written, hath sundrie obscure things, which doo require some further opening, for the better vnderstanding of the reader, I haue subnected and added to euerie chapter (so requiring) such notes and obseruations, as he shall be therewith the better instructed and satisfied. This thing thus by me doone, togither with so much as I my selfe haue penned from the death of king Henrie the eight vnto these presents: which although it maie seeme to be verie imperfect, and to want that fulnesse as the course of so manie yeares might affoord, or that some things maie be misreported and set downe, otherwise than the truth is, or that some things maie be mistaken, &c. let this be imputed vnto them, through whose default the same is so befallen, for manie things were promised and little performed, and some, who had and haue an interest in the matter, haue refused and would doo nothing. But for my selfe, according to such instructions and collections as are come to my hands, I haue after the method and nature of an historie, most sincerelie and faithfullie set downe what is materiall and woorthie the writing. And for as much as your selfe was a partie and a dooer in some part of the Desmonds wars, in which you were a painfull and a faithfull seruitor, and therefore can giue some report and testimonie to this discourse, and also for the loue and honour which I doo owe and beare vnto you, I thought it my part and dutie to offer and present, and presentlie in most humble maner I doo offer and present the same vnto your good fauour and protection. And albeit the thing it selfe be verie slender, and too farre an inferior present to be offered to one of your estate and calling, yet let your courtesie couer that, and accept my good will, which as time and occasion hereafter shall serue, I shall & will be most willing (as your lordships most deuout and assured) to supplie in all the good seruices I maie or shall be able to doo at your commaundement. The Lord blesse you and multiplie your daies, to the honor of God, the good seruice of hir maiestie, the benefit of the commonwealth, the comfort of your friends, and to your owne increase in all honour. Exon. Octob. 12. 1586.

Your L. verie good friend and alie at commandement,

IOHN HOOKER.

THE

THE

FIRST PREFACE OF

GIRALDUS CAMBRENSIS

VNTO HIS HISTORIE OF THE CONQUEST OF IRELAND.

FORSOMUCH as in our Topographie we haue at large set foorth and described the site of the land of Ireland, the natures of sundrie things therein conteined, the woonderous & strange prodigies which are in the same, and of the first origin of that nation, euen from the first beginning vntill this our time. it resteth, that at the request of sundrie men, and of some of great estate, we do now in a particular volume declare & set forth the conquest of the same land in these our daies, togither with the noble acts & gests therein doone. For if we haue well discouered the old & ancient times long before vs, how much more should we doo that which we haue seene, and for the most part are witnesses thereof, & which are yet in our fresh & perfect memorie? Our Topographie discouereth the things done in times past and long ago, but this present historie intreateth of the things presentlie doone, and in our daies But me thinketh I see some man to shrinke vp the nose, and as it were to snuffe, because I haue written all things so plainelie and euidentlie, and therfore in great scorne he reacheth the booke to one, & with as great disdaine casteth it to another. But let him know this, that I haue now written this cheflie for the laie people, and for such princes as be not of greatest learning, and are therefore desirous to haue things to be vttered in such a plaine and sensible speech as they may best vnderstand the same For whie, most plaine terms are most meet to be vsed, when the noble acts of noble men & worthie seruitors are to be published and set foorth to the notice and knowledge of all men. For this cause therefore haue I written this historie in as plaine & sensible maner as I can (leauing as much as may be) the darke & obscure maner of writing vsed in times past And forsomuch as euerie age hath his peculiar manner, I haue according to the mind of the philosopher (whose aduise is, that the liues of the old men, and the pleasant speeches of yoong men should be receiued and followed) I haue (I saie) of purpose written in that order and phrase of speech as now is most in vse. For sith that words are but messengers of a mans mind, and giuen onelie to that end he should without close couering and couching plainelie disclose his mind and meaning I haue purposelie indeuored my selfe, that seeing what others doo not see, and knowing what others doo not vnderstand, I might so write as I might of all men be vnderstood For whie, Seneca saith. It is better to be dumbe and not to speake at all, than so to speake as not to be vnderstood, so that the speech be framed in such phrases & order as are most meet to be vsed, & with the wise and learned do most affect But forsomuch as some men haue maliciouslie and slanderouslie depraued my Topographie, I haue thought good by the waie here to interlace a few words in defense therof All men generallie concerning the beginning of a good or a learned matter, doo consider and haue respect speciallie to three things; the first is, the author of the thing, then the matter it selfe, and lastlie, the ordering and well handling of the thing so begun. Concerning the first and last of these three, the enuious man

being

being afraid to vtter his malice, euen against his will giues praise & commendation to both. But yet as a staged man can not alwaies dissemble and cloke himselfe, so this man, who to haue his will ouer me & to depraue me, inueigheth against the second point, thinking and meaning by reproouing me to be a lier therein, to condemne all the rest, he obiecteth therefore and layeth to my charge the strange prodigies which I wrote, namelie how the woolfe spake and talked with a priest, of the man that in the hinder parts was like to an ox, of a woman that had a beard like a man, and a man like an horse, of a gote & a lion, which resorted and accompanied with a woman. But who so misliketh hereof, let him read in the booke of Numbers, & he shall find that Balaams asse spake and reprooued his maister. Let him examine the liues of the fathers, and he shall learne how that a satyre in the wildernesse did talke with Anthonie the heremite; and how Paule the heremite was fed in the desert by a rauen. Let him read also the workes of Ierome, the Exameron of Ambrose, and the dialog of Gregorie. Let him likewise read saint Augustine his booke of the citie of God, especiallie the xv. and xxi. bookes, which are full of strange prodigies and woonders: let him read Isodorus in the xi. booke of his Etymologies, concerning woonders, his xij. booke of beasts, & his xvi. booke of pretious stones, and of their vertues, let him also read Valerius Maximus, Trogus Pompeius, Plinius, and Solinus, & in euerie of these he shall find manie things which he may mislike and thinke to be vntruths, & so condemne the residue of all the writings of so noble and woorthie men. But let him be better aduised, & consider well, how that as S. Ierome saith, there are manie things conteined in the scriptures which seeme to be incredible, and to carie no truth in them, and yet neuerthelesse are most true. For whie, nature dooth not, nor can preuaile against the Lord of nature: and therfore euerie creature ought not loth, but to reuerence, and haue in great admiration the works of God. & as S. August. saith, How can that be against nature which is doone by the will of God? Bicause the will of so great a creator is the nature and beginning of euerie thing created. A portent then or a monster is not against nature, but against it which proceedeth from nature. And therfore as it is not impossible to God to ordeine and creat what natures or things he listeth, no more is it impossible to him to alter and change into what forms he listeth the things alreadie created. And yet I would not that euerie thing by me written, should foorthwith be credited and receiued as an vndouted truth: for whie, I my selfe do not so firmlie beleeue of them, as of things most certeine and true, sauing of such things which by experience I know to be true, and which also euerie other man may by proofe so find it to be. For as for all other things, I so account of them, that I neither do nor will stand either in the deniall or affirmation of them. The iewellers & such as haue, & be acquainted with the pretious stones come out of India, do not so strangelie thinke or haue admiration of them, as they who neuer saw them afore: & yet they hauing had once experience of them, do the lesse muse & wonder at the strangenes of them. For whie, the dailie vse taketh awaie all strangenes & admiration, and euerie thing be it neuer so strange & maruellous at the first, yet by dailie viewing of them they wax to be contemned and the lesse esteemed: euen as the Indians themselues do litle value or esteeme their commodities, which we do so much maruell & wonder at. S. Augustine therfore vpon the gospell, how the water was turned into wine hath these words: Maruellous great is the power of God in the creation of the heauen & earth, & of the gouerning of the same, & as great it is to see how the raine water, by the nature of the vine is turned into wine, and how of litle and small seeds great trees and fruits do spring and grow, and yet because we do see it this daie as it were by a naturall course, we do lesse esteeme & consider of them. But yet God aboue the common course hath reserued to himselfe some small things, & which seeme to be of of no value, to the end that his power might appeare in greater things, and driue vs the more to consider of them. Wherefore let the malicious & enuious be contented, & not to enuie against the Lord of nature, who of purpose in the sight of man hath doone manie things against the common course of nature: because it should be apparant, & euerie man should well see, that Gods power far exceedeth mans reach & knowledge, & his diuinitie surpasseth mans vnderstanding. Cassiodorus therfore saith: It is a great point of knowledge in man to vnderstand & haue the knowledge, that God can and dooth such great and woonderfull things as do far exceed and passe the capacitie & vnderstanding of man. For God alwaies of purpose dooth transpose and alter his great things into strange forms, that albeit men may in some respect discerne the same, yet fullie they can not comprehend the same. If then the old and ancient writers haue diligentlie and with good allowance noted & registred in their writings the strange prodigies in their times; whie are we doing the like (vnlesse the whole world be set in wickednesse) maligned and backbitten? For if there be anie new and strange thing in our worke, and which heretofore hath not beene heard of, yet let not the malicious & spitefull man forthwith, without further allowance condemne and depraue it, but rather suffer to remaine as it is. For as the poet saith: If our forefathers had reiected (as we do) all new things, what shuld now be old? Let him therfore cease to blame or carpe at new things, because in course of time they ceasse to be new, and wax to be old. He may therfore take his pleasure, and depraue the same: & yet no doubt our posteritie will allow therof. He may do what he can to hurt it, yet they will accept and read it. He may do what he can to disprooue and blame it, yet will they loue it. He may do what he can to reiect it, yet will they receiue and allow of it.

THE

SECOND PREFACE OF

GIRALDUS CAMBRENSIS

VNTO THE NOBLE EARLE OF POITIERS.

HAUING beene eftsoones, and by manie requested, to register and write the historie of such noble acts doone in our times, which I haue either seene my selfe, or haue heard it crediblie reported, I was for my excuse woont to alleage the wickednesse of the time, wherein, by reason of the excessiue riotousnesse which so aboundeth, all things are so farre out of order, and men so carefull to pamper vp the bodie, that the mind, which of his nature is free, is now in captiuitie, and cannot haue his libertie. Neuerthelesse, considering, and diligentlie aduising with my selfe, how necessarie the knowledge of those things will be to our posteritie, and how nothing is more pernicious and hurtfull to a good wit, and an honest disposition, than to lie wallowing in idlenesse and sloth, I did at length with much adoo yeeld my selfe to those requests, and resolued my selfe to satisfie the same. But yet what can be more presumptuous than to write when time serueth not, & leisure wanteth? Or to desire our owne bookes to be commonlie read, and yet at no leisure to read our selues? Or that we should be subiect to the examination and sifting of a malicious reader, and an enuious iudge, and yet we not at leisure to examine our selues? Tullius, the founteine and welspring of all eloquence, being on a time requested to make an oration, is said he did excuse himselfe, because he had not studied nor read the daie before. If so famous a man, and the father of all eloquence, did so esteeme the benefit of studieng, what shall others of a farre meaner estate and learning thinke of themselues? For true it is, the wit of man if it be not reuiued with continuall and dailie reading waxeth faint and dull, and with reading it is increased and nourished as it were with a naturall food and sustenance. For as the full barns are soone spent, if they be not new stored; and the stocke of great wealth and treasure soone wasted & consumed, if it be not repaired, euen so the knowledge of man being not dailie renewed by reading and perusing of other mens works dooth soone perish and decaie. We are compact and doo consist of two natures, the one temporall, the other eternall, and hauing respect to both are to nourish both, the earthlie part with things transitorie and earthlie according to the time, the heauenlie part with things perpetuall and euerlasting. The bodie for the time hath his cares, but the mind, which of his nature is free, and which cannot be shut vp, and as it were imprisoned, is neither vnder the power of vs, nor of anie others, let it therefore inioie his owne and proper libertie which to it apperteineth, and inioie the freedome to it belonging. As for the outward man, let him wander and straie, and be troubled about manie things, let him follow vaine and trifling toies, and doo all things as will lusteth: & let him be subiect to the miserable condition of the flesh: but the inward man, which as the kernell is inclosed in the shell, let him inioie that right and priuilege which God hath giuen vnto it, let it be so warded and defended, that being in troubles, it be not troubled, and being solitarie, it be not destituted. God and the king haue ech of them their seuerall power and empire ouer vs: the king hath power onelie ouer the bodie, but the secret and incomprehensible part within vs, namelie the soule, God onelie possesseth, and he alone knoweth and searcheth the same. For it is a most noble and excellent thing, passing all other the gifts of God vnder heauen, being incomprehensible, and yet comprehending all things, and most euidentlie declaring the diuine power which is in it. For by a certeine naturall agilitie which is in him he comprehendeth all the foure corners of the world, and in a maruellous secret celeritie dooth discerne the whole world and all that therein is: it hath the knowledge and vnderstanding of all arts, sciences & knowledges. he is onlie knowen to him that is vnknowen, seene of him that is not seene, & cōprehended of him which is incomprehensible. God forbid therefore, that the continuall exercises of this soule should be hindered with vaine and worldlie cares, whereby things for a time omitted or set aside should perish or be forgotten. for what is the bodie to the soule but a heauie burthen, a paine, & as it were a prison, which though not holding him, yet hindering him? For what the shell is to the kernell, the same is the flesh to the spirit, both of them carrieng his owne impediment and burthen. Wherefore right noble now earle of Poitiers, but shortlie which shall be king of England, & duke of Normandie, hauing the force and helpe of this, I haue yeelded my selfe, and haue now written and drawen out the historie of the conquest of Ireland, and the subduing of the barbarous nation of the same in these our daies, and haue dedicated the same vnto your highnesse: that by recording the gifts thereof, and seeing how your father did grow in renowme and honor, so the same also may increase in you: and as you are knowen to be the right heire of your fathers inheritance, so you may succeed him also in his vertues and victories to your great honor. I haue hitherto trauelled in this rude and rough matter after a grosse manner, but hereafter more fullie, and in better order to be expressed and set foorth, as time and yeares shall increase, and as I shall be more at full instructed.

TO HIS MOST REUEREND LORD AND BELOUED IN CHRIST,

IOHN

THE NOBLL AND WORTHIE

KING OF ENGLAND, LORD OF IRELAND, DUKE OF NORMANDIE AND OF AQUITAINE, AND EARLE OF ANIOU:

GIRALDUS OFFERETH THIS HIS SIMPLE WORKE, AND WISHETH ALL HEALTH BOTH OF BODIE AND OF SOULE, AND A PROSPEROUS SUCCESSE IN ALL THINGS ACCORDING TO HIS HEARTS DESIRE.

IT pleased your noble and excellent father king Henrie, to send me being then attendant vpon him, ouer with you into Ireland, where when I had noted sundrie notable things, and which were strange and vnknowne to other nations: then at my returne, I made a collection and choise of the chiefest matters therein and within three yeares, I made my booke of Topographie, of the woonders of Ireland, and of the description of that land, doone in and for the honor of your father, who hauing good liking, and being well pleased with those my trauels (for why, he was a prince (a thing rare in our times) verie well learned) his desire and pleasure was, I should also write out the historie of the last conquest of the same land, made by him and his Which renewing my former trauels I did but neither it, nor these my paines were considered For vertue commonlie is more commended than rewarded But because by negligence, or rather by reason of the great businesse, wherewith I was incumbred I had almost forgotten the site, nature, and maner of the west parts of the said land, which I had not seene a long time I thought it good to ouerrun, and peruse againe my said worke, and being better corrected, to dedicat the same vnto your highnesse Wherein our historie taketh his beginning from the time that Dermon mac Morogh prince of Leinster was driuen out of his countrie by his owne men, and fled to your father then being in Aquitane. most humblie crauing, and at length obteining aid and succor, vntill your first comming into that land, when I was with you and haue faithfullie declared in order, what things were there doone by euerie of these noble men and capteins, which then passed thither, euen from the first to the last, and what good or euill was doone by them.

In

In which historie as in a glasse a man may most apparantlie and euidentlie see and discerne truth, who and what they were which deserued the most honor in this conquest, whether the first aduenturers out of the diocesse of saint Dauids my cousins and kinsmen, or they of the diocesse of Landaff, who came next, and who in verie deed are gentlemen, but more in name than valiant in act, and who vpon the good successe of the first, hoping to haue the like themselues, went ouer: or else they which passed ouer the third time, who were well and fullie furnished at all points with good store of armor, vittell, and other necessaries. Surelie they deserued well, who gaue the first aduenture and they also are much to be commended, which continued the same but they deserued best, who went ouer last. For they not onelie did establish and confirme the authoritie and doings of the first and second, but also made a finall end, and brought the whole countrie into subiection. But alas, by reason of their too hastie returning from thense, and of the vnnaturall warres and rebellion of the sonnes against their father, the land could not be brought to a perfect order, nor the things begun could haue his full perfection. Wherefore, ô noble king, despise not the great trauels and labors of your father, nor yet my poore paines herein Doo not impart your honor and glorie to the vnworthie and vnthankefull. neither for the coueting of an Iland of siluer to hazard the losse of one of gold the one far passing and exceeding the other in value. For the gold of Arabia and the siluer of Achaia doo both fill a mans cofer alike but the one more in price and value than the other Besides this, there is another thing which might persuade you to be mindfull, and haue some regard of the land of Ireland It hath pleased God and good fortune to send you manie children, both naturall, and also legitimat, and more hereafter you may haue It were therefore verie good as you may, to appoint and place in those two kingdomes, two of your sonnes to be gouernors and rulers of them and vnder them to appoint a great number of your men, and endow them liberallie with great liuings and liuelehoods. and especiallie in Ireland, which as yet is rude, vnnurtured, and nothing to the purpose by our men inhabited. But if so be that neither for the increasing of your owne honor, the inriching of your treasurie, nor for the aduancing of your children, you will haue respect to your realme of Ireland, yet haue some consideration of your poore veterans and old seruitors, who haue most faithfullie and trustilie serued both you and your father, and by whose seruice that realme of Ireland was first conquered, and is yet kept and reteined, and yet are supplanted by such yoong nouices and yoonkers as are of late gone thither, to inioy and to succeed into the fruits of other mens trauels, fortune better fauouring them, than vertue commending And the follie of these men is growne to such a pride and arrogancie, that as it is said, they are greatlie to be suspected to aspire and to vsurpe the whole seigniorie and dominion to themselues, which it lieth you vpon to see to be quailed and abated.

And in following these your Irish affaires, you are to haue great care and regard, that when so euer you doo march and take anie iourneie, either for the vanquishing of the enimie, or for the reuenging of anie wrongs and iniuries, that you haue alwaies an eie backeward, and leaue all things behind you in such safe and sure order, that no danger thereof doo insue vnto you. For why, the houshold enimies be alwaies working of wiles and waiting for an aduantage, and doo but looke when time and place may serue for them to rebell and therefore you are to haue great care and good regard, that you doo leaue all things behind you in safetie, and out of danger. and that you doo not suffer the serpent to lurke and hide himselfe, as it

were

were in your bosome: nor to nourish and rake vp the fire as it were in your lap, the same being readie to breake out into great flames: for this shall not onelie be counted a great retchlesnesse, but also a great follie in you, and to your great reproch. It is verie expedient therefore to euerie prince, that in his land he doo not foster and mainteine anie such Hydras and venemous serpents. And for princes of Ilands, it should be good for them, that they in their dominions and realmes haue in no side anie other marches than the seas it selfe. But if it be so, that you will not be persuaded for anie of the foresaid reasons, to haue regard or remorse to your said land, being so oftentimes desolated, and almost vtterlie destroied, that it may be reduced to some better order and state, whereby it may be more profitable to your selfe and vnto yours: then I praie you to pardon vs Welshmen, notwithstanding we be of nature somewhat rash, and giue vs leaue to put you in remembrance touching which your father, for the aduancement of himselfe and of his posteritie, did promise to pope Adrian, when he first procured licence and libertie to inuade and to conquer the realme of Ireland. The first is, that you would set vp the true religion, and reforme the church of God in that realme: and then, as you doo now in England, so also in Ireland, you doo cause to be paied out of euerie house the Peter pence, according to the tenure of the said priuilege by your father obteined, and which remaineth in the treasurie of Winchester, that you maie so deliuer your fathers soule, and satisfie his promise. For why, as Salomon saith: A lieng toong beseemeth not a king, especiallie when he shall lie to God, and being a creature, wittinglie to offend his creator, for that is an offense verie heinous and dangerous.

And forsomuch as you are to answer before the high and strict iudge, hauing nothing for your excuse and defense than as before is said, for the so much innocent bloud by your father and your selfe alreadie shed, and which hereafter maie be shed: you ought to be verie carefull and diligent, that Gods anger maie be appeased, and your fathers promise be performed: that God being thus honored for this conquest, you maie haue a prosperous successe and all yours in this world: and also after this life inioie that perpetuall felicitie, which surpasseth all ioie and felicitie. And because you haue not kept nor performed these promises, these two defects by Gods iust iudgement are fallen vnto you. The one is, that this conquest could neuer be brought to his full effect and perfection. The other is, that they which were the cheefest and most principall seruitors in this conquest, namelie Robert Fitzstephans, who first entered into the land, and made waie vnto others, Henrie of monte Moris, Reimond, Iohn de Courcie, and Meilerius, neuer had anie lawfull issue of their bodies begotten. And no maruell: for notwithstanding the happie and fortunat successe of the conquest, the poore cleargie was neuer considered, but were driuen to beg, and the cathedrall churches which were richlie indued with great liuelehoods, possessions, and territories, were altogither wasted and spoiled. These things a good prince of his honor ought to see to be redressed, and to prouide that the cleargie, who are and ought faithfullie to assist and serue him in all weightie causes of councell and importance, should be releeued, and more the honor vnto them belonging, and that small portion which was promised vnto them, that God in some things in me be appeased and satisfied for these cruell and bloudie conquests. And moreouer, vnder your patience we sue also, that for the perpetuall memorie of this conquest made by Englishmen, and because in processe of time, and course of yeares, there happeneth great change of lords, and manie times the inheritance commeth to such as are furthest remoued in kinred, that therefore there be a yearelie tribute rated and yeelded vnto the king, to be

paied

paied in gold or such commodities as that land best yeeldeth: and that this be comprised in a publike instrument, that the whole world maie know how the realme and land of Ireland is subiect to the crowne of England. And forsomuch as things doone, being put and registred in writing, and to be read by an interpretor, are not sensible, nor so well vnderstanded of the hearer, as when he maie or dooth read the same in his owne speech and language, it were verie good (in my opinion) that some learned man, and skilfull in the French toong, should translate the same into French.

SYLVESTER GIRALDUS CAMBRENSIS,

HIS VATICINALL HISTORIE OF THE

CONQUEST OF IRELAND.

The figures of (1) (2) (3) &c set before certeine words of the chapters, are to be conferred with the like in the scholies or interpretations following euerie chapter, whereby the authors meaning is opened thus by the waie of a necessarie caueat to the reader in breuitie.

How Dermon Mac Morogh king of Leinster fled out of his countrie vnto Henrie the second king of England for aid and succour.

CHAP. 1.

DERMON (1) Mac Morogh prince of (2) Leinster & gouernour of the fift part or portion of Ireland, did in our time possesse & inioie the east part of the land, which bordereth and lieth towards England, being disseuered from the same by the maine seas This man from his verie youth, and first entrie into his kingdome, was a great oppressor of his gentlemen, and a cruell tyrant ouer his nobles which bred vnto him great hatred and malice Besides this, there befell to him an other mischéefe. for Ororike prince of (3) Meth was gone in a iornie, leauing his wife the daughter of Omolaghlin behind, in a certeine Iland in Meth there to remaine and tarie vntill his returne She (I saie) and this Dermon had béene long inamoured and in loue the one with the other and she watching a time how to haue loue and lust satisfied, taketh the aduantage of hir husbands absence, and yéeldeth hir selfe to be rauished, bicause she would be rauished for by hir owne procurement and intisings, she became and would needs be a preie vnto the preier Such is the variable & fickle nature of a woman, by whome all mischiefes in the world (for the most part) doo happen and come, as maie appeare by (4) Marcus Antonius, and by the destruction of (5) Troie King Ororike being aduertised hereof, was foorthwith maruellouslie troubled & in a great choler, but more grieued for shame of the fact than for sorow or hurt, and therefore is fullie determined to be auenged · and foorthwith assembleth all his people and neighbors, as also procured into his aid and for his helpe Rothorike king of (6) Connagh and then monarch of all Ireland The people of Leinster considering in what distresse their prince was, and how on euerie side he was beset of his enimies, they also call to mind the old sores and griefes, which they of long time had dissembled & to be auenged & awreeked thereof, they make league and become friends with their enimies, and vtterlie leaue and forsake their king. Dermon séeing himselfe thus forsaken and left destitute, and that fortune frowned vpon him (for he had oftentimes incountered with his enimies and euer had the woorst) determined at length, as to his last refuge to flie ouer the seas, and to séeke for some better chance. By this euent and sequele of this man, as also by manie other like examples it appeareth, that it is better for a prince to rule ouer a people, which of a good will and loue doo obeie him, than ouer such as be froward and stubborne. This (6) Nero well felt and (7) Domitianus well knew (8) and Henrie duke of Saxonie and Bauire well tried. It is more necessarie and expedient for a prince to be rather beloued than feared. In déed it is good to be feared, so that the feare doo procéed rather from a good will than of compulsion. For whatsoeuer is outwardlie onelie and to the shew loued and receiued, the same of consequence must be feared: but whatsoeuer is feared, that is not forthwith loued. Wherefore feare must be so tempered with loue, that neither a remisse good will doo wax into a coldnesse, neither feare grounded vpon a rash insolencie be turned and become tyrannie. Loue did inlarge the empire of (9) Augustus, but feare shortened the life of (10) Iulius Cesar. Well, Mac Morogh following fortune, and yet in hope that once againe she will turne hir whéele, hauing wind and wether at will, taketh ship, passeth ouer the seas, and went vnto Henrie the second king of England, and most humblie and earnestlie praieth his helpe and succor. Who being then in the remote places in France and Aquitaine, and busied in great and weightie affaires, yet most courteouslie he receiued him and liberallie rewarded him. And the king hauing at large and orderlie heard the causes of his exile and of his repaire vnto him, he tooke his oth of allegiance and swore him to be his true vassall and subiect, and therevpon granted and gaue him his letters patents in maner and forme as followeth.

Henrie the 2 king of Englands stile and letter

Henrie king of England, duke of Normandie and Aquitaine, and earle of Aniou, vnto all his subiects, Englishmen, Normans, Scots, and all other nations and people being his subiects sendeth greeting. Whensoeuer these our letters shall come vnto you, know ye that we haue receiued Dermon prince of Leinster into our protection, grace and fauour: wherefore whosoeuer within our iurisdiction will aid and helpe him, our trustie subiect, for the recouerie of his land, let him be assured of our fauour and licence in that behalfe.

(1) Dermon is in Latine *Dermitius*, and Morogh is in Latine *Murchardes*, and are méere Irish names, and for a difference giuen commonlie to a child at his birth or christening. Mac Morogh is a word compounded of Mac which is a sonne and of Morogh the proper name of a man, and so Mac Morogh is the sonne of Morogh: the Latine name is *Murchardides*, which is to saie *De Murcharde*, or of Morogh: according to the Welsh phrase in which the word ap is vsed in the same sense. And this is common to the Irish & Welsh, for they call not anie man by the name of his familie or nation as is vsed in England: but by the name of difference giuen to his father, as in this example, Dermon being Moroghs sonne is called Dermon Mac Morogh. But this name of Mac Morogh is since turned and become the name of a familie or nation: for by reason that this Mac Morogh was a noble and valiant man aboue all the rest of his nation in his daies, therefore his sequele and posteritie haue euer since and doo yet kéepe that name. Some are of the mind that Morogh and Maurice are one name, but the Latine differences importeth the contrarie, and the one is a méere Irish name, and the other a Welsh, and borowed out of Wales.

(2) Leinster in Latine *Lagenia*, is one of the fiue parts or portions of Ireland (for into so manie is the whole land diuided.) It lieth vpon the east seas, and extendeth in length from the further point of the territorie of Dublin, which is at the riuer of the Boine by Drogheda in the north, vnto the riuer of the Sure which fléeteth by the citie of Waterford in the south. In it are one and thirtie

cantreds

canteds otherwise named baronies or hundreds. It was sometimes diuided into fiue, but now into seauen counties, that is, Dublin, Kildare, Catherlogh, Kilkennie, Wexford, Leax now called the queenes countie, and Offalie called the kings countie. There are also in it one archbishop namelie Dublin, and foure bishopriks, that is, Kildare, Fernes, Leighlin, and Ossorie.

(3) Meth in Latine *Media* is one of the fiue portions of Ireland according to the first diuision. It is the least portion being but of eightéene canteds, but yet the best and most fertile, and lieth for the most part all within the English pale: and euer since the conquest of king Henrie the second, hath béene subiect and obedient to the English lawes and gouernement: and bicause it lieth as it were in the nauill or bowels of the land, it taketh the name accordinglie, being called *Media*, which is the middle. In it is but one bishop and the suffragan, and vnder the primat or archbishop of Ardmach. His see is at Trim and his house at Arbraghin. There was no prince sole gouernour of this as was of the other portions: bicause it was alwaies allowed & allotted to the monarch, whome they called *Maximum regem*, or *Regem Hiberniæ*, as a surplus towards his diet.

(4) Marcus Antonius was a famous and a noble Romane, excelling in wisdome, knowledge and learning all the Romane princes in his daies, as also a verie noble and a valiant man in the fields, hauing atteined to great victories and atchiued to sundrie conquests. And yet notwithstanding being maried to Cleopatra queene of Egypt, he so doted vpon hir, and was so bewitched in loue of hir, that leauing all his woonted manners, he consumed his whole time in hir companie, and in the end was more infamous for his vitious, disordered, and loose life, than before commended for his prowesse and vertue.

(5) Troia called also Ilion, was an ancient and a famous citie in Asia the lesse, and situated in the prouince of Dardania, builded by Tros the sonne of king Erichthonius, who called it after his owne name. It was a citie verie large, strong, and rich, and in those daies thought impregnable, & yet by meanes that Helena was rauished, the same was in the end vtterlie subuerted and destroied: the historie is this. Priamus the king of Troie had by his wife Hecuba a sonne named Paris or Alexander: he dreamed on a time that Mercurius should bring vnto him the thrée ladies, Venus, Iuno, and Minerua, that he should giue his iudgement which was the fairest and most beautifull of them. Then Venus, to haue the iudgement for hir and in hir behalfe, did promise him that he should haue for the same the fairest woman in all Gréece. Not long after, Paris being in his fathers court in Troie, there were great spéeches made of Helena and of hir passing beautie. She was wife to Menelaus king of Sparta in Gréece. Wherevpon Paris calling to memorie his former dreame, and also inflamed with a feruent desire to see so faire a ladie, maketh preparation both of ships and of men to saile into Greece. Howbeit, some write that he was sent by the king his father in an ambassage to king Menelaus: but whether it was so or not, certeine it is he went thither, and was receiued with all courtesie, and had his interteinement in king Menelaus house. Paris hauing viewed and beholden quéene Helena, he was not so much warmed before vpon the onelie report of hir, as now inflamed with hir passing forme and beautie, and taking the aduantage of king Menelaus absence, perforce taketh Helena, spoileth the kings house, and carieth all awaie with him. Menelaus at his returne home, being dismaied at so sudden a change and chance, and gréeued with such an iniurie, sendeth his messenger first to Paris, and then his ambassadours to king Priamus for restitution and amends. But when no intreatie could take place nor requests be heard, the Grecians not minding to beare with such an iniurie, doo all consent to be auenged thereof: and therefore with all their force and power doo prepare to giue warres vnto Troie, and make choise of Agamemnon the kings brother to be their

capteine. The warres were cruell and long, and endured for the space of ten yeares, but in the end Troie was taken, spoiled, and also destroied.

(6) Nero, whose name at the first was Claudius Domitius, was in his youthfull yeares well disposed to good letters, & giuen to honest exercises. And Claudius the emperor hauing good liking of him, adopted him to be emperour, and married him vnto his daughter. After the death of Claudius, he being emperour, did gouerne well enough the first fiue yeares: but thensefoorth he waxed so vicious, and became so horrible in all dissolute wantonnesse, prodigalitie, monstruous lecherie, couetousnesse, and all other most wicked vices, that he séemed to be borne to the destruction of the whole world. And in the end he was and became so odious to the whole world, that it was decréed by the senat, and sentence giuen, that he should be beaten and whipped to death. Which thing he perceiuing, fled out of Rome, and finding none that would kill him, did ranne himselfe thorough with his owne sword, saieng, "Most wickedlie haue I liued, and most shamfullie shall I die."

(7) Domitianus, the brother of Titus, and sonne of Vespasian the emperors, was nothing like vnto them, but altogither resembled & was of the nature and disposition of Nero: for at the first entrie into the empire, he did to his commendation sundrie good acts, but in the end he became so wicked a man and so cruell a tyrant, that he generallie was hated of all men, and abhorred of his owne familie, of whom some of them, to rid the common wealth from so wicked a member, did murther and kill him in his owne chamber.

(8) This Henrie was the sonne of Henrie the third of that name, and emperor of Rome, he was king of the Romans in his fathers time, and emperor next after him. His father died, he being verie yoong, and left him to the gouernement of the empresse his mother, who during his minoritie did rule and gouerne the empire in verie good order: but when he himselfe came to the sole gouernment, great dissentions fell betwéene him and his nobles, bicause he contemned, despised, & oppressed them. He gaue himselfe to wantonnesse and pleasure, and little estéemed the execution of iustice, by means whereof he had manie enimies, who sought what they might to depose him both of empire and of his life. The pope also and he were for the most part in continuall debates and strifes, and who was the chéefe cause whie he was so ouerset and hated of his nobles. And being thus ouermatched and in the hatred both of the temporall and ecclesiasticall estates, he for verie sorow languished and pined awaie, and so died.

(9) Augustus was the sonne of Octauianus a senator in Rome, who married Accia the daughter of Iulius Cesar, and was first named Octauianus Iulius Cesar. His vncle hauing no son, adopted him, made him his heire, and appointed him to be his successor in the empire. After the death of the said Iulius, the state by reason he was so cruellie murthered, was marueloushe troubled and in great perils. But this Octauianus hauing atteined to sit in Iulius Cesars seat, did so prudentlie order and direct his gouernement, that he did not onelie reduce and restore the citie and empire of Rome to a quietnesse; but also increased the same with the conquests of sundrie nations. Such also were his excellent vertues in wisedome, magnanimitie, courtesie, affabilitie, & liberalitie, and such others, that all people were not onelie rauished in loue with him, but also came and resorted of all nations vnto Rome, to visit, see, and heare him. And hauing stablished the empire in quietnesse, inlarged it with manie nations, & increased vnto himselfe the vniuersall loue of all people, the senat gaue him not onelie the name of Augustus, but gaue vnto him also the titles of the highest and greatest honors, and was called "Summus pontifex perpetuus dictator & pater patriæ," and yéelded vnto him the whole power and empire of the sole monarch of the world, now reposing that in him alone, which

which rested before in the senat and people of Rome. These be the fruites when a prudent magistrat and a wise gouernour ruleth in loue and gouerneth in wisedome

(10) Iulius Cesar was the sonne of Lucius Iulino a noble Romane, and came and descended of the ancient house of the Iulies, who were of the race of Aeneas. he was as noble a man as euer Rome brought fourth, and excellent in all respects. most valiant and fortunate in the warres, and verie prudent in the ciuill gouernement verie well learned, and a notable orator he deserued well of his common wealth, for he inriched the same with the conquests which he made ouer sundrie nations But his ambitious mind and immoderate desire to reigne alone, and to be the sole monarch of the world, drowned all the good vertues which were in him, and for which all the nations feared him, the citizens of Rome hated him, and the senators enuied him and in the end a conspiracie was made for the murthering of him, and by the senators executed For he on a certeine daie, vpon occasion being come into the senat house, and mistrusting nothing, although he wanted not sufficient warnings before giuen him, was there wounded in two and thirtie places to death, and so murthered

The returne of Dermon Mac Morogh from king Hearie through England, and of his abode at Bristow and other places in Wales.

CHAP 2

DERMON Mac Morogh, hauing receiued great comfort and courtesie of the king taketh his leaue, and returneth homeward through England. And albeit he had béene verie honourablie and liberallie rewarded of the king yet he comforted himselfe more with the hope of good successe to come, than with liberalitie receiued And by his dailie iorneng he came at length vnto the noble towne of (1) Bristow, where because ships and botes did dailie repaire and come from out of Ireland, and he verie desirous to heare of the state of his people and countrie, did for a time soiorne and make his abode and whilest he was there he would oftentimes cause the kings letters to be openlie red, and did then offer great interteinment, and promised liberall wages to all such as would helpe or serue him, but it serued not. At length Gilbert the sonne of Gilbert, earle of Chepstone (2) came to see him and to talke with him and they so long had conferred togither, that it was agréed and concluded betweene them, that the erle in the next spring then following, should aid and helpe him and in consideration thereof, the said Dermon should giue him his onelie daughter and heire to wife, togither with his whole inheritance, and the succession into his kingdome. These things orderlie concluded, Dermon Mac Morogh being desirous (as all others are) to sée his naturall countrie, departed and tooke his iourneie towards S. Dauids head or stone (3) in south Wales: for from thence is the shortest cut ouer into Ireland, the same being not a daies sailing, and which in a faire daie a man may ken and discerne. At this same time Rice Fitzgriffith was cheefe ruler vnder the king in those parties, and Dauid the second, then bishop of S Dauids, had great pitie and compassion vpon his distresse, miserie, and calamitie

Dermon thus languishing and lieng for passage, comforted himselfe as well as he might, sometime drawing and as it were breathing the aire of his countrie, which he séemed to breath and smell, sometimes viewing and beholding his countrie, which

which in a faire daie a man maie ken and descrie At this time Robert Fitzstephans vnder Rice had the gouernement, & was constable of Abertefie the cheefe towne in Caretica (4) and by the treacherie and treason of his owne men was apprehended, taken and deliuered vnto Rice, and by him was kept in prison thrée yeares, but now deliuered, vpon condition he should take part and ioine with Griffith against the king But Robert Fitzstephans, considering with himselfe that on his fathers side (who was a Norman) he was the kings naturall subiect, although by his mother the ladie Nesta, daughter to the great Rice Fitzgriffith, he were coosen germane to the said Fitzgriffith, chose rather to aduenture his life, and to séeke fortune abroade and in forren countries, than to hazard his faith, credit, and fame, to the slander, reproch, and infamie of himselfe, and of his posteritie At length by the earnest mediation and intercession of Dauid then bishop of S Dauids and of Maurice Fitzgerald, which were his halfe brothers by the mothers side he was set frée and at libertie: and then it was agréed and concluded betwéene them and Mac Morogh, that he the said Mac Morogh should giue and grant vnto the said Robert Fitzstephans, and Maurice Fitzgerald, the towne of (5) Wexford, with two (6) cantreds of land adioining, & to their heires in frée for euer and they in consideration thereof, promised to aid and helpe him to recouer his lands the next spring then following and to be then with him without all faile if wind and weather so serued. Dermon being wearie of his exiled life and distressed estate, and therefore the more desirous to draw homewards for the recouerie of his owne, and for which he had so long trauelled and sought abroad he first went to the church of S Dauids to make his orisons and praiers, and then the wether being faire, and wind good, he aduentureth the seas about the middle of August, and hauing a merrie passage, he shortlie landed in his ingratefull (7) countrie and with a verie impatient mind, hazarded himselfe among and through the middle of his enimies, and comming safelie to (8) Fernes, he was verie honorablie receiued of the clergie there who after their abilitie did refresh and succour him but he for a time dissembling his princelie estate, continued as a priuat man all that winter following among them

(1) Bristow in the old time was named Odera, afterwards Venta, and now *Bristolium*, and standeth vpon the riuer Hauinum which is nauigable, & fléeteth into Seuerne or the Seuerne seas in it there are two rodes, the one named Kingrode, fiue miles distant from Bristow, in which the ships doo ride The other is named Hongrode, a place where the ships lie bedded, and this is thrée miles from Bristow. It standeth vpon the borders or confines of the prouince or Glocestershire and Summersetshire / some would haue it to be in the marches and vnder the principalitie, but in the old times is was parcell of the vallie of Bath, which was the metropole of Summersetshire It is verie old, ancient and honorable, and sometimes named but a towne but since for desert and other good considerations, honoured with the name and title of a citie, as also is made a seuerall prouince or countrie of it selfe, being distinct from all others, hauing a maior and aldermen according to the ancient times, as also two shiriffes according to the latter grants, by whome the same is directed and gouerned It is the chéefest emporium in that part of England, the inhabitants being for the most part merchants of great wealth, aduentures, and trafikes with all nations great dealings they haue with the Camber people and the Irish nation, the one of them fast bordering vpon them, and the other by reason of the néerenesse of the seas, and pleasantnesse of the riuer, dailie resorting by water to and from them.

(2) Chepstone is a market towne in Wales, in that prouince named in old time Venta, being now vnder the principalitie of Wales. In times past it was named

Strigulia,

Strigulia, whereof Richard Strangbow being earle he tooke his name, being called *Comes Strigulensis*.

(3) S. Dauids head or stone is the promontorie in west Wales, which lieth and reacheth furthest into the seas towards Ireland: and the same being a verie high hill, a man shall the more easilie discerne in a faire daie the countrie of Wexford: for that is the neerest part of Ireland vnto that part of Wales. Not farre from this promontorie or point is the cathedrall church of saint Dauids, which is the sée of the bishop there: it was and is called Meneuia, and was in times past an archbishoprike. But as it is written in the annales of the said church, that in the time of Richard Carew and two of his predecessors bishops there, they were by the kings commandement made to yeeld, and submit themselues vnto the metropolitane sée of Canturburie.

(4) Aberteife is an old ancient towne standing vpon the mouth of the riuer of Teife, and thereof it taketh his name, that is to saie the mouth of Teife, but now it is called Cardigan. The countrie about it was in times past named Caretica, but now Cardiganshire, so Aberteife is Cardigan towne, and Caretica Cardiganshire.

(5) Wexford in Latine named *Guesfordia* is next after Dublin the chiefest towne in Leinster, it lieth full vpon the seas, but the hauen is a barred hauen and dangerous: from it is the shortest cut out of Ireland into England, if you doo touch and take land either at saint Dauids or at Milford.

(6) A cantred (as Giraldus saith) is a word compounded of the British and of the Irish toongs, and conteineth so much ground as wherein are one hundred villages: which in England is termed a hundred. Men of later time to declare the same more plainelie, doo saie that it conteined thirtie villages, & euerie village conteined eight plough lands. Other saie that a cantred conteineth twentie townes, and euerie towne hath eight plough lands arable, besides sufficient pasture in euerie for thrée hundred kine, and none to annoie another; and euerie plough land conteineth six score acres of land Irish, and euerie Irish acre farre exceedeth the content of the common acre.

(7) The place where Dermon landed is named Glasse caerge, it is a créeke or a baie lieng vpon the open seas, and in the countie of Wexford, sithence there was builded a monasterie which was and is dissolued.

(8) Fernes is the sée and cathedrall church of the bishop, whose diocesse is the countie of Wexford, it lieth néere in the middle of the prouince of Leinster, and was somtimes a church well adorned and mainteined, but now in great ruine and decaie, the bishop & chapiter not remaining there at all. There is also a strong fort of the princes, wherein sometimes was kept a garrison at the princes charges, but now onelie a constable is placed therein, and he hath the sole charge thereof.

The going ouer and landing of Robert Fitzstephans and of his companie in Ireland, and of the winning of the towne of Wexford.

CAP. 3.

IN the meane time Robert Fitzstephans, not vnmindfull nor carelesse of his word and promise, prepareth and prouideth all things in a readinesse, and being accompanied with thirtie gentlemen of seruice of his owne kinsfolks & * centeine armed men, * Thrée score other in iacks. and about thrée hundred of archers and footmen, which were all of the best chosen and piked men in Wales, they all ship and imbarke themselues in thrée sundrie barkes, and sailing towards Ireland, they land about the calends of Maie at the (1) Banne. Then was the old prophesie of Merlin fulfilled, which was, that A (2) knight

knight bipnted should first enter with force in arms & breake the bounds of Ireland If you will vnderstand the mysterie herof, you must haue respect to his parents, for his father was a Norman and an Englishman, his mother the noble ladie Nesta was a Camber or a Britaine, in his companie also was Hemere of Mont Maurice, a man infortunat, vnarmed, and without all furniture. but he trauelling in the behalfe of the earle Richard, to whome he was vncle, was rather a (3) spie than a souldier On the next daie following Maurice of Prendelgast a (4) lustie and a hardie man, and borne about Milford in west Wales, he with ten gentlemen of seruice, and a good number of archers imbarke themselues in two ships, and arriue also at the Banne These men thus landed at the Banne, and not standing well assured of their safetie, by reason their comming was blowen abroad through the whole countrie, they with all hast sent messengers to Dermon, aduertising him of their comming Whereupon diuerse of that countrie, who dwelling vpon the sea coasts, and who when fortune frowned had and did shrinke awaie from Dermon, now perceiuing that she fauored him againe, returned and fawned vpon him, according to the saieng of the poet in these words

 "As fortune so the faith of man doth stand or fall."

Mac Morogh, assoone as he heard of their landing and comming, sent his base son Donold, a valiant gentleman vnto them with fiue hundred men and verie shortlie after he himselfe also followed with great ioie and gladnesse And then when they had renewed their former couenants and leagues, and had sworne each one to the other, to obserue the same and to keepe faith then, though they were people of contrarie dispositions, yet now being good freends and all of one mind, they ioine their forces togither, and with one consent doo march towards the towne of Wexford, which is about twelue miles distant from the Banne When they of the towne heard therof, they being a fierce and vnrulie people, but yet much trusting to their woonted fortune, came foorth about two thousand of them, and were determined to wage and giue battell But when they saw their aduersaries armie to be better set in order than in times past, and that the horssemen were well armed with armour and shield shining bright then vpon new chances & changes taking new counsels, they set on fire and burned their suburbs, and retired into the towne

Fitzstephans minding and preparing to giue the assault, filleth the ditches with armed men, and setteth his archers to marke and watch well the turrets of the wals which things doone, he with great showtes and force giueth the assault. The townesmen within being readie to stand at defense, cast ouer the wals great peeces of timber & stones, and by that meanes hurting manie, made the rest to giue ouer and retire Among whom a lustie yoong gentleman named Robert Barrie, being hot and of a lustie courage, and nothing afraid of death, so he might atchiue vnto honour, giueth the first aduenture to scale the wals· but he was striken with a great stone vpon the headpeece, wherwith he fell headlong downe into the ditch and escaped verie hardlie, for with much adoo did his fellowes draw & pull him out of the place About sixteene yeares after, all his great teeth with the force and violence of this stroke fell out, and that which is verie strange, new teeth grew vp in their places Vpon this repulse they all retired and withdrew themselues from the wals, & assembled themselues vpon the sea strands, where foorthwith they set on fire all such ships and vessels as they could there find Among whome was one merchant ship latelie come out of England laden with wines and corne, which there laie then at anchor, and a companie of these lustie youths hauing gotten botes for the purpose, would haue taken hir which the mariners perceiuing, suddenlie cut their cabels and hoised vp their sailes, & the wind being westerlie and blowing a good gale, they recouered the seas. These youths still following them, had almost
 lost

lost all and marred the market for if others their fellowes had not made good shift and rowed a good pice after them they would scarselie haue recouered the land againe. Thus fortune, which is onlie constant in inconstancie, séemed to haue forsaken Morogh and Fitzstephans, and to haue left them destitute of all hope and comfort neuerthelesse on the next morow hauing heard diuine seruice through the whole campe, they determine with better aduise and circumspection to giue a new assault, & with lustie courages drew to the wals The townesmen within séeing this, began to distrust themselues, & to consider how most vnnaturallie and vniustlie they had rebelled against their prince & soueraigne wherevpon being better aduised, they send messengers to him to intreat for peace. At length by the earnest intercession and mediation of two bishops, and certeine good and peaceable men which were within the towne, peace was granted, and foure of the best & chiefest men within the towne were deliuered and giuen for pledges and hostages, for the true kéeping of the peace and their fidelitie. Mac Morogh, to gratifie his men in these his first successes, and to acquit the first aduenturors, did (according to his former promise and couenant) giue vnto Robert Fitzstephans and Maurice Fitzgerald the towne of Wexford, and the territories therevnto adioining and apperteining, and vnto Heruie of Mont Morice he gaue in fee two cantreds, lieng on the sea side betwéene Wexford and Waterford.

(1) The Banne is a little créeke lieng in the countie of Wexford, neere to Frther a fisher towne, which is belonging to the bishop of that diocesse, the open seas being on the east and not farre from the hauen mouth of Waterford on the south and as it should seeme, Fitzstephans and his companie mistooke the place or were driuen in there, the same being verie vnapt for a harborow but the same being the place of the first receipt of Englishmen, there were certeine monuments made in memorie thereof, and were named the Banna & the Boenne, which were the names (as the common fame is) of the two greatest ships in which the Englishmen there arriued.

(2) A knight biparted The prophesie was not onelie verified in respect of the parents of Robert Fitzstephans, the one being a Norman Saxon, and the other a Camber but also in respect of his armes and ensigne which were biparted being of two sundrie changes, namelie partie per pile gules, and ermine a saltier counterchanged For commonlie all prophesies haue their allusions vnto armes, and by them they are disconcred, though at the first not so appearing before the euent thereof

(3) Gentlemen The Latine word is *Milites*, which in the now common spéeches is termed knights, a name of worship and honour but the word it selfe importeth and meaneth men expert and skilfull to serue in the wars, whether it be on foot or horssebacke In times past when men ruled by the sword, then such as were valiant and of good experience grew into credit and estimation, and the people did make choise of such to gouerne, rule, and defend them, and who for their excellent vertues were called *Nobiles*, which in English is gentlemen. And then men being ambitious of honour, did contend who might best excell in feats of prowesse and chiualrie some deliting to excell in the seruice on foot and bicause they vsed chieflie the target and shield, they tooke their name thereof, & were called *Scutiferi* Some practised chieflie the seruice on horssebacke, and they (according to the manner of their seruice) were named *Equites* but both the one and the other were in processe of time called *Armigeri*, in English esquiers and this is taken for a degrée somewhat aboue the estate of a onelie gentleman. And for somuch as seruice in the fields did carie awaie with it the greatest honor and credit, and princes willing & desirous to incourage gentlemen to excell that waie and in that

kind of seruice, they deuised a third degree of honour named knighthood. And this, as it excelleth the others before and not to be giuen but for great desert so to increase the credit and estimation thereof, it was not to be giuen but with great solemnities and ceremonies, and the person so to be honored, was to be adorned with such ornaments as doo speciallie apperteine to the furniture of such seruice, as namelie a sword, a target, a helme, a paire of spurres, and such like and they which were thus aduanced were named *Milites* or knights, and thus the name of seruice was turned to the name of worship yea this degree did grow and was to be of such credit, honor and estimation, that kings and princes were and would be verie circumspect and aduised, before they would dub or promote anie man to this estate Wherefore considering the estate, nature & worship of a knight, and weieng also the course of this historie, it cannot be intended that all they which went ouer and serued in this conquest, though they were named *Milites*, that therfore they should be compted & taken for knights of worship and high calling but that they were such as were expert and skilfull to serue in warres according to the nature of the word *Miles* Wherefore I haue and doo English the word *Miles* in this historie a gentleman of seruice

(4) A spie, not to watch the doings of his countrimen, whereby to take them in a trip but to note, marke and consider the nature, maner, and disposition of the countrie and people whereby to aduertise the earle how he should prouide and order his doings against his comming ouer into the land

(5) Maurice of Prendalgast was doubtlesse a valiant gentleman, and borne and bred in west Wales, in or about the prouince of Penbroke He is not named nor mentioned in some books of this historie, but I finding in such exemplars as I haue of best credit, doo thinke I should haue doone wrong to haue omitted him There are yet of his race, posteritie and name, remaining at these daies in the countie of Wexford, and elsewhere

Of the ouerthrow giuen in Ossorie, and of the submission of the king thereof.

CHAP 4

THESE things thus doone and ended as they would themselues, they increase their armie with the townesmen of Wexford, and being then about thrée thousand men, they march towards (1 Ossorie, whereof Donald was then the prince, & who of all the rebels was the most mortall enimie which Mac Morogh had For on a time he hauing the said Dermons eldest son in his ward and handfast, was in gealousie of him, and mistrusted him with his wife wherevpon he did not onlie shut him vp in a closer prison, but also to be auenged thereof, and of other supposed iniuries, putteth out both of his (2) eies Iust then Dermon and his companie enter into Ossorie, but they durst not march or aduenture anie further than to the midst of the countrie, because the whole countrie else was full of woods, streicts, passes, and bogs, and no waie at all for men to trauell But when they met and incountered with the Ossorians, they found not cowards nor dastards, but valiant men, and who stood well to the defense of their countrie, and manfullie resisted their enimies For they trusted so much to their woonted good fortune and successe in such like affaires, that they shroonke not a whit from them, but draue them perforce out of the bogs and woods, and followed them into the champaine countrie

Robert Fitzstephans being in the plaine and open fields with his horsemen, and seeing that the Ossorians being there he had the aduantage of them, giueth most fiercelie

fiercelie the onset vpon them, and slue a great number of them; and such as straied and were scattered abrode, they either slue them or ouerthrew them: and such as were ouerthrowne, the footmen with their Galloglasses axes did cut off their heads. And thus hauing gotten the victorie, they gathered vp and brought before Dermon Mac Morogh three hundred of their enimies heads, which they laid & put at his féet, who turning euerie of them one by one to know them, did then for ioy hold vp both his hands, and with a lowd voice thanked God most highlie. Among these there was the head of one, whom especiallie and aboue all the rest he mortallie hated. And he taking vp that by the heare and eares, with his teeth most horriblie and cruellie bit awaie his nose and lips.

After this, they made a rode through the whole countrie, & marched almost to the vttermost parts, and still as they passed they murthered the people, spoiled, burned, and wasted the whole countrie. And therevpon the prince of Ossorie by the aduise of his friends, maketh sute and intreateth for peace: which obteined (although in verie déed it was but a coloured and a dissembled peace on both sides) they put in their hostages, made fealtie, and were sworne to bee faithfull and true to Mac Morogh, as vnto their lawfull and true lord. In these seruices, as in all other, Robert of Barrie, and Meilerius had the pricke and praise, and shewed themselues of all others the most valiant. Both these yoong gentlemen were nephues to Fitzstephans (4) the one being his brothers sonne, and the other his sisters sonne. They both were of like valiantnesse, but of sundrie dispositions and natures. For Meilerius being ambitious and desirous of honour, referred all his doings to that end, and whatsoeuer he attempted, was to aduance his fame and credit, making more account to be reported and haue the name of a valiant man, than to be so in déed. The other being of a certeine naturall disposition both noble and valiant, was neither a gréedie séeker of laud and praise, nor an ambitious crauer of fame and honour, but being alwaies among the best, did rather séeke and trauell to the best, than to be onelie counted the best.

Besides, he was naturallie indued with such a maidenlie shamefastnesse, and no bragger nor boaster, would neither glorifie his doings, nor yet like well of anie others which would so doo of him. By means whereof it came to passe, that the lesse ambitious and desirous he was of honour, the more the same followed him. for glorie and honour follow alwaies vertue, as the shadow the bodie, shunning them who doo most séeke for hir, & following them who do lest regard hir. And manie men are the more liked of manie, bicause they séeme not to like of anie. and praise, fame, and honour most commonlie, the lesse it is estéemed, the more sooner it is had & gotten. It fortuned on a time that the armie thus being in Ossorie, they did on a night incampe themselues about an old castell. These two gentlemen as they were euer woont, laie togither, and suddenlie there was a great noise, as it were of an infinit number of men, which séemed to breake in and rush in among them, with great force and a rage, destroieng all that euer was, and making a great noise with clashing of their harnesse, and striking of their bils togither, and therewithall such a noise and a showt, as though heauen and earth would haue come togither.

These kind of phantasmes and illusions doo oftentimes happen in Ireland, especiallie when there be anie hostings. With this noise the more part of the armie was so afraid and dismaid, that for the most part they all fled, some into the woods, and some into the bogs, euerie one séeking a place where to hide and succour himselfe. But these two onelie tarieng behind, raught to their weapons, and foorthwith full boldlie ran to Fitzstephans tents, and called againe togither all such as were thus scattered, and incouraged them to take their weapons, and to stand to defense. Robert of Barrie in all his hurlie burlie, standing alone by himselfe musing, except

a man

a man or two of his owne men about him, did aboue all others not without anie great admiration of manie, and to the great gréefe of such as enuied him, best acquit himselfe For among other good gifts which were in him, this was speciallie reported of him, that no feare, or force, no sudden mishap or misaduenture whatsoeuer, could at anie time make him afraid or discomforted, and to flie awaie. For howsoeuer things fell out and happened, he was alwaies at hand, and in a readines with his weapons to fight. And such a one as is alwaies readie to abide whatsoeuer shall happen, and to preuent what mischeefs maie insue, is by all mens iudgements counted the best and valiantest man This man was he, who in this Irish warres was the first who either was striken or hurt. As concerning the foresaid phantasme, this one thing is much noted of it, that in the morning following, when all things were pacified and quieted, the grasse and weeds which the night before stood there vpright and of a great height, did now in the morrow lie downe flat vpon the ground, as though the same had bin troden with great multitude of people, and yet was it most certeine that none had béene there at all.

(1) There be two Ossories, the one named the vpper Ossorie, which is of the ancient inheritance of the Macgnilfathrikes, and who are the barons therof, and this lieth in the diocesse of Leighling. the other lieth on the north of Ormond, and is vnder the iurisdiction of the earle of Ormond, who is also the earle thereof, being named earle of Ormond and Ossorie It is a diocesse of it selfe, and the bishop thereof is named the bishop of Ossorie, whose sée and house is at Kilkennie. It is parcell of the prouince of Leinster and vnder the obeisance then of Dermon Mac Morogh

(2) This was a courteous kind of punishing, for cōmonlie such is the reuenging nature of the méere Irishman, that albeit he can or doo laie neuer so manie plagues and punishments vpon his enimie yet is he neuer satisfied, vnlesse he haue also his life, yea and manie not therewith contented, but will vtter their wicked nature euen vpon the dead carcase, as dooth appeare in this chapter of the same Mac Morogh, who finding one of his enimies heads, was not satisfied, vntill in most cruell maner he did with his téeth bite awaie his nose and his lips

(3) There are in Ireland thrée sorts or degrées of soldiers the first is the horsseman, who commonlie is a gentleman borne, and he is armed with such armor as the seruice of that countrie requireth. the second degree is the Kernaugh, & he also is a gentleman or a frécholder borne, but not of that abilitie to mainteine a horsse with his furniture, and therefore he is a light souldier on foot, his armor is both light and slender, being a skull, a left gantlet or a target, a sword and skeine, and thrée or foure darts the third degree is the Galloglasse, who was first brought in to this land by the Englishmen, and thereof taketh his name. For Galloglas is to saie, an English yeoman or seruant, his armor is a skull, a iacke, an habergeon or shirt of male, a sword and a sparre, otherwise named a Galloglasse ax or halbert, & this man is counted the best souldier on foot, and the strength of the battell These in all hostings haue attending vpon them a number of boies and kernes, and who doo spoile and kill all such as be ouerthrowne and hurt in the fields

The

The conspiracie of Rothorike monarch of Ireland, and of the residue of the princes against Mac Morogh and Fitzstephans.

CHAP 5.

IN the meane time the wheele of fortune is turned vpside downe, and they which before séemed to stand aloft, are now afraid of sliding and they which were on high, in perill now to fall For assoone as it was noised through the whole land of the good successe of Dermon, and of the comming in of strangers into the land, and whereof they were much afraid Rothorike prince of (1) Conagh, and (2) monarch of the whole land, coniecturing how of small things great doo grow, and considering that by the comming in of strangers, the whole land was in some perill, sendeth abrode his messengers, and summoneth a parlement of the whole land who being assembled, and the matter at full debated, they doo with one voice and consent conclude and determine to make open warres, and to giue the battell vnto Mac Morogh And foorthwith euerie man hauing made readie both men and armor to his vttermost power, doo ioine all their forces and strengths togither, and with maine and strength doo inuade the countrie of Okensile in Leinster

Dermon Mac Morogh in this distresse was somwhat disquieted, and in a great perplexitie, parthe bicause some of his (but glosing) fréends distrusting the sequele, did shrinke from him, & hid themselues some of them most traitorouslie, contrarie to their oth and promise, were fled to his enimies and so in this his distresse he had verie few fréends, sauing onlie Robert Fitzstephans and the Englishmen with him. He therefore with such companie as he had, went vnto a certeine place not farre from Fernes, which was compassed and inuironed round about with great thicke woods, high stikle hilles, and with bogs and waters, a place so strong of it selfe, as it was in a maner inaccessible, and not to be entred into. And as soone as they were entred into the same, they foorthwith by the aduise of Fitzstephans (3) did fell downe trées, plashed the wood, cast great trenches and ditches round about, and made it so strict, narrow, crooked, and strong, that there was no passage nor entrie for the enimie and yet by their art and industrie it was made much more strong.

(1) Conagh, in Latine Conacia, is one of the fiue portions of the land, according to the ancient diuision In it are thirtie cantreds or baronies, and before and vntill the conquest they were vnder the gouernment of the sept of the O Conners, the eldest man of which sept by the Irish law was euer the prince but at the conquest it was giuen to certeine noble men of England, & by certeine descents it came to sir Walter de Burgo, who was lord of that whole prouince and earle of Wolster From these Burghs descend the Burghs now being in Conagh, they being of a base line, and first were put onlie in trust to kéepe that countrie to the vse of their lords, who then dwelled and remained in England This countrie lieth betwéene Vlster in the north, Mounster in the south, and the seas in the west The chéefest and onelie merchant towne or emporium thereof is Gallowaie

(2) There was alwaies one principall gouernor among the Irish, whom they named a monarch, and he was commonlie either of the Mac Carthies in Mounster, or of the Moroghs in Leinster, or of the O Connors in Connagh, as this Rothorike was He was elected & chosen by the common consent of all the nobilitie of the land. & being once chosen, all they did homage and fealtie vnto him The prouince of Meth, which was the least of the fiue seuerall portions was reserued alwais vnto him for his diet. For though the Omolaghlins did dwell in Meth, and were great

great inheritors or possessioners there, yet they were not counted for princes as the other were This monarch did gouerne the whole land vniuersallie, & all the princes were directed by him in him it laie whether it should be peace or warre, and what he commanded was alwaies doone

(3) The maner of the Irishrie is to kéepe them selues from force of the enimies, or in the bogs, or in the woods the one of his nature is so strong as no horsseman is to aduenture into the same, the other with industrie they make strong, by felling of trées & plashing of the woods, and by these means the horssemen (in whom is all the strength of their warres) can haue no passage nor entrie to the enimie, but must either retire, or go on foot, or séeke some other waie. If they will and must néeds passe that waie, they must of necessitie go on foot, and then they are too weake, and easilie to be ouercome by the Kernes, whose seruice is onelie on foot therefore they doo chéefelie kéepe themselues in such places, as where they can take the aduantage of others, and not others of them.

The description of Dermon Mac Morogh, and of the message of Rothorike O Connor sent vnto him for peace

CAP. 6.

DERMON Mac Morogh was a tall man of stature, and of a large and great bodie, a valiant and a bold warrior in his nation: and by reason of his continuall halowing and crieng his voice was hoarse he rather chose and desired to be feared than to be loued: a great oppressor of his nobilitie, but a great aduancer of the poore and weake To his owne people he was rough and greeuous, and hatefull vnto strangers, he would be against all men, and all men against him Rothorike minding to attempt anie waie whatsoeuer, rather than to aduenture and wage the battell, sendeth first his messengers with great presents vnto Fitzstephans, to persuade and intreat him that for so much as he made no chalenge nor title to the land, that he would quietlie, and in peace returne home againe into his owne countrie, but it auailed not. Then they went vnto Mac Morogh himselfe, & persuaded him to take part with Rothorike, and to ioine both their forces and armies in one, and then with might and maine to giue the onset vpon the strangers, and so vtterlie to destroie them And in this dooing he should haue Rothorike to his good fréend, and all Leinster in rest and quietnesse manie reasons also they alledged concerning their countrie and nation; but all was to no purpose

The speeches and oration which Rothorike O Connor made vnto his soldiors.

CHAP 7.

ROTHORIKE O Connor, seeing that by these his deuises and practises he could doo no good at all, and thinking that forsomuch as he could not auaile with words, he with force and armes, as his last remedie and helpe, prepareth his armor, and maketh for the battell and assembling his people togither, maketh vnto them these speeches. "Ye right noble and valiant defendors of your countrie and libertie, let vs consider with what people, and for what causes we are now to fight and wage the battell. That enimie of his owne countrie, that tyrant ouer his owne people, and

and an open enimie vnto all men, and who sometimes was an exiled man: sée how he being inuironed with the force of strangers, is now returned, & mindeth the vtter destruction of vs all, and of this his nation. He enuieng the safetie of his countrie and countrimen, hath procured and brought in a strange nation vpon vs, that by the helpe of a hatefull people he might satisfie and more effectuallie accomplish his malice, which otherwise by no means he could haue brought to passe. He then being an enimie, hath brought in that enimie which hath béene euer hatefull both vnto him, and vnto vs: and who are most gréedie to haue the souereigntie & dominion ouer vs all, protesting and openlie affirming, that by a certeine fatall destinie they are to be rulers ouer this land: yea, & so far hath he shed out his venome, and almost euerie man is so inuenomed therewith, that now no fauor nor mercie is to be shewed. O cruell beast, yea more cruell than euer was beast! for to satisfie his insatiable malice, and to be auenged with the bloudsheding of his owne people, he spareth neither himselfe, nor his countrie, nor sex. This is he who is a most cruell tyrant ouer his owne people: this is he who with the force and helpe of strangers vseth all force and crueltie against all men. He deserueth well therefore to be hated of all, which séeketh to be an enimie vnto all. Looke therefore (yee worthie citizens) well to your selues, I saie looke and consider well how by these meanes, I meane by ciuill discord, all realmes & nations haue for the most part béene ouerthrowen & vanquished. (1) Iulius Cesar minding to inuade Britaine had the repulse twise, & was driuen out by the Britons. But when Androgeus fell at variance with the king, he then to be reuenged, sent againe for Iulius, who thervpon returned and conquered the land. (2) The same Iulius also conquered all the west parts of the world, but when he waxed & became ambitious, & would be a sole monarch, & haue the whole gouernement in himselfe, then discord was raised, & debate was rife, & by that meanes all Italie was filled with murthers and slaughters. (3) The Britons being at discord with their king, procured Gurmundus, who then was a terror to all the ocean Iles, that he with the Saxons should pursue and make wars vpon their king, who so did: but in the end to their owne confusion and destruction. Likewise not long after (4) Isembertus the French king, being an enimie to his owne people, and at discord with them, he procured the said Gurmund to aid and helpe him to subdue his people, who so did: but thereof he had but bad successe. Wherfore let vs with one mind like to these Frenchmen stand stoutlie to the defense of our countrie, and couragiouslie giue the onset vpon our enimies. And whiles these strangers be but few in number, let vs lustilie issue out vpon them: for fire whiles it is but in sparkles is soone couered, but when it is in great flames, it is the harder to be quenched. It is good therefore to méet with things at the beginning, and to preuent sicknesse at the first growing: for diseases by long continuance hauing taken déepe root, are hardlie to be cured. We therefore, who are to defend our countrie and libertie, and to leaue to our posteritie an immortall fame, let vs valiantlie, and with a good courage aduenture and giue the onset, that the ouerthrow of a few may be a terror vnto manie, and that by this example all other forren nations may be afraid to aduenture the like attempt."

(1) Iulius Cesar hauing receiued two repulses, retired & tooke shipping, being in an vtter despaire & not minding to returne anie more. Wherevpon Cassibelan then king of the land called & assembled all his nobles to London, where for ioie he kept a great and a solemne feast, and at the same were vsed all such games and pastimes, as in those daies were most accustomed. And at a wrestling game then it chanced two yoong gentlemen, the one being nephue to the king, and the other cousine to the erle of London (Kent) to fall at variance, & in the end the kings nephue

nephue was slaine. The king much grieued therwith sent for the earle, whose name was Androgeus: and bicause he would not come vnto him he made wars vpon him. The earle considering in what distresse he was, and how farre vnable to incounter the power and withstand the displeasure of the king, sendeth his messenger with his letters vnto Iulius Cesar: and besought him most earnestlie to returne with his armie, and he would aid and helpe him against the king with all the power he had. Iulius Cesar glad of these tidings returneth with all spéed, and in the end hath the victorie: and thus by meanes of debate and diuision the relme, which otherwise was thought to be inpregnable, was subuerted and made tributarie.

(2) Iulius Cesar hauing happie and fortunate succese in all his affaires, grew into such a liking of himselfe, that he would needs be the sole monarch and emperor ouer the whole world, taking foule euill that according to the ancient gouernement of the Romans anie one should be ioined with him: and ambitiouslie séeking the same, he became dreadfull to the people, lothsome to his friends, and in the displeasure of the senat: who maligning at his aspiring and mistrusting the sequele thereof, conspired his death, and in the end he comming into the senat house, and mistrusting nothing, was murthered and slaine.

(3) At this time Careticus was king and ruled ouer Britaine, now named England, who was so vitious a man in all respects, that he became hatefull both to God and man: and his subiects not abiding his tyrannie, nor brooking his wickednesse, fell at diuision with him. Wherevpon Gurmundus then king of Ireland was procured (some saie by the Britons and some saie by the Saxons) who being entered into the land, and séeking by all the meanes they could to be the sole lords of the land, to inuade the land, which he did, and by the helpe of the Saxons droue the king out of his realme into Wales. And the Saxons hauing thus their wils droue also all the Britons out, who from thensefoorth hauing lost the land of Britaine, did inhabit themselues in Wales, Cornewall, and elsewhere, where they might haue refuge and succour. And thus though they were reuenged of their king, yet they themselues in the end felt the smart thereof: for they were all destroied or banished: such are the fruits of dissention and debate.

(4) This Isembertus was not king of France, but as (Gaufred saith) was nephue to the king: and the land being then in great troubles, this Isembert made title vnto it, and seeking by all the meanes and waies he could how to compasse the same, procured Gurmundus to helpe and aid him, promising him great rewards. Wherevpon Gurmundus passed ouer into France, where he had but an euill successe: for there was he slaine, Isembert ouerthrowne and the French nation preuailed. And herevpon Rothorike taketh an occasion to incourage his people to stand to their tackle, and valiantlie to withstand Mac Morogh, who as Isembert had procured in Gurmundus; so had he flocked in Englishmen to ouerrun his countrie.

The oration and speeches of Mac Morogh to his souldiors and people.

CAP. 8.

MAC Morogh beheld his men, & perceiuing them to be somewhat dismaied and out of heart, framed his speech to recomfort them, and thus saith vnto them: "Ye men of Leinster, truth and kindred in all aduentures hath hitherto ioined us in one fellowship: wherefore let vs now plucke vp our hearts and like men stand to our defense. For why, that wicked and ambitious man Rothorike, the author of all wickednesse & mischiefe, who desirous to haue the sole souereignetie and dominion dooth

dooth now determine (which God forbid) either to driue vs cleane out of our countrie, or vtterlie to destroie vs: and marke you now how he lifteth vp his head and looketh alofte. He is so proud and glorieth so much in his great multitude, that by ambition and pride he measureth & valueth his force and strength: but yet (for all that) manie times a small number being valiant and well appointed are better and haue preuailed against great troops, being but sluggards and vnarmed. If he make chalenge and pretend title to Leinster, bicause the same sometimes hath beene tributarie to some one king of Conagh, then by the same reason (1) we also maie demand and chalenge all Conagh: for both thereof and of all Ireland our ancestors haue beene the sole gouernors & monarchs. But to the purpose and to speake plainelie, he séeketh not to rule and to reigne as a monarch, but to vsurpe and destroie as a tyrant, to driue vs out of our countrie, to succéed into euerie mans right & inheritance, and so alone to rule the rost, and to be master ouer all.

"Manie there are which doo brag of their great multitudes, and put their trust therein: but let them be well assured that we Leinster men though we be but few in number, yet we neuer were nor yet are affraid to incounter euen with the best & proudest. For why, victorie is not gotten, neither dooth it stand alwaies in the great multitude of people, but in vertue and valiantnesse, in strength and courage. We on our sides against pride, haue humilitie: against wrongs, equitie: against arrogancie, modestie: and against intemperance, discretion & moderation: and these vertues are to fight for vs. Men doo not alwaie atteine vnto victorie by great troops and multitudes of people, but by vertues. The lawes of all nations doo grant and allow to resist and withstand force and iniurie with force and strength: it is a fauourable cause to fight for our countrie, and to defend our patrimonie. And forsomuch as they contend for the gaine, but we to eschew the losse, let vs be of a good courage: we stand vpon a good ground, and our seat is naturallie verie strong of it selfe, as also by our industrie made more strong: but by reason of the streictnesse thereof, the greater the companie is therin, the more comberous and troublesome it will be: and yet to win the victorie, a small companie being valiant, couragious, and of a good agréement shall serue and be sufficient."

(1) There be (as is said) fiue portions of Ireland, and euerie of them (except Meth which was reserued to the monarch for the time being for his diet) had their particular princes, & none of these did hold anie one of the other: but of some one of them choise was made by the whole estates of the land to be the monarch; and he for the time being did take and receiue homage and fealtie of all the others, not in respect that he was a particular prince, but bicause he was the monarch. And this Mac Morogh allegeth for him selfe, denieng that he held anie of his lands of the king of Connagh otherwise than in respect that he was the monarch.

The oration of Robert Fitzstephans made vnto his companions and souldiors.

CHAP. 9.

WHEN Dermon Mac Morogh had ended his speech, Robert Fitzstephans calleth his companie togither, & thus he speaketh vnto them: "Ye lustie yoong men and my companions in warres, which haue abiden with me in manie perils, & yet still of noble minds & valiant courages: if we would now consider with our selues, what we are, vnder what capteine, and wherefore we doo aduenture and attempt these great enterprises, no doubt we shall excell in our woonted valiantnesse, and good fortune shall be on our side We first came and descended from the (1) Troians, and since are of the French bloud and race of the one we haue these our noble and valiant minds, and of the other the vse and experience in feats of armes wherfore being thus descended of noble progenie by two maner of waies and in two respects as we be now well armed and appointed, so let vs also be of valiant minds and lustie courages and then no doubt this rascall and naked people shall neuer be able to resist nor withstand vs

"Besides you sée and know how that at home, partlie by the subtill and craftie dealings of our owne cousines and kinsmen, and partlie by the secret malice and deuises of our familiars and acquaintances, we are béereft & spoiled both of our countrie and patrimonie And now we are come hither, not as gréedie cormorants for large stipends, nor yet as couetous prollers for gaine and lucre but onlie in respect and consideration to haue and inioie the lands & townes to vs, and to our heires after vs, offered and promised We are not come hither like pirats or théeues to rob and spoile, but as faithfull friends, to recouer and to restore this noble and liberall gentleman to that his patrimonie, whereof he is spoiled and dispossessed. He it is that hath allured and flocked vs hither, he it is that loueth our nation and he it is who purposeth to plant and settle vs and our heires in this Ile And peraduenture by these meanes the whole land, which is now diuided into fiue prouinces or portions, maie be deduced and brought into one, and the same in time be wholie vnto vs and our heires if that by our valiantnesse and prowesse the victorie be gotten and Mac Morogh by our seruice, meanes, and industrie be restored, and then the whole dominion to vs and to our heires for euer to be reserued

"O how great were then our honor & glorie! yea so great, that with the perils of our bodies, losse of our liues, and the dangers of death, it is to be wished for, sought, & aduentured. For why should we be afraid? and what is death I praie you? Is it anie other than a short delaie or distance of time, & as it were a short sléepe betwéene this transitorie life and the life eternall to come? What is death (I saie) but a short passage from vaine and transitorie things to perpetuall and euerlasting ioies? And certeine it is we must all once die for it is that ineuitable destinie, which is common to all men, and can be eschewed of no man for be we idle, and doo nothing worthie of perpetuall fame and memorie, or be we well occupied, whereof insueth praise and honor yet die shall we Then the matter being so, let them be afraied of death, who when they die all things die with them but let not them shrinke nor be dismaied, whose vertue and fame shall neuer die but liue for euer Wherefore ye worthie men, who are enoblished for your valiantnes and famous for your vertues, let vs with bold minds and good courages giue the onset vpon our enimies, that in vs our noble race & progenie be not stained, but that either by a glorious victorie, or a famous death, we doo atchiue to perpetuall fame and honor"

How Rothorike intreateth for peace and obteineth the same.

CHAP. 10.

ROTHORIKE, when he had well considered with himselfe how the euents of wars are doubtfull and vncerteine, & that as the wiseman saith, "A man of wisedome and vnderstanding is to trie all manner of waies rather than the warres" and also being somewhat timorous to aduenture the battell with strangers, sendeth his messengers by all the waies they best might, to intreat for peace who at length through

through their industrie, and by the mediation of good men, and by Gods goodnesse who prospered the same, obteined the same, and which was concluded in this order. That Dermon Mac Morogh should haue and enioy all Lenster in peace and quietnesse, to him and to his heires, acknowledging Rothorike to be the chéefe king and monarch of all Ireland, and yéelding vnto him that seruice and dutie as vnto him therein apperteined And for the performance hereof, he deliuered his sonne Cunthurus in pledge and for an hostage To whome Rothorike then promised, vpon condition, that the peace and certeine other points obserued, he would giue his daughter vnto him in mariage These things being openlie published, each partie swore the one to the other, for the performance and kéeping of the same And yet whatsoeuer the vtter shew, it was secretlie agréed betwéene them, that Dermon Mac Morogh, when and assoone as he had quietlie setled Lenster in good order, he should returne and send home all the English people, as also in the meane time should not procure anie more to come ouer.

Of the comming of Maurice Fitzgerald into Ireland of the yeelding vp of Dublin to Dermon Mac Morogh, and of the warres betweene the two princes of Conagh and of Limericke

CHAP 11

THESE things thus doone & performed, and fortune seeming with a more fauorable countenance to smile vpon them, behold Maurice Fitzgerald, of whom we spake before, who was the halfe brother by the mothers side to Robert Fitzstephans, arriued at Wexford in two ships, hauing in his companie (which he brought) ten gentlemen of seruice, thirtie horssemen, and of archers and footmen about one hundred A man he was both honest and wise, and for his truth and valiantnesse verie noble and famous He was a man of his word, and constant of mind, and therewithall adorned with a certeine kind of womanlie shamefastnesse Mac Morogh being verie glad of this new repaire, as also much animated and incouraged therewith, beginneth to thinke vpon old sores, and to call to remembrance the great iniuries and wrongs which the citizens of Dublin had in times past doone both vnto his father and to himselfe, and minding to be reuenged thereof, bendeth his force, and marcheth with his whole armie to besiege the citie, but left Fitzstephans behind, who was then building a hold or castell vpon a certeine rockie hill called the (1) Carrike, about two miles from Wexford, which place although it were verie strong of it selfe, yet by industrie and labour it was made much stronger Morice Fitzgerald, with all the force and companie of the Englishmen, accompanied and attended Mac Morogh, who was his guide, and conducted him vnto Dublin Assoone as they were entred within the borders and confines of the territorie of Dublin they foorthwith burned, spoiled, and wasted the same, and the whole countrie thereto adioining The citizens of Dublin séeing and considering the same, began to quaile, and their hearts fainted, and doo seeke and intreat for peace, and hauing obteined the same, did sweare fealtie, and gaue in hostages for the true and firme kéeping of the same In this meane time there fell a great contention and quarell betwéene Rothorike of Connagh and Donald prince of Limereke And assoone as Rothorike was with all his force entered into the countrie of Limericke, Dermon Mac Morogh sent foorthwith Robert Fitzstephans with all his power, to aid and helpe the said Donald for he was Dermons sonne in law, by whose means he gat the victorie, and Rothorike with shame was driuen to retire out of the countrie, and to returne to his owne home and left the cheefrie which he demanded

In

In these and all other like seruices, Robert Barrie and Merlerius carried the best praise and commendations At this time was séene a woman who had a great beard, and a man vpon hir backe, as a horsse, of whom I haue alreadie spoken in my topographie.

(1) The said Carricke (as is written) is distant from the towne of Wexford about two English miles, and standeth vpon a high rocke, and is inuironed on two sides with the riuer which floweth to Wexford towne, and it is verie déepe and nauigable the other two sides are vpon the maine land, which is a verie fertile soile, and in height almost equall with the castell It was at the first made but of rods and turffes, according to the maner in those daies; but since builded with stone, and was the strongest fort then in those parts of the land. but being a place not altogither sufficient for a prince, and yet it was thought too good and strong for a subiect, it was pulled downe, defaced and raced, and so dooth still remaine.

Dermon Mac Morogh sendeth for the earle Richard, who foorthwith maketh great preparation for his comming.

CHAP. 12.

MAC Morogh, being by meanes of his good successe well quieted and satisfied, bethinketh himselfe now of greater matters, and deuiseth how and by what means he might recouer his old and ancient rights, as also purchase all Connagh to his subiection And herein he vsed a secret conference with Fitzstephans and Fitzgerald, vnto whome he vttereth and discouereth all his whole mind and intent who foorthwith gaue his answer that his deuise was verie easilie to be compassed, if he could get a greater supplie and aid of Englishmen Wherevpon he made most earnest requests vnto them, both for the procuring of their kinsmen and countriemen, as also for the furthering to effect his purpose and deuise And that he might the better persuade them herevnto, he offereth to either one of them his daughter and heire in marriage with the inheritance of his kingdome but they both being alreadie married, refused the offer And at length after much talke they thus concluded, that he should with all spéed send his messengers with his letters vnto the earle Richard, of whom we spake before, and vnto whome he the said Mac Morogh at his being at or about Bristow, had promised his daughter to wife, which letters were as followeth "Dermon Mac Morogh prince of Leinster, to Richard earle of Chepstone, and sonne of Gilbert the earle sendeth gréeting If you doo well consider and marke the time as we doo which are in distresse, then we doo not complaine without cause nor out of time for we haue alreadie seene the (1) storkes and swallows, as also the summer birds are come, and with the westerlie winds are gone againe, we haue long looked and wished for your comming, and albeit the winds haue béene at east and easterlie, yet hitherto you are not come vnto vs wherefore now linger no longer, but hasten your selfe hither with spéed, that it may thereby appeare not want of good will, nor forgetfulnesse of promise, but the iniurie of time hath béene hitherto the cause of your long staie All Leinster is alreadie wholie yéelded vnto vs and if you will speedilie come away with some strong companie and force, we doubt not but that the other foure portions will be reconciled and adioined to this the first portion Your comming therefore the more spéedie it is, the more gratefull, the more hastie, the more ioifull, and the sooner, the better welcome and then our mislike of your long lingering shall be recompensed

Mac Moroghs letter to earle Richard

pensed by your soone comming, for friéndship & good will is recouered and nourished by mutual offices, and by benefits it groweth to a more assurednesse." When earle Richard had read these letters, he taketh aduise with his friends, and taking some comfort and stomach of the good successe of Fitzstephans, whereof he was at the first both fearefull and doubtfull, fullie determineth to bend his whole force and power to follow this seruice and hostings This earle was a man of a verie noble parentage, and descended of verie honorable ancestors; but yet more famous in name, than rich in purse, more noble in blood, than endowed with wit, and greater in hope of succession, than rich in possessions. Well, he thought long yer he could wend himselfe ouer into Ireland, and therefore to compasse the same to good effect, maketh his repaire to king Henrie the second, and most humblie praieth and beséecheth him that he will either restore him to such possessions, as by inheritance did appertetne vnto him, or else to grant him the libertie to trie and séeke fortune in some other forren countrie and nation.

(1) The storke and the swallow are named *Aues semestres,* or the halfe yeares birds for they come at the spring, and depart againe awaie at the autumne or fall of the leafe, for in the winter they are not séene. And by this Mac Morogh alludeth and meaneth that he hath awaited that whole halfe yeare for the earles comming whose promise was, that in the spring of the yeare past he would haue come.

Of the arriuall of Reimond le grosse into Ireland, and of the fight which he had against the Waterford men at Dundorogh.

CHAP 13.

THE king hauing heard the earles requests, bethought himselfe a while thereof but in the end he alowed not of the one, nor granted the other, but fed him still with good spéeches, and nourished him with faire words, commending his noble mind, that he would aduenture so honorable an enterprise And in words the king seemed to giue him leaue to follow his deuise, but to saie the truth, it was rather in game than in earnest, for the king minded nothing lesse But the earle taking the aduantage of the kings words, and accepting the same for a sufficient leaue and licence, returneth home And the same being the winter season & verie vnfit to trauell into forren nations in martiall affaires, dooth now make preparation of all things fit to serue when time should require. And assoone as the winter was past, he sendeth ouer before him into Ireland, a gentleman of his owne houshold and familie named Reimond le grosse who had with him ten gentlemen of seruice, and three score and ten archers well appointed, and taking shipping about the kalends of Maie, then landed at the rocke of (1) Dundonolfe, which lieth south from Wexford, and about foure miles east from Waterford and there they cast a trench, and builded a little castell or hold, with turffes and wattell This Reimond was nephue to Robert Fitzstephans and to Maurice Fitzgerald, being the sonne vnto their elder brother named William, and was verie valiant, of great courage, and well expert in the warres and in all martiall affaires The citizens of Waterford, and Omolaghlin Ofelin, being aduertised of this their arriuall, and nothing liking the neighborhood of such strangers, take counsell togither what were best to be doone and finding it most necessarie and néedfull to withstand at the beginning, they doo conclude and determine to giue the onset vpon them, and being about thrée

thrée thousand men they take botes, and rowe downe the riuer of the Sure (which fléeteth fast by the wals of Waterford on the east, and diuideth Leinster from Mounster) and so came to the place where Reimond and his companie were, where they landed and set their men in order for the assaults, and marched boldlie to the ditches of Reimonds fortresse or castell but then it appeered how valiantnes can neuer be hid, lustie courage be daunted, nor yet prowesse or worthines be blemished For Reimond and his companie, although they were but few in number, and too weake to incounter with so great a companie as their aduersaries were yet being of couragious minds & lustie stomachs, went out to méet with their enimies, but when they saw that their small number was not sufficient nor able in the plaines to abide and indure the force of so great a multitude, they retired to their fort. The enimies thinking then to discomfit and cleane to ouerthrow them, followed and pursued them so shortlie, that the Englishmen were no sooner in at the gates, but the Irishmen were also at their heeles, and some of them within the gate. Which thing when Reimond saw, and considering also with himselfe what a distresse and perill he and all his were in, suddenlie turneth backe his face vpon his enimies, and the first of them which entred, he ranne him thorough with his sword (or as some saie claue his head asunder) and then with a lowd voice cried out to his companie to be of a good comfort Who forthwith as they turned and stood most manfullie to their defense so their enimies also being dismaied and afraid at the death of that one man, they all fled and ranne awaie and then they which in this doubtfull chance of fight, were thought should be vanquished and cleane ouerthrowne, suddenlie became to be the victors and conquerors. And these sharpelie then pursued their enimies, who were scattered abroad in the plaines and out of araie, that in a verie short time and space they slue aboue fiue hundred persons and being wearie with killing, they cast a great number of those whome they had taken prisoners headlong from the rocks into the sea, and so drowned them In this fight and seruice a gentleman named William Ferand did most valiantlie acquit himselfe. For albeit he were but of a weake bodie, yet was he of a verie stout stomach & courage he was diseased and sicke of the leprosie, and therefore desirous rather to die valiantlie, than to liue in miserie and for that cause would and did aduenture himselfe in places where most perill and danger was and séemed to be, thinking it good with a glorious death to preuent the gréefe and lothsomnesse of a gréeuous disease

Thus fell the pride of Waterford, thus decaied their strength and force, and thus began the ruine and ouerthrow of that citie, which as it bred a great hope and consolation to the Englishmen, so was it the cause of a great desperation and terror to the enimies It was a strange matter and neuer heard of before in those parties, that so great a slaughter should be made by so small a number neuerthelesse by euill counsell and too much crueltie, the Englishmen abused their good successe and fortune For hauing gotten the victorie, they saued seuentie of the best citizens, whom they kept prisoners, and for the ransome or redemption of these, they might haue had either the citie of Waterford yelded & surrendred vnto them, or such a masse of monie as they would themselues But Heruie of Mount Moris (who came ouer with thrée gentlemen of seruice, and ioined with his countrimen and Reimonds) being both of contrarie minds, striued the one with the other, what were best to be doone heerein.

(1) Dundonolfe is a rocke standing in the countie of Waterford vpon the sea side, lieng east from the citie of Waterford about eight English miles, and is from the towne of Wexford about twelue miles, lieng southwards from the same it is now a strong

a strong castell, and apperteining to the ancient house of the Powers of Kilmarthen, & called by the name of Dundorogh

(2) The citie of Waterford or Guaterford, named sometimes (as Ptolomeus writeth) Manapia, is a faire, ancient, and honorable citie, standing vpon the south side of the riuer of Suir, which fléeteth fast by the walles thereof and was first builded by one named Sitaratus, one of the thrée princes which came out of the east parts to inhabit that land It was at the first but a small pile, lieng in forme of a long triangle, but since & of late times inlarged by the citizens & inhabitants of the same It is the chéefest emporium in a manner of all that land, and standeth chéeflie vpon the trade of merchandize, they themselues being not onelie great trauellers into forren nations, but also great resort and dailie concourses of strangers are to it Concerning the gouernement, order, state and seruice of this citie, and of sundrie other things incident to the same, are at large described in the later historie of this land

The oration of Reimond for the deliuerie of the prisoners taken

CHAP 14.

REIMOND being verie desirous that the captiues taken might be deliuered, laboreth by all the waies he could how to compasse the same, & in presence of Herueie maketh these spéeches, and vseth these persuasions to all his companie. "Yée my noble and valiant companions and souldiers, for increase of whose honour, vertue and fortune séeme to contend, let vs now consider what is best to be doone with these our prisoners and captiues For my part I doo not thinke it good, nor yet allow that anie fauour or courtesie should be at all shewed to the enimie But vnderstand you these are no enimies now, but men, no rebels, but such as be vanquished and cleane ouerthrowen, and in standing in defense of their countrie, by euill fortune and a worse destinie they are subdued Their aduentures were honest and their attempts commendable, and therefore they are not to be reputed for théeues, factious persons, traitors, nor yet murtherers They are now brought to that distresse and case, that rather mercie for examples sake is to be shewed, than crueltie to the increasing of their miserie is to be ministred Sucrlie our ancestors in times past (although in déed it be verie hard to be doone) were woont in times of good successe and prosperitie, to temperat their loose minds and vnrulie affections with some one incommoditie or other Wherefore let mercie and pitie, which in a man is most commendable, worke so in vs, that we who haue ouercome others, may also now subdue our owne minds, and conquer our owne affections. for modestie, moderation, and discretion are woont to staie hastie motions, and to stop rash deuises O how commendable and honorable is it to a noble man, that in his greatest triumph and glorie, he counteth it for a sufficient reuenge, that he can reuenge and be wreaked?

"Iulius Cesar, whose conquests were such, his victories so great, and his triumphs so manie, that the whole world was noised therewith, he had not so manie fréends who reioised for the same, but he had manie more enimies who maligned and enuied at him, not onelie in slanderous words and euill reports, but manie also secretlie conspired, deuised, and practised his death and destruction and yet he was so full of pitie, mercie, and compassion, that he neuer commanded nor willed anie to be put to death for the same, sauing onelie one Domitius, whome he had of meere clemencie for his lewdnesse before pardoned, for his wickednesse released, and for

his

his trecherie acquited. And thus as his pitie did much increase h... ...ur, so did it nothing hinder his victories. O how beastlie then and impious is that crueltie, wherin victorie is not ioined with pitie? For it is the part of a right noble and a valiant man, to count them enimies which doo wage the battell, contend and fight for the victorie, but such as be conquered, taken prisoners, and kept in bonds and captiuitie, to take and repute them for men, that hereby fortitude and force may diminish the battell and end the quarrell, as also humanitie may increase loue & make peace. It is therefore a great commendation and more praiseworthie to a noble man in mercie to be bountious, than in victorie to be cruell, for the one lieth onelie in the course of fortune, but the other in vertue: and as it had béene a great increase of our victorie, and an augmentation of honour, if our enimies had béene slaine in the field and ouerthrowen in the battell: so they being now taken and saued, and as it were men returned from rebels to the common societie and fellowship of men, if we should now kill them, it will be to our great shame, dishonor, and reproch for euer. And for so much as by the killing and destroieng of them we shall be neuer the néerer to haue the countrie, nor neuer sooner to be the lords of the land, and yet the ransoming of them verie good for the maintenance of the souldiers, the good fame of vs, and the aduancement of our honour: we must néeds thinke it better to ransome them than to kill them. For as it is requisit and meet, that a souldier in the field fighting in armes, should then thirst for the bloud of his enimies, trie the force of his sword, and valiantlie stand to his tackle for victorie: so when the fight is ended, the wars are ceassed, & the armor laid downe, and all fiercenes of hostilitie set apart, then in a noble man must humanitie take place, pitie must be shewed, and courtesie must be extended."

The oration or speech which Herueie made.

CHAP. 15.

WHEN Reimond had ended his speech, & the whole companie being in a muttering, and as it were men well pleased and verie well allowing his mind and opinion: then Herueie stood vp and spake to them all in this maner. "Reimond hath verie exquisitlie discoursed with vs of pitie and mercie, and in set speeches vttering his eloquence, hath shewed his mind and declared his opinion, persuading and inducing vs to beléeue, that a strange land were to be conquered sooner by mercie and fond pitie than by sword and fire. But I praie you, can there be a worsse waie than so to thinke? Did Iulius Cesar or Alexander of Macedonie by such means or in such order conquer the whole world? Did the nations from out of all places run to submit themselues vnder their yoke and empire, in respect of their pitie & mercie, & not rather compelled so to doo for feare & perforce? For people, whiles they are yet proud and rebellious, they are (all pitie and mercie set apart) by all manner of waies and means to be subdued: but when they are once brought into subiection and bondage, and redie to serue and obeie, then they are with all courtesie to be intreated and dealt withall: so that the state of the gouernment may be in safetie and out of danger. Herein and in this point must pitie be vsed, but in the other seueritie or rather crueltie is more necessarie: here clemencie is to be shewed, but in the other rigour without fauour is to be exhibited and vsed. Reimond persuadeth that mercie is to be extended, as vpon a people alreadie subdued and subiected, or as though the enimies were so few and of so small a number, as against whome no valiant seruice nor chiualrie can be exploited,

exploited, and yet they redie to come with vs whereby our force may be increased, and our power augmented But alas! Doo not we sée how that the whole nation and people of Ireland are wholie bent, and not without cause altogither conspired against vs?

"Suerlie me thinketh Reimond is contrarie vnto himselfe, for why, his comming hither was not to dispute of pitie, nor to reason of mercie, but to conquer the nation and to subdue the people O what an example of impious pitie were it then, to neglect our owne safetie, and to haue remorse and compassion vpon others distresses? Moreouer, we haue here in the fields, and in armour more enimies than friends, we are in the middle of perils and dangers, our enimies being round about vs in euerie place and shall we thinke this to be nothing, but that we must be also in the like distresse and danger among our selues Round about vs our enimies are infinit, and within our selues some there be which practise our destruction. And if it should happen that our captiues and prisoners should escape and breake loose out of their bonds, which are but verie weake and slender, no doubt they will foorthwith take our owne armours and weapons against vs Well well, the mouse is in the cupbord, the fire is in the lap, and the serpent is in the bosome, the enimie is at hand readie to oppresse his aduersarie, and the gest is in place with small courtesie to requit his host And I praie you dooth not Reimond execute that in his facts and doongs, which he denieth in his words? Are not his spéeches contrarie to his deeds? Let him answer me to this If our enimies when they come in good araie and well appointed to giue the onset, and to wage the battell against vs, if they should happen to haue the victorie and the ouerhand ouer vs, would they deale in pitie & mercie? Would they grant vs our liues? Would they put vs to ransome? Tush what need manie words when the déeds are apparant? Our victorie is to be so vsed, that the destruction of these few may be a terror to manie wherby all others and this wild and rebellious nation may take an example, and beware how they meddle and incounter with vs Of two things we are to make choise of one, for either we must valiantlie and couragiouslie stand to performe what we haue taken in hand, and all fond pitie set aside, boldlie and stoutlie to ouerthrow and vanquish this rebellious and stubborne people or (if we shall after the mind and opinion of Reimond altogither be pitifull and full of mercie) we must hoise vp our sailes and returne home, leauing both the countrie and our patrimonie to this miserable and wretched people" Herueies opinion was best liked, and the whole companie allowed his iudgement, wherevpon the captiues (as men condemned) were brought to the rockes, and after their lims were broken, they were cast headlong into the seas, and so drowned.

The comming ouer of Richard Strangbow earle of Chepstow into Ireland, and of the taking of the citie of Waterford.

CHAP. 16.

IN this meane time Richard the earle, hauing prouided and made all things in readinesse fit for so great an enterprise, tooke his iournie, and came through Wales to S. Dauids: and still as he went he tooke vp all the best chosen and piked men that he could get. And hauing all things in place and in a readinesse méet and necessarie for such a voiage, he went to Milford hauen, and hauing a good wind tooke shipping and came to Waterford, in the kalends of September on the vigill

 of

of saint Bartholomew, and had with him about two hundred gentlemen of good seruice, and a thousand others Then was fulfilled Celidons prophesie, which was, that "A little firebrand shall go before a great fire, and as the sparkels inkindle the small wood, so shall the same set the great wood a fire" Likewise was fulfilled the saieng of Merlin, "A great forerunner of a greater follower shall come, and he shall tread downe the heads of Desmond and Leinster, and the waies before opened & made readie he shall inlarge." Reimond being aduertised of the earles arriuall, went the next morrow vnto him with great ioy, hauing with him in his companie fortie gentlemen of seruice And on the morrow vpon saint Bartholomews daie, being tuesdaie, they displaied their banners, and in good araie they marched to the wals of the citie, being fullie bent and determined to giue the assault the citizens & such others as had escaped at Dundorogh mantullie defending themselues, and giuing them two repulses Reimond who by the consent and assent of the whole armie was chosen and made generall of the field, and tribune of the host, hauing espied a little house of timber standing halfe vpon posts without the wals, called his men togither, and incouraged them to giue a new assault at that (1) place And hauing hewed downe the posts wherevpon the house stood, the same fell downe togither with a peece of the towne wall, and then a waie being thus opened, they entred into the citie, and killed the people in the streets without pitie or mercie, leauing them lieng in great heaps, and thus with bloodie hands they obteined a bloodie victorie. In the tower called (2) Reinolds tower they tooke two muitherers prisoners, whom they vnarmed and killed, also they tooke there Reinold, and Machlathlen Ophelan prince of the Decies: but these were saued by meanes of the comming and suite of Mac Morogh, who was also come thither with Maurice Fitzgerald and Robert Fitzstephans. And when they had set the citie and all other their things in good order, Mac Morogh gaue his daughter Eua, whom he had then brought thither with him, to be maried to the earle according to the first pact and couenant, and then the mariage solemnized and all things set in order, they displaid their baners & marched towards Dublin

Prophesies of Celidon and Merlin fulfilled

(1) In the verie place of the assault is now builded a strong fort and blockehouse, which is verie well furnished and appointed with ordinance and shot It is in the verie east angle or point of the walles of the citie: and within on the south side the walles dooth it appeere how the same was burned by the Englishmen at this their entrie

(2) The Reinolds tower is a little tower in the wall of the old citie, and is next or verie neere adioining to a late monasterie or friers there. it is a verie slender thing, and not worthie of any report, sauing that the author dooth alledge it as a fort in those daies vsed for a defense.

The besieging and taking of the citie of Dublin.

CHAP. 17.

DERMON being aduertised, and hauing perfect aduertisement that they of Dublin had procured & flocked all or the most part of the land to come to aid, helpe and to defend them; and that they had raied all the waies, passages and streicts about the citie, whereby no man could passe that waie, he left all those waies, and passing through the mounteines of Glundoloch, he brought his whole armie safe to (1) Dublin. And such was his mortall hatred towards the Dublians, that

that he could not forget the iniuries doon to himselfe, and the shamefull reproch doone to his father For his father being on a time at Dublin, and there sitting at the doore of a certein ancient man of the citie, they did not onelie there murther him; but for a further satisfieng of their malice, they cast him and buried him with a dog and therefore aboue all others he most mortallie hated them The citizens much mistrusting themselues, they send messengers to intreate for peace, and in the end by the mediation and meanes of Laurence then the archbishop of Dublin, a parlée and a treatie was obteined but whiles the old and ancient men were talking of peace, the yonger sort were busie in weapons For Remond and Miles of Cogan, two lustie yoong gentlemen, but more desirous to fight vnder Mars in the fields than to sit in councell vnder Iupiter; and more willing to purchase honor in the warres, than gaine in peace. They with a companie of lustie yoong gentlemen suddenlie ran to the walles, & giuing the assalt, brake in, entred the citie and obteined the victorie, making no small slaughter of their enimies but yet the greater number of them, with Hasculphus their captein, escaped awaie with such riches & iewels as they had, and recouered themselues vnto certeine ships which laie there, & so sailed to the north Ilands At this time there happened two strange miracles in the same citie, the one was of a crosse or a rood which the citizens minding to haue caried with them, was not nor would be remooued, the other was of a péece of monie which was offered to the same rood twise, & euer it returned backe againe, as you may sée more therof in our topographie When the earle had spent a few daies in the citie, about setting and setling the same in good order, he left the same to the charge and gouernance of Miles Cogan but he himselfe by the persuasion of Mac Morogh (who sought by all the waies he could, how to be reuenged vpon Ororike king of Meth) inuaded the borders of Meth, and wasted, spoiled, and destroied the same All Meth being in the end wasted by the sword and fire, Rothorike king of Connagh thought with himself what might hereof befall vnto him, bicause his neighbors house being set on fire, his was next to the like perill. he sent his messengers vnto Dermon Mac Morogh with this message "Contrarie to the order of the peace, thou hast procured, called, and flocked into this land a great multitude and number of strangers, and as long as thou didst staie and kéepe thy selfe within thy owne countrie of Leinster, we bare therwith, and were contented But forsomuch as now not caring for thy oth, nor regarding the safetie of thy hostages, thou hast so fondlie & lewdlie passed thy bounds. I am to require thee, that thou doo retire and withdraw these excurses of strangers; or else without faile I will cut off thy sonnes head, & send it thée." Mac Morogh when he heard this message, full stoutlie answered, and said he would not giue ouer that which he had begun, nor desist from his enterprise, vntill he subdued all Connagh his ancient inheritance, as also he had recouered the monarchie of all Ireland. Rothorike being aduertised of this answer, was somwhat warmed and offended therwith, & forthwith in his rage commanded Mac Moroghs sonne, who was his pledge, to be beheaded.

Two strange miracles

(1) Dublin is the oldest and ancientest citie in all Ireland, and was builded by one Amelaus, the eldest of three brethren named Ostmen or Easterlings. which came first out of Norwaie, or (as some write) out of Normandie, and did inhabit the land. It was first named Aghalia, that is, the towne of hurdels, for it standeth somewhat low and in a marish ground. and bicause when the same was first builded, the laborers were woont and did go vpon hurdels, it tooke the name thereof It was also called Doolin, which is to saie blacke water, for of that name is a certeine brooke, fleeting not farre out of the towne, but now is called Dublin or Diuelin; it standeth vpon the riuer named Anelipius or the Liffer, and it is a port towne,

being the chéefest citie and emporium of all that land. It is walled with stone round about, & at the east part therof is a verie old castle, builded first by Henrie Londers archbishop of Dublin, about the yéere 1212, which is now the quéenes castell, & wherein the lord deputie of that land most commonlie lieth, as also wherein the courts for the common law at the vsuall terms are kept. The citie it selfe stands most on trade of merchandize, & is by that means of good wealth. The inhabitants are méere Englishmen, but of Ireland birth. The gouernment thereof is vnder a maior and two shiriffes. And as concerning the order, gouernement, state, policies, and good seruices of the same, I shall more at large declare in my particular historie of this land.

The councell or synod kept at Armagh.

CHAP. 18.

THESE things thus ended & compleated, there was a synod or councell of all the clergie called and assembled at Armagh: there to intreat and examine what should be the causes and reasons, why & wherefore the realme was thus plagued by the resort and repaire of strangers in among them. At length it was fullie agreed, and euerie mans opinion was, that it was Gods iust plague for the sinnes of the people, and speciallie bicause they vsed to buie Englishmen of merchants and pirats, and (contrarie to all equitie or reason) did make bondslaues of them: and God now to auenge and acquit this their iniquitie, plagued them with the like, and hath set these Englishmen & strangers to reduce them now into the like slauerie and bondage. For the Englishmen, when their realme was at rest and peace, and their land in quiet estate, and they not in anie distresse, want, or penurie, their children and kinsmen were sold and made bondslaues in Ireland. And therefore it was most like, that God for the sin of the people would & did laie the like plague vpon the Irish people. It was therefore decreed by the said councell, and concluded by that synod, that all the Englishmen within that land, wheresoeuer they were, in bondage or captiuitie, should be manumissed, set frée and at libertie.

The proclamation of king Henrie the second against the earle, and of the sending of Reimond to the king.

CHAP 19.

WHEN tidings was caried abrode of the good successe which the Englishmen had in Ireland, & the news the further it went, the more it increased, and the king being aduertised that the earle had not onlie recouered Leinster, but had also conquered sundrie other territories, whereunto he had no title by the right of his wife, did set foorth his proclamation, forbidding and inhibiting that from thensefoorth no ship from out of any place, vnder his dominion, should passe or traffike into Ireland: and that all maner of his subiects which were within that realme, should returne from thense into England before Easter then next following, vpon paine of forfeiture of all their lands, as also to be banished men for euer. The earle when he saw him selfe in this distres, being in perill to lose his friends, and in hazard to want his necessaries, taketh aduise and counsell what were best

to

to be doone At length it was agreed and concluded, that Reimond should be sent ouer to the king then being in Aquitaine, with letters to this effect "My right honourable lord, I came into this land with your leaue and fauour (as I remember) for the aiding and helping of your seruant Dermon Mac Morogh And whatsoeuer I haue gotten and purchased, either by him or by anie others, as I confesse and acknowledge the same from and by meanes of your gratious goodnesse. so shall the same still rest and remaine at your deuotion and commandement"

The departure of Reimond to the king, and the death of Dermon Mac Morogh.

CHAP 20.

REIMOND (according to the order taken, and commandement giuen to him) made his repaire with all diligence to the king, & hauing deliuered his letters did await for his answer But the king being in some dislike with the earle, and not fauourable allowing his successe, differred the time, and lingered to giue anie answer About this time (1) Thomas the archbishop of Canturburie was murthered or slaine, and the yeare following about the kalends of Maie, Dermon Mac Morogh, being of a good age, and well striken in yéeres died, and was buried at Fernes

(1) The Romish or popish church make much a doo about this man, affirming him to be a man of much vertue and holinesse, and that he was martyred for the defending of the liberties of holie church, and for this cause the pope canonized him to be a saint But who so list to peruse and examine the course of the English histories, shall find that he was a froward and obstinat traitor against his master & soueraigne king and prince as amongst other writers it appeareth in the booke of the Acts and Monuments of Iohn Fox And forsomuch as the course of this chapter tendeth wholie in extolling of him, I haue omitted the same, and leaue to trouble the reader therewith.

The ouerthrow giuen to Hasculphus and the Easterlings or Norwaiemen at Dublin.

CHAP 21

AT this time about the feast of Pentecost or Whitsuntide, Hasculphus, who was sometime the chiefe ruler of Dublin, sought by all the waies he could how he might be reuenged for the reproch and shame which he had receiued when the citie of Dublin was taken, and he then driuen to flie to his ship, and to saue himselfe This man had beene in Norwaie, and in the north Ilands to séeke for some helpe and aid, and hauing obteined the same he came with threescore ships well appointed, and full fraughted with lustie men of warre vnto the coasts of (1) Dublin, minding to assaile the citie, and hoping to recouer the same And without anie delaiengs he landed and vnshipped his men, who were guided and conducted vnder a capteine named John Wood or John Mad, for so the word Wood meaneth They were all mightie men of warre, and well appointed after the Danish maner, being harnessed with good brigandines, iacks, and shirts of male, their shields, bucklers, and targets were round, and coloured red, and bound about with iron and as they were in armor, so in minds also they were as iron strong and mightie.

These

These men being set in battell araie, and in good order, doo march onwards towards the east gate of the citie of Dublin, there minding to giue th assault, and with force to make entrie. Miles Cogan then warden of the citie, a man verie valiant and lustie, although his men and people were verie few, and as it were but a handfull in respect of the others yet boldlie giueth the aduenture and onset vpon his enimies but when he saw his owne small number not to be able to resist nor withstand so great force and they still pressing & inforcing vpon him, he was driuen to retire backe with all his companie, and with the losse of manie of his men, and of them one being verie well armed, yet was his thigh cut oft cleane at a stroke with a Galloglasse axe But Richard Cogan brother vnto Miles, vnderstanding how hardlie the matter passed and had sped with his brother, suddenlie and secretlie with a few men issueth out at the south posterne or gate of the citie, and stealing vpon the backs of his enimies, maketh a great shout, and therewith sharplie giueth the onset vpon them At which sudden chance they were so dismaied, that albeit some fighting before, and some behind, the case was doubtfull, & the euent vncerteine yet at length they fled and ran awaie, and the most part of them were slaine, and namelie John Wood, whom with others John of Ridensford tooke and killed. Hasculphus fleeing to his ships was so sharpelie pursued, that vpon the sands he was taken, but saued, and for the greater honour of the victorie was caried backe aliue into the citie as a captiue, where he was sometime the chiefe ruler and gouernour. and there hée was kept till he should compound for his ransome. And then he being brought and presented to Miles Cogan, in the open sight and audience of all the people, and fretting much for this euill fortune and ouerthrow, suddenlie and in great rage brake out into these speeches, saieng. "We are come hither now but a small companie, and a few of vs, and these are but the beginings of our aduentures, but if God send me life, you shall sée greater matters insue and follow'. Miles Cogan when he heard these words (for in the toong standeth both life and death, the lord abhorreth the proud heart, and verie badlie dooth he ease his greefe which augmenteth his sorrow) commanded him to be beheaded And so the life to him before courteouslie granted, he by his fondnesse did foolishlie lose it.

(1) The port or hauen of Dublin is a barred hauen, and no great ships doo come to the towne it selfe but at a spring or high water, and therefore they doo lie in a certeine rode without the barre, which is about foure or fiue miles from the citie, and the same is called Ringwood, and from thence to Holie hed in Wales is counted the shortest cut betwéene England and Ireland.

Rothorike prince of Connagh and Gotred king of Man do besiege the citie of Dublin.

CHAP 22.

AFTER this, the Irishmen perceiuing that by reason of the kings late proclamation, the earles men and vittels did wast, decaie, and consume for want of their woonted supplies from out of England all their princes assembled themselues, and doo agree with all their power and force to besiege the citie of Dublin, being procured therevnto by Laurence then archbishop there, who for the zeale and loue of his countrie, did verie earnestlie trauell herein and ioining with Rothorike king of Connagh, they sent their letters to Gotred king of the Ile of Man, and to all others the princes of the Ilands, making earnest requests, vsing their persuasions, and promising liberall rewards, if they would come to helpe and aid them to besiege Dublin,

Dublin, they on the water, and the other at land: who were easilie to be persuaded thervnto, and forthwith yéelded to these requests, not onelie for the desire of gaines offered: but especiallie, because they doubted, and were afraid of the Englishmen, who hauing dailie good successe they feared least they in time would giue the onset on them, and make a conquest ouer their possessions. And therfore they foorthwith made themselues readie, and prepared their ships accordinglie. And as soone as the next good wind serued, they came in thirtie ships of warre, verie well appointed, and arriued into the hauen of Anelifle, or port of Dublin: whose comming was verie thankfull and gratefull. For whie? Whose helps are best liked when men in their affaires haue those to ioine with them which be or feare to be in the like perils and dangers? But the earle and his companie, who had béene shut vp now two moneths within the citie, and whose vittels failed, and were almost consumed by reason that vpon the kings commandement a restraint was made (and therefore none could be brought vnto them out of England) were in a great dumpe and perplexitie, and in a maner were at their wits end, and wist not what to doo. And in this their case see the course and nature of fortune, who when she frowneth, sendeth not one euill alone, but heapeth mischéefe vpon mischéefe, and trouble vpon trouble. For behold Donald Mac Dermon came from out of the borders of Kencile, & brought news that the men of Wexford & of Kencile to the number of thrée thousand persons had beseéged Robert Fitzstephans and his few men in his castell of the Karecke, and unlesse they did helpe and rescue him within thrée daies it would be too late, for they should and would else be taken. At this time there was with the earle within the citie Maurice Fitzgerald, and his cosine Reimond, who was latelie returned from the court, and these were not onelie now troubled in respect of their owne cause, but for the distres of others, and speciallie Maurice Fitzgerald, who tenderlie tooke and was gréeued with the distressed state of his brother Robert Fitzstephans, and of his wife and children, that they being in the middle of their enimies, should be in so weake a hold not able to kéepe out such a companie: and so rising vp maketh this spéech to the earle, and to such as were about him, as followeth.

The oration of Maurice Fitzgerald.

CHAP. 23.

"YE worthie men, we came not hither, nor were we called into this countrie to be idle, nor to liue deliciouslie: but to trie fortune, and to séeke aduentures. We stood somtimes vpon the top of the wheele, and the game was on our side; but now the whéele is turned, & we cast downe: and yet no doubt she will turne againe, and we shall be on the top. For such is the mutabilitie of fortune, & such is the uncerteine state & course of this world, that prosperitie and aduersitie doo interchangeablie, and by course the one follow the other. After daie commeth the night, and when the night is passed, the daie returneth againe. The sun riseth, and when he hath spred his beames all the daie time, then he commeth to his fall: and as soone as the night is past, he is againe come and returned to his rising againe. We who before this haue made great triumphs, & haue had fortune at will, are now shut vp on euerie side by our enimies. We be destitute of vittels, and can haue no reléefe neither by land nor yet by sea: our fréends cannot helpe vs, and our enimies readie to deuoure vs. Likewise Fitzstephans, whose valiantnesse and noble enterprise hath made waie vnto vs into this Iland, he now is also shut

shut vp in a weake hold and feeble place, too weake and slender to hold and kéepe out so great a force. Why then doo we tarie? And wherefore doo we so linger? Is there anie hope of reléefe from home? No no, the matter is otherwise, and we in woorse case. For as we be odious and hatefull to the Irishmen, euen so we now are reputed: for Irishmen are become hatefull to our owne nation and countrie, and so are we odious both to the one and to the other. Wherfore forsomuch as fortune fauoreth the forward, and helpeth the bold, let vs not longer delaie the matter, nor like sluggards lie still: but whiles we are yet lustie, and our vittels not all spent, let vs giue the onset vpon our enimies: for though we be but few in number in respect of them, yet if we will be of valiant minds and lustie courages, as we were woont to be, we may happilie haue the victorie and conquest of these naked wretches and vnarmed people." These spéeches he vsed as the sicke man is woont to doo, who in hope of recouerie of his health, dooth manie times beare out a good countenance, and dissemble his inward greefe and heauinesse. When he had fullie ended his talke and spoken his mind, Reimond, who was also in the like anguish and heauinesse spake thus.

The oration of Reimond.

CHAP. 24.

"YE renowmed, and worthie, & noble men, whose fame for valiantnesse and chiualrie is carried and spread beyond and through the ocean seas: we are now to looke well vnto our selues, and to haue good regard to our honor and credit. You haue heard how grauelie my vncle Maurice hath declared, how pithilie he hath aduised, and how prudentlie he hath counselled vs what we shall doo in this our distresse and present necessitie. Wherfore we are well to consider hereof, & to determine and resolue our selues what we will doo. The time is short, the perils imminent, and the dangers great, and therefore no delaies are now to be vsed. It is no time now to sit in long councels, nor to spend much time in speeches, but in present perils we must vse present remedies. Ye sée the enimies both at sea and land round about vs, and no waie is there to escape, but we must either giue the aduenture vpon them like men, or die here like beasts: for our vittels faile vs, and our prouision waxeth scant & short, and we know not how to renew the same. And how little comfort we are to looke for out of England, and what small helpe we shall haue from the king, I haue alreadie at large declared vnto you. I know his excellencie dispraiseth not our actiuities, but yet he fauoreth not our successes: he discommendeth not our valiantnesse, but yet enuieth at our glorie: in words he reporteth well of our seruices, but he yet secretlie hindereth the same: he feareth that which we meane not, and doubteth of that which we thinke not. To trust therefore vnto them, who care not for vs, to looke for helpe from them, who mind not anie, and to wait for reléefe where none is meant, it were but a meere follie, and a lost labor on our parts, and in the end like to returne to our owne shame, reproch, & confusion. Wherefore being out of all hope of anie further helpe or supplie; and out of all doubt of anie further comfort or reléefe: let vs as becommeth noble, lustie, and valiant men, trie the course of fortune, and prooue the force of the enimie. Let it appeere vnto them as it is knowen vnto vs, of what race we came, and from whom we descended. Camber (as it is well knowen) the first particular king of Cambria our natiue countrie, was our ancestor, and he the sonne of that noble Brutus, the first and sole monarch of all England, whose ancestor

ancestor was Tros the founder of the most famous citie of Troie, and he descended from Dardanus the sonne of Jupiter, from whom is deriued vnto vs not onlie the stemme of ancient nobilitie, but also a certeine naturall inclination of valiant minds, & couragious stomachs, bent to follow all exploits in prowesse and chiualrie, and wherein all our ancestors haue beene verie skilfull and expert And shall we now like sluggards degenerate from so noble a race, and like a sort of cowards be afraid of these naked and vnarmed rascals, in whome is no valor of knowledge nor experience in armes? Shall such a rabble of sauages pinne vs vp within the walles of this little Dublin, and make vs afraid of them, when in times past all the princes of Gréece kept warres for ten yeares & od moneths continuallie against our ancestors in the famous citie of Troie, and could not preuaile against them, vntill they vsed treasons and practised treacheries, which bred vnto them a more infamous victorie than a glorious triumph? Shall the honor of our ancestors be withered by our sluggishnesse, and the glorie of their prowesse be buried in our cowardnesse? Shall we be afraid of a few, and vnarmed, when they withstood infinit multitudes of the most worthiest and valiantest personages then in all the world? Let it neuer be said that the bloud of the Troians shall be stained in our pusillanimitie, and receiue reproch in our follie.

"And what though our enimies be neuer so manie, and we in respect of them but a handfull, shall we therefore be afraied, as though victorie stood in multitude, and conquest in great numbers? No no, kings be not so saued nor princes doo so conquer for a few men well disposed and a small number well incouraged, are sufficient to incounter with a greater number, being wretches and sluggards For fortune though she be purtraied to be blind, as one void of right iudgement, and to stand vpon a rolling stone, as being alwaies fléeting and mooueable yet for the most part she helpeth such as be of bold minds and of valiant stomachs If time did serue as matter is full and plentious, I could hereof recite manie yea infinite examples. (1) Thomiris the Scithian queene, did not she with a few hundreds incounter with the great monarch Cyrus, hauing manie thousands, and tooke him and slue him Alexander with a few Macedonians, did not he ouercome Darius the great monarch of the Persians, and take him, his wife, and daughters prisoners, & made a conquest of all Persia? (2) Leonides the Spartan, did not he with six hundred men breake into the campes of the mightie Xerxes, and there slaie fiue thousand of them? Let vs come a little néerer euen to our selues, who haue had in our owne persons, and in this land the like successes, namelie you my right honourable earle at Waterford, and my vncle Fitzstephans at Wexford, and I my selfe at Dundorogh small were our companies, and little was our force in respect of theirs, and yet we few thorough our valiantnesse ouercame and conquered them being manie

"What shall I trouble you with the recitall of examples sith time shall sooner faile than matter want and shall we then giue ouer and be white liuered? Shall we like cowards couer our progenie, our nation, and our selues also, with perpetuall shame and infamie? God forbid My mind then and opinion is, that we doo issue out vpon them, as secretlie and as suddenlie as we maie, and boldlie giue the onset vpon them And forsomuch as Rothorike of Connagh is the generall of the field, in whom lieth the chiefe force, and on whom all the rest doo depend, it shall be best to begin with him, and then if we can giue the ouerthrow vnto him, all the residue will flie, and we shall obteine a glorious victorie. but if we shall fall into their hands and be killed, yet shall we leaue an honourable report and an immortall fame to all our posteritie.' When Reimond had ended his spéeches and finished his oration, euerie one so well liked thereof, as with one consent they gaue ouer, and yéelded to his resolution and opinion

[illegible] lib 1

(1) Cyrus the sonne of Cambises the first monarch of Persia, after that he had subdued all Asia, he minding to doo the like in Scithia did inuade the same. Thomiris being then queene thereof And on a certeine time hauing pitched his tents in a faire and pleasant soile, suddenlie as though he had beene afraied of his enimies he fled, and left his tents full of wines and vittels Which when the queene heard, she sent hir onelie sonne a yoong gentleman with the third part of hir host and armie to follow and pursue Cyrus who when he came to the forsaken tents, and finding there such abundance & plentie of wine and vittels, whereunto the Scithians had not before beene accustomed, they fell so hungerlie to their vittels, and dranke so liberallie of the wines, that they were ouerladen and ouercommed with surfetting. Which when Cyrus heard of, he suddenlie and secretlie in the night came vpon them, and finding them all asléepe, killed them all Thomiris hearing of this, was not so much grieued with sorow for the death of hir sonne, as inflamed with the desire to be reuenged And she likewise faining hir selfe to flie, Cyrus by pursuing of hir was brought into certeine narrow streicts, where she taking the aduantage of him, tooke him, killed him, and slue all his companie, to the number of two thousand insomuch that there was not one left to returne with message to declare the same.

(2) Leonides was king of Sparta or Lacedemonia, who being aduertised that the mightie monarch Xerxes minding to continue the warres with his father Darius had appointed and begun against all Gréece, & that he had made preparation therefore fiue yeares togither, dooth also prepare himselfe to withstand the same. And notwithstanding that Xerxes had in his armie thrée hundred thousand of his owne subiects, and two hundred thousand of strangers yet Leonides hauing gotten Xerxes within the streicts of Thermipolis, and he hauing but foure thousand soldiers gaue the onset vpon the monarch, and fought the battels thrée daies togither with him, and at length gaue him the ouerthrow

How Rothorike of Connagh, and all his whole armie was discomfited

CHAP 25.

IMMEDIATLIE vpon the foresaid persuasions, euerie man with all spéed had made him selfe readie and got on his armor, thinking it too long yer they did bicker with the enimie and being all assembled and in good araie, they diuided them into thrée wings or wards, though in number they were verie few In the first was Reimond with twentie gentlemen and his few soldiers. In the second Miles Cogan with thirtie gentlemen and his other few soldiers. And in the third was the earle and Maurice Fitzgerald with fortie gentlemen and all their soldiors And in euerie ward were some of all the citizens, sauing such as were appointed for the gard and safetie of the citie Thus all things being set in an order, they suddenlie in the morning about nine of the clocke issued out, but not without some contention and controuersie for they striued among themselues, who should haue the fore ward, and giue the onset vpon the enimies, who were in number about thirtie thousand neuerthelesse they in the end agréed and appointed in order how all things should be doone and forthwith issued out and gaue the onset vpon their enimies, who then were out of araie and order, being vnwares of their comming. Reimond among the first being the first was foremost, & gaue the first aduenture, and striking two of his enimies through with his lance or staffe slue them both. Meilerius also and Girald and Alexander the two sonnes of Maurice, although they were in the rereward, yet they were so hot vpon the spurre, and followed in such lustie maner,

maner, that they were as forward as the foremost, and right valiantlie did ouerthrow and kill manie of the enimies

The like valiant minds were in all the whole residue, who now striued & serued all for the best game, and so lustilie they acquitted themselues, that the enimies being afraid, were faine to take their héeles and to run awaie But they still followed and pursued them euen vntill night, still murthering & spoiling them Rothorike the king himselfe trusted so much in the great troops and multitudes of his people, that he thought nothing lesse, than that so small a number as were within, would issue out and giue the onset vpon so manie as were without And therefore taking his pleasure and pastance, he was then a bathing but when he heard how the game went, and how his men were discomfited & the most part fled or flieng awaie, he neither taried for his chamberleine to apparell him, nor for his page to help him but with all the hast and post hast he could, he turneth a faire paire of heeles and runneth awaie and albeit he were verie sharplie pursued, yet (though hardlie) he escaped At night all the companie being returned, they recouered themselues into the citie againe not onelie with the honor of the field, but also with great booties and peeces of vittels, armor, and other trash. Immediatlie also were dispersed the other camps, namelie the archbishops, Machlaghlin, Machelewn, Gillemeholocke and Okencelos, who had all the force of Leinster, sauing a few of Kencile and Wexford and these were incamped on the south side Likewise Ororike of Meth, Okarell of Vriell, Mac Shaghline and Ocadise which were incamped on the north side raised their campes and shifted for themselues On the morrow, all things being set in good order, and good watch appointed for the safe kéeping and custodie of the citie, they march towards Wexford, and take the higher waie by Odrone

The guilefull and treacherous taking of Robert Fitzstephans at the Karecke

CAP. 26.

AFTER this good successe, fortune who cannot continue firme in one state, dooth now change hir course, and interlineth aduersitie with prosperitie For while, there is neither firth time, nor felicitie permanent vpon the earth. For the Wexford men and they of Kencile, forgetting their promise, and nothing regarding their faith which they had before made and assured vnto Robert Fitzstephans, doo now assemble themselues to the number of thrée thousand, and doo march toward the Kareke, there to besiege the same, where Robert Fitzstephans was then who mistrusting & fearing nothing, had but fiue gentlemen and a few archers about him The enimies giue the assalt, & not preuailing at the first, doo renew the same againe and againe but when they saw that all their labours were lost, bicause that Fitzstephans and his companie though they were but a few in number, yet they were verie nimble and verie readie to defend themselues, and especiallie one William Nott, who in this seruice did verie well and worthilie acquit himselfe, they now doo séeke to practise their old subtilties and guiles They leauing therefore to vse force and violence, doo now vnder colour of peace come toward the Kareke and bring with them the bishop of Kildare, the bishop of Wexford, & certeine other religious persons, who brought with them a massebooke, *Corpus Domini*, and certeine relikes and after a few speeches of persuasion had with Fitzstephans, they to compasse their matter, tooke their corporall othes, and swore vpon a booke, that the citie of Dublin was taken and that the earle, Maurice, Reimond, and all the Englishmen were taken and killed, that Rothorike of Connagh, with all the whole power and armie of Connagh & Leinster, was comming towards Wexford for the apprehension of him but for his sake, and for the good will which they bare vnto him, because they had alwaie found him a courteous and a liberall prince, they were come vnto him to conueie him awaie in safetie, and all his ouer into Wales, before the comming of that great multitude, which were his extreame and mortall enimies Fitzstephans giuing credit to this their swearing and auowries, did foorthwith yeeld himselfe, his people, & all that he had vnto them and their custodie but they foorthwith most traitorouslie, of them that thus yéelded into their hands some they killed, some they beat, some they wounded, and some they cast into prison But assoone as newes was brought that Dublin was false, and that the earle was marching towards them, these traitors set the towne on fire and they themselues with bag and baggage and with their prisoners gat them into the Iland Begorie, which they call the holie Iland, and which lieth in the middle of the hauen there.

The description of Robert Fitzstephans.

CHAP 27.

O NOBLE man, the onelie patterne of vertue, and the example of true industrie and labours. who hauing tried the variablenesse of fortune, had tasted more aduersitie than prosperitie! O worthie man, who both in Ireland and in Wales had traced the whole compasse of fortunes wheele, and had endured whatsoeuer good fortune or euill could giue! O Fitzstephans, the verie second an other (1) Marius, for if you doo consider his prosperitie, no man was more fortunate than he: and on the contrarie, if you marke his aduersitie, no man was or could be more miserable. He was of a large and full bodie, his countenance verie comelie and in stature he was somewhat more meane he was bountifull, liberall, and pleasant, but yet sometimes somewhat aboue modestie giuen to wine and women The earle (as is aforesaid) marched with his armie towards Wexford, fast by Odrone, which was a place full of streicts, passes, and bogs, and verie hardlie to be passed through: but yet the whole power, force, and strength of all Leinster came thither, and met him and gaue him the battell, betwéene whom there was a great fight, and manie of the enimies slaine. But the earle with the losse of one onelie yoongman recouered himselfe in safetie to the plaines, and there amongst others, Meilerius shewed himselfe to be a right valiant man

(1) This Marius was named Caius Marius, his father was borne in Arpinum, & from thence came to Rome, and there dwelt, being a poore artificer and handicrafts man, but much relieued by Metellus a noble Roman, in whose house, and vnder whom, both the father and the sonne were seruants. but being giuen altogither to martiall affaires, he became a verie valiant man, and did as good seruice to the citie of Rome as anie before or after him. Africa he conquered, and in his first triumph Iugurtha and his two sonnes were bound in chaines, and carried captiues to Rome before his chariot The Cambrians, Germans, and Tigurians wanting habitations, and thinking to settle themselues in Italie, trauelled thitherwards for the same purpose, but being denied by the Romans, they made most cruell warres vpon them, and slue of them at one time fourescore thousand souldiers, and thréescore thousand of others, wherewith the state of Rome and of all Italie was so broken, and ouerthrowne, that the Romans much bewailed themselues, & did thinke verelie that they should be vtterlie destroied. In this

distresse

distresse Marius tooke the matter in hand, and méeting first with the Germans, gaue them the battell, slue their king Teutobochus, and two hundred thousand men, beside fourescore thousand which were taken. After that he met with the Cambrians, and slue their king Beleus, and an hundred and fortie thousand with him, as also tooke fortie thousand prisoners. For which victorie he triumphed the second time in Rome, and was named then the third founder of Rome. Againe in the ciuill warre which grew by the means of Drusius, all Italie was then in armes, and the Romans in euerie place had the worse side (for all Italie began to forsake them) and in this distresse Marius hauing gotten but a small power in respect of the enmies, giueth the onset vpon the Marsians, and at two times he slue fourtéene thousand of them: which so quailed the Italians, and incouraged the Romans, that the Romans recouered themselues and had the maistrie. As in the warres so otherwise was Marius very fortunate: for being but of a base stocke, yet he maried Julia, a noble woman of the familie of the Julies, and aunt vnto Iulius Cesar: he passed thorough the most part of the offices in Rome: he was first *Legatus à senatu*, then *Præfectus equitum*, after that *Tribunus plebis*, *Prætor*, *Aedilis*, and seuen times was he consull. And as fortune séemed to fauour and countenance him aboue all other in Rome, so did she also checke him with great reproches, & burdened him with great miseries. For his pride was so excessiue, and his ambition so intollerable, that the best and most part of the Romans deadlie hated and enuied him: and therefore when he laboured to be *Aedilis*, *Pretor*, & *Tribune*, he was reiected; he was accused for ambition, and proclamed a traitor and an enimie to the common-wealth, he was inforced to forsake Rome and flie into Affrike. Also being at the seas, the mariners cast him on land among his enimies, and draue him to shift for himselfe. When he was pursued by his enimies, he was faine to hide himselfe in a bog, and couered himselfe with dirt & mire because he would not be knowne. Neuerthelesse he was taken and deliuered to a slaue to be killed. Manie other stormes of aduersitie and miserie did he abide and indure, and therefore it was said of him, that in miserie no man was more miserable, and in felicitie none more fortunate and happie than he.

The description of the earle Strangbow.

CHAP. 28.

THE earle was somewhat ruddie and of sanguine complexion and freckle faced, his eies greie, his face feminine, his voice small, and his necke little, but somewhat of a high stature: he was verie liberall, courteous and gentle: what he could not compasse and bring to passe in déed, he would win by good words and gentle spéeches. In time of peace he was more readie to yéeld and obeie, than to rule and beare swaie. Out of the campe he was more like to a souldior companion than a capteine or ruler: but in the campe and in the warres he caried with him the state and countenance of a valiant capteine. Of himselfe he would not aduenture anie thing, but being aduised and set on, he refused no attempts: for of himselfe he would not rashlie aduenture, or presumptuouslie take anie thing in hand. In the fight and battell he was a most assured token and signe to the whole companie, either to stand valiantlie to the fight, or for policie to retire. In all chances of warre he was still one and the same maner of man, being neither dismaid with aduersitie, nor puffed vp with prosperitie.

The

The earle leauing Wexford vpon the newes that Fitzstephans was in hold, went to Waterford, and from thence sailed into England, & was reconciled to the king

CHAP 29

AS the earle was marching towards Guefford, and was come to the borders therof, certeine messengers met him, and shewed to him the mischance happened vnto Robert Fitzstephans, and of the setting on fire the towne of Wexford adding moreouer, that the traitors were fullie determined if they trauelled anie further towards them, they would cut off all the heads of Fitzstephans and his companie, and send them vnto him Wherevpon with heauie cheare & sorrowfull hearts they change their minds, and turne towards Waterford Where when they were come, they found Herueie now latelie returned from the king with a message and letters from him vnto the earle, persuading and requiring him to come ouer into England vnto him Wherevpon the earle prepared and made himselfe readie, and as soone as wind and weather serued he tooke shipping, and caried Herueie along with him And being landed he rode towards the king, and met him at a towne called Newham néere vnto Glocester, where he was in readines with a great armie to saile ouer into Ireland Where after sundrie & manie altercations passed betweene them, at length by means of Herueie the kings displeasure was appeased, and it was agréed that the erle should sweare allegeance to the king, and yéeld and surrender vnto him the citie of Dublin, with the cantreds therevnto adioining, as also all such townes and forts as were bordering vpon the sea side. And as for the residue he should haue and reteine to him and his heires, holding the same of the king & of his heires These things thus concluded, the king with his armie marched along by Seuerne side, & the sea coasts of (1) Westwales, vnto the towne (2) of Penbroke, where he taried vntill he had assembled all his armie in (3) Milford hauen there to be shipped

(1) Westwales in Latine is named *Demetia*, and is that which is now called Penbrokeshire It reacheth from the seas on the north vnto the seas on the south In the west part thereof is the bishops sée of Meneue named saint Dauids and on the east side it bordereth vpon Southwales named Dehenbart In this part were the Flemmings placed first

(2) Penbroke is the chiefest towne of all *Demetia*, and lieth on the east side of Milford hauen, wherein was sometimes a verie strong castell builded (as some write) by a noble man named Arnulph Montgomer

(3) Milford is a famous and a goodlie harborough lieng in *Demetia*, or Westwales The Welshmen name it the mouth of two swords It hath two branches or armes, the one flowing hard to Hauerford west, and the other thorough the countrie named Rossia

Orooke prince of Meth besieging Dublin, is driuen off by Miles Cogan, and hath the woorst side

CHAP 30

IN the meane time Oroike, the one eied king of Meth, watching the absence of the erle as also of Reimond, the one being in England, and the other at Waterford,

Waterford he mustered a great number of soldiors and vpon a sudden about the kalends of September laieth siege to the citie of Dublin within the which there were then but few men, but yet they were valiant and verie men indeed And as the flame can not be suppressed, but that it will breake out euen so vertue and valiantnesse can not be shut vp, but that it will (when time and occasion serueth) shew it selfe. For Miles Cogan and all his companie vpon a sudden issue out vpon the enimies, and vnwares taking them napping, made a great slaughter of them among whom there was the sonne of Ororike a lustie yoong gentleman, and he slaine also And at this time the king of England, being at Penbroke in Wales, he fell out with the noblemen and gentlemen of the countrie because they had suffered the earle Richard to take his passage among them from thense into Ireland And remoouing such as had anie charge or kéeping of any forts there, he placed others therein but at length his heat being cooled, & his displeasure quailed, they were reconciled againe to his good fauour and grace

Whilest the king laie there, he had great pleasure in hawking, and as he was walking abroad with a goshawke of Norwaie vpon his fist, he had espied a falcon sitting vpon a rocke, and as he went about the rocke to view and behold him, his goshawke hauing also espied the falcon, bated vnto him, and therewith the king let him flie The falcon séeing hir selfe thus béset, taketh also wing and albeit hir flight was but slow at the first, yet at length she maketh wing and mounteth vp of a great height and taking the aduantage of the goshawke hir aduersarie, commeth downe with all hir might, and striking hir she claue hir backe asunder, and fell downe dead at the kings foot. wherat the king and all they that were then present had great maruell And the king hauing good liking, and being in loue with the falcon, did yearelie at the bréeding and disclosing time send thither for them. for in all his land there was not a better and a more hardie hawke.

The comming of king Henrie into Ireland.

CHAP. 31

THESE things thus doone, and all prepared in a readinesse fit for such a noble enterprise, and for which the king had staied a long time in Wales, he went to saint Dauids church, where when he had made his praiers and doone his deuotion, the wind and the wether well seruing, he tooke shipping and arriued vnto Waterford in the kalends of Nouember, being saint Luks daie hauing in his retinue fiue hundred gentlemen of seruice, and of bowmen and horssemen a great number This was in the seuentéenth yeare of his reigne, the one & fortith of his age, and in the yeare of our Lord one thousand one hundred seauentie & two, Alexander the third then pope, Frederike then emperor, and Lewes then French king And now was fulfilled the prophesie of Merlin, that "A fire globe shall come out of the east and shall deuour and consume all Ireland round about" and likewise the prophesie of saint Molin, that 'Out of the east shall come a mightie hurling wind, & rush thorough to the west, and shall run thorough and ouerthrow the force and strength of Ireland."

Prophesies of Merlin and Molin fulfilled.

·The

The citizens of Wexford present vnto the king Robert Fitzstephans, and sundrie princes of Ireland come and submit themselues to the king.

CHAP. 32.

THE king being thus landed at Waterford, and there resting himselfe; the citizens of Wexford, vnder colour and pretense of great humblenesse and dutie, and in hope of some thanks, they brought Robert Fitzstephans bound as a captiue and a prisoner, and presented him to the king as one who deserued small fauor or courtesie, that he had without his consent & leaue entered into Ireland, & giuen thereby an occasion to others to offend and to doo euill. The king not liking of him, fell out with him, and charged him verie déepelie and sharplie for his rash and hastie aduentures, and that he would take vpon him to make a conquest of Ireland without his assent and leaue: and forthwith commanded him to be handlocked and fettered, with an other prisoner, and to be safelie kept in Renold tower. Then Dermon Mac Arth prince of (1) Corke came to the king of his owne frée will, submitted himselfe, became tributarie, and tooke his oth to be true and faithfull to the king of England. After this the king remooued his armie and marched toward (2) Lismore, and after that he had tarried about two daies, he went to (3) Cashill, and thither came vnto him at the riuer of (4) Sure, Donold prince of (5) Limerike: where when he had obteined peace, he became tributarie and swore fealtie. The king then set (of his men) rulers and kéepers ouer the cities of Corke and Limerike.

Then also came in Donold prince of Ossorie, and Macleighlin O Felin prince of the Decies, and all the best & chiefest men in all Mounster, & did submit themselues, became tributaries and swore fealtie. Whome when the king had verie liberallie rewarded, he sent them home againe: and he himselfe returned backe againe to Waterford through (6) Tibrach. When he came to Waterford, Fitzstephans was brought before him, & when he had well beheld him, and considered with himselfe the valiantnesse of the man, the good seruice he had doone, & the perils & dangers he had beene in: he began to be mooued with some pitie and compassion vpon him, and at the intercession & by the mediation of certeine noblemen, he heartilie forgaue him, and released him from out of bonds, and restored him wholie to his former state and libertie, sauing that he reserued to himselfe the towne of Wexford, with the territories and lands thereunto adioining: & not long after some of those traitors, who thus had betraied him, were themselues taken and put to death.

(1) Corke, in Latine named *Corcagium*, is an ancient citie in the prouince of Mounster, and builded (as it should appeare) by the Easterlings or Norwaies. It standeth now in a marish or a bog, and vnto it floweth an arme of the seas, in the which are manie goodlie receptacles or harboroughs for ships, & much frequented as well for the goodlie commodities of fishings therein, as also for the trade of merchandize, by the which the citie is chieflie mainteined: for the inhabitants are not onlie merchants & great trauellers themselues; but also great store of strange merchants doo dailie resort & traffike with them. It is walled round about, and well fortified for a sufficient defense against the Irishrie. In it is the bishops sée of that diocesse, being called by the name of the bishop of Corke. The citie is gouerned by a maior and two bailiffes, who vsing the gouernement according to the lawes of England, doo keepe and mainteine the same in verie good order. They

They are verie much troubled with the enimie, and therefore they doo continuallie, as men lieng in a garison, keepe watch and ward both daie and night The prince of that countrie did most commonlie kéepe & staie himselfe in all troubles within that citie, vntill the time the same was conquered by the Englishmen, who euer since haue inhabited in the same.

(2) Lismore in times past was as faire a towne as it is ancient, and standeth vpon a goodlie riuer, which floweth vnto Youghall, and so into the maine seas. It was sometimes a bishoprike, but of late vnited to the bishoprike of Waterford, and so it lieth in the countie and diocesse of Waterford, but the soile it selfe was within the countie of Corke.

(3) Cashill is an old ruinous towne, but walled, and standeth vpon the riuer Sure In it is the see and cathedrall church of the bishop, bearing the name therof, who is one of the foure archbishopriks of that land, and vnder him are the bishops of Waterford, Corke, and seuen others

(4) The Sure is a goodlie and a notable riuer, and one of the chiefest in that land It hath his head or spring in a certeine hill called Blandina, but in Irish Sloghblome, for the pleasantnesse thereof Manie good townes are seated and builded vpon the same, & it is nauigable more than the one halfe It fléeteth from the spring or head fast by the towne of Thorleis, whereof the earle of Ormond is baron. from thense to the holie crosse and so to Clonmell, & from thense to Carig Mac Griffith, where is an ancient house of the earles, sometime named the earles of the Carig, but now earles of Ormond, and from thense fléeting by Tibrach, it commeth to Waterford, and fléeting by the wals thereof, it runneth into the seas

(5) Limerike is one of the first cities builded by the Norwaies or Easterlings, named sometimes Ostomen the founder whereof was the yoongest of thrée brethren whose name was Yuorus. It standeth vpon the famous and noble riuer of Shenin, which goeth round about it, the same being as it were an Iland The seat of it is such, as none can be more faire or more statelie It lieth in the maine land within the prouince of Mounster, called the north Mounster, and is from the maine seas aboue fortie miles, and yet at the wals euen the greatest ship at the seas maie be discharged and vnladen, and speciallie so there are for the citie it selfe is chieflie inhabited by merchants It is gouerned by a maior and bailiffes after and according to the English lawes and orders. It was in times past vnder a particular prince of it selt, but euer since the conquest it hath béene inhabited by the Englishmen, who doo so still continue therin

(6) Tibrach is an old towne, which in times past was rich and verie well inhabited, it lieth vpon the north side of the Sure, and about two miles from Carig Mac Griffith. In it is a great stone standing, which is the bound betwéene the counties of Kilkennie and Ormond.

Rothorike O Cōnnor the monarch and all the princes in Vlster submit and yeeld themselues vnto the king, as he passeth towards Dublin.

CHAP 33

THESE things thus doon at Waterford, the king left Robert Fitzbarnard there with his houshold, and marched himselfe to Dublin through the countrie of Ossorie and staieng somewhat by the waie in his iourneie, there came and resorted vnto him out of euerie place there the great men & princes, as namelie Machelan

Ophelan prince of Ossorie, Machc Talewie, Othwelie Gillemeholoch, Ochadese, O Carell of Uriell & Ororike of Meth: all which yeelded & submitted them selues to the king in their owne persons, & became his vassals, & swore fealtie. But Rothorike the monarch came no néerer than to the riuer side of the (1) Shenin, which diuideth Connagh from Meth, & there Hugh de Lacie and William Fitzaldeline by the kings commandement met him, who desiring peace submitted himselfe, swore allegiance, became tributarie, and did put in (as all others did) hostages and pledges for the kéeping of the same. Thus was all Ireland sauing Vlster brought in subiection, and euerie particular prince in his proper person did yéeld and submit himselfe, sauing onelie Rothorike, the then monarch of all Ireland; and yet by him and in his submission all the residue of the whole land became the kings subiects, and submitted themselues. For indéed there was no one nor other within that land, who was of anie name or countenance, but that he did present himselfe before the kings maiestie, and yéelded vnto him subiection and due obedience.

Prophesies of Merlin and Molin fulfilled.

And then was fulfilled the old and vulgar prophesie of S. Molin; "Before him all the princes shall fall downe, and vnder a dissembled submission shall obteine fauor and grace." Likewise the prophesie of Merlin; "All the birds of that Iland shall flée to his light, and the greater birds shall be taken & brought into captiuitie, and their wings shall be burned." Also the old prophesie of Merlin Ambrose; "Fiue portions shall be brought into one, & the sixt shall breake and ouerthrow the walles of Ireland." That which Ambrose nameth heere the sixt, Celidonius nameth the fift, as appeareth in his booke of prophesies. Now when the feast of Christmasse did approch and draw neere, manie and the most part of the princes of that land resorted and made repaire vnto Dublin, to sée the kings court: and when they saw the great abundance of vittels, and the noble seruices, as also the eating of cranes, which they much lothed, being not before accustomed therevnto, they much woondered and maruelled thereat: but in the end they being by the kings commandement set downe, did also there eat and drinke among them. At this time there were certeine soldiors, being bowmen, seassed at Finglas, and they hewed and cut downe the trees which grew about the churchyard, which had beene there planted of old time by certeine good and holie men: and all these soldiors suddenlie fell sicke of the pestilence and died all: as is more at large declared in our topographie.

(1) The Shenin is the cheefest and most famous riuer in that land, and dooth in a manner inuiron and inclose all Connagh, & diuideth it from the prouinces of Mounster and Meth: his head and spring is in the hill named Therne, which bordereth vpon O Connor Slegos countrie, not farre from the riuer of the Banne in Vlster, and in length is supposed to be about a hundred and twentie English miles. It is increased with sundrie brooks, and diuerse riuers run into the same; the chéefest whereof is that which riseth and commeth out of the logh or lake Foile. In it are manie loghs or lakes of great quantitie or bignesse, which are maruelouslie replenished and stored with abundance of fish: the chéefest of which are the logh Rie, and the logh Derigid. It is nauigable aboue thrée score miles, and vpon it standeth the most famous citie of Limerike. There is onlie one bridge ouer it, builded of late yeares at Alone, by the right honorable sir Henrie Sidneie knight, then lord deputie of the realme.

The councell or synod kept at Cashill.

CHAP. 34.

THE realme béeing now in good peace and quietnesse, and the king now hauing a care and a zeale to set foorth Gods honor and true religion, summoned a synod of all the clergie vnto Cashill, where inquirie and examination was made of the wicked and loose life of the people of the land and nation: which was registred in writing, and sealed vnder the seale of the bishop of Lismore, who being then the popes legat was president of that councell. And then & there were made and decréed sundrie good and godlie constitutions, which are yet extant, as namelie, for contracting of mariage, for paiment of tithes, for the reuerend and cleane kéeping of the churches, and that the vniuersall church of Ireland should be reduced in all things to the order and forme of the church of England. Which constitutions were foorthwith published throughout the realme, and doo here follow.

Constitutions made at the councell of Cashill

CHAP 35

IN the yere of Christs incarnation 1172, & in the first yéere that the most noble king of England conquered Ireland, Christianus bishop of Lismore, and legat of the apostolike see, Donat archbishop of Cashill, Laurence archbishop of Dublin, and Catholicus archbishop of Thomond with their suffragans and fellow-bishops, abbats, archdeacons, priors, deanes, & manie other prelats of the church of Ireland, by the commandement of the king did assemble themselues and kept a synod at Cashill: and there debating manie things concerning the wealth, estate, and reformation of the church, did prouide remedies for the same. At this councell were also for and in the behalfe of the king, whom he had sent thither, Rafe abbat of Buldewars, Rafe archdeacon of (1) Landaffe, Nicholas the chapleine, and diuerse other good clearks. Sundrie good statutes and wholesome laws were there deuised, which were after subscribed and confirmed by the king himselfe, and vnder his authoritie, which were these that follow. First, it is decréed that all good faithfull and christian people, throughout Ireland, should forbeare and shun to marie with their néere kinsfolke and cousins, & marie with such as lawfullie they should doo. Secondarilie, that children shall be catechised without the church doore, and baptised in the font appointed in the churches for the same. Thirdlie, that euerie christian bodie doo faithfullie and trulie paie yéerelie the tiths of his cattels, corne, and all other his increase and profits to the church or parish where he is a parishoner. Fourthlie, that all the church lands and possessions, throughout all Ireland, shall be frée from all secular exactions and impositions, and especiallie that no lords, earles, nor noble men, nor their children, nor familie, shall extort or take anie coine and liuerie, cosheries, nor cuddies, nor anie other like custome from thensefoorth, in or vpon anie of the church lands and territories. And likewise that they nor no other person doo hensefoorth exact out of the said church lands old, wicked, and detestable customes of coine and liuerie, which they were woont to extort vpon such townes and villages of the churches as were

Ecclesiasticall constitutions for Ireland.

neere and next bordering vpon them. Fiftlie, that when earike or composition is made among the laie people for anie murther, that no person of the cleargie, though he be kin to anie of the parties, shall contribute anie thing thereunto: but as they be guiltlesse from the murther, so shall they be frée from paiment of monie, for anie such earike or release for the same. Sixtlie, that all and euerie good christian being sicke & weake, shall before the priest and his neighbors make his last will and testament, and his debts and seruants wages being paid, all his mooueables to be diuided (if he haue anie children) into thrée parts: whereof one part to be to the children, another to his wife, and the third part to be for the performance of his will. And if so be that he haue no children, then the goods to be diuided into two parts, whereof the one moitie to his wife, and the other to the performance of his will and testament. And if he haue no wife, but onelie children, then the goods to be likewise diuided into two parts, wherof the one to himselfe, and the other to his children. Seuenthlie, that euerie christian being dead, and dieng in the catholike faith, shall be reuerendlie brought to the church, and to be buried as apperteineth. Finallie, that all the diuine seruice in the church of Ireland shall be kept, vsed, & obserued in the like order and maner as it is in the church of England. For it is méet and right, that as by Gods prouidence and appointment Ireland is now become subiect, and vnder the king of England: so the same should take from thense the order, rule, and maner how to reforme themselues, and to liue in better order. For whatsoeuer good thing is befallen to the church & realme of Ireland, either concerning religion, or peaceable gouernement, they owe the same to the king of England, and are to be thankefull vnto him for the same: for before his comming into the land of Ireland, manie and all sorts of wickednesses in times past flowed and reigned amongest them: all which now by his authoritie and goodnesse are abolished. The primat of Armagh, by reason of his weaknesse and great age, was not present at the synod: but afterwards he came to Dublin, and gaue his full consent to the same. This holie man (as the common saieng was) had a white cow, and being fed onelie by hir milke, she was alwaies carried with him wheresoeuer he went and trauelled from home.

The tempestuous and stormie winter.

CHAP. 36.

THE seas, which a long time had beene calme, began now to swell, and to be full of continuall storms and tempests, which were so raging, and so great, that in all that winter there arriued scarselie anie one ship or barke from anie place into that land: neither was there anie news heard from out of anie countrie during that winter. Whervpon men began to be afraid, and thinke verelie that God in his anger would punish them, and be reuenged for their wicked & sinfull life, and therefore had sent this plague vpon them. At this time in Southwales by reason of the extreme and continuall tempests, the sea sides and shores, which had manie yeares beene couered with great sand ridges, were now washed and carried awaie with the seas, and then there appeared the former fast and firme earth, and therin a great number of trees standing which did in times past grow there: and by reason they had béene so long couered, & as it were buried vnder the sands, they stood as trunked and polled trées, and were as blacke as is the Ebene. A maruelous alteration, that the place sometimes couered with seas, and a waie for ships to passe, is now become a soile of ground and drie land. But some suppose that this was

so

so at the first, and that those trées were there growing before or shortlie after the floud of Noah. The king remained at Wexford, still longing to heare news from beyond the seas and thus being solitarie he practised by all the means and sleights he could, how he might flocke and procure vnto him Reimond, Miles Cogan, William Makerell, & other of the best gentlemen, that he being assured of them to be firme of his side, he might be the stronger, and the earle the weaker.

The conspiracie made against the king by his sonnes, and the ambassage of the legat from the pope vnto him

CHAP 37

AFTER Midlent the wind being easterlie, there came and arriued into Ireland certeine ships, as well from out of England, as also from out of Aquitaine in France, which brought him verie ill & bad newes For there were come into Normandie from pope Alexander the third two cardinals in an ambassage, the one of them being named Albertus, and the other Theodinus, to make inquirie of the death of Thomas archbishop of Canturburie They were thought and taken to be iust and good men, and therefore were chosen of trust and of purpose for this matter. but yet for all that they were Romans, and who were fullie determined to haue interdicted, not onelie England, but also all the whole dominions subiect vnto the king, if he himselfe had not the sooner come and met with them Besides this, there was woorse newes told him, and a woorse mishap befell vnto him (for commonlie good lucke commeth alone, but ill haps come by heapes and by huddels) which was, that his eldest sonne whom he loued so deerlie, and whom he had crowned king, as also his two yoonger sonnes, with the consent and helpe of sundrie noble men, as well in England as beyond the seas, had confederated themselues, and conspired against the king in his absence. Which newes and secret conspiracie when he heard and vnderstood, he was in a maruellous perplexitie, and for verie anguish and greefe of mind did sweat. First it greeued him that he should be suspected and infamed of the crime whereof he was giltlesse. Also he feared of the great troubles which would grow and insue hereby to his kingdome, & all other his dominions. Yea, and it greeued him verie much, that he being minded and determined the next summer then following to settle Ireland in some good state, and to fortifie the same with holds and castels, he should now be compelled and driuen to leaue the same vndoone Wherefore sending some before him into England, as well to aduertise his comming homewards, as also of the safetie he had taken for Ireland, he bethought himselfe, as also tooke good aduise and counsell, what was best to be doone in these his weightie causes.

The king returneth homewards through Westwales, and of the speaking stone at saint Dauids

CHAP. 38

THE king being minded and determined to returne into England, set his realme of Ireland in good order, and left Hugh de Lacie (vnto whom he had giuen in fee the countrie of Meth) with twentie gentlemen, & Fitzstephans & Maurice Fitzgerald with twentie other gentlemen, to be wardens and conestables of Dublin Likewise he left Humfreie de Bohune, Robert Fitzbarnard, and Hugh de Gundeuile, with twentie gentlemen, to kéepe and gouerne Waterford Also he left William Fitzaldelme, Philip of Hastings, and Philip de Bruse, to be gouernors and rulers of Wexford they hauing also twentie gentlemen of seruice appointed vnto them And on the mondaie in the Easter wéeke, earlie in the morning at the sunne rising, he tooke shipping without the barre of Wexford, and the wind being westerlie and blowing a good gale, he had a verie good passage, and arriued about the noone-tide of the same daie vnto the baie of saint Dauids where he being set on land, he went on foot with a staffe in his hand in pilgrimage, and in great deuotion vnto the church of saint Dauids, whom the cleargie in procession met at the gate called the white gate, and with great honour receiued him. And as they were going verie orderlie and solemnlie in procession, there came vnto him a Welsh or a Camber woman, and falling downe at his feet, she made a great complaint against the bishop of that place which being by an interpretor declared vnto the king, albeit he vnderstood it well, yet he gaue hir no answer

She thinking that hir sute was not regarded, did wring hir fists, and cried out with a lowd voice, "Reuenge vs this day O Lechlanar, Reuenge vs I say, our kindred, and our nation, from this man" And being willed by the people of that countrie, who vnderstood hir speach, to hold hir peace, as also did thrust hir out of the companie, she cried the more, trusting and alluding to a certeine blind prophesie of Merlin, which was that 'The king of England the conqueror of Ireland, should be wounded in Ireland by a man with a red hand, and in his returning homewards through Southwales should die vpon Lechlanar' This (1) Lechlanar was the name of a certeine great stone which laie ouer a brooke, which fléeteth or runneth on the north side of the churchyard, and was a bridge ouer the same and by reason of the often and continuall going of the people ouer it it was verie smooth and slipperie In length it was of ten foot, in breadth six foot, and in thicknesse one foot And this word Lechlanar, in the Camber or Welsh toong, is to saie, The speaking stone For it was an old blind saieng among the people in that countrie, that on a time there was a dead corps carried ouer that stone to be buried, and the said stone spake, and foorthwith brake and claue asunder in the middle, and which clift so remaineth vnto this date And therevpon the people of that countrie, of a verie vaine and barbarous superstition, haue not since, nor yet will carie anie more dead bodies ouer the same

A prophesie of Merlin

A speaking stone

The king being come to this stone, and hearing of this prophesie, paused and staied a little while, and then vpon a sudden, verie hastilie he went ouer it which doone, he looked backe vpon the stone, and spake somewhat sharpelie, saieng "Who is he that will beleeue that lieng Merlin anie more? A man of that place standing thereby, and seeing what had happened, he to excuse Merlin, said with a lowd voice, "Thou art not he that shall conquer Ireland, neither dooth Merlin

meane

meane it of thée." The king then went into the cathedrall church which was dedicated to saint Andrew and to saint Dauid and hauing made his praiers, and heard diuine seruice, he went to supper, and rode after to Hauerford west to bed, which is about twelue miles from thense

(1) The writer hereof (of verie purpose) in the yeare 1575, went to the foresaid place to sée the said stone, but there was no such to be found, and the place where the said stone was said to lie, is now an arched bridge, vnder which fléeteth the brooke aforesaid, which brooke doeth not diuide the churchyard from the church, but the churchyard & church from the bishops and prebendaries houses, which houses in times past were verie faire and good hospitalitie kept therein. But as the most part of houses are fallen down and altogither ruinous, so the hospitalitie is also therwith decaied And for the veritie of the foresaid stone there is no certeintie affirmed, but a report is remaining amongst the common people of such a stone to haue béene there in times past.

The submission of king Henrie to the pope, and his reconciliation, as also the agreement betwéene him and the French king

CHAP 39.

THE king then tooke his iornie from Hauerford homewards along by the sea side, euen the same waie as before he came thither, and foorthwith in all hast he taketh shipping, and sailed into Normandie and immediatlie vnderstanding where the popes legats were, he repaired vnto them, and presented himselfe in most humble maner before them Where & before whome after sundrie altercations passed to and fro betwéene them, he purged himselfe by his oth, that he was giltlesse of the death of the archbishop Thomas neuerthelesse he was contented to doo the penance inioined him For although he did not kill, nor yet know, nor consent to the murthering of him, yet he denied not but that the same was doone for his (1) sake. The ambassadors & legats hauing thus ended with the king, with much honour returned backe, and homewards to Rome And then the king trauelled and went to the marches of France, there to talke and haue conference with Lewes the French king, betwéene whome then was discord and debate But after sundrie speeches past betwéene them, at length by the meanes and intercession of sundrie good men, and especiallie of Philip earle of Flanders (who was but then returned from Compostella, where he had bene in pilgrimage vnto saint Iames) the same was ended, and the displeasure which he had conceiued about and for the death of the archbishop of Canturburie was cleerelie released And by these means, the great malice and secret conspiracies of his sonnes and their confederats was for this time suppressed and quailed, and so continued vntill the yeare following.

(1) They which doo write and intreat of the life and death of this archbishop, doo affirme that the king after the death of this man, did send his ambassadors to pope Alexander at Rome, to purge himselfe of this fact And notwithstanding that he tooke a corporall oth, that he neither did it nor caused it to be doone, nor yet gaue anie consent, or was priuie thereof, nor yet was giltie in anie respect, sauing that he confessed he did not so well fauour the bishop as he had doone in times past yet could not his ambassadors be admitted to the presence and sight of the pope, vntill he had yéelded himselfe to his arbitrement and iudgement

ment which was that he should doo certeine penance, as also to performe certeine iniunctions which were as followeth That the king at his proper costs and charges should keepe and susteine two hundred souldiers for one whole yeare, to defend the holie land against the Turke That he should permit, and that it should be lawfull to all his subiects as often as them listed to appeale to the sée of Rome That none should be accounted thensefoorth to be lawfull king of England, vntill such time as he were confirmed by the Roman bishop That he should restore to the church of Canturburie all such goods and possessions as were taken and deteined from the same since the death of the archbishop That he should suffer all such people as were fled or banished out of the realme for his sake, to returne home without delaie or let, and to inioy and haue againe all such goods and lands whatsoeuer they had before. Other things this Romish antichrist did demand, and which the king was compelled to grant vnto before he could be released. whereby it dooth appeare how much they doo varie from the calling of Christs apostles, and how that (contrarie to the rule of the gospell) their onelie indeuour was to make and haue princes and kingdoms subiect to their becke and tyrannie

Iniunctions by the pope to the king of England

The vision which appeared vnto the king at his being at Cardiffe.

CHAP. 40

BUT before we doo proceed anie further, it were not amisse to declare what happened and befell vnto the king in his returning through Wales, after his comming from Ireland In his iournie he came to the towne of Cardiffe on the saturdaie in the Easter wéeke, and lodged there all that night. On the morrow being sundaie, and commonlie called little Easter daie or Low sundaie, he went somewhat earlie to the chapell of saint Perian, and there heard diuine seruice, but he staied there in his secret praiers behind all his companie, somewhat longer than he was woont to doo at length he came out, and leaping to his horsse, there stood before him one hauing before him a stake, or a post pitched in the ground He was of colour somewhat yellowish, his head rounded and a leane face, of stature somewhat high, and aged about fortie yeares, his apparell was white, being close & downe to the ground, he was girded about the middle, and bare footed This man spake to the king in Dutch, saieng, "God saue thée O king," and then said thus vnto him "Christ and his mother Marie, Iohn baptist, and Peter the apostle doo salute thée and doo strictlie charge and command thee, that thou doo forbid, that hensefoorth throughout all thy kingdome and domions, there be no faires nor markets kept in anie place vpon the sundaies and that vpon those daies no maner or person doo anie bodilie worke, but onelie to serue God, sauing such as be appointed to dresse the meat If thou wilt thus doo, all that thou shalt take in hand shall prosper, and thy selfe shalt haue a happie life" The king then spake in French to the gentleman, who held his horsse by the bridle, and whose name was Philip Merrios, a man borne in those parts, and who told me this tale "Aske him whether he dreame or not" Which when he had so doone the man looking vpon the king said. "Whether I dreame or not, marke well and remember what daie this is for if thou doo not thus, and speedilie amend thy wicked life, thou shalt before the yeere come about heare such euill news of those things which thou louest best, and thou shalt be so much vnquieted therwith, that thou shalt not find anie ease or end vntill thy dieng daie" With this word the king put spur to the horsse and rode awaie towards the towne gate, which was at hand but thinking vpon the words

words areigned his horsse and said, "Call me yonder fellow againe" Wherevpon the foresaid gentleman as also one William, which two were onelie then attending vpon him, first called and then sought him in the chappell, and finding him not there, sought him throughout the court, the towne, and in all the Ins, but could not find him The king being verie sad and sorie that he had not throughlie talked with the man, went abroad himselfe to seeke him, but finding him not, called for his horsses and rode from thence by Rempinbridge to Newberie And as this man had before threatned and said, it so came to passe before the yeare was ended: for his eldest sonne Henrie, and his two yoonger sonnes Richard earle of Aquitaine, and Geffreie erle of Britaine, in the Lent following forsooke and shroonke from him, and went to Lewes the French king. Whereof grew and insued vnto him such vexation and vnquietnesse as he had neuer the like before, and which by one means and other neuer left him vntill his dieng daie And suerlie it was thought the same by Gods iust iudgement so befell vnto him for as he had béene and was a disobedient sonne to his spirituall father, so his carnall sonnes should be disobedient and rebellious against their carnall father Manie such forewarnings the king had by Gods mercie and goodnesse sent vnto him before his death, to the end he should repent and be conuerted, and not be condemned which would to God that euerie prince and other man did not frowardlie and obstinatlie condemne, but rather with an humble and a penitent heart they would (as they ought to doo) receiue and imbrace the same! And therefore I haue and mind to write more at large in my booke, concerning the instruction and institution of a christian prince

The treason and killing of Ororike prince of Meth.

CHAP 41

IN the meane time Ireland was in good rest and peace, vnder such as vnto whom the charge thereof was committed And now on a time it happened, that the one eied Ororike of Meth, being at Dublin, complained vnto Hugh de Lacie of certeine iniuries doone vnto him, praieng redresse wherevpon the daie and a place of (1) parlée was betweene them appointed for the same. The night next before the daie of this parlée, a yoong gentleman named Griffith, the nephue of Robert Fitzstephans, and Maurice Fitzgerald, being the sonne to their eldest brother named William, dreamed in his sleepe that he saw a great heard of wild hogs to rush and run vpon Hugh de Lacie and his vncle Maurice, and that one of them being more horrible and greater than the rest, had with his tusks rent and killed them if he had not with all his force and strength rescued them, and killed the bore. On the morrow according to appointment, they came to the place appointed for the parlée, which was a certeine hill called Ororikes hill but before they came to the verie hill it selfe, they sent messengers the one to the other, requiring assurance and safetie. and hauing sworne on each part to kéepe faith and truth, they came to the place appointed and there met, but yet a small companie on either side For it was agréed vpon on both parties, & by couenant excepted, that on each part they should bring but a few and the like number, and they to be all vnarmed, the swords on one side and the spars on the other side, and for all the residue of the people and companie to stand aloofe and a farre off. But Griffith, who came to the said parlée with his vncle Maurice, was verie pensife and much troubled, concerning the vision which he saw in his sleepe, and doubting of the worst, made choise of seuen of the best gentlemen of his kindred. whome he knew to be

Griffiths dreame.

valiant, and in whome he had a speciall trust and confidence. These he draweth to the one side of the hill, but as néere to the place of parlée as he could, where euerie of them hauing his sword, spar and shield, lept and mounted vp to their horsses, and ranging the fields they made sundrie carreers and lustie turnaments, vnder the pretense and colour of plesantnes and pastime, but in verie déed to be in a readinesse if need should so require.

Hugh de Lacie and Ororike this meane while were talking and discoursing of manie things, but concluded not of anie thing, neither did Ororike meane anie such thing. For hauing a traitorous mind, and watching his time when he might best powre out his venem, fained himselfe to go out and abroad to make water, and vnder that colour beckened vnto his men, with whome he had concluded and agreed before, that with all hast they should come awaie vnto him, and they foorthwith in all hast so did, and he also then with a pale, grim, and murtherous countenance, hauing his ax or spar vpon his shoulder, returned backe againe. Maurice Fitzgerald, which was before warned by his cousine Griffith and aduertised of his dreame, gaue good eie and watched the matter verie narowlie, and therefore all the parlée time, he had his sword readie drawne about him and espieng the traitor to be fullie bent and about to strike Hugh de Lacie, he cried out vnto him, willing him to looke vnto himselfe, and to be at defense with himselfe, wherewith the traitor most violentlie strake vnto him, thinking verelie to haue murthered and dispatched him. But the interpretor of the parlée stepping in betwéene, saued Hugh de Lacie, but he himselfe was wounded to death, and his arme cleane cut off.

Then Maurice Fitzgerald with a lowd voice cried out to his companie, who with all hast came awaie, and then began a hot and a sharpe bickering of the English swords against the Irish spars. In which skirmishing Hugh de Lacie was twise felled to the ground, and had suerlie béene killed, if Maurice had not valiantlie rescued him. Likewise the Irishmen who were manie in number, they hauing espied the becking of the traitor, they came running in all hast out of the vallies with their weapons, thinking verelie to haue made a cleane dispatch and a full end of Hugh de Lacie and of Maurice Fitzgerald. But Griffith and his companions, still watching for that which indéed did happen, were at the first call of Maurice in a readinesse, and being on horssebacke they came awaie with all speed: which thing when the traitor saw, he gan to distrust, and thought to shift himselfe awaie and so to escape. But as he was leaping to his horsse, Griffith was come, and with his staffe or lance strake downe and ran through both horsse and man: who being thus striken downe and killed, as also thrée other of his men, who brought him his horsse and were in this bickering, they cut off his head from the bodie, and sent it ouer into England to the king. The residue of the Irishmen fled foorthwith and ranne awaie, but being hardlie pursued euen to the verie woods, there was a great discomfiture and slaughter made of them. Rafe the sonne of Fitzstephans, being a lustie and a valiant yoong gentleman, did well acquite himselfe, and deserued great commendation for his good seruice.

(1) The maner of the Irishrie was euer, and yet is, that when so euer there is anie controuersie amongst them, they will oftentimes appoint places where to meet and assemble themselues for conference, which commonlie is vpon some hill distant and farre from anie house, and this assemblie is called among them a parlée or a parlement. And albeit the pretense héereof is of some quietnesse and redresse: yet experience teacheth that there is not a woorse thing to be vsed among them: for lightlie and most commonlie there are most treacheries and treasons, most murthers and robberies, and all wickednesse imagined, deuised, and afterwards put in

practise

practise among them · and for the most part there is no parlée among them, whereof insueth not some mischéefe

(2) This hill lieth in the prouince of Meth, about twentie miles from Dublin, and is now called the Taragh . some thinke this to be the middle part or nauill of that prouince, it is a verie pleasant and a fertile soile, and also for the most part champion.

Sundrie examples concerning visions.

CHAP. 42.

FOR so much as there be sundrie opinions and iudgments concerning visions, it shall not be much amisse, or impertinent to our matter, to recite a few examples & true reports of the same. Valerius Maximus in his first booke and seauenth chapter writeth, that two men of Arcadia, iourneng togither in companie towards a towne named Megara, when they came thither, the one of them lodged himselfe with his fréend, but the other at a common Inne. He who laie in his fréends house being in bed and asléepe, dreamed that his companion came vnto him, and requested him to helpe him, bicause his hoast did oppresse him, wherewith he awooke, but verie shortlie he fell asléepe againe, and dreamed that his said companion came againe vnto him being verie sore wounded, and praied him that although he would not at the first time come and helpe him, yet that he would now reuenge his death, declaring that his host had taken his head and corps, and put it into a cart to be carried to the dunghill, and there to be buried. This man being awaked, and much troubled with this dreame, arose and sought for his fellow, and finding his dreame to be true, caused the hoast to be taken and apprehended, who for that his fact was executed and put to death. Aterius Rufus a gentleman of Rome likewise, being on a time at Siracusa, he dreamed that he was killed by a maister of fense, which came so to passe: for on the morrow after he was present at the plaie or game of swordplaiers or maisters of defense, whereas a (1) netcaster was brought in to fight with a swordplaier Wherevpon Aterius vttering his dreame to him that sat next by him, would haue gone and departed awaie, but being persuaded to the contrarie, did staie to his owne destruction. For the netcaster hauing ouerthrowne the swordplaier, and thinking to haue pearsed him through with his sword, missed him and stroke Aterius, who sat in place next therevnto, and so was he slaine Also Simonides the poet, being on a time set on land vpon the sea shore, he saw there a dead man lieng vnburied. The night following he dreamed that the said dead man did aduise and admonish him, that he should not take ship the daie following but his felowes minding not to lose anie time, and the weather seeming then to be faire, they went all abooord, and hoised vp their sailes, which Simonides refused to doo, and taried at land It was not long after but that the weather waxed to be fowle, and the seas to be high, and in the end both the ship and men to be all lost but Simonides crediting his dreame, was saued Moreouer Calphurnia, the wife vnto Iulius Cesar, the night before hir husband was slaine, dreamed that she saw him greatlie wounded to lie in hir lap . wherewith she being afraid did awake, and told Iulius hir dreame, requesting him that he would forbeare to repaire to the senat house that daie but he giuing small credit to a womans dreame, followed his mind and was slaine by the senators. But to leaue these examples fetched from out of other nations, let vs come neere home to our selues A brother of mine named Walter Barrie, a lustie yoong gentleman, making himselfe Prognosticall dreames.

selfe readie on a time to serue in a certeine hosting against his enimie; the night before he should take his iournie, he dreamed that my mother who was dead on long before, did come vnto him, and aduise & warne him, that if he loued his life he should in anie wise refraine and forbeare that iournie She in déed was not his naturall mother, but his mother in law, and yet loued him in hir lifè time as intirelie as hir owne child When he had told this his dreame to his father and mine, for indéed we were both brothers by one father, though we had not one mother. he also gaue him the like aduise and counsell, but he of his presumptuous mind, not regarding the same, followed his owne mind, and the same daie was killed by his enimie

(2) As dreames sometimes are good forewarnings to men to eschew euils which are towards, yet they are not alwaies to be so receiued, as prognostications infallible For sometimes the same fall out to the contrarie, as dooth appeere by Augustus the emperor, who hauing warres against Brutus and Cassius, and he by reason of his sicknesse carried in a litter, his physician Arterius dreamed that the goddesse Minerua did appeere vnto him, willing him to aduise and counsell the emperor, that he should not by reason of his sicknesse come into the field, nor be present in the battell, which he did. But the emperor notwithstanding entered into the field, being carried in his litter, and tooke maruellous great paines And albeit Brutus taking the emperors tents, séemed to haue the victorie, yet was he for all that vanquished, and the emperor had the conquest Likewise in west Wales, of late yeares, it happened a certeine rich man dwelling on the north side of a certeine mounteine, he dreamed thrée nights togither, that there was a chaine of gold hidden in the head stone, which couered and laie vpon a certeine well or founteine, named saint Bernaces well, and that he should go and fetch it This man at length, somwhat beléeuing the dreame, and minding to trie the same, went to the place, and did put his hand into the hole or place' but his hand was no sooner in, but that it was bitten, stoong, and enuenomed with an adder Wherefore a man may sée hereby what credit is to be giuen to dreams, and I for my part doo so credit of them as I doo of rumors. But concerning such visions as God dooth send by his angels to his prophets and holie men, we must otherwise thinke of them, bicause the effect of them is most vndoubted, certeine, and assured.

(1) The Romans had diuerse games, plaies, and exercises amongst themselues, and had for the same certeine amphitheaters and theaters made of purpose, wherein the people might sit to view and behold the same. Of these plaies or games some were of cruell beasts the one fighting with the other, some of men fighting with beasts, and some of men fighting the one with the other, and these plaies were called *Ludi gladiatorij*, games of sword plaieng or fighting for as in combates in England, so they being vnharnessed, did fight with their swords or weapons in the open sight of the people, indeuouring ech one to kill the other, which were spectacles of crueltie to harden the peoples hearts against killing in the warres Of these some were called *Mirmillones*, which were such as chalenged the fight, some were called *Gladiatores*, and these were such as we doo name masters of defenses, bicause they vsed onelie or cheeflie the sword, and some were called *Retiarij*, and these besides their weapons did vse a certeine kind of net, which in fighting they were woont to take and intrap their enimies, and such a one was this man, who fighting with a chalenger, did by chance misse him and kill Aterius

(2) In the old and first ages, men were much giuen to dreames and visions and oftentimes great forewarnings and prognostications were giuen thereby, as dooth appeare in the holie scriptures, as also in prophane histories. For Ioseph the son of

of Iacob, king Pharao, king Nabuchodonozor, Mardocheus, Daniell, Iudas Machabeus, Hercules, Pyrrhus, Cicero, Cassius, Parmensis, & manie others dreamed dreames, and the same came to passe. But yet these being but particular examples, and which it pleased God for some secret cause to vse: they are not to be drawne for presidents and examples to be dailie or in these daies vsed, but rather we must haue a respect and a regard to Gods speciall commandement, who by the mouths of his prophets hath vtterlie forbidden vs to listen to anie dreamer, or to giue credit vnto his words. "Thou shalt not (saith he) hearken to the words of a dreamer of dreames, for dreames haue deceiued manie a man, and they haue failed them who haue put their trust in them: for whie, they are full of deceipts and guiles, and inuented either for the mainteinance of superstition and error, or for the increasing of some filthie lucre and gaine." Phauorinus therefore inueighing against the Chaldeans, who were a people which were woont to relie much vpon dreames, willeth and aduiseth that no dreamer or interpreter of dreames should be sought or dealt withall. "For (saith he) if they tell thee of anie good thing, and in the end doo deceiue thee, thou shalt be in miserie to hope in vaine for the same. If they tell thée of some misfortune, and yet doo lie, yet shalt thou be in miserie, bicause thou shalt be still in feare least it may happen. And likewise if they shew thée of euill haps, and the same doo so follow, thou shalt be in miserie and vnquieted, that thy fortune and destinie is so euill. But if they tell thee of good things, and it be long yer the same doo happen, thou shalt be much vnquieted to looke so long for it, and alwaies in feare least thine expectation shall be frustrated: wherefore in no wise doo thou séeke anie such persons, nor giue anie credit vnto them."

The description of Maurice Fitzgerald.

CHAP. 43.

THIS Maurice was a man of much nobilitie and worship, but somewhat shamefast and yet verie well coloured, and of a good countenance, of stature he was indifferent, being seemelie and well compact at all points, in bodie and mind he was of a like composition, being not too great in the one, nor proud in the other; of nature he was verie courteous and gentle, and desired rather so to be in déed, than to be thought or reputed so to be. he kept such a measure and a moderation in all his doings, that in his daies he was a patterne of all sobrietie and good behauiour, a man of few words, and his sentences more full of wit and reason than of words and spéeches, he had more stomach than talke, more reason than spéech, and more wisedome than eloquence. And when so euer anie matter was to be debated, as he would take good leasure, and be aduised before he would speake: so when he spake he did it verie wiselie and prudentlie. In martiall affaires also he was verie bold, stout, and valiant, and yet not hastie to run headlong in anie aduenture. And as he would be well aduised before he gaue the attempt and aduenture, so when the same was once taken in hand, he would stoutlie pursue and follow the same. He was sober, modest, and chast, constant, trustie, and faithfull: a man not altogether without fault, and yet not spotted with anie notorious crime and fault.

The first dissention betweene the king and his sonnes.

CHAP. 44

IN the moneth of Aprill then next folowing, the yoong king sonne to king Henrie the elder, being no longer able to conceale or suppresse the wickednesse he had deuised against his father, he (I saie) and his two brethren the earls of Aquitaine and of Britaine suddenlie stole awaie into France, vnto Lewes the French king his father in law (for he had married his daughter), that hauing his aid he might ouer-run his owne father, and shorten his old yeares. And for his further helpe he had procured vnto him and on his side manie noble men both French and English, who openlie, but manie more, who secretlie did ioine with him to aid him. The elder king the father was verie much troubled and vnquieted for and about these and manie other sudden troubles, which on euerie side did grow vpon him; but yet he bare it out with a good face and countenance, dissembling that outwardlie which he conceiued inwardlie. And to stand firme and assured, he got and procured by all the meanes he could all such aid and helpe as was to be gotten and had. He sent into Ireland for his garrison, which he had left there, and being at Rone he committed the charge and gouernment of all Ireland vnto the earle Richard, but ioined Reimond in commission with him, bicause the earle without him would not doo anie thing, nor take the charge vpon him. And then the king of his liberalitie gaue also vnto him the towne of Wexford with the castell of Guikuilo.

Of the victories of king Henrie the second.

CHAP 45.

THE king hauing indured more than ciuill wars two whole years togither aswell in England as in Aquitaine, in great troubles, much wachings, & painfull trauels, yet at length most valiantlie he preuailed against his enimies, & surelie it was more of Gods goodnes, than by mans power, and (as it is to be thought) for the reuenge of the disobedience & wrongs doone by the sons against the father. But forsomuch as a mans owne houshold are commonlie the worst enimies; and of all enimies, the houshold & familiar enimie is most dangerous: there was no one thing which more troubled and grieued the king, than the gentlemen of his priuie chamber, and in whose hands in a manner laie his life or death, would euerie night secretlie and with treacherous minds run and resort to his sonnes, and in the morning when they should doo him seruice, they were not to be found. And albeit these warres in the beginning were verie doubtfull, and the king himselfe in great despaire: yet his hard beginning had a good ending, and he in the end had the victorie to his great honor and glorie. And God, who at the first seemed to be angrie with him, and in his anger to powre vpon him his wrath and indignation, yet now vpon his amendement and conuersion, he was become mercifull vnto him, and well pleased. And at the castell of Sandwich, whereof Reinulfe Glandeuill was then gouernor, who was a wise man, and alwaies most faithfull and trustie to the king, there was a generall peace proclamed, and all England in rest and quietnesse.

In this warre the king had taken prisoners the king of Scots, the earles of Chester and of Leicester, besides so manie gentlemen and good seruitors both English and French, that he had scarse anie prisons for so manie prisoners, nor so manie fetters for so manie captiues. But forsomuch as in vaine dooth a man triumph of the conquests vpon others, who cannot also triumph of the conquering of himselfe, and although the king had induted and abiden manie storms, great vnquietnesse, and much trouble, and at length hauing ouercommed both them and his enimies, he might the sooner haue béen wreaked and auenged of them: yet setting apart those affections euen in the middle of his triumphs vpon others, he also triumphed ouer himselfe, vsing such kinds of courtesies & clemencies as before had not beene heard. For suppressing his malice and reuenging mind, he gaue honor to his aduersaries, & life to his enimies. And the warres thus after two yeares ended, and all the great stormes ouercommed, he granted peace to all men, and forgaue ech man his offense and trespasse. And in the end also his sonnes repenting their follies, came and submitted themselues, with all humblenesse yéelding themselues to his will and pleasure.

The description of king Henrie the second.

CHAP. 46.

IT were not now amisse, but verie requisit that we should (for a perpetuall remembrance of the king) describe and set foorth as well the nature and conditions of his inward man as of his outward, that men which shall be desirous hereafter to learne and read his most noble acts in chiualrie, may also as it were before their eies conceiue his verie nature and liuelie portraiture: for he being so noble an ornament to this time and our historie, we might not well, neither dooth this historie permit vs to omit and passe him ouer in silence. Wherein we are to craue pardon that we may plainelie declare and tell the truth: for in all histories the perfect and full truth is to be alwaies opened, and without it the same wanteth both authoritie and credit: for art must follow nature. And the painter therfore, whose profession and art is to make his protraiture as liuelie as may be, if he swarue from the same, then both he and his worke lacke and want their commendation. And albeit no man be borne without his fault, yet is he most to be borne withall who is least spotted: & him must we account and thinke to be wise, who knowledgeth the same: for whie, in all worldlie matters there is no certeintie; and vnder heauen is no perfect felicitie, but euill things are mixt with good things, and vices ioined with vertues. And therefore, as things spoken in commendation either of a mans good disposition, or of his worthie doongs, doo delight and like well the hearer: euen so let him not be offended, if things not to be well liked be also recited and written. And yet the philosophers are of the opinion, that we ought to reuerence so the higher powers in all maner of offices and dueties, as that we should not prouoke nor mooue them with anie sharpe spéeches or disordered languages. For (as Terence saith) faire words and soothing speeches bréed fréendship, but plaine telling of truth makes enimies. Wherfore it is a dangerous thing to speake euill against him, though the occasion be neuer so iust, as who can foorthwith auenge the same. And it is a matter more dangerous, and he aduentureth himselfe verie far, which will contend in manie words against him, who in one or few words can wreake the same. It were suerlie a verie happie thing, and that which I confesse passeth my my reach if a man intreating of princes causes might tell the truth in euerie thing, and yet not offend them in anie thing But to the purpose

Henrie the second, king of England, was of a verie good colour, but somewhat red his head great and round, his eies were fierie, red, and grim, and his face verie high coloured, his voice or speech was shaking, quiuering, or trembling, his necke short, his breast brode and big, strong armed, his bodie was grosse, and his bellie somewhat big, which came vnto him rather by nature than by anie grosse feeding or surfetting For his diet was very temperat, and to saie the truth, thought to be more spare than comelie, or for the state of a prince and yet to abate his grossenesse and to remedie this fault of nature, he did as it were punish his bodie with continuall exercise, and did as it were keepe a continuall warre with himselfe For in the times of his warres, which were for the most part continuall to him, he had little or no rest at all and in time of peace he would not grant vnto himselfe anie peace at all, nor take anie rest, for then did he giue himselfe wholie vnto hunting, and to follow the same he would verie earlie euerie morning be on horssebacke, and then into the woods, sometimes into the forrests, and sometimes into the hilles and fields, and so would he spend the whole daie vntill night In the euening when he came home, he would neuer or verie seldome sit either before or after supper for though he were neuer so wearie, yet still would he be walking and going And forsomuch as it is verie profitable for euerie man in his life time, that he doo not take too much of anie one thing, for the medicine it selfe which is appointed for a mans helpe & remedie, is not absolutelie perfect and good to be alwaies vsed euen so it befell and happened to this prince, for partlie by his excessiue trauels, and partlie by diuerse bruses in his bodie, his legs and féet were swollen and sore And though he had no disease at all, yet age it selfe was a breaking sufficient vnto him He was of a resonable stature, which happened to none of his sons, for his two eldest sons were somwhat higher, & his two yoonger sons were somewhat lower and lesse than was he If he were in a good mood, and not angrie, then would he be verie pleasant and eloquent. he was also (which was a thing verie rare in those daies) verie well learned. he was also verie affable, gentle, and courteous, and besides so pitifull, that when he had ouercome his enimie, yet would he be ouercome with pitie towards him

In warres he was most valiant, and in peace he was as proouident and circumspect And in the wars mistrusting and doubting of the end and euent therof, he would (as Terence writeth) trie all the waies and meanes he could deuise rather than wage the battell If he lost anie of his men in the fight, he would maruellouslie lament his death, and séeme to pitie him more being dead than he did regard or account of him being aliue, more bewailing the dead than fauouring the liuing In times of distresse no man more courteous, and when all things were safe no man more hard or cruell Against the stubborne & vnrulie no man more sharpe, nor yet to the humble no man more gentle, hard toward his owne men and houshold, but liberall to strangers, bountifull abrode, but sparing at home whom he once hated, he would neuer or verie hardlie loue, and whom he once loued, he would not lightlie be out with him, or forsake him he had great pleasure and delight in hawking and hunting Would God he had béene as well bent and disposed vnto good deuotion!

It was said that after the displeasure growne betwéene the king and his sonnes, by the meanes and thorough the intising of the queene their moother, he neuer accounted to kéepe his word and promise, but without anie regard or care was a common breaker thereof. And true it is, that of a certeine naturall disposition he was light and inconstant of his word and if the matter were brought to a narrow streict or pinch, he would not sticke rather to couer his word, than to denie his déed.

déed. And for this cause he in all his doings was verie prouident and circumspect, and a verie vpright and a seuere minister of iustice, although he did therein greeue and make his friends to smart. His answers for the most part were peruerse and froward. Iustice which is God himselfe is fréelie and without rewards to be ministred. And albeit for profit and lucre all things are set to sale, and doo bring great gaines as well to the clergie as to the laitie: yet they are no better to a mans heires or executors, than were the riches of (2) Gehezi the seruant to Elizeus, whose gréedie takings turned himselfe to vtter ruine and destruction.

He was a great peacemaker, and a carefull keeper thereof himselfe: a liberall almes giuer, and a speciall benefactor to the holie land, he loued humilitie, abhorred pride, and much oppressed his nobilitie. The hungrie he refreshed, but the rich he regarded not. The humble he would exalt, but the mightie he disdained. He vsurped much vpon the holie church, and of a certeine kind of zeale, but not according to knowledge, he did intermingle and confound the prophane with holie things; for why, he would be all in all himselfe. He was the child of the holie church, and by hir aduanced to the scepter of his kingdome, and yet he either dissembled or vtterlie forgat the same: for he was slacke alwaies in comming to the church vnto the diuine seruice, and at the time thereof he would be busied and occupied rather in counsels and in conference about the affaires of his commonwealth, than in deuotion and praier. The liuelihoods belonging to anie spirituall promotion, he would in time of vacation confiscat to his owne treasurie, and assume that to himselfe which was due vnto Christ. When anie new troubles or wars did grow or come vpon him, then would he lash & powre all that euer he had in store or treasurie, and liberallie bestow that vpon a roister or a soldier, which ought to haue beene giuen vnto the priest. He had a verie prudent & forecasting wit, and therby forseeing what things might or were like to insue, he would accordinglie order & dispose either for the performance, or for the preuenting thereof: notwithstanding manie times the euent happened to the contrarie, and he disappointed of his expectation: and commonlie there happened no ill vnto him, but he would foretell therof to his friends and familiars.

He was a maruellous naturall father to his children, and loued them tenderlie in their childhood and yoong yeares: but they being growne to some age and ripenesse, he was as a father in law, and could scarselie brooke anie of them. And notwithstanding they were verie handsome, comelie, and noble gentlemen: yet whether it were that he would not haue them prosper too fast, or whether they had euill deserued of him, he hated them, & it was full much against his will, that they should be his successors, or heires to anie part of his inheritance. And such is the prosperitie of man, that as it can not be perpetuall, no more can it be perfect and assured: for why, such was the secret malice of fortune against this king, that where he should haue receiued much comfort, there had he most sorrow: where quietnesse & safetie, there vnquietnesse and perill: where peace, there enimitie: where courtesie, there ingratitude: where rest, there trouble. And whether this happened by the meanes of the (3) marriages, or for the punishment of the fathers sinnes: certeine it is, there was no good agréement, neither betweene the father & the sonnes, nor yet among the sonnes themselues.

But at length, when all his enimies and the disturbers of the common peace were suppressed, and his brethren, his sonnes, and all others his aduersaries as well at home as abroad were reconciled: then all things happened and befell vnto him (though it were long first) after and according to his owne will and mind. And would to God he had likewise reconciled himselfe vnto God, and by amendement of his life had in the end also procured his fauour and mercie! Besides this, which I had almost forgotten, he was of such a (4) memorie, that if he had once séene

 and.

and knowne a man, he would not forget him neither yet whatsoeuer he had heard, would he be vnmindfull thereof And hereof was it, that he had so readie a memorie of histories which he had read, as a knowledge and a maner of an experience in all things To conclude, if he had béene chosen of God, and béene obsequious and carefull to liue in his feare and after his laws, he had excelled all the princes of the world for in the gifts of nature no one man was to be compared vnto him Thus much brieflie, and yet not much besides the matter, I haue thought good to deliuer, that hauing in few words made my entrie, other writers maie haue the better occasion more at large to discourse and intreat of this so worthie an historie And therefore leauing the same to others, let vs returne to our Ireland, from whense we digressed

(1) The words are *Oculis glaucis* which some doo English to be greie eies, like the colour of the skie, with specks in it but some doo English it a bright red, as is the colour of a lions eie, which is commonlie a signe or an argument of a man which will be soone warmed & angrie. & so it is to be taken in this place for the words, which follow, be *Ad iram torvis*, which is to saie, grim looking eies disposed to anger which eies were answerable to the complexion and disposition of this king

(2) This historie is written in the fift chapter of the second booke of the kings, & in effect is this When the prophet Elisha or Elizeus had healed Naaman the Syrian of his leprosie, he would haue rewarded the prophet, & haue giuen great and rich gifts but he refused the same and would none thereof, wherefore Naaman departed awaie But Gehezi the seruant of the prophet, being touched with a greedie and a couetous mind, and angrie that his master had refused such rich presents, secretlie he ran after the Syrian; and ouertaking him, did aske of him in his masters name a talent of siluer, & certeine garments which he receiued doubled, and returned therewith But he was no sooner come home, but that his couetousnesse was rewarded, and he plagued with the leprosie of Naaman, which claue vnto him as white as the snow.

(3) The king maried Eleanor the daughter and heire to the erle of Poitiers (who before was maried to Lewes the eight and king of France, but diuorsed from him for néerenesse of blood) and after that he had continued with hir sundrie yeares, and receiued by hir six sonnes and thrée daughters, he fell in loue with a yoong wench named Rosamund, and then waxed wearie of his wife. And she to be awreaked, did not onelie in continuance of time find the means to find out this Rosamund, who was kept secret in a house builded like a labyrinth of purpose for hir safe kéeping at Woodstocke, where when the quéen had found hir, Rosamund liued not long after but also for a further reuenge, she by means of hir sonnes who were noble & valiant gentlemen, caused warres to be stirred and raised against the king to his great vnquietnesse and this is one of the mariages of which this author meaneth. The other was of his son named Henrie, whome he did not onelie make and crowne king in his life time, but also for a confirmation of a peace to be had betwéene him and Lewes the eight then French king, he maried his said sonne to the ladie Margaret daughter to the said French king By reason whereof his said sonne being once come to yéeres of age, and thinking it too long yer he could haue the sole gouernment, as also being by the quéene his mother intised, and taking hir part, he fled to the French king his father in law, and by his aid, as also of sundrie other noble men both English and French, who ioined with him, made warres vpon his said father · which bred vnto him no little trouble and vnquietnesse

(4) There is not a more commendable & more necessarie vertue in a king, than

is the gift of a quicke and good memorie: for by it knowledge dooth increase and experience is perfected. And therefore saith Cicero, that memorie is the treasurie of all good things, and most necessarie to the life of man: wherein the more the gouernor excelleth, the more prouident is his gouernment. For why, as Plutarch writeth, the remembrance of things past are speciall presidents and examples of things to come. Diuers and sundrie men haue béene famous, and much commended for their excellencie in this vertue. Mithridates king of Pontus in Asia had vnder his dominion two and twentie nations, and he was of such singular memorie, that he did not onelie vnderstand their seuerall languages, but also spake them perfectlie: and in iudgements would heare each man to speake in his owne language, and answer them in the same. Cyrus king of Persia, the sonne of Cambises, so excelled in memorie, that hauing an excéeding great multitude of men in his host, he would call euerie man by his proper name and surname. Cineas an ambassador from king Pyrrhus to the Romanes, was not in Rome aboue one whole daie, before he could salute euerie of the senators, and euerie noble man of Rome by his particular name. Likewise Iulius Cesar and Adrianus the emperors of Rome were of such excellent memories, that euerie of them at one instant could both read and write, as also speake and heare. The like also is said of the famous and most excellenthe learned man Erasmus Roterodamus, who hauing alwaies or for the most part sundrie and diuers clearks writing at one time and instant, of sundrie matters, would walke vp and downe among them, and indite to euerie one what he should write. And this thing is so necessarie in all princes, that in the old ages they were euer woont to haue about them such men as were of a speciall memorie, to put them in mind of all such things as to them should be méet and requisite, and these were called Nomenclatores. Whether this king had any such attending vpon him or not, it is certeine that he himselfe was of an excellent good memorie.

Thus far the first booke of the Conquest of Ireland.

SYLVESTER GIRALDUS CAMBRENSIS,

HIS SECOND BOOKE OF THE VATICINALL HISTORIE OF THE

CONQUEST OF IRELAND

The Proheme of the author.

WE haue thus farre continued our historie, in as perfect and full order as we could, hauing omitted nothing woorthie the memorie, as farre as the matter seemed to require: but being occupied and busied with the generall and necessarie causes in religion, although we had not sufficient leasure and time to follow and prosecute this our enterprise and matter begun, yet did not we thinke it meet to giue the same ouer, and to leaue it halfe vndoone. We haue therefore, and yet doo continue the historie but breefelie, not in anie high or eloquent stile, but in a common phrase and plaine speeches, giuing rather thereby an occasion to our posteritie for them to set foorth this historie, than to doo it our selues. For indeed our leasure is verie small, and such as it is, it is turned to troubles and vnquietnesse, our loue and zeale into hatred, our ioy into sorrow, and our rest to molestations.

For now flourish not the honest exercises of studies, but the busie policies of warres: now the good studies of the mind are contemned, and the lusts of the bodie imbraced: now we haue no leasure to serue the Muses, but to be hammering with weapons: quiet minds are not now at leasure, but glistering weapons and armors are in euerie mans hands. Wherefore let not the reader looke now at our hands for anie good order, eloquence, or pleasantnesse in this our writing: for place must be giuen of necessitie vnto time. And as the same is now verie troublesome, so can the same bring foorth but troublesome matters. In these troubled times, and wanting conuenient leasure and quietnesse, I haue trauelled with the more paines to absolue and end this my worke: not after the maner of a student, but as a trauellor, whose nature and condition is, that when he dooth set foorth on his iournie verie slacklie and slowlie, then dooth he make the more hast, and trauell the more speedilie. How soeuer it shall please God to deale with vs in the seruices now in hand, I haue as diligentlie as I can compiled this my historie as also my topographie, leauing the same as a monument of our will, to remaine to our countrie and posteritie for euer.

THE

SECOND BOOKE

OF THE

CONQUEST OF IRELAND.

The earle is sent backe againe into Ireland, and is made generall of the land, and Reimond is ioined in commission with him

CHAP I.

ERLE Richard, being now returned into Ireland, the people there being aduertised of the great trubles which were beyond the seas, they being a people constant onlie in inconstancie, firme in wauering and faithfull in vntruths; these (I say) and all the princes of that land, the earle at his comming found to be reuolted and to become rebels For the recouerie and suppressing of whom, the earle then wholie bestirred himselfe, and at length hauing spent and consumed all his treasure, which he had brought ouer with him, his soldiors who were vnder the guiding of Herueie being then constable, lacked their wages and were vnpaid and by reason of the emulation betwéene Herueie and Reimond, the seruice and exploits to be doon against the Irishrie was verie slacke and slender and by that meanes they wanted such preies and spoiles of neat and cattell as they were woont to haue for their vittels The souldiors in this distresse, wanting both monie for their wages and vittels for their food, assembled themselues and went vnto the earle, vnto whome with one voice they exclamed and said, that vnlesse he would make and appoint Reimond to be their capteine againe, they would without all doubt forsake him, and would either returne home againe, or (that which is worse) would go and serue vnder the enimies

In this distresse was Reimond appointed the capteine, & forthwith hauing mustered his souldiers, he made a rode or iourneie into Ophalia vpon the rebels there, where he tooke great preies, and were well recouered as well in horsse as in armor From thense they marched to Lismore, where when they had spoiled both the towne and countrie, they returned with great booties, taking the waie vnto Waterford by the sea side and being come to the sea shores, where they found thirteene botes latelie come from Waterford, as also others of other places; all these they laded with their preies, minding to haue passed by water vnto Waterford But tarieng there for a wind, the men of Corke, who had heard of their doings, and being but sixtéene miles from them, doo prepare two and thirtie barks of their owne towne, and doo well man and furnish them, being wholie determined to set vpon Reimond, and if they can to giue him the ouerthrow, which they did · betwéene whom was a cruell fight, the one part giuing a fierce onset

onset with stones and spaths, & the other defending themselues with bowes and weapons In the end the men of Corke were ouercome, and their capteine named Gilbert Mac Turger was there slaine by a lustie yoong gentlemen named Philip Welsh And then Adam Herford, who was the generall or admerall of that nauie, being well increased and laden with great preies, sailed with great triumph to the citie of Waterford

But Reimond himselfe was not present at this fight vpon the water, and yet hearing thereof, he came in all hast and marched towards them, taking his waie by the sea side, hauing in his companie twentie gentlemen, and thréescore horssemen. And by the waie in his iournee he met with Dermond Mac Artie prince of Desmond, who was comming with a great band of men to helpe and rescue the men of Corke where they fought togither but in the end Mac Artie had the worse side, and was ouerthrowne, and then Reimond hauing preied and taken about foure thousand head of neat, he marched and came to Waterford About this time also as they marched homewards, certeine Irishmen in those parties being skulking & lurking in the woods, when the preies and cattell passed by, they issued out, tooke and carried awaie certeine of the cattell into the woods, whereupon the crie was vp, and came as farre as Waterford Whereupon the souldiers and most part of the garison issued out, among whom Meilerius was the best and most forward. For he being come to the woods, and hauing in his companie then onelie one souldier, put spur to the horsse, and aduentured in the woods, following the Irishmen (by the abetting of the souldier who was with him) euen to the furthest & thickest part of the woods where he was so farre entered, that he was in danger of the enimie: and the souldier being not able to retire was there taken, killed and hewed in péeces Meilerius then séeing himselfe to be inuironed round about with the enimies, and he in the like perill as the other was, bicause he alone against a thousand was neither able to rescue his man, nor helpe himselfe, but in danger to be taken as was the other, like a valiant gentleman draweth his sword, and with a lustie courage, euen in despite of their téeth maketh waie through them And such as set vpon him he spared not, but cut off an arme of this man, a hand of that man, a head of one, and a shoulder of another, & he escaped throughout them without anie harme or hurt to his owne bodie, sauing that he brought two darts in his shield, and thrée in his horsse.

The ouerthrow giuen by the Irishmen against the souldiers which came from Dublin; and what the Ostomen were, of whom mention is made here and elsewhere.

CHAP 2.

WHEN these things were thus done, & the souldiers well refreshed by the booties and preies taken vpon the water and the land, Reimond being aduertised that his father William Fitzgerald was dead, he tooke shipping and passed ouer into Wales, there to take seisen, and to enter into the land descended vnto him. And in his absence Heruie was againe made lieutenant of the armie who in the absence of Reimond, thinking to doo some seruice and notable exploit, bringeth the earle vnto Cashill; and for their better strength and further helpe, sent his commandement vnto Dublin, that the souldiers there should come and méet them; who according came foorth. and in the iournee they passed thorough Ossorie, where on a certeine night they lodged themselues Donald then prince of Limerike, a man verie wise in his nation, hauing vnderstanding by his priuie espials

espials of their cōming, suddenlie and vnwares verie earlie in the morning with a great force and companie stale vpon them, and slue of them foure gentlemen which were capteins, and foure hundred (1) Ostomen in this sore discomfiture.

The earle as soone as he heard hereof, with great sorow & heauinesse returned vnto Waterford By means of this mishap, the Irishmen in euerie place tooke such a heart and comfort, that the whole nation with one consent and agréement rose vp against the Englishmen, and the earle as it were a man besieged, kept himselfe within the wals and citie of Waterford, and from whence he mooued not But Rothorike Oconor prince of Connagh, comming and passing ouer the riuer of Shenin, thinking now to recouer all Meth, inuadeth the same with sword and fire, and spoileth, burneth, and destroieth the same, & all the whole countrie euen to the hard walles of Dublin, leauing no castell standing or vndestroied.

(1) These Ostomen were not Irishmen, but yet of long continuance in Ireland. Some saie they came first out of Norwaie, and were called Ostomen, that is to saie Easterlings, or Easterne men, bicause that countrie lieth East in respect of England and Ireland Some thinke they were Saxons and Normans, but whatsoeuer they were, they were merchants and vsed the trade of merchandize, and in peaceable maner they came into Ireland; and there being landed they found such fauour with the Irishrie, that they licenced them to build hauen townes wherein they might dwell & vse their traffike These men builded the ancientest and most part of the cities and towns vpon or néere the sea side within that land, as namelie Dublin, Waterford, Corke, Limerike, and others And albeit they in processe of time grew to be mightie and strong, and for their safetie did build townes and castels yet they durst not to dwell among the Irish people, but still continued and kept themselues within their owne townes and forts, and thereof they are and were called since townesmen And of them were these, being the inhabitants of Dublin, which came to méet the earle, and were thus slaine.

The returning of Reimond into Ireland, and how he married Basilia the sister vnto the earle.

CHAP 3.

THE earle then seeing himselfe to be now in great distresse, and in a narrow streict, taketh aduise with his fréends and councellors what were best to be doone At length, as vnto his last refuge, he sendeth his letters to Reimond being yet in Wales, to this effect. "As soone as you haue read these our letters, make all the hast you can to come awaie, and bring with you all the helpe and force that you can make and then according to your owne will and desire, you shall assuredlie and immediatlie vpon your comming haue and marrie my sister Basilia." Reimond, as soone as he had read these letters, he was forthwith in hast to be gone, and thought it long yer he could be gone, not onlie in respect of the faire ladie, whom he had long wooed, loued, and desired, but also that he might helpe and succour his lord and maister in this distresse and necessitie Wherefore he maketh preparation accordinglie, and by means of friendship and otherwise, he had gotten thirtie lustie yoong gentlemen of his owne coosins and kindred, and one hundred horssemen, as also thrée hundred footmen and bowmen of the best and chosen men in all Wales all which were in a readinesse to go with him.

him. And as soone as the shipping for them was readie, and the wind seruing, he and his coosin Merlerius, with all the said companie tooke the seas, and shortlie after arriued in twentie barks vnto (1) Waterford

At the verie same time the townesmen of Waterford, being in a verie great rage and furie against the Englishmen there, were fullie minded and determined to haue killed them all wheresoeuer they could find them. But when they saw these barks comming in with their flags, hanging to their top masts, which to them were vnknowne, they were astonied at their so sudden comming, and their deuises were dashed Reimond foorthwith entered the towne with all his companie, and when all things were quieted and appeased, he & the earle went from thense vnto Wexford, with all their force and strength, leauing behind one (2) Precell or Purcell his lieutenant at Waterford But he verie shortlie minding to follow after the earle, tooke a boat, and as he passed ouer the riuer of the Suire, the maister of the boat and his companie which were townesmen of Waterford, slue this Purcell, and those few whom he had then attending vpon him Which murther when they had thus doone, they returned to the citie, and there without all pitie or mercie, spared neither man, nor woman, nor child, but slue as manie as they could find in the streets, houses, or anie other places Howbeit the citie it selfe was safelie kept by such as were then in Reinolds tower, who draue the traitors out of the citie, as also in the end compelled them to yéeld and submit themselues, and to intreat for peace, which they hardlie obteined, both with an euill credit and harder conditions

But Reimond still mindfull of the promise made vnto him, and he languishing vntill the same were performed, would not depart from out of Wexford, vntill messengers were sent to (3) Dublin to fetch and bring his louer Basilia to (4) Wexford to be married vnto him Which being doone, and he married, they spent all that daie and night in feastings & pastimes And as they were in their most iollitie, newes was brought vnto them, how that Rothorike prince of Connagh had destroied, wasted, & spoiled all Meth, and was entred into the borders of Dublin. Wherevpon Reimond on the next morrow, setting apart and giuing ouer all wedding pastimes, mustereth all his souldiors, and without anie delaiengs marcheth towards the enimies But Rothorike who had before tried his valiantnesse, and experimented his force, hearing of his comming and not minding to tarie or abide the same, retireth backe, and getteth him to his owne home and countrie Then Reimond recouereth againe all those countries, and foorthwith causeth all the forts and castels then before pulled downe and defaced, to be now reedified and repaired, as also the castels of Trim, and of Dunlences in Meth, of which Hugh Tirell was before the conestable, and for want of rescue and helpe compelled to leaue and forsake them And thus by the means of Reimond, all things being recouered and restored to their former and pristine estate, the whole land for feare of him continued a good time in peace and rest

(1) There is great varietie in such bookes and examples as I haue, and which I doo follow in this point some writing that Reimond did not land at Waterford, but at Wexford, and the tumult there being appeased, he went from thense vnto Waterford, and brought the earle vnto Wexford Some write againe (as is aforesaid) that he landed at Waterford, and not at Wexford but hauing saluted the earle, appeased the tumult, and set all things in order, he conducted the earle and the whole armie ouer land vnto Wexford Although there be some variance in the exemplars, yet concerning the substance of the historie it is not materiall

(2) There is also a varietie in the exemplars of this name, some write Fircellus, and some write Pricellus, and some Pircellus, or Purcell, it is like to be Purcell, for

for they of that name were seruitors in this conquest, and for their good seruice they were rewarded with lands and territories, and who are yet remaining about or néere the citie, and in the countie of Waterford

(9) It is certeine that this Basilia abode at Dublin, but whether she were there married or at Wexford it is doubted. Some hold opinion, that Reimond after that he had met and also saluted the erle, they foorthwith hearing the countries in Leinster, and especiallie about Dublin to be in an vprore, marched thither streightwaie without anie staie And there Reimond as a lustie soldior in his armor married the ladie Basilia, and they issued with aduantage vpon the enimie. But the writer of best credit saith that the marriage was at Wexford

The secret practise of Herueie against Reimond.

CHAP 4

BUT Herucie seeing the honor and credit of Reimond dailie to increase more & more, and he much gréeued therewith, deuiseth all the means he can how to stop and hinder the same and forsomuch as he could not compasse the same by anie open attempt, he practiseth it secretlie, and by secret deuises. Wherefore he is now a suter to marrie the ladie Nesta, daughter to Maurice Fitzgerald, and cousine germane to Reimond, that vnder the colour of this new affinitie, aliance, and vntained fréendship he might take Reimond in a trip Well, his secret deuises being to himselfe, and no such thing suspected nor mistrusted as he meant, he by his earnest sute obteineth this gentlewoman, and marrieth hir. And Reimond also to make freendship on all sides to be the more firme, procured that Aline the earls daughter was maried to William eldest son of William Fitzgerald And to Maurice Fitzgerald himselfe, who was lathe come out of Wales, there was giuen the halfe cantred of Ophelan, which he had before of the kings gift, as also the castell of Guindoloke and Meilerius bicause he was the better marcher had the other halfe cantred But the cantred of land which was neerest towards Dublin, and which the king had once giuen vnto Fitzstephans, was now bestowed vpon the two Herfords.

The obteining of the priuilege at Rome.

CHAP 5.

IN this meane time the king, though he were in great troubles, & much vnquieted with the wars, yet was he not vnmindfull of his realme of Ireland as also of the orders made and deuised at the councell of Cashill, for the redresse and reformation of the filthie and loose life of the Irishrie And therevpon sent his ambassadors vnto Rome to pope Alexander the third, of and from whom he obteined certeine priuileges, and vnder his authoritie, namelie, that he should be lord ouer all the realme of Ireland, and by his power and authoritie they to be reduced and brought to the christian faith, after the maner and order of the church of England This priuilege the king sent ouer into Ireland by one Nicholas Wallingford then prior, but afterwards abbat of Malmesburie, and William Fitzaldelme And then being at Waterford, they caused an assemblie and a synod to be had of all the bishops and clergie within that land, and then in the open audience of them, the said grant and priuilege was openlie read and published· as also one other priuilege before

 giuen

giuen and granted by pope Adrian an Englishman borne, at the sute of one John of Salisburie, who was made bishop of Karnoceus at Rome And by this man also he sent vnto the king for a token, and in signe of a possession thereof, one gold ring, which togither with the priuilege was laid vp in the kings treasurie at Winchester. The tenure of both which priuileges it shall not be amisse here to insert. And concerning the first, these are the words thereof

Two priuileges sent from Rome to the king of England

"Adrian the bishop, the seruant of the seruants of God, to his most déere sonne in Christ the noble king of England sendeth gréeting, and the apostolike benediction Your excellencie hath béene verie carefull and studious how you might inlarge the church of God here in earth, and increase the number of his saints and elects in heauen in that as a good catholike king, you haue and doo by all meanes labor and trauell to inlarge and increase Gods church, by teaching the ignorant people the true and christian religion, and in abolishing and rooting vp the weeds of sin and wickednesse and wherin you haue and doo craue for your better aid and furtherance the helpe of the apostolike sée, wherein the more spéedilie and discreetlie you doo procéed, the better successe we hope God will send For all they which of a feruent zeale, and loue in religion, doo begin and enterprise anie such thing, shall no doubt in the end haue a good and prosperous successe And as for Ireland and all other Ilands where Christ is knowen, and the christian religion receiued, it is out of all doubt, and your excellencie well knoweth, they doo all apperteine and belong to the right of saint Peter, and of the church of Rome And we are so much the more redie, desirous, & willing to sow the acceptable séed of Gods word, because we know the same in the latter daie will be most seuerelie required at our hands. You haue (our welbeloued in Christ) aduertised and signified vnto vs, that you will enter into the land and realme of Ireland, to the end to bring them obedient vnto law, and vnder your subiection, and to root out from among them their foule sins and wickednesse, as also to yéeld and paie yéerelie out of euerie house a yearelie pension of one penie vnto saint Peter and besides also will defend & kéepe the rites of those churches whole and inuiolate. We therefore well allowing and fauouring this your godlie disposition & commendable affection, doo accept, ratifie, and assent vnto this your petition and doo grant that you for the dilating of Gods church, the punishment of sin, the reforming of maners, planting of vertue and the increasing of christian religion, you doo enter to possesse that land, and there to execute according to your wisedome whatsoeuer shall be for the honor of God, and the safetie of the realme And further also we doo strictlie charge and require that all the people of that land doo with all humblenesse, dutifulnesse, and honor receiue and accept you as their liege lord and soueraigne, reseruing and excepting the right of the holie church, which we will be inuiolablie preserued, as

Peter pence

also the yeerelie pension of the Peter pence out of euerie house, which we require to be trulie answered to saint Peter, and to the church of Rome If therfore you doo mind to bring your godlie purpose to effect, indeuor to trauell to reforme the people to some better order and trade of life and that also by your selfe, and by such others as you shall thinke meet, true, and honest, in their life, maners and conuersation, the church of God may be beautified, the true christian religion sowed and planted, and all other things to be doone, that by anie meanes shall or may be to Gods honor and the saluation of mens soules whereby you may in the end receiue at Gods hands the reward of an euerlasting life, as also in the meane time, and in this life carrie a glorious fame, and an honorable report among all nations" The tenure and effect of the second priuilege is thus.

The second priuilege

"Alexander the bishop, the seruant of the seruants of God, to his déerelie beloued son the noble king of England sendeth gréeting, grace, and the apostolike benediction.

benediction. Forsomuch as things giuen and granted vpon good reasons by our predecessors, are to be well allowed of, ratified, and confirmed, we well considering and pondering the grant and priuilege, for and concerning the dominion of the land of Ireland to vs appertening, and latelie giuen by Adrian our predecessor, we following his steps doo in like maner confirme, ratifie, and allow the same: reseruing and sauing to saint Peter and to the church of Rome the yeerelie pension of one penie out of euerie house as well in England as in Ireland. Prouided also, that the barbarous people of Ireland by your meanes be reformed and recouered from their filthie life and abhominable conuersation, that as in name so in maners and conuersation they may be christians: that as that rude and disordered church by you being reformed, the whole nation also may with the profession of the name be in acts and life followers of the same."

The titles of the kings of England vnto Ireland.

CHAP 6.

LET then the enuious & ignorant cease and giue ouer to quarell and auouch that the kings of England haue no right nor title to the realme of Ireland. But let them well vnderstand that by fiue maner of waies, that is to saie, by two ancient titles, and three latter they haue to auouch and defend the same, as in our topographie is declared. First it is euident and apparent by the histories of England, that Gurguntius the sonne of Belin king of Britaine, as he returned with great triumph from out of Denmarke, he met at the Iles of the Orchades a nauie (1) of a certeine nation or people, named Baldenses, now Barons, and those he sent into Ireland, appointing vnto them certeine guides and leaders to conduct & direct them thither. Likewise the same histories doo plainlie witnesse, that king Arthur the famous king of Britaine, had manie of the Irish kings tributarie to him: & he on a time holding & kéeping his court at Westchester, Gillomarus king or monarch of Ireland, with other the princes thereof, came & presented themselues before him. Also the Irishmen came out of (2) Baron, the chiefe citie in Biscaie. And forsomuch as men, be they neuer so frée, yet they maie renounce their right and libertie, and bring themselues into subiection: so it is apparent that the princes of Ireland did freelie, and of their owne accord, submit & yéeld themselues to king Henrie of England: & swore vnto him faith and loialtie. And albeit such men of a kind of a naturall lightnesse and inconstancie, be not ashamed nor afraied to denie and renounce their faith: yet that can not so release and discharge them. Euerie man is at his owne choise and libertie how to contract and bargaine with anie one, but the same once made he can not fléet nor swarue from it. And finallie the holie pope, in whom is the effect of perfection, and who by a certeine prerogatiue and title requireth & claimeth all Ilands, bicause by him and by him and by his meanes they were first reduced and recouered to the christian faith, he I saie hath ratified and confirmed this title.

(1) The historie is this, that Gurguntius the son of king Belin made a viage into Denmarke, there to appease the people, who were then vp in rebellion against him: and hauing preuailed and ouercommed them, he in his returning homewards by the Iles of the Orchades, there met him a fléet or a nauie of thirtie or (as some saie) thrée score sailes of men and women latelie come and exiled from out of that part of Spaine, called then Baldensis, whereof Baron was the chiefe citie, but now

it

it is a part of the countrie of Gascoigne, whose capteine named (as some write) Bartholomew, did present himselfe before Gurguntius, and discoursing vnto him the cause of their trauels, besought him to consider of their distresse, and to grant vnto them some dwelling place, and they would béecome his subiects. Which their request the king granted, and taking their oth of allegiance sent and caused them to be conducted into Ireland, where as his subiects they remained and continued.

(2) These people were named Iberi, & before that they came to seeke vnto Gurguntius for a land to dwell in, they dwelled in that part of Spaine, whereof Baion is the metropole, which is now part of Biscaie, and this countrie before and long after the time of Gurguntius, was still subiect to the kings of Britaine, now called England.

The rebellion of Donald prince of Limerike, and of the taking of the citie of Limerike.

CHAP 7.

IN the meane while, Donald O Brin prince of Limerike waxed verie insolent, and nothing regarding his former promise and oth made to the king began & did withdraw his fealtie and seruice. Wherevpon Remond mustering his armie, gathered and picked out the best and lustiest men which he had. And hauing twentie and six gentlemen, thrée hundred horssemen, and thrée hundred bowmen and footmen in readinesse and well appointed, about the kalends of October marched towards Limerike to assaile the same. When they came thither the riuer of the Shenin, which inuironeth and runneth round about the citie, they found the same to be so déepe and stikle, that they could not passe ouer the same. But the lustie yoong gentlemen who were gréedie to haue the preie, but more desirous to haue the honor, were in a great agonie and gréefe, that they were thus abarred from approching to assaile the citie. Wherevpon one (1) Dauid Welsh so named of his familie and kinred, although otherwise a Camber or a Welshman borne, and nephue vnto Remond, who was a lustie and valiant yoong soldior, and a verie tall man aboue all the rest, was verie hot and impatient that they so long lingered the time about nothing. Wherevpon hauing a greater regard to win fame and honor than fearing of anie perill or death, taking his horsse and putting his spurres to his sides aduentureth the water, which being verie stikle and full of stones and rocks was the more dangerous: but yet he so wiselie marked the course of the streame, and so aduised and guided his horsse, that he passed the riuer, and safelie recouered the further side; and then he cried out alowd to his companie, that he had found a foord. But for all that there was neuer a one that would follow, sauing one Geffrie.

But they both returning backe againe to conduct ouer the whole companie, the said Geffreie his horsse being caried awaie with the violence of the streame, they were both drowned. Which when Meilerius (who was also come thither) did sée, he began to fret with himselfe, partlie for that his cousine & kinsman of so noble an enterprise had so bad a successe, partlie also disdaining that anie should atchiue to honor but himselfe. Wherevpon being mounted vpon a lustie strong horsse, setteth spurre to his side, and being neither dismaied with the stiklenesse and danger of the water, nor afraied with the mishap fallen to the gentleman, who was then drowned, more rashlie than wiselie aduentureth the riuer & recouereth the further side & banke. The citizens some of them watching and méeting him at the waters side,

side, and some standing vpon the towne wals fast by the riuer side, minding and meaning to haue driuen him backe againe, or to haue killed him in the place, hurled stones a good pace vnto him. But this noble and lustie gentleman, being thus sharplie and hardlie beset in the middle of perils and dangers, his enimies on the one side hardlie assailing, and the riuer on the other side stopping and closing him vp from all rescue, standeth to his tackle, and as well as he could couering his head with his shield, defendeth and saueth himselfe from his enimies. Whilest they were thus bickering there was great showting and noise on both sides of the water. But Reimond being then the generall of the field, and in the rereward, knowing nothing hereof, as soone as he heard of it, came in all hast through the campe vnto the waters side. Where when he saw his nephue on the other side, to be in the middle of his enimies, and like to be vtterlie cast awaie and destroied vnlesse he had some spéedie helpe and succour, was in a maruellous griefe & agonie, & verie sharplie crieth and calleth out to his men, as followeth.

(1) This Welsh was so called, the same being the name of his familie and kindred, and not of the countrie of Wales, wherein he was borne. He was a woorthie gentleman, and of his race there are yet remaining manie good and woorthie gentlemen, who are chéeflie abiding in the prouince and citie of Waterford: for there were they first planted.

The oration and speech of Reimond vnto his companie, and of the recouerie of the citie of Limerike.

CHAP. 8.

"O YE worthie men, of nature valiant, and whose prowesse we haue well tried, come ye awaie. The waie heretofore not knowne, and the riuer hitherto though not passable, by our aduentures a foord is now found therein: let vs therefore follow him that is gone before, and helpe him being now in distresse. Let vs not suffer, nor sée so woorthie a gentleman, thus for our common cause and honor oppressed, to perish and be cast awaie before our eies and in our sights for want of our helpe, and by meanes of our sluggishnesse. It is no time now to vse manie words, nor leisure serueth to make manie spéeches. The shortnesse of the time, the present necessitie of this noble gentleman, & the state of our owne honors vrgeth expedition, & requireth hast." And euen with these words he put spurres to the horsse, and aduentureth the riuer: after whome followed the whole companie, euerie one striuing who might be formost. And as God would they passed all safe ouer, sauing two souldiors and one gentleman named Guido, who were drowned. They were no sooner come to land, but that their enimies all fled and ran awaie, whome they pursued, and in the chase slue a number of them, as also entered and tooke the towne. And hauing thus gotten both the citie and the victorie, they recouered their small losse with great spoiles & riches, as also reaped great honor and fame.

Now reader, which of these thrée thinkest thou best valiant, and best woorthie of honor? Him who first aduentured the riuer, and taught the waie? Or him who séeing the losse of his companion, the perill of the riuer, and the multitude of the enimies, did yet (not fearing death nor perill) aduenture himselfe in the midle of his enimies? Or him who hastilie setting all feare apart, did hazard himselfe and all his hoast to saue the friend, and to aduenture vpon the enimie? And this one thing by the waie is to be noted, that on a tuesdaie Limerike was first conquered, on a tuesdaie it was againe

A note concerning tuesdaie or the date of Mars.

againe recouered, on a tuesdaie Waterford was taken, on a tuesdaie Wexford was gotten, and on a tuesdaie Dublin was woone. And these things came not thus to passe, as it were by a set match, but euen of a common course of fortune, or by Gods so appointment. And it is not altogither against reason, that martiall affaires should haue good successe vpon Mars his daie.

The description of Reimond.

CHAP. 9.

REIMOND was big bodied and brode set, of stature somwhat more than meane, his haire yellow and curled, his eies big, greie, and round, his nose somewhat high, his countenance well coloured, pleasant, and merie. And although he were somewhat grosse bellied, yet by reason of a certeine liuelinesse which was in him, he couered that fault: and so that which seemed to be a blemish in his bodie, he couered with the vertue of his mind. He had such a speciall care of his men and soldiors, that he would be a spie ouer his watchmen, and in his trauell that waie he watched manie whole nights, ranging and walking abroad in the camps. And in this he was verie happie & fortunate, that he would neuer or verie seldome laie violent hands vpon anie, of whom he had charge or were vnder his gouernement, although he had rashlie or vnaduisedlie ouerthrowne himselfe, & straied out of the waie.

He was verie wise, modest, and warie, being nothing delicat in his fare, nor curious of his apparell. He could awaie with all wethers, both hot and cold, and indure anie paines: he was also verie patient, & could verie well rule his affections. He was more desirous to doo good to such as he gouerned, than to be glorious of his gouernement: for he would shew himselfe more like to be a seruant than a master. Finallie and to conclude, he was a verie liberall, wise, gentle, and a circumspect man. And albeit he were a verie valiant capteine, and a noble soldior: yet in all martiall affaires, he passed and excelled in wisedome & prouidence. A man doubtles in both respects much to be praised and commended: hauing in him whatsoeuer apperteined to a valiant souldior, but excelling in all things belonging to a good capteine.

The description of Meilerius.

CHAP. 10.

MEILERIUS was a man of a browne hew and complexion, his eies blacke, his looke grim, and his countenance sowre & sharpe, and of a meane stature, his bodie for the bignesse verie strong, broad brested, & he was small bellied. His armes and other lims more sinewous than fleshie, a stout and a valiant gentleman he was and emulous. He neuer refused anie aduenture or enterprise which were either to be doone by one alone, or by mo, he would be the first that would enter the field, and the last that would depart from the same. In all seruices he would either haue the garland or die in the place, and so vnpatient he was in all exploits, that he would either haue his purpose, or lie in the dust: and so ambitious and desirous he was to haue honor, that to atteine therevnto, there was no means nor mild thing but

but that he would suerlie haue the same either in death or in life for if he could not haue it and liue, he would suerlie haue it by dieng And verelie both he and Reimond haue béen worthie of too too much praise and commendation, if they had beene lesse ambitious of worldlie honors, and more carefull of Christes church, and deuout in christian religion, whereby the ancient rights thereof might haue béene preserued and kept safe and sound and also in consideration of their so manie conquests and bloudie victories, and of the spilling of so much innocent blood, and murthering of so manie christian people, they had béene thankefull to God, and liberallie contributed some good portion for the furtherance of his church and religion But what shall I saie? It is not so strange but much more to be lamented, that this vnthankefulnesse euen from our first comming into this land, vntill these presents, this hath béene the generall and common fault of all our men.

The commendation and praise of Robert Fitzstephans, and of his cousins.

CHAP. 11.

WHAT shall we speake or saie, how well Robert Fitzstephans and his sonnes haue deserued? What of Maurice Fitzgerald? What shall I saie of Robert of Barrie, a man verie honest and valiant, whose worthie commendations by the premisses are to be knowne? What shall be said of Miles of Cogan, the nephue vnto Fitzstephans and Maurice, who as he came ouer with the first, so in commendation and for his seruice deserueth to be the chéefe and first? What shall we saie of Robert Fitzhenrie, & the brother vnto Meilerius, who if he had not so soone beene dead and cut, he would doubtlesse haue béene nothing behind his brother? What shall we speake of Reimond of Kantune & of Robert Barrie the yoonger they both were verie worthie, tall, handsome, and worthie men? What also shall be said of Reimond Fitzhugh, who although he were but of a little statute, yet for his honestie & prudence not to be forgotten? These thrée lastlie spoken of for their valiantnesse and prowesse doone in the parties of Desmond, deserue great honor and commendation, and great is the pittie that through too much hardinesse their daies were so shortened, and their time so cut off? What did also a number of our gentlemen of the same their kindred & cousenage deserue, whose noble acts were such, and deserued such a perpetuall fame and memorie, that if I had a hundred toongs, a hundred mouthes, and so manie voices of yron, yet could I not vtter and at full declare their worthinesse and deserts. O kindred, O nation, which in double respects art noble! for of the Troians by a naturall disposition thou art valiant, of the French nation thou art most expert and skilfull of armes and chiualrie O worthie nation and kindred! which of thy selfe art sufficient and able to haue conquered anie nation, if enuie and malice had not maligned at thy worthinesse Well then Reimond had taken order for the kéeping of the citie, and had well vittelled the same, he left therein a garison of his owne men, fiftie gentlemen, two hundred horssemen, and two hundred bowmen, ouer whome he appointed Miles of S Dauids his cousine to be leiutenant and so as a noble conqueror he safelie returned into the borders of Leinster But sée the nature of enuie, who neuer ceaseth to persecute vertue For Herime of Mount Maurice, notwithstanding by meanes of the late affinitie he were thought to be a good friend, yet could he not forget his old malicious mind and wicked deuises for still he secretlie from time to time sent his messengers and letters to the king of England, and full vntrulie did aduertise the state, euent, and successe of all things, affirming that Reimond contrarie to the kings

kings honor and his owne allegiance had determined to haue assumed and chalenged vnto himselfe not onelie the citie of Limerike, but also the whole land of Ireland. And to make this the more probable, and himselfe of more credit, he aduertiseth that Reimond had placed and appointed garrisons for the purpose, and had sworne the whole armie to obserue certeine articles by him prescribed, to the great preiudice of the king. Which his aduertisment being interlined with manie good words, the king so credited the same, that he beleeued it to be most true: for as it is well seene, a little suspicion of an iniurie doone or offered to be doone vnto a prince, dooth more sticke in his mind, than manie benefits and good seruices before doone. The king therefore after the winter following sent ouer foure of his seruants in message to Ireland, namelie Robert Powre, Osbert of Herloter or Herford, William Bendeger, and Adam of Gernemie: of which, two of them to come awaie and to bring Reimond with them, and the other to tarie and remaine behind with the earle.

The description of Heruie.

CHAP. 12.

AS we haue of others, so let vs also now make and set foorth the description of Heruie. He was of stature a tall and a comelie man, his eies graie and somewhat big, amiable of face and pleasant of countenance, an eloquent man, hauing a long and a round necke, his shoulders somewhat low, his armes and hands somthing long, he was broad brested, but small in waste, though the same being big in others is thought to be commendable, his bellie was somewhat big and round, his thighes, legs, and féet being well proportionated and answerable to his bodie, of stature he was indifferent. But as in bodie he was well beset & compact, so on the contrarie, his mind, life, and conuersation were corrupt & disordered. For euen from his childhood he was giuen to lecherie, being readie and forward to performe in wanton & filthie actions, whatsoeuer liked him or anie others, who were of the like disposition: and therefore he forbare neither incest nor adulteries, nor anie other such like filthinesse. Besides, he was a priuie and an enuious accuser, and a double man, vncerteine, vaine, and altogither vnconstant, sauing in inconstancie, a verie subtill man and a deceitfull: vnder his toong he had both milke and honie, but both of them were mixed with poison. He was sometimes in great prosperitie, and all things fell out according to his owne desire, and suddenlie fortune turning hir whéele, he had such a fall, that he did neuer recouer the same againe. He was sometimes a verie good soldior, and had good experience in the feats of warre after the maner vsed in France: but he was so suddenlie altred & changed, that he became more skilfull in malice than valiant in prowesse, more full of deceit than renowmed in honor, more puffed vp in pride than endowed with worship, more hastie than happie, and more full of words than abounding in truth.

The succouring of the garrison at Limerike.

CHAP. 13.

REIMOND hauing receiued the kings determination by the foresaid foure messengers, prepared all things in a readinesse for his passage ouer accordinglie, and nothing

nothing wanted therevnto but onelie a west wind But before the same happened, messengers came from the garrison at Limerike, aduertising that Donold prince of Thomond had besieged the citie round about with a great armie, and that their vittels which they had in the towne, aswell that which they found at their comming thither, as also what so euer was else prouided, were all spent and consumed, and therefore requested that they might with all spéed be rescued and holpen The earle, who was verie sorie & pensife for these newes, and deuising all the waies he could to helpe them caused a muster to be taken of all his souldiers, who were so gréeued for the going awaie and departure of Reimond, that they vtterlie denied and refused to go and to serue that waie, vnles Reimond were their capteine and lieutenant Whervpon they tooke aduise with the kings messengers what were best to be doone in this distresse At length it was thought best, that Reimond should take the enterprise in hand, and he though verie loth, yet at the request of the earle and the foresaid gentlemen, yéeldeth himselfe to that seruice, and marched foorth toward Limerike, hauing with him foure score gentlemen of seruice, two hundred horsmen, & thrée hundred archers, besides Morogh of Kencile, and Donold of Ossorie, and certeine other Irishmen, who serued and attended him. And as he was marching and comming toward Cashill, tidings was brought him that the prince of Thomond had raised his siege and was comming towards him to méet him, and was now come to the passe of Cashill which passe although naturallie of it selfe it were verie strong, yet by means of new trenching, plashing of trées, and making of hedges, it was made so strong, that no horsmen could either enter or passe through the same.

The oration of Donold to his soldiers, the recouerie of the citie of Limerike.

CHAP 14

REIMOND being now almost come to the place where his enimies laie, diuided his hoast or armie into thrée parts or companies, and determined to giue the onset or aduenture Wherevpon Donold prince of Ossorie, who was a mortall enimie to the prince of Thomond, and now verie desirous that some good exploit shuld be doone, and beholding the Englishmen now also set in good araie, for though they were but few in number in respect of the others, yet they were piked men, valiant and couragious he also to incourage them, to shew themselues like valiant men, vseth and maketh these spéeches vnto them "Yee worthie, noble, and valiant conquerors of this land, you are this daie valiantlie to giue the onset vpon your enimies, which if you doo after your old and accustomed maner, no doubt the victorie will be yours, for we with our spars, and you with your swords, will so sharplie them pursue, as they shall verie hardlie escape our hands, and auoid our force But if it so fall out, which God forbid, that you be ouerthrowne and haue the woorse side be you assured that we will leaue you and turne to our enimies, and take part with them. Wherefore be of good courages, and looke well to your selues, an dconsider that you are now far from anie fort or place of refuge, and therefore if you should be driuen to flee, the same will be long and dangerous to you, as for vs yée may not trust vnto vs, for we are determined to sticke to them who shall haue the victorie, and will pursue and be on the racks of them who shall flée and run awaie, and therfore be no longer assured of vs than whilest yee be conquerors" Meilerius who had the fore ward, hearing these words, being varmed with the same, suddenlie like a hurling and a blustering wind entered into the passe, pulled downe the fastnesse, and brake downe the hedges, and so made waie, with no small slaughter of the enimies, whereby the passe was recouered and the enimies ouercome And they then marched without perill vnto Limerike, where they entered the third daie in the Easter wéeke, being on tuesdaie And as the first conquest of Limerike was vpon a tuesdaie, so was the second also, where for a time they staied, and restored all things by the enimies before spoiled, & set the same in good order The enimies finding themselues to be too weake, and that it was better to bow than to breake, practise to haue a parlée and a communication with Reimond & in the end the messengers of Rothorike king of Connagh, and of Donold of Thomond, did obteine the same, and a parlée was appointed for them both, which was in one daie, but not in one place, for Rothorike of Connagh came by boates vpon the riuer of Shenin, as far as the great logh of Dirgid, & there staied And Donold not far from thense kept himselfe and his companie in a certeine wood. But Reimond chose a place not far from Killaloo, which is about seauentéene miles from Limerike, and in the midle betwéene them both. The parlée betweene these continued a pretie while, but in the end both kings submitted & yéelded themselues, gaue hostages, made fealtie, and were sworne to be true from thensefoorth for euer, to the king of England and to his heires

These things thus doone and concluded, Reimond returneth in great triumph and iolitie vnto Limerike And by and by there came messengers vnto him from Dermon Mac Artie prince of Desmond, praieng and requesting him to aid and helpe him, being the king of Englands faithfull and liege man against his eldest sonne Cormon Olechan, who went about to driue and expell him out of his land and dominion & promised him good interteinment both for himselfe and for his souldiors for the same Reimond nothing refusing the offer, and verie desirous of honor, taketh aduise of his fréends and companions, and by all their consents, the iorneie towards Corke was liked Wherevpon Reimond displaieth his banner, and marcheth thitherwards, and taketh by the waie great preies and booties of neat, cattell, and other things of the cattels he sent a good portion backe vnto Limerike for vittelling of that citie, & in the end he conquered the whole countrie, subdued the rebellious sonne, and restored Dermon the prince to his estate and right And thus by reason of Reimond Mac Artie, he was restored and recouered, who otherwise had beene in vtter despaire, and out of all remedie And now to recompense his son Cormach, who before this, by waie of a peace and an intreatie, both vniustlie & guilefullie had taken and imprisoned him, he to acquite guile with guile, and the like with the like, tooke his sonne and cast him into prison, and not long after smote off his head

The death of the earle Strangbow.

CHAP. 15.

WHILEST these things were thus adooing in Desmond, there came a messenger in all hast from Dublin, with letters to Reimond from his wife Basilia, the effect whereof the messenger knew not These letters Reimond foorthwith deliuered to a familiar fréend of his to read them vnto him secretlie, and apart from all others, the tenure of them was as followeth "To Reimond hir most louing lord and husband, his owne Basilia wisheth health as to hir selfe. Know yee my déere lord that

The ladie Basilias letter to hir husband Reimond.

that my great cheeketooth, which was woont to ake so much, is now fallen out, wherefore if yée haue anie care or regard of me, or of your selfe, come awaie with all spéed" Reimond hauing considered of this letter, did by the falling of the tooth fullie conjecture the death of the earle, for he laie verie sicke at Dublin before his comming awaie from thense But he being thus deceased, which was about the kalends of Iune, they at Dublin did what they could to képe the same secret, for feare and in doubt of the Irishmen, vntill that Reimond were come with his band of souldiers vnto them Reimond himselfe foorthwith returned vnto Limerike and notwithstanding he were verie sorie and much gréeued with this newes, yet dissembling the same, and bearing it out with a good countenance, would not nor did vtter or disclose it to anie bodie, sauing to a few wise and discréet men of his familiars and trustie councellors And then vpon good aduise and deliberation had among them, it was concluded and agréed vpon, that forsomuch as the earle was dead, and that Reimond also was to depart awaie ouer into England, that the citie of Limerike which was so farre remoted and in the middle of manie enimies, should for the time be left, and the garrison to be conducted and brought from thense into Leinster, for the defense and safe keeping of the townes and forts vpon the sea coasts. There Reimond full much against his will yéelded to this their aduise and counsell, being much gréeued that hauing taken paines to recouer the citie of Limerike, he was now neither able to képe it himselfe, nor yet had any to leaue behind him, who would take charge vpon him But at length he sent for Donald prince of Thomond, being the kings baron & sworne subiect, and vnto him he committed the custodie and charge of the citie: who foorthwith pretending all truth and fidelitie was contented therewith; and did not onelie put in hostages, but also tooke a corporall oth, and was solemnlie sworne for the safe keeping and the restitution of the same at the kings will and pleasure, as also in the meane time to képe the peace

Then Reimond and all his companie departed and went awaie but they had not so soone passed ouer the one end of the bridge, but that the other end was foorthwith broken downe, euen at their heeles; and the citie which was well walled, defended and vittelled, was set on fire in some sundrie parts, which they saw and beheld with no small greefe of mind. The false traitor then openlie shewing and teaching what credit was to be giuen thenseforth to the Irish nation, who so wickedlie, impudentlie, and perfidiouslie did periure themselues. The king of England not long after, being aduertised héereof, is said to haue thus said "Noble was the enterprise in the giuing of the first aduenture vpon the citie, but greater was the rescuing and recouering thereof againe: but it was onelie wisedome, when they left and forsooke it" Reimond then returned vnto Dublin with his whole garrison in safetie, and then the erle, whose corps by his commandement was reserued vntill Reimonds comming, was buried in the church of the Trinitie at Dublin, before the rood there, by the appointment of Laurence the archbishop, who did execute all the funerall seruices and obsequies

The comming of William Fitzaldelme and others ouer into Ireland

CHAP 16.

THESE things thus doone, the kings messengers vpon these new changes and chances were to take new aduises, and hauing throughlie debated the state of the countrie, and the necessitie of the time, they thought it best and did conclude that Reimond should tarie behind, and kéepe the countrie in good state and order; but they themselues to returne backe to the king. Who accordinglie prepared themselues, and at the next westerlie wind then following, they tooke shipping and passed ouer into England, and being landed, did in post and with all the hast they could, make their repaire vnto the king, vnto whom they declared the death of the earle, & all other things concerning the state of that land. The king then vpon aduise and deliberation had in this matter, sent ouer William Fitzaldelme, with twentie gentlemen of his houshold, to be his lieutenant, & ioined Iohn de Courcie in commission with him, who had attending vpon him ten men. Likewise Robert Fitzstephans and Miles Cogan, who had noblie serued him in his wars two yeeres, were also sent with them, hauing twentie men attending vpon them. These assoone as they were arriued, and come to land, and Reimond hauing vnderstanding of the same, assembleth his companie and soldiors, which was a companie well beséene, and marcheth towards Wexford, and there in the confines or marches of the same he met Fitzaldelme and the rest of his companie, whom he verie louinglie saluted and imbraced: and forthwith according to the kings pleasure he yéelded and deliuered vp vnto Fitzaldelme, then the kings lieutenant, all the cities and townes, as also all such hostages as he had within that land.

Fitzaldelme when he saw and beheld so iolie and lustie a companie about Reimond, and well marking also Meilerius, and others the nephues of Reimond, about the number of thirtie persons, mounted vpon their horsses, verie lustie and braue, and well beséene in like armor, with their shields about their necks, and their staues in their hands, coursing vp & downe after their maner about the fields. He enuied thereat, and turning backe to his men, said secretlie vnto them, "I will shortlie cut off this pride, and quaile this brauerie." Which in the end it partlie so came to passe, for both he and all the rest which followed him in that office, did as it were by a secret conspiracie, enuie and maligne at Reimond, Meilerius, Fitzmaurice, sonnes to Fitzstephans, and all other of their race and kindred. For this was alwaies the lucke and fortune of this kindred and familie.

In all seruices of warres they were then the foremost, and had in best price, and in all martiall affaires they were the best and most valiant men: but when there was no such seruice in hand, and no néed of them, then were they contemned and no account was made of them, but by a secret malice they were abased, reiected and refused. And albeit great was their malice, yet was their nobilitie so honorable and great, that by no meanes, doo what they could, was the same to be extirpated or rooted out. For euen at this daie, such good successe hath their noble beginnings had, that their ofspring hath euer since (1) continued in that land, in much honor, force and power. And to saie the truth, who persed the force of the enimies in that land? Euen the Geraldines. Who did best kéepe & prefer the land in safetie? The Geraldines. Who made the enimies to go backe & be afraid? The Geraldines. Who be they which for their good deserts are most maligned and enuied at? The Geraldines. Surelie, if it had pleased the prince to haue considered of them according to their deserts and worthinesse, no doubt the whole state of Ireland long yer this had béene quieted and established. But causelesse were they alwaies had in suspicion, & their worthinesse still had in gelousie: and they put in trust, as in whome was neither valiantnesse of seruice, nor assurednesse of trust. But yet ye worthie and noble men, who for to atteine to honor, haue not béene afraid of death, and for to obteine fame and renowme, haue not estéemed your selues, be not dismaid, though ye be vncourteouslie considered, and without your deserts disdained and maligned at: but go ye onwards,

and

and procéed in your woonted steps of vertue And if my pen can go according to worthinesse, I shall be happie, and receiue the guerdon of vertue & immortall fame for vertue cannot faile nor die, but either in this life or in the life to come, or in both, shall haue his iust reward and desert And albeit your valiant seruice and worthinesse, either by the slackenes of the king, or by meanes of other mens secret and enuious practises, haue not beene hitherto considered nor rewarded yet shall not I faile, with my pen to publish, and in my writings to remember the same And therefore shrinke not now neither doo you giue ouer to labor and trauell from daie to daie to grow and increase in honor, fame and renowme For the memoriall thereof (farre surpassing all the treasuries in the world) for a time through malice maie be couered, but neuer suppressed nor extincted but as fire long hid, shall in the end breake out into great flames, and for euer remaine in perpetuall memorie.

About this time was borne in Gwendelocke a monstrous man, begotten by a wicked man of that countrie vpon a cow, a vice then too common in that wicked nation It had the bodie of a man, but all the extreame parts of an oxe, for from the ankles of the legs and the wrists of the armes, he had the hoofes of an oxe, his head was all bald, sauing a few small & thin heares heere and there his eies great, round and blacke, like an oxe, nose he had none but onelie two holes, speake he could not but onelie bellowed like a cow This monster did dailie resort vnto the house of Maurice Fitzgerald, about dinner times, and such meate as was giuen him he would take in his hoofes, and put to his mouth, and so feed himselfe, &c but to returne to the matter William Fitzaldelme, being now in high authoritie, and hauing the gouernement and charge of the land in his hands, marcheth along the sea coasts, and vieweth all the townes, forts and castels that waies but for the inner countrie, the mounteines and hils vpon the maine land, and bordering vpon the Irishrie, he neither cared nor passed for the same but yet misliked not the welth and riches thereof For being a verie greedie and a couetous man, and especiallie hungrie to haue gold and treasure, whereof was good store in that land, he gréedilie scraped and scratched togither whatsoeuer was to be gotten

A monstrous man begotten vpon a cow.

About this time, Maurice (2) Fitzgerald in the kalends of September died at Wexford, whose death was lamented, & his departure bewailed of all the countrie For whie, he was a verie graue & a valiant man, & who for his constancie, truth, courtesie & loue left not his like behind After his death, William Fitzaldelme sent for the sonnes of the said Maurice, and so dealt with them, that he neuer left them, vntill by one means or other he had craftilie gotten from them the castell of Guendoke Howbeit afterwards he gaue them Fernes in exchange which albeit it were in the middle of their enimies, yet like lustie and couragious gentlemen, they builded there a strong castell, which they kept & inhabited maugre all their enimies Walter Almane, so called in name, and not for that he was either in nature or stature an Almane, being nephue to William Fitzaldelme, was made seneschall of Wexford, who nothing degenerated from the maners & conditions of his vncle, but was one who was a corrupt man in all his actions & doings, being couetous, proud, malicious and enuious And surelie it is commonlie séene, that there is none lightlie woorse, than when a beggerlie rascall from nothing, and from a base estate, is aduanced to wealth, credit and estimation For such a one alwaies doubting and mistrusting all things, suppresseth all things, & thinking all things to be lawfull for him to doo, vseth all extremities at his will and pleasure There cannot be (I saie) a woorse beast, than when a cruell rascall and proud begger is raised to estate, and made a ruler ouer his betters.

This Walter entered into acquaintance with Morogh prince of Kencile, and by him

him being corrupted with great bribes, did what he could to procure the vtter destruction of Reimond and all his foresaid coosins and kinsmen. And to begin the execution of their practises, the foresaid William first tooke awaie from Reimond all his lands about Dublin, and about Wexford. And whereas he receiued letters of commandement from the king, to restore vnto Fitzstephans a cantred of land which he had in Ophelan, he being well bribed, detracted and lingered the execution thereof: but yet in the end appointed and assigned vnto them other places which were further off and remoted, and the same the more perillous, because they were in the middle of the enimies.

(1) It is verie true, that these Geraldines euen euer since haue continued in this land of Ireland, and did dailie grow and increase to much honour, there being at this instant two houses aduanced to the titles of earledoms, and sundrie to the estates of barons. And so long as they continued in the steps of their ancestors, they were not so honourable as terrible to the Irish nation: but when they leauing English gouernment, liked the loose life of that viperous nation, then they brought in coine and liuerie, and a number of manie other Irish and diuelish impositions, which hath béene the ruine of their honour, the losse of their credit, & in the end will be the ouerthrow of all their houses and families.

(2) This Fitzgerald was buried, and yet lieth in a monasterie of Greie friers without the walles of the towne of Wexford, which house is now dissolued, and the monument of his buriall almost destroied: there wanting some good and woorthie man to restore the same againe. He deserued well of his prince and countrie: and therefore lamentable it is, that in so vnkind a countrie no one good man is to be found, that of so woorthie a knight will not restore so woorthie a monument.

The description of William Fitzaldelme.

CHAP. 17.

THIS Fitzaldelme was a grosse and corpulent man, as well in stature as in proportion, but of a reasonable height, he was verie liberall and courtlike. And albeit he were of great courtesie, and would giue to anie man much honour and reuerence, yet was the same altogither with wiles and guiles: for vnder honie he gaue venem, and his sugred words were mingled with poison. And as a venemous serpent couered with gréene leaues, he with an outward shew of courtesie couered his mindfull trecherie. For to the outward shew he was liberall and courteous, but inwardlie full of rancor and malice. In countenance pleasant, but in a stinking breast was hid a stinking vapor: outwardlie as méeke as a lambe, but within as wilie as a fox: carieng vnder swéet honie most bitter venem. His words as smooth as oile, and yet indeed they were deadlie strokes: whome he honoured and reuerenced this daie, he would either spoile or destroie the next daie. A cruell enimie against the weake and feeble, and a flatterer vnto the rebell and mightie: gentle to the wild and sauage, and courteous to the enimie, but extreame to the good subiect, and cruell to the humble; and by that means he was not fearefull to the one, nor trustie to the other. A man full of flatterie, and yet altogither craftie and deceitfull.

full He was also much giuen vnto wine and to women He was a grédie couetous man, and an ambitious flatterer, being altogither bent to the one and the other

(1) This William was the sonne of Aldelme father to Burke erle of Kent (as some saie) and his son Richard was sent into Ireland, and there greatlie aduanced, and of him (being lord of Connagh) descended the burgesses called Clanricards, who were the best blood of the foresaid Richard, and these doo yet remaine in Connagh, of whom is the earle of Clanrike now liuing

How Iohn de Courcie inuadeth Vlster

CHAP 18

IOHN Courcie, who (as is before said) was ioined in commission with William Fitzaldelme, when he saw the course and maner of his dealings, who as he was couetous, and did nothing but for monie, so was he timerous, and did all things in craft and deceit as also that the enimie feared him not, and the good subiect loued him not. And considering also that the souldiers and garrison at Dublin, by means of their capteins couetousnesse were vnpaid of their wages, and by reason of his slouth and sluggishnesse the vittels waxed scant, & none went & scouted anie more abrode as they were woont to get anie booties or preies, he secretlie dealeth with some of them, and by his wise conference, and wittie persuasions, allureth and intiseth vnto him euen such as were the valiantest, honestest, and chosen men of them all. who were content and verie glad to accompanie and follow him And hauing so gotten into his companie two and twentie gentlemen, and about three hundred others, he boldlie entreth and inuadeth into the prouince of Vlster, a countrie which hitherto had not tried the force and strength of the English nation And then was fulfilled the prophesie of Merlin Celodine (as is said, howbeit I will not so affirme it) "A white knight sitting vpon a white horse, bearing birds in his shield, shall be the first which with force of armes shall enter and inuade Vlster" A prophesie of Merlin fulfilled

This Iohn Courcie was somewhat of a browne colour, but therewith somewhat whitish, and at that time he rode vpon a white horsse, as also did beare in his shield thrée painted (1) birds After that he had passed thrée daies iourneie through the countrie of Vriell, he came the fourth daie (being the kalends of Februarie) to the citie of (2) Downe, without anie resistance of the inhabitants thereof he being an enimie and a ghest vnlooked for And (3) Odonell then the ruler of that countrie, being astonied and amazed at their so sudden comming, fled awaie The souldiers which before then comming from Dublin were halfe pined with famine, and hunger starued, hauing now recouered great booties and preies of neat and cattels, were full and well refreshed.

At this verie present time, there was come thither out of Scotland a legat from Rome named Viuianus, & he tooke great pains to intreat & make a peace betwéene Odonell & Iohn de Courcie, vsing all the persuasions that he could, affirming that if he would depart and go awaie, there should be a yearelie tribute paid to the king of England but all his words auailed nothing. Odonell séeing that words could little auaile, assembleth all the forces of the countrie and within eight daies hauing gotten about ten thousand souldiors, with force inuadeth, & with great courage commeth

commeth to enter & breake into the citie of Downe For in Ireland, as it is commonlie also in all other lands, they which inhabit in the north, are more warlike and cruell than anie others in other parts Iohn Courcie séeing the course and bent of the enimies, who not onelie vpon a hope and confidence of their great multitude against so few enimies, but also their valiant and couragious minds, who were fullie determined to inuade the citie thought it better with his small companie (which though they were but few in respect of their aduersaries, yet they were souldiors valiant, couragious, and of good seruice) to issue out and aduenture the fight with them, than to be pinned & shut vp in a beggerlie wall made with turffes in a corner of the citie, and there for want of vittels to be famished Wherefore he issued out and ioined the battell with them, where the fight was hot, the bowes a farre off on the one side, and the darts on the other side then lance against lance, and the bill against the spar, and the sword against the skeine who buckled so lustilie the one against the other, that manie a man fell that daie to the dust And in this terrible fight and buckling, he that had séene how valiantlie each man shewed himselfe, and speciallie how Iohn Courcie most valiantlie with the stroke of his sword mangled manie a man, killing some, but wounded and maimed manie, would and must néeds haue commended him for a right woorthie, noble, and right valiant warrior.

(1) He giueth thrée birds as this author saith, which by heralds are thus blasoned. Argent thrée griphs or genes gules crowned gold. this griph or gene is a kind of an eagle, but such as is rauenous, and feedeth more vpon carren than vpon anie foule of his owne preieng: & for his cowardnesse carrieth neither the name nor praise apperteining to the true eagle

(2) Downe is a towne lieng in the Ards, which is in Vlster, a profitable and a fertile soile. it is the sée of the bishop of that diocesse, who beareth his name of the said towne, being called the bishop of Downe

(3) The Latine word is *Dunlenus*, which I doo find to be Englished Odonell, which is the name of a great familie or nation in the prouince of Vlster, but whether this Latine be trulie so interpreted, I referre it to the reader, or such as be expert in such Irish names

The commendation of Roger Power, and the victorie of Iohn de Courcie, and of the prophesies of Colodine.

CHAP 19

IN this fight there was manie a woorthie man, which valiantlie acquited himselfe. but if it might be said without offense, there was no one man who did more valiant acts than (1) Roger le Power, who albeit he were but a yoong man and beardlesse, yet he shewed himselfe a lustie, valiant, & couragious gentleman, & who grew into such good credit, that afterwards he had the gouernment of the countrie about Leighlin, as also in Ossorie This fight was verie long & doubtfull, each partie manfullie defending themselues, and none yeelding the one to the other But as the common prouerbe is, be the daie neuer so long, yet at the length it ringeth at euensong. so likewise this fierce, long, and cruell fight had his end, and the victorie fell to Iohn de Courcie, and a great multitude of the enimies were slaine

slaine in the field, as also vpon the woars of the seas as they were fléeing and running awaie. Then was fulfilled the old prophesie of Celodine the Irish prophet, who forespeaking of this battell said, that there should be such a great bloudshed therein of the Irish people, that the enimies perceiuing them should wade vp to the knees in bloud. Which thing came so to passe, for the Englishmen perceiuing them and killing them vpon the woars, the same were so soft, that with the weight of their bodies they sunke downe vp to the hard knées or twisels, and so the bloud fléeting and lieng vpon the woars, they were said to be therein vp to the knées.

A prophesie of Celodine fulfilled.

The same man also (as is said) did write that a poore stranger, and one come out from other countries, should with a small power come to the citie of Downe, and against the will of the gouernor thereof should take the same. Manie other things also he wrote of sundrie battels to be waged, and of the euents thereof, which were all fulfilled in Iohn de Courcie. This booke the said Iohn had, and he so esteemed the same, that still he had it about him, and in his hands, and did manie times, yea and for the most part direct his doongs by the same. It was also written in the same booke, that a yoong man with force and armes should breake and enter in through the wals of Waterford, and conquer the same with the great slaughter of the townsmen: moreouer, that the same man should come to Wexford, & from thense to Dublin, where he should enter in without anie great resistance; & all these things (as is apparant) were fulfilled in earle Richard. Likewise he wrote in the same booke, that the citie of Limerike should be twise left and forsaken by the Englishmen: but the third time it should be kept, which thing came so to passe. For first (as is before written) Reimond had it and gaue it ouer: the second was, when the king had giuen the same to Philip de Bruse, for he being brought thither by Fitzstephans, and Miles Cogan, to take and enter into the same, and being come to the riuer side of Shenin for the same purpose, was there vtterlie discoraged to procéed anie further, and so without anie thing doone, leaueth the same as he found it, and came backe againe, as hereafter in his place it shall be shewed. And thus (according to this vaticine) twise it was left, but the third time it shall be kept.

But this is to be implied and meant of Hamon de Valognies the iusticiarie there appointed, in whose time the said citie being vnder his gouernment, was by treacherie and treason destroied, and so forsaken and left, but afterwards recouered by Meilerius: euer since which time it hath remained and béene kept in the possession of the Englishmen. Well then to the battels of Iohn de Courcie, first he had the victorie in two notable battels or fights at Dublin, the one in Februarie, and the other in Iulie: in which he hauing but a small companie of men, fought against fifteene hundred of his enimies, of whome he slue and ouerthrew a great number, and had the victorie. The third was at Ferlie about the taking of a preie, where by reason of the streict & narrow passes, he was too much and euerie estsoones ouerset by the enimies, and so had the woorse, some of his men being killed, and some scattered and dispersed abroad in the woods and fields, so that he had scant eleuen persons left with him. And notwithstanding that he had thus lost his men and horsses, yet was he of such a valiant mind and courage, that with those few which were left, he went through his enimies, and in spite of them all trauelled two daies and two nights on foot in their armour without meat or drinke thirtie long miles, vntill he was past danger, & so came safelie vnto his owne castell againe. The fourth battell was at Vriell, where manie of his men were killed and manie fled. The fift was at the bridge of Yuor, after and vpon his comming from out of England, and yet therein he had the victorie and conquest. So in three battels he had the victorie, but in two he receiued both the losse and hurt; and yet in them did more annoie the enimie, than was hurted himselfe.

(1) The race & issue of the Powers hath euer since and yet dooth remaine in Ireland, who nothing degenerating from this their ancestor, haue for their part shewed themselues valiant and men of good seruice, for which they haue béene honorablie rewarded, and are now barons and peeres of the realme. Their habitation and dwelling is in the prouince or countie of Waterford, and not far from the citie of Waterford.

The description of Iohn de Courcie.

CHAP. 20.

THIS Iohn de Courcie was white and pale of colour, but verie fierce and arrogant, he was sinowous and a verie strong made man, verie tall and mightie, and of a singular audacitie: and being from his verie youth bent to the wars proued a verie valiant souldior. He would be the first in the field and formost in the fight; and so ambitious and desirous he was of honor, that were the enterprise neuer so perillous, and the seruice neuer so dangerous, yet he would giue the aduenture. And albeit he were the generall or capteine, yet setting the prioritie thereof apart, he would be as a common souldior, and serue in the place of a priuat seruitor, and manie times being more rash than wise, and more hastie than circumspect, he had the woorst side and lost the victorie. And although in seruice he were thus forward, earnest, and vehement, yet in time of peace and rest he was verie sober, modest, and altogither giuen and disposed to serue God, and hauing the victorie of his enimies and good successe in his affaires, he would ascribe the honor vnto God, and be thankefull for the same. But as Tullius writeth, nature neuer made anie thing perfect and absolute in all points. And so it appeared in this man, for through his too much pinching and sparing, and by reason he was verie vncerteine and vnconstant, his vertues (otherwise great, and deseruing great praises and commendations) verie much impeirshed and blemished. He maried the daughter of Gotred king of Manne. And after that he had waged manie battels, and fought sundrie times with his enimies, he at length had the masterie and conquest ouer them: and then hauing brought the whole countrie to a good peace and rest, he builded sundrie and diuerse castels throughout Vlster, in such méete and conuenient places as he thought best. And by the way this one thing me thinketh is The three chiefe posts of Ireland without issue lawfull verie strange, that these thrée notable & the chiefest posts of Ireland, namelie Herueie, Reimond, and this Iohn de Courcie, by Gods secret, (but not vniust iudgement) neuer had anie lawfull issue. I might also say the like of Meilerius, who as yet hath no lawfull issue by his wife. Thus much hauing bréeflie and by the waie spoken of the noble acts of Iohn de Courcie, and leauing the same vnto others to be more at large set forth and described, we will now returne againe to Dublin.

The

The councell or synod kept at Dublin, of Viuian the popes legat, and of Miles Cogans issuing into Connagh.

CHAP. 21.

IN this meane time, Viuianus the popes legat remained still in Ireland, and held a synod at Dublin of all the clergie, in which he openlie confirmed and published the right which the king of England hath to the realme of Ireland, as also the popes ratification and confirmation of the same, commanding and charging euerie person, of what estate, degrée, or condition soeuer he were, that vpon paine of excommunication he should not denie his loialtie, nor breake his allegiance vnto him. And moreouer (1) forsomuch as the manner and custome was among the Irishrie, that whensoeuer anie goods, corne, or vittels, were put and kept in anie church, no man would medle or deale to carrie the same awaie, yet neuerthelesse, he gaue licence and libertie to all Englishmen, that whensoeuer they went, or were to go in anie hosting, and could not elsewhere be prouided of anie vittels, that they might lawfullie take what they found in anie church, so that they left with the church-wardens, or such as had the charge thereof, the true and iust value of so much as they tooke awaie. These things thus doone, Miles of Cogan, who was lieutenant of the bands of soldiors vnder William Fitzaldelme, as also conestable of the citie of Dublin, he with 40 gentlemen, whereof 20 were vnder the conduct of Ralph the son of Fitzstephans, as also his lieutenant, and they hauing with them 200 horssemen & 300 footmen, passed ouer the riuer of Shenin, & inuaded Connagh, which hitherto no Englishman had aduentured. The Connagh men foorthwith set on fire and burned all their townes, villages, and churches, as also all such corne as they had in their haggards, and in their caues, and could not carrie with them. Likewise they tooke downe the images and crucifixes, and hurled them abroad in the fields. Neuerthelesse, the Englishmen marched onwards, till they came to the towne of Thomond, where they staied eight daies togither, and finding the countrie forsaken of the people, and barren of vittels, they returned backe againe ouer the Shenin: and by the waie they met with Rothorike prince of Connagh, who laie in a wood neere the Shenin watching for them, and he had thrée great troops and companies with him of the best fighting men of Connagh. Betwéene them there was a long and a cruell fight, in which Miles lost but thrée of his owne companie, but manie of his enimies were slaine. Which doone, he recouered ouer the riuer, & so came safelie to Dublin.

(1) This vsage and custome is yet at this present obserued, and euerie church in the countrie stuffed and filled with great chests full of corne, which the husbandmen doo for safetie kéepe therein: and this lieth safe at all times, euen in the verie warres among themselues: howbeit the same is not so religiouslie kept and obserued in these daies as in times past.

How William Fitzaldelme is sent from home into England, and Hugh de Lacie put in his place: and how Miles Cogan and Robert Fitzstephans haue the kingdome of Corke giuen vnto them.

CHAP. 22.

WILLIAM Fitzaldelme, who during his abode and being in this land, had doone nothing worthie the commendation, sauing that he caused the staffe called Iohns staffe to be fetched from Armach, and brought to Dublin, he (I saie) and Miles Cogan, with Robert Fitzstephans were sent for by the king to come home. In whose roome the king sent ouer Hugh de Lacie, and made him his deputie ouer the whole land, ioining in commission with him Robert Powre then seneschall of Wexford and Waterford. The king, after the returne of the aforesaid Fitzaldelme and others, thinking and considering with himselfe the good seruice of Miles Cogan, Robert Fitzstephans, and others; as also how necessarie it were, that such noble seruitors and valiant men were placed among the Irish people, wherby to keepe them in good order and dutifull obeisance, he gaue to Robert Fitzstephans, and to Miles Cogan in fée for euer to be equallie diuided betwéene them all south Mounster (1) that is to saie, the whole kingdome of Corke, from the west part of the riuer at Leismore vnto the seas, sauing and reseruing the citie of Corke, and one cantred of land therevnto adioining. Also he gaue vnto Philip de Bruse all the north Mounster, that is to saie, the kingdome of Limerike, sauing and excepting the citie of Limerike it selfe with one cantred therevnto adioining, to haue vnto him and to his heires for euer in fée These men thus rewarded, confederated themselues togither to ioine and helpe one another, and euerie of them maketh the best preparation that he can. Which being in redinesse they tooke shipping and arriued into Ireland in the moneth of Nouember, and landed at Waterford from thense they coasted along vnto Corke where they were receiued with much honor both by the citizens, and also by an English gentleman named Richard of London, who was deputie there vnder Fitzaldelme

As soone as they had pacified and quieted Dermon (2) Mac Artie prince of Desmond, and the residue of the noble men and gentlemen in those parties, Fitzstephans and also Miles Cogan diuided betwéene them the seauen cantreds, which were néerest to the towne for these they kept and held in best peace and rest. Fitzstephans had the thrée cantreds which laie in the east part, and Cogan had the foure which laie in the west, the one hauing the more because they were the worser, and the other had the fewer cantreds that were the better soile and ground. The citie it selfe remained in their ioint gouernement, and the residue of the cantreds being foure and twentie remained in common, and the profits thereof growing they equallie diuided betwéene them A cantred both in English and in Irish is so much land as conteineth one hundred villages, as is in our topographie declared, which is commonlie called an hundred. These things thus doone, they bring and conduct Philip de Bruse vnto Limerike Fitzstephans had with him twentie gentlemen and fortie horssemen, Miles Cogan had twentie gentlemen & fiftie horsemen, Philip de Bruse had twentie gentlemen & thrée score horssemen, besides a great number of bowmen & footmen, which they all had when they were come to Limerike, which was about fortie miles from Corke, & onlie the riuer of

What a cantred is.

Shenin

Shenin was betwéene them and the citie the same at their comming was set on fire before their eies by the citizens themselues. Neuerthelesse, Stephans and Miles offered to aduenture ouer the water, and to enter the towne, or if Philip thought it so good, they would there build a castell vpon the riuers side right ouer against the towne But Philip albeit he were a valiant and a good man, yet considering with himselfe how dangerous the place was, being in the middle of the enimies, and farre remoted from all succors and helpe, without which he was not able with his small companie to defend and kéepe the same, as also being partlie persuaded by the counsell and aduise of his companie, thought it better to returne home in safetie, than to dwell in the middle of his enimies in continuall perill and danger. And it is not to be much maruelled that in this iourneie he had so euill successe for whie he had gathered & reteined to him the notablest murtherers, théeues, & seditious persons that were in all Southwales, and the marches of the same, and these were of best credit with him, and he most ruled by them

About this time Amere duke Fitzstephans son, a lustie yoong gentleman and a towardlie, died at Corke in March, to the great sorrow and gréefe of all his fréends. Neere about this time was found and seene a great tode at Waterford, wherof was made much woondering, as is in our topographie declared. Also within the space of thrée yeares there was seene thrée eclipses of the sun, howbeit these were not vniuersall, but particular eclipses seene onelie in the land. After that Fitzstephans and Miles Cogan had quietlie and peaceablie gouerned and ruled the kingdome of Desmond fiue yéeres togither, and by their prudence and modestie had restrained the hastie forwardnesse, and rash disposition of their yoong men, Miles and Rafe the sonne of Fitzstephans a lustie yong gentleman, and who had married Miles daughter, went toward Lismore, there to méet & to haue a parlée with Waterford men· as they sate in the fields waiting and looking for them, one Machture with whome they should and had appointed to haue lien at his house the next night following, suddenlie and vnwares came stealing vpon them, and there traitorouslie slue them, and fiue of their companie. By meanes whereof the whole countrie foorthwith was in an vproare, insomuch that Dermon Mac Artie, and all the Irishrie in those parties, as also the traitor Machture, were out. and denieng to be anie longer the kings loiall subiects, made wars against Fitzstephans, who now once againe felt the course of fortunes disposition. And these so much annoied him, that he could neuer recouer himselfe againe, vntill that his nephue Reimond, who succéeded him in the gouernement there, came and rescued him. yet that notwithstanding, he was neuer his owne man, neither could he be at a perfect peace and rest

Three eclipses of the sun in three yeres

And by the waie this is to be noted and considered, that as the northerne men be warlike and valiant, so are the southerne men craftie and subtill, the one seeking honor, the other deliting in craft & deceit, the one valiant, the other wilie; the one of great courage, the other set all on treason and falshood. But to the matter. When Reimond hard how fortune frowned vpon his vncle Fitzstephans, and what distresse he was in, being shut vp in the citie of Corke, and his enimies assailing him round about, forthwith assembleth his companie, and hauing in readinesse twentie gentlemen, and one hundred of footmen and bowmen, he taketh shipping at Wexford, and sailing along the coasts, maketh towards Corke with all the hast he can, that he might relieue and comfort his friends, and be a terror vnto his enimies. And in the end hauing ofttimes incountered with the enimies, some he killed, some he droue out of the countrie, and some he compelled (which was the greater number) to submit themselues and to sue for peace and thus in the end after great stormes and tempest followed a faire wether and a calme Verie shortlie after Richard of Cogan, brother

brother vnto Miles, & nothing inferior vnto him in valiantnesse, or anie other respect came into Ireland with a iollie picked companie and chosen men, being sent to the king to supplie his brothers roome. Also in the end of the same winter, and in the moneth of Februarie (3) Philip Barrie nephue to Fitzstephans, a verie honest and a wise gentleman, came ouer with a lustie companie of chosen men, as well for the aid of his vncle, as also for the recouerie of his land in Olethan, which was perforce taken awaie (4) from Fitzstephans, as also afterwards from Rafe Fitzstephans sonne. In the same passage also came Gerald an other nephue of Fitzstephans, and brother vnto vnto Philip Barrie, who with his good aduise and counsell did verie much pleasure and helpe both his vncle and brother. for he was learned and a great trauellor, in searching to learne the site and nature of that land, as also the first origine of that nation, and whose name the title of the booke beareth About this time Herrie of Mont Morris professed himselfe a moonke in the monasterie of the Trinitie in Canturburie, and gaue to the same in franke and pure almes all his patronages and impropriations of all his churches, lieng by the sea coasts betwéene Waterford & Wexford, and so became a moonke, & liued a solitarie life in a religious habit who as he changed his habit, so would God he had changed his mind! & as he hath laid awaie his secular weeds, had cast off his malicious disposition!

(1) The gift which the king gaue vnto these two gentlemen of this countrie is yet extant vnder his broad seale, and was giuen by the name of the kingdome of Corke, being bounded from the riuer which fléeteth by Lismore towards the citie of Limerike, vnto Knocke Brendon vpon the seas on the west, to be holden of the king, and of his heires by thrée score knights fées. The citie it selfe without cantred of land was reserued to the king, sauing that they two had the custodie thereof. This kingdome in course of time for want of heires male of them, came to two daughters The one of them was married to Carew and the other to Courcie, & they in the right of their wiues inioied the same during their liues; and after them their heires, vntill such time as by a diuision growing amongest the Englishmen, the Irishrie expelled them, and recouered the countrie vnto themselues

(2) These Mac Arties are yet remaining in the said prouince of Corke, and they be now dispersed into sundrie families, but the chiefest of them is named Mac Artie More, and he in the time of king Henrie the eight was aduanced to the honor and degree of an earle, being called the earle Clan Artie, which in common speech by interposition of the letter C is pronounced Clancartie

(3) In this point there is a varietie among the writers, some writing that Fitzstephans should take awaie the land from Philip Barrie, and giue it to his son Rafe, and to recouer this out of their hands, the said Philip came ouer with such power and force as he could make Some write againe that the land after that it was giuen to Philip Barrie, he departing into England left it in the custodie and charge of Robert Fitzstephans, who when he listed not or could not keepe it anie longer, deliuered the custodie thereof to his sonne Rafe who as his father so was he wearie to kéepe the same. And for that cause Philip Barrie minding to more, and to make the best therof, with such force and helpe as he had gotten, came ouer both to helpe his vncle, & also to fortifie & build holds & castels vpon his said land, whereby he might be the better able to defend and kéepe the same and this séemeth to be the truth of the historie

(4) This Philip of Barrie, hauing seized vpon lands and possessions in Ireland, his posteritie haue euer since continued in that land, and nothing degenerating from their

their first ancestor, haue from age and to age béene noble and valiant gentlemen, and who for their fidelitie and good seruices, were aduanced to honour and made vicounts. and in that title of honor doo continue still But would to God they were not so nuzled, rooted, and altogither seasoned in Irishrie! the name and honor being onelie English, all the rest for the most part Irish.

How Hugh de Lacie builded castels, and fortified in Leinster and Meth

CHAP. 23.

WHILEST these things were thus a dooing in Desmond, Hugh de Lacie a good and a wise man buildeth sundrie castels both in Leinster and Meth, and fortifieth the same verie stronglie and among others he builded one at (1) Leighlin vpon the riuer of (2) Barrow besids Ossorie, a place naturallie of it selfe verie strong, which place Robert Powre by the kings commandement had the charge of, vntill he gaue the same ouer and forsooke it. O what worthie champions and fit marchmen were this Powre & Fitzaldelme, to be sent to dwell and rule in a nation, which is destituted and wanteth noble and valiant men! But a man maie sée the course of fortune, who when she is disposed to smile, how she aduanceth and raiseth vp men from base estate to high degrées for why, these two had more pleasure in chambering and plaieng the wantons with yoong girls, and to plaie vpon a harpe than to beare a shield or staffe, or to weare armour And trulie it was to be maruelled, that so noble a prince could send such cowards to beare rule, and haue authoritie in places of seruice. But to the matter. Hugh de Lacie being a verie wise man, all his care was to bring all things to a peace and quietnesse and therefore such as were oppressed or driuen out of their lands and territories, he restored them, and with such courteous behauiour and gentle spéeches he dealt with all men, that in a verie short time he drew vnto him the hearts of the people, who desirous to dwell vnder his gouernment, manured the grounds, which being then wast and vntilled, was in short space full stored and fraughted both with corne and cattell. And then for the safetie of the people and defense of the countrie, he builded townes and erected castels in euerie place, made orders & established lawes for the gouernment of the people. And by this it came to passe, that ech man inioied the labours of his owne hands, and euerie man liued in peace one with the other, and euerie bodie loued him, and he assured of all men But hauing thus by his wisedome, policie, and good gouernement recouered that nation to good conformitie and obedience, behold enuie (which alwaies maligneth vertue) he was had in a gealousie and suspicion, that his drift and policie was to appropriat the whole land to himselfe, and as the lawfull king and monarch would crowne himselfe king of Ireland Which opinion was so receiued & false rumour so spred, that it was in a short time carried into England, which when it came to the kings eares, you maie not thinke that he at all liked thereof, or could brooke the same.

(1) This Leighlin standeth full vpon the riuer of Barrow, and it is a verie old & ancient castell called by the name of the Blake castell, a fort in those daies verie strong it standeth in the baronie of Odrone, which is the ancient inheritance of the Carews, who being barons of Carew in Wales, one of them maried the daughter and heire of the baron of this Odrone, & so the Carews became & were for the course of sundrie yeares, vntill in the troublesome times, in king Richard the seconds

time

time they were expelled, as all others or the most part of the English were. But being dwelling there, some one of them builded a religious house of Greie friers neere adioining to the said castell, which being since dissolued in king Henrie the eights time, the same fell into the kings hands, who made thereof a fort, and kept there a perpetuall garison, and thus was it disseuered from the baronie. There is also one other Leighlin distant from this about an English mile, where is the cathedrall church of that diocesse and whereof the bishop taketh his name being called the bishop of Leighlin, but for difference sake the same is called old Leighlin, and this other Leighlin bridge, by reason of a bridge builded of stone ouer the riuer at that place, and whereof the one end butteth vpon the foresaid Blake castell.

(2) The Barrow is a goodlie and a notable riuer, hauing his head or spring in the hill called Mons Blandina or Slogh Blome, in which also are the heads or springs of the two other notable riuers Suire and the other Fore. This Barrow kéepeth & hath his course through the countie of Lex, and passeth by the market towne of Athie vnto Carlow, and from thense vnto Leighlin, and so to Rosse, a little aboue which towne it méeteth and ioineth with the Fore, and they togither kéepe their course about six miles, vntill they méet with the Suire, which is neere vnto the late abbeie of Dunbrodie: and as they all doo spring and rise out of one mounteine, so after they haue taken their seuerall courses, they meet togither and take one waie into the seas. They are all nauigable, and all a like replenished with sundrie sorts and kinds of fishes.

The description of Hugh de Lacie

CHAP 24

IF you will know what manner of man Hugh de Lacie was, you shall vnderstand his eies were blacke and déepe, and his nose somewhat flat, and the right side of his face from the chin vpwards by a mischance was shrewdlie skalled: his necke was short, and his bodie hairie, as also not fleshie but sinewish and strong compact; his stature was but small, and his proportion deformed, but in conditions he was verie sober, trustie, and modest. He was verie carefull in his owne priuat matters, but in causes of gouernment and in all publike affaires he was most vigilant and carefull. And albeit he were a verie good souldier, and one of great experience in martiall affaires, yet in his sundrie aduentures wherein he was sometimes rash and verie hastie, he sped not alwaies best nor had the best successe. After the death of his wife he was somewhat lose of life, being much giuen to women, of whom he made no great choise: he was verie gréedie and couetous of wealth and possessions, but ouermuch ambitious of honour and reputation. At this time in Leinster florished Robert Fitzhenrie brother vnto (1) Meilerius, who in his youthfull yeares was verie lustie like the flower of the garden, which when the winter draweth and is cold, dooth vade and wither awaie. Likewise (2) Alexander and Giraldus the two sonnes of Maurice. And albeit Girald were a man but of meane stature, yet verie wise, sober, and honest. Also Roger le Powre conestable of Leighlin, Hugh de Lacie, and William le Powre seneschall of Waterford, Robert Barrie the yoonger sonne of Philip Barrie, and both the Reimonds were of best fame and credit in these daies. About this time befell and happened the two strange woonders at Fother in Meth, whereof we haue spoken in our topographie, namelie, of the woman violentlie and perforce abused in a mill by a souldier, and of the otes there stolen and caried awaie.

(1) Nesta

(1) Nesta the daughter of the great Rhesus had thrée husbands, by the first named Henrie she had a sonne, who being named after his name, was named Fitzhenrie, who was father to Henrie, Robert, and this Meilerius

(2) This same Nesta had to hir third husband one Gerald of Windsore, and by him had issue hir fourth son named Maurice, who was father to William Gerald and this Alexander This Gerald was a valiant and a noble gentleman, and who had wars against Rhesus the father of this Nesta, and kept the towne and castell of Penbroke against him and all his force but in the end after a peace concluded betwéene them, he maried this ladie, and had worthie issue by hir.

How Hugh de Lacie vpon a vaine suspicion was sent for into England, and of his returne, againe from thense.

CHAP. 25.

THE suspicion conceiued of Hugh de Lacie dailie increased more & more, and as is before said came to the kings eares, who as princes in such causes was verie gelous, and could not like thereof, and therefore foorthwith sent for Hugh de Lacie by John conestable of Chester and Richard Pet, whome he appointed to tarrie and serue in his place, & to be the gouernors or lords iustices of the land But before he should depart and go awaie, it was agréed by a common consent, that there should diuerse castels and sundrie forts be builded in Leinster for Meth was alredie méetlie well and indifferentlie fortified & incastelled First therefore they builded two castels in Fotheret of Onolan, the one for (1) Reimond, and the other for Griffith his brother: the third was at (2) Tresseldermont néere to Moroghs countrie for Walter of Ridensford: the fourth for John (3) Clauill vpon the riuer of Barrow not far from Leighlin the fift at Collach for John Herford And as for Kildare, which with the countrie adioining was before by the earle in his life time giuen to Meilerius, was taken from him, & in exchange the countrie of (4) Lex was giuen to him, which was a wild and sauage countrie, full of woods, passes, and bogs, and in the middle of the enimies, as also from anie succour or rescue. howbeit not vnfit for this such a champion of Mars and so worthie a souldier

These things being thus doone in the summer time, Hugh de Lacie tooke his passage ouer to England, and made his spéedie repaire to the kings presence, where he so wiselie and dutifullie behaued himselfe, that the king not onelie was resolued of his truth and fidelitie, but also putting especiall confidence in him, he sent him backe againe And calling home the foresaid John de conestable and Richard Pet, made him his generall and deputie of the land, and tooke assurance of him for his truth in this behalfe howbeit he ioined in commission with him one Robert of Salisburie, who should in the kings behalfe be a councellor and a trustie assistant vnto him in all his doings Now Hugh de Lacie being returned backe againe into Ireland, and there settled and placed, thinketh vpon his first deuises, how to fortifie the countrie and to kéepe it in good order. And the more castels he builded, and the more Englishmen he did bestow and place therein, the sooner and better did he thinke to bring the same to passe and effect Among manie castels therfore which he builded, he made one at Tachmeho in Lex, which he gaue to Meilerius, as also gaue him his néece to wife, also one castell néere to Abowie which he gaue to Robert Bigaret, and not farre from thense an other castell which he deliuered to Thomas Fleming And not farre from thense he builded one other castell at the Norach on the riuer of the Barrow, which Robert Fitzrichard had

besides in Meth he builded the castels of Dunach and of Kilaue, as also Adam Fucepoit and Gilbert Migents castels, and manie others, which were now too long to be particularlie repeted and recited

Talke betweene a priest and a woolfe

And about this time was that strange talke and communication in a wood in Meth, betwéene a priést and a woolfe, whereof we haue spoken in our topographie. which thing though it may seeme verie strange & most incredible, yet the same is not to be discredited For as S Jerome saith, you shall find in scripture manie strange things, & which to a mans iudgement shall seeme to be nothing true at all. and yet neuertheles they are most true For nature cannot preuaile nor doo anie thing against the Lord of nature neither ought anie creature to contemne or scorne, but rather with great reuerence and honour to consider the workes of God his creator Not long after this king Henrie the yoonger, the son of king Henrie the elder, being seduced & carried (the more was the pitie) by lewd and naughtie counsels, rebelled the second time against his father, and had gotten vnto him the most part of the best noble men in all Poitiers, & the lustiest gentlemen in all France besides his brother Geffreie the earle of Britaine the chiefe author and cause of this rebellion, and manie others of his confederates But in the end, by Gods iust iudgement and vengeance for his vnnaturall ingratitude against his father, who though he were a verie valiant and a lustie gentleman, yet against death nothing can helpe, and so died about June at Marels to the great sorrow of manie And verie shortlie after also the foresaid Geffreie, a noble and a valiant gentleman, & who for his worthinesse and prowesse might haue béene the sonne of Vlysses or Achilles, who now reuolting the third time from his father, and rebelling against him, was by Gods iust iudgement about the kalends of August taken out of his life, and so died.

(1) Nesta the daughter of the great Rhesus prince of Wales had thrée husbands, the third of them was Gerald of Windsore, and these had to their first sonne William Fitzgerald the father vnto this Reimond, and Griffith

(2) Tresseldermont is a castell about a fiue miles from Catherlough, & somtimes a verie faire towne and walled round about, and bordering néere to the baronie of Odrone The English writers doo saie that this castell was not builded in this Tresseldermont, but at Kilken, a castell about thrée miles from this, and both now belonging to the earle of Kildare. But the Latine bookes, which are of eldest writing and credit, and whom I doo herein follow, doo write it by expresse words, Tresseldermont

(3) This castell of Clauill not far from Leighlin, is supposed to be that which is now called Carlough or Catherlough howbeit the common fame of the countrie dooth attribute this castell of Carlough to Eua the earls wife, and the ladie and heire of Leinster, and that she should build the same But there appeereth no such things of hir doings, for by the course of the historie it is plaine, that the castels builded in Leinster were doone by the Englishmen onelie, and for their defense and safetie

(4) The countrie of Lex is parcell of Leinster, & lieth in the marches and extreame confines of the same by the west it is verie strong and fast, being full of woods and bogs, and therefore a safe receptacle for rebels and outlawes It is within the diocesse of Leighlin, and before now of late no shire ground, but inhabited by the Mores, who were alwaies rebels and traitors. But in hope to reforme the same it was made a countie of it selfe, by an act of parlement in the third and fourth yeares of Philip and Marie, and named the Queenes countie.

The

The death of Laurence archbishop of Dublin, and of Iohn Comin made archbishop in his place.

CHAP 26.

IN this meane time Laurence archbishop of Dublin died at the castell of Angiers in Normandie, about the kalends of December 1180 He was a (1) iust and a good man, but somwhat in displeasure with the king, who had him in suspicion bicause he was at the councell of (2) Laterane, and there inueighed much against the king of England and his honour, & for that cause in his returne homewards through Normandie was staied, and in the end there died, where he was buried in the high church of our ladie After him John Comin an Englishman borne, and a monke in the abbeie of Euenham, was by the kings means elected orderlie by the clergie of Dublin archbishop, and afterwards confirmed by pope Lucius at Viterbe, where he was also made a cardinall A man he was verie well learned and eloquent, and verie zealous in causes of the church, wherein he would haue doone verie much good, if that he had not beene too worldlie, & haue sought to haue pleased worldlie princes, and to haue beene in the kings fauour.

(1) This one thing is and was a common obseruation in the Romish church, that if anie one had receiued the charact thereof, that although he were neuer so rebellious nor so great a traitor against his prince, yet the same was to be interpreted to be in defense of the holie church, and such a one was counted a godlie and a holie man, though by the scriptures he who resisteth his prince is said to resist God himselfe

(2) The councell of Laterane is said to be one of the greatest synods or generall councels that hath bin, it was kept at Rome vnder pope Innocent the third An 1204. Manie decrées were there made for the aduancing of the Romish antichrist. but yet the councell could not be brought to his full perfection by reason of the ciuill wars in Italie But among other decrées this was concluded, that all controuersies betwéene kings and princes, the correction therof should apperteine to the pope as also no man should be counted emperour, except the pope had admitted him and crowned him

The comming of Iohn the kings sonne into Ireland.

CHAP 27.

THE king to aduance his yoonger sonne named Iohn had giuen him the dominion ouer Ireland, and he thereupon had taken homage of sundrie persons for the same · and now minding to bring the same to a finall end & perfect order, sendeth ouer into Ireland before his sonne Iohn the new archbishop of Dublin, who as a fore-runner vnto his sonne should prepare all things in readinesse against his comming, who foorthwith tooke his iournie about the kalends of August, and sailed ouer into Ireland Also in the moneth of September then next following, he sent ouer Philip of Worcester, a valiant souldier, a sumptuous and a liberall man, with fortie gentlemen, who was commanded to send ouer (1) Hugh de Lacie, and he to staie there

there as gouernour of the land vntill Iohn his sonne came ouer. This Philip being thus placed in authoritie, the first thing he did he resumed and tooke into the kings vse the lands in Ochathesie, and diuerse other parcels which Hugh de Lacie had before sold, and these he appointed to serue for the kings prouision and diet. And after the winter was past, he assembled and mustered all his men and companie, & began to trauell from place to place, and in March about the middle of Lent he came to (2) Armagh, where when he had extorted and perforce exacted from the cleargie there a great masse of monie and treasure, he returned vnto the citie of Downe, and from thense to Dublin in safetie. being well laden with gold, siluer, and monie, which he had exacted in euerie place where he came for other good he did none In this iournie there happened two strange miracles, the one at Armach concerning the great anguish and griefe of (3) Philip when he departed and went out of the towne, the other was of a (4) fornace which Hugh Tirell tooke away from the poore priests at Armagh, as more at large is declared in our topographie.

Two strange miracle.

(1) This Hugh de Lacie albeit he were thus sent for, yet he went not ouer, as it appéereth by the course of the histories of this time he was about building of a castell at Deruagh, and there being among his labourers, and séeing one not to frame verie well in his worke, taught him what he should doo, taking his pickeax in both his hands and brake the ground. This wicked Irishman when he saw his lord and master thus stooping and labouring, suddenlie came behind him, and with his ax or weapon strake him in the head and slue him, but his inheritance and possessions came & descended to his two sonnes Walter and Hugh.

(2) In Ireland there are foure archbishoprikes, one at Dublin for the prouince of Leinster, another at Cashill for the prouince of Mounster, the third at Thomond for the prouince of Connagh, & the fourth at Armagh for the prouince of Vlster The chiefest of them is the archbishop of this Armagh, for although euerie one of the others be named a primat of Ireland, yet this one alone is named primat of all Ireland, which title he hath partlie bicause he is successour to S Patrike, who first conuerted Ireland to the christian faith, and had his see and church at this Armagh, one other cause is bicause this archbishop was the first that receiued a pall from the pope This pall is a certeine inuesture of cloth, which the pope haloweth and giueth or sendeth to euerie archbishop, who weareth the same vppermost vpon his garment The nature of this pall, of the first inuention thereof and the causes whie it is giuen to euerie archbishop, is not incident nor apperteining to the course and nature of this historie, and therfore I will omit it This Armagh was somtimes a faire towne, and therein a faire cathedrall church, lieng faire and remote from all good neighbors, and in the middle of the Onels and other sauage people, the same hath beene and still is and lieth wast and the archbishop remooued to a house of his named Terseekam, which lieth néere the towne of Drogheda, being a place of better safetie

What the bishops pall is

(3) The historie is, that this Philip of Worcester being well landed with great riches exacted from the cleargie and departed, he was no sooner out of the towne, but that he was taken with a sudden pang, which for the time was so vehement, that it was supposed he would neuer haue recouered it.

(4) This Hugh Tirell among other the spoiles which he tooke, he had a great brueing fornace or pan which serued for the whole house, for which his dooing the priests cursed him, and he caried this along with him vntill he came to the citie of Downe And on a night he being in his lodging, the same was entred with fire, and the horsses which drew the said pan, as also much goods which they brought with them, and a great part of the towne was burned. In the morning, when he saw the great

great spoile, and yet the said pan as nothing hurt nor perished, he began to repent and be sorie, and so restored the pan againe.

The comming of Heraclius the patriarch into England.

CHAP. 28.

WHILE these things were dooing in Ireland, Heraclius the reuerend patriarch of Ierusalem, hauing gone a long iourneie from the east to the west, came into England about the beginning of Februarie, who brought with him the keies of the holie citie and sepulchre, with the kings ensigne and martiall signe, in the behoofe of all the states of the holie land, as well of the brethren of th' order of the temple as hospitall: and with the consent of all the cleargie and laitie, making supplication to king Henrie the second, falling at his féet with teares, and humblie desiring him, that he would be pitifullie mooued to the aid of the holie land, and Christes patrimonie, desperatlie afflicted by the infidels: otherwise affirming (which within two yeares happened) that the whole kingdome would fall shortlie into the hands of the Soldane of the Saracens and of Egypt. Oh what a glorie was it to this king and kingdome, that he passing so manie emperours, kings and princes, as though there were no helpe in the middle part of the world, should come into this corner of the earth, & as it were into an other world to require aid! O how worthie, perpetuall and incomparable had the kings glorie béene, if he setting aside other businesse, and forsaking his kingdoms, had taken without delaie (at this calling of Christ) Christes crosse, and haue followed him! Verelie, he should haue receiued of him the euerlasting kingdome, if he had serued him in this necessitie of whom he receiued his kingdome, and so glorious a grace of gouernement on earth. Oh if he would haue defended here (for his abilitie) the patrimonie of so worthie a kingdome in this point of necessitie, and this triall of deuotion, he might haue béene worthilie fortified in earth by such a patrone and tutor in all his affaires and necessities whatsoeuer.

The answer of the king to the patriarch.

CHAP. 29.

A DAIE for answer herof being appointed at last by the king at London, manie as well knights as of common sort, by the admonishments of the patriarch, as the sermons of Baldwin the archbishop were croised to the seruice of Christ. At the last the patriarch receiued this answer of the king, that it was not good to leaue his realme without defense and gouernement, & leaue open his lands beyond sea to the rapacitie of the Frenchmen that hated him: but as concerning monie, he would giue both that which he sent thither, to be reserued for him, and more also for the defense of the holie land. To whome the patriarch answered, by following this aduise. "O king you doo nothing: and by this meanes you shall neither saue your selfe, nor rescue Christes patrimonie. We come to séeke a prince, and not monie. Euerie part of the world almost sendeth vs monie, but none sendeth vs a prince. Therfore we desire a man that may want monie, and not monie that may want a man." But, when the patriarch could get no other answer of the king, he taketh This was the saieng of Themistocles.
an

an other deuise he desireth him to giue to their aid one of his sonnes, and if none other, yet his yoongest sonne Iohn, that the bloud descending from the Anjowes might in a new branch raise vp the kingdome.

Iohn himselfe, albeit he was readie to passe into Ireland giuen him by his father, with a great armie, (prostrating himselfe at his fathers féet) desired (as they saie) that he might be sent to Ierusalem, but he obteined it not So the patriarch séeing he could doo nothing, and draw no oile out of the hard stone, hée spake thus against the king, in th audience of manie, with a threatfull and propheticall spirit. "O glorious king, thou hast reigned hitherto among the princes of the world with incomparable glorie, and your princelie honour hath hitherto dailie increased to the type of highnesse But now doubtlesse is this triall being forsaken of God, whom you forsake, and destitute of all heauenlie grace From hensefoorth shall your glorie be turned into sorrow, and your honor to reproch so long as you liue. I would to God the king had auoided this threat by penance, like the king of Niniuie, and had caused this sentence to be altered!"

The holie man spake this thing thrise, first at London, then at Douer, and lastlie at Chinon castell beyond the sea And I would to God the patriarch had béene a man without that propheticall spirit, & had rather spoken a lesing, that we may for more euidence touch such things brieflie as were before spoken by that true fore-speaker, which we saw shortlie to take effect. Whereas the king reigned thirtie and fiue yeares, thirtie years were granted him for worldlie glorie, expectation of his conuersion, & triall of his deuotion, but the last fiue years fell vpon him, as vpon an vngratefull, reprobate, and abiect seruant, in reuengement, sorrow, & ignominie For in the two and thirtith yeare of his reigne, immediatlie after the comming of the patriarch, his first enterprise of sending his sonne Iohn into Ireland, both the labour and cost was frustrate and lost The thrée and thirtith yeare, whereas he neuer lost land before, he lost to king Philip (being but a child) almost all Aniou. The foure and thirtith yéere he lost the castell Rader, and welnéere all Berre The fiue and thirtith yeare of his reigne, and the fourth yéere after the comming of the patriarch, not onelie king Philip of France, but his son Richard of Poitiers rising against him, he lost the cities of Towres and Maine, with manie castels, and himselfe also, according to that in saint Gregorie. "Those that the Lord hath long forborne, that they might be conuerted, if they doo not conuert, he condemneth them the more greeuouslie"

The crossing of kings.

CHAP 30.

BUT perchance the king was reserued by heauenlie disposition to the victorie of deserued loue How much greater is it to repare things cast downe, than to vnderprop things likelie to fall? And who had knowne Hector, if Troie had continued in prosperitie? By so much as aduersitie is more instant and vrged, by so much the glorie of valiantnesse will shine the brighter For by the secret iudgement of God, within two yeares after the victorie was giuen to the pagans and Parthians, against the christians, either to reuenge the cold deuotion of the east church, or to trie the deuout obedience of the westerne men, the worthie Richard earle of Poitiers hearing this ouerthrow, tooke deuoutlie the crossine vpon him at Towres, giuing an example to other princes in that matter. Wherevpon the king of England, the earles father, and Philip king of France, who had bin before at variance (with Gods grace,

grace, and the archbishop of Towres persuasion) in that place and that houre, at their conference at Guisors were croised, with manie other great men of the clergie and laitie. And as kings folowed the example of the erle, so after them example the emperour Frederike, through the persuasion of the duke of Alba, with manie states of Almane were croised in the lords court at Mentz So as it is thought, the king of England being reserued more than all other to the restoring of the decaied state of the holie land, if he had finished his life in this victorie, doubtlesse that famous prophesie of Merlin Ambrosius had beene verified in him "His beginning (saith he) shall wauer with wild affections, and his end shall mount to heauen" A prophesie of Merlin touching the king

The discord of the kings.

CHAP 31.

A SUDDEN discord rose betwene the kings and that (which was woorse) betwéene the father and the earle, through the working of the old enimie, & their sinnes deseruing the same, to the great hinderance of their noble enterprise as though they being vnfit for it, the honor thereof was reserued for other, or perchance according to the sentence of Gregorie Aduersitie, which is obiected against good vowes, is a triall of vertue, and not a signe of disproofe Who is ignorant how happie a thing it was that Paule was driuen into Italie, and yet he suffered shipwracke? But the ship of his heart was safe among the surges of the sea. Likewise therfore as vertue is perfected in infirmitie, and gold tried in the fire so the constancie of faith that cannot be craized with tribulations, dooth increase more as sinapis, and the courage of the mind is more valiant againe than troublous assaults of fortune O how much rather would I, that these kings accompanied with a few men acceptable to God, had taken vpon them this laborious, but yet a glorious iourneie, than to wax proud for the great wealth that they had gathered of manie people to this end Read ouer the whole bible, and consider these latter times, and you shall find, that victorie hath béene gained, not with force and humane power, but with Gods grace and store of vertues For as Cassiodorus saith "An armed people without the Lord is vnarmed" And as Seneca saith, "Not the number of the people, but the vertue of a few get the victorie" Of the foure before named, the emperour Frederike, albeit he was the last croised, yet in the execution thereof he was the first whome therefore I account so much the more woorthie of victorie in heauen, and glorie in earth, that he forsaking large kingdomes and his empire, delaied not out the matter

A vision and exposition thereof.

CHAP 32.

THERFORE I thought it not inconuenient to set downe a vision, which he that hideth much from wisemen & reuealeth it to babes visited me withall, being a most simple and vile wretch In the miserie of this time, in that ciuill and detestable discord betwéene the king and the erle of Poitiers, I being with the king at Chinon castell the seuenth ides of Maie at night in my sléepe about the cocke crowing, me thought I saw a great multitude of men looking vp into heauen, and as it were woondering

woondering at somewhat. So I lifting vp mine eies to sée what the same was, I saw A strange vision. a bright light breake out betweene the thickenesse of the clouds, and the clouds being incontinentlie seuered asunder, and the lower heauen as it were being opened, and the sight of mine eies pearsing through that window to the empereall heauen, there appeered the court thereof in great multitude, wide open as it were to be spoiled, all kinds of munition being bent against it. You might haue séene there a head cut from one, an arme from another, and some striken through with arrowes, some with lances, and some with swords. And when manie of the beholders either for the brightnes, or terror, or pitie, had fallen flat on their faces, me thought that I (to see the end of the matter) did view it longer than the rest. So they hauing gotten the victorie ouer all the other, the bloudie slaues fell vpon the prince of the heauenlie orders, sitting in his throne as he was woont to bee pictured, and drawing him from the throne on the right hand, hauing his breast naked, they thrust him through the right side with their lances, and immediatlie there followed a terrible voice in this maner, Woch, woch, O Holi-ghost! But whether it came frō heauen, or was vttered by the people beneath, I can not tell; and so the terror of this voice & the vision awakened me.

I call him here to witnesse, to whome all things are apparant and manifest, that immediatlie as I sat in my bed, & reuolued these things in my mind, I was in so great an horror both of bodie and mind, for halfe an houre and more, that I feared least I should haue fallen besides my selfe. But recoursing deuoutlie to the onlie refuge of humane saluation, & blessing my forehead with the crosse eftsoones, & fortifieng my mind thereby, I passed the rest of the night without sléepe, & so through Gods grace returned fullie to my selfe: yet to this daie I can neuer remember that vision without horror. What may be more terrible to a creature than to see his creator smitten through with weapons? What man without gréefe can abide to see the seruants of God, & patrons of men to be murthered? Who can behold the Lord of nature to suffer, & dooth not suffer therewith? What this vision portendeth, The meaning of the foresaid vision. without preiudice to anie I will shew brieflie. He that suffered once in his owne person for all, giueth vs to vnderstand, that he now suffereth againe, but that in his flocke. And he that by triumphing ouer the crosse, and ascending to the right hand of his father, hath victoriouslie entered his kingdome, his enimies now go about to depriue him of his kingdome, and subuert his church, which he gathered vnto him by the shedding of his bloud. Therefore, as I doo suppose, this passion did not appeare vpon the crosse, but his maiestie: as though the crosse now being taken awaie, his enimies go about to take that glorie from him, which he got on the crosse. Or else that his faithfull had suffered, not in the crosse, but with weapons in that holie land, which he after so manie miracles had consecrated with his bloud. So likewise he declared this his passion which he for his susteined, not in the crosse, but in his maiestie: so he signified, that all the court of heauen suffered with the like compassion, mouing his to reuengement with the shewing of so great gréefe. As concerning that voice beginning in a barbarous language and ending in Latine, what I thinke I will shew. Woch, woch, in the Germane toong, is a signe of gréefe doubled. And where that wofull mourning voice began in the Germane toong, and ended in Latine, it maie be signified thereby, that onelie the Almans and the Italians take this the affliction of their Lord more grieuouslie than other nations, as their hasting declareth. God forbid that the passion or lamentation be here vnderstood by anie slaughter of the christians and people in this expedition.

The

The memorable euents of our time.

CHAP. 33.

I THINKE it not impertinent to set downe here (by occasion) the aduentures and notable euents in England: and first of all, the sudden death of the deteiners of the kingdome of England against the lawfull heire, the nephue of Henrie by his daughter Matild: as well the death of the woorthie knight Eustathius the son of king Stephan, and son in law to Lewes the French king: as of his mother quéene Matild the countesse of Bullogne. Then the concord adoption made betwéene king Stephan, and Henrie duke of Normandie. And then after the death of king Stephan, the mariage of queene Elianor, and the translation from crowne to crowne. Immediatlie, the aduancement of the duke to the kingdome, and the coronation of king Henrie the second. The assiege of the castell of Bridgenorth vpon Seuerne, and the compulsion of the woorthie knight Hugh Mortimer to dedition, to the terrible example of all. What néedeth manie words? To confound the mightie, and to make euen the rugged, there were prosperous successes. And as destruction fell vpon the deteiners of the kingdome, so likewise it fell vpon the peacebreakers of the same, as well of the brethren, as also of the sons.

The subduing of prince Oene at Colshull in Northwales in a wooddie streict, not without the losse of manie knights. A sumptuous expedition to Tholouse, albeit it was vnprofitable. An altercation & warre betwéene the king of England and Lewes of France, through the doting of both parts. The yéelding vp of prince Rhese by the means of his vncle Oene at Pencador in Southwales, the king of England comming thither. The vnwilling & wrested confession onelie by word & by writing (as some say) of Thomas of Canturburie, and his suffragans at Clarendon, as concerning annates: when that prophesie of Merlin Ambrosius seemed to be fulfilled, "The buls toongs shall be cut out." The iniurious crieng out of all the court at Northampton against the father, bearing the crosse, & mainteining the rights of the crucifix, and the priuie departure of him to exile that night. The ambassage of Reinold archbishop of Cullen, & chancellor to the emperor, from the said emperor to the king of England: who was an effectuous persuader of mariage to be had betwéene Henrie the emperors nephue duke of Saxonie and Bauier, and Matild the kings eldest daughter: he mooued also, but in vaine, to set cleare the Almains schisme. Not long after the publike periurie through out all the realme, by the kings proclamation against the sée of saint Peter, and the archbishop of Canturburie. And incontinentlie the countie Gunceline, and other states of Saxonie came from the duke into England for the kings daughter. A prophesie of Merlin fulfilled.

The coronation of king Henrie the third, son to king Henrie, solemnized in London by the archbishop of Yorke, to the preiudice of the church of Canturburie. Ambassadors came from Spaine, and obteined the kings daughter Elianor, to be maried vnto Ansulfo, king of Toledo and Castile. The comming of Dermicius (being expelled) to the king, and the sailing ouer into Ireland of Fitzstephans, & earle Richard. The expedition of the lord of *Oswalstre in Powes, and his returne by occasion of raine: not without his hurtfull dismembring of the pledges, and great slaughter of his enimies. The martyrdome of Thomas. The often shining miracles. The departure of the noble Henrie bishop of Winchester, descended of the kings bloud at Winchester. The viage of the king into Ireland. The conspiracie of the states against their prince, and the children against their father. * Albimonasterie.

The comming of two cardinals into Normandie, to make inquirie of the death of the martyr. The sudden returne of the king out of Ireland into Wales, and so into England, thense into Normandie, with an appeasing of the said cardinals, and the French king. The first departure of the yoong king with his two brethren from his father into France. The victorie of the ciuill and two yeares warre, and the kings mercie towards the vanquished, as we haue shewed before. The comming of Huguntio Petie Leon cardinall of the title of saint Angelo into England, and the celebration of a councell vnder him of all the cleargie of England, at London, as concerning the contention of supremasie betweene Richard archbishop of Canturburie, and Roger of Yorke but the allegations on both sides with fists and staues brake it off. The bishop of Capua, and Diaferus elect of Ciora, and earle Florius, came from William king of Sicill, to haue mariage betwéene him and Ioane the kings yoonger daughter.

The ambassadors of the kings of Spaine, Castile, and Nauar, came into England: who as concerning lands and castels (whereof they contended) promised altogither to stand vnto the king of Englands arbitrement. Wherefore the king assembling at London all the lawyers & wise men in the land of both orders; when the cause was proposed and the allegations heard on both sides, by famous aduocats, among whome, Peter of Cardon, that came in the behalfe of the king of Nauar, excelled in eloquence the king vsing wise counsell, and intending to end the contention by transaction, that giuing somewhat from one, and keeping somewhat from an other, he would hurt neither partie much. But as he was appointed iudge by both, so he was carefull for the commoditie of both as much as could be. So making a transaction, and ingrossing it in writing, he writ the iudiciall examination for a prouiso, That if either part refused to stand to his arbitrement, the definitiue strife might be dirempted by sentence. The comming of Lewes king of France into England, who went on pilgrimage to Canturburie, to the martyr Thomas, to require his helpe deuoutlie, whome he in the time of his exile had helped and offering a cup pretious both for matter & substance in the place where the holie bodie was buried, when he had declined a while prostrat on his face, and had laid his bare head a while in the right side hole of the marble stone that standeth therby, at last, rising from his praier (that he might confirme the memorie of his pilgrimage with euerlasting record) in the presence of the king of England, the earle of Flanders, the archbishop of the see, the prior of the couent, and other men of state, he gaue yearelie vnto Canturburie abbeie an hundred tuns of wine.

The second defection of king Henrie the third, and earle Geffreie, with the sudden death of the yoonger king at Marcels. The comming on pilgrimage of Godfrie archbishop of Cullen, and Philip earle of Flanders vnto Canturburie. The death of earle Geffreie. The comming of Heraclius the patriarch, and the sailing of earle Iohn into Ireland. Almost all things as they be here set in order, chanced in our time, in no great distance betwéene, in and about the space of thrée and thirtie yeares. O how glorious had all these things béene, if they had sorted to a good end! Which surelie would haue hapned, if he setting other things aside, had followed Christ, when he was called, of whome he receiued all these benefits, and had spent the last fiue yeares reigne in his seruice. But these things being before rehearsed by the way, let vs returne to the historie.

The

The recapitulation of sundrie acts, and of the comming of Iohn the kings sonne to Ireland, with his successe there.

CHAP 34.

NOW omitting the building of three castels, one at Tipporarie, the other at Archphin. & the third at Lismore, after the comming of earle Iohn, & speaking nothing of the euill fortune of thrée woorthie yoong men, Robert Barrie at Lismore, Reimond Fitzhugh at Olethan, and Reimond Cantitinensis at Odrona Of part of the garrison of Archphin slaine in the wood there, by the prince of Limerike on Midsummer daie, & foure knights there killed, not without manfull defense Of them of Limerike, and the noble man Ograine slaine at Tipporarie Of them of Archphin slaine againe by those of Limerike in taking of a préie Of Dermucius Mac Arthie prince of Desmond, with others slaine in parlée neere Corke by them of Corke, and the garrison of Theobald brother to Walter Of the slaughter of them of Kencolon, with their prince inuading Meth by the men thereof, & William Litle, and one hundred of their heads sent to Dublin Of the finding out of the bodies of Patrike, Brigid, & Columbe at Dundalke, & their translation from thense by the procurement of Iohn de Curcie

Of the heading of Hugh Lacie at Dornach, through the treason of his owne Irishmen Of the killing of twelue noble knights vnder Iohn de Curcie, in the returne from Connagh Of the traitorous and lamentable slaughter of Roger Powre, and manie others in Osserie and thorough that occasion, the priuie conspiracie of all Ireland against the Englishmen, manie castels being therewith destroied. All which things are not vnwoorthie to be recorded, when the dominion was translated to the kings son But assigning these doings to other writers, we will proceed to more profitable matters How and wherefore this first enterprise of the kings son had no good successe I thought good to declare brieflie: that this small addition (albeit it can not be a cure to that which is past) yet it may be a caueat for things to come. ¶ This recapitulation followeth in a more absolute forme, pag 223 which being deliuered out of sundrie copies, doo perfect one another] Note.

When all things méete and necessarie for so great a iournie or voiage were at the king his commandement and charges made readie, then Iohn the kings yoonger sonne a little before made lord of Ireland, was sent ouer, and in the Lent time (1) he tooke leaue of his father, and as he trauelled towards saint Dauids to take shipping, he passed and rode along by the sea coasts of Southwals, and so came to (2) Penbroke There brought and accompanied him vnto the ship a noble and a worthie man named Reinulfe Glanuile, one of the K his most priuie councell in all weightie matters, as also cheefe iustice of England And on wednesdaie in the Easter weeke, the wind being at east and blowing a good gale, he tooke ship in Milford hauen, but for hast he left to doo his deuotion and oblation at saint Dauids, which was but an euill halsoning neuerthelesse on the next morrow about noonetide he arriued in safetie vnto Waterford with all his companie, which were about thrée hundred gentlemen, and of bowmen, footmen, horssemen, and others a great number Then was fulfilled the vaticine or prophesie of old Merlin · "A burning globe shall rise out of the east, & shall compasse about the land of Ireland, and all the foules of that Iland shall flée round about the fire " And hauing spoken these words of the father, he continueth his speech, and thus speaketh of his sonne "And of this fire shall rise a sparkle, for feare of which all the inhabiters of the land shall tremble and be afraid · Prophesie of Merlin fulfilled

 and

and yet he that is absent shall be more estéemed than he that is present, and better shall be the successe of the first than of the second."

Iohn at this his first arriuall into Ireland was of the age of 12 yeres, which was from the first arriuall of his father thirtéene yeares, of the landing of the earle Strangbow fouretéene yeares, and from the first entrance of Robert Fitzstephans fiftéene yeares, and the yeare of our Lord one thousand one hundred eightie and fiue, Lucius then Romane bishop, Frederike the emperor, and Philip the French king. There passed ouer with the king in the same fléet manie good clerks, among whome (3) one was speciallie commended vnto this yoong lord by his father, for that he was a diligent searcher of naturall histories, as also had béene before two yeares in the same land, and there collected sundrie notes, and sufficient matter as well for his historie, as for his topographie and which after that he was returned home, and attending in the court, did (as leisure serued him) digest and set in good order of a booke, the same being his labor of thrée yéeres. A trauell to him painefull, but to his posteritie profitable, although much misliked and enuied at by such as then were liuing the one liked it well, but the other dispraised it, the one reaped a benefit and commoditie, but the other of a secret malice maligning the same, fretted in his humor, and was grauelled in his owne follie

(1) The first voiage of the king his sonne, being then but a child of twelue yéeres of age the English chronicles doo make small mention thereof But such as doo write thereof, doo report that the king brought his sonne as farre as Glocester on this iorne, and there dubbing and honoring him with the degree of knighthood, sent him on his iorne.

(2) Penbroke is an old and an ancient towne, builded by a noble man named Arnulph Montgomerie the ancestor of the Carews, whose names are Montgomeries, & lieth in Westwales named Demetia, but now of this towne is called Penbrokeshire. It standeth vpon a créeke of Milford hauen, about two miles from the castell Carew. of which castell the Montgomeries builded, and there dwelling tooke the name thereof, & were called Carews, which name that familie dooth yet reteine In this towne of Penbroke standeth a goodlie and a strong castell, which hath béene in times past the seat and house of manie a noble man bearing the name of the earles of Penbroke In this was king Henrie the seuenth borne. It is now in great ruine and in decaie.

The ancient house of the Carews.

(3) This man ment here is Giraldus Cambrensis the author of this booke, who (as it appeareth by this and other his works) was learned and much giuen to studie He was archdeacon of saint Dauids, and descended from Girald of Windsore, and the ladie Nesta his wife, for he was the son of Maurice, and the sonne of the foresaid Girald and Nesta. and so this Girald of Windsore was his Proauus or great grandfather.

The praise and commendation as also the excuse of Robert Fitzstephans and the earle Strangbow.

CHAP 35.

ROBERT Fitzstephans was the first who taught and shewed the waie to the earle, the earle to the king, and the king to his sonne Great praise-worthie was he that gaue the first aduenture, and much was he to be commended who next followed and increased the same. but aboue all others he deserued best, who fulfilled, absolued,

absolued, and ended the same And here is to be noted, that albeit both Fitzstephans and the earle did helpe Dermon Mac Morogh to recouer his countrie of Leinster, as also defended and kept the same from robbers, théeues, & enimies. yet they did it in diuerse respects The one in respect of his faith and promise, the other for loue of Eua, & of the (1) inheritance, which by hir should grow and come vnto him. But as concerning the intruding vpon Waterford, and the conquests of sundrie territories as well in Desmond as in Meth, I can not excuse them. The earle, who in right of his wife was lord of Leinster, the fift part or portion of Ireland, surrendred and yéelded vp all his right and title there vnto the king himselfe, and tooke it againe to hold of him The like also did all the princes of the land Whereby as also by other old and ancient records it is apparant, that the English nation entred not into this land by wrong and iniurie, (as some men suppose and dreame) but vpon a good ground, right, and title.

(1) The course of this historie in the beginning dooth plainelie declare, how that Dermon after his departure from the king came to the citie of Bristow, and there hauing conference with Richard Strangbow erle of Chepstow, did offer vnto him his onelie daughter and heire in marriage, with the inheritance of all Leinster conditionallie that he would passe ouer into Ireland, and to helpe him to recouer his land, which conditions were accepted and afterwards performed Afterwards he lieng at saint Dauids for passage, there he met with Robert Fitzstephans, & did condition with him, that if he would passe ouer into Ireland to helpe him, he would giue him the towne of Wexford with certeine cantreds therevnto adioining, which conditions were then accepted and afterwards performed Thus it appeareth that the one for loue of the gentlewoman, and the other in respect of his promise did passe ouer into that land and realme.

The causes of lets whie this conquest could not nor had his full perfection.

CHAP 36.

HAPPIE and for euer happie had Ireland béene, which being valiantlie conquered, well replenished with townes, and fortified with castels from sea to sea of the first (1) aduenturers, who were then minded to haue established a good order and gouernment, had not they through the secret malice and treacherie of some men béene called awaie and sent from home Yea happie had it béene, if the first conquerors (being noble and valiant men) might according to their deserts haue had the charge of gouernment committed vnto them. For whie, a nation which at the first comming ouer of our men, when they were galled with our arrows, and afraid of our force, they were then easie to be reclamed. But partlie by meanes of trifling and delaieng of time, which is alwaies dangerous, and partlie by reason that the best seruitors being called home from thense, new rulers tooke too much ease, and liued in too much securitie, nothing was doone to anie purpose and therevpon the people of that countrie tooke hart of grace, and practised our manners in shooting and the vse of our weapons: and by little and little they became so well expert and skilfull therein, that whereas at the first they were easie to be ouercommed, were now strong and hardie, and not onlie able to resist, but also readie to put vs in danger and hazard And the causes herof whoso listeth to search, shall easilie find out the same. for if you will read ouer the bookes of the kings & prophets, examine the course of the old testament, and well consider the examples of these our latter

daies;

daies; you shall find it most certeine and true, that no nation, no state, no citie, nor common-wealth was euer ouerthrowne by the enimie, nor ouercome by the aduersarie but onelie for sinne and wickednesse. And albeit the Irish people and nation for their sinfull and abhominable life did well deserue to be ouerthrowne and ouerrun by strangers; yet was it not Gods will and plesure that they should vtterlie be brought into subiection: neither was it his good will & pleasure that the Englishmen, though they had brought some of them into subiection, yet they should not therefore haue the whole empire and entire soueraigntie ouer them: for both were sinfull people and merited not anie fauour at Gods hand, but deserued to be seuerelie punished, and therfore neither the one (albeit he were a conqueror, and had the ouer hand) could yet obteine a seat (2) in Pallas castell, nor yet the other be fullie subdued & broght into perfect subiection. The Irish people are said to haue the foure men whome they account to be great prophets, and whome they haue in great veneration and credit (3) Merlin, Bracton, Patrike, and Columkill, whose books and prophesies they haue among themselues in their owne language, and all they intreating and speaking of the conquest of this land, doo affirme that the same shall be assailed with often warres, the strifes shall be continuall, and the slaughters great. But yet they doo not assure nor warrant anie perfect or full conquest vnto the English nation (4) not much before dooms daie. And albeit the whole land of Ireland, from sea to sea, haue for the most part béene in the power of the Englishmen, and by them fortified and replenished with sundrie and manie castels, though sometimes to their perilles and smarts: yet Bracton saith, that the king who shall make the absolute and finall conquest, shall come from out of the deserts and mounteins of saint Patrike, and vpon a sundaie at night shall with force breake into a castell builded in the fastnesse of Ophalie: and vntill that time the English nation shall from time to time be in continuall troubles with the Irishrie, sauing that they shall hold and inioie the whole land bordering vpon the east coasts of the seas.

Sin the cause of ouerthrows by the enimie.

The foure Irish prophets.

(1) The course of this historie dooth at full declare in particulars, how the first aduenturers were maligned, & as much as might be discredited. First Robert Fitzstephans, whose seruice was counted notable, and his fidelitie to his prince and king trustie and assured: yet fell he into the kings displeasure, was cast into prison, and albeit deliuered out againe, yet the king conceiuing some gelousie of him, had him ouer into Normandie, where he serued two yeares in his warres: and although he were againe afterward sent ouer into Ireland, yet was he not in anie authoritie or office. The earle Strangbow although he came ouer with the king his speciall licence, yet his good successe was so enuied at, that the king made proclamation, that all his subiects being in Ireland with the earle, should returne & come home; and that no vittels, no munition, nor anie reléefe should be transported out of anie of his dominions into Ireland. And albeit the earle afterwards were reconciled to the king, yet was he faine to yéeld vnto him all his land and dominion of Leinster vnto the kings deuotion, & to receiue the same againe to be holden of the king. Reimond who could not be charged, nor spotted with anie vntruth: yet the treacherous Heruie with his false informations so inucigled and falselie informed the king against him, that he was sent for home, and not trusted with anie gouernement. Hugh de Lacie, who (as the historie saith) was the first that made waie into Vlster, who fortified the prouince of Leinster and Meth with manie strongs holds & castels, and brought all the countrie to a peaceable state; he was suspected to haue meant the impropriation of the whole land to his owne vse, and was dismissed of his charge and gouernement, and sent for home: and in place and lieu of these were sent ouer William Fitzaldelme, Philip of Chester, and others, in whome was no value

at

at all, but onelie to pill and poll the people, and to heape vp treasure and riches

(2) Pallas was the daughter of Iupiter, who for hir excellent gift in inuention, is said and fained by the poets to be borne of the braine of Iupiter without anie moother, she inuented the order of warres, and deuised the manner of fightings, she maketh men to be bold, and giueth the victorie. And bicause Englishmen could not obteine a full and a perfect victorie: therefore they were said not to sit in Pallas castell.

(3) There were two Merlins and both were prophesiers the one was named *Merlinus Calidonius*, or *Syluestris*, bicause his dwelling and habitation was néere or by a wood called *Calidonia*, he was borne in the marches of Scotland, but a man verie excellentlie well learned in philosophie, and in knowledge of all natural causes; and by diligent obseruations he would gesse maruellouslie at the euents of manie things Whervpon he was taken for a prophesier, and reputed for a magician or a diuinor He was in the time of king Arthur, about the yeare fiue hundred and thréescore, and of this Merlin it is spoken in this historie The other Merlin was before this man and in the time of Vortiger, about the yeare of our Lord foure hundred and thréescore, and he was named *Ambrosius Merlinus*, who was also excellentlie well learned, both in philosophie and the art magike, but his sentences were so darkelie couched, that nothing could be conceiued nor vnderstood by them before the euent

(4) Much adoo there hath béene, and manie books written, concerning the full conquest of this land so manie heads, so manie reasons But if men would haue the truth plainelie told, it is soone to be séene how the verie cause proceedeth and is continued for want of a generall reformation. But Pluto hath so blinded mens eies, that séeing they can not nor will not see: but hereof I shall more at large write in an other place.

A breefe repetition of certeine things done within the course of the historie that are omitted

CHAP 37.

HERE by the waie it were not amisse breflie to touch & declare of certeine things which happened, & which (for certeine causes) are not at full discoursed in this storie, as we wished that we might haue had the oportunitie so to haue doone. First therefore you shall vnderstand that Iohn the kings sonne at his first comming ouer builded three castels, one at Tibrach an other at Archephinan, and the third at Lisemore Likewise thrée worthie gentlemen were lost and killed, namelie, Robert Barrie at Lisemore, Reimond Fitzhugh at Olthan, and Reimond Kantune at Ossorie. Also how Donald the prince of Limerike secretlie stole vpon the earles armie in Ossorie, as they were comming from Dublin towards Limerike, and slue foure hundred Ostomans, and foure noble gentlemen, which were their capteines, among whom was Ogranie an Irishman. And also Dermond Mac Artie prince of Desmond, being at parlee with certeine men of Corke not farre from the said towne, was there set vpon by the said Corkemen & (1) Theobald Fitzwalter, and there was he and the most part of his companie slaine The like happened in Meth, where they of Kencole & their capteine made a rode, and being set vpon by one William the iustice of that countrie, they were all slaine and a hundred of their heads sent vnto Dublin. Moreouer Iohn de Courcie found the bodies of saint Patrike, saint Brigid, and saint Colome at Downe, and remooued them from thense. Hugh de Lacie builded his castell

castell at Derach, was there traitorouslie slaine Iohn de Courcie at his returne from out of Connagh lost sixtéene of his best gentlemen. Roger le Powre a valiant, and a lustie yoong gentleman, was by treason taken and murthered in Ossorie, wherevpon the Irishmen foorthwith brake out from their due obeisance to the king of England, and rebelled against the Englishmen, destroied manie castels, and set the whole realme in a great sturre and vnquietnesse Other sundrie things happened which were too long to recite and therefore leauing the same, we will returne to our historie

(1) This Theobald Fitzwalter, who by his nation was named Becket but by his office Butler, was the sonne of Walter the sonne of Gilbert & was the first Butler that came into Ireland, who being a wise and an expert man, was first sent with William Fitzaldelme Afterwards he was sent ouer by king Iohn to view and serch the countrie, and in the end he grew into such credit, that he was infeoffed with great liuings there, as also aduanced (and his posteritie after him) to great honors & promotions, which now are named earles of Ormond and Ossorie

The causes why England could not make the full and finall conquest of Ireland.

CHAP. 38.

IT were not amisse, that we now did consider the causes, and declare the impediments, why the kings sonne had not the best successe in this his so honourable a iournie, and wherefore his so famous attempt tooke not effect that albeit the same can not reuoke and remedie that which is past and doone, yet that it maie be a forewarning to that which maie follow and insue The principall and chiefe cause I suppose and thinke to be, bicause that whereas the patriarch of Ierusalem named Heraclius came in an ambassage vnto him, in the name and behalfe of all the whole land of Palestine called the holie land, requesting that he would take vpon him to be their helpe, and defending the same against the Saladine then king of Egypt and of Damasco who hauing bent his whole force against them, was like within two yeares following vtterlie to be ouerrun, the said holie land, vnlesse some rescue in the meane time and with expedition were prouided: he vtterlie denied and refused the same And being further vrged to send one of his sonnes, although it were the yoongest he denied that also making no account neither of the cause it selfe, which was Christ, nor of the people, which were christians neither yet of the person, which was a reuerend and honourable personage.

And yet neuerthelesse he sent foorth his yoonger sonne in a iournie or hosting, more sumptuous than are néedfull or profitable? And whither I praie you? Was it into the east and against the Saracens and miscreants? No, no, it was into the west, & against his euen christian, nothing séeking the aduancing of Gods glorie, nor promoting of his cause, but onelie for his owne priuat lucre and singular commoditie An other cause was this At the first landing and entrie of the kings sonne at Waterford, a great manie of the chiefest of the Irishmen in those parties, and who since their first submission to king Henrie had continued faithfull and true, they being aduertised of this his arriuall, did come and resort vnto him in peaceable maner, and after their best order to salute him, and congratulate his comming But our new men & Normans, who had not before béene in those parties, making small account of them, did not onelie mocke them, and laugh them to scorne for the manner of their apparell, as also for their long beards and great glibs,

glibs, which they did then weare and vse according to the vsage of their countrie but also they did hardlie deale and ill intreat manie of them. These men nothing liking such interteinment shifted themselues out of the towne, & with all hast sped themselues home: euerie one into his owne house; & from thense they with their wiues, children, and houshold, departed and went some to the prince of Limerike, some to the prince of Corke, some to Rothorike prince of Connagh, and some to one lord, and some to an other. and to these they declared orderlie how they had béene at Waterford, and what they had séene there, and how they were intreated, and how that a yoong man was come thither garded with yoong men, and guided by the counsels of yoong men: in whom there was no staie, no sobrietie, no stedfastnesse, no assurednesse, whereby they and their countrie might be assured of anie safetie.

These princes and namelie they thrée of Connagh, Corke, and Limerike, who were the chéefest, and who were then preparing themselues in a readinesse to haue come and saluted the kings sonne, and to haue yéelded vnto him the dutifull obeisance of faithfull subiects when they heard these newes, they began streightwaies to imagine, that of such euill beginnings woorse endings would insue. and reasoning the matter among themselues, did conclude, that if they thus at the first did deale so discourteouslie with the humble, quiet, and peaceable men what would they doo to such as were mightie and stout, and who would be loth to receiue such discourtesies at their hands? Wherefore with one consent they concluded to stand and ioine togither against the English nation, and to their vttermost to aduenture their liues, and to stand to the defense of their countrie and libertie And for the performance thereof, they enter into a new league among themselues, and swore each one to the other, and by that means enimies before are now made fréends and reconciled. This we know to be true, and therefore we speake it, and that which we saw we doo boldlie witnesse. And for so much as we thus fondlie and in our pride did abuse them, who in humblenesse came vnto vs therefore did we well deserue by Gods iust iudgement (who hateth the proud and high minded) to lose the others, for by this example they were vtterlie discouraged to like of vs And this people and nation though it be barbarous and rude, not knowing what perteineth vnto honour yet most and aboue all others doo they desire to be exalted and honoured And although they be not ashamed to be found false of their word, and vntrust in their dealings yet will they greatlie discommend lieng and commend truth, louing that in others, which is not to be found in themselues But to the matter. What great euils and inconueniences doo grow by such follies and insolencies, a wise man may soone learne by the example of Rehoboam the sonne of Salomon, & so by an other mans harme learne to beware of his owne (2) For he being lead and carried by yoong mens councels, gaue a yoong mans answer vnto his people, saieng vnto them, "My finger is greater than was my fathers loins, and whereas he beat you with rods, I will scourge you with scorpions," by reason whereof ten tribes forsooke him for euer, and followed after Ieroboam Another cause is this, when Robert Fitzstephans came first ouer, and also the earle, there were certeine Irishmen which tooke part with them, and faithfullie serued vnder them and these were rewarded and had giuen vnto them for recompense certeine lands, which they quietlie held and inioied, vntill this time of the comming ouer of the king his sonne: for now the same were taken from them, and giuen to such as were new come ouer, contrarie to the promise & grant to them before made Wherevpon they forsooke vs and fled to our enimies, and became not onelie spies vpon vs, but were also guiders and conductors of them against vs: they being so much the more able to hurt and annoie vs, bicause they were before our familiars, and knew all our orders and secrets. Besides this, the cities and townes vpon and néere the seacoasts, with all such lands, reuenues, tributes, and commodities as to the same did belong and apperteine, and which before was imploied and spent for the defense of the commonwealth & countrie, and in the seruice against the enimies, were now all assigned and bestowed vpon such as were giuen to pilling and polling, and who laie still within the townes, spending their whole time, and all that they had in drunkennesse and surfetting, to the losse and damage of the good citizens and inhabitants, and not to the annoiance of the enimies. And besides sundrie other commodities, this was one, and a speciall one, that at the verie first entrie of the king his sonne into this vnrulie and rebellious land, the people being barbarous, and not knowing what it was to be a subiect, nor what apperteineth to gouernment, such men were appointed to haue the charge, rule and gouernement, as who were more méet to talke in a parlor than to fight in the fields, better skill to be clad in a warme gowne than to be shrowded in armor, and who knew better how to pill and poll the good subiects than to resist and incounter the enimie. yea for their valiantnesse and prowesse they might well be resembled vnto William Fitzaldelme, vnder whose gouernement both Ireland and Wales were almost vtterlie destroied & lost. For whie, they were neither faithfull to their owne people nor dreadfull to their enimies, yea they were vtterlie void of that affect, which is naturallie ingraffed in man, which is to be pittifull to the humble and prostrate, and to resist the proud and obstinat, but rather of the contrarie, they spoiled their owne citizens, and winked at their enimies: for to resist and withstand them nothing was doone, no castels nor fortresses builded, no passes for safetie made, no waies for seruice opened, but althings went to ruine, and the common state to wracke. Moreouer, the seruing men and the soldiers which were in garrison, they liking well of their capteins and masters maners and loose life, gaue themselues to the like, spending their whole time in rioting, banketing, whoredome, and all other dissolute and wanton orders, tarrieng still within the townes and places far off from the enimies. For as for the marches (so called bicause the same bordered vpon their enimies, or rather of Mars, bicause in those places martiall affaires were and are woont to be most exercised) they would not come néere the sight thereof, and by that means the people there dwelling and seated, the soiles there manured, the castels there builded, were altogether destroied, wasted, spoiled, and burned. And thus the prowesse of the old capteins, the good seruices of the veterans & well-experimented soldiers by the insolent, distemperat, and lewd life of these new comes was discredited. whereof was nothing else to be awaited for but after such calmes must néeds insue stormes and tempests. And albeit they thus lieng in the townes in securitie and at rest, wallowing in lose and wanton life, euerie daie being a holie daie to Bacchus and Venus: yet the state of the land at large was most miserable and lamentable. For euerie where was howling and wéeping, the manured fields became waste, the castels destroied, and the people murthered, and no newes but that the vtter destruction of the whole land was at hand. And in this distresse and necessitie it had béene verie requisit and néedfull that the souldiers should haue taken vp their weapons, serued against the enimie, and haue defended the common state: but it was farre otherwise, for there was such lawing & vexation in the towns, one dailie suing and troubling another, that the veterane was more troubled with lawing within the towne, than he was in perill at large with the enimie. And thus our men, giuen ouer to this trade and kind of life, became fainthartet, and afraid to looke vpon the enimie: and on the contrarie the enimie most strong, stout, and bold. Thus was the land then gouerned, and thus the same posted towards the destruction of the English nation and gouernment, which had doubtlesse verie shortlie followed and insued, had not the king prouided a speedie remedie for the same. For the king being aduertised how disorderlie things framed,

The inconueniences following euill gouernement.

Lawing woorse than warring

framed, and considering with himselfe in what perill the state of his realme and people stood, he with all spéed sendeth for all these new come souldiors, in whome (other than the name of a souldior was nothing of anie value and commendation) and commandeth them to repaire and come home, and sendeth ouer in their places these old beaten and well tried soldiors, by whose seruice the land before had beene conquered and kept, among whome one and the cheefest was Iohn de Courcie, who was made lord deputie, and had the gouernement of the land committed vnto him who, according to his office and dutie, setteth in hand the reformation of all things méet and requisit to be redressed who the more valiant and forward he was in his said affaires and seruices, the more the land grew to good order, and inioied peace & quietnesse For whie, he would not be idle himselfe, neither would he suffer his souldiers to lie idle like loiterers and sluggards. but was alwaies labouring and trauelling abroad, and marching still towards the enimies, whome he followed and pursued euen through the whole land, to the vttermost parts thereof, as well in Corke, Thomond, Connagh, and elsewhere, and if by any means he could haue anie aduantage of them, he would surelie giue the onset and aduenture vpon them which for the most part was to their ouerthrowe, though he and his sometimes were galled, and felt the smart. And would to God he had beene as prudent a capteine as he was a valiant souldior, and as proudent in the one as skilfull and hardie in the other! But to my former purpose. Among the manie and sundrie inconueniences happened by euill gouernment of these new officers (as is before said) there was none greater, nor more to be lamented than was this. that notwithstanding God of his goodnesse did giue the victorie, and send the happie successe in this noble conquest. yet was there neither due thanks attributed vnto God, nor anie remembrance giuen vnto his church, but to increase a further ingratitude, they tooke and spoiled awaie from the same their lands and possessions, as also minded to abridge them of their old and ancient priuileges & liberties Too great a note of ingratitude, and an argument of too much vnthankfulnes whereof what vnquietnesse and troubles did insue, the sequele therof (for the course of sundrie years) did shew and declare

Aha Giraldus! could you see that cursed fault and abuse?

So manie outrages & disorders, which did créepe in by the disordred gouernement vnder the king his sonne, were not so much to be imputed to his yoong and tender yeares, as vnto the euill counsels and directions of such as were about him, and had the speciall charge thereof, for such a sauage, rude, and barbarous nation was by good counsels, discréet directions and prudent gouernement to haue béene gouerned and reduced to good order and conformitie For whie, if a realme which by wise and prudent gouernement is brought and reduced to a perfect state, yet being committed to the gouernement of a child is cursed and brought to manifold distresses, troubles and miseries (5) how much more then is it to be so thought of that land, which of it selfe being rude and barbarous, is committed to the gouernement of such as be not onelie rude and barbarous, but also lewd and euill disposed. And that this did so happen and come to passe in Ireland, all wisemen doo know it, and the elder sort doo confesse it to be true; although yoong men to couer their folies, would reiect it to some other causes & impediments. For whie, such of them as had procured vnto themselues great liuings, lordships and territories, they pretended at the first that they would be readie to serue the king his sonne, to defend the countrie, to resist the enimie, and that they would doo this and that with manie good morowes. But when they had gotten what they would, and had that they sought for, then it manifestlie appeared that it was singular gaine & priuat profit which they shot at. for hauing obteined that, they neuer remembred their oth to their lord, nor cared for the common state, nor passed for the safetie and defense of the countrie, which in dutie they ought chiefelie to haue considered.

(1) The Irish nation and people euen from the beginning haue béene alwaies of a hard bringing vp, & are not onelie rude in apparell but also rough & ouglie in their bodies: their beards and heads they neuer wash, clense, nor cut, especiallie their heads; the haire whereof they suffer to grow, sauing that some doo vse to round it: and by reason the same is neuer kembed, it groweth fast togither, and in processe of time it matteth so thicke and fast togither, that it is in stéed of a hat, and kéepeth the head verie warme, & also will beare off a great blow or stroke, and this head of haire they call a glibe, and therein they haue a great pleasure.

(2) The historie is written in the first booke of the kings the twelfe chapter, and in the second of the chronicles the tenth chapter: the effect therof is, that after the death of Salomon the people of Israell requested Rehoboam his sonne, to ease them of the grieuous burdens and heauie yoke which his father laied vpon them, who leauing the counsell of the old counsellors, gaue them answer by the aduise of yoong heads, as in this place is recited.

(3) What these Irishmen were, there are diuerse opinions. Some thinke that they were such as did inhabit about Wexford, some thinke that they were they of Kencelo, for they faithfullie serued the Englishmen vnder their capteine named Morogh at Limerike, when the earle of Reimond recouered the same. But I find it to be noted of the Orians, who are now dwelling within the baronie of Odron, and had a seat there by the gift of the Kauenaughs, but since resisting against them and denieng to paie their accustomable cheuerie, yéelded themselues vnto the earle of Ormond, paieng vnto him a certeine blacke rent to be their defendor against the said Keuenaughs, but in right they are tenants to the barons of Odron.

(4) This is meant of that which is before spoken in the twentie chapter in the description of this Iohn de Curcie, where his too much rashnes is noted to be a great fault in him.

(5) It is written by the preacher, or Ecclesiastes; "Wo be vnto thee O thou land whose king is but a child." Which is not ment absolutelie of a child, but of such a one who (as a child) hath an euill affection, and is void of that grauitie, wisedome, and maiestie as is required in a prince and gouernour. For Iosias when he was crowned king of Iehuda, was but eight yeares of age; and yet bicause he did that which was right in the sight of God, and ruled the land godlie and vprightlie, he is commended in the scriptures for the same.

Three sorts of people which came and serued in Ireland.

CHAP. 39.

THERE were three sundrie sorts of seruitors which serued in the realme of Ireland, (1) Normans, Englishmen, and the Cambrians, which were the first conquerors of the land: the first were in most credit and estimation, the second were next, but the last were not accounted nor regarded of. The Normans were verie fine in their apparell, and delicate in their diets, they could not féed but vpon deintics, neither could their meat digest without wine at each meale; yet would they not serue in the marches, or anie remote place against the enimie, neither would they lie in garrison to kéepe anie remote castell or fort, but would be still about

The Normans fine in their apparell and delicat in their diet.

about their lords side to serue and gard his person; they would be where they might be full and haue plentie, they could talke and brag, sweare and stare, and standing in their owne reputation, disdaine all others. They receiued great interteinement and were liberallie rewarded, and left no meanes vnsought how they might rule the rost, beare the sway, and be aduanced vnto high estate and honour. In these things they were the first and formost, but to serue in hosting, to incounter with the enimie, to defend the publike state, & to follow anie martiall affaires, they were the last and furthest off. And for asmuch as those noble and worthie seruitors, by whose seruice, trauels and industrie, the said land was first entred into and conquered, were thus had in contempt, disdaine, and suspicion, and onelie the new comes called to counsell, and they onelie credited and honored, it came to passe that in all their doings they had small successe, & by whole and little their credit decaied, and nothing came to effect or perfection which they tooke in hand.

(1) This king, besides England and Scotland, had in his rule and gouernement the duchie of Normandie, and the earledomes of Gascoine, Guien, Aniou, & Poitiers, beside the losse of that which came to him by the right of his wife. And albeit he trusted the Englishmen well inough, yet being borne on the other side of the seas, he was more affectionated to the people of those prouinces there subiect vnto him: for of them he chose both them which were of his councell in peaceable gouernment, as also his seruitors in martiall affaires. And albeit he had of euerie of these prouinces some, yet bicause Normandie was the cheefest, and he duke thereof, they went all vnder the name of Normans, and so called Normans.

How or by what manner the land of Ireland is throughlie to be conquered.

CHAP. 40.

IT is an old saieng, that euerie man in his owne art is best of credit & most to be beléeued: & so in this matter they are speciallie to be credited, who haue béene the chiefest trauellers and seruitors in and about the first recouerie of this land, doo know and can best discouer the natures, manners, and conditions of these people and nation: for as the matter speciallie toucheth them, so none can doo it better than they. For which, by reason of their continuall warres with them, being their most mortall enimies, none can better saie than they how they are either to be conquered or vanquished. And here by the waie happie had Wales bin, I meane that Wales which the English people doo inhabit, if the king therof in gouerning the same or when he incountred with his enimies had vsed this deuise & policie. But to the matter. These Normans although they were verie good souldiers and well appointed, yet the manner of the warres in France far differeth from that which is vsed in Ireland and Wales, for the soile & countrie in France is plaine, open, & champaine; but in these parts it is rough, rockie, full of hils woods, & bogs. In France they weare complet harnesse, and are armed at all points, not onelie for their honor, but especiallie for their defense and safeties, but to these men the same are combersome & a great hinderance. In France they kéepe standing fields & trie the battels, but these men are light horssemen & range alwaies at large. In France they kéepe their prisoners and put them to ransomes, but these chop off their heads and put them to the sword. And therefore when the battell is to be waged in the plaine, open, & champaine countrie, it behoueth all

Great ods betweene the warres in France and Ireland or Wales.

all men to be armed, some in complet harnesse, some in iackes, some in Almaine riuets, & some in brigandines & shirts of maile, according to their places of seruice. So on the contrarie, where the fight & triall is in narow streicts, rockie places, & where it is full of woods & bogs, & in which footmen are to serue and not horssemen, there light armor and slender harnesse will best serue. To fight therefore in such places and against such men, as be but naked and vnarmed men, and whome at the first push and aduenture, either the victorie must be had or lost, light and easie armor is best and conuenient. And againe these people are verie nimble & quicke of bodie, and light of foot, and for their safetie and aduantage they séeke waies through streicts and bogs, and therefore it is not for anie man laden with much armor to follow and pursue them. Moreouer, the Frenchmen and Normans most commonlie are horssemen, and doo serue on horssebacke, & these men haue their sadles so great and déepe, that they cannot at ease leape vp and downe, and being on foot by reason of their armor, they cannot serue nor trauell. And you shall further vnderstand, that in all the seruices and hostings, both in Ireland & in Wales, the Welsh seruitors, and especiallie such as doo dwell in the marches, by reason of their continuall wars, they are verie valiant, bold, and of great experiences, they can endure anie paines and trauels, they are vsed to watchings and wardings, they can abide hunger and thirst, and know how to take aduantage of their enimie, and their seruice by horse is such, that they are readie to take aduantage of the field, being quicke & readie to take and leape to the horsse, as also to leaue the same, & to folow the enimie at their best aduantage, whether it be on horsse or on foot. And such kind of seruitors and souldiers were they, which first gaue the aduenture and first preuailed in Ireland. and by such also in the end must the same be fullie conquered, that when the battell is to be fought & waged in the plaine and champaine countrie, and against such as be throughlie armed and appointed for the same, it is reason that the aduerse part be likewise armed and appointed. But when the matter is to be waged in stéepe places, rough fields, rockie hils, or in marish and boggie grounds, and against such as be quicke of foot, and doo séeke others to tops of hils, or to bogs, and woods, then men of the like exercise, and hauing light armour, are to be allowed. And in the Irish wars this one thing is to be considered, that you doo in euerie wing ioine your bowmen with your footmen and horssemen, that by them they may be defended from the Kerns, whose nature and conditions are to run in and out, and with their darts are woont shrewdlie to annoie their enimies, who by the bowmen are to be kept off. And moreouer, that the hither part of the land lieng on the east side, or part of the Shenin which diuideth the thrée other parts from this, and this being the fourth part must be well fortified with castels and forts: but as for Connagh & Thomond, which lie in the further side of the Shenin, and all those parties (sauing the citie of Limerike which must needs be recouered and kept in the English gouernement) must for a time be borne withall, and by little and little by fortifieng of the frontiers in méet places be gotten and recouered, and so by little and little to grow in vpon them as occasion shall serue.

The Kernes vsage in battell

How

How the Irish people being vanquished are to be gouerned.

CHAP. 41.

AS there be means and policies to be vsed in conquering this people, who are now more light in their bodies than inconstant in mind: so when they are vanquished, they must in an order be ruled and gouerned. First and principallie therefore it is to be considered, that whosoeuer shall be gouernor ouer them, that he be wise, constant, discreet, and a staied man; that in time of peace, and when they are contented to liue vnder law and in obedience, they maie be gouerned by law, directed by right, and ruled by iustice; as also to be stout and valiant, readie and able with force seuerelie to punish all such as (contrarie to their dutie and allegiance) shall either rebell and breake out, or otherwise liue in disordered maner. Moreouer, when anie haue doone amisse, and contrarie to dutie haue rebelled, and doo yet afterwards knowledge their follie, and yeelding themselues haue obteined pardon; that in no wise you doo afterwards euill intreat them, neither yet laie their former faults to their charges, neither cast them in the teeth of their follies: but hauing taken such assurance of them as you maie, to intreat them with all courtesies and gentlenesse, that by such good means they maie the better be induced and incouraged to kéepe themselues within their dutie, for loue of their good gouernement which they sée: and yet be afraid to doo euill for feare of punishment, which they are to receiue for their euill and lewd doongs. And if they will not thus order and gouerne them, but confound their doongs, being slacke to punish the euill, and quicke to oppresse the good and obedient, to flatter them in their rebellions and outrages, and to spoile them in peace, to fauor them in their treasons and treacheries, and to oppresse them when they liue in loialtie, as we haue seene manie so to haue doone: surelie these men so disorderedlie confounding all things, they in the end shall be confounded themselues. And bicause harms foreséene do least annoie & hurt, let them which be wise looke well, that in time of peace they doo prepare for the warres. For after the Alcion daies and calme seas doo follow stormes and tempests: and therefore, when they haue vacant times and leisure, let them build and fortifie castels, cut downe and open the passes, and doo all such other things as the nature of warres requireth to be preuented. For this people being vncerteine, craftie, and subtill, vnder colour of peace, are woont alwaies to be studieng and deuising of mischiefs. And also bicause it is good to be wise by another mans harme, & warie by other mens examples. For nothing dooth better teach a man than examples, and the paterns of things doone afore time. Let not them forget what became of these woorthie men, Miles of Cogan, Rafe Fitzstephans, Hugh de Lacie, Roger Powre, and others, who when they thought of least danger they were in most perill: and when they thought themselues in most safetie, they were intrapped and destroied. For as we haue said in our Topographie, this people is a craftie and a subtile people, and more to be feared when it is peace, than when it is open warres: for their peace indéed is but enmitie, their policies but craft, their friendships but coloured, and therefore the more to be doubted and feared. And by experience the same in some part hath béene prooued: and therfore, as Euodius saith, "Let the fall and ruine of things past be forewarnings of things to come."

No better teachers than examples

And bicause herein a man can not be too wise nor warie, it were good that an order were taken (as it is in Sicilia) that none of them should weare anie weapon at all, no not so much as a staffe in their hands to walke by. For euen with that weapon,

pon,

pon, though it be but slender, they will (if they can) take the aduantage, and bewreake their malice and cankered stomachs. Finallie, forsomuch as the kings of England haue a iust title, and a full right to the land of Ireland in sundrie and diuerse respects; and considering also that the same is chieflie mainteined by the intercourse and traffike of merchandizes out of England; and without the same cannot releeue and helpe it selfe; it were verie expedient that for the acknowledging of the one, and for the inioieng of the other, as also for the supporting of the continuall charges of the king of England there yearelie bestowed: that there be a yearelie tribute paied and answered vnto the kings of England, either in monie, or in such commodities as that land breedeth, aswell for the continuance of the title in memorie, as also for the auoiding of manie inconueniences. And because time weareth awaie, and men doo dailie perish and die, that this order for the perpetuall honour of the king and of his realme, and the memoriall of this conquest, the same be ingrossed and registred in a publike instrument to indure for euer. And thus hauing spoken what we know, and witnessed what we haue séene, we doo here end this historie, leauing vnto others of better knowledge and learning, to continue the same as to them shall be thought most néedfull and conuenient.

Thus farre Giraldus Cambrensis.

THE

PROCESSE OF IRISH AFFAIRES

(BEGINNING WHERE GIRALDUS DID END) VNTILL THIS PRESENT AGE, BEING A WITNESSE OF SUNDRIE THINGS AS YET FRESH IN MEMORIE.

WHICH PROCESSE FROM HENSEFORWARD IS INTITULED

THE CHRONICLES OF IRELAND.

LEAUING at the conquest of Ireland penned by Giraldus Cambrensis, we are now to proceed in that which followeth. wherin our authour (as he himselfe writeth) vsed such notes as were written by one Philip Flatsburie, out of a certeine namelesse author, from this place vnto the yeare 1370. and we hauing none other helpe besides (except onelie Henrie of Marleborow) do set downe that which we find in our oft mentioned authour, and in the same Marleborow in all the whole discourse that followeth, except in some certeine particular places, where we shew from whense we haue drawne that which we write as occasion serueth.

THE

CHRONICLES OF IRELAND, &c.

HUGH de Lacie (of whom such memorable mention is made heretofore) the rather to méet with such hurlie burlies as were like to put the state of the Irish countrie in danger, if the same were not the sooner brought to quiet, erected and built a number of castels and forts in places conuenientlie seated, well and sufficientlie garnished with men, munitions, and vittels, as one at Derwath, where diuerse of the Irish praied to be set on worke for wages. Lacie came sundrie times thither to further the worke, full glad to sée them fall in vre with anie such exercise, wherein might they once begin to haue a delight, and tast the swéetnesse of a true mans life, he thought it no small token of reformation: for which cause he visited them the oftner, and merilie would command his gentlemen to giue the laborers example to take their tooles in hand, and to woorke a season, whilest the poore soules looking on might rest them. But this pastime grew to a tragicall end. For on a time, as each man was busilie occupied, some lading, some heauing, some plastering, some grauing, the generall also himselfe digging with a pickaxe: a desperat villaine among them whose toole the noble man vsed, espieng both his hands occupied, and his bodie inclining downwards, still as he stroke watched when he so stooped, and with an axe cleft his head in sunder, little esteeming the torments that for this traitorous act insued. This Lacie was reputed to be the conqueror of Meth, for that he was the first that brought it to anie due order of obedience vnto the English power. His bodie the two archbishops, Iohn of Dublin, and Matthew of Cashill buried in the monasterie of Beetie, and his head in saint Thomas abbeie at Dublin.

A castell built at Derwath.

1186

Lacie is traitorouslie slaine.

By occasion of this murther committed on the person of Hugh Lacie, Iohn Curcie, and Hugh Lacie the yoonger, with their assistants, did streight execution vpon the rebels, and preuenting euerie mischiefe yer it fell, staied the realme from vprores. Thus they knitting themselues togither in friendship, continued in wealth and honor vntill the first yeare of king Iohns reigne, who succéeding his brother king Richard, tooke his nephue Arthur, son to his brother Geffreie earle of Britaine, and dispatched him (some said) with his owne hands, because he knew what claime he made to the crowne, as descended of the elder brother. And therefore not onelie the French king, but also certeine lords of England and Ireland fauored his title: and when they vnderstood that he was made awaie, they tooke it in maruelous euill part. And Curcie either of zeale to the truth, or parcialitie, abhorring such barbarous crueltie, whereof all mens eares were full, spake bloudie words against king Iohn, which his lurking aduersaries (that laie readie to vndermine him) caught

Curcie and Hugh Lacie the yoonger keepe the realme in quiet.

1199

King Iohn slaieth his nephue Arthur.

Curcie vttereth displeasant words against King Iohn.

by

by the end, and vsed the same as a meane to lift him out of credit: which they did not onelie bring to passe, but also procured a commission to attach his bodie, and to send him ouer into England.

He is accused.

Earle Curcie mistrusting his part, and belike getting some inkeling of their drift, kept himselfe aloofe, till Hugh Lacie lord iustice was faine to leuie an armie and to inuade Vlster, from whense he was oftentimes put backe.

He is proclaimed traitor.

Whervpon he proclaimed Curcie traitor, and hired sundrie gentlemen with promise of great recompense, to bring him in either quicke or dead. They fought once at Downe, in which battell there died no small number on both parts, but Curcie got the vpper hand, and so was the lord iustice foiled at Curcies hands: but yet so long he continued in practising to haue him, that at length Curcies owne capteins were inucitied to betraie their owne maister: insomuch that vpon Good fridaie, whilest the earle out of his armour visited barefooted certeine religious houses for deuotion sake, they laid for him, tooke him as a rebell, & shipped him ouer into England the next waie, where he was adiudged to perpetuall prison.

He is taken.

One Seintleger addeth in his collections (as Campion saith) that Lacie paied the traitors their monie, and foorthwith therevpon hanged them.

Translation of prebendaries to monks.

This Curcie translated the church and prebendaries of the trinitie in Downe, to an abbeie of blacke moonks brought thither from Chester, and caused the same to be consecrated vnto saint Patrike: for which alteration, taking the name from God to a creature, he déemed himselfe woorthilie punished. Not long after (as saie the Irish) certeine French knights came to king Iohns court, and one among them required the combat for triall of the right to the duchie of Normandie.

A chalenge for a combat made by certeine French knights.

It was not thought expedient to ieopard the title vpon one mans lucke, yet the chalenge they determined to answer. Some friend put them in mind of the earle imprisoned, a warrior of notable courage, and in pitch of bodie like a giant. King Iohn demanded Curcie whether he could be content to fight in his quarell?

Curcies answer to king Iohn.

"Not for thee" said the erle, "whose person I estéeme vnwoorthie th'aduenture of my bloud, but for the crowne & dignitie of the realme, in which manie a good man liueth against thy will, I shall be contented to hazard my life."

He taketh vpon him to defend the chalenge.

These words were not construed in the woorst part, as procéeding from an offended mind of him that was therein estéemed more plaine than wise. Therefore being cherished and much made of, he was fed so woonderfullie (now he came to so large allowance in diet after hard keeping) that the French chalenger tooke him for a monster: and fearing to deale with him, priuilie stole awaie into Spaine. It is further reported, that the French king, being desirous to sée Curcie, requested king Iohn that he might come before them, and shew of what strength he was by striking a blow at an helmet. Herevpon foorth he was brought, and presented before the kings, where was an helmet set vpon a blocke. Curcie taking a sword in his hand, and with a sterne & frowning countenance cast vpon the kings, gaue such a stroke to the helmet, that cleauing it in sunder, the sword sticked so fast in the log, that no man there was able to plucke it foorth except Curcie himselfe. When he therefore had plucked foorth the sword, the kings asked him what he meant to looke vpon them with such a grim & froward countenance before he gaue the blow to the helmet? He answered, that if he had missed in his stroke, he would haue killed all the whole companie, as well the kings as others. Then was he released of bonds, and crossing the seas towards Ireland whither he was bound, was fifteene times beaten backe againe to the English shore, & going into France to change the coast died there.

Curcie departeth this life.

The description of Curcie.

This Curcie was white of colour, mightie of lims, with large bones and strong of sinews, tall & broad in proportion of bodie, so as his strength was thought to excéed, of boldnesse incomparable, and a warrior euen from his youth, the formost in the front of euerie battell where he came, and euer readie to hazard himselfe in place of most danger, so forward in fight, that oftentimes forgetting the office

office of a capteine, he tooke in hand the part of a souldior, pressing foorth with the formost, so that with his ouer rash violence, and desire of victorie, he might séeme to put all in danger. But although he was thus hastie and hot in the field against his enimies, yet was he in conuersation modest and sober, and verie religious, hauing churchmen in great reuerence, ascribing all to the goodnesse of God, when he had atchiued anie praise woorthie enterprise, yéelding thankes to his diuine maiestie accordinglie. But as seldome times anie one man is found perfect in all things, so these vertues were spotted with some vices, namelie, too much nigardnesse in sparing, and inconstancie. He maried the daughter of Godred king of Man, and after manie conflicts and battels had against the Irish, he conquered (as before ye haue heard) the countrie of Vlster, and building diuerse strong castels therin, he established the same vnder his quiet rule and gouernment, till he and Lacie fell out, as before is expressed.

After Curcies decease, because he left no heires, the earledome of Vlster was giuen vnto Hugh Lacie in recompense of his good seruice. There was one of the Curcies remaining in Ireland that was lord of Rathermie and Kilbarrocke, whome (as an espiall of all their practises and informer thereof to the king) Walter and Hugh the sons of Hugh Lacie slue, by reason whereof great trouble and disquietnesse insued, those Lacies bearing themselues (now after the decease of their father) for gouernors out of checke. To set the realme in quiet, king Iohn was faine to passe thither himselfe in person with a maine armie, banished the Lacies, subdued the residue of the countrie yet not conquered, tooke pledges, punished malefactors, established the execution of English lawes, coined monie of like value currant sterling in both realmes. The two Lacies repenting their misdemeanors, fled into France disguised in poore apparell, and serued there in an abbeie as gardeners, till the abbat by their countenance and behauior began to gesse their estates, and opposed them so farre that they disclosed what they were, beséeching the abbat to keepe their counsels, who commending their repentant humblenes, aduised them yet to make sute for their princes fauor, if it might be had, promising to doo what he could in the matter, and so tooke vpon him to be a suter for them vnto the king that was his godcept and well acquainted with him. He trauelled so earnesthe herein, that at length he obteined their pardons, but yet they were fined, Walter at foure thousand, and Hugh at fiue and twentie hundred markes: and herevpon Walter was restored vnto the lordship of Meth, and Hugh to the earledome of Vlster.

King Iohn went into Ireland.

See more hereof in England

They fled into France

They are pardoned, and put to their fines

King Iohn appointed his lieutenants in Ireland, and returning home, subdued the Welshmen, and soone after with Pandulfus the legat of pope Innocentius the third, who came to release him of the censure, wherin he stood excommunicat, to whom as to the popes legat he made a personall surrender of both realmes in waie of submission, and after he was once absolued, he receiued them againe. Some adde, that he gaue awaie his kingdoms to the see of Rome for him and his successors, recognising to hold the same of the popes in fée, paieng yearelie therefore one thousand markes, as seauen hundred for England, and three hundred for Ireland. Blondus saith, "Centum pro vtroque auri marchias." Sir Thomas More (as Campion saith) a man both in calling & office likelie to sound the matter to the depth, writeth preciselie, that neither such writing the pope can shew, neither were it effectuall if he could. How farre foorth, and with what limitation a prince may or may not addict his realme feodarie to another, Iohn Maior a Scotish chronicler, and a Sorbonist not vnlearned, partlie scanneth, who thinketh three hundred markes for Ireland no verie hard penworth. The instrument (as Campion thinketh) which our English writers rehearse, might happilie be motioned and drawen, and yet not confirmed with anie seale, nor ratified: but though the copie of this writing remaine in record, yet certeine it is, king Iohns successors neuer paid it. After Iohn Comin

An hundred marks of gold *Blondus*

Iohn Bale in his apologie against vowes

Comin archbishop of Dublin, and founder of saint Patriks church succéeded Henrie Londores in the sée, who builded the kings castell there, being lord chéefe iustice of Ireland, him they nicknamed (as the Irish doo commonlie giue additions in
respect of some fact or qualitie) Scorchuillein, that is, Burnebill, because he required to peruse the writings of his tenants, colourablie pretending to learne the
kind of ech mans seuerall tenure, and burned the same before their faces, causing
them either to renew their takings, or to hold at will.

In the yeare one thousand two hundred and sixtéene king Iohn departed this
life. In his daies diuerse monasteries were builded in Ireland, as (besides those
that before are mentioned) in the fourth yeare of his reigne the abbeie of
Douish was founded, in the sixt the abbeie of Wetherham in the countie of Limerike, by Theobald le Butler lord of Carrackie, and in the twelfe yeare Richard
Henrie the third Oute builded the monasterie of Grenard. In the daies of Henrie the third that
Warres betwixt Lacie and Marshall succéeded his father king Iohn great warres were raised in Ireland betwixt Hugh
Lacie & William Marshall, so that the countrie of Meth was gréeuouslie afflicted.
1228 In the yeare of our Lord 1228, after the death of Londores archbishop of Dublin,
that was lord chéefe iustice, king Henrie the third vnderstanding the good seruice
The Giraldines doone by the Giraldines euer since their first comming into Ireland, although by
wrong reports the same had beene to their preiudice for a time sinisterlie misconstrued, so as the gentlemen had still béene kept backe, and not rewarded according
Morice Fitzgerald to their deserts. The king now informed of the truth made Morice Fitzgerald the
sonne of Morice aforesaid lord chéefe iustice of Ireland. Lucas succeeded Lon-
Lucas archbishop dres in the archbishops sée, and was consecrated. In the yeare one thousand two
1230 hundred and thirtie, Richard Marshall was taken prisoner in battell at Kildare.
1234 Some write that he was wounded there, and within few daies after died of the
hurt at Kilkennie, and was buried there in the queere of the church of the friers
preachers, néere to the place where his brother William was interred, who departed
this life in the yeare one thousand two hundred thirtie and one.

1241 In the yeare one thousand two hundred fortie and one, Walter Lacie lord of Meth
departed this life in England. he left two daughters behind him that were his heires,
The lord Verdon Margaret married to the lord Verdon, and Matild the wife of Geffrie Genuill.
Geffreie Genuill. 1252 King Henrie in the six & thirtith yeare of his reigne, gaue to Edward his eldest
1253 sonne, Gascoigne, Ireland, and the countie of Chester. In the yeare following,
Hugh Lacie earle of Vlster departed this life, and was buried at Cragfergus, in the
church of the friers minors, leauing a daughter behind him, that was his heire,
whome Walter de Burgh or Bourke married, and in right of hir was created earle
of Vlster, as after shall appeare. Morice Fitzgerald lord iustice of Ireland, being
requested by this prince to come and assist him with a power of men against the
The castell of Sligath Welsh rebels, left a sufficient garrison of men in the castell of Sligath, which he
had latelie builded, and then came ouer with Phelin Ochonher, and a lustie band of
souldiers & meeting the prince at Chepstow, behaued themselues so valiantlie,
that returning with victorie, they greatlie increased the fauor of the king and
prince towards them, and vpon their returne into Ireland, they ioined with Cor-
macke Mac Dermot Mac Rorie, and made a notable iournie against Odonill the
Irish enimie, that when Lacie was once dead, murdered & sore annoied the kings
Odonill subiects of Vlster. Odonill being vanquished, the lord iustice forced pledges and
tribute of Oneale to keepe the kings peace and diuerse other exploits praise-worthie did he during the time of his gouernment, as Flatsburie hath gathered in his
notes for the lord Girald Fitzgerald earle of Kildare, in the yeare one thousand fiue
hundred and seuentéene. After Morice Fitzgerald succeeded in office of lord iu-
Iohn Fitzgeffrie lord iustice stice, Iohn Fitzgeffrie knight, and after him Alarne de la Zouch, whome the earle of
Alarne de la Zouch lord iustice Surrie Fitzwarren slue. And after de la Zouch, in the yeare one thousand two hundred

dred fiftie and eight, being the two and fortith of Henrie the third his reigne, was
Stephan de long Espée sent to supplie that roome, who slue Oneale with thrée hun- Stephan de long Espe
dred fiftie & two of his men in the stréets of Downe, and shortlie after departed William Dene
this life, then William Dene was made lord iustice, and Gréene castell was de- lord iustice Greene castell
stroied. Also Mac Carene plaid the diuell in Desmond. destroied Mac Carene
In the yeare one thousand two hundred sixtie and one, sir William Dene lord 1261
iustice of Ireland deceased, and sir Richard Rochell (or Capell as some copies haue) Sir Richard Capell lord iustice.
was sent to be lord iustice after him, who greatlie enuied the familie of the Giral-
dins, during his gouernement the lord Iohn Fitzthomas and the lord Morice his Lord Iohn Fitzthomas slaine
son were slaine. In the yeare one thousand two hundred sixtie and foure, Walter
de Burgh was made earle of Vlster, and Morice Fitzmorice tooke the lord iustice The lord iustice taken.
of Ireland togither with Theobald Butler, Miles Cogan, and diuerse other great
lords at Tristildermot, on saint Nicholas daie. And so was Ireland full of warres,
betwixt the Burghs and Giraldins. In the yeare one thousand two hundred sixtie 1266
and six, there chanced an earthquake in Ireland. In the yeere following, king 1267
Henrie tooke vp the variance that was in Ireland betwixt the parties, and discharging
Dene, appointed Dauid Barrie lord iustice in his place, who tamed the insolent Dauid Barrie lord iustice
dealings of Morice Fitzmorice, cousine germane to Fitzgerald.

In the yeare one thousand two hundred sixtie and eight, Conhur Obren was 1268
slaine by Dermot Mac Moncrd, and Morice Fitzgerald earle of Desmond was
drowned in the sea, betwixt Wales & Ireland. And Robert Vffort was sent ouer Robert Vffort
to remaine lord iustice of Ireland, and Barrie was discharged, who continued till
the yeare one thousand two hundred sixtie and nine, and then was Richard de Ex- Richard de Excester
cester made lord iustice. And in the yeare following, was the lord Iames Audleie 1270
made lord iustice. Richard Verdon, and Iohn Verdon were slaine, and Fulke arch- 1271
bishop of Dublin deceased. Also the castels of Aldlecke, Roscoman, & Schelirgagh,
were destroied. The same yeare was a great dearth and mortalitie in Ireland. In
the yeare one thousand two hundred seuentie & two, the lord Iames Audleie was The lord Audleie
slaine by a fall from his horsse in Thomond, and then was Morice Fitzmorice made
lord iustice of Ireland, and the castell of Randon was destroied. In the yeare one Randon
thousand two hundred seauentie and two, king Henrie the third departed this life, The decease of king Henrie the third
and the lord Walter Genuill latelie returned home from his iournie into the holie 1272
land, was sent into Ireland, and made lord iustice there. In the yeare one thousand Walter Genuill.
two hundred seuentie and fiue, the castell of Roscoman was eftsoones repared and 1275
fortified.

In the yeare one thousand two hundred seuentie and six, there was an ouerthrow 1276
giuen at Glenburie, where William Fitzroger, prior of the knights hospitalers, & An ouerthrow at Glenburie
manie other with him, were taken prisoners, and a great number of other were
slaine. The same yeare, Iohn de Verdon departed this world, and Thomas de Clare
married the daughter of Morice Fitzmorice. In the yeare following, Robert Vffort
was appointed to supplie the roome of Genuill, being called home, and so was
this Vffort the second time ordeined lord iustice of Ireland. He hauing occasion
to passe into England, made his substitute Fulborne bishop of Waterford till his
returne, and then resumed the gouernement into his owne hands againe. In the
yeare one thousand two hundred seauentie and seauen, Thomas de Clare slue Obren- 1277
roth king of Tholethmond, and yet after this the Irish closed him vp in Slewbany,
togither with Maurice Fitzmaurice, so that they gaue hostages to escape, and the
castell of Roscoman was woone. In the yere next insuing, was Iohn de Der- 1278
lington consecrated archbishop of Dublin. There was also a councell holden at
Grenoke, and Mac Dermot slue Cathgur Oconthur king of Connagh. In the
yeare one thousand two hundred seuentie and nine, Robert Vffort vpon occasion of
busines

busines came ouer into England, and left frier Fulborne bishop of Waterford to supplie his roome, and Rafe Pipherd and Ohanlan chased Oneale in a battell.

1280 In the yeare one thousand two hundred and foure score, Robert Vffort came the third time to occupie the roome of lord chiefe iustice in Ireland, resuming that

1281 roome into his hands againe. In the yeare following, the bishop of Waterford was established by the king of England lord iustice of Ireland. Adam Cusacke the yoonger slue William Barret, and manie other in Connagh. And in the next yeare, to wit, one thousand two hundred foure score and two, Penquett slue Murertagh, & his brother Art Mac Murgh at Athlon. Also the lord Iames de Birmingham, and Piers de Tute departed this life. Also the archbishop Derlington deceassed. And about the same time, the citie of Dublin was defaced by fire, and the steeple of Christs church vtterlie destroied. The citizens before they went about to repare

Christ church repared their owne priuat buildings, agreed togither to make a collection for reparing the ruines of that ancient building first begun by the Danes, and continued by Citrius

Donat bishop of Dublin. prince of Dublin at the instance of Donat sometime bishop of that citie, and dedicated to the blessed trinitie.

At length Stranghow earle of Penbroke, Fitzstephans, & Laurence, that for his vertue was called saint Laurence archbishop of Dublin, and his foure successors, Iohn of Euesham, Henrie Scorichbill, and Lucas, and last of all Iohn de saint Paule finished it. This notable building, since the time that it was thus defaced by

Strangbows toome restored by Henrie Sidneie. fire, hath béene beautified in diuerse sorts by many zealous citizens. Stranghowes toome defaced, by the fall of the roofe of the church, sir Henrie Sidneie, when he was lord deputie, restored; & likewise did cost vpon the earle of Kildares chappell for an ornament to the quier, ouer the which he left also a monument of capteine

Capteine Randolfe. Randolfe, late coronell of the English bands of footmen in Vlster that died there valiantlie, fighting in his princes seruice as after shall appeare. In the yeare one thousand two hundred foure score and three, Fulmund chancellor of Ireland, and Richard Tute departed this life, and frier Stephan Fulborne was made lord iustice of Ireland.

1285 In the yeare 1285, the lord Theobald Butler fled from Dubline, and died shortlie after, and the lord Theobald Verdon lost his men and horsses as he went towards

John Samford consecrated archbishop of Dublin. Offalie, & the next day Gerald Fitzmaurice was taken, and Iohn Samford was consecrated archbishop of Dublin. Moreouer at Rathod, the lord Geffreie Geneuill

An ouerthrow at Ratod. fled, and sir Gerard Doget, and Rafe Petit were slaine, with a great number of

Norwagh and Ardscoll burnt. others. The Norwagh and Ardscoll with other townes and villages were burnt by

1286 Philip Stanton the sixteenth daie of Nouember, in the yeare 1286. Also Calwagh was taken at Kildare. In the yeare 1287, diuerse nobles in Ireland deceased, as Richard Deceter, Gerald Fitzmaurice, Thomas de Clare, Richard Taffie, & Nicholas

1288 Teling knights. The yeare next insuing, deceased frier Fulborne lord iustice of

Samford archbishop of Dublin lord iustice. Ireland, and Iohn Samford archbishop of Dublin was aduanced to the roome of lord iustice. Also Richard Burgh earle of Vlster besieged Theobald Verdon in the castell of Athlon, and came with a great power vnto Trim, by the working of Walter Lacie.

1290 In the yeare 1290, was the chase or discomfiture of Offalie, & diuerse Englishmen slaine. Also Mac Coghlan slue Omolaghelin king of Meth, and William Burgh was discomfited at Delum by Mac Coghlan. The same yeare 1290, William

William Vescie lord iustice. Vescie was made lord iustice of Ireland, and entered into that office on S. Martins daie. Vnto this iustice, Edward Balioll king of Scotland did homage for an earledome which he held in Ireland, in like maner as he did to king Edward for the

1292 crowne of Scotland. In the yeare 1292, a fifteenth was granted to the king, of all the temporall goods in Ireland, whilest Vescie was as yet lord iustice. This Vescie

was

was a sterne man and full of courage, he called Iohn earle of Kildare before him, charging him with foule riots and misdemeanors, for that he ranged abroad, and sought reuenge vpon priuat displeasures out of all order, and not for anie aduancement of the publike wealth or seruice of his souereigne.

The earle as impatient to heare himselfe touched as the iustice to suffer euill The earle of Kildare
dooing, answered thus: "By your honor and mine (my lord) and by king Edwards hand (for that was accompted no small oth in those daies among the Irish) you would if you durst appeach me in plaine termes of treason or felonie: for where I haue the title, and you the fléece of Kildare, I wote well how great an eiesore I am in your sight, so that if I might be handsomlie trussed vp for a fellon, then might my master your sonne become a gentleman." "A gentleman" quoth the iustice, "thou proud earle? I tell thée the Vescies were gentlemen before Kildare was an earledome, and before that Welsh bankrupt thy cousine fethered his nest in Leinster. But seeing thou darest me, I will surelie breake thy heart." And therwith he called the earle a notorious theefe and a murtherer. Then followed facing and bracing among the souldiers, with high words, and terrible swearing on both sides, vntill either part appeased his owne.

The lord iustice shortlie after, leauing his deputie William Hare, tooke the sea, and hasted ouer to the king. The earle immediatlie followed, and as heinouslie as the lord iustice accused him of felonie, Kildare no lesse appealed him of treason. For triall héereof, the earle asked the combat and Vescie refused not: but yet when the lists were prouided, Vescie was slipt awaie into France, and so disherited of all his lands in the countie of Kildare, which were bestowed vpon the earle and his heires for euer. The earle waxing loftie of mind in such prosperous successe,
squared with diuerse nobles, English and Irish of that land. The same yeare died 1294
Iohn Samford archbishop of Dublin, and Iohn Fitzthomas earle of Kildare, and The death of the archbishop Samford
Iohn de la Mare tooke prisoners, Richard Burgh earle of Vlster, and William Burgh
within the countie of Meth, and the castell of Kildare was taken, and all the The earle of Vlster taken prisoner.
countrie wasted by the English on the one side, and the Irish on the other, and Calwagh burnt all the rolles and talies concerning the records & accompts of that
countie. Great dearth and death reigned in Ireland this yeare, and the two yéeres Great dearth and death.
next insuing. The earle of Kildare deteined the earle of Vlster prisoner, vntill by authoritie of a parlement holden at Kilkennie, he was deliuered out of the castell of Leie, for his two sonnes, and for the inuasion which the earle of Kildare had made into Meth, and other his vnrulie and misordred parts, was disseized of the castell of Sligagh, and of all his lands in Connagh.

William Dodingsels, being this yeare made lord iustice of Ireland, after Vescie William Dodingsels lord iustice
died, in the yéere next following, that is 1295, and the thrée and twentith of king
Edward the first. After him succéeded in that roome the lord Thomas Fitzmaurice. 1295
In the yeare 1296, frier William de Bothum was consecrated archbishop of Dublin. Thomas Fitzmaurice lord iustice.
In the yeare 1298, and six and twentith of Edward the first, the lord Thomas Fitz- 1296
maurice departed this life, and an agréement was made betwixt the earle of Vlster 1298
and the lord Iohn Fitzthomas earle of Kildare, by Iohn Wogan that was ordeined *Ric. Turris.*
lord iustice of Ireland. In the yéere 1299 William archbishop of Dublin departed 1299
this life, and Richard de Fringis was consecrated archbishop in his place. The king went vnto Iohn Wogan lord iustice, commanding him to giue summons vnto the nobles of Ireland, to prepare themselues with horsse and armor to come in their best araie for the warre, to serue him against the Scots: and withall wrote vnto the same nobles, as to Richard de Burgh earle of Vlster, Geffreie de Geneuill, Iohn Fitzthomas, Thomas Fitzmaurice, Theobald lord Butler, Theobald lord Verdon, Piers lord Birmingham of Thetemore, Eustace lord Powre, Hugh lord Purcell, Iohn de Cogan, Iohn de Barrie, William de Barrie, Walter de Lastice, Richard de

Excester, Iohn Pipurd, Walter Lenfant, Iohn of Oxford, Adam de Stanton, Simon
de Pheibe, William Cadell, Iohn de Vale, Maurice de Carre, George de la Roch,
Maurice de Rochford, and Maurice Fitzthomas de Keito, commanding them to be
with him at Withwelaun the first of March. Such a precept I remember I haue
read, registred in a close roll among the records of the tower. But where Marlburrow saith, that the said Iohn Wogan lord iustice of Ireland, and the lord
Iohn Fitzthomas, with manie others, came to king Edward into Scotland, in the
nine and twentith yeare of king Edwards reigne, Campion noteth it to be in the
yere 1299, which fell in the seuen & twentith of the reigne of king Edward:
& if my remembrance faile me not, the close roll aforementioned beareth date of
the foure and twentith yeare of king Edwards reigne. All which notes may be
true, for it is verie like, that in those warres against the Scots, the king sent diuerse times to the Irish lords to come to serue him, as it behooued them to doo by
their tenures: and not onelie he sent into Ireland to haue the seruices of men, but
also for prouision of vittels, as in close rolles I remember I haue also séene recorded
of the seauen and twentith and thirtith yeare of the said king Edward the first his
reigne. For this we find in a certeine abstract of the Irish chronicles, which should
Chr Pembrig séeme to be collected out of Flatsburie, whom Campion so much followed, that in
1301 the yeare 1301, the lord Iohn Wogan lord iustice, Iohn Fitzthomas, Peter Bir-
Irishmen inuade Scotland mingham, & diuerse others went into Scotland in aid of king Edward, in which
yeare also a great part of the citie of Dublin, with the church of saint Werburgh
was burnt in the night of the feast daie of saint Colme. Also the lord Geneuill
married the daughter of Iohn de Montfort, and the lord Iohn Mortimer married
the daughter and heire of Peter Geneuill, also the lord Theobald de Verdon married
the daughter of the lord Roger Mortimer. The same yeare in the winter season,
the Irish of Leinster raised warre against the townes of Wicklow and Rathdon,
dooing much hurt by burning in the countrie all about: but they were chastised
for their wickednesse, loosing the most part of their prouision and cattell. And
in the Lent season the more part of them had béene vtterlie destroied, if discord
and variance had not risen among the Englishmen, to the impeachment of their
purposed enterprises.

In haruest there were thrée hundred théeues slaine by the Phelanes. Also Walter
Walter Power. le Power wasted a great part of Mounster, burning manie farmes and places in that
1302 countrie. In the yeare 1302, pope Boniface demanded a tenth of all the spirituall
liuings in England and Ireland, for the space of thrée yeares, to mainteine wars in
1303 defense of the church of Rome, against the king of Arragon. In the yeare 1303,
The earle of Vlster. the earle of Vlster, and Richard Burgh, and sir Eustace le Power, with a puissant
armie entered Scotland. The earle made thrée and thirtie knights at Dublin, before he set forwards. The same yeere Girald, sonne and heire to the lord Iohn
Fitzthomas departed this life, and likewise the countesse of Vlster. William de
Wellisleie, and sir Robert de Persiuall were slaine the two and twentith of October.
1304 In the yeare 1304, a great part of the citie of Dublin was burnt by casuall fire.
In the yeare next insuing, Iordane Comin with his complices slue Mauragh Oconhur king of Offalie, and his brother Calwagh, with diuerse others within the court
of Piers de Birmingham at Carricke in Carbrie. Also sir Gilbert Sutton steward
of Wexford was slaine by the Irishmen, néere to the farme of Hemond de Grace,
which Hemond bare himselfe right valiantlie in that fight, and in the end through
his great manhood escaped.

1306 A discomfiture at Offalie In the yeare 1306 a great slaughter was made in Offalie néere to the castell of
Geschill, the thirteenth daie of Aprill vpon Oconhur and his fréends by the Odemp-
sies, in the which place were slaine a great number of men. Also Obrien king of
Thomond was slaine. Moreouer, Donald Oge Mac Arthie slue Donald Russe king
of

of Desmond. And vpon the twelfe of Maie in the confins of Meth, a great ouerthrow chanced to the side of the lord Piers Butler, and Balmore in Leinster was *Balmore burnt.*
burnt by the Irish, where Henrie Celfe was slaine at that present time. Hereof
followed great warres betwixt the English and Irish in Leinster, so that a great *Warres in Leinster.*
armie was called togither foorth of diuerse parts of Ireland, to restreine the malice
of the Irish in Leinster, in which iournie sir Thomas Mandeuill knight entred into
a conflict with the Irish néere to Glenfell, in the which he bare himselfe right manfullie, till his horsse was slaine vnder him, and yet then to his great praise and high
commendation he saued both himselfe and manie of his companie. The lord chan- *The lord chancellor consecrated bishop of Imalcie.*
cellor of Ireland, Thomas Caucocke, was consecrated bishop of Imalcie within the
Trinitie church at Dublin, and kept such a feast as the like had not lightlie beene
séene nor heard of before that time in Ireland, first to the rich & after to the poore.
Richard Ferings archbishop of Dublin deceased on the euen of saint Luke the *The archbishop of Dublin deceased.*
euangelist, to whom succéeded Richard de Hauerings, who after he had continued
in that sée about a fiue yeares, resigned it ouer by dispensation obteined from Rome,
and then his nephue Iohn Léech was admitted archbishop there.

In the yeare 1307 the first of Aprill, Murcod Ballagh was beheaded néere to 1307
Merton by sir Dauid Caunton knight, and shortlie after was Adam Daune slaine.
Also, a great discomfiture and slaughter fell vpon the Englishmen in Connagh by *A discomfiture in Connagh.*
the Oscheles the first daie of Maie, and the robbers that dwelt in the parties of
Offalie raised the castell of Geischell, and in the vigill of the translation of Thomas
Becket, being the sixt of Iulie, they burnt the towne of Leie and besieged the
castell: but they were constreined to depart from thense shortlie after, by Iohn
Fitzthomas and Edmund Butler that came to remoue that siege. In the yeare 1308 1308
king Edward the first departed this life the seuenth of Iulie.

Edward the second.

RICHARD archbishop of Dublin, after that he had gouerned that sée the space
of fiue yeares, by reason of a vision that he saw in his sléepe, féeling himselfe
troubled in conscience, with consideration of that dreame, resigned the next morrow
all his title to the archbishops dignitie (as before ye haue heard) and contented himselfe with other ecclesiasticall benefices as seemed conuenient to his estate. This 1300
yeare by vertue of letters directed from the pope to the king of England, he caused *The order of the Templers suppressed.*
all the Templers as well in England as Ireland to be apprehended, and committed
to safe kéeping. The profession of these Templers began at Ierusalem, by certeine
gentlemen that remained in an hostell néere to the temple, who till the councell of
Trois in France were not increased aboue the number of nine, but from that time
foorth in little more than fiftie yeares, by the zealous contribution of all christian
realmes, they had houses erected euerie where, with liuings bountifullie assigned to
the same for their maintenance, in so much as they were augmented vnto the number of thrée hundred, that were knights of that order, beside inferiour brethren
innumerable: but now with wealth they so forgot themselues, that they nothing
lesse regarded, than the purpose of their foundation: and withall being accused
of horrible heresies (whether in all things iustlie or otherwise, the Lord knoweth)
they were in the councell at Lions in France condemned, and their liuings transposed
to the knights Hospitalers, otherwise called the knights of the Rhodes, and now
of Malta. The manner of their apprehension and committing was sudden, and so
generall in all places vpon one daie, that they had no time to shift for themselues.

For first, the king sent foorth a precept to euerie shirife within the realme of

England, commanding them within each of their roomes to cause a prescribed number of knights, or rather such men of credit, on whose fidelities he might assure himselfe to assemble at a certeine towne named in the same writ, the sundaie next after the Epiphanie, & that ech of the same shiriffes failed not to be there the same daie, to execute all that should be inioined them by anie other writ, then and there to be deliuered. The shirifle of Yorke was commanded to giue summons to foure and twentie such knights, or other sufficient men to méet him at Yorke The shiriffe of Norffolke and Suffolke, to summon twentie to meet him at Thetford. The other shiriffs were appointed to call to them some ten, some twelue, or some fourteene, to méet them at such townes as in their writs were named The date of this writ was from Westminster the fiftéenth of December, in the first yeare of this king Edward the seconds reigne The other writ was sent by a chapleine authorized both to deliuer the same writ, and to take an oth of the shiriffe, that he should not disclose the contents, till he had put the same in execution, which was to attach by assistance of those aforementioned knights, or as manie of them as he thought expedient to vse, all the Templers within the precinct of his roome, and to seize all their lands, goods, and cattels into the kings hands, and to cause an inuentarie of the same indented be made in presence of the warden of the place, whether he were knight of the order or anie other, and in the presence of other honest men neighbours thereabouts, keeping the one counterpane with himselfe, sealed with his seale that made the seizure, and leauing the other in the hands of the said warden and further to sée the same goods and cattels to be put in safe kéeping, and to prouide that the quicke goods might be well kept and looked vnto, and the grounds manured to the most profit, and to cause the bodies of the Templers attached, to be so deteined in all safetie, as that they be not yet committed to irons nor to streict prison, but to remaine in some conuenient place other than their owne houses, and to be found of the goods so seized accordinglie as falleth for their estates, till he haue otherwise in commandement from the king · and what is doone herein, to certifie into the excheker the morrow after the purification The date of this second writ was from Biflet the twentith of December There was likewise a writ directed to Iohn Wogan lord iustice of Ireland, signifieng vnto him what should be doone in England, touching the apprehension of the Templers, and seizure of their lands and goods, commanding him to procéed in semblable manner against them in Ireland · but the daie and place when the shiriffes should there assemble, was left to the discretion of the said iustice and treasuror of the excheker there, but so as the same might be doone before anie rumour of this thing could be brought ouer out of England thither Also a like commandement was sent vnto Iohn de Britaine earle of Richmond, lord warden of Scotland, and to Eustace Cotesbach chamberleine of Scotland, also to Walter de Pedet on lord iustice of west Wales, to Hugh Aldighleigh *alias* Auderleie lord iustice of north Wales, and to Robert Holland lord iustice of Chester Thus much for the Temples. But now to other doings in Ireland

1308 In the yeare 1308 the twelfe of Aprill deceased Peter de Birmingham a noble warriour, and one that had béene no small scourge to the Irish The eleuenth of Maie the castell of Kennun was burnt, and diuers of them that had it in kéeping were slaine by William Macbalther, and other of the Irish, and likewise the towne of Courcoulie was burnt by the same malefactors And the sixt of Iune, Iohn lord Wogan lord iustice was discomfited néere to Glindelorie, where Iohn de S Hogelin, Iohn Norton, Iohn Breton, and manie other were slaine The sixtéenth of Iune, Dunlouan, Tobir, and manie other townes were burnt by the Irish rebels About this season, Iohn Decer maior of Dublin builded the high pipe there, & the bridge ouer

This Macbalther was after hanged at Dublin

The lord iustice discomfited 1308

Iohn Decer maior of Dublin.

ouer the Liffie towards S Vlstons, and a chappell of our ladie at the friers minors, where he was buried, repared the church of the friers preachers, and euerie fridaie tabled the friers at his owne costs.

Iohn Wogan hauing occasion to passe into England, William Burgh did supplie his roome, vnto whom king Edward recommended Piers de Gaueston, when (contrarie to the kings mind) he was banished by the lords of England, and about the natiuitie of our ladie he came ouer into Ireland, being sent thither by the king with manie iewels and beside the letters which he brought of recommendation from the king, he had assigned to him the cōmodities roiall of that realme, which bred some trouble and bickerings there, betwixt Richard Burgh earle of Vlster, and the said Gaueston, who notwithstanding bought the good willes of the souldiers with his liberalitie, slue Dermot Odempsie, subdued Obren, edified sundrie castels, causeies, and bridges, but the next yeare he was reuoked home by the king, as in the historie of England it maie appeare. Burgh Piers Gaueston sent into Ireland.

In the vigill of Simon and Iude, the lord Roger Mortimer landed in Ireland with his wife, right heire to the seigniorie of Meth, as daughter to Piers Genuill, that was sonne to the lord Geffreie Genuill, which Geffreie became a frier at Trim of the order of the preachers by reason whereof, the lord Mortimer and his wife entered into possession of the lands of Meth In the yeare 1309, on Candlemas day, the lord Iohn Bonneuill was slaine néere to the towne of Ardscoll, by the lord Arnold Powre and his complices, his bodie was buried at Athie in the church of the friers preachers. In the yere following, at a parlement holden at Kildare, the lord Arnold Powre was acquit of that slaughter, for that it was prooued it was doone in his owne defense In the yeare 1311, or (as some bookes haue) the yeare 1309, Wogan lord iustice summoned a parlement at Kilkennie, where diuerse wholesome lawes were ordeined, but neuer executed There fell the bishops in contention about their iurisdictions, namelie the bishop of Dublin forbad the primat of Armagh to raise his crosier within the prouince of Leinster. Lord Roger Mortimer. 1309 Lord Iohn Bonneuill slaine. 1310 1311 A parlement at Kilkennie. *Campion*

Shortlie after, Rowland Ioice the primat stale by night (in his pontificals) from Howth to the priorie of Grace Dieu, where the bishops seruants met him, & with force chased him out of the diocesse This bishop was named Iohn a Léekes, and was consecrated not long before he kept this sturre. Richard earle of Vlster with a great armie came to Bonrath in Thomond, where as sir Robert or rather sir Richard de Clare discomfited his power, tooke sir William de Burgh prisoner, or (as some bookes haue) the earle himselfe. Iohn Lacie the sonne of Walter Lacie, and diuerse others were slaine. The twelfe of Nouember this yere, Richard de Clare slue six hundred Galloglasses, and Iohn Morgoghedan was slaine by Omolmore. Also Donat Obren was murthered by his owne men in Thomond Sir Richard de Clare Iohn Lacie slaine

The one and twentith of Februarie began a riot in Argile by Robert Verdon, for the appeasing wherof an armie was lead thither by Iohn Wogan lord chiefe iustice in the beginning of Iulie, but the same was discomfited, and diuerse men of account slaine, as sir Nicholas Auenell, Patrike de Roch, & others. At length yet the said sir Robert Verdon, and many of his complices came and submitted themselues to prison within the castell of Dublin, abiding there the kings mercie. The lord Edmund Butler was made deputie iustice vnder the lord Iohn Wogan, who in the Lent next insuing besieged the Obrens in Glindelow, and compelled them to yeeld themselues to the kings peace Also in the yeare abouesaid 1312, Maurice Fitzthomas maried the ladie Katharine, daughter to the earle of Vlster at Gréene castell, and Thomas Fitziohn maried an other of the said earles daughters in the same place, but not on the same daie for the first of those two mariages was celebrated the morrow after saint Dominikes daie, and this second mariage was kept 1312 Robert Verdon raiseth a riotous tumult Iohn Wogan lord iustice.

the

the morrow after the feast of the assumption of our ladie. Also Robert de Bruse ouerthrew the castell of Man, and tooke the lord Donegan Odowill on saint Barnabies daie.

1313 Campion. In the yeare 1313, Iohn a Leekes archbishop of Dublin departed this life, after whose decease were elected in schisme and diuision of sides two successors, Walter Thorneburie lord chancellor, and Alexander Bignor treasuror of Ireland. The chancellor to strengthen his election, hastilie went to sea, and togither with an hundred and fiftie and six persons perished by shipwracke. The other submitting his cause to the processe of law, taried at home and sped. Moreouer, the lord Iohn de Burgh, sonne and heire to the earle of Vlster, deceased at Galbie on the feast daie of saint Marcell & Marcelline. Also the lord Edmund Butler created thirtie knights in the castle of Dublin on saint Michaels daie being sundaie. The knights hospitalers or of saint Iohns (as they were called) were inuested in the lands of the Templers in Ireland. The same yeare was the lord Theobald Verdon sent lord iustice into Ireland.

The earle of Vlsters sonne and heire deceaseth.

1314

1315 In the ninth yeare of king Edwards reigne, Edward Bruse, brother to Robert Bruse king of Scots, entered the north part of Ireland with six thousand men. There were with him diuerse capteins of high renowme among the Scotish nation, of whome the chiefe were these: the earles of Murrie and Mentith, the lord Iohn Steward, the lord Iohn Campbell, the lord Thomas Randolfe, Fergus de Andressan, Iohn Wood, and Iohn Bisset. They landed néere to Cragfergus in Vlster the fiue & twentith of Maie, and ioining with the Irish, conquered the earledome of Vlster, and gaue the English there diuerse great ouerthrowes, tooke the towne of Dundalke, spoiled & burnt it, with a great part of Vrgile: they burnt churches & abbeies, with the people whom they found in the same, sparing neither man, woman nor child. Then was the lord Edmund Butler chosen lord iustice, who made the earle of Vlster and the Giraldines friends, and reconciled himselfe with sir Iohn Mandeuill, thus seeking to preserue the residue of the realme which Edward Bruse meant wholie to conquer, hauing caused himselfe to be crowned king of Ireland. The lord iustice assembled a great power out of Mounster, and Leinster, and other parts therabouts, and the earle of Vlster with another armie came vnto him néere vnto Dundalke, where they consulted togither how to deale in defending the countrie against the enimies: but hearing the Scots were withdrawne backe, the earle of Vlster folowed them, and fighting with them at Coniers, hée lost the field.

Edward Bruse inuadeth Ireland.

Capteins of name with Bruse.

Dundalke taken and burnt.

Edmund Butler lord iustice.

Théere were manie slaine on both parts, and William de Burgh the earls brother, sir Iohn Mandeuill, and sir Alane Fitzalane were taken prisoners. Herewith the Irish of Connagh and Meth began foorthwith to rebell against the Englishmen, and burnt the castell of Athlon and Randon. And the Bruse comming forward burnt Kenlis in Meth, and Granard, also Finnagh, and Newcastell, and kept his Christmas at Loghsudie. From thense he went through the countrie vnto Rathimegan and Kildare, and to the parties about Tristeldermot and Athie, then to Reban, Skether, & néere to Ardskoll in Leinster: where the lord iustice Butler, the lord Iohn Fitzthomas, the lord Arnold Powre, and other the lords and gentlemen of Leinster and Mounster came to incounter the Bruse: but through discord that rose among them, they left the field vnto the enimies, sir William Pendergast knight, and Hemond le Grace a right valiant esquier were slaine there. And on the Scotish side sir Fergus Andressan and sir Walter Murrie, with diuerse other that were buried in the church of the friers preachers at Athie.

After this the Bruse in his returne towards Meth burnt the castell of Leie, and so passed foorth till hee came to Kenlis in Meth. In which meane time Roger lord Mortimer, trusting to win himselfe fame if he might ouerthrow the enimies, called

foorth

forth fiftéene thousand men, and vnderstanding that the Scots were come to Kenlis, made thitherwards, and there incountering with them, was put to the woorse, his men (as was supposed) wilfullie shrinking from him, as those that bare him hollow hearts. With the newes of this ouerthrow, vpstart the Irish of Mounster, the Otoolies, Obrens, Omores, and with fire and sword wasted all from Arclow to Leix. With them coped the lord iustice, and made of them a great slaughter, fourescore of their heads were sent to the castell of Dublin.

The lord Mortimer discomfited by the Scots.

In time of these troubles and warres in Ireland by the inuasion thus of the Scots, certeine Irish lords, faithfull men and true subiects to the king of England, did not onelie promise to continue in their loiall obeisance towards him, being their soueraigne prince, but also for more assurance deliuered hostages to be kept within the castell of Dublin. The names of which lords that were so contented to assure their allegiance were these, Iohn Fitzthomas lord of Offalie, Richard de Clare, Morice Fitzthomas, Thomas Fitziohn le Power baron of Donoille, Arnold le Power, Morice de Rochford, Dauid de la Roch, and Miles de la Roch. These and diuerse other resisted with all their might and maine the iniurious attempts of the Scots, although the Scots had drawne to their side the most part of the wild Irish, and no small number also of the English Irish, as well lords, as others of meaner calling: so that the countrie was miserablie afflicted, what by the Scots on the one part, and the Irish rebels on the other, which rebels notwithstanding were ouerthrowne in diuerse particular conflicts. But yet to the further scattering of the English forces in Ireland, there rose foure princes of Connagh, but the Burghes and Birminghams discomfited them, and slue eleuen thousand of them beside Athenrie. Amongst other were slaine in this battell Fedelmicus, Oconhur king of Connagh, Okellie, and diuerse other great lords and capteins of Connagh and Meth. The lord Richard Birmingham had an esquier that belonged to him called Iohn Husseie, who by the commandement of his maister went foorth to take view of the dead bodies, and to bring him word whether Okellie his mortall fo were slaine among the residue. Husseie comming into the field with one man to turne vp and suruere the dead carcases, was streight espied by Okellie, that laie lurking in a brake bush thereby, who hauing had good proofe of Husseie his valiancie before that time, longed sore to traine him from his capteine, and presuming now vpon his good opportunitie, discouered himselfe, not doubting, but either to win him with courteous persuasions, or by force to worke his will of him, and so comming to him said: "Husseie, thou séest that I am at all points armed, & haue mine esquire here likewise furnished with armour & weapon readie at mine elbow, thou art naked with thy page, a yoongling, & not to be accounted of: so that if I loued thée not, and meant to spare thée for thine owne sake, I might now doo with thée what I would, and slea thée for thy maisters sake. But come & serue me vpon this request here made to thée, and I promise thée by saint Patrikes staffe to make thée a lord in Connagh, of more possessions than thy maister hath in Ireland." When these words might nothing were him, his owne man (a great stout lubber) began to reproue him of follie, for not consenting to so large an offer, which was assured with an oth, wherevpon he durst gage his soule for performance.

Assurance giuen by the lords of Ireland for their loialtie.

A great ouerthrow.

The king of Connagh slaine.

Now had Husseie thrée enimies, and first therefore turning to his knaue, he dispatched him. Next he raught vnto Okellies esquier such a knocke vnder the pit of the eare, that downe he came to the ground and there he laie. Thirdlie, he laid so about him, that yer anie helpe could be looked for, he had also slaine Okellie, and perceiuing the esquire to be but astonied he recouered him, and holpe him vp againe, and after he was somewhat come to himselfe, he forced him vpon a trunchion, to beare his lords head into the high towne before him, who did so; and

and Husseie presented it to Birmingham, who after the circumstances declared, he dubbed Husseie knight, aduancing him to manie preferments. The successors of that familie afterwards were barons of Galtrim. Sir Thomas Mandeuill and others in this meane while made oftentimes enterprises against the Scots, and slue diuerse of them in sundrie conflicts. But howsoeuer it chanced, we find recorded by Henrie Marlburrow, that either the said sir Thomas Mandeuill (that thus valiantlie behaued himselfe against the Scots) or some other bearing the same name, and his brother also called Iohn Mandeuill were both slaine shortlie after at Downe, vpon their comming foorth of England, by the Scots that were readie there to assaile them.

Sir Thomas Mandeuill slaine.

Thus may we see, that those lords and knights, which had giuen pledges for their loialtie to the king of England, sought by all waies and meanes how to beat backe the enimies, which they might haue doone with more ease, if the Irish had not assisted the Scots, and presuming of their aid, rebelled in sundrie parts of the countrie; who neuerthelesse were oftentimes well chastised for their disloiall dealings, as partlie we haue touched; although we omit diuerse small ouerthrowes and other particular matters, sith otherwise we should increase this booke further than our first purposed intent would permit. Whilest the Scots were thus holden vp in Ireland, that they could not in all things worke their wils, Robert le Bruse king of Scots came ouer himselfe, landed at Cragfergus to the aid of his brother, whose souldiors most wickedlie entred into churches, spoiling and defacing the same of all such toomes, monuments, plate, copes, & other ornaments which they found, and might laie hands vpon.

Campion
1316
The king of Scots in Ireland

The castell of Cragfergus, after it had béene strictlie besieged a long time, was surrendred to the Scots, by them that had kept it, till they for want of other vittels were driuen to eate leather, and eight Scots (as some write) which they had taken prisoners. The lord Thomas, sonne to the earle of Vlster departed this life. And on the sundaie next after the natiuitie of our ladie, the lord Iohn Fitzthomas deceased at Laragh Brine néere to Mainoth, and was buried at Kildare, in the church of the friers preachers. This Iohn Fitzthomas, a little before his death, was created earle of Kildare, after whome succéeded his sonne Thomas Fitziohn a right wise and prudent personage. The fourteenth of September, Conhor Mac Kele, & fiue hundred Irishmen were slaine by the lord William de Burgh, and lord Richard Birmingham in Connagh. Also on the mondaie after the feast of All saints, Iohn Loggan and sir Hugh Bisset slue a great number of Scots, among the which were one hundred with double armors, and two hundred with single armors, so that of their men of armes there died thrée hundred beside footemen.

Cragfergus deliuered vp to the Scots.
Men eaten

Iohn Fitzthomas the first earle of Kildare deceasseth

Scots ouerthrowne

The fiftéenth of Nouember chanced a great tempest of wind and raine, which threw downe manie houses, with the stéeple of the Trinitie church in Dublin, and did much other hurt both by land and water. On the fift of December, sir Alane Steward that had béene taken prisoner in Vlster by Iohn Loggan, and sir Iohn Sandale, was brought to the castell of Dublin. After Canlemas, the Lacies came to Dublin, & procured an inquest to be impanelled to inquire of their demeanor, for that they were accused to haue procured the Scots to come into Ireland: but by that inquest they were discharged, and therewith tooke an oth to keepe the kings peace, and to destroie the Scots to the vttermost of their power. In the beginning of Lent, the Scots came in secret wise vnto Slane, with twentie thousand armed men, and with them came the armie of Vlster, destroieng all the countrie before them. Moreouer, on mondaie before the feast of S. Matthias the apostle, the earle of Vlster lieng in the abbeie of S. Marie néere to Dublin, Robert Notingham maior of that citie, with the communaltie of the same went thither, tooke the earle, and put him in prison within the castell of Dublin, slue seuen of his men, and spoiled the abbeie.

A great tempest

1317

The earle of Vlster apprehended.

The

The same wéeke, Edward Bruse marched towards Dublin, but herewith, turning to the castell of Knoke, he entred the same, and tooke Hugh Tirrell the lord thereof, togither with his wife, and ransomed them for a summe of monie. The citizens of Dublin burnt all their suburbs for feare of a siege, and made the best purueiance they could to defend their citie, if the Bruse had come to haue besieged them but he turning another waie, went vnto the towne of Naas, and was guided thither by the Lacies, contrarie to their oth. From thense he passed vnto Tristeldermot, and so to Baliganam, and to Callan, at length he came to Limerike, and there remained till after Easter. They of Vlster sent to the lord iustice lamentable informations of such crueltie as the enimies practised in those parts, beséeching him to take some order for their reliefe in that their so miserable estate. The lord iustice deliuered to them the kings power with his standard, wherewith vnder pretense to expell the Scots, they got vp in armor, and ranging through the countrie, did more vexe and molest the subiects, than did the strangers. The Scots procéeded and spoiled Cashels. & wheresoeuer they lighted vpon the Butlers lands, they burnt and spoiled them vnmercifullie

Hugh Tirrell taken by the Scots.

The kings standard deliuered to them of Vlster.

In this meane while had the lord iustice and Thomas Fitziohn earle of Kildare, Richard de Clare, and Arnold le Powre baron of Donnoill leuied an armie of thirtie thousand men, readie to go against the enimies, and to giue them battell, but no good was doone For about the same time the lord Roger Mortimer was sent into Ireland as lord iustice, and landing at Yoghall, wrote his letters vnto the lord Butler, & to the other capteins, willing them not to fight till he came with such power as he had brought ouer with him. Whereof the Bruse being warned, retired first towards Kildare. But yet after this he came within foure miles of Trim, where he laie in a wood, and lost manie of his men through famine, and so at length about the beginning of Maie he returned into Vlster

Roger Mortimer iustice of Ireland.

The lord Edmund Butler made great slaughter of the Irish néere to Tristledermot, and likewise at Balithan he had a good hand of Omorch, and slue manie of his men The lord Mortimer pacified the displeasure and variance betwixt Richard earle of Vlster, and the nobles that had put the said earle vnder safe kéeping within the castell of Dublin, accusing him of certeine riots committed to the preiudice and losse of the kings subiects, whereby the Scots increased in strength and courage, whose spoiling of the countrie caused such horrible scarsitie in Vlster, that the soldiors which the yeare before abused the kings authoritie, to purueie themselues of ouer fine diet, surfetted with flesh and *Aquavitæ* all the Lent long, prolled and pilled insatiablie wheresoeuer they came without need, and without regard of the poore people, whose onelie prouision they deuoured. These people now liuing in slauerie vnder the Bruse, starued for hunger, hauing first experienced manie lamentable shifts euen to the eating of dead carcasses.

Slaughter of Irishmen.

1317

The earle of Vlster deliuered out of prison

Scarsitie of vittels in Vlster

The earle of Vlster was deliuered by maineprise and vpon his oth, by the which he vndertooke neuer to seeke reuenge of his apprehension otherwise than by order of law, and so had daie giuen him vnto the feast of the natiuitie of saint Iohn baptist: but he kept not his daie, whether for that he mistrusted to stand in triall of his cause, or through some other reasonable let, I cannot tell. A great dearth this yeere afflicted the Irish people: for a measure of wheat called a chronecke was sold at foure and twentie shillings, & a chronecke of otes at sixteene shillings, and all other vittels likewise were sold according to the same rate, for all the whole countrie was sore wasted by the Scots and them of Vlster, insomuch that no small number of people perished through famine.

The earle of Vlster deliuered

Great dearth

About the feast of Pentecost the lord iustice Mortimer tooke his iornie towards Drogheda, and sent to the Lacies, commanding them to come vnto him, but they refused so to do. Wherevpon he sent sir Hugh Crofts vnto them, to talke with them

 about

Sir Hug Crofts slaine

about some agréement of peace but they slue the messenger, for whome great lamentation was made, for that he was reputed & knowne to be a right woorthie knight The lord iustice sore offended herewith, gathereth an armie, & goeth against the Lacies, whome he chased out of Connagh, so that Hugh Lacie withdrew to Vlster, & there ioined himselfe with Edward Bruse. Whervpon, on the thursdaie next before the feast of saint Margaret, the said Hugh Lacie and also Walter Lacie were proclamed traitors This yeare passed verie troublesome vnto the whole realme of Ireland, as well through slaughter betwixt the parties enimies one to another, as by dearth and other misfortunes Hugh Canon the kings iustice of his

The Lacies reuolt to the Scots

1318 bench was slaine by Andrew Birmingham betwixt the towne of Naas and castell Marten Also in the feast of the purification, the popes bulles were published, whereby Alexander Bignor was consecrated archbishop of Dublin About the same time was great slaughter made of Irishmen, through a quarrell betwixt two great lords in Connagh. so that there died in fight to the number of foure thousand men on both parties

Bignor consecrated archbishop of Dublin

Walter Islep treasuror of Ireland

After Easter Walter Islep treasuror of Ireland was sent ouer into that realme, who brought letters to the lord Mortimer, commanding him to returne into England vnto the king: which he did, and departing foorth of Ireland, remained indebted to the citizens of Dublin for his prouision of vittels in the summe of a thousand pounds, whcrof he paid not one farthing, so that manie a bitter cursse he carried with him to the sea, leauing William archbishop of Cashell lord chancellor gouernor of the land in his place: and so by this meane was the said archbishop both chancellor and iustice, and so continued till the feast of saint Michaell At what time Alexander Bignor archbishop of Dublin arriued at Yoghall, being constituted lord iustice, and came to Dublin on saint Denise daie, being the seauenth of October. But here is to be remembred, that a little before the departure of the lord Mortimer foorth of Ireland, to wit, the fift of Maie, the lord Richard de Clare with foure knights, sir Henrie Capell, sir Thomas de Naas, sir Iames Caunton, and sir Iohn Caunton, also Adam Apilgard and others (to the number of foure score persons) were slaine by Obren and Mac Arthie. It was said that the enimies in despite caused the lord Richards bodie to be cut in péeces, so to satisfie their malicious stomachs, but the same péeces were yet afterwards buried in the church of the friers minors at Limerike. Also before the lord Mortimers returne into England, Iohn Lacie was had foorth of the castell of Dublin, and carried to Trim, where he was arreigned and adiudged to be pressed to death, and so he died in prison.

The lord Richard de Clare slaine

The lord Birmingham and other capteins against the Scots

But now to returne vnto the dooings in time of Bignors gouernment. Immediatlie vpon his arriuall, the lord Iohn Birmingham being generall of the field, and hauing with him diuerse capteins of worthie fame, namelie sir Richard Tute, sir Miles Verdon, sir Hugh Trippetton, sir Herbert Sutton, sir Iohn Cusacke, sir Edmund Birmingham, sir William Birmingham, Walter Birmingham the primat of Armagh, sir Walter de la Pulle, and Iohn Maupas led forth the kings power, to the number of one thousand thrée hundred foure and twentie able men against Edward Bruse, who being accompanied with the lord Philip Mowbraie, the lord Walter de Soules, the lord Alaine Steward, with his thrée brethren, sir Walter, and sir Hugh, sir Robert, and sir Aimerie Lacies, and others, was incamped not past two miles from Dundalke with thrée thousand men, there abiding the Englishmen, to fight with them if they came forward which they did with all conuenient spéed, being as desirous to giue battell as the Scots were to receiue it

The primat of Armagh

The primat of Armagh personallie accompaneng the English power, & blessing their enterprise, gaue them such comfortable exhortation, as he thought serued the time yer they began to incounter. And herewith buckling togither, at length the Scots

Scots fullie and wholie were vanquished, and two thousand of them slaine, togither with their capteine Edward Bruse. Maupas that pressed into the throng to incounter with Bruse hand to hand, was found in the search dead aloft vpon the slaine bodie of Bruse. The victorie thus obteined vpon saint Calixtus daie, made an end of the Scotish kingdome in Ireland, & lord Birmingham sending the head of Bruse into England, or as Marlburrow hath, being the messenger himselfe, presented it to king Edward, who in recompense gaue to him and his heires males the earledome of Louth, and the baronie of Ardich and Athenrie to him and his heires generall for euer. Shortlie after sir Richard de Clare with foure other knights of name, and manie other men of warre were slaine in Thomond. The lord Roger Mortimer came againe into Ireland to gouerne as lord iustice there now the second time, and the townes of Athessell and Plebs were burned by the lord Fitzthomas brother to the lord Maurice Fitzthomas. And about this season the bridge of Kilcolin was builded by Maurice Iakis.

The battell of Armagh. *The Scots vanquished.* *Edward Bruse slaine.* *Birmingham made earle of Louth.* *Sir Richard de Clare slaine.* 1319

In the yeare following, to wit, one thousand thrée hundred and twentie, which was the fouretéenth yeare of king Edwards reigne, Thomas Fitziohn earle of Kildare was made lord iustice of Ireland. Here is to be remembred, that about this time also Alexander Bignor archbishop of Dublin sent to pope Iohn the two and twentith, for a priuilege to institute an vniuersitie within the citie of Dublin, and his sute tooke effect: and the first thrée doctors of diuinitie did the said archbishop himselfe create, William Hardite a frier preacher, Henrie Cogie a frier minor, and frier Edmund Bernerden: and beside these one doctor of canon law, to wit, Richard archdeacon of saint Patrikes that was chancellor of the same vniuersitie, who kept their terms and commensements solemnlie: neither was this vniuersitie at anie time since disfranchised, but onlie through change of times discontinued, and now since the dissoluing of monasteries vtterlie decaied.

1320 *The earle of Kildare lord iustice.* *An vniuersitie erected at Dublin.*

A motion was made (as Campion hath noted) in a parlement holden there, whilest sir Henrie Sidneie was the quéenes lieutenant, to haue it againe erected, by waie of contributions to be laid togither: the said sir Henrie offering twentie pounds lands, and an hundred pounds in monie. Other there were also, that according to their abilities and deuotions followed with their offers. The name was deuised; A worthie plantation of Plantagenet & Bullogne. But while they disputed of a conuenient place for it, and of other circumstances, they let fall the principall.

In the yeare one thousand three hundred twentie and one, there was a great slaughter made of the Oconhurs at Balibagan, by the English of Leinster and Meth. 1321
And Iohn Birmingham earle of Louth was lord iustice of Ireland. Vnto this man, whilest he was lord iustice, the king wrote, commanding him to be with him at Carleill in the octaues of the Trinitie, in the fiftéenth yeare of his reigne, with thrée hundred men of armes, one thousand hobellars, and six thousand footmen, ech of them armed with an aketon, a sallet, and gloues of maill, which number was to be leuied in that land: besides thrée hundred men of armes which the earle of Vlster was appointed to serue within that iournie, which the king at that time intended to make against the Scots. The date of the letter was the third of Aprill. In the yeare one thousand thrée hundred twentie and two, diuerse nobles in Ireland departed this life, as the lord Richard Birmingham, the lord Edmund Butler, and 1322
the lord Thomas Persiuall. Moreouer, the lord Andrew Birmingham, and sir 1323
Richard de la Lond were slaine by Onolan. In the eighteenth yéere of king Edward the second his reigne, the lord Iohn Darcie came into Ireland to be lord iustice, and the kings lieutenant there. In these daies liued in the diocesse of Ossorie the ladie Alice Kettle, whome the bishop ascited to purge hir selfe of the fame of inchantment and witchcraft imposed vnto hir, and to one Petronill and Basill hir complices. She was charged to haue nightlie conference with a spirit called

Rec. Turris. *Iohn Darcie lord iustice.* *The ladie Alice Kettle accused of sorcerie.*

called Robin Artisson, to whome she sacrificed in the high waie nine red cocks, and nine peacocks eies. Also that she swept the streets of Kilkennie betwéene compleine and twilight, raking all the filth towards the doores of hir sonne William Outlaw, murmuring & muttering secretlie with hir selfe these words:

To the house of William my sonne,
Hie all the wealth of Kilkennie towne.

At the first conuiction they abiured & did penance, but shortlie after they were found in relapse, & then was Pentionill burnt at Kilkennie, the other twaine might not be heard of. She at the houre of hir death accused the said William as priuie to their sorceries, whome the bishop held in durance nine wéeks, forbidding his keepers to eat or to drinke with him, or to speake to him more than once in the daie. But at length, thorough the sute and instance of Arnold le Powre then seneschall of Kilkennie, he was deliuered, and after corrupted with bribes the seneschall to persecute the bishop, so that he thrust him into prison for thrée moneths. In rifling the closet of the ladie, they found a wafer of sacramentall bread, hauing the diuels name stamped thereon in stéed of Iesus Christ, and a pipe of ointment, wherewith she greased a staffe, vpon the which she ambled and gallopped thorough thicke and thin, when and in what maner she listed. This businesse about these witches troubled all the state of Ireland, the more, for that the ladie was supported by certeine of the nobilitie, and lastlie conueied ouer into England, since which time it could neuer be vnderstood what became of hir. In the yeare one thousand three hundred twentie and six, & last of king Edwards the seconds reigne, Richard Burgh earle of Vlster departed this life.

Edward the third.

1326 VNNETH was the businesse about the witches at an end, when it was signified,
that a gentleman of the familie of the Otoolies in Leinster, named Adam Duffe,
1327 possessed by some wicked spirit of error, denied obstinatelie the incarnation of our sauior, the trinitie of persons in the vnitie of the Godhead, & the resurrection of the flesh; as for the holie scripture, he said it was but a fable: the virgin Marie he affirmed to be a woman of dissolute life, and the apostolike sée erronious. For such assertions he was burnt in Hogging greene beside Dublin. About the same time, Fitzarke Macmorch, and sir Henrie Traherne were taken prisoners. In the yeare following, the lord Thomas Fitziohn erle of Kildare, and the lord Arnold Powre & William earle of Vlster were sent ouer into Ireland, & Roger Outlaw prior of saint Iohns of Ierusalem in Ireland, commonlie called the prior of Kilmaman, was made lord iustice. This man by reason of variance that chanced to rise betwixt the Giraldins, the Butlers, and Birminghams, on the one side, and the Powres & Burghs on the other for terming the earle of Kildare a rimer, to pacifie the parties called a parlement, wherein he himselfe was faine to make his purgation of a slander imposed to him, as suspected of heresie.

Adam Duffe an heretike

The prior of Kilmainan lord iustice.

Arnold Powre accused of heresie

The bishop of Ossorie had giuen an information against Arnold le Powre, conuented & conuicted in his consistorie of certeine hereticall opinions, but bicause the beginning of Powrs accusation concerned the iustices kinsman, and the bishop was mistrusted to prosecute his owne wrong, and the person of the man rather than the fault: a daie was limited for the iustifieng of the bill, the partie being apprehended and respited thereunto. This dealing the bishop (who durst not stirre out of

Kilkennie

Kilkennie to prosecute his accusation) was reputed parciall and when by meanes hereof the matter hanged in suspense, he infamed the said prior as an abbettor and fauourer of Arnolds heresie The prior submitted himselfe to the triall, and therevpon were seuerall proclamations made in court, that it should be lawfull to anie man to come into the court, and to inferre, accuse, and declare what euidence he could, against the lord iustice but none came Then passed a decrée by the councell, commanding all bishops, abbats, priors, and the maiors of Dublin, Corke, Limerike, Waterford, and Droghedagh, the shirifs, knights, & seneschals of euerie shire, to appeare at Dublin. From amongst all these, they appointed six inquisitors, which examining the bishops and other persons aforesaid singularlie one by one, found that with an vniuersall consent they deposed for the prior, affirming that (to their iudgements) he was a zelous and a faithfull child of the catholike church In the meane time, Arnold le Powre the prisoner deceased in the castell, & bicause he stood vnpurged, long he laie vnburied

In the yeare one thousand thrée hundred twentie and nine, Iohn de Birmingham earle of Louth, and his brother Peter, with many other of that surname, and Richard Talbot of Malahide were slaine on Whitsun euen at Balibragan by men of the countrie Also the lord Thomas Butler, and diuerse other noblemen were slaine by Mac Gogoghdan & other Irishmen néere to Molinger For the Irish as well in Leinster as in Meth made insurrections in that season, and so likewise did they in Mounster vnder the leading of Obren, whom William earle of Vlster and Iames earle of Ormond vanquished So outragious were the Leinster Irish, that in one church they burnt foure score innocent soules, asking no more but the life of their priest then at masse, whome they notwithstanding sticked with their iauelins, spurned the host, and wasted all with fire, neither forced they of the popes interdiction, nor anie ecclesiasticall censures denounced against them (matters of no small consideration among them namelie in those daies) but maliciouslie perseuered in the course of their furious rage, till the citizens of Wexford somewhat tamed them, and slue foure hundred of them in one skirmish, the rest fleing were all drenched in the water of Slane In the yeare one thousand thrée hundred and thirtie, the earle of Vlster with a great armie made a iournie against Obren, and the prior of Kilmainan lord iustice put Maurice Fitzthomas earle of Desmond in prison in the marshalseie, out of the which he fréelie escaped, and the lord Hugh Lacie returned into Ireland, and obteined the kings peace and fauour.

1329 — *The earle of Louth slaine.* — *The lord Butler slaine* — 1330 — *The prior of Kilmainan lord iustice*

In the yeare one thousand thrée hundred thirtie and one, the earle of Vlster passed ouer into England, and great slaughter was made vpon the Irish in Okenslie Also the castell of Arclo was taken by the Irishmen, and great slaughter made of the English in the Cowlagh by Otothell and others Also the lord Anthonie Lucie was sent ouer lord iustice into Ireland, and great slaughter was made of the Irish at Thurlis by the knights of the countrie, & at Finnath in Meth, there were manie of them slaine by the English, but yet was the castell of Fernis taken and burnt by the Irish On the feast daie of the assumption of our ladie, which falleth on the fifteenth of August, Maurice Fitzthomas earle of Desmond was apprehended at Limerike by the lord iustice, and sent vnto the castell of Dublin Moreouer, the lord iustice tooke sir William Birmingham at Clomell by a wile, whilest he was sicke in his bed, & sent him (togither with his sonne Walter Birmingham) vnto the castell of Dublin, the thirtith of Aprill In the yeare one thousand three hundred thirtie and two the said sir William was hanged at Dublin, but Walter was deliuered by reason he was within orders

1331 — *Anthonie Lucie lord iustice* — *The earle of Desmond apprehended.* — 1332 — *William Birmingham executed*

Campion following such notes as he hath séene, writeth that the death of this William Birmingham chanced in time of the gouernement of William Outlaw prior

Campion.

of Kilmainan, being lieutenant vnto Iohn lord Darcie, that was made lord iustice (as the said Campion hath noted) in the yeare one thousand thrée hundred twentie and nine. Although Marlburrow affirmeth that he came thither to beare that office, in the yeare one thousand thrée hundred thirtie and two, after the lord Lucie was discharged, as hereafter shall be recited. But whensoeuer, or vnder whome soeuer Birmingham was executed, he was accounted an od knight, and such a one as for his valiancie, his match was not lightlie to be anie where found. The castell of Clonmore was taken the same yeare by the Englishmen, and the castell of Bonrath was destroid by the Irish of Thomond. Also Henrie de Mandeuill was taken and sent prisoner to be safelie kept in Dublin. Likewise Walter Burgh with two of his bretheren were taken in Connagh by the earle of Vlster, and sent to the castell of Norburgh.

The lord Darcie iustice. This yeare the lord Antonie Lucie was discharged of his roome by the king, and so returned with his wife & children into England, and the lord Iohn Darcie was sent ouer lord iustice in Lucies place, and great slaughter was made vpon Brien Obren, and Mac Arthie in Mounster, by the English of that countrie. This Iohn Darcie (as should appeare by gifts bestowed vpon him by the king) was in singular fauour with him. Amongst other things which he had of the kings gift, we find that he had the manors of Louth, and Bahogarie, and other lands in Ireland which belonged to The earle of Ew the earle of Ew. And for that the said earle was a Frenchman, and tooke part with Philip de Valois the kings enimie, they were seized into the kings hand. The earle of Desmond vpon suerties was set at libertie, and by the parlement holden at Dublin 1333 A parlement in this yeare 1333, was sent ouer into England vnto the king, and William erle of Vlster a yoong gentleman of twentie yeares of age, in going towards Knockfergus the seauenth of Iune, was slaine neere to the foords in Vlster by his owne people, but his wife and daughter escaped into England: and the daughter was after maried vnto the lord Lionell the kings sonne. She deceased afterwards at Dublin, and left a daughter behind hir that was his heire, maried to Roger Mortimer earle of March, and lord of Trim.

This murther was procured by Robert Fitzmartine Mandeuill, who was the first that presumed to giue to the earle anie wound. To reuenge the death of this earle of The earle of Vlster slaine Vlster (slaine as yée haue heard beside Knockfergus) the lord iustice Darcie with a great power went into Vlster, to pursue those that through Mandeuils seditious tumults had so traitorouslie murthered their lord. At his setting forward, the said Sir Thomas Burgh iustice Darcie appointed sir Thomas Burgh treasuror, to gouerne as lieutenant to him in his absence. When the lord iustice had punished the traitors in Vlster, he passed The lord iustice inuadeth Scotland. ouer into Scotland, there to make warre against the Scots that were enimies at that present to the king of England, and on the feast daie of saint Margaret, great slaughter was made of the Scots by the Irishmen: and so what by the king in one part, and the lord iustice of Ireland in another, Scotland was in maner wholie conquered, and Edward Balioll was established king of Scotland. The lord iustice might haue possessed the Iles if they had béene worth the kéeping: into the which Iles, except the said Darcie and the earle of Sussex late lieutenant of Ireland, no gouernor at anie time yet aduentured. At Darcies comming backe into Ireland, and exercising the office of lord iustice, he deliuered Walter Birmingham out of the castell of Dublin.

1336 In the yeare 1336, and tenth of Edward the thirds reigne, on S. Laurence daie, the Irish of Connagh were discomfited and put to flight by the Englishmen of the 1337 countrie there, with the losse of one Englishman, and ten thousand of the enimies. The lord Iohn Charleton baron came into Ireland to be lord iustice, and with him Sir Iohn Charleton iustice his brother Thomas bishop of Hereford lord chancellor, and Iohn Rice lord treasuror, and

and two hundred Welshmen souldiors. The bishop was ordeined afterward lord 1338
iustice, in whose time all the Irish of Ireland were at defiance with the English, and The bishop of Hereford lord
shortlie brought againe into quiet by the earles of Kildare and Desmond. The lord iustice
Iohn Darcie by the kings letters patents was (during life) ordeined lord iustice of 1340 Iohn Darcie lord
Ireland, in the fourteenth yeare of king Edward the thirds reigne, which king abused iustice during life
by euill counsell and sinister informers, called in vnder his signet roiall, the fran- Calling in of liberties
chises, liberties and grants, whatsoeuer had béene deuised, made and ratified to the
realme of Ireland, and to euerie each person thereof. This reuoking of liberties was
displeasantlie taken. The English of birth and the English of blood falling at words,
were diuided into factions about it, for which contention the Irish still waited, so as
the realme was euen vpon the point to giue ouer all, and to rebell. For redresse
whereof, the lord iustice called a parlement at Dublin, to the which the nobles
refused to come, and in quiet wise assembled themselues togither at Kilkennie,
where they with the commons agreed vpon certeine questions to be demanded of the
king by waie of supplication, signifieng in the same partlie their greefes. Which
questions were in effect as followeth.

1. How a realme of warre might be gouerned by one both vnskilfull and vnable Articles or questions
in all warlike seruice?

2. How an officer vnder the king, that entered verie poore, might in one yeare
grow to more excessiue wealth, than men of great patrimonie and liuelihood in
manie yeares?

3. How it chanced, that sith they were all called lords of their owne, that the
souereigne lord of them all was not a pennie the richer for them?

The cheefe of them that thus seemed to repine with the present gouernment, was
Thomas Fitzmaurice earle of Desmond, through whose maintenance and bearing
out of the matter, the countrie was in great trouble, so as it had not lightlie beene
séene, that such contrarietie in minds and disliking had appeared amongst those of
the English race, in that realme at anie time before. Héerewith Rafe Vffort was sent 1343
ouer lord iustice, who bringing his wife with him, the countesse of Vlster arriued Rafe Vffort lord
about the thirtéenth of Julie. This man was verie rigorous, and through persuasion iustice
(as was said) of his wife, he was more extreame and couetous than otherwise he The countesse of Vlster.
would haue béene, a matter not to be forgotten. For if this ladie had beene as
readie to mooue hir husband to haue shewed himselfe gentle and mild in his
gouernement, as she was bent to pricke him forward vnto sharpe dealings and rigorous procéedings, she had beene now aswell reported of, as she is infamed by their
pens that haue registred the doomings of those times. But to the purpose. This
Vffort lord iustice, in paine of forfeiture of all his lands, commanded the earle of The earle of Desmond
Desmond to make his personall appearance at a parlement, which he called to
be holden at Dublin, there to begin the seuenth of Iune. And bicause the earle
refused to come according to the summons, he raised the kings standard, and with
an armie marched into Mounster, and there seized the earles possessions into
the kings hands, letting them foorth to farme for an annuall rent vnto other
persons.

And whilest he yet remained in Mounster, he deuised waies how to haue the earle
of Desmond apprehended: which being brought to passe, he afterward deliuered
him vpon mainprise of these suerties whose names insue. William de Burgh earle of Suerties for the earle of Desmond.
Vlster, Iames Butler earle of Ormond, Richard Tute, Nicholas Verdon, Morice
Rochford, Eustace le Powre, Gerald de Rochford, Iohn Fitzrobert Powre, Robert
Barrie, Maurice Fitzgerald, Iohn Wellesleie, Walter le Fant, Richard Rokelleie,
Henrie Traherne, Roger Powre, Iohn Lenfant, Roger Powre, Matthew Fitzhenrie,
Richard Walleis, Edmund Burgh sonne to the earle of Vlster, knights. Dauid Barrie

William,

William Fitzgirald, Foulke de Fraxinus, Robert Fitzmaurice, Henrie Fitzberkleie, Iohn Fitzgeorge de Roch, Thomas de Lees de Burgh. These (as yée haue heard) were bound for the earle. And bicause he made default, the lord iustice verelie tooke the aduantage of the bond against the mainpernours, foure of them onelie excepted, the two earles and two knights.

Vffort euill spoken of. The lord iustice is charged with strict dealing by writers in this behalfe, for that the same persons had assisted him in his warres against Desmond. But trulie if we shall consider the matter with indifferencie, he did no more than law and reason required. For if euerie suertie vpon forfeiture of his bond should be forborne, that otherwise dooth his duetie, what care would men haue either to procure suerties or to become suerties themselues? But such is the affection of writers, speciallie when they haue conceiued anie misliking towards those of whome they take occasion to speake, so as manie a worthie man hath béene defamed, and with slander greatlie defaced in things wherein he rather hath deserued singular commendation. But

Ioie conceiued for the death of the lord iustice Vffort. howsoeuer this matter was handled touching the earle of Desmond, vpon the death of the lord iustice, which insued the next yeare, bonfiers were made, and great ioy shewed through all the relme of Ireland. His ladie verelie (as should appeare) was but a miserable woman, procuring him to extortion and briberie. Much he abridged the prerogatiues of the church, and was so hated, that euen in the sight of the countrie he was robbed without rescue by Mac Cartie, notwithstanding he gathered power, and dispersed those rebels of Vlster. Robert Darcie was ordeined iustice by

1346 Robert Darcie lord iustice. the councell till the kings letters came to sir Iohn Fitzmaurice, who released Fitzthomas earle of Kildare left in durance by Vffort at his death. Fitzmaurice continued

Iohn Fitzmorice iustice. I. Birmingham iustice. not long, but was discharged, and the lord Walter Birmingham elected to succeed in that roome, who procured a safe conduct for Desmond to plead his cause before the king, by whom he was liberallie intreated, and allowed towards his expenses there twentie shillings a day at the princes charge. In consideration of which courtesie shewed to his kinsman, the earle of Kildare, accompanied with diuerse lords, knights, and chosen horssemen, serued the king at Calis, a towne thought impregnable, & returned after the winning thereof in great pompe and iollitie.

1347 *Record Tur.* We find that Thomas Berkeleie, and Reinold lord Cobham, and sir Morice Berkleie became mainpernours for the said earle of Desmond, that he should come into

1348 England, and abide such triall as the law would award. Iohn Archer prior of Kil-

The prior of Kilmainan. Baron Carew iustice. Sir Thomas Rokesbie iustice. *Record Tur.* mainan was substituted lieutenant to the lord iustice. To whom succéeded Baron Carew, and after Carew followed sir Thomas Rokesbie knight, vnto whom was assigned aboue his ordinarie retinue of twentie men of armes, a supplie of ten men of armes, and twentie archers on horssebacke, so long as it should be thought néedfull. Great mortalitie chanced this yeare, as in other parts of the world, so espe-

1349 ciallie in places about the seacoasts of England and Ireland. In the yeare following departed this life Alexander Bignor archbishop of Dublin. And the same yeare was

Iohn de S. Paule archbishop of Dublin. Iohn de saint Paule consecrated archbishop of that sée. This yeare deceased Kem-

1350 Kemwrike Shereman. wrike Shereman sometime maior of Dublin, a great benefactor to euerie church and religious house within twentie miles round about the citie. His legacies to the poore and others, beside his liberalitie shewed in his life time, amounted to thrée thousand marks.

Sir Robert Sauage. In this season dwelled in Vlster a welthie knight one sir Robert Sauage, who the rather to preserue his owne, began to wall and fortifie his manor houses with castels and piles against the Irish enimie, exhorting his heire Henrie Sauage to applie that worke so beneficiall for himselfe & his posteritie. "Father (quoth yoong Sauage) I remember the prouerbe 'Better a castell of bones than of stones.' Where strength & courage of valiant men are prest to helpe vs, neuer will I (by the grace of God) cumber

cumber my selfe with dead walles. My fort shall be where soeuer yoong bloods be stirring, & where I find roome to fight." The father in a fume let lie the building, and forsware to go anie further forward in it. But yet the want therof and such like hath beene the decaie as well of the Sauages, as of all the English gentlemen in Vlster: as the lacke also of walled townes is one of the principall occasions of the rude wildnesse in other parts of Ireland.

This Sauage, hauing prepared an armie against the Irish, allowed to euerie souldier before they should buckle with the enimie, a mightie draught of *Aqua vitæ*, wine, or old ale, and killed in prouision for their returne, béefe, venison, and fowle, great plentie: which doings diuerse of his capteins misliked, bicause they considered the successe of warre to be vncerteine, and therefore estéemed it better policie to poison the cates, or to doo them awaie, than to kéepe the same: and happilie to féed a sort of roges with such princelie food, if ought should happen to themselues in this aduenture of so few against so manie. Herat smiled the gentleman and said, "Tush ye are too full of enuie: this world is but an in, to the which ye haue no speciall interest, but are onelie tenants at will of the Lord. If it please him to command vs from it as it were from our lodging, and to set other good fellowes in our roomes, what hurt shall it be for vs to leaue them some meat for their suppers? Let them hardlie win it & weare it. If they enter our dwellings, good maner would no lesse but to welcome them with such fare as the countrie bréedeth, and with all my heart much good may it doo them. Notwithstanding I presume so far vpon your noble courages, that verelie my mind giueth me we shall returne at night, & banket our selues with our owne store." And so did, hauing slaine 3000 Irishmen.

1355
The earle of Desmond lord iustice deceased.
Thomas Rokesbie lord iustice his saieng.

In the yeare 1355 deceased Maurice Fitzthomas earle of Desmond lord iustice of Ireland, who had that office of the kings grant for terme of life. After him succeeded in that roome Thomas de Rokesbie, a knight, sincere and vpright of conscience, who being controlled for suffering himselfe to be serued in tréene cups, answered: "Those homelie cups & dishes paie trulie for that they conteine: I had rather drinke out of tréene cups & paie gold and siluer, than drinke out of gold & make woodden paiment." This yeare began great variance betwixt Richard Rafe primat of Armagh, & foure orders of begging friers, which ended at length by the deaths of the said Richard Rafe, and Richard Kilminton, in the yeare 1360. Rafe deceasing in the popes court, and Kilminton in England. Almerike de S. Amand, Iohn or (as other haue) Iames Butler earle of Ormond, and Maurice Fitzthomas earle of Kildare, were appointed lord iustices of Ireland by turnes. In Ormonds time, and in the thrée and twentith yeare of king Edward the thirds reigne, order was taken that the Irish lords should remaine and dwell in their houses on the marches, to defend the subiects from inuasions of enimies. And further, proclamation went foorth, that no meere Irish borne should be made maior, bailiffe, porter, officer, or minister in anie towne or place within the English dominions: nor that anie archbishop, abbat, prior, or anie other being of the kings allegiance, vpon forfeiture of all that he might forfeit, should aduance anie that was méere Irish borne to the roome of a canon, or to haue anie other ecclesiasticall benefice that laie among the English subiects.

1357
Dissention betwixt the primat of Armagh, & the foure orders of friers.
Thrée lord iustices.
Record Tur.

The earle of Kildare lord iustice.

To Maurice Thomas earle of Kildare, when he was ordeined lord iustice, the kings letters assigned in yearelie fee for his office 500 pounds, with condition, that the said gouernour should find twentie great horsses to serue in the field, he himselfe to be the twentith man in going against the enimie: which allowance and conditions in those daies (so farre as I can gesse) should séeme to be ordinarie to the office.

Lionell duke of Clarence.

Lionell duke of Clarence sonne to king Edward the third, came ouer into Ireland to be be lord iustice there, and was in right of his wife earle of Vlster. He published an inhibition to all of the Irish birth not once to approch his armie, nor to be in anie wise imploied in seruice of the wars. He vanquished Obren, but yet sudenlie (no man vnderstanding how) an hundred of his souldiers were wanting as they laie in garrison, the losse of whom was thought to be occasioned by that displeasant decree afore rehearsed. Wherevpon he tooke better aduise, and receiued the Irish into like fauour, as other lieutenants had them in before that present, shewing a tender loue towards them all, and so euer after prospered in his affaires. He created diuerse knights, as Preston, now knowne by the name of the familie of Gormanston, Holiewood, Talbot, Cusac, de la Hide, Patrike, Robert and Iohn de Fraxinis, all these being gentlemen of worthie fame in chiualrie. The exchequer he remooued to Catherlagh, & bestowed in furnishing that towne fiue hundred pounds.

1362 In the yeare 1362 Iohn de S. Paule archbishop of Dublin departed this life the fift ides of September. And in the yeare following was Thomas Minot consecrated archbishop of that place. Girald Fitzmaurice earle of Desmond was appointed lord iustice, vntill the comming of the lord Windsor, the first lieutenant in Ireland, who came ouer in the yeare 1369. This Windsore called a parlement at Kilkennie, in the which was granted to the king a subsidie of three thousand pounds to be leuied of the people, subiects to the king in that land. And in an other parlement holden by him at Baldoill they granted two thousand pounds to be likewise leuied. Which said sums were granted of the méere and frée good wils of the nobles and communaltie of the land, towards the maintenance of the kings expenses in his warres. Yet the king in the three and fortith yeare of his reigne, directing his letters vnto the said lord Windsor, cōmanded him to surcease from leuieng the foresaid monie, although afterwards he commanded againe that the arrerages should be leuied and paid to his lieutenant the said Windsor.

1367 The lord Windsor lieutenant. 1369. *Record Turris.* A parlement. A subsidie.

The third pestilence in Ireland made awaie a great number of people. In the yeare 1370 the lord Gerald Fitzmorice earle of Desmond, and the lord Iohn Fitzrichard, and the lord Iohn Fitziohn, and manie other noble men were slaine by Obren, and Mac Connard of Thomond in the moneth of Iulie. In the yeare 1372 sir Richard Ashton was sent ouer to be lord iustice in Ireland. In the yeare following great warre was raised betwixt the English of Meth, and Offeroll, in the which manie vpon both sides were slaine. In Maie, the lord Iohn Husseie baron of Galtrim, Iohn Fitzrichard shiriffe of Meth, and William Dalton were slaine in Kinaleigh. In the yeare 1375 Thomas archbishop of Dublin departed this life, and the same yeare was Robert de Wikeford consecrated archbishop there.

Mortalitie of people. 1370. Conhur. 1372. Sir Richard Ashton lord iustice. 1373. Slaughter. 1375.

Richard the second.

1381 EDMUND Mortimer earle of March & Vlster was made the kings lieutenant in Ireland. In the yeare 1383 a great mortalitie reigned in that countrie. This was called the fourth pestilence. In the yéere 1385 Dublin bridge fell. Beside Edmund Mortimer earle of March, Campion affirmeth, that in this Richard the seconds daies, there are iustices and lieutenants of Ireland speciallie recorded, Roger Mortimer sonne to the said Edmund, Philip Courtneie the kings cousine, Iames earle of Ormond, and Robert Vere earle of Oxford, marquesse of Dublin lord chamberleine, who was also created duke of Ireland by parlement, and was credited with the whole dominion of the realme by grant for tearme of life, without paieng anie thing therefore, passing all writs, and placing all officers, as chancellor, treasuror, chiefe iustice, admerall, his owne lieutenant, and other inferiour charges vnder his owne Teste. In the

The earle of March the kings lieutenant. 1383. 1385.

the yeare 1390, Robert de Wikeford archbishop of Dublin departed this life, and the 1390
same yeare was Robert Waldebie translated vnto the archbishop of Dublin an Augustine frier.

In the yeare 1394, king Richard sore afflicted and troubled in mind with sorrow 1394
for the decease of his wife queene Anne, that departed this life at Whitsuntide last King Richard goeth ouer into Ireland
past, not able without teares to behold his palaces and chambers of estate that represented vnto him the solace past, & doubled his sorow, sought some occasion of businesse, and now about Michaelmas passed ouer into Ireland, where diuerse lords and princes of Vlster renewed their homages, & placing Roger Mortimer erle of Roger Mortimer
March his lieutenant, returned about Shrouetide. In the yeare 1397, Richard de lord lieutenant. *Thom. WalS.*
Northalis archbishop of Dublin departed this life, that was the same yeare from 1397
another see remooued thither: he was a frier of the order of the Carmelites.

The same yeare Thomas de Cranlie was chosen and consecrated archbishop of Dublin. Also sir Thomas de Burgh, and sir Walter de Birmingham, slue six hun- Six hundred
dred Irishmen, with their capteine Macdo vne Morcouer. Edmund earle of March Irishmen slaine.
lord deputie of Ireland, with the aid of the erle of Ormond, wasted the countrie of an Irish lord called Obren, and at the winning of his cheefe house he made seuen knights, to wit, sir Christopher Preston, sir Iohn Bedlow, sir Edmund Londores, sir Iohn Londores, sir William Nugent, Walter de la Hide, and Robert Cadell. But after this it chanced, that on the Ascension daie, certeine Irishmen slue fortie Englishmen, and among them these were accounted as principall, Iohn Fitzwilliams, Thomas Talbot, and Thomas Cambrie. But shortlie after Roger Mortimer earle of March and Vlster the kings lieutenant was slaine, with diuerse other, by Obren and other Irishmen of Leinster at Kenlis. Then was Roger Greie elected lord iustice of Roger Greie lord iustice of Ireland
Ireland.

The same yeare on the feast daie of saint Marke the pope, the duke of Surreie landed in Ireland, and with him came sir Thomas Cranlie the archbishop of Dublin. King Richard informed of the vnrulie parts and rebellious sturres of the Irishmen, minded to appease the same, and speciallie to reuenge the death of the earle of 1398
March: wherevpon with a nauie of two hundred sails he passed ouer into Ireland, King Richard passeth the second time ouer into Ireland
and landed at Waterford on a sundaie, being the morrow after saint Petronilla the virgins day. The fridaie after his arriuall at Ford in Kenlis within the towne of Kildare, there were slaine two hundred Irishmen by Ienicho de Artois a Gascoigne, and such Englishmen as he had with him: and the morrow after, the citizens of Dublin brake into the countrie of Obren, slue thirtie & three of the enimies, and tooke fourescore men with children.

The fourth kalends of Iulie, king Richard came to Dublin, and remained there The king commeth to Dublin
for a time, during the which diuerse lords and princes of the countrie came in and submitted themselues vnto him, by whome they were courteouslie vsed, and trained to honourable demeanor and ciuilitie, as much as the shortnes of time would permit, See more hereof in England
as in the English historie you maie find set foorth more at large. Whilest king Richard thus laie in Dublin to reduce Ireland into due subiection, he was aduertised that Henrie duke of Lancaster, that latelie before had beene banished, was returned, & ment to bereaue him of the crowne. The sonne of which duke, togither with the duke of Gloucesters sonne, the king shut vp within the castell of Trim, and then taking the seas, he returned and landed in Wales, where he found his defense so weake, and vnsure, that finallie he came into his aduersaries hands, and was deposed by authoritie of parlement, and then was the said duke of Lancaster admitted to reigne in his place.

Henrie the fourth.

1400 AT Whitsuntide in the yeare 1400, which was the first yeare of the reigne of
Henrie the fourth, the conestable of Dublin castell, and diuerse other at Stanford
in Vlster, fought by sea with Scots, where manie Englishmen were slaine and
1401 drowned. In the second yeare of king Henrie the fourth, sir Iohn Stanleie the
Sir Iohn Stanleie lord lieutenant. kings lieutenant in Ireland returned into England, leauing his vnder lieutenant there
Sir Stephan Scroope. sir William Stanleie. The same yeare on Bartholomew éeuen, sir Stephan Scroope,
deputie vnto the lord Thomas of Lancaster the kings brother, and lord lieutenant of
Ireland, arriued there to supplie the roome of Alexander bishop of Meth, that
exercised the same office vnder the said lord Thomas of Lancaster, before the
comming of this sir Stephan Scroope, which sir Stephan for his violence and extortion before time vsed in the same office vnder king Richard, was sore cried out vpon
by the voices of the poore people, insomuch that the ladie his wife hearing of such
exclamations, would in no wise continue with him there, except he would receiue a
solemne oth on the bible, that wittinglie he should wrong no christian creature
in that land, but dulie and trulie he should sée paiment made for all expenses: and
hereof (she said) she had made a vow to Christ so determinatlie, that vnlesse it were
on his part firmelie promised, she could not without perill of soule go with him.
Hir husband assented and accomplished hir request effectuallie, recouered a good
opinion for his vpright deling, reformed his caters & puruerors, enriched the countrie, mainteined a plentifull house, remission of great offenses, remedies for persons
indangered to the prince, pardons of lands and liues he granted so charitablie and
so discréetlie, that his name was neuer recited among them without manie blessings
and praiers, and so chéerefullie they were readie to serue him against the Irish vpon
all necessarie occasions. The lord Thomas of Lancaster the kings sonne, and lord
lieutenant of Ireland, arriued the same yeare at Dublin, vpon saint Brices daie.
The Irish ouerthrowne by the maior of Dublin. The maior of Dublin Iohn Drake, with a band of his citizens neere to Bre, slue
foure thousand of the Irish outlawes (as Campion noteth out of the records of
Christs church) but Marburrow speaketh onelie of 493, and these being all men of
warre. The verie same daie that this victorie was atchiued, to wit, the eleuenth
day of Iulie, the church of the friers prechers of Dublin was dedicated by the archbishop of that citie. The same yeare in September, a parlement was holden at
Dublin, during the which in Vrgile sir Bartholomew Verdon knight, Iames White,
Stephan Gernon, and other their complices, slue the shriffe of Louth Iohn Dowdall.
1403 In the yere 1403, in Maie, sir Walter Betterleie steward of Vlster, a right valiant
knight was slaine, and to the number of thirtie other with him. The same yeare
about the feast of saint Martin, the lord Thomas of Lancaster the kings sonne
Stephan Scroope. returned into England leauing the lord Stephan Scroope his deputie there: who also
The earle of Ormond lord iustice. in the beginning of Lent sailed ouer into England, and then the lords of the land
chose the earle of Ormond to be lord iustice.
1404 In the fift yere of Henrie the fourth, Iohn Colton archbishop of Armagh the seuen
The archbishop of Armagh deceased. & twentith of Aprill departed this life, vnto whom Nicholas Sloning succéeded.
The same yeare on the daie of saint Vitale the martyr, the parlement of Dublin
began before the earle of Ormond then lord iustice of Ireland, where the statutes
of Kilkennie and Dublin were confirmed, and likewise the charter of Ireland. In
1405 the sixt yeare of Henrie the fourth, in the moneth of Maie, thrée Scotish barks
were taken, two at Green castell, and one at Alkeie, with capteine Macgolagh.
The same yeare the merchants of Drodagh entered Scotland, and tooke preies and
pledges. Also on the éeuen of the feast day of the seuen brethren, Oghgard was
burnt

burnt by the Irish. And in Iune sir Stephan Scroope that was come againe into Ireland, returned estsoones into England, leauing the earle of Ormond lord iustice of Ireland. About the same time they of Dublin entered Scotland at saint Ninian, and valiantlie behaued themselues against the enimies, and after crossing the seas, directed their course into Wales, and did much hurt to the Welshmen, bringing from thense the shrine of saint Cubins, & placed it in the church of the Trinitie in Dublin. Iames Butler earle of Ormond died at Baligam, whilest he was lord iustice, vnto whom succeeded Gerald earle of Kildare.

The citizens of Dublin inuade Scotland. *They inuade Wales.* *The earle of Ormond deceased.*

In the seuenth yeare of king Henrie on Corpus Christi day, the citizens of Dublin with the countrie people about them, manfullie vanquished the Irish enimies, and slue diuerse of them, and tooke two ensignes or standards, bringing with them to Dublin the heads of those whom they had slaine. The same yeare the prior of Conall, in the plaine of Kildare, fought manfullie with the Irish, & vanquished two hundred that were well armed, slaieng part of them, and chasing the residue out of the field, and the prior had not with him past the number of twentie Englishmen: but God (as saith mine author) assisted those that put their trust in him. The same yeare after Michaelmas, Stephan Scroope deputie iustice to the lord Thomas of Lancaster the kings sonne, and his lieutenant of Ireland, came againe ouer into Ireland. And in the feast of saint Hilarie was a parlement holden at Dublin, which in Lent after was ended at Trim. And Meiler de Birmingham slue Cathole Oconhur about the end of Februarie. In the yere 1407, a certeine false and heathenish wretch an Irishman, named Mac Adam Mac Gilmore, that had caused fortie churches to be destroied, as he that was neuer christened, and therefore called Corbi, chanced to take prisoner one Patrike Sauage, and receiued for his ransome two thousand markes, though afterwards he slue him, togither with his brother Richard.

Hen. Marlb. *A parlement at Dublin.* 1407 *Corbi what it signifieth.*

The same yeare in the feast of the exaltation of the crosse, Stephan Scroope deputie to the lord Thomas of Lancaster, with the earles of Ormond and Desmond, and the prior of Kilmainan, and diuerse other capteins and men of warre of Meth, set from Dublin, and inuaded the land of Mac Murch, where the Irish came into the field and skirmished with them, so as in the former part of the daie they put the English power to the woorse, but at length the Irish were vanquished and chased, so that Onolan with his son and diuerse others were taken prisoners. But the English capteins aduertised here, that the Burkens and Okeroll in the countie of Kilkennie, had for the space of two daies togither doone much mischiet, they rode with all spéed vnto the towne of Callan, and there incountering with the aduersaries, manfullie put them to flight, slue Okeroll, and eight hundred others. There went a tale, and beleeued of manie, that the sunne stood still for a space that daie, till the Englishmen had ridden six miles: so much was it thought that God fauoured the English part in this enterprise, if we shall beléeue it.

Okeroll slaine.

The same yeare the lord Stephan Scroope passed once againe ouer into England, and Iames Butler earle of Ormond was elected by the countrie lord iustice of Ireland. In the daies of this K. Henrie the fourth, the inhabitants of Corke being sore afflicted with perpetuall oppressions of their Irish neighbors, complained themselues in a generall writing directed to the lord Rutland and Corke, the kings deputie there, and to the councell of the realme then assembled at Dublin: which letter bicause it openeth a window to behold the state of those parties, and of the whole realme of Ireland in those daies, we haue thought good to set downe here, as it hath beene enterd by Campion, according to the copie deliuered to him by Francis Agard esquire, one of the queenes maiesties priuie councell in Ireland.

A letter

A letter from Corke out of an old record that beareth no date

"IT may please your wisedomes to haue pittie on vs the kings poore subiects within the countie of Corke, or else we are cast awaie for euer. For where there are in this countie these lords by name, beside knights, esquiers, gentlemen, and yeomen, to a great number that might dispend yearelie eight hundred pounds, sixe hundred pounds, foure hundred pounds, two hundred pounds, one hundred pounds, an hundred markes, twentie markes, twentie pounds, ten pounds, some more, some lesse, to a great number, besides these lords. First the lord marques Caro, his yearelie reuenues was beside Dorseie hauen and other creekes, two thousand two hundred pounds sterling. The lord Barnewale of Béerhauen, his yearelie reuenue was beside Bodie hauen and other creekes, one thousand six hundred pounds sterling. The lord Wogan of the great castell, his yearelie reuenue beside his hauens and creekes, thirtéene thousand pounds. The lord Balram of Enfort, his yearelie reuenue beside hauens and creekes, one thousand three hundred pounds sterling. The lord Curcie of Kelbretton his yearelie reuenue beside hauens and creekes, one thousand two hundred pounds sterling. The lord Mandeuile of Barenstelie, his yearelie reuenue beside havens and creekes, one thousand two hundred pounds sterling. The lord Arundell of the Strand, his yearelie reuenue beside hauens and creekes, one thousand fiue hundred pounds sterling. The lord Barod of the gard, his yearelie reuenues beside hauens & creekes one thousand one hundred pounds sterling. The lord Stemeie of Baltimore, his yearelie reuenue beside hauens and creekes, eight hundred pounds sterling. The lord Roch of Poole castell, his yearelie reuenues besides hauens and creekes, ten thousand pounds sterling. The kings maiestie hath the lands of the late yoong Barrie by forfeiture, the yearelie reuenue whereof, besides, two riuers and creekes, and all other casualties, is one thousand eight hundred pounds sterling.

I thinke rather Greene castell

"And that at the end of this parlement, your lordship, with the kings most noble councell may come to Corke, & call before you all these lords, and other Irishmen, and bind them in paine of losse of life, lands and goods, that neuer one of them doo make warre vpon an other, without licence or commandement of you my lord deputie, and the kings councell, for the vtter destruction of these parts is that onelie cause. And once all the Irishmen, and the kings enimies were driuen into a great vallie called Clane onght, betwixt two great mounteines called Maccort, or the leprous Iland, and there they liued long and manie yeares with their white meat, till at the last these English lords fell at variance amongst themselues, and then the weakest part tooke certeine Irishmen to take their part, and so vanquished their enimies. And thus fell the English lords at warre among themselues, till the Irishmen were stronger than they, and draue them awaie, and now haue the countrie whole vnder them, but that the lord Roch, the lord Barrie, and the lord Curcie onelie remaine with the least part of their ancestors possessions: and yoong Barrie is there vpon the kings portion, paieng his grace neuer a pennie rent. Wherefore we the kings poore subiects of the citie of Corke, Kinsale, and Yoghall, desire your lordship to send hither too good iustices to sée this matter ordred, and some English capteins with twentie Englishmen that may be capteins ouer vs all: and we will rise with them to redresse these enormities all at our owne costs. And if you will not come nor send, we will send ouer to our liege lord the king, and complaine on you all." Thus far that letter.

The citie of Corke.

And (as saith Campion) at this daie the citie of Corke is so incumbred with vnquiet neighbors

neighbors of great power, that they are forced to gard their gates continualle, &
to kéepe them shut at seruice times, at meales, and from sun setting to sun
rising, not suffering anie stranger to enter the towne with his weapon, but to
leaue the same at a lodge appointed. They dare vnneth at anie time walke abroad
far from the towne for their recreation, except at seasons, and then with strength
of men furnished with armor and weapon for their safegard. They match in wedlocke
among themselues, so that welnéere the whole citie is alied and ioined togither in consanguinitie. But now to returne vnto the doomgs of the earle of Ormond that was
placed lord iustice in Scroops roome. We doo find that in the yeare 1408 he 1408
called a parlement at Dublin, in which the statutes of Kilkennie and Dublin A parlement at Dublin
were eftsoones renued, and certeine ordinances established vnder the great seale
of England against purueiors. The same yeare, the morrow after Lammas daie, The lord Thomas of Lancaster commeth ouer into Ireland
the lord Thomas of Lancaster sonne to king Henrie the fourth, lord lieutenant of
Ireland, landed at Carlingford, and in the wéeke following he came vnto Dublin,
and put the earle of Kildare vnder arest, comming to him with three of his
familie. He lost all his goods, being spoiled & rifled by the lord lieutenant his
seruants, & himselfe kept still in prison in the castell of Dublin, till he had paid 300
marks fine.

On the daie of saint Marcell the martyr deceased the lord Stephan Scroope at Tristel- The lord Scroope deceaseth
dermot. The same yeare also was the lord Thomas of Lancaster at Kilmainan wounded
(I know not how) and vnneth escaped with life, and after caused summons to be
giuen by proclamation, that all such as ought by their tenures to serue the
king, should assemble at Rosse. And after the feast of saint Hilarie, he held a
parlement at Kilkennie for a tallage to be granted. And after the thirtéenth of The lord Thomas returneth into England
March, he returned into England, leauing the prior of Kilmainan for his deputie
in Ireland. This yeare also Hugh Macgilmore was slaine in Cragfergus within
the church of the friers minors, which church he had before destroied, and broken
downe the glasse windowes to haue the iron bars, thorough which his enimies the
Sauages entred vpon him. This yeare being the tenth of Henrie the fourth, in 1409
Iune, Iames de Artois with the Englishmen slue foure score of the Irish in Vlster. Iames de Artois
This yeare king Henrie gaue the sword to the citie of Dublin, which citie was The sword giuen to the citie of Dublin
first gouerned (as appeareth by their ancient seale called *Signum præpositura*) by
a pronost, and in the thirtéenth of Henrie the third by a maior and two bai- Bailiffes changed into shiriffes
liffes, which were changed into shiriffes, by charter granted by Edward the sixt,
1547.

This maioraltie, both for state and charge of office, and for bountifull hospitalitie,
exceedeth anie citie in England, London excepted. In the yeare following, the 1410
one and twentith daie of Maie, a parlement began at Dublin, which lasted thrée
wéekes, the prior of Kilmainan sitting as lord iustice. The same yeare, the two
and twentith of Iune, the same iustice tooke the castels of Mibraclide, Oferoll,
and de la Mare. Ireland this yeare was sore afflicted for want of corne. The lord
iustice entred into the land of Obren with 1500 Kernes, of which number eight hundred A iournie made by the lord iustice
reuolted to the Irish, so that if the power of Dublin had not beene there, it had
gon euil with the lord iustice, and yet he escaped not without losse, for Iohn Der-
patrike was slaine there. In the yeare 1411, marriages were celebrated among the 1411
nobilitie in Ireland. William Preston married the daughter of Edward Paris, and Iohn Marriages
Wogan matched with the eldest daughter of Christopher Preston, and Walter de
la Hide with the second daughter of the same Christopher. In the yeare 1412, about 1412
the feast of Tiberitius and Valerianus, which falleth on the tenth of April, Oconthir Oconthir
did much mischiefe in Meth, and tooke 160 Englishmen. The same yeare Odoles
a knight, and Thomas Fitzmorice fought togither, and either slue other. The foure
and twentith of Maie, Robert Mounteine bishop of Meth departed this life, to The bishop of Meth deceaseth.
whome

The death of Henrie the fourth. whome succéeded Edward de Audiscie sometime archdecon of Cornwall. This yeare
on saint Cutberts daie king Henrie the fourth departed this life.

Henrie the fift.

1413 In the first yeare of this king, the fiue and twentith of September, landed in
Iohn Stanleie the kings lieutenant in Ireland. Ireland at Clawcarte, Iohn Stanlie the kings lieutenant of that land. He departed
this life the 18 of Ianuarie next insuing at Athird, in Latine called *Atrium Dei*.
Thomas Crauleie archbishop of Dublin. After his decease, Thomas Crauleie archbishop of Dublin was chosen lord iustice of
Ireland. Ianico de Artois led foorth a power against Magmors, a great lord of Ireland, but néere to a place called Inor manie Englishmen were slaine. The morrow
A parlement. after saint Matthias daie, a parlement began againe at Dublin, which continued
for the space of fiftéene daies, in which meane time the Irish did much hurt by
inuasions made into the English pale, and burning vp all the houses afore them
that stood in their waie, as their vsuall custome was in times of other parlements.
1414 Wherevpon a tallage was demanded, but not granted. In the yeare 1414, the Englishmen fought with the Irish neere to Kilka, and slue an hundred of the enimies, whilest
the archbishop being lord iustice in Tristeldermot, went in procession with his
cleargie, praieng for the good spéed of his men and other of the countrie
that were gone foorth to fight with the aduersaries. In the feast of saint Gordian
and Epimachus, to wit the tenth of Maie, were the English of Meth discomfited
by Oconthur and his Irish, where they slue Thomas Maureuar baron of Serin, and
Englishmen slaine. there were taken prisoners Christopher Fleming, Iohn Dardis, and diuerse others,
beside manie that were slaine.

Iohn lord Talbot of Sherfield. On saint Martins éeuen sir Iohn Talbot of Holomshire, lord Furniuale landed at
Dalkeie, the kings lieutenant in Ireland, a man of great honor. In the yeere one
1415 Robert Talbot deceaseth. thousand foure hundred and fiftéene in Nouember, Robert Talbot, a right noble
man that walled the suburbs of Kilkennie, departed this life. Also Patrike Baret
bishop of Fernis deceased, and was buried among the canons at Kenlis. This
yeare on the feast daie of Geruasius and Prothasius which falleth on the ninetéenth
of Iune, the lord lieutenants wife the ladie Furniuall was brought to bed at Finglasse
1416 of a sonne named Thomas. About the same time also Stephan Fleming archbishop
The archbishop of Armagh deceaseth. of Armagh departed this life, after whome succéeded Iohn Suanig. On the daie of
saint Laurence the lord Furniuals sonne Thomas Talbot that was borne at Finglasse in
Nouember last past, departed this life, and was buried in the quéere of the friers preachers
church in Dublin. About the same time the Irish fell vpon the Englishmen, and slue
manie of them, among other Thomas Balimore of Baliquelan was one. The par-
The parlement remooued to Trim. lement which the last yeare had béene called and holden at Dublin, was this
yeare remooued to Trim, & there began the eleuenth of Maie, where it continued
for the space of eleuen daies, in the which was granted to the lord lieutenant a
A subsidie. subsidie in monie.

In the yeare following, the archbishop of Dublin passed ouer into England, and
1417 The archbishop of Dublin deceased. deceased at Faringdon, but his bodie was buried in the new college at Oxford.
This man is greatlie praised for his liberalitie, he was a good almesman, a great
His praise. clerke, a doctor of diuinitie, an excellent preacher, a great builder, beautifull, tall
of stature, and sanguine of complexion. He was foure score and ten yeares of age
when he died, and had gouerned the church of Dublin in good quiet for the
1418 space of twentie yeeres. This yeare shortlie after Easter, the lord deputie spoiled
the tenants of Henrie Crus, and Henrie Bethat. Also at Olane on the
feast daie of saint Iohn and saint Paule, the erle of Kildare, sir Christopher
Preston,

Preston, and sir Iohn Bedlow were arrested and committed to ward within the castell of Trim, because they sought to commune with the prior of Kilmainan.

The nine and twentith of Iune Matthew Husseie baron of Galtrim deceased, & was buried at the friers preachers of Trim. In the yeare one thousand foure hundred

1419 & nineteene a roiall councell was holden at Naas, where was granted to the lord lieutenant a subsidie in monie. The same yeare vpon Cenethursdaie Othoell tooke foure hundred kine that belonged vnto Balmore, so breaking the peace contrarie to his oth. The fourth ides of Maie, Mac Murch chéefe capteine of his nation, and of all the Irish in Lemster was taken prisoner, and the same daie was sir Hugh Cokeseie made knight. The last of Maie the lord lieutenant, and the archbishop of Dublin with the maior rased the castell of Kenmie. The morrow after the feast daie of Processus and Martinianus, that is the twentith of Iune, the lord William de Burgh and other Englishmen slue fiue hundred Irishmen, & tooke Okellie. On the feast daie of Marie Magdalen the lord lieutenant Talbot returned into England, leauing his deputie there the archbishop of Dublin. This yeare about saint Laurence daie, diuerse went foorth of Ireland to serue the king in his warres of Normandie, as Thomas Butler that was prior of Kilmainan, and manie others. Iohn Fitzhenrie succéeded the said Butler in gouernment of the priorie of Kilmainan. The archbishop of Dublin that remained as lord deputie slue thirtie Irishmen néere vnto Rodiston. Also the thirteenth of Februarie Iohn Fitzhenrie prior of Kilmainan departed this life, and William Fitzthomas was chosen to succéed in his place, and was confirmed the morrow after saint Valentines daie.

A councell or parlement holden

Mac Murch taken prisoner.

Okellie taken.

The prior of Kilmainan went to serue the king in France.

1420 Iames Butler earle of Ormond appointed the kings lieutenant in Ireland, in place of Iohn lord Talbot and Furniuall, landed at Waterford about the fourth ides of Aprill and shortlie after his comming ouer, he caused a combat to be fought betwixt two of his cousins, of whom the one was slaine in that place, and the other carried awaie sore wounded. On saint Georges daie, he held a councell in Dublin, & summoned a parlement to begin there the seuenth of Iune. In the meane while he fetcht great booties out of the countries of the Irish lords, Oralie, Mac Mahun, and Magnois. But first yer we go further to shew what Marlburrow hath noted of the doings, whilest this earle of Ormond gouerned as the kings lieutenant in Ireland, we haue thought good to set downe what Campion also writeth thereof, as thus.

Iames Butler erle of Ormond lord lieutenant

A parlement summoned

In the red moore of Athie (the sunne almost lodged in the west, and miraculouslie standing still in his epicicle by the space of thrée houres, till the feat was accomplished, and no hole nor quakemire in all that bog annoieng either horsse or man of his part) he vanquished Omore and his terrible armie with a few of his owne meinie, and with the like number he ouercame Arthur Mac Morogh, at whose might & puissance all Lemster trembled. To the instruction of this mans worthinesse, the compiler of certeine precepts touching the rule of a common-wealth exciteth his lord the said earle in diuerse places of that worke incidentlie, eftsoons putting him in mind that the Irish are false by kind, that it were expedient, and a worke of charitie to execute vpon them wilfull and malicious transgressors the kings lawes somewhat sharplie, that Odempsie being winked at a while, abused that small time of sufferance to the iniurie of the earle of Kildare, intruding iniustlie vpon the castell of Leie, from whense the said deputie had iustlie expelled him, and put the earle in possession thereof, that notwithstanding their oths and pledges, they are yet no longer true than they féele themselues the weaker. This deputie tamed the Briens, the Burghs, Mac Banons, Oghaghucaght, Moris Mac Mahun, all the capteins of Thomond: & all this he did in thrée months, the clergie twise euerie weeke in solemne procession praieng for his good succes against those disordered persons, which now in euerie part of Ireland.

Iames Young an author alleaged by *Campion*

The sunne staieth his course

land degenerated from the English ciuilitie, to their old trade of life vsed in that countrie, repined at the English maner of gouernment. So far Campion.]

Diuerse parlements vpon prorogations were holden in time that this earle of
1420 Ormond was gouernor. The first began at Dublin the seauenth of Iune in this
The parlement began. yeare one thousand foure hundred and twentie, which continued about sixtéen
daies. At this parlement was granted to the lord lieutenant a subsidie of seauen hundred marks. At the sixtéene daies end this parlement was adiorned till the mondaie after saint Andrews daie. In the same parlement the debts of the lord Iohn Talbot which were due to certeine persons for vittels and other things, taken vp whilest he was lord lieutenant there, were reckoned vp, which lord Talbot verelie, for that he saw not the creditors satisfied before his comming awaie, was partlie euill spoken of in the countrie. The morow after the feast of Simon and Iude, the
The castell of Colmolin. castell of Colmolin was taken by Thomas Fitzgirald. And on saint Katharins euen,
The earle of Ormonds son and heire borne. the sonne and heire of the earle of Ormond lord lieutenant was borne, for the which there was great reioising. In the parlement begun againe at Dublin the mondaie after saint Andrews daie, an other subsidie of thrée hundred marks was granted vnto the lord lieutenant. And after they had sat thirtéene daies, it was eftsoons adiorned vntill the mondaie after saint Ambrose daie. Then rumors were spred abrode, that Thomas Fitz-Iohn earle of Desmond was departed this life at Paris vpon saint Laurence daie, after whome succéeded his vncle Iames Fitzgirald, whome he had three seuerall times renounced, as one that was a waster of his patrimonie both in England and Ireland, and not like to come to anie good proofe.

1421 In the yeare one thousand foure hundred twentie and one, the parlement began
A parlement. againe vpon the last prorogation, the mondaie after saint Ambrose daie: in which parlement it was ordeined that certeine persons should be sent to the king, to sue that a reformation might be had in matters touching the state of the land. The chéefe of those that were thus sent, were the archbishop of Armagh, and sir
The bishop of Cashill accused. Christopher Preston knight. Moreouer Richard Ohedian bishop of Cashill was accused by Iohn Gese bishop of Lismore and Waterford, who laid thirtie articles vnto his charge. Amongst other, one was for that he loued none of the English nation, and that he bestowed not one benefice vpon anie Englishman, and counselled other bishops that they should not bestow anie within their diocesse vpon anie Englishman. Moreouer, another article was for counterfeting the kings seale. And another, for that he went about to make himselfe king of Mounster, and had taken a ring from the image of saint Patrike (which the earle of Desmond had offered) and giuen it to his lemman. Manie other crimes were laid to him by the said bishop of Lismore and Waterford, which he exhibited in writing. Also in the same parlement there rose contention betwixt Adam Paine bishop of Clone, and another prelat, whose church he would haue annexed vnto his see. At length, after the parlement had continued for the space of eightéene daies, it brake vp. Herewith came
The duke of Clarence slaine in France. newes of the slaughter of the lord Thomas of Lancaster duke of Clarence, that had béene lord lieutenant of Ireland. And vpon the seuenth of Maie certeine of the earle of Ormonds men were ouerthrowen by the Irish, néere to the abbeie of Leis, and seuen and twentie Englishmen were slaine there: of whom the cheefe were two gentlemen, the one named Purcell, & the other Grant. Also ten were taken prisoners, and two hundred escaped to the foresaid abbeie, so sauing themselues. About
Mac Mahun. the same time Mac Mahun an Irish lord did much hurt within the countrie of Vigile, by burning & wasting all afore him. Also vpon the morrow after Midsummer daie, the earle of Ormond lord lieutenant entred into the countrie about Leis

vpon

vpon Omordis, and for the space of foure daies togither did much hurt, in slaieng and spoiling the people, till the Irish were glad to sue to peace.

Henrie the sixt.

LIEUTENANTS to Henrie the sixt ouer the relme of Ireland were these, Edmund earle of March, and Iames earle of Ormond his deputie, Iohn Sutton, lord Dudleie, and sir Thomas Strange knight his deputie, sir Thomas Stanleie, and sir Christopher Plunket his deputie. This sir Thomas Stanleie on Michaelmasse daie, in the twelfe yeare of king Henrie the sixt, with all the knights of Meth & Uriell, fought against the Irish, slue a great number, & tooke Neill Odonell prisoner.] Here endeth *Marlburrow* and all that followeth is taken out of *Campion.*

Lion lord Wels, and the earle of Ormond his deputie. Iames earle of Ormond by himselfe, Iohn earle of Shrewesburie, and the archbishop of Dublin lord iustice in his absence. Richard Plantagenet duke of Yorke, father to king Edward the fourth & earle of Vlster, had the office of lieutenant by the kings letters patents during the terme of tenne yeares, who appointed to rule vnder him as his deputies at sundrie times the baron of Deluin, Richard Fitzeustace knight, Iames earle of Ormond, and Thomas Fitzmorice earle of Kildare. To this Richard duke of Yorke and Vlster then resident in Dublin, was borne within the castell there his second sonne the lord George that was after duke of Clarence. His godfathers at the fontstone were the earles of Ormond and Desmond. Whether the commotion of Iacke Cade an Irishman borne, naming himselfe Mortimer, and so pretending cousinage to diuerse noble houses in this land, procéeded from some intelligence with the dukes fréends here in Ireland, it is vncerteine: but surelie the duke was vehementlie suspected, and immediatelie after began the troubles, which through him were raised. Which broiles being couched for a time, the duke held himselfe in Ireland, being latelie by parlement ordeined protector of the realme of England: he left his agent in the court, his brother the earle of Salisburie, lord chancellor, to whom he declared the truth of the troubles then toward in Ireland: which letter exemplified by sir Henrie Sidneie lord deputie, a great searcher and preseruer of antiquities, as it came to Campions hands, and by him set downe we haue thought good likewise to present it here to your view. *Campion* out of the records of Christs church. George duke of Clarence borne at Dublin. Iacke Cade.

"*To the right worshipfull, and withall mine heart entierelie beloued brother, the earle of Salisburie.*

"RIGHT worshipfull, & with all my hart entierelie beloued brother, I recommend me vnto you as heartilie as I can. And like it you to wit, sith I wrote last vnto the king our soueraigne lord his highnesse, the Irish enimie, that is to saie Magoghigam, and with him thrée or foure Irish capteins, associat with a great fellowship of English rebels, notwithstanding that they were within the king our soueraigne lord his peace, of great malice, and against all truth haue maligned against their legiance, and vengeablie haue brent a great towne of mine inheritance in Meth, called Ramore, and other villages thereabouts, and murthered and brent both men, women, and children, withouten mercie: the which enimies be yet assembled in woods and forts, awaighting to doo the hurt and gréeuance to the kings subiects, that they can thinke or imagine. For which cause I write at this time vnto the kings highnesse, and beséech his good grace for to hasten my paiment for this land, according vnto his letters of warrant now late directed vnto the treasuror of England, to the intent I may wage men in sufficient number for to resist The copie of a letter.

 the

the malice of the same enimies, & punish them in such wise, that other which would doo the same for lacke of resistance, in time maie take example. For doubtlesse, but if my paiment be had in all hast, for to haue men of warre in defense and safegard of this land, my power can not stretch to kéepe it in the kings obeisance: and verie necessitie will compell me to come into England to liue there vpon my poore liuelihood. For I had leauer be dead than anie inconuenience should fall therevnto by my default: for it shall neuer be chronicled nor remaine in scripture (by the grace of God) that Ireland was lost by my negligence. And therefore I beséech you right worshipfull brother, that you will hold to your hands instantlie, that my paiment maie be had at this time in eschewing all inconueniences. For I haue example in other places (more pitie it is) for to dread shame, and for to acquit my troth vnto the kings highnesse, as my dutie is. And this I praie and exhort you good brother, to shew vnto his good grace, and that you will be so good, that this language maie be enacted at this present parlement for mine excuse in time to come, and that you will be good to my seruant Roger Ro the bearer of these, and to my other seruants, in such things as they shall pursue vnto the kings highnes, and to giue full faith and credence vnto the report of the said Roger, touching the said matters. Right worshipfull, and with all my heart entierlie beloued brother, our blessed Lord God preserue and keepe you in all honour, prosperous estate, and felicitie, & grant you right good life and long. Written at Dublin the fiftéenth daie of June. "Your faithfull true brother

"RICHARD YORKE."

Roger Ro.

Of such power was Magoghigam in those daies, who as he wan and kept it by the sword, so now his successors in that state liue but as meane capteins, yéelding their winnings to the stronger. This is the miserie of lawlesse people, resembling the rudenesse of the rude world, wherein euerie man was richer and poorer than other, as he was in might and violence more or lesse inabled. Here began factions of the nobilitie in Ireland, fauouring diuerse sides that stroue for the crowne of England. For the duke of Yorke, in those ten yeares of his gouernement excéedinglie wan the hearts of the noblemen and gentlemen of that land, of the which diuerse were slaine with him at Wakefield; as the contrarie part was the next yeare by his sonne Edward earle of March at Mortimers crosse in Wales. In which meane time the Irish grew hardie, & vsurped the English countries insufficientlie defended, as they had doone by like oportunitie in the latter end of Richard the second. These two seasons set them so aflote, that hensforward they could neuer be cast out from their forcible possessions, holding by plaine wrong all Vlster, and by certeine Irish tenures no small portions of Mounster and Connagh, least in Meth and Leinster, where the ciuill subiects of the English bloud did euer most preuaile.

Magoghigham his power

Edward the fourth and Edward the fift

THOMAS Fitzmorice earle of Kildare, lord iustice till the third yeare of Edward the fourth, after which time the duke of Clarence, brother to the king, had the office of lieutenant while he liued, & made his deputies by sundrie times, Thomas earle of Desmond, Iohn Tiptoft earle of Worcester the kings cousine, Thomas earle of Kildare, and Henrie lord Greie of Ruthin. Great was the credit of the Giraldins euer when the house of Yorke prospered, and likewise the Butlers thriued vnder the bloud of

Lieutenants and deputies in king Edward the fourth his daies

The Butlers

of the Lancasters. for which cause the earle of Desmond remained manie yeres deputie to George duke of Clarence his good brother but when he had spoken certeine disdainefull words against the late mariage of king Edward with the ladie Elizabeth Greie, the said ladie being now queene, caused his trade of life after the Irish maner, contrarie to sundrie old statutes enacted in that behalfe, to be sifted and examined by Iohn erle of Worcester his successor, so that he was atteinted of treason, condemned, and for the same beheaded at Droghedagh. *The earle of Worcester* 1467

Iames the father of this Thomas earle of Desmond, being suffered and not controlled during the gouernment of Richard duke of Yorke his godcept, and of Thomas earle of Kildare his kinsman, put vpon the kings subiects within the countries of Waterford, Corke, Kerrie, and Limerike, the Irish impositions of quinto and liuerie, cartings, carriages, lodgings, cocherings, bonnaght, and such like, which customes are the verie breeders, mainteiners, and vpholders of all Irish enormities, wringing from the poore tenants euerlasting sesse, allowance of meat and monie, whereby their bodies and goods were brought in seruice and thraldome, so that the men of warre, horsses, and their Galloglasses lie still vpon the farmers, eat them out, beggar the countrie, foster a sort of idle vagabonds, readie to rebell if their lord command them, euer nuzled in stealth and robberies. *Campion out of Sertleges in his collectoris* *Irish impositions*

These euill presidents giuen by the father, the son did exercise, being lord deputie to whome the reformation of that disorder speciallie belonged. Notwithstanding the same fault being winked at in other, and with such rigor auenged in him, was manifestlie taken for a quarrell sought and procured. Two yeares after, the said earle of Worcester lost his head, whilest Henrie the sixt taken out of the tower was set vp againe, and king Edward proclamed vsurper, and then was Kildare inlarged, whom likewise attemted, they thought also to haue rid, and shortlie both the earles of Kildare & Desmond were restored to their bloud by parlement. Sir Rowland Eustace, sometime treasuror and lord chancellor, was lastlie also lord deputie of Ireland. He founded saint Francis abbeie beside Kilcollen bridge. King Edward a yeare before his death honored his yoonger sonne (Richard duke of Yorke) with the title of lieutenant ouer this land, which he inioied till his vnnaturall vncle bereft both him and his brother king Edward the fift of their naturall liues. 1469 *Restitution to bloud* 1470 *Flatsburie.*

Richard the third.

WHEN this monster of nature & cruell tyrant Richard the third had killed his two yoong nephues, and taken vpon him the crowne & gouernement of England, he preferred his owne sonne Edward to the dignitie of lord lieutenant of Ireland, whose deputie was Girald earle of Kildare that bare that office all the reigne of king Richard, and a while in Henrie the seuenth his daies. *Richard the third.*

Henrie the seuenth.

TO which earle came the wilie priest sir Richard Simon, bringing with him a lad that was his scholer, named Lambert, whome he feined to be the sonne of George earle of Clarence, latelie escaped foorth of the tower of London. And the boie could reckon vp his pedigrée so readilie, & had learned of the priest such princelie behauiour, that he lightlie mooued the said earle, and manie others the nobles of Ireland (tendering as well the linage roiall of Richard Plantagenet duke of Yorke, and his *Henrie the seuenth* *Sir Richard Simon priest.* *Lambert counterfeit to be the earle of Warwike.*

sonne

sonne George their countrieman borne, as also maligning the aduancement of the house of Lancaster in Henrie the seuenth) either to thinke or to faine, that the world might beleeue they thought verelie this child to be Edward earle of Warwike, the duke of Clarence his lawfull sonne.

And although king Henrie more than halfe marred their sport, in shewing the right earle through all the streets of London, yet the ladie Margaret duches of Burgognie, sister to Edward the fourth, hir nephue John de la Poole, the lord

The lord Louell. Sir Thomas Broughton.

Louell, sir Thomas Broughton knight, and diuers other capteins of this conspiracie, deuised to abuse the colour of this yoong earles name, for preferring their purpose: which if it came to good, they agreed to depose Lambert, and to erect the verie earle indeed now prisoner in the tower, for whose quarell had they pretended to fight, they deemed it likelie he should haue beene made awaie. Wherefore it was blazed in Ireland, that the king to mocke his subiects, had schooled a boie to take vpon him the earle of Warwikes name, and had shewed him about London, to blind the eies of the simple folke, and to defeat the lawfull inheritour of the good duke of Clarence their countriman and protector during his life, vnto whose linage they also deriued title in right to the crowne.

Lambert crowned.

In all hast they assembled at Dublin, and there in Christs church they crowned this idoll, honoring him with titles imperiall, feasting and triumphing, raising mightie shouts and cries, carrieng him from thense to the castell vpon tall mens shoulders, that he might be seene and noted, as he was sure an honorable child to looke vpon. Herewith assembling their forces togither, they prouided themselues of ships, and imbarking therein, they tooke the sea, and landing in Lancashire, passed forwards, till they came to Newarke vpon Trent. Thereupon insued the battell of Stoke, commonlie called Martin Swarts field, wherein Lambert and his maister were taken, but yet pardoned of life, and were not executed. The erle of Lincolne, the lord Louell, Martin Swart, the Almaine capteine, and Maurice Fitzthomas capteine of the

1489
Jasper duke of Bedford lieutenant.

Irish, were slaine, and all their power discomfited, as in the English historie it may further appeare. Jasper duke of Bedford, and earle of Pembroke lieutenant, and Walter archbishop of Dublin his deputie.

In this time befell another like Irish illusion, procured by the duchesse aforesaid, and certeine nobles in England, whereby was exalted as rightfull king of England, and vndoubted earle of Vlster, the counterfeit Richard duke of Yorke, preserued

Perkin Warbecke.

from king Richards crueltie (as the adherents faced the matter downe) and with this margame lord, named indeed Peter, (in scorne Perkin) Warbecke, they flattered themselues manie yeares after. Then was sir Edward Poinings knight sent ouer lord de-

1494
Sir Edward Poinings lord deputie.
Perkin Warbecke taken.

putie, with commission to apprehend Warbecks principall parteners in Ireland. amongst whom was named Girald Fitzgirald, whose purgation the king (notwithstanding diuerse surmising and auouching the contrarie) did accept. After much adoo, Perkin being taken, confessed by his owne writing the course of his whole life, and all his proceedings in this enterprise, whereof in the English historie, as we haue borowed the same footh of *Halles* chronicles, yee may read more, and therefore heere we haue omitted to speake further of that matter.

1501
Henrie duke of Yorke, after king Henrie the eight, lord lieutenant.

In the yeare 1501, king Henrie made lieutenant of Ireland his second sonne Henrie, as then duke of Yorke, who after reigned by the name of Henrie the eight. To him was appointed deputie the foresaid Girald erle of Kildare, who accompanied with Iohn Blake maior of Dublin, warred vpon William le Burgh, Obren, and Mac Nemarre, Ocarroull, and fought with the greatest power of Irishmen that had

The field of Knocktow.

beene togither since the conquest, vnder the hill of Knocktow, in English the hill of the axes, six miles from Galowaie, and two miles from Belliclare Burghes manour towne.

towne. Mac William and his complices were there taken, his souldiers that escaped the sword were pursued fleeing, for the space of fiue miles: great slaughter was made of them, and manie capteins caught, without the losse of one Englishman. The earle of Kildare at his returne was made knight of the noble order of the garter, and liued in worthie estimation all his life long, as well for this seruice, as diuerse other his famous exploits.

The earle of Kildare, knight of the garter.

Thus farre the Irish Chronicles continued and ended at Henrie the seauenth.

TO THE

RIGHT HONORABLE

Sir HENRIE SIDNEIE Knight,

LORD DEPUTIE OF IRLLAND, LORD PRESIDENT OF WALES, KNIGHT OF THE MOST NOBLE ORDER OF THE GARTER, AND ONE OF HIR MAIESTIES PRIUIE COUNCELL WITHIN HIR REALME OF ENGLAND.

HOW cumbersome (right honorable) and dangerous a taske it is, to ingrosse and diuulge the doings of others, especiallie when the parties registred or their issue are liuing both common reason sufficientlie acknowledgeth, and dailie experience infallibile prooueth For man by course of nature is so partiallie affected to himselfe and his bloud, as he will be more agreeued with the chronicler for recording a peeuish trespasse, than he will be offended with his friend for committing an heinous treason Ouer this, if the historian be long, he is accompted a trifler if he be short, he is taken for a summister if he commend, he is twighted for a flatterer if he reprooue, he is holden for a carper if he be pleasant, he is noted for a iester if he be graue, he is reckoned for a drooper if he misdate, he is named a falsifier if he once but trip, he is tearmed a stumbler: so that let him beare himselfe in his chronicle as vprightlie and as conscionablie as he may possible, yet he shall be sure to find them that will be more prest to blab foorth his pelfish faults, than they will be readie to blaze out his good deserts Others there be, that although they are not able to reprooue what is written, yet they will be sure to cast in his dish what is forgotten. Heere, saie they, this exploit is omitted there that policie is not detected heere this saieng would haue beene interlaced. there that trecherie should haue beene displaied These & the like discommodities, with which historiographers are vsuallie cloid, haue borne backe diuers and sundrie willing minds, who taking the waie to be thornie, the credit slipperie, the carpers to be manie, would in no case be medlers, choosing rather to sit by their owne fire obscurelie at home, than to be baited with enuious toongs openlie abroad.

Others on the contrarie side, being resolute fellowes, and trampling vnder foot these curious faultfinders, would not sticke to put themselues foorth in presse, and maugre all their hearts, to buskle forward, and rush through the pikes of their quipping nips, and biting frumps. But I taking the meane betweene both these extremities, held it for better, not to be so faint and peeuish a meacocke, as to shrinke and couch mine head for euerie mizeling showre, nor yet to beare my selfe so high in heart as to pranse and iet like a proud gennet through the street, not weighing the barking of currish bandogs. And therefore, if I shall be found in mine historie sometime too tedious, sometime too sparе, sometime too fawning in commending the liuing, sometime too flat in reproouing the dead I take God to witnesse, that mine offense therein proceedeth of ignorance, and not of set wilfulnesse But as for the passing ouer in silence of diuerse euents (albeit the law or rather the libertie of an historie requireth that all should be related, and nothing whusted) yet I must confesse, that as I was not able, vpon so little leasure, to know all that was said or doone, so I was not willing for sundrie respects, to write euerie trim tram that I knew to be said or doone. And if anie be ouerthwartlie warwarded, as he will sooner long for that I haue omitted, than he will be contented with that I haue chronicled; I cannot deuise in my iudgement a better waie to satisfie his appetite, than with one Dolie, a peintor of Oxford, his answer: who being appointed to tricke out the ten commandements, omitted one, and pourtraied but nine. Which fault espied by his maister that hired him, Dolie answered, that in verie deed he peinted but nine howbeit, when he vnderstood that his master had well obserued and kept the nine commandements that alreadie were drawne, he gave his word at better leisure throughlie to finish the tenth. And truelie so must I saie. I haue laid downe heere to the reader his view, a breefe discourse, whereof I trust he shall take no great surfet And when I am aduertised, that he will digest the thin fare that heere is disht before him: it may be (God willing) heereafter, that he shall find my booke with store of more licorous deinties farsed and furnished, leauing to his choise, either nicelie to pickle, or greedilie to swallow, as much as to his contentation shall best beseeme him. Wherefore my good lord, sith I may not denie, but that the worke is painfull, and I doo forecast that the misconstruction may be perilous the toilesomnesse of the paine I refer to my priuat knowledge, the abandoning of the perill, I commit to your honorable patronage, not doubting thereby to be sheelded against the sinister glosing of malicious interpretors. Thus betaking your lordship to God, I craue your attentiuenes, in perusing a cantell or parcell of the Irish historie that heere insueth.

RICHARD STANIHVRST

A CONTINUATION

OF THE

CHRONICLES OF IRELAND,

COMPRISING THE REIGNE OF

KING HENRIE THE EIGHT.

GIRALD Fitzgirald earle of Kildare, son to Thomas Fitzgirald, of whō mention hath béene made in the latter end of the former storie, a mightie man of stature, full of honor & courage, who had béene deputie & lord iustice of Ireland first & last 33 yéeres, deceased at Kildare the third of September, & lieth intoomed in the queere of Christes church at Dublin, in a chappell by him founded. Betwéene him & Iames Butler earle of Ormond (their owne gelousies fed with enuie & ambition, kindled with certeine lewd factious abettors of either side) as generallie to all noblemen, so especiallie to both these houses verie incident, euer since the ninth yeare of Henrie the seuenth, bredsome trouble in Ireland. The plot of which mutuall grudge was grounded vpon the factious dissention, that was raised in England betweene the houses of Yorke & Lancaster, Kildare cleauing to Yorke, and Ormond relieng to Lancaster. To the vpholding of which discord, both these noble men laboured with tooth and naile to ouercrow, and consequentlie to ouerthrow one the other. And for somuch as they were in honour peeres, they wrought by hooke and by crooke to be in authoritie superiours. The gouernement therfore in the reigne of Henrie the seuenth, being cast on the house of Kildare, Iames earle of Ormond a deepe and a farre reaching man, giuing backe like a butting ram to strike the harder push, deuised to inueigle his aduersarie by submission & courtesie, being not then able to ouermatch him with stoutnesse or preheminence. Wherevpon Ormond addressed his letters to the deputie, specifieng a slander raised on him and his, that he purposed to deface his gouernement, and to withstand his authoritie. And for the cleering of himselfe and of his adherents, so it stood with the deputie his pleasure, he would make his spéedie repaire to Dublin, & there in an open audience would purge himselfe of all such odious crimes, of which he was wrongfullie suspected. 1514

The occasion of the dissention betweene Kildare and Ormond

To this reasonable request had the lord deputie no sooner condescended, than Ormond with a puissant armie marched towards Dublin, incamping in an abbeie in the suburbs of the citie, named saint Thomas court. The approching of so great an armie of the citizens suspected, and also of Kildares councellors greatlie disliked, lastlie the extortion that the lawlesse souldiers vsed in the pale by seuerall complaints detected: these three points, with diuerse other suspicious circumstances laid and put togither, did minister occasion rather of further discord, than of anie present agreement. Ormond persisting still in his humble sute, sent his messenger to the lord deputie, declaring that he was prest and readie to accomplish the tenour of his letters, and there did attend (as became him) his lordship his pleasure. And as for the companie, he

Ormond marcheth to Dublin

he brought with him from Mounster, albeit suspicious braines did rather of a malicious craftinesse surmise the worst, than of charitable wisedome did iudge the best, yet notwithstanding, vpon conference had with his lordship, he would not doubt to satisfie him at full in all points wherewith he could be with anie colour charged, and so to stop vp the spring, from whense all the enuious suspicions gushed. Kildare with this mild message intreated, appointed the méeting to be at saint Patrike his church where they were ripping vp one to another their mutuall quarels, rather recounting the damages they susteined, than acknowledging the iniuries they offered: the citizens and Ormond his armie fell at some iar, for the oppression and exaction with which the souldiers surcharged them. With whom as part of the citizens bickered, so a round knot of archers rushed into the church, meaning to haue murthered Ormond, as the capteine and belweddet of all these lawlesse rabble. The earle of Ormond suspecting that he had béene betraied, fled to the chapiter house, put to the doore, sparring it with might and maine. The citizens in their rage, imagining that euerie post in the church had beene one of the souldiers, shot hab or nab at randon vp to the roodloft and to the chancell, leauing some of their arrowes sticking in the images.

The citizens in an vprore.

Kildare pursuing Ormond to the chapiter house doore, vndertooke on his honor that he should receiue no villanie. Wherevpon the recluse crauing his lordships hand to assure him his life, there was a clift in the chapiter house doore, pearsed at a trise, to the end both the earles should haue shaken hands and be reconciled. But Ormond surmising that this drift was intended for some further treacherie, that if he would stretch out his hand, it had béene percase chopt off, refused that proffer, vntill Kildare stretcht in his hand to him, and so the doore was opened, they both imbraced, the storme appeased, and all their quarels for that present rather discontinued than ended. In this garboile, one of the citizens, surnamed Blanchfield was slaine. This latter quarell being like a gréene wound, rather bungerlie botcht than soundlie cured, in that Kildare suspected that so great an armie (which the other alledged to be brought for the gard of his person) to haue béene of purpose assembled, to outface him & his power in his owne countrie. And Ormond mistrusted, that this treacherous practise of the Dublinians was by Kildare deuised. These and the like surmises lightlie by both the noble men misdéemed, and by the continuall twatling of fliring clawbacks in their eares whispered, bred and fostered a malice betwixt them and their posteritie, manie yeeres incurable, which caused much stir and vnquietnesse in the realme, vntill the confusion of the one house and the nonage of the other ended and buried their mutuall quarels.

The earles reconciled.

Blanchfield slaine.

Ormond was nothing inferiour to the other in stomach, and in reach of policie far beyond him. Kildare was in gouernement mild, to his enimies sterne, to the Irish such a scourge, that rather for despite of him than for fauor of anie part, they relied for a time to Ormond, came vnder his protection, serued at his call, performed by starts (as their manner is) the dutie of good subiects. Ormond was secret and of great forecast, verie staied in spéech, dangerous of euerie trifle that touched his reputation. Kildare was open and plaine, hardlie able to rule himselfe when he were moued to anger, not so sharpe as short, being easilie displeased and sooner appeased. Being in a rage with certeine of his seruants for faults they committed, one of his horssemen offered master Boice (a gentleman that reteined to him) an Irish hobbie, on condition, that he would plucke an haire from the earle his beard. Boice taking the proffer at rebound, stept to the earle (with whose good nature he was throughlie acquainted) parching in the heat of his choler, and said. "So it is, and it like your good lordship, one of your horssemen promised me a chosse horsse, if I

The description of Ormond.

The description of Kildare.

Boice.

snip

snip one haire from your beard." "Well," quoth the earle, "I agree therto, but if thou plucke anie more than one, I promise thée to bring my fist from thine eare."

The branch of this good nature hath beene deriued from him to an earle of his posteritie, who being in a chafe for the wrong sawcing of a partridge, arose suddenlie from the table, meaning to haue reasoned the matter with his cooke. Hauing entred the kitchen, drowning in obliuion his chalenge, he began to commend the building of the roome, wherein he was at no time before, & so leauing the cooke vncontrold, he returned to his ghests merilie. This old earle being (as is aforesaid) soone hot and soone cold, was of the English well beloued, a good iusticier, a suppressor of the rebels, a warriour incomparable, towards the nobles that he fansied not somewhat headlong and vnrulie. Being charged before Henrie the seuenth, for burning the church of Cashell, and manie witnesses prepared to auouch against him the truth of that article, he suddenlie confessed the fact, to the great woondering and detestation of the councell. When it was looked how he wold iustifie the matter, "By Jesus (quoth he) I would neuer haue doone it, had it not béene told me that the archbishop was within." And bicause the same archbishop was one of his busiest accusers there present, the king merilie laughed at the plainnesse of the noble man, to see him alledge that thing for excuse, which most of all did aggrauate his offense.

The last article against him they concerned in these tearmes, Finallie all Ireland can not rule this earle. "No?" quoth the king, "then in good faith shall this earle rule all Ireland." Thus was that accusation turned to a ieast. The earle returned to his countrie lord deputie, who (notwithstanding his simplicitie in peace) was of that valour and policie in war, as his name bred a greater terror to the Irish, than other mens armies. In his warres he vsed for policie a retchlesse kind of diligence, or a headie carelesnesse, to the end his souldiors should not faint in their attempts, were the enimie of neuer so great power. Being generall in the field of Knocktow, where in effect all the Irish rebels of Ireland were gathered against the English pale, one of the earle his capteins presented him a band of keins, euen as they were readie to ioine battell, and withall demanded of the erle in what seruice he would haue them imploied? "Marie (quoth he) let them stand by and giue vs the gaze." Such was his courage, that notwithstanding his enemies were two to one, yet would he set so good a face on the matter, as his souldiors should not once suspect, that he either néeded, or longed for anie further helpe.

Kildare returneth lord deputie

Kildares policie in war

Hauing triumphantlie vanquished the Irish in that conflict, he was shortlie after, as well for that, as other his valiant exploits, made knight of the garter: and in the fift yeare of Henrie the eight in that renowme & honour he died, wherein for the space of manie yeares he liued. No maruell if this successe were a corsie to the aduerse part, which the longer it held aloofe, and bit the bridle, the more egerlie it followed the course, hauing once got scope and roome at will, as shall be hereafter at full declared. Ormond bearing in mind the trecherie of the Dublinians, procured such as were the grauest prelats of his clergie, to intimate to the court of Rome the heathenish riot of the citizens of Dublin, in rushing into the church armed, polluting with slaughter the consecrated place, defacing the images, prostrating the relicks, rasing downe altars, with barbarous outcries, more like miscreant Saracens, than christian catholikes. Wherevpon a legat was posted to Ireland, bending his course to Dublin, where soone after hee was solemnelie receiued by Walter Fitzsimons, archbishop of Dublin, a graue prelat, for his lerning and wisedome chosen to be one of king

1514

The Dublinians accused

A legat sent from Rome

Walter Fitzsimons

king Henrie the seuenth his chapleins, in which vocation he continued twelue yeares, and after was aduanced to be archbishop of Dublin.

The legat vpon his arriuall indicted the citie for his execrable offense: but at length, by the procurement as well of the archbishop as of all the cleargie, he was weighed to giue the citizens absolution with this caueat, that in detestation of so horrible a fact, and *Ad perpetuam rei memoriam*, the maior of Dublin should go barefooted thoroughout the citie in open procession before the sacrament, on Corpus Christi daie: which penitent satisfaction was after in euerie such procession dulie accomplished. Girald Fitzgirald, sonne and heire to the aforesaid erle of Kildare, was shortlie after his fathers decease constituted lord deputie of Ireland, before whome in the seuenth yeare of Henrie the eight, there was a parlement holden at Dublin, wherein it was established, that all such as bring out of England the kings letters of priuat seale, for particular causes against anie of the king his subiects in Ireland, should find sufficient sureties in the king his chancerie in Ireland, to bée bound by recognisance, that the plaintife shall satisfie the defendant, that purgeth or acquiteth himselfe of the matter to him alledged, for his costs and damages susteined by such wrongfull vexation. This noble man being valiant and well spoken, was nothing inferior to his father in martiall prowesse, chasing in the time of his gouernment the familie of the Tooles, battering Ocarrell his castles, and bringing in awe all the Irish of the land.

Penance inioined to the citizens of Dublin.

The earle of Kildare lord deputie.

A parlement holden at Dublin.

This earle of good meaning, to vnite the houses in friendship, matched his sister Margaret Fitzgirald with Piers Butler earle of Ossorie, whome he also helped to recouer the earldome of Ormond, into the which, after the decease of the earle Iames, a bastard Butler had by abatement intruded. Great and manifold were the miseries the ladie Margaret susteined, hir husband Piers Butler being so egerlie pursued by the vsurper, as he durst not beare vp hed, but was forced to houer and lurke in woods and forrests. The noble woman being great with child, and vpon necessitie constreined to vse a spare diet (for hir onelie sustenance was milke) she longed sore for wine, and calling hir lord, and a trustie seruant of his, Iames White vnto hir, she requested them both to helpe hir to some wine, for she was not able anie longer to indure so strict a life. "Trulie Margaret," quoth the earle of Ossorie, "thou shalt haue store of wine within this foure and twentie houres, or else thou shalt feed alone on milke for me."

Piers Butler and Margaret Fitzgirald espoused.

Iames White.

The next daie following, Piers hauing intelligence that his enimie the base Butler would haue trauelled from Donmore to Kilkennie, notwithstanding he were accompanied with six horssemen: yet Piers hauing none but his lackie, did forestall him in the waie, and with a couragious charge gored the bastard through with his speare. This prosperous calme succeeding the former boisterous storme, the ladie Margaret began to take heart, hir naturall stoutnesse floted, as well by the remembrance of hir noble birth, as by the intelligence of hir honorable match. Kildare all this while kept in authoritie, notwithstanding the pushes giuen against him by secret heauers that enuied his fortune, and sought to nourish the old grudge, was at length by their priuie packing fetched vp to the court of England by commission, and caused him to be examined vpon diuerse interrogatories touching the affaires of Ireland.

The bastard Butler slaine.

Kildare sent for into England.

He left in his roome Maurice Fitzthomas of Lackiagh lord iustice: and shortlie after came ouer lord lieutenant Thomas Howard earle of Surreie, who was after duke of Norffolke, grandfather to the last duke, accompanied with two hundred yeomen of the crowne: before whome, shortlie after his repaire thither, there was a parlement holden

Maurice Fitzthomas lord iustice.

Surrie lord lieutenant of Ireland.

holden at Dublin, in which there past an act, that all wilfull burning of corne, as 1521
well in réekes in the fields, as also in villages and townes, should be high treason A parlement holden at Dublin.
Item, an act against loding of woolles & flox, vpon paine of forfeiture of the double value of the same, the one halfe to the king, and the other halfe to him that will sue therefore. Item, that anie person seized of lands, rents, or tenements in possession or in vse, vnto the yearelie value of ten markes aboue the charges, in fee simple, fée taile, or for terme of life, copie hold, or ancient demeane, shall passe in euerie attemt. While the lord lieutenant sat at dinner in the castell, of Dublin, The Moores in rebellion
he heard news that the Moors with a maine armie were euen at the entrie of the borders, readie to inuade the English pale. Immediatlie men were leuied by Iohn Fitzsimons. John Fitzsimons.
Fitzsimons then maior of Dublin, and the next morrow ioining them vnto his band, the lieutenant marched towards the frontiers of Leix.

The Moores vpon the lieutenant his approch, seuered themselues into sundrie companies, and vnderstanding that the cariage was dragging after the armie, and slenderlie manned, certeine of them charged the lieutenat his seruants, and such of the citizens as were appointed to gard the cariage Patrike Fitzsimons, a strong sturdie Patrike Fitzsimons
yoonker, kept the enemies such tacke, as he chased part of them awaie, rescued the cariage, slue two of the rebels, and brought the heads with him to maister maior his tent The next morning, two of the lieutenant his men, that slunke awaie from Fitzsimons, thinking that the cariage had béene lost, aduertised their lord that Fitzsimons fled awaie, and the Moores were so manie in companie, as it had béene but follie for two to bicker with so great a number The lieutenant posted in a rage to the maior his pauillion, telling him that his man Fitzsimons was a cowardlie traitor in running awaie, when he should haue defended the cariage.

"What am I, my lord" (quoth Patrike Fitzsimons) skipping in his shirt out of the tent, with both the heads in his hand? "My lord, I am no coward, I stood to my tacklings when your men gaue me the slip, I rescued the cariage, and haue here sufficient tokens of my manhood,' tumbling downe both the heads. "Saist thou so Fitzsimons?" quoth the lieutenant, "I crie thée mercie, and by this George, I would A valiant wish.
to God it had beene my good hap to haue béene in thy companie in that skirmish." So drinking to Fitzsimons in a boll of wine, and honourablie rewarding him for his good seruice, he returned to his pauillion, where hauing knowledge of Omore his recule, he pursued him with a troope of horsmen The lieutenant thus passing forwards, The earle of Surreie in danger to haue béene slaine
was espied a gunner of Omors, who lodged close in a wood side, and watching his time, he discharged his péece at the verie face of the lieutenant, strake the visor off his helmet, and pearsed no further, as God would.

This did he (retchlesse in maner what became of himselfe, so he might amaze the armie for a time) and surelie hereby he brake the swiftnesse of their following, & aduantaged the flight of his capteine, which thing he wan with the price of his owne bloud For the souldiors would no further, till they had ransacked all the nookes of this wood, verelie suspecting some ambush thereabout, and in seuerall knots ferretted out this gunner, whome Fitzwilliams and Bedlow of the Roch were Fitzwilliams Bedlow
faine to mangle and to hew in péeces, because the wretch would neuer yéeld In the meane while, defiance was proclamed with France and Scotland both at once, which 1523
mooued the king to call home Surreie out of Ireland, that he might imploie him in those wars. Surreie sent for home
His prowesse, integritie, good nature, and course of gouernment, the countrie much commended Piers Butler earle of Ossorie was appointed lord deputie Piers Butler earle of Ossorie lord deputie
In the meane time, Kildare attending the king his pleasure for his dispatch, recouered fauour through the instance of the marques Dorset, whose daughter dame Elizabeth Greie he espoused, and so departed home. Now was partaker of all the deputies 1524
counsell

Robert Talbot at Belgard

counsell one Robert Talbot of Belgard, whome the Giraldines deadlie hated him they procured to kéepe a kalendar of all their doings, who incensed brother against brother In which rage, Iames Fitzgirald méeting the said gentleman beside Ballimore, slue him euen then vpon his iournie toward the deputie to kéepe his Christmas with him

Margaret countesse of Ossorie

With this despitefull murther both sides brake out into open enimitie, and especiallie the countesse of Ossorie, Kildare his sister, a rare woman, and able for wisedome to rule a realme, had not hir stomach ouerruled hir knowledge. Here began informations of new treasons, passing to and fro, with complaints and replies But the marques Dorset had wrought so for his sonne in law, that he was suffered to rest at home, and onelie commissioners directed into Ireland, with authoritie to examine the root of their griefes wherein if they found Kildare anie thing at all purged, then instructions were to depose the plaintiffe, and to sweare the other lord deputie Commissioners were these, sir Rafe Egerton, a knight of Cheshire, Anthonie Fitzherbert, second iustice of the common plées, and Iames Denton, deane of Litchfield, who hauing examined these accusations, suddenlie tooke the sword from the earle of Ossorie, sware Kildare lord deputie, before whome Con Oneale bare the sword that daie.

Commissioners sent to Ireland.

Kildare sworne lord deputie

Cardinall Woolseie enimie to the Giraldines

Concerning the murtherer whom they might haue hanged, they brought him prisoner into England, presented him to the cardinall Woolseie, who was said to hate Kildare his bloud. and the cardinall intending to haue put him to execution, with more reproch and dishonor to the name, caused him to be led about the streets of London haltered, and hauing a taper in his hand. which asked so long time, that the deane of Lichfield stepped to the king, and begged his pardon The cardinall was sore inflamed herewith, & the malice not hitherto so ranke, was throughlie ripened, and therfore henseforward Ossorie brought foorth diuerse proofes of the deputie his disorder, for that (as he alledged) the deputie should winke at the earle of Desmond, whome by vertue of the king his letters he ought to haue attached Also, that he sought for acquaintance and affinitie with meere Irish enimies, that he had armed them against him, then being the king his deputie, he hanged and headed good subiects, whome he mistrusted to leane to the Butlers friendship. Kildare was therfore presentlie commanded to appeare, which he did, leauing in his roome his brother Fitzgirald of Leixlip, whom they shortlie deposed, and chose the baron of Deluin, whome Oconor tooke prisoner, & then the earle of Ossorie (to shew his abilitie of seruice) brought to Dublin an armie of Irishmen, hauing capteins ouer them Oconor Omore, and Ocaroll, & at S. Marie abbeie was chosen deputie by the kings councell

Pardon granted

Kildare accused The articles

Fitzgirald lord iustice

The earle of Ossorie chosen lord deputie

In which office, being himselfe (saue onelie in feats of armes) a simple gentleman, he bare out his honor, and the charge of gouernement verie worthilie, through the singular wisedome of his countesse, a ladie of such a port, that all estates of the realme crouched vnto him, so politike, that nothing was thought substantiallie debated without hir aduise manlike and tall of stature, verie liberall and bountifull, a sure friend, a bitter enimie, hardlie disliking where she fansied, not easilie fansieng where she disliked the onelie meane at those daies whereby hir husband his countrie was reclamed from sluttishnesse and slouenrie, to cleane bedding and ciuilitie But to these vertues was linked such a selfe liking, such an ouerwéening, and such a maiestie aboue the tenure of a subiect, that for assurance thereof, she sticked not to abuse hir husbands honor against hir brothers follie Notwithstanding, I learne not that shée practised his vndooing (which insued, and was to hir vndoubtedlie great heauinesse, as vpon whome both the blemish thereof, and the substance of the greater part of that

The Countesse of Ossorie.

that familie depended after) but that she by indirect meanes lifted hir brother out of credit to aduance hir husband, the common voice, and the thing it selfe speaketh All this while abode the earle of Kildare at the court, and with much adoo found shift to be called before the lords to answer suddenlie. They sat vpon him diuerslie affected, and namelie the cardinall lord chancellor misliking the earle his cause, comforted his accusers, and inforced the articles obiected, in these words Kildare conuented before the councell

The cardinall lord chancellor chargeth Kildare

"I wot well (my lord) that I am not the méetest at this boord to charge you with these treasons, because it hath plesed some of your pufellows to report that I am a professed enimie to all nobilitie, & namelie to the Giraldines· but séeing euerie curst boy can say as much when he is controlled, and séeing these points are so weightie, that they should not be dissembled of vs, and so apparant, that they can not be denied of you, I must haue leaue (notwithstanding your stale slander) to be the mouth of these honorable at this present, and to trumpe your treasons in your waie, howsoeuer you take me. First you remember, how the lewd earle of Desmond your kinsman (who passeth not whome he serueth, might he change his maister) sent his confederats with letters of credence vnto Francis the French king and hauing but cold comfort there, went to Charles the emperor, proffering the helpe of Mounster and Connagh towards the conquest of Ireland, if either of them would helpe to win it from our king How manie letters, what precepts, what messages, what threats haue bin sent you to apprehend him, and yet not doone? Why so? 'Forsooth I could not catch him' Nay nay earle, forsooth you would not watch him If he be iustlie suspected, why are you parciall in so great a charge? If not, why are you fearefull to haue him tried? Yea, for it will be sworne and deposed to your face, that for feare of meeting him, you haue winked wilfullie, shunned his sight, altered your course, warned his friends, stopped both eares and eies against his detectors, and when soeuer you tooke vpon you to hunt him out, then was he sure afore hand to be out of your walke

"Surelie, this iugling and false plaie little became either an honest man called to such honor, or a noble man put in so great trust Had you lost but a cow or a horsse of your owne, two hundred of your reteiners would haue come at your whistle to rescue the preie from the vttermost edge of Vlster all the Irish in Ireland must haue giuen you the way But in pursuing so néedfull a matter as this was, mercifull God, how nice, how dangerous, how waieward haue you béene? One while he is from home, another while he kéepeth home, sometimes fled, sometimes in the borders, where you dare not venture I wish my lord, there be shrewd bugs in the borders for the earle of Kildare to feare· the earle nay the king of Kildare, for when you are disposed, you reigne more like than rule in the land where you are malicious, the truest subiects stand for Irish enimies where you are pleased, the Irish foe standeth for a iust subiect hearts & hands liues & lands are all at your courtesie who fauneth not thereon cannot rest within your smell, and your smell is so ranke that you trake them out at pleasure" ¶ Whilest the cardinall was speaking, the earle chafed and changed colour, and at last brake out, and interrupted him thus.

"My lord chancellor, I beséech you pardon me, I am short witted, and you I perceiue intend a long tale if you procéed in this order, halfe my purgation will be lost for lacke of cariage I haue no schoole trickes, nor art of memorie except you heare me while I remember your words, your second processe will hammer out the former." Kildare interrupteth the cardinals tale

The lords tender Kildare

He answereth the cardinals objection

former." The lords associat, who for the most part tenderlie loued him, and knew the cardinall his manner of tawnts so lothsome, as wherewith they were inured manie yeares ago, humblie besought his grace to charge him directlie with particulars, and to dwell in some one matter, untill it were examined throughlie. "That granted, it is good reason, (quoth the earle) that your grace beare the mouth of this boord: but my lord, those mouths that put these things into your mouth, are verie wide mouths, such in déed as haue gaped long for my wracke, and now at length, for want of better stuffe, are faine to fill their mouths with smoke. What my cousine Desmond hath compassed, as I know not, so I beshrew his naked heart for holding out so long. If he can be taken by mine agents that presentlie wait for him, then haue mine aduersaries bewraied their malice, and this heape of heinous words shall resemble a scarecrow, or a man of straw that séemeth at a blush to carrie some proportion, but when it is felt and peised, discouereth a vanitie, seruing onelie to feare crowes: and I verelie trust, your honors shall sée the proofe by the thing it selfe, within these few daies. But go to: suppose he neuer be had? What is Kildare to blame for it, more than my good brother of Ossorie, who notwithstanding his high promises, hauing also the kings power, is yet content to bring him in at leasure? Can not the erle of Desmond shift but I must be of counsell? Cannot he hide him except I winke? If he be close am I his mate? If he be friended am I a traitor? This is a doubtie kind of accusation, which they urge against me, wherein they are stabled and mired at my first deniall. You would not see him (saie they.) Who made them so familiar with mine eiesight? Or when was the erle within my view? Or who stood by when I let him slip? Or where are the tokens of my wilfull hudwinke? But you sent him word to beware of you. Who was the messenger? Where are the letters? Conuince my negatiue, see how loose this idle geare hangeth togither. Desmond is not taken. Well, you are in fault. Whie? Because you are. Who prooueth it? No bodie. What coniectures? So it seemeth. To whome? To your enimies. Who told it them? They will sweare it. What other ground? None. Will they sweare it my lord? Whie then of like they know it, either they haue mine hand to shew, or can bring foorth the messenger, or were present at a conference, or priuie to Desmond, or some bodie bewraied it to them, or they themselues were my cariers or vicegerents therein. which of these parts will they choose, for I know them too well. To reckon my selfe conuict by their bare words or headlesse saiengs, or frantike othes, were but mere mockerie. My letter were soone read, were any such writing extant, my seruants & friends are readie to be sifted: of my cousine of Desmond they may lie lowdly, since no man here can well contrarie them. Touching my selfe, I neuer noted in them much wit, or so fast faith, that I would haue gaged on their silence the life of a good hound, much lesse mine owne. I doubt not, may it like your honors to appose them, how they came to the knowledge of those matters, which they are so readie to depose: but you shall find their toongs chained to another man his trencher, and as it were knights of the post, suborned to saie, sweare and stare the uttermost they can, as those that passe not what they saie, nor with what face they saie it, so they saie no truth. But of another side it gréeueth me that your good grace whom I take to be wise and sharpe, and who of your blessed disposition wisheth me well, should be so farre gone in crediting these corrupt informers that abuse the ignorance of your state and countrie to my perill. Little know you (my lord) how necessarie it is, not onelie for the gouernor, but also for euerie noble man in Ireland to hamper his uncivill neighbors at discretion, wherein if they waited for processe of law, and had not those liues and lands you speake of within their reach, they might hap to lose their owne liues and

and lands without law. You heare of a case as it were in a dreame, and féele not the smart that vexeth vs. In England there is not a meane subiect that dare extend his hand to fillip a péere of the realme. In Ireland except the lord haue cunning to his strength, and strength to saue his crowne, and sufficient authoritie to take théeues & varlets when they stir, he shall find them swarme so fast, that it will be too late to call for iustice. If you will haue our seruice take effect, you must not tie vs alwaies to these iudiciall procéedings, wherewith your realme (thanked be God) is inured. Touching my kingdome, I know not what your lordship should meane thereby. If your grace imagine that a kingdome consisteth in seruing God, in obeieng the prince, in gouerning with loue the common-wealth, in shouldering subiects, in suppressing rebels, in executing iustice, in bridling blind affections, I would be willing to be inuested with so vertuous and roiall a name. But if therefore you terme me a king, in that you are persuaded that I repine at the gouernment of my soueraigne, or winke at malefactors, or oppresse ciuill liuers, I vtterlie disclame in that odious terme, maruelling greatlie that one of your grace his profound wisedome, would séeme to appropriat so sacred a name to so wicked a thing. But howsoeuer it be (my lord) I would you and I had changed kingdoms but for one moneth, I would trust to gather vp more crummes in that space, than twise the reuenues of my poore earledome. but you are well and warme, and so hold you, and vpbraid not me with such an odious terme. I slumber in an hard cabin, when you sléepe in a soft bed of downe. I serue vnder the king his cope of heauen, when you are serued vnder a canopie. I drinke water out of my skull, when you drinke wine out of golden cups: my coursor is trained to the field, when your genet is taught to amble: when you are begraced and belorded, & crouched and knéeled vnto, then find I small grace with our Irish borderers, except I cut them off by the knees."

In what case stand the noble men of Ireland with rebels

At these girds the councell would haue smiled, if they durst. but ech man bit his lip, & held his countenance, for howsoeuer some of them leaned to the erle of Ossorie, they all hated the cardinall, who perceiuing that Kildare was no babe, rose in a fume from the councell table, committed the erle, & deferred the matter till more direct probations came out of Ireland. The duke of Norffolke, who was late lieutenant in Ireland, perceiuing the cardinall to be sore bent against the nobleman, rather for the deadlie hatred he bare his house, than for anie great matter he had wherewith to charge his person, stept to the king, and craued Kildare to be his prisoner, offering to be bound for his foorth comming, ouer and aboue all his lands, bodie for bodie. Whervpon, to the cardinall his great griefe, the prisoner was bailed, and honorablie by the duke interteined. During his abode in the duke his house, Oneale and Oconor, and all their fréends and alies, watching their time to annoie the pale, made open insurrection against the earle of Ossorie then lord deputie of Ireland, insomuch that the noble man mistrusting the ficklenesse of Desmond on the one side, & the force of these new start vp rebels on the other side, stood halfe amazed, as it were betwéene fire & water. For remedie whereof, letters thicke and thréefold were addressed to the councell of England, purporting that all these late hurlie burlies were of purpose raised by the meanes of Kildare, to the blemishing and staining of his brother Ossorie his gouernment. And to put the matter out of doubt, it was further added, that Kildare commanded his daughter Elice Fitzgirald, wife to the baron of Slane, to excite in his name the aforesaid traitors to this open rebellion.

The cardinall not beloued

The duke of Norffolke bound for Kildare

1528 The Irish in rebellion.

Kildare afresh impeached

The cardinall herevpon caused Kildare to be examined before the councell, where he pressed him so déepelie with this late disloialtie, that the presumption being (as

 the

the cardinall did force it) vehement, the treason odious, the king suspicious, the enimie eger, the fréends faint (which were sufficient grounds to ouerthrow an innocent person) the earle was repriued to the tower. The nobleman betooke himselfe to God & the king, he was hartilie beloued of the lieutenant, pitied in all the court, and standing in so hard a case, altered little of his accustomed hue, comforted other noble men prisoners with him, dissembling his owne sorrow. On a night when the lieutenant and he for their disport were plaieng at slidegrote or shoofleboord, suddenlie commeth from the cardinall a mandatum to execute Kildare on the morrow. The earle marking the lieutenants deepe sigh: "By saint Bride lieutenant (quoth he) there is some mad game in that scroll; but fall how it will, this throw is for an huddle." When the woorst was told him: "Now I praie thee (quoth he) doo no more but learne assuredlie from the king his owne mouth, whether his highnesse be witting thereto or not?" Sore doubted the lieutenant to displease the cardinall: yet of verie pure loue to his freend, he posteth to the king at midnight, and deliuered his errand: for at all houres of the night the lieutenant hath accesse to the prince vpon occasions. The king controlling the saucinesse of the priest (for those were his termes) deliuered to the lieutenant his signet in token of countermand, which when the cardinall had seene, he began to breath out vnseasoned language, which the lieutenant was loth to heare, & so left him pattring & chanting the diuell his *Pater noster*. Thus brake vp the storme for that time, & the next yeare Woolseie was cast out of fauour, and within few yeares sir William Skeffington was sent ouer lord deputie, and brought with him the erle pardoned and rid from all his troubles.

The earle of Kildare committed.

A mandatum to execute Kildare.

The cardinall his presumptuousness blamed of the king.

1529

Sir William Skeffington deputie of Ireland.

When it was bruted, that Skeffington, the earle of Kildare, and Edward Staples bishop of Meth landed néere Dublin, the maior and citizens met him with a solemne procession on saint Marie abbeis gréene, where maister Thomas Fitzsimons recorder of Dublin made a pithie oration to congratulate the gouernor and the earle his prosperous arriuall, to whome Skeffington shaped an answere in this wise: "Maister maior and maister recorder, you haue at length this noble man here present, for whom you sore longed, whilest he was absent. And after manie stormes by him susteined, he hath now to the comfort of his fréends, to the confusion of his foes, subdued violence with patience, iniuries with sufferance, and malice with obedience: and such butchers as of hatred thirsted after his bloud, are now taken for outcast mastiues, littered in currish bloud. How well my master the king hath beene of his gratious inclination affected to the earle of Kildare (his backe fréend, being by his iust desert from his maiestie wéeded) the credit wherein this noble man at this present abideth, manifestlie declareth. Wherefore it resteth, that you thanke God and the king for his safe arriuall. As for his welcome, maister recorder his courteous discourse, your great assemblies, your chéerefull countenances, your willing meetings, your solemne processions doo so far shew it, as you minister me occasion on his lordship his behalfe, rather to thanke you for your courtesie, than to exhort you to anie further ceremonie."

Edward Staples bishop of Meth.

Thomas Fitzsimons.

Skeffington his answere.

He glanseth at the cardinall who was taken to be a butcher his sonne.

Hauing ended his oration, they rode all into the citie, where shortlie after the earle of Ossorie surrendred the sword to sir William Skeffington. During the time that Kildare was in England, the sept of the Tooles making his absence their haruest, ceased not to molest and spoile his tenants, and therefore the erle meaning not to wrap vp so lightlie their manifold iniuries, was determined presentlie vpon his arriuall to crie them quittance: to the spéedinesse of which seruice he requested the aid of the citizens of Dublin: & expecting in Christs church their answere touching this motion, the maior & his brethren promised to assist him with two hundred archers. The late come bishop of Meth being then present, mooued question, whether the citizens were pardoned for crowning Lambert contrarie to their

Kildare inuadeth the Tooles.

Meth his question.

their dutie of allegiance, and if they were not pardoned, he thought they might aduantage the king thereby. Whereat one of their sagest and expertest aldermen, named Iohn Fitzsimons, stept foorth and said: "My lord of Meth, may I be so bold as to craue what countrieman you are?" "Marie sir (quoth the bishop) I would you should know it, I am a gentleman and an Englishman." "My lord (quoth Fitzsimons) my meaning is to learne, in what shire of England you were borne?" "In Lincolnshire good sir" (quoth Staples.) "Why then my lord (quoth Fitzsimons) we are no traitors, because it was the earle of Lincolne and the lord Louell that crowned him: and therefore if you be a gentleman of Lincolnshire, sée that you be pardoned, for God and our king be thanked we haue néed of none." At this answer Meth was set, and such as were present were forced to smile, to sée what a round fall he caught in his owne turne.

Iohn Fitzsimons answereth Meth.

In the second yeare of Skeffington his gouernement, it happened that one Henrie White, seruant to Benet a merchant of Dublin, was pitching of a cart of haie in the high street; and hauing offered bores plaie to passengers that walked to and fro, he let a bottle of his haie fall on a souldiors bonet, as he passed by his cart. The souldior taking this knauish knacke in dudgeon, hurled his dagger at him, and hauing narrowlie mist the princocks, he sticked it in a post not farre off. White leapt downe from the cart, and thrust the souldior through the shoulder with his pike. Wherevpon there was a great vprore in the citie betwéene the souldiors and the apprentises, insomuch as Thomas Barbie being the maior, hauing the king his sword drawne, was hardlie able to appease the fraie, in which diuerse were wounded, and none slaine. The lord deputie issued out of the castell, and came as farre as the pillorie, to whome the maior posted thorough the prease with the sword naked vnder his arme & presented White that was the brewer of all this garboile to his lordship, whome the gouernour pardoned, as well for his courage in bickering as for his retchlesse simplicitie and pleasantnesse in telling the whole discourse. Whereby a man maie sée how manie bloudie quarels a bralling swashbuckler maie picke out of a bottle of haie, namelie when his braines are forebitten with a bottle of nappie ale.

Henrie White raised an vprore in Dublin.

Thomas Barbie maior.

White pardoned.

About this time there was a great stirre raised in England, about the king his diuorse, who thinking it expedient in so fickle a world to haue a sure post in Ireland, made Kildare lord deputie, Cromer the primat of Armagh lord chancellor, and sir Iames Butler lord treasuror. Skeffington, supposing that he was put beside the cushin by the secret canuassing of Kildare his friends, conceiued therof a great gelousie, being therein the deeper drenched, bicause that Kildare hauing receiued the sword, would permit Skeffington, who was late gouernour, now like a meane priuat person, to danse attendance among other suters in his house at Dublin, named the Carbrie. Skeffington plaieng thus on the bit, shortlie after sailed into England, vpon whose departure the lord deputie summoned a parlement at Dublin, where there past an act against leasers of corne: also for the vniting and appropriation of the parsonage of Galtrim to the priorie of saint Peters by Trim. In the parlement time, Oneale on a sudden inuaded the countrie of Vriell, rifling and spoiling the king his subiects, at which time also was the earle of Ossorie greatlie vexed by the Giraldins, by reason of the old quarels of either side afresh reuiued.

Kildare lord deputie. Cromer. Butler.

Skeffington offended with Kildare.

He saileth into England.

1532

A parlement summoned at Dublin.

Vriell inuaded by Oneale.

The next yeare, the lord deputie going against Ocarroll, was pitifullie hurt in the side with a gun, at the castell of Birre, so that he neuer after inioied his lims, nor deliuered his words in good plight, otherwise like inough to haue béene longer forborne in consideration of his manie noble qualities, great good seruices, and the state of those times. Straightwais complaints were addressed to the king of these

Kildare hurt.

enormities,

Kildare accused. enormities, and that in most heinous maner that could be deuised, boulting out his dooings as it were to the last brake of sinister surmises, turning euerie priuat iniurie to be the king his quarrell, & making euerie puddings pricke as huge in shew as Samson his piller. Wherevpon Kildare was commanded by sharpe letters to repaire into England, leauing such a person for the furniture of that realme, and the gouernance of the land in his absence, for whose dooings he would answer. Being vpon the sight of this letter prepared to saile into England, he sat in councell at Dublin, and hauing sent for his sonne & heire the lord Thomas Fitzgirald (a yoong strippling of one and twentie yeares of age, borne in England, sonne to the lord Zouch his daughter, the earle of Kildare his first wife) in the hearing of the whole boord thus he spake.

He is sent for to England.

Thomas Fitzgirald.

The earle of Kildare his exhortation to his sonne the lord Thomas.

"SONNE Thomas, I doubt not, but you know that my soueraigne lord the king hath sent for me into England, and what shall betide me God knoweth, for I know not. But howsoeuer it falleth, both you and I know that I am well stept in yeares: and as I maie shortlie die, for that I am mortall, so I must in hast decease, bicause I am old. Wherefore insomuch as my winter is welneere ended, and the spring of your age now buddeth, my will is that you behaue your selfe so wiselie in these your gréene yeares, as that to the comfort of your friends you maie inioie the pleasure of summer, gleane and reape the fruits of your haruest, that with honour you maie grow to the catching of that hoarie winter, on which you sée me your father fast pricking. And wheras it pleaseth the king his maiestie, that vpon my departure here hense, I should substitute in my roome such one, for whose gouernement I would answer: albeit I know, that your yeares are tender, your wit not settled, your iudgement not fullie rectified, and therefore I might be with good cause reclamed from putting a naked sword in a yoong mans hand: yet notwithstanding, forsomuch as I am your father, and you my sonne, I am well assured to beare that stroke with you in stéering your ship, as that vpon anie information I maie command you as your father, and correct you as my sonne for the wrong handling of your helme.

"There be here that sit at this boord, far more sufficient personages for so great charge than you are. But what then? If I should cast this burthen on their shoulders, it might be that hereafter they would be so farre with enuie carried, as they would percase hazzard the losse of one of their owne eies, to be assured that I should be depriued of both mine eies. But forsomuch as the case toucheth your skin as néere as mine, and in one respect nigher than mine, bicause (as I said before) I rest in the winter, and you in the spring of your yeares, and now I am resolued daie by daie to learne rather how to die in the feare of God, than to liue in the pompe of the world, I thinke you will not be so brainesicke, as to stab your selfe thorough the bodie, onelie to scarifie my skin with the point of your blade. Wherefore (my sonne) consider, that it is easie to raze, and hard to build, and in all your affaires be schooled by this boord, that for wisedome is able, and for the entier affection it beareth your house, will be found willing, to lesson you with sound and sage aduise. For albeit in authoritie you rule them, yet in councell they must rule you. My sonne, you know that my late maimes stifleth my talke: otherwise I would haue grated longer on this matter. For a good tale maie be twise told, and a sound aduise (eftsoones iterated) taketh the deeper impression in the attentiue hearer his mind. But although my fatherlie affection requireth my discourse to be longer, yet I trust your

your good inclination asketh it to be shorter, and vpon that assurance, here in the presence of this honourable assemblie, I deliuer you this sword." ¶ Thus he spake for his last farewell with trickling teares, and hauing ended, he stood, imbrased the councell, committed them to God, and immediatlie after he was imbarked. Kildare saileth into England

But although with his graue exhortation the frosen hearts of his aduersaries for a short spirt thawed, yet notwithstanding they turned soone after all this gare *Gloria patri* vnto a further fetch, saieng that this was nothing else but to dazell their eies with some iugling knacke, to the end they should aduertise the king of his loiall speeches, adding further, that he was too too euill that could not speake well. And to force the prepensed treasons they laied to his charge, with further surmises they certified the councell of England, that the earle before his departure furnished his owne piles and forts with the king his artillerie and munition taken foorth of the castell of Dublin. The earle being examined vpon that article before the councell, although he answered that the few potguns and chambers he tooke from thense, were placed in his castell to strengthen the borders against the inrodes of the Irish enimie, and that if he intended anie treason, he was not so foolish, as to fortifie walles and stones, and to commit his naked bones into their hands; yet notwithstanding he deliuered his speeches by reason of his palseie, in such staggering and mafling wise, that such of the councell as were not his friends, persuading the rest that he had sunke in his owne tale, by imputing his lisping and dragging answer rather to the gilt of conscience, than to the infirmitie of his late maime, had him committed, vntill the king his pleasure were further knowne. His oration misconstrued. He is accused for taking the king his artillerie. Kildare committed

But before we wade anie further in this matter, for the better opening of the whole ground, it would be noted, that the earle of Kildare, among diuerse hidden aduersaries, had in these his later troubles foure principall enimies that were the chiefe means & causes of his ouerthrow, as in those daies it was commonlie bruted. The first was Iohn Alen archbishop of Dublin, a gentleman of a good house, chapleine to cardinall Wolseie, & after by the cardinall his means constituted archbishop of Dublin, a learned prelat, a good housholder, of the people indifferentlie beloued, and more would haue béene, had he not ouerbusied himselfe in supplanting the house of Kildare. And although it were knowne, that his first grudge towards the Giraldins procéeded from the great affection he bare his lord and master the cardinall, insomuch as he would not sticke, were he able, for the pleasuring of the one to vndoo the other; yet such occasions of greater hatred after insued (namelie for that he was displaced from being lord chancellor, & Cromer the primat of Armagh by Kildare his drifts setled in the office) as notwithstanding the cardinall his combe was cut in England, yet did he persist in pursuing his woonted malice toward that sée. Kildare his chiefe enimies. Iohn Alen archbishop of Dublin

The second that was linked to this confederacie, was sir Iohn Alen knight, first secretarie to this archbishop, after became master of the rolles, lastlie lord chancellor. And although sir Iohn Alen were not of kin to the archbishop, but onelie of the name, yet notwithstanding the archbishop made so great reckoning of him, as well for his forecast in matters of weight, as for his faithfulnesse in affaires of trust, as whatsoeuer exploit were executed by the one, was foorthwith déemed to haue béene deuised by the other. The third of this crew was Thomas Canon, secretarie to Sketfington, who thinking to be reuenged on Kildare for putting his lord and master beside the cushin, as he surmised, was verie willing to haue an ore in that bote. The fourth that was suspected to make the muster, was Robert Cowlie, first bailiffe in Dublin, Sir Iohn Alen knight. Thomas Canon. Robert Cowle

Dublin, after seruant to the ladie Margaret Fitzgirald, countesse of Ormond and Ossorie, lastlie master of the rolles in Ireland, and finallie he deceased at London.

This gentleman for his wisdome and policie was well estéemed of the ladie Margaret countesse of Ossorie, as one by whose aduise she was in all hir affaires directed. Wherevpon some suspicious persons were persuaded and brought in mind, that he was the sower of all the discord that rested betwéene the two brethren Kildare and Ossorie: as though he could not be rooted in the fauour of the one, but that he must haue professed open hatred vnto the other. These foure, as birds of one feather, were supposed to be open enimies to the house of Kildare, bearing that swaie in the commonwealth, as they were not occasioned (as they thought) either to craue fréendship of the Giraldines, or greatlie to feare their hatred and enimitie. There were beside them diuerse other secret vnderminers, who wrought so cunninglie vnder the thumbe, by holding with the hare, and running with the hound, as if Kildare had prospered, they were assured, their malice would not haue béene in manner suspected: but if he had béene in his affaires stabled, then their fine deuises for their further credit should haue beene apparented. Wherefore the heauing of his backe fréends not onelie surmised, but also manifested by Kildare, the lord Thomas being iustice or vicedeputie in his fathers absence, fetcht both the Alens so roundlie ouer the lips, as well by secret drifts as open taunts, as they were the more egerlie spurd to compasse his confusion. For the lord iustice and the councell, with diuerse of the nobilitie, at a solemne banket discoursing of the ancientie of houses, and of their armes, sir Iohn Alen spake to the lord iustice these words.

The lord Thomas inkindleth the Alens against him.

"My lord, your house giueth the marmoset, whose propertie is to eat his owne taile." Meaning thereby (as the lord Thomas supposed) that Kildare did vse to pill and poll his fréends, tenants & reteiners. These words were no sooner spoken, than the lord Thomas striking the ball to Alen againe, answered, as one that was somewhat slipper toonged, in this wise. "You saie truth sir, indéed I heard some saie, that the marmoset eateth his owne taile. But although you haue béene fed by your taile, yet I would aduise you to beware, that your taile eat not you." Shortlie after this quipping gamegall, the lord iustice and the councell rode to Drogheda, where hauing for the space of three or foure daies soiourned, it happened that the councellors awaited in the councell chamber the gouernour his comming, vntill it was hard vpon the stroke of twelue. The archbishop of Dublin rawlie digesting the vicedeputie his long absence, said: "My lords, is it not a prettie matter, that all we shall staie thus long for a boie?" As he vttered these speeches, the lord iustice vnluckilie was comming vp the staires, and at his entrie taking the words hot from the bishop his mouth, and iterating them verie coldlie, he said: "My lords, I am heartilie sorie, that you staied thus long for a boie." Whereat the prelat was appalled, to see how vnhappilie he was gald with his owne caltrop. These & the like cutting spéeches inkindled such coles in both their stomachs, as the flame could not anie longer be smouldered, but at one clift or other must haue fumed. The enimies therefore hauing welnigh knedded the dough that should haue béene baked for the Giraldines bane, deuised that secret rumors should sprinkle to and fro, that the earle of Kildare his execution was intended in England, and that vpon his death the lord Thomas and all his bloud should haue beene apprehended in Ireland. As this false muttering flie abroad, it was holpen forward by Thomas Canon, and others of Skeffington his seruants, who sticked not to write to certeine of their fréends, as it were, verie secret letters, how that the earle of Kildare their maister his secret enimie (so they tooke him, bicause he got the gouernement ouer his head) was alreadie cut shorter, as his issue

The propertie of the marmoset.

The archbishop his taun

The enimies conspire the ouerthrow of the Giraldins

The occasion of Thomas Fitzgirald his rebellion

issue presentlie should be: and now they trusted to sée their maister in his gouernment, after which they sore longed, as for a preferment that would in short space aduantage them. Such a letter came vnto the hands of a simple priest, no perfect Englishman, who for hast hurled it amongest other papers in the chimnies end of his chamber, meaning to peruse it better at more leisure. The same verie night, a gentleman reteining to the lord Thomas, the lord iustice or vicedeputie, as is before specified, tooke vp his lodging with the priest, and sought in the morning when he rose for some paper, to draw on his strait stockings, and as the diuell would, he hit vpon the letter, bare it awaie in the heele of his stocke, no earthlie thing misdéeming. At night againe he found the paper vnfretted, and musing thereat he began to pore on the writing, which notified the earle his death, and the apprehension of the lord Thomas. To horsse goeth he in all hast, brought the letter to Iames de la Hide, who was principall councellor to the lord Thomas in all his doings. De la Hide hauing scantlie ouerread the letter, making more hast than good spéed, posted to the lord Thomas, imparted him that letter, and withall putting fire to flax, before he diued to the bottome of this trecherie, he was contented to swim on the skum and froth thereof: as well by soothing vp the tenor of the letter, as by inciting the lord Thomas to open rebellion, cloking the odious name of treason with the zealous reuengement of his fathers wrongfull execution, and with the warie defense of his owne person.

Iames de la Hide.

The lord Thomas being youthfull, rash, and headlong, and assuring himselfe that the knot of all the force of Ireland was twisted vnder his girdle, was by de la Hide his counsell so far caried, as he was resolued to cast all on six and seauen. Wherefore hauing confederated with Oneale, Oconor, and other Irish potentats, he rode on saint Barnabies daie, accompanied with seauen score horssemen in their shirts of maile, through the citie of Dublin, to the Dam his gate, crost ouer the water to saint Marie abbeie, where the councell according to appointment waited his comming, not being priuie to his intent: onelie Cromer the lord chancellour excepted, who was secretlie aduertised of his reuolt, and therefore was verie well prouided for him, as héereafter shall be declared. This Cromer was a graue prelat, and a learned, well spoken, mild of nature, nothing wedded to factions, yet a welwiller of the Giraldines, as those by whose means he was aduanced to dignitie. When the lord Thomas was set in councell, his horssemen and seruants rusht into the councell chamber armed and weaponed, turning their secret conference to an open parlée. The councell hereat amazed, and silence with securitie commanded, the lord Thomas in this wise spake.

Cromer lord chancellor.

Thomas Fitzgirald his rebellious oration.

"HOWSOEVER iniuriouslie we be handled, and forced to defend our selues in armes, when neither our seruice nor our good meaning towards our princes crowne auaileth: yet saie not héereafter, but in this open hostilitie which héere we professe and proclame, we haue shewed our selues no villaines nor churles, but warriours and gentlemen. This sword of estate is yours, and not mine, I receiued it with an oth, and haue vsed it to your benefit. I should staine mine honour, if I turned the same to your annoiance. Now haue I need of mine owne sword, which I dare trust. As for the common sword, it flattereth me with a painted scabberd, but hath indéed a pestilent edge, alreadie bathed in the Giraldines bloud, and now is newlie whetted in hope of a further destruction. Therefore saue your selues from vs, as from open enimies, I am none of Henrie his deputie, I am his fo, I haue more mind to conquer than to gouerne, to meet him in the field than to serue him in office. If all the hearts of England and Ireland, that haue cause thereto, would ioine in this quarell (as I hope they will) then should he soone abie (as I trust he shall) for his crueltie and tyrannie, for which the age to come may lawfullie score him vp among the ancient tyrants of most abhominable and hatefull memorie."

Hauing added to this shamefull oration manie other slanderous and foule tearmes, which for diuerse respects I spare to pen, he would haue surrendered the sword to the lord chancellor, who (as I said before) being armed for the lord Thomas his comming, and also being loath that his slacknesse should séeme disloiall in refusing the sword, or his frowardnesse ouer cruell in snatching it vpon the first proffer, tooke the lord Thomas by the wrist of the hand, and requested him for the loue of God, the teares trilling downe his chéekes, to giue him for two or thrée words the hearing, which granted, the reuerend father spake as insueth.

The chancellor his oration.

"My lord, although hatred be commonlie the handmaiden of truth, bicause we sée him that plainelie expresseth his mind, to be for the more part of most men disliked: yet notwithstanding I am so well assured of your lordship his good inclination towards me, and your lordship so certeine of mine entire affection towards you, as I am inboldned, notwithstanding this companie of armed men, fréelie and frankelie to vtter that, which by me declared, and by your lordship followed, will turne (God willing) to the auaile of you, your friends, alies, and this countrie. I doubt not (my lord) but you know, that it is wisedome for anie man to looke before he leape, and to sownd the water before his ship hull thereon, & namelie where the matter is of weight, there it behoooueth to follow sound, sage, and mature aduise. Wherefore (my lord) sith it is no margame for a subiect to leuie an armie against his prince, it lieth your lordship in hand to breath longer on the matter, as well by forecasting the hurt whereby you may fall, as by reuoluing the hope wherwith you are fed. What should mooue your lordship to this sudden attempt, I know not. If it be the death of your father, it is as yet but secretlie muttered, not manifestlie published. And if I should grant you, that your zeale in reuenging your father his execution were in some respect to be commended: yet reason would you should suspend the reuenge vntill the certeintie were knowne. And were it, that the report were true, yet it standeth with the dutie and allegiance of a good subiect (from whom I hope in God you meane not to disseuer your selfe) not to spurne and kicke against his prince, but contrariwise, if his soueraigne be mightie, to feare him: if he be profitable to his subiects, to honour him: if he command, to obeie him: if he be kind, to loue him: if he be vicious, to pitie him: if he be a tyrant, to beare with him: considering that in such case it is better with patience to bow, than with stubburnnesse to breake. For sacred is the name of a king, and odious is the name of a rebellion: the one from heauen deriued, and by God shielded, the other in hell forged, and by the diuell executed. And therefore who so will obserue the course of histories, or weigh the iustice of God in punishing malefactors, shall easilie sée, that albeit the sunne shineth for a time on them that are in rebellion: yet such swéet beginnings are at length clasped vp with sharpe & sowre ends.

The subiect's dutie towards his king.

The name of a king sacred.

Rebellion from whense it springeth.

"Now

"Now that it appeareth, that you ought not to beare armour against your king, it resteth to discusse whether you be able (though you were willing) to annoie your king. For if among meane and priuat foes it be reckoned for follie, in a secret grudge to professe open hatred, and where he is not able to hinder, there to shew a willing mind to hurt: much more ought your lordship in so generall a quarell as this, that concerneth the king, that toucheth the nobilitie, that apperteineth to the whole commonwelth, to foresée the king his power on the one side, & your force on the other, and then to iudge if you be able to cocke with him, and to put him beside the cushion, and not whilest you striue to sit in the saddle, to lose to your owne vndoing both the horsse and the saddle.

"King Henrie is knowne to be in these our daies so puissant a prince, and so victorious a worthie, that he is able to conquer forren dominions: and thinke you that he cannot defend his owne? He tameth kings, and iudge you that he may not rule his owne subiects? Suppose you conquer the land, doo you imagine that he will not recouer it? Therefore (my lord) flatter not your selfe ouermuch, repose not so great affiance either in your troope of horssemen, or in your band of footmen, or in the multitude of your partakers. What face soeuer they put now on the matter, or what successe soeuer for a season they haue, bicause it is easie for an armie to vanquish them that doo not resist: yet hereafter when the king shall send his power into this countrie, you shall see your adherents like slipper changelings plucke in their hornes, and such as were content to beare you vp by the chin as long as you could swim, when they espie you sinke, they will by little and little shrinke from you, and percase will ducke you ouer head and eares. As long as the gale puffeth full in your sailes, doubt not but diuerse will auerre vnto you and féed on you as crowes on carion: but if anie storme happen to bluster, then will they be sure to leaue you post alone sticking in the mire or sands, hauing least helpe when you haue most néed. And what will then insue of this? The branches will be pardoned, the root apprehended, your honour distained, your house atteinted, your armes reuersed, your manours razed, your doings examined, at which time God knoweth what an hartburning it will be, when that with no colour may be denied, which without shame cannot be confessed. My lord, I powre not out oracles as a soothsaier, for I am neither a prophet, nor the sonne of a prophet. But it may be, that I am some frantike Cassandra being partener of her spirit in foretelling the truth, and partaker of hir misfortune in that I am not (when I tell the truth) beléeued of your lordship, whom God defend from being Priamus. Cassandras prophesie

"Weigh therefore (my lord) the nobilitie of your ancestors, remember your father his late exhortation, forget not your dutie vnto your prince, consider the estate of this poore countrie, with what heaps of cursses you shall be loden, when your souldiers shall rifle the poore subiects, & so far indamage the whole relme, as they are not yet borne that shall hereafter féele the smart of this vprore. You haue not gone so far but you may turne home, the king is mercifull, your offense as yet not ouer heinous, cleaue to his clemencie, abandon this headlong follie. Which I craue in most humble wise of your lordship, for the loue of God, for the dutie you owe your prince, for the affection you beare the countrie, and for the respect you haue to your owne safetie, whom God defend from all traitorous & wicked attempts."

Hauing ended his oration, which he set foorth with such a lamentable action, as his chéekes were all bebiubbered with teares, the horssemen, namelie such as vnderstood

stood not English, began to diuine what the lord chancellor ment with all this long circumstance; some of them reporting that he was preaching a sermon, others said that he stood making of some heroicall poetrie in the praise of the lord Thomas. And thus as euerie idiot shot his foolish bolt at the wise chancellor his discourse, who in effect did nought else but drop pretious stones before hogs, one Bard de Nelan, an Irish rithmour, and a rotten shéepe able to infect an whole flocke, was chatting of Irish verses, as though his toong had run on pattens, in commendation of the lord Thomas, inuesting him with the title of Silken Thomas, bicause his horssemens iacks were gorgeouslie imbrodered with silke: and in the end he told him that he lingred there ouerlong. Whereat the lord Thomas being quickned, did cast his eie towards the lord chancellor, & said thus.

Bard de Nelan.

Silken Thomas.

The replie of Silken Thomas.

"My lord chancellor, I come not hither to take aduise what I should doo, but to giue you to vnderstand what I mind to doo. It is easie for the sound to counsell the sicke: but if the sore had smarted you as much as it festereth me, you would be percase as impatient as I am. As you would wish me to honour my prince, so dutie willeth me to reuerence my father. Wherefore he that will with such tyrannie execute mine innocent parent, and withall threaten my destruction, I may not, nor will not hold him for my king. And yet in truth he was neuer our king, but our lord, as his progenitors haue beene before him. But if it be my hap to miscarie, as you séeme to prognosticat, catch that catch may, I will take the market as it riseth, and will choose rather to die with valiantnesse and libertie, than to liue vnder king Henrie in bondage and villanie. And yet it may be, that as strong as he is, and as weake as I am, I shall be able like a fleshworme to itch the bodie of his kingdome, and force him to scratch déepelie before he be able to pike me out of my seame. Wherefore my lord, I tkanke you for your good counsell, and were it not that I am too crabbed a note in descant to be now tuned, it might be that I would haue warbled swéeter harmonie than at this instant I meane to sing." ¶ With these words he rendered vp the sword, and flung awaie like a bedlem, being garded with his brutish droue of brainesicke rebels."

Henrie lord of Ireland.

Thomas rendereth vp the sword.

The councell sent secretlie vpon his departue to master maior and his brethren, to apprehend (if they conuenientlie might) Thomas Fitzgirald and his confederats. But the warning was so Skarborrow, the enimie so strong, the citie (by reason of the plage that ranged in towne and in countrie) so dispeopled, as their attempt therein would seeme but vaine and friuolous. Ouer this, the weaker part of the rebels would not pen vp themselues within the citie wals, but stood houering aloofe off toward Ostmantowne gréene, on the top of the hill where the gallowes stood (a fit centre for such a circle) till time they were aduertised of their capteine Thomas his returne. This open rebellion in this wise denounced; part of the councell, namelie Alen archbishop of Dublin & Finglasse chiefe baron hied with bag and baggage to the castell of Dublin, whereof Iohn White was constable, who after was dubbed knight by the king in England, for his worthie seruice doone in that vprore.

Alen. Finglasse. Iohn Walter.

Thomas & his crew, supposing that in ouerruning the whole land, they should find no blocke to stumble at sauing the earle of Ossorie, agreed to trie if by anie allurements he could be traind to their confederacie. And forsomuch as the lord Iames

Iames Butler was linked with Thomas Fitzgirald in great amitie and friendship, it was thought best to giue him the onset, who if he were woon to sware with them, they would not weigh two chips the force of his father the earle of Ossorie. Thomas foorthwith sent his messengers and letters to his cousine the lord Butler, couenanting to diuide with him halfe the kingdome, would he associat him in this enterprise. Wherevpon the lord Butler returned Thomas his brokers with this letter.

The lord Butler his letter to Thomas Fitzgirald.

"TAKING pen in hand to write you my resolute answer, I muse in the verie first line by what name to call you, my lord, or my cousine, séeing your notorious treason hath distained your honour, and your desperate lewdnesse shamed your kindred. You are so liberall in parting stakes with me, that a man would wéene you had no right vnto the game: so importunat in crauing my companie, as if you would persuade me to hang with you for good fellowship. Doo you thinke that Iames was so mad, as to gape for gogions, or so vngratious, as so sell his truth for a péece of Ireland? Were it so (as it cannot be) that the chickens you reckon, were both hatched and feathered, yet be thou sure, I had rather in this quarell die thine enimie, than liue thy partener. For the kindnesse you proffer me, and good loue in the end of your letter, the best waie I can I purpose to requite, that is, in aduising you, though you haue fetcht your feare, yet to looke well yer ye leape. Ignorance and errour, with a certeine opinion of dutie, haue caried you vnawares to this follie, not yet so ranke but it maie be cured. The king is a vessell of bountie & mercie, your words against his maiestie shall not be accounted malicious, but rather belched out for heat and impotencie, except your selfe by heaping offenses discouer a mischeefous and willfull meaning. Farewell."

Thomas Fitzgirald netled with this round answer, was determined to inuade the countrie of Kilkennie, first forcing an oth vpon the gentlemen of the pale: and such as would not agree thereto he tooke prisoners. Fingall, which was not before acquainted with the recourse of the Irish enimie, was left open to be preided and spoiled by the Tooles, who were therein assisted by Iohn Birnell of Balgriffin, a gentleman of a faire liuing, setled in a good battle soile of Fingall, taken for one not deuoid of wit, were it not that he was ouertaken with this treason. The Dublinians hauing notice that the enimie made hauocke of their neighbors of Fingall, issued out of the citie, meaning to haue intercepted them at the bridge of Kilmainan. And hauing incountered with the Irish néere the wood Salcocke, what for the number of the rebels, and the lacke of an expert capteine to lead the armie of Dublin in battell raie, there were fourescore of the citizens slaine, and the preide not rescued. In this conflict, Patrike Fitzsimons, with diuerse other good housholders, miscaried.

Fingall spoiled. Iohn Birnell of Belgriffin. The Dublinians discomfited. Patrike Fitzsimons slaine.

This victorie bred so great an insolencie in Thomas Fitzgirald, as he sent his messengers to the citie, declaring that albeit they offered him that iniurie, as that he could not haue frée passage with his companie to & fro in the pale, & therefore would he vse the benefit of his late skirmish, or be answerable in iust reuenge to their due desert, he might by law of armes put their citie to fire and sword: yet this notwithstanding, if they would but permit his men to laie siege to the castell of Dublin, he would enter in league with them, and would vndertake to backe them in such

Messengers sent from Thomas to Dublin.

fauourable

fauourable wise, as the stoutest champion in his armie should not be so hardie, as to offer the basest in their citie so much as a fillip. The citizens considering that the towne by reason of the sickenesse was weakened, and by this late ouerthrow greatlie discouraged, were forced to make a vertue of necessitie, by lighting a candle before the diuell, till time the kings pleasure were knowne, to whom with letters they posted one
Francis Herbert sent into England. of their aldermen named Francis Herbert, whom shortlie after, the king for his seruice dubbed knight, infeoffing him with part of Christopher Eustace of Balicutlan
Eustace of Balicutlan. his lands, who had vnaduisedlie a foot in this rebellion. But before the citizens would returne answer to Thomas as touching this message, they secretlie aduertised maister Iohn White conestable of the castell of this vnlawfull demand.

The conestable weighing the securitie of the citie, little regarding the force of the enimie, agreed willinglie therto, so that he might be sufficientlie stored with
The archbishop of Dublin meaneth to saile into England. Bartholomew Fitzgerald. men and vittels. Iohn Alen archbishop of Dublin, fearing that all would haue gone to wracke in Ireland, being then in the castell, brake his mind touching his sailing into England, to one of his seruants named Bartholomew Fitzgerald, whom notwithstanding he were a Geraldine, he held for his trustiest and inwardest councellor. Bartholomew vndertaking to be the archbishop his pilot, vntill hee were past the barre, incouraged his maister to imbarke himselfe hard by the Dams gate. And as they were hulling in the channell that euening, they were not ware, vntill the barke strake on the sands néere Clontarfe.

The archbishop with his man stale secretlie to Tartaine, there meaning to lurke vntill the wind had serued to saile into England, where he scarselie six houres soiourned, when Thomas Fitzgerald knew of his arriuall, and accompanied with Iames de la Hide, sir Iohn Fitzgerald, Oliuer Fitzgerald his vncles, timelie in the morning, being the eight and twentith of Iulie, he posted to Tartaine, beset the
1534 Teling. Waffer. house, commanded Iohn Teling and Nicholas Waffer to apprehend the archbishop, whome they haled out of his bed, brought him naked in his shirt, barefooted, and bareheaded, to their capteine. Whom when the archbishop espied, incontinentlie he knéeled and with a pitifull countenance & lamentable voice, he besought him for the loue of God not to remember former iniuries, but to weigh his present calamitie, and what malice soeuer he bare his person, yet to respect his calling and vocation, in that his enimie was a christian, and he amongst christians an archbishop.

As he spake thus, bequeathing his soule to God, his bodie to the enimies mercie, Thomas being stricken with some compassion, & withall inflamed with desire of reuenge, turned his horsse aside, saieng in Irish (*Beir uaim è bodde ugh*) which is as much to saie in English, as Away with the chürle, or Take the chürle from me: which doubtles he spake, as after he declared, meaning the archbishop should be deteined as prisoner. But the caitifs that were present rather of malice than of igno-
Alen archbishop of Dublin murthered at Tartaine. rance, misconstruing his words, murthered the archbishop without further delaie, brained and hacked him in gobbets, his bloud with Abell crieng to God for reuenge, which after befell to all such as were principals in this horrible murther. The place is euer since hedged and imbared on euerie side ouergrowne and vnfrequented for detestation of the fact. This Alen (as before is declared) was in seruice with cardinall Woolseie, of déepe ingenie, in the law canon, the onelie match of Stephan Gardiner, an other of Woolseies chapleins, for auoiding of which emulation he was preferred in Ireland, rough and rigorous in iustice, deadlie hated of the Geraldines for his maisters sake & his owne, as that he crossed them diuerse times, and much bridelled both

father

father and son in their gouernements, not vnlike to haue promoted their accusations, and to haue béene a forger of the letter before mentioned, which turned to his small destruction.

The rebels hauing in this execrable wise imbrued their hands in the archbishop his blood, they rode to Houth, tooke sir Christopher lord of Houth prisoner, & vpon their returne from thense, they apprehended maister Luttrell chiefe iustice of the common plées, conueieng him with them as their prisoner. The Dublinians during this space, hauing respit to pause, sent into the castell by night sufficient store of vittels, at which time, Iohn Fitzsimons, one of their aldermen, sent to master conestable twentie tun of wine, foure & twentie tun of béere, two thousand drie ling, sixteene hogsheads of poudered beefe, and twentie chambers, with an iron chaine for the draw bridge of the castell that was newlie forged in his owne house for the auoiding of all suspicion. The castell being with men, munition, and vittels abundantlie furnished, answer was returned to Thomas Fitzgerald, purporting a consent for the receiuing of his souldiors. Which granted, he sent Iames Field of Luske, Nicholas Waffer, Iohn Teling, Edward Rouks (who was likewise a pirat scowring the coast, and greatlie annoieng all passengers) Broad and Pursell, with an hundred souldiors attendant on them, as on their capteins. These valiant Rutterkins planted néere Preston his innes, right ouer against the castell gate two or thrée falcons, hauing with such strong rampiers intrenched their companie, as they litle weighed the shot of the castle. And to withdraw the conestable from discharging the ordinance, they threatened to take the youth of the citie, and place them on the top of their trenches for maister conestable to shoot at, as at a marke he would be loth to hit.

The lord of Houth taken prisoner. Iustice Luttrell taken. Iohn Fitzsimons. The castell of Dublin besieged. Field. Waffer. Teling. Roukes.

The English pale in this wise weakened, the citizens appeased, and the castell besieged, Thomas Fitzgerald and his confederats were resolued to trie if the lord Butler would stand to his doughtie letter, and sith he would not by faire means be allured, hée should be (maugre his head) by foule means compelled to assist them in this their generall attempt. Thomas vpon this determination, being accompanied with Oneale, diuerse Scots, Iames de la Hide, his principall councellour, Iohn de la Hide, Edward Fitzgerald his vncle, sir Richard Walsh parson of Loughsewdie, Iohn Burnell of Balgriffin, Iames Gernon, Walter Walsh, Robert Walsh, Maurice Walsh, with a maine armie, inuaded the erle of Ossorie and the lord Butler his lands, burnt and wasted the countrie of Kilkennie to Thomas towne, the poore inhabitants being constreined to shunne his force, rather than to withstand his power.

Thomas Fitzgerald inuadeth the countrie of Kilkennie.

Fitzgerald his approch towards these confines bruted, the earle of Ossorie, and his son the lord Butler, with all the gentlemen of the countrie of Kilkennie, assembled néere Ierpon, to determine what order they might take, in withstanding the inuasion of the rebels. And as they were thus in parlée, a gentleman of the Butlers accompanied with sixtéene horsmen, departed secretlie from the folkemote, & made towards Thomas Fitzgerald and his armie, who was then readie to incampe himselfe at Thomas towne. When the chalenger was escried, and the certeine number knowne, sixtéene of Fitzgerald his horssemen did charge him, and presentlie followed them seuen score horssemen, with two or three banners displaied, pursuing them vntill they came to the hill where all the gentlemen were assembled, who being so suddenlie taken, could not stand to bicker, but some fled this waie, some that waie, the earle was scattered from his companie, and the lord Butler vnwares was hurt: whom when such of the rebels knew as fauoured him, they pursued him but coldlie, and let him escape on horssebacke, taking his waie to Downemore (neére Kilkennie) where he laie at surgerie.

The earle of Ossorie fleeth. The lord Butler wounded.

During

Francis Herebert commeth from England. Shillingforth.

During the time that Thomas with his armie was ransacking the erle of Ossorie his lands, Francis Herebert returned from England to Dublin with the king and councels letters to maister Shillingforth then maior, and his brethren, with letters likewise to maister White the constable, to withstand (as their dutie of allegiance bound them) the traitorous practises of Thomas and his complices, and that with all spéed they should be succored vpon the sight of these letters. Maister Thomas Fitzsimons recorder of the citie, a gentleman that shewed himselfe a politike and a comfortable councellor in these troubles, paraphrasing the king his gratious letters, with diuerse good and sound constructions, imboldened the citizens to breake their new made league, which with no traitor was to be kept. The aldermen and communaltie, with this pithie persuasion easilie weighed, gaue forthwith order, that the gates should be shut, their percullices dismounted, the traitors that besieged the castell apprehended, flags of defiance vpon their wals placed, and an open breach of truce proclamed.

Thomas Fitzsimons.

No league to be kept with traitors. The Dublinians breake with Thomas Fitzgirald.

Field and his companies (who did not all this while batter aught of the castell, but onelie one hole that was bored through the gate with a pellet, which lighted in the mouth of a demie canon, planted within the castell) vnderstanding that they were betraied, began to shrinke their heads, trusting more to their héeles than to their weapons: some ran one way, some another, diuerse thought to haue béene housed and so to lurke in Lorels den, who were thrust out by the head and shoulders: few of them swam ouer the Liffie, the greater number taken and imprisoned. Forthwith post vpon post rode to Thomas Fitzgirald, who then was rifling the countrie of Kilkennie, certifieng him that all was mard, the fat was in the fire, he brought an old house about his owne eares, the Paltocks of Dublin kept not touch with him, the English armie was readie to be shipt, Herebert with the king his letters returned; now it stood him vpon to shew himselfe a man or a mouse. Thomas with these tidings amazed, made spéedie repaire to Dublin, sending his purseuants before him, to command the gentlemen of the English pale to méete him with all their power néere Dublin. And in his waie towards the citie, his companie tooke diuerse children of the Dublinians, that kept in the countrie (by reason of the contagion that then was in the towne) namelie Michaell Fitzsimons, Patrike Fitzsimons, William Fitzsimons, all sons to Walter Fitzsimons late maior, at which time was also taken Iames Stanihurst, with diuerse other yoonglings of the citie.

Field and his companie taken.

The youth of Dublin taken prisoners.

Hauing marched néere Dublin, he sent doctor Trauerse, Peter Lince of the Knoke, and Oliuer Grace, as messengers (for I maie not rightlie tearme them ambassadors) to the citizens, who crossing the Liffie from the blacke friers to the keie, explaned to the maior and aldermen their errand, the effect whereof was, either to stand to their former promise, or else to restore to their capteine his men, whom they wrongfullie deteined in goale. The first and last point of this request flatlie by the citizens denied, the messengers returned, declaring what cold interteinment they had in Dublin. Thomas herewith frieng in his grease, caused part of his armie to burne the barke wherin Herebert sailed from England: which doone without resistance, the vessell road at anchor néere saint Marie abbeie, they indeuored to stop all the springs that flowed vnto the towne, and to cut the pipes of the conduits, whereby they should be destitute of fresh water. Shortlie after, they laid siege to the castell in the Shipstréet, from whense they were hastilie by the ordinance feazed, and all the thatcht houses of the stréet were burnt with wild fire, which maister White deuised, because the enimie should not be there rescued.

Messengers sent to Dublin. Trauerse. Lince. Grace.

Dublin besieged.

The shipstreet fired.

When no butter could sticke on their bread, in that part of the citie, the greater number of the rebels assembled to Thomas his court, and marched to saint Thomas his

his

his street, rasing downe the partitions of the row of houses before them on both sides of the street, finding none to withstand them for the inhabitants fled into the citie, so that they made a long lane on both the sides like a gallerie, couered all ouer head, to shield as well their horssemen as their footmen from gunshot This doone they burnt the new street, planted a falcon right against the new gate, and it discharged, pearsed the gate, and kild an apprentise of Thomas Stephens alderman, as he went to bring a bason of water from the high pipe, which by reason the springs were damd vp, was at that time drie Richard Stanton, commonlie called Dicke Stanton, then gailor of the new gate, a good seruitor, an excellent markeman, as his valiant seruice that time did approue For besides that he gald diuers of the rebels as they would skip from house to house, by causing some of them with his peece to carrie their errands in their buttocks, so he perceiued one of the enimies, leueling at the window or spike at which he stood but whether it were, that the rebell his ponder failed him, or some gumboll or other was out of frame, Stanton tooke him so truelie for his marke, as he strake him with his bullet full in the forehead vnder the brim of his scull, and withall turned vp his héeles

Richard Stanton.

Stanton not satisfied with his death, issued out at the wicket, stript the varlot mothernaked, and brought in his péece and his attire The desperatnesse of this fact disliked of the citizens, and greatlie stomached by the rebels, before Stanton returned to his standing, the enimies brought faggots & fiers to the new gate, and incontinentlie fired them The townesmen perceiuing that if the gate were burnt, the enimies would be incouraged vpon hope of the spoile, to venter more fiercelie, than if they were incountred without the wals, thought it expedient presentlie to charge them To this exploit they were the more egerlie mooued, because that notwithstanding Thomas his souldiors were manie in number, yet they knew that the better part of his companie bare but hollow hearts to the quarell · for the number of the wise gentlemen of the pale did little or nothing incline to his purpose. And therefore when he besieged the citie, the most part of those arrowes, which were shot ouer the walles, were vnheaded, and nothing annoied them: some shot in letters, and foretold them of all the treacherous stratagems that were in hammering

Faggots laid vnto the new gate.

That espied the citizens, and gathering the faintnesse of his souldiors thereby, blazed abroad vpon the walles triumphant newes, that the king his armie was arriued and as it had béene so in déed, suddenlie to the number of foure hundred rushed out at the new gate, through flame and fire vpon the rebels, who (at the first sight of armed men) wéening no lesse but the truth was so, otherwise assured, that the citie would neuer dare to rencounter them, gaue ground, forsooke their capteins, dispersed and scattered into diuerse corners, their falcon taken, an hundred of their stoutest Galloglasses slaine Thomas Fitzgirald fled to the graie friers in S Francis his stréet, there coucht that night, vnknowen to the citie, vntill the next morning he stale priuilie to his armie not far off, who stood in woonderfull feare that he was apprehended. Thomas his courage by this late ouerthrow somewhat cooled, and also being assuredlie told, that a fleete was espied a farre off bearing full saile towards the coast of Ireland, he was soone intreated, hauing so manie irons in the fire, to take egs for his monie & withall, hauing no forren succor, either from *Paulus Tertius*, or Charles the fift, which dailie he expected he was sore quailed, being of himselfe, though strong in number of souldiors, yet vnfurnished of sufficient munition and artillerie, to stand & withstand the king his armie in a pitcht field, or a maine battell. Vpon this & other considerations, to make as faire weather as he could, he sent Iames de la Hide, Lime of the Knocke, William Bath of Dollarstowne, doctor Trauerse, Thomas Field of Painstowne, as messengers to the citizens, to treat with them of a truce, who being let in at

The citizens bicker with the rebels.

Thomas Fitzgerald fleeth

De la Hide. Lime Bath Trauerse. Field

at the new gate, repaired to William Kellie his house, where maister maior and his brethren were assembled. The articles propounded by them to the citizens, were these.

The articles propounded to the citizens.

1 That Thomas Fitzgerald his men, who were deteined in prison, should be redeliuered.

2 Item, that the citizens should incontinentlie deliuer him at one pament, a thousand pounds in monie.

3 Item, that they should deliuer him fiue hundred pounds in wares.

4 Item, to furnish him with munition and artillerie.

5 Item, to addresse their fauorable letters to the king for their capteine his pardon, and all his confederats.

The citizens answer these articles.

The maior and aldermen, hauing ripelie debated the tenour of these articles, agréed, that maister Fitzsimons their recorder should answer vnto the first, that they would not sticke to set his seruants at libertie, so he would redeliuer them the youth of the citie, which was nothing else in effect, but tit for tat. As for the second and the third demand, they were so greatlie by his warres impouerished, as they might hardlie spare monie or wares. And as touching implements for warre, they were neuer such fond niddicockes, as to offer anie man a rod to beat their owne tailes, or to betake their mastiues vnto the custodie of the woolues, maruelling much that their capteine would so farre ouershoot himselfe, as to be taken with such apparent repugnancie. For if he intended to submit himselfe to the king his mercie, and to make them humble meanes to his highnesse for the obteining of his pardon, he ought rather to make sute for some good vellam parchment for the ingrossing thereof, than for munition and artillerie to withstand his prince. Wherfore, that thrée vnlawfull demands rejected, they would willinglie condescend to the first and last, as well requesting him to deliuer them the youth of the citie, as to submit himselfe and his companie to the king his mercie: promising not onelie with their fauourable letters, but also with their personall presences to further, as far as in them laie, his humble sute to the king and councell.

William Bath.

As they parled thus to and fro, William Bath of Dollarstowne a student of the common lawes spake: "My maisters, what néedeth all this long circumstance? Let vs all drinke of one cup." Which words were shortlie after vpon Skeffington his arriuall so crookedlie glosed, as by drinking of a sowre cup he lost the best ioint of his bodie. For albeit vpon his triall he construed his words to import an vniforme consent towards the obteining of Fitzgerald his pardon, yet all this could not colour his matter in such wise, but that he and Eustace of Balicutlan were executed at the castell of Dublin. The messengers knowing their capteine to be at a low eb, were agréed to take the offers of the first & last conditions, and that to the accomplishing of these articles hostages should be giuen of either part. The messengers deliuered to the citizens doctor Trauers & others, the citizens deliuered them Richard Talbot, Aldreman, Rochford, & Rerrie. These were committed to the custodie of Dauid Sutton of Rabride, who redeliuered them to the citizens immediatlie after vpon the certeine rumor of Skeffington his repaire.

Eustace of Balicutlan.

Hostages taken. Doctor Trauerse. Talbot. Rochford. Rerrie. Dauid Sutton.

Thomas growne to this point with the Dublinmans raised his siege, caused his artillerie to be conueied to Houth, marching after with his armie, to the end he might as well bulch the English ships if they durst anerre the coast, as to bicker with the soldiors vpon their arriuall. But before he tooke his iorneie vnto Houth, he rode to Mainoth, to see that the castell should be of all sides fortified, where being doone to vnderstand, that a companie of white cotes with red crosses landed at Dublin secretlie in the dead of the night, and also that another band arriued

The white cotes landed at Dublin.

at

at Houth, and were readie to march towards Dublin, he posted incontinentlie with two hundred horssemen towards the water side, incountred néere Clontarfe, the Hamertons, two valiant and couragious gentlemen, hauing in their companie foure score souldiors, where they fought so valiantlie for their liues, as so few footmen could haue doone against so great a troope of horssemen: for they did not onlie mangle and hacke diuerse of the rebels, but also one of the Hamertons wounded Thomas Fitzgirald in the forehead. Some report that one of the Musgraues, who was of kin to Fitzgirald, was slaine in this conflict, whose death he is said to haue taken greatlie to hart. The rebelles fleshed with the slaughter of the English, hied with all spéed to Houth, shot at the ships that rode at anchor, caused them to flée from thense, & to make towards Skerrish, where landed both the Eglebées, and the Dacies, with their horssemen. Rouks, Fitzgerald his pirat, was sent to scowre the coast, who tooke an English barke laden with verie faire geldings, and sent them to his capteine. After that Thomas had returned with this bootie, and the spoile of such as were slaine to Manoth, sir William Brereton knight, with his sonne Iohn Brereton, was inshored at Houth with two hundred & fiftie soldiors verie well appointed, and maister Salisburie with two hundred archers.

The Hamertons slaine.

Thomas Fitzgirald wounded. Musgraue.

Eglebees. Dacies. English geldings taken.

Sir William Brereton. Iohn Brereton. Salisburie.

Lastlie landed at the slip, neare the bridge of Dublin, sir William Skeffington knight lord deputie, whome the Irish call the gunner, because he was preferred from that office of the king his maister gunner to gouerne them, and that they can euill brooke to be ruled of anie that is but meanlie borne. The maior and aldermen receiued the gouernor with shot, and great solemnitie, who yéelding them hartie thanks for their true and loiall seruice, deliuered them the king and councell his letters, purporting the same effect in writing that he before expressed in words. Barnwell lord of Trimlestowne, who had the custodie of the sword, did surrender it to sir William Skeffington, according to the meaning of the king his letters patents on that behalfe.

Sir William Skeffington lord deputie landeth.

Letters of thanks from the king to the Dublinians.

The lord of Trimlestowne surrendreth the sword.

Thomas Fitzgirald hauing intelligence that the whole armie was arriued, warded the castell of Manoth so stronglie, as he tooke it to be impregnable. And to the end he might giue the gouernor battell, he rode towards Connagh, to leuie all such power of the Irish, as either for wages, or for goodwill he could win to assist him. The lord deputie forewarned of his drift, marched with the English armie, and the power of the pale to Manoth, and laid siege to the castell on the north side towards the parke. But before anie péece was discharged, sir William Brereton, by the deputie his appointment, did summon the castell: offering such as kept it to depart with bag and baggage, and besides their pardon to be liberallie rewarded for their good and loiall seruice. But such as warded the castell, scornefullie scoffing the knight his offer, gaue him hartie thanks for his kindnesse which they said procéeded rather of his gentlenesse than of their deseruing, wishing him to keepe vp in store such liberall offers for a deere yeare, and to write his commendations home to his fréends, and withall, to kéepe his head warme, for at their hands he was like to haue but a cold sute. Finallie not to take such keepe of their safetie, in that they were assured, that he and his fellowes should be sooner from the siege raised, than they from the hold remooued.

Thomas Fitzgirald goeth toward Connagh.

The castell of Manoth besieged.

Sir William Brereton summoneth the castell.

Vpon this round answere the ordinances were planted on the north side of the castell, which made no great batterie for the space of a fortnight: yet the castell so warilie on ech side inuironed, as the rebelles were imbard from all egresse and regresse. Christopher Parese fosterbrother to Thomas Fitzgirald, to whome of speciall trust the charge of the castell was chieflie committed, profering his voluntarie seruice (which for the more part is so thanklesse and vnsauorie as it stinketh)

Christopher Parese betraieth the castell of Manoth.

Profered seruice stinketh.

stinketh) determined to go an ase beyond his fellows, in betraieng the castell to the gouernor. In this resolution he shot a letter indorsed to the lord deputie, the effect whereof was, that he would deuise means the castell should be taken, so that he might haue a summe of monie for his paines, and a competent state during his life. This motion by letters to and fro agréed vpon, Parese caused such as kept the ward, to swill and boll so much, as they snorted all the night like grunting hogs, litle misdeeming that whilest they slept, anie Iudas had beene waking within the castell.

The occasion of this extraordinarie excéeding was colored, for snatching into the castell a field péece the daie before from the armie, for which they kept such potreuels, and triumphant carousing, as none of them could discerne his beds head from the beds feet. Parese, taking his tide and time, made signe to the armie, betwéene the twilight and dawning of the daie, who hauing scaling ladders in a readinesse, would not ouerslip the opportunitie offered.

Holland petit capteine to Salisburie. The castell taken.

Holland, petit capteine to Salisburie, was one of the forwardest in this exploit, who leaping downe from the wall, fell by mishap into a pipe of feathers, where he was vp to the arme pits, so stiffelie sticking therein, and also vnwealdie in his armor, as there could not helpe himselfe neither in nor out.

Brereton scaleth the wals.

Sir William Brereton and his band hauing scaled the wals cried on a sudden, "Saint George, saint George." Thrée drunken swads that kept the castell thought that this showt was nought else but a dreame, till time they espied the walles full of armed men, and one of them withall perceiuing Holland thus intangled in the pipe, bestowed an arrow vpon him, which by good hap did misse him. Holland forthwith rescued by his fellows, shot at the other, and strake him so full vnder the skull, as he left him spralling. The resistance was faint, when the souldiors entered, some yeelding themselues, others that withstood them slaine.

Brereton aduanceth his standard.

Sir William Brereton ran vp to the highest turret of the castell, & aduanced his standard on the top thereof, notifieng to the deputie, that the fort was woone. Great and rich was the spoile, such store of beds, so manie goodlie hangings, so rich a wardrobe, such braue furniture, as trulie it was accounted (for houshold stuffe and vtensiles) one of the richest earle his houses vnder the crowne of England.

The lord deputie entereth the castell. Iames de la Hide. Haward.

The lord deputie entred the castell in the after noone, vpon whose repaire, Iames de la Hide, and Haward, two singing men of the earle his chappell, that were taken prisoners, prostrated themselues on the ground, pitifullie warbling a soong, named *Dulcis amica*.

Girald Ailmer.

The gouernour rauished with the sweet and delicat voices, at the instance of Girald Ailmer chiefe iustice, and others of the councell pardoned them.

Parese commeth before the gouernour.

Christopher Parese not misdoubting but that he should haue beene dubd knight for his seruice doone that daie, presented himselfe before the gouernour, with a chéerefull and familiar countenance, as who should saie, Here is he that did the déed. The deputie verie coldlie & halfe sternelie casting an eie towards him said: "Parese, I am to thanke thee on my master the king his behalfe, for this thy proffered seruice which I must acknowledge to haue beene a sparing of great charges, and a sauing of manie valiant soldiors liues to his highnesse: and when his maiestie shall be thereof aduertised, I dare be bold to saie that he will not sée thée lacke during thy life. And bicause I maie be the better instructed how to reward thée during my gouernement, I would gladlie learne, what thy lord and master bestowed on thee." Parese set a gog with these mild spéeches, and supposing the more he recited, the better he should be rewarded, left not vntold the meanest good turne that euer he receiued at his lords hands. "Why Parese (quoth the deputie) couldest thou find in thine heart to betraie his castell, that hath beene so good lord to thée? Trulie, thou that art so hollow to him, wilt neuer be true to vs." And therewithall, turning his

his talke to his officers, he gaue them commandement to deliuer Parese the summe of monie that was promised him vpon the surrender of the castell, and after to chop off his head. Parese at this cold salutation of "Farewell & be hanged," turning his simpering to wimpering said: "My lord, had I wist that you would haue dealt so streictlie with me, your lordship should not haue woone this fort with so little bloudshed as you did."

A notable iudgement

Whereat master Boise, a gentleman of worship, and one that reteined to that old earle of Kildare, standing in the preasse, said in Irish, *Antragh*, which is as much in English as Too late, wherof grew the Irish prouerbe, to this daie in the language vsed, Too late quoth Boise, as we saie, Beware of had I wist, or After meat mustard, or You come a daie after the faire, or Better doone than said. The deputie asked them that stood by what was that he spake? Master Boise willing to expound his owne words, stept foorth and answered, "My lord, I said nothing, but that Parese is seized of a towne néere the water side named Baltra, and I would gladlie know how he will dispose it before he be executed." The gouernour not mistrusting that master Boise had glosed (for if he vnderstood the true signification of the terme, it was verie like that too late had not beene so sharpe to Parese, but too soone had beene as sowre to him) willed the monie to be told to Parese, and presentlie caused him to be cut shorter by the head: declaring thereby, that although for the time he imbraced the benefit of the treason, yet after he could not digest the trecherie of the traitor.

Boise

Antragh

The prouerbe Too late quoth Boise

Baltra.

Parese beheaded

The deputie hauing left a garrison in the castell, returned with the armie triumphantlie to Dublin. Thomas Fitzgirald not misdoubting but such as he left in the castell were able to stand to their tackle, leuied a huge armie in Oconhur his countrie, and in Connagh, to the number of seuen thousand, marching with them towards Mainoth, minding to haue remooued the king his armie from the siege: but being certified, that Parese his fosterbrother yéelded vp the castell to the deputie, the better part of his companie gaue him the slip. All this notwithstanding he made with such as would sticke to him to Clane. The lord deputie hauing intelligence of his approch, left sir William Brereton at Dublin to defend the citie, & marched with the armie to the Naas, where he tooke seuen score of Thomas his Galloglasses, and lead them all vnarmed toward Iohnstowne. The scout watch espieng Thomas to march néere, imparted it to the gouernour, who presentlie commanded each man to kill his prisoner before the charge, which was dispatcht, onely Edmund Oleine escaping mother-naked by flight to Thomas his companie, leauing his shirt in his kéepers hands. Both the armies aduanced themselues one against the other, but the horssemen of either side could not charge, by reason of a marish or quakemire that parted them. Wherfore the deputie caused two or thrée field péeces to be discharged, which scattered Thomas and his rablement, insomuch as he neuer in such open wise durst after beare vp head in the English pale, but rather by starts and sudden stratagems would now and then gall the English. As when the castell of Rathimgan was woone, which was soone after the surrender of Mainoth, he caused a droue of cattell to appeare timelie in the morning hard by the towne. Such as kept the fort, suspecting it to be a bootie, were trained for the more part out of the castell, who were surprized by Thomas, that laie hard by in ambush, and the greater number of them slaine.

The deputie returneth to Dublin

Thomas Fitzgirald marcheth towards Mainoth.

Brereton left to defend Dublin

Galloglasses taken and slaine

Edmund Oleine escapeth

Thomas and his companie fléeth

Fitzgirald his stratagems

Another time he fired a village hard by Trim, and deuised such of his horssemen that could speake English, being clad and horssed like northerne men, to ride to Trim, where a garrison laie with hue and crie, saieng that they were capteine Salisburie his souldiors, and that the traitor Thomas Fitzgirald was burning a village hard by. The souldiors suspecting no cousinage issued out of the towne,

who

who were by his men charged, & a great number of them slaine, some chased to the towne, and forced to take sanctuarie in the churchyard, which in those daies was highlie reuerenced. These and the like knacks vsed Thomas, being for his owne person so well garded, and for defect of a maine armie so naked, as neither he was occasioned to feare the English, nor the English forced to weigh him. During this time, there arriued with a fresh supplie of horssemen & archers, sir William Sentlo knight & his son, sir Rice Manswell knight, sir Edward Griffith knight, who were dispersed to sundrie parts of the pale to defend the countrie from the enimies inuasion. When the heat of this rebellion was in this wise aswaged, the lord deputie finding out no deuise to apprehend the capteine, imploied his industrie to intrap his confederats. Burnell of Balgriffin perceiuing all go to wracke fled to Mounster, where he was taken by the lord Butler viscount Thurles, and being conueied to England was executed at Tiburne. Doctor Trauers, who was left as hostage with the citizens, was by them deliuered to the lord deputie, and after with Rouks the pirat executed at the gallows on Ostmantowne gréene.

William Sentlo. Rice Manswell. Edward Griffith.

Burnell of Balgriffin taken and executed. Trauers executed.

Rouks executed.

Walter de la Hide and his ladie Gennet Eustace apprehended.

Sir Walter de la Hide knight and his wife the ladie Gennet Eustace were apprehended, & brought as prisoners by master Brabson vicetreasuror from their towne of Moiclare to the castell of Dublin, bicause their sonne and heire Iames de la Hide was the onelie bruer of all this rebellion: who as the gouernor suspected, was set on by his parents, & namelie by his moother. The knight & his wife, lieng in duresse for the space of twelue moneths, were at seuerall times examined, & notwithstanding all presumptions and surmises that could be gathered, they were in the end found giltlesse of their sonne his follie. But the ladie was had in examination apart, and intised by meanes to charge hir husband with hir sonne his rebellion, who being not woone thereto with all the meanes that could be wrought, was menaced to be put to death, or to be rackt; and so with extremitie to be compelled, whereas with gentlenesse she could not be allured to acknowledge these apparent treasons, that neither hir husband nor she could without great shew of impudencie denie.

Gennet Eustace dieth.

The gentlewoman with these continuall storms heartbroken, deceased in the castell: from thense hir bodie was remooued vnto the greie friers with the deputie his commandement, that it should not be interred, vntill his plesure were further knowne; adding withall, that the carcase of one who was the moother of so arrant an archtraitor, ought rather to be cast out on a dunghill to be carrion for rauens and dogs to gnaw vpon, than to be laid in anie christian graue. The corps lieng foure or fiue daies in this plight, at the request of the ladie Gennet Golding, wife to sir Iohn White knight, the gouernor, licenced that it should be buried. Sir William Skeffington a seueare and vpright gouernour died shortlie after at Kilmainan: to whome succeeded lord deputie the lord Leonard Greie, who immediatlie vpon the taking of his oth marched with his power towards the confines of Mounster, where Thomas Fitzgirald at that time remained. With Fitzgirald sir William Brereton skirmished so fiercelie, as both the sides were rather for the great slaughter disaduantaged, than either part by anie great victorie furthered. Master Brereton therefore perceiuing that rough nets were not the fittest to take such peart birds, gaue his aduise to the lord deputie to grow with Fitzgirald by faire meams to some reasonable composition. The deputie liking of the motion, craued a parlée, sending certeine of the English as hostages to Thomas his campe with a protection directed vnto him, to come and go at will and pleasure. Being vpon this securitie in conference with the lord Greie, he was persuaded to submit himselfe to the king his mercie, with the gouernours faithfull and vndoubted promise that he should be pardoned vpon his repaire into England. And to the end that no trecherie might haue

Skeffington deceased.

Leonard Greie lord deputie.

Brereton skirmisheth with Fitzgirald.

Thomas Fitzgirald submitteth himselfe to the deputie.

haue béene misdeemed of either side, they both receiued the sacrament openlie in the campe, as an infallible seale of the couenants and conditions of either part agréed.

The sacrament receiued.

Héerevpon Thomas Fitzgirald sore against the willes of his councellors, dismist his armie, & rode with the deputie to Dublin, where he made short abode when he sailed to England with the fauourable letters of the gouernour and the councell.

Thomas saileth into England. 1535

And as he would haue taken his iournie to Windsore, where the court laie, he was intercepted contrarie to his expectation in London waie, and conueied with hast to the tower.

He is committed to the tower.

And before his imprisonment was bruted, letters were posted into Ireland, streictlie commanding the deputie vpon sight of them, to apprehend Thomas Fitzgirald his vncles, and to sée them with all speed conuenient shipt into England. Which the lord deputie did not slacke. For hauing feasted thrée of the gentlemen at Kilmainan, immediatlie after their banket (as it is now and then séen, that swéet meat will haue sowre sauce) he caused them to be manacled, and led as prisoners to the castell of Dublin: and the other two were so roundlie snatcht vp in villages hard by, as they sooner felt their owne captiuitie, than they had notice of their brethrens calamitie.

Thomas his vncles taken.

The next wind that serued into England, these fiue brethren were imbarked, to wit Iames Fitzgirald, Walter Fitzgirald, Oliuer Fitzgirald, Iohn Fitzgirald, and Richard Fitzgirald. Thrée of these gentlemen, Iames, Walter, and Richard, were knowne to haue crossed their nephue Thomas to their power in his rebellion, and therfore were not occasioned to misdoubt anie danger. But such as in those daies were enimies to the house, incensed the king so sore against it, persuading him that he should neuer conquer Ireland, as long as anie Giraldine breathed in the countrie: as for making the pathwaie smooth, he was resolued to lop off as well the good and sound grapes, as the wild and fruitlesse berries. Whereby appeareth how dangerous it is to be a rub, when a king is disposed to swéepe an allie.

Thus were the fiue brethren sailing into England, among whom Richard Fitzgirald being more bookish than the rest of his brethren, & one that was much giuen to the studies of antiquitie, wailing his inward griefe, with outward mirth comforted them with chéerefulnesse of countenance, as well persuading them that offended to repose affiance in God, and the king his mercie, and such as were not of that conspiracie, to relie to their innocencie, which they should hold for a more safe and strong barbican, than anie rampire or castell of brasse.

Innocencie a strong fort.

Thus solacing the sillie mourners sometime with smiling, sometime with singing, sometime with graue and pithie apophthegmes, he craued of the owner the name of the barke, who hauing answered, that it was called the Cow, the gentleman sore appalled thereat, said:

The Cow.

"Now good brethren I am in vtter despaire of our returne to Ireland, for I beare in mind an old prophesie, that fiue earles brethren should be caried in a Cowes bellie to England, and from thense neuer to returne."

Whereat the rest began afresh to howle and lament, which doubtlesse was pitifull, to behold fiue valiant gentlemen, that durst méet in the field fiue as sturdie champions as could be picked out in a realme, to be so suddenlie terrified with the bare name of a woodden cow, or to feare like lions a sillie cocke his combe, being mooued (as commonlie the whole countrie is) with a vaine and fabulous old wiues dreame. But what blind prophesie soeuer he read, or heard of anie superstitious beldame touching a cow his bellie, that which he foretold them was found true. For Thomas Fitzgirald the third of Februarie, and these fiue brethren his vncles, were drawne, hanged, and quartered at Tiburne, which was incontinentlie bruted as well in England and Ireland, as in forren soiles.

1536. Thomas Fitzgirald & his vncles executed. Dominicke Powre.

For Dominicke Powre, that was sent from Thomas to Charles the fift, to craue his aid towards the conquest of Ireland (like

Charles Reinold. (like as Chale in Grauill, otherwise called Charles Reinold, was directed to *Paulus tertius*) presenting the emperour with twelue great haukes and fourteene faire hobbies, was aduertised by his maiestie that he came too late, for his lord and master and fiue of his vncles were executed at London the third of Februarie: howbeit the emperour procured king Henrie to pardon Dominicke Powre. Which notwithstanding he obteined, yet would he not returne to Ireland, but continued in Portingale, hauing a ducket a daie of the emperour during his life, which he ended at Lisborne.

James de la Hide. James de la Hide the chiefe councellor of Thomas Fitzgirald, fled into Scotland and there deceased. To this miserable end grew this lewd rebellion, which turned to the vtter vndooing of diuers ancient gentlemen, who trained with faire words into a fooles paradise, were not onelie dispossessed of their lands, but also depriued of their liues, or else forced to forsake their countries. As for Thomas Fitzgirald, who (as I wrote before) was executed at Tiburne, I would wish the carefull reader to vnderstand that he was neuer earle of Kildare, although some writers, rather of errour than of malice, terme him by that name. For it is knowne that his father liued in the tower, when he was in open rebellion, where for thought of the yoong man his follie he died; and therefore Thomas was attainted in a parlement holden at Dublin, as one that was déemed, reputed, and taken for a traitour before his fathers decease, by the bare name of Thomas Fitzgirald. For this hath béene obserued by the Irish historiographers euer since the conquest, that notwithstanding all the presumptions of treason, wherewith anie earle of Kildare could either faintlie be suspected or vehementlie charged; yet there was neuer anie erle of that house read or heard of, that bare armour in the field against his prince. Which I write not as a barrister hired to plead their cause, but as a chronicler moued to declare the truth.

Thomas Fitzgirald was not earle of Kildare.

L. St. pag. 404.

No earle of Kildare bare armour at anie time against his prince.

The description of Thomas Fitzgirald. This Thomas Fitzgirald (as before is specified) was borne in England, vpon whom nature powred beautie, and fortune by birth bestowed nobilitie: which had it beene well emploied, & were it not that his rare gifts had béene blemished by his later euill qualities, he would haue proued an impe worthie to be ingrafted in so honorable a stocke. He was of stature tall and personable, in countenance amiable, a white face, and withall somewhat ruddie, delicatlie in each lim featured, a rolling toong & a rich vtterance, of nature flexible and kind, verie soone caried where he fansied, easilie with submission appeased, hardlie with stubbornnesse weied, in matters of importance an headlong hotspur: yet neuerthelesse taken for a yoong man not deuoid of wit, were it not (as it fell out in the end) that a foole had the keeping thereof.

The aduentures of the yoong Fitzgirald son to the ladie Grey countesse of Kildare. But to returne to the course of the historie. When Thomas and his vncles were taken, his second brother on the father his side, named Girald Fitzgirald (who was after in the reigne of quéene Marie restored to the earledome of Kildare, in which honour as yet he liueth) being at that time somewhat past twelue, and not full thirteene yeares of age, laie sicke of the small pocks in the countie of Kildare, at a towne named Donoare, then in the occupation of Girald Fitzgirald. Thomas Leurouse, who was the child his schoolemaster, and after became bishop of Kildare, mistrusting vpon the apprehension of Thomas & his vncles, that all went not currant, wrapt the yoong patient as tenderlie as he could, and had him conueied in a cléefe with all spéed to Ophalie, where soiourning for a short space with his sister the ladie Marie Fitzgirald, vntill he had recouered his perfect health, his schoolemaster caried him to Odon his countrie, where making his aboad for a quarter of a yeare, he trauelled to Obren his countrie in Mounster, and hauing there remained for halfe a yeare, he repaired to his aunt the ladie Elenor Fitzgirald, who then kept in Mac Cartie Reagh hir late husband his territories.

Donoare. Thomas Leurouse.

Elenor Fitzgirald.

This

This noble woman was at that time a widow, alwaies knowne and accounted of each man, that was acquainted with hir conuersation of life, for a paragon of liberalitie and kindnesse, in all hir actions vertuous and godlie, and also in a good quarell rather stout than stiffe. To hir was Odoneil an importunate suter. And although at sundrie times before she seemed to shake him off, yet considering the distresse of hir yoong innocent nephue, how he was forced to wander in pilgrimwise from house to house, eschuing the punishment that others deserued, smarted in his tender yeares with aduersitie, before he was of discretion to moore anie prosperitie, she began to incline to hir wooer his request, to the end hir nephue should haue béene the better by his countenance shouldered, and in fine indented to espouse him, with this caueat or prouiso, that he should safelie shield and protect the said yoong gentleman in this calamitie. This condition agréed vpon, she rode with hir nephue to Odoneil his countrie, and there had him safelie kept for the space of a yeare.

But shortlie after the gentlewoman either by some secret friend informed, or of wisedome gathering that hir late maried husband intended some treacherie, had hir nephue disguised, storing him like a liberall and bountifull aunt with seuen score porteguses, not onelie in valour, but also in the selfe same coine, incontinentlie shipped him secretlie in a Britons vessell of saint Malouse, betaking him to God, and to their charge that accompanied him, to wit, master Leurouse, and Robert Walsh sometime seruant to his father the earle. The ladie Elenor hauing thus to hir contentation bestowed hir nephue, she expostulated verie sharpelie with Odoneil as touching his villanie, protesting that the onlie cause of hir match with him procéeded of an especiall care to haue hir nephue countenanced: and now that he was out of his lash that minded to haue betraied him, he should well vnderstand, that as the feare of his danger mooued hir to annere to such a clownish curmudgen: so the assurance of his safetie should cause hir to sequester hirselfe from so butcherlie a cutthrote, that would be like a pelting mercenarie patch hired, to sell or betraie the innocent bloud of his nephue by affinitie, and hirs by consanguinitie. And in this wise trussing vp bag and baggage, he forsooke Odoneil and returned to hir countrie. The ladie Elenors liberalitie. Fitzgerald saileth to France.

The passengers with a prosperous gale arriued at saint Malouse, which notified to the gouernour of Britaine, named monsieur de Chasteau Brian, he sent for the yoong Fitzgirald, gaue him verie hartie interteinement during one moneths space. In the meane season the gouernour posted a messenger to the court of France, aduertising the king of the arriuall of this gentleman, who presentlie caused him to be sent for, and had him put to the Dolphin named Henrie, who after became king of France. Sir Iohn Wallop (who was then the English ambassadour) vnderstanding the cause of the Irish fugitiue his repaire to France, demanded him of the French king, according to the new made league betweene both the princes: which was, that none should kéepe the other his subiect within his dominion, contrarie to either of their willes, adding further, that the boie was brother to one, who of late notorious for his rebellion in Ireland was executed at London. Chasteau Brian. Sir Iohn Wallop demandeth Fitzgerald.

To this answered the king, first that the ambassador had no commission from his Prince to demand him, & vpon his maiestie his letter he should know more of his mind: secondlie that he did not deteine him, but the Dolphin staied him: lastlie, that how grieuouslie soeuer his brother offended, he was well assured, that the sillie boy neither was nor could be a traitor, and therefore there rested no cause whie the ambassador should in such wise craue him, not doubting that although he were deliuered to his king, yet he would not so far swarue from the extreame rigor of iustice, as to imbrue his hands in the innocent his bloud, for the offense that his The king denieth him.

brother had perpetrated. Maister Wallop herevpon addressed his letters to England, specifieng vnto the councell the French kings answer. And in the meane time the yoong Fitzgirald hauing an inkling of the ambassador his motion, fled secretlie to Flanders, scantlie reaching to Valencie, when Iames Sherelocke, one of maister Wallop his men, did not onelie pursue him, but also did ouertake him as he soiourned in the said towne.

Fitzgirald fleeth to Flanders.

Iames Sherelocke pursueth Fitzgirald.

Wherevpon maister Leurouse, and such as accompanied the child, stept to the gouernor of Valencie, complaining that one Sherelocke a sneaking spie, like a pikethanke promoting varlet, did dog their master from place to place, and presentlie pursued him to the towne: and therefore they be sought the gouernour, not to leaue such apparant villanie vnpunished, in that he was willing to betraie not onelie a guiltlesse child, but also his owne countriman, who rather ought for his innocencie to be pitied, than for the desert of others so egerlie to be pursued. The gouernor vpon this complaint sore incensed, sent in all hast for Sherelocke, had him suddenlie examined, and finding him vnable to color his lewd practise with anie warrantable defense, he laid him vp by the héeles, rewarding his hot pursute with cold interteinment, and so remained in gaole, vntill the yoong Fitzgirald requiting the prisoner his vnnaturall crueltie with vndeserued courtesie, humblie besought the gouernor to set him at libertie. This brunt escaped, Fitzgirald trauelled to Bruxels, where the emperour kept his court.

Sherelocke imprisoned.

Crueltie requited with courtesie.

Doctor Pates being ambassador in the low countries, demanded Fitzgirald of the emperour on his maister the king of Englands behalfe. The emperor hauing answered that he had not to deale with the boy, and for ought that he knew was not minded to make anie great abode in that countrie, sent him to the bishop of Liege, allowing him for his pension an hundred crownes monethlie. The bishop interteined him verie honorablie, had him placed in an abbeie of moonks, & was so careful of his safetie, that if anie person suspected had trauelled within the circuit of his gléebe, he should be streictlie examined whither he would, or from whense he came, or vpon what occasion he trauelled that waie. Hauing in this wise remained at Liege for halfe a yere, the cardinall Poole (Fitzgirald his kinsman) sent for him to Rome. Whervpon the gentleman as well with the emperor his licence, as with surrendring his pension, trauelled to Italie, where the cardinall would not admit him to his companie, vntill he had atteined to some knowledge in the Italian toong. Wherfore allowing him an annuitie of thrée hundred crownes, he placed him with the bishop of Verona, and the cardinall of Mantua, and after with the duke of Mantua. Leurouse in the meane while was admitted through the cardinall Poole his procurement, to be one of the English house in Rome, called saint Thomas his hospitall.

Doctor Pates.

The emperor bestoweth a pension on Fitzgirald.

Cardinall Poole sendeth for Fitzgirald.

Leurouse placed in the English hospitall.

Robert Walsh, vpon his maisters repaire to Italie, returned to Ireland. Fitzgirald hauing continued with the cardinall, and the duke of Mantua, a yeare and an halfe, was sent for by the cardinall Poole to Rome, at which time the duke of Mantua gaue him for an annuall pension 300 crownes. The cardinall greatlie reioised in his kinsman, had him carefullie trained vp in his house, interlacing with such discretion his learning and studies with exercises of actiuitie, as he should not be after accounted of the learned for an ignorant idiot, nor taken of actiue gentlemen for a dead and dumpish meacocke. If he had committed anie fault, the cardinall would secretlie command his tutors to correct him, and all that notwithstanding, he would in presence dandle the boie, as though he were not priuie to his punishment; & vpon his complaint made, he vsed to checke Fitzgirald his maister openlie for chastising so seuerelie his pretie darling.

Robert Walsh returneth to Ireland.

Cardinall Poole his order in training yoong Fitzgirald.

In

In this wise he rested thrée yeares togither in the cardinall his house, and by that time hauing stept so far in yéers (for he was pricking fast vpon ninetéene) as he began to know himselfe, the cardinall put him to his choise, either to continue his learning, or by trauelling to seeke his aduentures abrode. The yoong stripling (as vsuallie kind dooth créepe) rather of nature addicted to valiantnes, than wedded to bookishnesse, choosed to be a trauellér: and presentlie with the cardinall his licence repaired to Naples: where falling in acquaintance with knights of the Rhodes, he accompanied them to Malta, from thense he sailed to Tripolie (a fort apperteining to the aforesaid order, coasting vpon Barbarie) and there he abode six weekes with Mounbrison, a commander of the Rhodes who had the charge of that hold.

Fitzgirald trauelleth to Naples Tripolie

Mounbrison

At that time the knights serued valiantlie against the Turks and miscreants, spoiled and sacked their villages and townes that laie neere the water side, tooke diuerse of them prisoners, and after sold them to the christians for bondslaues. The yoong Fitzgirald returned with a rich bootie to Malta, from thense to Rome, hauing spent in this voiage not fullie one yeare. Proud was the cardinall to heare of his prosperous exploits: and for his further aduancement he inhansed his pension of thrée hundred crownes, to three hundred pounds, ouer and aboue thrée hundred crownes that the duke of Mantua allowed him. Shortlie after he preferred him to the seruice of the duke of Florence, named Cosmo, with whom he continued maister of his horsse thrée yeares, hauing also of the duke thrée hundred duckets for a yearelie pension during life, or vntill he were restored: in like maner as the cardinall Poole and the duke of Mantua in their annuities had granted him.

Fitzgirald returneth to Rome

The cardinall inhanseth Fitzgiralds pension

He is master of the horsse to the duke of Florence

During the time that he was in seruice with the duke of Florence, he trauelled to Rome a shrouing, of set purpose to be merrie: and as he rode on hunting with cardinall Fernese the pope his nephue, it happened that in chasing the bucke he fell into a pit nine and twentie fatham déepe, and in the fall forsaking his horsse within two fathams of the bottom, he tooke hold by two or three roots, griping them fast, vntill his armes were so wearie, as he could hang no longer in that paine. Wherefore betaking himselfe to God, he let go his gripe by little and little, and fell softlie on his horsse, that in the bottom of the pit laie starke dead, and there he stood vp to the ancles in water for the space of thrée houres. When the chase was ended, an exceeding good greihound of his named Grifhound, not finding his maister in the companie, followed his tract vntill he came to the pit, and from thense would not depart, but stood at the brim incessantlie howling. The cardinall Fernese and his traine missing Fitzgirald, made towards the dog, and surueieng the place, they were verelie persuaded that the gentleman was squised to death.

He falleth into a deepe pit.

His greihound findeth him out

Hauing therefore posted his seruants in hast to a village hard by Rome (named Trecappan) for ropes and other necessaries, he caused one of the companie to glide in a basket downe to the bottome of the hole. Fitzgirald reuiued with his presence, and willing to be remooued from so darkesome a dongeon to the open aire, besought the other to lend him his roome, whervpon he was haled vp in the basket: as well to the generall admiration of the whole companie, as to the singular gratulation of the cardinall and all his friends, rendering most hartie thankes vnto God his diuine maiestie, for protecting the gentleman with his gratious guerdon. And thus surceassing to treat anie further of his aduentures, vntill the date of time traine my pen to a longer discourse, I will returne to the inhabitants of the English pale, who after the death of Thomas Fitzgirald, through rigor of iustice and the due execution of lawes were greatlie molested. For ouer this, that such as were knowne for open and apparant traitors in the commotion, were for the more part executed, or with round sums fined, or from the realme exiled: certeine gentlemen of wor-

Trecappan

 ship

Commissioners sent to Ireland. ship were sent from England, with commission to examine each person suspected with Thomas his treason, and so according to their discretion, either with equitie to execute, or with clemencie to pardon all such as they could proue to haue furthered him in his disloiall commotion. Commissioners were these: sir Anthonie Sentleger knight, sir George Paulet knight, maister Moile, and maister Barnes. Much about this time was there a parlement holden at Dublin before the lord Leonard Greie lord deputie, beginning the first of Maie, in the eight and twentith yeare of the reigne of king Henrie the eight.

Their names.

A parlement. 1539

In this parlement there past these acts following.

An act
- For the attaindor of the earle of Kildare, and Thomas Fitzgirald, with others.
- For the succession of the king & queene Anne.
- Of absenties, wherein was granted to the king the inheritance of such lands in Ireland, wherof the duke of Norffolke & George Talbot earle of Waterford & Salop were seized, with the inheritances of diuerse other corporations and couents demurrant in England.
- For the repeale of Poinings act.
- Authorising the king his heirs and successors to be supreame head of the church of Ireland.
- That no subiects or resiants of Ireland shall pursue or commense, vse or execute anie maner of prouocations, appeales or other processe from the see of Rome, vpon paine of incurring the premunire.
- Against such as slander the king, or his heires apparant.
- For the first fruits.
- Of sir Walter de la Hide knight his lands in Carbeire granted to the king.
- How persons robbed shall be restored to their goods.
- Restreining tributs to be granted to Irishmen.
- Against proctors to be any member of the parlement.
- Against marieng or fostering with or to Irishmen.
- Against the authoritie of the see of Rome.
- For the twentith part.
- For the English order, habit, and language.
- For the suppressing of abbeis.
- For the lading of wooll & flockes.
- For the proofe of testaments.
- Of faculties.
- Declaring th'effect of Poinings act.
- Of penall statutes.
- For the weres vpon Barou, and other waters in the countrie of Kilkennie.
- For the personage of Dongaran.
- For leasers of corne.

The old earle of Kildare his wish before his death.

As for the old earle of Kildare, who in this parlement was atteinted for diuerse presumptions, in the preamble of the said act rehearsed, certeine it is, that the reuolt of his sonne Thomas Fitzgirald smot him so déepelie to the heart, as vpon the report thereof he deceased in the tower, wishing in his death-bed that either he had died before he had heard of the rebellion, or that his brainelesse boy had neuer liued

liued to raise the like commotion. This earle, of such as did not stomach his procéedings, was taken for one that bare himselfe in all his affaires verie honorablie, a wise, deepe, and far reaching man: in war valiant without rashnesse, and politike without treacherie. Such a suppressor of rebels in his gouernement, as they durst not beare armor to the annoiance of anie subiect, whereby he heaped no small reuenues to the crowne, inriched the king his treasure, garded with securitie the pale, continued the honor of his house, and purchased enuie to his person. His great hospitalitie is to this daie rather of each man commended, than of anie one followed. He was so religiouslie addicted vnto the seruing of God, as what time soeuer he trauelled to anie part of the countrie, such as were of his chappell should be sure to accompanie him. Among other rare gifts, he was with one singular qualitie indued, which were it put in practise by such as are of his calling, might minister great occasion as well to the abandoning of flattering carie tales, as to the staied quietnesse of noble potentates.

His seruice.

His hospitalitie and deuotion.

For if anie whispered, vnder *Benedicite*, a sinister report or secret practise, that tended to the distaining of his honor, or to the perill of his person, he would strictlie examine the informer, whether the matter he reported were past, or to come. If it were said or doone, he was accustomed to laie sore to his charge, where, and of whome he heard it, or how he could iustifie it. If he found him to halt in the proofe, he would punish him as a pikethanke makebate, for being so maliciouslie caried, as for curriеng fauour to himselfe, he would labor to purchase hatred to another. But if the practise were future, and hereafter to be put in execution, then would he suspend the credit, vsing withall such warie secrecie, as vntill the matter came to the pinch, the aduersarie should thinke that he was most ignorant, when he was best prouided. As being in Dublin forewarned, that Iohn Olurkan with certeine desperate varlets conspired his destruction, & that they were determined to assault him vpon his returne to Mainoth, he had one of his seruants named Iames Grant, that was much of his pitch, and at a blush did somewhat resemble him, attired in his riding apparell, and namelie in a scarlet cloake, wherewith he vsed to be clad. Grant in this wise masking in his lords attire, rode as he was commanded in the beaten high waie towards Mainoth, with six of the earle his seruants attending vpon him. The conspirators awaiting towards Lucan the comming of the earle, incountered the disguised lord, and not doubting but it had béene Kildare, they began to charge him: but the other amazed therewith, cried that they tooke their marke amisse, for the earle rode to Mainoth on the further side of Liffie. Wherewith the mutherers appalled, fled awaie, but incontinentlie were by the earle apprehended, susteining the punishment that such caitifes deserued.

The old earle of Kildare his policie when his death was conspired.

Iohn Olurkan.

Iames Grant.

This noble man was so well affected to his wife the ladie Greie, as he would not at anie time buy a sute of apparell for himselfe, but he would sute hir with the same stuffe. Which gentlenesse she recompensed with equall kindnesse. For after that he deceased in the tower, she did not onelie euer after liue as a chast and honorable widow, but also nightlie before she went to bed, she would resort to his picture, & there with a solemne congée she would bid hir lord goodnight. Whereby may be gathered with how great loue she affected his person, that had in such price his bare picture. An other act that did passe in this parlement touching absenties, procéeded of this occasion. Maister Girald Ailmer, who first was chiefe baron of the excheker, after chiefe iustice of the common plees, was occasioned, for certeine his affaires, to repaire vnto the court of England. Where being for his good seruice greatlie countenanced by such as were in those daies taken for the pillers of the weale publike, namelie of the lord Cromwell, it happened that through his lordship his earnest meanes, the king made maister Ailemer chiefe iustice of his bench in Ireland.

The ladie Greies kindnesse to hir husband.

Girald Ailmer.

land. This aduancement disliked by certeine of Waterford and Weisford, that were not friended to the gentleman, they debased him in such despitefull wise, as the earle of Shrewesburie, who then was likewise earle of Waterford, was by their lewd reports caried to chalenge the king, so far as with his dutie of allegiance he durst, for bestowing so weightie an office vpon so light a person, being such a simple Iohn at Stile as he tearmed him, no wiser than Patch the late lord cardinall his foole.

The king herevpon expostulated with the lord Cromwell, who being throughlie acquainted with the gentleman his rare wisedome, answered: that if it would stand with his maiesties pleasure to enter into conference with him, he should be sure to find him no babe, notwithstanding the wrong informations of such as labored to thwart or crosse him. Whereto the king vpon further leasure agréed, and shortlie after (according to his promise) bestowed two or thrée houres with maister Ailmer: who vpon the lord Cromwell his forewarning, was so well armed for his highnesse, as he shewed himselfe in his discourse, by answering *Ad omnia quare*, to be a man woorthie to supplie an office of so great credit. In this conference the king demanded him, what he tooke to be the chiefe occasion of disorder in Ireland, and how he thought it might best be reformed? "Trulie and it like your maiestie, (quoth Ailmer) among sundrie reasons that might be probablie alleged for the decaie of that your kingdome, one chiefe occasion is, that certeine of your nobilitie of this your realme of England are seized of the better part of your dominion in Ireland, whereof they haue so little kéepe, as for lacke of their presence, they suffer the said lands to be ouerrun by rebels and traitors. Wherefore if your highnesse would prouide by act of parlement, that all such lands, which by reason of their absence may not be defended, should be to your highnesse by the consent of the nobilitie and communaltie granted, you might thereby enrich your crowne, represse rebels, and defend your subiects from all traitorous inuasion."

The king tickled with this plausible deuise, yéelded maister Ailmer hartie thanks for his good counsell, and in this parlement had the tenure thereof put in effect. Which redounded chéeflie to the lord of Shrewesburie his disaduantage, as one that was possessed of diuerse ancient lordships and manors in that countrie. Soone after this parlement, Oneale imagining that he was able to make his partie good against the English pale, conspired with Odoneale Maggadnesh, Ocaghan, Mac Kwilen, Ohanlan, and other Irish lords, and on a sudden inuaded the pale, came to the Nauan, burnt all the townes of ech side confining, after marched to Taragh, mustering with great pride his armie vpon the top of the hill: and hauing gathered togither the spoile of the pale without resistance, he began to recule northwards, making his full account to haue gone his waie scotfrée.

Oneale rebelleth.

The lord Leonard Greie being then lord deputie, forecasting the worst, certified the king & councell of Oneale his rebellion, and withall humblie besought a fresh supplie of souldiors to assist the pale in resisting the enimie, and that sir William Brereton (who was discharged & returned to England) should be sent into Ireland, as one that for his late seruice was highlie commended of the countrie. The king and councell condescending to the deputie his request, appointed sir William Brereton to hie thither with speed, hauing the charge of two hundred and fiftie souldiors of Cheshiremen. In which seruice the gentleman was found so prest and readie, that notwithstanding in mustering his band he fell by his mishap off his horsse, and therewithall brake his thigh in two places, yet rather than he would retire homewards, he appointed the mariners to hale him vp to their barke by pullies, and in such impotent wise arriued in Ireland, suppressing the féeblenesse of his bodie with the contagious valor of his mind.

Sir William Brereton sent for into Ireland.

Sir William Brereton sent into Ireland.

The

The lord deputie in the meane while marched with the force of the pale, the maior & the citizens of Dublin to Drogheda: from thense likewise accompanied with the maior & townesmen, he marched northward to Bellahoa, where Oneale & his companie on the further side of the water laie incamped with the spoile of the pale. The deputie by spies and secret messengers hereof certified, caused the armie to trauell the better part of the night, insomuch as by the dawning of the daie they were neere to the riuers side: where hauing escried the enimies, namelie Maggadnesh, and the Galloglasses that were placed there to kéepe the streicts (for Oneale with a maine armie lurked not farre off) they began to set themselues in battell araie, as men that were resolued with all hast and good speed to supprise the enimie with a sudden charge.

The foord of Bellahoa

At which time Iames Fleming baron of Slane (commonlie called Blacke Iames) garded with a round companie, as well of horssemen as of footmen, humblie besought the deputie to grant him that daie the honor of the onset. Whereto when the lord Greie had agréed, the baron of Slane with chéerefull countenance imparted the obteining of his sute, as plesant tidings to Robert Halfepennie, who with his ancestors was standardbearer to the house of Slane. But Halfepennie séeing the further side of the water so beset with armed Galloglasses as he tooke it, as likelie an attempt to rase down the strongest fort in Ireland with a fillip, as to rush through such quicke iron walles, flatlie answered the baron, that he would rather disclame in his office, than there to giue the onset where there rested no hope of life, but an assured certeintie of death. And therefore he was not as yet so wearie of the world, as like an headlong hotspur, voluntarilie to run to his vtter and vndoubted destruction. Wherefore he besought his lordship to set his heart at rest, and not to impute his denial to basenesse of corage, but to warinesse of safetie, although he knew none of staied mind, but would sooner choose to sléepe in an whole shéepe his pelt, than to walke in a torne lion his skin, namelie when all hope of life was abandoned, and the certeintie of death assuredlie promised.

Iames Fleming baron of Slane.

Robert Halfepennie

The baron with this answer at his wits end rode to Robert Betoa of Downore, brake with him as touching Halfepennie his determination, & withall requested him (as he did tender his honor) now at a pinch to supplie the roome of that dastardlie coward, as he did terme him. Betoa to this answered, that though it stood with good reason, that such as heretofore tasted the sweet in peace, should now be contented to sip of the sowre in war: yet notwithstanding, rather than the matter should to his honor lie in the dust, he promised to breake through them, or else to lie in the water, & withall being surpassinglie mounted (for the baron gaue him a choise horsse) he tooke the standard, & with a sudden showt, hauing with him in the forerancke Mabe of Mabestowne (who at the first brunt was slaine) he floong into the water, and charged the Irish that stood on the further shore. After followed the gentlemen and yeomen of the pale, that with as great manhood charged the enimies, as the enimies with corage resisted their assault. To this stoutnesse were the enimies more boldlie pricked, in that they had the aduantage of the shore, and the gentlemen of the pale were constreined to bicker in the water.

Robert Betoa

Mabe of Mabestowne slaine.

But the longer the Irish continued, the more they were disaduantaged, by reason that the English were so assisted with fresh supplies, as their enimies could not anie longer withstand them, but were compelled to beare backe, to forsake the banke, and to giue the armie free passage. The English taking hart vpon their faintnesse, brake through the Galloglasses, slue Maggadnesh their capteine, pursued Oneale with the remnant of his lords, leauing behind them for lacke of safe carriage the spoile of the pale, scantlie able to escape with his owne life, being egerlie pursued by the armie vntill it was sunne set. In this hot conflict Matthew King, Patrike Barnewall

The Irish discomfited Oneale put to flight

King Barnewall.

Basnet *Fitzsimons*

wall of Kilmallocke, sir Edward Basnet priest, who after became deane of saint Patriks in Dublin, and was sworne one of the priuie councell, and Thomas Fitzsimons of Curdufte, were reported to haue serued verie valiantlie. Moreouer, Iames Fitzsimons maior of Dublin, Michaell Cursete maior of Drogheda, Girald Ailmer cheefe iustice, and Thomas Talbot of Malahide, were dubbed knights in the field.

The maiors of Dublin and Drogheda dubbed knights *Ailmer* *Talbot*

The valiantnesse of the lord Greie

But of all others, the lord Greie then lord deputie, as he was in authoritie superior to them all, so in courage and manlinesse he was inferior to none. He was noted by the armie to haue indured great toile and paine before the skirmish, by posting bareheaded from one band to an other, debasing the enimies, inhansing the power of the pale, depressing the reuolt of rebellious traitors, extolling the good quarell of loiall subiects, offring large rewards, which with as great constancie he performed, as with liberalitie he promised. Ouer this, he bare himselfe so affable to his souldiors, in vsing them like fréends and fellows, and terming them with courteous names, and mooning laughter with pleasant conceipts, as they were incensed as well for the loue of the person, as for the hatred of the enimie, with resolute minds to bicker with the Irish. In which conflict the deputie was as forward as the most, and bequit himselfe as valiant a seruitor as the best.

The gouernor, turning the oportunitie of this skirmish to his aduantage, shortlie after rode to the north, preieng & spoiling Oneale with his confederats, who by reason of the late ouerthrow were able to make but little resistance. In this iornie he rased saint Patrike his church in Downe, an old ancient citie of Vlster, and burnt the monuments of Patrike, Brigide, and Colme, who are said to haue beene there intoomed, as before is expressed in the description of Ireland. This fact lost him sundrie harts in that countrie, alwaies after detesting and abhorring his prophane tyrannie, as they did name it. Wherevpon conspiring with such of Mounster as were enimies to his gouernment, they booked vp diuerse complaints against him, which they did exhibit to the king and councell. The articles of greatest importance laid to his charge were these.

The lord Greie accused.

The articles that were laid to his charge

1 Inprimis, that notwithstanding he were strictlie commanded by the king his maiestie, to apprehend his kinsman the yong Fitzgirald, yet did he not onlie disobeie the kings letters as touching that point by plaieng bopéepe, but also had priuie conference with the said Fitzgirald, and laie with him two or thrée seuerall nights before he departed into France.

2 Item, that the cheefe cause that mooued him to inuegle Thomas Fitzgirald with such faire promises, procéeded of set purpose to haue him cut off, to the end there should be a gap set open for the yoong Fitzgirald to aspire to the earledome of Kildare.

3 Item, that he was so gréedilie addicted to the pilling and polling of the king his subiects, namelie of such as were resiant in Mounster, as the beds he laie in, the cups he dranke in, the plate with which he was serued in anie gentlemans house, were by his seruants against right and reason packt vp, and carried with great extortion awaie.

4 Item, that without anie warrant from the king or councell, he prophaned the church of saint Patrikes in Downe, turning it to a stable, after plucked it downe, and ship tthe notable ring of bels that did hang in the steeple, meaning to haue sent them to England, had not God of his iustice preuented his iniquitie, by sinking the vessell and passengers wherein the said belles should haue béene conueied.

These and the like articles were with such odious presumptions coloured by his accusers, as the king and councell remembring his late faults, and forgetting his former seruices (for commonlie all men are of so hard hap, that they shall be sooner

for

for one trespasse condemned, than for a thousand good deserts commended) gaue commandement that the lord Greie should not onelie be remooued from the gouernment of the countrie, but also had him beheaded on the tower hill the eight and twentith of Iune. But as touching the first article, that brought him most of all out of conceipt with the king, I mooued question to the erle of Kildare, whether the tenor therof were true or false? His lordship thereto answered *Bona fide*, that he neuer spake with the lord Greie, neuer sent messenger to him, nor receiued message or letter from him. Whereby maie be gathered, with how manie dangers they are inwrapped that gouerne prouinces, wherein diligence is twhackt with hatred, negligence is loden with tawnts, seueritie with perils menaced, liberalitie with thanklesse vnkindnesse contemned, conference to vndermining framed, flatterie to destruction forged, each in countenance smiling, diuerse in heart pouting, open fawning, secret grudging, gaping for such as shall succéed in gouernment, honouring magistrates with cap and knee as long as they are present, and carping them with toong and pen as soone as they are absent.

The lord Greie beheaded. 1541

The lord Greie guiltlesse of the first article.

The dangers that happen to gouernors of prouinces.

The lord Leonard Greie (as is aforesaid) discharged, sir William Brereton was constituted lord iustice, whose short gouernement was intangled with no little trouble. For albeit he and Oneale fell to a reasonable composition, yet other of the Irish lordings, namelie Oconhur and his adherents, that are content to liue as subiects, as long as they are not able to hold out as rebels, conspired togither, and determined to assemble their power at the hill of Fowre in west Meth, and so on a sudden to ransacke the pale. The lord iustice foorthwith accompanied with the armie, and with two thousand of the pale, of which no small number were ecclesiasticall persons, made towards the rebels, who vpon the approch of so great an armie gaue ground, and dispersed themselues in woods and marishes. The lord iustice this notwithstanding inuaded Oconhur his countrie, burnt his tenements, & made all his trenches with the multitude of pioners so passable, as foure hundred carts, beside light carriage, were led without let thorough the countrie. Oconhur soone after submitted himselfe, & sent his sonne Cormach to the lord iustice as hostage for his future obedience and loialtie to the king his highnesse. After this iournie was ended, sir Anthonie Sentleger knight of the order was constituted lord deputie, and sir William Brereton lord high marshall, who within one halfe yeare after he was preferred to be marshall, trauelling by the lord deputie his appointment to Limerike, to bring in Iames earle of Desmond, who stood vpon certeine tickle points with the gouernor, ended his life in that iournie, and lieth intoomed at Kilkennie in the quier of saint Kennie his church. In the thrée and thirtith yeare of the reigne of Henrie the eight, there was a parlement holden at Dublin before sir Anthonie Sentleger, in which there passed these statutes following, namelie.

Sir William Brereton lord iustice.

Oconhur submitteth himselfe to the lord iustice.

Sir Anthonie Sen leger lord deputie.

Sir William Brereton lord high marshall.

He dieth.

1542

An act:

- That the king and his successors to be kings of Ireland.
- For graie merchants.
- That the plantife maie abridge his plaint in assise.
- That consanguinitie or affinitie being not within the fift degree, shall be no principall chalenge.
- That maketh it felonie to anie man to run awaie with his master his casket.
- For the adnihilating of precontracts in mariage.
- For all lords to distreine vpon the lands of them holden, & to make their auowrie, not naming the tenant, but their land.
- For capacities.

An act
- For seruants wages.
- For ioint-tenants.
- For recouerie in auoiding leases.
- For tithes.
- For attournements.

This parlement was proroged vntill the fiftéenth of Februarie, and after was continued at Limerike before the said deputie, at which time there passed

An act
- For the adiournment of the parlement, and the place to hold the same, and what persons shall be chosen knights and burgesses.
- For the election of the lord iustice.
- Touching mispleding and ieofailes.
- For lands giuen by the king.
- For the suppression of Kilmainan and other religious houses.

1543 This parlement was likewise proroged, and after was continued and holden before the said gouernour at Dublin, the sixt daie of Nouember, in the foure and thirtith yeare of the reigne of king Henrie the eight, wherein there passed these acts; namelie.

An act
- For the diuision of Meth into two shires.
- For persons standing bound in any court for their appeerance, and being in seruice, to be discharged by writ.

This parlement was further proroged vntill the seuentéenth of Aprill, and at that time before the said gouernor it was holden and ended: in which there passed an act touching the manour and castell of Dongiruan to be vnited and annexed to the crowne for euer. To this parlement resorted diuerse of the Irish lords, who submitting themselues to the deputie his mercie, returned peaceablie to their countries. But Iames earle of Desmond sailed into England, and before the king and councell purged himselfe of all such articles of treason as were falselie laid to his charge: whose cleare purgation and humble submission the king accepted verie gratefullie. Shortlie after Desmond his returne homeward, the great Oneale was created earle of Tiron, and his base sonne Matthew Oneale baron of Dongiruan. For in those daies Iohn Oneale, commonlie called Shane Oneale, the onelie sonne lawfullie of his bodie begotten, was little or nothing estéemed.

Iames earle of Desmond.

Oneale earle of Tiron.

Oneale hauing returned to Ireland with this honour, and the king his fauor, Obrien with certeine other Irish lords sailed into England, submitting their liues and lands to the king his mercie. This Obrien was at that time created earle of Clencare, in which honour his posteritie hitherto resteth. Shortlie after the returne of these lords to their countrie, king Henrie being fullie resolued to besiege Bullongne, gaue commandement to sir Anthonie Sentleger deputie, to leuie an armie of Irishmen, and with all expedition to send them to England. To these were appointed capteins the lord Powre, who after was dubd knight, Surlocke & Finglasse, with diuerse others. They mustered in saint Iames his parke seuen hundred. In the siege of Bullongne they stood the armie in verie good sted. For they were not onelie contented to burne and spoile all the villages thereto adioining, but also they would range twentie or thirtie miles into the maine land: and hauing taken a bull, they vsed to tie him to a stake, and scorching him with faggots, they would force him

Obren created earle of Clencare.

1544 The Irish sent for to the siege of Bullongne.

Their policie in purueieng for the armie.

him to rore, so as all the cattell in the countrie would make towards the bull, all which they would lightlie lead awaie, and furnish the campe with store of béefe.

If they tooke anie Frenchman prisoner, lest they should be accounted couetous, in snatching with them his entier bodie, his onelie ransome should bée no more but his head. The French with this strange kind of warfaring astonished, sent an ambassador to king Henrie, to learne whether he brought men with him or diuels, that could neither be woone with rewards, nor pacified by pitie: which when the king had turned to a ieast, the Frenchmen euer after, if they could take anie of the Irish scatering from the companie, vsed first to cut off their genitals, and after to torment them with as great and as lingering paine as they could deuise.

After that Bullongne was surrendred to the king, there incamped on the west side of the towne beyond the hauen an armie of Frenchmen, amongst whome there was a Thrasonicall Golias that departed from the armie, and came to the brinke of the hauen, and there in ietting and daring wise chalenged anie one of the English armie that durst be so hardie, as to bicker with him hand to hand. And albeit the distance of the place, the depth of the hauen, the neerenesse of his companie imboldened him to this chalenge, more than anie great valour or pith that rested in him to indure a combat, yet all this notwithstanding, an Irishman named Nicholl Welsh, who after reteined to the earle of Kildare, loathing and disdaining his proud brags, flung into the water, and swam ouer the riuer, fought with the chalenger, strake him for dead, and returned backe to Bullongne with the Frenchman his head in his mouth before the armie could ouertake him. For which exploit, as he was of all his companie highlie commended, so by the lieutenant he was bountifullie rewarded.

A Frenchman chalenger and slaied.

Nicholl Welsh.

Much about this time the earle of Lennox, verie wrongfullie inquieted in Scotland, and forced to forsake his countrie, became humble petitioner to king Henrie as well to releeue him in his distressed calamitie, as to compasse the means how he might be restored to his lands & liuing. The king his highnesse mooued with compassion, posted the earle ouer to Ireland, with letters of especiall trust, commanding sir Anthonie Sentleger then deputie, to assist and further the Scotish outcast, with as puissant an armie as to his contentation should séeme good. The deputie vpon the receipt of these letters, sent for Iames Butler earle of Ormond and Osserie, a noble man, no lesse politike in peace, than valiant in warres, made him priuie to the king his pleasure, and withall in his maiesties name did cast the charge hereof vpon the said earle, as one that for his tried loialtie was willing, and for his honour and valour able to attempt and atchiue so rare and famous an exploit. The lord of Ormond as willing to obeie, as the gouernour was to command, leuied of his tenants and reteiners six hundred Gallowglasses, foure hundred Kearnes, thrée score horssemen, and foure hundred and fortie shot: so in the whole he mustered on Osmantowne greene néere Dublin, fiftéene hundred souldiours.

1545

The earle of Lennox assisted by king Henrie.

Iames Butler earle of Ormond.

The lord deputie yéelding his honour such thanks in words, as he deserued indéed, leuied in the pale fifteene hundred souldiours more, to be annexed to the earle his companie. Ouer them he constituted sir Iohn Trauers capteine, but the erle of Ormond was made generall of the whole armie. When the souldiours were with munition and victuals aboundantlie furnished, the earle of Ormond and the earle of Lennox tooke shipping at Sherise, hauing in their companie twentie and eight ships well rigged, sufficientlie manned, and stronglie appointed. From thense they sailed northwards, and rode at anchor without the hauen of Oldfléet beyond Karregfergus. Where hauing remained hulling without the mouth of the hauen, contrarie to the aduise of the masters of their ships (who prognosticated the spéedie approch of a storme, and therefore did wish them to take a good harbrough) it

Sir Iohn Trauers knight.

The earle of Ormond and the earle of Lennox in danger to be drowned.

 hapned

hapned that the said night there arose so boisterous a tempest, that the whole fleet was like to haue béene ouerwhelmed. The mariners betaking their passengers and themselues to the mercie of God, did cut their maine masts, let slip their anchors, and were weather driuen to the hauen of Dunbritaine in Scotland, whereas they were like to run their ships on ground, and consequentlie they all should either haue béene plunged in the water, or else haue béene slaine on the land by a great number of Scots that awaited their approach. God with his gratious clemencie preuenting their imminent calamitie, sent them not onelie a wished calme, but also a prosperous gale of wind, that blew them backe in safetie to the Irish coast, from whense they were scattered.

The earle of Ormond his propertie.

The earle of Lennox aduertised by certeine of his fréends that met with him on the sea, that the Scots (contrarie to their promise) dealt verie doublie with him (for although they gaue their word to surrender vp to him the castell of Dunbritaine, yet they did not onelie fortifie that hold, but also were readie to incounter with his souldiors vpon their arriuals) he concluded to returne to Ireland. The earle of Ormond verie loath that so great an attempt should take so little effect, dealt with him verie earnestlie, notwithstanding his counsell were bewraied to inuade his enimies, and his lordship should be sure to find the armie so forward in assisting him in so famous an enterprise, as they would shew themselues more willing to bicker with his foes in Scotland, than without skirmishing to returne to Ireland. For the earle of Ormond was of this nature, that as he would not begin anie martiall broile rashlie or vnaduisedlie, so he would not séeme to put it vp lightlie or easilie.

The lord of the out Iles saileth to the earle of Lennox.

Further, whereas the earle of Lennox stood in hope, that the lord of the out Iles would aid him, it was thought by Ormond not to be amisse, to expect his comming, and so ioining his companie to the armie, there rested no doubt, but that the Scottish enimies would be forced to plucke in their hornes, although at the first blush they séeme to set a good face on the matter. Lennox somewhat with this persuasion carried, gaue his consent to expect the lord of the out Iles determination, who notwithstanding all the fetch of the enterprise were descried, would not slip from his word, but personallie sailed to the Irish fléet, with thrée gallies well appointed. The noble man with such martiall triumphs was receiued, as warlike souldiors could on the sea afoord him. But of all others, both the earls gaue him heartie interteinment for his true & honorable dealing, that to be as good as his word, would not séeme to shrinke from his fréend in this his aduersitie. And shortlie after as they craued his aduise what were best to be doone, either to land in Scotland, or else to returne homeward, his flat resolution was at that time to retire, bicause their drift was detected, their feined friends fainted, the castels were fortified, and the shoares on all parts with swarms of Scots peopled. Wherefore he thought it better policie to giue out in open rumors, that they meant not at anie hand to inuade Scotland, but to retire to their countrie.

Ormond and Lennox land.

The lord of the out Iles dieth.

And after that the Scotish souldiors should be dismist, which would be incontinent vpon their returne, by reason of the excessiue charges: then might the earle of Lennox with lesse preparation, and more secrecie giue a fresh onset, that the enimies should sooner féele his force, than heare of his arriuall. Ormond and Lennox vpon this determination landed with the greater part of the armie, and appointed the ships to bend their course to Dublin. The lord of the out Iles and his three gallies sailed with the fléet, for he was not able by reason of the féeblenesse of his bodie to trauell by land, or scantlie further to prolong his life, which he ended at Houth presentlie vpon his arriuall, and was with great solemnitie buried in saint Patrike his church at Dublin, vpon whose death this epitaph following was framed:

"Vique

His epitaph.

"Vtque manúque mea patriæ dum redditur exsul,
Exsul in externa cogor & ipse mori."

The Irish skirmish with the earle of Lennox

The earle of Ormond his toilsome trauell

Both the earles marched with the armie on foot to Carregfergus, where they brake companie. For Lennox and sir Iohn Trauers taking as he thought the shorter but not the safer waie, trauelled through the Ardes with the number of fiue hundred souldiers, where the Irish inhabitants skirmished with them, and put them to such streict plunges (for they would gladlie haue seene what a clocke it was in their budgets) as they wished they had not parted from the rest of the armie. The earle of Ormond with his souldiers (which were a thousand fiue hundred, as before is expressed) marched on foot to Belefast, which is an arme of the sea, a quarter of a mile broad or little lesse. And albeit then wether were bitter and ouernipping, and no small parcell of the water were congeled with frost, yet the earle and his armie waded ouer on foot, to the great danger as well of his person, as of the whole companie, which doubtlesse was a valiant enterprise of so honorable a personage. From thense he passed to Strangford, and through Lecale to Dondalke, where he discharged his souldiers, and hauing presented himselfe to the gouernour at Dublin, he rode homewards to the countie of Kilkennie.

The deputie and Ormond at debate

Ormond his letters intercepted.

Shortlie after sir Anthonie Sentleger lord deputie and the earle of Ormond fell at debate, insomuch as either of them laid articles of treason one to the others charge. The chiefe occasion of their mutuall grudge procéeded of certeine new and extraordinarie impositions, wherewith the deputie would haue charged the subiects. Whereat the earle of Ormond as a zelous defendor of his countrie began to kicke, & in no sort could be woone to agree to anie such vnreasonable demand. Herevpon Ormond, perceiuing that the gouernour persisted in his purpose, addressed letters of complaint to such as were of the priuie councell in England: which letters were by one of sir Anthonie his friends intercepted at sea, and presented to him to be perused. Sir Anthonie hauing ouer read the writings, sent master Basnet in post hast with the packet to Kilkennie, where the earle of Ormond kept his Christmasse, requesting his lordship to take in good part the opening of his letters. Which was doone rather to learne the effect of his complaint, than in anie sort to imbar his writings from comming to the councels hands.

The lord deputie and Ormond sent for to England

They are made freends

The earle answered that his quarell was so good, his dealing so open, as he little weighed who tooke a view of his letters. And for his part what he wrote he meant not to vnwrite, but in such sort as they came from the gouernour, they should be sent to the councell: and if their honours would allow anie subiect to be so hardie, as to intercept and open letters that were to them indorsed, he could not but digest anie such iniurie that they would seeme to beare. With this answer Basnet returned, and the earle performed his promise. Wherevpon the gouernour and he were commanded to appeare before the priuie councell in England, where they were sundrie times examined, and their accusations ripelie debated. In fine, the councell equallie to both parts in their complaints affected, and weighing withall rather the due desert of both their loiall seruices, than the vaine presumption of their mutuall accusations, wrapped vp their quarels & made them both fréends, with such indifferencie as neither part should be either with anie conquest exalted, or with anie foile debased.

Sir Iohn Alen lord chancellor committed to the Fleet

And for so much as sir Iohn Alen knight then lord chancellor of Ireland, was found to limpe in this controuersie, by plaieng (as it was supposed) more craftilie than wiselie, with both the hands, in that he séemed to be rather a fosterer of their malice, than an appeaser of their quarels, he was likewise sent for into England and being tript by the councell in his tale, was committed to the Fleet, wherin he

remained

remained a long time. In this trouble the earle of Ormond was greatlie aided by sir William Wise knight a worshipfull gentleman, borne in the citie of Waterford, who deseruing in déed the praise of that vertue, whereof he bare the name, grew to be of great credit in the court, and stood highlie in king Henrie his grace, which he wholie vsed to the furtherance of his friends, and neuer abused to the annoiance of his foes. This gentleman was verie well spoken, mild of nature, with discretion stout, as one that in an vpright quarell would beare no coles, seldome in an intricate matter grauelled, being found at all assaies to be of a pleasant and present wit. Hauing lent the king his signet to seale a letter, who hauing powdred ermintes ingrailed in the seale, "Why how now Wise (quoth the king) what, hast thou lice here?" "And if it like your maiestie," quoth sir William, "a louse is a rich cot by giuing the louse. I part armes with the French king, in that he giueth the floure de lice." Whereat the king hartilie laughed, to heare how pretilie so biting a taunt (namelie proceeding from a prince) was suddenlie turned to so pleasant a conceipt.

Sir William Wise knight.

Anon after the agreement made betwéene Ormond and Sentleger, the earle his seruants (which he kept at that time in his liuerie to the number of fiftie) besought his lordship to take at the Limehouse his part of a supper, which they prouided for him. The noble man with honour accepting their dutifull offer, supped at their request, but not to their contentation at the place appointed. For whether it were that one caitife or other did poison the meat, or that some other false measures were vsed (the certeintie with the reuenge whereof to God is to be referred) the noble man with thirtie and fiue of his seruants presentlie that night sickened: one James White the earle his steward, with sixteene of his fellowes died, the remnant of the seruants recouered. But their lord, whose health was chieflie to be wished, in the floure of his age deceased of that sicknesse at Elie house in Holborne, much about the eight and twentith of October, and was buried in saint Thomas of Acres his church, whose death bred sorow to his friends, little comfort to his aduersaries, great losse to his countrie, and no small griefe to all good men.

The earle of Ormond deceaseth. 1546

This earle was a goodlie and personable noble man, full of honour, which was not onelie lodged inwardlie in his mind, but also he bare it outwardlie in countenance: as franke & as liberall as his calling required, a deepe and a farre reaching head. In a good quarell rather stout than stubborne, bearing himselfe with no lesse courage when he resisted, than with honorable discretion where he yéelded. A fauourer of peace, no furtherer of warre, as one that procured vnlawfull quietnesse before vpright troubles, being notwithstanding of as great wisedome in the one, as of valour in the other. An earnest and a zealous vpholder of his countrie, in all attempts rather respecting the publike weale than his priuat gaine. Whereby he bound his countrie so greatlie vnto him, that Ireland might with good cause wish, that either he had neuer beene borne, or else that he had neuer deceased, so it were lawfull to craue him to be immortall, that by course of nature was framed mortall. And to giue sufficient proofe of the entire affection he bare his countrie, and of the zealous care he did cast thereon, he betooke in his death-bed his soule to God, his carcase to christian buriall, and his hart to his countrie, declaring thereby, that where his mind was setled in his life, his hart should be there intoomed after his death. Which was according to his will accomplished. For his hart was conueied to Ireland, and lieth ingraued in the quéere of the cathedrall church in Kilkennie, where his ancestors for the more part are buried. Vpon which kind & louing legacie this epitaph following was deuised.

His description.

His epitaph.

"Cor patriæ fixum viuens, iam redditur illi
Post mortem, patriæ quæ peracerba venit.

Non

Non sine corde valet mortalis viuere quisquam,
  Vix tua gens vita permanet absque tua.
Quæ licèt infœlix extincto corde fruatur,
  Attamen optato viuere corde nequit.
Ergò quid hæc faciat? Quem re non possit amorem
  Cordi vt tam charo reddere corde velit?"

The effect of which said epitaph is thus Englished:

"The liuing hart where laie ingrauen
  the care of countrie deere,
To countrie liuelesse is restord
  and lies ingrauen here
None hartlesse liues, his countrie then
  alas what ioie is left,
Whose hope, whose hap, whose hart he was
  till death his life bereft
And though the soile here shrowds the hart,
  which most it wisht t enioie,
Yet of the change from nobler seat,
  the cause dooth it annoie
What honour then is due to him,
  for him what worthie rite?
But that ech hart with hartiest loue,
  his worthiest hart may quite?"

This earle was of so noble a disposition, as he would sooner countenance and support his poore well willer in his aduersitie, than he would make or fawne vpon his wealthie friend in prosperitie. (The kindnes of Iames erle of Ormond to his friends.) Hauing bid at London (not long before his death) the ladie Greie countesse of Kildare to dinner, it happened that a souldier, surnamed Powre, who latelie returned fresh from the emperour his warres, came to take his repast with the earle before the messenger When the earle and the countesse were set, this roisting Rutterkin wholie then standing on the soldado hoigh, placed himselfe right ouer against the countesse of Kildare, hard at the earle of Ormond his elbow, as though he were haile fellow well met The noble man appalled at the impudent saucinesse of the malapert soldier (who notwithstanding might be borne withall, bicause an vnbidden ghest knoweth not where to sit) besought him courteouslie to giue place. The earle, when the other arose, taking vpon him the office of a gentleman vsher, placed in Powre his seat, his cousine Edward Fitzgerald, now lieutenant of hir maiesties pensioners, (Edward Fitzgirald) who at that time being a yoong stripling, attended vpon his mother the countesse, and so in order he set euerie gentleman in his degree, to the number of fifteene or sixteene and last of all the companie, he licenced Powre, if he would, to sit at the lower end of the table, where he had scantlie elbow roome.

The countesse of Kildare, perceiuing the noble man greatlie to stomach the souldior his presumptuous boldnesse, nipt him at the elbow, and whispering softlie, besought his lordship not to take the matter so hot, bicause the gentleman (she ment Powre) knew that the house of Kildare was of late atteinted, and that hir children were not in this their calamitie in such wise to be regarded "No ladie (quoth the earle with a lowd voice, and the tears trilling downe his chéeks), saie not so, I trust to sée the daie, when my yoong cousin Edward, and the remnant of your children (as little reckoning as he maketh of them) shall disdaine the companie of any such skipiacke' Which prophesie fell out as trulie as he foretold it, onelie

saiing

sauing that it stood with God his pleasure to call him to his mercie before he could see that daie after which doubtlesse he longed and looked, I meane the restitution of the house of Kildare

Sir Anthonie Sentleger returneth lord deputie

After this noble earle his vntimelie decease, sir Anthonie Sentleger was returned to Ireland lord deputie, who was a wise and a warie gentleman, a valiant seruitor in war, and a good iusticer in peace, properlie learned, a good maker in the English, hauing grauitie so interlaced with pleasantnesse, as with an exceeding good grace he would atteine the one without pouting dumpishnesse, and exercise the other without loathsome lightnesse There fell in his time a fat benefice, of which he as lord deputie had the presentation. When diuerse made suit to him for the benefice, and offered with dishonestie to buie that which with safetie of conscience he could not sell, he answered merilie, that he was resolued not to commit simonie yet notwithstanding he had a nag in his stable that was worth fortie shillings, and he that would giue him fortie pounds for the nag, should be preferred to the benefice Which he rather of pleasure vttered, than of anie vnconscionable meaning purposed to haue doone

Sentleger his simonie

His gouernement had beene of the countrie verie well liked, were it not that in his time he began to assesse the pale with certeine new impositions, not so profitable (as it was thought) to the gouernors, as it was noisome to the subiects The debating of which I purpose to referre to them, who are discoursers of publike estates, and the reformers of the commonwealth, praieng to God, that he with his grace direct them so faithfullie to accomplish the duties of good magistrates, that they gouerne that poore battered Iland to his diuine honour, to hir maiesties contentation, to the suppressing of rebels, to the vpholding of subiects, and rather to the publike weale of the whole countrie, than to the priuat gaine of a few persons, which oftentimes falleth out in proofe to the ruine and vndoing of the seeker.

Thus farre (gentle reader) as mine instructions directed me, and my leasure serued me, haue I continued a parcell of the Irish historie, and haue stretched it to the reigne of Edward the sixt Whereupon I am forced to craue at thine hands pardon and tollerance pardon for anie error I shall be found to haue committed, which vpon friendlie admonition I am readie to reforme tollerance, for that part of the historie which is not continued, till time I be so furnished and fraught with matter, as that I maie emploie my trauell to serue thy contentation

FINIS

THE

SVPPLIE OF THIS

IRISH CHRONICLE,

CONTINUED FROM THE DEATH OF

KING HENRIE THE EIGHT, 1546,

VNTILL THIS PRESENT YEARE 1586,

IN THE 28 YEARE OF HIR MAIESTIES REIGNE,

SIR IOHN PEROT RESIDING DEPUTIE IN IRELAND.

BY IOHN VOWELL alias HOOKER

OF THE CITIE OF EXCESTER, GENTLEMAN.

AS from the time of *Giraldus Cambrensis* (the best deserued and exact writer of the conquest and state of Ireland in his time, few or none haue followed and continued any perfect course of that historie vntill the death of king Henrie the eight, and the beginning of king Edward the sixt 1546; and therefore no certeine knowledge nor assurance can be yelded, nor set downe either of the quiet gouernement in time of peace, or of the troublesome state in time of warres and rebellions; but that which is collected either out of the records, which were verie slenderlie & disorderlie kept, or out of some priuat mens collections and pamphlets, remaining in some od and obscure places. euen so the like from that time vnto these presents hath happened and is fallen out, euerie gouernour neglecting, and verie few others for want of due obseruations willing, to commit vnto writing what was doone, and woorthie the memoriall, sauing the things so latelie doone are not altogither out of remembrance, and some yet liuing that can remember some things doone in their times. And yet that is so vncerteiné, and euerie man so varieth one from the others reports, that no man can well therevpon set downe a perfect and so exact a course as the nature of an historie requireth, and as it ought to be doone. He therefore that vpon such vncerteinties shall intermedle and vndertake the penning, much more the printing of such an vncerteine, confused, and intricate discourse, must looke and be assured to be subiect to manie cauils and reproches: which thing discouraged me the writer hereof to intermedle at all in this historie. Neuerthelesse, this worke requiring a supplie, and my selfe being earnestlie required to doo something herein, haue aduentured the matter, and by all the meanes I could, haue searched and collected to set downe in this short discourse and rhapsodie, what by writings or reports I could learne and find to be true, and worthie the memoriall: which albeit, it be not so full as the worke requireth, nor so sufficient as to the satisfaction of the reader, nor yet so answerable to the nature of an historie as is necessarie and requisit: yet let the good will of the writer be his discharge from reproch, and be an occasion to the learned to amend the thing thus in a good affection begun, and to reduce it to a more full measure in matter and truth: that this historie may haue his perfection, the reader satisfied, and this writer acquited.

IOHN HOOKER, aliâs VOWELL.

The

SVPPLIE

OF THE

IRISH CHRONICLES

EXTENDED TO THIS PRESENT YEARE OF OUR LORD 1586,

AND THE 28 OF THE REIGNE OF

QUEENE ELISABETH.

AFTER the death of king Henrie the eight, sir Anthonie Sentleger knight, was reuoked, who deliuered vp the sword at his departure vnto sir William Brabston knight, and he was lord iustice, vntill such time as sir Edward Bellingham was sent ouer to be deputie. This man was seruant to king Edward the sixt, and of his priuie chamber a man verie well learned, graue and wise, and therewith stout & valiant, and did verie worthilie direct his gouernment. In his time there was a mint kept in the castell of Dublin, which being at his commandement, he was the better able to doo good seruice to the king his maiestie, and to the benefit of that realme. In the ciuill gouernment he was carefull to place learned and wise magistrats, vnto whome he had a speciall eie for the dooing of their offices, as he had the like care for good and expert capteins, to serue in the martiall affaires. And for the more spéedie seruice to be doone therein at all times needfull, he kept sundrie stables of horsses: one at Leighlin, one at Lex, and some in one place and some in another, as he thought most méet for seruice. And whatsoeuer he had to doo, or what seruice soeuer he meant to take in hand, he was so secret, and kept the same so priuie, as none should haue anie vnderstanding thereof, before the verie instant of the seruice to be doone, and for the most part, whensoeuer he tooke anie iournie in hand, his owne men knew not whither, or to what place he would ride, or what he would doo. It happened that vpon some occasion he sent for the earle of Desmond, who refused to come vnto him. Wherevpon calling vnto him his companie as he thought good, and without making them acquainted what he minded to doo, tooke horsse & rode to Leighlin bridge. The abbeie there (being suppressed) he caused to be inclosed with a wall, and made there a fort. In that house he had a stable of twentie or thirtie horsses, and there he furnished himselfe and all his men with horsses and other furniture, and foorthwith rode into Mounster, vnto the house of the

Sir Anthonie Sentleger reuoked.
1547
Sir Edward Bellingham made lord deputie.
A mint in Dublin.
Sir Edward Bellinghams carefulnesse in gouernement.
Sundrie stables of horsses kept.
His secrecie in his seruice.
Leighlin abbeie inclosed with a wall and made a fort.

 earle,

The earle of Desmond taken in his house

earle, being then Christmas, and being vnlooked and vnthought of, he went in to the earle, whome he found sitting by the fire, and there tooke him, and caried him with him to Dublin

The earle is rude without nurture

The earle instructed in ciuilitie

This earle was verie rude both in gesture and in apparell, hauing for want of good nurture as much good maners as his Kerns and his followers could teach him. The deputie hauing him at Dublin, did so instruct, schoole and informe him, that he made a new man of him, and reduced him to a conformitie in maners, apparell, and behauiours appertening to his estate and degree, as also to the knowledge of his dutie and obedience to his soueraigne & prince, and made him to kneele vpon his knées sometimes an houre togither, before he knew his dutie This though it were verie strange to the earle, who hauing not béene trained vp in anie ciuilitie, knew not what apperteined to his dutie and calling neither yet of what authoritie and maiestie the king his soueraigne was, yet when he had well digested and considered of the matter, he thought himselfe most happie that euer he was acquainted with the said deputie, and did for euer after so much honor him, as that continuallie all his life time at euerie dinner and supper, he would praie for the good sir Edward Bellingham and at all callings he was so obedient and dutifull, as none more in that land.

The earle praieth for sir Edward Bellingham

The lord deputie would be chargeable to none.

This sir Edward lord deputie, when and where soeuer he trauelled he would be chargeable to no man, but would be at his owne charge It happened that trauelling the countrie, he was lodged on a night in vicount Baltinglasses house, where all things were verie plentifullie prouided for him which the vicount thought to haue giuen and bestowed vpon his lordship but at his departure, he commanded his steward to paie & discharge all things, thanking the vicount for his courtesie, but refused his interteinement, saieng "The king my maister hath placed me here to serue him and alloweth me therein for my charges and expenses wherefore, I neither maie nor will be burdenous nor chargable to anie other man" He was verie exquisit & carefull in the gouernement, as few before him the like, aswell in matters martiall, as politike, magnanimous and couragious in the one, to the appalling of the enimie, and as seuere & vpright in the other, to the benefit of the commonwelth. For neither by flatterie could he be gained, nor by briberie be corrupted, he was feared for his seueritie, and beloued for his integritie, and no gouernor for the most vniuersallie better reported of than was he But as vertue hath the contrarie to enimie, so he found it true for he was so enuied at, and that rebellious nation not brooking so woorthie a man, who trauelled all the waies he could to reduce them to the knowledge of themselues, and of their duties, and also to reforme that corrupt state of gouernement, that great practises and deuises were made for his reuocation, and matters of great importance informed and inforced against him Wherevpon, before two yeares ended of his gouernement, he was reuoked, and sir Francis Brian made lord iustice At his comming into England, great matters were laid vnto his charge but he so effectuallie did answer the same, that his maiesties doubtfulnesse was resolued, & he not onlie cléered, but also better liked than euer he was before, & should haue béene sent backe againe, had he not alleged his infirmitie, the which was a fistula, and other good reasons, which were accepted for his excuse Sir Francis Brian had maried the countesse of Ormond, and by that meanes he was a dweller in that land where he died & was buried in the citie of Waterford. His time of iusticeship was but short, & no great matters could in so short a time be doone by him After his death, sir William Brabston had the sword deliuered vnto him, and he continued lord iustice, vntill that sir Anthonie Sentleger came ouer, who was now lord deputie the second time who notwithstanding by his knowledge & experience he had good skill and did well gouerne yet there remained some

The good gouernement of this deputie

Sir Edward Bellingham well beloued.

1548

Sir Francis Brian lord iustice

Sir Francis Brian maried the countes of Ormond, died and was buried at Waterford

1549

Sir William Brabston lord iustice

1550

Sir Anthonie Sentleger lord

some coles of the fire in his first gouernement vnquenched, and within a shorter time than thought of, he was reuoked and sir James Crofts was sent ouer to supplie the place, his euill successes in good attempts did not answer his valour and good deserts. *deputie the second time* 1551 *Sir James Crofts lord deputie*

And albeit the time of his gouernement were not long, yet it continued vntill the death of king Edward the sixt, and then he was called home, and sir Thomas Cusacke and sir Gerard Elmer were appointed lords iustices, who iointlie gouerned the estate, vntill quéene Marie sent ouer sir Anthonie Sentleger, who now the third time was lord deputie. This man ruled and gouerned verie iustlie and vprightlie in a good conscience, and being well acquainted in the courses of that land, knew how to meete with the enimies, and how to staie all magistrates and others in their duties and offices: for which though he deserued well, and ought to be beloued and commended, yet the old practises were renewed, and manie slanderous informations were made and inueighed against him, which is a fatall destinie, and ineuitable to euerie good gouernor in that land. For the more paines they take in tillage, the worse is their haruest, and the better be their seruices, the greater is the malice and enuie against them, being not vnlike to a fruitefull apple trée, which the more apples he beareth, the more cudgels be hurled at him. Well, this man is called home, and the lord Thomas Fitzwaters was made lord deputie. At sir Anthonies comming ouer, great matters were laid to his charge, and manie heauie aduersaries he had, which verie eagerlie pursued the same against him: wherein he so answered, that he was not onelie acquited, but also gained his dischaige for euer to passe ouer anie more into so vnthankefull a land. 1552 *Sir Anthonie Sentleger lord deputie the third time* *A fatall destinie to euerie good gouernor to be slandered* 1555 *The lord Fitzwaters made lord deputie*

The lord Fitzwaters being lord deputie, after a short time of his being there, was sent for into England. And in his absence, sir Henrie Sidneie then treasuror at warres, and doctor Corwen, were for a time ioint lords iustices: but verie shortlie after, a commission was sent to sir Henrie Sidneie to be sole lord iustice, and so continued alone vntill the lord Fitzwaters, now earle of Sussex, came againe and resumed his former office of deputie. After that he was come ouer, he had somewhat to doo with the Oneile. For the whole north part of Ireland began to be vnquieted, and for preuenting of sundrie inconueniences, which might grow by the Scotish Ilanders in aiding the said Oneile, the lord deputie made a iourneie and voiage into the said Iles, to ioine them into his friendship. In his absence, he constituted sir Henrie Sidneie lord iustice, but after that he had doone his businesse he returned againe to Dublin, where he remained and continued in his office vntill the death of quéene Marie, and then he passed ouer into England, and left sir Henrie Sidneie to be lord iustice now the fourth time. And after some time spent there, and quéene Elisabeth now setled in the imperiall crowne of England, she sent ouer the said earle as lieutenant of Ireland to performe those seruices, which before he had taken in hand: who did verie great good seruice against the Irishrie, and by meanes he tooke the Oneile, and kept him prisoner in the castell of Dublin: but yet before he could or did bring the same to perfection, he was reuoked into England, and left the land in a verie broken state, which was committed to sir Nicholas Arnold, & he was made lord iustice. But his gouernement being not well liked, choise was made by hir maiestie and the councell of sir Henrie Sidneie, now knight of the honorable order of the garter, to supplie that place, who then was lord president of Wales. 1555 *Sir Henrie Sidneie and Corwen lords iustices* *The Oneile and all the north be vnquiet* 1556 *Sir Henrie Sidneie lord iustice the fourth time* 1557 *The earle of Sussex lord lieutenant* *The Oneile taken and kept in prison* 1564 *Sir Nicholas Arnold lord iustice* 1565 *Sir Henrie Sidneie lord deputie*

This man had béene before a long seruitour to that realme, hauing for sundrie yeares béene treasuror at warres, which is the second office vnder the lord deputie in that land, as also had béene lord iustice solie and iointlie foure times. Great was his knowledge, wisedome, and experience both of that land, and of the nature, manners,

manners, and disposition of the people: wherein the more he excelled anie others in those daies, the more apt and fit was he to haue the gouernement of them. He was therefore called from out of Wales, where he then resided in his gouernement vnto the court: and there after conference had with hir highnesse, and with the councell, he was appointed to be lord deputie of Ireland, being the seuenth yeare of hir maiesties reigne, in the yeare of our Lord 1565. And then he receiued of hir maiestie a booke of instructions signed with hir owne hand, dated the fift of October 1565, the seuenth yeare of hir reigne aforesaid, concerning the principall articles for his gouernement & direction, which cheefie consisted in these points.

Sir Henrie Sidneie lord president of Wales.

A booke of articles deliuered to sir Henrie Sidneie for his gouernement.

First, that there should be a bodie of a councell established, to assist him being lord deputie, in the gouernement of the same realme in times of peace and of warre, and whose names were then particularlie set downe: and order giuen, that euerie of them should before their admission be sworne by the said lord deputie, according to the accustomed manner: with an exhortation, that for somuch as hir maiestie had reposed a speciall trust and confidence in their wisedomes, aduises, good counsels, and seruices: he the lord deputie should vse their aduises, assistance, and counsels in all matters of treatie and consultation, concerning the state of that realme.

A councell to be established.

Euerie councellor to be sworne.

And they likewise, considering the place and authoritie wherevnto hir maiestie had called the said sir Henrie Sidneie, to hold hir place in that realme: they should yéeld that obedience and reuerence vnto him, as to such a principall officer dooth apperteine. And then they both togither, to haue a speciall care and regard to the gouernement, which was comprised in foure articles that doo orderlie hereafter follow.

The said foure articles were these.

1 First, that they should faithfullie and earnestlie regard the due and reuerend obseruation of all Gods lawes and ordinances, made and established for the mainteinance of the true christian faith and religion among hir people, and that all meanes should be vsed, aswell by doctrine and by teaching, as by good examples, that deuotion and godlinesse might increase, and contempt of religion might be restreined, punished, and suppressed. That learning in the scriptures might be mainteined and increased among the cleargie, and that for the releefe of the ecclesiasticall state, no alienations nor wasts of the lands perteining to anie church or colledge, should be alienated: neither anie impropriations of benefices be put in vre: besides sundrie other articles incident to this effect.

Gods lawes to be kept, and christian religion to be vsed.

Learning of the scriptures to be mainteined.

The church lands not to be alienated.

2 The second was, that the administration of law and iustice should dulie and vprightlie be executed, without respect of persons: that inquirie be made what notable faults are in anie of the iudges, or other ministers of the law: that vnfit persons maie be remoued from their places, and some sufficient persons of English birth be chosen to supplie the same. That shiriffes be appointed and renewed in euerie countie, and to execute their offices vprightlie, according to the lawes of England.

The lawes to be dulie administred.

Shiriffes to be appointed in euerie shire.

3 The third, that the garisons and men of warre be well ordered to the benefit of the realme, and repressing of disordered subiects and rebels: that they doo liue according to the orders appointed, without oppression of the good and true subiects. That there shall be once within a moneth at the least a muster made either by the lord deputie, or by such commissioners as he shall appoint méete and indifferent for that purpose, who shall make inquirie of the number of the souldiors vnder euerie capteine, for the sufficiencie of their persons, their horsses, armors, and

The garisons to be looked vnto.

A muster to be kept euerie moneth.

and weapons, and other their necessaries: and how they were paied of their wages, and whether they were Englishmen or not.

4 The fourth article was, whether there had béene had a due care & regard to the preseruation of the reuenues of the crowne, & for the recouerie of that which is withdrawne. And whether euerie of the officers appointed for the receiuing of anie part of the said reuenues, as namelie the receiuers of rents, shiriffes, eschetors, collectors of the subsidies, customors, clerks of the crowne, of the hamper, and of the first fruits, and the farmers of customes and such others, did yearelie make and answer their accounts, and besides sundrie other articles incident to euerie of these principals.

A due regard to be had of hir maiesties reuenues.

That euerie officer of receipts doo yearelie make his account.

After that he had receiued this booke, and his commission, he prepared himselfe with all the expedition he could to follow the great charge committed vnto him: which being doone, he repaired to hir maiestie and tooke his leaue: and to his farewell, she gaue him most comfortable spéeches and good counsels, promising hir fauor and countenance to all his well doings, and a consideration for the same when as time should serue. The like leaue he tooke also of the lords of the councell, who in like order gaue him the like farewell: and these things doone, he departed towards the sea side, where after he had taried a long time for a good wind and passage, he tooke ship, and arriued in Ireland the thirtéenth of Ianuarie, about fiue miles from Dublin, and from thense he trauelled to Dublin, where he was most honorablie receiued by sir Nicholas Arnold then lord iustice, and the whole councell, togither with the maior and his brethren of that citie. And the people in great troops came and saluted him, clapping and shooting with all the ioie that they could deuise.

Sir Henrie Sidnie taketh his leaue of the quéene and councell.

Sir Henrie Sidneie ioifullie receiued into Dublin.

The next sundaie then next following, being the seuenth daie of his arriuall, and the twentith of the moneth, he accompanied with the lord iustice and councell, repaired to the high church in the citie named Christes church, where after that the diuine seruice was doone, he tooke his oth, receiued the sword, and assumed vpon him the gouernement: and wherewith he made a most pithie, wise, and eloquent oration, which consisted vpon these speciall points. The first, what a pretious thing is good gouernement, and how all realmes, commonwealths, cities, and countries doo flourish and prosper, where the same is orderlie, in equitie, iustice, and wisedome, directed & gouerned. Secondlie, what a continuall care the quéenes highnesse hath had, and yet hath, not onelie for the good guiding & ruling of the realme of England, but also of Ireland, which she so earnestlie desireth, and wisheth to be preserued, as well in peace as in warre: that she hath made great choise from time to time of the most graue, wise, and expert councellors for the one, and the most valiant, skilfull, and expert men of armes for the other: that both in peace and warres, the publike state of the commonwealth, and euerie particular member therein might be conserued, defended, and kept in safetie vnder hir gouernement. And for the performance thereof, hir maiestie ouer and besides the reuenues of the crowne of Ireland, did yearelie far aboue anie of hir progenitors, expend of hir owne cofers out of England, great masses of monie, amounting to manie thousand pounds. All which hir excessiue expenses and continuall cares she made the lesse account of, so that hir realme and subiects of Ireland might be preserued, defended, and gouerned.

The benefit of good gouernement.

The quéenes maiesties continuall care for Ireland.

The quéenes maiestie expendeth yearelie out of hir owne cofers for Ireland sundrie thousands of pounds.

Lastlie, notwithstanding hir maiestie might haue made better choise of manie others, who were better able to hold hir place in this realme, both for honor, wisedome, and experience: yet hir pleasure was now to cast this heauie charge and burden vpon him. Which he was the more vnwilling to take vpon him, because the greater the charge was, the more vnable & weake he was to susteine the same. Neuerthelesse,

Neuerthelesse, being in good hope, and well promised of hir highnesse fauor and countenance in his well doings, and hauing his confidence in them hir highnesse councellors associated vnto him, to ioine, aid, and assist him in this gouernement; he was and is the more readie to take the sword in hand, in hope that this his gouernement shall be to the glorie of God, the honor of hir maiestie, the benefit of the commonwelth, and the preseruation of the whole realme and people of the same. And so making his earnest request to the said lords present, for their concurring with him, and the aiding and assisting of him in this hir maiesties seruice, he made an end of his speeches.

The said councellors, hauing well considered the great value and weight of this his graue and wise oration, did most humblie thanke his lordship for the same, and promised in all dutifulnesse, faith, and obedience to performe and attend whatsoeuer to them in anie wise should apperteine. These things doone, they all conducted the said lord deputie in all honorable manner vnto the castell of Dublin: the common people in euerie street and corner meeting him, and with great acclamations and ioie did congratulat vnto his lordship his comming among them in that office. Immediatlie after the performance of all the solemnities, perteining to these actions, he called and assembled all those persons which hir highnesse had appointed, admitted, and allowed to be of hir maiesties priuie councell for that realme, and did sweare them according to the accustomed manner. Then from time to time they assembled and met, consulting and deliberating what waie and order were best to be taken for repairing of that broken commonweale and ruinous state, being as it were a man altogither infected with sores and biles, and in whose bodie from the crowne of the head to the sole of the foot there is no health. And surelie if the state of that land was euer miserable and in perill to be ouerthrowne, it was neuer more like than at these presents, for as for the English pale, it was ouerwhelmed with infinite numbers of caterpillers, who dailie by spoiles and robberies haue deuoured and wasted the same: whereby the people vniuersallie were so poore, and the commons in such extreame penurie, that they had not horsses, armor nor weapons to defend them, nor apparell, vittels, nor anie other necessaries to releeue them, the soldiors so beggerlie that they were most intollerable to the people, and so rooted in insolencie, loosenesse and idlenesse, that vnlesse the remedie were the more speedie, they would bée past correction: and so much the worsse, bicause manie of them were allied in mariage, and companies of the Irish: who the more they were affected to them, their truth and seruice more doubtfull to hir maiestie. The prouince of Leinster and they altogither most miserable, the Tools, Obirnes, Kinsbelaghes, Odoiles, Omoroughs, Cauenaughs, the Moores, and the residue in their accustomable manners wholie bent to spoiles and all mischiefs, no place of anie safetie remaining for the good subiect: especiallie in the countie of Kilkennie, which being sometimes a fertile rich soile, and well manured and inhabited, became of all others most desart and beggerlie, verie few being left to inhabit the same.

The congratulation of the people. *The broken state of Ireland.* *The English pale wasted and spoiled.* *Soldiors beggerlie and out of order.* *The miserable state of Leinster.* *The fertile soile of the countie of Kilkennie made wast.*

Mounster, the inhabitants there likewise for the most part being followers to the earle of Desmond, and following his warrs against the erle of Ormond, made that prouince, and especiallie the counties of Tipperarie and Kirrie, being wealthie and rich, to become bare and beggerlie, and verie few of whom hir maiestie was or could be assured. Notwithstanding experience had taught them, and they assured, that no waie was for their recouerie and safetie so good and assured, as to humble themselues, and to become hir highnesse loiall and obedient subiect: yet as swine delighting in their durt and puddles, contented themselues rather with a beggerlie life to be miserable, than in dutifull obedience to be at peace and assured. The prouinces also of Thomond altogither almost wasted by the warres betwéene the earle there

Mounster by ciuill war destroied. *Thomond all wasted by ciuill warres.*

there

there and sir Donell Obrien. Ormond likewise by reason of dissention betwéene the earles of Desmond and Ormond, and by the dailie inuasions and preies of Piers Grace was almost wasted and vnhabited.

Connagh, one of the goodliest, pleasantest, and most fertile soiles of that land, & in times past verie rich and wealthie, and well inhabited, is wasted with the wars betwéene the erle of Clanrichard and Mac William Enter the Irish countries all wasted and impouerished, partlie by reason of their dissimulations, societies, and conferences with the rebelles, and partlie by the particular discords among themselues. Finallie, all the gentlemen throughout, woont in times past to be képers of hospitalitie, were by the dailie preies made vpon them and their tenants so impouerished & distressed, that they were not able to mainteine and reléeue themselues nor their families. The prouince of Vlster for wealth and plentie was well stored, not onlie of themselues, but by reason that it was the receptacle and place of receipt of all the preies and spoiles from out of the other prouinces: but as for loialtie, dutifulnesse, and obedience to hir maiestie, they were most disloiall, rebellious, and disordered. For after that Shane Oneile by blood and murther had gotten the maisterie, he alone then ruled the rost, who in pride exceeded all the men vpon the earth, abiding no superior, nor allowing anie equall. And héere it were not amisse, but verie expedient to set downe the first origin and cause whie the said Shane did first breake out from his due obedience, and did shake off the gouernement of hir maiestie, which (as farre as the writer hereof hath gathered and collected) is as here followeth.

Connagh deuoured by ciuill warre.

The gentlemen all impouerished.

Vlster wealthie and rich.

Shane Oneile.

The cause of Shane Oneiles rebellion.

Con Oneile, the first earle of Tiron, had two sonnes, Matthew and this Shane or Iohn. And king Henrie the eight hauing good liking of this Con Oneile, and to reteine and keepe him a good subiect, he being a mightie man, and of great power in his countrie, he made and created him earle of Tiron, and his eldest son Matthew he made baron of Dunganon, and the remainder of the said earledome to the said Matthew, and to the heirs male of his bodie. This Shane being the second brother, and of an aspiring mind, enuied his elder brother, and in no wise could he brooke him, but from time to time séeketh occasions to quarell and fall out with him, and in the end most traitorouslie and vnnaturallie murthered him: their father yet liuing, who did not so much lament and bewaile the same, but began much more to distrust of his owne safetie. Neuerthelesse, it is not knowen that the said Shane did offer him anie violence, but when he was dead, although he had no right to succéed into the earledome, by reason that Matthew his elder brother had left sons behind him, who by the letters patents and course of the common law were to succeed the grandfather: yet Shane vsurped the name of Oneile, and entred into his fathers inheritance according to the Irish manner, among whome the custome is, that the eldest in yeais of the name of anie house or familie dooth succéed his ancestor, vnlesse at the time of his death he had a son of the full age of one and twentie yéers. And thus hauing perforce entred into his fathers inheritance, he scorneth at the English gouernement, and after the Irish manner proclaimeth himselfe Oneile, and the capteine of his countrie, refuseth likewise all obedience to hir maiestie, and breaketh out into open rebellion.

Con Oneile made earle of Tiron.

Shane vsurpeth the name of Oneile.

The Irish custome in succession.

Shane Oneile breaketh into rebellion.

Sir Henrie Sidneie then lord iustice, in the absence of the erle of Sussex, being aduertised of these stirs, taketh aduise of the councell what was best to be doone. And then it was agreed, that the said lord iustice should take his iorneie towards Dundalke, for the fortifieng of the English pale, and should send a messenger to Shane Oneile, who then laie at a lordship of his about six miles from Dundalke, and to will him come to Dundalke to his lordship: which was doone. But Shane returned his answer, praieng pardon, and also most humblie requested his lordship

 that

> Shane Oneile praieth sir Henrie Sidneie to be his gossip

that it would please him to christen a son of his, & be his gossip, & then he would come to his lordship to doo all things in seruice for hir maiestie, as his lordship should command and appoint. This answere at the first was not thought good, nor yet honorable to the lord iustice so to doo, vntill the said Shane had first come and submitted himselfe. But when it was considered what great inconueniences might insue, if his request were denied, it was agréed that the said lord iustice should condescend vnto his request. And accordinglie vpon the last of Ianuarie, one thousand fiue hundred fiftie and eight he went vnto the said Shanes house, and there his lordship and Iaques Wingfield were godfathers, and hauing performed the baptising of the child, they both had conference of the matter: where the said Shane, to excuse his doings, did allege for his defense sundrie articles as followeth.

> 1558

> Shane excuseth himselfe why hee came not to the lord iustice.

First, he said that Matthew baron of Dungannon was the sonne of one Kellaie of Dundalke, a smith by occupation, begotten and borne during the spousals of the said Kellaie, and one Alson his wife, and that the said Matthew was alwaies taken and reputed to be the sonne of the said Kellaie, vntill he was of the age of sixtéene yeares or thereabouts: at which time Con Oneile his father, vpon the saieng of the said Alson, that he was the father of the said Matthew, did accept and take the said Matthew to be his sonne, & gaue him the name of Fardarough. And here vnderstand you the wickednesse of this countrie, which is, that if anie woman doo mislike hir husband, and will depart from him, he shall haue all such children as were borne of hir bodie during their abode togither, except such as she shall name to be begotten by anie other man: which man so named shall by their custome haue the said child: and so it should séeme to be meant of this point. Also the said Matthew did vpon this the affirmation of his mother séeke to vsurpe the name of a seignorie of the Oneiles, and the dominions apperteining to that seignorie and surname. Also that there be aboue a hundred of that name, which will not in anie wise yéeld to this the claime of Matthew, although he for his owne part would be contented therewith. Also he saith that the letters patents (if anie such be) that should intitle the sonne of the said baron to the said lands are vtterlie void, because that Con Oneile father to the said Shane had no other right nor interest to that countrie, but during his owne life: and therefore without the consent of the lords and inhabitants of that countrie, could make no surrender nor conueiance, wherby he might be inabled to take and haue the said lands by force of letters patents.

> Matthew was Kellaies sonne.

> The obiections of Shane Oneil against the title of Matthew to be Oneile.

> The wicked custome of the Irishrie.

> Matthew seeketh the seigniorie of Oneile.

Also he saith, that by the lawes in the English pale of Ireland, no letters patents, made to anie person, be of anie force or value, vntill that an inquisition be taken of the lands so giuen before that the letters patents doo passe: which in this case neither was, nor could be doone, sith the countrie of Tiron is no shire ground. Also if the said lands should according to the quéens lawes descend to the right heire, then in right it ought to descend to him, as next heire being mulierlie borne, and the other not so borne. Also he saith, that vpon the death of his father lord of the countrie, the whole countrie according to the custome of the countrie did assemble themselues togither, and by a common consent did elect and choose (without anie contradiction) him the said Shane to be Oneile, as the most worthie and ablest of that countrie. Which election by the custome of the countrie hath beene alwaies vsed without anie confirmation, asked of the kings and quéenes of England. Also he saith that as Oneile he claimeth such authorities, iurisdictions, and duties vpon his men & countrie, as are due time out of mind to his predecessors, and which duties for the most part are recorded, and remaine in writing. When the lord iustice had at full heard these articles, and considered well of them togither with the councell, made answer vnto Shane that the matter was of great weight and importance, & which neither he nor the councell cold determine of themselues, before hir maiestie were made priuie and acquainted therewith;

with, and therefore in the meane time willed and required him to be quiet, and to shew himselfe a dutifull subiect vnto hir maiestie, nothing doubting but that he should haue and receiue at hir hands, what should be found méet, right, and iust.

And so hauing vsed manie good and freendlie spéeches and exhortations vnto him, the said Shane promised to vse and behaue himselfe well and honestlie, & as to his dutie should apperteine: they departed in verie freendlie maner. And thus in such wisedome and politike maner the lord iustice handled the matter, that by temporising and gaining of time all matters were pacified, and so continued vntill the comming ouer of the earle of Sussex lord deputie: who then of a new tooke the matter in hand, and he did so streictlie and seuerelie follow the same, that he ouermatched Shane Oneile. But it so greeued the said Shane, that notwithstanding he dissembled and gaue a good countenance, & promised well, yet in the end being once at libertie, he performed nothing: but as the woolfe which often casteth his haires but neuer changeth his conditions, was one and the same man or rather worse, and thenseforth tyrannized and vsed most crueltie, and of all others most disloiall and disobedient, to the deputie would he not come, nor would he in anie wise conferre with him, but at his owne pleasure.

Shane Oneile promiseth to be quiet.

Shane Oneile become a tyrant and a rebell.

The quéenes maiestie in some termes he would honor, but in déeds he denied all obedience, subtill and craftie he was especiallie in the morning: but in the residue of the daie verie vncerteine and vnstable, and much giuen to excessiue gulping and surfetting. And albeit he had most commonlie two hundred tunnes of wines in his cellar at Dundrum, and had his full fill therof, yet was he neuer satisfied, till he had swallowed vp maruellous great quantities of Vskebagh or Aqua vite of that countrie: whereof so vnmeasurablie he would drinke and bouse, that for the quenching of the heat of the bodie, which by that meanes was most extremelie inflamed and distempered, he was eftsoones conueied (as the common report was) into a déepe pit, and standing vpright in the same, the earth was cast round about him vp to the hard chin, and there he did remaine vntill such time as his bodie was recouered to some temperature: by which meanes though he came after in some better plight for the time, yet his manners and conditions dailie worse. And in the end his pride ioined with wealth, drunkennesse, and insolencie, he began to be a tyrant, and to tyrannize ouer the whole countrie, greatlie it was feared that his intent was to haue made a conquest ouer the whole land. He pretended to be king of Vlster, euen as he said his ancestors were, and affecting the maner of the great Turke, was continuallie garded with six hundred armed men, as it were his Ianisaries about him, and had in readinesse to bring into the fields a thousand horssemen, and foure thousand footmen. He furnished all the pesants and husbandmen of his countrie with armour and weapons, and trained them vp in the knowledge of the warres: and as a lion hath in awe the beasts of the field, so had he all the people to his becke and commandement, being feared and not beloued.

Shane Oneil a drunkard and a surfetter.

Shane Oneil buried in the ground after his drunkennesse.

Shane Oneils force.

The pesants in Vlster trained vp in warre.

Diuerse meanes and waies were practised and vsed by the lord deputie and councell for the pacifieng and recouerie of him, and commissioners from time to time sent vnto him, for and about the same, who sometimes would be verie flexible, but foorthwith as backwards and vntoward. Of all the residue of Ireland there was the lesse doubt to recouer them, by reason that they by their owne ciuill warres had consumed and spoiled the one and the other: but of this man, small or no hope at all, vnlesse he might be chastised, and with force be reduced to conformities. Which in the end it pleased the Lord God to take the matter in hand, and to performe the same by taking of him awaie. And bicause in these troublesome times, it were méet aduertisements should go to and from hir maiestie and councell to the lord deputie, & so likewise from his lordship to them, order was taken for the more spéedie conueiance of letters reciproke, there

Posts set betweene Ireland & London.

should be set posts appointed betwéene London and Ireland. This was then the present state of all Ireland, altogethers deuoured with robberies, murders, riots, treasons, ciuill and intestine warres, and few or none assured and faithfull to hir highnesse out of the English pale, and out of cities and townes: and yet the one being gentlemen and liuing by their lands, by continuall spoiles and robberies were decaied; the other by the losse of their traffike being merchants impouerished, and brought to such extremities, as not able to relieue and mainteine themselues.

The miserable state of Ireland

And among all other the most intollerable miseries vniuersallie reigning, this one excéeded all the rest, that there was scarse a God knowen, and if knowen, not all honored in the land, for the churches for the most part were all destroied & vncouered, the clergie scattered, the people vntaught, and as shéepe without their pastour wandering without knowledge and instruction. Then where neither God is knowen, the prince obeied, no lawes currant, no gouernement accepted, and all things infolded in most extreme miserie; how lamentable and dolefull is that state and kingdome? Wherefore sir Henrie Sidneie now lord deputie, & the councell pondering this distressed state, and the great burden which laie them vpon to helpe and redresse the same, dailie assembled themselues, & deuised the best waie what might be to be taken herein. Wherin his lordships cause so much was the weaker, as that such as were chiefest of the councell, then ioined to assist him in councell and seruice, were for the most part spent and decaied men, and the lord deputie himselfe driuen to deuise, to inuent, to dispose, and in the end to execute all himselfe. Well, neuerthelesse it was concluded and agréed, that the English pale should be fortified and defended from the inuasion of the Oneile and all his complices, and that the deuises set downe for the staie and recouerie of the rest of the land should be followed from time to time, as matter, time, and oportunitie would serue therevnto.

No God nor religion in Ireland

At this present time the earles of Ormond and Desmond were in England, and the quarrels and controuersies growen betwéene them were dailie examined before the lords of the councell, and their allegations produced in writing by the one against the other. And bicause their assertions were so contrarious and vncerteine in denieng and affirming, as no procéeding could be had for a finall end and order, it was thought good and necessarie that their complaints and answers should be examined in the realme of Ireland, where their doings were best knowen, and where their misorders were committed. And then by the aduise of the councell both the said earles submitted themselues to the quéenes maiesties order & determination: and for performance thereof, they both by waie of recognisance in the chancerie were bound ech of them in twentie thousand pounds. And then a commission vnder hir highnesse broad seale of England was sent to the lord deputie for taking of the forsaid examinations. But in the meane time whilest these things were in dooing in England, sir John of Desmond, in verie outragious and disordered manner, fired & spoiled the tenements of the earle of Ormond, which things were verie shortlie after appeased. In these troublesome daies Mac Artmore an ancient gentleman of the Irish race, the principall man of his sept in Mounster, hauing verie great possessions, and laie still in peace and did nothing at all, neither tooke he partie with one whom he liked not, neither holpe he the other whom he feared not, but to the outward appéerance misliked both their doings.

The earles of Ormond and Desmond submit themselues to the queens order

Sir Iohn of Desmond spoileth the earle of Ormonds lands

This man made his humble sute to hir maiestie, that he might surrender all his lands, possessions and territories vnto hir maiesties highnesse, and to recognise his dutie and allegiance to hir, and so to resume and haue a new estate therof from hir againe, according to the orders and laws of England. Which hir maiestie did accept; and foorthwith made him a new estate of inheritance: and for the better his staie in all obedience and dutie to hir crowne, did for the worthinesse of his bloud & stocke, & for

Mac Artimore surrendereth all his lands to the quéene & taketh it of hir

& for the greatnesse of his gouernement make him a baron of the parlement in that relme, & for his further aduancement created him an earle vnder hir letters patents by the name of the earle of Clancare. These newes being reported to Shane Oneile, he scoffed at it, nothing liking the choise of hir highnesse in aduansing such a one to that honour, and enuied and maligned him that he was so honored. And therefore not long after, when the commissioners were sent to intreat with him vpon sundrie points, they found him most arrogant & out of all good order, braieng out spéeches not méet nor séemelie. "For (saith he) you haue made a wise earle of Mac Artimore, I kéepe as good a man as is he. And albeit I confesse the quéene is my soueraigne ladie, yet I neuer made peace with hir, but at hir séeking." And where he had required to haue his parlement robes sent vnto him as earle of Tiron, which title he claimed and required (which if it were denied him, then he required a triall to be made in parlement) yet now he cared not for so meane an honour as to be an earle, except he might be better and higher than an erle. "For I am (saith he) in bloud and power better than the best, and I will giue place to none of them, for mine ancestors were kings of Vlster. And as Vlster was theirs, so now Vlster is mine and shall be mine. with the sword I wan it, and with the sword I will kéepe it." Which his words fell out true, though long he inioied not the same. and foorthwith he fell into most horrible tyrannies and cruelties, wherby he became execrable and hatefull vnto all his people and countrie who were wearie of him.

Mac Artimore made earle of Clancare

Shane Oneile scoffeth at the earle of Clancare

The proud taunts of Shane Oneile

Shane Oneile for his pride and tyrannie becometh hatefull before God & man

Now hir maiestie, being gréeued and annoied with his treasons and rebellions of long time, was fullie minded either to haue him clearelie rooted out, or chastised but therein she was staied, being borne in hand that the best waie to bring him to reformation, was to yéeld to him in sundrie things of him desired. But now she seeing him to haue manifested himselfe a notorious traitor, and past all grace, she gaue commandement to the lord deputie to imploie his whole care, consideration and wisedome, how such a cankred and dangerous rebell might be vtterlie extirped. And séeing the matter also to haue so manie accidents and circumstances belonging vnto it, as which by letters to and fro could not bée well concluded: therefore she sent ouer, sir Francis Knolles vicechamberleine, to conferre with the lord deputie, who arriued at Dublin the seuenth of Maie 1566, aswell concerning these matters of warre, as the whole state and gouernment of this realme. Who when he was arriued, and hauing at large conferred with him about the same, the time betwéene them was concluded and appointed, that the seruice should be in the winter, & accordinglie things necessarie, as well monie, men, munitions, and vittels were sent ouer, and Edward Randolph colonell of the footmen, and sundrie other capteins arriued with their souldiers from out of England, and all things were disposed both for the garrison and the campe, as it was conuenient to be.

Sir Francis Knolles sent into Ireland 1566

Likewise the archtraitor knowing what preparation was made against him, he dooth the like also on his part against hir maiestie, and at a lordship or manour of his, about six miles out of Dundalke, he mustreth all his whole armie, which was of foure thousand footmen, and seuen hundred horssemen. And glorieng much in himselfe of such his great force and puissance, which he thought to suffice to haue conquered all Ireland withall, and that no man durst to aduenture vpon him: he marcheth vnto the towne of Dundalke, where he incampeth himselfe, & beseegeth the same. He was no more busie to giue sundrie attempts of inuasion, and to enter the towne, but the souldiers within were as valiant to resist and defend: which in the end turned to his reproch, and hée had the repulse, being with shame driuen to raise his siege, and to depart with the losse.

Shane Oneile beseegeth Dundalke & is repelled

The like successe he had at Whites castell, and when he made his rode and inuasion into the English pale, when his great multitude stood him not in so much stead,

stead, as a farre smaller companie of the English souldiers deserued commendation: which perforce and maugre of his teeth compelled him to retire with shame, and to returne with losse. About this time in the moneth of Iulie 1565, and the first yeare of the deputation of sir Henrie Sidneie, Edward Randolph, a verie expert and a valiant souldier, was sent ouer out of England, and arriued at the Dirrie with seuen hundred men vnder his regiment, and he himselfe by the councell in England appointed to be the coronell. This man as soone as he was landed, intrenched himselfe at the Dirrie, where he remained in garrison without dooing of anie thing, vntill the comming of the lord deputie from Dublin, with the residue of hir maiesties forces, appointed to be ioined with the said coronell, for the better seruice against the arrogant traitour Shane Oneile.

1565

Coronell Randolph arriueth at the Dirrie where he intrencheth himselfe.

And after that the said lord deputie was come, and had staid there about six daies, and had set all things in such good order as that seruice required, he returned backe to Dublin through Odonels countrie and so thorough Connagh, leauing the coronell accompanied with one band of fiftie horssemen vnder the leading of capteine George Heruie the elder, and with seuen companies or hundreds of footmen vnder the charges of capteine Robert Cornewall, and capteine Iohn Ward, and others, all well furnished, both with munitions, vittels, and all other necessaries meet and requisit. Shane Oneile who knew well of the garrisons, of their forces & numbers, and he not minding that they should there rest in peace, but standing now vpon his honor and reputation, incamped himselfe about two miles from the garrison, hauing then in his armie two thousand fiue hundred footmen, & thrée hundred horsmen. And frō daie to daie he would continuallie with his horssemen houer and range the fields, and shew himselfe readie to trie the matter if the Englishmen durst to aduenture the same.

The lord deputie cometh to the Dirrie and setteth all things in order for the seruice.

Oneil incampeth néere the Dirrie and offereth skirmish.

The coronell not liking these dailie offers, and thinking it to be a verie great dishonour vnto him, and all the English nation, which were come ouer to serue against him, and now would doo nothing, but were dailie bearded by the enimie: notwithstanding that his forces when they were at the best, were but small in respect of the enimie, and by reason of the sicknesse in the campe, that his small companie was much weakened and vnable to serue: yet he was determined with a full resolution to take the offer of the enimie, and either he would lose his life, or remooue him from his so neere a seat. Wherevpon he drew out of his companie to the number of thrée hundred men, whome he thought most méet to serue, and being accompanied with fiftie horssemen vnder capteine George Heruie, marched toward Oneils campe, who pretending a great ioy to see the forwardnesse of the Englishmen, he with all his forces issued out, and with speed prepared to incounter with them, persuading himselfe that he should that daie be maister of the field, and haue a conquest to his hearts desire.

The coronell prepareth to fight with Oneile.

The coronell made choise of the ground to fight in, and prepared himselfe to stand and abide their charge. Oneile in great furie, and with a great multitude charged the coronels footmen, and his maine battell, but he was so receiued with the English shot and so galled, that he made some staie. Wherevpon capteine Heruie taking his oportunitie, most valiantlie with his small band of horssemen brake in to the battell of Oneile. Likewise coronell Randolph with his few horssemen gaue the charge vpon the left wing of them. The one of them being well followed and accompanied with his band, did the seruice which he desired: but the coronell verie valiantlie making waie through the enimies, and no man following him, was in fighting wounded to death, and whereof immediatlie he died. The rebels being astonied and amazed at the valour of the Englishmen, fled and turned their backs, whome the souldiers followed, and had the slaughter of them so long as their weapons lasted in this con-

The valiant seruice of capteine George Heruie.

The coronell Randolph is slaine.

Oneile and his companie flie, and are pursued.

flict

flict. The rebels were slaine that daie in this chase aboue foure hundred persons, besides the like number of such as were hurt and wounded. The coronell onelie was slaine, but capteine Herne and diuerse of the horssemen were verie sore hurt and wounded.

Killed & hurt about 800.

After the death of this valiant coronell, whose funerall the lord deputie did afterwards celebrate with great honour at Dublin, Edward Sentlow was made coronell: vnder whose gouernement the garrison liued verie quietlie. For this last ouerthrow so quailed the spirits and courages of Oneile and his companie, that they had no desire of anie further incountering with the Englishmen. And thus all the winter following little was doone: and being determined in the spring to aduenture some peece of seruice, but the lord otherwise appointed it. For about the foure and twentith of Aprill, by a misfortune neuer yet knowne by what means, the fort and towne of the Dirrie was all burned, and the storehouses where the munitions and vittels laie were blowne vp with the gunpowder, and twentie men killed with the same: and so manie of the souldiers as laie sicke there were burned in their beds. Whervpon the coronell calling all his capteins togither, and considering the distresse which they now were in, by the losse of their vittels and munitions, and not knowing where to be furnished otherwise, they all concluded and determined to abandon that place, and to imbarke themselues for Dublin, which immediatlie they all did, sauing capteine George Herne: for he rather did choose to hazard his life to returne by land, than to impouerish his souldiers by killing their horsses (which perforce they must needs haue doone) for want of shipping. And therefore euen almost against all hope he returned towards Dublin through the enimies countrie, who followed and chased him foure daies togither without intermission, both with horssemen and footmen: but at length he recouered Dublin, not without great woonder and admiration. The lord deputie he wanted not his espials, both about Oneile, and in all places throughout Vlster: and thereby knew the forces, bent, and determinations of euerie of them, whereby he knew how to meet with them euerie waie for the best seruice of hir maiestie. And yet considering the great importance of the seruice, he could not be satisfied herein, but that he would make a iournie into Vlster himselfe. And being accompanied with the earle of Kildare, and certeine of the councell, and with such capteins and souldiers as he thought good: he aduanced & set foorth out of Drogheda the seuentéenth of September 1566, and incamped that night at Rosse Keagh, & so from thense he trauelled throughout Vlster, and passed thense vnto Athlon in Connagh, where he came the six and twentith of October.

The lord deputie keepeth the coronell Randolphs funerals.

The Dirrie and all the vittels and munitions are burned.

The coronell abandoneth Dirrie, and returneth to Dublin by seas.

Capteine George Herne returneth by land in great danger.

The lord deputie maketh a iournie into Vlster.

1566

In this iournie the rebell neuer durst (for all his brags) once to shew his face, nor to offer anie fight at all, sauing once at and néere a wood not far from Clogher, where he offered a skirmish, and gaue the charge with horssemen, footmen, and certeine Scotish shot: which continued a good space, and sundrie hurt on both sides, but none died of his lordships men. He shewed himselfe also once with a great multitude of horssemen and footmen, not farre from the castell of Erlough Lenough, called the Salmon, but tooke his ease and durst not to giue the aduenture. In this iournie the lord deputie restored Odonell to the possession of his lands and castels, kept by Oneile from him, & sundrie lords and men of the best sort submitted themselues. By which this his lordships iournie he recouered to hir highnesse a countrie of foure score miles in length, and eight and fortie miles in bredth, without losse of anie man sauing Mac Gwier, who being sicke died in this iournie, and sauing a few persons which by the waie vpon an occasion would aduenture the winning of a certeine Iland in the middle of a lough, wherein was supposed to be great store of wealth and vittels of the enimies, and in assailing of it they were drowned.

The pusillanimitie of the Oneile.

Odonell restored vnto his possessions.

The lord deputie recouereth a great countrie in Vlster vnto the crowne.

Immediatlie vpon the discharge of the armie at Athlon, the lord deputie fortified

all

The earle of Desmond is in campe and doth no hurt

all the frontiers of the English pale with garrisons sufficient for the same. And as concerning the troublesome state of Mounster, the earle of Desmond was in the field with two thousand men, and incamped himselfe in places indifferent to annoie at his pleasure the earle of Ormond, the lord Barrie, the lord Roch, and sir Moris Fitzgerald of the Decies, but he did not hurt anie man at all, sauing one Mac Donogh a rebell and a disloiall sauage man. The lord deputie being ouerlaied with the continuall cares to resist Oneile, could not in person trauell into Mounster, nor yet without great perill diuide his armie: wherefore he sent capteine Herne constable of Leighlin vnto the said earle, whereby he might be aduertised of his intendement and meaning: which appeared to be but a méere insolencie and an outrage to be reuenged vpon the earle of Ormond, although the rumor was, that he would conioine with Oneile.

The earle of Desmond maketh his repaire to the lord deputie.

Which report when it came to his eares, and being aduertised that the lord deputie was offended with him that he had gathered such a force, and was in the fields: He for his purgation herein, without further delaie, tooke his horsse, and hauing in his companie onelie the baron of Dunboine, and capteine Herne, with their companies, made hast to present himselfe before the lord deputie: where and before whome for purging of himselfe, and to declare his dutie, he offered himselfe to his lordships deuotion, either to go and attend him vnto Vlster in that sort as he then was, or else to follow him with all such force as he could get, the lord deputie finding him vittels and then to abide & serue in Vlster in despite of Shane Oneile, or else that he would in his lordships absence remaine vpon the borders there, with such a number of horssemen, as should be appointed vnto him, shewing also and pretending such dutifulnesse to hir maiestie, as was méet for a subiect to shew to his soueraigne. The deputie hauing some liking of his offers, and considering the fickle state of these presents, accepteth his last offer, willing him to go backe againe, and to prepare a crew of one hundred horssemen, at the least, and so to returne againe

The earle of Desmond serueth in the English pale

within fourteene daies: which he did, and with him came sir Iohn Desmond, his vncle the baron of Dunboine, the lord Powre and others: who accompanied with the baron of Deluin, sir Warham Sentleger, and capteine Herne, did remaine vpon the borders, vntill his lordships returne from out of his iournie in Vlster.

Oliuer Sutton complaineth against the earle of Kildare

And as the realme at large was much infested with the cruell warres of Oneile and the troubles in Mounster, so also there wanted no daily complaints of griefs vnto the lord deputie of sundrie persons one against an other. For Oliuer Sutton, a gentleman dwelling in the English pale, did exhibit a certeine booke in writing, conteining an information of sundrie notorious disorders in that realme, hurtfull to the good policie of the same, and contrarie to sundrie good lawes and acts of parlement, whereof a great part did touch the earle of Kildare. The matter was referred by hir maiesties order to the hearing of the lord deputie and councell.

The ladie of Dunboine complaineth against the Butlers

Likewise sir Edmund Butler and Piers his brother were greeuouslie complained vpon by the ladie of Dunboine, Mac Brian Arra, Oliuer Fitzgerald, sir William Occarell, and others, for their dailie outrages, robberies, murthers, preies, and spoiles taken. For the hearing and appeasing of such matters, and for the better ministration of iustice, the lord deputie had beene a long sutor to hir maiestie and councell for a chancellor to be sent ouer, who at length were resolued vpon doctor Weston, deane of the

1567
Doctor Weston is made lord chancellor of Ireland

arches, who arriued at Dublin in Iulie 1567, a notable and a singular man, by profession a lawyer, but in life a diuine, a man so bent to the execution of iustice, and so seuere therein, that by no meanes would he be seduced or auerted from the same: and so much good in the end insued of his vpright, diligent, and dutifull seruice, as that the whole realme found themselues most happie and blessed to haue him serue among them. Now he taking vpon him to deale in all matters of com-

plaints

plants, both eased the lord deputie of a great burthen, and did most good to the countrie, and acquited himselfe against hir maiestie.

But to returne to the lord deputie, who immediatlie vpon the dismissing of the armie at Athlon, he tooke order (as is aforesaid) for placing of his garrisons in such conuenient places vpon the frontiers, as then apperteined and was most méet & conuenient. The rebell on his part leaueth nothing vndoon, which might be for the furtherance of his enterprises: and being in great iollitie of himselfe deuised manie things, and to make some shew of his abilitie, entered into the English pale, with sword and fire wasted the countrie, slue manie of hir maiesties subiects, and in the end besieged hir highnesse towne of Dundalke: where his pride and treason were iustlie scourged, who came not with so much glorie to besiege it, as he did returne with shame to leaue and loose it. The lord deputie not abiding the same, nor sleeping his matters, determined to make a new rode vpon him: and in the meane time, he so handled the matter, that he had vnfethered him of his best friends, aids, and helps. For besides the whole countrie, as is before said, gained from him the last iournie, Mac Gwier, a mightie man in his countrie forsooke him, and submitted himselfe to hir maiestie, offering all loiall obedience and faithfull seruice, and to receiue his lands and countrie at hir highnesse hands.

The Oneile entereth the English pale with sword and fire.

The Oneile besiegeth Dundalke the second time, and departed with great dishonor.

The Oneile forsaken of friends. Mac Gwier forsaketh Oneile, and so doo the Scots.

Alexander Og and Mac Donell offer to serue hir maiestie, with all the Scots vnder them against the rebell. Con Odonell late deliuered from the rebell, offereth seruice against him. Tirlogh Lenough with the helps of his neighbours dailie backed the said Oneile, that his force was quailed that waie. The lord deputie had continuallie foure regiments residing neere the English pale, who continuallie as it were by turnes were occupied in persecuting of the rebell: & his lordship being at Drogheda did also issue out, and in one morning tooke a preie of two thousand kine, 500 garrons, and innumerable other small beasts and cattell. The rebell seeing himselfe thus distressed of his goods, and forsaken of his helps and followers, his men, some by Odonell, and some by others to the number of thrée or foure thousand persons at times slaine, himselfe discomfited, his passages stopped, and all places of his refuge preuented, and now but one poore castell left wherein he trusted to commit himselfe vnto, he being thus weakened, and beholding his declination and fall towards, was fullie bent and determined to disguise himselfe, and so as not knowne to come with a collar or halter about his necke to the presence of the lord deputie, and in all humble and lowlie maner to submit himselfe: hoping that by this kind of humilitie to find mercie at hir maiesties hands. But his conscience was so cauterised, and his hands so imbrued with infinit and most horrible murthers, bloudsheds, treasons, whoredomes, drunkennesse, robberies, burnings, spoiles, oppressions, and with all kinds of wickednesse, that his heart was ouerlaied and ouerladen with an vtter despaire to obteine anie grace or fauor: and therefore was the more easilie persuaded by those whome he tooke to be his friends, to the first and to intreat the Scots for friendship, and that they would come and aid him in his most wicked rebellion. Wherevpon he tooke his iournie towards Clandeboie, where Alexander Og and his companie, to the number of six hundred persons, were then incamped: and for the better gaining of his purpose, he had a little before inlarged Charleie Boie brother to the said Alexander, and who had béene prisoner with him.

The lord deputie taketh a great preie vpon the Oneile.

The Oneile distressed of all comfort is in doubt what to doo.

Oneile his owne conscience condemneth him to seeke submission.

Oneile seeketh for helpe of the Scots.

The Scots disguised the matter with him, pretending and promising him aid and assistance: which they ment not. For assoone as Oneile togither with Odonels wife, whom he kept, & the small companie which he brought with him were come into the tent, and they assured of him, they called to remembrance the manifold iniuries which they had receiued at his hands, and namelie the murthering of one Iames Mac Conell, & one Mac Guilie then néere cousins and kinsmen, and being inflamed with mali-

The Scots doo disguise with Oneil.

Shane Oneil slaine by the Scots by a draught made by capteine Piers.

Shane Oneils head set vpon the top of the castell of Dublin.

cious minds to reuenge their deaths, they fell to quarelling with the said Shane Oneile, and with their slaughter swords hewed him to peeces, and slue all those of his companie that were with him. His bodie they wrapped in a Kernes shirt, and so without all honor was carried to a ruinous church not farre off, and there interred, but after a few daies he was taken vp againe by capteine Piers, by whose deuise this stratagem or rather tragedie was practised, and his head was sundried from the bodie, and sent to the lord deputie, who caused the same to be set vpon a stake or pole on the top of the castle of Dublin. A fit end for such a beginning, and a iust reward for such a wicked traitor and sacrileger: who began his tyrannie in bloud, did continue it with bloud, and ended it with bloud. The lord deputie being then at Drogheda, and aduertised of the death of this Shane, and of the iust iudgements of God laid vpon him; for the same prostrated himselfe before the high and eternall God, and gaue his most humble and hartie thanks for the deliuerie of that land from so wicked a tyrant, sacrileger and traitor; and with all the conuenient spéed that might be, he dispatched the messengers to hir maiestie and councell, aduertising this hap and good successe. Which doone, his lordship with all spéed made his repaire into Vlster, and incamped himselfe in the middle and heart of the countrie, vnto whome all the noblemen and gentlemen of Tiron, being glad that they were deliuered from the tyrant, made their repaire vnto his lordship: and especiallie all they which were competitors of the capteinrie of Tiron, who most humblie and obedientlie presented and submitted themselues vnto hir highnesse. And when his lordship had set all things in such order as the time required, he assembled all the gentlemen of the countrie, and most pithilie and effectuallie instructed and persuaded them to obedience, teaching them the great blessings of God which commeth thereby, as also putteth them in mind what inconueniences, miseries and calamities they had felt by the contrarie: and for their greater quietnesse and peace, he promised shortlie to send commissioners amongst them, who should haue authoritie to decide all controuersies betweene partie and partie (title of land and death of man excepted.)

The queene aduertised of Shane Oneils death.

The noblemen of Vlster, being glad of Oneils death do submit themselues.

Orders giuen by the lord deputie to the noblemen of Vlster.

Also he proclamed and commanded hir maiesties peace to be kept, and commanded all churchmen and husbandmen to returne to their accustomed exercises: and that all men of warre should liue vpon their owne, or vpon that which their fréends with a good will would giue them: and so publishing peace vniuersallie, euerie man departed home ioifullie. The lord deputie likewise returned to Dublin, and commanded the sonne of the late rebell, who laie for an hostage of his father, to be safelie kept in the castell of Dublin, according to hir maiesties letters of commandement in that behalfe, dated the sixt of Iulie 1567. The queenes maiestie being deliuered from this traitorous rebell, and hauing all Vlster at hir commandement and disposition, was verie desirous to haue a true plot of the whole land, wherby she might in some sort see the same, & did send ouer into Ireland one Robert Léeth, skilfull in that art, and that he should make the perfect descriptions of the same. Likewise also she being aduertised of the outragious dealings of the earle of Desmond, in mainteining proclamed rebels, and continuing of warres against the earle of Ormond (whose insolencie to séeke to be reuenged vpon the said earle, was the disturbance of the whole realme, the spoile of the whole countrie, and the onelie cause of great murthers, bloudshed, and vndooing of manie people) she willed the lord deputie by hir letters to apprehend the said Desmond, and to commit him to the castell of Dublin, which was so doone. And after both he and his brother sir Iohn of Desmond were sent into England, and there committed to the tower.

Oneils sonne is cōmitted to safe custodie.

Robert Léeth sent into Ireland to draw a true plot of the whole land.

The earle of Desmond committed to ward, and sent to the tower, together with his brother sir Iohn Desmond.

After all the foresaid broiles and ciuill wars were appeased, and the realme set in quietnesse and good order, the lord deputie hauing receiued hir maiesties letters for his repaire into England vnto hir presence, he did accordinglie prepare himselfe thervnto, and by a commission vnder hir broade seale of Ireland did appoint doctor

1567

Waston

Doctor Weston and sir William Fitzwilliams made lords iustices.

Weston then lord chancellor, and sir William Fitzwilliams treasuror at wars, to be lords iustices in his absence: the one of them being verie well learned, iust, and vpright; the other verie wise, and of great knowledge and experience in the affaires of that land. Both which two being like well minded to doo hir maiestie seruice, did most louinglie and brotherlie agree therein, each one aduising and aduertising the other according to the seuerall gifts which God had bestowed vpon them: by which meanes they passed their gouernment verie well and quietlie to the great contentation of hir maiestie, the commendation of themselues, and the common peace of the countrie. And so the said sir Henrie hauing placed the said iustices, he passed the seas into England, and carried with him the earle of Desmond and Oconnor Sligo, he was with great honor receiued at the court, and the other was sent to the tower. Hir maiestie lay at this time at Hampton court, and looking out at a window, she saw him to come in with two hundred men attending vpon him, and not knowing at the first sight who it was, it was told hir that it was sir Henrie Sidneie hir deputie in Ireland. "Then it is well (quoth she) for he hath two of the best offices in England." So he presented himselfe before hir highnesse, and was welcome to hir.

Sir Henrie Sidneie lord deputie passeth into England, and carried with him the earle of Desmond.

Ed. Moliueux.

Neuerthelesse, after his departure, the particular grudges betweene some certeine men brake out into great and outragious disorders, as sir Edmund Butler with great hostilitie maketh inuasion vpon Oliuer Fitzgirald, being accompanied with Piers Grace. The outlawes of the Oconnors and Omores proklamed traitors, and hauing in the field a thousand of Galloglasses, horssemen, and kernes, threaten to burne the towne of Kilkennie, and spoile Ocarell of his countrie. But they as also Oliuer Fitzgirald, a man not apt in times past to complaine, but rather bent to satisfie himselfe with double reuenge, leauing to séeke reuenge by armes, made their recourses to the lords iustices, and by law requested redresse.

Sir Edmund Butler breaketh out into outrages.

The erle of Clancart was puffed vp with such insolencie, that he named himselfe king of Mounster, and did confederate with the Mac Swaines, Osoliuan More, and others of the Irishrie of that prouince, and in warlike maner and with banners displaied inuadeth the lord Roches countrie, and in burning of his countrie, he destroied all the corne therein, seuen hundred sheepe, and a great number of men, women and children, and carried awaie fiftéene hundred kine, and a hundred garons. Also Iames Fitzmoris of Desmond maketh cruell warres against the lord Fitzmoris baron of Lixenew, which albeit they were but priuie displeasures, yet troublesome to the whole countrie: and the lords iustices being not prepared to stop the same, they did yet so temporise with them, as they gained time, till further order might be taken vpon aduertisement of hir maiesties pleasure herein.

The pride of Mac Artie More earle of Clancart.

The earle of Clancart maketh warres vpon the lord Roch.

Iames Fitzmoris maketh warre vpon the baron of Lixenew.

About this time one Morice a runnagate préest, hauing latelie béene at Rome, and there consecrated by the popes bull archbishop of Cashell, arriued into Ireland, and made chalenge to the same sée: which being denied vnto him by the archbishop which was there placed by hir maiestie, the said supposed bishop suddenlie with an Irish skaine wounded the bishop, and put him in danger of his life.

The archbishop of Cashel in danger to be killed.

This yeare sir Peter Carew of Mohonesotrie in the countie of Deuon knight, one descended of a noble and high parentage, whose ancestors for sundrie hundred of yeares were not onelie barons of Carew in England, but marquesses of Corke, barons of Odron, and lords of Maston Twete, and sundrie other seignories in Ireland. When he had looked into his euidences, and had found how by right these great inheritances were descended vnto him, he made the quéens maiestie and councell acquainted therewith, and praied that with their fauor and furtherance he might haue libertie to follow, and by order of law to recouer the same. Which was granted vnto him, as also he had hir highnesse and their lordships seuerall letters to them, their lords iustices and officers there to that effect, and willing them to aid and

Sir Peter Carew maketh sute to hir maiestie for the recouerie of his lands in Ireland.

assist him with all such hir maiesties euidences remaining in the records of the castell of Dublin, or else where in that land, and by all such other good meanes they might. Wherevpon he sent the writer hereof to be his agent: who hauing by search found his title to be good, and confirmed by sundrie records and presidents, found in hir maiesties treasurie and castell of Dublin, answering and agréeing with the euidences of sir Peter Carew: then the said sir Peter passed in person into Ireland, and made title and claime to the lordship of Maston, then in the possession of sir Christopher Chiuers knight, and to the baronie of Odron, then in the occupation of the Cauenaughs.

Sir Peter Carew passeth into Ireland.

The first, when it was found good in law, and sir Christopher Chiuers yéelded, and compounded for it: the other was trauersed before the lord deputie and councell, and vpon good and substantiall euidences, records, and proofes, a decree passed by the lords of the councell, in the behalfe of sir Peter Carew, and the same confirmed by the lord deputie, and by that meanes he recouered the possession of the baronie, which was before taken from his ancestors, as the records doo impart, about the eighteenth yeare of king Richard the second. But as for the marqueship of Corke, being a matter of great weight and importance, and the prouince of Mounster then not setled in anie quietnesse: he would not as then nor yet thought it good to deale therein. Sir Henrie Sidneie, hauing spent a long time in England, was commanded to returne to his charge in Ireland, where he arriued at Crag Fergus, in September 1568. and tooke the sword of gouernement vpon him, and so discharged the lords iustices. And then he and the councell by their letters of the fourth of Nouember 1568, did aduertise hir maiestie of the state that the said realme of Ireland then stood in. Which in briefe consisted in these points immediathe following.

Sir Peter Carew by a decree recouereth the baronie of Odron.

1568

Sir Henrie Sidneie returneth lord deputie.

That sir Edmund Butler had made a preie in Shilelagh vpon Oliuer Fitzgarret, and doone sundrie murders, burnings, and great spoiles vpon his countrie: who was forthwith sent for, and refuseth to come, excusing that he had businesse about the execution of certeine seruices in the counties of Kilkennie, and Tipporarie, and that the residue of all Leinster was quiet. That Connagh was in indifferent good order, sauing some contention betwéene the earle of Clanricard, and Mac William Enter, and an old controuersie renewed betwéene Odonell and Oconner Sligo for the title of a rent in Enter, Connaghs countrie. In Thomond great complaints made against the earle thereof, by Oshaghnes, who by reason of the oppression of the said earle, he was compelled with his followers to forsake his countries. As for Mounster, it was all in disorder by the warres of Iames Fitzmoris of Desmond, against Fitzmoris baron of Lixenew: and of the earle of Clancart, against the baron of Roch: and also by the disorders of Edward Butler, who being combined with Piers Grace and certeine outlawes, did disorderlie spoile and preie the countries to féed their bellies.

The state that Ireland stood in.

Connagh in reasonable peace.

Mounster out of order.

The present state of Vlster the lord deputie being desirous to know the certeintie thereof, immediatlie vpon his landing in Ireland he made a iourneie throughout the same, and found the Irishrie to stand in wauering terms: wherevpon he sent for Turlogh Lenogh Oneile, who yéelding himselfe somewhat giltie, because he somewhat swarued from his dutie, and differed from the articles in his lordships absence before, concluded with him in making a iourneie vpon Ferneie, and in combining with the Scots, of whome he had in reteinue about one thousand, he desired pardon: which it was long and verie hardlie obteined, and not vntill his lordship had caused the pledges to be executed, which the Scots had put in for their loialtie. Odoneile quietlie possessed the countrie of Tirconell, and continued a dutifull subiect to hir maiestie, sauing the old grudge betwéene him and Turlogh did rather increase than decaie. Ochan lord of the land betwéene Loghfoile and the Ban, being

Turlogh Lenogh breaketh the peace, but submitteth himselfe.

being for the same sometime molested by Turlogh Lenogh, did beare with all iniuries, and desired to be exempted from Turlogh, and to hold the same of the queenes maiestie. The like did the two principall men, eligible for the capteinrie of Tiron, desire for their parts all the residue of Vlster in good state and quietnesse.

The lord deputie after this iourneie returned to Dublin, and there, when by the aduise of the councell he had disposed all things in good order concerning the gouernement, he caused the writs for summons of the parlement to be awarded out vnto euerie noble man for his appéerance, & to euerie shiriffe for choosing of knights and burgesses for their like appéerance at Dublin the seuentéenth of Ianuarie, in the eleuenth yeare of hir maiesties reigne, at which time and daie appéerance was then and there made accordinglie. On the first daie of which parlement, the lord deputie, representing hir maiesties person, was conducted and attended in most honorable manner vnto Christes church, and from thense vnto the parlement house, where he sat vnder the cloth of estate, being apparelled in the princelie robes of crimson veluet doubled or lined with ermin. And then & there the lord chancellor made a verie eloquent oration, declaring what law was, of what great effect and value, how the common societie of men was thereby mainteined, and each man in his degrée conserued, as well the interior as the superior, the subiect as the prince: and how carefull all good common-wealths in the elder ages haue béene in this respect: who considering the time, state, and necessitie of the common-wealth, did from time to time ordeine and establish most holsome lawes, either of their deuises, or drawen from some other good common-wealth: and by these meanes haue prospered and continued.

A parlement summoned at Dublin

The lord chancellor his oration

And likewise, how the quéenes most excellent maiestie, as a most naturall mother ouer hir children, and as a most vigilant prince ouer hir subiects, hath béene alwaies, & now presentlie is verie carefull, studious, & diligent in this behalfe: hauing caused this present parlement to be assembled, that by the councell and aduise of you hir nobilitie, & you hir knights and burgesses, such good lawes, orders, and ordinances maie be decréed, as maie be to the honor of almightie God, the preseruation of hir maiestie, and of hir imperiall crowne of this realme, and the safetie of the common-wealth of the whole realme: for which they were not onelie to be most thankefull; but also most carefull to doo their duties in this behalfe. And then he the lord speaker directing his speeches to the knights and burgesses, who were there in the behalfe of the whole commons of the realme, willed them that for the auoiding of confusion, and for an orderlie procéeding in this action, they should assemble themselues at and in the house appointed for that assemblie, and there to make choise of some wise and sufficient man to be their mouth & speaker. And then concluding with an exhortation of obedience and dutifulnesse, he ended, and the court adiourned vntill thursdaie next, the twentith of Ianuarie. In the meane time, the knights and burgesses met in the lower house, and appointed for their speaker one Stanihurst, recorder of the citie of Dublin, a verie graue, wise, and learned man; who vpon thursdaie aforesaid was presented to the lord deputie, and to the lords of the higher house: & then he hauing doone most humblie his obedience and dutie, made his oration and speech, first abasing himselfe, being not a man sufficientlie adorned and furnished with such gifts of knowledge and learning, as to such an office and calling dooth apperteine: wherein he was so much the more vnfit, as the cause he had in hand was of great weight and importance. And therefore he wished, if it might so séeme good to his lordship, some man of more grauitie, and of better experience, knowledge, and learning might supplie the place. Neuerthelesse, for somuch as he might not refuse it, he was the more willing, because he did well hope his seruice being

Stanihurst chosen to be speaker of the lower house

Stanihursts oration

doone

doone with his best good will, and in all dutifulnesse, it would be accepted. And againe his comfort was the more, bicause he had to deale in such a cause, as was for the establishing of some good and holsome lawes, wherof he was a professor.

And herevpon he tooke an occasion, according to the argument that was before handled by the lord chancellor, speaker in the higher house, to discourse of the nature and good effect of lawes, and what good successe there insueth to all such realmes, countries, and common-wealths, as by lawes are well ruled & gouerned. And when he had spoken at large hereof, there he declared what great causes that realme of Ireland had, to giue for euer most hartie thanks and praises to God for his goodnesse, in sending such a vertuous, noble, and a most godlie prince, as was hir maiestie, who not onlie was carefull by the sword to stand in their defense against all enimies, traitors, and rebels, in times of wars and rebellions: but also for their conseruation in times of peace would haue such lawes, statutes, and ordinances to be made in a parlement of themselues, as should be most expedient for the common-wealth of the same land. When he had at large discoursed of this matter, then he concluded with an humble petition, that it might please hir maiestie to grant vnto them their liberties and fréedoms of old belonging to euerie assemblie of a parlement. The first was, that euerie man being a member of the lower house, should and might haue frée comming and going to and from the parlement, and during their abode at the same without molestation or impeachment of anie person or persons, or for anie matter then to be laid against anie of them. The second, that they and euerie of them might haue libertie to speake their minds fréelie to anie bill to be read, & matter to be proposed in that parlement. Thirdlie, that if anie of the said house shuld misorder and misbehaue himselfe in anie vndecent manner, or if anie other person should euill intreat or abuse anie of the said house, that the correction and punishment of euerie such offendor should rest and remaine in the order of the said house. When he had ended his spéech, and in most humble maner doone his obeisance, the lord deputie hauing paused vpon the matter, made answer to euerie particular point in most eloquent and effectuall manner, which consisted in these points: Nothing misliking with the speaker for so much abasing of himselfe, bicause he knew him to be both graue, wise, and learned, and verie sufficient for that place, doubting nothing but that he would performe the same in all dutifulnesse, as to him apperteined. And concerning the benefit which groweth to all nations and common-wealths by the vse of the lawes, besides that dailie experience did confirme the same generallie, so no one nation particularlie could better auouch it than this realme of Ireland: and therefore he did well hope that they would accordinglie frame themselues to liue accordinglie, and also to praie for hir maiesties safetie and long life, whereby vnder hir they might inioie a peaceable and a quiet life in all prosperitie. And concerning the priuileges, which they requested to be allowed, forsomuch as the same at the first were granted to the end that they might the better and more quietlie serue hir highnesse in that assemblie, to hir honor, and to the benefit of the common-wealth, it pleased hir maiestie so long as the were not impeached, nor hir imperiall state derogated, that they should inioie the same. And so after a long time spent in this oration the court was adiourned.

The requests of the speaker for allowance of the liberties of the parlement house.

The lord deputie answereth Stanihursts oration.

The next daie following being fridaie the lower house met, and contrarie to the order of that house, and dutie of that companie, in stéed of vnitie there began a diuision, and for concord discord was receiued. For all, or the most part of the knights and burgesses of the English pale, especiallie they who dwelled within the counties of Meth and Dublin, who seeing a great number of Englishmen to haue place in that house began to except against that assemblie as not good, nor warranted by law.

A mutinie in the lower house.

law. Their vantparler was sir Christopher Barnwell knight, who being somewhat learned, his credit was so much the more: and by them thought most méetest and worthie to haue béene the speaker for that house. And he being the spokesman alleged thrée speciall causes, whie he and his complices would not yéeld their consents. The first was, bicause that there were certeine burgesses returned for sundrie townes, which were not corporat, and had no voice in the parlement. The second was, that certeine shiriffes, and certeine maiors of townes corporat had returned themselues. The third and chéefest was that a number of Englishmen were returned to be burgesses of such towns and corporations, as which some of them neuer knew, and none at all were resiant & dwelling in the same, according as by the lawes is required.

Sir Christopher Barnwell excepteth against the choise of the burgesses.

These matters were questioned among themselues in the lower house for foure daies togither, and no agréement: but the more words, the more choler, and the more spéeches, the greater broiles, vntill in the end, for appeasing the matter, the same was referred to the lord deputie and iudges of the realme: vnto whom the said speaker was sent to declare the whole matter, and to know their resolutions. And they hauing at large discoursed and conferred of this matter, returned their answer, that concerning the first and second exceptions, that the burgesses returned for townes not corporat, and for such shiriffes, maiors, and soueraignes as haue returned themselues shall be dismissed out of the same: but as for such others as the shiriffes and maiors had returned, they should remaine, and the penaltie to rest vpon the shiriffes for their wrong returnes. The messenger of this answer, howsoeuer he were liked, his message could not be receiued nor allowed: which being aduertised vnto the lord deputie and the iudges, then Lucas Dillon hir maiesties attorneie generall was sent vnto them, to ratifie and confirme their resolutions: and yet could not he be credited, neither would they be satisfied, vnlesse the iudges themselues would come in persons and set downe this to be their resolutions. Vpon this answer the speaker commanded a bill to be read, but the foresaid persons would not suffer nor abide the reading thereof: but rose vp in verie disordered manner, farre differing from their duties in that place, and as contrarie to that grauitie and wisedome, which was or should be in them. Wherefore, for pacifieng of the same, the chéefe iustices of the quéenes bench, and the chéefe iustices of the common plées: the queenes sergeant, attornie generall, and sollicitor, the next daie following came to the lower house, and there did affirme their former resolutions, which thought it might haue sufficed. Yet certeine lawiers who had place in that house, did not altogither like thereof.

The resolution of the iudges.

The disliking of the iudges opinions.

The selfewill and frowardnesse of the burgesse of the English pale.

And albeit this matter were orderlie compassed, and sufficient to haue contented euerie man: yet the same was so stomached, that the placing of the Englishmen to be knights and burgesses, could not be digested, as did appéere in the sequele of that assemblie, where euerie bill furthered by the English gentlemen was stopped and hindered by them. And especiallie sir Edmund Butler, who in all things which tended to the quéenes maiesties profit or common-wealth, he was a principall against it: fearing that their capteinries should be taken awaie, and coine, and liuerie be abolished, and such other like disorders redressed, which he and his complices misliking, it did euen open it selfe of a rebellion then a brewing and towards. Which in déed followed. For immediatlie after the parlement, he returned home with a discontented mind, and gathered his forces, and followed his purpose. But to the purpose.

Sir Edmund Butler misliketh with the parlement.

There were two billes put in of moment & great consequence. The one was concerning the repeale of an act for that sessions, onelie made in the time of sir Edward Poinings lord deputie, in the tenth yere of king Henrie the seuenth, which though

The repeale of Poinings act.

though it were meant most for their owne benefit and common-wealth of that realme: yet so gelous they were, that they would not in long time enter into the consideration thereof. The other was for the granting of the impost for wines then first read. And in this matter they shewed themselues verie froward & so vnquiet, that it was more like a bearebaiting of disordered persons, than a parlement of wise and graue men. Wherewith a certeine English gentleman (the writer hereof) being a burgesse of the towne of Athenrie in Connagh, who had before kept silence, and still so meant to haue doone, when he saw these foule misorders and ouerthwarting, being grieued, stood vp, and praied libertie to speake to the bill, who made a preamble, saieng, that it was an vsage in Pithagoras schooles, that no scholers of his should for certeine yeares reason, dispute, or determine, but giue eare and keepe silence: meaning that when a man is once well instructed, learned, and aduised, and hath well deliberated of the things he hath to do, he should with more discretion and wisdome, speake, order, and direct the same. Notwithstanding, now he being but a man of small experience, and of lesse knowledge in matters of importance, and therefore once minded to haue beene altogither silent, is inforced euen of a verie zeale and conscience, and for the discharge of his dutie, to praie their patience, and to beare with his speeches. And then vpon occasion of the bill read, and matter offered, he entred into the discourse what was the office & authoritie of a prince, and what was the dutie of a subiect: and lastlie, how the queenes maiestie had most honorablie and carefullie performed the one, and how vndutifullie they had considered the other: for that she neither found that obedience in that land, which still liued in rebellion against hir, neither that beneuolence of the better sort, which for hir great expenses spent for their defenses and safeties they ought to haue yéelded vnto hir. It appeered manifest in sundrie things, and speciallie in this present assemblie, namelie one bill concerning the repeale of Poinings act, for this time onelie meant for your owne benefit, and for the common-wealth of this realme: and the other concerning the bill now in question, the one by you denied, and the other liketh you not. And yet hir maiestie, of hir owne roiall authoritie, might and may establish the same without anie of your consents, as she hath alreadie doone the like in England, sauing of hir courtesie it pleaseth hir to haue it passe with your owne consents by order of law, that she might thereby haue the better triall and assurance of your dutifulnesse and goodwill towards hir. But as she hath and dooth find your bent farre otherwise, so dooth the right honorable the lord deputie find the like. For notwithstanding his long seruices in times past, his continuall and dailie trauels, iorneies, and hostings, with the great perill of his life against the rebels for your sake and safetie, and his endlesse turmoiles and troubles in ciuill matters and priuat sutes for your quietnesse, and to you well known, he hath deserued more than well at your hands: yet as the vnthankfull Israelites against Moses, the vnkind Romans against Camillus, Scipio, and others: and as the vngratefull Athenians against Socrates, Themistocles, Meltiades, and others, you haue and doo most vngratfullie requite and recompense this your noble gouernor: against whome and his doongs you doo kicke and spurne what in you lieth. But in the end it will fall vpon you, as it hath doone vnto others to your owne shame, ouerthrow, and confusion. And when he had spent a long time in this matter, and prooued the same by sundrie histories of other nations, he procéeded to the bill, which by sundrie reasons and arguments he prooued to be most necessarie, and méet to be liked, allowed, and consented vnto.

Now when he had thus ended his spéeches, he sat downe, the most part of the house verie well liking and allowing both of the person and of the matter, sauing the persons before named, who did not heare the same so attentiuelie as they did digest

digest it most vnquietlie, supposing themselues to be touched herein. And therfore some one of them rose vp and would haue answered the partie, but the time and daie was so far spent aboue the ordinarie houre, being well néere two of the clocke in the afternoone, that the speker and the court rose vp and departed. Howbeit such was the present murmurings and threatnings breathed out, that the said gentleman for his safetie was by some of the best of that assemblie conducted to the house of sir Peter Carew, where the said gentleman then laie and resided. The lord deputie in the meane time, hearing that the lower house were so close, and continued togither so long aboue the ordinarie time, he doubted that it had béene concerning the questions before proponed, and therefore did secretlie send to the house to learne and know the cause of their long sitting. But by commandement of the speaker, order was giuen to the doore-kéepers, that the doores should be close kept, & none to be suffered to come in or out, so long as the gentleman was in deliuerie of his speeches, and after the court was ended, it was aduertised to the said lord deputie, who thanked God that had raised vp vnknowen fréends vnto him in that place.

The next daie following being fridaie, assoone as the court of the lower house was set, sir Christopher Barnewell, and the lawiers of the English pale, who had conferred togither of the former daies spéeches, stood vp and desired hearing: who hauing the matter in question, did in most disorderlie manner inueigh against the said gentleman, affirming, auouching, and protesting, that if the words spoken had béene spoken in anie other place than in the said house, they would rather haue died than haue borne withall. Whervpon the speaker by consent of the residue of the house commanded them to silence, and willed that if they had anie matter against the said gentleman, they should present and bring it in writing against mondaie then next following. And for somuch as their dealings then were altogither disordered, being more like to a bearebaiting of lose persons than an assemblie of wise and graue men in parlement, motion and request was made to the speaker, that he should reforme those abuses and disordered behauiours, who not onelie promised so to doo, but also praied assistance, aduise, and counsell for his doings therein, of such as were acquainted with the orders of the parlements in England. Which was promised vnto him and performed, and also promised that a booke of the orders of the parlements vsed in England should in time be set forth in print, which the said gentleman did, and presented & bestowed the same among them in forme following.

A booke of the orders of a parlement house imprinted for Ireland.

The order and vsage how to keepe a parlement in England in these daies, collected by John Vowell alias Hooker gentleman, one of the citizens for the citie of Excester at the parlement holden at Westminster, Anno Domini 1571, & Elisabethæ Reg. decimo tertio. and the like vsed in hir maiesties realme of Ireland.

And here you must note, that what the kings and queenes of England do in their persons in England, the same is done in Ireland by the lord deputie, and who in the like parlement robes and vnder the like cloth of estate representeth hir maiestie there in all things.

By whom and for what cause a parlement ought to be summoned and called.

The king, who is Gods annointed, being the head and chiefe of the whole realme, and vpon whom the gouernement and estates thereof doo wholie and onelie depend, hath the power and authoritie to call and assemble his parlement, and therein to séeke and aske the aduise, counsell, & assistance of his whole realme, and without this his authoritie no parlement can properlie be summoned or assembled. And the king, hauing this authoritie, ought not to summon his parlement but for weightie and great causes and in which he of necessitie ought to haue the aduise and counsell of all the estates of his realme, which be these and such like as foloweth.

First for religion, forsomuch as by the lawes of God and this realme, the king next and immediatlie vnder God is his deputie and vicar in earth, and the chiefest ruler within his realms and dominions his office, function, and dutie is, aboue all things to seeke and sée that God be honored in true religion and vertue, and that he and his people doo both in profession and life liue according to the same

Also that all idolatries, false religions, heresies, schismes, errors, superstitions, & whatsoeuer is contrarie to true religion, all disorders and abuses, either among the cleargie or laitie, be reformed, ordered, and redressed

Also the assurance of the kings and queenes persons, and of their children, their aduancement & preferment in mariages, the establishing of succession, the suppression of traitors, the auoiding or eschewing of warres, the attempting or mouing of wars, the subduing of rebels, and pacifieng of ciuill wars and commotions, the leuieng or hauing anie aid or subsidie for the preseruation of the king and publike estate: also the making and establishing of good and wholesome lawes, or the repealing and debarring of former lawes, as whose execution may be hurtfull or preiudiciall to the estates of the prince or commonwealth

For these and such like causes, being of great weight, charge and importance, the king (by the aduise of his councell) may call and summon his high court of parlement, and by the authoritie thereof establish and order such good lawes and orders as then shall be thought most expedient and necessarie.

The order and maner how to summon the parlement.

The king ought to send out his writs of summons to all the estates of his reamd at least fortie daies before the beginning of the parlement, first to all his lords an barons, that is to wit, archbishops, bishops, dukes, marquesses, earls, vicounts and barons; and euerie of these must haue a speciall writ Then to the clergie, and the writ of their summons must be addressed to euerie particular bishop for the clergie of his diocesse All these writs which are for the clergie, the king alwaies sendeth to the archbishops of Canturburie and Yorke, and by them they are sent and dispersed abroad to euerie particular bishop within their seuerall prouinces, and so the bishops giue summons to the clergie

Lastlie, for the summoning of the commons, he sendeth his writ to the lord warden of the fiue ports, for the election of the barons thereof, and to euerie seuerall shiriffe for the choise and election of knights, citizens, and burgesses within his countie.

How and what persons ought to be chosen for the clergie, and of their allowances

The bishop ought vpon the receipt of the writ sent vnto him for the summoning of his clergie, foorthwith to summon and warne all deanes and archdeacons within his diocesse to appéere in proper person at the parlement, vnlesse they haue some sufficient and reasonable cause of absence, in which case he may appéere by his proctor, hauing a warrant or proxie for the same

Then must he also send the like summons to the deane and chapter of his cathedrall church, who shall foorthwith assemble their chapter, and make choise of some one of themselues to appéere in their behalfe, and this man thus chosen must haue their commission or proxie.

He

He must also send out his summons to euerie archdeaconrie and peculiar, requiring that the whole clergie doo appeere before him, his chancellor or officer, at a certeine daie, time, and place: who being so assembled, shall make choise and election of two men of the said clergie to appeere for them, and these shall haue their commission or proxie for the same.

These proctors thus to be chosen ought to be graue, wise, and learned men, being professors either of diuinitie or of the ecclesiasticall lawes, and that can, will, and be able to dispute in cause of controuersie, conuincing of heresies, appeasing of schismes, and deuising of good and godlie constitutions concerning true religion and orders of the church.

These proctors (thus elected) ought to haue reasonable allowances for their charges, according to the state, qualitie, or condition of the person, as also a respect had to the time. The proctors of the deane and chapter are to be paid out of the exchekcr of the cathedrall church. The proctors of the clergie are to be paid of the clergie, among whom a collection is to be leuied for the same, according to an old order vsed among them.

How and what maner of knights, citizens, and burgesses ought to be chosen, and of their allowances.

The shiriffe of euerie countie, hauing receiued his writs, ought foorthwith to send his precepts and summons to the maiors, bailiffes, and head officers of euerie citie, towne corporate, borough, and such places as haue béene accustomed to send burgesses within his countie, that they doo choose and elect among themselues two citizens for euerie citie, and two burgesses for euerie borough, according to their old custome and vsage. And these head officers ought then to assemble themselues & the aldermen and common councell of euerie citie or towne, and to make choise among themselues of two able and sufficient men of euerie citie or towne, to serue for and in the said parlement.

Likewise at the next countie daie to be holden in the said countie after the receipt of this writ, the shiriffe ought openlie in the court of his shire or countie, betwéene the houres of eight and nine of the forenoone, make proclamation; that euerie freeholder shall come into the court, and choose two sufficient men to be knights for the parlement; & then he must cause the writ to be openlie & distinctlie read. Wherevpon the said freeholders, then and there present, ought to choose two knights accordinglie, but he himselfe cannot giue anie voice, neither be chosen.

These elections aforesaid so past and doone, there ought to be seuerall indentures made betwéene the shiriffe & the fréeholders of the choise of the knights, and betwéene the maior and the head officers of euerie particular citie & towne of the choise of their citizens & burgesses & of their names, & of their mainperners and suerties. Of these indentures, the one part being sealed by the shiriffe, ought to be returned to the clerke of the parlement, and the other part of the indentures, sealed by such as made choise of the knights, & such as made choise of the citizens & burgesses vnder the seuerall common seales of their cities and townes, ought to remaine with the shiriffe, or rather with the parties so elected and chosen.

The charges of euerie knight and citizen was woont to be a like, which was thirteene shillings and foure pence by the daie: but now by the statute it is but eight shillings, that is, to euerie knight and euerie citizen foure shillings, and to euerie burgesse the old vsage to haue fiue shillings: but now it is but thrée shillings and foure pence limited by the statute, which allowance is to be giuen from the first daie of their iourneie towards the parlement, vntill the last daie of their returne from thense. Prouided, that euerie such person shall be allowed for so manie daies as by iourneieng six and twentie miles euerie daie in the winter, and thirtie miles in the summer, he may come & returne to and from the parlement.

In choise of these knights, citizens, and burgesses, good regard is to be had that the lawes and customs of the realme be herein kept and obserued: for none ought to be chosen, vnlesse he be resiant and dwelling within the shire, citie, or towne for which he is chosen. And he ought to be graue, wise, learned, skilfull, and of great experience in causes of policie, and of such audacitie as both can and will boldlie vtter and speake his mind according to dutie, and as occasion shall serue; for no man ought to be silent or dum in that house, but according to his talent he must and ought to speake in the furtherance of the king and commonwealth.

And the knights also ought to be skilfull in martiall affaires, and therfore the words of the writs are that such should be chosen for knights as be *Cincti gladio*: not bicause they shall come into the parlement house in armour, or with their swords: but bicause they should be such as haue good experience and knowledge in feats of warre and martiall affaires, whereby they may in such cases giue the king and relme good aduise and counsell. Likewise they ought to be laie men, and of good fame, honestie, and credit, being not outlawed, excommunicated, or periured, or otherwise infamous: for such persons ought not to haue place or be admitted into the parlement house.

The degrees of the parlement.

In times past there were six degrées or estates of the parlement, which euerie of them had their seuerall officers and ministers of attendance; but now the same are reduced into foure degrées.

The first is the king, who in his personage is a full and whole degrée of himselfe, and without whom nothing can be doone.

The second degree is of the lords of the clergie and of the temporaltie, and are all called by the names of barons.

The third is of knights, citizens, and burgesses, & these be called by the names of the communaltie.

The fourth is of the clergie, which are called by the name of conuocation, & these persons haue no voice in the parlement; neither can they doo anie thing other than to intreat in causes of religion, which from them is to be commended to other estates.

Of the places and houses of the parlement.

As it lieth in the king to assigne and appoint the time when the parlement shall begin, so that he giue at the least fortie daies summons: so likewise he maie name and appoint the place where it shall be kept. But wheresoeuer it be kept, the old vsage and maner was, that all the whole degrees of the parlement sat togither in one house; and euerie man that had there to speake, did it openlie before the king and his whole parlement. But hereof did grow manie inconueniences, and therfore to auoid the great confusions which are in such great assemblies, as also to cut off the occasions of displeasures which eftsoones did happen, when a meane man speaking his conscience fréelie, either could not be heard, or fell into the displeasure of his betters; and for sundrie other great gréefs, did diuide this one house into thrée

thrée houses, that is to wit, the higher house, the lower house, and the conuocation house.

In the first sitteth the king, and his lords spirituall and temporall, called by the name of barons, and this house is called the higher house.

The second is where the knights, citizens and burgesses doo sit, and they be called by the name of commons, and this house is called the lower house.

The third is, where the prelats and the proctors of the cleargie, being called by the name of the cleargie, and this house is called the conuocation house. Of euerie of these houses, their orders and officers, we will bréeflie subiect and declare particularlie in order as followeth.

Of the higher house.

The higher house (as is said) is where the king and his barons doo sit in parlement, where the king sitteth highest, and the lords & barons beneath him, each man in his degrée the order is this. The house is much more in length than in breadth, and the higher end thereof in the middle is the kings seat or throne hanged richlie with cloth of estate, and there the king sitteth alwaies alone. On his right hand there is a long bench next to the wall of the house, which reacheth not so farre vp as the kings seat, and vpon this sit the archbishops and bishops, euerie one in his degrée. On his left hand there are two like benches, vpon the inner sit the dukes, marquesses, earles and vicounts. On the other, which is the hindermost & next to the wall, sit all the barons euerie man in his degrée. In the middle of the house, betwéene the archbishops seat and the dukes seat, sitteth the speaker, who commonlie is lord chancellor, or keeper of the great seale of England, or the lord chiefe iustice of England, as pleaseth the king, who dooth appoint him: and he hath before him his two clerks sitting at a table before them, vpon which they doo write and laie their bookes. In the middle roome beneath them sit the chiefe iustices and iudges of the realme, the barons of the escheker, the kings sergeants, and all such as be of the kings learned councell, either in the common lawes of the realme, or of the ecclesiasticall laws, and all these sit vpon great wooll sacks, couered with red cloth.

At the lower end of all these seats is a barre or raile, betwéene which & the lower end of the house is a void roome seruing for the lower house, and for all sutors that shall haue cause and occasion to repaire to the king or to the lords. This house as it is distinct from the others, so there be distinct officers to the same belonging and appertaining, which all be assigned and appointed by the king and all haue allowances for their charges at the kings hands, of which officers what they are, what is euerie of their offices, and what allowances they haue, shall be written in order hereafter.

Of the officers of the higher house and first of the speaker, and of his office.

The chéefest officer of the higher house is the speaker, who is appointed by the king, and commonlie he is the lord chancelor or keeper of the great seale, or lord chéefe iustice of England, his office consisteth in diuerse points.

First, he must on the first daie of the parlement make his oration in the higher house, before the king, his lords and commons, and then and there declare the causes why the king hath summoned that parlement, exhorting and aduising euerie man

man to doo his office and dutie, in such sort as maie be to the glorie of God, honor of the king, and benefit of the commonwealth.

Also he must make one other oration, but in waie of answer to the speakers oration, when he is presented to the king.

Likewise he must make the like on the last daie of the parlement. And you shall vnderstand, that vpon these three daies he standeth on the right hand of the king neere to his seat, at a barre there appointed for him, but at all other times he sitteth in the middle of the house, as is before said.

When he hath ended his oration vpon the first day, he must giue order vnto the lower house in the kings behalfe, willing them to repaire vnto their house, and there (according to their ancient orders and customs) make choise of their speaker.

All bils presented vnto the higher house he must receiue, which he hath foorthwith to deliuer vnto the clearks to be safelie kept.

All bils he must cause to be read twise before they be ingrossed, and being read thrée times he must put the same to question.

If anie bill put to question doo passe with their consent, then the same must be sent to the lower house, vnlesse it came first from thense, and in that case it must be kept vntill the end of the parlement.

If anie bill be denied, impugned, and cleere ouerthrowne, the same is no more to be thensefoorth receiued.

If any bill be put to question, & it be doubtfull whether side is the greater, & giueth most voices, then he must cause the house to be diuided, and then iudge of the bill according to the greater number.

If anie bill be vnperfect, or requireth to be amended, he must choose a certeine number of that house, as he shall thinke good, and to them commit that bill to be reformed and amended.

If anie bill or message be to be sent to the lower house, it is his office to make choise of two of the kings learned councell there being, to be the messengers thereof.

If any bill or message be sent from the lower house, he must come from his place to the bar, and there receiue the same, and being returned to his place, and euerie stranger or messenger departed, he must disclose the same to the lords.

Item, if anie disorder be committed or doone in the house by anie lord or other person, he ought with the aduise of the lords to reforme the same: but if it be among the lords, and they will not be reformed, then he must foorthwith aduertise the king.

Item, he ought at the beginning of the parlement, to call by name all the lords of the parlement, & likewise at other other times as he séeth occasion, whose defaults ought to be recorded, & they to paie their fines, vnlesse they be dispensed withall by speciall licence from the king, or haue some iust and reasonable cause of absence.

Item, he must see and cause the clearks to make true entries & true records of all things doone there, and to see that all clearks doo giue and deliuer the copies of all such bils there read, to such as demand for the same.

Item, he shall keepe the secrets, & cause & command euerie man of ech degrée in that house to doo the like.

Also he ought not to go anie where, but the gentleman sergeant ought to attend vpon him, going before him with his mace, vnlesse he be the lord chancellor, for then he hath a sergeant of his owne.

This allowance that he hath is at the kings charges.

Also

Also for euerie priuat bill that passeth and is enacted, he hath ten pounds for his part.

Of the chancellor of the higher house

The chancellor is the principall clearke of the higher house, and his charge is safelie to kéepe the records of the parlement, & the acts which be past

All such statutes as be enacted, he must send to the kings seuerall courts of records to be inrolled, as namelie the Chancerie, the Kings bench, the Common plees, and the Excheker

All such acts as are to be imprinted, he must send to the printer

All such priuat acts as are not imprinted, if anie man will haue the same exemplified, he must transmit the same to the lord chancellor to be ingrossed and sealed, and for the same he to take the fees appointed and accustomed

He hath for his allowance an ordinarie fée for terme of life of the king

Of the clearks of the parlement.

There be two clearks, the one named the clearke of the parlement, & the other named the clearke of the crowne The clearke of the parlement his office is to sit before the lord speaker, and to read such bils presented as he shall be commanded.

He must kéepe true records, and true entries of all things there doone and to be entred

If anie require a copie of anie bill there, he ought to giue the same, receiuing the ordinarie fees

If anie bill after his ordinarie readings be to be ingrossed, he must doo it.

The councell of the house he maie not disclose.

At the end of the parlement he must deliuer vp vnto the chancellor all the acts and records of that house, sauing he may keepe a transumpt and a copie thereof to himselfe

He hath his allowance of the king.

Also for euerie priuat bill which is enacted, he hath thrée pounds

Also for euerie bill whereof he giueth a copie, he hath for euerie ten lines a penie, according to the custome

¶ The clearke of the crowne, his office is to supplie the place and roome of the clearke of the parlement in his absence, & hath in all things the like charges and profits as the clearke ought to haue.

He must giue his attendance to the higher house from time to time, & doo what shall be inioined him

All such acts as be not imprinted, if anie man will haue them exemplified vnder the brode seale, he must exemplifie them, and haue for the same his ordinarie fees.

These two clearks, at the end of the parlement, ought to be present in the house, and within the lower bar at a boord before them, their faces towards the king and there the one must read the bils which are past both houses, and the other must read the consent or disagreement of the king

Of the sergeants or porters of the higher house.

There is but one sergeant, which hath the charge of keeping of the doores: for

for though there be diuerse doores, yet the kéepers thereof are at his assignment.

He ought to sée the house be cleane & kept swéet.

He ought not to suffer anie maner of person to be within the house, so long as the lords be there sitting, other than such as be of the learned councell, and of that house, and except also such as come in message from the lower house with bils or otherwise, and except also such as be sent for, and be admitted to haue anie thing there to doo.

Also he must attend and go alwaies with his mace before the speaker, vnlesse he be lord chancellor, or kéeper of the great seale for then he hath a sergeant of his owne.

He ought to kéepe safelie such prisoners as be commanded to his ward, and to fetch or send for such as he shall be commanded to fetch.

This porter or sergeant hath (besides his ordinarie fee) a standing allowance for euerie daie of the parlement.

Also he hath for euerie priuat bill which is enacted, fortie shillings.

Also he hath for euerie prisoner committed to his ward, a certeine allowance for his fees.

Also he hath of euerie baron or lord of that house, a certeine reward.

Of the lower house.

The lower house (as is said) is a place distinct from the others, it is more of length than of breadth, it is made like a theater, hauing foure rowes of seates one aboue an other round about the same. At the higher end in the middle of the lower row, is a seat made for the speaker, in which he alwaies sitteth before it is a table boord, at which sitteth the clarke of the house, and therevpon laieth his bookes, and writeth his records. Vpon the lower row on both sides the speaker, sit such personages as be of the kings priuie councell, or of his chiefe officers, but as for anie other, none claimeth, nor can claime anie place, but sitteth as he commeth, sauing that on the right hand of the speaker, next beneath the said councels, the Londoners, and the citizens of Yorke doo sit, and so in order should sit all the citizens accordinglie. Without this house is one other, in which the vnder clearks doo sit, as also such as be sutors and attendant to that house. And when soeuer the house is diuided vpon anie bill, then the roome is voided, and the one part of the house commeth downe into this to be numbered.

The office of the speaker of the lower house.

The chiefe or principall officer of this house is the speaker, and is chosen by the whole house, or the more part of them, he himselfe being one of the same number, and a man for grauitie, wisedome, experience, and learning, chosen to supplie that office, during the time of the parlement, and is to be presented to the king the third daie folowing.

His office is to direct and guide that house in good order, and to sée the ordinances, vsages, and customs of the same to be firmelie kept and obserued.

When he is presented vnto the king, sitting in his estate roiall in the parlement house for the purpose, he must then and there make his oration in commendation of the lawes and of the parlement, which doone, then he hath (in the name of the house of the commons) to make to the king the thrée requests.

First, that it maie please his maiestie to grant, that the commons assembled in the

the parlement, may haue and inioie the ancient priuileges, customes, and liberties, as in times past haue appertemed, and béene vsed in that house

Then, that euerie one of that house maie haue libertie of speech, and fréelie to vtter, speake, and declare his mind and opinion to anie bill or question to be proponed

Also, that euerie knight, citizen, and burgesse, and their seruants, maie haue free comming and going to and from the said parlement, as also during the said time of parlement, & that they, nor anie of their seruants or retinue to be arrested, molested, sued, imprisoned, or troubled by anie person or persons

And lastlie, that if he or anie other of that companie, béeing sent or come to him of anie message, and doo mistake himselfe in dooing thereof, that his maiestie will not take the aduantage thereof, but gratiouslie pardon the same

He must haue good regard, and sée that the clearke doo enter and make true records, and safelie to keepe the same, and all such bils as be deliuered into that house

He must on the first and third daie, and when soeuer he else will, call the house by name, and record their defaults.

All bils, to be brought and to be presented into that house, he must receiue & deliuer to the clearke

He ought to cause and command the clearke to reade the bils brought in, plainelie, and sensiblie, which doone, he must bréefle recite and repeat the effect and meaning thereof

Of the bils brought in he hath choise, which and when they shall be read vnlesse order by the whole house be taken in that behalfe

Euerie bill must haue thrée readings, and after the second reading he must cause the clearke to ingrosse the same, vnlesse the same be reiected and dashed

If anie bill or message be sent from the lords, he ought to cause the messengers to bring the same vnto him, and he to receiue the same openlie, and they being departed and gone, he ought to disclose and open the same to the house.

If when a bill is read, diuerse doo rise at one instant to speake to the same, and it cannot be discerned who rose first, then shall he appoint who shall speake neuerthelesse, euerie one shall haue his course to speake if he list

If anie speake to a bill and be out of the matter, he shall put him in remembrance, and will him to come to the matter

If anie bill be read thrée times, and euerie man haue spoken his mind, then shall he aske the house whether the bill shall passe or not? saieng thus As manie as will haue this bill passe in maner & forme as hath béene read, saie Yea then the affirmatiue part saie Yea As manie as will not haue this bill passe in maner and forme as hath beene read, saie No If vpon this question the whole house, or the more part, doo affirme and allow the bill then the same is to be sent to the higher house to the lords But if the whole house, or the more part doo denie the bill, then the same is to be dashed out, and to be reiected but if it be doubtfull vpon giuing voices, whether side is the greater, then must a diuision be made of the house, and the affirmatiue part must arise and depart into the vtter roome, which (by the sergeant) is voided before hand of all persons that were there. And then the speaker must assigne two or foure to number them first which sit within, and then the other which be without, as they doo come in, one by one: and as vpon the triall the bill shall be allowed or disallowed by the greater number. so to be accepted as is before said

If vpon this triall the number of either side be like, then the speaker shall giue his voice, and that onelie in this point. for otherwise he hath no voice

Also if anie of the house doo misbehaue himselfe, & breake the order of the house, he hath to reforme, correct, and punish him, but yet with the aduise of the house.

If anie forren person doo enter into that house, the assemblie thereof being sitting, or doo by arresting anie one person thereof, or by anie other meanes breake the liberties and priuileges of that house, he ought to sée him to be punished.

Also during the time of the parlement, he ought to sequester himselfe from dealing or intermedling in anie publike or priuat affaires, and dedicat and bend himselfe wholie to serue his office and function.

Also he ought not to resort to anie noble man, councellor, or other person, to deale in anie of the parlement matters but must and ought to haue with him a competent number of some of that house, who maie be witnesses of his doings.

Also during the time of parlement, he ought to haue the sergeant of armes with his mace to go before him.

Also he hath libertie to send anie offendor, either to sergeants ward, or to the tower, or to anie other prison at his choise according to the qualitie and quantitie of the offense.

He hath allowance for his diet one hundred pounds of the king for euerie sessions of parlement.

Also he hath for euerie priuat bill passed both houses, and enacted, fiue pounds.

At the end, and on the last daie of the parlement, he maketh his oration before the king in most humble maner, declaring the dutifull seruice and obedience of the commons then assembled to his maiestie, as also most humblie praieng his pardon, if anie thing haue béene doone amisse.

Of the clearke of the lower house.

THERE is onelie one clearke belonging to this house, his office is to sit next before the speaker at a table, vpon which he writeth & laieth his bookes.

He must make true entrie of the records and bils of the house, as also of all the orders thereof.

The bils appointed vnto him by the speaker to be read he must read openlie, plainelie, and sensiblie.

The billes which are to be ingrossed, he must doo it.

If anie of the house aske the sight of anie bill there, or of the booke of the orders of the house; he hath to deliuer the same vnto him.

If anie desire to haue the copie of anie bill, he ought to giue it him, receiuing for his paines after ten lines a pennie.

He maie not be absent at anie time of sitting, without speciall licence.

He ought to haue for euerie priuat bill passed and enacted, fortie shillings.

He hath allowed vnto him for his charges (of the king) for euerie sessions, ten pounds.

Of the sergeant or porter of the lower house.

THE sergeant of this house is commonlie one of the kings sergeants at armes, and is appointed to this office by the king. His office is to kéepe the doore doores of the house: and for the same he hath others under him, for he himselfe kéepeth the doore of the inner house, where the commons sit, and séeth the same to be cleane.

Also he maie not suffer anie to enter into this house, during the time of the sitting there; vnlesse he be one of the house, or be sent from the king or the lords, or otherwise licenced to come in.

If anie such person doo come, he ought to bring him in, going before him with his mace vpon his shoulder.

If anie be committed to his ward, he ought to take charge of him, and to kéepe him in safetie vntill he be required for him.

If he be sent for anie person, or to go in anie message, he must leaue a substitute behind him, to doo his office in his absence.

He must alwaies attend the speaker, and go before him, carieng his mace vpon his shoulder.

His allowance (during the time of the parlement) is twelue pence the daie of the kings charges.

Also he hath of euerie knight and citizen, two shillings six pence; and of euerie burgesse, two shillings.

If anie be commanded to his ward, he hath of euerie such prisoner, by the daie, six shillings and eight pence.

If anie priuat bill doo passe and be enacted, he hath for euerie such bill, twentie shillings.

Of the conuocation house.

THE conuocation house is the assemblie of the whole clergie, at and in some peculiar place appointed for the purpose.

But as the barons and lords of the parlement haue their house seuerall and distinct from the commons: euen so the archbishops and bishops doo sequester themselues, and haue a house seuerall from the residue of the clergie. And this their house is called the higher conuocation house, the other being named the lower conuocation house. Both these houses haue their seuerall officers, orders, and vsages; and each officer hath his peculiar charge and function; as also certeine allowances, euen as is vsed in the parlement houses of the lords and commons.

The archbishops and bishops doo sit all at a table, and doo discourse all such causes and matters as are brought in question before them, either of their owne motions, or from the higher court of parlement, or from the lower house of conuocation, or from anie priuat person. Euerie archbishop and bishop sitteth & taketh place according to his estate and degrée, which degrees are knowne by such degrées & offices in the church as to euerie of them is assigned: for one hath the personage of a priest, an other of a deacon, this is a subdeacon, he is a sexton, and so foorth, as such officers were woont to be in the church.

The bishops doo not sit at forenoone, but onelie at afternoone, because they, being barons of the higher house of parlement, doo resort and assemble themselues there at the forenoones with the temporall lords.

The conuocation house of the rest of the clergie doo obserue in a manner the like orders as the lower house of the commons doo vse. For being assembled togither on the first daie, with the bishops, are by them willed to make choise of a speaker for them, whom they call the prolocutor: when they haue chosen him, they doo present him vnto the bishops: and he thus presented, maketh his oration, and dooth all things as the speaker of the lower house for the commons dooth, as well for the ordering of the clergie & of the house, as for the order in sitting, the order in speaking, the order of recording things doone among them, and all other such like things.

And this is to be vnderstood, that the whole clergie can deale and intreat but onlie of matters of religion, and orders of the church, which their doings and conclusions can not bind the whole realme, vnlesse they be confirmed by act of parlement: but yet sufficient to bind the whole clergie to the kéeping thereof, so that the king (who is the supreme gouernor of both estates) doo consent and confirme the same. And forsomuch as by knowing the orders of the parlement house, you may also know the orders of both the conuocation houses, which are like & correspondent to the others: these shall suffice for this matter.

Of extraordinarie persons which ought to be summoned to the parlement.

Besides the personages of the former degrées, which ought to be summoned to the parlement: the king also must warne and summon all his councellors both of the one law and of the other; and these haue their places onelie in the higher house, namelie the two chéefe iustices and their associats of the kings bench and the common plées, the barons of the excheker, the sergeants, the attornie, the sollicitor, the maister of the rolles, and his fellows of the chancerie.

The offices of these personages are to giue councell to the king and parlement, in euerie doubtfull cause according to the lawes.

Also if anie bill be conceiued and made disorderlie, they ought to amend and reforme the same, vpon order and commandement to them giuen.

Also they must attend to come and go at the commandement of the king and parlement.

Also they may not speake nor giue aduise, but when they be asked and put to question.

Also they haue no voice in parlement, because they are commonlie councellors to the same.

They are all reteined at the kings charges.

Likewise all officers of the parlement are to be summoned, as namelie the chancellor of the parlement, the clerks, the sergeants, the porters, and such others, who likewise are reteined at the kings costs. Of their offices and charges it is alreadie particularly declared.

Of the daies and houres to sit in parlement.

All daies of the wéeke are appointed, sauing and excepted the sundaies and all principall feasts, as namelie the feast of Alhallowes daie, Christmas, Easter, Whitsuntide, and saint Iohn the baptists daie, and also such other daies as the parlement by consent shall appoint and assigne.

The beginning is at eight of the clocke in the morning, and dooth continue vntill eleuen of the clocke.

They doo not sit at afternoones, for those times are reserued for committées and the conuocation house.

In the morning they beginne with the common praier and the letanie, which are openlie read in the house.

Of

Of the king, his office and authoritie.

HAUING declared of all the estates, degrees, and personages of the parlement, it resteth now to speake also of the king, and of his office, who is all in all, the beginning and ending, and vpon whome it resteth and dependeth the effect & substance of the whole parlement. For without him and his authoritie nothing can be doone, and with it all things take effect. Neuerthelesse, when he calleth & assembleth his parlement, there are sundrie orders which of him are to be obserued, and which he ought to see to be kept and executed, or else the parlement ceasseth to be a parlement, and taketh not his effect, of which orders these be the chéefe which doo insue.

First, the king ought to send out his summons to all the estates of his realme, of a parlement, assigning and appointing the time, daie, and place.

Also his summons must be at the least fortie daies before the beginning of his parlement.

Also he must appoint and prouide all such officers as ought to attend the parlement, who must be found at his charges.

Also the king ought not to make anie choise, or cause anie choise to be made of any knight, citizens, burgesses, proctors of the clergie, speaker of the common house, or prolocutor of the conuocation house: but they must be elected and chosen by the lawes, orders, and customs of the realme, as they were woont and ought to be, and the kings good aduise yet not to be contemned.

Also the king ought to grant, permit, and allow to all and euerie of the estates, and to euerie particular man lawfullie elected, and come to the parlement, all and euerie the ancient fréedoms, priuileges, immunities, and customs, during the parlement, as also during the times and daies, comming and going to and from the parlement: but yet the same humblie to be requested of his highnesse by the speaker in his oration at the beginning of the parlement.

Also the king in person ought to be present in the parlement thrée daies at the least, during the time of the parlement, that is to saie, the first daie, when the whole estates according to the summons make their appearance, which is called the first daie of the parlement. On the second daie, when the speaker of the common house is presented, which is counted the beginning of the parlement. And the third daie, which is the last day, when the parlement is proroged or dissolued: for vpon these daies he must be present, vnlesse in case of sicknes, or absence out of the realme, for in these cases the king may summon his parlement by commission, and the same is of as good effect as if he were present in person: and as for anie other daies, he is at his choise and libertie to come or not to come to the parlement.

Also the king ought to propone to the parlement house in writing all such things & matters of charge, as for which he calleth the said parlement. And accordinglie as the same shall then by the consent of all estates be aduised, concluded, and agréed: so the king either hath to allow or disallow the same, for he can (of himselfe) neither adde nor diminish anie bill, but accept the same as it is presented vnto him from the estates of the parlement, or else altogither reiect it.

Also the king as he dooth prefix and assigne the daie and time when the parlement shall begin, so also he must assigne & appoint the time when the same shall be proroged or dissolued: which ought not to be as long as anie matters of charge, weight, or importance be in question, and the same not decided nor determined.

Of

Of the dignitie, power, and authoritie of the parlement, and of the orders of the same

THE parlement is the highest, cheefest, and greatest court that is or can be within the realme: for it consisteth of the whole realme, which is diuided into thrée estates, that is to wit, the king, the nobles, and the commons, euerie of which estates are subiect to all such orders as are concluded and established in parlement.

These thrée estates may ioinctlie and with one consent or agreement establish and enact anie lawes, orders, and statutes for the common wealth: but being diuided and one swaruing from the other, they can doo nothing. For the king, though he be the head, yet alone can not make anie law, nor yet the king and his lords onelie, nor yet the king and his commons alone, neither yet can the lords and the commons without the king doo anie thing of auaile. And yet neuerthelesse, if the king in due order haue summoned all his lords and barons, and they will not come, or if they come they will not yet appéere, or if they come and appéere, yet will not doo or yéeld to anything, then the king with the consent of his commons (who are represented by the knights, citizens, and burgesses) may ordeine and establish anie act or law, which are as good, sufficient, and effectuall, as if the lords had giuen their consents.

But of the contrarie, if the commons be summoned and will not come, or comming will not appéere, or appéering will not consent to doo anie thing, alleging some iust, weightie, and great cause, the king (in these cases) cannot with his lords deuise, make, or establish anie law, the reasons are these. When parlements were first begun & ordeined, there were no prelats or barons of the parlement, and the temporall lords were verie few or none, and then the king and his commons did make a full parlement, which authoritie was hitherto neuer abridged. Againe, euerie baron in parlement dooth represent but his owne person, and speaketh in the behalfe of himselfe alone.

But in the knights, citizens, and burgesses are represented the commons of the whole realme, and euerie of these giueth not consent onlie for himselfe, but for all those also for whome he is sent. And the king with the consent of his commons had euer a sufficient and full authoritie to make, ordeine, and establish good and wholesome lawes for the commonwealth of his realme. Wherefore the lords being lawfullie summoned, and yet refusing to come, sit, or consent in parlement, can not by their follie abridge the king and the commons of their lawfull proceeding in parlement.

The lords and commons in times past did sit all in one house, but for the auoiding of confusion they be now diuided into two seuerall houses, and yet neuerthelesse they are of like and equall authoritie, euerie person of either of the said houses being named and counted a péere of the realme (for the time of the parlement) that is to saie, equall: for *Par* is equall. And therefore the opinion, censure, and iudgement of a meane burgesse, is of as great auaile as is the best lords, no regard being had to the partie who speaketh, but the matter that is spoken.

They be also called péers, as it were fathers, for *Pier* is a father, by which is meant that all such as be of the parlement should be ancient, graue, wise, lerned, and expert men of the land: for such were the senators of Rome, and called *Patres conscripti*, for the wisedome and care that was in them in gouerning of the commonwealth. They are also called counsellors, because they are assembled and called to the parlement for their aduise and good councell, in making and deuising of such good orders and lawes as may be for the commonwealth.

They therefore which make choise of knights, citizens and burgesses, ought to be well aduised

aduised that they doo elect and choose such as being to be of that assemblie, and thereby equall with the great estates, should be graue, ancient, wise, learned, expert and carefull men for their commonwealth, and who (as faithfull and trustie councellors) should doo that which should turne and be for the best commoditie of the commonwealth, otherwise they doo great iniurie to their prince and commonwealth.

Also euerie person of the parlement, during the times of the parlement, and at his comming and going from the same, is frée from all troubles, arrests and molestations. no action or sute taking effect which during that time is begun, entred, or commensed against him, in what court so euer the same be, except in causes of treason, murther, and fellonie, and except also executions in law, awarded and granted before the beginning of the parlement.

Also euerie person hauing voices in parlement, hath free libertie of speach to speake his mind, opinion, and iudgement, to anie matter proponed, or of himselfe to propone anie matter for the commoditie of the prince and of the commonwealth: but hauing once spoken to anie bill, he may speake no more for that time.

Also euerie person once elected & chosen a knight, citizen or burgesse and returned, cannot be dismissed out of that house, but being admitted, shall haue his place and voice there, if he be a laieman. But if by error a man of the cleargie be chosen, then he ought and shall be dismissed, also if he be excommunicated, outlawed, or infamous.

Also euerie one of these houses ought to be incorrupt, no briber nor taker of anie rewards, gifts or monie, either for deuising of anie bill, or for speaking of his mind, but to doo all things vprightlie, and in such sort as best is for the king and commonwealth.

Also euerie one ought to be of a quiet, honest and gentle behauiour, none taunting, checking, or misusing an other in anie vnséemelie words or deeds: but all affections set apart, to doo and indeuour in wisedome, sobrietie and knowledge, that which that place requireth.

Also if anie one doo offend or misbehaue himselfe, he is to be corrected and punished by the aduise and order of the residue of the house.

Also all the prisons, wards, gailes, within the realme and the kéepers of the same are at the commandement of the parlement, for the custodie and safekeeping or punishment of all and euerie such prisoners, as shall be sent to anie of them by the said parlement houses, or anie of them: howbeit most commonlie the tower of London is the prison which is most vsed.

Also if anie one of the parlement house is serued, sued, arrested, or attached by anie writ, attachment, or minister of the Kings bench, Common plees, Chancerie, or what court so euer within this realme: the partie so troubled and making complaint thereof to the parlement house: then foorthwith a sargeant at armes is sent to the said court, not onelie aduertising that the partie so molested is one of the parlement house, but also inhibiting and commanding the officers of the said court to call in the said processe, and not to deale anie further against the said partie: for the parlement being the hiest court, all other courts as inferior yéeld and giue place to the same.

Also as euerie one of the parlement house is free for his owne person, for all maner of sutes to be commensed against him: so are also his seruants frée, and not to be troubled nor molested, but being troubled, haue the like remedie as the maister hath or may haue.

Also no manner of person, being not one of the parlement house, ought to enter or come within the house, as long as the sitting is there, vpon paine of imprisonment,

imprisonment, or such other punishment as by the house shall be ordered and adiudged.

Also euerie person of the parlement ought to kéepe secret, and not to disclose the secrets and things spoken and doone in the parlement house, to anie manner of person, vnlesse he be one of the same house, vpon paine to be sequestred out of the house, or otherwise punished, as by the order of the house shall be appointed.

Also none of the parlement house ought to depart from the parlement, without speciall leaue obteined of the speaker of the house, and the same his licence be also recorded.

Also no person, being not of the parlement house, ought to come into the same, during the time of the sitting: so euerie one comming into the same oweth a dutie and a reuerence, to be giuen when he entreth and commeth in.

If a baron or a lord come and enter into the higher house, he ought to doo his obeisance before the cloth of estate, and so to take his place.

Also when he speaketh, he must stand bareheaded, and speake his mind plainlie, sensiblie, & in decent order.

If anie come in message or be sent for to the higher house, they must staie at the inner doore vntill they be called in, and then being entred, must first make their obeisance: which doone, to go to the lower end of the house, and there to staie vntill they be called: and being called, they must first make one lowe courtesie and obeisance, and going forwards, must in the middle waie make one other lowe courtesie, and then being come foorth to the barre, must make the third courtesie, the like must be doone at the departure.

Also when anie knight, citizen or burgesse dooth enter and come into the lower house, he must make his dutifull and humble obeisance at his entrie in: and then take his place. And you shall vnderstand, that as euerie such person ought to be graue, wise, and expert, so ought he to shew himselfe in his apparell. For in time past, none of the councellors of the parlement came otherwise than in his gowne, and not armed nor girded with weapon. For the parlement house is a place for wise, graue, and good men, to consult, debate, and aduise, how to make lawes and orders for the commonwealth, and not to be armed as men readie to fight, or to trie matters by the sword. And albeit the writ for the election of the knights haue expresse words to choose such for knights as be girded with the sword, yet it is not meant thereby that they should come and sit armed: but be such as be skilfull in feats of armes, and besides their good aduises can well serue in martiall affaires. And thus the Romane senators vsed, who being men of great knowledge and experience, as well in martiall affaires, as in politike causes, sat alwaies in the senat house and places of councell in their gownes and long robes. The like also was alwaies and hath béene the order in the parlements of this realme, as long as the ancient lawes, the old customes and good orders thereof were kept and obserued.

Also if anie other person or persons, either in message or being sent for, doo come: he ought to be brought in by the sergeant, and at the first entring must (following the sergeant) make one lowe obeisance, and being past in the middle waie, must make one other, and when he is come before the speaker, he must make the third, and then do his message, the like order he must kéepe in his returne. But if he doo come alone, or with his learned councell, to plead anie matter, or to answer to anie obiection: he shall enter, and go no further than to the bar within the doore, and there to doo his three obeisances.

Also when anie bill is committed, the committées haue not authoritie to conclude, but onelie to order, reforme, examine, and amend the thing committed vnto them, and

and of their doings they must giue report to the house againe, by whome the bill is to be considered

Also euerie bill, which is brought into the house, must be read three seuerall times, and vpon thrée seuerall daies.

Also euerie bill, which vpon anie reading is committed and returned againe, ought to haue his thrée readings, vnles the committées haue not altered the bill in anie substance or forme, but onelie in certeine words

Also when anie bill vpon reading is altogither by one consent reiected, or by voices after the third reading ouerthrown, it ought not to be brought anie more to be read, during the sessions of parlement.

Also if anie man doo speake vnto a bill, and be out of his matter, he ought to be put in remembrance of the matter by the speaker onelie and by none other, and be willed to come to the matter

Also whensoeuer anie person dooth speake to anie bill, he ought to stand vp, and to be bareheaded, and then with all reuerence, grauitie, and séemelie spéech to declare his mind But whensoeuer anie bill shall be tried either for allowances, or to be reiected then euerie one ought to sit, bicause he is then as a iudge

Also euerie knight, citizen, and burgesse, before he doo enter into the parlement, and take his place there, ought to be sworne and to take his oth, acknowledging the king to be the supreme and onelie gouernour of all the estates within this realme, as also to renounce all forren potentates.

The order of the beginning and ending of the parlement

ON the first daie of the summons for the parlement, the king in proper person (vnlesse he be sicke or absent out of the realme) being appareled in his roiall and parlement robes, ought to be conducted and brought by all his barons of the cleargie and laitie, and the commons summoned to the parlement, vnto the church, where ought a sermon to be made by some archbishop, bishop, or some other famous learned man The sermon ended, he must in like order be brought to the higher house of parlement, and there to take his seat vnder the cloth of estate: likewise euerie lord and baron (in his degrée) ought to take his place

This doone, the lord chancellor, or he whom the king appointeth to be the speaker of that house, maketh his oration to the whole assemblie, declaring the causes whie and wherefore that parlement is called and summoned, exhorting and persuading euerie man to doo his best indeuour in all such matters as shall be in the said parlement proponed, as shall be most expedient for the glorie of God, the honor of the king, and the commonwealth of the whole realme Then he directeth his talke vnto the knights, citizens, and burgesses, aduertising them that the kings pleasure is, that they doo repaire to their house, and there according to the old and ancient custome, doo choose and elect some one, wise, graue, and learned man among themselues to be speaker for them, and giueth them a daie when they shall present him to the king And these things thus doone, the king ariseth, and euerie man departeth This is accounted for the first daie of the parlement

The second or third daie after, when the speaker is to be presented the king with all his nobles (in like order as before) doo assemble againe in the higher house, and then come vp all the commons of the lower house, and then and there doo present their speaker vnto the king. The speaker foorthwith maketh his dutifull obeisances, beginneth and maketh his oration before the king, and prosecuteth such matters as occasion serueth, and as is before recited in the office of the speaker, and this doone, euerie man departeth. And this is accounted for the beginning of the parlement, for before the speaker be presented, and these things orderlie doone, there can no bils be put in, nor matters be intreated of.

Lastlie, when all matters of weight be discussed, ended, and determined, the king commandeth an end to be made. And that daie the king, his nobles, and commons doo againe assemble in the higher house in their robes, and in like order as is before recited, where the speaker maketh his oration, and is answered by the lord chancellor or speaker of the higher house. Then all the bils concluded and past in both houses, that is to saie, in the higher house of the lords, and in the lower house of the commons, are there read by the titles: and then the king giueth his consent or dissent to euerie of them as he thinketh good. And when the titles of all the bils are read, the lord chancellor or lord speaker, by the kings commandement, pronounceth the parlement to be proroged or cleane dissolued. And this is called the last daie or the end of the parlement, and euerie man is at libertie to depart homewards.

The mondaie following, sir Christopher Barnewell and his complices, hauing better considered of themselues, were quiet and contented, and the parlement begun with some troubles had his continuance and end with better successe. In the time of this parlement, and after the same, sundrie grieuous complaints were exhibited to the lord deputie and councell by the late wife of the deceased baron of Dunboin, Mac Birin Arra, Oliuer Fitzgirald, sir William Occuell, and diuerse others the quéenes good subiects, against sir Edmund Butler and his brethren, for sundrie routs and riots, spoiles and outrages which they were charged to haue doone vpon hir maiesties subiects. Wherevpon first letters and then commissioners were sent in to the counties of Kilkennie and Tipporarie for the hearing and redressing thereof: but they returned without dooing of anie thing. For sir Edmund, conceiuing some hard dealings to be meant toward him by the lord deputie, and minding to stand vpon his defense and gard, did not appéere before the said commissioners, but both he and his brethren combined themselues with Iames Fitzmoris Odesmond, Mac Artie More, Mac Donagh, and the seneschall of Imokilie and others of Mounster, who before (and vnwitting the Butlers) had sent the vsurped bishops of Cashell and Emelie togither with the yoongest brother of the erle of Desmond vnto the pope & to the king of Spaine, for reformation of the popish religion, & for fréeing the land from the possession of hir maiestie and of the imperiall crowne. Which mater in the end brake out into an open and actuall rebellion, and the lord deputie by proclamation published them all to be traitors, and against whom he prepared an hosting. But before the same was fullie prepared, he sent his letters and commandement vnto sir Peter Carew knight then being at Leighlin, to enter into the action of warres against sir Edmund Butler, who being accompanied with capteine Gilbert, capteine Malbie, capteine Basnet, and others, latelie sent vnto him from the lord deputie, followed his commandement, and first assaulted the castell of Cloughgrenan in the Dullogh belonging to sir Edmund Butler, and tooke it, and gaue the spoile vnto the souldiers.

Commissioners sent to heare the cōplaints made against the Butlers.

The noblemen and gentlemen in Mounster sent their messengers to the pope.

The noblemen & gentlemen in Mounster proclamed traitors. Sir Peter Carew is cōmanded to serue against the Butlers.

Cloughgrenan taken.

From thense they remooued to Kilkennie towne, where they laie for a time, where a man of the earle of Ormonds, espieng vpon a certeine daie sir Peter Carew to be walking in the garden of the castell of Kilkennie alone, he charged his péece, and leueled the same vnto the said Peter Carew, and minded to haue discharged it vpon him out of a window in the castell. At which verie instant a chapleine of the said earls & his steward, comming by him, & suspecting some euill thing towards, turned vp the mouth of the péece, which therewith was discharged, and so no bodie hurt, and vnderstanding the thing was meant against sir Peter Carew, blamed the fellow, and

Sir Peter Carew in danger to haue beene killed.

and for a time thrust him out of the house. Whilest these capteins laie at Kilkennie, it was aduertised vnto them, that a great companie of the rebels were incamped about thrée miles out of the towne, & were there marching in verie good order. Whereupon sir Peter Carew, being then the generall, assembled all the capteins, and taking their aduise what was best to be doone, they concluded that Henrie Dauels a verie honest and a valiant English gentleman, who had serued long in that countrie, and was verie well acquainted, especiallie in those parts, for he had maried his wife out of that towne, and him they sent out to discouer the matter, who about thrée miles off had the view, and espied a great companie of about two thousand, resting vpon a little hill in the middle of a plaine, being all armed and marching in battell araie. When he returned with this report, then sir Peter Carew appointed the voward to capteine Gilbert, who togither with Henrie Dauels and twelue other persons of his companie galloped before the rest, and finding as it was before aduertised, gaue the charge. The residue of the companie followed with the like hast vnder sir Peter Carew, and then capteine Malbie, and capteine Basenet, séeing and assured that all things were cleere behind them, followed so néere, that all the companie euen as it were at one instant gaue the like charge, where they slue foure hundred Gallowglasses at the least, besides others. The residue of the companie were fled into the mounteins fast by, and none or few escaped but the horsemen and Kerns. And of hir maiesties side no one man slaine, but a man of capteine Malbies was hurt.

Henrie Dauels sent to discouer the enimie.

Sir Peter Carew and the English capteins giueth charge vpon the rebels & haue the victorie.

Sir Peter Carew, hauing had and obteined this victorie, and marching in good order, did returne with all his companie to the towne of Kilkennie, euerie capteine and souldier carieng two Gallowglasses axes in his hand, but left the spoile to their followers. Sir Edmund Butler at this instant was not in the campe, but was at his vncles house at dinner. The townesmen of Kilkennie were verie sorie for this the slaughter of so manie men. And yet neuerthelesse not long after, Iames Fitzmoris came to this towne, and besieged it, but the towne being well garonised with certeine soldiers, & they themselues well appointed, did so carefullie and narowlie looke to themselues, that they defended and kept the towne, notwithstanding all his force. But yet the countrie and other small townes did not so escape, for the countie of Waterford, and the lord Powre, the countie of Dublin, and all the countrie were spoiled, preied, and ouerrun, and among all others the old Fulco Quimerford a gentleman, of long time seruant to thrée earles of Ormond, was robbed in his house at Callon of two thousand pounds, in monie, plate, and houshold stuffe, besides his corne and cattell. When they had taken their pleasure in this countrie, they went to the countie of Wexford, which thing had not lightlie béene séene before, and at a faire kept there at Enescorth, there the souldiers committed most horrible outrages, lamentable slaughters, filthie rapes, and defloures of yoong women, abusing mens wiues, spoiling the towne, & slaughtering of the men, and such as did escape the sword were caried captiues & prisoners. From hense they went into Osserie and into the quéenes countie, and spoiled the countrie, burned townes and villages, murthered the people and then they met with the earle of Clancare, and Iames Fitzmoris Odesmond, with whom they then combined, and agreed to cause Tirlough Lennough to procure in the Scots, they sent new messengers to the pope, and to the king of Spaine. Finallie, nothing was left vndoone, which might anie waies tend to the subuersion of hir maiesties imperiall crowne of Ireland, and to discharge that land from all Englishmen and English gouernement, and by these means (the English pale and the good cities & townes excepted) the most part, if not the whole land, was imbrued & infected with this rebellion.

Iames Fitzmoris besiegeth Kilkennie.

Fulco Quimerford spoiled & robbed.

A wicked massacre at Enescorth.

A wicked conspiracie and combining of the traitors.

The earle of Ormond himselfe, a man of great honour and nobilitie, was all this

time

time in England but from time to time was aduertised of the troublesome state in that land: and whereof no little detriment redounded to his lordship, by reason that a great and most part of all his lordships throughout that land were spoiled and wasted, which did not so much gréeue him as the follies of his brethren For great were his griefs, & verie much was he vnquieted therewith for when he bethought himselfe of his brethren, nature mooued him, and reason persuaded him, that no such outragious parts could proceed from them, which in anie waies should either concerne hir maiestie, or the dishonour of him and his house, which hitherto hath beéne alwaies found sound and true Wherefore, when he heard of anie matter against them herein, he would plead their innocencies, and defend their causes, vntill such time as by credible letters, aduertisements, and reports, he saw apparant matter and manifest proofes of the contrarie Which reports albeit they grieued him verie much, yet (as I said) nothing greeued him more, than their disloialtie and breach of dutie against hir maiestie, and the dishonour of his owne house Wherefore to acquite himselfe and his dutie towards hir highnes he offereth to serue against them & others, by the sword, or by some other means, to reconcil and reclaime them

The earle of Ormonds lands spoiled

The good affection of the earle of Ormond to his brethren

The earle of Ormond offereth to serue against his brethren

Whervpon hir maiestie, standing assured of his fidelitie, and hauing a speciall trust in him, sent him ouer into Ireland, who arriued at Wexford the fouretéenth of August 1569, at that verie time when that wicked massaker was committed and doone at the faire at Innescorth Immediatlie vpon his landing, he aduertiseth vnto the lord deputie his comming, and with all conuenient spéed maketh his repaire vnto him, who then was incamped and laie néere Limerike and then and there offereth his seruice with all his best power, and brought with him his brother Edmund Butler, who in the open view and sight of the whole campe did yeeld and submit himselfe simplie to hir maiesties mercie, confessing his follie and crauing pardon. And then was he deliuered to the earle his brother vpon his bonds, to bée foorth comming before the said lord deputie at his comming to Dublin and also promised to doo the like with his two other brothers, which he did vpon the sixtéenth of October 1569 At which time when they all appeared before the lord deputie and councell, they were charged with manie and sundrie things but sir Edmund Butler for himselfe alledged, that others were the causers whie he did that which he did And for himselfe he alledged, first that the lord deputie did not brooke nor like him, for he could haue no iustice at his hands, nor against sir Peter Carew, who clamed and had entered vpon some part of his lands, nor yet against any other person Then that the said lord deputie had threatned him that he would lie in his skirts, and would pull downe his loftie lookes. Thirdlie, that the said lord deputie should go about to kill all the Butlers in Ireland, and would then go into England, and there would doo manie things

The earle of Ormond arriueth at Wexford

The earle repaireth to the lord deputie

Edmund Butler submitteth himselfe

Sir Edmund Butlers excuses

When all these things were heard at full, and nothing in proofe falling out as was auouched, the thrée brethren were committed to ward into the castell of Dublin, out of which sir Edmund escaped, and made breach neuerthelesse the earle brought him againe. And vpon the last of Februarie 1569 he brought also his two other brethren, for whome he had vndertaken, and presented them before the lord deputie and councell, where the matter being heard at large, the councell conferred hereof among themselues, and in the end they all the thrée brethren were againe called before the lord deputie and councell, and then and there knéeling vpon their knées, did confesse their follies, and submitted themselues in all dutifulnesse and simplicitie to the quéens mercie where the earle not onlie naturallie as a brother made humble petition for them but grauelie as a father recited their errors, reprooued them of their outrages, and counselled them to their duties and in the end condescended in the due consideration of hir maiesties roiall estate. And therevpon they were

1569

The loue and grauitie of the earle of Ormond to his brethren were committed to safe kéeping within hir maiesties castell of Dublin, at hir highnesse disposition, and not long after vpon hope of amendment were pardoned. But to the matter againe.

The lord deputie followed his first begun hosting, who when he was incamped néere Clonmell, where it was thought he should haue béene fought withall, he wrote to the maior and his brethren of the citie of Waterford, to send vnto him the assistance of a few souldiers onelie for thrée daies, who did verie insolentlie and arrogantlie returne an answer by waie of disputing their liberties with hir maiesties prerogatiue, and so sent him no aid at all. Wherein the more they shewed their affection to the rebels, the more was their ingratitude & disloialtie to hir highnesse, the reward whereof they felt in the end. The camp at this time being within half a mile of Clonmell, the lord deputie before his dislodging from thense went into the towne, where the soueraigne and his brethren receiued him with all the honour they could, and gaue him a banket in their towne-house, where, vnto them & the whole multitude then present, he made a verie eloquent speach, teaching them the dutifulnesse and obedience of a subiect, and the great inconuenience which groweth by the contrarie to all commonwealths, and each member of the same: and therefore laieng before them their present estate for example, did mooue and persuade them to hold fast the dutie & obedience which they ought to hir maiestie, and not to be dismaid at the doings of the rebels and disobedient: who though for a time they had their will and pleasure, yet God, in whose hand is the heart of the prince, and vnder whome all kings and princes doo rule, hath béene alwaies, is, and will be, a swift reuenger against them for the same: euen as of the contrarie he sendeth his manifold blessings of peace, wealth and prosperitie to the obedient and dutifull subiect. And so hauing vsed sundrie and notable sentences and examples to this effect, he left them and returned to his campe.

The citie of Waterforus standing vpon their liberties refuse to send aid to the lord deputie.

The lord deputie went into Clonmell & setteth verie good speaches vnto them

And from thense he remooued and marched towards Cashell, which lieth in the countie of Tipporarie, néere vnto which place Edmund Butler had warded a castell: who when he saw the armie approching, he set all the out houses on fire, and prepared themselues to defend the pile. The lord deputie taking the same as a defiance, approched therevnto and besieged it: and whilest the assault was in preparing, it was yéelded by composition, and after restored to one Cantrell the owner thereof. From thense by iourneies he marched and went to Corke, being met in the waie by the vicounties of Roch and Barrie, and by sir Corman Mac Teege: and being aduertised that Fitzedmund seneschall of Imokillie, a principall rebell, and combined with Iames Fitzmorris, had spoiled and preied the whole countrie: and had also warded and vittelled his castell of Barie martyr, which by his tenure he was of himselfe bound to mainteine and defend it, he marched thither and laid siege to the same, and in the end tooke it full of vittels. But the seneschall in the dead of the night fled out through a hole of the house in a bog, and there escaped.

Barie martyr a castell of the seneschals besieged and taken.

The seneschall escapeth out of his castell

The spoile was giuen to the souldiers, & the castell with a gard of twentie men was giuen to Iasper Horseie, & so he returned to Corke, and from thense he tooke iourneie to Kilmallocke, and finding that place most necessarie for a fort, he appointed and named Humfreie Gilbert hir maiesties seruant to be coronell, and besides his owne band of an hundred horssemen he appointed foure hundred footmen, and certeine Kernes there to remaine. And there he did knit and compone vnto him by oth, and vnder good pledges, the vicounties of Roch and Dessis, with the lord Powre, the lord Courcie, sir Corman Mac Téege, sir Donogh Clancartie, and Barrie Oge, and the most part of the fréeholders in the counties of Limerike and Corke. And this doone he passed by iourneies to Limerike, and from thense he went to Gallewaie, and there established a president and a councell, and placed sir Edward Fitton to be lord president,

Humfreie Gilbert made coronell of Mounster.

Sir Edward Fitton made president of Connagh.

sident, the earles of Thomond and Clanricard, and all the noble men & septs of gentlemen of that prouince yéelding to the same.

Capteine Gilberts good seruice

Thense he marched to Athlon, taking in the waie the castell of Rosocomen, which he left with the ward of twentie horssemen, to Thomas le Strange, and then dismissed the armie, but himselfe by iourneies trauelled and came to Dublin, and there remained Capteine Gilbert in the meane time, hauing a speciall respect and regard to his charge, his valiancie and courage was such, and his good hap so well answering his woorthie and forward attempts, that he in short time broke the hearts, and appalled the courages of all the rebels in Mounster, and no rebell knowne left in effect, which dare to withstand and make anie resistance against him. And to such an obedience he brought that countrie, that none did or would refuse to come vnto him, if he were sent for but by a horsse boy: for all yéelded vnto him, some by putting in recognisances, & some by giuing of pledges, and all in séeking mercie and pardon.

The earle of Clancare submitteth himselfe to capteine Gilbert

And that proud earle of Clancare, which in his glorie not long before vsurped this name to be king of Mounster, euen he now, and Mac Donagh his chiefe follower, went to Limerike vnto him, and there falling vpon their knées acknowledged their treasons, and most humblie desired hir maiesties pardon: and offered to put in his eldest sonne, and the sonnes of his chiefest fréeholders for pledges and hostages.

The good seruice of sir Edward Fitton lord president of Connagh

Likewise the president of Connagh in such wisedome, courage, & vprightnesse, directed his gouernement, that he was obeied of all the whole people in that prouince, as well the nobilitie as the commons. The wicked he spareth not, but being found faultie either in open sessions, or by martiall inquisition, he causeth to be executed: and by these meanes hauing rid awaie the most notable offendors and their fosterers, the whole prouince rested in good quietnesse and in dutifull obedience to hir maiestie and hir lawes.

The Cauenaghs submissions

The Cauenaghs, the ancient enimies to the English gouernement, and who in the rebellion were conioined with the Butlers: these bordering vpon the frontiers appointed to sir Peter Carew, were so by him chased and persecuted, that finding no place of rest or quietnesse, he hath brought them to submit themselues simplie to hir maiesties mercie, and haue put in their pledges to abide such orders and conditions as shall be laid vpon them.

Turlogh shot through with two bullets

Turlogh Lennogh in Vlster, being at supper with his now wife, aunt to the earle of Argile, was shot through the bodie with two pellets out of a caliuer, by a iester or rimer of the Donloghs. Wherevpon the Scots whome he reteined were in a maze, and the countrie standing vpon the election of a new capteine: howbeit, he was in hope of recouerie. And thus after long troubles was the state of the whole realme recouered to quietnesse. Wherevpon capteine Gilbert, when he had setled Mounster in outward appéerance in a most perfect quietnesse, and brought it to good conformitie: he made his repaire to Dublin to the lord deputie, where he aduertised and recounted all his doings at full.

And hauing matters of great importance in England, he desired licence to depart ouer: whome the said deputie did not onelie most courteouslie receiue, but also most thankefullie did accept his good seruice, and in some part of recompense, vpon New-

Drogheda

Capteine Gilbert dubbed knight

yeares daie in the church at Drogheda, he did bestow vpon him the order of knighthood, which he well deserued, and at his departure gaue him letters of credit to hir highnesse, and to the lords of the councell. And now by the waie, if without offense a man maie, after the maner of Cambrensis in his historie, and after the vsage of noble gouernors and capteins in other realmes, who for the increase of vertue, and incouraging of woorthie persons, doo attribute to such as doo deserue well their due praises & commendations, I hope it shall not be offensiue to the reader, nor impertinent to the historie, to set downe somewhat of much, what maie be said of these two woorthie personages,

personages, sir Peter Carew, and sir Humfreie Gilbert: both which were of one countrie and birth, borne in the countie of Deuon, and of néere bloud, kinred, and consanguinitie.

Sir Humfreie Gilbert, he was a second brother, and borne of a great parentage, whose ancestors came and descended from the earle of Cornewall, a man of a higher stature than of the common sort, & of complexion cholerike, from his childhood of a verie pregnant wit and good disposition: his father died leauing him verie yoong, and he conceiuing some great good thing to come of his towardnesse, prouided some portion of liuing to mainteine and kéepe him to schoole. And after his death, his mother, being no lesse carefull of him, did cause him to be sent to schoole to Eton college: from thense, after he had profited in the elements & principall points of grammar, he was sent to Oxford, & did there prosper & increase verie well in learning and knowledge. And being (as his friends thought) verie well furnished, they would haue put him to the ins of court. But an aunt of his, named mistres Katharine Ashleie, who was attendant to the queenes maiestie, after that she saw the yoong gentleman, and had had some conference with him, she fell in such liking with him, that she preferred him vnto hir maiesties seruice: and such was his countenance, forwardnesse, and behauiour, that hir maiestie had a speciall good liking of him, and verie oftentimes would familiarlie discourse and conferre with him in matters of learning. After a few yeares spent in the court, he passed ouer into Ireland, being commended by hir highnesse to sir Henrie Sidneie then lord deputie: who gaue him interteinement, and made him a capteine ouer an hundred horssemen: wherein he so well acquited himselfe, that he was also made coronell of Mounster, and had appointed vnto him, besides his owne band of one hundred horssemen, foure hundred footemen, besides such Geraldines as Thomas of Desmond, brother to the erle of Desmond had procured, & vpon his oth of loialtie and pledges had promised his faithfull seruice. *The description of sir Humfreie Gilbert, and his descent.*

And albeit he were but yoong of yeares, which might séeme to hinder his credit: yet such was his deuout mind to serue hir maiestie, and so effectuallie to his great praise he followed the same; that with manie good gifts and excellent vertues he so supplied euen as much as manie men of elder yeares & greater experience did not commonlie atteine vnto. For in seruice vpon the enimie he was as valiant and couragious as no man more, and so good was his hap to answer the same: for he alwaies for the most part daunted the enimie, and appalled their courage, as did appéere in the ouerthrow giuen néere Kilkennie in the Butlers warres, when he with twelue persons gaue the onset vpon a thousand men, of which six hundred were armed Gallowglasses, who then were ouerthrowne: and likewise in Mounster, which was altogither vp in rebellion, and he coronell, did not onelie in martiall affaires shew himselfe most valiant, and in short time reduced the whole troope of the rebels, and the proudest of them to obedience, hauing vnder him but fiue hundred against sundrie thousands, and inforced that proud earle of Clancart to follow him to Limerike, and there humblie vpon his knees to aske pardon and mercie: but also, after that he had subdued and ouercome them, did most vprightlie order and direct his gouernement, and with all indifferencie would heare, decide, and determine the complaints & griefs, and compound all the causes of euerie sutor. Which was so rare a thing in one of his yeares, as scarse was credible, had not eiewitnesses and dailie experience prooued and iustified the same. *The valiantnes in seruice, and the wisedome in gouernement of sir Humfreie Gilbert.*

After that he had established peace and tranquillitie in that countrie, he went to Dublin: where when he had recounted all his seruices, and the good successe thereof, and in what quiet state he had left the countrie, he desired leaue to passe ouer into England, for and about certeine matters of great importance, which he had to follow, which he did

he did obteine: as also in reward of his seruice, and for his good deserts he (as is before said) was honored and dubbed a knight, and with letters in his praise and commendation to hir maiestie, and the lords of the councell, he departed. Assoone as he had presented himselfe before hir highnesse, hir good countenance and fauour, in respect of his good seruice to hir maiestie was increased and doubled, and he speciallie aboue all others magnified and well accepted. Not long after, he was maried to a yoong gentlewoman, and an inheritrix: and thensefoorth he gaue himselfe to studies perteining to the state of gouernement, and to nauigations. He had an excellent and readie wit, and therewith a toong at libertie to vtter what he thought. Which being adorned with learning and knowledge, he both did and could notablie discourse anie matter in question concerning either of these, as he made good proofe thereof, as well in familiar conference with the noble, wise, and learned, as also in the open assemblies of the parlements, both in England and in Ireland: in which he shewed the great value of knowledge, wisedome, and learning which was in him, and the great zeale he had to the commonwelth of his countrie. He had a great delight in the studie of cosmographie, and especiallie in nauigations, and finding out by his studies, certeine nations and vnknowne lands, which being found, might redound to the great benefit of his countrie: he made hir maiestie acquainted therewith, and obteined of hir a licence to make a nauigation, which he tooke in hand. But before he could compasse the same to effect, he was in a foule storme drowned at the seas. Onelie he of all his brethren had fiue sonnes and one daughter, children by their countenances giuing a hope of a good towardnesse. And albeit he in person be deceassed, yet in their visages, and in the memoriall of his great vertues, and a life well spent, he shall liue in fame immortall. Thus much without offense, and not altogither impertinent, concerning this gentleman, and now to the historie.

Sir Humfreie Gilbert is drowned.

Turlogh Lenough prepareth to inuade the English pale.

Turlogh Lenough thinking to inuade vpon the English pale, for the bending of the lord deputies force against him, he was repressed, and driuen to kéepe himselfe within his owne limits, and by that meanes brought to disperse his power: for being not able to paie and satisfie the Scots, the one was wearie of the other: and his wife and he not agréeing, they were vpon a point to sunder. The earle of Thomond reuolteth from his due obedience, and becommeth a rebell: whome the earle of Ormond so hardlie pursued, that he draue him out of that land, and he fled into France, and from thense into England. For the discouerie of whose treasons and rebellions to hir maiestie & to the lords of the councell, one Rafe Rockeleie chiefe iustice of Connaugh was sent into England, where after long sute made for his submission, he was sent backe into Ireland, there to receiue according to his deserts: hir maiesties pleasure yet being such, that if he were not found culpable of treason against the state, that he should be spared from iudgement of death.

The earle of Thomond revolteth.

The earle of Ormond followeth the earle of Thomond, and driueth him out of the land.

Lucas Dillon made chiefe baron.

This yéere the queenes maiestie, considering the good seruice of Lucas Dillon hir generall attorneie in Ireland, was vpon the death of baron Bath made chéefe baron of the exchecker there, & capteine Piers for his good seruice at Knockfergus was liberallie considered and countenanced by hir maiestie. And likewise after manie motions, sutes, and requests made to hir maiestie for a president and councell to be established in Mounster, and the same once determined and appointed: but by the sicknesse and vnabilitie of sir Iohn Pollard, appointed to be the president, it was lingered and deferred, is now reuiued and renewed, and sir Iohn Perot knight was made lord president, and a councell of good assistants chosen, as also his diet houses, interteinment, and all other things necessarie ordered, assigned, and appointed. This knight was borne in Penbrokeshire in Southwales, and one of great reuenues and worship, valiant, and of great magnanimitie, and so much the more meet to gouerne and tame so faithlesse and vnrulie a people, as ouer whome he was now made ruler.

Sir Iohn Perot appointed to be lord president of Mounster.

They

They heard no sooner of his comming, but as a sort of waspes they fling out, and reuolting from their former fened obedience, became open rebelles and traitors vnder Iames Fitzmoris an archtraitor, and as dogs they returne to their vomit, and as swine to their durt and puddles. The rebelling of Mounster against the president.

And here may you sée the nature and disposition of this wicked, effrenated, barbarous, and vnfaithfull nation, who (as Cambrensis writeth of them) they are a wicked and peruerse generation, constant alwaies in that they be alwaies inconstant, faithfull in that they be alwaies vnfaithfull, and trustie in that they be alwaies trecherous and vntrustie. They doo nothing but imagin mischeefe, & haue no delite in anie good thing. They are alwaies working wickednes against the good, and such as be quiet in the land. Their mouths are full of vnrighteousnesse, and their toongs speake nothing but cursednesse. Their feet swift to shed blood, & their hands imbrued in the blood of innocents. The waies of peace they know not, & in the paths of righteousnesse they walke not. God is not knowne in their land, neither is his name called rightlie vpon among them. Their quéene and soueraigne they obeie not, and hir gouernment they allow not, but as much as in them lieth doo resist hir imperiall estate, crowne, and dignitie. It was not much aboue a yeare past, that capteine Gilbert with the sword so persecuted them, and in iustice so executed them, that then they in all humblenesse submitted themselues, craued pardon, and swore to be for euer true and obedient: which, so long as he maistered and kept them vnder, so long they performed it; but the cat was no sooner gone, but the mise were at plaie; and he no sooner departed from them, but foorthwith they skipped out, and cast from themselues the obedience and dutifulnesse of true subiects. For such a peruerse nature they are of, that they will be no longer honest and obedient, than that they cannot be suffered to be rebelles. Such is their stubbornesse and pride, that with a continuall feare it must be brideled, and such is the hardnesse of their hearts, that with the rod it must be still chastised and subdued: for no longer feare, no longer obedience, and no longer than they be ruled with seueritie, no longer will they be dutifull and in subiection, but will be as they were before, false, trucebreakers & traitorous. Being not much vnlike to Mercurie called quicke siluer, which let it by art be neuer so much altered and transposed, yea and with fire consumed to ashes, yet let it but rest a while vntouched nor medled with, it will returne againe to his owne nature, and be the same as it was at the first. And euen so dailie experience teacheth it to be true in these people. For withdraw the sword, and forbeare correction, deale with them in courtesie, and intreat them gentlie, if they can take anie aduantage, they will surelie skip out: and as the dog to his vomit, and the sow to the durt & puddle they will returne to their old and former insolencie, rebellion, and disobedience. This is to be meant of the Irishrie and sauage people, who the further they are from the prince and court, the further from dutie and obedience, the more they are vnder their Obrian gouernment, the lesse dutifull to their naturall soueraigne and prince. But concerning the inhabitants in the English pale, and all cities and townes, the contrarie (God be praised) is dailie seene. The nature of the Irish men. The nature of quicke siluer.

Well, this worthie knight knowing that he should haue to doo with a sort of netles, whose nature is, that being handled gentlie, they will sting; but being hard crushed togither, they will doo no harme: euen so he began with them. The sword and the law he made to be the foundation of his gouernement, by the one he persecuted the rebell and disobedient, and by the other he ruled and gouerned in iustice and iudgement. Great troubles he had in both, but little he did preuaile in the latter, before he had ouercome the first: and therefore minding to chastise the rebelles, and to bring them to obedience, he followed and chased them from place to place: in the bogs he pursued them, in the thickets he followed them, in the plaines he fought with them, and The gouernment of sir Iohn Perot. His seruice against the rebelles.

in their castels and holds he beseeged them, and would neuer suffer them to be at rest and quietnesse, vntill he had tried and wearied them out, and at length inforced Iames [Iames Fitzmoris seeketh for peace and submitteth himselfe.] Fitzmoris and his complices to come vnto Kilmalocke vnto him, and there simplie to submit himselfe, and vpon his knees in the open sight of all the people to confesse his disloialties, and in all humble manner to craue mercie and pardon. Whome though vntill hir maiesties pleasure knowne he did forbeare, yet the residue he spared not, but after their deserts he executed in infinit numbers. And hauing thus rid the garden from these wéeds, and rooted vp the fields from these thornes, he entreth into the gouernement by order of law, and from place to place throughout all Mounster [The ciuill gouernement of sir Iohn Perot.] he trauelleth and kéepeth his sessions and courts, hearing euerie mans complaints, and redresseth their griefs, and in short time brought the same to such a quietnesse and peaceable estate, that whereas no man before could passe through the countrie, but was in danger to be murdered and robbed, and no man durst to turne his cattell into the fields without watch, and to keepe them in barnes in the night time: [The quietnes and safetie in Mounster.] now euerie man with a white sticke onelie in his hands, and with great treasures might and did trauell without feare or danger where he would (as the writer hereof by triall knew it to be true) and the white shéepe did kéepe the blacke, and all the beasts laie continuallie in the fields, without anie stealing or picking.

Now when he had thus quieted this prouince, and setled all things in good order, then he beginneth to reforme their maners in life and common conuersation and apparell, suffering no glibes nor like vsages of the Irishrie to be vsed among the men, nor the Egyptiacall rolles vpon womens heads to be worne. Whereat though the ladies and gentlewomen were somewhat greeued, yet they yéelded, and giuing the same ouer, [Sir Iohn Perots assistants.] did weare hats after the English manner. In this his seruice he had two verie good & notable assistants, the one concerning the martiall affaires, and the other for his [George Burchier his birth and seruices.] gouernement by the course and order of the law. Concerning the affaires martiall George Bourchier esquier was ioined with him in commission, and did him notable good seruice, he was the third sonne to Iohn earle of Bath, whose ancestors were descended from out of the loines of kings, and men of great honor and nobilitie, and they were no more noble of bloud than valiant, wise and prudent in all their actions, both in the seruices of chiualrie and matters of policies, and whereof the histories of England in manie places doo make mention and report. And this gentleman, hauing some motion of the valure and valiantnesse of his ancestors deriued and descended vpon him, was affected and giuen to all feats of chiualrie, and especiallie to the seruice in the warres, wherein he prooued a verie good souldior, and an expert capteine, both as an horsseman, and as a footeman, both which waies he serued, as the seruice and time required. If he serued vpon foot, he was apparelled in the manner of a Kerne and a foot souldior, and was so light of foot as no Kerne swifter: for he would pursue them in bogs, in thickets, in woods, in passes, and in streicts whatsoeuer, and neuer leaue them, vntill he did performe the charge and seruice committed vnto him. If he were to serue vpon his horssebacke, his dailie seruice can witnes sufficientlie how much, and how often he preuailed against the enimie, and appalled their courages, and with whome he would incounter if he might by anie meanes.

Notwithstanding, as couragious and circumspect as he was, that he would not be lightlie intrapped in the field, yet was he deceiued in the house. For vnder the colour of a parlée, and vpon a truce taken, he was inuited to a supper, and little think- [George Burchier taken prisoner.] ing that anie breach of the truce should be made, he went into the castell whereas he was bidden. But in his being there, he was taken prisoner, and handfasted, and so kept for a space, but yet not long after he was restored and set at libertie. Concerning his other assistant, [George Welsh a lawier, well learned, and vpright.] his name was George Welsh borne in Waterford, and a gentleman of an ancient familie, he was brought vp in learning, and was a student in the

innes

innes of court at London, and prospered verie well therein: and albeit his yeares were but yoong, yet his knowledge, grauitie, and sinceritie counteruailed the same with an ouerplus. In deciding of all matters he was vpright and iust, being not affectionated nor knowne to be corrupted for anie mans pleasure. In iudgement vpright, in iustice seuere, and without respect of persons would minister what the law had prescribed, he spared neither partie, nor would be affected to anie; by which meanes he did maruellous much good in that seruice, and happie was that gouernor that had so good a counsellor.

Immediatlie vpon the placing of this gouernement in Mounster, sir Henrie Sidneie had libertie and licence to returne ouer into England, and receiued hir maiesties letters dated the thirtéenth of December one thousand fiue hundred seuentie and one, 1571
& in the thirtéenth yeere of hir maiesties reigne, for the placing of sir William Fitzwilliams to be lord deputie in his place. Which when he had doone, he passed ouer the seas, and by iourneies came to the court. He was verie honorablie receiued, and by hir highnesse well commended, there being sundrie noblemen and gentlemen of the court, which met him before he came to Whitehall, where hir maiestie then laie, who (as time conuenient serued) did recount vnto hir the whole estate in all things of the realme of Ireland, which hir maiestie liked verie well.

Sir William Fitzwilliams made lord deputie.

But this sir John Perot president of Mounster continued still in his office, and there remained for certeine yeares vntill he was reuoked, which was too soone for that countrie. For neuer man was more fit gouernour for that effrenated and hardnecked people than was he, nor was that countrie euer in better estate for wealth, peace and obedience, than he in the time of his gouernement did reduce the same vnto. Happie was that prouince, and happie were those people, which being eaten out, consumed and deuoured with caterpillers, he had brought and reformed to a most happie, peaceable, and quiet estate, and he left it euen in the same maner. Which if it had béene continued by the like, to haue followed him in the gouernement, the same would so haue continued: but the want of the one was in short time the decaie of the other, and that reformed countrie brought to a most miserable estate, as by the consequence may appéere.

Sir William Fitzwilliams, hauing a speciall care and respect to his charge and office, disposeth all things in the best order he could by the aduise of the councell, and finding the state somewhat quiet, sauing Mounster, his care and studie was so to keepe and mainteine it. And he being a wise and a graue man, and of so great experience in that land, he draweth the plot of his gouernement into certeine speciall points and articles. First, that the religion established according to Gods holie word, should haue a frée passage through the whole land, and by euerie man aswell of the clergie as of the laitie to be receiued, imbraced and followed. Then that the common peace and quietnesse thorough out the whole land might and should be conserued, and all occasions of the breach thereof, and of all mutinies and diuisions to be cut off. Thirdlie, that hir maiesties great and excessiue charges to the consuming of hir treasure might be shortened, and hir reuenues well husbanded and looked vnto, according to hir sundrie commandements tofore giuen. Lastlie, that the lawes and iustice might haue their due course and be current thoroughout the whole land, and the iudges and officers should vprightlie minister iustice to each man according to his desert, and that all the souldiers should be kept in that discipline as to them apperteineth.

The points of sir William Fitzwilliams lord deputies gouernement.

Religion.

The common peace.

The sauing of expenses.

Lawes to be executed.

Souldiers to be kept in their discipline.

These considerations and such like, being ordered and established with the consent and aduise of the whole councell, and well liked of euerie good subiect, bicause the same was grounded vpon verie good reasons: yet it tooke not that effect as it was meant and wished it should. For that wicked race of the Irishrie, in whom was no zeale in religion, and lesse obedience to hir maiestie, and least care to liue in an honest conuersation and common societie, but alwaies watching the best opportunitie and time to breake out into their woonted outrages, robberies, and rebellions: these (I saie) in sundrie places begin to plaie their pagents. The first was Brian Mac Kahir of Knocking in the countie of Caterlough Cauenagh, who vpon certeine wrongs which he complained he had receiued by one Robert Browne of Malrenkam, he tyrannized ouer the whole countrie, committed manie outrages and spoiles, preied the countrie, & burned sundrie towns. Likewise the gentlemen of the countie of Wexford, and namelie sir Nicholas Deuereux knight, being grieued with the death of Robert Browne, who was his nephue, being his sisters sonne, were as vnquiet on their parts, and all rose vp in armour against Brian Mac Kahir, and each one with all the forces they could make did resist the other, so that all the whole countrie was thereby in a verie troublesome state, and no end could be had before they had tried it with the sword. For the Wexford men following their matters verie egerlie, and being in a great companie well appointed, they sought out Brian Mac Kahir, and gaue the onset vpon him, but he so watched the matter, and tooke them at that aduantage, that although he and his companie were but small in respect of the others, yet he gaue them the foile and ouerthrow, and killed the most principall gentlemen of that shire about or aboue thirtie persons.

Brian Mac Kahir his warres in Wexford

Brian Mac Kahir hath the victorie of the Wexford men

In this companie was an English gentleman, who after was in great credit & office among them, and he in danger to haue drunken of the same cup, was driuen to leape vp on horssebacke behind another man, and so escaped, or else he had neuer béene seneschall of that prouince. After this fight, though the grudge were not forgotten nor a reuenge vnsought, yet by little and little it quailed. About two yeares after, Brian Mac Kahir made humble sutes to the lord deputie for his pardon, and submitted himselfe to his lordships deuotion, confessing in writing his foule disorders and outrages, and yet firmlie auouching that the quarell did not begin by him nor by his meanes: his submission was such and in so humble sort, as that he obteined the same. And according to his promise then made, he did thenseforth vse and behaue himselfe most dutifullie, and liued in a verie good order. This Brian was a Cauenaugh, and the sonne of Charels, the sonne of Arthur, which Arthur was by king Henrie the eight made a baron for terme of his life: for he was a man of great power within the counties of Wexford & Catherlough. And this Brian Mac Kahir Mac Arthur was a yoonger sonne to Charels, but the chiefest for valiantnesse, magnanimitie and wisedome, and none of all the sept of the Cauenaughs, though they were manie and valiant men, to be compared vnto him euerie waie, and vnto whom they all would giue place.

Thomas Masterson

Brian Mac Kahir his submission

Brian Mac Kahir what he was

Now he being assured of them, and also being alied by marriage vnto Hewen Mac Shane, whose daughter he married, he was also assured of the Obrinnes and of the Omoroughs, & so a man of great strength and abilitie. He became in the end to be a follower vnto sir Peter Carew, with whom he neuer brake his promise, but stood him in great stéed aswell in matters of counsell, as of anie seruice to be doone in those parts. A man (which is rare among these people) verie constant of his word, and so faithfullie he serued, and so much he honoured sir Peter Carew, that after his death, being as one maimed, he consumed and pined awaie, and died in peace.

The strength of Brian Mac Kahir

Brian Mac Kahir is a follower to sir Peter Carew

The Omores, notwithstanding the earle of Kildare was waged by hir maiestie to persecute and chastise them, yet without anie resistance or impeachment they rage and outrage in all traitorous manner and rebellious disorders. They inuaded the English pale, spoiled and burned sundrie townes and villages, and carried the preies and pillage with them without anie resistance. The whole prouince of Connagh was

The Omores rebell

All Connagh in actuall rebellion

was altogither in actuall rebellion by the earle Clanricard sonnes, and they for their aid had called & waged a thousand Scots. And though they and the Irishrie were of diuerse nations, yet of one and of the same dispositions and conditions, being altogither giuen to all sinne and wickednes, and their harts were altogither imbrued in bloud and murther. The earle himselfe was at this time prisoner in the castell of Dublin for the same rebellion: who hearing of the outrages of his sonnes, made sute to the lord deputie, that if he might be set at libertie, he would vndertake to bring in his sons, and to quiet the countrie.

The false dissembling of the earle of Clanricard

The lord deputie, desiring nothing more than peace, after sundrie conferences had with him, did by the aduise of the councell inlarge him, in an assured hope that he would effectuallie performe in déed what he had promised in word. But he came no sooner home among his people, and had conferred with his sonnes, but he forgat his promise and performed nothing at all. Likewise the Ochonners and the Omores, accompanied with a rable of like rebels, fall into open rebellion, spoile the countrie, deuoure the people, and make all wast and desolate. Tirlough Lenough in Vlster was readie to reuolt, but that he stood in doubt of the earle of Essex, who lieng vpon the fines and marches in Vlster, was not onelie in readinesse to haue bearded him, but also he had set Odoneile in open warres against him. Mounster was likewise in open rebellion. But sir Iohn Perot then president so coursed and followed them, that notwithstanding a great combination and league was betwéene Iames Fitzmoris and all the rebels in Connagh and Leinster, yet he kept them asunder and so sharpelie pursued Iames, that he left him no one place to rest in, nor anie followers to follow him. Besides these vniuersall troubles, which were sufficient to haue apalled the best and wisest gouernour, these three things increased his griefe and sorow. First the losse of a most faithfull councellor and one of his chiefest and trustiest assistants doctor Weston then lord chancellor, whom it pleased God to call out of this miserable life, a man in his life time most godlie, vpright and vertuous, and such a one as that place was not possessed of the like in manie currents of yeares, in his life most vertuous and godlie, in matters of councell most sound and perfect, in iustice most vpright and vncorrupted, in hospitalitie verie bountious and liberall, and in manners and conuersation most courteous and gentle, faithfull to his prince, firme to his friend, and courteous to all men. And as was his life so was his death, who a little before the same called his houshold, and gaue them such godlie instructions, as to their callings apperteined. Then he set his priuate things in order, and he spent all the time that he had in praiers and exhortations.

The Ochonners and the Omores rebell

The distressed mind of the lord deputie

The death of doctor Weston lord chancellor.

At last, feeling a declination towards, he appointed a generall communion to be had of his houshold and friends in his chamber, vnto which all the councell came and were partakers. And then these godlie actions finished, he gaue a most godlie exhortation to the councell, persuading them to be vertuous and zelous in Gods true religion: then to be mindfull of their duties to hir maiestie, and lastlie remembring their callings and estate, and the great charge of the gouernement laid vpon them and committed vnto them, that they would be valiant, carefull, and studious to performe the same, as might be to the glorie of God, honor to the quéene, & benefit to the whole realme. Which points he handled so godlie, learnedlie & effectuallie, that he made their teares to trill, and their hearts to be heauie. After this doone he bid them farewell, and not long after he being feruent in his praiers, he died most godlie, vertuouslie, and christian like.

The next was the breach of the earle of Desmond, who was a prisoner in the castell of Dublin, and he hauing giuen his faith and oth to be a true prisoner, and to shew himselfe a dutifull subiect, did yet make his escape: which being doone in

The earle of Desmond breaketh prison.

so troublesome a time, it was doubted verie much what would insue thereof. Wherefore not onelie in that land, but in England also, hir maiestie vpon knowledge did cause musters to be made in all the parts vpon and towards the south and west parties, and men to be in readinesse to be transported, if anie occasion by his escape should happen to follow. For it was greatlie doubted what would follow of that his breach, sauing that the president in Mounster was thought to be sufficientlie prepared and furnished against him, if he did or would attempt anie disorder that waie.

The reuocation of the erle of Essex.

The third was the reuocation of the earle of Essex, who had taken vpon him to recouer the whole prouince of Vlster to obedience, with hir maiesties aid. And he hauing with great charges brought the same to a great likelihood and towardnesse, the armie was cashed, and he dismissed and discharged, and the enterprise dissolued. These with sundrie other accidents of the like nature, were sufficient to haue swallowed vp anie man in the gulfe of despaire, had not the lord God looked vpon him, and hir maiestie most gratiouslie pondered his manie & sundrie most humble requests for his reuocation, which hir highnes by hir letters vnto him granted, and immediatlie wherevpon he (after foure yeares painfull seruice) was discharged of his office, & returned into England. Manie good & notable things were doone in the time of this mans deputation worthie to be remembred, and for euer to be chronicled. But forsomuch as the records and presidents of the same cannot bee had, and the imprinter cannot staie his impression anie longer time, the same with patience must be borne withall, vntill a better opportunitie shall serue as well for it, as for the commendation of this honorable & ancient gentleman, who hath deserued well and honourablie of his prince and countrie for his seruice and gouernment.

Sir William Fitz-williams discharged of the deputiship.

1575

Sir Henrie Sidneie lord deputie the third time.

After that this man was cleane discharged, the sword and office was deliuered vnto sir Henrie Sidneie, who now the third time entred into the gouernment of this cursed land, and arriued at the Skirries the twelfe of September 1575, who at his comming found the infection of the plague so generallie dispersed, and especiallie in the English pale, that he could hardlie find a place where to settle himselfe without danger of infection. And euen as this plague reigned, so the old rebellious minds of the northerne Vlsterians brake out. For he was no sooner knowne to be entred into the land, but for a bien veneu to welcome him into the countrie, Serlo Boie with his companie came to Knockfergus, there to make preie of the towne, & so proudlie assailed the same, that he slue a capteine named Baker, and his lieutenant, with fortie of his souldiers, besides diuerse of the townsmen, of whome some were hurt, some maimed, and some slaine, and yet neuerthelesse by the valour & courage of the rest of the souldiers and townsmen, the preie was rescued, and the Scots perforce driuen awaie.

The pestilence great in the English pale.

Serlo Boie assaulteth Knockfergus.

The lord deputie, considering with himselfe that of such beginnings euill would be the euents and sequels thereof, if the same were not out of hand preuented, and knowing also by his owne experience, how perillous delaies be in such cases, thought it verie necessarie and expedient (according to the old saieng *Principijs obsta serò medicina paratur, &c.*) foorthwith to withstand the same. And therefore by the aduise of so manie of hir maiesties priuie councell, as could in that quesie time be assembled, he tooke order for the safe kéeping of the English pale, and committed the custodie thereof in his absence, to certeine gentlemen of best account and wisedome, to sée the same to be kept and quieted. And he himselfe in his owne person, taking with him hir maiesties armie, which was then about six hundred horssemen and footmen, and accompanied with such gentlemen and councellors as he had appointed for that seruice, tooke his iourneie towards Vlster. And as he passed, he found the whole countrie throughout wasted, spoiled, and impouerished, sauing the

The lord deputie maketh a iourneie into Vlster.

the Newrie, which sir Nicholas Bagnell knight marshall did inhabit, and the Glins and Routs which Sorlo Boie with the Scots possessed, and Killultagh.

Now in all that iorneie few came to submit themselues, sauing Mac Mahon, and Mac Gwier, & Tirlough Lenough, who first sent his wife, and she being a woman verie well spoken, of great modestie, nurture, parentage, and disposition, and aunt to the then earle of Argile, was verie desirous to haue hir husband to liue like a good subiect, and to be nobilitated. Tirlough himselfe followed verie shortlie after his wife, & came before the lord deputie without pledge, promise or hostage, and simplie & without anie condition did submit himselfe in all humblenesse and reuerence to his lordship, making the like sutes as his wife before his comming had motioned vnto his lordship, referring himselfe neuerthelesse to be ordered and directed by his lordship in all things. And after that he had spent two daies, vsing himselfe in all the time of his abode in all dutifulnesse, subiection, and reuerence, did in like maner take his leaue, and returned to his owne home. And as for Odonell lord of Tirconell, and Mac Gwier lord of Farmanaugh, albeit they came not in persons, yet they wrote their most humble letters of submission, and offered all such rents and seruices, as to them apperteined to yéeld, making request that they might onelie serue vnder hir highnesse, and be discharged from the exactions of all others.

Tirlough Lenough submitteth him in all humilitie.

After that the lord deputie had performed this iourneie, and was returned to Dublin, then he made the like iourneies towards the other parts of the land. And beginning in Leinster, he found the whole countie of Kildare, and the baronie of Carberie, extreamelie impouerished by the Omories, both in the time of the late rebellion, and also since, when they were vnder protection. The kings and queenes counties were all spoiled & wasted by the Oconnors and the Omores, the old natiue inhabiters of the same, and of them Rorie Og had gotten the possession and the setling of himselfe in sundrie lands there, whether the tenants will or no, and as a prince occupieth what he listeth, and wasteth what he will. Neuerthelesse, vpon the word of the earle of Ormond, he came to the lord deputie at his being in Kilkennie, and in the cathedrall church there he submitted himselfe: and in outward appearance repented his former faults, and promised amendment: but how well he kept and performed it, his rebellions in the yeare following can witnesse.

The iourneie of the lord deputie in Leinster.

Rorie Og vpon the word of the earle of Ormond came vnto the lord deputie, and submitted himselfe.

The lord deputie at his comming to Kilkennie was receiued by the townsmen in all the best maner they could, and the earle of Ormond himselfe feasted and intreated him most honourablie, and had great care that his lordship and all his traine should not want anie thing. At this towne the two cousins and kinsmen of sir Peter Carew late deceassed, that is, Peter Carew, and George Carew, and the gentleman who had béene his agent in all his causes within that land, came before the lord deputie, and there communicated with his lordship the state of the deceassed knight, and of his countrie, submitted the same to his order and direction, as also made humble sute vnto his lordship for his presence at the funerals at Waterford, where it was appointed he should be buried. Whose lordship as vpon the first newes of this knights death, so now also vpon the new recitall thereof, maruellouslie lamented and bewailed the losse of so worthie a knight, and the want of so wise and faithfull an assistant and councellor. And then he tooke order therein, shewing most honourablie not onelie the offices of a faithfull and good friend to the dead, but also the like good will to the two yoong gentlemen, of which one was then his heire, and to inioy his baronie. And according as things were determined, the corps was remooued from Rosse where he died, and carried to Waterford against his comming thither, where it was buried in verie honourable maner, as shall hereafter appeare, being not impertinent to the historie to set downe some short discourse of this most woorthie gentleman and of his life.

The lord deputie interteined verie well in Kilkennie.

Sir Peter Carew his death.

Sir Peter Carew died at Rosse, & was buried at Waterford verie honourablie.

Sir

Sir Peter Carew his life, birth and conditions.
His descent

Sir Peter Carew was descended of noble and high parentage, whose first ancestor was named Montgomercie, and in the time of king Henrie the second he married the ladie Elisabeth daughter to Roesius prince of Southwales, by which mariage he was aduanced to honour, and made baron of the castell of Carew, whereof

Baron of Carew

his posteritie in time tooke their surnames, being called Carews. And some of them passing into Ireland did grow to be mightie men, and of great honor and possessions in that land, being marquesses of Corke, barons of Hidron and Lexnew, lords of Maston, and inheritors to sundrie great lordships and seigniories in that land. And likewise in England they were men of great credit, seruice, and honour, and by waie of mariages matched and combined with honourable and great houses.

His stature
His disposition

This foresaid sir Peter, who was lineallie descended from them, was of stature meane, but verie stronglie and well compacted, of complexion cholerike, from his childhood vpwards bent and giuen to an honest disposition, and in his tender yeares he serued vnder, and was page to the prince of Orenge beyond the seas, and by

His skill and seruice in the warres

that means had the greater delight & skill in martiall affaires, wherein he had good knowledge, as did well appeare in the manifold seruices he did vnder king Henrie the eight, king Edward the sixt, and quéene Elisabeth, in sundrie places beyond as

His trauels

also on this side the seas. He was in his yonger yeares a great traueller, and had béene at Constantinople in the Turkes court, at Vienna in the emperours palace, at Venice, and in the French kings court, and in the houses of the most of all christian princes, in euerie of which places he left some tokens of his value. He was blessed of God with manie singular good gifts, as well of the mind as of the bodie, being

His religion
His qualities

vertuouslie disposed euen from his verie infancie, sincere in religion (and for which he was partlie an exiled man in the Marian daies) dutifull to his prince, and faithfull to his countrie, vpright in iustice, politike in gouernement, and valiant in armes,

His learning

skilfull in the Italian and French toongs, and a great student in such bookes as those toongs did yéeld, and by that means some knowledge ioined with his pregnancie of wit, he would discourse verie substantiallie in anie matter concerning policie or

His cōditions

religion, peace or warres, good to euerie man, hurtfull to no man, bountifull & liberall, abhorring couetousnesse and whordome, a great housekéeper, and of great hospitalitie. And if anie fault were in him, it was rather of too much spend-

His anger without malice

ing, than in reasonable sauing, he would be soone warme, but without gall, and against his enimie most stout and valiant. finallie such was his vpright dealing,

His zeale

honest conuersation, and zeale to the commonwealth, as no man was more honoured nor vniuersallie beloued than was he.

His title to his lands in Ireland

When he had spent the greater part of his age, he bethought himselfe vpon such lands as his ancestors had in Ireland, and which in right did descend vnto him and finding his title to be good, he acquainted hir highnesse therewith, and obteined hir fauour and good will to passe ouer into Ireland, to follow the recouerie

He recouereth some part of his lands in Ireland

thereof. Which he did, and made such good proofes of his title, as well by records as by euidences, that he recouered so much as he did then put in sute, namelie the lordship of Maston, of which he had béene dispossessed of about seauen score yeares, which he departed with vnto sir Christopher Chiuers knight, then tenant to the same, and the baronie of Hidron then in the possession of the Cauenaughs, the ancient enimies of the English gouernment, and who had expelled his ancestors

His good dealing with his tenants

about two hundred yeares past. But being put once in possession, he dealt in such good order with them, and so honourablie vsed himselfe, that they all voluntarilie yeelded vp their lands, and submitted themselues to his deuotion, and finding him to be a verie rare man in manie and sundrie respects, as of the like they had not heard nor knowne, they much reioised of him, and counted themselues happie and blessed

blessed to be vnder his gouernment. At his first comming he resumed the whole baronie into his owne hands, and thereof he gaue some péeces in frehold, to such gentlemen as he thought good; and for the residue euerie of them what he had before, he tooke it againe vnder writing by lease. He diuided the baronie into certeine manors and lordships, and in euerie one he did erect a court baron, and there all matters in variance betwéene them were ended and determined after the English maner, according to iustice & truth. He would not suffer anie wrong to be doone vnto them, neither would he beare with anie of them dooing wrong. Their complaints he would heare, and with indifferencie he would determine them: he dwelled among them, and kept a verie liberall and a bountifull house, and such hospitalitie as had not béene tofore knowne among them; and for which he was marueloushe beloued, and his fame spred throughout that land. His housekéeping and hospitalitie.

He kept continuallie of his owne priuat familie, aboue or néere a hundred persons in house, he had alwaies in readinesse fortie horssemen well appointed, besides footmen, & commonlie one hundred Kerns, and all that his countrie at commandement; by which meanes he chased and pursued such as laie vpon the frontiers of his countrie, that they if anie had offended, would come and submit themselues simplie to his mercie: & the residue willing to serue him at all néeds. If anie noble man or others did passe by his house, there he first staied and was interteined according to his calling, for his cellar doore was neuer shut, & his butterie alwaies open, to all commers of anie credit. If anie garrison either came to assist and attend him, or passed through his countrie, he gaue them interteinment, and vittelled them at his owne charges, and paied readie monie both for it, and for all things taken of the countrie; for without present paiment he would haue nothing: which was a rare thing and not heard of in that land. Readie paiment for all things. And as concerning hir maiesties seruice, it was so honourable for hir highnesse, and so profitable to the countrie, and accomplished with such a disposition and a good will, as all and euerie the gouernours in his time thought themselues happie to be assisted with such a man. In matters of counsell he was verie graue and considerate, in matters of policie verie wise and circumspect, and in martiall affaires verie valiant and noble, and in all of great knowledge and experience: in euerie of which (as occasion serued) his seruice was readie and at commandement, so long as his abode was in that land.

In the Butlers warres, vpon commandement from the deputie, he did first serue at Cloghgreman, a castell of sir Edmund Butlers, where being accompanied with capteine Gilbert, capteine Malbeie, and capteine Basnet, and Henrie Dauels, and their bands, assaulted the castell, tooke it, and gaue the preie to the souldiers. His seruice in the Irish wars. Then they went to Kilkennie where they issued out and made a sallie vpon the whole armie of sir Edmund Butler: which being about thrée miles from the towne, gaue them the ouerthrow, and put all the Gallowglasses and the rest to the sword, sauing the horssemen and Keirnes which fled into the woods: and then méeting the lord deputie, attended him in the whole iourneie and seruice of the said warres vntill the same was ended. In which he assisted the said deputie with his faithfull aduise and counsell, and with all such dutifull seruice as which his lordship could not lacke, and which he so aduertised to hir maiestie. Likewise in Vlster he was in the whole or the most part of that seruice with the earle of Essex, whom he aduised and assisted with all the best seruice and counsell he could, to the great comfort of the earle, and commendation of himselfe. Sir Peter Careus seruice in Vlster.

The fame and report of this noble gentleman, for his wisedome, valiantnesse, experience, vprightnes, houskéeping, bountifulnesse, liberalitie, and his iust dealings with euerie man, was spred through out all that nation, and he fauoured and beloued of all men. And certeine gentlemen in Mounster, knowledging and confessing that His title to his lands in Mounster.

he had a iust title to their lands and possessions: and that he (as descending lineallie from the marquesse of Corke) was then lawfull lord, and to whome they ought to yéeld their lands, some of them made their repaire, and some wrote their letters vnto him: and all with one consent acknowledged him to be their right and lawfull lord, and offered not onelie truelie to instruct and to aduertise him throughlie of his whole inheritance, but if it would please him to come to the citie of Corke, they would all appeare before him, and submit themselues, and yéeld vp their lands into his hands.

The offer of the gentlemen to be his tenants.

Sir Peter Carew, when he had considered and well bethought of these offers, and had taken aduise with his fréends, thought it not good to refuse the same; and that so much the sooner, bicause he had made hir highnesse acquainted with his title, and had before obteined hir letters to sir William Fitzwilliams then lord deputie of Ireland, and to sir Iohn Parret then lord president of Mounster, that they should assist him in his sutes, and to call the contrarie parts, and to persuade them with all quietnesse to yéeld to his iust titles. And againe, finding that part of the realme to be now verie quiet, & the people well disposed, he sent first his agent the writer heereof to Corke, where and before whome there came Mac Artie Riogh, Corman Mac Teege, Barrie Og, the Omahons, the Odriscots, the Odallies, & sundrie others, who of their owne fréewill offered to giue in recompense of that which was past, and towards the setting vp of his house, if he would come and dwell among them, thrée thousand kine; and so manie shéepe and hogs and corne, as according to that proportion, and would also yéerelie giue him in the like maner such a portion as should be to his contentation and good liking. When his agent had aduertised these things vnto him, and according to his order had prepared a house in Kinsale, and one other in Corke for him: the said sir Peter did set the house of Leighlin to his kinsman and cousine Peter Carew, who afterwards was his heire, and prepared his ship to passe himselfe with his houshold stuffe to Corke. And being in readinesse for the same, it pleased God to call him to another passage, for falling sicke at the towne of Rosse, he died the seauen and twentith of Nouember 1575, and was buried verie honorablie and in warlike manner at Waterford, the fiftéenth of December in the cathedrall church, with all such ensignes of honor as to his degrée apperteined, there being then present sir Henrie Sidneie lord deputie, and the councell. And thus much concerning that worthie knight sir Peter Carew.

The death of sir Peter Carew 1575.

His buriall.

The receiuing of the lord deputie at Waterford.

The lord deputie, being accompanied from Kilkennie with the earle of Ormond vnto the citie of Waterford, he was verie honourablie receiued at his entrie into the citie, by the maior & his brethren, and an oration congratulatorie made vnto him in the Latine toong by a yoong scholar clad in white attire, verie well and eloquentlie pronounced. Great triumphes were made, both vpon the land and vpon the water; with all such shewes and tokens of ioie and gladnesse, as could be deuised. And whiles he remained in the citie, there wanted not anie thing méet and conuenient for the interteinement of his lordship, and of all his traine: which his lordship did verie well accept and take in good part, as also aduertised it to the lords of hir maiesties honourable priuie councell in England. This citie is a verie ancient citie, and first builded (as the common opinion is) by Sitiracus one of the thrée brethren, which came out of Norwaie, called Easterlings. It standeth and is situated vpon the riuer of Suire, which riseth in the hill or mount Blandina, named in Irish Slough blome: and fléeteth by Thurles in Tipporarie, whereof the earles of Ormond are vicounts: from thense to the Holie crosse, Ardmale, Cahir Doweske, Ardfinan, Inislouagh, Clonmell, Carricke Mac Griffin, and so to Waterford.

The description of the citie of Waterford.

The situation.

It was of it selfe a verie little pile, but strong and well walled, and of late yeares vpon occasion of warres inlarged in the time of king Henrie the seuenth and in-

closed

closed with a strong wall: when Lamberd (named Perkin Warbecke) was crowned king at Dublin, about which king fell great controuersies betwéene them and Gilbert erle of Kildare. For the said erle being then lord deputie sent his letters to the said maior & his citizens, requiring them to receiue into their citie the new king, as other good cities had doone: who refusing to acknowledge anie other king, than king Henrie of England, he threatened them that he would take their citie perforce and hang the maior. Wherevpon hot words grew on euerie side, & the same like to haue growne to hand fight: the Waterfordians offering to wage the battell where the erle would appoint. Which their truth at that time auailed them much afterwards, and they in speciall fauour with king Henrie the seuenth and king Henrie the eight, by whome their liberties and franchises were inlarged.

A controuersie betwéene the earle of Kildare and the Waterfordians.

The Waterfordians refuse to acknowledge Perkin to be their king.

The Waterfordians in fauor with the kings of England.

The soile about it is verie barren and full of hils and rocks, and the lesse profitable for lacke of good manurance and husbandrie: but what faileth in the land, is recompensed with the sundrie commodities which the riuer yéeldeth, which is not onlie plentifull and abundant of all sorts and kinds of fishes, but also it is a goodlie hauen and a receptacle for all sorts of ships: & for this it is called *Larga porta*, The great or large hauen. The resort of merchants from out of all countries to this citie maketh the same verie populous and rich, & is the chiefest *Emporium* of that prouince. Great be the priuileges which the kings of England gaue to the maior & citizens, as well concerning the riuer as the citie, by king Iohn, king Henrie the third, and king Edward the first.

The commodities of the riuer.

Larga porta.

The riuer was bounded and limited from the mouth of the seas, betwéene Rirdowan where Hoke tower standeth vpon the east side, and Rodibanke vpon the west side, and from thense vnto Carricke vpon Sure: and so farre beyond, as the said riuer ebbeth and floweth that waie. & from the said mouth vnto the Inostiage vpon the riuer of Ore, and so far as the same water ebbeth and floweth, and likewise from the said mouth, vnto saint Molins vpon the riuer of Barrow, and so farre beyond the same, as the water ebbeth & floweth. Yet notwithstanding great controuersies haue beene betwéene this citie and the towne of Rosse, which lieth vpon the riuer of Barrow, concerning the bounds and limits that waie, bicause they of Rosse doo claime a priuilege vpon that riuer as of the gift and grant of Roger Bigod earle marshall: who married Isabell the eldest daughter of Walter earle marshall, and in hir right was lord of Rosse and of the riuer of the Barrow. Wherevpon certeine inquisitions were taken in the time of king Edward the third, and of king Richard the second: and then at Clonmell vpon the othes of six knights and eighteene esquiers, it was found for the citie of Waterford. And these are the bounds of the port or hauen of Waterford, within the which bounds and limits the citie of Waterford, by the grants of sundrie kings vnder their charters, haue these priuileges. That no ship shall be laden nor vnladen, but at the citie of Waterford, and there to paie all such customes and duties as belong and are due for their merchandize. Also that they haue the prisage wines and the iurisdiction of the admeraltie, within the limits of the said riuer.

The riuer of Water[illegible]

A controuersie betwéene the Waterfordians and the towne of Rosse for the riuer of Barrow.

A verdict passed in the behalfe of the Waterfordians.

The priuileges of Waterford vpon the water.

The citie it selfe was first incorporated by king Henrie the second, & after confirmed by king Iohn, Henrie the third, and king Edward the first with augmentations. The maior hath the sword borne before him by the gift of king Edward the fourth, and king Henrie the seauenth, by the name of the sword of iustice. They haue cognisance of all maner of plées as well reall, personall, & mixt. They are iustices of oier and determiner, & maie sit vpon triall of treasons, murthers, and felonies, without anie speciall commission to be sued out for the same. Also that no officer nor officers of the kings or queenes of England, nor their deputies shall intermeddle, nor exercise anie authoritie nor iurisdiction, within the citie and liberties,

The incorporation of the citie.

The priuileges of the citie of Waterford.

The sword of iustice.

but

but onelie the maior & officers of the same. Also they haue a maior and officers of the staple yearelie to be chosen, who haue the liberties for taking of statutes and recognisances staple, not onelie within their owne towne & concerning themselues, but also of sundrie townes in Leinster and Mounster, and the counties of Waterford, Kilkennie, Wexford, and Tipperarie. Also they haue libertie from time to time to transport, lade, and carrie awaie corne, vittels, wooll, horsses, & hawks, and to licence anie other within the limits of their iurisdiction to doo the like. Also all forfeitures, amerciaments, fines, felons goods, and deodands goods, they haue to their owne vse. Also that in all doubts, the words of their charters should be expounded to the best sense, and if then there were anie further doubt, the same should be determined and decided by the king or his councell in the realme of England. Also that they should not at anie time be compelled to go and serue in anie hosting, except the king himselfe or anie of his sonnes were present in person.

These and manie other like priuileges of the kings of England from time to time, of their bounteous liberalitie, and in consideration of their dutifull and good seruices, did giue and bestow vpon them. All which, O you the inhabitants of Manapia and citizens of Waterford, the ofspring of so good ancestors, ought to be lessons and presidents vnto you, for your continuance in the like offices and duties: that you maie thereby shew your selues to be as were your predecessors, faithfull, loiall, and obedient: and that your apophthegme maie be for euer found true, *Waterfordia semper manet intacta*. Otherwise brag neuer so much of your worthinesse, & glorie neuer so much of your values (as the Iewes did of their father Abraham) yet it shall so little auaile you, that their honour shall be your reproch, and their glorie your shame, if you doo not also the like, and in the end your vtter confusion. For as the holie scripture saith: If you be the children of light, then as children walke you in the light, otherwise that light which is in you shall be darkenesse. If you be the children of Abraham, then doo you the workes of Abraham: otherwise God, who is able and will raise vp the verie stones to be sonnes to Abraham, shall reiect you, and giue your citie to a people which shall bring foorth the fruits of dutie and obedience. For so did he with his owne peculiar people, the Iewes, whom for their disobedience against himselfe, and against his annointed princes, did after sundrie punishments and no amendment giue them ouer vnto their enimies hands: who put their yoong men to the sword, & their priests to slaughter, their virgins were deflowred, their widows defiled, their citie vtterlie destroied, and not one stone left vpon an other, and all the people which escaped the sword, carried awaie captiues & made vagabonds, euen to this daie vpon the face of the earth. If he did this to his owne peculiar people, doo not you of Waterford, whom God hath blessed manie waies, thinke that you dooing the like wickednesse, shall escape the like iudgements. Wherefore if you will eschew the wrath to come, beware by their examples, and humble your selues in all dutifulnes & obedience to God and to your prince. Examine not his authoritie, nor decipher his power: compare not your priuileges with his authoritie, nor doo you dispute your liberties with his prerogatiue. For notwithstanding your priuileges, liberties, and grants be great and manie: yet they can not abate nor impugne the least part of the princes prerogatiue: which is so great, as nothing can be greater, if you will take the view of Gods owne ordinances, when he first erected and established a king, who gaue him so high and so absolute authoritie, that (as the apostle saith) it must be with all humblenesse obeied: bicause he is Gods minister especiallie when it concerneth the interest of hir maiesties imperiall crowne of that land, the suppression of rebels and traitors, & the deliuerie of your selues and that realme from the enimies and rebels.

An admonition to the citizens of Waterford.

Waterford a semper manet intacta.

An exhortation to the citizens of Waterford.

The princes prerogatiue.

And

And doo not you thinke that this digression is impertinent to the historie. For as your ancestors good doings are set downe to their praises and commendations, so the same shall be doone of yours, either to your praises for your well doings, or for your reproch to the contrarie. But to the historie. When the lord deputie had giuen thankes to the maior and his brethren for his good interteinement, he departed thense by iournies towards Corke, and by the waie at Dungaruon the earle of Desmond came vnto him, and verie humblie offered him all the seruice he was able to doo to hir maiestie, and did accompanie him from thense vnto the citie of Corke, where the said lord deputie was receiued in the best manner the citizens could, with all humblenesse, and with all such triumphs and other shewes and tokens of good will and dutifulnesse as they could giue, without grudging or complaining either of the townesmen or of the souldiers. To this towne resorted vnto him the earles of Desmond, Thomond, Clancar, and all the noblemen and best gentlemen in all Mounster, and their wiues, and there kept their houses the whole Christmasse. During his being there, manie complaints were made of great outrages, murthers, spoiles, and thefts doone throughout that prouince, whervpon dailie sessions were kept, and the malefactors of which thrée and twentie verie notable and notorious offendors were executed and put to death.

The earle of Desmond humblie offereth his seruice to the lord deputie.

The lord deputie receiued honorablie into Corke.

All the noblemen in Mounster repaire to the lord deputie.

Executions at Corke.

It was also ordered, that for the cutting off and abolishing of the great swarmes and clusters of the idlers, which like waspes troubled the whole land, and liued onelie by spoile and rapine, that euerie nobleman and gentleman should giue and deliuer in the names of euerie seruant and follower which he had, and should sée the same to be booked and registred. And if any of them were found vnbooked and not registred, that he should be vsed as a fellon where so euer he was taken, and for all such, as whose names were registred, his lord and master should answer for him. To this order all the noble and gentlemen gaue their full consents, and foorthwith the same was openlie proclamed in their presence, who séemed to receiue it with all ioy, and promised that it should be followed with effect, and immediatlie they gaue in their pledges. When all things were thus in these parts setled in good and quiet order, he tooke his iournie towards Limerike, and there he was receiued with much more pompe and shewes than in anie place before. But as before, so here he spent a few daies in kéeping of sessions, in executing of iustice, and in hearing of poore mens complaints, and tooke the like order for registring of euerie noble and gentlemans follower, as he had doone at Corke. Which when he had doone, he rode thense vnto Thomond where he was complained vnto of manie great murthers, rapes, thefts, and other outrages, whereof he found great plentie. And for want of sufficient time to proceed throughlie to doo iustice and iudgement therein, he referred the same to certeine commissioners appointed for the purpose: sauing that he committed the principall offendors to ward, and some he banished and abandoned out of those parts, vntill further order were taken for them.

Euerie nobleman and gentleman to answer for his men.

The lord deputie honorablie receiued at Limerike.

Thomond is cleane out of order.

From thense he entred into Connagh, and came to the towne of Gallewaie, where he found the towne much decaied and almost desolated, sundrie of the good housholders hauing sought new habitations vnder Mac William Eughter: and the countrie through out altogither spoiled and deuoured by the Mac an Earles, the hopeles (but much better if they had beene hoplesse) sonnes of the earle of Clanricard, whose outrages were most heinous and horrible. But when these gracelés impes perceiued of the great complaints made against them, and doubting what would be the sequele if some waie were not taken, they voluntarilie went to Gallewaie towne, and came to the church vpon a sundaie at the publike seruice, where the lord deputie then was, and there knéeling vpon their knées confessed their faults,

The towne of Gallewaie in great decaie.

The earle of Clanricards sonnes submit themselues.

faults submitted themselues, and most lamentablie craued pardon, promising vnfeinedlie amendment, and neuer to reuolt more from their dutifull obedience to hir maiestie and hir lawes. The deputie mooued herewith, and hoping the best, did by the aduise of hir maiesties councell thinke it good, with some sharpe reprehensions and a little punishment for this time to release them, & so he tooke his

1576 iourneie towards Dublin, where he came the thirtéenth of Aprill 1576, but kept sessions in euerie place as he passed through the countrie, and placed his garrisons in places conuenient.

In this his iourneie he found a verie ruinous state and most lamentable disorders, which required a spéedie reformation. And though the outrages in the ciuill gouernment were great, yet nothing to be compared to the ecclesiasticall state, for

The ruine of the ecclesiasticall state.

that was too too far out of order, the temples all ruined, the parish churches for the most part without curates and pastors, no seruice said, no God honored, nor Christ preached, nor sacraments ministred. And therefore it appéered, yea and it was openlie preached before the lord deputie himselfe, that manie were borne which neuer were christened: and the patrimonie of the church wasted & the lands imbezelled. A lamentable case, for a more deformed and a more ouerthrowne church there could not be among christians. The deputie considering and bethinking with himselfe, how the church of God was abused, and that God had in store some wrath and indignation for this defiling of his holie sanctuarie, did for the auoiding thereof write his letters of aduertisement to hir highnesse, and most earnestlie praied hir princelie authoritie for redresse thereof, and therewith most humblie requested, that the commonwealth being destitute of a chancellor, and other most necessarie magistrates for the gouernement, might likewise with all spéed be sent ouer. When hir maiestie and councell had considered this aduertisement, and had entered into

Manie in Ireland not christened.

The spoile of the churches.

An order for the reformation of religion.

the depth thereof, order for a redresse was taken foorthwith: and the matters concerning religion and reformation of the church, it was committed to the said lord deputie, and to archbishops and certeine bishops, with others, to sée the same to be put in execution. And for the gouernment one William Gerard esquier a professor of the laws was sent to be lord chancellor, & sir William Drurie to be president of Mounster, which arriued at Dublin, the one the sixteenth of Iune, and the other the thrée and twentith of the same 1576. The lord chancellor he did foorthwith settle and place in his roome. And then his lordship prepareth to take a iourneie towards Waterford, to doo the like with sir William Drurie. But when he was passed a daies iourneie, word was brought vnto him from the bishop of Meth, who laie then vpon the confines of Meth and Connagh for ordering of matters in these parties, and the like from the maior of Gallewaie, and from diuerse others, who affected well the state, crieng out with trembling termes and dolefull reports, that the earle of Clanricard his sonnes that basterlie brood, which not scarse two moneths past had humbled themselues to the lord deputie, confessed their faults, and craued pardon, and had most firmelie protested and sworne most dutifull and continuall obedience.

William Gerard to be lord chancellor.

Sir William Drurie to be lord president.

1576

The earle of Clanricards sonnes brake out into rebellion.

These (I saie) not without the counsell and consent of their father, were on a night stollen ouer the riuer of Shennon, and there cast awaie their English apparell, and clothed themselues in their old woonted Irish rags, and sent to all their old friends to come awaie to them, and to bring the Scots whom they had solicited, and their Gallowglasses, and all other their forces with them. Who when they met togither, they foorthwith went to the towne of Athenrie, and those few houses which were newlie builded, they sacked, set the new gates on fire, beat awaie the masons and labourers which were there in working, brake and spoiled the quéenes armes, and others, there made and cut to be set vp. Bad and wicked they were before,

The earle consented to his sonnes disloialtie.

Athenrie spoiled.

fore, but now ten times worse than euer they were, being come, euen as it is said in the scriptures, that the wicked spirit was gone out of the man, and wanting his woonted diet, returneth vnto the house from whense he came, and finding the same swept cleane, he goeth and séeketh out other seuen wicked spirits, and entreth and dwelleth where he did before, and the last state of that man is woorse than the first. And if a man should aske of these bastardlie boies, and of their sier, what should be the cause that they should thus rage, and so wickedlie and suddenlie reuolue, as dogs to their vomits, so they to their treasons and trecheries, hauing beene so courteouslie vsed, so gentlie interteined, so friendlie countenanced, so fatherly exhorted, so pithilie persuaded, & so mercifullie pardoned in hope of amendment: surelie nothing can they answer, but that they would not be honest, nor in anie part satisfie a little of infinite the robberies, thefts, and spoiles which they had made. For bastardlie slips cannot bring foorth better fruits, neither can thornes bring foorth grapes. It is the good trée onelie that bringeth foorth good fruits, & which is to be cherished, and to be much made of; but thornes and briers are prepared for the fire, and to be burned. For let the husbandman bestow neuer so much husbandrie vpon the thorne, he will still be but a thorne. yea let him graffe neuer so good a peare vpon him, the same shall be but a stonie peare, and lacking continuall husbandrie, will reuolt to his old nature againe. As the husbandman then prospereth best, when his fields and gardens are weeded and clensed from thornes, brambles & briers, prepared for the fire: euen so shall the magistrate inioie the quiet state of a commonwealth, when iustice taketh place, and iudgement is executed; when the good are preserued and cherished, and the wicked (prepared for the gallowes) according to their deserts are punished.

Selfewill cause of the rebellion.

Punishment of the wicked maketh a quiet common wealth.

The instrument, when euerie string is stretched to his proper tune, then the musike is sweet, and the harmonie pleasant; but if that one string be out of order, the discord of that one marreth and disgraceth all the whole musike of the rest: euen so is it in a commonwealth, when euerie subiect is dutifull to his prince, obedient to his magistrate, and liueth according to his vocation and calling, the same prospereth and flourisheth; but let the wicked be left at libertie, and be vnpunished, the whole state is disturbed, & the commonwealth (as a garden ouergrowne with wéeds) in perill and danger to be ouerthrowne. The best commonwealth in all ages then prospered best, when the wicked were as well punished, as the good conserued. And experience teacheth, that a théefe, murtherer, a traitor, & such malefactors doo neuer better seruice to their prince & commonwealth, than when they be hanged on the gallowes, and so fastened to a gibbet. But to the matter.

The lord deputie vpon these aduertisements, finding the matter to be of such importance, which required some expedition to withstand the same, or else the whole land like to be in danger, altereth his intended iourneie, and returneth to Dublin, vsing such expedition, that within three daies following he was entered into Conagh. The brute thereof when it was blowne abrode, it was scarse credited by the rebels, bicause it was so sudden and with such spéed. But finding it to be true, and they afraid of their shadowes, they all one and other fled into the mounteins, sauing certeine gentlemen of the earls countrie, which left the traitorous boies, & came to the deputie, and offered their loialtie and seruice with fidelitie. The earle their father would faine haue excused himselfe, but in the end when no excuses could be accepted, his castels were taken, and he brought to the lord deputie. who notwithstanding his humble submissions and crauing of pardons, he was sent to the castell of Dublin, and there kept in close prison. But the lord deputie he passed thense to Gallewaie, and after he had there staied a few daies, for the comforting of the townesmen, who stood much dismaied of their estate, and in feare to be surprised and

The lord deputie altereth his course, and entreth into Conagh.

The earle of Clanricard is sent to the castell of Dublin and kept in close prison.

Sir William Drurie placed to be lord president in Munster.

and taken for pledges he passed through Thomond, and came to Limerike, where he setled sir William Drurie (who had accompanied him in all this seruice) to be the lord president. And from thense being accompanied and attended vpon with him and the nobilitie of that prouince and diuerse gentlemen of account, they passed to Corke, & there the lord president remained.

The gouernment of sir William Drurie.

Now he the said president, being thus placed in the gouernement of that prouince, did beare himselfe so vprightlie, and in so honourable a sort, that he reformed the same maruellouslie both in life and maners: and of a fierce people he tamed them to obedience. For the euill men he spared not, but by law and iustice in the open sessions, or by sword without respect of persons he punished according to their deserts: euen as of the contrarie the good subiects he would fauour and protect. If anie seruice were to be doone vpon the enimie and rebell, he would be the first in the field, and neuer ceasse to pursue him, vntill he had either taken him, or driuen him out of the countrie. If anie matters were in variance betwéene man and man, or anie bils of complaints exhibited vnto him, the same he would either determine, or referre them to the law, for which he kept courts continuallie, & where the same were heard and ended, and at which for the most part he would be present. The rude people he framed to a ciuilitie, & their maners he reformed and brought to the English order. And by all these means he did maruellouslie reforme that whole prouince to a most peaceable, quiet and ciuill estate, sauing the countie palatine in Kerie: which the earle of Desmond claimed to be his libertie, and that no person was to intermeddle nor yet to vse anie iurisdiction there, other than his owne officers. But when his lordship had looked into the most loose and dissolute life there vsed, and that it was a sanctuarie for all lewd and wicked persons, and how that liberties granted at the first for the maintenance of iustice was now become a cloke and a shrowd for all licentiousnesse: he purposed and was fullie determined to make a iourneie into that priuileged place, to make a passage for law and iustice to be there exercised, euen as he had tofore doone in other places, knowing that it could not be safe among a great flocke to leaue a scabbed sheepe, nor good for a commonwealth to haue nursseries for sinne.

The earle of Desmond will haue no officer to intermeddle in his countie palatine.

The countie palatine a sanctuarie of sinne and wickednesse.

The lord president purposeth to doo iustice in Kerrie.

The erle, when he perceiued this, he was in a great furie and agonie, and vsed all the waies he could to dissuade the lord président from the same. Which when he by no means could compasse, then according to his accustomable dissimulations he maketh faire weather, and offereth all the seruice he could doo to his lordship, and requested him that it would please him to vse his house and countrie at his pleasure, and that it would likewise please his lordship to lie at his house at Tralie when he passed that waie, the earle minding nothing lesse than his welcome thither, but practising in the end openlie what he had dissemblinglie and in secret deuised and determined. The lord deputie, nothing mistrusting anie secret practise to be imagined against him, granteth the earles request, and when he saw time, he taketh his iourneie into Kerrie, hauing no more men with him than sufficient, to the number of six score, or seuen score persons: and as he passed through the countrie, he kept courts and sessions, and heard euerie mans complaint: and at length as his iourneie laie, he rode vnto Tralie, where he minded to lodge with the earle. The earle hauing the gouernor (as he thought) within his clooches, and minding to practise that openlie, which he had deuised secretlie, had appointed in a readinesse seuen hundred, or eight hundred of his best followers to haue intrapped his lordship, and in sted of a bien venu into the countrie, to haue cut him off for euer comming more there. Which his villanous treacherie when his lordship saw and vnderstood, and considering that he was so néere vpon them: as that he was either to aduenture vpon them, or with dishonor to hazard himselfe and his companie: he calleth all his companie

The lord president entreth into Kerrie.

The treacherous practise of the earle to haue intrapped the lord president.

The lord president giueth the

companie togither, and with verie good and pithie words incourageth them to giue the onset vpon them: and foorthwith with a good courage they all march forwards, and gaue the charge vpon them. But they, notwithstanding they were all well armed, and seuen to one of the other: yet being as it were astonied at the boldnesse of this noble man, and at his great courage, for which he was famous in & through all that land, both the earle and his companie turned their heeles, forsooke the field, and dispersed themselues into the woods, and elsewhere, for their best safetie.

Charge vpon the earle of Desmond.

The countesse, when she heard hereof, fell in a great sorow and heauinesse for hir husbands so bad dealings, and like a good Abigaell went and met the lord president, fell vpon hir knées, held vp hir hands, and with trilling teares praied his lordships patience and pardon, excusing as well as she could hir husbands follie, saieng that he had assembled all that companie onelie for a generall hunting, nothing thinking vpon his lordship, and that the men séeing his lordship could not be persuaded to make anie staie, and so praied his lordship to take it. And herein she so wiselie and in such modestie did behaue hir selfe, that his lordship granted hir request, and temporised with the earle. But he followed his determination, and vsed his authoritie to decide matters in and throughout the palantine of Kerrie. This gréeued the earle to the hart, who hauing no other waie to be reuenged, he deuiseth certeine articles against the president, which he with great exclames exhibited vnto the lord deputie. The lord deputie, when he departed from Corke, he returned to Dublin, where he was aduertised that the Mac an Earles in Connagh had hired a new supplie of two thousand Scots and were in actuall rebellion. Wherevpon he prepared a new iourneie thitherwards, and being come thither, he found the matter to be true, and that they were vp in campe and in outragious maner spoiling the countries. But before his comming they had besieged Bailie Riogh which was the earles their fathers house, and for his treacherous dealings confiscated.

The earle complaineth against the lord president.

The Mac an Earles in Connagh rise in rebellion.

The earls sons doo besiege Bailie Riogh.

In this house the lord deputie, at his last departure from thense, had placed Thomas le Strange, and capteine Colier with one hundred footmen, and fiftie horssemen to lie in garrison, but the earls sons, thinking themselues of sufficient strength to recouer the same againe, laid siege vnto it, and inuironed it round about. but they were so resisted, that they did not onelie not preuaile; but the garrison within did make sundrie assaults vpon them, and slue at sundrie times six of their principall capteins, and one hundred and fiftie of their men. And in the end, when they saw they could not preuaile, they raised their siege, and followed their accustomed robbing and spoiling of the countrie, but especiallie vpon Mac William Eughter, from whome they tooke sundrie of his castels, and spoiled him of his goods and cattels. The lord deputie, not slacking nor slowing his businesse, followed out of hand the foresaid rebels, who skipped to and fro in such sort, that in no case could he find them at any aduantage. Wherfore he did disperse his companies, and according as intelligence was giuen, he caused pursute to be made vpon them. And by that meanes, although he could not méete with the whole troope of them, whereby to haue a full aduantage vpon them, yet manie times he met with some of them, slue them, hanged and executed them, tooke their peeces from them, and gained awaie their holds and castels. And at length hauing good espials, it was aduertised vnto him, that the Scots were incamped in the confins and marches of Mac William Eughters countrie, and therevpon he forthwith marched thitherwards, and in his waie manie of them fell into his lap, who had their rewards. Vnto whose lordship resorted the said Mac William with all the force he had & could make, who in this rebellion, being the onelie man of power in Connagh, & yet not able to saue himselfe a hole from their inuasions, did shew himselfe

Maister William Eughter his countrie spoiled.

The lord deputie followeth the rebels.

The Scots incamped in Connagh.

Mac William Eughter commeth with all the force he could make vnto the lord deputie.

himselfe most loiall, and did the best seruice that was doone vpon the rebels: and by the meanes of the said deputie, he recouered, and was repossessed of sundrie his castels, which in this rebellion had béene taken from him.

The Scots forsake Connagh and returne home.

The Scots, when they heard of the approching of the deputie towards them, they raised their campe, and suddenlie dispersed themselues, and the most of them, being wearie of their abode and interteinment, fled into the rout in Vlster. The residue like vnto the bare arssed rebels sculked to and fro, but in the end, they and the others were all dispersed, & durst not to appeare. Wherefore the deputie, when he had broken the galles of them, & had thus dispersed them, he by iournies returned towards Dublin, and hauing a little before receiued hir maiesties letters in the behalfe of Nicholas Malbie hir seruant, whome she commended for his sufficiencie, both for martiall and ciuill causes, and as well for the incouragement of him, as for the nourishing of the like vertues in others of his profession, hir pleasure was to commit vnto him the chéefe charge and gouernement vnder the said deputie in Connagh, and willed that he should be forthwith established in that office, & to be sworne one of hir priuie councell, & to haue that countenance, authoritie, & interteinement as was méet, conuenient & agréeable for the place, office, & person. Which the said deputie most willinglie & gladlie performed, dubbed him knight, and made him gouernor by the name of a coronell of Connaugh, thinking himselfe most happie, that he was assisted with such a man, as who for his experience in iudgement, his discretion in gouernement, and his painefulnesse and skill in martial seruice was sufficient and compleat, and best able, partlie by force, partlie by persuasion, and chieflie by ministring of iustice, was (I saie) best able, and would frame the rude and barbarous people of that prouince to ciuilitie and good order. And thus much he aduertised vnto hir maiestie by his letters, with thankes for hir choise of so méete and apt a man. During the time of this seruice and being of the lord deputie in Connagh, the earle of Essex, a man of great nobilitie and parentage died in Dublin. Great doubts were made of his death, some thinking that he should be poisoned, because he was then in the best time of his age, of a verie good constitution of bodie, and not knowne to haue beene sicke anie time before his death. But the matter examined by all the meanes that could be deuised, there was no such thing then found: but supposed, that for so much as he had a flux, which was a spise of a *Dysenteria*, and wherewith he had beene oftentimes before troubled, by the inspection and iudgement of such physicians & others who were present, it was iudged and found that it was some cause of his death. Some thought rather that he should be bewitched, as that countrie is much giuen to such dailie practises. But how far is that from all christianitie, all wise and godlie doo know, and euerie good christian should vnderstand. It is against the word of the Lord and all christian religion, and therefore not to be credited. It was thought and so affirmed by the most part of all men, that some inward griefe of the mind and secret sorow of the hart had hastened that, which no infirmitie of the bodie nor anie other deuises extraordinarie could compasse. For where that maladie is once entered, and hath seized and taken possession, and which by no physicke can be releeued or cured, it is but in vaine to minister the same to the bodie, which can not indure when the other faileth, no more than can an accident remaine, when the substance is gone, or else as the imbers or ashes giue heat, when the wood is burned and consumed.

Sir Nicholas Malbie appointed gouernor of Connagh.

The death of the earle of Essex.

Dysenteria

The sundrie opinions of his death. Poisoning. Witchcraft.

Sorrow and griefe of mind.

No physicke against the sorow of the mind.

He was no more honorable of birth and parentage by his ancestors, of whome some descended out of kings loines; but as singular a man for all the gifts both of mind and bodie, as that age had not manie better. Towards God he was most deuout and religious, whome he serued according to his holie word in all truth and sinceritie, and his whole life according to his vocation he framed after the same; being

The vertues of the earle of Essex.

being not spotted with drunkennesse, couetousnesse, whoredome, incontinencie, or anie other notorious crime: a great fauourer of the godlie, a friend to the professors of the gospell, & an extreame enimie to the papists & enimies of the true religion: to his prince & soueraigne most dutifull and humble, faithfull & obedient: his superiors he honored, his elders he reuerenced, his equals he loued, his inferiors he fauored: to his countrie trustie, to the commonwealth zealous, to all men courteous, and to the poore and oppressed bounteous and liberall.

In matters of policie he was verie prudent, and of a great reach: in causes of counsell sound, and of a déepe iudgement: in martiall affaires most valiant and of great courage, and of so heroicall a mind, that if his abilitie had answered his good will, he had not bin a second, neither to Lacie, nor to Courcie, nor to anie the first conquerors of Vlster to the crowne of England. For such a plot he had laid for the regaining thereof, that it could not be denied, but if the same had béene followed, great good would haue insued in processe of time to hir maiestie, in obedience and reuenues, and a great suertie to that estate, and the like increase of benefit to the whole commonwealth. The more noble were his good and worthie attempts, the more he was crossed and contraried: but by such secret meanes, as which he did rather for the most part coniecture amisse, than hit aright: but yet such was the great valour of his mind, and the magnanimitie of his stomach, that his good meanings & attempts, for the honor of his prince, and the benefit of the commonwealth, being so contraried and ouerthwarted, he whome no trauels, no paines, no seruice, no hardnesse could breake, the verie griefe of mind and sorrow of heart (as it was thought) did onelie consume and ouerthrow. He was also verie learned, and of great reading, and sometimes a scholer in the vniuersitie, and had verie good knowledge in all kind of letters, as well theologicall as humane, and of a verie quicke wit to conceiue, of a good capacitie to vnderstand, and of a readie toong to vtter and deliuer in a verie good order what he had conceiued, and so well he would discourse and argue anie matter, as few scholers better, and not manie so skilfull in anie one, as he was generallie in all good vertues. A more noble man euerie ware, not England, nor anie other nation hath lightlie affoorded. And certeinlie, if it had pleased God that Lachesis had bene idle, or had spun a longer thread, that he might haue liued to haue béene imploied according to his excellent vertues, either in matters of counsell, of policie, or martiall, no doubt he would haue prooued a most worthie and beneficiall member vnto hir maiestie, and hir whole commonwealth. As his life was, so also was his death most godlie, comfortable, and vertuous, the one answerable to the other, euen as S. Augustine writeth, *Vix malè moritur qui benè viuit*. In all the time of his sicknesse, which was about twentie or one and twentie daies, although he were manie times tormented with greeuous pangs in the bellie: yet was he neuer heard to grudge or murmur, nor to speake anie angrie or idle word, but most patientlie and méekelie tooke all things in good part. After he perceiued that nature began to faile and defect, he yéelded himselfe to die, and was verie desirous that his friends and welwillers should haue accesse vnto him, and to abide by him at their pleasure. And by that meanes he had continuallie about him diuerse men of all degrees, as well of the clergie, as of the laitie, both men and women, gentlemen & seruants, before whom he did shew most apparant arguments of a godlie and vnfeined repentance of his life past, and of a most christian and perfect charitie with all the world, freelie forgiuing euerie offense doone vnto him, and asking the like of all others. His faith he openlie confessed, and witnessed a most vndoubted assurance of his saluation in Christ Iesus, purchased for him in his bloud and death: and manie times he would with a lowd voice saie, *Cupio dissolui & esse cum Christo*. He spent most part of the time, when the extremitie of his sicknesse did not let him,

A plot for the regaining of Vlster

The earle of Essex contraried in all his attempts.

The earle verie well learned.

A godlie life hath a godlie end.

His patience in his sicknes

His repentance and charitie

He confesseth his faith

His praieng and hearing the word.

in praiers, and in hearing the word read vnto him, and would vse such godlie admonitions, such pithie persuasions, & so graue instructions, as he neuer did, nor thought he could doo in all his life time: for he neuer séemed in all his daies to be halfe so wise, learned, and eloquent. The néerer that death drew, the more feruent he was in praier, and requested all his companie to doo the like; and the verie last words that he spake was, The lord Iesus. And when his toong gaue ouer to speake anie more, he lifted vp his hands & eies to the Lord his God, vntill most swéetlie, mildlie, and godlie he did yéeld vp his ghost, which manie times before he had commended to his Lord and God. And thus this noble man vpon the two and twentith daie of September, and in the yere of our Lord one thousand fiue hundred seuentie and six, left this world, to the great sorow of his fréends, and losse of the commonwealth; but to the gaine of himselfe, who by all apparant arguments and testimonies of his vndouted faith, dooth assure vs of his euerlasting ioie, and eternall felicitie.

See more of this earle of Essex in the chronicles of England.

His letters to the lord deputie.

About thrée daies before his death, he wrot his last letters to the lord deputie, being then in the remote parties of Connagh; and verie desirous he was to haue spoken with him. In which letters he gaue his lordship most hartie thanks for all the good freendships past betweene them, and wished that the good and faithfull dealings betweene them were knowne as well in England as elsewhere. Then he commended to him all his seruants generallie, and some by particular name; and therein a speciall request for his sonne and heire, that though he himselfe should die to his freends, yet his sonne the earle of Essex might liue to the seruice of his prince, and the good of the commonwealth. And lastlie, he touched somewhat concerning his buriall, and herewith he sent vnto his lordship a little George and a garter, the ensignes of the order of the garter, whereof they both were knights and companions, to be a memoriall of the loue and goodwill past betweene them. And now leauing this honorable earle in his heauenlie ioie and blisse: let vs returne to the historie of this effere and effrenated nation.

The effect of the earles letters to the deputie.

The disagréements betwéene the earls of Desmond and Thomond.

The prouince of Mounster was indifferent quiet, but some repinings were betwéene the earles of Thomond and Desmond, the one not abiding nor digesting the orders, which vpon sundrie complaints were made against him, which he refused to obeie, vntill *Volens nolens* he were pressed therevnto by the lord president: the other, who was alwaies a verie wilfull man, notwithstanding he had at Corke yéelded himselfe (of his owne frée consent) to abide the orders there made for the quietnesse of the countrie, yet now hauing taken the aduise of his disordered folowers, he would not be withdrawen from his woonted exactions, and therefore repined to beare further anie cesse; and wrote his letters to the lords of hir maiesties priuie councell in England, complaining much, and proouing nothing, and aggrauating the taking of the cesse, with most manifest vntruths. And so far he was carried in misliking the gouernment, bicause he saw his owne woonted swaie was much abated, that he would verie faine haue slipped out if he could. And it was verelie thought that he was combined in a secret conspiration with the forelorne sonnes of the earle of Clanricard, as was his brother sir Iohn of Desmond, who for his conference had with Shane Burke, was suspected to haue ioined with him in his rebellion; as also because he had promised him aid out of Mounster, if he would hold out, and for which he was committed to ward. Which caried the more likelihood, bicause his intention was to put awaie his owne wife, & to haue matched himselfe in marriage with Shanes sister, who was Orwackes wife, & of late forsaken by him. Neuerthelesse, the erle was fearefull to offend the state, for the president was so watchfull to espie out both his and all the rest of their doings, and in such a readinesse to be at inches with them, and vpon their bones if they started out neuer so little, that he kept himselfe quiet,

The earle of Desmond repineth against all good orders, and complaineth against the cesse.

Sir Iohn of Desmond committed to ward.

Sir P. Desmond putteth away his wife and marrieth another mans wife.

quiet, and came in to the said president, and deliuered in his men that were demanded, & which before he denied, being verie notorious malefactors and practisers of vnquietnesse.

And now that the whole land was (as was thought) in quiet, or at least in outward shew more quiet than in times past, the noblemen & gentlemen in the English pale, of whome least suspicion of anie euill was thought, they begin verie inconsideratlie to repine against the cesse. who if they had entred into the due consideration thereof, they (although somewhat to their further charge) should haue mainteined it because that the same was procured for the defense of themselues, and they onelie had the benefit thereof. For you shall vnderstand that the lord deputie, being a man of great wisdome, knowlege, and experience, when he considered the fickle state of that wauering and rebellious nation of the Irishrie, who notwithstanding they had neuer so firmly promised, sworne, and vowed all allegiance and obedience to hir maiestie yet vpon euerie light occasion, without anie respect of faith and dutie, would fling out into secret conspiracies, and so into open rebellion, and then for the appeasing thereof, and the preseruation of hir good subiects, hir highnesse was driuen to inlarge hir garrisons, and to increase hir armie to hir excessiue charges, and all which companies were vittelled by the English pale and further, considering that the benefit which grew hereby, was generallie extended to the whole pale, who in equitie should be contributorie to the burthen, as they were partakers of the ease, and yet manie of them, pretending to haue liberties and priuileges, clamed to be exempted from anie contribution at all, whereby the residue were the more grieued, & the greater burthened, to their impouerishing, & the hinderance of their seruice the lord deputie caused a through search to be made in hir highnesse court of the exchekers in Ireland, of all the records, for and concerning all and all manner of liberties which at anie time had tofore bin granted to anie person or persons whatsoeuer · and in the end found that (verie few ancient liberties excepted) all were vsurped, or by statute repealed.

The gentlemen in the pale begin to repine against the cesse.

Liberties claimed to be discharged of the cesse

The records searched for liberties.

Wherevpon to ease the oppressed, and to make the burthen to be borne more vniuersallie, and so more indifferentlie, and for the better furtherance of hir highnesse seruice he commanded by proclamation all such liberties and fréedoms to be dissolued, as which either had no grant at all, or which had not that continuance of times out of memorie of man. And of this latter sort were manie made by a statute but to indure onelie for ten yeares, and all which were expired. And for this cause they neuer found fault before now that they are greeued, and therefore doo repine against cesse, and with open mouths crie out, that they were so poore that they could not beare anie césse, and that it was against the law. And here for your better vnderstanding what cesse is, and what is meant thereby, it is a prerogatiue of the prince, to impose vpon the countrie a certeine proportion of all kind of vittels for men and horsse, to be deliuered at a reasonable price called the quéens price, to all and euerie such souldiors as she is contented to be at charge withall, and so much as is thought competent for the lord deputies house, and which price is to be yeerelie rated and assessed by the lord deputie and the councell, with the assistants and assent of the nobilitie of the countrie, at such rates and prices as the souldiors may liue of his wages, and the said deputie of his interteinment.

Liberties dissolued by proclamation

What cesse is

These things although they were orderlie doone, yet certeine malecontents, finding themselues gréeued, bicause they should also now beare a portion, and be contributaries first they draw their heads togither, and make there supplication to the lord deputie and councell, which was receiued verie willinglie, and offer made that conference should be had with them, how and what waie it might best be deuised to ease there griefes, & not to charge the quéene. Wherevpon at a time appointed they all met,

The malecontents make their supplication to the lord deputie & councell to be discharged of the cesse.

met, and came in persons before the deputie and councell, where the said malecontents first opened their griefes, that they had certeine old and ancient priuileges and liberties which were taken from them, then that they were compelled to yeeld to an vnreasonable cesse, which they were not able to beare, and that was will and pleasure onlie, and contrarie to all law and reason, that anie such charge should be imposed vpon them without a parlement or grand councell.

When the lord deputie and councell heard them at full, they appointed a daie, when they should come and receiue their answer. In the meane time the lord deputie and councell consulted and considered of the matter, and resolued themselues vpon an answer. And when the daie came and they appeered, answer was made vnto them by the mouth of the lord chancellor, that they had no charters nor liberties at all to be found in hir highnesse records, other than such as were expired and of no validitie. And as for the greatnesse of the cesse, the burden whereof they had alleged to be vnreasonable and not to be borne, bicause they said & auouched that it was ten pounds & twelue pounds of ech plough land; it was offered that they should be discharged, if they would paie but fiue markes for euerie plough land. And whatsoeuer they said in deniall of the paieng of the cesse, it was and is to be proued, that it was not onelie hir maiesties prerogatiue which may not be impeached, but also to be prooued by most ancient records, that euer since the time of king Henrie the fourth, for the space of eight or nine score yeares, there hath bin still from time to time, as occasion hath required, the like charges imposed by the name of cesse by the deputie and councell, and such nobilitie as were sent for and did come to the same, now in question and by them repined at. Neuerthelesse, they repined and flatlie denied that they would yéeld to anie cesse, saieng and alledging as before, that it was against reason and law, and therefore praied that they might haue his lordships libertie to make their repaire ouer into England, and to acquaint hir highnesse with their case. Whereunto he answered, that he would neither giue any such leaue nor denie them to go. Whereupon they assembled themselues togither againe, and by the aduise of certeine busie headed lawiers and malecontented gentlemen, who had stirred and set them a worke to combine themselues to follow this sute, and contributed a masse of monie amongst themselues, for the charge of the said lawiers, namelie Barnabie Scurlocke, Richard Neteruill, and Henrie Burnell, who hauing béene sometimes students in the ins of the court in London, & acquainted with Littletons tenures, thought themselues so well fraughted with knowledge in the laws, as they were able to wade in all matters of the deepest points of the law. But if they had first (as it becommeth dutifull subiects) to haue looked in the booke of God, they should haue found it written there, that it was God himselfe who first made kings and established their thrones, and gaue them most excellent preeminences next to himselfe, that they should be vnder him the supreme gouernours vpon the earth, and haue that authoritie and prerogatiue, that all inferiors and subiects should and ought in all humblenesse and dutifulnesse submit themselues vnto the obedience of them for the Lords sake, bicause so is it the will of God, without sifting of his authoritie or examining his gouernment. For there is no power (as the apostle saith) but of God, & they are ordeined of God, wherfore who so resisteth them, resisteth God, and whose resistances & disobediences the Lord himselfe hath reuenged oftentimes on the disobedient. Wherfore euerie man is to be subiect in all humilitie & obedience vnto them in all maner of ordinances, being not against God, not onlie bicause of wrath, but also for conscience sake, especiallie in matters being well considered, & which doo concerne their one benefit and safetie. If this be the infallible truth, how farre were these men ouershot, that thus would dispute the princes prerogatiue with their Littletons tenures, and measure the same with their owne rules

The prerogatiue of a prince by the law of God.

rules and deuises? It had bin much better for them, & more to their commendations, if they had (as the scholers of Pythagoras) kept silence and had held their peace, vntill such time as they had beene better studied in their owne lawes and then they should haue found it written that the prince or king is the head and most excellent part of the bodie of the commonwealth, and through his gouernance the preseruer and defender of the whole bodie, and (as the prophet termeth them) to be nourishing fathers of the people which are the rest of the bodie, and for which causes the lawes doo attribute vnto him all honor, dignitie, prerogatiue, and preeminence aboue all others, and which his prerogatiue dooth not onelie extend to his owne person, and all that which he hath of his owne, but also to all his subiects. And the lawyers themselues doo so far stretch this for a *Maxime*, that whatsoeuer lawes be made and established either for the benefit of holie church or common profit, it is alwaies implied *Salua in omnibus regis prærogatiua*, and that nothing shall be intended to be preiudiciall to his crowne and dignitie But by all likelihood these men were not so faire read, or if they had, then malice or desire of some pelting lucre, which blindeth manie of that profession, had made them forgetfull of themselues & of their duties Well, these great lawiers beare the malecontented lords & gentlemen in hand, that their cause & sute was good and reasonable, and by the law to be warranted, & not to be doubted but the same would haue good successe Wherevpon they made vp their supplication and letters to hir maiestie, with the like letters to hir honorable priuie councell, dated the tenth of Ianuarie, 1576, and vnder the hands of Rowland vicount of Baltinglas, Ed of Deluin, Christopher of Hoth, Peter of Trimleston, Iames of Kellew, and Patrike Naugle barons, sir Oliuer Plunket, sir Thomas Nugeat, sir Christopher Chiuers, and sir William Searefield knights, Edward Plunket, Patrike Naugle, Patrike Husseie, George Plunket, Francis Nugeat, Laurence Nugeat, Nicholas Tasse, Iames Nugeat, and William Talbot, in the names of all the inhabitants within the English pale, had subscribed And then also they deliuered in the like order their letters of atturneie vnto their said agents, and so much monie for their expenses as was thought sufficient, with their order and promise to supplie what soeuer they should need And thus being furnished with all things to their contentments, they past ouer the seas, and made their repaire vnto the court of England, and there at time conuenient did exhibit their supplications and letters to hir maiestie and the lords of the councell, which in effect consisted in these points

The kings prerogatiue by the lawes of the realme

The impaled gentlemen send into England their agents to complaine.

First, that where there was a cesse imposed by the lord deputie and councell vpon the English pale for hir maiesties garrisons, they finding themselues grieued therewith, made their complaint thereof vnto the said lord deputie and councell for redresse, and could not be heard 1

The effect of the letters & complaints exhibited to hir maiestie and councell

Secondarilie, they affirmed that the said cesse, or anie other like to be imposed vpon them, was against the lawes, statutes, and vsages of that realme 2

Thirdlie, that the cesse was a most intollerable and grieuous burden, there being exacted out of euerie plough land ten and twelue pounds 3

Fourthlie, that in the leuieng and exacting, there were manie and sundrie abuses doone and committed. 4

When hir maiestie had throughlie read both the complaints and letters, she foorthwith sent and set them ouer to the lords of hir priuie councell to be considered, and the same to be throughlie examined; who foorthwith assembled themselues, and hauing read and heard the contents thereof, did compare them with the like letters sent vnto them from the said malecontented lords & gentlemen, as also with the instructions and aduertisements, which they likewise had receiued from the lord deputie and councell out of Ireland, concerning the same And after long debating of

The matter is referred to the councell

of the matter, that they might the better proue and vnderstand the greatnesse therof did by hir highnesse commandement call before them the earles of Kildare and Ormond, the vicount of Gormanstone, and the baron of Dunsanie, who then were attendant at the court, and declared vnto them the whole matter, and the maner of these mens procéedings both héere and in that realme, whose intent and meaning was in verie déed, vnder color to séeke some reliefe, to haue taken awaie wholie the imposing of anie cesse, and so consequentlie to haue taken awaie the right & prerogatiue, which hir maiestie & predecessors haue alwaies inioied, and without which that realme could not be defended, nor themselues preserued

These foure noblemen, when they had heard the whole matter, séemed to be sorie, and to mislike of their vnaduised procéedings they confessing and acknowledging that cesse hath beene alwaies vsed to be taken, and they thought him not to be a dutifull subiect, who would denie or impugne the same although they wished and did praie, that the poore inhabitants in times of scarsitie might be eased of some part of the burthen which they now presentlie did beare When the lords of the councell had proceeded herein so farre as they could, they deliuered vp their opinions to hir maiestie, aduertising that concerning the first article they could say nothing, but that they supposed that the doings of hir highnesse deputie was not so strict as was complained, bicause he had written otherwise

The answers of the councell to the articles of the complainers.

To the second their opinion was, that it touched hir maiesties prerogatiue, so much to be denied of that imposition, which hath béene vsed, allowed, and continued for manie yeares, and in times of hir sundrie predecessors, that now it might not be suffered to be impeached, vnlesse hir highnesse would loose and forgo hir title, right, and interest to the crowne of Ireland, or else support the whole burthen and charge to defend the same of hir owne pursse neither which extreamities could or might in anie wise be tollerated

To the third, that the cesse was intollerable, and not able to be borne, they thought that to be true, if ten pounds and twelue pounds should be demanded out of euerie plough land, as they complained: but they vnderstood by credible informations from the deputie and councell the contrarie, & that they were offered at fiue marks the plough land. which was supposed to be verie easie and reasonable.

To the fourth article their opinion was, that if anie such abuses were doone, it were good the same were set downe and knowne, and a redresse therof to be ordered

Hir maiestie offended with the complainers

When hir highnesse had read and thoroughlie considered their opinions and resolutions, and finding hir selfe vndutifullie to be handled by hir subiects, commanded by the aduise of hir councell the said agents which followed their sute, to be committed to the Fleet, and foorthwith wrote hir letters to the said hir deputie and councell, finding hir selfe grieued with the said hir subiects of the pale, that the reléeuing of hir armie with vittels by waie of cesse, should be auouched to be a matter against law, and ancient custome. and yet the same both in hir time and in the times of hir progenitors, hath vsuallie béene imposed, and now impugned by some such as in times past had subscribed therevnto, in preiudice of hir prerogatiue, and hinderance of hir seruice. And therfore she did not onelie mislike, & was greatlie offended with these their presumptuous and vndutifull maner of procéeding; but also found fault with the said deputie and hir councell there, that they would and did suffer hir prerogatiue in contempt of hir highnesse and authoritie to be so impugned, & the parties not committed & punished by which meanes the matter at the first and in the beginning might haue beene remedied And therefore as hir highnesse had alreadie giuen order for committing them to the Fléet, for the punishment of the agents which were sent ouer with the complaints and letters, for such their iustifieng and mainteining

The agents of the complainers sent to the Fleet

Hir maiestie offended with the lord deputie and councell for suffering the complainers vnpunished mainteining the imposition of the said cesse to be against the lawes and customes of that hir realme, and therefore séeking to impeach hir prerogatiue and roiall authoritie: but also willed and commanded him and all hir whole councell to send for those lords and gentlemen, which subscribed the letters sent vnto hir highnesse, who if they will stand to mainteine their assertions, and auow the imposition of the cesse to be against the lawes and customes of the realme, and not warrantable by hir prerogatiue, that then hir pleasure was, that these persisting and auowing to be likewise committed.

The complainers which subscribed to be sent and committed to ward.

And concerning the abuses perpetrated in the maner of the leuieng the said cesse, hir commandement and order was, that whosoeuer were culpable therein, he should be punished with all seueritie. And herewith also she was contented, and had giuen order for some qualification to be yeelded vnto, as by the said hir deputie and councell should be thought méet, considering the scarsitie and the dearth which was then in the said English pale. And in case the said lords and gentlemen vpon better consideration will be contented to acknowledge their offenses, and submit themselues simplie, and vnder their hand-writings: that then they to receiue fauour. And as for those and such hir learned men, as were present at the debating of the matter, and did forbeare (contrarie to their dutie & knowledge) to stand in mainteinance against the said prerogatiue, to be displaced and discharged out of hir fée, and their places to be supplied by such others as by the deputies shall be thought méet. Immediatlie vpon the receipt of hir maiesties letters, and the like from the councell, the lord deputie and councell by their letters sent not onelie for those malcontents, which had before subscribed to the letters sent to hir highnesse and councell, but also in discretion for such others who for their disguised and cunning manner of dealings were speciallie noted to be councellors, ringleaders, and procurors of these letters to hir maiestie and the lords of hir councell: who when they were come, and then being dealt withall, touching their claime of fréedome from cesse: their answers were arrogant and wilfull, and repining against hir maiesties prerogatiue, and affirming boldlie in plaine spéeches and without anie sticking, that no cesse could be imposed but by parlement or a grand councell, and whatsoeuer was otherwise set downe, was against the law: and so stubbornelie they were bent therein, that they would not yeeld to anie conference: wherevpon they were all committed to the castell of Dublin, notwithstanding some of them (after they had better aduised themselues) yéelded a submission and praied mercie.

The complainers acknowledging their faults to be gentlie vsed.

The lawyers of her maiesties fee mainteining the complaints, to be displaced.

The malcontents & their abbettors sent for.

The proud answers of the malcontents.

The malcontents are all committed to prison.

Which doings when the lord deputie and councell had foorthwith aduertised to hir highnesse & the councell in England, they nothing liking these arrogant and disloiall parts of these impaled malecontents, sent for their agents, and hauing the like conference with them, found them of like disposition, being as a fit couer to the pot, verie froward, arrogant, and wilfull: wherevpon they were remooued from the Fléet to the Tower, a place appointed for the offendors in capitall causes, and for such (being impugners of hir prerogatiue) as be supposed to offend in the néerest degrée to the highest. These things when were notified vnto the lords and gentlemen in Ireland, they were maruellouslie gréeued, but not the one nor the other would giue ouer, vntill their arrogancies and insolencies were by apparant matter and good records fullie conuinced, and condemned: for which the lord chancellor of verie purpose was sent ouer into England, who so fullie, effectuallie, and discréetlie did resolue hir maiestie and councell in euerie point, which the parties agents could not denie.

The agents for their frowardnesse sent to the Tower.

The lord chancellor of Ireland sent into England.

Now in the end they considered better of themselues, and sent their humble submission in writing vnder their hands to the said lords of hir maiesties priuie councell, confessing that they had disloiallie and insolentlie, both in words and

The agents submit themselues.

writings offended most greeuouslie, protesting yet that their intent was neuer to denie hir roiall prerogatiue, to vse the same as occasion should serue, but onelie to redresse certeine abuses, and therefore most humblie praied they might find some mercie, and that the hard and painfull imprisonment which they had susteined, might be a sufficient punishment for the same. Wherevpon they were released, putting in bonds of one thousand pounds, that within fiue daies they should depart homewards into Ireland, and after their transportation & arriuall thither, should make their immediat repaire, without staie or lingering, to the lord deputie and councell, and there to giue their attendance, vntill by them they should be licenced to depart. At their comming home they performed the conditions of their obligations, and most humblie in like order submitted themselues to the lord deputie and councell, and then (according to an order thought good by the lords of the councell in England, and referred to the liking of the lord deputie and councell in Ireland) the same was after long trauerse ended and determined. But heere to set downe what practises, informations, & deuises were made against the said deputie, by the said malecontents, and some (by their means) of no small calling had informed that he had alienated the hearts of the subiects from loiall obedience, that he had farmed all the whole relme, that he had wasted hir maiesties treasures and reuenues, that he wanted policie in his gouernement, that he should for this dealing with hir subiects be reuoked, that he did all things by his owne mind without the aduise of others, contrarie to the course of other deputies before him, that he did grant manie pardons, to the imboldening of manie which offended the more.

The agents were released vpon their bonds to appeare before the lord deputie and councell.

The false accusations made against the lord deputie.

These and manie such other like vntruths they spred. But truth, which is the daughter of time, did manifest it to the whole world, that their ouerthrow was his credit, and his preuaile was to their reproch and shame. And albeit manie were the pangs and inward greefes, which for a time by the meanes of their false suggestions he susteined, and with great paines he couered: yet in the end it turned to his great ioy and comfort. And here by the way, if a man without offense should fall into the consideration of this their resistance, and repining against the cesse, which was then enterprised and taken in hand, when the whole land stood in a broken and doubtfull state, and the time verie dangerous, when the earle of Desmond frowardlie kicked at the like, and all the lords in Mounster had contrarie to their owne orders and promises, denied, and commanded their tenants to denie after the manner of the English pale, to paie anie cesse, when Iames Fitzmoris being furnished with men, monie, and munition, by the pope and king of Spaine, was dailie looked for to come and inuade the land, and when the great ones hauing hollow harts, and addicted to papistrie, did dailie gape and expect for the same, when the disloiall Irishrie in Mounster and Connaugh were combined and ioined in these conspiracies, when Rorie Og, Omore, Connor Mac Cormake, Oconnor & others, animated by the forsaid conspiracies, were vp in open rebellion, and vsed most execrable outrages, when some of the best townes in Leinster did aid, comfort, and mainteine these rebels, and besides manie other circumstances concurring heerewith: might it not be well presumed (and as it was so doubted) that the cause being like, they should also be combined and linked alike? And might not the whole world iudge that neither barrell was the better herring? And yet notwithstanding it fell in the end to a better effect. For the lords and inhabitants in the English pale, since the time of the conquest by king Henrie the second, and since their first arriuall into this land, it hath not béene lightlie knowne that they had broken their faith and their allegiance, and not to rebell in anie waies against the crowne of England, and the kings of the same, sauing as now in respect to saue their purses, rather than meaning anie breach of dutie, had ouer shot themselues

The fidelitie of the English pale to the crowne.

which

which vpon a further consideration of the truth they repented, and vpon their submission were pardoned, in hope and vpon their promise that they would neuer thensefoorth offend, nor be found faultie with the like. During the trauerse about the cesse, manie things happened in the land worthie to be reprehended (as great and sundrie were the aduertisements from out of France by such Englishmen as were there imploied) of an intention of Iames Fitzmoris to inuade Ireland, who had béene at Rome with the pope, and there was he princelie interteined, and returned from thense with a good masse of treasure, making his returne through Spaine, and by the king thereof was furnished with men, munitions, & treasures, and all things necessarie. Which things were by letters from him signified vnto the chéefest of all Mounster his secret confederats, and they being papists both in bodie & soule, desirous of change of gouernement, and to be vnder a prince of their owne superstition, did dailie languish and expect his comming. Wherefore hir maiestie and councell, hauing the like intelligences, doo also prepare monie, munitions, vittels, and men, and all other things necessarie for the withstanding of him.

Rorie Og, Omore, and Connor Mac Cormake, Oconnor, and their coparteners, contrarie to their othes, submissions, and promises, hoping for aid out of Connaugh, began anew to gather their fréends and confederats out of seuerall places, to the number of a hundred swords, which with his owne made aboue seauen score; and being animated by Shane Burke to continue a rebell, he burned diuerse mens haggards, poore mens houses, and sundrie villages, and committed manie outrages: and being not resisted, he tooke such incouragement of his successe, that leauing poore villages, he went to great towns, as to the Naas, distant from Dublin about ten miles. The verie same daie that he came thither at night, was the patrone daie of the said towne, commonlie called the church holie daie, which daie after the maner of that countrie, and not much vnlike the festiuall daies which the Ethniks and Pagans were woont to celebrate to their idoll gods of Bacchus and Venus, they spent in gluttonie, drunkennesse, and surfetting. And after they had so filled their panches, and the daie was gone, they somewhat late in the night went to their beds, hauing forgotten to make fast their towne gates, or put anie watch to ward them. Which thing Rorie Og when he knew, and hauing intelligence that euerie man was in his bed asléepe, then he in the dead night came to the towne with all his companie, who like vnto a sort of furies and diuels new come out of hell, carried vpon the ends of their poles flankes of fier, and did set as they went the low thatched houses on fier. And the wind being then somewhat great and vehement, one house tooke fier of another, and so in a trise and moment the whole towne was burned; and yet in the towne supposed to be fiue hundred persons in outward appearance, able to haue resisted them: but they being in their dead sléeps, suddenlie awaked, were so amazed, that they wist not what to doo, for the fier was round about them and past quenching, and to pursue the enimie they were altogither vnfurnished, and durst not to doo it, neither if they would they could tell which way to follow him. For he taried verie little in the towne, sauing that he sat a little while vpon the crosse in the market place, and beheld how the fire round about him was in euerie house kindled, and whereat he made great ioy and triumph, that he had doone and exploited so diuelish an act. And then after a short space he arose and departed with great triumph according to his accustomed vsage in all his euill actions, but yet contrarie to his vsage, he killed no one person in the towne. As he returned he preied and spoiled the countrie, and ranging to and fro, as his wauering head carried him, he came verie shortlie vnto the towne at Leighlin bridge, and there burned part of the towne.

The burning of the Naas by Rorie Og.

Rorie Og burneth the towne at Leighlin bridge.

But George Carew brother vnto Peter Carew, then constable of the said towne and

George Carew with twelue persons against 840 setteth vpon them & driueth them to flie

and fort, hauing then but a small ward to defend the violence of the enimie, and yet thinking it should be too great a dishonour vnto him to be bearded with a traitor, and to let him depart vnfought withall he issued out vpon him, hauing with him onelie seuen horssemen and fiue shot, and gaue the charge vpon the said rebels, being two hundred and fortie, with such a courage and valiantnesse (and they astonied bicause it was so sudden and in the night time) that he killed some of them and then they with the losse of those men began to flie. But at last when they perceiued his force to be but small, and too weake to resist their great number, they returned and chased him to the verie walles of the castell, where if he and his small companie had not like valiant and good souldiers acquited themselues, the rebels had entred into the house, for they were within the gate and there fought, but driuen out and the gate shut. At this bickering they lost sixtéene men, and one of their chiefe capteines named Piers Mornagh, who died verie shortlie after of his hurt. Capteine Carew lost but two men and one horsse, but euerie one of the rest of his companie was hurt.

The castell in danger to be taken

The enimie, nothing triumphing nor liking this interteinement, presentlie retired and departed, by which meanes the one halfe of the towne was saued. After their returne from hense, they spoiled sundrie townes and villages vpon the confines & borders of the English pale. And albeit they were verie egerlie followed and pursued, and oftentimes with losse of his companie, yet he was so mainteined, and his watch and spiall was so good, that partlie by the helpe of his acquaintance, and partlie by meanes of the water bogs and fastenesse in euerie place, he was in safegard and safetie. In this pursute made vpon him, it happened that a parlée was appointed betwéene capteine Harington and him, vnto whom Rorie Og swore and promised most faithfullie to yeeld himselfe to some conformitie and order. The capteine nothing mistrusting him, gaue too much credit to his subtill promises, and did so open himselfe vnto him, that through his owne follie Rorie tooke aduantage, and perforce tooke him and Alexander Cosbie, who was with him in hand, both which he handfasted togither, and caried them along with him as his water spaniels, thorough woods and bogs, threatening them still to kill them. This thing being knowne, great sorow and greefe was conceiued of the lord deputie, and of all good Englishmen, and dailie practises were deuised for their deliueries, and at length by treatie of friends an agreement was in a manner concluded. But before the same was fullie perfected, a draught was made by Robert Harepole constable of Catherlough, to intrap and to make a draught vpon Rorie: for he knowing where the said Rorie was woont to hant, and by good espials learning where his couch and cabine was, he being accompanied with Parker lieutenant to capteine Furse and fiftie of his band, earelie in the morning, about two houres before daie, he went and marched to the verie place where Rorie laie, and beset the same. Rorie hearing an vnwoonted noise, and suspecting the worst, he came suddenlie vpon Harington and Cosbie, thinking to haue slaine them, and gessing in the darke to the place where they laie, gaue him diuerse wounds, but none deadlie, the greatest was the losse of the little finger on his left hand. Robert Harepole when he had broken open the doore of the cabin, he tooke as manie as were within prisoners: but Rorie himselfe and one other priuilie in the darke stole awaie and crept among the bushes, so that he could not be found. The souldiers in the meane time, making spoile of all such goods as they found, killed all the men who were there, but saued capteine Harington and Cosbie.

The enimie is driuen to retire and flie awaie

Rorie Og by slight and deceipt taketh capteine Harington prisoner

A draught made vpon Rorie Og by Harepole

Capteine Harington is hurt.

Rorie Og escapeth

Rorie Og albeit he was glad that he was so escaped, yet in a great griefe for the losse of his prisoners, and minding to be reuenged, priuilie with all the companies which he could get, besides them which Shane Burke had sent vnto him out of Connagh,

Capteine Harington is deliuered.

Connagh, he went to Catherlough earlie in the morning, and burned a few haggards of corne and a few houses, and so retired. Robert Harepole hearing hereof, foorthwith followeth them with ten or twelue horsses which he had in a readinesse, and at a foord not far off he ouertooke them, and killed sixtéene or seuentéene of his best men, and Rorie himselfe escaped verie narowlie, and so continued still in his former outrages, vntill he was intrapped and taken by a deuise of his owne to intrap others, which was in this manner. Vpon the nine and twentith of Iune 1578, he set foorth of purpose an espiall, whom he had cunninglie framed, and made apt for the purpose to go to sir Barnard Fitzpatrike lord of vpper Osserie, and to tell him by the waie of great friendship and in secrecie, that Rorie Og had béene of late in the countie of Kilkennie, and there had taken a great preie and spoile, of pots, pans, and other houshold-stuffe, which he might easilie take if he would aduenture the matter, and if he did wiselie handle it, he might also take Rorie himselfe and all his companie, which as he said (but vntrulie) that they were but few in number. The lord of vpper Osserie, neither beléeuing nor yet mistrusting this newes, and yet forecasting the worst, did put himselfe in readinesse to follow the occasion that was offered, and taking with him a good companie of horssemen and footmen, went towards the place where the bait was laied, and being come néere vnto it made staie, or else he had beene intrapped, and sent thirtie of his men into the woods to serch for Rorie. But the baron himselfe with certeine of his horssemen and shot staied in the plaines, to attend the issue of the matter. The companie were no sooner entered into the woods, but Rorie the rebell shewed himselfe with a thirtie persons, the rest lieng in ambush, and he was of the opinion that his fame and estimation was so great, and of such value among the Irishrie, that no man durst to aduenture vpon him if he once saw his presence. But he was deceiued. For at the first sight and view of him, the lord of Osseries Kerne gaue the charge vpon him, and at their incounter one of them lighted vpon him, and with his sword presentlie thrust him through the bodie: which was no sooner doone, but two or three hacked vpon him, & gaue him such deadlie wounds that he fell downe and died, the same being the last daie of Iune beforesaid, and so this bloudie caitife, deliting all in bloud, perished and died in his owne bloud.

Rorie Og burneth Catherlough.

1578

A bait laid for the lord of vpper Osserie

Rorie Og is slaine.

But before Rorie Og was thus brought to destruction, the lord deputie made a iournie to the borders of Offalie and Lex, to haue met with the foresaid Rorie Og & his companions the Oconnors for the suppressing of their insolencie, who were growen into such a pride by taking of capteine Harrington, and their strength so increased, that with most vndutifull termes they breathed out slanderous spéeches against hir maiestie, as which were not to be indured. Wherefore he beset the whole countrie & confines as he thought best, to stop their passage and to annoie them, & so he went to Kilkennie, and there by sundrie examinations found people of all degrees in that towne to haue relieued the said Rorie with vittels and all other necessaries, for his feeding and defense, with whome he tooke order according to their deserts. At his being there he sent for the earle of Desmond to come vnto him, bicause he had refused to come to the lord president when he sent for him sundrie times, and for which cause the said lord president was there to complaine vpon him, as also that he had of his owne authoritie, without anie warrant, gathered togither a rable of lewd and vnrulie followers, which harried vp and downe the countrie, eating and spending vpon the same, contrarie to all good orders, and which was not to be suffered.

The lord deputie maketh a iournie vpō Rorie Og.

The earle of Desmōd sent for to come to the lord deputie to Kilkennie

Which earle foorthwith, vpon the receipt of the said letters, came to Kilkennie to the lord deputie, and there being examined of those his vnséemelie parts, confessed some part: and for excuse he alledged and much mistrusted and doubted the president, least he would haue staied him, and haue vsed him hardlie, for which he

The earle of Desmond and the lord president of Mounster are reconciled

he was blamed and reprooued by the lord deputie. But in the end, when they came togither, they were reconciled and made good friends, and then he promised vpon his returne home to disperse abroad his companions, and to obeie the president as hir maiesties principall officer of that prouince, and to come vnto him at all commandements, and which things he performed. For not long after he vttered and

The earle of Desmond discouereth to the lord president Iames Fitzmoris his practises

bewraied to the said lord president the practises of Iames Fitzmoris, who by the arriuall of certeine Frenchmen and Irishmen vnto Sligo, in a ship of saint Malowes, did what he could to stirre & make a rebellion in Mounster and Connagh whereby a plot was laied for the staie of those Frenchmen, and the apprehension of the Irishmen These were good demonstrations to the vtter shew of the obedience and loialtie of the said earle, but in truth méere dissimulation, as afterwards it appeared

Connagh was in some part troubled, by means of Orwarke capteine of his sur-

Comers in Connagh

name, in whose countrie there were certeine comers of moine and mainteined by him. The coronell vnderstanding hereof, he sent vnto Orwarke for them, and who

Orwarke refusing to deliuer the comers his castell is taken, and he submitteth himselfe

denied to deliuer anie of them wherefore to correct that his pride, disobedience, and insolencie, he sent a priuat band of footmen, who distressed Orwarke, slue his men, tooke his castell, and put all the ward to the sword Wherevpon he came with all humilitie and submitted himselfe, and craued pardon. All the residue of Connagh was verie quiet, and increased hir maiesties reuenues to the yearelie summe of eightéene hundred pounds by the yeare, with good contentation And now when it was thought that all things were quiet throughout all Ireland, behold sudden aduertisements were giuen both vnto hir maiestie and councell in England,

Tho Stukeleie suspected to come into Ireland.

and to the lord deputie in Ireland, that Thomas Stukeleie was arriued out of Italie vnto Cadis in Spaine, with certeine men, ships, and munitions assigned vnto him by the pope And being accompanied with certeine strangers attending vpon him, he was come to the seas, to land vpon some part of the realme of Ireland, in traitorous maner to inuade the same, and to prouoke the people to ioine with him in

Great preparation made against Stukeleie

rebellion. All things, as well men, munitions, monie, vittels, and all other things necessarie were prouided and prepared for the preuenting of them, as well by sea as by land but in the end, aduertisement was giuen from out of Portugall, that his enterprise was directed another waie, and to another purpose, and so all things were

The pope his fauour to Stukeleie

quiet Neuerthelesse, it appeared that he was in great fauour with the pope, and was appointed to some speciall seruice against hir maiestie, if opportunitie would haue serued, & all other things had fallen out as it was deuised And for the incouraging of him, the pope besides great treasures liberallie bestowed vpon him, he gaue him sundrie titles of honour, and made him knight, baron of Rosse and Idron, vicount

Stukeleie his honour and titles.

of the Morough & Kenshlagh, and earle of Wexford and Catherlough, and marquesse of Lemster, and generall to the most holie father Gregorie the seuenth *Pontifici maximo*

In the middle of these broiles, the vicount Baltinglasse, one of the chiefe impugners and malecontents against the cesse, wrote his letters to the earle of Or-

The vicount Baltinglasse complaineth to the earle of Ormond against sir Nicholas Bagnoll

mond, then attendant at the court of England, and complaineth of great iniuries and spoiles to the value of two hundred pounds in monie, besides numbers of shéepe and kine, doone vpon him and his tenants by the English souldiers, vnder sir Nicholas Bagnoll knight marshall, when they were lodged one night in his house at Baltinglasse, in the time that they serued vpon the rebell Rorie Og Which

The earle of Ormond aduertiseth the complaint of the vicount to hir maiestie and councell.

letter was by the said earle shewed to hir maiestie, and to the lords of hir most honourable priuie councell. Vpon which complaint, bicause it seemed somewhat pitious and lamentable, and hir maiestie partlie persuaded (as a matter verie likelie to be true) that such gréeuous extortions suffered vncorrected, made hir gouernement

ment more hatefull to that nation, than did anie of the Irish exactions letters were sent to the lord deputie, to take care with all diligence, that the poore oppressed might be satisfied, and the offendors also be punished, according to the quantities and qualities of their offenses.

Hir maiestie sendeth letters in the behalfe of the vicount B. Itinglasse

The lord deputie, before the receipt of these letters, was complained vnto by the said vicount, and sir Nicholas Pagnoll was called to answer such hurts as were obiected against him. And vpon the replication of the vicount, sir Lucas Dillon and sir Thomas Fitzwilliams knights were appointed to examine all such witnesses, as were brought foorth for proofe of the surmises, which in the end fell out to none effect, for nothing could be prooued to anie purpose. But it appeared manifest of the contrarie, by the report and testimonie of sundrie gentlemen of verie good credit, and how that the said marshall at his first comming to that towne, had giuen great charge to euerie capteine, to foresee that no iniurie should be offered, no spoiles committed, nor anie thing to be taken by anie souldier or other person without present paiment, protesting and proclaiming execution according to marshall law, vpon such as should doo the contrarie.

The vicount Baltinglasse complaineth to the lord deputie against sir Nicholas Bagnoll.

Likewise at his departure from thense, he made the like proclamation, that if there were anie which had anie cause of complaint for anie wrong or iniurie doone, or that anie thing were taken and not paied for, he should come and be heard, and be satisfied. And by this it dooth appeare, that the surmises were made rather to aggrauat his greefe conceiued against the imposition of the cesse, than for anie good matter in truth. Wherefore as he and his complices preuailed little in the one, no more had he successe or credit in the other. For the matter was fullie certified vnto the lords of the councell, and a request therewith made verie earnestlie, that the said vicount might be reprooued, and also terrified to proffer or practise any such vntrue and indirect dealings. By these and other the like practises of the said vicount, that bicause he did not brooke nor like of the cesse, he thought by waie of exclames to aggrauat his owne case, that thereby the lord deputie might fall into the dislike of hir maiestie, and be out of fauour, but the contrarie in the end fell out to his owne reproofe and discredit.

The vicount Baltinglasses complaints are vntrue

When the lord deputie had ended and finished all his businesse, and had set the whole realme in order and peace, being now deliuered from inward and ciuill warre, and from the feare of Stukeleies inuasion, he prepared (according to hir maiesties former letters of the six and twentith of March last past) to take his passage for England, and to make his repaire to hir highnesse. And so when all things were accordinglie prepared, and the wind & weather so seruing, he deliuered vp the sword according to hir maiesties commandement, the six & twentith of Maie 1578, vnto sir William Drurie, then lord president of Mounster. And then being conducted by the said now lord iustice and councell, and all the nobilitie, citizens & people to the waters side, he imbarked himselfe, taking his leaue in most honourable, louing, and courteous maner of euerie man. And at his verie entring into the ship for his farewell vnto that whole land and nation, he recited the words of the 114 psalme, "In exitu Israel de Aegypto, & domus Iacob de populo barbaro," alluding thereby to the troublesome state of Moses in the land of Aegypt, and of his departure from out of the same: who notwithstanding he had in great wisedome, care, and policie gouerned the stiffnecked people of Israell, had doone manie miracles and woonderous works to their comfort, had deliuered them from manie great perils and dangers, had preserued and also kept them in peace and safetie, had in the end through the mightie hand of God brought them out of the hands of Pharao, and from out of the land of Aegypt, and had giuen them the sight of the land of promise: yet he found them alwaies a froward and peruerse generation, a stiffenecked and an vngratefull

The whole land in peace

1578

The sword is deliuered to sir William Drurie as lord iustice

The departure of sir Henrie Sidneie, and of his last saiengs.

The notable works of Moses, & yet he not accepted

vngratefull people euen no lesse as this noble man, and most woorthie gouernour hath found of the people of this most cursed nation. Who notwithstanding he was a verie painfull traueller both by daie and night, in fowle and in faire weathers, in stormes and in tempests, in troubles and in dangers, in scarsitie and in penurie, in danger of the enimie and perill of his life and yet continuallie studieng, deuising, trauelling, toiling, and labouring to doo them good (as he did full manie and often times) which so long as they felt the ease & comfort, so long were they contented and quiet: but otherwise most vngratefull and vnthankefull And offering vnto him the like reward as Licurgus receiued of the most vnthankfull Lacedemonians, who when he had recouered that sauage nation to a ciuill life, and a politike gouernement, and in the end reduced them to that order and maner, as they became to be feared of all their neighbors, they in recompense euill intreated him in verie bad speaches, and strake out one of Licurgus his eies But these men for thousands and infinit commodities, would not onelie haue bereft his lordship of both his eies, but also doone him a further inconuenience (if successe had happened) according to their malice

The painfull trauels of the lord deputie not considered

The ingratitude of the Lacedemonians to Licurgus.

And now here by the waie, let it not be offensiue to set downe somewhat of much concerning this woorthie and noble man for the course of his life He was borne and descended of a noble house and parentage, his father named sir William Sidneie, a knight of great reputation and credit in the countie of Kent, and in great fauour with king Henrie the eight, in whose time, and with his great good liking, he and others lustie yoong gentlemen of the court trauelled into Spaine and other nations, to visit and to sée the maner of the emperours and other princes courts: his mother descended of the house of Charles Brandon duke of Suffolke, vnto whom she was verie néere alied This yoong gentleman, his father being deceassed, and he of verie tender and yoong yeeres, was brought vp in the court vnder the same maister as was king Edward the sixt, and profited verie well, both in the Latine and French toongs, for he had a verie good wit, and was verie forward in all good actions, and whereof was conceiued some good things would come of him: his countenance was verie amiable, and his behauiour verie gentle and courteous, in whome king Henrie the eight (being his godfather) had a verie great liking, and made him be attendant and plaiefellow with prince Edward

The parentage of sir Henrie Sidneie

Sir Henrie Sidneie was brought vp in the court

The prince fell in such a good familiaritie and good liking of him, that he vsed him not onelie as a companion, but manie times as a bedfellow, and so delighted in his companie, that for the most part they would neuer be asunder, neither in health, nor in sickenesse, vntill the dieng daie of the prince who then departed his life in this gentlemans armes Somewhat before his death, the king gaue the order of knighthood to this gentleman, for a memorie and a recompense of his good will and loue: vpon which daie also he did the like vnto sir William Cicill, now lord Burghlie and lord high treasuror of all England by meanes of which their conioined aduancement, there entred a verie feruent affection and good will betwéene them, with a reciproke answering of beneuolence each one to the other, vntill their dieng daies This noble gentleman for his forwardnesse in all good actions, was as it were the paragon of the court, by reason of the manie good gifts which God had bestowed vpon him euerie waie For concerning the bodie, he was goodlie of person and well compact, and well beseene, he was comelie and of a good countenance, he was so courteous and of so good behauiour, he was so wise and so modest, so vertuous and so godlie, so discréet and so sober, as he was another Scipio: being but yoong in yeares, and old in behauiour, and finallie so rare a man, as that age had not affoorded manie better This man for his excellent good gifts, he was made ambassador into France, being but about one and twentie yeares of

Sir Henrie Sidneie the king his companion and bedfellow.

The king died in sir Henrie Sidneis armes

The king dubbeth sir Henrie Sidneie and sir William Cicill knights in one daie

Edm. Molineux

Sir Henrie Sidneie an ambassador sundrie times

of age; and twise in one yeare after that into Scotland and by quéene Marie ioined in commission with others to attend king Philip his comming into England, for the mariage betwéene their maiesties. And now in this hir maiesties reigne, he was sent ambassador into France, to treat a peace or pacification betwéene the prince of Condie and the duke of Guise.

In the beginning and about the second or third yeare of hir maiesties reigne, he was made knight of the garter, and lord president of Wales, and after one of hir maiesties most honorable priuie councell. But before this immediatlie vpon his returne from out of Spaine, he accompanied the lord Thomas lord Fitzwaters his brother in law into Ireland: where he was made treasuror at the warres, one of the principall offices in the land: and in course of time & yeares for his excellencie in knowledge and experience in that land, he was made lord iustice fome times, and was lord deputie thrée times. In which offices, how he did most honorablie acquite himselfe his acts doo declare, and the summarie recitall shall partlie discouer and set downe. He was no sooner placed in gouernement, but first and foorthwith he laid downe his plot, wherevpon he would ground & laie the foundation of his gouernement, and according to it would he frame and direct all his actions: which plot and deuise consisteth in these points, religion towards God, obedience to the prince, the peace of the people, and the well gouernement in all things concerning the commonwealth, either in causes ciuill or martiall.

Sir Henrie Sidneie lord president of Wales and knight of the garter.

Sir Henrie Sidneie lord treasuror at armes.

He was lord iustice fome times.

The plot of sir Henrie Sidneies gouernement.

Concerning religion, he was no more carefull in his owne person, but the like also in his priuat familie, where he had dailie exercises of praiers, both earlie and late, morning & euening, neither would he haue anie to serue him, who was not affected to religion, and of an honest conuersation. Atheists and papists he detested, dronkards and adulterers he abhorred, blasphemous and dissolute persons he could not abide. And at his first being in authoritie in Ireland, & finding the whole land generallie (a few priuat places excepted) to be either of no religion, or of papisticall religion, and being openlie by a preacher out of a pulpit aduertised, that in the remote places of that land, manie a soule was borne which neuer receiued baptisme, nor knew anie christening, great was his gréefe and much was he vnquieted, vntill he had found the redresse thereof. Wherefore he aduertised hir maiestie, & most earnestlie sued & praied for redresse & reformation, which in the end was granted, & a commission sent to him for the same: which foorthwith he committed to the archbishops & bishops to execute, with whom he ioined, furthered and holpe them accordinglie to the vttermost. But yet it tooke not that good effect as he wished and willed it might. And as for ecclesiasticall liuings which were of his gift and disposition, he would neuer bestow, but vpon such, as of whome he conceiued a good opinion, both for his religion and honestie.

Religion.

Manie borne in Ireland neuer christened.

The prince, who was scarse knowne in manie places in that land, he brought both to knowledge and obedience. The wild he tamed, the froward he reformed, the disobedient he punished, the traitors he persecuted, the rebels he chastised, the proud he made to stoope, and that arrogant and most insolent Shane Oneile, who could abide no equall, nor acknowledge a superior, by a draught was brought to his deserued confusion, & whose head for a trophie, & for the example of Gods iustice laied vpon him, was set vpon a pole vpon the gate of the castell of Dublin. The whole prouince of Vlster, with all the mightie personages of the same, he brought to the quéenes peace & obedience. The earle of Clanricard he tooke and imprisoned, and his vntamed springals he draue to submission, and to sweare dutie and obedience. The vnconstant earle of Desmond and all his Gnaldines and followers, and the proud and vngratefull earle of Clancar, and all the Irishrie of his adherents, he made them perforce to submit themselues, and to craue pardon. The Cauenaghs, the Otooles, the Obirnes, the Ocomores, the Omores, and a rable of other like septs, togither

Shane Oneile slaine.

All Vlster brought to obedience.

The earle of Clanricard imprisoned.

The mightie earles in Mounster brought to submission.

The rebels in Leinster tamed

with Rorie Og, Pheon Mac Hew, and other their leaders and guides in Leinster he tamed, and perforce compelled to sweare loialtie and subiection. Lastlie, the malecontents against hir maiesties prerogatiue for the cesse in the end cried *Peccaui*, and conformed themselues in all dutifulnesse.

The malecontents against the cesse reformed

And when he had trauelled long in these affaires, which he saw could not haue continuance, vnlesse they by some other meanes might be kept vnder gouernement: he by pithie persuasions, sound arguments, great reasons, and continuall sutes to hir maiestie and councell, obteined to haue rulers and gouernors to be placed in the remote prouinces, and sound, learned, and vpright iust lawiers out of England to be sent ouer, for the direction of the gouernement, according to the lawes of England: which in the end hir maiestie most gratiouslie granted, and he most ioifullie obteined.

Sir Humfreie Gilbert coronell in Mounster

Sir Iohn Perot, Sir William Drurie lord presidents in Mounster

In Mounster therefore first he placed a coronell to breake the ise, namelie sir Humfreie Gilbert, a valiant, a worthie, and a notable man, both for his martiall seruice, and his ciuill gouernement: after him followed the like and worthie gentleman sir Iohn Perot knight: and lastlie the valiant and prudent sir William Drurie: which both were lord presidents. This man was afterwards lord iustice, and the other at these presents is lord deputie of that land.

Sir Edward Fitton and sir Nicholas Malbie gouernors in Connagh

In Connagh sir Edward Fitton knight, a verie wise and a modest gentleman, late treasuror at armes, was lord president: and after him was sir Nicholas Malbie knight, a valiant and expert man in martiall matters, and verie wise and of good knowledge in publike and ciuill causes: who could verie exactlie handle the sword, and vse the pen, he (I saie) was made coronell of all Connagh. And how well the foresaid rulers and gouernors did rule by the sword, with the assistance of their capteins, and how vprightlie they ministred law and iustice by the aduice of the councellors in their seuerall prouinces, the records and registers of their dooings doo at large witnesse and set foorth. The like order he tooke also at Dublin, which being the metropole and chiefe citie of the whole land, and where are hir maiesties principall and high courts, to answer the law to all sutors throughout the whole realme: and he considering that a great defect was in the administration of iustice in those courts, by reason of kinred, affinitie, and priuat affections among the chiefe iudges and officers of that countrie birth:

English lawyers placed to be iustices in the courts

he by his like earnest sutes to hir maiestie, procured them to be remoued, and their roomes to be supplied with such wise, graue and learned Englishmen, as were sent from out of England to be chiefe iustices, atturneie, and sollicitor.

The statutes to be reviewed and printed

And further also, whereas there were manie good lawes & statutes established in the realme, which hitherto were laid vp and shrouded in filth and cobwebs, and vtterlie vnknowne to the most part of the whole land: and euerie man ignorant in the lawes of his owne natiue countrie, he caused a through view, and a review to be made, and then a choise of all such statutes as were most necessarie to be put in vse and execution: which being doone, he caused to be put in print, to the great benefit of that whole nation.

The records searched and set vp in places conuenient

And likewise for the records, which were verie euill kept, not fensed or defended from raine and foule weather, but laie all in a chaos and a confused heap, without anie regard, he caused to be viewed and sorted, and then prepared méete roomes, presses, and places for the kéeping of them in safetie, and did appoint a speciall officer with a yearelie fée for the kéeping of them:

The castell chamber duelie kept

and for all such matters as were to be heard and determined in the castell chamber, before the lords, as it is in the starchamber in England, he would be for the most part present at euerie court, and alwaies would haue the assistants and persons of hir maiesties learned councellors. Neuerthelesse, he himselfe had a maruellous head to conceiue, a déepe iudgement to vnderstand, and a most eloquent toong to vtter whatsoeuer was requisit to be spoken, either in that place, or in anie other assemblie, which he would deliuer in such an eloquent phrase, and so pleasantlie it would flow from him, with such pithie reasons, sound arguments, and effectuall discourses, as that the

the lesse learned he was, the more strange it was that such great good things could come out of his mouth. And such was his amiable countenance, his comelie behauior, his commendable personage, that he would and did conquer their hearts, and game the loue of euerie man, and the people of all sorts would and did fall in loue with him for his vprightnesse, indifferencie, and iustice, in determining of euerie mans cause. And he knowing the nature and disposition of that people, who could not abide anie long sutes in law, he was so affable and courteous, that euerie sutor should haue accesse vnto him, and foorthwith he would heare his cause, and with such expedition would cause the same to be determined, that he purchased to himselfe the vniuersall loue of all the Irishrie, who thought themselues the more happie, if their causes might be once brought to his hearing & the more willing to leaue their Obrian law, & to imbrace the course of the English lawes. Wherevpon he deuised, and consequentlie with great policie and wisedome executed the diuision and distribution of the wild sauage, and Irish grounds into shire grounds and counties, appointing in euerie of them shiriffes, constables, and all such kind of officers as are vsed to be in all other counties: by which meanes hir maiesties writ had passage amongest them, and they brought to the order of the English lawes & gouernement, which neuer tofore was heard or knowne among them.

Edm. Molin.

The Irish grounds reduced into counties and shires.

When he had doone all such things as are before recited, for and concerning the due course of gouernment by order of law: then also he bethought himselfe vpon such other things as were necessarie in sundrie respects to be doone, as the castell and house of Dublin, which before his comming was ruinous, foule, filthie, and greatlie decaied. This he repaired, and reedified, and made a verie faire house for the lord deputie or the cheefe gouernor to reside & dwell in. The towne of Carigfergus, being open to the northerne rebelles, he began to inclose with a wall and to fortifie, which for shortnesse of time he could not finish. A gaole at Molengar he builded, a verie necessarie thing in those parties, for restreining and safe kéeping of malefactors. The towne of Athenrie in Connagh he caused to be reedified, & the faire bridge of Athlon vpon the déepe and great riuer of the Shenin he builded with masonrie and frée stone, and raised vp the walles & battlements verie faire. By building of which bridge a passage (neuer tofore had) was made open & frée betwéne the English pale and Connagh, which more danted, apalled, and kept the rebelles in awe and obedience than any thing before had doone. Sundrie like common workes he made and did, and more would, if his residing there had continued. All which his forsaid doings, no doubt, were verie chargeable to hir maiestie. And for easing whereof he (as it became him) & in verie deed had also promised and deuised how, and by what means these charges might be answered, and hir highnesse be reléeued of the great and intollerable charges which she dailie was at in that land, he did by good means inlarge and increase hir reuenues and yearelie receipts to about eleuen thousand pounds by the yeare more than he found it, and much more would he haue doone, if he had staied there but a short time longer than he did.

The castell of Dublin repared.

The towne of Carigfergus fortified.

A gaole at Molengar builded.

The towne of Athenrie reedified.

The bridge of Athlon new builded.

The queenes great charges to be releeued.

Hir maiesties reuenues increased.

Thus much brieflie of his generall actions, and concerning his priuat dealings and conuersation. He was godlie disposed, & a zelous promoter of the true religion, a notable orator & out of whose mouth flowed such eloquent spéeches, such pithie sentences, such persuasorie reasons, as it was verie strange, that he by a naturall course should performe that which manie by learning could not reach nor atteine vnto. He had some sight in good letters and in histories and armories, and would discourse verie well in all things, he was affable and courteous to all men, verie familiar with most men, and strange to none, verie temperat and modest, seldome or neuer in anie distempered or extraordinarie choler, vpright in iustice, frée from corruption, and liberall to euerie deseruing person, a bounteous housekéeper, and of great hospitalitie, and had all officers in verie honorable

The good vertues and disposition of Sir Henrie Sidneie.

Religious.

Eloquent.

Affable.

Temperat.

Liberall.

A housekeeper.

notable order, according to his estate & honor; a thing much allowed and liked in that nation: verie familiar, and a louer of all such as were learned and were men of vnderstanding, whome he would honor and estéeme verie much, gratefull to all men, and a most louing maister to all such as serued him, whom he loued full

See more of this sir Henrie Sidneie in the English chronicles, An. Dom. 1580, noted by Iohn Molineux.

dearlie. And albeit he were a man of a great reach and iudgement, yet he would not doo anie thing without aduise & counsell, for which purpose he made a speciall choise of two singular men, who were priuie to all or most part of his actions, sir Lucas Dillon knight, and Francis Agard esquier: the one a lawier, and yet not ignorant in anie thing perteining either to the marshall affaires, or to the ciuill gouernement: the other a verie wise man, and of a déepe iudgement and experience in all matters of policies. And so true and trustie these were, that he named the one *Meus fidelis Lucas*, and the other *Meus fidus Achates*. And notwithstanding in sundrie and almost infinit respects, as partlie by the course of this historie it dooth appeare, he hath deserued most hartie thanks, and a gratefull remembrance for euer

The ingratitude of Ireland.

amongst them: yet most vnnaturallie and vngratefullie they haue requited and recompensed him. Not much vnlike the viper, who when he hath doone the act of generation with his female, which (as the writers of naturalles saie) it is doone by the

The nature of the viper.

mouth, she immediatlie biteth off his head, and so destroieth him, and likewise the yong, conceiued with the death of their sire or father, and nourished in the wombe of their mother, and readie now to be borne & brought foorth, they not abiding their due time, most vnnaturallie doo knaw out hir wombe and bellie to hir confusion, and so they are conceiued with the destruction of their father, and borne with the confusion of their mother. This vngratfull people (I saie) notwithstanding the innumerable benefits bestowed vpon them and that whole com-

This was a troublesome parlement.

monwealth, yea and the dailie purchasing of their wealth, preseruation, and safetie, could nor would be euer thankfull. As besides manie examples it appeared at the parlement holden in the eleuenth yeare of hir maiesties reigne, where when lawes were to be established for their benefit, and the abolishing of certeine wicked and lewd vsages, which were among the Irishrie, they not onelie did impugne and resist that assemblie, as much as in them laie: but recompensed the good things (for their benefits established) with open war and rebellion against hir maiestie.

The cesse impugned.

Also, when a reasonable and a vsed cesse was to be set and leuied for the benefit of the inhabitants and dwellers in the English pale, and for the represse of their enimies which thirsted after their confusion: they immediatly repine and doo resist

The corrupt and vngratful nature of the Irishmen.

the same. For this is their corrupt nature, that if he did at anie time pursue the enimie for their peace and quietnesse, and did aduenture neuer so great dangers for them, were his successe neuer so good, yet would they enuie at him. If he by the aduise of the councell did determine anie thing for their behoofe, yet would they mislike it. If anie thing well meant had euill successe, they would like it, and vpon neuer so little occasion offered they would make their complaints, libels should dailie be exhibited, and accusations be deuised, with open mouths they would exclame, and nothing would they leaue vndoone which might turne to his discredit and impeachment of his gouernement. But truth the daughter of time, which in the end was manifested, and when he had yéelded before hir highnesse and councell a true and a perfect account of all his doings, and had trulie manifested the course of his gouernement, then their glittering gold was found to be worse than copper, not abiding the hammar, he according to his desert receiued thanks, and they reproch and ignominie. Wherefore great good cause had he to be glad and ioifull, that he

The fatall destinie vpon all gouernors in Ireland.

was to be deliuered from so vngratfull a people and vnthankfull a nation. But shall a man saie the truth? It is a fatall and an ineuitable destinie incident to that nation, that they cannot brooke anie English gouernor, for be he neuer so iust, vpright, & carefull for their benefit, they care not for it: let him be neuer so beneficiall to their

commonwealth

commonwealth, they account not of it, let him be neuer so circumspect in his gouernement and aduised in his doomings, they will discredit and impeach it. If he be courteous and gentle, then like a sort of nettles they will sting him: if he be seuere, they will cursse him, and let him doo the best he can, he shall neuer auoid nor escape their malice and spite.

This noble and worthie man, who aboue all others had best triall thereof, thought himselfe most happie when he was deliuered from them and gone out of their Egypt, and now returned to his owne natiue countrie of Chanaan, who thensefoorth sometimes attended the court, and serued hir maiestie as a most faithfull, graue, and wise counsellor: sometimes he followed his charge and calling of president in Wales, which office he did most honorablie vse and discharge. In the end, when Lachesis had spun out the thread of his life, and Atropos readie to execute hir office, he fell sicke at Worcester: and féeling a decaie of nature, and that he did dailie wax weaker and weaker, he yeelded and humbled himselfe to die, and holding vp his hands, and lifting vp his eies, he continued in most hartie and incessant praiers vnto God, crauing with a most penitent hart, pardon for his sins, and commending his soule into the hands and mercie of God, thorough the bloud of Iesus Christ. And when his hands gaue ouer, his toong ceassed, and his sight failed, he yéelded vp his spirit, and departed this life in a most godlie and christian maner the fift daie of Maie, one thousand fiue hundred eightie and six. His bodie was imbowelled, and his entrails were buried in the deans chapell of the cathedrall church in Worcester: his hart was carried to Ludlow, & there intoomed in the toome that his welbeloued daughter Ambrosia was buried, which he had builded in the collegiat church of the same towne, wherin he had erected a certeine monument for a perpetuall remembrance to that town & to Tikenhill, to which he was verie much affected, & made his most abode during the time of his presidencie. And from thense his bodie by easie iournies was verie honorablie caried to his house of Peneshurst in Kent, & in his parish church there he was interred in all honorable maner, as to his estate did agrée vpon the one and twentith of Iune, in the yeare one thousand fiue hundred eightie and six, he being then about the age of seauen and fiftie yeares. And thus this noble and worthie knight, who had spent the whole course of his life in the dutifull seruice of his prince, and to the great benefit of the commonwealth, is now deliuered vnto the euerlasting seruice of the eternall God, in whose celestiall heauens he resteth in blisse and ioie with the foure and twentie elders, who there are now beholding the face of God, and praising his holie name for euer.

The death of sir Henrie Sidneie

Edm. Molineux.

But to returne to the lord iustice, who being entered into the gouernement, and finding it in some quiet state, did by the aduise of the councell follow that course as néere as he could, as which was left vnto him, and by that meanes kept the whole land verie quiet and in peace. For almost a yeare after his entrie into that office and gouernement, vntill that Romish cockatrice, which a long time had set abrood vpon hir egs, had now hatched hir chickins, which being venemous as were their sire, raised, wrought, and bred great treasons, open warres, and hostilitie through out that land. For Iames Fitzmoris a Geraldine & cousine germane to the earle of Desmond, who not manie yeares before had béene an archtraitor, and a principall capteine of the warres and rebellion in Mounster, and wherein he was then so followed at inches and pursued by sir Iohn Perot, then lord president of Mounster, that after manie and sundrie conflicts, he was in the end compelled and inforced to yeeld and submit himselfe, and to craue hir maiesties gratious pardon: insomuch that he came in simple into the towne of Kilmallocke, and there in the church before all the people did

Sir William Drurie the lord iustice followeth the course of his predecessor to rule in peace.

Iames Fitzmoris an arch traitor.

Iames Fitzmoris submitteth himselfe and sweareth obedience.

did humble and prostrate himselfe before the said lord president, and asked pardon, swearing and promising then all dutifulnesse, truth, & obedience for euer to hir highnesse, and to the crowne of England.

James Fitzmoris hath his pardon sent vnto him.

Euen this periured caitife, who for his treasons and great outrages, villanies, and bloudsheds, had deserued a thousand deaths, and yet in hope of amendement hir maiestie gaue him his pardon, and sent it vnto him by hir seruant Francis Agard esquier: euen this man (I saie) most traitorouslie fled into France, and there comming into the kings presence, did offer to deliuer into his hands the whole realme and land of Ireland, if that his maiestie would giue him aid, and furnish him with men and monie, and such furniture as he should haue néed of in such an action. The king at the first gaue him good countenance, great rewards, & liberall interteinement, and accepted his offer: but when he had well considered the matter, and had further looked into the same, he changed his mind. James Fitzmoris, who had staied there in the French court about two yeares, and saw nothing go forward, & the French king waxed cold, who in the end gaue him no other answer, but that he would commend him by his letters to his sister the queene of England, for obteining of a pardon for him, and for hir good countenance towards him: he forsooke France, and made a iournie into Spaine vnto king Philip. The king who had receiued the gift of Ireland of the pope by meanes of the bishop of Cashell, being not willing to deale therein, without his assistance & aduise, James Fitzmoris made his iourneie from thense to the pope, vnto whom he declared that he had béene with king Philip, as dooth appeare by his letters of credit to his holinesse, and that he would deliuer and cause to be deliuered the kingdome of Ireland vp into their hands, and reduce the same againe to the holie church of Rome, if he might haue men, monie, and such furniture of munitions, & other necessaries as should be requisit in that seruice. The pope was verie glad of this sute, and liked it verie well, and did accept this offer, as also gaue him good countenance and interteinement. And in the end vpon sundrie conferences betwéene the pope and king Philip, it was agréed betwéene them, that Fitzmoris should be furnished with men, monie, and all things necessarie for this seruice. James Fitzmoris during his being in Rome, he fell acquainted with doctor Sanders an English Iesuit, & doctor Allen an Irish Iesuit, and both traitors to hir maiestie and crowne, and these two men being glad of such a sute, & they in great fauor with the pope, folowed the sute verie earnestlie, and promised to follow it to the vttermost in their owne persons.

James Fitzmoris fleeth into France and offereth the crowne of Ireland to the French king.

The French king misliketh to deale in Ireland matters.

James Fitzmoris séeketh to king Philip and to the pope.

James Fitzmoris his promise to king Philip and the pope.

The pope is glad of James Fitzmoris offer.

James Fitzmoris falleth acquainted with doctor Sanders and doctor Allen.

Now when all things were concluded betwéene the pope and king Philip, doctor Sanders, doctor Allen, and James Fitzmoris made their last repaire to the pope, who foorthwith made Sanders his legat, & gaue him the holie ghost, with authoritie to blesse and curse at his will and pleasure, and to him and the others he gaue then also his blessing, and therewith his letters of commendation to king Philip, who according to the conclusion made betwéene them both, he was furnished with all things méet and necessarie for them. Whervpon when time serued they imbarked themselues, and their companie in thrée ships well appointed for the purpose, and arriued at Smereweeke, *aliàs* saint Marie wéeke, in the beginning of Iulie 1579, néere the Dingle a cush in Kerrie in Ireland: where he landed, and all his companie, being about the number of foure score Spaniards, besides a few Englishmen and Irishmen, and there builded a fort in the west side of the baie for their safetie, and drew their ships close vnder the said fort.

James Fitzmoris is furnished with ships and all necessaries.

James Fitzmoris landeth at Saint Marie weeke in Ireland with foure score Spaniards.

The two doctors, when they had hallowed the place after their popish maner, promising all safeties, and that no enimie should dare to come vpon them, and trouble them: neuerthelesse they were beguiled. For at that instant, there was in

Kensale

Kensale a Deuonshire gentleman and a man of warre, named Thomas Courtneie, and he hearing of the landing of this Iames Fitzmoris, and of the popes traitorous legats, was contented, and by the persuasion of Henrie Dauels, being then in those parts, and hauing a good wind, did come about and doubled the point, came into the baie of Saint Marie weeke or Smerwecke; and finding the three ships of Iames Fitzmoris at anchor, was so bold in the waie of good speed to take them. And after that he had staied there a while in that seruice, he tooke them all along with him: whereby Iames Fitzmoris and his companie lost a péece of the popes blessing, for they were altogither destituted of anie ship, to ease and reléeue themselues by the seas, what need soeuer should happen. As soone as they were thus landed, newes was sent and carried abrode foorthwith to Iames & Iohn brethren to the earle of Desmond, and so consequentlie to the whole countrie. These two brethren, who had long looked for the arriuall of this their cousine, and archtraitor, assembled all their tenants, folowers, and friends, and out of hand made their present repaire vnto him: whose commings and companies he accepted verie thankefullie, saieng that he had not a thorough and a full liking of his cousine sir Iohn of Desmond. Which when sir Iohn perceiued, he deuised how he would salue that sore, as most wickedlie afterwards he did.

Iames Fitzmoris ships are taken awaie by one Thomas Courtneie a gentleman of Deuon.

Sir Iames and sir Iohn of Desmond the earles brethren come to Iames Fitzmoris.

The earle of Desmond at this time was in reedifieng of a castell, which he had in the confines of Brenne Agonessis countrie, who assoone as he heard of the arriuall of his cousine Iames Fitzmoris, he foorthwith did discharge and dismisse his whole companie of workemen and labourers, pretending in outward shew what he neuer meant, that he was to withstand and resist his cousine and all his companie, and foorthwith maketh his repaire into Kerrie, and there assembleth all his followers and force, as though he would doo great things and worke miracles. And foorthwith likewise he sent his letters to Mac Artie More earle of Clancar, & willeth him in all hast to assemble all the force he could make, and to make his spéedie repaire to him, for vanquishing (if they could) of the enimies now landed at S. Marie weeke. The earle of Desmond in the meane time had receiued a péece of the popes blessing, and his heat was abated. But the erle of Clancar returned his answer, that he would come vnto him with all spéed, and hem campe with him where he would, as néere to the Dingle as he might: and accordinglie he came to the place appointed. Which Desmond séemed to like well though it were against the splene, neuerthelesse when he saw the forwardnes of Clancar, albeit he would not, nor yet well could in open termes fall out with him, yet he deuiseth matters whereupon he might haue some occasion to dislike with him, & to make him wearie of his companie. Which when Clancar perceiued, and saw the vnwillingnesse of Desmond to doo anie seruice against the rebels, but rather inclined towards them, he tooke the best opportunitie he could, and departed awaie from him, and dismissed his companie.

The erle hearing of the landing of Iames Fitzmoris leaueth ouer his buildings.

The earle of Desmond pretending some seruice against the rebels sendeth to the earle of Clancar to come with him.

The earle of Clancar attendeth the earle of Desmond.

Desmond liketh not Clancars readinesse.

Clancar departeth from Desmond.

The lord iustice, who was at Dublin, as soone as he was aduertised of Iames Fitzmoris landing, he maketh all the preparation he can, & marcheth with all the queenes force towards Mounster, dispatching also a messenger to hir maiestie of these towardlie broiles and rebellion. But before he could prepare all things, as to such a great action did apperteine, he sent Henrie Dauels an English gentleman before him, that he being verie well acquainted with the earle of Desmond and his brethren, should practise with them to prepare themselues to be in a readinesse to assist his lordship, for the resisting against those enimies. Who being accompanied with one Arthur Carter prouost marshall of Mounster, made his spéedie repaire to the earle of Desmond & his brethren being in Kerrie, and aduertised vnto them the lord iustices pleasure, as also as much as in him laie did persuade them to the like, who as then had all his force and souldiers about him. From thense he departed to the

The lord iustice prepareth to march into Mounster.

Henrie Dauels sent to the earle of Desmond.

Henrie Dauels persuadeth Desmond to serue against the rebels.

the fort, wherof when he had taken the view, & saw the force as yet not so great but might be easilie as yet ouerthrowne, he returned backe to the earle, and gaue him aduise to draw all his force and companie towards the fort, persuading him to assaile it while it was but weake, of small force, and easie to be taken, and that in so dooing it should be greatlie to his honour. But the earle being not of so good a mind, or bent to doo so good a péece of seruice, answered, that he would not aduenture to take so great an enterprise in hand with so small a companie as he then had. Then Dauels went to sir Iames and to sir Iohn of Desmonds the earles brethren, and persuaded them to aduise their brother the earle, either to doo that seruice which would be to his great honour and commendation, or else that they would take it in hand; which if they would also refuse it, that then the earle would spare to him a companie of his Gallowglasses, and about thrée score of his shot, and he would ioine with capteine Courtneie who laie then within the baie with his marriners, & he would giue the assault by land, and the other should doo the like by sea.

Desmond refuseth to giue the onset vpon Iames Fitzmoris.

But the earle, being mooued hereof, would not yéeld to this motion, but answered that his shot was more meet to shoot at foule than fit to aduenture such a péece of seruice and his Gallowglasses were good men to incounter with Gallowglasses, and not to answer old soldiers. Wherevpon when he saw the bent and disposition of the earle, that he minded not to annoie, but rather to ioine, aid, and helpe the traitors: he togither with the prouost marshall tooke their leaue of the earle, and minded to returne backe vnto the lord iustice, to giue his lordship to vnderstand how all things stood, & what successe he had had in his message. And by the waie they laie that night at Traleigh, which is about fiue miles from castell Maine, and laie that night in one Rices house, who kept a vittelling house and a wine tauerne, the house being both strong and defensible, but so little that their companies and seruants were dispersed, and laie abroad in other places where they might haue lodging. But sir Iohn of Desmond, whose hart was imbrued with a bloudie intent, followed him, but somewhat late, and came to the towne of Traleigh, and immediatlie set spies vpon Dauels, as also had corrupted the man of the house which kept the gate, that he should leaue the doores open. Henrie Dauels mistrusting no hurt, and least doubting of that tragedie which was so néere at hand, especiallie to be done by him, whom of all the men borne in that land he least doubted, & best trusted, gat him to his bed, & Arthur Carter the prouost marshall with him. Now about the dead of the night, when they were in their déepe sléepes sir Iohn according to his wicked deuise came to the house, the castell doore being left open for the purpose, with all his companie, euerie one being armed and their swords drawne, and went foorthwith vp into the chamber where Dauels & his companie were in their beds fast asléepe, but with the noise they were suddenlie awaked. When Dauels saw sir Iohn of Desmond armed and his sword drawn, he was somwhat astonied at that sight, and rising vp in his bed said vnto him (as he was euer woont to saie verie familiarlie) "What sonne, what is the matter?" But he answered him, "No more sonne, nor no more father, but make thy selfe readie, for die thou shalt." And foorthwith he & his companie strake at him & his companion, both naked in their shirts, and most cruellie murthered them both. Then they searched the whole house & spared none, but put all to the sword, sauing a boie named Smolkin, who laie in the chamber, and had béene a continuall messenger betwéene Dauels and this Iohn Desmond. This boie séeing his maister to be thus murthered ran vpon Iohn of Desmond, and held him by the armes as well as he could, crieng, "What wilt thou kill my maister?" But he answered, "Go thy waies Smolkin, thou shalt haue no harme." But the boie seeing blowes still to be giuen, cast himselfe downe vpon his maister, crieng "If thou wilt kill him then kill me also." And so saued him as well, and so long

The earle refuseth to doo anie seruice.

Henrie Dauels departeth from Desmond.

Sir Iohn of Desmond followeth Dauels and corrupteth the porter.

Henrie Dauels most cruellie murthered.

The faithfulnesse of a boie to his maister.

long as he could. But it auailed not, for slaine and most cruellie he was there mur-thered.

This Henrie Dauels was a gentleman, borne in Deuon, and descended of a verie ancient and a worshipfull house, and being but a yoonger brother, and hauing but a verie small portion left vnto him, when he came to some yeares and knowledge, he gaue himselfe to serue in the warres. And king Henrie the eight, hauing then warres against the French king, he entred into France to séeke his aduenture: and there he had verie good interteinment, and prooued to be a verie good souldiour. After whose warres he serued in Scotland, and was in garrison at Barwike: and from thense he was remooued into Ireland, where he serued vnder sir Nicholas Herne knight conestable of Leighlin, and seneshall of Wexford, and so well he behaued himselfe there, that he was commended for his good seruice towards the prince, well beloued of his countriemen, and in maruelous fauour of the Irish people, for no seruice was too hard for him in the kings causes, and so well he was acquainted with the coun-trie, as no man better knew and had the skill to serue than he could there. As for his countrimen, he was so déere and louing towards them, as he was more like a father than a fréend, and more like a fréend than an vnacquainted countriman: for he was an host and a harborer to euerie one of them, of what estate and condition so euer he were of. For were he rich or poore, a gentleman or a begger, he was fréendlie to euerie one, and no man did or could lacke that interteinment, that he was by anie manner of waie able to giue and afoord: which a number of English-men tried and found to their great comfort, and to his euerlasting fame.

Henrie Dauels what he was, and of his conditions.

The loue of Dauels to his countrimen.

And as for the Irishmen, the longer he liued the better beloued among them: for as he would not iniurie them, no more would he suffer them to be oppressed or iniuried: a great housekéeper amongst them, which they maruelouslie estéemed. When he was in office among them, he was vpright and iudged righteouslie, if out of office, louing & fréendlie to euerie man, and by that means so well (as no man better) beloued and trusted. For what he had once said and promised, that would he surelie keepe and performe, and thereof it came into a bie-word in the countrie where he dwelled, that if anie of them had spoken the word, which was assuredlie looked to be performed, they would saie, Dauels hath said it: as who saith, it shall be performed. For the nature of the Irishman is, that albeit he kéepeth faith for the most part with no bodie, yet will he haue no man to breake with him. But Henrie Dauels, he was so carefull of his word, that if he once promised, he would not breake it for anie mans pleasure, and by that means he was so well beloued, that his verie horsseboies had frée passage euen through the enimies, if he were knowne to be Dauels man. And that which is more, as the writer hereof speaketh vpon knowledge, that if anie Englishman had anie occasion to trauell in that countrie thoroughout Lemster or Mounster, if he had but a horsseboie of his, he should not onelie passe fréelie thorough the countries without impeachment, but should haue also verie good and fréendlie interteinment. Among the noblemen he was greatlie estéemed, and was in great fauour with the earles of Ormond and Desmond: who although they were for the most part at iarres and contentions, yet Henrie Dauels was in such fauour, as he could and did passe to and fro in the greatest matters of importance betwéene them: wherein he bare so indifferent a hand, as both parties imbraced him for his vprightnesse and indifferencie. The erle of Ormond himselfe loued him so well, as no Englishman better, and all his brethren found such a fréend of him, and such interteinment with him and especiallie sir Edmund Butler, that at all needs and in all distresses they were sure to haue him to their fréend, and manie times it stood them in good stéed.

The credit of Dauels word.

And as for the earle of Desmond, though he were a verie vncerteine and a mutable man, yet Henrie Dauels could preuaile with him, and were his fume neuer so hot, and he neuer so hastie, yet could he appease and quiet him. And as for sir Iohn of Desmond the earles brother, such was his profession and outward affection towards him, of a most firme freendship, that it was thought to be impossible, that the loue and goodwill betweene them could by anie meanes be dissolued. For in what distresse so euer sir Iohn of Desmond was (as he was in manie) Henrie Dauels did alwaies helpe him, and at sundrie times redéemed him out of prison, yea out of the castell of Dublin, when he was committed for capitall crimes, and became suertie for him in great sums of monie, and became pledge bodie for bodie for him. Dauels purse was at his commandement, his house at his deuotion, and what he had at his disposition. And so farre this good will grew betweene them, that Iohn of Desmond, as one knowledging himselfe most bounden to him, did call him father, euen as the other called him sonne. And now sée, when treason and trecherie was entred into him, how contrarie to all faith, fréendship, and humanitie, the sonne most vnnaturallie bereft the father of his life, and most cruellie murthered him. Wo worth to so wicked a villaine, that so bereft the prince of so faithfull a subiect, the gouernors of so trustie a seruitor, the commonwealth of so good a member, of a man most dutifull to his superiors, vpright in iustice, trustie in seruice, expert in the warres, faithfull vnto his freend, louing to his countrie, fauoured of all men, hurtfull to no man, of great hospitalitie to all good men, good to all men, a father vnto the distressed, and a succorer of the oppressed, finallie such a rare man of his degree and calling, as few like haue béene found in that land, and yet against all pittie and mercie, most cruellie murthered by a traitor to God and his prince, euen to the gréefe of the traitors of his owne blood. But here it falleth out that is of old said; Saue a murtherer or a theefe from the gallowes, and he shall be the first that shall cut thy throte.

Henrie Dauels alwaies a trust freend to sir Iohn of Desmond

When this bloudie murtherer had executed this crueltie vpon his good freend, he foorthwith made his repaire to Iames Fitzmoris, and to his doctors and companie in great brauerie, recompting vnto them what a noble act and a valiant seruice he had doone in murthering of an honest, faithfull, & friendlie gentleman, saieng, I haue now killed an English churle (for so maliciouslie the Irishmen terme all Englishmen) & said to his cousine Iames, Now thou maist be assured of me and trust me, for now that I haue begun to dip my hand in blood, I will now stand to the matter with thee to my vttermost. Iames Fitzmoris when he had heard him at full, although both he and his doctors, and the whole companie of the Spaniards did reioise and were glad of his death, yet Iames did blame and abhorre the maner of his death, blaming and reproouing him verie much, that he should murther him in his bed, being naked and scarse awaked out of his sléepe, which he said was too cruell, bicause he might otherwise haue had aduantage vpon him either by the high waies or otherwise to his commendation. Howbeit, doctor Sanders terming his bloudie murther to be a sweet sacrifice before God, did both allow it, and gaue him plenarie remission of all his sinnes. The earle himselfe likewise, when he heard hereof, he was maruelouslie gréeued and offended with his brother, and gaue him such sharpe spéeches and reproofes, as it was thought they would not so soone haue beene fréends againe: but wicked doongs amongst the wicked establish and confirme them in their wickednesse. At this present time, there was with the earle (as verie often he had béene) one Appeslete an English capteine, who could doo verie much with him, and vpon the hearing of the death of his good friend Henrie Dauels, he began to doubt and mistrust of himselfe and of his owne assurance. Wherefore he goeth to the earle, and

The brags of John Desmond for killing of Dauels

His crueltie misliked

The popes doctors doo allow and commend the murther

and dissembling his griefe, persuadeth him to draw his companie togither, and to remooue from thense to his house of Asketten, which is about fourtéene miles from Limerike, and there to abide the comming of the lord iustice, and to ioine with him in this seruice against the enimie. The earle, who minded nothing lesse than so to serue, dissembled the matter, and followed this counsell, and remooued from thense to Asketten, where he laie close and did nothing, but still séemed in speeches and outward shewes to mislike with Iames Fitzmoris and all his companie, and yet dailie his best followers and soldiers flocked and repaired to Iames Fitzmoris, manie of them for zeale to the popish religion, wherin they were as deuout as the popes legates and the Spaniards: but manie of them knowing the earles intent, did it for feare and auoiding of his displesure. The Spaniards, who had continued there in the fort and elsewhere, and not finding the repaire of the souldiers, nor yet anie other thing answerable to that seruice as it was promised them, began to mislike it and distrusting of anie good successe, did repent and were sorie, wishing themselues at home againe: but such was then case, that they could not shift for themselues to escape neither by sea nor by land, and therefore necessitie so compelling, they resolued themselues to abide the brunt.

The earle of Desmond remooueth to Asketten.

The earles chiefe men turne to the enimie.

The Spaniards like not their comming.

Iames Fitzmoris, perceiuing their discontented minds, had conference with them & persuaded them to be of a good comfort, for they should verie shortlie haue a greater supplie and companie which he dailie looked for, and all things should be had according to their owne minds: aduertising them that in the meane time he was to take a iournie to a place of thrée or foure daies iournie from thense, called the holie rood or crosse in Tipporarie, and there to performe a vow which he had before made when he was in Spaine, praieng their patience. But in verie truth his intent was to trauell into Connagh and into Vlster, and in both his waies, his neerest waie was through Tipporarie, and there to flocke and draw vnto him all and so manie of the rebels as he could wage to ioine with him, whereof he made no doubt, but assured himselfe to find as manie readie to go as he willing to haue. And so taking his iournie with thrée or foure horssemen, and a dozzen Kernes, he passed through the countie of Limerike, & came into the countrie of sir William Burke his verie néere cousine and kinsman, and who before in the last rebellion did ioine with him, to the great danger of his life and losse of all his goods.

Iames Fitzmoris persuadeth the Spaniards to patience.

Iames Fitzmoris pretendeth a pilgrimage.

And when he came so farre in his iournie, being now about thrée score miles from S. Marie wéeke, his carriage horsses (which they terme garons) waxed faint, and could not trauell anie further: wherefore he commanded some of his men to go before, & looke what garrons they first found in the fields, they should take them and bring them vnto him. And as it fell out they espied a plow of garrons plowing in the field, which they foorthwith tooke perforce from the poore husbandmen two of them, and carried them awaie. Wherevpon according to the custome of the countrie, the hobub or the hue and crie was raised. Some of the people followed the tract, & some went to their lords house, which was sir William Burke being néere at hand to aduertise the matter, who hauing thrée or foure of his sonnes and verie tall gentlemen at home with him, they tooke their horsses and a few Kernes and two shot with them, and followed the tract, and ouertooke them at a fastenes fast by the woods side, where they found Iames Fitzmoris, whome before they knew not to be come into those parties, to make head to answer them. But when he saw that it was his cousine Theobald Burke and his brother and his companie, who had beene his companions in the late rebellion when sir Iohn Perot was lord president of Mounster, he spake ouer vnto them, and said, "Cousine Theobald (who was the eldest son to his father) two carriage horsses shall be no breach betweene vs two, and I hope that you which doo know the cause that I haue now in hand, you will take my part therein,

Iames Fitzmoris stealeth garrons.

The Burkes follow the preie.

This was a draught made by the lord president.

Iames Fitzmoris maketh head to resist.

Iames Fitzmoris persuadeth tee

Burkes to rebellion

in, and doo as I and others will doo:" and so continuing some spéeches, did what he could to draw him and all his companie to be partakers in this rebellion. But he answered that he and his father had alreadie dealt too much that waie with him, and that he will neuer doo the like againe: for his father, he, and all his brethren, had sworne to be true, obedient, and faithfull to the quéenes maiestie, and which oth they would neuer breake: cursing the daie and time that euer they ioined with him in so bad a cause against hir maiestie, and therefore required to haue his garons againe, or else he would come by them aswell as he could.

James Fitzmoris slaine

Some thinke that this peece of seruice was a draught made by sir William Drurie lord iustice.

The conditions of Iames Fitzmoris.

Iames Fitzmoris standing vpon his reputation, thought it too much dishonorable vnto him to depart with that which he had in hand, and therfore vtterlie denied the deliuerie, and thervpon each partie set spurre to the horsses and incountered the one the other. The skirmish was verie hot and cruell, and Theobald Burke & one of his yoonger brethren were slaine, & some of their men. Iames Fitzmoris likewise and his companie had the like successe, for he himselfe was first hurt and wounded, and then with a shot striken thorough the head, and so was slaine, with sundrie of his companions: wherein he found that the popes blessings and warrant, his *Agnus Dei*, and his graines had not those vertues to saue him, as an Irish staffe or a bullet had to kill him. Thus was hir highnesse most happie, and that whole land most happiest, that they were deliuered from so wicked and bloudie a traitour, and that the great & venemous hydra was thus shortened of one of his heds. For otherwise it was to be doubted that if he had liued, he would haue bin the cause of much bloudshed, and all the rebels in that land would haue ioined with him. For he was of verie good credit & estimation through the whole land, he was of a verie good gouernement, and of a great reach, but a déepe dissembler, passing subtill, and able to compasse anie matter which he tooke in hand, familiar to all men, and verie courteous, valiant, and verie expert in martiall affaires, but so addicted to poperie and that baggage religion, that he became a most horrible traitour to hir maiestie, and a mortall enimie to euerie good man: and so far he was imbrued herein, that a man might saie that he was borne to the same end, euen to be a traitor and a rebell to God, to his prince, and to the whole commonwealth.

Iames Fitzmoris his quarters set vpō the gates of Kilmallocke.

Sir William Burke being made a baron sowned for ioy & shortlie after died.

After that he was thus dead, and the same made knowen to the lord iustice, he gaue order that he should be hanged in the open market of Kilmallocke, & be beheaded & quartered, & the quarters to be set vpon the towne gates of Kilmallocke, for a perpetuall memoriall to his reproch for his tresons and periuries, contrarie to his solemne oth taken in that errour. Hir maiestie, when she was aduertised of this péece of good seruice of sir William Burke and the losse of his eldest sonne, she wrote hir letters of the good acceptation of his seruice, comforted him for the losse of his son, and in recompense did create him baron of the castell of Connell by hir letters patents dated the fourth of Maie, the twentith yeare of hir reigne, & gaue him the yearelie pension of a hundred marks, to be paid at hir maiesties excheker yearelie during his life, wherof he tooke so sudden ioy that he sowned, and séemed to be dead.

The Spaniards amazed with the deth of Fitzmoris.

Sir Iohn of Desmond supplieth Iames Fitzmoris roome.

Sir William Drurie lord iustice maketh a iournie into Mounster.

When newes of the death of Iames Fitzmoris was brought to the fort at S. Marie weeke, great sorow was amongest them all, they being all amazed and wist not what to doo, especiallie the Spaniards who depart could not, and to submit themselues they would not, and yet they were of the mind to giue ouer and to intreat for a licence to depart. Which purpose they would haue followed, if that sir Iohn of Desmond had not taken the matter in hand: for he hauing imbrued himselfe so vnnaturallie in bloud, and doubting the same would neuer be pardoned, did follow the matter. The lord iustice (as is aforesaid) immediatlie vpon the newes of the arriuall of these Spaniards, and of the death of Henrie Dauels, made his preparation of all the forces

forces which hir maiestie had in that land, which was but foure hundred footmen and two hundred horssemen, a verie small companie for so great seruice towards: yet considering that the victorie consisteth not in the arme of man, nor in horsse or mule, but onelie in the good gift of God, he marcheth foorth in his iournie, hauing in his companie of Englishmen sir Nicholas Bagnoll knight marshall, sir Nicholas Malbie coronell of Connagh, Iaques Wingfield master of the ordinance, and Edward Waterhouse one of hir maiesties seruants, Edward Fitton, Thomas Masterson, and others. And of the Irish lords he was accompanied with the earle of Kildare, sir Lucas Dillon chiefe baron, the vicount Mountgarret, the baron of vpper Osserie, and the baron of Dunboine, who had of themselues two hundred horssemen, besides footmen and Kernes: and so they marched forward by iournies vntill they came to Kilmallocke, where not farre from the towne they all incamped: & then he sent from thense a messenger to the earle of Desmond, and so likewise to all the principall gentlemen of the best accompt in those parties, to come vnto him.

The lord iustice incampeth neere to Kilmallocke.

The earle in outward appéerance seemed verie willing to come, but vntill he had receiued some promise of fauour from the lord iustice, he still lingered and trifled the time and came not. But in the end his lordship being verie well accompanied with horssemen and footmen, he went to the campe, and presented himselfe before the lord iustice, and made a shew of all dutifulnesse, obedience, & fidelitie, whereas indéed no such thing was ment. For though his bodie were there, his mind was elsewhere: for whiles he was in the campe, sundrie trecheries were practised by him, yet they were not so secretlie doone but they came to light, & were discouered to the lord iustice. Wherevpon he was committed to the custodie of the knight marshall. Whiles he was in his ward, and fearing least some greater matters would be reuealed against him, he praied accesse to the lord iustice, and then he humbled himselfe verie much, and promised and sware vpon his honour & allegiance, that he would faithfullie and to the vttermost of his power serue hir highnesse against the rebels. Whose humblenesse and promise the lord iustice by the aduise of the councell did accept, and so inlarged him: which was in the end the vtter confusion of the earle himselfe and all his familie, and in the meane time great troubles, causes of much bloudshed, and vndooing of all Mounster.

The earle of Desmond commeth to the lord iustice to the campe.

The earle of Desmond is cōmitted to ward.

The earle of Desmond dooth humble himselfe and sweareth to serue rulie.

Whiles the lord iustice laie thus in campe about Kilmallocke, newes was brought vnto him, that sir Iohn of Desmond was incamped with a great companie of the rebels vpon the borders of Slewlougher. Wherevpon his lordship remooued and marched thitherwards, the earle then promising that he would in person incounter and fight hand to hand with his brother. Now when they were come to the place of seruice, the earle being best acquainted with the countrie, gaue aduise to the lord iustice, that he should diuide the armie into two parts, and the lord iustice should take one waie, and he the earle would take another waie: which aduise was followed. But bicause that place of the present seruice is adioining to a great wood, and wherein were manie fastnesse, the lord iustice did diuide the rest of his companie into two other parts, and so euerie of these thrée companies tooke waie into the wood & serched it throughout, but there they found no bodie. For sir Iohn had some secret knowledge of the lord iustices comming, and so was gone before.

Iohn of Desmond incampeth at Slewlougher.

The daie being spent to small purpose, & the night drawne towards, he incamped that night in the same places where the rebels had bin before, & there he remained somewhat longer than he thought: bicause he would spend and wast the forrage of that countrie, which was one of the chiefest places of reliefe that the enimies had. And from thense he went backe againe towards Kilmallocke, where he incamped himselfe at a place called Gilbons towne, which lieth in the plaines betwéene Limerike and Kilmallocke towards Emelere and Harlo, & there he continued about nine

wéekes

wéekes in continuall toiling and trauelling to and fro, in all such seruices as was dailie offered to be doone vpon the enimie, from which he had no rest neither day nor night. Wherevpon for the better seruice he diuided his bands, and tooke out of the Irish companies one hundred, and deliuered them to the guiding of capteine Iohn Herbert, a man of verie good seruice, and one other hundred to capteine Prise.

These two capteins had made spoill vpon certeine rebels, which shrowded themselues in the great wood called the blacke wood, vpon whom they made a sallie, and did verie good seruice vpon them. But as they were to returne to the campe, which laie beside Getenbre castell, the said Iohn of Desmond, who laie in ambush for them, met and incountered them, where was a sharpe fight betwixt them, and the two capteins with the most part of their companie slaine: & Iohn of Desmond himselfe was there hurt in the nose. The losse of those two capteins and their men was a great weakening to the lord iustice his armie, his enimies being strong and manie, and his companie weake and few, sauing at that instant the souldiers sent out of Deuon and Cornewall arriued at Waterford to the number of six hundred men, vnder the leading of capteine George Bourchier, capteine Peter Carew, capteine George Carew his brother, and capteine Dowdale, whose comming at so present a distresse was both ioifull and also gladsome.

Sir Iohn of Desmõd lieth in an ambush for the English capteins and discomfiteth them.

The Deuonshire souldiers arriue at Waterford.

And néere about this time, it was aduertised vnto the lord iustice, that Iohn of Desmond was at Connell, which was about sixteene miles from the campe: and his lordship being well furnished & prepared, and he minding to doo some peece of seruice vpon him, made verie secretlie a iourneie thither: but Desmond wanting not his good espials, had an inkling and a knowledge thereof, and so shifted himselfe awaie, wherevpon the lord iustice returned to his campe. The queens maiestie and councell, being alwaies mindfull of hir Ireland, and by reason of the newes that the enimies were dailie stronger and stronger, she sent ouer sir Iohn Perot late president of Mounster, with six ships well furnished and appointed, whereof he was admerall, and William Gorge master porter of the tower and a pensioner, viceadmerall: and all these arriued vnto the citie of Corke. Whereof the lord iustice being aduertised, was verie glad, and did appoint one hundred vnto sir William Stanleie, who before was capteine of certeine horssemen, and one other hundred he assigned vnto capteine Hind. And seeing now some good seruice towards, and to incourage certeine gentlemen to be the more willing to follow the same, called before him George Bourchier, William Stanleie, Peter Carew, and Edward Moore, and vsing vnto them verie good spéeches, to incourage and persuade them to doo hir maiestie good seruice in these hir affaires, and in hope they would performe the same, he dubbed them knights: who accordinglie did acquit themselues, and some of them with the losse of their liues ended their daies in this seruice.

Sir Iohn Perot sent to serue on sea.

Knights dubbed in the field.

And he further also for his owne part, the more hée bethought himselfe of the great seruice and charge laid vpon him, the more carefull he was to doo what the same required: where, in his owne person he so toiled and trauelled, and so ouercame himselfe with studieng, watching, labouring and trauelling, that he ouerthrew his owne health, and was no longer able to indure the same: but being ouercome by sicknesse, and driuen to yéeld therevnto, was determined to haue dissolued his campe, and so to haue returned to Waterford, and there to staie for a time. But the capteins séeing the necessitie of the present seruice, persuaded him not to dissolue the armie, but to take some order herein for hir highnesse seruice, and he to sequester himselfe for a time for his health. Vpon whose aduises he prepared himselfe to trauell towards Waterford, and for the continuance of the seruice did commit the gouernement to sir Nicholas Malbie, who was then gouernour by the name of coronell of Connagh,

Sir William Drurie falleth sicke & goeth to Waterford.

Sir Nicholas Malbie made gouernor of Mounster.

Connagh and then by easie iourneies hée came to Waterford, and there he found himselfe euerie daie more weaker than other, and in the end did distrust his owne recouerie.

And yet mindfull of hir maiesties seruice, he to incourage other therein sent & called before him William Pelham esquier, William Gorge esquier viceadmerall of the six ships, Thomas Perot sonne and heire to sir Iohn Perot, and Patrike Welsh maior of the citie of Waterford, and gaue vnto them the order of knighthood, vsing the like persuasions as heretofore he had doone vnto others in the like case. And albeit he were of a good heart and courage, yet that was no sufficient physicke to recouer his helth of bodie, but that still decaied. And douting verie much of his recouerie, he sent to Dublin to the lord chancellor, and to the ladie Thamine his wife, for their speedie comming vnto him, who accordinglie satisfied his request. But he inioied their companie a verie short time: for he died within two daies after their comming, being the last of September 1579, and after his death his bodie was carried vnto Dublin, where it was buried.

Knights dubbed at Waterford.

Sir William Drurie lord iustice dieth.

But here by the waie (which should before haue béene said) as he came towards Waterford through Tipporarie, the countesse of Desmond met with him, and brought with hir hir onelie sonne and heire to the earle, and being a sutor in the behalfe of hir husband, presented him to the lord iustice to be a pledge for the truth and fidelitie of the earle hir husband. For after the time that he was set at libertie in the campe néere Kilmallocke, he neuer repaired any more to the lord iustice, but stood vpon his owne kéeping, notwithstanding by his letters he professed all loialtie and obedience, which he neuer meant. For in verie truth he was (notwithstanding his dissembling) a verie ranke traitor, as in open fact and action did verie shortlie appeare, to his owne deserued confusion.

The countesse of Desmond giueth hir son to be a pledge for his father.

But to returne to sir Nicholas Malbie, who immediatlie vpon the departure of sir William Drurie vnto Waterford, according to the office & charge laid vpon him, he set in hand foorthwith to follow and performe the same. For he was able to do it, being of great experience in martiall affaires, hauing béene seruitor that waie vnder sundrie kings, & in strange nations, as also was verie wise, lerned, and of great knowledge in matters of policie, hauing béene a student in good letters, and a great trauellor in sundrie nations, & therein did obserue the maner of the seuerall gouernments in euerie such place as where he trauelled. He had vnder him in the whole an hundred and fiftie horssemen, and nine hundred footmen, to command, and diuiding them according to the seruice then in hand, he sent sir George Bourchier, capteine Dowdall, and capteine Sentleger, vnto Kilmallocke with thrée hundred footmen, and with fiftie horsmen, there to lie in garrison, and a speciall place méet for the same, & which the enimie most speciallie coueted to possesse. But the more his care was that waie, the like was their diligence, vigilancie, & care of the other waie to kéepe the same. Then with the residue of the companie he marched himselfe to the citie of Limerike, where he staied and remained for a time to refresh his souldiors.

The commendation of sir Nicholas Malbie.

During his abode and being there, it was thought good by him and his capteins, to send vnto the earle of Desmond for his repaire vnto him, and to haue conference with him, to vnderstand his bent and aduise for hir maiesties seruice against the enimies. The earle hauing receiued the gouernors letters, gaue verie good woords, & promised much, but performed nothing. Wherefore he was againe and againe sent for from time to time, but he came not, but laie still at his house of Asketten, which is about fourtene miles from Limerike. For albeit as yet he was not in anie actuall rebellion, yet it was not vnknowne but that he was secretlie combined with his two brethren, which as open traitors were in open rebellion and in armes against hir maiestie. Which the earle, suspecting the same might be laid vnto his charge, would not

The gouernor sendeth for the earle of Desmond.

The earle giueth good words and dissembleth.

not aduenture himselfe to come in person to the gouernor, but still fed him with faire words and friuolous answers. Wherefore the gouernor thought good to spend no more time in vaine to looke for him, but left Limerike, and went into the fields, where he incamped himselfe, and so set forwards to doo some seruice vpon the enimie, hauing then in his companie six hundred footmen vnder the ensigns of sir William Stanleie, capteine George Carew, capteine Fisher, capteine Furse, capteine Piers, & capteine Hind, and he himselfe and capteine Apeslie reserued one hundred horssemen betweene them. Now being aduertised that a great companie of the rebels were incamped in Connilo vnder their capteine Iohn of Desmond, he marched towards them. And being come néere to an abbeie or monasterie called Monaster Neuagh seuen miles from Limerike, there appeared a great companie in a plaine field both of horssemen and footmen, in estimation two thousand or there abouts, marching in battell araie, and had cast out their wings of shot, and placed euerie thing verie well and orderlie.

The gouernor remoueth from Limerike to Conilo.

When the gouernor perceiued and beheld this, being verie glad that some péece of seruice was towards, he likewise conferreth with his capteins, and by their aduises setteth his companie in like good order, and brought them into a quadrant proportion, setting out his flankers in seuerall places according to the seruices, & appointed verie good leaders for the same: but his cariages he placed in the rereward, with shot sufficient for their safegard. Now when all things were thus ordered, he marched forwards to the enimies. Iohn of Desmond, when he saw that he must fight or flie, and that brags would not beare out the matter, by the councell of doctor Allen, who had the holie ghost at commandement, to giue them the victorie caused the popes banner to be displaied, and then marching forwards in verie good order, hee tooke a plaine ditch in the open field: and minding to abide the fight, disposeth his horssemen, footmen, Galowglasses, and his shot for his best strength and aduantage.

The gouernor marcheth to incounter with Iohn of Desmond.

The popes banner displaied.

The gouernor setteth onwards, & giueth the onset vpon them with his shot, who valiantlie resisted the first & second volées, & answered the fight verie well, euen to the couching of the pikes, that the matter stood verie doubtfull. But the Englishmen so fiercelie & desperatlie set vpon them afresh with the third volée, that they were discomfited and had the ouerthrow giuen them, and fled. Iohn of Desmond, as a woorthie Xerxes, who (as the historiographers write of him) was *Primus in fuga, postremus in bello*, sat vpon his horsse all this while and gaue the looking: who soeuer turned first, he was the first that was gone: for he put spur to the horsse & fled awaie as fast as he could, shewing a faire paire of héeles, which was better to him than two paire of hands. In this fight were manie slaine, of which doctor Allen was one, and thrée score others of good account. And in the chase, there were slaine and hurt, which died shortlie after, about two hundred men. This doctor Allen was an Irish man borne, and the chiefest cause of this fight. For he trusting to the Spaniards, whom he knew to be verie skilfull, and also dreaming the victorie by his inchantments to be at his commandement, incouraged Iohn of Desmond forwards: and in the campe in the waie of good spéed would néeds saie masse, and as the prophets of Baal in the time of king Achab, he offered to his God Mazim, and cried out for his aid, but none would come, for his God was asléepe and could not heare. Notwithstanding, he stood so much vpon the credit of his offrings and sacrifices, that he assured them of a victorie, and that he himselfe would be the first that should that daie giue the first blow, but whether he so did or not, there was he slaine: where he had the iust reward of a traitor, who most wickedlie and disloiallie forsooke the dutie and allegiance, which by the word of God he did owe vnto hir highnesse, and deuoted himselfe a professed Iesuit to the Romish antichrist, and an open

The battell betweene the gouernor and sir Iohn of Desmond

The Irish lost the field

Doctor Allen is slaine

Doctor Allen incouraged the campe to fight.

opén traitor vnto his lawfull prince. The earle of Desmond himselfe was not present in this fight, but he and the dissembling baron of Lexnew stood in the view & sight of it, vpon a little hill in a wood about a quarter of a mile from thense: but the whole companies were there, and had part of the breakefast.

The earle of Desmond was in view of the fight

This baron of Lexnews eldest sonne, named Patrike, was seruant to hir maiestie and sworne, and serued in the court, but had leaue of hir maiestie to come into Ireland to see his father: but he was no sooner come, and entred into his fathers house and home, but he forsooke his faith and oth to hir highnesse, and became a wicked rebell, and most traitorouslie bare armes against hir, and so continued a rank traitor to the verie end. Wherein appeareth the nature of himselfe, and of the blood of that cursed generation, among whome there is neither faith, nor truth. And therefore they maie be verie well resembled to an ape, which (as the common prouerbe is) an ape is but an ape, albeit he be clothed in purple and veluet: euen so this wicked impe. For notwithstanding he was trained vp in the court of England, sworne seruant vnto hir maiestie, in good fauour and countenance in the court, and apparelled according to his degree, and dailie nurtured and brought vp in all ciuilitie: he was no sooner come home, but awaie with his English attires, and on with his brogs, his shirt, and other Irish rags, being become as verie a traitor as the veriest knaue of them all, & so for the most part they are all, as dailie experience teacheth, dissemble they neuer so much to the contrarie. For like as Iupiters cat, let hir be transformed to neuer so faire a ladie, and let hir be neuer so well attired and accompanied with the best ladies, let hir be neuer so well estéemed and honored: yet if the mouse come once in hir sight, she will be a cat and shew hir kind: but to the historie.

The baron of Lexnews son, seruant to the queene and sworne, beareth armes against hir

No faith nor regard of an oth among the Irishrie

Iupiters cat.

When the battell was ended, & the retreat sounded, the gouernor incamped himselfe fast by the riuer side of the monasterie aforesaid, and there laie that night. About midnight, when all things were quiet, & euerie man was at his rest: euen then the often named earle of Desmond sendeth a messenger with letters of congratulation vnto the gouernor, bearing him in hand that he was verie glad and ioifull of his good successe and victorie: and like an hypocrite pretending verie good will to hir maiestie, gaue him aduise that for the auoiding of hir great charges, he should dislodge himselfe from that place, which as he thought was not best for an armie to lie in. The gouernor answered his letters with the like, and requested him to come vnto him, that they might haue conference togither, and ioine in this hir maiesties seruice, and wherein he would be glad to follow his aduise in anie thing that might further hir highnesse seruice: but to withdraw himselfe and his companie from thense, vnlesse he could giue him a good reason, he would not yéeld to his motion, nor take his warrant for anie warrantise. And therefore he remained thensefoorth in the same place thrée or foure daies, expecting still the earles comming: but he so little meant anie such thing, that thensefoorth he became a rebell in open action, and in armes against the gouernor, finding nothing in the earle but dissembling, and to vse delaies and faire spéeches to gaine time to serue his turne, remoued from thense to a towne of the earles named Rekell, and there incamped himselfe. They were no sooner settled, but the scoutmaister, hauing béene abroad, declareth to the gouernor that he had discouered a great companie of horssemen and footmen which were within a mile of the campe, & therewith was the alarum made, & sundrie horssemen & shot according to the direction of the gouernor issued out, & met with the enimies, and skirmished with them, of whom they killed manie, and tooke some prisoners.

The earle of Desmonds dissembling, & his counsell

The earle of Desmond sheweth himselfe to be an open rebell

The gouernor remoueth to Rekell

These men, being examined, declared that the earle was now in the fields and in armes, and so had béene euer since the last ouerthrow of his brother Iohn of Desmond, and likewise declareth the whole bent of the earle and his brother. This péece of seruice being doone, and the night drawing néere, the watch was charged,

The earle of Desmond in open rebellion

The earle of Desmond secretlie in the night stealeth to the gouernors campe to intrap it.

and euerie man tooke his rest. But the earle and his brother minding to doo some mischiefe, they watched, and in the dead of the night then following, taking aduantage of the time, when men were wearie and in their sléepes, came with all their companies, and meant to haue set vpon the whole campe. But they came too short and missed of their purpose: for the campe was too well warded for them to take anie aduantage. The gouernor considering the intent of the enimies was to doo what they could to remoue him from that place, which could not be kept but to the great damage of the enimies sundrie waies, and that the same was a verie necessarie place for a garison and a ward, whereby to stop the continuall intercourse of the enimies, which by the means of a bridge ouer that water, they had a continuall recourse to & fro that waie: he before his departure from thense did plant & place a ward in the castell adioining to the bridge, which did from that time annoie the enimies verie much: and then from hense he marched towards the earles house of Asketten, and by the waie he met with sundrie of the earles companie, and skirmished and fought with them to the losse of manie of them.

A garison placed at Kekell.

Asketten the earle of Desmonds chiefest house.

This house of Asketten is a verie strong castell, standing vpon a rocke in the verie midst of the riuer, and the chiefest house of the earles, wherein he had a strong ward: but he himselfe at this present time and his brother Iohn were assembled vpon a little hill on the further side of the riuer, standing there vpon their whole force. The gouernor hoping of some good seruice towards, drew all his companie into the abbeie house of Asketten, not far from the castell house, and there conferring with the capteins what were best to be doone, it was agréed and thought good, that a letter or two more should be written to the earle, and to persuade him to submission. The gouernor, who was a verie good secretarie, and could pen a letter verie excellentlie well, did draw a letter, vsing manie good words, termes, and reasons to persuade him to conformitie and obedience to hir maiestie: & that he should not be the occasion of the vtter fall & end of so noble a house, which descended from Roesus the great prince of South-wales by his mother Nesta daughter vnto the said Roesius, as Giraldus one of the same familie writeth. And herewith by the waie of a parenthesis, it dooth not appeare by anie sufficient authoritie, vnlesse a sonet and a deuise of a noble man be a sufficient authoritie, that the Giraldines came out of Italie, but perhaps out of Normandie: and the first of them placed in England had some interteinement and liuing at Windesor, and thereof was called Giraldus de Windesora: and he gaue not the armes of Richard Strangbow earle of Chepstow, as some haue written: but as he was a gentleman of himselfe, gaue the armes incident to his owne house, which is argent a salter gules.

A letter sent to the earle of Desmond to persuade him to submission.

The house of Desmond.

For certeine it is, he was and is a verie ancient gentleman, whose ancestors were planted and placed in that land by king Henrie the second, and haue euer since continued in this land in much honor, wishing, aduising, and persuading, that if there were anie feare of God, obedience to the prince, or regard of himselfe, and of his name and familie, that he would reclaime himselfe vnto dutie and obedience: and that the honor of his ancestors might not be buried in his trecheries and follies. These letters being well penned were sent vnto him. But notwithstanding the most pithie, true, and effectuall reasons and arguments were sufficient to haue persuaded anie honest or reasonable man: yet was his Pharaos heart so hardened and indurated in disobedience, rebellion, and trecherie, that nothing could make him to yéeld and relent: but leauing his former and woonted dissimulations, returneth the messenger with a flat deniall that he will not yeeld anie further obedience to hir highnesse. And foorthwith to confirme the same, he fortifieth his strongest and best houses and castells: as namelie Asketten with his chosen followers and men of best trust, the castels of Carigofoile and Strangicallie with Spaniards and some Irishmen. The gouernor,

The earle of Desmond will not be persuaded.

The earle of Desmond fortifieth his castels.

uernor, vpon the receipt of the earles answer, and minding to frame his seruice accordinglie, news was brought him that sir William Drurie lord iustice was dead, who deceassed at Waterford vpon the third of October 1579, which was a dolefull hearing to all good Englishmen, and a great hinderance vnto hir highnesse seruice.

Sir William Drurie dieth.

This sir William Drurie was verie valiant, wise, and a gentleman of great experience, descended of a verie ancient and a worshipfull house, being a yoonger brother, but the birthright excepted, nothing inferior to his elder brother anie kind of waie in the gifts of wisedome, valiantnesse, knowledge, and experience of matters politike or martiall. In his youth he was a page, and serued in the court, and as in yeares, so in knowledge of all courtlie seruices he did grow and increase, and became to be as galiant a courtier as none lightlie excelled him. He was verie deuout, and a follower vnto the then lord Russell lord priuie seale, and after earle of Bedford, who gaue him good countenance and interteinment: for vnder him he serued in France at Muttrell and Bullongnois, and after the warres ended, he went to Calis, and oftentimes being there he issued out, and did manie good seruices about Cambraie and in Artois: and in the end about Bruxelles he was taken prisoner. Not long after he was redéemed and ransomed, and then he would néeds serue at the seas, and hauing gotten a ship well appointed for the purpose, he aduentureth that seruice. The beginning of it was so hard, that in nine daies he was in a continuall storme, and in great despaire for euer to recouer: neuerthelesse, whom the sword could not make afraid, the seas could not dismaie; but was euer one and the same man, of a good mind and great corage: and the storme being past, he followed the seruice which he had taken in hand, and became to be an excellent maritimall man, and verie expert in all seruices at the seas. When the time of this his seruice was expired, he returned into England, & attending vpon the earle of Bedford, he accompanied him in the seruice against the rebels of Deuon, at the commotion or rebellion in the third yeare of the reigne of king Edward the sixt one thousand fiue hundred fortie and nine, and did there verie good seruice. After which in course of time, he went to serue at Berwike, where his valor and behauior was such, that he was made prouost marshall vnder the earle of Sussex being lord lieutenant, and for his sundrie notable good seruices he rewarded him with the degrée of knighthood.

The conditions and manners of sir William Drurie. *His seruice in Bullongne.* *He is taken prisoner.* *He serueth at seas.* *His seruice at the commotion in Deuon.* *His seruice at Berwike.* *He is prouost marshall.* *He is dubbed knight.*

Not long after that, there was a péece of necessarie seruice to be doone in Scotland by the said earle vpon the quéenes commandement, but he was verie sicke, and at that time he could not performe the same: wherfore he deputed in his place this worthie knight, whome he then made generall of the armie: and with such forces as were thought méet he entreth into the seruices appointed vnto him, being accompanied with the earle of Lennox, sir Thomas Manners, sir George Carie, and sir Robert Constable, with sundrie other capteins, to the number of twelue hundred footmen. And his commission being to serue at Edenborough, which then by the reason of the diuision among the noblemen, about the murthering of the earle of Murreie, he tooke, spoiled, and burned sundrie forts and castels: and in the end besieged and tooke the towne and castell of Edenborough, and deliuered the same, according as he was commanded, to the vse of the king: and so he returned againe to his old charge, with great praise and commendation, as in the chronicles of England and Scotland is at large recorded.

He is generall of the armie, and dooeth a good peece of seruice in Scotland. *He besiegeth and taketh Edenborough castell.*

In verie short time after, hir maiestie hauing good experience of the valor of this knight euerie waie, as well for his valiantnes in martiall affaires, as for his wisedome in ciuill gouernement, she calleth and draweth him from his office and charge at Berwike, and remooueth him into Ireland, there to be imploied in the office of a lord president, and assigneth vnto him the gouernement of the whole prouince of Mounster, where he shall

Sir William Drurie sent into Ireland to be lord president of Mounster.

shall haue sufficient matter and occasion to vse both the sword & the law, iudgement and mercie. And hauing receiued hir highnes commandement in this behalfe, he maketh his voiage & repaire into Ireland: & being now settled in his roome and office by the right honorable sir Henrie Sidneie lord deputie, he acquiteth himselfe verie well euerie waie, being as seuere a iudge and earnest persecutor of the wicked and rebellious, as a zealous defender of the dutifull and obedient, to the great good liking of hir maiestie, the terror of the wicked, the comfort of the good, and the benefit of the commonwealth. After some time of his triall in this office, and sir Henrie Sidneie lord deputie being reuoked into England, he who had serued well in part, is called now to serue in all: and from a particular president is called to be a generall gouernor: and is in place of the departed deputie made lord iustice. He was no sooner entred into the office, but forthwith the rebellion and warres of the Desmonds began in Mounster vnder Iames Fitzmoris, and the Italians latelie come from the pope, and vnder the earle of Desmond and his brethren, who had long breathed and looked for this time. For the pacifieng, or rather subduing of this wicked rebellion, he tooke such continuall trauels and troubles, & so brused his bodie, that being not able to hold out any longer, he fell sicke & died (as is beforesaid) in the citie of Waterford, and from thense his corps was remooued to Dublin, and there buried, his bodie resting in peace, his soule in euerlasting blisse, and his fame in this world for euer immortall.

Sir William Drurie is made lord iustice of all Ireland.

The rebellion of the Desmonds in Mounster.

The death of sir William Drurie.

Sir Nicholas Malbie, who was cheefe gouernor of Mounster, now that his commission by the death of sir William Drurie was expired and ended, gaue ouer to follow anie actuall warres or ciuill administration in Mounster, but remooued himselfe and the whole campe vnto Lougher, and there dispersed them abrode in townes and villages to lie in garrison, and vpon their owne gards, vntill it were knowne who should haue the sword, and be the principall officer. Amongest the capteins thus dispersed into seuerall places, sir William Stanleie and capteine George Carew were assigned to lie at Adare. The traitors & rebels, hearing of the death of the worthie knight of whose prowesse and valiantnesse by the sword, & of whose wisedome & vprightnes in gouernement, they had good triall, yet not abiding to be alienated from their old leauened and wicked vsage, they were not a little glad that he was dead, euen as the other were most sorowfull for the losse & lacke of him. Wherefore now they pull vp their spirits, & confer togither how they may in this inter-reigne win the spurs, and be vtterlie deliuered from the English gouernement. Wherefore it is agreed among them, that vpon euerie seuerall garrison of the most principall capteins, they would set seuerall companies to watch & keepe them in their holds, that they should not issue out, but to their perill. Some therefore are appointed at Kilmalocke, some at Carigofoile, some at Asketten, and some at one place, and some at another. And at Adare, where these two gentlemen sir William Stanleie & George Carew laie, sir Iames of Desmond brother to the earle with foure hundred Kerns and fiftie horsses was appointed to serue and watch, which he did so carefullie & narowlie, that none durst to peepe nor looke out but in danger of some perill. But when vittels waxed short within doores, the souldiors, who could nor would be pined, gaue the aduenture to fetch that which was without doores: and as want of vittels did increase, so did their issuings out vpon the enimies grow and increase. And so often were their sallies and incountrings with the enimies, that in the end they finding & feeling the courage of the Englishmen, they had alwaies the worst side, and at euerie bickering euer lost some of their companie. Wherevpon they raised their siege, gaue place to the garrisons, and returned to the earle of Desmond. For albeit as yet they wanted a generall gouernor to rule aboue all, yet the capteins were not to seeke, nor yet failed to doo the seruice which vnto them did apperteine, either for seruice or safetie

The campe is dissolued and dispersed into garrisons.

Sir William Stanleie and capteine George Carew are assigned to Adare.

The garrisons are besieged and inuironed by the Irishrie.

Sir Iames of Desmond besiegeth Adare.

The Irishmen leaue to inuiron the garrison.

safetie. And among all the rest sir William Stanleie and capteine George Carew (as is before said) lieng in garrison at Adare, and vpon an occasion minding to doo a peece of seruice, verie earlie, and before the breake of the daie, they tooke a bote or a cote trough, which could not hold aboue eight or ten persons at a time, and passed ouer their soldiors vnto the other side of the riuer, which lieth betwéene Adare and the Kerrie, minding to haue burned & wasted all the lands and countrie belonging & apperteining to the knight of the valleie, who then was in actuall rebellion against hir maiestie, with the earle of Desmond and his brethren, where they then laie at a castell named Balliloghan, the chiefest & strongest place which the enimie had in that place and countrie, and this was furnished with a strong ward of the Spaniards. After that these two capteins had burned and spoiled the countrie, and put to the sword whomsoeuer they thought good in their returne before they could recouer the riuer, sir Iames of Desmond, the knight of the valleie, and the foresaid Spaniards with all their forces, to the number of foure hundred footmen and thirtie horssemen, gaue the charge vpon these two ensignes verie fiercelie, they hauing not in their companie aboue six score persons to the vttermost. These two capteins answered the charge, and most valiantlie skirmished with them at the push of the pike without intermission aboue eight hours, and killed of them aboue fiftie shot and Kernes, and sir Iames himselfe with others gréeuouslie hurt and wounded, without the losse of anie one of their owne men, sauing sundrie were shrewdlie hurt and wounded. At length these two capteins recouered their bote, and caused all the souldiors to be transported, they themselues being the verie last that passed ouer, and the enimies doubting of the safetie, stood afterwards vpon a better force.

The knight of the valleie his countrie spoiled.

The knight of the valleie a rebell.

Sir William Stanleie and capteine George Carews seruice at Adare.

The lords of the councell at Dublin in the meane time, considering the distressed state of the whole land for want of a principall officer, did assemble themselues, and tooke aduise for the choise of some one wise man, méet and fit for the gouernement. And in the end they resolued vpon sir William Pelham, whom they chose to be lord iustice. And vpon sundaie being the eleuenth of October 1579, he receiued the sword and tooke his oth in Christs church of Dublin: there being present the lord chancellor, the archbishop of Dublin, the earles of Ormond and Kildare, and the whole councell, besides a great number of barons, knights, and gentlemen. The sermon being ended, he returned to the castell, before whome sir Nicholas Bagnoll knight, marshall of Ireland, by his office did beare the sword before him, & the whole companie there did attend him: being come to the castell, he was receiued with the shot of all the great artillerie. As soone as he was entered into the chamber of presence, and the sword there deliuered, he called the lord chancellor before him: and in consideration of his good seruices in causes of councell, and of hir maiesties good acceptation of the same, he rewarded & honoured him with the degrée of knighthood, by the name of sir William Gerard.

Sir William Pelham chosen to be lord iustice.

1579

Sir William Pelham hauing taken the sword, dubbeth the lord chancellor knight.

Likewise, he called Edward Fitton the sonne and heire of sir Edward Fitton, late treasuror of Ireland, and dubbed him knight. After dinner the counsell sat, consulting vpon causes of the estate: and for quieting of the realme, letters were sent vnto all the noblemen and gentlemen of anie countenance and calling, persuading them to the continuance of their loialties and dutifull obedience. And for the gouernement of the prouince of Mounster, in absence of the lord iustice, a patent was sealed and deliuered to the earle of Ormond: who hauing the keeping and custodie of the yoong lord Girald sonne and heire to the earle of Desmond, was by a warrant willed to deliuer him to capteine Mackworth, and he to bring or conueie him to the castell of Dublin. Likewise, a warrant vnder the brode seale was sent to sir Warham Sentleger, to be knight or prouost marshall of all Mounster. These and other things doone concerning the kéeping of the English pale in quiet: the lord iustice, who

The earle of Ormond made gouernor of Mounster.

Sir Warham Sentleger made prouost marshall of Mounster.

had

had a speciall eie to the troublesome state of Mounster, prepareth to make presentlie a iournie into Mounster. But first it was concluded and agreed, that the lord chancellor should passe ouer into England, with letters of aduertisement to hir maiestie and councell of the present state of Ireland, and of his lordships iournie towards against the rebels: who had also in commission to vtter by speech what was to be aduertised & answered vpon hir maiesties demands and councels. When all things were prepared for his iournie, he appointed the erle of Kildare to defend the borders northward, and his lordship marched southward toward Mounster, taking with him the three bands latelie come from Berwike, vnder the leading of capteine Walker, capteine Case, and capteine Pikeman: with so manie others as he thought méet and necessarie for that seruice. And when he came in his waie to Kilkennie, being the nineteenth of October, there he remained two daies and kept sessions, whereat he sat in person, and determined manie matters, and did cause Edmund Mac Neile a notable traitor, & sundrie other malefactors, to be executed to death: and also he made a peace and reconciliation betwéene the earle of Ormond and sir Barnabie Fitzpatrike, baron of vpper Ossorie, betwixt whome was a mortall hatred. And bonds were taken betwéene them for restoring ech one to the other the preies, which either of their men had taken. During his abode and being in Kilkennie, the earle gaue his lordship verie honorable and good interteinment.

The lord iustice maketh a iournie into Mounster. The lord chancellor sent into England.

The lord iustice keepeth sessions at Kilkennie.

The earle of Ormond and the baron of vpper Osserie reconciled and made freends.

From this towne he departed the two and twentith of October, and by iournies he came to Cashell, where the earle of Ormond with a band of two hundred and thirtie men came and met him. And here the lord iustice sent his letters of the foure and twentith of October to the earle of Desmond, for his repaire vnto him, for the appeasing of the quarell and controuersie betwéene him & sir Nicholas Malbie, referring vnto him to come either to Cashell or to Limerike. And from this towne he rode to Limerike, and about a mile before he came to the citie, sir Nicholas Malbie and sundrie other capteins & gentlemen met his lordship, and for his welcome gaue him a braue volée of shot: and so brought him to the citie, where the maior in all dutifull maner receiued him, and presented him with a thousand well weaponed and appointed men of the same citie. The next daie he departed thense, and went to a towne name Fanings, where sir Nicholas Malbie presented vnto his lordship a letter, which he receiued from Vlike Burke: the same being the letter of doctor Sanders sent vnto the said Vlike, and with most pestilent reasons persuaded him to rebellion. And to this towne came the countesse of Desmond from hir husband, with letters of hir husband to the lord iustice, in excusing his not comming vnto him.

The earle of Desmond is sent for to come to the lord iustice.

The lord iustice honorablie receiued into Limerike.

Doctor Sanders wicked letters to Vlike Burke.

The lord iustice séeing the earle to vse but delaies, tooke aduise of the councell which was with him, what was best to doo. And in the end it was concluded, that the earle of Ormond should go vnto him, and to conferre with him vpon such articles as were deliuered, and now sent by him vnto the said Desmond, and to require his resolute answer.

The said articles were in summe as followeth.

FIRST, that he should deliuer vnto the said lord iustice, doctor Sanders, and certeine strangers of diuerse nations, now remaining in the said earles countries, and mainteined by such traitors and in such castels, as be at his deuotion and commandement.

The earle of Desmond is required to deliuer doctor Sanders and the Spaniards.

That he shall deliuer vp into hir maiesties hands one of his castels of Carigofoile or Asketten, for the pledge of his good behauiour: which vpon sundrie and diuerse reasons is suspicious, and he for his disloialtie greatlie suspected.

The earle to deliuer one of his castels.

That

That he doo foorthwith come and simplie submit himselfe vnto hir maiestie, and to referre his cause to the iudgement of hir maiestie and councell in England, or vnto him the lord iustice and councell in Ireland. The earle to submit himselfe.

That he doo foorthwith repaire to the lord iustice, and come with his lordship with all his forces, to prosecute his brethren and other traitors, and to assist and aid the earle of Ormond, lord generall in this seruice. That he prosecute his brethren and rebels.

Which conditions if he will hold, then he shall be reputed as a nobleman, and be receiued into fauour notwithstanding his errours past, but if he refuse, that then let him know, that immediatlie by open proclamation he shall be published a traitor.

The earle of Ormond, according to the order, went to the said Desmond, and deliuered vnto him both the letters and the said articles, and required his resolution and answer. Which when he had ouer read and considered, he returned his answer by a letter dated at Crogh the thirtith of October 1579, vsing therein nothing but triflings and delaies, requiring restitution for old wrongs and iniuries, and iustifieng himselfe to be a good subiect, though he doo not yeeld to the foresaid articles. During the time of this parlée, the lord iustice was remooued to Crome, where he expected the returne of the erle of Ormond, and to that place sir William Stanleie & capteine George Carew came vnto his lordship with their two hundred footmen. The earle sendeth letters but commeth not.

The earle of Ormond being returned, & hauing little preuailed with Desmond, notwithstanding his sundrie persuasions, there were other letters sent vnto him to induce him to the consideration of himselfe and his estate. but when no reason, no persuasion, nor counsell could preuaile, then it was thought good by the lord iustice & councell to procéed to their former determination, and to proclame him a traitor. The lord iustice remooued from Crome to Rathkill, and he was no sooner incamped, but alarum by the traitors was raised which was answered foorthwith by the lord iustice and the earle of Ormond & in that skirmish thrée or foure of the traitors were slaine, of which the earle of Desmonds butler was one, the earle himselfe being then incamped within a mile of his brothers and notwithstanding his iustification to be a good subiect, he dailie accompanied and conferred with them. The lord iustice séeing that neither counsell nor delaie of time could auaile with the earle of Desmond, then by the generall consent of the nobilitie, the councell, gentlemen, and the whole armie, a proclamation was openlie published against the said earle and all his confederats, in the highest degrée of treason at Rathkill the second of Nouember 1579. The effect of which treasons and proclamation was as here vnder followeth. The second letter sent to the earle of Desmond for his comming in. The earle of Desmonds butler taken and slaine. The earle of Desmond proclamed traitor.

The earle of Desmonds treasons articulated.

THE the erle of Desmond hath practised most vnnaturallie the subuersion of the whole state.

2 That he practised to bring in strangers, and practised with foren princes to bring and allure in strangers to inuade this land.

3 That he fostered and mainteined doctor Sanders, Iames Fitzmoris, and others beyond the seas to worke these feats.

4 That albeit to the vtter shew of the world, he seemed at the first to dislike with them at their landing yet were they secretlie interteined by the said earles permission, throughout all his countie of palantine in Kerrie.

5 That when his brethren most traitorouslie had murthered Henrie Dauels and others

others at Traleigh, he did let his said brethren slip, without reproouing or blaming of them, and had also commended speciallie the slaughter of Edmund Duffe an Englishman, who at the said murthering laie in the next bed vnto Dauels

6 That when the strangers at Smerweeke had no waie to escape by sea, at the comming of sir William Drurie, he gaue place vnto them for their escape by land, and gaue his tenants and followers libertie, to aid, helpe, and mainteine them

7 That contrarie to the commandement giuen vnto him by the lord iustice, he returned into Kerrie, and caused the strangers to leaue the fort, and to repaire to the towne of the Dingle and to other places which were at his deuotion, & had there interteinements

8 That he distributed the ordinances and artillerie of the forts vnto the rebels, as dooth appéere by a note found in the port mantien of doctor Allen latelie slaine in the incounter executed by sir Nicholas Malbie

9 That he hath set at libertie such strangers as he kept colourablie as prisoners, and hath appointed them to gard his houses and castels

10 That he hanged most abhominablie Richard Eustace, Simon Burn, and others the quéenes subiects, for whome he vndertooke to the late lord iustice to be safelie brought vnto him

11 That he sent sundrie of his principall men, seruitors, and followers, and his houshold seruants, as also his chiefe capteins, which vnder the popes banner displaied most traitorouslie in the fields, did assaile sir Nicholas Malbie knight hir maiesties lieutenant of all Mounster, at Mounster Enagh, and which banner Nicholas Williams the earles butler did that daie carrie

12 That he hath vtterlie refused manie persuasions, friendlie counsels, sundrie messages, and all the good means vsed and wrought to reduce and to bring him to obedience

13 That he hath not onelie refused to deliuer vp doctor Sanders and the Spaniards, which doo dailie accompanie him, but hath broken downe his castels, burned his townes, and desolated his countries aforehand, to the intent hir maiesties forces and subiects shall not be succoured nor refreshed

14 That he dailie looketh for a further aid and a new supplie of forreners, & dailie solliciteth the chiefe men of the Irish countries to ioin with him in this his most execrable and rebellious enterprise.

15 That he openlie protested & sent a message to the lord iustice that he would disturbe the whole state of Ireland. Wherfore they did pronounce, proclame, and publish him to be a most notorious, detestable, and execrable traitor, and all his adherents, against hir maiesties crowne and dignitie, vnlesse within twentie daies after this proclamation he did come in, and submit himselfe Vnto which proclamation there subscribed the earle of Ormond, the baron of Dunboine, the bishop of Waterford, the vicount Mountgarret, sir Nicholas Malbie, sir Edmund Butler, Edward Waterhouse, Theobald Butler, Edward Butler, and Piers Butler

The proclamation against Desmond is sent to all the cities in Ireland

This proclamation was foorthwith sent and dispersed to Dublin, Waterford, Corke, Limerike, and other principall townes to be in like order proclamed Immediatlie and within an houre after this proclamation, the countesse of Desmond came to the campe, but the campe was before dislodged from the towne, and all his countrie foorthwith consumed with fire, and nothing was spared which fire & sword could consume From this place the lord iustice remooued to Pople Brian, wherevpon the third of Nouember he tooke a generall muster of the whole armie and then he deliuered to the erle of Ormond two hundred and fiftie horssemen, and also eight ensignes of footmen,

footmen, of the which companie George Bourchier went to Kilmallocke, and sir William Stanleie and capteine George Carew to Adare. And then he remooued and tooke his iournie vnto Limerike, being accompanied with the earle of Ormond, who the next daie left the lord iustice and returned to his charge. After which departure of the lord iustice, the proclamed traitor of Desmond and his brothers, not able anie longer to shrowd his treacheries, went with all his forces to the towne of Youghall, where against his comming the gates of the towne were shut, but yet it was thought but colourablie: for verie shortlie after, without deniall or resistance, the earle and all his troope of rebels entered the towne and tooke it, and there remained about fiue daies, rifling and carrieng awaie the goods and houshold stuffe to the castell of Strangicallie and Lefinnen, the which then were kept by the Spaniards.

The towne of Youghall taken & spoiled.

The earle of Ormond, assoone as he was aduertised hereof, he caused a barke well appointed to be dispatched from Waterford, & to come to Youghall: the capteine of which bark was named White, a man of that countrie birth, verie valiant and of a stout stomach. Assoone as he was come to the wals of the towne, and had anchored his ship, he recouered from the rebels certeine ordinances of the said townes, and being put to vnderstand that the seneshall of Imokellie was comming towards the towne, he set all his men on land, and setting his men in good order, he entered into the towne at the watergate, and marched in good order through the towne, till he came where the rebels were togither, and then more rashlie than considerathe, gaue the charge and onset vpon them: but the number of them being great, and his but a handfull to them, he was in verie short time inclosed and ouerlaied, and there slaine, and with much adoo did a few of his companie recouer their ship againe. The lord generall and gouernour in the meane time, not slacking his businesse, did assemble and muster all his companie,& being accompanied with sir George Bourchier, sir William Stanleie, capteine Dowdall, capteine Furse, and others, made a iournete into Connilo, which was then the chéefest place of trust that the earle had, both for safetie and strength, and for vittels and forage, and there his greatest force and strength of his souldiors were seized in the townes and villages. And they then little thinking and lesse looking for anie such ghests, were vnawares and vpon a sudden intrapped and taken napping, and the most part of them taken and slaine, and the villages for the most part burned and spoiled. The earle of Desmond at this present time was there but not knowne in his castell called the New castell, and escaped verie narowlie. This péece of seruice being doone, the lord gouernour marched towards Mac Willies countrie, and being to go through a certeine passe, he met with the seneshall, vpon whome he gaue the charge, who answered the same verie valiantlie, and the skirmish was verie hot, in which the seneschals brothers and sundrie of his men were slaine, and the like also befell vpon the lord gouernours men, though not so manie, amongest whome capteine Zouches trumpetor was one, which so greeued the lord generall, that he commanded all the houses, townes, and villages in that countrie and about Lefinnen, which in anie waie did belong to the earle of Desmond, or of anie of his fréends and followers, to be burned and spoiled.

A barke well appointed at Waterford is sent to Youghall.

The ordinances recouered from the rebels.

White, capteine of the barke is slaine.

The earle of Ormond maketh a rode into Connilo, and killeth a number of the rebels.

The earle of Desmond in danger to be taken.

From this he tooke his iournete towards Corke, and in his waie at Drunfening he tooke a preie of one thousand fiue hundred kine or cowes, which were all driuen and sent vnto Corke, at which citie assoone as his lordship was come, and had rested a small time, then by the aduise of the capteins he diuided and bestowed his companie into sundrie garrisons and places conuenient, as which might best answer the seruices. And his lordship being accompanied with capteine Dowdall and capteine Furse, he went to Cashell, and by the waie he tooke the maior of Youghall, whome foorthwith he examined, and for his treasons and treacheries, in that he would yéeld vp the towne vnto Desmond, and had before refused a band of Englishmen which was appointed to lie in garrison in that towne, for the defense thereof, and had promised that he would kéepe and defend the same against all men, he carried him along with him vnto Youghall, and there before his owne doore hanged him. The lord gouernour when he came into the towne, found it all desolate, rifled and spoiled, and no one man, woman or child therein, sauing one frier, whome he spared, bicause he had fetched the corps of Henrie Dauels from Traleigh, and had carried it to Waterford, where it was buried in the chancell of the cathedrall church. And his lordship much pitieng the desolate estate of the towne, did take order for the reedifieng of the wals and gates, and placed therein a garrison of thrée hundred footmen vnder capteine Morgan and capteine Piers, who did verie good seruice in the countrie, and by good means drew home the people and old inhabitants, and impeopled the towne againe. And the lord gouernour departed thense, and followed his seruice, as time, place, and opportunitie did serue, and taking aduise with the capteins for some speciall seruice, and remembring that the Spaniards had hitherto lien in rest and quietnesse, in garrison at Strangicallie, and hitherto nothing doone or said vnto them, it was agréed betwéene his lordship and the capteins, to doo some seruice vpon them, and to trie their value: wherevpon they marched thither and laid siege therevnto.

The maior of Youghall hanged before his owne dores

The towne of Youghall all desolate

The inhabitants reuoked to dwell and inhabit the towne

The Spaniards, who kept alwaies good watch, and had also verie good espials abrode, they were forthwith aduertised that a companie of souldiers were drawing and marching towards the said castell, and when they themselues saw it to be true, and had discouered them, they began to distrust themselues, and to doubt of their abilitie how to withstand them. Wherefore abandoning & forsaking the castell, they passed ouer the water, thinking to recouer the woods and so to escape that present danger. But sir William Stanleie, capteine Zouch, capteine Dowdall, capteine Piers, capteine Roberts, and all their companies did so egerlie follow and pursue them, that in the end they ouertooke them, and slue all or the most part of them, and so tooke the castell, wherein the lord gouernour placed a ward. Likewise when he laie at Adare, and vnderstanding that the erle of Desmond was abrode, the garrison minding to doo some seruice vpon him, they issued out. Whereof he hauing some intelligence, notwithstanding his companie was but small in comparison of the others, yet he laie in an ambush to méet them in their returne, and vpon an aduantage he gaue the onset vpon them, and gaue a verie hot charge, in which the souldiers of the garrison were so hardlie assailed, that they brake the most part of their pikes, and were inforced with their swords and with the stumps of their staues to stand to their defenses, which they did so valiantlie, that the earle in the end with the losse of his men was driuen to giue ouer and to flée.

The Spaniards lieng in Strangicallie forsake their fort and in fleeing are slaine

The earle of Desmond lieth in an ambush

The like seruice did sir Henrie Wallop, who then laie at Limerike, sir George Bourchier, capteine Dowdall, capteine Holingworth, and all the residue of the capteins in their seuerall charges and garrisons, who though of themselues they were verie forward, yet the lord gouernour neuer slept his time, but was alwaies in readinesse, being the first with the formost, and the last with the hindermost. In the moneth of August 1580, he remooued and dislodged himselfe from Adare, and marched to Boteuant a house of the lord Barries, where a péece of seruice was appointed them to be doone: but suddenlie such a sicknes came among the souldiers which tooke them in the head, that at one instant there were aboue thrée hundred of them sicke, and for thrée daies they laie as dead stockes, looking still when they should die, but yet such was the good will of God, that few died, for they all recouered. This sicknesse not long after came into England & was called the gentle correction. Now the companie being thus recouered, his lordship minding to follow a péece of seruice, diuideth his companie into two parts, the one he tooke himselfe,

The diligent seruice of the earle of Ormond

A sicknesse in the campe

and

and tooke the waie by the Iland, & the other he appointed to go directlie vnto Traligh, and there they met and diuided their companies into thrée parts, & so marched to Dingle a cush. And as they went they draue the whole countrie before them vnto the Ventrie, & by that means they preied and tooke all the cattell in the countrie to the number of eight thousand kine, besides horsses, garrons, shéepe, and gotes, and all such people as they met they did without mercie put to the sword. By these meanes the whole countrie hauing nor cattel nor kine left, they were driuen to such extremities, that for want of vittels they were either to die and perish for famine, or to die vnder the sword. Neuerthelesse, manie of them vnderstanding that sir William Winter viceadmerall of England was newlie arriued with the quéenes ships at the Ventrie, and that he had receiued a commission to vse marshall law, they made their repaire vnto him, and obteined protections vnder him. Which the souldiers did verie much mislike, the same to be somewhat preiudiciall to hir maiesties seruice, bicause they persuaded themselues, that if they had folowed the course which they began, they should either haue taken or slaine them all.

All the countrie is preied

Sir William Winter giueth protection.

Sir William, viceadmerall of England, vpon the newes reported to hir maiestie that a new supplie was prepared to come into Ireland from out of Spaine, was commanded to kéepe the seas and to attend their comming, and as occasion serued to doo his best seruice vpon them. Who when he had so doone certeine moneths, his vittels waxed scant, and séeing no such matter, and also that the winter was drawing onwards, thinking nothing lesse than that the Spaniards would so late in the yeare arriue thither, he hoised his sailes and returned into England. But he was mistaken & deceiued: for not long after they came and landed at Smerwéeke, as hereafter shall be at full declared. And now leauing the soldiers in their garisons, let vs returne to the lord iustice, who when he departed from Limerike the fift of Nouember 1579, being accompanied with the Berwike bands, he went into Thomond, where the earle and his sonne with two bad horssemen met his lordship, and from thense he trauelled by iournies vnto Gallewaie, where he was verie honorablie receiued. And to the end to incourage them to persist and continue in dutifull obedience, he confirmed vnto the corporation certeine branches and articles, whereof some before this were granted vnto them in the time of sir Henrie lord deputie, and some now newlie set downe and granted, which in effect were these as followeth.

Sir William Winter kéepeth the seas.

The lord iustice with the Berwike bands goeth into Thomond

The lord iustice is verie honorablie receiued in Gallewaie

The charter of Gallewaie with new liberties confirmed.

First that no writ of *subpœna* shall be warded out of the chancerie against anie inhabitant in Gallewaie, vntill the partie which sueth out the writ, haue put in good and sufficient sureties before the lord chancellor, or the maior of Gallewaie to performe the same with effect.

That no new office nor officer be erected in the towne of Gallewaie by anie deputie or gouernour, otherwise than as they in times past haue vsed to doo.

That the maior by the aduise of foure aldermen, and other foure discreet men of the towne vpon good considerations may grant safe conduct and protection to English rebels and Irish enimies.

That the merchants of the towne which shall buie anie wares or merchandize of strange merchants shall put in good and sufficient bands before the maior that he will well and trulie make paiment vnto the said merchant stranger for his debt and dutie.

That if anie inhabitant in the towne doo vse anie vndecent & vnreuerent speach to the maior, that he shall be punished according to the qualitie of the fault and offense.

That the maior, bailiffes, and inhabitants shall inioy, vse, and exercise all their ancient liberties, vsages, and customes.

That in all actions tried before the maior, the partie condemned shall paie reasonable costs, and the said maior shall not take anie fee for anie sentence, called Oleigethe

That no dead bodie shall be interred or buried within the towne and walles of Gallewaie

That when anie strange merchants come to their port and hauen, that the same be serched and viewed for weapons and munitions, and that none aboue the number of ten persons of the said ship shall come into the said towne

That no stranger be suffered to take the view of the strength of the towne, nor to walke on the wals

That the maior from time to time doo take the muster and view of all the able men, and of their furniture and armour

That all vnserviceable people in time of seruice be sent out of the towne.

That sufficient vittels from time to time be prepared to serue the towne for ten moneths at the least before hand.

That a storehouse be prouided alwais in the towne for a staple of vittels to be kept there at all times

William Noris newlie come out of England meeteth the lord iustice

From thense his lordship by sundrie iournies came to Athlon and so to Dublin; where about thrée miles before he came to the citie, William Noris newlie arriued out of England, and accompanied with certeine gentlemen, met him with a hundred and fiftie horssemen, well furnished and well horssed with English geldings, euerie man wearing a red cote with a yellow lace, who attended his lordship into the citie, and from thense he was assigned and sent vnto the Newrie, where he died verie shortlie after vpon the fiue and twentith of December 1579 His hart was consumed, his splene corrupted, and his braine mixt with filthie matter His bands were diuided and deliuered to other capteins And immediatlie vpon his entrance into the citie, he sent for Iaques Wingfield master of the ordinance, and by order he was commanded as prisoner to kéepe his chamber for his contempt, bicause he did not attend the lord iustice into Mounster as he was commanded, but vpon his submission after foure daies he was released And vpon the death of Francis Agard esquier, sir Henrie Harington, who had married one of his daughters and heires was by vertue of certeine letters from out of England, appointed to be seneshall of the Obirnes, as his father in law before was The earle of Desmond and his two brethren sent a proud and an arrogant letter vnder their hands, dated the nine and twentith of Nouember 1579, to the lord iustice, aduertising, that they were all entered into the defense of the catholike faith, with great authoritie both from the popes holinesse and king Philip, who haue vndertaken to defend and mainteine them, and therefore persuaded the lord iustice to ioine with them.

Capteine Noris sent to lie at the Newrie

Sir Henrie Harington is made seneshall of the Obirnes

The proud letters of the earle of Desmond

The lord iustice entreth a new iournie into Mounster

The lord iustice, hauing set the pale in some order, & hauing committed the same to the gouernement of the erle of Kildare, he made a new iournie into Mounster, and departed out of Dublin the eightéenth of Ianuarie 1579, with such companies and forces as he thought good for that seruice, and tooke his iournies along by the sea coasts, and being come to Waterford, there he kept sessions, & sat in person at the same And from thense taking Tinneterne in his waie he came to Wexford, the fiue and twentith of Ianuarie 1579 by water from Ballihacke in certeine botes verie well appointed by the maior of the citie And before he came thither, sir William Stanleie, sir Peter Carew, and capteine George Carew, and capteine

The lord iustice keepeth sessions at Wexford

teine Peirs, issued out of the citie with their foure bands, and neere to the shore in the view of his lordship, they presented him with a iollie skirmish, and so retired themselues, to make ward against his landing. The bulworks, gates, and curteins of the citie were beautified with ensignes and shot in warlike maner, and then all the shot of the ships in the hauen, and a great ranke of chambers vpon the keie, togither with the shot of the souldiers, were discharged, and gaue his lordship a lustie and a great thundering peale.

At his landing the maior and aldermen araied in their scarlet gownes met him, and presented vnto his lordship the sword and the keies of the gates, which foorthwith he redeliuered vnto them againe, and the sword the maior bare and caried before his lordship. He went first to the church, and by the waie vpon two seuerall stages made for the purpose, there were two orations made vnto him in Latine, and at his returne from the church, he had the third in English at the doore of his lodging. And to this citie the earle of Ormond came vnto him, and they being togither, letters were sent from sir William Morgan of aduertisement, that the traitors were come downe about Dungaruon and Yoghall. Wherevpon one hundred horssemen vnder capteine Zouch, and Sentleger, and foure hundred footmen vnder sir William Stanleie, sir Peter Carew, capteine George Carew, & capteine Peirs were dispatched to serue against them.

The lord iustice receiued honourablie into Waterford.

The lord iustice from Waterford, vpon notice of the trouble dailie increasing, sent a commission of the eleuenth of Februarie, to sir Warham Sentleger to be prouost marshall, authorising him to procéed according to the course of marshall law against all offendors, as the nature of his or their offenses did merit and deserue; so that the partie offendor be not able to dispend fortie shillings by the yeare in land, or annuitie, or be not woorth ten pounds in goods: also that vpon good causes he maie parlée and talke with anie rebell, and grant him a protection for ten daies: that he shall banish all idlers & sturdie beggers: that he shall apprehend aiders of outlawes and theeues, and execute all idle persons taken by night: that he shall giue in the name and names of such as shall refuse to aid and assist him: that in dooing of his seruice, he shall take horsse-meat and mans-meat where he list, in anie mans house for one night: that euerie gentleman and noble man doo deliuer him a booke of all the names of their seruants and followers: that he shall put in execution all statutes against merchants and other penall lawes, and the same to sée to be read and published in euerie church by the parson and curat of the same: and that he doo euerie moneth certifie the lord iustice how manie persons, and of their offenses and qualities, that he shall execute and put to death: with sundrie other articles, which generallie are comprised in euerie commission for the marshall law.

The articles of a comission for the marshall law.

The lord iustice, after that he had rested about thrée weekes at Waterford, he remooued and went to Clonmell, where the earle of Ormond met him, being the fiftéenth of Februarie 1579, and from thense he went by iourneies vnto Limerike, where the chancellor of Limerike vpon suspicion of treason was committed to prison, and his lodging being searched, manie masse bookes and other popish trash, togither with an instrument of the earle of Desmonds libertie palantine of Kerrie was found. He was after indicted, arreigned, and found guiltie, but in the end pardoned. And the bishop likewise was vpon some suspicion committed prisoner vnto his owne house.

The chancellor of Limerike sent to ward for treason.

The bishop committed prisoner to his owne house.

And out of Limerike he marched the tenth of March to Rathkell, where within one houre the erle of Ormond came vnto him, and there consulted for the maner of the persecution of the enimie. Which when they had agréed vpon, they passed the next morning ouer the bridge of Adare, and by the waie they burned and spoiled the countrie, and went to Rathkell. Now when they had amended the bridge

which

which the rebels had destroied and made passable, they passed ouer the same into Conillo, where the lord iustice and the earle of Ormond diuided their companies, and as they marched they burned and destroied the countrie, and they both that night incamped within one mile at Kilcolman. And there it was aduertised, that Nicholas Parker lieutenant vnto capteine Fenton, comming from Limerike with fiue horssemen, and thrée shot which were of the garrison at Adare, he was set vpon at Rathkell by a hundred traitors, which did discharge sixtéene or eightéene shot at him, and sundrie darts, before he espied them: but he and Iames Fenton the capteins brother, and Guidon, so bestirred themselues, that they gaue the enimie the repulse, and slue their leader, with fiue or six others, and so came safe to the campe, but with the hurt of one of their horsses.

Nicholas Parker [illegible] valiantlie [illegible]

The souldiers likewise in the campe were so hot vpon the spurre, & so eger vpon the vile rebels, that that day they spared neither man, woman, nor child, but all was committed to the sword. The same daie, a souldier of the marshals incountered with two lustie Kernes, the one of them he slue, and the other he compelled to carrie his fellows head with him to the campe: which when he had doone, his head also was cut off and laid by his fellowes. The next daie following, being the twelfe of March, the lord iustice and the earle diuided their armie into two seuerall companies by two ensignes and thrée togither, the lord iustice taking the one side, and the other taking the other side of Slewlougher, and so they searched the woods, burned the towne, and killed that daie about foure hundred men, and returned the same night with all the cattell which they found that daie.

And the said lords, being not satisfied with this daies seruice, they did likewise the next daie diuide themselues, spoiled and consumed the whole countrie vntill it was night. And being then incamped néere togither, the baron of Lexnew came to the earle of Ormond, whome the earle in the next morning brought before the lord deputie, where he in most humble maner yéelded, and submitted himselfe to his lordships deuotion, promising and presenting his seruice with all dutifulnesse. And then, when after great trauels they had maruellouslie wasted and spoiled the countrie, they appointed to march to Carigofoile, and to laie siege to the same: for in it laie the greatest force of the Desmonds, and which was garded and kept by the Spaniards. This castell standeth in the riuer and at euerie full sea both it and the bawnes about it are inuironed with the said floods and flowing waters. As soone as they were incamped, the lord iustice approched the castell so néere as he could, to take the view thereof, that accordinglie he might consider the most fittest places for the laieng of the shot for the batterie: and then he commanded capteine George Carew to take out certeine shot, and to go with him in this seruice. Now the Spaniards hauing espied them, spent manie shot vpon them, and where the lord iustice verie hardlie escaped with his life, and from being slaine with a musket shot. When his lordship vpon this view had determined what he would doo, he caused the canon shot to be planted in the place most fit for the batterie, for otherwise the fort was not to be assaulted.

The baron of Lexnew submitteth himselfe.

The castell of Cargofoile is besieged.

The lord iustice and capteine Carew take the view of the castell.

The castell besieged.

In the same were sixtéene Spaniards and fiftie others vnder one Iulio an Italian, who at the request of the countesse of Desmond vndertooke the kéeping of it, and who reported himselfe to be a verie notable enginer. & standing vpon his reputation, he plied the campe with continuall shot, putting out an ensigne and railing with manie bad speeches against hir maiestie, declaring also that they kept it for the king of Spaine and so still would, vntill further aid were sent from him: and which in verie déed was dailie looked for. Before the canons and other battering péeces could be vnladen, they spent the time, occupieng the one the other with such deuises as they thought good for the seruices. And the Spaniards, hauing the aduantage,

The proud brags of the Spaniard.

uantage, did by their often shot hurt and kill some Englishmen, namelie a souldior of sir George Bourchiers, one of sir Henrie Wallops, & one of capteine Zouches: and sir William Stanleie comming with his companie to the trenches to take the ward of capteine George Carew, which kept the watch that night past, was hurt with a musket shot out of the castell in the necke. Assoone as the ordinance was vnladen and planted, they began forthwith to batter the fort with three canons, a culuering, and a demie culuering, and in short time they so beat it, that the house fell and filled the ditches, by meanes wherof the same became to be assaultable.

The castell is battered with shot.

Capteine Macworth, who had the ward of that daie, entred into the vtter bawne by a doore that the souldiors had broken, and was maister of it presentlie. The Spaniards thervpon retired to a turret that was vpon the wall of the barbican, & some sought other places to hide and to saue themselues, but that part of the castell was beaten downe: and then capteine Macworth recouered the possession of the whole, and did put fiftie to the sword, of which nineteene were found to be Spaniards, and six others he tooke, wherof one was a woman, which were executed in the campe. None were saued that daie but onelie the capteine Iulio, whome the lord iustice kept for certeine considerations two or three daies: but in the end he was hanged as the rest were before him. The next daie, being the first of Aprill one thousand fiue hundred and fourescore, the ordinances were remoued and caried to the ship, which with all such souldiors as were sicke and hurt were sent to Limerike, to be relieued and cured. This castell one of the principallest and chiefest forts thus recouered, there resteth onelie the house and castell of Asketten: and the lord iustice, and the earle of Ormond thought nothing more necessarie, than euen forthwith to march to Asketten, and to incampe there and to besiege it, euen as they had doone to this fort of Carrigofoile. Where when they came, the two lords diuided themselues, the one taking the one side, and the other taking the other side of the water: and vpon the third of Aprill they incamped at the said castell, the lord iustice lieng in the abbeie, and the earle of Ormond vpon the further side of the riuer.

Capteine Macworth first entreth the castell.

The castell of Carrigofoile is taken.

The bragging Spaniard is taken and hanged.

1580

The castell of Asketten appointed to be besieged.

The lord iustice viewed the place, and found no waie possible to place anie watch or ward neere to the castell, by reason of the great disaduantage of the rockes which laie altogither vpon the castell. While the campe laie there, sir William Stanleie, capteine George Carew, and capteine Walker went to giue siege vnto the castell of Balliloghan, a strong house of the Desmonds, and which was warded vntill this time against hir maiestie. The ward had no sooner the sight and view of these three ensignes, but that they fired the house and fled: but they were so narrowlie pursued, that the leader of them and some of his companie were ouertaken and slaine. Whilest the siege laie at Asketten, sir Henrie Wallop treasuror at warres came from Limerike to the campe the fourth of Aprill 1580: and the verie same night following, being a verie darke and close night, the warders of the castell fearing the example of the execution doone at Carrigofoile, and doubting the sequele of the lord iustice preparation made for the batterie to be laid against it, did abandon and forsake the castell verie secretlie about midnight, leauing a traine of pouder to set it on fire, which consumed & burned a great part of the same: but the principall towers remained vntouched. The warders by fauor of the darke night escaped into the woods.

Sir William Stanleie and capteine George Carew besiege the castell of Balliloghan.

The warders forsake the castell.

The warders of Asketten forsake the castell and by a traine set it on fire.

This castell thus recouered, the earle of Desmond had neuer a castell in all Mounster which was warded against hir maiestie: but all were now at hir deuotion. The lord iustice being possessed of Asketten, he appointed a strong garrison to reside there, and placed sir Peter Carew, and sir Henrie Wallops companie in the castell, and capteine George Carew, and capteine Hollingworth to be in the abbeie, and so vpon the fift of Aprill he dislodged with the rest of the armie, and went vnto Lime-

The castell of Asketten is taken.

A ward placed at Asketten.

rike

rike: commanding the capteins to cut down the woods on both sides of the riuer, that the botes might passe fréelie to and fro. At his comming to Limerike, all things now séeming to be at peace, the earle of Ormond returned home to Kilkennie, & certeine of the councell which had followed in this iourneie rode to Dublin: and sir Nicholas Malbie departed into Connagh. And notwithstanding that the most part of the armie was now dispersed into garrisons: yet the seruices of euerie of them neuer abated. For alwaies as the time of seruice required, the Irishmen were issued out vpon, and most commonlie had the worst side. And the lord iustice himselfe taking an occasion to visit the ward at Adare, he passed by water, and capteine Case went by land, and after a time spent in searching the woods, they returned with a preie of one thousand and two hundred kine, and verie good store of shéepe, besides the slaughter of manie traitors.

The armie is dispersed, and the garrisons are sent to their places appointed.

At his being and during his abode in Limerike, vpon the fifteenth of Maie, he receiued hir maiesties commission vnder the broad seale of England to be lord iustice (where before he held the same by the election and order of the councell) and therewith also one other commission, for creating of sir William Burke baron of castell Connall, with a yearelie pension of one hundred markes during his life. And from this time, the lord iustice spent this summer in Mounster, trauelling to and fro through out the whole prouince: he himselfe and euerie other capteine in his seuerall garrison dooing such seruice vpon the rebels as by occasion was offred. The lord iustice vpon the fiftéenth of Iune, after that he had marched a few miles in Mac Aulies countrie, spoiling, defacing, and burning the same, he passed through the boggie mounteine of Slewlougher into Kerrie, and there he discouered a great preie of the countrie; and pursuing the same, by the voward of his horssemen, and he himselfe in person tooke about two thousand kine, besides store of shéepe and garons, with part of the traitors masking apparell. The earle of Desmond, the countesse his wife, and doctor Sanders little thinking of this matter, escaped verie hardlie; and their priest for hast was faine to leaue his gowne behind. The like seruice he did the next daie, being the fiue and twentith of Iune at Castelmange. But at this time, a great mutinie began amongest the souldiors vnder sir George Bourchier, capteine Macworth, and capteine Dowdall, by reason of their wants: but his lordship with such lenitie and courtesie handled the matter, that they departed from him well satisfied. Likewise sir Cormac Mac Teige shiriffe of the countie of Corke did notable seruice vpon sir Iames of Desmond; which sir Iames vpon the fourth of August made a roade into Muskroie, and tooke a great preie from the foresaid sir Cormac. Wherevpon his brother Donnell assembleth his brothers tenants and countrie and followed the preie, and recouered the same: sir Iames, who thought it to be too great a dishonor and reproch to depart with anie thing which he had in hand, withstanding the matter.

A commission to create sir William Burke to be baron.

The earle of Desmond and his wife and doctor Sanders in perill to be taken.

A mutinie among the souldiors for lacke of vittels.

Sir Cormac Mac Teige dooth a peece of seruice vpon sir Iames of Desmond.

Wherevpon they fell at hand-fight. In which conflict and fight the said Donnell behaued himselfe so valiantlie, and his companie so lustilie stucke to the matter, that the preie was recouered, and sir Iames himselfe mortallie wounded and taken prisoner, and all his force, being aboue a hundred and fiftie persons, were slaine and ouerthrowne. He that tooke him was a smith, and seruant to sir Cormac, who foorthwith handfasted him: and for auoiding of certeine inconueniences, he kept him close, and secretlie hid him in a certeine bush in the fastnesse there, and bound him so fast and sure, that he could not escape nor run awaie. And when all the companie was gone, then he tooke him and carried him to sir Cormac his maister, who kept him in safe custodie, vntill, by letters of commandement from the lord iustice and councell, he did deliuer him vnto sir Warham Sentleger then prouost marshall, and to capteine Raleigh; who (according to a commission in like order to them addressed) was

Sir Iames of Desmond in taking of a preie is taken prisoner and executed.

Sir Iames of Desmond sent to sir Warham

was examined, indicted, arreigned, and then vpon iudgement drawen, hanged and quartered: and his bodie being quartered, it was togither with the head set on the towne gates of the citie of Corke, and made the preie of the foules. And thus the pestilent hydra hath lost an other of his heads.

Sentleger & to capteine Raleigh, and was executed to death.

This seruice of this knight was maruellouslie well accepted, and first from the lord iustice and councell, and then from hir maiestie he receiued verie fréendlie and thankfull letters. This man was a yonger house vnto Mac Artie Reough, and they both a yonger house vnto Mac Artie More now earle of Clancar; and whose ancestors (as is said) were kings before the conquest of Mounster. They are all men of great power, and greatlie estéemed in those parties. But this sir Cormac, in dutie and obedience to hir maiestie and hir lawes, and for his affection to all Englishmen, surpasseth all his owne sept & familie, as also all the Irishrie in that land. For albeit a méere Irish gentleman can hardly digest anie Englishman or English gouernment, & whatsoeuer his outward appearance be, yet his inward affection is corrupt and naught: being not vnlike to Iupiters cat, whome though he had transformed into a beautifull ladie, and made hir a noble princesse, yet when she saw the mouse, she could not forbeare to snatch at him: and as the ape, though he be neuer so richlie attired in purple, yet he will still be an ape. This knight, after he did once yéeld himselfe to hir maiesties obedience, and had professed his loialtie, he euer desired to ioine himselfe vnto the companie of the Englishmen, and became in time a faithfull and fréendlie man vnto them, liued according to hir maiesties lawes, and did so good seruice at all times when it was requisit and required, as none of that nation did euer the like. And if at anie time he were had in suspicion, he would by some kind of seruice purge & acquite himselfe, euen as he did in this present seruice in taking of sir Iames of Desmond, to his great praise & commendation, and to his acquitall against the reprochfull reports of his aduersaries. And sir William Fitz-williams in the time of his deputiship, hauing had a verie good triall of his fidelitie, truth, and good seruice, did giue vnto him the order of knighthood, and made him shiriffe of the countie of Corke: euen as the lord iustice now did commend this his seruice vnto hir maiestie by his letters of the twelfe of August, a thousand fiue hundred and eightie, and praieng that the same might be so acceptablie receiued, as that the enobling of him might be both an ornament to his house, an incoraging vnto others to doo the like, and a testimonie against others of his sort, who haue neglected a number of occasions (at greater aduantages) to haue doone the like seruices.

Iupiters cat.

The loialtie of sir Cormac Mac Teige.

Sir Cormac Mac Teige made knight.

The death of Iames of Desmond, and the quartering of his bodie did maruelouslie dismaie the earle himselfe, sir Iohn his other brother, and doctor Sanders, and all their confederats. And by reason of the continuall persecuting of the rebels, who could haue no breath nor rest to reléeue themselues, but were alwaies by one garrison or other hurt and pursued, and by reason the haruest was taken from them, their cattels in great numbers preied from them, and the whole countrie spoiled and preied, the poore people, who liued onelie vpon their labors, and fed by their milch cowes, were so distressed, that they would follow after the goods which were thus taken from them, and offer themselues, their wiues, and children, rather to be slaine by the armie, than to suffer the famine wherewith they were now pinched. And this great calamitie made also a diuision betweene the earle of Desmond and his brother sir Iohn, either of them excusing that whereof they were both guiltie. The earle himselfe (without rest) fléeth from place to place, and findeth small comfort, and séeing no other remedie, sent his ladie and wife vnto the lord iustice, who in great abundance of teares bewraied the miserable

The miserie of the people.

The sute of the countesse of Desmond.

estate of hir husband, hir selfe, and their followers, making (with most lamentable requests) sute, that hir husband might be taken to submission.

Sir Iohn of Desmond minded to ioine with the vicount Baltinglasse.

Sir Iohn of Desmond, being in the like distresse, he togither with doctor Sanders gaue the aduenture, to passe for their refuge to the vicount Baltinglasse, then being in the countie of Kildare. The garrison which laie at Kilmallocke, making an issue out by night to doo some seruice, by chance met the said Iohn and Sanders in the darke night, and not knowing them did set vpon them, and of foure of them they tooke two, the one being a frier named Iames Haie and standardbearer to the late Iames Fitzmoris, who vpon his examination confessed that the earle of Desmond was author of all these warres, and the other was Sanders man, who was slaine, and the frier was reserued, but sir Iohn and the doctor by the benefit of the darknesse verie hardlie escaped, & cut off from their iournie. The lord iustice being at Newcastell, and being aduertised that the earle of Desmond and Sanders were in Kerrie he foorthwith sent for the garrisons of Adare and Asketten to come to him, and for the garrison of Kilmallocke to méet him at the place, daie and time appointed, for a speciall peece of seruice then to be doone. Whose commandement being doone and obeied, they tooke their waie into Kerrie, and there they had taken the earle, and his countesse, and doctor Sanders, had not a false brother bewraied the matter, and yet for hast they left their breakfast behind them halfe dressed. Neuerthelesse, they tooke two preies, the one of fiftéene and the other of eightéene kine, and the next daie they tooke another preie of two hundred kine, slue diuerse traitors, and tooke two friers, whose gownes were too long for them to follow the earle and the popes nuntio, they being poore bare footed friers, and he a lustie horsman: and then his lordship returned to Asketten, where he left maister Parker conestable of the place, and from thense he went to Limerike, where he receiued news by maister Zouch, and after by letters from the lord Greie lord deputie, of his arriuall to Dublin. And then his lordship minding to make his spéedie repaire to Dublin, did set the countrie in some good order, and by the aduise of the councell at Limerike, he appointed sir George Bourcher coronell of all Mounster, and instructions were deliuered vnto him, both for certeine speciall seruices to be doone, & also for the generall gouernement of the whole prouince, & had left vnto him the charge (vnder his gouernement) of the whole forces in Mounster, which of footmen were two thousand eight hundred & twentie, and of horssemen thrée hundred fourescore and fiftéene: the whole, thrée thousand two hundred and fiftéene men. Likewise he had sent the like instructions to sir William Sentleger, and the erle of Clancar. And these & other like things doone, he tooke his iournie through Conaugh for the like establishing of the countrie, & came to Dublin the sixt daie of September one thousand fiue hundred fourescore and one, and the next daie he deliuered vp the sword to the lord Greie, as to the lord deputie of Ireland, in saint Patrikes church in presence of the councell, noble men, and gentlemen, which were for the same purpose there assembled.

Sir Iohn of Desmond and doctor Sanders in fléeing, were in danger to be taken.

The earle and his countesse in danger to haue beene taken.

Sir George Bourcher coronell of Mounster.

This force is both of the princes paie, and of the lord of the prouince.

The vicount of Baltinglasse lieth in the Glinnes with the rebels.

And within six daies after the lord Greie his arriuall, it was giuen his lordship to vnderstand, that the vicount of Baltinglas, and Pheon macke Hugh, the chéefe of his sex of the Obrins, were lieng in the Obrins countrie, and were now of great force and strength, by meanes of the companie of capteine Fitzgirald, kinsman to the earle of Kildare, who had a band of footmen committed vnto him in the beginning of this rebellion, for the defense of the countie of Kildare, which bordereth fast by the Obrins. And he nothing regarding now, either the dutie of a subiect, or his owne credit, most traitorouslie reuolteth from his lawfull prince, and conioineth himselfe with traitors and rebels. And with these he practiseth and persuadeth

persuadeth to resist and make head against hir maiesties forces, because they could not (as he said) withstand or preuaile against them: who without anie reward promised, were easilie persuaded, because they would be persuaded, and were most willing to exercise anie maner of outrage. All these thus combined, drew one string, & incamped themselues in the fastnes of the Glinnes, about 20 miles from Dublin, where they kept all their goods & cattell. This fastnesse was by nature so strong as possible might be: for in it is a vallie or a combe lieng in the midle of the wood, of a great length, betweene two hils, & no other waie is there to passe through. Vnder foot it is boggie and soft, and full of great stones and slipperie rocks, verie hard and euill to passe through; the sides are full of great & mightie trees vpon the sides of the hils, & full of bushments and vnderwoods. The strength of the fastnesse in the Glinnes.

The lord deputie, being not yet acquainted with the custome of the countrie, nor with the Irish seruices, and thinking himselfe in honor to be touched, and the whole armie to be discredited, if a companie of traitors should lie so néere vnto him, and not be touched nor fought withall: resolued himselfe to haue a péece of seruice to be doone vpon them. Wherfore he with all his whole armie marcheth vnto the said Glinnes, & giueth order to sir William Stanléie, sir Peter Carew, sir Henrie Bagnoll, capteine Awdleie, and to Iohn Parker, lieutenant to capteine Furse with all their footmen, and to Francis Cosbie capteine of the kerne, and George Moore an old veteran of Berwike, coronell of all the footmen, to take this seruice vpon them. But Cosbie, who had beene a long seruitor, and knew what to that kind of seruice did belong, did foresée the danger which would follow hereof, and so declared it to his companie: notwithstanding to auoid the reproches which might be laied to his charge, followed the said seruice, and vpon the next daie, being the fiue & twentith of August, they entered the Glinnes. A seruice appointed to be doone against the Obrins.

The lord deputie being accompanied with the earle of Kildare, Iaques Wingefield, capteine George Carew, capteine Denie, and others on horssebacke staied vpon the mounteine side hard by the wood. The archtraitor Fitzgirald, hauing some secret intelligence of the seruice towards, he bestoweth and placeth all his men with their peeces amongst the trées, and there couered themselues, vntill the Englishmen were entered and passed into the fastnesse, about halfe a mile or more, and could not easilie returne: and he hauing them at aduantage vpon euerie side of the hill, with great furie assaileth them with his shot, and in verie short time did kill the most part of the vowarde, both capteins and souldiors. The residue which followed, being in despaire to recouer what was lost, and distrusting themselues, fled at all hands, and ran backe as fast as they could in so bad a waie. And yet such was the nimblenesse of the traitors, and their skill of seruice in such places, that they were like to haue béene killed, if the lord deputie, and the horssemen had not rescued them: vpon whose comming they retired into their fastnesse. The lord deputie staied vpon the mounteins.

In this conflict, George More, capteine Audleie, Francis Cosbie, and sir Peter Carew coronell, were then murthered and slaughtered, which sir Peter was verie well armed, and with running in his armor, which he could not put off, he was halfe smothered, and inforced to lie downe: whome when the rebels had taken, they disarmed him, & the most part of them would haue saued him, and made request for him, they thinking that more profit would grow among them by his life than benefit by his death. Notwithstanding, one villaine most butcherlie, assoone as he was disarmed, with his sword slaughtered and killed him; who in time after was also killed. Before the entrie into this seruice, Iaques Wingfield being acquainted with this kind of bold and rash hardinesse, and foreséeing the euill successe which was feared would insue, persuadeth with his two nephues, sir Peter The Englishmen slaine in the Glinnes. Sir Peter Carew slaine. Iaques Wingfield his wisdome towards his nephues.

and capteine George Carew, to staie and to forbeare to aduenture into the woods. But sir Peter could not listen thereunto, nor be persuaded; but would néeds go in. His brother would haue doone the like, but his vncle perforce kept him, saieng: "If I lose one, yet I will keepe the other:" and so by that meanes he was by Gods goodnesse saued and preserued.

This blacke daie was a dolefull and a gréeuous daie to the lord deputie and all his companie: notwithstanding, hoping of a hard beginning would follow a better ending tooke the matter as patientlie as he could, and made his returne vnto Dublin, abiding the comming of the lord iustice; who as soone as he was returned, then the lord Greie was sworne, and had the sword deliuered vnto him. The earle of Ormond in this meane time, being verie desirous to doo some seruice vpon the Spaniards, being nothing afraid of their force and multitude, marcheth towards the fort, and incampeth at Traleigh, where the scout the same night espied a light in the enimies campe, and by reason of the darke night, the companie of them seemed to be the greater: which caused the gouernor to be more watchfull and circumspect. Wherefore in the morning, like a wise and a politike capteine, setteth all his companies in battell araie, & so marcheth forwards in his strength & verie good order ouer the strand of Traleigh towards the fort, euerie man being at a full resolution to doo his best seruice that day against the enimie. When these strangers had knowledge of the approching of the lord gouernor, and his companie, albeit their fort was verie strong, both by nature and by art; yet they distrusted themselues, and forsooke the fort, and by the guiding of the Irishrie, they remoued themselues from thense to Glanningell, whome the gouernor pursued, & ouertooke some of them, vpon whome he gaue the onset, and skirmished with them: diuerse of them he slue, and manie he tooke, whome he caried along with him: the residue of them fled into the fastnesse of Glanningell, which is a verie strong place and couert, by reason of the great woods and of the mounteines adioining. Wherevpon the daie being spent, and no seruice for that time to be doone anie further, the lord gouernor incamped there that night, fast to their enimies nose, to trie him what he would, or durst doo.

The earle marcheth in order of battell to the fort.

The Spaniards leaue their fort.

The earle followeth the Spaniards and putteth them to the foile.

Assoone as he was incamped, he calleth the prisoners (who were taken) before him, and they confessed that they were in number, not aboue seuen hundred men; but had brought with them pikes, caliuers, munitions, and all kinds of artillerie, sufficient for fiue thousand men: because they knew that the Irishmen were of bodies sufficient, but that they lacked furniture and training; & in these two things they minded to furnish them: and further also they said, that they had sent backe two of their ships into Spaine, to aduertise that they were safelie arriued, and how that they were interteined: requesting that the supplie appointed before their comming from home, might with all spéed be sent awaie, and for which they did dailie looke: because it was throughlie concluded betwéene the pope and king Philip, to make a through conquest of all Ireland; and so consequentlie as time should serue, to doo the like with England. And moreouer, that they had brought with them a great masse and store of monie and treasure, which according to their commission they had deliuered to the earle of Desmond, sir Iohn his brother, & to doctor Sanders the popes nuntio; and more is promised to be sent.

The companie of the Spaniards not aboue seuen score.

The determinations of the pope and king Philip, to make a through conquest of Ireland.

After these things thus doone, it was giuen to the said gouernor to vnderstand, that the same night there were three hundred souldiors of the enimies companie returned & gone backe to the fort. Wherevpon he returned also, and followed them the next morning, and came to Dingle, where he incamped as néere to the fort as he could; and there choosing to himselfe capteine Dowdall, capteine Piers, and

The earle of Ormond incampeth at the fort.

and certeine shot, he drew so neere to the fort as he had the whole discouerie and sight of the fort and companie therein, which séemed to be easie to be gotten, if he had anie shot and munitions for the same. But as neither the scholer without his booke, nor the artificer without his tooles, can doo anie thing in his profession: no more can the souldior fight without his meet weapons, nor serue without his necessaries: and therefore for want of things necessarie for this batterie, the lord gouernor was driuen to returne, and to leaue the fort.

The earle for lacke of munition could no preuaile against the fort.

The Spaniards perceiuing this, or mistrusting some other matter, made a sallie of thréescore men, and the gouernor seeing their aduantage, thought to follow the aduise of his capteins, and not to haue dealed at all with them. But one Andrew Martin more hastie than aduised, and more rash than wise, procured a skirmish with them, in which he was slaine; and the lord gouernor compelled of force to answer the skirmish. But it was not long, but that he sounded the retract, and being not able to annoie the enimie, nor preuaile at the fort, he returned backe againe, and by iourneies he came to Rekell: where he met the lord deputie, vnto whom he yéelded vp all his companie, and his commission, and then made prouision of his men, and for victuals, to follow the said lord deputie. The lord deputie had now in his companie about eight hundred men, horssemen and footmen, vnder the leadings of capteine Zouch, capteine Walter Raleigh, capteine Denie, who had also capteine George Carews companie vnder his ensigne, capteine Macworth, capteine Achin, and others: and then he marched towards the fort where the Spaniards and Romans were setled.

The Spaniards issue out and giue a skirmish.

The lord deputie commeth to Rekell, and is there met by the earle of Ormond.

Capteine Raleigh, notwithstanding that the lord deputie had raised his campe at Rekell, and was gone towards the fort, yet he taried and staied behind, minding to practise some exploit. For it was not vnknowne vnto him, that it was a maner among the Irish kerns, that whensoeuer anie English campe was dislodged and remooued, they would after their departures come to those camps to take what they there found to be left. Thus therefore lieng, and kéeping himselfe verie close, taried and abode the comming of the said kerns, who suspecting no such trap to be laid for them, came after their maners and old vsages to the said place, and there tooke their pleasure, who when they were in their securitie, the capteine and his men came vpon them, and tooke them all. Among them there was one, who caried and was laden with withs, which they vsed insted of halters: and being demanded what he would doo with them, and whie he caried them; gaue answer, that they were to hang vp English churls; for so they call Englishmen. "Is it so (quoth the capteine) well, they shall now serue for an Irish kerne:" and so commanded him to be hanged vp with one of his owne withs, the residue he handled according to their deserts.

The lord deputie incamped himselfe as néere the fort as he could. And at this present was sir William Winter also newlie returned from out of England: but he arriued at Kinsale, and his vice admerall capteine Bingham came into the baie of saint Maries weeke or Smerewéeke, and not long after, sir William Winter himselfe followed. And by these means the said lord deputie was so well furnished of all things necessarie, that he at land, and sir William Winter at sea besieged the fort. But before anie assault giuen, he first summoned the fort; requiring of them who they were, what they had there to doo, by whom they were sent, and whie they fortified in hir maiesties land, & required therewith to yéeld vp the fort. But they answered, that they were sent some from the holie father, which had giuen that realme to king Philip, and some from king Philip, who was to receiue and recouer that land to the holie church of Rome, which by hir maiesties means was become

The lord deputie marcheth to the fort, and besiegeth it.

The fort is summoned.

The answer of the fort.

come schismaticall, and out of the church, with other reprochfull speeches: and that therfore they were in that respect to kéepe what they had, and to recouer what they yet had not. Wherevpon the lord deputie sent to sir William Winter, to haue conference with him, how, in what sort, and by what waies they were to worke for the dispossessing of these strangers from their fort, and how their artillerie and munitions might be best placed and laied for the batterie; and betwéene whom it was then determined how all things should be doone.

The Spaniards make a sallie vpon the Englishmen.

Whiles they were thus in speeches, and consulting of the matter, the Spaniards thinking to take some aduantage, made a sallie vpon the Englishmen: which was forthwith answered by capteine Denie (who as then had but a doozzen shot) and by Michaell Butler lieutenant to capteine Raleigh: & these so valiantlie behaued themselues, and so worthilie followed the fight, that they made the Spaniards with more hast than with good speed to returne againe to their fort. The same night following, sir William Winter, according to the conclusion betwéene the lord deputie and him, he did cause to be vnloden certeine culuerings, and like péeces of ordinance out of hir maiesties ships, which then laie in the rode of Smereweeke, and then there being a great banke betweene the shores side and the fort, through which the ordinance were to be caried, they did in the same night cut through that banke, caried their ordinance through it, and mounted them in the place appointed, before the breake of the daie, and before it was open daie the batterie was readie to be giuen. A péece of seruice (the place and time considered) thought woorthie great commendations. The lord deputie likewise had doone the like vpon the land side, & so being on both sides in readinesse to follow the seruice, his lordship summoned them by the shot of a péece of ordinance, offering vnto them mercie if they would yéeld. But they knowing nothing what was doone that night, answered as before, that they would kéepe what they had, and would increase what they could get. Wherevpon they began to batter the fort on both sides, both by land and by water. This first daie of batterie was captaine Raleighs ward daie. But the Spaniards made their brags, that they cared not for this; and to set a good face vpon it, some of them sallied out, and offered the skirmish, but verie faintlie and fearefullie: and so both vpon the first daie, the second daie, and the third daie, little was doone, but onelie the continuance of the batterie. The fourth daie was capteine Zouches ward daie, vnder whom was a lustie yoong gentleman named Iohn Chéeke, who drew so néere the fort, that he looked ouer the purport into it, which being séene and perceiued, one of the Spaniards leuelled a péece at him, & with his shot strake him in the head, wherewith he died. About the end of these foure daies, the trenches for the full batterie were drawne and brought so néere vnto the fort, that now they left to dallie anie longer with the fort, but verie hotlie and sharpelie they battered at it on both sides. The Spaniards, who had staied themselues vpon the hope of some further supplie, to come out of their countrie, and thinking of some better aid of the erle of Desmond, & of his brethren, than yet they had receiued; and séeing also the batterie to be such as they could not be able to withstand and hold out, they desired a parlée with the lord deputie, who vtterlie denied it: saieng, that his seruice was against traitors and rebels, with whom no spéeches nor parlées are allowed. And forsomuch as they (though strangers by birth) otherwise did confederat with them in such a traitorous action, they were in the like predicament with them. Then they requested that they might haue libertie to depart with bag & baggage, which also would not be granted. Then they requested that certeine particular men among themselues might haue their frée passage, and certeine other conditions: but my lord refused both this, and all other conditions,

The diligent seruice of the mariners.

The fort is beset vpon the land side.

Iohn Chéeke is slaine.

The fort is battered on euerie side.

The Spaniards desire a parlée.

conditions, requiring an absolute yéelding, or nothing at all. When they saw that they could not preuaile anie waie, then at the length they hanged out a white flag, and with one voice they all cried out *Misericordia, misericordia,* and offered to yéeld both themselues and the fort, without anie condition at all. Which thing when it was aduertised to his lordship, he sent capteine Iaques Wingfield master of the ordinance to the fort, and to make triall whether this their offer were true and vnfeigned: who when he came to the fort, he was receiued in, and foorthwith the capteine of the fort came vnto him, and in all humble maner yéelded himselfe to be brought, and to be presented vnto the lord deputie: and at the commandement of the said Iaques Wingfield he disarmed himselfe, and caused all his companie to doo the like, and to bring all the armour in the fort into one place, and there they laied their pikes acrosse vpon the same. Which being doone, the said capteine Wingfield came out of the fort, and brought the capteine with him, promising him safe conduct to the lord deputie. But by the waie, his lordship sent some to receiue him at his hands, and willed the said Iaques Wingfield to returne againe to the fort.

Capteine Wingfield is sent to the fort.

In this fort sir Iames Fitzgirald knight, and lord of the Decies, was a prisoner by the order of the earle of Desmond, and one Plunket an Irishman, and one Englishman, which came and accompanied the traitors out of Spaine. The knight was set at libertie, but the other two were executed. When the capteine had yéelded himselfe, and the fort appointed to be surrendered, capteine Raleigh together with capteine Macworth, who had the ward of that daie, entered into the castell, & made a great slaughter, manie or the most part of them being put to the swoord. And when all things were cléere, the lord deputie came to the fort, and hauing doone what pleased him, his lordship returned, and manie of the capteins he saued. The fort foorthwith was rased, the armor and munitions were dispersed abroad, and all things doone as it pleased the lord deputie: he sent the coronell and campemaister ouer into England by capteine Denie, and dismissed the armie, and sent euerie capteine to his garrison. And his lordship went from thense to Dingham, which is a long scattering waste towne, and in it foure or fiue castels, which the earle of Desmond had caused to be defaced in the beginning of this rebellion.

The prisoners in the fort deliuered.

And heere the earle of Ormond met with the lord deputie with a new supplie of his owne men, being readie to haue followed the seruice if need had so required. In this towne the lord deputie made capteine Zouch gouernor of Kerrie and Desmond, and appointed vnto him thrée hundred men, and accompanied him with capteine Cash, who had one hundred men, and capteine Achin, who had fiftie horssemen, and commanded these to lie in garrison in that towne, or where they thought good. And these had to them giuen all the victuals which were found in the fort. And from hense his lordship went to Limerike, and came thither the seauen and twentith of Nouember, in the yeare of our Lord one thousand fiue hundred & eightie. At which time there arriued out of England six new bands of soldiers, vnder the leading of capteine Berkleie, capteine Cruse, capteine Herd, and capteine Tanner, all which his lordship bestowed in seuerall garrisons, and in such places as were most meet for seruice; capteine Berkelie onelie of the capteins remained in Mounster, and was placed in the house of Asketten, the chéefest castell of the earle of Desmond with two hundred men. The others went into Connagh, where the wicked sonnes of the earle of Clanricard were now vpon their keeping. For notwithstanding that the Spaniards were ouerthrowne, and thereby a sufficient warning was giuen to the rebels, to bethinke themselues, that if they did persist in their rebellions, the like would also insue vpon them: yet see how that the

Capteine Zouch made the gouernour of Desmond.

Capteine Berkeleie came into Ireland, and laie at Asketten.

the venemous Hydra had no sooner lost one of hir heds, but in steed of one, sundrie and manie others are sproong vp. For at the verie instant, the bastardlie brood of the earle Clanricard, the vicount of Baltinglasse, associated with the Obirns, Omores, and Keuenaghs in Leinster, & with sundrie others of that wicked nation, conspire, and are vp in open rebellion, and so now at this one instant, Mounster, Connagh, and a great péece of Leinster are in arms and actuall rebellion: onelie Vlster (which was woont to be the woorst) is now the best and most quietest.

Connagh, Leinster and Mounster, are all vp in rebellion.

The earle of Ormond is the gouernour of Mounster.

The lord deputie being at this present in Limerike, & aduertised of these troubles, setteth all things in order for the seruice in Mounster, and committed the whole gouernement of that prouince vnto the earle of Ormond, and then he returned vnto Dubline, where he tooke order for Connagh & Leinster. And about this time there arriued out of England 150 horssemen set out at the charges of the cleargie of England, vnder the leadings of William Russell sonne to the earle of Bedford, and of Brian Fitzwilliams, which were dispersed according to the seruice.

The cleargies band doo arriue into Ireland.

The earle of Kildare, and the baron of Delvin had in suspicion, and are committed to ward.

The lord deputie being returned vnto Dubline, the earle of Kildare, and the baron of Delvin his sonne in law, were had in suspicion to be partakers and secret dealers in these rebellions, and therevpon were committed to ward vnder the custodie of Iaques Wingfield maister of the ordinance. Immediatlie vpon whose apprehensions, the lord Henrie Fitzgirald, sonne and heire to the said earle, and of the age about seauentéene yeares, being persuaded by his fosterfathers and followers, he fled into Ophalia whereof he was baron, and there (as it was said) he was taken by the Oconhours, and kept against his will for his safetie, vntill they did heare further what should be become of the earle.

The earls sonne is kept by the Oconhours.

This thing being aduertised to the lord deputie, he coniectured that this was but a surmised and colorable kind of dealing, to bleare his lordships eies: wherefore by order and good aduise he first willed the earle to send for his sonne, who did so. But his messenger returned with an answer, that the yoong lord was willing to come, but the Oconhours, who were in doubt what should be become of the earle, would in no wise suffer his sonne to depart, vnlesse they might haue good assurance for his safe returne againe vnto them. The lord deputie not liking these kind of fond excuses and disordered dealings, sent the earle of Ormond then being in Dubline, to deale with the Oconhours, who being accompanied with sir Edmund and Piers his brethren, Nicholas White maister of the rolles, capteine George Carew, capteine Macworth, and sundrie other capteins and gentlemen, made their repaire to the borders and marches of Ophalia, whense after much talke to no purpose, they all returned without the yoong lord. Neuertheles afterwards the Oconhours when they had better considered of the matter, and had had some conference with Hussey and others the earles men, and mistrusting that some further troubles would insue, euen as the earle of Ormond had partlie threatened them, and doubting also least the staieng of the sonne might be preiudiciall to the father, then in all hast did send the yoong lord to the erle of Ormond, who carried him to Dubline, and deliuered him to the lord deputie: and his lordship foorthwith sent him to the ward, where he remained with his father, vntill they both and the baron of Delvin were sent into England, where the earle and the baron were sent to the Tower, and the yoong lord committed to the custodie of the erle of Bedford. The earle died after in London, and his bodie was carried into Ireland, and there buried amongest his ancestors.

The earle of Ormond is sent for the yoong lord Fitzgirald.

The yoong lord is sent to the earle of Ormond.

The earle of Kildare and his sonne and sonne in law are sent into England.

The earle died in London.

Capteine Walter Raleigh, being in garrison at Corke, and nothing liking the outrages, bodrages, and villanies dailie practised by Burie, Condon, and others vpon the good subiects and hir maiesties garrisons, whereof sundrie complaints had béene made,

Capteine Raleigh complaineth against the sufferance of the rebel.

made, and small redresse had, he rode himselfe to Dubline vnto the lord deputie, and made his complaints thereof, alledging that the outrages of the Barries and his consorts were such, that vnlesse they were proclamed traitors, and with all diligence followed and pursued the euent therof would be verie euill, to the aggreeuance of good subiects, & to the incouragement of the wicked whose insolence and pride was growne to such a heigth, that the swoord with extremitie was the onelie meane now to redresse the same.

The lord deputie and councell, when they had heard and well considered this, they sent him backe againe with a commission vnto himselfe, to seize and enter vpon the castell and house of Barrie court, and all other the lands of the said Barrie and likewise to pursue and follow him in the best maner as he thought good: and for his better seruice to be doone herein, he had certeine horssemen in wages also giuen vnto him, and added vnto his ensigne of footmen: wherevpon he returned. But before he was come backe to Corke, the case was altered, for the matter was so ordered and handled by such as there and then were in authoritie, and so manie delaies were vsed to hinder the good seruice purposed, that his commission auailed him verie little or nothing, for the castell of Barrie Moore was committed and deliuered to the custodie of the mother of the said Dauid Barrie, and by hir set ouer vnto him hir sonne: and who foorthwith burned and defaced the said castell being his principall house, as also wasted the whole countrie, and became more woorse and outragious than he was before. This capteine making his returne from Dubline, & the same well knowne vnto the seneschall of Imokellie, through whose countrie he was to passe, laie in ambush for him to haue intrapped him betwéene Youghall and Corke, lieng at a foord, which the said capteine must passe ouer with six horssemen, and certeine keine. The capteine little mistrusting anie such matter, had in his companie onelie two horssemen and foure shot on horssebacke, which was too small a force in so doubtfull and dangerous times: neuerthelesse he had a verie good guide, which was the seruant of Iohn Fitzedmunds of Cloue, a good subiect, and this guide knew euerie corner and starting hole in those places.

Capteine Raleigh hath a commission, & the inlargement of a band of horssemen to pursue the enimie

Dauid lord Barrie burneth and spoileth his owen house

Capteine Raleigh is laid for by the seneschall.

The capteine being come towards the foord, the seneschall had espied him alone, his companie being scattered behind, and verie fiercelie pursued him, and crossed him as he was to ride ouer the water, but yet he recouered the foord and was passed ouer. The Irishman who was his guide, when he saw the capteine thus alone, and so narrowlie distressed, he shifted for himselfe and fled vnto a broken castell fast by, there to saue himselfe. The capteine being thus ouer the water, Henrie Moile, riding alone about a bowes shoot before the rest of his companie, when he was in the midle of the foord, his horsse foundred and cast him downe, and being afraid that the seneschals men would haue folowed him and haue killed him, cried out to the capteine to come and to saue his life, who not respecting the danger he himselfe was in, came vnto him, and recouered both him and his horsse. And then Moile coueting with all hast to leape vp, did it with such hast and vehemencie, that he quite ouer leapt the horsse, and fell into a mire fast by, and so his horsse ran awaie, and was taken by the enimie. The capteine neuerthelesse staid still, and did abide for the comming of the residue of his companie, of the foure shot which as yet were not come foorth, and for his man Jenkin, who had about two hundred pounds in moneie about him, and sat vpon his horsse in the meane while, hauing his staffe in one hand, and his pistoll charged in the other hand. The seneschall, who had so fiercelie followed him vpon spur, when he saw him to stand and tarie as it were for his comming, notwithstanding he was counted a man (as he

The seneschal followeth capteine Raleigh.

The distressed state of Henrie Moile

The cowardnesse of the seneschall.

he was indeed) of great seruice, and hauing also a new supplie of twelue horssemen and sundrie shot come vnto him, yet neither he nor anie one of them, being twentie to one, durst to giue the onset vpon him, but onelie railed and vsed hard speeches vnto him, vntill his men behind had recouered and were come vnto him, and then without anie further harme departed.

It happened that not long after, there was a parlee appointed betwéene the lord gouernor and the rebels, at which the seneschall was present, and stood much vpon his reputation. Capteine Raleigh being present began to charge him of his cowardnesse before the earle of Ormond, that he being twentie of his side, to him alone, durst not to incounter with him. Wherevnto he gaue no answer. But one of his men standing by, said, that his maister was that daie a coward, but he would neuer be so forgetfull againe, if the like seruice were to be doone, and in manie great termes exalted his maister the seneschall for his valiantnesse and seruice. The earle of Ormond hearing those great spéeches, tooke the matter in hand, and offred vnto the seneschall, that if he and sir Iohn of Desmond there present, and thrée or foure others, the best they could choose, would appoint to meet him, capteine Raleigh, and such foure others as they would bring with them, they would come to the same place and passe ouer the great riuer vnto them, and would there two for two, foure for foure, or six for six, fight and trie the matter betwéene them, but no answer was then giuen: wherevpon the white knight was afterwards sent vnto him with this chalenge, but the rebels refused it. Not long after this, there were spéeches made, that the earle of Ormond was to depart from this long and wearie seruice into England, & capteine Zouch should in his place be the generall. Betwéene the remoouing of the one, and the placing of the other, sir William Morgan, capteine Raleigh, and capteine Piers had a commission to be gouernors of that part of Mounster, where they spent all that summer, and laie for the most part at Lismore, and in the countrie and woods thereabouts, in continuall seruices vpon the enimies from time to time, as occasion and oportunitie serued.

The chalenge made by the earle of Ormond to the seneschall.

Capteine Raleigh a commissioner in Mounster.

And when the summer was spent, capteine Raleigh returned with all his band vnto Corke, being in number eight horssemen and foure score footmen. And as he passed through the countrie, it was aduertised to him, that Dauid Barrie an archtraitor was at Cloue with a great troope of sundrie hundreds of men. Wherevpon he thought good to passe that waie through the towne of Cloue, minding to trie the valor of Dauid Barrie, if by anie meanes he might méet with him. And euen at the verie townes end he found Barrie and all his companie, and with a lustie courage gaue the onset vpon him. But Barrie refused it, and fled. And then this capteine passing from thense, in his iorneie he espied in a plaine néere adioining to a woods side, a companie of footmen by themselues, vpon whome with six horssemen he gaue the charge: but these being cut off from the wood wherevnto they were fléeng, and hauing not succor now to helpe & relieue themselues, they turned backe, & conioining themselues togither to withstand this force and onset made vpon them, in which they behaued themselues verie valiantlie, and of the horsses they killed fiue, of which capteine Raleigh his horsse was one, and he himselfe in great danger, and like to haue béene slaine, if his trustie seruant Nicholas Wright a Lackshire man borne had not bin. For he perceiuing that his maisters horsse was galled and stricken with a dart, and plunged so much, that to his séeming he was past seruice, the said Nicholas willed and called to an Irishman there, whose name was Patrike Fagaw, that he should looke to his capteine, and either to rescue him, or to giue charge vpon the enimie. Wherevpon the said Fagaw rescued his capteine,

Capteine Raleigh followeth [illegible] Barrie.

Capteine Raleigh in danger [illegible].

The good [illegible] of Nicholas Wright.

teine, & the said Nicholas Wright forthwith gaue the onset vpon six of the enimies and slue one of them. And therewith came one Iames Fitzrichard an Irish gentleman with his keine to the rescue of the capteine, but his keine was slaine, and himselfe in danger. For Wright not looking on them followed the enimie verie egerlie, and recompensed the losse of one with the slaughter of others. Which capteine Raleigh perceiuing cried out to his man, saieng, "Wright, if thou be a man, charge aboue hand & saue the gentleman." Who at his maisters commandement pressed into the middle of the enimies, and slue one of them, and so saued the gentleman: and in which skirmish his horsse leg was cut vnder him. Diuerse footmen were slaine of the enimies, and two were taken prisoners, whome they caried with them to Corke.

At his being in Corke there were sundrie péeces of seruices doone by him, all which doo verie well deserue to be for euer registred. And amongst all others this one point of his seruice deserueth both commendation and perpetuall remembrance. The lord Roch was growen into a suspicion that he was not sound of his loialtie. Whervpon capteine Raleigh by commandement was to fetch him and his ladie to Corke vnto the generall. This thing was not so priuilie determined, but that the seneschall and Dauid Barrie had knowledge thereof, and minding verelie to take the capteine at some aduantage, they had assembled a great companie of themselues to the number of seuen or eight hundred men to haue met with him either comming or going. The capteine perceiuing and forethinking how dangerous his enterprise was against so noble a man in that countrie as the lord Roch was, who was verie well beloued, commanded vpon a sudden all his men one and other, both horssemen and footmen, which in the whole were not aboue foure score and ten persons, to be in a readinesse vpon the paine of death betweene ten and eleuen of the clocke of the same night. At which time euerie man being in a readinesse, he tooke his iorneie and marched toward the lord Roches house called Ballie in Harsh, which is about twentie miles out of Corke, and came thither somewhat earlie in the morning. At his comming he went foorthwith to the castell gate.

The lord Roch is had in suspicion, and is sent for.

Capteine Raleigh commeth to the lord Roches house.

The townsmen when they saw their lords house and castell thus suddenlie beset, they doubting the worst, did arme about fiue hundred of themselues. Whervpon capteine Raleigh placed and bestowed his men in battell raie in the towne it selfe, & marched againe to the castell gate, with certeine of his officers and gentlemen of his band, as by name Michaell Butler, Iames Fulford, Nicholas Wright, Arthur Barlow, Henrie Swane, & Pinking Huish, and they knocked againe at the gate. And after a while there came thrée or foure of the said lord Roches gentlemen, & demanded the cause of their comming, vnto whome the capteine answered, that he was come to speake with my lord: which was offered he should, so that he would bring in with him but two or thrée of his gentlemen, which the capteine was contented with, yet in the end (but with much adoo) he came in with all these few persons before named. When the capteine was once come within the castell, and had entred into some speeches with the lord Roch, he so handled the matter by deuises and meanes, that by little and little, and by some and some, he had gotten in within the iron doore or gate of the courtlodge all his men. And then hauing the aduantage, he commanded his men to stand and gard the said gate, that no man should passe in or out: and likewise charged euerie man to come into the hall with his péece well prepared, with two bullets. The lord Roch when he saw this, he was suddenlie amazed & stricken at the hart with feare: but dissembling the same, he set a good face vpon the matter, and calling for meat, requested the capteine and his foresaid gentlemen to sit downe, & to kéepe him companie at dinner.

Capteine Raleigh being receiued into the castell getteth in all his men.

After dinner, the capteine falling into speeches with the said lord Roch, declared plainlie vnto him the cause of his comming, and shewed that he and his wife were accused to be traitors, and that he had a commission (which he shewed vnto them) to take and carie them along with him to Corke: which he was to performe, and so would. The lord Roch alledged manie excuses for himselfe and for his wife, saieng in the end that he neither could nor would go: the capteine answered, that if they would not go with a good will, they should perforce go against their will. The lord Roch séeing that there was no remedie, he yéelded: and then the capteine minding to lose no time, willed him to command and cause all those of the towne, and all such as were about the house, to attend and be in readinesse to aid him, and to set him foorth in his iorneie: which he did, and verie willinglie shewed himselfe to abide and obeie the capteines commandement: saieng that he would answer the matter well inough, and discharge whatsoeuer should be laid to his charge, for he knew himselfe to be cleare. And so he made himselfe and his wife redie to take the iorneie in hand, as the capteine did appoint and command: and towards night they did set forward to Corke. But the night fell out to be verie tempestuous and foule, and therewith so darke, that no man could sée hand or foot, nor yet discerne one another: and the waies also were so fowle, so full of balks, hillocks, pits, and rocks, that the souldiors thereby were maruellouslie troubled and incombred, some stumbled among the stones, some plunged into holes, and some by their often fals were not onelie hurt, but also lost their armour: and were maruellouslie spoiled: and besides that, they were among and in the middle of the enimies, who laie in sundrie ambushes, thinking verelie to haue intercepted them, and to haue set vpon them: but the darke night which was cumbersome to themselues, was a shadow to shrowd them from their enimies. And in the end, though with much trouble, they came to Corke in safetie, sauing one soldier named Iohn Phelum, who by his often falling and stumbling among the stones and rocks, did so hurt one of his feet, that he could neuer recouer the same, but did in the end consume and rot awaie.

The lord Roch yeeldeth to go with capteine Raleigh.

The capteine being come to the towne somewhat earlie in the morning, he was receiued in, and presented his prisoners to the generall, with no little admiration that he had escaped so dangerous a iorneie, being verelie supposed of all men that he could neuer haue escaped. The lord Roch being brought to be examined, did so well answer for himselfe, that in the end he was acquited, and taken for a true and a good subiect, and which in time was well tried and knowne. For not he himselfe onlie, but all his sons and followers, did attend and performe all such seruices as were laid vpon them, and in which, thrée of his sonnes were killed by the enimie in hir maiesties seruice.

The L. Roch acquiteth himselfe.

The L. Roch and his sonnes good seruices.

Capteine Zouch (as is afore said) laie at the Dingham, among whose companie there fell a dangerous and an extreme sicknesse: few or none escaped it, howbeit manie died therein. And in which distresse it was aduertised him, that the earle of Desmond and Dauid Barrie was assembled at Aghado with thrée thousand men, and he being verie desirous to doo some seruice vpon them, drew all his full force of horsemen and footmen vnto Castelmange. And then by the aduise of his capteins Achim and Cash, he suddenlie made an onset vpon his enimies, before they wist of anie such thing, and slue a great companie of them: and draue the erle to such a push, that he in his shirt was driuen to shift for himselfe, in the middle of his gallowglasses, and by that means he escaped. The earle nothing liking this coorse successe, sought a better place of safetie, and remooued himselfe to Harlow wood, and passed by the waie to Kilmallocke. Which when the garrison there did vnderstand,

Capteine Zouch putteth the earle of Desmond in danger to be taken.

stand, they pursued and followed him, namelie capteine Bourchier, capteine Dowdall, capteine Makworth, and capteine Norris, thrée miles togither vpon the plains betwéene Kilmallocke and the wood, and slue manie of the rebels. And capteine Dowdall who was acquainted verie well with that wood, and in it had serued sundrie times, he would néeds, and did enter into the wood, where he met with the earle of Desmond now the second time, and gaue the onset vpon him, killed a great number of his men, tooke from them their carriages, and droue awaie a great preie of kine, and brought them to Kilmallocke to the garison. Neere about this time the seneschall came to Lismore, and preied that countrie, and droue awaie their cattell. Which when the garison heard, and were aduertised thereof, they issued, and followed the preie to recouer it, but they were so incountered and skirmished withall, that they lost the preie, and fiue and twentie of their men were slaine. Diuerse skirmishes were dailie doone vpon the enimie, and manie iorneies made vpon them to their great damages and hurts.

Capteine Dowdall preieth the erle of Desmond.

The seneschall preieth the garison of Lismore.

In the moneth of August next following, in the yeare of our Lord one thousand fiue hundred eightie and one, the lord deputie made a iorneie into Mounster, where when he had taken an account of all their doings and seruices, he established capteine Zouch to be gouernour of all Mounster, and generall at armes, and then his lordship returned through Conagh vnto Dublin. This now new gouernor, being accompanied with capteine Raleigh and capteine Dowdall, trauelled from place to place to see all things in good order: but the certeine place of their resting was at Corke, where for the most part they laie in garison: making in the meane time sundrie iorneies, as occasion of seruice did require. And they being in Corke, newes was brought vnto the gouernour that there was a great quarell fallen out betwéene Dauid Barrie and the seneschall and that they were mortall enimies, and at a deadlie food, and they laie both in Dunfrinnen side, not far from the blacke water. The earle of Desmond and Iohn his brother laie in Patrike Condons countrie, being on the further side of the said water, who were verie sorie for this quarell, and would haue come vnto them, but the waters were so great, they could not, yet they sent their messengers to and fro among them for some pacification, but it was to no effect. Capteine Dowdall vpon these newes sent out an Irish man which he had, and who was a notable spiall, named Richard mac Iames, and willed him to séeke out where the seneschall was, to the end that he might make a draught vpon him. This Richard drawing himselfe to the companies of the rebels, and lieng among them in their cabins where they laie in the woods, he fell in companie, and then entred into a great familiaritie of one which was a messenger from the Desmonds vnto the seneschall, and he thinking nothing but that this Richard was one of the said companie, began to discourse vnto him the businesse which he had there to doo: and told him that the next daie following, sir Iohn of Desmond did appoint to come thither, and to make a peace and an agréement betwéene Barrie and the seneschall. When as Richard mac Iames had heard at full all his spéeches, then he intreated him that he would go to Corke with him, which in the end the fellow was contented so to doo. And in the next morning they went togither to Corke, and at their comming thither, did declare vnto capteine Dowdall the whole matter, and he foorthwith aduertised the same to the gouernour: who albeit he did not altogither beléeue what was told, yet he agréed that it was best that some seruice should be doone vpon them, and concluded that himselfe and capteine Dowdall should doo the same, vnder the colour that they were to make a iourneie vnto Limerike, and so they caused it to be said: for in no wise would they be knowne of that which they had determined. And hauing prepared all things necessarie for this seruice, the same night they left the charge of the garison vnto capteine Raleigh lieutenant: and

The lord deputie establisheth capteine Zouch gouernour of all Mounster.

The L. Barrie and the seneschall fall out.

Capteine Dowdall maketh a spiall vpon the seneschall.

Sir Iohn of Desmond appointed to make a league betweene Barrie and the seneschall.

The gouernor Zouch and capteine Dowdall make a secret iourneie.

and themselues taking their leaue, as though they were bound for Limerike, they marched out at the gates, and by breake of the daie they came to castell Lions, the weather being verie mistie and thicke, and in the castell they found but one poore man, who told them that Dauid of Barrie was gone but a little before them vnto Humacquilliam. The gouernour and the capteine being verie eger, and desirous to doo some seruice, they followed the tract of the horsse a good prettie waie, but the capteine mistrusting that no good seruice would be doone, that waie, persuaded the gouernour that he should rather enter and search the woods, which were fast by, where as he thought some good seruice would be doone: whose aduise the gouernour followed: and they had ridden but a little waie, but they saw two horssemen come riding toward them, but as soone as they had séene the said gouernour and capteine, they returned backe againe.

Then the capteine told him that there was a bog in the wood, and his aduise and counsell was, that some of his shot should be sent to stand betwéene the bog and the wood, which being doone, they followed those two men so short, that they were driuen to forsake their horsses, and to run on foot towards the bog. But the lose shot being in a readinesse, did put them backe againe vpon the horssemen, who gaue the onset vpon them, and the one of them, which was sir Iohn of Desmond they sore hurted with a horssemans staffe, that he spake verie few words after. And the other whose name was Iames Fitziohn of Strongeculle, they tooke: and both they carried with them to Corke. Sir Iohns head was sent to Dublin, but his bodie was hanged vp by the héeles vpon a gibbet, and set vpon the north gate of Corke. And Iames Fitziohn was drawne, hanged, & quartered. And thus haue you the third head of the venemous Hydra cut off, who had his iust reward and merit, if not too too good for so villanous & bloudie a traitor: who respecting neither the honor of God, the obedience to his prince, the credit of his owne house, the faith to his friend, nor the state of the commonwealth, was wholie imbrued in bloud and villanie, and in bloud he died, and had his reward by Gods iust iudgement.

Sir Iohn of Desmond killed, and his bodie hanged vpon a gibbet by the heels

Not long after this, it was agreed that a draught should be made vpon Dauid Barrie, for the preie which he and Goren mac Swene had made in Carbrere, and passed with the same by Bentrie, where laie a garrison vnder the leading of capteine Appeslere: but he being deceassed, the same was committed to capteine Fenton, whose lieutenant named Richard Cant minding to crosse the preie, fell into the fight with Barrie and his companie: but he was slaine and all his companie, there being but one man the drumslager left aliue, who by swiftnesse of his foote escaped. The foresaid Appeslere was a verie proper man, a gentleman borne, and of a good house, and brought vp in learning, he could write verie well, and also deliuer his speeches verie orderlie and eloquentlie. When he grew to some ripe yeares, he fell acquainted with some lose companions, who persuaded him to accompanie them to the seas, promising him the sun and the moone, and all the wealth in the world. And he being soone intised and persuaded, was contented, and went to the seas, and became as bad as the baddest, whereof great troubles insued: and he at length was driuen to leaue the seas, and to wander a long time on the seacoasts in the prouince of Mounster: where by occasion he fell to come to acquaintance of the earle of Desmond, with whome he found such fauor, that no Englishman could doo more with him than he could. Afterwards, when the narrow searching for him was quailed and forgotten, he fell to be acquainted with the good Henrie Dauels, whome he found rather a father than a friend vnto him: and then his behauiour was such, that he grew to be in good fauour with all Englishmen, and in the end put in trust to doo sundrie seruices in Mounster, and was become and made a capteine, in which office he discharged himselfe verie honestlie and faithfullie.

faithfullie. The gouernor continuing still in one and the same mind, to doo some seruice vpon Barrie, who then laie in Dunfiennin, he togither with capteine Dowdall marched to Barries campe, and earlie in the morning (they being vnlooked for) entred into the campe and there made a great slaughter vpon Barries men, but Barrie himselfe was gone and fled. After this time, the said Barrie considered his distressed case, and how continuallie he was pursued and followed by the gouernour and the English garisons, whose force he saw that he could by no means auoid, but that at one time or other they would take him at some aduantage. He maketh humble petition to the gouernour that he might be vnder his protection, and to liue thenseforth in some dutifull and restfull order; which he in the end did obteine.

The gouernor and capteine Dowdall spoile and enter into Barries campe and kill his men.

Barrie sueth for a protection.

The lord deputie, thinking that by the death of Iohn of Desmond, and the silence of the earle his brother, who what was become of him no man could tell, but supposed that he was fled beyond the seas, or that he was dead, and that all things were well and in quiet in all Mounster; he thought good to ease hir maiesties charge, and so cashed sundrie bands and discharged sundrie garisons, leauing for the seruice of Mounster in the whole but 400 footmen & 50 horssemen, of which, 200 were vnder the leading of the gouernor, one hundred vnder capteine Dowdall, and one hundred vnder Sir George Bourcher, and the first horssemen were vnder capteine Achin, who laie in garrison at Adare in Kerrie. When all things (I saie) séemed to be at rest and in peace, and all things well, behold a new stirre (and vnlooked for) is now raised: for Fitzmoris baron of Lexna, who had hitherto dissembled the matter, and pretended to haue béene a dutifull subiect, when he saw the weakenesse of the Englishmen, & how that the garrisons were discharged, & therefore the few men left were scarse able well to saue and kéepe themselues, much lesse to hurt others: he breaketh out into open rebellion, and ioineth with him his wicked, traitorous, and periured sonne. This baron of Lexna his first ancestors were seruants to the barons of Carew, and of Odron, and lords of Lexna, and had the chiefe rule and gouernment vnder him of all his countrie in Mounster, which was verie great and large: his eldest sonne he kept in the court of England. And this Fitzmoris, who by the authoritie vnder his master was growen into great credit in the countrie, and standing in hope to haue their friendship and assistance in all his businesse, watched his time, and killed the lord Carew his maister, at a table which yet remaineth in the house, and entred into all his baronie of Lexna & his other possessions in Mounster, euen as the like was doone by the Kauenaghs in Odron in Leinster. And the heire of Carew in England, who had great and large possessions in Deuon and in sundrie shires elsewhere in England, made the lesse and little account of his lands in Ireland, and so by little and little they lost all their lands in Ireland.

The l. deputie casheth sundrie bands in Mounster.

Fitzmoris baron of Lexna breaketh into open rebellion. The cause of this his breaking out, some do impute it to the hard dealing of the gouernor, who so narowlie watched him that he alwais tooke from him what he had, and so intercepted him from his prouision, that he had nothing left to eat.

Fitzmoris seruant to Carew lord of Lexna killeth his maister.

This new baron of Lexna, the first thing that he tooke in hand, was to cleanse and to rid his owne countrie from all Englishmen and their garisons, and in the end, taking capteine Achin at an aduantage, slue him, and recouered the ward of Adare. After that, he went to the ward kept in the castell of Lesconile, in which were but eight Englishmen, and the castell being verie hard to be gained, he vsed this stratagem. He laid verie close & secretlie a companie of his men in an old house fast by the castell, & then he practised with an old woman, which was woont euerie morning to bring a great basket of coles or turffe into the ward, that as soone as she was betwéene the two gates of the castell, she should let fall hir basket and crie out: which she did. For when she was come to the castell, and had after hir accustomable maner called to the ward, one of them came and loosed the vtter iron doore, and then he did open the inner doore for hir to come in. When she was come betwéene the two doores, she let fall hir great basket of coles and cried out. The companie foorthwith lieng in the said old house came, and the ward being not able to draw vnto them,

The baron of Lexna destroieth all the English in his countrie, and taketh the queenes forts.

A stratagem vsed in taking the castell of Lesconile.

them the vtter iron doore, nor to shut fast the inner doore, the enimie entred, tooke the castell, killed all the ward, and cast them ouer the wals. The good successe of this stratagem caused him to practise & to put in vse other like deuises for the regaining of the castell (as I remember) of Adnagh. For he supposing that hungrie soldiors would be contented to accept anie courtesie, he procured a yoong harlot, who was somewhat snowtfaire, to go to the castell, pretending some iniurie to haue béene doone to hir, and to humble hirselfe to the capteins deuotion, being supposed, that he by these meanes would fall into the liking and fantasieng of hir, and so would reteine hir. And by these meanes, she by hir cunning handling of the matter, according vnto the plot before contriued betwéene Fitzmoris and hir, she should at one time or other find the occasion or opportunitie to betraie the castell. The capteine receiued hir into the castell, and not forgetting the late former practise at Lesconile, caused him to be the more warie and circumspect, and to looke vnto himselfe. Wherevpon he so handled the matter with this harlot, that he in the end found out all the deuise, and foorthwith he carried hir vp vnto the top of the castell and cast hir ouer the wals, where with the fall she was crushed and died. Fitzmoris being disappointed of his purpose, departed from thense, and ranged ouer all the countries of Tipporarie, Ormond, and Waterford, where were no garrisons to resist him, and there plaied his parts.

A stratagem at Adnagh.

The gouernor, who laie at Corke, being aduertised of these outrages, called his companie togither, which (as is before said, was not aboue foure hundred persons) and other reported (but vntrulie) to be about foure thousand: yet minding not to suffer an iniurie, marched with such companie as he had into Clanmoris, which is the said Fitzmoris countrie, and distant from Corke about thrée daies iourneie. The baron by his espials being aduertised of their comming, forsooke his castell at Adaire, and defaced his castell at Lexna, and drew his goods, and all his forces into the wood of Lesconile. When the gouernor was come to Adaire, he found the towne burnt, and the few Englishmen (which were in the abbeie) greatlie distressed. From thense he went to Lesconile, which is ten miles further, where he discouered the baron and all his companie, which then laie in a plaine bottome in the said wood, hauing then in his companie of gallowglasses, kerne, shot, and horssemen, about seuen hundred men.

The gouernor marcheth from Corke to Clanmoris to incounter with Fitzmoris.

The gouernor taking aduise what was best to be doone, because that place was full of fastnesse, and no passage for anie horssemen, but all rested vpon the seruice of the footmen, they diuided their companie. And capteine Dowdall being verie desirous to aduenture the seruice vpon him, he had six score footmen appointed and deliuered vnto him, and the residue he reserued to himselfe. The capteine entred into the wood, and followed vntill he came into the plains where Fitzmoris was, who hauing a great companie, and the capteine but (as it were) a handfull to his, he diuided his whole companie into foure parts, thinking to haue inclosed the capteine, and to haue his will vpon them. The capteine perceiued it, and forthwith brake vpon one of the companies, and had such a hand vpon them, that he slue a number of them. Which when Fitzmoris saw, like a valiant man turned his backe and fled awaie into the mounteins of Sloughlougher, and left all his goods behind, which the capteine tooke, and also all the cattell there, and brought the same to the gouernor. From thense they marched to the castell of Clan, of which Oliuer Stephanson had the ward and kéeping: and there newes was brought vnto him, that the lord deputie had sent vnto him two bands of footmen, of which one hundred were sir Henrie Wallops, and the other capteine Norris. Wherevpon he trauelled vnto Limerike, and left the whole charge of Clanmoris, and of Kerrie vnto capteine Dowdall. And the said capteine being put to wéet that the baron was incamped at

Capteine Dowdall entereth vpon Fitzmoris, and giueth him the foile.

The baron of Lexna fleeth into the hils of Sloughlougher.

A supplie of two hundred men sent to the gouernor.

at Glanflish with two hundred and fortie gallowglasses, two hundred kerne, foure-score shot, and thirtie horssemen, and he himselfe hauing then but the lieutenant Wingfield in his companie, made a sallie vpon them, and killed with the sword, and draue into the riuer aboue seuen score of them, and recouered a preie of eight hundred kine, fiue hundred horsses and mares, besides a great number of shéepe and gotes: and in the taking of the baron, he found store of monie and plate, and massing garments. And from hense he marched with his cattell, and incamped besides Alough, néere vnto the earle of Clancar his house, and from thense to Castellmange, and so to Adare, and furnished as he went euerie ward and garison with store of vittels, and with the goods he rewarded his souldiors. From this time, the baron Fitzmoris hauing lost all his prouision & store, was neuer able to recouer himselfe, neither to credit nor to wealth, nor yet to hold vp his head, but was forsaken of all his fréends and followers: and being ashamed of himselfe, and of his bad and disloiall trecheries, walked and wandred abroad as a forlorne man, not knowing what to doo, whither to go, or where to seeke for succor and helpe.

Capteine Dowdall setteth vpon Fitzmoris in Glanflish and giueth him the ouerthrow.

The baron Fitzmoris with a few is ouerthrowne to his vtter fall, and forsaken of all his fréends.

At length being wearie of himselfe, and of his distressed miseries, bethinketh vpon the earle of Ormond, whome notwithstanding that without cause he had verie much iniuried, hauing most outragiouslie preied his countries, burned his villages, and killed his people: yet he maketh his recourse vnto his lordship, acknowledgeth his fault, confesseth his follies, and being most sorie for the same, desireth his lordship to pardon and remit him, and most humblie requested him to haue vnder him a protection. This honorable man, notwithstanding the great iniuries doone vnto him, and he of a great courage and stomach, and of a noble mind, and loth to put vp so great iniuries, yet (as it is attributed to the lion, *Parcere prostratis*) when he had shewed the great gréefes of the said Fitzmoris, he forgat all his owne wrongs, and granted him his request. Capteine Dowdall, leauing the gouernors souldiors and companie at Adare, vnder the leading of capteine Smith, he marcheth towards Corke, where he rested and laie in garison. Now when all these broils were ended, and verelie supposed that all things had béene at rest, and the whole prouince of Mounster at peace, behold the earle of Desmond, who was thought to be either dead or fled, beginneth to appeare, and to shew himselfe, and hauing assembled a great companie, came to Adare, where the garison issued out vpon him: betwéene whom the fight was hot, and manie slaine on both sides. Among whom, Smith serjeant of the band, and Morgan the lieutenant were both slaine: but yet the English souldiors recouered the abbeie. About this time one Thomas Birne lieutenant to the notable archtraitor Fitzgirald, being wearie of the wicked actions which hitherto he had followed among the rebels, sent his messenger to capteine George Carew, requesting him to deale with the lord deputie for his pardon, and for so manie of his companie as would ioine with and accompanie him in a péece of seruice to be doone: which he promised to recompense with the price of his capteins head, which he would in a bag present to his lordship, as also would kill so manie of his companie as would not consent with him therevnto.

The baron being distressed of all helps, seeketh to the earle of Ormond for a protection.

The courtesie of the earle of Ormond.

The earle of Desmond thought to be dead dooth now shew himselfe.

The fight at Adare.

A draught made to kill Fitzgirald.

When this deuise was readie to be practised, the clearke of the band, who was one of the confederats, verie trecherouslie did discouer the same vnto Fitzgirald, who immediatlie tooke and hanged his lieutenant, the sergeant of his band (who was an Englishman) and so manie of the souldiors as were of that confederacie. Not long after, Fitzgirald bethinking vpon the extreame miseries, which in this rebellion he had indured, and the small hope which he had to preuaile in these his bad and traitorous actions, but chiefie being afraid of his owne life, least at one time or other he should be slaine by his souldiors: he sent a messenger to the then lord iustices, requiring his pardon, and which he would redéeme with the head of his best

Fitzgirald executed to death so manie as conspired against him.

Fitzgirald practiseth the death of Pheon mac Hugh.

best fréend and fellow in armes Pheon mac Hugh, the verie gall of all the wars and rebellion in Leinster.

Fitzgerald is hanged for his conspiracie.

This was not so couertlie doone, but that Pheon mac Hugh had knowledge of the practise, and he foorthwith intreated Fitzgerald in the like manner as he before had doone with the lieutenant, and so hanged him vp. The lord deputie after long sute for his reuocation, receiued hir maiesties letters for the same, and then he sent for capteine Zouch gouernor of Mounster to come to Dubline: and in the end of August 1582, after that he had serued full two yeres he deliuered vp the sword vnto the archbishop of Dubline then lord chancellor, and to sir Henrie Wallop then treasuror at armes, and tooke shipping, hauing with him capteine Zouch, who was after slaine by one of his most familiar acquaintance, and sundrie other gentlemen. The said lord Greie was a man of great nobilitie, and of as honourable and ancient descent, one that feareth God in true religion, and dutifull to hir maiestie in all obedience. And albeit he had deserued well of that Irish nation, and had sowed the good seeds of notable seruices, as well for his martiall seruices, as for his ciuill gouernment, yet he reped (as his predecessors before him) but darnell and cockle. For they had among them not onelie conspired his death, for which some paid déerelie, but made also sundrie complaints against him, to which he answered to his commendation and acquitall, and to their reproch for their ingratitude.

The lord Greie yéeldeth vp the sword & returneth into England. 1582.

The lord chancellor and sir Henrie Wallop are lord iustices.

These two lords iustices being fallen into a broken time, the warres being not ended, the people not quieted, and the gouernement not staied nor setled, yet they both ioining their wisedoms, seruices, and good wils, were so blessed therein, that by them that land was reduced to some perfection and quietnesse. For not long after they had taken the sword in hand doctor Sanders the popes nuncio and legat, who came from that holie sée of Rome, the sea of all wickednesse, with Iames Fitzmoris in Iulie in the yeare of our Lord one thousand fiue hundred seuentie and nine, to beare arms in this land against hir maiestie, after that he had wandered vp and downe thrée yeares togither with the earle and his brethren sir Iohn, in woods and bogs, and had liued with them a most miserable and wretched life, and had béene partaker of their most cruell bloudsheds, outrages, murthers, and robberies, a life good and too good for a traitor and a rebell. He fell sicke of an Irish ague and of the bloudie flix, and laie in the wood of Clennelisse, which is a wood full of allers, withies, briers, & thornes, and through which is no passage, where partlie of his sicknesse, but chéefelie for famine and want he died. Euen in this filthie place, that most miserable wretch and traitor was lodged and died, bequeathing his treasons, trecheries, and disloialties against his soueraigne mistresse and ladie hir maiestie vnto the pope, reseruing the punishment to the Lord himselfe, who is a swift and iust iudge vpon all traitors and disobedient persons, and his bodie (as some said) was deuoured vp of woolues, but (as some doo thinke) that so much as was left was buried at Clincairne, not farre off from the place where he died.

The death of doctor Sanders.

The two lords iustices being entred into this broken gouernement, did what they could to kéepe the same in peace, and vnderstanding the wilfull disposition of Desmond, they did vse all the means and waies they could to pacifie him, but so farre was he imbrued and poisoned with the venom of treason and rebellion, that no reason, no dutie, nor anie other respect could persuade him to be a loiall and dutifull subiect. Wherefore he continued still in his old accustomed spoiling and wasting the countries, and trusting to no house nor castell, did shrowd himselfe in woods and bogs, and in the winter following he kept his Christmasse in the wood of Kilquieg néere to Kilmallocke. And about the fourth of Ianuarie then following, one Iohn Welsh a valiant and a good souldior, was resolued to make a draught vpon the

The earle of Desmond kéepeth his Christmas in the woods.

the said earle, and he made acquainted therewith capteine Dowdall, capteine Bungor and George Thornington prouost marshall of Mounster, all which lie then in garrison in Kilmallocke, and according to the order betweene them then agréed vpon, they marched in the night time to the place and wood where the earle laie.

A draught made vpon the earle by Iohn Welsh.

But being come thither, they were to passe ouer a great riuer, before they could come to enter into the wood of Kilquieg, & by reason of the great raines then falling, it was impossible for man or horsse to passe ouer the same, which thing Iohn Welsh did before mistrust. Wherefore the night before, he went thither verie closelie with such few persons as he had chosen for the purpose, and there he caused a number of flakes and hurdels to be made of halson, allers, and withie rods which he caused to be drawne ouer the riuer by one, whom he had there of purpose which could swim verie well. And this fellow when he had fastened some of the hurdels to a trée in the further side of the water, and then by a rope drew ouer the residue one after another, did so fasten and tie one vnto another, and so cunninglie handled the matter, that when the capteins came, they passed ouer the riuer verie well without danger or perill. And so from thense the said Welsh did guide and bring them by the breake of the daie vnto the earles cabin: but the wood was so full of thickets, and so mirie, that they were faine to go a speares length wide from the cabin to come vnto it. The earle hearing a great noise, and suspecting some extraordinarie and a greater companie to be in place more than his owne, and doubting the woorst, ran out of his bed in his shirt, and ran into the riuer fast by his cabin, and there hid himselfe close vnder a banke hard vp to his chin, by which meanes he escaped and his wife with him. The souldiors made diligent search for him both by searching of the riuer and of the wood, but could not find him, wherevpon they did put to the sword so manie as they found there, and carried awaie the goods with them, and so returned to Kilmallocke.

A deuise how to passe ouer a great riuer.

The earle escapeth verie hardlie.

At this time the seneschall secretlie with all the force which he could make, came vnto the towne of Youghall, & entred into the end of the same towne. Wherevpon the alarum was raised, and foorthwith Caluerleigh being lieutenant to capteine Morgan, hauing all his soldiors togither, of which he had fortie shot, went vnto that end of the towne where the seneschall scaled the wals, & there he made a sconse, or a little bulworke, and by that meanes saued the towne, and draue the seneschall from his purpose, and killed aboue fiftie of his men: and so being disappointed of his purpose he departed awaie. In the end of this moneth of Ianuarie the earle of Ormond arriued from out of England to Waterford with a new supplie of foure hundred men, whome he diuided and committed vnto the seuerall leadings of sir George Bourcher, sir William Stanleie, capteine Edward Berkleie, and capteine Roberts. And being now lord generall by hir maiesties appointment ouer all Mounster, and hauing obteined an augmentation of two pence by the daie for euerie soldiors wages, he assembleth all the soldiors and euerie capteine which had anie charge, and tooke order with euerie of them for such seruices as were to be doone, furnisheth them with vittels, munitions, monie, and all things necessarie and meet for them, requesting euerie one of them to shew themselues like good and valiant soldiors, in the pursuing of the rebels, and vanquishing of the enimies: and such grace and loue he found among the soldiors, that he was no more desirous than they most glad and willing to performe the same. Such a good affection euerie one did beare to this honorable man.

The seneschall assaulteth & entreth into Youghall and hath the repulse.

The earle of Ormond arriueth to Waterford and is generall of Mounster.

The loue of the capteins and soldiors to the earle of Ormond.

At this time aduertisement was giuen vnto his lordship, that the earle of Desmond was incamped in the fastnesse of Harlo wood with a great number of rakehels & rebels. His lordship mustered all his companies, and minding to doo some seruice vpon the said rebels, marcheth towards the said fastnesse of Harlo wood. And

being

being come thither, he diuideth his companies into foure parts, and they entered into some seuerall places of the wood at one instant: and by that meanes they scowred the wood throughout, in killing as manie as they tooke, but the residue fled into the mounteins. The rebels being thus narrowlie followed and pursued, they neuer after met togither in the like companies, nor assembled themselues in such great numbers: but the most part of them, which were the chiefest followers and greatest fréends vnto Desmond, as Fitzmoris of Lexna before named, the seneschall, the lord Barrie, Condon, Donnell mac Knought, & sundrie others, some and some came awaie, and sought for protection. And albeit their manifold and infinit outrages, murthers, bloudsheds and spoiles, had deserued a thousand deaths: yet his lordship considering their repentance, sorrows, and humble submissions, and respecting more hir maiesties godlie disposition to mercie than their deserts, did (for the most part) grant vnto euerie of them their requests. The soldiors after this péece of seruice were dispersed abroad into their seuerall garrisons. And albeit the greater parts of the rebels were some by sword, and some by protection abated, and much decreased, yet none of them laie altogither idle, but did follow the seruice as time and occasion offered. For the earle himselfe, though he were thus vnfeathered of his greatest helps, yet he was one & the same man, a most ranke traitor and rebell: and therefore vpon him dailie were draughts and pursutes made, and neuer left, vntill in the end he came vnto confusion.

The lord generall scoureth Harlo wood.

Desmond is forsaken of all his followers and friends.

In the moneth of August, in the yeare of Christ one thousand fiue hundred eightie and thrée, it was aduertised to the garrisons in Kilmallocke and Cashell, that the erle of Desmond was come againe to harborough himselfe in Harlo wood, and had aboue thrée score gallowglasses besides kerne a great number, vpon whom capteine Dowdall hauing good espials, made a iornie thither, and being entred into the wood verie earlie, laie close all the forenoone. For these gallowglasses had bin so dared from time to time, that now like a sort of déere they laie vpon their kéepings, and so fearefull they were, that they would not tarie in anie one place anie long time, but where they did dresse their meat, thense they would remooue, and eat it in another place, and from thense go vnto another place to lie. In the nights they would watch, in the forenoones they would be vpon the hilles and mounteins, to descrie the countrie, and in the afternoone they would sléepe. The capteine breaking time with them, made staie in the wood accordinglie, and in the afternoone he learned by his espials, that they were returned from the mounteins, and were entred into their cabins, where some of them were asleepe, and some of them occupied in dressing of a horsse for to eat, for other vittels were scant. The capteine suddenlie entred vpon them, and tooke them at such aduantage, that they were all, for the most part, put to the sword: of which, fiue and twentie were taken in their cabins. After the dispatch of these Gallowglasses, which are counted the best men of warre among the Irishrie: the residue of the Irish rebels were so dismaid, that a man might without anie great danger passe throughout Mounster.

A draught made vpon the gallowglasses in Harlo wood.

The gallowglasses in Harlo wood put to sword.

About a moneth after this, in September, in the yeare one thousand fiue hundred foure score & thrée, it happned that certeine of the lord Roches men, being in Dowall néere to Trusham, were riding about certeine businesse, and met with the earle of Desmond, hauing in his companie two or thrée horssemen and a priest. The kerns which attended the said lord Roches men, enuironed & compassed them about, but the earle and his men being well horssed, escaped, onelie the priest they tooke, by reason of his bad horsse, and him the lord Roch sent the next daie vnto the lord gouernour, and being examined, he confessed in what great distresse and

The L. Roch his men discouer Desmond.

miserie

miserie the erle was, and that for feare he lurked in corners, & would not be séene. And further, that he had his onelie reléefe and was fostered by Goron mac Swene, a capteine of the gallowglasses, and who was then vnder protection. And by these meanes, the erle (who had not béene heard of since he was gained out of Harlo wood) is now discouered. Wherevpon the lord generall commanded a barke to be foorthwith vittelled, and to be dispatched into Dingle a Cush: and foorthwith commanded capteine Dowdall to repaire thither, and there to be in garison, which he did foorthwith performe. The earle of Desmond when he heard how that he was discouered, and how that vittels and a garison were sent to Dingle a Cush to the working of his wo, he was assured that he should be surelie pursued by capteine Dowdall, who of all other capteines and sir George Bourchier did from time to time gall and most earnestlie pursue him. Wherefore now as for his last helpe, by the helpe and friendship of Goron mac Swene, & Morle Morough mac Swene his brother, he gathereth a new companie, and maketh himselfe as strong as he can, and getteth himselfe into Desmond, and there standeth vpon his gard. Goron mac Swene in the meane time entreth into Carberie, and taketh a great preie of kine, which he droue foorthwith into Desmond toward the earle, but the iorneie was so long, that he laie short of the earle that night about thrée or foure miles.

The Desmond is reuealed by Goron mac Swene

A garison appointed to be at the Dingle

Desmond feareth Dowdall

Goron preith all Carberie for Desmond

The men of the countrie, who had thus lost their goods, thrée of them with their swords and targets followed the tract a far off, minding to haue stollen awaie their owne kine if by anie means they could, and if opportunitie would so serue, for by force or by intreatie they knew it to be impossible for them to recouer anie thing at all. The foresaid Goron, when he had lodged himselfe for all night, it was his pleasure to walke abrode in the fields, and suspecting no harme, went alone, hauing onelie one kerne with him (and both without weapon) about ten or twelue score off from his lodging. About which place it happed the foresaid thrée men had hidden and couched themselues in a bush, and taking the occasion offered, they went also betwéene him and his lodging, and fell vpon him and his kerne, & killed them both: and as soone as they had cut off their heads, they shifted for themselues. Gorons companie, finding their maister lacking, went abrode to séeke him, and in the end found him and his man without heads, lieng dead vpon the ground, which cast them into such a maze, as they wist not what to thinke or to doo: neither could they imagine nor deuise how this should come to passe, for garison there was none in those parts, and they knew of no person thereabouts whome they could suspect. But this is the iust iudgement of God, who in his iustice looketh vpon the periured and wicked, and in mercie beholdeth his seruants. For if this man had liued, it was feared that by his means the earle would haue increased a new force, and haue dighted the lord gouernour and all the garisons to greater troubles. The erle being aduertised of the losse of this his friend, his cheefe and onelie staie, was in a great agonie, and maruellouslie dismaid, and séeing no other remedie, he prepareth the best for himselfe, and taking the aduantage of the time, before the garison should be placed at the Dingle, he made a draught into Kerrie neere Traleigh, minding to take a preie from such as had forsaken him and had receiued their protections. Wherefore in the euening he sent two horssemen with a certeine kerne ouer the strand of Traleigh vnto a castell there, & commanded them to take their preie from thense, which they did, and brought the same awaie with them.

Goron mac Swene is killed

The erle commandeth preie to be taken in Kerrie.

Among those kine thus driuen awaie, a poore woman of that countrie lost all those few that she had, and being distressed of that which was the cheefe, and in a maner the onelie reléefe of hir and hir children and houshold, and not knowing how she could by anie meanes recouer them, she bethought hir selfe vpon a brother which

she

she had, dwelling on the other side of the mounteine, in a castell named Drome, which was one of the Morettos, and to him she runneth in all the hast she could, and declareth hir estate and case, praieng him to helpe hir, and that he would follow the tract for the recouerie of hir kine. Who when he was aduertised that there were but two horssemen & a few kerne which had drouen the preie awaie, he to pleasure his sister tooke three other of his brethren, and followed the tract, till he came to Castelmange, which castell was in the waie. And when he came thither, he went to the castell, and desired the constable (whose name was Cheston, and not long before lieutenant to capteine Berkeleie) that he would spare him some shot and a few of his kerne to helpe him to follow the preie which was driuen that waie. The constable and the souldiors were verie glad to pleasure him, and so he had seuen shot and a doozzen of kerne which dwelled in an out house fast vnder the castell, & so they went altogither to Traleigh, they being in number three and twentie persons: one of these was an Irish man borne, named Kellie, but serued alwaies vnder Englishmen, and could speake verie good English. This man, when they came to Traleigh, they appointed & made him their leader or capteine, and Moretto because he was borne in those parties, and best knew the countrie, they appointed to be their guide: and from thense they followed the tract vntill they came to the side of a mounteine, where there was a glan, and in it a little groue of wood: and the night being come vpon them, there they staid and rested themselues for that night. And in the darke night one of them had espied through the trées a fire not farre off, wherevpon they drew themselues close together, and caused one of themselues closelie and secretlie to draw towards the fire and to discouer what companie was there, and how manie was of them, which man did so. And when he returned backe vnto them, he told them that there was an old bad house, and about fiue or six persons therein: wherevpon they all determined and agreed to repaire to that place to know the whole matter. Moretto was the guide to bring them to the house, and Kellie did set his companie in order and good araie, as was most for their seruice, if néed should so require. And when they were come to the house, they found in it but onelie one old man, for the residue were gone. Then Kellie drew his sword and strake the old man, with which blow he had almost cut off one of his arms, and then he strake him againe, and gaue him a great blow on the side of his head, wherewith the said old man cried out, desiring them to saue his life, for he was earle of Desmond, and then Kellie staied his hands: but the erle bled so fast, that he waxed verie faint, and could not trauell anie further: wherevpon the said Kellie bid and willed him to prepare himselfe to die, and then he strake off the earls head.

The earle of Desmond taken in an old house alone and slaine

The residue of the companie in this meane time spoiled and rifled the house, and tooke what them listed: and then they all departed and went to Castelmange, and carried the earles head with them, but left the bodie behind, and whether the same were deuoured by the woolues or buried by his kerne it is not certeinlie knowne. As soone as they came to Castelmange, they sent the said earles head vnto the lord generall, who foorthwith sent the same into England for a present to hir maiestie, which foorthwith was put vpon a pole, and set on London bridge. When this his death was noised and knowne, there was no more seruice to be doone: for euerie rebell cast awaie his weapon, and sought all the waies they could to humble themselues and to become good subiects: sauing one Iohn Bourke, who stood vpon his protection, and yet neuerthelesse he and his companie went to Adare, there to haue taken a preie. But as he passed by the castell, a bowe therein discharged his peece vpon the said Bourke, & strake him in the head, whereof he died. The common people, who had felt the great smart of this troublesome time reioised and were glad

The earle of Desmonds head sent into England and set vpon London bridge

Iohn Bourke hauing a protection made a stealth, and was killed

of

of the death of the erle, being in a good hope that the long troubles should haue an end, and they to be the more at rest. During these continuall troubles in Mounster, the two lord iustices which laie at Dublin were much eased from all martiall affaires elsewhere, and were troubled but with the clamorings, exclamations, and brabling of the Irish people, not woorth the remembring: sauing that a certeine combat was fought and tried before them in the castell of Dublin, betwéene two Oconhours, verie neere coosens & kinsmen: the one was named Teig mac Guill Patrike Oconhour appellant, the other was named Con mac Cormake Oconhour defendant. One of these appealed and charged the other for sundrie treasons in the late rebellion, and which could haue no other triall but by combat, which was granted vnto them. Wherevpon, according to the lawes and orders of England for a combat to be tried, all things were prepared, the daie, time, and place appointed, and according to the same, the lord iustices, the iudges, and the councellors came and sat in the place appointed for the same, euerie man in his degree and calling. And then the court was called, and the appellant or plantife was brought in before the face of the court, being stripped into his shirt, hauing onlie his sword and target (which were the weapons appointed) and when he had doone his reuerence and dutie to the lord iustices and to the court, he was brought to a stoole set in the one of the ends within the lists, and there sat. After him was the defendant brought in, in the like maner and order, and with the like weapons: and when he had doone his dutie and reuerence to the lord iustices and to the court, he was brought to his chaire placed in the other end of the lists. Then were their actions and pleadings openlie read, and then the appellant was demanded whether he would auerre his demand or not? who when he had affirmed that he would, the partie defendant was likewise asked whether he would confesse the action, or stand to the triall of the same? who did answer as did the other, that he would auerre it by the swoord.

A combat betwéene two Oconhours.

The maner of the combat.

Upon this their seuerall answers, they were seuerallie called the one after the other, euerie of them taking a corporall oth that their quarell was true, and that they would iustifie the same both with sword & blood. Thus they being sworne are brought backe againe euerie of them to their seuerall places as before. And then when by the sound of a trumpet a signe was giuen vnto them when they should enter into the fight, they arose out of their seats, and met ech one the other in the middle within the lists, and there with the weapons assigned vnto them, they fought: in which fight the appellant did preuaile, and he not onlie did disarme the defendant, but also with the sword of the said defendant did cut off his head, and vpon the point of the same sword did present it to the lord iustices, and so with the victorie of his enimie he was acquitted. Thus much I thought good to saie somwhat of much, of the maner of a combat, which together with manie circumstances therevnto belonging is now for want of vse almost cleane forgotten, and yet verie necessarie to be knowne. And as for this combat it was so valiantlie doone, that a great manie did wish that it had rather fallen vpon the whole sex of the Oconhours, than vpon these two gentlemen.

The vicount of Baltinglas, being aduertised of the death of the earle of Desmond, which was no small griefe vnto him: and he also verie wearie of his trotting and wandering on foot amongst bogs, woods, and desert places (being altogither distressed, and in great miserie, and now destitute of all his friends and acquaintances, and not able to hold head anie longer against hir maiesties force) did imbarke himselfe for Spaine, in hope to haue some reléefe and succor, and to procure some aid from the king of Spaine; and by that meanes to be of some abilitie to renew his force and rebellion. But he found in the end verie small comfort. And therefore of

The vicount of Baltinglasse wearie of his life.

The vicount Baltinglasse imbarketh himselfe for Spaine.

of a verie melancholie gréefe & sorrow of mind, as it is thought, he died, being in verie extreame pouertie and need. Not long after this, the two lord iustices, who had ruled and gouerned the land in these troublesome and broken times in great wisdome, care, & circumspection, when they had brought the whole land to a peaceable & quiet gouernment, and deliuered the same from all open or knowne rebellion; they cashed and discharged all the garrisons in Mounster, onelie two hundred souldiors excepted: they kept it in good quietnesse, vntill the arriuall of sir Iohn Perot knight, who was sent ouer to be lord deputie, and landed at Dublin about the middle of Iune, one thousand fiue hundred fourescore and foure, the six and twentith yeare of hir maiesties reigne vnto whome they deliuered the swoord: who being entered into his office, begun such a course, that of his good beginnings a great hope was conceiued of the like to insue. For he was a right woorthie seruitor in that land, when he was lord president in Mounster: and by whome Iames Fitzmoris was subdued, and the whole prouince maruellouslie well reformed: whose notable and most noble acts as they doo well deserue, so when the same shall come to his full measure, they shall be registred to his perpetuall fame and immortall honor. And yet in the meane time, it shall not be offensiue to remember some speciall points of his late seruice, which doo deserue to be remembred: as also for the incouraging of this noble man to continue the good course which he hath begun; which doo halson and giue a hope that he will *Addere colophonem,* and bring that land to a full and perfect gouernment & regiment; which Giraldus Cambrensis would not warrant could be doone much before doomesdaie.

Sir Iohn Perot arriueth into Ireland to be lord deputie.

Not long after the arriuall of this man, the Scots after their accustomed maner, for a bien venu or welcome to his lordship, they began a rebellion, and are vp in armes readie for the warre. His lordship hauing notice and knowledge thereof, maketh himselfe forthwith in a readinesse to méete with them, and to stop them of their purpose: and therein he so ordered and handled the matter, that the Scots were driuen to séeke peace, to craue pardon, to submit themselues, and to sweare allegiance, faith, and obedience to hir maiestie. Which when they had obteined, then they tooke the lands wherein they dwelled, of hir highnesse, yéelding a yearelie rent, which before they had not béene accustomed nor woont to dooe. And by these meanes, if there be any truth in them, the state of that countrie standeth the better assured.

The Scots rebell and are subdued.

Then when he was from this seruice returned to Dublin, his speciall care, studie, and indeuor was to deuise and studie how to reduce and reforme the whole realme and the gouernment, according to the laws of England. Wherevpon he would and did verie often assemble the whole councell, or so manie of them as were there, for their aduise herein; whose names are these. The archbishop of Dublin lord chancellor, the earle of Ormond lord treasuror, the primat of Armagh, the bishop of Meth, the bishop of Kilmore, sir Iohn Noris lord president of Mounster, sir Henrie Wallop treasuror at armes, sir Nicholas Bagnoll knight marshall, Robert Gardner chiefe iustice of the bench, sir Robert Dillon knight chiefe iustice of the common plées, sir Lucas Dillon knight chiefe baron, sir Nicholas White knight master of the rols, sir Richard Bingham knight chiefe commissioner in Connagh, sir Henrie Cowleie knight, sir Edward Waterhouse knight, sir Thomas le Strange knight, Edward Brabesbie, Geffreie Fenton secretarie, sir Warham Sentleger & sir Valentine Browne knights; but discontinued. By the good aduise, helpe, and councell of these wise and prudent councellors, he first thought it best to bring the whole land into shire grounds, whereby the laws of England might haue a through course and passage. Wherefore, what sir Henrie Sidneie before had doone in a few counties, that he performed

The councell in Ireland.

The whole realme brought into shire grounds.

formed in the whole realme, and brought the same into such & so manie seuerall counties, as was thought best and most fit for that purpose. To euerie of which new counties he appointed and assigned seuerall shiriffes, and all such inferior officers as were most requisit, and to the same incident and apperteining. All and euerie which shires hitherto not registred, nor published in chronicle, togither with such as tofore were knowne, I thought it good to set downe by their seuerall names, and in their prouinces as followeth.

The shires in Ireland.

Counties in Mounster.	Limerike	
	Corke	Old counties.
	Kerrie	
	Tipporaria	
	Crosse	
	Waterford	
	Desmond	New countie.
Counties in Vlster.	Louth	Old counties.
	Downe	
	Antrim	
	Monahon	New counties.
	Tiron	
	Armagh	
	Colrane	
	Donergall	
	Farmanagh	
	Cauon	
Counties in Leinster.	Dublin	Old counties.
	Wexford	
	Catherlogh	
	Kilkennie	
	Kildare	
	Kings countie	
	Queenes countie	
	Meth & West-Meth	
	Longefford	New counties
	Wickelow	
	Fernes	
Counties in Connagh	Clare	Old counties.
	Letrimme	
	Gallowaie	New counties.
	Roscommin	
	Maio	
	Sligo	

When he had performed this, and established the same by act of parlement, then hir maiesties writs and processe had a frée passage, and were currant through out the

English lawes currant through Ireland.

the whole land, and hir maiestie knowne to be soueraigne ladie and quéene of the same. Then the Irishrie by little and little gaue ouer their Brehon laws, and their Irish vsage, and became obedient vnto the English laws, vnto which they referred themselues to be tried, and to haue all their quarels to be decided and determined: whereof at these presents is extant a verie notable president & example betweene two of the most principall and chiefe personages in the prouince of Vlster. The one is he, who nameth himselfe Onele, and the other is the earle of Tiron, the heire to the great Con Onele. These two and their ancestors, and all other noble men in that prouince, when so euer anie discord or enimitie did fall out among them, they had no peacemaker but the sword, and by wars and bloudshed was the same decided. Neuerthelesse, these two noble men leauing to pursue their quarels, as in times past with the sword & in hostile maner, doo refer themselues to the triall of the laws, and each one of them sueth the other at the common laws, and in the chancerie in hir maiesties court at Dublin, and there as dutifull subiects doo abide the triall of their cause. A thing so much the more to be considered, as the parties be of that nobilitie and stoutnesse, and a thing so rare, as heretofore not heard nor knowne. Which course if it haue so happie a progresse and successe, as it hath a good enterance and beginning; no doubt, but that partlie by the laws, and partlie by the sword, an vniuersall obedience shall through that land be established: the common societie shall be preserued, the whole realme shall florish and prosper, hir maiestie shall be obeied, the reuenues shall be increased, and in the end, peace shall be vpon Israell. And as this example giueth some manifest good hope thereof, so the same is confirmed and increased by the happie victorie of late in Connagh, where a number of Scots, hauing made an inuasion, were met and incountered withall, by the right worthie sir Richard Bingham knight, chiefe commissioner of that prouince, and by him they were vanquished & ouerthrowne, to the number of fifteene hundred persons, so that verie few or none escaped the sword, to returne home with the news of their successe: but were either killed or drowned.

Onele and the earle of Tiron sue each one the other at law.

Sir Richard Bingham his victorie vpon the Scots.

Thus much hitherto generallie concerning the gouernment of that land of Ireland, since the death of king Henrie the eight, vntill these presents. In the course of which time, manie more notable things haue beene doone, worthie to be registred in the chronicles of perpetuall fame and memorie. For the atteining to the knowledge whereof, though Iohn Hooker the writer hereof haue béene a diligent traueller and a searcher for the same, yet he wanted that good successe, as both the historie it selfe requireth, and he himselfe wisheth. And yet the most part of all the actions in that age consisted most in continuall warres, rebellions, and hostilitie, either against their most sacred kings and queenes, or amongst themselues. But whatsoeuer tofore hath beene doone, none were so tragicall, impious, and vnnaturall, as were the last warres of the Giraldines of Desmond in Mounster. For of the Giraldines of Kildare, who were not acquainted, nor consenting to these wicked actions, nothing is meant. Whereinto who so listeth to looke, and well to consider, he shall find and sée most euident and apparant examples of Gods iustice & iudgement, against such as doo rebell against the Lords annointed, whome the Lord by his expresse word hath commanded to be honored and obeied in all humblenesse and dutie: because they are his vicars, substitutes, and vicegerents vpon the earth, to defend the good, and to punish the euill, and who so resisteth them, doo resist his ordinances, and shall receiue hard iudgement, as most manifestlie it dooth appeare in this the earle of Desmonds rebellion. All which if it should be set downe particularlie, as in course it fell out, it would be verie tedious: but much more lamentable and dolefull to be read.

And

And therefore leauing the large discourse, it shall suffice to shut and conclude this historie, with the briefe recitall of the most speciall points, to mooue ech man to consider the mightie hand of God against traitors and rebels, and his louing mercie and kindnesse vpon the dutifull and obedient. First therefore Iames Fitzmoris, the first ringleader in this pageant, and who most vnnaturallie had flocked in strangers and forreiners to inuade the land, for establishing the antichristian religion, and the depriuing of hir maiestie from hir imperiall crowne of the realme of Ireland: this man (I saie) was he who yeelded the first fruits of this rebellion. For in his idolatrous pilgrimage to the holie crosse, and his traitorous iournie to practise with all the rebels and inhabitants in Connagh and Vlster to ioine with him, he did commit a robberie, and being pursued for the same, he was slaine by a gentleman, and one of his owne kinsmen Theobald Burke, and his head & quarters set vpon the gates of the towne of Kilmallocke.

Then Iames of Desmond brother to the earle, hauing done a robberie vpon sir Corman mac Teige, was likewise taken and carried to Corke, where he was drawne, hanged, and quartered, and his head and quarters set vpon the gates and wals of the citie of Corke. After him, sir Iohn of Desmond, one other brother to the said earle, who was a speciall champion of the pope, from whom he had receiued manie blessings, buls, and Agnus dei, which should keepe and preserue him from all harme: yet for all this his holie cote armour, he was met withall by capteine Zouch and capteine Dowdall, and by them he receiued his iust reward of a bloudie traitor, and a fréendkiller, being killed and then carried dead to Corke, where his bodie was hanged by the héeles, and his head sent to Dublin, and there set vpon the top of the castle. And in the end, the earle himselfe was also taken, and with the sword the head was diuided from the bodie: the one was sent to London, and there set vpon London bridge; and his bodie vncerteine whether it were buried or deuoured by the wild beasts. And thus a noble race and ancient familie, descended from out of the loines of princes, is now for treasons and rebellions vtterlie extinguished and ouerthrowne, onelie one sonne of the said earles is left, and yet prisoner in the Tower of London. The two doctors, Allen & Sanders, who were the holie fathers legats and nuncios, and in their foolish fantasies dreamed that they had the Holie ghost at commandement, and yet most errant traitors against the lords annointed: the one of them lifting vp his swoord against hir sacred maiestie, vnder the popes banner at Mounster, one thousand fiue hundred thréescore and ninetéene, was slaine and killed: the other after that he had followed the heeles of the Desmonds almost foure yeares, wandering to and fro in the woods & bogs, died most miserablie in the wood of Cleneles, in such diseases as famine and penurie vse to bring. The Romans and Spaniards, and the strangers which were sent from the pope and king Philip, with all their consorts and companies, verie few left of them to returne home, and to carie news of their successe, but were all put to the sword. And as for the great companies of souldiors, gallowglasses, kerne, & the common people, who followed this rebellion, the numbers of them are infinit, whose bloods the earth dranke vp, and whose carcases the foules of the aire and the rauening beasts of the féeld did consume and deuoure. After this folowed an extreme famine: and such as whom the sword did not destroie, the same did consume, and eat out, verie few or none remaining aliue, sauing such as dwelled in cities and townes, and such as were fled ouer into England: and yet the store in the townes was verie far spent, and they in distresse, albeit nothing like in comparison to them who liued at large. For they were not onelie driuen to eat horsses, dogs and dead carions, but also did deuoure the carcases of dead

Iames Desmond taken in a robberie, hanged, drawne, & quartered.

Sir Iohn of Desmond slaine, and his bodie hanged by the heeles.

The earle of Desmond slaine, and his head sent to London and set vpon London bridge.

Allen and Sanders died, the one with the sword, the other of famine.

All strangers slaine.

After the wars folowed a famine.

men, whereof there be sundrie examples namelie one in the countie of Corke, where when a malefactor was executed to death, and his bodie left vpon the gallows, certeine poore people secretlie came, tooke him downe, and did eat him. Likewise in the baie of Smeerewicke, or saint Marie wicke, the place which was first seasoned with this rebellion, there happened a ship to be there lost through foule weather, and all the men being drowned, were there cast on land.

A man hanged was eaten.

Men drowned and eaten.

The common people, who had a long time liued on limpets, orewads, and such shelfish as they could find, and which were now spent, as soone as they saw these dead bodies, they tooke them vp, and most greedilie did eat and deuoure them: and not long after, death and famine did eat and consume them. The land it selfe, which before those wars was populous, well inhabited, and rich in all the good blessings of God, being plentious of corne, full of cattell, well stored with fish and sundrie other good commodities, is now become wast and barren, yéelding no fruits, the pastures no cattell, the fields no corne, the aire no birds, the seas (though full of fish) yet to them yéelding nothing. Finallie, euerie waie the curse of God was so great, and the land so barren both of man and beast, that whosoeuer did trauell from the one end vnto the other of all Mounster, euen from Waterford to the head of Smeerewéeke, which is about six score miles, he should not meet anie man, woman, or child, sauing in townes and cities, nor yet sée anie beast, but the verie woolues, the foxes, and other like rauening beasts: manie of them laie dead being famished, and the residue gone elsewhere. A heauie, but a iust iudgement of God vpon such a Pharoicall and stifnecked people, who by no persuasions, no counsels, and no reasons, would be reclamed and reduced to serue God in true religion, and to obeie their most lawfull prince in dutifull obedience, but made choise of a wicked idoll, the god Mazim to honor, and of that wicked antichrist of Rome to obeie, vnto the vtter ouerthrow of themselues and of their posteritie. This is the goodnesse that commeth from that great citie vpon the seuen hils, and that mightie Babylon, the mother of all wickednesse & abhominations vpon the earth. These be the fruits which come from that holie father, maister pope, the sonne of sathan, and the man of sinne, and the enimie vnto the crosse of Christ, whose bloodthirstinesse will neuer be quenched, but in the blood of the saints, and the seruants of God, and whose rauening guts be neuer satisfied, but with the death of such as doo serue the Lord in all godlines, & who will not be drunke in the cup of his fornications: as it dooth appere by the infinit & most horrible massacres, and bloodie persecutions, which he dailie exerciseth throughout all christian lands. Which bicause he can not performe also within the realmes of England & Ireland, what practises hath he made by inchantments, sorceries, witchcrafts, & tresons to bereaue hir maiestie of hir life? What deuises hath he vsed to raise vp hir owne subiects to rebellions and commotions, to supplant hir of hir roiall estate and gouernment? What practises hath he vsed with forren princes and potentats, to séeke occasions of breaches of peace and raisings of warres? And how craftilie hath he suborned his vnholie & traitorous Iesuits, vnder colour of holines, to range from place to place through hir maiesties realmes, and to mooue and persuade hir people from dutifull obedience vnto hir highnesse, and to denie hir supreme authoritie and gouernment? Finallie, how dooth he from time to time like a rauening woolfe séeke the deuouring of hir, and of all hir good subiects, which liue in the feare of God, and in the religion established vpon his holie word and gospell? Whereof hath insued the losse of infinit thousands of people, as whereof manie apparant examples are set downe and recorded in the histories of England, but of them all, none more lamentable than is this historie of Ireland, and especiallie this tragedie

The fruits which come from the pope.

The wicked practises of the pope.

tragedie

tragedie of Mounster. In which it dooth appeare, how that for the maintenance of the popes quarels, the earth hath drunke vp the bloud, the fouls of the aire haue pierced, and the beasts of the field haue deuoured the carcases of infinit multitudes & numbers of people. Which if euerie man would well looke into and consider, the vngodlie shall sée the great iudgements of God, and his seuere iustice against all such as shall dishonor his holie name, and against such as shall rebell and resist against his annointed: that thereby they may repent, amend their liues, and be conuerted vnto the Lord, both in true religion towards him, and in all dutifull obedience to his annointed. And the good and godlie shall sée, and thereby consider the great good mercies shewed vpon them, in that he hath and continuallie dooth preserue and kéepe them from out of the iawes of the lion in all safetie, that they should dailie more and more grow from grace to grace, and liue in all holinesse and vertue towards him, and persist in all dutifull obedience vnto hir maiestie our soueraigne ladie and queene, whose daies the Lord God continue and prolong to reigne ouer vs to his good will and pleasure: and so shall we hir people sée good daies, liue in securitie, and the peace of Israell shall be vpon vs.

Thus farre the chronicles of Ireland, continued by Iohn Hooker aliàs Vowell, Gent.

THE END.

GENERAL INDEX.

ABBASIE of Winchester obteined for monie, vol ii page 35
Abbat of Ferne burnt, v 306.
—— Of Kilwinning slaine, v. 651
—— Of Tulrie murthered, v. 509
—— Agelonthus. ¶ Sée Agelonthus.
—— Of Battell in rescuing Winchelseie is put to flight, ii 731.
—— Of Glastenburie an erls son, ii 71.
—— Egelsin ¶ Sée Egelsin.
—— Eglewine ¶ Sée Eglewine
—— Fecknam of Westminster installed, iv. 85
—— Frederike ¶ Sée Frederike.
—— Ioachim, a man of great fame, ii. 219.
—— Losanage ¶ Sée Losanage.
—— Paule ¶ Sée Paule.
—— Of saint Augustine capteine of an armie, ii 3
—— Of S Edmunsburie, Robert Lon an earls sonne, ii 33
—— Thurstan ¶ Sée Thurstan
—— Of Westminster died suddenlie, iii. 13.
—— ¶ Sée Conspirasie.
Abbats ordeined by William Rufus, ii 33
—— They and priors depriued, and whie, ii 1.
—— Not to be made knights, &c note ib.
Abbeie of Bangor, vi. 86.
—— Now plowed ground, i 141
—— Of saint Augustine at Canterburie built, i. 596
—— Of Rippon burnt by K Edred, i 692
—— Of Founteins famous how seated, i 160
—— Of moonks Benedictine suppressed, i 174.
—— Of Osneie by whom and wherevpon it was begun to be built, i 250
—— Of Battell with the roll thereof, ii 5 6 7 8
—— The first of white moonks when and by whom founded, ii 44
—— Of S. Albons repaired by Lanfranke, ii. 30.
—— Of Charterhouse moonks built, ii 30 v 423
Abbeis in France how many, i 234
—— Built by Adelstane, i 688
—— Founded by Allured, i 655.
Abbeis Building of them thought a full satisfaction for sins, vol. i page 701
—— What their state was in the daies of John of Beuerlie and Beda, i. 643
—— Builded thrée by duke William, ii. 25.
—— Founded in king Stephans time, ii 110
—— Eleuen let out to farme, ii 43
—— Searched and ransacked at duke Williams commandement, ii 14.
—— Suppressed, iii 807 810.
—— Their lands promised by quéene Marie to be restored note, iv 75
—— ¶ See Churches and Nunneries
—— Founded, v 306, 300, 287, 295, 288, 313.
—— Giuen up by vnlawfull meanes, v 451
—— In Englishmens hands, v. 331.
Aber in Brittish is the mouth or fall of euerie riuer, i 117
Aberden towne burned by the English, v 376.
Abertaw the Brittish name of Berstable, i. 112.
Abertifie, vi 127.
Abircorne wall and the manner how built, v. 129.
—— Ouerthrowne, ib.
Abiuration for speking against the popes authoritie, iii 722
—— Of bishop Pecocke, iii. 242
—— ¶ Sée Bishop Pecocke
Aborigenes, and the opinion cōcerning them gainsaid, i 432
Aboundance ¶ Sée Plentie
Absolution to be purchased from Rome, ii. 371.
—— Of the clergie sued for from Rome, ii. 348.
—— Of Oxford by legat Otho, ii 383
—— For vowes and other offences, ii 445
—— For an oth obteinied, ii 540
—— For the offence of disobedience, ii 348.
—— Pronounced by cardinall Poole to the parlement house, iv 67.
Abstinence of the north Britons, i 279
Aburgauennie lord arreigned at Westminster, iii 675
—— Assembleth a power against Wiat, and putteth them to flight, iv 11

Acca bishop of Hexham, vol i. page 611.
Accusation false for a time preuailed but in time frustrate note, ii 386
——— Of a iustice for taking of bribes, ii. 121.
——— Of two noble men that had the custodie of the king and quéene of Scots, ii 433
——— Against prince Henrie to king Henrie the fourth his father, iii 53.
——— Uniust redoundeth to the accusants shame, iii 792.
——— Interchangable and doubtfull tried by combat. note, ii 890
——— False punished, iii 846
——— False punished by pillorie note, iv 85
——— Of a maister against his seruant whereof followeth secret vengeance, iii 1065
Achaius king of Scotland maketh the nobles agree, v 185
——— Deceaseth, v 193
Achelnotus archbishop of Canterburie, i 782
Acho king of Norwaie landed in Albion, v 313, 314
——— The cause of his comming into Scotland, v 315
——— His demands and exhortation to his people, ib.
——— His nephue slaine, v 316
——— The losse of his ships and mariners, his flight into Orkeneie, v. 317.
——— Prepareth to make a new inuasion, but dieth before purbision was readie, ib
Ackwold king of Eastangles, i 641.
Aeon See Acres
Acres besieged, v 302.
Acton knight his rebellion, surprised, he and his complices condemned of treason and heresie, iii 63.
Ada the son of Ida king of Brenitia, i. 58
——— The daughter of Aurelius and wife of Conranus, v 149
Adam of Hereford admerall of the English fleet, discomfiteth and spoileth the Irish fleet, vi 182.
Adamant stones, i 402
Adder in the Saxon toong described Atter, i 383.
Adders without hurt, v 303
Adela married to Richard Henrie the second his son, ii 162
Adelicia ¶ Sée Quéene
Adelike castell taken, vi 259
Adeliza the daughter of duke William, whome Harold should haue married, i 757
Adelme rebelling against his king, and pardoned, dooth good seruice in the field, i 61?
Adelstan king of England crowned and consecrated at Kingston vpon Thames, i 684
——— Sorie too late for exiling his brother, i 687
——— He goeth out of his waie to sée where S. John Beuerlie was buried, i. 687
——— His victories against diuerse kings conspiring against him, i 686
Adelstan his victorie against six kings, all slain with diuerse others, vol i page 688.
——— Entered into Deira, v 191
——— Pursueth Hungus, his cruell proclamation, doth challenge his enemies, is slaine, v. 191, 192.
——— Described, his death, and what presents were sent him, i. 688
——— His buriall, v 192
——— ¶ Sée Athelstane
Adelstan bishop of Shireburne, cõmended, i 665.
——— Of K. Egberts councell, i 661
Adelwold king of Sussex receiueth the Ile of Wight as a gift vpon condition, i 624
——— He causeth the Essex men to yéeld vnto him, i 679.
——— He is slaine, ib.
Adelwold K. Edwards brother taketh part with the Danes, i 678
——— Bishop of Winchester builded Elie abbie, i. 697.
Admerall, and the reason of the name, i. 337.
Admonition ¶ Sée Warning.
Adonthus master of the horsse to king Harold slaine in fight, ii 10
Adraste worshipped and praied vnto, i. 498
Adrian abbat of Augustines at Canterburie commended, i 626
——— He that came with Theodore, and died, i. 642
Adrian the emperor passeth into Britaine, i 513
——— His wall undermined and ouerthrowne, i 514; v 131.
——— Prepareth to go into Britaine, transported, findeth nothing abrode in the country of his enemies, beginneth to make a wall for safegard of the Britons, commeth to London, v. 88, 89.
Adrian the pope sendeth legats into England, i 651.
——— Confirmeth the priueleges of the church and realme of Ireland, vi 186
Aduancement of a bondman disdained, i 502.
Aduentuters, iii 681.
——— Soldiers and whie so called, iii 690
——— their capteine slaine, and they discomfited, iii 693
——— Good seruitors, iii 694
——— Slaine and discomfited, their finall end, iii 696.
——— ¶ Sée Kréckers,
Adulfe ¶ Sée Emperour
Adulterie punished with hanging, ii 365
——— Seuerlie corrected in a maiores time in London, ii 754
——— ¶ Sée Incest, Fornication, and Whoredome.
——— Cause of warres, vi 121
Adulterer mainteined by an adulteresse: note, i 492.
Adwin bishop of Winchester cõmitted to prison, i. 740.

Aegypt how many cities it cōtained, now decaied, vol i page 324
Aegyptus and his fiftie sonnes, i 134.
Aeuum ¶ Sée Age
Affinitie ¶ Sée Fréendship and Marriage.
Affliction maketh men religious, vi 81
Agamppus a prince of France married Ceadeilla, i 447
Agard Francis sent to Iames Fitzmoris with his pardon, vi 406
—— His death, vi 428.
Agatha and Christine renounce the world, v 281
Agatha the mother of Edgar Etheling driuen by tempest into Scotland, ii 9
Agathysi ¶ Sée Picts.
Age of thirtie and thrée score, &c yeares, and what Epaminondas said thereof, i 191
—— In Latin Seculū or Aeuū and what that word signifieth, i 411
Agelmarus bishop of Thetford deposed and whie, ii 14
Agelonthus abbat of Glastenburie, ii 8
Agilbert bishop of Paris, i 618
Agincourt battell, iii 78
—— When fought, iii 196.
—— The number of the slaine, noblemen prisoners, iii 82, 83
Agneda ¶ Sée Edenburgh, v 43.
Agnerus and Dubba two Danish capteines brethren, i 667
Agricola inuadeth Leneux, returneth to Pictland, pursueth his enterprise against the Scots, v 78
—— His name dredfull to the Scots and Picts, v 93
—— Maketh a bridge, &c passeth with his host and incampeth néer the foot of the mountein of Granberie, v 81
—— Commeth to the succor of his men, v 80
—— Discomfiteth his enimies, ib
—— Sendeth foorth his nauie of ships to discouer the furthest point of Britaine northward, v 81
—— Subdueth Angus and wintereth there, certified of the mischance of his nauie, v 83.
—— He is sent for to Rome, ib
Aid forren and the hurt thereof, i 11, &c
Aidan bishop, i 616.
—— A Scot commeth into England to preach the gospell, i 615.
—— His coniecture touching Oswin fell out true, i 618
—— Commeth to the kingdome of Scots by surrender, v 165
—— Appointeth sessions to be kept yearlie in thrée parts of the realme, in warrs against Brudeus, ib
—— Reproued, repenteth, v 166
—— His diligence to resist his enemies, v 167, 168.
—— His death, v 169.
Ailmer lord iustice of the common plées, vi 309
—— made chéefe iustice of the Kings bench, vi. 309
Ailmer he is discommended to the king, vol vi page 310
—— The king hath speeches with him and liketh him well, ib
—— He is the cause whie the lands of all nobles absenting out of the land are giuen to the king, ib
Aire red as though on fier, ii 64
—— Full of clouds red, yellow, and gréene, ii 177.
—— Ruddie of colour as though it burned and of a sanguine hue, ii 245
—— Séemed to be on a bright fier, ii 289
—— ¶ Sée Lights.
Aire of Ireland, vi 9
Aire castell besieged and woone, v. 134.
Aiske a towne, burned by the English, iii 564.
Aitiles stone, i 402
Alabaster white where to be had, i. 395
Alan the son of Stephan, ii 12
Alan earle of Britaine aduanced by duke William his vncle, ii 11
—— The blacke earle, issulesse, ii 12
—— le Rous, issulesse, ib
Alanson besieged and yéelded vp, iii 93.
Alarike ¶ Sée Athaulfe
Albanact the yoongest sonne of Brute had Albania giuen him, i 196
—— His death reuenged by his brethern, i 197
Alban a citizen of Werlancester martyred vnder Dioclesian, i 527
Albania now Scotland, i 470
—— By whom built, i 444.
—— How first called Scotland, i. 196
—— What it conteined as Brute left it, ib
—— The portion of Albanactus the yoongest son of Brutus, i 157
—— Diuided by Fergus among his capteins and soldiers, i 198
Albemarle besieged by French king, ii 254
—— Woone by the earle of Flanders, ii 152.
—— William, whose son should haue béene made king of England, ii 36
Alberike ruler of Northumberland, ii. 21
Albertus de Lasco, &c his comming into England. iv 505
—— Prepareth for his returne into Poland, iv 507
—— Described, ib
—— Intertemed at Oxford, iv. 507, 508.
—— His departing thense, iv. 508
—— ¶ Sée Polander
Albion a noble man his relation, v 187.
Albine treatise against Charles his articles, i. 652.
—— ¶ Sée Alcwine
Albion how long he gouerned Britaine, and by whome he was slaine, i 8
—— He with a companie of his race proceeding from Cham, i 9.
Albion and Bergion ioined powers against Hercules, i 7
—— His name died not though he were slaine in fight, i 8

Albion the name of Britaine, and why so called as some coniecture, vol 1 page 6.
——— The ancient religiõ vsed therein, i 33
——— The name thereof how long it remained, i 8
——— How long it was so called, ib
——— The name of it better known to the Gréeks than that of Britaine, i 9
——— What sundrie natiõs had dwelt in it, i. 10
——— ¶ Sée Britaine and England
——— Now England, why so named as Bodin saith, i 430
——— Diuerse opinions of the name, i 432, 433.
——— The giant comming into this Iland, i 432.
——— The son of Neptune, subdueth the Celts, i 431.
——— He and Bergion slaine with the most part of their armie, i 433
Albions and Saxons incounter, v 143
Albren the sepulture or graue of Danes, v 258
Alchfled daughter of Oswic maried to Peda, i 620
Alchumie a mettall worthie to be banished out of England, i 400
Alcluide a famous citie, i 119
——— Anciẽt and how seated, i 321
——— Destroied by the Danes, i 663
——— Whether in Scotland or no, i 160
Alcwine a famous clerke an Englishman, i 647
Alder growing in England whose barke serueth to die blacke, i 358
Aldermarie church in London why so named, i 190.
Aldelme archbishop of Canturb i 681
——— Bishop of Worcester in fauour with K Edward the third, i 749
——— Archbishop of Yorke, i 681, 756
——— Slaine by duke Chorthmond, i 655.
Alderware a town about Tame and why so named, i 190
Alderman of London his authoritie, ii 207.
——— Seuen deceased within the space of ten moneths, ii 85, 231
——— ¶ Sée Almshouses, Charitie, Londoners, and Schoole
Aldghitha quéene, sister to Edwin and Mercia sent to Chester, ii 1
Aldelme bishop of Shireburne, i 612
Aldinus Ealdbright.
Aldred archbishop of Yorke, ii. 1.
——— Crowneth duke William, ii 1
——— And Mawd quéene, ii. 11
——— Dieth for griefe, ii 10
Aldroenus king of litle Britaine in France, i 543
Aldulfe king of Eastangles departeth this life, i 641.
Ale sold by weight, v 304
— It and wine sold by the pound, v. 423
— Diuerslie termed for the strẽgth, i. 340
— What slights are vsed for the vtterance of it, i 286.
Alectus counted a ringleader of théeves note, i 521
——— Killeth Caransius and succéedeth him in rule ouer Britaine, i 520.
Alectus usurped the title and dignitie of king of Britaine, vol i page 520
Alen the east and west, riuer described, i 153
Alexander king of Scotland his valiancie, v 316
——— With his wife came to London, v 320.
——— Goeth into England, v 311.
——— Commended of the pope, v 310
——— Maried, v 321.
——— Marieth the daughter of the lord Coucie, v 311.
——— His answer to a legats message, v. 319.
——— His wisedome praised, ib
——— Taken by the Cumins, v 313
——— Set at libertie, ib
——— In armes against the Danes and Norwegians, v 314
——— In battell against king Acho of Norwaie, v. 315
——— His manhood, his death and buriall, v. 286, 287.
——— Manner of his death, ii 188
Alexander ¶ Sée Pope
Alexander the fierce crowned king note, v 286.
Alexander the second crowned king, v 306
——— He passeth to London, ib
——— He is accused, v 307
——— Returneth into his countrie, ib
——— In armes against the English, ib
——— Deceaseth, v 311
Alexander pope the second fauored duke Williams conquest of England, i 760
Alexander the third crowned, an interview betwixt the king of England and him, v 312
——— His lawes, v 322.
——— His sudden and strange death, v 321.
Alexander prince of Scotland maried, v 320
——— His death, ib
Alexander of the Iles arrested, v 420
——— Commeth to the king and asketh pardon, ib
Alexander Canon a valiant man note, v 287.
Alexander ouerthrew and killed a lion, i 380.
Alexander Phereus and his dog, i 389
Alexander bishop of Lincolne fled into Scotland, ii. 15
Alexander Robert See Iusts triumphant
Alfer ¶ Sée Elfer.
Alfin bishop of Winchester, i 697
Alfled the daughter of Offa king of Mercia, i 654
Alfred first diuided England into shires, i 257
——— King of Northumbers and the place of his buriall, i 158
——— His death laid to earle Goodwins charge, and how he was slaine, i 222
Alfred the son of Egelred maketh chalenge to the crowne, i 733
——— Striueth in vaine to kéepe Adelstane from the gouernment, i 684.
——— Taken prisoner, his eies put out, his death, i. 733

Alfred suspected persons for his death examined, vol i page 737
——— ¶ Sée Alured
Alfred the beautifull daughter of Horgerius note, i. 695
——— The wife of king Edgar dieth, and what offense it caused him to doo, ib.
——— Hir wicked purpose to kill hir sonne, i. 700.
Alfreda the daughter of K Offa of Mercia maried to Ethelbert, i 648.
——— Gréeued at the death of hir husband, becometh a nun, i 649.
Alfride king of Northumbers, i. 641.
——— A bastard, i. 635.
Afrije the seuenth abbat of S Albons, i 323.
Alfrike duke of Mercia, banished, i. 704.
——— Wise admerell of king Egelreds nauie a traitor to his countrie, i 706
Alfrike archbishop of Yorke, i 737
Alfwald king of Northumbers his death, i 652.
——— His sonnes miserablie slaine by Ethelbert, i 654
Alfwen sister to Elfleda, i 682
Algar the sonne of earle Leofrike hath Harolds lands giuen him, i. 749.
——— His intended rauishing reuenged, i 649
——— His eies put out for his fathers treason, i. 706
Algar made earle of Chester, exiled, he recouereth it by force, i. 751
Algar earle of Oxford, i 748
——— Banished, i 749
Aliance aduisedlie to be made, i. 556
——— ¶ Sée Mariage.
Alice the daughter of erle Morieine, sold for monie, ii 144.
Alkes and Vres, i 380.
Allaine Zouch lord iustice slaine by the earle of Surrie lord Fitzwarren, vi 238
Allegiance ¶ Sée Loialtie.
Allen archbishop of Dublin enemie to the Giraldines, was murthered, vi 234
Allen sir Iohn knight, enemie to the erle of Kildare, vi 287.
Allen doctor acquainted with James Fitzmoris, vi 206.
——— Ioineth with him in conspirasie, vi. 406
——— He arriueth into Ireland, ib
——— He causeth the popes banner to be displaied, vi 416
——— He incourageth the traitors, ib.
——— He is slain, ib.
Alleluia note, a stratagem, i 562.
——— ¶ Sée Germaine
Allered archbishop of Yorke, i 742.
Allum decre, iii. 532
Alma daughter to erle Strangbow, married vnto William Fitzirald, vi 185
Almaricus a traitorous deacon, i. 712.
Almaine great and tall incountred withall by the duke of Suffolke, iii 606
Alman Walter, vi 197
Alman Walter seneshall of Wexford, vol. vi. page 197.
——— Corrupt and couteous, ib
——— A secret enemie to Reimond, vi 198.
Almes Charitie
Almeshouses for the poore, iv 427.
——— Within Bishopsgate, iii 1024.
——— Of Dauid Smith for poore widows, iv. 548.
——— For the reliefe of the poore, iv 551.
Almiramolt king of the Saracens feineth himselfe dead, ii 214
Alpine crowned king of Scots, inuadeth Pictland, v 195.
——— Refuseth anie treatie of peace, v 197.
——— The incamping of his armie, ib
——— Constrained by the nobles, taketh vpon him to be crowned king, v 193
——— Unwilling to receiue it, fled, ib.
——— Ioifullie receiued of Dongall, ib.
——— His excuse, v 194
——— Taken by his enemies and after beheaded, v. 198.
——— His head stolen and solemnlie buried with his bodie, ib
Alps, and that sundrie cities and holdes were placed among them, i 7.
Alps or hils of Snowdonie, not less famous than the transmarine Alps, i 136.
Alricke the son of Herbert slaine in fight, i. 655.
——— ¶ Sée Wichtred
Alstan bishop of Shireburne a warrior, i 667.
Alswald. ¶ Sée Alfwald.
Alswine the brother of king Egfrid slaine, i. 631.
Altars taken downe and tables set in their roome, iii 1024
Altred king of Northumbers, i. 648
Alume note, i 397
Alured sent ambassadours to king Gregorie about a peace, v 221.
Alured king of West Saxons and the greatest part of England, i 668
——— Persecuted by the Danes, ib
——— He vanquished them by sea, i 669
——— By their meanes put to his shifts, i 670
——— Disguiseth himselfe like a minstrell, i 671.
——— King Ethelwulfes sonne and consecrated king at Rome, i 662
——— His prouision for the saftie of his land against the Danes, i 674
——— Learned, and what workes he wrote, i 675.
——— Described and commended, i 674
Alured his court learned, i 675.
——— How he diuided the time for his necessarie vses, ib
——— His death, i 674
——— Last will and epitaph, i 675.
Alwin ¶ Sée Adwin
Ambassadour into Denmarke, iii. 711.
——— Sent into France, iii 67, 634, ii 831, 816, 602, 577, 443, 365, 351, 289, 191, iv 266, 79, 557, 560
——— ¶ Sée Sackuill.

Ambassadour sent to the generall councell, they come to the councell, vol ii page 409.
——— At Cambreie, ii 119
——— Sent into Germanie, ii 501.
——— Sent to the king of Almaigne, ii 450.
——— To Philip archduke of Burgogne, iii 506
——— To the pope, ii 418, 626, 651, 651, 109, 323, 354, 53, 48, iii 16.
——— Sent to the king of Scots, ii 513, 280, 282, iv 600
——— Sent into Spaine, ii 429
——— To the emperour Charles, iii 720
——— The answer which they receiue, iii 722
——— Sent from Alfonse king of Castile, &c ii 174.
——— Sent from the king of Connagh in Ireland, ii 106
——— Sent from the emperour, ii 59, 61, 128, iii 530, 616, 709, 714, 834, iv 10
——— From the K of Spaine, iii 561, 714
——— From the French king with a traine, ii 187, 574, 602, 813, iii 16, 37, 195, 632, iv 435
——— From the good townes in Flanders, ii. 632
——— From the king of Hungarie, iii 713
——— Out of Muscouie, iv 66, 235
——— From the duke of Burgogne, iii. 329
——— From the pope, ii 577
——— Out of Scotland, ii 276, iii 681, 349, 16
——— From Swethen about a marriage, ii 186
Ambassadorlieger of Spaine ¶ Sée Mendoza
Ambassadors into Denmarke, v 450
——— Into England, v 530, 606, 610, 745, 614
——— Out of England, v 665
——— Out of France, 665, 666.
——— Into England, v 722
——— Into Scotland, v 731
——— Out of England into Scotland, v 665, 666
——— Into France to consummate the mariage of Marie queene of Scots to the Dolphin, v 435.
——— from an I into France, v 488
——— Out of France into England, v 602
——— Out of England to Scotland, v 603, 722
——— From the king of France, v 618
——— Out of England, v 619.
——— Out of France, v 710
——— Out of Scotland into France, ib
——— Into France, v 511.
——— To the king of the Romans, v. 158
——— From Spaine, v 464
——— From Swethen, v 614
——— Shire, v 257
Ambassage disdainefull, ii 64.
Ambassage roiall into France, vol ii page 817.
Amber great stone to be had in certeine Ilands of Scotland, i 76
——— A kind of great stone, i 101
——— Riuer described, i 165
Amberuilliers castell taken, iii 113
Ambition ¶ Sée Makbeth
——— Bréedeth dissention, vi 77, 78.
——— Cause of bloudshed, ib
——— To rule alone, what mischeefe it inferreth, i 452
——— It causeth bloudshed, i 431
——— It causeth slaughter, i 415
——— Cause of dissention betwéene brethren note, i 450.
——— Rewarded with shame, i 148
——— Of nephues for monarchie or sole regiment note, i 448
——— In noblemen, i 574
——— Of Bassianus note, i. 519.
——— Of Carausius but a mean man séeking to be a king, i 516
——— Of Hengist the Saxon, i 555
——— Of Leirs two sons in law, i 447
——— Of Romans, i 192
——— Of the old emperor Seuerus, i 516, 517
——— Of Ueranius discoured at his death, i 495.
——— Of Uortigerne, i 552
——— Was Anselme loth to be suspected of, ii. 47
——— Of earle Robert of Northumberland, ii. 37.
——— Of earle John, ii 230.
——— In the French and Spanish kings aspiring to the empire, iii 698
——— Of archbishop Thurstane notable, ii 65.
——— Of bishop Longchampe, ii 225
——— Of an old aged Durham note, ii 207.
——— Of earles suing to be kings, ii 1.
——— Of two archbishops, ii 17
——— Of bishops, ii 65
——— Contentious, ii 209
——— Of two moonkes labouring for an abbaie, ii 31
——— Of mans nature, ii 130, iii 634
——— The working thereof, iii 410
——— The fruits thereof noted in Robert, ii 19.
——— It will haue a fall, iii 404 note, the whole storie, from 1066, 1067
——— ¶ Sée Selim and Turke
Ambiskeleth king of Scots turned from vertue to licentiousnesse, gathereth an armie, v 179
——— His death, ib
Abrie now Salisburie, i 561
Amneie riuer his course, i 82.
Amcolme and Witham riuers of which goeth a byword, i 169
Amercduke Fitzstephans sonne, vi. 205
——— Instituted S Albon, i 527
——— Born in Caerlon, i 156
——— Martyred at Redburne, i 529.

Amphibalus his bodie found and buried at saint Albons, vol ii page 175
Amphibalus abbie at Winchester, i 552
Amphibologie of the woord daughter, ii 271
Amphibologie of the woord swords, i 132
Amsterdam a towne of great concourse and commerce, inexpugnable, iv 652, 653
Anabaptists doo penance and are burned, iii 807
———— Their heresies, recantation and penance at Pauls crosse, iv 326
———— Banished, iv 328
———— Burned in Smithfield, ib.
———— Manie in Amsterdam, iv 652
Analassus hath Northumberland giuen him, v 229
———— Fled into Westmerland, rifled the Ile of Man, and got him into Ireland, ib
———— ¶ Sée Norwegians
Anandale taketh his name of the riuer Anand, i 149
Ancarig or Crowland Isle, why so called, i 173.
Ancaster séemeth to haue béen a great thing, i 365
Anchors of wood cōmon to Gothlanders and others, i 7
Ancres bore great swav in time past in Ancarig, i. 171
Andates the goddesse of victorie worshipped of the Britains, i 517
Andragatius killeth Gratian by treason, i 537
Andredeschester, i 173
Andredecester, i 569.
———— A citie in Britaine, ib
Androgeus abandoneth Britaine because the people hated him as a traitor, i 479
———— Aided Cassibelane against Cesar, i 470.
———— Duke of Troinouant, i 476
———— ¶ Sée Earle
Andrew Boord writ of fantastical Englishmen, i 289.
Angell ¶ Sée Vision
Anger what mischiefes it procureth men vnto, i 733
—— What the heat thereof driueth a man vnto note, ii 365
—— ¶ Sée Enuie
Angiers citie taken, ii 274
———— Woone of king John by assault, ii 294
———— Repared by king John, ii 295
Angles one of the six nations that came with the Saxons into Britaine, i 9, 553, 556
Angles land one of the names of Britaine, ib.
Anglesie why so named, i 63
———— Cut from Wales by working of the sea, i 62
———— Lost in the conquerors time and recouered againe in William Rufus time, i 64
———— Fullie as great as the Wight, i 63
———— Inuaded by the Romans and wone, i. 194
———— Yéelded to Agricola, i. 505
———— Inuaded by Suetonius, v 71
———— Inuironed with the sea, ii 38
Angli, quasi Angeli, vol i page 591
———— Of authoritie in Germanie, i. 556.
Anglia, why so called, i 588
Angolesme recouered by the Frenchmen, ii 633.
Angus erle commeth into England, v. 713
—— Returned into Scotland, v. 726
—— Entereth Sterling, v 730
—— Sent into Scotland, v. 530
—— Committed to ward, v 535
—— His dissimulation, v. 555.
—— Put to flight, ib.
—— ¶ Sée Earle
Angus the thane of Galloway raiseth a commotion, discomfited, besieged, yéeldeth, becommeth a canon, v 291
Angusian king of Scots beareth king Arthurs sword before him in signe of homage, i 202
Angusianus with vpright dealing purchaseth the more friendship, vanquished, proclamed king, v 109
———— He, Fethelmarus, and Romacus, sons to three seuerall brethren pretend right to the estate, ib
———— Sueth for feare, v. 110.
———— In armes, ib
———— Slaine, ib
Aniou, a rode made thereinto by the duke of Clarence, iii 126.
Anna king of Eastangles slaine by Penda, i 620
—— His daughters professed nuns, i. 617
Annand deliuered vnto the gouernour, v. 634.
———— The church vndermined, v 552.
———— Blowne vp with powder, v 553
Annates forbidden to be paid to the pope, iii 775
Anne Askew and others arreigned and acquitted, iii 817.
Anne Bullen created marchionesse of Pembroke, iii. 776
Anne Bullen. ¶ Sée Quéene
Anne of Cleeue, a marriage betwéene hir and king Henrie the eight concluded, iii 810
———— She is receiued at Calis, landeth in Kent, the order of hir receiuing on Black heath, iii. 811
———— The meeting of hir and the king, hir chariot wherein she rode all hir iournie, hir welcome to Gréenewich, iii 813
———— She is married to king Henrie the eight, iii 811
———— At quéene Maries coronation, iv 6.
———— Deceaseth, iv 88
Annuities ¶ Sée Patents
Anselme archbishop of Canterburie elected, ii 33
———— Pretending an vnwillingnesse to be placed in the sée of Canterburie, i 224.
———— At strife with William Rufus and whie, ii. 40.
———— His shift for his paiment to William Rufus, and his honest satisfaction, ii 37.
———— ¶ Sée Archbishop
———— Prepareth to auoid the realme by ship, and

complaineth to the pope of William Rufus, vol ii page 43.
Anselme his admonition from Rome to William Rufus, returneth into England, ii 46
——— At the instance of Hugh earle of Chester commeth ouer into England, ii 47
——— Restored home, ib
——— Goeth to Rome, ii 53
——— Denieth to doo homage to Henrie the first note, ii 48
——— Holdeth a councell at Westminster note, and what was there decréed, ii 51
——— Refuseth to consecrat the bishops inuested by the king, ii 52
——— Banished, and his sée seized vpon into the kings hands, ii 53
——— Receiued into Henrie the firsts fauour and returneth home, ii. 56
——— Held a synod, and what was there decréed, ii 58.
——— Writeth to pope Paschall that he would not send archbishop Thomas of Yorke his pall, ii. 59
——— His cursse feared of king Henrie the first and his bishops, ii 62
——— He falleth sicke, ii. 60
——— His death, and what countrie man he was, ii 61
Antedating of the kings seale tresonable and so executed, iii 819.
Anthropophagi of the Irish in Britaine, i 10.
Anticipation. ¶ Sée Subsidie
Antigonus brother of Pandrasus taken prisoner, slain, i 438
Antimonie, i 397
Antipape, ii 813, 41, iii 46
——— ¶ Sée Fitzled, Pope, and Schisme
Antiquitie reuerenced note, the meaning of the proclamation, iv 416.
——— Presented vnto quéene Elisabeth at Norwich, iv 361, 393
Antiquities found in sundrie places of England, i 364, 365 366
Antoninus his thorow fares, i 418
——— In hope to be emperor concludeth a peace with the enimies, v 97.
Antoninus Pius emperor sendeth Lollius Urbicus to kéepe the Britains in order, i 514
Antwerpe, the first Scotish house there builded, v 349
——— Entered into by the Spaniards who plaied the cruell tyrants, iv 331
——— Interteineth the duke of Alanson right roiallie note, iv. 466, 467, 468
——— Reioiceth at the duke of Alansons comming, 463
——— ¶ Sée duke of Alanson
Anwicke castle woone by the English, v 282
Apeman enimie to yong children, i 382
Apostastasie ¶ Sée Idolatrie, and Sighere
Apparell of clergie men in England, i 233
——— And of the laie people, i 289.
Apparell of king Henrie the eight at his coronation, vol iii page 547, 548
——— Running at the ring, iii 556
——— Of him and his nobles going to méet Maximilian, iii 581
——— After the taking of Tornaie, iii. 586
——— Sumptuous at quéene Anne's coronation, iii. 780
——— Of the duke of Alanson whereat the French woondered, iv 474
——— Of William Rufus counted gorgious then, but now verie simple, ii 46.
——— Of Edward the second gorgious and triumphant, ii 553
——— Sumptuous of Richard the second, ii. 858.
——— Of sir John Arundell verie sumptuous, ii. 725.
——— Strange of prince Henrie, sonne to Henrie the fourth, iii 53
——— Gorgious of Richard the seconds court note, at the verie end of this storie, iii 62
——— Of Edward the fourth at an interview with the French king, iii. 339.
——— Sumptuous of the earle of Northumberland, iii 531
——— Sumptuous of the duke of Buckingham, iii 547
——— Of great estates, iii 590, 591.
——— Statelie in France at a tilt, iii. 607.
——— Of the earle of Surrie receiuing the French kings ambassadors, ii 257.
——— Statelie of the duchie of Brabant, iv. 472
——— Of the monsieur of Brabant, iv 468
——— Of the king of England and France at an interuiew, iii 617, 648, 619
——— Right gorgious in a shew, iii 539
——— Faire sutes giuen by king John and the archbishop of Canturburie to their seruants note, ii. 282
——— Disguised souldiers in womens apparell note, iv 192
——— Of women wherein a bishop disguiseth himselfe, ii 228
——— Costlie forbidden, ii 193
——— An act for it, ii 605, 678
——— Of a knight all not worth foure shillings, iv 21
——— Changed from robes to rags note, ii 788.
——— ¶ See Maske
Apparition ¶ Sée Uision
Appeales to Rome, ii 169, 233, 362, 368
——— Forbidden, &c ii 126
——— Of the prince of Wales before the French king, ii 687.
Appesleie a capteine mistrusteth himselfe, vi 410
——— He withdraweth the earle of Desmond, vi. 411
Appletrée ¶ Sée Gun.
Apprentises at what time admitted to fellowships of companies, ii 207

Aques besieged by earle Richard, Henrie the seconds sonne, vol ii. page 172
Aquitane full of warre, ii. 690
—— The graunt thereof to the duke of Lancaster reuoked, ii. 831
—— Recouered by the French, the dignitie and state of that dukedome, iii 236.
Arbitrement of eight graue councellors to end controuersies, i. 570
—— Of certeine graue persons in the strife betwéene William Rufus and his brother Robert reiected, and whie, ii 35.
Arbogaster a Goth slaieth Flauius victor Nobilissimus, i. 538
Arcadian dogs, i 390
Archbishop of Canterburies title and office at kings coronatiōs, &c i 222.
—— He crowneth the king, i 226.
—— Beereaued of his pall, i 240.
—— Of Yorks authoritie extended thorough out all Scotland, i 202
—— Fighteth against the king of Scots, i 212
—— Crowneth the quéene whose perpetuall chapleine he is, i 226
—— His chappell called Cawood, and the vse thereof, i 161.
—— Cranmer of Canturburie spitefullie abused as being thought an ostler, i 256.
—— Of London named Fastidius, i 48
—— Richard of Canturburie misliked exemption of clergymen from the court and councell, i. 227.
—— Robert of Canturburie a Norman, i 12.
—— Ambitious and malicious, i 222.
—— Expelled out of England, i 12
—— Aldelme of Canturburie, i 684.
—— Athelred of Cāturburie, i 678.
—— Athelnotus of Canturburie, i. 732.
—— Alured of Yorke, i 681.
—— Alfrike of Yorke, i 737
—— Allered of Yorke, i 742
—— Augustine the moonke of the English nation, i 793
—— Bertuald of Canturburie, i 642.
—— Brightwald of Canturburie, i 637.
—— Bosa of Yorke, i 636.
—— Ceadda of Yorke, i 625
—— Damianus of Cant i 620.
—— Deusdedit of Cantur ib.
—— Eaubald of Canturb i 656.
—— Edsinus of Canturburie, i 739
—— Elonthus of Canturburie, i 733
—— Elphegus of Canturb. murthered by the Danes, i 712
—— Egbert of Yorke note, i 644
—— Euethelme of London ambassador for Britains, i 563
—— Honorius of Canturburie, i. 609
—— he receiueth his fall, ib.
—— Iohn of Yorke resigneth, i 636.
—— Lambert of Canturb i 651
—— Depriued, i 646.
Archbishop Laurence of Canturb. ¶ Sée Laurence
—— Nothelmus of Canturb vol i page 644.
—— Oswald of Yorke, i 697.
—— Pleimund of Canturb i 675
—— Paul of Yorke receiueth his pall, i 609.
—— Robert of Canturburie, i. 741.
—— Siricius of Canturb i 705
—— Stigand of Canturburie an intrudor. note, i 747
—— Tackwine of Canturburie, i. 642.
—— Theodore of Canturburie created vpon condition, i 626.
—— Wilfride the second of Canturburie, i 641
—— Wolfhere, i 677
—— Wolstan of Yorke, i 688.
—— Resigneth, v. 454
—— Abused, depriued, put in prison, v. 451.
—— Sent vnto Rome, v 455
—— Of Glasgow dieth, v 468
—— Of S Andrews executed, v 650
—— Deceaseth, v 493
—— of Cashill like to be killed, vi 339
—— Aldred submitted himself to duke William, ii 1
—— ¶ Sée Aldred Anselme.
—— Arundell of Canturburie his answer for the clergie, he chafeth, the kings answer to him, iii 30
—— Baldwin of Canturburie exhorted men to go to war against the Saracens, ii 188
—— Deceaseth, ii 226.
—— Boniface of Canturburie vncle to quéene Elenor, ii 389
—— Described and how he came to be aduanced, ii 390
—— Courtneie of Canturburie his visitation, ii 828.
—— He excommunicateth of the Wiclenists: note, ib.
—— Authorised by the pope to leuie foure pence of the pound, &c note, ii 830.
—— Cranmer of Canturburie, iii 778.
—— ¶ Sée Cranmer
—— Edmund of Canturburie getteth him to Pontneie to remaine in voluntarie exile, ii. 383.
—— What caused him to depart England, his death and surname, reputed a saint, ib
—— Grindall of Canturburie elected, iv. 329
—— Deceaseth, iv 305
—— Heath of Canturburie his words vttered in the parlement house touching the proclamation of quéene Elisabeth, iv 155.
—— Lord Chancellor, iv 82.
—— Hubert elected of Canturburie, lord chéefe iustice, ii 242, 252
—— Complained of the pope, ii. 265
—— His words at the Coronotion of king John, ii 275.
—— Lord Chancellor to the mislike of some note, ii. 276.
—— Deceaseth, ii 292

Archbishop Lanfranke ¶ Sée Lanfranke
——— Langdon of Canturburie elected whiles two others were striuing for it, vol ii page 295
——— Neuill of Canturburie commended, ii 303
——— His conditions, ib
——— Parker of Canturburie deceaseth, iv. 327
——— His commendation, ib
——— A benefactor diuerse waies, iv. 328
——— ¶ Sée Parker
——— Rafe of Canturburies returne into England out of Normandie, i 69
——— Dieth, ii 71
——— Reignolds election of Canturburie bred much discord, ii 292
——— Richard of Canturburie receiueth his pall, ii 63
——— His consecration disturbed, ii. 147
——— His death and conditions note, ii 187
——— Robert of Canturburie accused by Edward the first to the pope, suspended, ii 540
——— Roger of Canturburie, ii 110
——— Sauage of Canturburie deceaseth, iii 538
——— Stephan of Canturburie deceaseth, ii. 362
——— Stigand ¶ Sée Stigand
——— Stratford of Canturburie in Edward the the thirds displesure, he writeth vnto him, refuseth to come to the court, ii 619.
——— Sudburie of Canturburie made lord Chancellour, ii 726
——— Theobald of Canturburie consecrated, ii 85
——— Deceased, ii 117
——— Thomas, ii 14 ¶ Sée Thomas Wethersheid elected to Canturburie, ii 362
——— Whitegift doctor of diuinitie, thankful for his aduancements, the armes of both sées which he inioied blasoned, his posie answerable to his propertie, iv 509, 580.
——— Made of the priue councell, iv 660
——— William of Canturburie, ii 71
Archbishop of Canturburie primate of Ireland, ii 38
——— Made the popes legat, ii 236
——— Besieged Marelburgh castell, ii 246
——— Flieth out of the realme, ii 101
——— Goeth to Rome, ii 67
——— Hath power legatine, ii 117
——— He and king William at contention and whie, ii 40
——— Capteine of an armie, ii 3
Archbishop of Canturburie put by from crowning the king, vol ii page 1
——— Accused of treason by the speaker in parlement, ii 539
——— Condemned to perpetuall imprisonment, ii 840
——— His words at a parlement in the behalfe of the clergie, that would be exempted from paieing of subsidies, ii 520
——— His goods confiscat, his obstinacie, ii 521.
——— Purchaseth a grant of the pope to leuie monie, ii 411
——— Restored to his sée, iii 8
——— His cursse, ii 416
——— He and Winchester made fréends, ii 427
——— Standeth against Henrie the third in defence of his clergie, at contention with the earle of Kent, appealeth to Rome, dieth in his returne from thense, ii 368
——— Readie to broch new contention, ii. 353
——— legat and lord chéefe iustice of England, ii 256
Archbishop of Yorke acknowledged primat of all Scotland, ii. 15
——— His subiection to the archbishop of Canturburie note, ii 15
——— Sent ouer to Guisnes to be kept in safe custodie, iii 329
——— Inconstant and variable note, iii 310, 311
——— A conspirator, he is in armes, iii 37.
——— Forbidden to be at Richard the firsts coronation, ii 218
——— The estimation that was had of him, his protestation whie he put on armes, ii 218
——— He and others arrested, put to death, reputed a martyr, iii 38
——— Of councell with the Persies conspiracie, iii 23
——— Made cardinall, resigneth his archbishoprike, ii 182
——— Crowneth Henrie the first and whie, ii 47
——— Depriued of his crosse, ii 105
——— Accurssed by the pope, his constancie note, ii 413.
——— Gouernour of the realme, ii. 396
——— Proud, deposed, and out of fauour with Richard the first, ii 255
——— Accused but to no purpose, ii 247
——— His presumptuous demeanor, ii 169
——— He and Elie reconciled by Richard the firsts meanes, ii 230

Archbishop of Yorke he and Durham at strife, vol ii page 231
——— Sicke and his place supplied, ii 84
Archbishop Geffreie bastard of Yorke, ii 206
——— Obteineth his pall, ii 226
——— Commited to prison note, ib
——— Depriued and whie, ii. 280.
——— Restored to all his dignities, ii. 283
——— Stealeth out of the realme, ii. 295
——— Deceaseth, ii 305.
——— Gerard of Yorke consecrateth the bishops of Henrie the firsts inuesting, ii 52
——— Receiueth his pall, ii 53
——— Deceaseth, ii 59
——— Greie of Yorke, ii 315.
——— Gréenwich, and what summes of monie the pope had from him, ii 542
——— Roger sent to the pope, ii 128
——— Forbidden the vse of the sacraments, ii. 130
——— Deceaseth, ii. 182.
——— Sands, iv. 110
——— ¶ Sée Sands.
——— Thomas sometimes Henrie the firsts chapleine and much adoo about his consecration, ii 59
——— Refuseth to come to Canturburie to be consecrated, ii 59.
——— Suspended, &c ii 60
——— Hath his pall sent him from the pope, ii. 61
——— Submits himselfe to Canturburie, note the forme, ib.
——— Dieth, ii 63.
——— Thurestine of Yorke, ib.
——— Restored vpon condition, ii. 69
——— Made lieutenant of the north parts, ii 83
——— In armes against the Scots, ii 83
——— Deceaseth, iv 233.
——— Of Cullen visiteth Beckets toome, ii. 186.
——— Of Rone chéefe gouernour of England, ii 229.
——— Of saint Andrews in Scotland receiueth his staffe from an altar, ii 69
——— A deadlie enemie to Henrie the eight, iii. 851
——— Of Vienna the popes legat not receiued as legat, and whie, ii 48
Archbishops appointed in Ireland, vi. 42, 95.
——— and their suffragans, vi 42
Archbishops striue for preheminence, v 461
——— Of S Andrewes, their catalog v 741
——— There authoritie at the first equall, i 226
——— Thrée in Britaine in times past, i. 221, 512.
Archbishops of London their names, vol i page 237.
Archbishops so manie as are extant to be had from the fith first receiued, i 247
——— Their authoritie exemplified note, i. 731
——— They fléeе with their clergie into woods and mounteins note, i 589
——— The sée of Canturb monks refuse, i. 626
——— The sée remoued to Lichfield, i 612.
——— Of Canturburie & Yorke with a decrée concerning their election, i 609
——— The sée restored to Canturburie, i 653
——— The sée of Canturburie void, i 651
Archbishops at contention for primasie note, ii 11
——— Decided by the king and bishops of the lands, ii 15
——— Sentenced by decrée of the pope, ib.
——— Go both to Rome, and whie, ii 53
——— At strife, ii 59
——— At strife for the primasie note, ii. 63
——— Thorough ambition, ii 67
——— Sue both personallie for their consecration to the pope, ib
——— At strife for a péece of seruice about king Henrie the first, ii. 73
——— At strife for carrieng of their crosses, ii 246.
——— Of Canturburies sée void foure yeares, and in Henrie the firsts hands, ii 63
Archbishops of Canturburie from the first to the last, their names and liues, &c. set downe in a collection, iv 660
Archbishops of England are in no respect to deale with the pope note, ii. 40.
——— Their authoritie notablie exemplified in Anselme note, ii 41
——— Their election annulled vpon good causes note, ii 362
——— Six at London in time of the parlement, ii 142
Archbishoprike of Canturburie void more than thrée yeares, ii 389
——— Uoid foure yeares note, ii 30
——— Let out to farme, ii 219.
——— Of Caerlheon vtterlie extinguished, i 222
——— Of London translated to Canturburie, i 221
——— Of Yorkes restitution, circuit, and valuation, i 214
Archbishopriks in France how manie, i. 234
——— Giuen to strangers by duke William, ii 14
Archdecons should be decons, ii 51.
——— Under bishops and called the bishops eies, their office, i 278.
——— Belonging vnto the bishoprike of London, foure, i 237
Archdeacorie of Canturburies iurisdiction, i. 236.

Archdeacōnie of S Albons, vol i page 237
Archdeconries not to be let out to farme, ii 51
Archer good was Henrie the eight, iii 556
Archer English of the Garrison of Cais, a notable peece of seruice against the enemie, ii 632
Archerie ¶ Sée Bowes
Archers of England driue the French from their siege, ii 622
—— Notable seruice against the Genowaies note, ii 633
—— Uictorious against the French, ii 640
—— Seruice against the Scots, iii 880
—— Fulfill a prophesie note, ii 665
—— Force against the French, ii 666
—— Worthie actiuitie, i. 679
—— Ualiancie against the Spaniards, ii 683.
—— Good seruice vnder sir Hugh Caluerlie, ii 724.
—— Under the conduct of a préest, ii. 760.
—— Shot killeth in a quarell, ii 766
—— Great seruice against the Spanish & French, ii 767
—— Good seruice against the Saracens, ii 810
—— In the time of a conspiracie note, iii. 12.
—— The greatest force of the English armie note, iii 79
—— Good seruice at Teukesburie field, iii 319
—— Good seruice vnder sir Humfreie Talbot, iii 494.
—— Good seruice against the enemies, iii 495.
—— Of the Cornish rebels, whose arrowes were in length a full cloth yard, iii 515.
—— Game made with laieng wast of gardens in Moorefield, iii 720.
—— A shew of two hundred in a mai-game before king Henrie the eight, iii 611, 612
—— Gall the French horssemen, iii 843
Archers Irish, iii 878
—— Discomfited, iii 875
—— ¶ Sée Inclosures
Archflamines (like bishops) cōstituted, i 198
—— Conuerted into Bishops, i 199.
Archigallus king of Britaine giuen to dissention, and depriued, i 460
Ard assaulted by the Englishmen, iii 35
Arden murthered by the meanes of his wife a notable whoore note, iii. 1024.
Arden ¶ Sée Sumeruill
Ardescoll towne burned, vi 240
Ardmagh enemie to rats, vi 41
Ardulfe made king of Northumberland and consecrated, i. 655.
—— His acts & déeds, ib
Areani, and their charge note, i 546.
Arelius Ambrose ¶ Sée Aurelius
Argadus is sent forth to apprehend rebels, v 91
—— Created lord president of the councell, ib
—— Chosen to gouerne Scotland, vpright, rebuked, confesseth his faults, permitted to continue in his office, and amendeth his former misgouernment, v 90, 91
—— Slaine by ambush v 94
Argathelia when first so named, vol v. page 37
Argentine sir Giles knight slaine in fight note, v 348
Argile, for Argathtle, v 125.
—— The earle at dissention with earle Huntleie, v 602
—— Infested by the Iland men, v 94.
—— ¶ Sée Argathalia
Arks besieged, iii 579
Arlete duke Robert of Normandies paramour, that bare him duke William the conqueror, and of hir pleasantnesse and daliance, i 761
Arlet duke William Conquerors mother the daughter of a burgesse, ii 33
Armach in Ireland, where the sée metropolitane is, ii 173
Armenia, the king thereof commeth ouer into England for aid against the Turkes, ii 768.
—— Sueth for a safeconduct to come into England, which is denied him, ii. 777
—— Would gladlie that a peace betwéene England and France should be concluded, ii 823.
Armetrida the wife of Hugh Lou earle of Chester, ii. 33
Armie called the armie of the God and the holie church, ii 320
—— Of able men that England can leauie, i. 333.
Armour and munition in England, io
—— Differing from that of other nations, and wherein it consisteth, ib
Armour and an ordinance for the same, ii 181.
—— ¶ Sée England
Armorie of the prince and of the nobilitie, i 334.
Armorica by whom first peopled, i. 537.
—— Giuen to Conan Meridoc, & the plot to people it disappointed, i 534
—— The etymon or reason of the name, i. 539.
Armorica in France where it lieth, i 445.
Arnalt knight his valiantnesse, iii. 907
Arnold sir Nicholas lord iustice, 6 325
—— Bred the best horsses in England, i 371.
Arnulfe ¶ Sée Ardulfe.
Arrane earle would exchang lands with Morton, v. 712
—— Flieth, v. 729, 730.
—— Breaketh his faith, v 533.
—— ¶ Sée Erle.
Arrogancie of Becket blamed, ii 132.
—— ¶ Sée Ambition and Pride.
Arasicide ¶ See Saracens.
Arthur begotten out of wedlock, i 575
—— Of whom begotten, i 571
—— He beginneth to reigne, i 574.
—— Of a mightie making, i. 577.
—— What is left written of him, i 579
—— He had two wiues, i 580
—— His exploits, i 576
—— His twelue battels against the Saxons i 574.
—— He is wounded and dieth, his buriall note, i 577
—— Held a parlement at Chester, i 125
—— His feast roiall held at Caerleon whereat were present all the king his subiects, i 202.

Arthur his bodie higher by two foot than anie mans that came to sée the feast roiall, vol i page 18
—— His last and fatall conflict, & where fought, i. 111.
—— Receiueth homage at Westchester for the realme of Ireland, vi 77, 187
—— The great whose sonne, v 150
—— Proclamed king of Britaine, v 153
—— Goeth foorth against the Saxons, raiseth a power against the Picts, ib
—— Returneth to London, v. 154
—— Discomfiteth the Saxons, vseth victorie with gentlenes, ib
—— Causeth churches to be repared, purposeth to destroie the whole race of the Saxons in Albion, his badge, his exhortation to his people, v 156
—— Upon conditions receiueth the Saxons vpon their submission, v. ib
—— His victorious conquests, v 159
—— His munificence, v 157.
—— He with thirtie thousand Britains slaine, v 161.
Arthur king of England receiued homage at Westchester for the realme of Ireland, vi 67, 187.
Arthur prince deceasseth, v 470
Arthur mac Morough discomfited by the earle of Ormond, 6 265.
Arthur made awaie by meanes of his vncle king Iohn, and whie, ii 12
Arthur the eldest and first son of Henrie the seuenth borne, iii 492
—— Had carnall knowledge with his wife, he is sent into Wales, iii 527
—— Deceaseth, iii 529.
Arthur Plantagenet created viscount Lisle, iii 686
—— Deceaseth in the tower, iii 823, 824
—— ¶ Sée Plantagenet
Arthur of Britaine ¶ Sée Duke.
Arthurs horse note, v 337.
Articles concluded at the synod of Cashill, 6. 163, 164
——— For gouernment, 6, 326.
——— For martiall law, 6 291.
Artificers diet, i 282
Aruiragus sendeth messengers to Uespasian, v 65
——— Giueth his enemies an ouerthrow, v 62.
——— Reuolteth, v 64
——— Would disinherit his owne children which he had by Uoada, promised aid to the Britons, v. 62, 63.
——— Restored to his former dignitie, v 65
——— Forsaketh his lawfull wife, v. 62
——— K. of Britaine, i 478
——— He surueieth this land & repareth the ruines of it, i. 484
——— His valiantnesse, ib.
——— In what state Britaine was in his reigne, i 502.
——— King of the Iceni, i 495.
——— He putteth the Romans to flight, i 484
——— He is most villanouslie abused by the Romans, i 495.
Aruiragus he is buried at Glocester, vol. i page 186
Arundell of the Strand his reuenues one thousand fiue hundred pound, 6 262
——— Castell besieged, ii 5.
——— Knight drowned, his excesse and sumptuous apparell, ii 725
——— Iohn archbishop of Canturburie fled to Rome for feare of his head, i 226
Arundell towne and the castell so named of the riuer Arun, i 93.
Asburga a gentlewoman maried to king Ethelwulfe, i 660
Asclepiodotus ¶ Sée Duke
Ash commeth vp naturallie of it selfe euerie where in England, i 358.
Ashbert protector or gouernor of yoong king Kenelme bribed, murthered his lord and maister, i 659
Ashton sir Richard lord iustice, 6 258.
Aske a notable rebell pardoned note, iii 803
—— He and others practise to raise a new rebellion, ib
—— He with his copartners is executed, iii. 804.
Asketen the earle of Desmonds house, 6. 418.
——— His house is besieged, 6 421.
——— Capteine Birklie late in garrison at his castle, 6. 439.
Aspe growing in England whereof fletchers doo make their arrowes, i 358.
Assaracus interteineth Brute, i. 438
Assassini ¶ Sée Saracens
Assemblies vnlawfull an act there against, iii 1021.
Asses none yéeldeth England, i. 370
Asserius Meneuensis bishop of Shirborne, i. 675.
Assise of bread published by proclamation note, ii 287.
Assurance giuen for loialtie by the lords of Ireland, vi 24
Astronomers deceiued, and how they excused their false predictions, iii 693.
——— Deceiued in their predictions, iv 510.
Asturians, i 479
Athaulfe and Alrike kings of Goths, v 120
Athelnotus archbishop of Canturburie, i. 736.
Athelon castell burned, vi 48
Athelon bridge builded, vi 246
Athelred Archbishop of Canturburie, i 678.
Athelstane chéefe priuileger of Berstable, i 112.
Athelstane K. of Britaine subdueth Scotlãd whole & gaue land thereof by déed, i 204.
Athelstane ouerthroweth thousands of aliens at Seton in Deuonshire, i 101
Athelstane base sonne to king Edward against the Scots, v 227.
——— Tooke Northumberland, v. 228.
——— ¶ Sée Adelstane
Athelstane king of Kent & duke Ealhere vanquish the Danes by Sea, i 661
——— ¶ Sée Adelstane
Atheniens, when they began their yeare, i. 410.
Athirco king of Scots regardeth not his nobles, abuseth a noble mans daughter, v 98.

Athirco conspired against, vol v page 99.
——— Killeth himselfe, ib
Atholl assigned to the Picts, v. 123
—— The earle made lord chancellor, v 086
Attaindors at parlement, i 262 iii 808, 823
——— ¶ Sée Treason
Atturnies multiplied how inconuenient, i 262
Atwater the bishops purpose in beginning to clense the Fosse dike, i 170
Aualon Ile now Alpes Ile, i 578
Audelie lord chéefe capteine of the Cornish rebels ignominiouslie drawne vnto Tiburne and executed, iii 504.
——— Slaine, iii. 251.
——— Knight lord chancellor, iii 777
——— Keeper of the great seale, iii. 776
Augustine the moonke his conuerting of the Saxons from paganisme, i 47
——— One and twentie hundred moonkes slaine in his quarell, i 62
——— Ordeined archbishop of the English nation, i. 593
——— His see at Canturburie, i 595.
——— He receiueth the pall, i 594
——— Surnamed the Englishmens apostle, i. 5'6.
——— He requireth thrée things of the Britains to be obserued, ib
——— His miracles, his acts and déeds, i 595.
Augustinus and Mellitus sent into Albion, v. 169.
Augustus the emperour, vi 124.
——— Is denied his tribute out of Britaine, his acts and déeds note, i 579
Aulafe K of Norweie baptized, i. 706
—— Banded with Danes & others maketh against Adelstane, discōfited, i. 687
—— Chased by king Edmund, he returneth into Northumberland & expelled by the people, i 691.
—— He taketh vpon him the rule of the Northumbers, i 689
—— Disguised he commeth to view the English campe, i 687
—— King of the Danes of Northumberland attempteth war against king Edmund, his death, i 689.
Aulus Atticus a Romane capteine slaine, i. 509
Aulus Didius sent into Britaine to supplie the roome of Ostorius, i 592.
——— Commeth into Britaine, v 70.
——— Dieth at London, v 71
Aulus Uictorinus lieutenant of Britaine, v 89
Aulus Plautius with his armie arriueth in Britaine, i 481
Auon riuer, and his course described, i 98
——— The third by sundrie occasions growne famous, i 115.
Auon or Nene riuer giueth Hampton his name, i. 171.
Aurelius Ambrosius & his brother Uter arriue in Britaine with their powers against Uortigerne, i 564.
Aurelius Ambrosius he and Uter Pendragon flée into little Britaine, vol i page 553
——— He with his Britains encounter the Saxons, i 571
——— He putteth Saxons out of Britaine, i. 565.
——— He falleth sicke at Winchester, i 566
——— ¶ See Uter Pendragon.
Aurelius Ambrose purposeth warres against the Saxons, v 147.
——— His oration, v 148
——— Proclaimed king of Britaine, ib
——— Hasteth foorth to London, by whose meanes he got the victorie as himselfe confesseth, v 148, 149
——— He and Uter sonnes to king Constantine, v 144
—— Falleth sicke of a consumption, deceaseth, v. 150
Arelius Conanus made king of Britaine, & described, i 583
——— He killeth Constantine, i ib
——— He is noted by Gyldas to be a verie bad man, i 582
Auricular confession. ¶ Sée Confession
Authoritie ¶ Sée Magistrates
Authun ¶ See Berthun
Auxerre citie taken by sir Robert Knols, ii. 670.
Ax riuer in Summersetshire described, i. 101
Ax riuer the secōd described, i 115.

B.

Babington and his confederats ¶ See Traitors.
Bacchanalia, v 154
Bacon knight lord keeper deceaseth, iv. 346.
——— His epitaph in Paules, ib
——— ¶ Sée more of him, iv 374
——— ¶ Sée Chancellors.
Bach a capteine, v 559
Badbie his notable constancie, iii 48, 49
Badge of the bright sunne the earle of Marches badge, iii 270
——— Of the earle of Warwike worne in euerie mans cap note, iii 302.
——— Of Richard the second, ii 857
——— Of Quéen Elizabeth note, iv 382
——— Of King Arthur, v 156
Badges a bill against the wearing of them, ii 809.
Badgers in Englād, i 379.
Badon hill, i 571
Bagnoll sir Nicholas complained against by Baltinglasse, he beareth the sword, vi 398, 399.
——— A bill is exhibited against him, vi 399.
——— The matter of a bill against him examined, ib.
——— He is in the hosting with sir William Drurie, vi 413
Bagot knight and prisoner discloseth the secrets of trouble, iii 4, 5
Bailiffes office, i 261.
——— First that bare rule in London, ii 207.
—— ¶ Sée London and Officers
B[illegible]ds castell, when and by whom builded, i 329.

Bainards castell new built, vol. iii. page 525.
Baion yéelded to the Englishmen, ii. 506.
Bakers sell bread lacking six or seuen ounces weight in a penie lofe, ii. 488.
——— Punished by the pillorie, ii. 448.
Baldred vsurped the kingdome of Kent & departeth into exile, i. 659.
——— ¶ Sée Ualdred.
Baldud. ¶ Sée Bladud.
Baldwin earle of Flanders commethe into England to visit Edw. 3. his brother in law, i. 742.
——— Earle of Flanders aided duke William to conquer England,
Baldwine archbishop of Canturburie, i. 380.
Baledgar castell finished, v. 286.
Bales writing within the compass of a penie, v. 330.
Balford sir Iames submitteth himselfe to the regent, v. 669.
Balic martyr castell taken, vi. 365.
Balimore in Leimster burned, vi. 343.
Balioll his line and title to the crowne, v. 323.
——— Crowned, v. 367.
——— His resignation to Bruse, v. 357.
——— Commeth into England, his promise to the king of England, landeth in Scotland, v. 366.
——— Withdraweth into England, v. 380.
——— He hath all the fortresses of Scotland in his hands, foure excepted, v. 371.
——— Resigneth his right, and whie, to Edward king of England, v. 386.
——— Promiseth and dooth homage to king Edward, v. 327.
——— He answerth a sute commensed against him in the parlement of England, as an inferior person, v. 327.
——— Resigneth all his right to king Edward, v. 330.
——— Kept as prisoner in England, ib.
——— His returne into Scotland, renounceth the administration, ib.
——— Goeth to France, ib.
——— Dooth homage for his earldome in Ireland, vi. 240.
——— Obteineth the kingdome of Scotland, ii. 498.
——— The forme of his fealtie to the king of England, ib.
——— His homage, ii. 499.
——— Crowned king of Scotland, ib.
——— Chased out of Scotland, ii. 600.
——— Doth homage to Edward the third, ii. 601; v. 330.
——— Departeth this life, ii. 58.
Baltinglas. ¶ Sée Poer.
Balram lord of Eufort his reuenues one thousand and thirtie pounds, vi. 268.
Banbourgh. ¶ Sée Castell.
Bangor bishopriks erectiõ, circuit, and valuation, i. 244.
Bangor abbie, vi. 86, 87.
Bangor monastrie now ploughed grouned, i. 141.
Banke of Chesill and the strange nature thereof, i. 100.
Banket roiall: note, vol ii. page 439; iii. 590.
——— Of two hundred and thrée score dishes, iii. 634.
——— Of two hundred dishes vpon the sudden, iii. 756.
——— Of thirtie or fortie dishes and not one of them fish nor flesh, iv. 200.
——— Fatall, i. 556.
Banketing house of French king described, iii. 634.
——— Of Henrie the eight in his palace at Guisnes, iii. 648, 649.
——— Within the town of Calis, iii. 655.
——— At Westminster builded, iv. 434.
——— How garnished and decked, iv. 434, 435.
——— The costs and charges thereof, iv. 435.
Bankerupts practise, iii. 568.
Banishment of bishops and other English in duke Williams time, ii. 13.
——— By whome ordeined, ii. 57.
——— For twelve moneths, ii. 465.
——— Of the earle of Cornewall out of the realme, ii. 549.
——— Perpetuall, ii. 796.
Banister the duke of Buckinghams seruant receiueth the duke in perill of life into his house, iii. 416.
——— Bertaieth him into the hands of his enemies for monie, Gods secret iudgements vpon him and his children: note, iii. 418.
Banne and Begabunne, vi. 2.
Banne the riuer, vi. 40.
Banneret, vi. 57.
——— An order of knights, i. 273.
Bannocksborne whie so named, v. 344.
Banquho a vanisher of the Danes: note, v. 268.
——— The father of manie kings, v. 268, 269.
——— Slaine, v. 271.
Baptisme without préests, i. 72.
——— Ministered to a great fort at once, i. 76.
——— Of bondmen and bondwomen and making them frée, i. 631.
——— How gratious being receiued: note, ib.
——— Receiued of the British armie and how beneficiall, i. 563.
——— At the ministring thereof godfathers were in vse, i. 616.
——— Ministred to ten thousand in the riuer of Suale, i. 593.
——— Eglered defiled the font with his ordure when he was baptised, i. 703.
Bardi, their vsage and profession, i. 430.
Bards and whervpon they had their name, i. 36.
——— Degenerate from their first institution, ib.
——— A name contemptuouslie ascribed to idiots and fooles, i. 37.
Bardus the son of Druis, ib.
——— The fift king of ye Celts, i. 36.
——— A Celtik word and what it signifieth, i. 37.
Barie Robert his valiantnesse, vi. 131, 140.
——— Philip nephue to Fitzstephans, vi. 206.

Barre Girald Cambrensis, vol vi page 206.
—— His issue remaineth in Ireland, vi 206
—— Og sweareth fealtie, vi 365.
Barkeleie Edward arriueth into Ireland, vi 439
——— He lieth in Askeren, ib.
Barnabie Fitzpatrike baron of Upperossorie taketh Rorie Og and killeth him, vi 397
——— He and the earle of Ormond are reconciled, vi 442
Barnabées daie kept holie daie all London ouer, iii 1024
Barnacles, nor fish nor flesh, vi 18, 20
——— Generation verie strange, i 374
——— Great plentie in Mona and Ireland, being neither fish nor flesh, i 66
——— Their generation by diligent inquirie partlie knowen, i. 67
Barnard of Newmarch a Norman, ii 28
Barnes doctor and two merchants of the Stilliard did penance at Paules crosse for heresie, iii. 711
——— For a sermon inuectiue against bishop Gardiner, asketh him forgiuenesse iii 815.
——— He and others executed, iii 818
Barnet towne how seated, iii 312
Barnet fielde ¶ Sée Battell
Barnet & Sullomain all one or not far in sunder, i 322
Barnewell baron of Trimelston, vi 55
——— He deliuereth the kings sword to the deputie, vi 299
——— Of Beere hauen his reuenues one thousand six hundred pounds, vi 262
——— Sir Christopher, a wise and a learned knight, vi. 55
——— He excepteth against the Englishmen to be burgesses, vi 343
——— Offended with the speech of an English gentleman in parlement, vi. 345
——— Is commanded to silence, vi 345
Barnwells first arriuall in Ireland, vi 55.
Baro a word yet in vse, and commonlie pronounced Barnes, i 264
Barod lord of the gard his reuenues one thousand and one hundred pounds, vi 262
Baron whereof he beareth his name, & his dignitie, ib
—— Who is so created, i 266
—— Chéefe lord of excheker, i 265
Barons in England how manie, i 277.
—— Foure under the earle of Chester, ii 33.
Barow riuer, vi 207
Barretors taken and put to death, v 232
David lord iustice burneth his own house, vi 441
——— He is set vpon by capteine Raleigh, vi. 442
——Iland went fiftie yéers ago for ten pounds, i 128
——— Of certeine strange noises to be heard at a rift thereof, i. 217
Bartholenus inhabiteth Ireland, vol vi, page 74.
Barton the Scotish pirat, ii 730
——— Incountereth the lord Howard, he is slaine, iii 565
Basilia earle Strangbowes daughter married to Reimond, vi 182
—— Hir dreame, vi 191
Basreeg ¶ Sée Halden
Bassianus borne of a British woman ruleth Britaine, i 518
——— He practises with physicians to poison his father Seuerus, ib
——— Entereth into Westmerland, v 105.
Bassinatas, v 217
Baston Robert a Carmelite note, v 344
——— His verses, v 349
Bastard of Burgogne ambassadour into England, iusts betwixt him and the lord Scales, iii 285.
Bastard to a king made a bishop, ii 172.
Bastards made legitimat, ii 834
——— Made kings as Alfrida king of Northumberland, i 635
——— Morindus admitted to rule Britain, i 458.
Bataui now Hollanders, i 544
Bath taken by the bishop of Constance, ii 28
—— It and Welles when and by whome vnited, ii. 46
—— Of Dullerdstowne executed, vi 298.
—— How called in the Romãs time, i 321.
—— Of the ancientness of the same, i. 361.
—— And Welles counted but one citie, i. 319
—— Bishoprikes election, circuit, and valuation, i. 388
—— Called Carbadon, i 449
—— Besieged by the Saxons and Germans, but ouerthrowne and slaine, i 575
—— ¶ Sée Caerbran
Baths hot when first made or repared and by whome, i 446
—— Their number, names, and colour of their water, &c i 362
—— Whether naturall or artificiall, i 361, 362.
—— Cold in Summersetshire, i 360
—— ¶ Sée Welles.
Battell first on the water that euer was fought, i. 6
—— Cruell betwéene Hercules, Albion, and Bergion, &c i 74.
Battell on Bloreheath ¶ Sée Bloreheath, Conflict, & Warre
—— Of Deglaston, v 167
—— Of Folkirke note, v 333.
—— Of Witton vpon Swale, v 353.
—— Of Blackborne, v 379
—— Of Poitiers, v. 387
—— Of Shrewesburie, v 406.
—— Of Otterborne, v 399.
—— Of Bauge, v 412
—— Of Harlow, v. 410.
—— Of Piperdan, v 425
—— Of Banocksburne, v 459
—— Fought against James the fourth note, v 481.

Battell of thirtie against thirtie: note: vol. v. page 402.
—— Betwixt fishes, ii. 390.
—— Of herrings, iii. 163.
—— Betwixt flies and gnats, ii. 797.
—— Their slaughter, ib.
—— ¶ Sée Warres.
—— Of Agincourt, iii. 78.
—— At Barnet, iii. 312.
—— Of Bloreheath, iii. 251.
—— Of S. Edmundsburie, ii. 156.
—— Of Northampton, iii. 260.
—— Of Palmesundaie, iii. 277.
—— Of Saxton. ¶ Sée Palmesundaie.
—— At Hedgcote or Banberie, iii. 291.
—— At Exham, iii. 281.
—— At Teukesburie, iii. 319.
—— The first at saint Albons, iii. 240, 241.
—— At Wakefield, iii. 268.
—— Of thrée long houres betwéene the English and French, great losse on the English side, iii. 165.
—— Second at saint Albons, iii. 270.
—— Of Mortimers crosse, iii. 269.
—— Of Uerneull, iii. 141.
—— Of Ferribrig the thirtéenth of March, one thousand foure hundred thrée score and one, wherein twentie thousand were slaine, most knights and gentlemen, iv. 277.
—— Betwéene duke William and his sonne Robert: note, ii. 19.
—— Betwéene the Danes and Normans verie fierce, ii. 11.
—— Begun with praier: note, ii. 637.
—— Of Kenils crosse, ii. 644.
—— Of Aubroie, ii. 679.
—— Of Sluise where the English where victors, ii. 614.
—— Of Banokesburie, ii. 553.
—— Called the white battell and whie, ii. 558.
—— Of Boroughbridge,
—— Of Comeran in Ulster, ii. 554.
—— At Dunbar betwéene the English and Scots in Edward the first time, ii. 516.
—— Betwéene the earle of Lincolne and the earle of Arthois, ii. 521.
—— Of Fowkirke, ii. 530.
Battell betwéene Henrie the third and his barons: note, ii. 461, 462.
—— Of Euesham, ii. 466.
—— Of Chesterfield, ii. 469.
—— Betwéene king Richard the third and the earle of Richmond, Bosworth field, iii. 443.
—— At Stoke néere to Newarke betwéene the earle of Lincolne, &c. and Henrie the seuenth, iii. 487.
—— Of saint Aulbin in Britaine betwéene the duke of Britanie and the French king, iii. 491.
—— At Blackheath, iii. 515.
—— Of Spurs, iii. 585.
—— Of Pauia, iii. 697.
—— At Muckleborow. ¶ Sée Leith and Scotland.
—— Staid by Gods prouidence: note, iii. 802.
—— Of the bridge of Bouins, ii. 317.
Battell sharpe and bloudie betwéene duke Robert and Henrie the first brethren, vol. ii. page 55.
—— Thrée things to be foreséene by them that shall give it, ii. 90.
—— Of Monadmore in Ireland, ii. 101.
—— Of Ashdon fought betwéene K. Edmund Ironside and Cnute with his Danes, i. 723.
—— Of foure houres continuance betwéene the English and the Danes, ib.
—— At Ardmagh against the Scots, vi. 251.
—— At Knocktow, vi. 270.
—— Against the giants, vi. 201.
—— Ground, v. 457.
—— Abbie, why so called and by whom built, ii. 25.
—— Church to what saint dedicated, ii. 35.
—— Abbie roll, ii. 5, 6, 7, 8.
Baulbason a French knight valiant fighteth with Henrie the fift hand to hand, iii. 121.
Beasts wild deuour rulers of Britaine, i. 445.
—— Sauage in England, i. 378.
—— Uenemous, i. 382.
Beatrice put to death hir stepsons for poisoning hir husband, i. 685.
Beauchampe Henrie crowned king of Wight, &c. i. 56.
Beaumont. ¶ Sée Strife.
Beautie a snare to intrap: note, i. 555.
—— A bait, and also a deadlie baine, i. 695.
—— Abused to a shamefull end, i. 740.
—— It helped not to saue life, i. 713.
—— Edgina most excellent, i. 682.
—— ¶ Sée Ronise.
Becket Thomas archdecon of Canturburie, ii. 110.
—— Lord chancellour, ii. 111.
—— Sent into France, ii. 114.
—— His and Henrie the seconds first falling out, ii. 116.
—— His authoritie, ii. 117.
—— A better courtier than a preacher, ib.
—— Practiseth secret treason, ii. 118.
—— Receiueth an oth, ii. 120.
—— Repenteth him thereof and would haue fled the realme, ib.
—— Cited to appéere the king and sentence against him, ib.
—— Condemned in fiue hundred markes, ii. 121.
—— Called to an account, ib.
—— Will not be persuaded to submit himselfe to the king, appealeth to Rome, goeth to court, is reputed a traitor, and disallowed to be archbishop, ii. 121, 122.
—— Writieth proudlie to king Henrie the second, i. 224.
—— His stout courage, ii. 122.
—— His flight by night, ii. 123.
—— His complaint to the pope, ii. 124.
—— Resigneth his pall, ii. 125.
—— His cursse, ii. 127.
—— An edict against him, ii. 126.
—— Six yéears in exile, ii. 131.
—— His arrogance and wilfulnesse in opinion, in fauour with the French king, reconciled to

Henrie the second king of England, vol. ii page 132, 133
——— Is aduised by the French king, returneth into England, is complained of to Henrie the second by the archbishop of Yorke, he is killed, ii. 133, 134, 135, 136
——— His death discussed, ii 141
——— The king purgeth himselfe of his death, ii 143.
——— Canonized a saint, his holie daie and collect for the same, ii 146
——— His toome visited by the French king, ii 178
——— His toome visited by the archbishop of Cullen, ii 186
——— His shrine visited by the earle of Flanders, ii 264
——— His sword in the ministration of an oth, ii. 523
——— His shrine taken awaie and his dead bones burnt, iii 807
Becons and the vse of them in countries néere the sea, iii. 732
Beda a famous préest and where he was brought vp, i. 154
—— Where he was borne and dwelt, ib
—— The first doctor that euer was in Cābridge, i. 256.
—— Dieth, diuerse things noted concerning him, i 643.
Bedford castell besieged, i. 356.
——— Deliuered to the barons, ii 320
Béere and the maner of brewing thereof, i. 285.
—— What water best to make it, i 280
—— March béere, i. 282
—— ¶ Sée Ale.
Bées how ingendered, i 384, 620
—— ¶ Sée Honie
Beggers termed idle, who they be, i. 308
Bele doctor an vndiscréet and seditious preacher, iii. 619.
Belesme. ¶ See Erle
Belforrest his opinion touching the name Anglia, i 9.
——— Maketh but foure parts of the earth, i 3.
Beline and Bren made fréends, i 454.
——— ¶ Sée Brennus
——— Part the whole empire betwixt them, i 197
Belinesgate, i. 320
Belins gate (now Billingsgate) whereupon the ashes of Belins bodie were kept in a vessell of brasse, i 456
Belinus his sonne claimed Ireland by descent, vi. 76
Bell of S Fllutus note, i 697
——— Generall of Cassibelans armie valiant, i 470
Bell a seditious préest arreigned, condemned, his prophesie, his sermon to the rebels, his seditions, his execution at saint Albons, ii 749.
Bell roong at eight of the clocke at night by whom appointed, and whie, vol. ii page 9.
—— ¶ Sée Chime
—— Vsed in battell caused terror note, i 478
Bell castell assaulted and yéelded vp to the English, iii 688
Bellingham sir Edward, lord deputie, vi 323
——— He keepeth a mint, ib
——— His carefulnesse for his gouernment, ib.
——— His readinesse to serue, ib
——— He builded a fort at Leighlin, vi 323.
——— He taketh the earle of Desmond napping, vi 324
——— He carrieth the earle of Desmond to Dublin, and causeth him to be nurtered and instructed, ib
——— The earle of Desmond alwaies praied for him, vi 324
——— He was neuer chargeable to anie subiect, ib.
——— His vprightnesse and sinceritie, ib.
——— Was verie well beloved, ib
——— Is reuoked, ib
Belman ¶ Sée Common criei.
Benbrike doctor poisoned at Rome, iii 610.
Benedict bishop the moonke, i 315
Bendish Hall confined from the Bendishes by the moonks of Feuersham, i. 179
Bendishes gentlemen of an ancient and seruisable house, ib.
Benefices bestowed, v 487
——— Belonging to strangers their valuation taken, ii 408.
——— The value of them in strange hands, iv 427.
——— Bestowed without consent of patrons, ii. 386.
——— Impropriat, ii 371
——— With request to the pope that would not meddle with reseruations, ii 700, 701
——— Inhibited by the king and how. note, ii. 626.
——— The best in strangers hands, ii 627
——— A proclamation that all Englishe beneficed men in Rome should returne into England, ii 813
——— ¶ Sée Abbies, Bishops, Churches, Clergie, Pope, Sequestration
——— In England so small that they will not mainteine a scholar much lesse a learned man i. 229
——— Diuerse waies flesed, i ib. 230
——— Tenths paid out of thē yearly to the prince, i. 323
——— Two by dispensation how they may be held, i 229
——— A direction for patrons to bestow them well in yē vicanage, i 251
——— ¶ Sée Ministers.
Benefit of good gouernment, vi 326
Beneuolence granted to Edward the fourth, iii 694.
——— Put into Henrie the seuenths head to be leuied ouer the whole land, iii. 532.

Beneuolence an exaction of monie of whose deuise, vol. iii page 496
——— ¶ Sée Subsidie
Beneuolence of the French king to the earle of Richmond note, iii 120
Beningfield knight his churlish vsing of the ladie Elisabeth his prisoner and in his kéeping, iv 129.
——— He is too streict and seuere in his office against the ladie Elisabeth, iv 128
——— He grudgeth at the genle intertemement of hir, his rude and vngentle behauiour, iv. 56.
——— His cruell dealing towards hir, iv. 131
Berebeating on sundaie reuenged by Gods iust iudgment, iv 504
Berds shauen, and rounded haire in vse with the Normans, ii 8
Berengaria daughter to the king of Nauarre, king Richard the firsts wife, ii 219, 220
Bergion brother to Albion kept Ireland and the Orkneis, i 453
——— Reigned ouer the Orchades as supreme lord, i 7
——— He and Albion slaine by Hercules, ib
——— ¶ Sée Albion
Bericus expelled out of Britain, his counsell to Claudius, i 481
Berill in vse of glasse for windowes, i 316
Berkhamstéed castell surrendered, ii. 342
Berking, and who built the abbeie there, i 630
Berklie sir Dauid knight, slaine, v 255.
Berne iudge burned for crueltie, i 651
Berne an earle maliciouslie slaine by his cousin, i 742
Berne a noble man about Yorke, the rauishing of whose wife bred much mischéefe, i 668
Berne K of Estangles, i 641
Bernicia otherwise called Northumberland, i 202.
——— ¶ Sée Bernicia and Northumberlãd
Bernred by murther vsurpeth the kingdome of Mercia, he is slaine, i 640
Bernhulfe of Mercia slaine, i 657
——— He stomacheth king Egbert, i 658
Berstable towne somtime walled with foure gates note, i 112.
Bertha a towne drowned by inundation, v 203
Bertha king of Cheriberts daughter wife to Ethelbert king of Kent, i 590
Berthfride a valiant Northumber capteine, i. 641
Berthun a duke of Sussex slaine, i 634
Berrockshire now Barkeshire, i 666
Bertie, husband to the duchesse of Suffolke attached by bishop Gardiner note, iv 104
——— ¶ Sée duchesse Katharine of Suffolke
Bertwald archbishop of Canturburie, i 642.
Bertwolfe K of Mercia tributarie to the Westsaxons, chased out of his countrie by the Danes, i 663
Berwike vpõ Twéed by whom builded, i 198
Berwike yéelded vp to ye king of England without resistance, i 213
——— Woone by the Scots but not the castell, i 212
Berwike woone by king Henrie, vol v page 307.
——— Besieged, defended against the English, their policie to win it, v. 328, 329
——— Besieged, v 353
——— Deliuered to the Scots, v 447
——— Recouered by the Scots, v 352
——— Woone with shedding of much bloud note, v 329, 386
——— Rased, v. 386
——— Repaired againe by king Edward, ib
——— Taken by Scots, and recouered, v. 392.
——— Besieged, v 392
——— Yéelded to king Edward the third, v 371
——— Assieged by an armie of English, v 453
——— The castell taken, ib
——— ¶ Sée Danes and Gregorie.
——— Fortified, ii 550
——— Taken by the Scots, ii 657.
——— Besieged, ii 600
——— Surrendered, ii 601
——— Betraied to the Scots, ii 556
——— Summoned and woone by Edward the first, ii 513
——— Fortified by Edward the first, ii 515
——— Chéefie regarded, iii 692
——— Yeelded to Henrie the fourth, iii 39
——— The castell woone by the Scots, ii 761
——— Recouered by the earle of Northampton, ib
——— Woone by the Scots, ii 721
——— Recovered by the earle of Northumberland, ib
——— Woone by the Scots, recouered by the English, ii 716.
——— The capteine thereof will not suffer the duke of Lancaster to enter, ii 751
——— Deliuered to the French king and of him possessed, iii 279
——— Woone by the Englishmen, iii 350
——— Deliuered to lord Stanlie, &c. iii. 352
Beston ¶ Sée Castell
Beton James archbishop of S Andrews dieth, v 515.
——— Dauid forgeth the kings will, v 529.
——— The protestants espie his iugling, v 530
——— Committed to ward, ib
——— He is murthered, v 546
Betrice Henrie the thirds daughter borne, ii 398
Beuchamps iournie to the holie land against the Saracens, ii 37
——— His valiantnesse, ii 151
Beuclerke Henrie why so called, ii 25.
Beuer no where to be found in Britaine, but in ye riuer Teifie, i 135
——— His hinder féet and tail supposed to be fish, i 379
Beuer castell to whom it appertemed, ii. 326
Beuerlie how called in old time, and how it came to the present name, i 158
——— Towne burned, ii 196
——— Iohn the first doctor that euer was in Oxford, i 253
——— First teacher of diuinitie in Oxford, i 154

Beaumont vicount his daughter married vnto the Scotish king, vol i page 190
——— Discomfited by the Scots, ii 555.
Beaumont lord of Heinault note, ii 595, 596
——— Forsaketh the king of Englands seruice, ii 579, 631
——— Lord high constable of England, iii 211
Bible in euerie church commanded to be read, iii 806
——— The necessarie vse and benefite thereof, iii 959
——— Presented to quéene Elisabeth which she promiseth the citie often to read ouer, iv. 166
Bigod Roger his spoiles and booties, ii 28.
——— Hugh sometime steward to Henrie the first, ii 79
——— Knight procureth a commotion, iii 803
——— Apprehended and executed, iii 803, 804.
Bignorke archbishop of Dublin, vi 251
——— He dooth erect an vniuersitie in Dublin, ib
——— He képeth termes and commensements, ib.
Bilneie burned, iii. 775
Bingham sir Richard cheefe commissioner in Connagh his great victorie vpon the Scots, vi 458
Birds ¶ Sée Fowles.
Birinus a bishop Italian conuerteth the Westsaxons to the christian faith, i 616
Birmingham sir Walter slue six hundred men, vi 259.
Birmingham Iohn generall of the field against the Scots, vi 250.
——— He vanquisheth them and killeth Edward Bruse, vi 251
——— Made baron of Athenrie, and erle of Louth, ib
——— Is made lord iustice, ib
——— Is slaine, ib
Birmingham Richard ouerthroweth the Irish in Connagh, ib
Birmingham Meiler sleieth Cathell Ochonner, vi 261
Biscop a moonke builded two abbies, and what artificers he brought into England that were not in it before, i 629
Bisi. ¶ Sée Bishop
Bishop first of the Ile of Man, i 67
——— But a bishops shadow, and why, ib
Bishop of Orchades whose sée is at Pomona, i 76
——— Of Shireburne slaine in the battell of Athelstane, i 101
——— Of Winchester perpetuall prelat to the honourable order of the garter, i 237
——— Of Aberden a builder, v. 490
——— Deceseth, v. 481
Bishop Adam of Cathnesse slaine by the people, note, v 309.
Bishop Acca of Hexham, i 641
——— Adelstan of Shireburne of K Egberts councell, i 661
Bishop Adelwold of Winchester, vol i page 710
——— Aldhelme bishop of Shireburne, i 642.
——— Alfin of Winchester, i 697.
——— Asserius of Shireburne, i 655
——— Adrian an Italian of Hereford, Bath and Wels, iii 195
——— Agelmarus ¶ Sée Agelmarus
——— Alexander ¶ Sée Alexander.
——— Anthony of Durham, summoned to appear before Edward the first, refuseth, the conclusion of the strife betwéene him and the moonk, ii 512
——— Athelmarle Henrie the thirds halfe brother bishop of Winchester, ii 419
——— Of S Andrews made archbishop, primat and metropolitane, v 451
——— Taken, v 731.
——— Of Bueux earle of Kent, v. 280.
——— Bisi of the Eastangles, i. 629
——— Bonifacius of the Eastangles, ib
——— Brightelme of Dorchester, i 697.
——— Beauchampe of Salisburie is sent to the duke of Yorke, &c to know the lords meaning that were vp in armes, 251
——— Beaufort of Winchester sonne to Iohn duke of Lancaster, iii 146, 147
——— Otherwise called the rich cardinall, deceased, and described, iii 212.
——— Camelgaret taken prisoner of the Danes, and redéemed by K. Edward, i 697.
——— Cedda of the Eastsaxons, i 621
——— Christianus ¶ Sée Christianus
——— Cox of Elie deceaseth, his epitaph, iv 416.
——— Coifi in armes on horsbacke destroieth idols, i 607
——— Colman of Northũbers, i 624.
——— Cutbert of Lindesferne, i 635.
——— Of Dunblane deceased, v 614
——— Of Durham in armes against the Scots, v. 399
——— Daniell of Winchester, i. 642.
——— Diuma first bishop of Mercia, i 623.
——— Dunstane of Worcester and London, i. 695
——— Edhidus of Lindseie, i 631.
——— Eata of Hexham, i 636
——— Edmund of Shireburne slaine in battel, i. 667
——— Eadulfus of Litchfield, adorned with the pall, i 646
——— Egwine of Worcester, i 640
——— Elutherius of Westsaxons, i 612
——— Elphegus of Winchester, i. 704, 706.
——— Erkenwald of the Eastsaxons, his sée at London, i 629
——— Ethelwold of Winchester, i 696.
——— Egelwinus. ¶ Sée Eglewinus
——— Ermenfred ¶ Sée Ermenfred
——— Finan of Northumbers, i 624.
——— Fisher of Rochester complained of to king Henrie the eight, iii. 745
——— Beheaded, iii 793

Bishop Foliot of London ambassador to the French king, vol ii page 123
——— Fox of Durham owner of Horham castell, iii 516
——— Of Excester ambassadour into Scotland, iii. 489
——— Of Winchester, iii 617
——— ¶ Sée Corpus Christi college.
——— His wisedome in procuring the clergie to be contributors of monie for Henrie the seuenths behoofe, iii 532
——— Gardiner bishop of Winchester ambassador into France, iii 795
——— ¶ Sée Gardiner.
——— Geffreie of Lincoln king Henries base sonne, ii 172
——— His letter to the archbishop of Canterburie, he resigneth his bishoprike, ii. 180
——— Gifford of Winchester refuseth to be consecrated at the archbishop of Yorks hands, and therefore banished and depriued, ii 53
——— ¶ Sée Gifford
——— Godfreie of Winchester sonne to the lord Richard de Lucie deceaseth, ii. 291
——— Graie of Norwich lord lieutenant of Ireland, ii 302
——— Graie of Norwich president of the councell, ii 293
——— Grosted of Lincolne deceased, his praise, ii 430
——— Harvie first bishop of Elie, ii. 61.
——— Horne of Winchester deceaseth, iv. 106
——— Hugh of Lincolne his bold courage to king Richard the first, ii. 249.
——— Deceaseth, a description of his doings, and life presumptuous, ii 281
——— Admitted into the number of saints, ii 282
——— Of Coventrie restored to his sée, ii. 255
——— Iewell of Salisburie deceaseth, iv 262
——— Lisle of Elie and the ladie Wake at variance, ii 671
——— Longchampe of Elie the popes legat, his statelie port, ii 223
——— Depriueth bishops, meaneth to keep earle Iohn low, besiegeth the castell of Lincolne, raiseth his siege with dishonour, breaketh agreements concluded, ii 123, 124
——— Lord chancellor of England, ii 209.
——— Morton of Elie commended, iii 430.
——— Buildeth vpon the dukes ambition, iii 406
——— Deuiseth to be at his owne libertie in his bishoprike of Elie, he saileth into Flanders to the earle of Richmond, iii 413
——— What pagents he plaid, the high honour wherein he was placed, his subtill vndermining of the duke of Glocester, iii 404.
——— Defeated the practises of king Richard the third and Peter Landoise, iii 434
Bishop Morton abureth duke Richard to release the realme by some deuise from the present euill estate, vol iii page 407
——— A new conference betwéene them, iii 408.
——— Made archbishop of Canturburie, cardinall and lord chancellor, iii 488
——— Odo ¶ Sée Odo
——— Osmond ¶ Sée Osmond
——— Pecocke of Chichester abiured at Paules crosse note, iii 245
——— Peter of Winchester gouernor of king Henrie the third, ii. 349
——— Rafe of Durham his warlike exhortation, ii 84
——— Ralegh of Winchester consecrated by the pope, he stealeth out of the realme, he giueth to the pope six thousand marks, ii 400
——— Ranulfe ¶ Sée Ranulfe
——— Remelid of Hereford inuested by the king. note, ii 52
——— Remigius. ¶ Sée Remgigeus Sée Remigius
——— Richard of London translated to the Archbishoprike of Canturburie, ii 63
——— Roger of Salisburie put in trust with the gouernement of the realme, ii. 77.
——— Ruthall of Durham, one of king Henrie the seuenths priuie councell, his booke of priuat affaires vnaduisedlie deliuered in stéed of the kings, disaduantageable to himselfe, iii 540, 541
——— He died with griefe, iii 541.
——— Samson of Worcester the mouth of the bishops, ii 61.
——— Tunstall. ¶ Sée Tunstall
——— Wainfléet of Winchester founder of Magdalen college in Oxford, iii 213
——— Walkhelme ¶ Sée Walkhelme
——— Walkher ¶ Sée Walkher
——— Walter of Alba bringeth Anselme his pall. ii. 43
——— ¶ Sée Walter, ii I
——— Waltham of Salisburie buried at Westminster among the kings, ii 230
——— Warlewarts words to the pope Paschall in behalfe of Henrie the first, ii 53
——— Watson of Winchester deceaseth, iv 533
——— Wickham of Winchester remembred and commended note, iii 32, 33.
——— Made lord chancellor, ii. 790
——— William ¶ Sée William
——— Wolstane ¶ Sée Wolstane.
——— Ebmound of Rochester, i 630.
——— Ieroman is sent to the Eastsaxons to reduce them to the faith, i 627.
——— Lincolne slaine in the battell of Ashdon, i 726
——— Oswald of Worcester, i 695
——— Pitts of Rochester a good musician, i 626
——— Of Rochester and king Egelred at strife, i 704
——— Seibulfe of Mercies, i. 623

Bishop Swithune of Winchester of king Egberts councell, vol i page 661
——— Tida of Northumbers, i 625
——— Waldher of London, i 630.
——— Werefridus of Worcester, i 675
——— Wilfrid of Northumbers his diligence, i 625
——— William of London banished, i 747
——— William the poor bishop of Rochester, i 630
bishop not disgraded and yet liuing a priuat life, i 626
——— None of Westsaxons for the space of seuen yéeres, i 663
——— A kings son and heire a bishop, i 663
——— One ioineth his power to Adelstans armie, is slaine by the enemie, i 67
Bishop of Beauuois taken prisoner, ii 261
——— An aduersarie to Richard the first, two of his chapleins come to Richard the first to intreat that they might wait vpon their maister, but are denied, ib.
Bishop of Carleill bold and faithfull, commended, iii 5
——— The first was a prior and the kings confessor, ii. 75
——— Of Constance with others taketh Bath, ii 28
——— Of Couentrie committed to prison, ii 546
——— Of Dublin made archbishop, ii 101.
——— Of Durham created an earle, ii 207.
——— Besieged the castell of Tickhill, ii 246
——— Lost his earledome, ii 249
——— Restrained of his libertie, ii 212
——— Chiefe ruler of the north parts, ii 209
——— He and earle Patrike at strife, ii 278
——— By letters asswageth the Scotish kings displeasure, hée goeth into Scotland, iii 521.
——— Of Elies taking vp of horses to k. Richard the firsts vse, ii 212
——— Summoned to appeare at Reading, his returne to London, a declaration against him, he yéeldeth vp the tower, ii 227
——— His letter to the shiriffe of Kent, ii 226.
——— Disguiseth himselfe in womans apparell, he flieth, is betraied, and committed to prison, complaineth of his wrongs to the pope, ii 228
——— He deceaseth, ii 262
——— Of Elie imprisoneth archbishop Geffreie of Yorke, ii 227
——— Arriueth in England as a simple bishop, ii 241
——— Sent ambassadour to the emperour, ii 256
——— Banished, ii 86
Bishop Blind of Excester sent to Rome from Henrie the first, vol ii page 63
——— Put in charge with the citie of London, beheaded by the Londoners, ii 681
——— Hereford arrested for treson, ii 575
——— His deuise to get monie of the bishops, ii 131
——— Of Ireland elected out of England, ii 36
——— Of Léege murthered, ii 242
——— Of Lincolne visited abbeies, and is suspended by the pope, ii 246, 121
——— Capteine of a band of men, ii 50
——— Of London taken vp with reproachfull words, and reuenged by the Londoners, ii 705
——— His palace, where Richard second kept open house, ii 811
——— His stout words to an earle, ii. 784
——— Made lord chancellor, ii 755
——— Ambassadour to the emperour, ii 291
——— Deane to the archbishop of Canturburie, ii 60
——— Of Norwich in armes against the antipope, ii 756, 757
——— Couragious and warlike, ii 760.
——— Setteth forward with his armie, and inuadeth Flanders, ii 757
——— The order of his battell against the Flemings, ii 758
——— His disobedience punished, ii. 762
——— His armie of fiue hundred footmen and manie horsmen, ii 305
——— Returneth out of Flanders into England, ii 761
——— Of Rosse an enmie to the English estate, iv 537
——— Of Salisburies men and the Londoners in a riot, he maketh a great complaint of them to the king, ii 818
——— Made lord chancellor, ii. 86
——— Dieth for thought, ib
——— Of Whiteherne consecrated. ii 206.
——— Of Winchester lent Henrie the fift two hundred thousand pounds, iii 128
——— Made a cardinall, iii 156
——— Legated and vnlegated by the pope, iii 166, 167.
Bishop earle of Kent, ii 21
——— Capteine of an armie, ii 12
——— Wiped of fiue thousand pounds by William Rufus note, ii 31
——— Depriued of his staffe by the king, ii 35
——— ¶ Sée Herbert.
——— One reuengeth anothers death, ii 20
Bishop of Rosse taken in Germanie, v. 690.

Bishop of Rosse his testimoniall left with the duke of Bauier, vol v. page 690
—— Wardlaw inueigheth against superfluous fare, v 422.
—— —— Died of greefe, v 452.
Bishop and his clerks, certeine dangerous rockes, so named, i 133
Bishops and bishoprikes in Ireland, vi. 42, 94.
Bishops married were onelie made archbishops, vi. 87
Bishops of Limericke committed to ward, vi 429
Bishops in their ancientie as they sat in parlement An. 5 reg. Elisab i. 78
—— They preach diligentlie, though their predecessors in times past were occupied in temporall affaires, i 227
—— They are called honorable, and lords, i. 265
—— Greatlie esteemed in times past, i 365
—— Their liuings fléesed, & sundrie actions of theirs against this spitefull age defended, i 233
—— Italians fiue succéeded each other in Worcester sée, i 239
—— Of Durham sometimes earls Palantine, i. 244
—— Of Lichfield for a while called bishops of Chester, i 240
—— Of London so manie as are extant to be had from the faith first receiued, i. 247.
—— Thrée chiefe in Britaine, v 42
—— Preferred from the pulpit to the keeping of the kings wardrobe, i 240
—— ¶ See Clergie
—— Authoritie exemplified note, i 621.
—— Went to war & aid the king, i 658.
—— Foure of Mercies, i 624
—— Two notable in Ethenwulfes daies. note, i 661
—— Two elected in place of one, i 630
—— Prosperouslie conduct British host against the Saxons note, i 562.
—— Of Northumbers held their see at Lindesferne, i 624
—— Two elected and consecrated for one, i. 629
—— Creat archbishops, i. 625.
—— How to be ordered, i 594.
—— Ordeined for auoiding the pope's displesure, i 683
—— What maner of men they haue béene, i. 747
—— In Britaine twentie eight, i 512
—— What prouinces they gouerned in 731 yeares, i 642
—— ¶ Sée Synod
—— First sée in Scotland, v 107
—— Foure erected, v 288
—— Twelve in Scotland, v 151.
—— How manie, v 28
—— Summoned to a conuocation at Northampton, v 399
—— Their death, v 541.
Bishops chosen principall iustices of the realme, vol ii page 199
—— Sent ambassadours to the French king, ii. 195
—— Forbidden the vse of the sacrament, ii 130
—— Disallow archbishop Thomas Becket, ii 122.
—— Thinke to please God in breaking their oth, ii 79
—— Of Man first and second, ii 101
—— Threatened, ib
—— In suspicion to be disloiall, ii. 86.
—— Inuesting doone by the kings of England, ii 19
—— ¶ Sée William Rufus
—— At strife about crowning the king, and saieng masse before him, ii 62
—— Translation from sée to sée, ii 61
—— Of priuie councell and ambassadors at Rome, ii 53
—— Fiue consecrated by Anselme in one daie, ii. 57
—— Inuestitures giuen awaie from the king by the popes sentence, ii 53.
—— Of a late election Salisburie and Hereford, ii 51.
—— Depriued by the bishop of Elie, ii 223
—— Contentious and ambitious, ii 209.
—— Elected and consecrated, ii 206.
—— Quarell with the moonks of Canturburie, ii 293
—— Thrée dead in one yeare, iii 526.
—— Restored and others depriued, iv 2.
—— Trauell to make peace, ii. 457
—— Would rather become martyrs than lose their monie, ii 436
—— Practise to disappoint the archbishop of Canturburie of his purpose, ii 120
—— Readinesse to resist the Saracens, ii 362.
—— Ambassadors, ii 354
—— Cannot tell what to saie in the contention betwéene king William Rufus and Anselme: note, ii 41, 42
—— Of Ireland their names and sées, ii 38
—— Seditious and ranke warriors, ii 28
—— In fault that duke William was king of England, ii 1.
—— Submit themselues to duke William, ib.
—— Sworne to be loiall, ii 2
—— Flie into forren lands and countries, ii 9.
—— Sées remoued from small towns to cities of more fame, ii 19
—— In arms against rebellious earls, ii 18
—— Of Scotland consecrated by the archbishop of Yorke, ii 15
—— Of Excester from the first to the last set downe in a catalog, iv 406
—— Six receiue the communion, iv. 186
—— Depriued, & others succéeding, iv 181
—— Sée Ambition, Archbishops, and Consecration.
Bishoprike of London why called honorable, i 248.

Bishoprike in the Ile of Man and whose donation, vol i page 216
——— Of Carleils erection, ii 75
——— Of Elie first erected, ii 61
——— Of Lincolne void seventéene, ii 128, 189
——— Of Waterford in Ireland erected, ii 37
——— At Donwich, i 609
——— At Dorcester, i 616
——— Two made of one, i 612.
——— Two vnder one bishop, i 695
Bishoprikes in England their elections and their severall circuits, &c i 245
——— Their tenths & to what sums they yearlie amounted, ib
——— Under the sée of Canturburie twentie one, and Yorke, foure, i. 227
——— They beare the names of cities, and why, i 323
——— Ouerthrowne and now out of name, which in old time were famous, i 246
——— Bought and sold as other meaner liuings, i 231.
——— Thrée thorough out all this land, i 199
——— How manie in England with archbishoprikes, i. 319
——— In Wales their erection, circuit, & valuation, i 245
——— In France how manie, i 234.
——— Bestowed by king Henrie his gift thought insufficient, ii 52
——— Bought of king William Rufus, ii 35
——— Let out to farme, ii. 43
Bishopsgate new builded, iii 345.
Biskains and Englishmen togither by the eares, iii 570
Bitumen, i 397.
Blacke Agnes of Dunbar a manlie woman, v 378
Blacke Will a notorious murthering ruffian, iii 1025.
——— Receiueth ten pounds in reward for murthering of Arden, iii 1028
——— Burnt at Flushing, iii 1030
Blacknesse and of what bredth the sea is there, i 5
——— Betraied, v 665.
——— A hauen towne on the south shore of Scotland, iii 884.
Blackheath field, iii 515
Blackwagon that followed euill Maie daie, iii 625
Blackwell hall in old time called the temple of peace, i 451.
Blackwell knight smothered to death in a throng, ii 548
Bladud the ninth ruler of Britaine, i. 446
——— Presuming to flie is dasht to péeces with a fall, ib
Bladus king Orkneie killeth himselfe, v 57
Blasing starre, ii 353, 435, 479, iv. 132, 458
——— Of thrée moneths continuance, i. 630, v 445.
——— What ensued note, i 631, 692.
——— Séene in England or the of seuen daies continuance, i 757.
Blasing starre the yeare before Edward the third, death note, vol i page 751
——— Two, one appéering in the morning, the other in the euening, and what insued, i 612
——— Of fourtéene daies appearance, v. 295, 296
——— Séene at noone daies, v 321, 322
——— With fierie rnes, v 217
——— Uerie terrible, v 305, 306.
——— Two verie dreadfull, v 203
——— Of strange appéerance, ii. 63
——— With other strange sights, iii 19
——— Uerie dreadfull for thurtie daies space togither, ii 390
——— In the north of a moneths continuance, ii 574
——— With long and terrible streames, ii 605.
——— Appéering in a faire & cleare daie, ii 19.
——— ¶ Sée Comet and Starre
Blasphemie of pope Iulie against God, iv 77
——— Of a popish preacher seuerelie punished by God, iv 78
——— Punished, v 225
Blecca gouernor of the citie of Lincolne, i 609
Bledenke duke of Cornewall, i 509
Bleothgent king of Wales partaker with a rebell, ii 8.
Blewbeard, capteine of rebels, iii. 220
Blockhouses ¶ Sée Castels
——— And bulworks builded, iii 808
Bloreheath field, iii 251
Bloreheath battell betwéene Henrie the sixt and the duke of Yorke purposed, but not executed, i. 119.
Bloud stone, i. 402.
Bloud rained, i 118.
Bluet Robert bishop of Lincolne note, ii 31
Blunt knight, his notable seruice against the French, iii 56
Boarinke lands and whie so named, v 287.
Boclough the lard enterpriseth to take the king from the erle of Angus, v 502
Bodgers suborned and licenced note, i 340.
Bodinus and whense he deriueth the name Albion, i 6
——— Put to flight, v. 502.
Bogdale the reson of the name, v. 125
Boghan castell surrendered, v 634
Bohune Iohn, his wife and issue, ii 33
Boid lord, beareth all the rule about the king, v 449
——— Accused, refuseth to be tried by waie of arraignment flieth into England, passeth to Denmarke, his vain hope to obteine pardon, goeth into Italie, is murthered, v 449, 451
Boise seruant to the erle of Kildare his pretie request, vi 274
——— His adage Antragh, Too late quoth Bois, vi. 301.
Boier maior of Bodmin in Cornwall hanged note, iii 925

Boldnesse. ¶ Sée Magnanimitie, and Words.
Bolton prior of S. Bartholomewes builded an house at Harrow on the hill to auoid floods prognosticated that yeare, vol. iii. page 693.
Bonagh a wicked Irish imposition, vi. 269.
Bondage. ¶ Sée Seruitude.
Bondmen made truly free, i. 631.
——— By letters reuocatorie disfranchised, ii. 748.
——— Letters of manumission called in, ii. 750.
Bondslaue in honor, i. 504.
Boner bishop of London emploied about the controuersie of Henrie the eights unlawfull marriage, iii. 767.
——— Beareth with the enemies of the L. Elisabeth, iv. 136.
——— His god was the rood of Paules, iv. 63.
——— Writeth to cardinall Poole concerning persecution, iv. 144.
——— Head broken: note.
Bones of dead men of greater statue thā is credible found in Godmancester, i. 173.
——— ¶ Sée Giants.
Bonifarius a godlie preacher, v. 171.
Bonifacius bishop of Eastangles, i. 629.
Bonifacius B. of Mentz his epistle to Ethelbald, i. 640.
Bonneuile lord Iohn slaine at Ardscole, vi. 245.
——— Is buried at Athie, ib.
Bookes anie waie impairing the popes dignitie are forbidden, iv. 83.
——— Seditious scattered, and the offendors executed, iv. 505.
——— Printed and the printer executed, iv. 511.
——— Popish dangerous and damnable to read or listen vnto, iv. 579.
——— Seditious published against the state, and the offendors executed, iv. 620.
——— ¶ Sée Libels.
Boorne doctor preaching at Paules crosse hath a dagger throwne at him, iv. 3.
Bores nature, & how he is to be hunted being wild, i. 380.
——— Tame made brawne, i. 373.
Borsholder, i. 259.
Borthwicke capteine accused of heresie, v. 516.
Bosa archbishop of Yorke, i. 636.
Bosworth field. ¶ Sée Battell.
Botes guided by the ferrymen by a rope without ores, i. 100.
——— What number of them & water men are kept and mainteined vpon the Thames, i. 82.
——— Made of rushes and reeds, i. 7.
Bothwell erle made chancellor, v. 731.
——— Conuicted, v. 508.
——— Banished the realme, ib.
——— Flieth, v. 613.
——— Escapeth out of prison, ib.
——— Set at libertie, v. 552.
——— He keepeth himselfe in ambush at Haltwell Sweire, v. 585.
——— Returned home, v. 613.
Bothwell erle hurt with a caliuer, vol. v. page 619.
——— Murthereth the king, ib.
——— Cléered from the murther of the king, v. 620.
——— Taketh the quéene by force, ib.
——— Diuorced from his wife, ib.
——— Marieth the quéene, ib.
——— Flieth to Dunbar, v. 625.
Bothwell Adam deceasseth, v. 468.
——— ¶ Sée Erls.
Boudicia. ¶ Sée Uoadicia.
Bounarme with his ten spears all at once about him, iii. 607.
Bourat castle destroied in Thomond, vi. 245.
Bowes long of great vse sometimes in Englād, i. 333.
——— ¶ Sée Archerie.
Bowes Rafe. ¶ Sée Iusts triumphant.
Bowes sir Robert knight, sent into Scotland, v. 689.
——— Inuadeth the borders, v. 526, 527.
Bow stéeple builded, iii. 574.
Brabanters and the reason of their name: note, ii. 170.
——— Ouercome by earle Richard, Henrie the seconds sonne, ii. ib.
——— The number of 20000 reteined by Henrie the second to beare armor, ii. 150.
Brabeston vice treasurer bringeth sir Walter dela Hide and his wife to Dublin, vi. 302.
Brachara. ¶ Sée Eathelus.
Bracklie sometime a noble towne, now scarce a good village, i. 171.
Brackwort, i. 285.
Braie knight of garter commended, iii. 530.
Brambre knight executed with an ax of his owne deuise, ii. 794.
Brandon knight standbearer to the earle of Richmond slaine, iii. 444.
——— Knight his pompe at iusts, iii. 559.
——— He is created vicount Lisle, iii. 574.
Brawne of the bore, wherein note the termes, i. 373.
——— A meat not vsuallie knowne to strangers, ib.
——— Eaten in Lent by a papist that tooke it to be fish, ib.
Bread whie it holdeth not ovt the size, i. 283.
——— Of diuerse sorts, ib.
——— Not looked vnto either for ẏ size or stuffe, i. 339.
——— Made of bran and puffens, iii. 952.
——— Made of ferne rootes, iii. 193.
——— ¶ Sée Assise.
Breame. ¶ Sée Bruistar.
Brechus the first crowned king of Scots in Ireland, v. 37.
Bremicham towne by what artificers chieflie mainteined, i. 164.
Bren Obren in Mounster discomfited, 6. 253.
Bren maried the duke Alobrogs daughter, i. 453.
——— He and Beline ioining forces take Rome, i. 454.

Bren and Beline their ioint gouernment intollerable, vol i page 452.
Brendon the abbat, vi 86
Brendon the name of the chiefe Irish lawiers, vi 57
——- What matters he doth determine, ib
——- The Brehons law giuen ouer ib
Brenicii kingdome when it began, i 583
Brennicia, alias Northumberland, a kingdome, i 29
—— Whereof it sometime tooke that name, i 153
Brennich riuer whereof Brennicia kingdome tooke ẏ name, i 150
Brennus king of Britaine called into Ireland, vi 76
Brereton capteine of the aduenturers taken and slaine, iii 693
Brereton sir William arriueth at the Houth in Ireland with 250 soldiers, vi 299
——- He summoneth the castle of Mainoth, vi 300
——- He scaleth and entereth the castle and setteth vp the kings standard, ib
——- He is made custos and keeper of Dublin, vi 301
——- He is made lord iustice, vi 313
——- He inuadeth Oconhors countrie and discomfiteth the Irish rebels, ib
——- He compelleth them to submission and to put in pledges, ib
——- He is made lord marshall of Ireland, ib
——- He is sent to fetch in the earle of Desmond, ib
——- He dieth by the waie, and was buried at Kilkennie, ib
——- He skirmished with Fitzgerald, vi 302
Brereton blockes neuer séene but against some mischéefe to befall to that house, i 115
Brest yéelded vp to the duke of Britaine, ii 834
—— Besieged by the duke of Lancaster, and the maner how, ii 769
—— Force intended against it, iv 117
Bretamous castell beyond sea built by the Britons, i 526
Brethren at strife and banded one against another, i 450
——- Slaine, ib
——- At dissention, vi 205.
——- At deadlie hate & pursuing one another, ii 55
——- Set at variance by factious persons, ii 54
——- In armes one against another, ii 31
——- Forces vnited how valiant and effectuall in warre, ii. 10, 11.
Brethrens mutuall crueltie, v 324
Briake in Britaine assaulted and taken, iii 16
Brian sir Francis lord iustice, vi 324
—— He marrieth the countesse of Ormond, ib
—— He died and was buried in Waterford ib
Brian mac Cahir Cauenagh breaketh out in wars against Wexford men, vi 372
—— They follow and pursue him, ib
—— He submitteth him selfe, ib
—— His parentage, ib.
Brian mac Cahir Cauenagh marrieth the daughter Hewen mac Schan, vol vi. page 372.
—— His strength and power, ib
—— He is a follower to sir Peter Carew, ib
—— He was a wise man, ib.
—— He died, ib
Bribe of fiue hundred markes giuen to come to the popes presence, ii 158
Bribes the ouerthrow of lawes & good orders note, iii 657.
—— Of a iustice seuerelie handled for taking them, ii 421
——- Hinder the execution of good orders & statutes note, ii 652.
——- Refused, ii 31
Briberie how it tempteth mens minds note, ii 620
—— ¶ Sée Gifts and Rewards
Bricke burning a decaie of wood, i 394
Bride or Briged base daughter to Dubtactus, vi. 85
—— She is deliuered to a Pet or a magician to be trained vp, ib
—— Is instructed in christian religion by S. Patrike, ib
—— Hir great iudgement and estimation, ib.
—— Hir answer to the king, vi. 85, 86
—— She professeth virginitie, vi 86
—— She died and was buried at Down, ib
—— The concordance of the foure euangelists found amongst hir monuments, ib
Bride riuer mouth naturallie placed betwéene two hils, fit for a hauen, i 100.
Bridge of London a continuall stréet situate ouer ẏ Thames, i 82
——- Of Rochester by whome begun and by whome finished, i 91
——- Uske ouerthrowne by the rage of a riuer, i 127
Bridges made with hard shift, iv 97
—— In England borne downe with land-floods, ii 65
—— ¶ Sée Floods
Bridgenorth besieged, ii. 50.
Bridewell a place which Henrie the eight put to vse at plesure, iii 713, 714
—— Henrie the eights new palace, a place receiuing noblemen, iii 678
—— The maior and aldermen enter and take possession thereof, iv 82
—— When it became a place to punish vagrant and lewd persons, iii 1061, 1062.
Brigantia now Compostella, v 34.
Brigantines ¶ Sée Ordouices.
Brigants now Yorkshire, disdaine to be subiect to a womans gouernment, i 493
Brightnod earle of Essex gaue battell to the Danes, slaine, i 705
Brighthelme bishop of Dorchester, i 697
Brightrike K of Westsaxons, i 652
——- His policie to rule quietlie, ib
——- Marieth Ethelburga K Offas daughter, i 646
——- His dcth, i 654.

Brightwold chosen to be archbishop of Canturb vol i page 637.
Brinchild a prince of Henaud his valiantnesse, i 145
Bristow taken by the earle of Glocester, ii 83
——— ¶ Sée Faire
——— How called in the Romans time, i. 321
——— Bishoprike thereof, erection, circuit, and valuation, i 213
Britaine whether an Iland at the first or no, i. 427.
——— Gouerned by lieutenants and treasurors of Romane emperours, i 487
——— Diuided from Scotland by the emperor Adrian note, i 514
——— Gouerned by British rulers, i 437.
——— First inhabited by the Celts, i 428.
——— Rulers and kings bitterlie inueied against by Gyldas, i 582, 583.
——— The state of it during Aruiragus reigne, i 502
——— Afflicted by the inuasion of barbarous nations, i 549
——— Spoiled pitifullie by Eurmudus, i 588
——— Kings thrée of it slaine in one battell at once, i 587.
——— The state of it vnder Marius, i 503.
——— Ruled by women, i 141.
——— Gouerned by kings of their owne nation, i 458, 459, 460, 461
——— Gouerned by fiue kings at once, i. 550
——— The state of it vnder kings, i 451, 452, 453, 454
——— In France, i 535.
——— So called by cōmandment of the subduer, i 443
——— It receiueth faith note, i 486
——— Diuerse people inhabiteth diuerse portiōs of it, i 461
——— Diuided into realms, i 461.
——— Unknowne to the Romans but by report, i. 465.
——— Whether the kings of it were kings or rulers of the commonwelth or tyrants, &c. i. 464.
——— A part of it called Ualentia, i 546
——— The success on of the kings thereof orderlie in their yeares to Elourus, i 461
——— Of whom first inhabited, i. 427.
——— Pentarchie, i 450
——— Sometimes called Samothea, i 429.
——— The subiection of it to the Romans when it was, i 477
——— A monarchie how long after Brutes death, i. 471
——— The state of it touching gouernment when Cesar did conquer it, ib
——— The state of it vnder rulers, i. 454, 455, 456, 457.
——— It tasted the crueltie of Dioclesian, &c i. 527
——— It receiueth the faith, i 512
——— The state of it vnder British kings, i. 531.
Britaine was the first name of England & Scotland, vol iii page 912
——— ¶ Sée Earles
——— When not cut frō the maine by Noahs floud, i 379
——— The first conquest therof, i 6.
——— The gospell preached there and by whome, i 10.
——— Diuided by the Romans into fiue prouinces, i 30
——— The manifold alterations and cōuersions of the estate therof since the time of Samothes, i 49
——— How it lieth from the maine, i 4.
——— Unto what portion of the earth it is referred, ib
——— Why called Albion (as some cōiecture), i 6
——— Ships wrought of wicker sometime vsed in it, ib
——— The kings therof from Samothes to Brute, and so forwards, i. 31, 32, 33
——— Of Paules presence there, i. 10
——— It hath néed of no nation but of itselfe, i. 398
——— Subdued by Iulius Cesar, i 199
——— Edgar king thereof rowed in a barge by six or seuen kings, i 206
——— Inioied by Brute & his posteritie during two and fiftie descents, i 196
——— Why named the great, i 199
——— The soucreingtie thereof how it remaineth to the princes of the same, i. 196.
——— Of the people there, their constitution of bodie, age, &c i 193
——— How first diuided into thrée portions, i. 195
——— Generallie commended in an ancient monument, i 188
——— The foure high waies sometime made in it by the princes of the same, i 189
——— The aire, soile, and commodities thereof, i 183
——— Under the Celts thrée hundred and fourtie one yeares, i 6
——— The distance of it from the maine, i 5.
——— The name of it knowne to some of the Gréeks, i. 9.
——— The longitude & latitude thereof, i. 4.
——— A long while called Samothea, i. 6
——— The anciēt names of it, ib.
——— Promontories thereof, i 5
——— The forme of it thrée cornered, i 4
——— Uariance among writers about the cōpass therof, i 5
——— A parcell of it inhabited sometime by the Irish, i 10
——— Pestered with manie sorts of people, i 11
——— What sundrie people and nations setled themselues in it, i 9, 10, 11, 12
——— Called Angles land by an edict, i 9
——— Ilāds to be séene vpon the coasts of it, i. 52.

Britaine the first prouince that receiued the gospell generallie, vol 1 page 45
——— Into how manie kingdoms it hath bin diuided, 1 26, 27, 28, 29
——— What nations came with the Saxons into it, 1 11
——— At the first one intire kingdome, 1 26
——— How soone inhabited after the diuision of the earth, 1 6.
——— The differing opinions of men touching the name of it, ib
——— Whether it were sometime parcell of the maine, ib
——— How long it was called Albion, ib.
——— Deliuered of a tyrant by Hercules, 1 7.
——— ¶ Sée Albion, England, Picts, Romans, & Scots.
——— Inhabited with the Picts, vi 79
——— It is halfe bigger than Ireland, vi 1.
Britaine erle of Richmond and lord warden of Scotland commanded to suppresse the templers, vi 244
Britains plagued by the lord admerall, iii 571, 572.
——— Repine to be gouerned by men of base degrée, 1 414.
——— Commonlie called Welshmen, 1 638
——— The sauge sort, their vsage & attire note, 1 517
——— Outrageous crueltie hauing gotten victorie against the Romans. note, 1 500
——— Their lamentable case after ouerthrow by I Agricola, 1 509
——— They, the Scots, and Picts in a league, 1 532
——— They of Caledarwood assault the Romans vpon aduantage, 1 507
——— Their miseries manifold note, 1 491
——— They go to Rome and complaine of Perhennis to Cōmodus the emperor, 1 514
——— What practices Agricola vsed to traine them to crueltie, 1 505
——— Skilfull in swimming, ib
——— Admitted as well women as men to publike gouernment, 1 496
——— Readie to defend their countrie against Cesar, 1 466
——— They refuse to paie tribut to Augustus, 1 479
——— Their maner of fighting in chariots, 1 168
——— Susteined a sore oue throw at the hands of Scapula, 1 191
——— Persecuted by the Scots and Picts, 1 541
——— An armie of them newlie christned, 1 562
——— They choose a place of aduantage to encounter the Romans, 1 189
——— The ridiculous voiage of Caligula attempted against them, 1 480
——— Driuen by Romans out of their wood of refuge, 1 472
——— Plagued by the Saxons from time to time at appointment of God for their foule sins, 1 585
——— Made tributarie to the Romans, 1 175
Britains at contention among themselues after the death of Lucius, vol. 1 page 513
——— By consent giue rule of all things in the wars to Cassibelane, 1 472
——— Pursued by Centwine K of Westsaxons by fier and sword, 1 682
——— Defended the christian faith euen with the sheding of their bloud, 1 529
——— Their fiercenesse against the Romans, 1 167
——— Not all vanquished by Cesar, 1 447
——— They send to Cesar about a treatie of peace, 1 466
——— Utterlie disabled by Plautius and his power, 1 482
——— Their maner of fighting in war, 1 473
——— Remoued into Wales and Cornwall, 1 589
——— Receiued into the subiection of the Eastangles & British kings, 1 645
——— Discomfited, leaue their countrie a prie to the Saxons, 1 559
——— They lost the more part of their ancient seats, 1 589
——— They lie armor aside, & betake them to the reading of the holie scriptures 1 643.
——— Seruing in war vnder Cōstertine fortunat, 1 532
——— Under the conduct of Uoadicia giue the Romans a shamefull discōfiture, 1 199
——— They obteine the field against the Saxons, 1 558
——— Miserable state vnder Uortigerne, 1 555
——— They rebell against Alectus & his Romans, 1 520
——— Oppressed of Saxons, craue aid of two bishops & preuaile note, 1 562
——— Their good zeal to religion in their troubles by Hengist note, ib
——— Ouerthrowne by the Saxons & slaine in great numbers, ib
——— Their disloialtie to Uter Pendragon, 1 570
——— Their kings seek to rule in this land, 1 558
——— At variance among themselues after the death of Lucius, 1 513
——— For lacke of skill gaue place to the Romans, 1 522
Britannia, why it ought rather to be called Bridania, 1 632
——— ¶ Sée Britaine
Brithriks profered seruise hath ill successe, 1 711
Britons through rest and ease became vnapt for wars, v 155
——— Aided by the Scots, refuse aid being offered, v. 58
——— Ouerthrowne, ib
——— Soiorning in warre giue themselues to banketting and voluptuousnes, v 154
——— Ouerthrowne by the Saxons, v 153
——— Refuse to receiue either Loth or anie of his sonnes to reigne ouer them, ib
——— They win London, ib.

Britons aid against the Scots, about to deceiue the Picts, vol v page 39
——— Rebell, require aid of Caratake, chased, v 67
——— Kept possession of Cumberland and those other countries being by the coast of the West seas, v 210
——— Request to haue one of their owne nation appointed to succeed king Arthur, v 159.
——— Repent them of the league made with the Scots, v 220
——— Send ambassadors to the Picts, v 38
——— At no hand admit peace, v 161
——— Discomfited by the Picts and Scots, v 49
——— Spite shewed vnto the Romans, v 94
——— Recieue the christian faith, v 95
——— At the appointment of Uictorine make a wall, v 123
——— Loth to breake peace with the Scots and Picts, their seruilitie, they conspire against their nobles, send into Britaine Armorike for aid, v 134, 135, 136
——— The tenor of their letters sent to Etius with the answer, v 131
——— Leaue Pictland, and get themselues to the riuer Tine, require aid at the hands of Etius, forsaken of the Romans, v 130
——— Dout to ione with the maine armie of Scots and Picts, v. 133
——— Their crueltie in slaieng the Saxons, v 157
——— Come to Adrians wall & pull it downe to let in the Scots, v 96
——— Rebell and choose one Fulgentius their capteine, ib
——— Chaced, know not whither to go, v 139
——— Giue themselues to all kind of vice and abhominations, v 151
——— Receiue a great ouerthrow, ib
——— Require aid of the Scots and Picts against the Saxons, v 144
——— Distressed, v 141, 142.
——— Ouerthrowne, v 65
——— Their great earnestnesse to recouer their libertie, v 136
——— Rebell, appeased, v 75
——— Reuolt from their obedience to the Romans and whie, v 84.
——— Make themselues strong, assemble at Shrewesburie, & confederat, v 62
——— Their desperat hardinesse, v 64
——— Weried with trauell, v 63
——— Bet vp Romans, yeeld themselues to Carantius, v 106
——— Send for aid against the Romans to the Scots, v 58
——— When they first inhabited Ireland, vi. 76
Britons Armorike, v 148
——— Aid king Arthur, v. 153.
——— ¶ Sée Englishmen & Picts
Britons expert in art magike, i 429
——— Why they vsed to paint their faces, i 441.
Britons suing for aid to the Romans against the Scots & Picts could get none, vol i page 512
——— Welshmen, i 560.
——— Utterlie subdued by the Romans but not without much slaughter & bloudshed, i 473
——— In great miserie spoile one another, i 541
——— Where the line and gouernment of their kings ended, i 637.
——— ¶ Sée Britains
Britons diuided this Iland into cantreds, i 297
——— Their abstinence, i 279
——— They had some vse of Logike and Rhetorike from the Galles, i 35
——— The speach of ye ancient sort and of the Celts much alike, i 22.
——— They and the Celtes indifferentlie called Cimbri, i 23
——— They are driuen into Wales & Cornewall by the Saxons, &c i. 11
——— Diligent and readie in pedegrees, i 23
——— Their industrie in the vse and application of the benefits of their countrie, i 187
——— Defended against their slanderers, i 193, 191
——— Valourous, i 192
——— The constitution of their bodies, ib
——— Their slight building, i 314
——— ¶ Sée Welshmen
Brocmale earle of Chester defender of the moonks of Bangor against the Northumbers discomfited, i 598
Brocmale. ¶ Sée Brocmale.
Bromleie esquire his manhood, iii 75
Bromleie knight his decease, iii 101
——— Made capteine of Dampfront, iii 97
——— The old armes of their house, iii 98
——— Knight lord chancellor, iv 346, 374
Brookes ¶ Sée Riuers
Brotherton Thomas K Edward the first his sonne, 533
Broughtie Crag woone by the French, v 552, 561.
——— The fort builded there by the English, v 560
——— Besieged by the earle of Argile, v 553
——— The siege raised, v 560
——— Besieged by the gouernor, v 554
——— ¶ Sée Broughtie Crag
Broughton sir Thomas confederated with Parkin, iii 270
Browne his seditious bookes procure losse of life, iv 505
——— ¶ Sée Murther
Brudeus king of Picts killeth Egfride, i. 634.
——— By denieng to deliuer the Scotish outlawes procureth warres to himselfe and his countrie, v 165, 166
——— Maketh slaughter of the Scots v 167
——— Hurt in the thigh, ib.
Brudus king of Picts sent to Alpine for renewing league sendeth for aid into England, v 196, 197
——— Entreth into Angus, v 197

Brudus politike, vol v page 197
——— Deceaseth, v 198
Bruing. ¶ Sée Beere
Bruister and Marie Breame smoothered to death, iv 505
Brunkard Henrie ¶ Sée Iusts triumphant
Bruse king in armes against Edward of Carnaruan, v 344.
——— His wife restored vnto him by exchange, v. 349
——— Treason against him note, v 350
——— Giueth discomfitures to rebels, v. 342.
——— Recouereth castels, v 343
——— Inuadeth England, ib
——— Offended with his brother, ib
——— His exhortatiō to his armie, v. 345, 346
——— His miserable state in the beginning of his reigne, v 340
——— His wife taken, ib
——— His brethren put to death, ib.
——— His inuincible hart in trouble, ib.
——— Getteth ouer into the Iles, ib
——— Commeth to Glenneske, v 341.
——— Inuadeth England, v 355.
——— Burning and wasting, ib
——— With an armie in Scotland, ib.
——— Inuadeth the north parts of England approching almost to Yorke, v 356
——— His second mariage & issue, v 350
——— Killeth an Englishman, v 348
——— Gouerneth by deputation, v 357, 358.
——— He deceaseth, v 360
——— His fame and praise amongst his enimies, ib
——— The aduice giuen by him to his nobles before his death, v. 361
——— His desire to haue his hart borne to the holie sepulchre, ib.
——— ¶ Sée Antwerpe
Bruse Robert the first crowned, v 339
——— Discomfited at Meffen, ib
——— Maried to Martha daughter to the earle of Caricke, v. 320
——— King of Scotland, ib
——— The occasion of the Scots ouerthrow at Dunbar, v 329
——— Submitteth himselfe, ib
——— His ancestors, v. 323.
——— Landed in Ireland to aid his brother, vi 248
——— Besiegeth Cragfergus, ib
——— Crowned king of Scotland, in armes against prince Edward and the English power, put to flight by the erle of Pembroke, fled into Kentrie, his wife and his brethren taken, his words to his wife, he is executed, and his lands giuen awaie by the king Edward the first, wherein note the end of his disloialtie, v 510, 511, 512
Bruse inuadeth England, ii 571.
——— His ill dealing with Welshmen, ii 164.
——— His wife whose daughter she was, ii. 541.
——— Pronounced accursed, ii 557.
Bruse thriueth in his successe, inuadeth England, & raiseth his siege, vol ii page 553, 554
Bruse and Cumine conspirators, their end, v 337.
Bruse Edward proclamed K of Ireland, v. 351.
——— Slain, ib
——— ¶ Sée Wallase
——— Brother to king of Scots inuadeth Ireland, vi. 246
——— Proclameth himselfe king, burneth Dundalke, ib
——— Spoileth the countrie, ib
——— Discomfiteth the English men, vi 247.
——— He and his companie vanquished and slaine, vi 251
Brute the sonne of Syluius arriueth in Britaine with his ships, i 9.
——— What time he arriued in Britaine, i 8
——— He subdueth all Britaine, i 195
——— He diuided all Britaine to his thrée sonnes, ib.
——— From whense he learned his religiō, i 39
——— His death the maner thereof not certeinlie knowen, i 195.
——— Intered at his new citie, i 196
——— His descent, arriuall in Britaine, killing of his father, &c i 437
——— He & his wife Innogens arriuall in Leogitia, &c i 439
——— He was not the first that inhabited this Ile, i. 436
——— Incountered by the giants of the Ile, i 443
——— His line ended, i 550
——— His letter to king Pendrasus, with certeine martiall exploits of his, i 438
——— His thrée sonnes, their names, & how vpon his dethbed he diuideth all Britaine among them, i 443.
——— His arriuall in this Ile, i 442.
——— He and Corineus ioine companies, i 441.
——— He with his companie landed in Affrica, i. 440
——— His death and buriall, i 443
Brute Gréeneshield the sixt ruler of Britaine, i. 455
Bruton Iohn bishop of Hereford kéeper of yᵉ kings wardrobe, i 240
Bubali olim in Anglia, i 347
Buchanan pathe followeth the error of Goropius about Britaine, i 6
——— Reprouing and reproued, ii 193
——— Hath the gentle checke and reproofe, v. 414.
Bucke, and what names he hath before he be so called, i 380
Buckingham & Bedfordshires haue the riuer Clée rising in their verie confines, i 173
Buckhurst lord made of the priuie councell, iv 660.
——— ¶ Sée Sackuill
——— Ambassador to the French king in Henrie the seuenths time, i. 388
Buckquhane, the reason of the name, v 125
Buggerie committed by a lord and punished, iii. 818

Buieng and selling on the sundaie a law against it, vol. iii page 205.
——— ¶ Sée Selling
Building and furniture of houses in England described, i 314
——— With stone now cōmonlie vsed therein, ib.
——— New and curious deuises vsed therein, i 356.
——— Quarries of stone seruing thereto, i. 394
Buildings in Englãd of what manner, i 397
——— Of William Rufus verie great and famous, ii 39
Buls wild sometimes in England, i 379
Bull seditious hanged on the bishop Londons gate, and the partie executed as a traitor, iv. 252
——— ¶ Sée Felton and Pope
Bullen besieged, assalted, deliuered vp, the number of them than that foorth of the towne, iii 839,840
——— Manie feats of armes exploited by the English and French, iii 853
——— The Frenchmen busie to build a fort there, iii 850
——— To be restored to the French king by accord note how, iii. 856.
——— Bullenois restored to the French vpon certeine conditions: note, iii 1023
——— Deliuered vp and entired into, ib.
——— By the French king, ib
——— Besieged by the Englishmen the king himselfe being present, iii 502
——— The Base, a camuasado giuen vnto it, the French haue an overthrow, iii 844
Bullocke a mercilesse murtherer hanged within Bishopsgate note, iv 266.
——— ¶ Sée Murther
Bulmar knight rebuked for refusing K Henrie the eights seruice, and taking the seruice of the duke of Buckingham, iii 640.
Burchet gentleman of the middle temple hanged note, iv 324
Burchier George is in commission with sir Iohn Perot for Mounster, vi 370
——— His parentage, ib
——— His valientnesse and good seruice, ib.
——— Is restored againe, ib
——— He arriueth in Ireland with a supplie of Deuonshire souldiers, vi 414
——— He is dubbed knight, ib
——— He is sent to lie in garrison in Kilmallocke, vi 415
——— He is assigned to serue vnder the earle of Ormond, vi 425.
——— He maketh a rode into Connell, ib
——— Is colonel of Mounster, vi 434
——— His seruice vpon Desmond, vi 125.
——— A mutinie among the souldiers, vi. 432
Burchier sir Rafe knight his deuise of casting alabaster in moolds, i 395.
Burdet knight his valiantnesse against the enimie note, iii 145.
Burdet knight slaine, iii 195
Burdet for a word spoken beheaded, iii 345.
Burdens yéelded againe to the French king, iii 236.
Burgenild ¶ Sée Quendred
Burgesse of the parlement arrested, and what mischéefe thereof insued: note, vol iii page 824
Burgesses & citisens, i 236
Burgh or Bourke earle of Clanricard, vi 53
——— Warres betwéene him and Mac William Eughter, vi 329, 340
——— Submitteth to sir Edward Fitton lord precident, vi 366
——— His sonnes rebell and wage Scots, vi 372, 373
——— He is prisoner in the castell of Dublin, vi 373
——— He promiseth vpon enlargement to reclaime his sonnes, ib.
——— He performeth nothing, ib
——— His sonnes spoile all Connagh, vi 381
——— They breake out againe into rebellion, ib
——— His sonnes flie, vi 383
——— He is committed to close prison in the castell of Dublin, ib
——— His sonnes rebell againe and do reteine Scots, vi 385
——— His sonnes besiege Balie Riogh, ib
——— They preuaile not, ib
Burgh Richard earle of Ulster besiegeth Athlone, in which is Theobald Uerdon, vi 240
——— Is taken prisoner, vi 241.
——— Is disseized of his lands in Connagh, ib.
——— Is discharged, ib
——— He entereth into Scotland, vi 242
Burgognians ioine with the English host and make it stronger, iii. 680.
Buriall of duke Williams bodie not suffered without satisfaction to the lord of the soile, ii 25
——— Of more than two hundred dead corpses in the Charterhouse yard, ii 651
——— Christian forbidden préests concubines, ii 358.
——— Of nobles and great men in a moonks cowl: note, ii 337
——— Neglected note, ii 272.
——— Of the dead doone with honour and reuerence, iii. 120
——— For the dead, iv 234
——— Of dead bodies within their owne parishes, ii 52
——— Of the Iewes at London, ii 175
——— ¶ Sée Churchyard new.
——— Ancient maner of in Anglesere, i 64.
——— Of Scotish princes, an ordinance therefore, v 19
——— Of soldiors slaine, v. 115
——— Of one quicke, v 70, 115
Burials of the kings of Ireland, i 70.
——— Of the kings of Scotland, ib
Burhred K of Mercia marieth king Ethelwulfes daughter, i. 662.
——— Aided against the Danes, i 666
——— Fleeth his countrie and dieth, i 669.

Burke lord William slue Okellie and fiue hundred Irishmen, vol vi page 248
—— He is lord deputie, vi 245
—— Peers Gaueston is recommended vnto him, ib.
—— Is taken prisoner, vi 241.
Burke sir William and his sons doo follow Iames Fitzmoris for a preie, vi. 411
—— They incounter with him, and kill him, vi 412
—— Theobald is slaine, ib
—— Sir William is made baron of Connell Lath an yearlie pension of one hundred markes, vi 412
—— Swowndeth for ioie, ib
Burkens of Kilkennie rob and spoile the countrie, vi 261
—— They are discomfited, ib
Burlie knight and the earle Uere in faithfull freendship, ii 791
—— What the same Burlie was note, ib
Burnell of Balgriffen confederated with Kildare, vi 302
—— Fleeth into Mounster, ib
—— Is taken prisoner by the vicount Tharles, ib
—— Is sent into England and executed at Tiburne, ib
Burnell Henrie a student at the lawes, vi 390
—— A councellour and agent against the cesse, ib
—— Passeth ouer into England vnto the court, ib
—— Is sent to the fleet, vi 392
—— Remoued to the tower, vi 393.
—— Submitteth himselfe, ib
Burning in the hand when maried, iii 521.
Burrow, i 258
Burrow what kind of custome, i 303
Burrowes how they were walled about with stone walles, i 265
—— To what vse the Britons put them, ib
Bursse, ground purchased to build it, the first stone thereof laid, iv 230
—— Finished & named The roiall exchange by the now queene Elisabeth, iv 258
Bushie knight, ii 847
—— ¶ See Flatterie
Butcher strangelie saued from drowning, ii 70
—— Hanged for fauouring rebels, iii 802
Bute Ile taken v 339
Butler sir Edmund dubbed knight, vi 53
—— Made lord iustice, vi 246
—— He dubbeth knights, ib
—— Discomfiteth the Irishie at Tristeldermon, vi 249
—— He died vi 248
Butler sir Edmond breaketh out into rebellion, vi 339
—— He misliketh the English burgesses, vi 343
—— Great complaints against him, vi 362
—— Refuseth to come before the commissioners, ib.
—— His castle of Cloghirinam taken, ib
Butler committed to the castle of Dublin, vol vi. page 361
—— Broke out from thense, ib
—— Submitteth himself, ib
—— He accuseth the lord deputie of hard dealing, vi. 362.
—— Committed againe to the castle of Dublin, vi 365
—— Pardoned, ib
Butler James lord iustice, vi 53
—— Dubbed knight, ib.
—— He married the earle of Herefords daughter, ib.
—— Is earle of Tipporaria, ib.
—— Pledge for the earle of Desmond, vi 255
—— Created earle of Ormond, vi 53.
—— He is lord iustice, vi 53, 261
—— Died, vi 261
Butler James earle of Ormond, lord lieutenant, vi. 265
—— He summoneth a parlement at Dublin ib
—— In his gouernment, the sunne staid his course three houres, ib
—— His notable seruices in taming and vanquishing the Irishie, vi 267
—— He kept by prorogation sundrie parlements, vi 266
—— His sonne and heire born, ib
—— Lieutenant to king Henrie the sixt, vi 267
—— Godfather to George duke of Clarence, ib
Butler James earle of Ormond his contention with the earle of Kildare, vi 275
—— He releeth to the house of Lancaster, ib
—— He is a deepe reaching man, ib
—— He marcheth to Dublin with a puissant armie, ib
—— He praieth to purge himself, ib
—— The citizens of Dublin fall at iarre with him, vi 276
—— He is in danger to be killed, ib
—— He is rescued by the earle of Kildare, ib.
—— They are reconciled, ib
—— The description of him, ib
Butler Peers earle of Ossorie marrieth the ladie Margaret Fitzgerald sister to the earle of Kildare, vi 278
—— His bastard brother Iames intrudeth vpon the erldome of Ormond, ib
—— He gaue charge vpon his brother and killeth him, ib
—— Was lord deputie, vi 279
—— The sword taken from him, vi 280
Butler lord Iames, lord treasuror, vi 285
Butler Thomas prior of Kilmain serueth king Henrie the sixt in France, vi 265.
Butler Thomas earle of Ormond his troubles with the earle of Desmond, vi 352.
—— His countrie spoiled, vi 363
—— Submitteth himselfe to the queenes order, vi. 332
—— His affection to his brethren, vi. 364.

Butler Thomas arriueth at Wexford, vol. vi. page 364
—— He repaireth to the lord deputie at Limerike and offereth his seruice, ib.
—— He yeeldeth and presenteth his brother sir Edmund vnto him, ib
—— He vndertaketh for him and for his appearance at Dublin, ib
—— His graue behauiour at place of councell, ib.
—— He serueth vpon the earle of Thomond and driueth him out of the land, vi. 368
—— He was gouernour of Mounster, vi 421
—— He hath the custodie of the young lord Girald sonne to the earle of Desmond, ib
—— He maketh iournie into Connilo, vi 425.
—— He meeteth with the maior of Youghall, ib
—— He carrieth him to Youghall and hangeth him before his owne dore, vi 426
—— He and the baron of vper Ossorie are reconciled, vi 422
—— He is sent to the earle of Desmond to persuade him to submission, ib
—— He subscribeth to the proclamation against the earle of Desmond, vi 424
—— He causeth the towne of Youghall to be inhabited and new peopled, vi 426
—— He besiegeth the castle of Strangcallie, ib
—— He taketh their castle and putteth a ward in it, ib
—— His seruice vnder the lord iustice, vi 429
—— He receiueth the submission of Fitzmoris baron of Leraw, vi 430
—— He is at the siege and taking of the castle of Cargfoile, ib
—— He returneth home to Kilkenie, vi 432.
Butler lord Thomas is slaine by Gogaghadon, vi 253
Butler Theobald, lord Butler fled out of Dublin, vi 240
—— Died, ib
—— He founded the abbie of Wetherham, vi 238
Buttermen and the cause that butter riseth in the p ce,
Butterwife set on the pillorie, iii 345
Buxton bains, 330.

C

Cadall of Gallowaie, gouernour, sent with an armie into Ireland, v 56
—— Rewarded for his good seruice, ib.
—— Deceaseth, v 57
Cador earle of Cornwall, i 580
—— Duke of Cornwall, killeth Theldrike, i 576
Cadwall vanquished, restored to his kingdome, v 170
Cadwalline ¶ Sée Cadwallo
Cadwallo K of Britaine rebelleth against Edwine, i 610
—— What the British writers report of him, i 612.
Cadwallo his image of brasse set on a brasen horsse set vpon Ludgate, vol i page 611
—— Terrible both in nature and countenance, i 612
—— Slaine by Oswald at Denisburne, ib
Cadwallader king of Britons constreined to forsake the land, i 633.
Cadwaller prince of Wales slaine, ii 179
Cadwan chosen K of Britaine after 24 yeares space without anie one speciall gouernment, i 601
—— His acts and deeds, ib
—— K. of Northwales, i 599
Caen taken by the English, iii 91
—— Besieged and yéelded to the French king, iii 216
Caerbardon now called Bath, i 449
Caerbran now Bath, when first built, i 416
Carbrank, i. 41
—— ¶ Sée Yorke
Caergrant, now Cambridge, i 459
Caerguent, i 116.
—— ¶ Sée Winchester.
Caerleir now Leicester when first built, ib
Caerleon by whom erected and built, i 436, 485, 492
—— See Chester
Caerlud, now London, i 46.
Caermarlet, i 488
Caesar made a tabber of English pearle, i 401
Cages and stocks ordeined, iii 532
Caim an English saint and of his effectuall praiers, i 116
Cair Caridor a strong place of incamping, i 328
Cairmarder how called in the Romans time, i 321
Caius de canibus Anglicis, i 386
Caius Trebonius leutenant of thrée legions, i 473
Caius Uolusenus came ouer into Britaine to view the Ile i 465
Calaminarie stones, i 402.
Calaterwood in Scotland, i 152
Calcedonie stone, i 402
Caldorus a Briton reioiseth as well at the slaughter of his owne people as his enimies, v 9
Caldwell doctor in physicke founder of surgerie lecture in London note, iv 196, 197
—— Deceaseth, his distributions in his life, and bequests after his death, his commentaries vpon Paulus Aegineta and other books, his infirmitie that was his end, his age, iv 531
—— His armes blasoned, his epitaph, iv 231
Calen his graue counsell taketh place, v 211
Calendar of England how it might be the more perfect, i 112
Calendar Romane, i 408
—— Papisticall in vse in the arches, i 306
—— Generallie corrected by the pope, i 410
Calendar of the greatest fures in England, i 112
—— Of the greatest trauelled thorowfares and townes in England, i 415.
—— ¶ Sée Kalendar
Calendarwood, i 507
Calends of the moneth consecrated to Iuno, and the reason of the name, i 408.

Calice a towne in Picardie, & how far distant from Rome, vol i page 5
Caligula emperour of Rome purposeth to search the vttermost bounds of Britaine, i 480
Calis ¶ Sée Itius portus
Calis, the French commissioners would haue rased to the ground, ii 822
—— Preparatiō made to win it, the enimies frustrated, ib
—— Besieged, note the commodiousnesse of that towne, ii 640
—— Surrendered to Edward the third, vpon what conditions, ii 617
—— Inexpugnable note, ii 542
—— Six burgesses thereof presented to Edward the third, ii 648
—— Yéelded to the king of England, ib
—— Made a colonie of England, a practise to betraie it, Edward the third passeth ouer secretlie thither, ii 648, 649.
—— Not furnished with a sufficient number of men, deliuered to the French, iv 90
—— Rifled and spoiled by the French, the poorest auoid out of the same, conquered and lost in lesse than eight yéers, how long in possession of the kings of England, iv 92, 93.
—— Hauen, the Frenchmens meaning to destroie the same disappointed, iii 687
—— How the French were in loue with it after it was lost, note the words of the lord Cordes, iii. 495
—— King Henrie the seuenth saileth thither, iii 525
—— The mart of all the English commodities kept there, iii 505
—— The duke of Burgognies armie of 40000 men, iii 187
—— Besieged, he breaketh vp his seige and flieth, iii 187, 188
—— A report that Richard the second went to resigne it into the French kings hands, ii 791
—— The ioie that the French made euerie waie for the getting of it, iv 93
—— The French king goeth to visit Calis, iv 102
—— The losse thereof with what indignation quéene Marie taketh it, iv 117
—— Might haue béene recouered from the French, iv 119.
—— The eleuenth king from the conquest got it, and the eleuenth againe after him lost it, iv. 139
—— Quéene Marie pensife for the losse of it, the cause of hir sicknesse and death, iv 121
—— Triumphs in France for the getting thereof, iv 101
—— Besieged by Edward king of England, v. 382
—— ¶ Sée Calis, Duke, and Uictorie
Calphurnius Agricola lieutenant of Britaine, i 514.
———— Is sent into Britaine, entereth into the borders of his enimie, returneth to Yorke, v 92
———— Studieth to reforme the state of Britain, returneth to Rome, v. 93.
Caltrops of iron inuenomed and cast among people, vol i page 481.
—— Cast vpon the ground to annoie the Danes, vi 91
Caluerleie knight a valiant capteine, ii. 717.
—— He recouereth Marke castell, ib.
—— His exploits against the French, ii 718.
—— His valiantnes, ii. 724
Camaletum, i 488
Camber the second sonne of Brute had Cambria giuen, i. 195.
Cambria why so called, i 117.
Cambridge how called in the Romans time, i 321.
—— Uniuersitie erected by Sigibert, i 242
—— Fortie six miles from London, i 250
—— Not long since burned, ib.
—— Colleges with their founders names, i. 255.
—— Kings college chappell of what stone it is builded, i 394
—— ¶ Sée Uniuersities
—— Quéene Elisabeths progresse thither, iv 225
—— Presenteth a faire and statelie cup to quéene Elisabeth, iv. 404
—— ¶ Sée Emanuell college
—— By whome builded, i 459
—— The uniuersitie by whom founded, i. 619
—— Fauoured of king Sigebert and bishop Felix, i 460
—— Pestered with the Danes a whole yeare, i 699
—— The towne and uniuersitie when first founded, i 460
—— Burnt by Danes, i 711.
—— The uniuersitie found before Oxford 265 yeares, v 242
Camedolon a citie belonging to the Trinobants, i. 488
Camelgaret a Welsh bishop taken prisoner of the Danes, & redeemed, i 679
Camelodunum whether Colchester or no, i 488, 489.
—— Supposed of Polyd Virg to be Doncaster or Pontfret, i 488
—— (Now Colchester) taken by the Romans, i 483
—— Peopled with souldiers by Osorius Scapula, i 488
Camelon the principall citie of Picts, ouerthrowne by Iulius Cesar, i 199
—— Besieged by Uespasian, surrendered, peopled with Romans, v 65
—— Taken by force, v 128
—— The citie throwne downe, v 205
—— The gentelwomen there are preserued, v. 203, 204
—— Require a truce for thrée daies, v 204.
Campbell a Scotish pirat or rouer taken on the sea, iii. 676.
Campeius refuseth to giue iudgement in the matter

of Henrie the eight his vnlawfull mariage vnto quéen Katharine, vol iii page 740.
——— ¶ See Cardinall
Campians description of cardinall Woolseie, iii 756.
——— ¶ Sée préests seminarie
Candels of tallow eaten vp of an Isleand gentlewoman, i 589
Candida Casa, v 181, 501
Cangi inhabitants of Denbighshire, i 487.
Cannus a Danish capteine landeth at the Red braies, marcheth through Angus, v 260
——— Incourageth his Danes, he is slaine, v 260, 261.
Canon Robert secretarie to sir William Skeuington an enimie to Kildare, vi 287
Canon Hugh Richard the kings iustice slaine, vi 250
Canons regular put in préests places, ii. 172
——— Of Yorke refuse to receiue the archbishop of Canturburie as their primat, ii. 256.
——— ¶ Sée Préests
Canonizing of kings déere, iii 325.
Cantaber a Spaniard begun the vniuersitie of Cambridge, i 249.
——— Whether builder of Cambridge or no, i. 459
Cantabrians, i 479.
Cāting ¶ Sée Pedlers Frēch
Canton sir James and Canton sir Iohn slaine, vi. 250.
——— Sir Dauid beheaded Murcod Ballough, vi 243
Cantred what it is, vi 126
Canturburie ¶ Sée Archbishop
——— How called in the Romans time, i. 320
——— The chiefe citie of the kingdome of Kent, i 28
——— One of the two onlie prouinces now of England, i 221.
——— Bishoprikes vnder the said sée twentie one, i 227
——— Bishop of Rochester crossebearer in times past the archbishop of the said see, i 236
——— Archbishoprike when and by whom first erected, & the circuit of the same, i 236
——— Archbishops of the popish stampe, proud, ambitious contentious, &c i. 222, 223, 224.
——— In old time Kaerkir, by whome first builded, i 446
——— Of saint Agnes church built there by Eadbald, i 603
——— The sée of archbishop Augustine, i 595.
——— Like to haue been taken by the Danes but for composition, i 711.
——— Taken of the Danes by treason, i 712.
——— Citizens & the earle of Bullongne togither by the eares, i 742.
——— The archbishoprike void, i 626.
Canute brother to Swane generall against the Scots, v. 262
Canute his words to Edmund Ironside, vol v. page 266.
Canute alias Knought the Dane is slaine, vi 92.
Canutus lawes for his forrest, i 346, 347
——— His authorising the clergie to punish whoredome, i 212
——— He was a glutton, i 287
——— Ment to haue attempted a subduing of London, and hindred, ii 11
——— Discomfited by the Normans retireth to his ships, ib
——— ¶ Sée Osborne.
Captintie right happie, v 408.
Capons made of gelded cocks a practice brought in by the Romans, i 375
Car Thomas, v 663
Car Walter sent to defend Iedworth, v 611.
——— Ioineth with William Ruthwin, ib
Caradocks a linage of great honor, antiquitie and seruice, i 118
Carantius troubleth the estate of Britaine, v. 101
——— His wilie practise, v 105.
——— Offereth to come to make answer vnto such matters he was charged with, requireth to be aided against the Romans, vsurpeth the kingdome of Britaine hauing got the victorie, diuideth the game in assigning to his confederats their due portions, v 105, 106.
Caransus maketh peace betwéene the Scots and the Picts, vi 82
Caratake chosen capteine of the Britons, v 62
——— Proclamed king of Scots, borne in Carike, v 61.
——— His answer to the Romane ambassadors, v 63
——— Assembleth an armie, v 65
——— The strength of the place where he was incamped, ib.
——— Assembleth an armie, v 68
——— Escapeth, flieth vnto Dunstafage, vtterlie refuseth to become a subiect, v 66
——— Exhorteth his to fight, ouerthrowne, betraied by his stepmother, sent to Rome, shewed in triumph, dieth, v 66
——— Renowned in Italie & Rome, i 490
——— His wife and daughter taken prisoners by the Romans, ib
——— His couragious words (being captiue) to Claudius the emperor, ib
——— His prowesse against the Romans, i 489
Caratіcus king of Britaine hated of his people, vi 84
Carausius a Britaine of low birth killed Bassianus in fight, i. 516
——— Of a bondman made king of Britaine, i. 520
——— Slaine, ib
——— ¶ Sée Carantius.
Carburne hill, v. 621
Carcer Aeoli an hole so called in old-time, i 115.
Cardane king of Demarke, v 214.
Cardans fond opinion touching dogs become wolues, and wolues dogs, i 390.

Cardinall Gualo summoneth the Scottish cleargie, vol v page 308

—— His auarice, condemned in a summe of monie, the Scots sore offended at him, his practise, v 307

—— Commeth into England furnished with the popes authoritie note, ib

Cardinall Hugh of saint Angelo the popes legat, v. 299

Cardinall Campeius sent into England about Henrie the eight his vnlawfull mariage, iii 736

—— Sent from the pope and the cause of his staieng at Calis, receiued with great pompe, what trash was inclosed in his chests, the pomp of him and Woolsie going to the court, iii 626, 627

—— Of Canturburie thought the fittest man to deale with the quéene for surrendering hir sonne, iii 370

—— He vseth another waie to persuade hir, iii 376

—— De Comus letter to Parrie, touching resolution to kill the quéene, iv 753

—— Gualo commeth ouer into England, ii. 351.

—— A couetous prelat and fauourer of king Iohn, ii 324

—— Iohannes de Anagnia, prohibited to passe no further into England than Douer, ii 208

—— Nicholas sent into England to take awaie the interdiction, ii 313

—— Octauianus legat into Ireland, ii 191

—— What words Richard the first vsed to him against Rome, ii 214

—— Otho commeth into England, the lords grudge at his receiuing without their knowledge, he is praised for his sober behauiour, strifes by him are compounded, ii 382, 383.

—— He holdeth a synod at London, he goeth to Oxford, a fraie betwixt his men and the scholers, his cooke slaine, he complaineth to the king, he curseth the misdooers, ii 383

—— Made to blush at Chater-house moonks words, ii 389

—— Lieth in the wind still for the popes profit, ii 387

—— Beginneth to looke to his owne commoditie, ii 386

—— His persuasions to the English cleargie, touching tribute to the pope, frustrate, ii 359

—— Peito become a begging frier, iv 527

—— Petrus Hispanus sent from the pope, the cause of his comming, his demand of monie of religious houses, ii 543

—— He preacheth, & curseth Bruse the vsurper, ii 513

—— Pierget his trauell to treat a peace betwéene both kings of England and France note, ii 663

—— Poole made archbishop of Canturburie, iv. 84.

Cardinall Poole was to reduce the church of England to the popes obedience, vol iv page 7, 8

—— Sent for home into England, iv 9

—— The councell diuided about the receiuing of him, ib

—— Arriueth at Douer, his restitution in bloud, commeth to the parlement house, his oration there tending to the publike estate, iv 64, 65.

—— Against the pope, iv 527

—— Cômeth to Pauls crosse in great pompe, iv 73

—— A supplication exhibited vnto him, his authoritie apostolike note iv 66, 67

—— His malice against Henrie the eight, iv 89, 90.

—— Boners letter touching persecution vnto him, staieth Boners crueltie somewhat, a papist but no bloudie papist, halfe suspected for a Lutheran at Rome, an errant traitor, seditious and impudent, his treasons detected by his owne brother, woorse than a pagan, iv 144, 145, 146.

—— Vnkind to Henrie the eight that brought him vp, the manner of his death and distribution of his goods, iv 146, 147

—— Disceaseth, described, iv 141, 142

—— Earnest in burning the bones of the dead, iv 141

—— Articles touching the cleargie to be inquired of in his visitation, iv. 141, 142

—— And the laietie, iv 142

—— Of Praxed, liberall of the faculties note, ii 734

—— Vmano of S Stephans in mount Celio, ii 173

—— Of Winchester complained against the duke of Glocester, iii. 199.

—— Otherwise called the rich cardinall, deceaseth note, iii 212

—— Woolseie ¶ Sée Woolseie

Cardinall commeth into England, receiuing an oth not to preiudice the realme, ii 414

—— He maketh shift for monie, ib.

—— Two, Iohn and Peter sent into England in commission from the pope, ii 14.

—— Two robbed and the robbers executed, ii 555.

—— They cursse the Scots, ii 5.

—— Two from the pope to accord the two kings of England and France, ii 647.

—— Two come into England about a treatie of peace, ii 607

—— Their returne to Rome, ib

—— Appointed to treat a peace betwéene England and France, ii 696

—— Sent to the king of England and France to treat of peace, they gather monie, ii 508

Cardinals of England all from the first to the last, collected iv. 147 to 153

—— Onlie two in Scotland, v 736

—— Sent to king Henrie the second, ii. 165.

Careie George knight desirous of combat with the lord Fleming, his letter of challenge, and replie to a former answer, vol iv page 246, 247
Careticus made K. of Britaine full of dissention, i 588.
———— His acts and deeds, i 589
Carew baron slaine with a bullet shot, iii 576.
——— Knight taken of French, iii 833
——— Beheaded note, iii 808.
——— Used as an instrument to appease rebellion in Deuon, iii 940.
——— Charged with the in Deuonshire, iii. 953
——— ¶ Sée Dinham
——— Carew baron of Carew lord iustice, vi 256.
——— Marquesse of Corke, his reuenues in Ireland two thousand two hundred pounds, vi. 262.
——— Sir Peter lord of Odron, vi 207
——— Sueth for a licence to recouer his lands in Ireland, vi 339, 340.
——— He recouereth so much as he had in suit, ib
——— He serueth in the Butlers wars, vi 363
——— He was in danger to haue bin murthered, vi. 362
——— He giueth a hot charge vpon the enimie and hath the victorie, vi 363
——— His seruice in Ulster, vi 377
——— His seruice in the Butlers wars, vi 377.
——— His parentage, vi. 376.
——— His title to great seignories in Mounster, ib
——— His manie and most excellent vertues and qualities, ib
——— A short discourse of his life, vi 376, 377.
——— He died at Rosse and was buried at Waterford, vi 375.
Carew sir Peter the Yoonger, his being in Ireland, ib.
——— His place in Leighlin, vi 378.
——— He arriueth at Waterford with a band of Deuon souldiers, vi 411
——— Is dubbed knight, ib
——— He receiueth the lord iustice at Waterford, vi 429
——— Is slaine vi 435
Carew George his being in Ireland, vi 376
——— His seruice against Rorie Og, vi 396.
——— His arriuall at Waterford with a band of Deuon souldiers, vi 414.
——— His seruice against sir Iohn Desmond, vi 416.
——— He lieth in garrison at Adare, vi 420
——— Is besieged there, ib
——— Is set on by the Desmonds and Spaniards, vi 421
——— He receiueth sir William Pelham, lord iustice at Waterford, vi 429
——— He taketh the view of Cargfoile, vi 430
——— He besiegeth and taketh the castle of Balie Lougham, vi 431
Carike, vi 139.
Carleill by whom builded, i 416
———— How called in the Romans time, i 320
———— Sometimes named Cardoill, i 215
Carleill standeth betwéene two streams or riuers, vol i page 149.
———— The bishopriks erection, circuit, and valuation, i 245.
Carlill woon by the Scots, v 307.
——— Repaired, v 290
——— Destroied by the Danes, repaired and peopled by William Rufus, ii 32, 33.
——— Assalted by the Scots, ii 766
Carmichell laird, v 650.
Carolus Clusius, i 352
Carolus Magnus in league with the Scots, v. 185
Carpenters of England highlie comended, i 316
———— The passe in their new frames the finest of old, i. 356
Carpes latelie brought into England and later into the Thames, i 81
Carpwald slaine by Richbert his countriemant, i 609
Carron riuer runneth with bloud, v 123
Cartandes quéen of Scots, v 116
———— Lamenteth hir infortunate estate, ib
Carter an Englishman seruing among the French, but to their disaduantage, an hardie souldiour, and good seruitor, iii 907
Carthamus bastard saffron, i 393.
Cartimandua buried quicke, v 70
———— Quéene of Brigants betraieth Caratake into the Romans hands, i 490
———— At square with hir husband Henatius note, v 432
Cassels earle committed into ward, v 648
——— Slaine, v 503
Cassibilane king of Britaine requireth aid of the Scots against the Romans, v 58
———— Protector of the Britains, i 464
———— He sendeth to foure kings of Kent for aid against Cesar, i 470
———— He ruled Oxfordshire, Berkeshire, Buckinghamshire, Hamshire, Bedfordshire, i 472
———— Chose chéefe gouernor of the British armie, ib
———— Vanquished by Cesar, i 475.
———— His noble acts and stratagems against the Romans, i 476
———— He opposeth himselfe against Cesar in behalfe of Britaine, i 465
———— His sharpe stakes pitcht and set on the Thames banke, i 476
———— His towne taken by Cesar, ib
———— The time of his regiment & vanquishment, i 477
Cassimere ambassador from the emperor Maximilian note, iii 530
———— His comming into England, receiuing at London, going to the court, made knight of the garter, iv 315
Castell of Bungle & Leicester, &c. when and by whom defaced, i 328
———— Of Bestons prophesie, ib.

Castell of Cambridge higher than that of Oxford, vol i page 250
—— Of Blackenesse woone, v 600.
—— ¶ Sée Blackenesse.
—— Of Banbourgh how woone and gotten, ii. 56
—————— Yéelded vnto king William Rufus, ib
—— Of Leauer summoned to yéeld to king Iohn, ii 327
—— Of Bihaus yéelded, ii 350
—— Chartleie and Beston built, ib
—— Of Doll in Britaine belonging to earle Rafe, besieged, ii 19
—— Of Douer and Windsor could Lewis neuer subdue, ii 332
—————— Yéelded vnto the quéene, ii 83.
—————— Dooth Lewis the French labour to get but in vaine, ii 333.
—— Of Durham by whom built, ii 17.
—— Of Faringdon built, ii 96
—— Of Fodringheie taken by dissimulation, ii. 350
—— Galiard besieged and woone by the French, ii. 288.
—————— Builded by Richard the first, ii. 269
—— Of Horne ouerthrowne by William Rufus, ii 29
—— Of Huntington woone, ii 158.
—— Of Maluaisin built by William Rufus, and whie, ii 36.
—— Of Montgomerie built, ii 351
—————— Woon by the Welshmen, ii 36.
—— Of Newarke in whose keeping, ii 333
—————— Where king Iohn died, ib
—— Of Newberrie woone, ii 102
—— Of Norham by whome begun, ii 71
—— Of Notingham woone by Richard the first, ii 246
—————— In whose keeping, ii 333
—— Of Ramseie where Odo laie fortified against William Rufus, ii 29.
—— Of Richmout néere Gillingham builded, ii 11
—— Of Rochester. ¶ Sée Rochester.
—— Of Rockingham, ii 41.
—— Of Rutland builded, ii 141
—— Of Tickhill yéelded, ii 246
—— Of Tunbridge yéelded into William Rufus his hands, ii 29
Castell séene in the aire and armed men, ii 677.
Castels surrendered and taken by force of the English, v 336
—— Repaired, v 135.
—— In pledge, v. 289.
—— ¶ Sée their proper names dispersed in this table
—— Besieged and surrendered to Lewis the French king's sonne, ii 342.
Castels woone by the bishop of Durham, vol iii. page 529
—— Builded by duke William for the suppressing rebellions, ii 9
—— Fortified by king Iohn, ii 338.
—— Besieged by bishops, ii 216
—— Deliuered to king Richard the first, ii 222.
—— Deliuered by the king of Scots, ii. 163.
—— Woone by the Scots, ii 157
—— Held by great men against king Stephan, ii 83
—— Licenced to be builded, ii. 80
—— Manie builded in king Stephans daies, ii. 110.
—— In number 1115 to be rased, ii 105
—— Fortified by the bishop of Winchester, ii 92.
—— Built by the bishop of Salisburie, ii 8
—— Recouered by K. Stephan, ii 85.
—— Of Bristow and Cardiff, &c by whome builded, ii. 63.
—— Fortified against Henrie the first, ii. 50.
—— And holds in England, i 326.
—— Manie and by whom sometimes builded, i. 327
—— What and where mentioned, ib
—— The ruine of manie cities, i 326.
—— The cause of their ruine and decaie, i 327.
—— At Cambridge and Oxford by whom builded, i. 250.
Casteller. ¶ Sée Shoomaker.
Castile inuaded by the duke of Lancaster, and the king of Portingale, ii 770, 771.
—— Philip king thereof saileth out of Flanders into Spaine, cast by casualtie of sea vpon the English coasts, promiseth to deliuer Henrie the seuenth the earle of Suffolke, iii 535, 536
Castins lieutenant of Britaine, v 126
—— Raised an armie, ib
Cat hanged at Cheape disguised like a massing préest, iv. 28.
Catara ¶ Sée Forbisher
Catagrine ¶ Sée Catigerne
Cataratacus vanquished by the Romans, i. 482.
Catalog of Irish saints, vi 222
—— Of lerned men, v 57.
—— Of noblemen, vi 46.
—— Of bishoprikes and bishops of Kildare, vi. 41, 45
Catesbie and his conditions described, iii 379
Cathnisse the earle passeth into Orkenie, v. 508.
—— Slaine, ib
Catherlow alias Carlow or Clauill, vi 208
—— By whome it was builded, vi 210.
—— How far distant from England, i 191.
Catigerne the brother of Uortimer killeth Horsus, i. 568
Catell kept for profit, i 369
—— Somtimes féed vpon saffron, i 390
—— In England of diuerse sorts, i 186.
Catus Decianus taketh flight, i 499
—— Procurater fled into France, v 71.
—————— Wounded, v 72.

Charitie of Iohn Ligh a préest, vol iii page 539
——— Of Kneisworth maior of London, iii 532
——— Of sir Iohn Allen, twise maior of London, iii 831
——— Of George Monex maior of London, iii 599
——— Of Thomas Huntlow shiriffe of London, iii 810
——— Of Thomas Gibson shiriffe of London, iii 807
——— Of sir Thomas White, iv 8
——— Of sir Iohn Gresham, iv 83
——— Preached before Edward the sixt, and the effects that followed note, iii 1060
——— It and concord in a commonwealth be things most necessarie note, iii 852
——— ¶ Sée Almeshouses, Pittie, and Mercie
——— Of Oswald to the poore note, i 616
——— ¶ See Hospitalitie
Charles the fourth emperour glased church windows with geat stone, i 401
Charles de Ualois chaseth the Englishmen, his returne into France, ii 507
——— Sent to Bruges, and disappointed of his preie, ii 525
——— ¶ Sée French King
Charles Iames yoong prince of Scots christened, iv 231.
Charta de Foresta, ii 357, 527
Charter of Alexander king of Scotland made to Henrie the third, ii 40?
——— The same confirmed by the pope, ii 406, 407
——— Of articles concerning a league betwéene Henrie the third & the nobles of Wales, ii 391, 392
——— Of the articles of Dauid of Wales his submission, ii 393
——— When Edward the first is acknowledged superior lord of Scotland ii 494, 495, 496
——— Of king Iohns submission, as it was conceiued to the pope at Rome, ii 307
——— Of Richard the first concerning turnaments, ii 253
——— Conteining articles of the peace and agréement concluded betwixt the two kings read in S Peters church in Yorke, ii 165
——— Of agréement betwéene the king of England and the king of Conagh, ii 167
——— Of king Stephan and the pacification of troubles betwixt him and Henrie Fitzempresse, ii 106
——— Of manumission granted to the rebels by Richard the second, ii 743
——— Blanke sealed note, ii 848
——— Confirmed vnder Henrie the thirds acknowledgment and subscription of witnesses, ii 381
——— Cancelled and much grieued at, ii 360
Chartres taken by treason notwithstanding the truce, iii 173
Charugage a certeine dutie for euerie plowland, ii 296
Chase and parke how they differ, vol i page 316.
Chases & what beasts to them properlie belonged, ib.
Chastitie of the ladie Grue, and her wisdom, ii 387.
——— Should such professe as would be admitted subdeacons, ii 51
——— ¶ Sée Clergie
——— ¶ Sée Uirginitie
Chatalon in Touraine deliuered to the Scots, v. 412
Chaucer the English poet in what kings time he liued, iii. 59. 59
——— ¶ Sée Dukes
Chaumount Hugh taken prisoner, ii 263
Cheapside conduit builded, iii 348
Cheddeihole or Cheddei rocke in Summersetshire in English woonder, i 217
Chécke knight his deserued commendation note, iii 1011
——— His treatise shewing how greeuous sedition is to a commonwealth note, iii 989 to 1011.
Cheinie knight, lord warden of the cinque ports, authorised by Henrie the eight to the christening of the Dolphins daughter, iii 856
——— An enimie to Wiat note, iv 12.
——— Henrie the eights letter to him for a prescript forme of demeanor in the English towards the French, iii 856, 857, 858
——— Lord warden of the Cinque ports his death, his old seruices at home and abroad, much spoken to his praise and honor note, iv 157.
Cheldrike K of Germaine commeth in aid of Colgrime, i 475
Chelmesford or Chelmecford so named of the riuer Chelmer, i 180
Cherwald K. of Westsaxons ouercomme of Penda, i 618
——— Admitteth bishops and expelleth them again, ib
——— Unuanquished by Uulfhere, i 621.
Cheolred K of Mercia, i 639
Chepstow, vi 126
Cheribert. ¶ Sée Bertha
Cherwort ¶ Sée Béere
Cheshire made a prince palatine, ii 813
Cheshiremen gard Richard the second, ii 838.
——— Slaine note, iii 26
Chesill riuer described, being like a narrow banke note, i 110
Chesholme Iohn commeth out of France, v 651.
Chester how called in the Romans time and when it was an vniuersitie, i 320
——— How seated, why called Caerleon or Ciuitas legionum, and how statlie in old time, i 125
——— Raced to the ground and not since reedified, i 62
——— Bishopriks erection, circuit, and ualuation, i 214
——— A colonie of Romans note, i 191
——— Taken by the Danes, i 673
——— Builded by Marius, as some thinke, i 510
——— Conquered by Egbert, i 658
——— Defaced by the Danes, i 681

Chester two churches there built by earle Leofrike, vol 1 page 750
——— Supposed to haue been begun to be builded by Osto ius, 1 491
——— Repaired by I eill, & when first so called, 1 416
Chester abbeie by whome builded, ii 46.
——— Who gaue the order therto, ii 47
——— Earledome by whome possessed and inioied, ii. 38.
Chestershire & Lancastershire diuided by the riuer Tame, 1 142
Cheuiot hils twentie miles in length, 1 184
Cheuling encountereth with Britans & vanquisheth them, 1 586.
——— K. of Westsaxons endeth his life in exile, 1 589
——— ¶ Sée Kenrike
Chichester how called in the Romans time, 1 321
——— Bishoprike when first begun, & the circuit thereof, 1 237
Cherburgh besieged by the English, iii 96
——— Yéelded to the Englishmen, ib
——— Deliuered to the English, ii 719
——— Possessed by the English, iii 98
Child of eleuen yeais old speaking strange spéeches, iv 433
Children 50 of Ebranke, 1 445
Chime of saint Giles without Criplegate to be mentioned, iv 428
——— ¶ Sée Bels.
Chimmage ¶ Sée Subsidie
Chimnies how manie, in times past, 1 317
Chinon taken by force of assault, ii 293
Chipping Walden, why so named, 1 347
Chorea Gigantum, 1 571
Christ and of a portion of his bloud shewed in a solemne procession, ii 414
Christ counterfet whipped, iv 202
——— False apprehended and punished, ii 351.
Christ Iesus his birth, 1 479 v 60, 61
——— Diuerse things that were occupied about him crucified sent to Adelstane for presents, 1 668
Christening not knowne nor vsed in some places in Ireland, vi 382
Christian bishop of Lisemore, vi 94
Christians preuaile against the Saracens at Damieta, ii 349
——— At enmious discord, ii 232
——— Beheded by the Turks, ii 230
——— And Saracens are at peace, ii 234
——— Two hundred and thréescore deliuered from the captiuitie of the Turks, by means of one Iohn Fox note, iv. 428
——— ¶ Sée Saracens.
——— Saued from the furie of the sword, 1 204
——— Gréeuouslie afflicted after Cowins death, 1 610.
——— Persecuted vnder Dioclesian, 1 527
——— Honored and cherished in Constantines time, 1. 531.
Christians in word but not in déed & how Peda thought of them, vol 1 page 620
——— ¶ Sée Constantineus and Dioclesian
Christianitie abiured for monie note, ii 15.
Christiannus a bishop of the Danes, & capteine in warre, ii 12
Christine a quéenes sister, a nun. ¶ Sée Margaret.
Christmas roiall, iii 558
——— Shewes, iii 514
——— Called The still Christmasse, iii 711
——— Bankets resembling the feasts of Bacchanalia, v 151
Christes church in Dublin burned, vi 240
——— New reedified and restored, ib
——— First builded by the Danes, ib.
——— Hospitall erected, iii 1062
Chronicles of Barnwell, 1 190
——— Of Burton, 1. 41
——— Of Cogshall, 1 21.
——— Whereof and whie so named, and their necessarie vse, iv 311, 312
——— And other books burned, v. 337
Chroniclers deserue a dutifull reuerence, and whie, iv 311, 312
Chrysocolla, 1 397
Chrystal stone, 1. 402
Church of England more beneficial to the princes coffers than the state of the laitie, 1 231
——— The ancient and present state thereof, 1 221.
——— It is become the asse whereon euerie market man is to ride and cast his wallet, 1 231
——— Lands of it and college possessions pried after by dingthriefts, 1 256
——— Whether that which Lucius builded at London stood at Westminster or in Cornehill, 1 42.
——— That of S Martins turned into a barne, 1. 97
——— ¶ Sée Vniuersitie
Church neglected whiles the Danes kept such a sturre in England note, 1. 683
——— Inriched by Cnute and his wife Emma, 1. 732
——— Gouernement thereof prescribed by Gregorie, 1 593
——— Articles of reformation for it from pope Adrian note, 1 651
——— Of saint Anthonies in London, when and by whom builded, iii 710
——— Of saint Dunstans in the east defiled with bloud note, iii 95
——— Of Ely dedicated note, ii 425.
——— Of Hales solemnlie dedicated, ii 423
——— Of Scotland obedient to the church of England, 1 168
——— Of England sore fléesed of hir wealth, ii. 30.
——— Ruinated by the Danes in the north parts, and verie scant note, ii 15
——— Depriued of temporall prosperitie, ii 112.
——— Impropriat, & that the bishop of Linco ne

had authoritie to institute vicars in them, vol ii. page 121
Church occupied by incumbents strangers of the popes preferring, what grudge it bred note, ii 370
——— Spoiles aduantage not the getter note, ii 535.
——— That for feare of the censure thereof the English pledges were released, ii 255
——— Iewels &c turned into monie for Richard the first his ransome, ii 241
——— The state thereof in Beckets time, ii 132
——— Liuings restored by act of parlement note, iv 80
——— Cathedrall to inioie the right of their elections, ii 700.
——— Ouerthrowne by an earthquake, ii 754.
——— In London stricken and broken by tempest, iv. 185
——— Made a kenell of hounds, reuenged, ii 38
——— ¶ Sée Consecration, Fines, Inuestitures, Lands, Schisme
——— Inriched & the crowne impouerished note, v 289
——— Cathedrall of Murrie burnt, v 401.
Church discipline, i 594
Churches in England scowred and cleansed from all relikes of idolatrie, and how beautifull, i 232
——— Priuileges granted to them and church yards, i 332
——— Stone in times past was vsed and dedicated to thē, i 394
——— The old estate of cathedrall churches, i 234
——— Exercises kept in them, i 227
——— Why so called, ib.
——— In part conuerted into markets & shops, and why, ib.
——— Collegiat diuers in England, i 234
——— Parish churches wherevpon they began & were erected, i 227.
——— Exercises vsed ordinarilie in them, i 232
——— Decaied in Lelands time, i 325
——— In Lincolne fiftie two in times past, i 324.
——— In France how manie, i 234.
——— ¶ Sée Clergie and Parishes
——— Built euerie where in Northumberland when Aidan preached, i 616.
——— Repared by Aurelius Ambrose, i. 616.
——— Destroied, i 588
——— How bountifull king Ethewulfe was to them, i 662
——— First builded, vi 85
——— Spoiled, vi 382.
——— Repared, v 263
——— Indowed by king William, v 305.
Churchmen ¶ Sée Clergie
——— Fauoured, v 136.
——— Their liuings demanded, v 609, 610
Churchyard new néere Bedlem first made, iv. 234.
Cicero matched by Fronto, i. 522
Cicester, the situation thereof, iii 520
Cicester how called in the Romans time, vol. i. page 320
Cicill knight commissioner into Scotland, about an accord of peace, iv 198
——— Created lord treasuror, iv 285
——— His descent, iv 317
Cidmouth hauen whereof so named, i 101
Cinegiscus & his sonne Richelius reigne iointlie ouer the Westsaxons, i 600
Cinevulfus ¶ Sée Kinewulfe
Cingetorix king of Kent taken prisoner of Romans, i 475
Cinnabarum, i 397
Cipriots resist Richard the first his landing, and are pursued, vanquished, ii 121
——— Their offers in respect of his discontentment and losse, ii 221
——— Submit themselues and are receiued as his subiects, ii 222.
——— Their king submitteth himselfe to Richard the first, ii 221
——— Stealeth awaie, & submitteth himselfe againe, is committed prisoner and chained in giues of siluer, ii 222
Circumcision for loue of a Jewish woman, ii. 352.
Cirencester, now Cicester taken by Gurmundus, i 588.
Cirus monarch of Persia, vi 153
Cissa sonne to Ella the Saxon, i 573.
Cisteaux moonks. ¶ Sée moonks white.
Citie whereof it consisteth, iii 996
Cities their necessarie vse and seruice note, iii 997.
——— First builded, vi 91
Cities, townes & monasteries ouerthrowne with wind, i 652
——— Defaced with fire, i 648
——— That stood in this land in the Romans time, i 320.
——— When first builded and multipled, i 319
——— Greater in times past, when husbandmē were all citizens, ib
——— That send knights, citizens, burgesses and barons to parlemēt, i 294
——— Southerlie builded were ancient, faire & great, i 319
——— Ancient so decaied as that their ruins are no where to be séene, i 321.
——— The names of them in England, i 324.
——— ¶ Sée Towns
Citizens & burgesses, i 274.
——— Sée Londoners
Ciuilis a mainteiner of iustice, i 515.
Ciuilitie in Ireland, vi 4.
Claie of diuerse sorts occupied in building, i. 315.
Clanricard ¶ Sée Bourgh & Borgh.
Clare sir Richard discomfiteth the earle of Ulsters power, vi 245
——— He slue six hundred gallowglasses, ib
——— Giueth hostages to assure his allegiance, vi. 247
——— He leuieth an armie against the Scots, vi. 249.
——— He slaine, vi 250.

Clare Thomas married the daughter of Moris Fitzmoris, vol vi page 239
—— He slue Ovrentoth king of Thomond, ib
—— He died, vi. 240
Clarens duchie whense it had the denomination, i 177
Claudia Rufina a British ladie, i 40
Claudianus report of Britaine in the decaie of the Romane empire, i. 518.
Claudiocestria, now Glocester, i 485
Claudius the emperor moueth war against Britaine, & why, i 481
—— He sendeth legions of soldiers into Ireland, i. 481
—— He giueth his daughter Cenissa in mariage to Aruiragus, ib
—— He woone Portchester, ib
—— He setteth Caratake, his wife & kindred at libertie, i 490
—— He in person commeth into Britaine, i 484 v 61.
Claudius temple builded, v 65
—— At Colchester, v 237.
Cleanders hatred against Perhennis, i. 514
Cle hils in Shropshire, i 184
Clee riuer rising in the verie confines of Buckingham & Bedfordshire, i 173
Clemencie of Iames the fourth vnto rebels and murtherers, v 460
Clere sir Iohn slaine in the ile of Orkneie, v 585.
Clergie fauour Cnute for their oth sake, i 721
—— Of England reuerentlie thought of in foren regions, i 246
—— Fauourable in punishing whoredome, i 312.
—— Their presumptuous authoritie restreined by acts, ii 414.
—— Large offer to Henrie the third in a parlement, ii 441
—— Depriued of their liuings and liberties, ii 14.
—— And Normans preferred, ib
—— Kicked at by Duke William, against whome note his malice, ib
—— Pinched by their pursses, fret and fume against the popes procéedings in that behalfe, ii 436
—— Resist duke Williams decrées, and are banished, ii 12
—— Hardlie delt withall, and out of order note, ii 40
—— Of England complain to pope Urban against William Rufus, ii 30.
—— Cardinall Pools articles concerning them, iv 141
—— Grant halfe of all their spirituall reuenues for one yeare to Henrie the eight, iii 684.
—— Complained of by the commons, iii. 741
—— Both head and taile one with another against them, iii 745
—— In danger of a premunire, their offer to Henrie the eight, iii 766
—— The same pardoned, ib.
Clergie their submission to Henrie the eight note, vol iii page 766
—— Speake euill of Henrie the eights procéedings in the reformation of religion, iii 795
—— Conuocation for the reforming of religion, ib
—— Complained of for their crueltie Ex officio, iii 775
—— The cause whie so heinouslie offending was so fauoured, iii 523
—— Of two sorts and both desirous to spare their pursses, iii 532
—— Of Excester againt Henrie the sixt and the duke of Summerset in defense of their ecclesiasticall priuileges, iii 229
—— A bill exhibited against them in the parlement, iii 65
—— Libels against the in cast abrode, iii. 86.
—— Sorelie bridled, ii 813
—— Inueied against of the Wickleuists, ii 825
—— They complaine of them to the king, ib
—— Ignorant and couetous in Richard the seconds time note, ii 869.
—— Mainteined by archbishop Arundell of Canturburie, iii 30
—— Fauoured of Henrie the fourth, iii. 48
—— Displeased by Henrie the firsts doomgs, ii. 52
—— Of England consisted most of préests sonnes, ii. 57
—— Exempted from dealing in anie temporall cause or office, ii 51
—— To kéepe no woman in their house except, &c ii. 58.
—— Of liberties obteined for them, ii 171
—— Against Henrie the second, whome he laboureth to bridle, ii 119
—— A heauie time for them note, ii 297
—— In what awe they had K Iohn, ii 312
—— Repining against K. Iohn, ii 317
—— More malicious to king Iohn than he deserued, ii 339
—— Complaine to Henrie the third against the collections for the pope, ii 388
—— Of Durham glad to flie into the holie Iland, ii 12.
—— Paid a tenth sooner than the time appointed, ii 609
—— Deposed for denieng the subsidie, ii 696
—— Presumptuous demenors, ii 575
—— Without head note, ii 503
—— Grant halfe part of their liuings to king Edward the first, ib
—— Grant the eleaueuth part of ecclesiasticall things to Edward the first, ii 492
—— Grant tenths of spirituall liuings to Edward the first, ii 493
—— Continue in deniall of a subsidie, ii 520
—— Excuse to be frée from subsidies, &c ii 519
—— Their pride abhorred of Edward the first, ii 511

Clergie oppressed complaine, & the same redressed, vol ii page 513
——— Fined, but the temporaltie pardoned note, ii 348.
——— In a miserable case, ii 520
——— Pinched with courtesies, beneuolences, and aids note, ii 512
——— Mainteined and defended by archbishop Richard of Canturburie, ii 308
——— Sore gréeued at the popes exactions, ii 388.
——— ¶ Sée Bishops, Churchmen, Ferebeth, & Préests
Clergieman slaine and what seuere execution insued, v 309, 310
Clergie men vsed kings as they listed, i 224, 225, 226.
——— Had the best wine in old time, i 281, 282
——— Immunitie of them greater vnder idolatrie than vnder the gospell, i 36.
——— ¶ Sée Preests
Clerke knight, a valiant capteine, ii 723
Clinton lord admerall, sent against the rebels in the north, iv 336
——— Sent out against Brest, iv 118
——— His seruice in Scotland, iv 881.
——— Deceaseth, iv 554
Clinton Gefferie, a noble man accused of treason, ii 74
Clinton Atkinson ¶ Sée Pirats
Clippers of gold ¶ Sée Coine.
Clocks, i 405
Clodius Albinus lieutenant of Britaine, i 515.
Cloten inheritor to the whole empire, and why he diuided it, i 197.
——— K of Cornwall, i 450
Cloth carried out to be shorne, i 397
Clothiers in diuerse places reléeued, iv 427
——— In Barton had two hundred pounds lent gratis for euer, iv 534
Clothworkers starue and beg, i 367
Clontars field by Kilmainham, vi 94
Clowne deriued of the word Colom, vi 4
Cneus Trebellius appointed in Agricoh his place, v 83
——— Lieutenant of Britaine, i 510, 513
Cnute the son of Sweine succeeds his father in England, i 716.
——— Absolute K of England, i 726
——— He passeth into Denmarke to subdue the Uandals & Swedeners that annoied his land, i 729
——— His diuerse acts politike, and memorable saiengs, i 731
——— He refuseth combat proffered him by K Edmund Ironside, i 721.
——— At Gilingham in Dorsetshire he is put to flight, i 722
——— He is maried to the widow of Egelred, i 727
——— He sendeth awaie his Danish nauie into Denmarke, i. 728.
Cnute his endeuor to establish himselfe in the kingdome, vol i page 717
——— He taketh vpon him the rule of all England, i 727
——— He causeth Edriks throte to be cut, i 728.
——— What countries he passed through, i. 719
——— He returneth into England, ib
——— He & K Edmund Ironside fight a combat, i 724.
——— His lawes, i 732
——— He is forced to forsake England, i 717
——— He would command the sea in his pride, & is taught humilitie, i 731
——— He renounceth the wearing of a crowne roiall anie more, ib.
——— His children, ib
——— His death, i 730
Cnuto with certeine Danes, arriueth in England: note, ii 18
Cobham lord Iohn begun to build Rochester bridge, i 91.
Cobham lord with his new supplie of soldiers, valiant, iii 909.
——— Condemned note, ii 843.
——— Unable to resist Wiat and his power, iv. 14
——— Made of the priue councell, iv. 666.
——— His lineall descent, iv 790
Cobham Thomas bishop of Worcester note, i 289.
Cobois capteine, v 562
Cocke of Westminster ¶ Sée Casteller
Coell traitorouslie slaine in his bed, i 198.
Coelus gouernment in Britaine, i 527.
Cogan Miles with others assaulted Dublin and taketh it, vi 147
——— Hath the custodie of the citie, ib
——— He is besieged therein by Hasculphus, ib
——— He taketh him and cutteth off his head, ib.
——— He is made lieutenant of the armie and constable of Dublin, vi 203
——— He first entereth into Conagh, vi 203
——— He and Robert Fitzstephans haue the kingdome of Cork giuen to them, vi. 204
——— He is slaine, vi 205.
Cogan Miles is taken prisoner, vi 239
Cogan Richard brother to Miles, his good seruice and valiantnesse, vi 150
——— He commeth to Cork with a companie to supplie his brothers place, vi 205, 206
Cogidunus king of Britaine, i 478
——— Faithfull to the Romans, i 492
Cognisances. ¶ Sée Badges
Coifi an heathenish bishops zeal to destroie idolatrie, i 607
Coillus king of Britaine described, i 511.
——— His subtiltie, entered into Scotland with an armie, slaine, and his armie discomfited, v 41, 42
Coine imbased, v 453
——— Base, iii 838.
——— New, v. 5
——— Of small péeces, as six pence, &c iv 203.
——— New of sundrie sorts, iv 202

Coine thirtie barrels carried ouer sea for soldiours paie, vol ii page 396
—— Of sundrie sorts in England currant, prohibited by proclamation, ii 532.
—— ¶ Sée Monie, & Romans
—— Of Edward the first amended, ii 483
—— Of grotes and halfe grotes, first coined, ii 632
— — To be inhansed or abased, ii 636
— — Disanulled, and degrées of Florens made, ii 629.
—— New of gold called the Floren, ii 627.
—— Of Ireland reformed, ii 302
—— Altered, ii 114
—— Of Henrie the seconds changed in forme, & whie, ii 180
—— Cricket, wherein note Henrie the firsts art, ii 77
—— Changed, iii 55
—— Imbased, iii 1031
—— New stamped, iii 283
—— Diuerse sorts newlie ordeined, iii 532
—— Of gold set at their valuation, iii 713
—— Salute, iii 124
—— Clipped an ordinance for the same note, ii 416
—— And lucerne not to be vsed, vi 163
Coine clippers, washers, &c searched for, ii. 482
—— Both gold and siluer, executed as traitors, iv 329, 343
Coine counterfettors executed, iv. 234, 545
Coiner executed, iii 532
Coiners in Connagh, vi 398.
—— Of England in times past, & now present, ib
Coines forren both of gold and siluer, i. 367
Colchester. v 65
—— Builded, i 533
—— Walled by Helen, ib
—— Whereof Eldad was bishop, ii 565
—— In old time called Camalodunum, i 178.
—— Wan by the Romans, i 181
—— Whether so named of the riuer Colne or Colonia Romanorum, i 178
—— How called in the Romans time, i 320
—— Named a long time Colonia, i. 368
—— Castell besieged, and deliuered to king Iohn, ii 329
Colemines, i 397
Colewort medicinable, i 352.
Colgerne a Saxon is sent for by Occa, v 151, 152
—— Landeth in Northumberland, v 152.
—— Created duke of Northumberland, v 153
—— Reprooueth Loth, is run through by his aduersarie, v 155
Colier capteine his seruice in the Butlers warre, his seruice at castle Balie Riogh, vi 385.
College ¶ Sée Uniuersitie
Collect deuised in honour of Thomas Becket note, ii 146
Collect ¶ Sée Praiers
Collection ¶ Sée Officers.
Collet Iohn deane of Paules, founder of Paules schoole, vol i page 248
Collingborne a fauourer of the earle of Richmond, his purpose to aid him at Poole in Dorchester, indicted to be a libellor against the king, he is executed, iii 422, 423
Collingham a valorous gentleman of Sussex, ii 332
Colman bishop of Northumbers, i 624
—— Conuerted the Saxons, v 175
—— Erected a monasterie, v 176
—— Gouernor of Marre, a wise counsellor, his oration before king Achaius. note, v. 187.
Colme king of Leinster, vi 86
Colmekill, v 125
Colmes inch Ile woone by the English, v. 551
Colonie of southerne men planted in Carlell, ii 32
—— What it is, i 322
Combat, vi 245
—— Betwéene two Oconhers, vi 455
—— In a case of treason, v 234
—— ¶ Sée Iusts
—— Betwéene Catigerne & Horsus, i 558.
—— Offered by K Edmund Ironside to Cnute the Dane, i 721
—— Fought betwéene K Edmund Ironside & Cnute, i 724.
—— Purposed of Edgar against the king of England & Kenneth king of Scots, i 698
—— Betwéene Corineus & Thomagot, i 15
—— ¶ Sée Conflict
—— Appointed at Tuthill, in a controuersie of land, but not tried note, iv 261
—— With the lord Fleming, sued for by sir George Carew, iv 246
—— Fought at Westminster, ii 651
—— In a case of debate, appointed and disappointed, ii 653
—— Required betwixt the king of England and France, for triall of all matters of controuersie betwéene them, ii 263
—— Purposed in a controuersie of lands, ii. 174
—— Betwixt Henrie de Essex and Robert de Montfort, ii 114.
—— Fought betwixt esquires of differing nations, ii 671
—— Betwéene two dukes, staied by Richard the second, ii 871
—— Appointed betwéene the duke of Lancaster and the duke of Norfolke, ii 186, 187
—— Betweene a knight and an esquire, with the maner thereof note, ii 727
—— For triall of treason, in what care lawfull note, ib
—— Betwéene two Scotish gentlemen, accusing each other, iii 890.
—— Betwéene Henrie the fift, and monsieur Baulbason, iii 122
—— Upon triall of manhood, betwéene an Englishman and a French, iii 214.
—— Appointed and disappointed, iii. 210.

Combat betwéene Iulian Romerou, and Marow, vol iii page 808.
——— The French king challengeth the emperor thereto, and giueth him the lie, iii 231
Combination of traitors, vi 369.
Comes ¶ Sée Earle
Comet. ¶ Sée Blasing Starre
Comin archbishop of Dublin, founder of saint Patrikes church, vi 237, 238
——— Sute made to king Henrie the second that he should be bishop, vi 236
Comius of Arras ambassadour from the Romans staid of the Britons as prisoner, i 467
Commandement bloudie executed on the English, i 16
Commissioners for examining the matters betweene the earles of Ossorie and Kildare, vi 280
——— Sent into England, v 648.
Commodus the emperor sendeth Ulpius against the Britains, i 514
——— He enuieth the renowne of Ulpius, ib
Common crier for sale of houshold stuffe, iv 226
Commons proponed certeine articles against the duke of Suffolke, iii 218
——— In England to what vse they serued, and how their vse is peruerted, i 188
——— Incroched vpon by the erecting of tenements i 189
Commotion of the commons in diuerse parts of the realme, by reason of the great subsidie, and other oppressions, i 735
——— In Summersetshire and other places note, iii 907
——— In Yorkeshire, iii 290
——— In Norwich against the prior of the plase note, iii 209
——— ¶ Sée Insurrection, Rebellion, and Subsidie
——— Against Arunagus, v 65
——— Betweene the earles of Murrie and Huntleie, v 486.
——— In Scotland, note the end, v 244.
——— ¶ Sée Angus, Uariance
Communion booke and common praier published, iii 906
——— Confirmed, ii 1031
Communion in both kinds, ii 869
——— Receiued of six bishops, iv 186
Companie lewd, and what mischéefe and disorder it worketh, ii 517.
——— With ill counsell how mischéefous, ii. 502
Compassion of an Englishman to a French, iii 214
——— Of Perken Wardbecke counterfet, iii 513.
Compiegne surrendered to the English by a policie, recouered from the French iii 140
Composition vnwise, v 343
Compostella ¶ Sée Brigantia
Complaint out of England to Rome against Henrie the third, ii. 384.
Complaint made to the pope by the monks of Christs church of their archbishop, vol ii page 265
——— Of Becket to the pope, ii 124
——— Of Anselme to the pope against William Rufus, ii 43
——— ¶ Sée Clergie
——— First tendered out of England to Rome, i 12
Complexions of people according to the climat where they dwell, i 193
Compremise ¶ Sée Arbitrement
Compulsion voluntarie, iii 910
Con Onele beareth the sword before the lord deputie, vi 280.
——— Created earle of Tiron, vi 329
——— He kept Alson the wife of Kelleie a smith, vi 330.
——— He had no right to the countrie but for his life, ib
Conan the sonne of Alane earle of Britaine, maried to a kings daughter, ii 12
Conan Meridoc duke of Cornwall, i 533.
Conanus chosen king of Scotland, persecuteth offenders, renounceth the estate, v 50
——— Giuen to excessiue gluttonie, conspired against, committed to close keeping, his officers punished, v 89, 90
——— Dieth, v 91
Conanus Camber counselleth the Britons to seeke peace with the Scots, and slaine amongst them, v. 130, 131
——— Goeth about to persuade his countrie to breake the peace with the Scots and Picts, v 134
Concordance of the foure euangelists found among S Brides monuments, vi 87
Concubine of the duke of Lancaster maried vnto him, ii 831
——— Of the duke of Glocester, whom he marieth, iii 145
——— Thrée of Edward the fourth, iii. 384.
——— ¶ Sée Shores wife, Perers, Préests, and Daisie
Concubines loue to hir paramour, notable, ii. 259.
Concupisence, v 182.
Conduit at Walbrooke new built, vi 231
——— In Holbourne founded and finished, iv. 428
——— In Cheapside builded, iii 348.
——— At Bishopsgate builded, iii 533.
Connewaie sir Iohn lord president of Ulster, vi 85.
Confession of a murthering queene note, v 183
——— Of the duke of Suffolke at his beheading, iv 21
——— Of sir Thomas Palmer on the scaffold at Tower hill, iv 5
——— Uoluntarie of Francis Throckmorton the traitor, written to queene Elisabeth, with his letters of submission note, iv 544, 545
——— Uoluntarie of Parrie the notable traitor that ment to haue murthered the quéene, iv. 566 to 570.

Conspirasie and murther, vol v page 89
——— Against king William Rufus, to put him beside the crowne, ii 28
——— Of Robert earle of Northumberland, and whie, ii 36
——— In Northfolke towards, and how extinguished note, iv 253, 254.
——— Of the lords against Henrie the third, ii 361
——— Of Foukes de Brent, against Henrie the third, and his foule end, ii 356
——— Against the lord chéefe iustice, ii 354
——— To set prisoners at libertie, ii 572
——— Of lords against king Iohn, ii 318, 319, 320
——— Of lords binding themselues against king Iohn, ii 319
——— Of great men against king Stephan, ii 83.
——— Disclosed, and the discloser slaine, iii. 10
——— What an ill euent it hath, iii 37, 38
——— A fresh against Henrie the fourth, by the earle of Northumberland others, iii 36
——— Of the Persies with Owen Glendouer, iii 22, 23, 21
——— Deuised but not practised, and yet punished. note, iii 19
——— Against Henrie the fourth and the parties executed, iii 12, 13
——— Of the noblemen strangelie disclosed· note, iii 10
——— Of the abbat of Westminster against Henrie the fourth note, iii 9
——— Betwéene the duke of Glocester and the abbat of saint Albons, their purpose, & is disclosed, ii. 836.
——— Richard the second against the duke of Glocester, ii 387
——— Of Frenchmen against the English, iii 107
——— Of nobles against Edward the fourth note, iii 288, 289, 290
——— Of the Parisiens against the duke of Bedford punished with death, iii 138
——— At Excester against Richard the third, some of the parties executed, iii 121
——— Of the duke of Buckingham against Richard the third, had ill successe note, iii. 416, 417
——— Against Henrie the seuenth, and what an ill end it had, iii 481, 486, 487
——— Against the prince falleth out alwaie against the cōspirators shamefull death, iii 529.
——— Traitorous note, iii 798
——— Vpon a malcontentment. ¶ Sée Lincolnshiremen
——— Against the ladie Elisabeth whiles she was in trouble, iv 182
——— Against quéene Marie, sorting to an euill end note, iv 84
Conspirasie of quéene Maries death, and the offendors executed, vol iv page 54
——— ¶ Sée Duke of Buckingham, Noblemen, Rebellion, Heresies, & Treson
Conspirators ouerthrowne and discomfited note, ii 29.
——— Extreamlie punished, and that diuerslie, ii 36.
——— Vanquished and punished. note, ii. 325
——— In league, and inuade Henrie the seconds dominions, ii 150
——— Against Henrie the first, to put him beside the crowne, ii 49
——— Of king Iames the first his death, v 425
——— Search made for them, their execution, v. 127.
——— Drowned and otherwise reprochfullie executed note, ib
——— Put to a most horrible death note, v 230
——— Discouered and pardoned. note, v 278
Constable Iohn sent for Lacie, vi 209
——— ¶ Sée France
Constables of England, called high constables, the office ending in the duke of Buckingham, iii 663
——— High and petie their offices, i 261.
Constance the mother of duke Arthur ¶ Sée Duke.
Constance wife to Eustace sent home, ii. 104
Constancie of the Picts when they were besieged, v 204
——— Of the archbishop of Yorke, ii 443
——— Of the earle of Carlill at his death, ii 574
——— In martyrdom, iii 49
——— Of a good Iew in christianitie, ii 46.
Constantia the daughter of Margaret countesse of Britaine, how married, ii 12
Constantine cousine to Arthur reigneth ouer Britaine, his exploits, i 581
——— Gyldas, to be a verie ill man, i 539, 582
——— Slaine in battell, i 581
Constantine brother to Aldoenus K of Britaine vpō couenant, i 551
——— His thrée sons, & his death by treason, i 552.
——— A Britaine borne, his regiment in this Ile, why surnamed Great, i 530
——— An assured branch of the British race, i 533
——— Commended, i. 532
——— His decease, i 533
Constantine the emperour & his sonne slaine, i 552
Constantine aspired vnto the crowne, v 248, 249
——— Crowned by force of fréends, v 249.
——— In armes against Malcolme and Kenneth, ib

Constantine assembleth a mightie armie, vol. v. page 214
———— Proceedeth against his enimies, v. 215
———— Is slaine, v 250
Constantine crowned king of Scots at Scone, v. 212
———— He would faine recouer his predecessors losses, he deuiseth a reformation of disorders, v 212, 213
———— Conspired against, & the conspirators executed, v 213
Constantine placeth his soldiers and incourageth them, v 216
———— He is taken and murthered, ib
Constantine proclaimed king of Britaine, v 121.
———— Slaine, ib
Constantine proclaimed heire apparent and prince of Britaine, v. 160.
———— Crowned king of Britaine, v 162
———— Forsaketh his earthlie kingdome in hope of the heauenlie, entereth into religion, v 163.
———— Murthered, ib.
Constantine the first king of Scots, nothing like his vncle in noble conditions, v 137
———— Slaine by one whose daughter he had rauished, v 138
Constantine the third, king of Scots beginneth his reigne, v 226
———— Becometh a canon, v 228
———— His decease, ib
Constantinople the emperor thereof commeth into England, ii 381
Constantius his reigne ouer Britaine, i 528.
———— A simple K and slaine by his gard, i 552.
Constantius the Romane lieutenant taketh Coels daughter a Britaine to wife, i 627
———— His notable talke and behauior on his death bed, i 529
Constantius a monke elected of Britaine, v 138
———— Murthered, ib
Constantius persecuteth the Christians, v 106
———— ¶ Sée Dioclesian
Contention about succession to the crowne of England, i 699
———— ¶ Sée Discord
———— About the inioieng the sée of saint Andrews, v 485
———— Betwéene earles and other states, v. 490, 491
———— Betwéene kinsmen for the crowne, v. 328.
———— ¶ Sée Dissention, & Variance
———— Greeuous betwéene the king of England & Lilo bishop of Elie note, i 241.
———— Betwixt the earles of Leicester and Glocester, ii 451
———— Betwéene the two princes of Wales pursued. note, ii 391
———— Betwixt prelats, ii 422.
Contention betwéene Henrie the third, and the bishop of Lincolne, vol ii page 395.
———— Betwixt Frederike the emperour and pope Innocent, ii 388
———— Betwixt two Welsh princes for the principalitie, ii. 387
———— Betwéene the archbishop of Canturburie and the earle of Kent, ii 368
———— Newlie broched by the archbishop of Canturburie, ii 353.
———— Betwixt the earles of Leicester and Glocester, ii 447
———— About the choosing of the emperour, ii. 268
———— Betwéene bishops for superioritie, ii 231.
———— Betwixt two ambitious bishops, ii. 209.
———— Betwéene Henrie the second and Thomas Becket, ii 116
———— Betwéene bishops, ii 62
———— About the election of the maior of London, ii 762
———— Hot betwéene William Rufus and Anselme, ii 40, 41, 42, 43
———— Betwéene the archbishops of Ardmagh & Dublin, vi 245
———— About Burgesses, vi 342
Contracts of marriage to be void without witnesses, ii 51
———— ¶ Sée Marriage
Contribution appointed by Henrie the second, ii. 127
Controuersie betwixt king Henrie the third, and the bishop of Winchester, ii 400, 401
———— About the crowne of Scotland, ii 493, 491.
———— Betwéene the archbishop of Canturburie and the moonks, ii 208
———— Betwixt the nobles and peeres appeased by Henrie the first, ii 65
———— ¶ Sée Combat and Contention
Controuersies to be ended by arbitrement, i 570, 571
Conuall elected king of Scots, his deuotion to the crosse, v 163.
———— Towards churchmen, & Churches, ib
———— Deceaseth, v 164
Conuall succéedeth Achaius, and is king of Scots, deceaseth, v 193
Conuocation at Westminster called by bishop Longchamp, ii 223
———— ¶ Sée Councell and Synod
Cooke Anthonie ¶ Sée Iusts triumphant.
Coopers, i 397
Copa ¶ Sée Eopa
Cope Allan his wrong iudgement, vi 11.
Copiholders oppressed, i 318.
Copland refuseth to deliuer his prisoner the king of Scots to anie except to the king of England, ii. 645
Copper, ii 400
Copsi slaine by Osulfe, ii 21
Corbie neuer christened, vi 261.

Corbreid king of Scots, vol v page 69
——— His thrée sonnes v 73
——— Deceaseth, ib
——— ¶ See Gald
Corbrigge sometimes inhabited by the Romans, ii 154
Cordeilla gouerneth Britaine & killeth hir selfe, i 448
——— Regan & Gonorilla, the three sole daughters of Leir, i 447
Cordes lord a Frenchman maketh aduantage of occasion, iii 494
——— His malicious and foolish words, iii 495
Corineus duke of Cornewell, i 444.
——— He wrestleth with Gogmagog, i 443.
——— He killeth Imbert, i 442
——— ¶ See Brute
——— Tewelue cubits high that is eightéene foot, i 15
Corke citie the fourth citie of Ireland, vi 30
——— An ancient citie builded by the Esterlings, vi 160, 183
——— The gouernement of it, vi 161
——— It is an euill neighbourhad, vi 30, 261
——— They match in marriage among themselues, vi 30
——— The kingdome of Corke giuen to Fitzstephan and Cogan, vi 201
——— The bounds of the countrie, vi 206
——— The receiue the lord deputie with all honour, vi. 381.
——— The Corkemen and their prince discomfited and their countrie preied, vi 182
Cormach bishop of Dublin went to king Gregorie about peace, v 224
Cormake Olegham riseth against his father to expell him out of his kingdome, vi 194
——— He is subdued, ib
——— He is beheaded, ib
Cormake mac Dermont mac Rorie pursueth Odonell, vi 238
——— He vanquisheth him, ib
Cormake mac Tiege knight, shiriffe of Corke, vi 132
——— His seruice vpon sir Iames Desmond, ib
——— He taketh him prisoner, ib
——— He is well accepted of the quéene and of the lord iustice, vi 133
——— He is a yoonger house vnto mac Artie Righo, ib
——— His fidelitie and loialtie, ib
——— He is dubbed knight, ib
——— He offereth to acknowledge sir Peter Carew to be his lord, vi 378
——— Cormans preaching among the Northumbers taking small effect, maketh him depart, i 614, 615
Cormorants about the Ile of Thé, i 382
Corne in England and other kinds of graine, i 185
Corne what obseruations are kept in the countrie for the price thereof the yeare following, vol i page 341
——— What great abuse is suffered therein both for price, &c, i 340, 341
Cornelius and his hugh armie, v. 228.
——— He is sore wounded, ib
Cornewall whie giuen to Corineus, i. 443
——— Called the promontorie of Helenus, and why, i 60
——— The Britons call it Cernuw, i 25
Cornishmen their seruice against the Romans, i 170
——— Subdued by Adelstan, i 688.
——— Strong archers, iii 515
——— Rebell against Henrie the seauenth, their shamefull end, iii 513, 514
Corona ciuica, à ciuem redimendo, i. 487
Coronation solemn and statelie of Richard the second, ii 713, 714
——— Of Richard the first roiall, ii 204
Corpus Christi feast first instituted, v 313
——— College in Oxford, by whome and when founded, iii. 617
Corrall white, i 402.
Correction doone vnnaturall by a mother on hir son, i 703
Cosneie besieged by the Dolphin, & rescued by the duke of Bedford, iii 132
Cotten capteine of Iniskith, v 563
Cotteshold shéepe transported into Spaine, iii. 285.
Couentrie made frée of toll and custome, i 750.
——— The quéenes Henrie the sixts wife secret harbour, iii 260
——— She is a better capteine than the king hir husband, ib.
——— The church when and by whom ioined to the sée of Chester, i 46
Couetousnesse hath a pretense, v 174
——— The root of all mischiefe, v 174, 275
——— Linked with crueltie, v 182.
——— Of Henrie the first note, ii. 63
——— Of Cardinall Uiuiano noted, ii 172, 173
——— Of the emperour hauing Richard the first his prisoner, ii 273.
——— Of the emperor notable against honour and honestie, ii 244, 245.
——— To be noted in Richard the firsts demands, ii 215
——— Of king Iohn, ii 319
——— Of cardinall Gualo, ii 321
——— Of Gualo notable, ii 333
——— Of duke William, ii 13, 14.
——— Of William Rufus, ii 30
——— Purchased Henrie the seventh hatred among his people, iii 431
——— Of two moonks, ii 31
——— Of officers in a collection, ii 241.
——— Inueighed against, ii 368
——— Of monie the cause of murther note, iv 266
——— Cloaked with an excuse, ii 63

Couetousnesse. ¶ Sée Flemings, and Rome
———— How dangerous, vol i page 455
———— Of bishop Adelstan, i. 665
———— Of Harold in diuiding spoiles of the Norwegians, i 759
———— It caused murther, i 718
Councell held at London, v 139
———— Without the cleargie, v 608
———— Called by Constantine the third, v. 228.
———— ¶ Sée Parlement
———— Holden at Ardmagh, vi 148.
———— At Cashill, vi 163
———— At Waterford, vi 185
———— At Laterane, vi. 211.
———— At Grenocke, vi 239.
———— At Dublin, vi. 203
———— Held at Rockingham castell and whie, ii. 41.
———— Held at London, ii 353
———— Generall summoned by the pope, ii. 408
———— In Edward the thirds slip, ii 631
———— Of the cleargie called by the cardinall, ii 314.
———— At Yorke, ii 553.
———— At Westminster by the archbishop of Canturburie, ii 280.
———— At Winchester and traitors proclamed, ii. 248
———— At Canturburie, ii 208
———— At Pipewell, ii 206.
———— At London by king Henrie the first, ii. 57
———— At Oxford, ii 116
———— At Clarendon, ii 119.
———— At Towers, ii 118
———— Generall at Rome; ii 177
———— At Westminster, ii 146
———— At Gaitington, ii 193
———— Of bishops, ii. 121
———— At Cassill called by K Henrie the second, ii 146
———— Of lords at Clerkenwell, ii 187
———— Generall at Pisa, iii 46
———— Prouinciall, iii 46.
———— At Stamford, ii 317
———— At Nottingham, and who present, ii 781.
———— Generall at Constance, iii 68
———— Generall the prerogatiue of the English nation, iii 88
———— Of Henrie the sixt most spirituall persons note, iii 208
———— ¶ Sée Assemblie, Folkmote, Parlement, & Synod
Counsell good, the want whereof a cause of committing foule sins, ii 30
———— Euill of nobles to duke Robert to put king William his brother from the crowne, ii 28
———— Good of Lanfranke to William Rufus to win and keepe fauour of people, ii 27
———— Of strangers followed, homebred refused ii 399
Counsell good giuen and safely followed note, vol ii page 371.
———— That bred grudge and mislike betwéene Henrie the third and his nobles, ii 455
———— Euill turneth to the hurt of the counsellor, ib
———— Euill of a bishop to his soueraigne against the commonwelth, ii 553.
———— Euill falleth out to the counsell giuer note, ii 352
———— Euill and lewd companie how mischéeuous, ii 552
———— Good giuen ill rewarded, ii 570
———— Good not to vse crueltie, ii 325.
———— Good ill requited, ii 319
———— Giuen for the which the counsellors were cursed, ii 291, 292
———— Of euill persons to the sonne against the father, ii 148
———— Euill sorteth ill to the counsellor, ii 191
———— Lewd falleth ill to the counsellor, ii 18
———— Euill and dangerous, ii 737
———— Good neglected, ii 767
———— Euill and what inconuenience followeth it. note, ii 868
———— Taken how to deale with the lords that conspired against Richard the second, ii 784
———— Euill how preualent and mischéeuous, iii 288
———— Of the lord Hastings to his acquaintance note, iii 297
———— Of a damsell to the duke of Clarence, iii 296.
———— Good regarded of a king, iii 639.
———— Ill giuen to a king, ii 429
———— Euill giuen and followed note, ii 19.
———— Couetous and mischéeuous of the earle of Hereford practised, ii 14.
———— ¶ Sée Warnings
———— Graue taketh place, v 211
———— Good of graue men despised, v 198.
———— Euill of a wicked woman followed with destruction note, v 231
———— Ill of a woman to reuenge, &c note, v 214
———— Good of capteins not regarded, v. 181
———— In issue vnhappie, 554
———— Tending to safetie, neglected bréedeth danger, i 690
———— Pestilent of a wicked wife, i 619.
———— Of yoong heads pernicious, i 152
———— Good giuen of a woman i 599
———— Good neglected, & what insued, i 655
———— For safetie neglected with losse and ieopordie, i 679
———— Unaduisedlie taken, hurteth, i 655
———— Euill what mischéefe it worketh, i. 740
———— Euill falleth out ill to the counsellor, i 741
———— Good ill requited, i 64
———— Euill followed procureth hurt, i 749.
Counter in Woodstréet not ancient, iv 80.
Counterfet of Richard Plantaganet, iii. 503.

Counterfet earle of Warwike, vol. iii page 525
Counterfet king Edward the sixt, whipped, and executed as a traitor, iv 75
Counterfet king Richard the second, iii 11, 29
Counterfet duke of Yorke ¶ See Perkin Wardbecke
Counterfet Christ whipped, iv 202
Counterfet to be possessed with the diuell, punished by dooing open penance, iv 325.
Counterfet spirit in a wall without Aldersgate, iv 70
——— ¶ See Dissimulation and Dissemblers.
Counterfetting of licences, and antedating them, iii. 819
——— ¶ See Antedating
——— Of queene Elisabeths hand, punished as an offense tresonable, iv 264
Countesse of Bierne a woman receiueth soldiers paie, ii 397
——— Of Broughan for setting the crowne on Robert Bruse his head note, ii 540
——— Of Oxford practise to brute that Richard second was aliue, iii 29
——— Committed to prison, ib
——— Deceaseth, ii 410, iii 315
Countesse of Prouance commeth ouer into England, ii. 400, 415
——— Dealeth vnnustlie with Henrie the third his sonne in law, ii 411
Countesse of Richmond and Derbie, &c, mother to Henrie the seuenth, iii 302
Countesse of Salisburie beheaded, being the last of the right line and name of Plantagenet, iii 820
Countesse of Warwike taketh sanctuarie, iii 315
Countesse of Ulster, vi 255
——— Married to Rafe Ufford lord iustice, ib
——— She persuadeth hir husband to extremitie, ib
Countesse of Leneux borne, v 486.
——— ¶ See Margaret, and Leneux.
Counties ¶ See Shires
Couper ¶ See Follie
Court, certeine lords, ladies, and others put out of Richard the seconds court, ii 793.
Court misliked, ii 819
Court of England alwaies kept where the prince lieth, i 330
——— Punishment of such as smite within the bounds of it forbidden, i 332.
Court kept at Kingshill in Rochford after midnight note, i 263
Courtiers the best learned and worst liuers, i 330
Courtneie lord, prisoner in the Towre, he hath priuie enimies, iv. 25, 26
Courtneie earle of Deuonshire goeth ouer into Italie, deceaseth descended of the bloud roiall, iv 79
Courts of some princes beyond sea compared vnto hell, i. 331.
Courts of chancerie at Yorke and Ludlow, i. 301
Cow the name of ship, vi 503.
——— The prophesie of the Cowes bellie, ib
Cowleie Robert an aduersarie to the earle of Kildare, vol vi. page 287
——— Bailiffe in Dublin, vi 287, 288.
——— Master of the rolles, vi 288
——— Died at London, ib.
Cox doctor the duke of Summersets ghostlie father at his death, iii. 1033
Crab a pirat and a reueller note, v 368
Craftsmen brought into Scotland to instruct the people, &c v 49
Cragfergus yeelded vnto the Scots, vi 248
——— It is inclosed with a wall, vi. 403
Cragmiller prouost of Edenburgh, v. 625.
Cranestane capteine ouerthrowne, v. 711
Cranmer archbishop of Canturburie supposed to be an ostler note, i 256.
——— Arreigned of treason, iv 10
——— Nominated archbishop of Canturburie, iii 777.
——— He, Latimer and Ridlie sent to Oxford to dispute, iv 28
——— Committed to the tower, iv 5
——— Examined, condemned, burned, described, iv 83
Crathlint cheefe conspirator to the murthering of Donald, procureth the nobles to oppress the seruants of Donald, v 103
——— Reioseth to heare that Carantius was aliue, resolueth to aid him and to certifie him, cometh to a communication with the king of Scots, v 105
——— Made king of Scots, his politike gouernment, goeth to hunt, promiseth to obserue the ancient amitie betweene the Scots and Picts, v. 103, 104
——— Destroieth the temples of God and man, v 106, 107
——— Dieth, v. 107
——— Causeth a commotion, instigated to reuenge, v 244
——— Taken and executed, v 245.
Credulitie how mischeefous, iii. 511 512
Creekes noted by seafaring men for their benefit vpon the coasts of England, i 181.
——— ¶ See Hauens and Riuers
Creichton William a Scot imprisoned in England, v 710
——— Apprehended with diuerse plots for inuasion of this realme, iv 571, 572
Creplegate builded, iii. 350
Cressingham Hugh regent of Scotland, v. 331
Crida first K of Mercia, i 587.
Crispine William taken prisoner, i 56
Crocus (in English Saffron) with the occasion of the name, i 390
Crofts sir Hugh slaine by the Lacies, vi 249, 250.
Crofts sir Iames lord deputie, vi 325.
Crofts knight, generall of Habington, iii 907
——— Examined touching the ladie Elisabeth, iv 126
——— Went to talke with the queene of Scots, iv. 191

Crofts his militarie seruice in Scotland, vol iv page 189.
Crokers, or saffron mens obseruation, i 392
Crome at Paules crosse recanteth, iii 856
Crome primat of Ardmagh lord chancellor, vi 285
—— His oration, vi 290
—— His graunt, vi 289
Cromwell sometimes cardinall Wolseis seruant, aduanced to Henrie the eights seruice, iii 748
—— Maister of the iewell house, iii 778
—— Created lord and keeper of the priuie seale, iii 798.
—— Made knight of the garter, iii 804
—— Lord earle of Essex, & great chamberlaine of England, iii 815
—— Committed to the Towre, iii 816
—— The words he spake at his death, iii 817.
—— A description of him by sundrie circumstances, ib.
Crosbie knight his gift to the citie of London, iii 344
Crosse called the black crosse, ii 596, v 279
—— Of the bishop of Elie and the print thereof, ii 228
—— The signe thereof solemnlie vsed by the duke of Lancaster, ii 865
—— And the priuilege of those that tooke vpon them the same, ii 330
—— Preached against Manfred, ii 436
—— Séene in the aire long and large, with a crucifix, ii 197
—— In Cheape defaced note, iv 445, 446.
Crosse borne before them that came to conuert Ethelbert & the English Saxons to the faith, i 593
—— Erected in full hope to be an ensigne or trophie of victorie note, i. 611.
—— Reuerenced by Constantine, i 532.
Crosses of bloudie colour fell frõ heauen on mens garments signifieng affliction, i 653
—— Of wood foũd about Halidon, i 219.
—— Red, white, and gréene differences of nations note, ii. 192
—— How they came there, i 219.
Crossing bringeth sight of the diuells, and crossing driueth them awaie, i 691.
Crotoie beseiged by the duke of Burgognie and rescued, iii 192
Crowdan what it signifie note, v 265
Crowdon his reaching to the borders of Scotland, i 184
Crowes cur rõ, i 382
—— White, i 375
—— Tame crowes of a tinminer and a shoemaker strange tales of them, i 399
Crowne of Scotland changed, v 44
—— Intaled, v 350
—— An act for the succession thereof, v 357, 391
—— ¶ Sée Angusianus, Contention, Scotland.
Crowne of gold the first that was euer worne in this nation, vol i page 197
—— Roiall set on a crucifix, and renounced of Cnute, i 731
—— Of England recouered out of the hands of Danes, i 727
—— Of gold what king did first weare, i 197.
—— Controuersie for that of England, i. 732
Crowne called Corona ciuica, i 487.
Crowne established by act of parlement note, iii 791
—— And what king Iohn did for feare to be depriued thereof, ii 12
—— Intailed, iii 8
—— ¶ See Oth, Parlement, Succession
Crowne of sedges and bulrushes set vpon the duke of Yorkes head in derision, iii 269
Crownes shauen controuersed, i 625.
Crueltie paid with sudden mischéefe, vi 277
—— Of the Britains and Flemings, iii 29.
—— Beastlie and barbarous, iii 34
—— Restreined by Gods iudgment, ii 265
—— Without direction of iustice, ii 300
—— Of king Iohn by preching of Cementarius a preacher, ib
—— Of duke William against the English, ii 12, 23
—— Of the Scots, ii. 516
—— Of king Malcolme against the English, ii 16
—— Of the papists in quéene Maries time toward the martyrs, iv 523
—— Ioined with victorie, ii 38
—— And extremitie shewed vnto gentlemen by rebels, iii 1006.
—— ¶ Sée Frenchmen
—— Of the Scots, v 131, 205.
—— Of Summerleid, v 293
—— Makbeth, v 274.
—— Of Britons extreme, v 162
—— In warre, v 377.
—— Of a theefe to a widow, v 121.
—— Barbarous and unnaturall note, v 145
—— Of one brother to another, v 324
—— Of rebels, v 294
—— Caused through feare, v 273, 274
—— ¶ Sée Britons, Danes, Makbeth, Théeues
—— Of the Britains too outrageous, i 500
—— Executed vpon Beatrice king Edwards daughter, i 685
—— In gouernment purchase malice and death, i 680.
—— In an extreme kind, i 728
—— Of Cnute against the English pledges, i. 716
—— Unspeakable vsed against Alfred by his tormentors, i 735.
—— Of the Danes in winning of Canturburie, i 712
—— Of earle Tostie, i 753
—— For vsing whereof iudge was burned, i 657

Cruceltie of Penda and Cadwallo, vol i. page 610.
——— ¶ Sée Tyrannie
Cubit geometricall, i 16
Culen crowned king, requireth public praiers to be had, his oth, v 236
—— Continued not as his beginning was, v 237.
—— His lewd and wicked inclination, v 238
—— He is murthered, v 239
Culpepper under marshall of Calis, iii. 580
Culuerings seauen, called the seauen sisters, taken from the Scots, iii. 593
——— ¶ Sée Guns
Cullen capteine taken, v 651
Cumberland and Westmerland by what riuer deuided, i 116
Cumberland sore spoiled by the Scots, ii 760
——— Inuaded, v 305.
——— It and Westminster do homage vnto England, v 229
——— Giuen to the king of Scots to hold in homage, i 630
——— Wasted by the Danes, i 707
Cumbre slaine for speking truth and giuing good counsell, i 645
Cumin Robert capteine against the Northumbers in a rebellion, ii 10
Cumins Dauid. ¶ Sée Earle of Atholl, Bruse.
Cummins kindred when they had their beginning, v 287
——— Complained of and put to the horne, v 312
——— Great of power and honor note, v 313
Cunedag sole ruler of Britaine, i 448
Curcie Iohn winneth Dun in Ulster, ii 172.
——— His valiantnesse, ii 173
Curcie Robert slaine, ii 111.
Curcie Iohn arriueth into Ireland, vi 196
——— In commission for lord iustice with Fitzaldelme, vi 199.
——— Inuadeth Ulster, ib
——— Uanquisheth Odonell, vi 200
——— His valiantnes, ib
——— He marrieth the king of Maines daughter, vi 202
——— The description of him, ib.
——— Carefull to serue God, ib
——— He keepeth the whole land in quiet, vi 235
——— His irreuerend speeches to the king, ib.
——— Is accused and proclamed traitor, vi 236
——— He foiled the lord iustice at Dowre, vi 236.
——— Is taken and committed to perpetuall prison, ib
——— He answereth the French combat, ib
——— The French king requesteth to see him, ib.
——— He is set at libertie, & dieth, ib
——— He left no lawfull issue, vi 237
Curfue, or couer fue, when and where first instituted, ii 9
Curres. ¶ Sée Dogs.
Curse of duke William against Robert his rebellious sonne, ii 19
——— Of archbishop Gefferie of Yorke, ii. 295.
Cursse of Thomas Becket for curtailing his horsse, vol. ii. page 136
——— Of the pope against the archbishop of Yorke note, ii. 443
——— Against the troublers of peace, ii 471
——— Upon the people of the south parts of England, ii 370.
——— Against the breakers of Oxford statutes, ii. 452
——— For oppressing of the poore, and how feared note, ii 303
——— Of a legat to Lewis the French kings sonne, ii 345
——— A great péece of ecclesiasticall discipline in old time note, ii 60
——— Euerie sundaie to be read, ii 52
——— ¶ Sée Pope
——— Of the pope when first thundered out at England note, i 688
——— Of the Irishmen when thought to take place, i 634, 635
Cursses of the oppressed heard and reuenged. note, iii 1030
Curthose Robert, Henrie the first his brother, dieth for gréefe, ii 76
Cusake Adam his seruice in Connagh, vi 240.
Cusake sir Iohn serueth the Scots, vi 250.
Cusake sir Thomas lord iustice, vi 325
Custome that the kings of Englands eldest sonnes were euer made dukes of Normandie, ii 64
——— Of bieng and selling of men like oxen and kine, ii 52
——— Of wooll, and augmentation thereof grudged at note, ii 521
——— Raised to an higher price, ii 522
Custome of Halifax, i 312.
——— ¶ Sée Law
Custome paid out of Britaine to the Romans, i. 480.
Custome of Northumberland, to sell their néere kinsfolks for a small price, i 591
Cutberd bishop of Lindesferne, i 722.
Cutha fighteth with the Britains at Bedford, i. 586.
Cuthred king of Westsaxons his exploits, i 644.
Cymbri of likelihood came out of Britaine, i. 23.
Cynike yeare note, i. 410

D

Dacres lord warden of the west marches of England, v 195
——— Arreigned but found cléere to his great honor, iii 792
——— Arreigned for murther, executed at Tiburne: note, iii 821, 822
——— Rebelleth, iv 237
——— Flieth into Scotland, ib
Daie naturall when it beginneth, i 405.
——— Longest in some parts of Britaine, i 4.
——— Of how manie hours it consisteth. note, i. 405
——— Diuerslie accounted by hours, ib.

Dale artificiall, vol i. page 405
Daies of the wéeke named after the English, Saxonish, and Scotish maner, i. 411.
—— Called Atri among the Romans, why, i. 408
—— Diuerslie accounted and named of diuerse people, i. 407
Daisie the concubine of Iames the third, v. 453
Dale pewterer his fault and releasment after long imprisonment. note, iii. 847.
Dales then names changed, v. 203.
—— Thrée men doubted whether théeues or true men doo most abound in them, i. 154
Dalmatia now Slauonia, i. 479, 488
Damianus consecrated archbishop of Canturburie, i. 620
—— ¶ Sée Fugatius.
Damieta, ii. 349
—— ¶ Sée Saracens.
Dampfront yéelded to Henrie the fift, iii. 96.
Danaus & his fiftie daughters, i. 434.
—— The murthering of their husbands how reuenged and their names, i. 435.
Danes how they first came into Britaine, i. 11
—— Prospered not in their purpose establishing of themselues in Britaine, and whie, ib.
—— Arriue in Scotland & kill king Constantine, i. 204.
—— Sometimes lords of Pomona an Ile in Scotland, i. 75
—— Arriue vpon the English coasts, & how much mischéefe in K. Egelreds time. i. 703
—— Ouer all England like grasshoppers, i. 705.
—— Wintered at London, i. 668
—— Enuiron K. Edmund in Formingham castell, & pitifullie put him to death, i. 667
—— Cause of their comming into Northumberland, i. 668
—— That first arriued on the English coasts, & when, i. 653
—— How manie shires they wasted, i. 712.
—— Norwegians and they encounter, i. 452.
—— Sought the destruction of this land, i. 660
—— Ioine with the Welsh and are vanquished, i. 658.
—— Landed and spoiled the abbeie of Lindesferne, & did much hurt in Northumberland, i. 655
—— How long the persecution of them lasted, i. 661
—— With a nauie of 35 ships arriue on the English coasts, i. 658
—— Entering vpon diuerse parts of England are vanquished and slaine, i. 661
—— Come to Reading are put to flight, i. 667
—— Come within 17 miles of Bristow, i. 669.
—— Compelled to flee to their ships wt shame and losse enough, i. 655
—— Forced to paie tribut to the king of Britaine, i. 457
—— Slaine by multitudes at Tenet, i. 669
—— Lose one of their kings and fiue earles in a discomfiture, i. 666
—— Grow in puissance, i. 665
Danes fauoured of K. Edgar, vol. i. page 694.
—— Truce breakers, i. 669
—— Their campe viewed by Alured disguised like a minstrell, i. 671
—— Besiege Nottingham, i. 666.
—— Soiorne at London, i. 670
—— Went into Northumberland, i. 669
—— Wast all the east part of Kent, i. 664
—— Nine earles & one of them slaine in Ethelreds time, ib
—— Diuerse méetings & encounters betwéene them & K. Edwards forces, i. 679
—— Remained at Cambridge a whole yeare, i. 669
—— Besiege Rochester, i. 672
—— Build them a castell in the borders of Wales, i. 673
—— With their armies come into Yorkshire, i. 665
—— Diuerse baptised, i. 671.
—— Wintered in Circncester, i. 672.
—— Constreined to eat horseflesh, i. 673.
—— Wintered in Lindseie, i. 677
—— Meant to inhabit Northumberland, ib
—— Arriue in Essex, i. 673
—— Their armie diuided into three parts, i. 673, 674
—— Take preies about Chichester, i. 673
—— Beereved Alured almost of all his kingdome, i. 670
—— Destroie Winchester, i. 661.
—— Assembled in Staffordshire, i. 680
—— Had the whole gouernment from the Thames Northward, i. 668
—— Crueltie in the winning Canterburie citie, i. 712
—— Ouercome at Brentford, i. 722
—— Inuade the west parts of this Iland, i. 707.
—— Trucebreakers, i. 710
—— Wast this land in all parts after Dunstans death, i. 705.
—— First entrie of them controuersed among writers and all their attempts impeached, i. 702.
—— Deliuer to king Alured hostages & couenants to depart his dominions, i. 671
—— Egenelds deuise to murther them all in one daie, i. 708
—— Ouercome by sea and otherwise vanquisht, i. 661
—— In great miserie for lacke of vittels, i. 680
—— Rule & persecution when it ceassed in England, i. 738
—— Kings & earles of their armie slaine, i. 679.
—— Tributarie to the Britains, i. 453
—— Utterlie expelled out of England by decree, i. 187, 710
—— Rob the English merchants and win great prises, ii. 830.
—— Arriue in England to ioine with the rebels against duke William, and returne dooing nothing, ii. 18
—— Winter betwixt Ouse and Trent, ii. 11.

GENERAL INDEX.

Danes wasted and ruinated religious places in north parts, vol ii page 18.
—— Under the conduct of Canute, &c preuaile mightilie in the North, ii 10, 11
—— ¶ See Normans Sweine
—— Shot quarels and threw darts, v 216
—— Their crueltie in such places where they came, v 217.
—— Prepare to battell, v 219
—— Their cheefe generall, ib.
—— Led to their camp, ib
—— Their apparell, weapons, and proportion of bodie, take flight, v 215
—— The cause that made them arere warre against England and Scotland, v 214
—— They vse great crueltie, ib
—— Séeke to reuenge old losses, v 241
—— Consult to go into England, to saile into Kent, land at Montrosse, come to the riuer of Taie, v 241, 242
—— Forsake the fields, v 243
—— Procure war against England, v 231
—— Breakers of faith and promise, v 257.
—— Their crueltie, ib
—— Their bones séene in diuerse places, v. 261
—— Slaine néere vnto Gemmer, v 262
—— Put to flight, v 259
—— Slaine at Abirlemnon, v 261.
—— Their bones of great bignesse, v 263
—— Put to flight by the Scots, v 232.
—— To be baptised, v 226.
—— Discomfited, v 227
—— Conceiue hope of good successe, ib
—— Vanquished and buried in saint Colmes church, v 268.
—— Ouercome with drinke, fall asléepe, v 267
—— Slaughtered, ib
—— They and the Norwegians come to aid the Scots and Picts, v 80
—— They and the Picts ioine themselues togither, fled into Northumberland, their nobilitie slaine at Berwicke, v 218, 219
—— The order of placing their armie, v 215.
—— They and the Norwegians chased by the Scots, v. 316
—— ¶ Sée Acho, Englishmen, Scots
—— They and the Norwegians arriue in Ireland, vi. 88
—— They inuade it the second time, vi 89.
—— They made sundrie inuasions at sundrie times, vi 91
—— They besiege Dublin, ib.
—— They winne Dublin, ib
—— They roue the ocean seas for inlarging their conquests, vi 91
—— They traffike with the Irishrie, ib.
—— They build towns and castles, vi 91.
—— They are mingled in blood with the Irish, ib
—— They become lords, ib
—— Danes, Esterlinges, Norwegians, and Normans are all one nation, ib
Danefield and why so named, i 158
Danegilt, vol i page 705
——— Ceased in England, i 752
Daniall bishop of Winchester, i 642.
Dasers a kind of dogs, i 389
Dansing ¶ Sée Woonder.
Darbie towne so named of the riuer Darwent, i 164
Darcie sir Anthonie knight, v 466
Darcie sir Arthur knight sent to the borders, v. 510
Darcie Iohn lord iustice sent into Ireland, vi. 254
——— Receiued great liuings of the king, ib.
——— He svbdueth in Ulster, ib
——— He inuadeth Scotland, ib
——— He maketh a great slaughter vpon the Irishrie in Mounster, ib
——— He only was the first that ventured vpon the Scotish Iles, ib
——— He is made lord iustice for terme of his life, vi 255
——— He causeth liberties and franchises to be called in, ib
——— He calleth a parlement for the same, ib
Darcie Robert lord iustice, vi 256
Darcie lord knight of the garter, generall of a power sent against the Moores, iii 561
——— His companie readie at Plimmouth, honourablie receiued of the king of Aragons councell, discontented at a bishops declaration, iii. 562, 563
——— His returne out of Spaine, iii. 563
Dardan king of Scots, v 73
——— Falleth into all kind of vices, beheaded, ib.
Daris an earle in Mounster, vi 84, 85
—— He fauoured Patrike and gaue him a dwelling place called Sorta, ib
Darlington knight, lord gardian of London, remooued, ii 819
Dartford by whome builded, now a palace roiall, i 329
Darwēt riuer described, i 158
Daubeneie lord with others sent against the French king, his feats of armes, iii. 494
——— Henrie the seauenths chéefe chamberleine, iii 510
——— Deceaseth, iii 538
Daughters vnkind to their father, i 447.
Dauels Henrie, a gentleman of Deuon, vi. 409
——— His training vp in the wars, ib
——— His comming into Ireland, ib
——— He is sent to the earle of Desmond, vi 407
——— He doth persuade the earle to resist the rebels, ib
——— His counsell is refused, vi 408.
——— He departeth homewards from the earle, he is murdered in his bed by sir Iohn and sir Iames Desmond the earles brethren, ib
——— His state and conditions, vi 409
——— His skill in the seruice of that countrie, ib.
——— His loue to his countrie, ib

Dauels his notable good vertues, vol. vi page 409
—— The credit of his word, ib.
—— His credit with the erle of Ormond and with the Butlers, ib
—— His fast friendship to sir Iohn of Desmond, vi 410
Dauid king of Scots earle of Huntington, i. 207.
—— Conueied ouer into France, v 367.
—— The north parts of Scotland obeie him, v. 376
—— Returneth to Scotland, v. 381
Dauid of Wales reuolteth, and becommeth a rebell, ii. 484
—— Condemned of treason, & executed, ii 487
Dauid king his liberalitie, inuadeth Northumberland, v. 382
—— The borders of England, ib
—— With a great armie, 383
—— His valiance, taken by Iohn Copland, v 384.
—— Deceaseth after he had repented him of his mariage, v 389.
Dauid the fierce and the first of that name king of Scotland, v 288
—— His care for the poore, ib.
—— A builder of abbeies, ib
—— Inuadeth Northumberland, v 290
—— Mortified from the world, his oration to his nobles, testifieng how patientlie hée tooke the death of his sonne note, v 290.
—— His exhortation to his nobles, his departure out of this life, v 292
Dauid Fauconer slaine, v 507
Dauid Richio the quéenes secretarie slaine, v 617
Deacons in the church of England but no subdeacons, i 229.
Deanes of cathedrall churches not knowne before the conquest, i. 227
—— Of Paules in their succession to the last named Alexander Nowell, i 248
Debate betwixt the dukes of Lancaster and Brunswike, ii 653
—— Betwixt the townsmen and scholars of Oxford, ii 654
—— How it was ended and taken vp, ii 655.
—— ¶ Sée Contention
Debt of Henrie the third, thrée hundred thousand markes, ii 435.
—— Henrie the thirds sparing to bring him out of it, ii 419
—— Maketh foes of fréends note, ii 537
Deceit in saffron, and how to be perceiued, i 392
Decima a surname of a Romane legion wherein the eagle was painted, i. 467
Dée or Deua a noble riuer rising in Merionethshire, i 139
—— Troublesome streame when the wind is at southwest note, i 140
Dedication of Churches ¶ Sée Church.
Déed of gift after the old forme and fashion, v 393.
—— The forme thereof in duke Williams time, ii 11.
Deglaston battell, v 167.
Deira kingdom when it began, vol i page 584.
—— Now Northumberland, i 591.
—— Deliuered De ira Dei, ib
—— Wasted by fire and sword, v. 191.
Dela his sonne a Grecian conquered Ireland, vi. 75
Dela Hide sir Walter troubled for conspiracie, vi. 300.
Dela Hide Iames a chéefe coūsellor to Thomas lord Fitzgerald, vi 289
—— Sent to Dublin to intreat for a submission, vi 297.
—— Fled into Scotland and died, vi 304
Delaies did not William Rufus vse, but exceeding speed note, ii 39
—— Breedeth losse note, ii 29.
Dele and old Saxon word signifieng a bottome or vale, i 346
Demands of the pope a large tenth, ii 364
—— Out of spirituall liuings in England, ii. 359.
—— In a treatie of peace, ii. 277.
—— Moderated, ii 822
—— Hard, that hindered the peace betwéene England and France, ii 703
—— Too large, and hinder the concluding of peace, ii 621
—— Verie large for a dowerie of gold and siluer, ii 215
—— Unreasonable, ii 403
—— Presumptuous of the French king concerning peace, ii 665.
Demetia now Southwales, i 456, 470.
Demetrius his vaine tales told in his treatises, i. 316
Denbighshire spoiled by Ostorius, i 487
Denie Edward ¶ Sée Iusts triumphant
Denmarke king arriueth in England, the citie of London banket him, he departeth into Flanders, iii 686
—— Inuested into the order of the garter, iv. 495
Denmarke and Scotland in amitie, v 424
—— Munition for warre sent from thense, v. 473.
—— The king thereof commeth into Scotland, restored vnto his kingdome, v. 466.
Derision of the English gentlemen in a rime, ii 595
—— Of quéene Ione, called Ione makepeace, ii. 596
—— Of the duke of Yorke aspiring to the crowne, iii 269
—— Lewis his fame, iii 316, 653.
Dermond king of Corke submitteth himselfe to king Henrie the second, vi 160
Dermond mac Arthie prince of Desmond is ouerthrowne by Reimond, vi. 182
—— — Is aided and restored by Reimond, vi. 194.
Dermond mac Rorie inuadeth Ulster, vi 238
Dermond mac Morough king of Leinster, vi. 121, 133.

Dermond mac Morough an oppressor of his people, vol. vi. page 134.
——— He is hated, ib.
——— He seeketh to king Henrie for aid, vi. 122.
——— He sweareth allegiance to the king, ib.
——— He hath the kings letters of protection, ib.
——— The etymologie of his name, ib.
——— He commeth to Bristow, vi. 125.
——— His acquaintance and composition for a marriage with the Strangbow earle of Chepstow, ib.
——— He returneth into Ireland, vi. 126.
——— He compoundeth with Fitzstephans and Fitzmoris for their aid, ib.
——— He is honorablie receiued at Fernes by the clergie, ib.
——— His immanitie and cruell nature, vi. 131.
——— He is set vpon by Rothorike of Conagh, vi. 133.
——— His stature and conditions, vi. 134.
——— He inuadeth Ossorie, vi. 130.
——— He preuaileth, vi. 131.
——— His oration to his souldiers, vi. 136.
——— He besiegeth and taketh Dublin, vi. 147.
——— Is threatened by Ororike king of Conagh, ib.
——— He inuadeth Meth, ib.
——— He is reconciled with Rothorike of Conagh, vi. 139.
——— His eldest sonnes eies are put out, vi. 130.
——— He dieth, vi. 149.
——— Buried at Fernes, ib.
Derth, ii. 653.
——— Of corne, ii. 333, 504, 810.
——— Increaseth, ii. 449, 555.
——— By means of raine, ii. 99, 693.
——— By extreame cold weather, ii. 376.
——— After a wet season, iii. 722.
——— Of vittels: note, ii. 410; iii. 192, 831.
——— For space of three yeares, ii. 271.
——— Made markets deere, ii. 491.
——— Through out all England, ii. 261.
——— Exceeding great, ii. 444.
——— In Henrie the thirds campe: note, ii. 429.
——— And plentie, iv. 86.
——— Without scarsitie and plentie to them that had monie, iv. 324.
——— Where none needed, ii. 816.
——— Great, v. 313.
——— Extreme and lamentable: note, v. 330.
——— Exceeding, & after that a plentie, v. 304.
——— And famine extreme, v. 342.
——— And how helped, v. 332.
——— It and deth, v. 292, 378.
——— By pestilence, v. 429.
——— In England by means of tempest, i. 174.
——— It and mortalitie in Britaine and Ireland, i. 625.
——— It and death, ii. 374, 445, 554, 649, 693.
Desire hard to be brideled: note, vol. iii. page 119.
——— ¶ Sée Bruse.
Desmond the earle. ¶ Sée Girald Fitzgirald.
Desmond sir Iohn spoileth the earle of Ormonds countries, vi. 332.
——— Is sent into England, and offereth to serue against Oneale, vi. 336.
——— Committed to the tower, vi. 338.
——— Is committed to the castle of Dublin, ib.
——— He conioineth with Iames Fitzmoris, vi. 407.
——— He murthereth Henrie Dauels, vi. 408.
——— His brags and vaunts for the said his slaughter, vi. 410.
——— He is pardoned by the popes legat for the same, ib.
——— He supplieth Iames Fitzmoris his roome, vi. 412.
——— He incampeth at Slulougher, vi. 413.
——— He lieth in ambush at Getenbre castle, vi. 414.
——— He priuilie stealeth awaie at Connell, vi. 416.
——— He encountereth with the lord gouernor, ib.
——— Hath the worst side and fléeth, vi. 416.
——— He giueth the battell to the gouernor, ib.
——— He fléeth to the vicount Baltinglasse for aid, vi. 434.
——— Is in danger to be taken, ib.
——— He intreateth a peace betweene Barrie and the Seneshall, vi. 445.
——— He is killed and then hanged, vi. 446.
Desmond Iohn is miserable end: note, iv. 528.
——— ¶ Sée more in Earle of Desmond.
Desmond sir Iames conioineth in rebellion with Iames Fitzmoris, vi. 407.
——— He is one of the murtherers of Dauels, vi. 408.
——— He is pardoned by the popes legats for the same, vi. 410.
——— Besiegeth the castle at Adare, vi. 420.
——— Raiseth his siege and departeth, ib.
——— Taketh a preie and is taken prisoner, vi. 432.
——— Is drawn hanged and quartered, vi. 432, 433.
Desmond Girald earle of Desmond his wars with the earle of Ormond, vi. 328.
——— He is in England, vi. 332.
——— The quarels betweene him and the erle of Ormond referred vnto the quéenes order, ib.
——— He incampeth himselfe, vi. 336.
——— Repareth to the lord deputie, ib.
——— Serueth and offerth to serue against Oneile, ib.
——— Is committed to the castell of Dublin, vi. 338.
——— Is carried into England and sent to the Towre, ib.
——— Breaketh prison at Dublin, vi. 373, 374.

Desmond Gerald he submitteth himselfe and yeeldeth all his to the lord deputie, vol vi. page 381
———— He will not permit the lord president to intermeadle within his liberties, vi 384
———— Is set vpon by the lord president, vi 384, 385
———— Complaineth to the lord deputie against him, vi 385
———— His disagreement with the earle of Thomond, vi 388
———— Repineth against the cesse, ib
———— Commeth to the lord deputie to Kilkennie, vi 397
———— He and the lord president are reconciled, vi 398
———— Discouereth the treacherie of Iames Fitzmoris, ib
———— He is perforce made to submit himselfe, vi 401
———— Dischargeth his workmen vpon the arriuall of Iames Fitzmoris, vi 407
———— He pretendeth to serue against him, ib
———— Refuseth it, vi 40[illegible]
———— Commeth to the lord iustice at the campe, vi 413
———— Is committed and submitteth himselfe, vi 413
———— His sonne is deliuered for a pledge, vi 415.
———— The gouernor sendeth for him, vi 415
———— Dissembleth, ib
———— He sheweth himselfe an open rebell, vi 417
———— He is persuaded to yeeld himselfe and will not, vi. 418
———— He fortifieth his castels, ib
———— Is sent for to come to the lord iustice, vi 422
———— The articles demanded of him, ib
———— His treasons, ib
———— Is proclamed traitor, vi 124
———— He is in danger to be taken, vi 425
———— Lieth in ambush, vi 426
———— His castels at Caregfoile and Asketten taken, vi 431
———— Supposed to be dead, vi 149.
———— Keepeth his Christmas in a wood, vi 150
———— Is forsaken, vi 152
———— Is in danger, vi 153
———— Is slaine, vi 151
Desmond Girald Fitzgerald the earle of Desmonds sonne is deliuered for a pledge, vi 421
Desperation, iii 229
Dessée monsieur flieth from Iedworth, v 562
———— Returneth into France, v 564
Destinie cannot be auoided, iii 233
Deth after derth, i 741, iii 809, 999
——— And derth, ii 167, 145, 555, 556
——— Of great personages, ii 186, 348, 387, 395, 400, iii 530, 538, 805, 815, iv 158, v. 468, 107, 413, 415, 116, 428, 604, 823, 538, 510, 426, 156
Deth in Spain through heat of that countrie, vol ii. page 771
——— And multitudes of people, ii 702.
——— Of learned bishops, ii 430
——— In one yeare, iii 509.
——— Of seuen aldermen in London in the space of ten moneths, iv 231
——— ¶ Sée Aldermen
——— Preferred before losse of monie, ii. 436.
——— Great by the flix, iii 50
——— Of people, ii 35
——— Desperate of Summeruile, iv 528
——— In winter, iv 528
——— Of much people in London, iii 591
——— By strange diseases note, iv 85.
——— By the sword prefered before famishment, i 288
——— Of old people, iv 103
——— After a great derth, ii. 167.
——— Of horsse and men in the English host, ii 763
——— In the north counteries, with spoile doone by the Scots, ii 724.
——— In Yorke and sundrie other places, ii 314.
——— Of men and beasts, called the third mortalitie, ii 693
——— After a sort sudden, ii 681
——— Most men, few women, ii 676
——— Of people betwixt Candelmas and Easter, ii. 651
——— Lamentable, ii. 556
——— It endeth discord note, ii 677
——— ¶ Sée Buriall.
——— Sudden of sir Thomas Gresham, iv 426.
——— Of a woman that forsware hir selfe ¶ Sée Periurie
——— Of a sorcerer note, iv. 314
——— Of quéene Anne, the wife of Richard the third, iii. 431
——— Sudden and dreadfull of a blasphemous preacher, iv 79
——— Of a mercilesse and tyrannicall bishop, iv. 81.
——— Of the erle of Suffolke note, ii 753
——— ¶ Sée Abat
——— Of kings, v 411
——— Of noblemen, v 412
——— Sudden, v 44
Deuereux earle of Essex his honor, vertues, and nobilitie, vi 386
———— His life and deth, vi 387, 388
Deuiaticus king of the Swessions held Britaine in subiection, i 10
Deuonshire parted from Cornwall by the intercourse of the riuer Thamar, i 104
———— The bredth of it and Cornwall, i 113
Deuonshiremen vanquish the Danes, i 661
Deuotion supperstitious of Henrie the yoong prince note, ii 185
———— ¶ Sée Moore knight
Deusdedit archbishop of Canturburie, i 620
Dials, i 405
Diamond stones, i 402

Diamond found in a marble quarrie at Naples, vol i page 396.
Diana honored of the Scots, the goddesse of hunting, v 15
Diches about London clensed, i 528
Didanus the father of Friswide, i 649
Diet of frée cost note, iv 613
—— Moderated by an ordinance made by the maior and aldermen, iii 831
—— Excessiue restreined, ii 193
—— A statute cōcerning it note, ii 678
—— Superfluous and excessiue restreined · note, v 213
—— Fine cooke re banished, v 91
—— Delicat spoken against, redressed, and when baked meat began in Scotland, v 422.
—— ¶ Sée Surfeiting
—— Of the nobilitie, i 278
—— Of merchants, i 281.
—— Of artificers, i 382
—— Of the ancient Gentiles, i 287
Digblie Edward ¶ See Iusts Triumphant
Digeon ¶ Sée Gun
Dillon Lucas the quéenes atturnie sent to the parlement house, vi 345
———— Made baron of the excheker, vi 368
———— Examineth vicount Baltinglasse of complaints, vi 399.
Dimmocke knight his challang at Richard the thirds coronation, iii 400
———— The kings champion, the manner of his tenure at a coronation, iii 549
———— His championlike office, ii 176
Dinas Bren a castell note, i 381.
Dindimus & Uerianianus brethren slain in battell by Constans, i 539
Dinham esquier high tresuror of England, iii 253
———— Ualiant, ii. 254
———— He and baron Carew with their powers come to Excester, iii 295
Dinnune burned, v 539
Diocleslan a tyrant, i 512
———— He and Maximian emperors, i 528
———— Persecuter of the christians, v 106
Dionethus duke of Cornwall, i 535
———— Reputed for the second person in the realme, v 128
———— Ioineth with the Scots against the Romans, proclamed king of Britaine, escapeth slaughter, v 126, 127
Diram and Culpepper quéene Catharines paramors, arreigned at Guildhall, executed, iii 822, 823
Dirrie and all the vittelles and munitions burned, vi 355
Dis one of the sons of Iaphet originall beginner of Britaine, i 6
Disciplme sent for to Eleutherius from Lucius, i 43.
———— Uerie necessarie in the church, ib.
———— Wished, i 358
———— ¶ Sée Church
Discord bringeth decaie, i 571
Discord of brethren · note, vol. i pages 752, 678, 679
———— Ciuill openeth a gap to the forein enimies, i 665
———— Bringeth miseries manifold, i 683
———— Amongst a companie harteneth the enimie, i 83
———— ¶ Sée Contention, Dissention, and Malice.
———— What commeth of it, ii. 693
———— Unnaturall of brethren abhorred, ii 50
———— Betwéene the French king and his nobles, ii 179
———— Betweene Henrie the second and the French king, ii 186
———— Causing ciuill warre that might haue béene foreséene, ii 112
———— Manteined betwéene sonnes by the mother, ii 149
———— Sowne betwixt Henrie the father and Henrie the son ii 141
———— Increseth betwéene Henrie the second and Thomas Becket note, ii 119
———— Enuious among the christians, ii 232
———— Betwixt the pope and the emperor, ii. 129
———— Betwixt the cardinall and the archbishop of Canturburie, ii 315
———— Betwixt king Iohn and his barons with the causes, ii 319
———— It and concord with their differing effects, iii 1009
———— What it bréedeth, iii 291
———— Ciuill, & inconueniences thereof, iii 227
———— Among the French nobles, iii 86
———— Giueth opportunitie to the enimie note, ii 32
———— Offereth occasion of inuasion note, ii. 34.
———— How inconuenient, ii 1
———— About trifles and how vnhappie it fell out, ii 22.
———— Betwixt Sauerie de Mauleon and the earle of Salisburie, ii 355
———— Betwixt the Norman warriors and them of Baion, ii 197
———— Betwixt Edward the firsts men and the Cautners, ii 527
———— Betwixt préests and friers, ii 671
———— Of thrée or foure yeares ended by the death of one man, ii 677.
Disdain how dangerous, i 145
Disloialtie, v 371
———— ¶ Sée Disobedience
Disme granted of clergie, ii 700
———— To Edward the first and his brother, ii. 277
———— To Henrie the third by the pope, for one whole yeare, ii 168
Disobedience in the Dowglasse, v 428.
———— Punished, v 332
———— Punished by fier and sword, i 692
———— Punished with wasting and spoiling, i. 690.

Disobedience of the bishop of Norwich to Richard the second punished, vol ii page 762
———— Of the archbishop of Thurstane against Henrie the first, ii 65
———— To Richard the firsts commandement, ii. 243
———— Mainteined, i 148, 149
———— Of earle Robert of Leicester, ii 154
———— In Henrie the sonne to Henrie the second his father, i. 131.
———— To the prince a sin most abominable, iii 991
———— To the king, is disobedience to God, iii 921
———— Of a subiect against his king sending for him, ii 36
———— Of the nobles to Edward the first note, ii 521
———— It and presumption of the bishop of Durham against Edward the first. note, ii 542, 171
———— ¶ Sée Rebellion
Dispensation from Rome to marrie with the lord Derneleie, v 614
———— ¶ Sée Marriage and Pope
Disputation of grammer scholers, iv 79, 80
Dissemblers punished, ii 351.
Dissention betweene the earle Morton and the lord Iohnstone, v 711
———— Amongst the nobilitie, v 688.
———— Betwéene the pope and king Iohn, v 305.
———— In England, v 443.
———— A present destroier, v 58
———— ¶ Sée Contention, Nobles, Discord, Warres Ciuill.
———— Cause of confusion, vi 77, 81, 88, 257.
———— Betweene Kildare & Ormond, vi 275
———— Damnifieth the author, i 460
———— Among the noblemen, ii 773
———— Betwéene Richard the second and the parlement house, ii 775
———— Betweene Richard the second and his nobles, ii 784
———— The fruits thereof, iii 1006
———— In France, made the earle of Richmond renew his sute, and put him to his shifts, iii 433
———— He hath men and monie of the French king for hostages, he is gréeved at the newes of king Richard the thirds intended marriage with his néece, iii 433
———— Ciuill among noblemen, prosecuted with sword and slaughter note, iii 290
———— Betwixt the duke of Glocester and the bishop of Winchester, iii 146
———— Order taken by the lords for the pacifieng thereof, iii 153, 154, 198
———— Ciuill and the inconuenience thereof, iii. 244
———— Among the Scotish nobilitie iii 10
———— Betwixt prince Edward and the earle of Glocester, ii 153
Dissimulation of Edward the seconds wife, vol ii. page 578
———— To auoid danger, ii 854.
———— Of yoong king Henrie note, ii 184.
———— Notable of a wench counterfetting a spirit, iv 56
———— Of Wolseie, iii 740
———— Of the French king, v. 501
———— Of the duke of Glocester dangerous, v 366
———— To auoid imminent danger, ii 214
———— Of Richard the first did him no good note, ii 235
———— Most profound and notable, iii. 318
———— Singular of duke Richard the third, iii 395
———— Of the earle of Warwike, iii 283
———— Of the king of Cipres, ii 221
———— Of Edward the fourth, to passe the countereies without danger, & bring his purpose to passe, iii 303
———— Of the duke of Clarence, iii 308.
———— Of the high constable of France, iii. 332
———— Of the French king vpon a naughtie meaning, iii 338
———— With other ill qualities note, iii. 163.
———— Notable, iii 70
———— Of Pirrie notorious, iv 582, 561.
———— ¶ Sée Flatterie and Policie
———— And deliting in lies, v 275, 276
———— Craftie and cloked, v 53.
———— Requited with dissimulation, i. 740
———— Of Edrike brought him vnto a shamefull end i 729
———— Of earle Goodwin, i 733, 734, 735
———— Of Hengist notable, i 560
———— Of Herculeus Maximianus, i 530.
———— Of quéen Alfred, i 700
———— Of Uortigerne notable, i 553.
———— Of Edrike, i 710
———— ¶ Sée Edrike
Diuell waits at the table when Dunstan sat with the king, i. 691
—— He laugheth at Dunstans exile, i 693.
—— Appeareth in the likenesse of a frier, iii 20
Diuision in a realme and the mortall mischéefe, iii 218.
———— ¶ Sée Dissention
Diuma the first bishop of Mercia, i 623.
Diuorse betwéene the quéene and the earle of Angus, v 502
———— Betwéene Henrie the eight and queene Katharine ¶ Sée Quéene Katharine
Dobegnie lord dieth, v 468
Doctrine confirmed by miracle, i 563
———— What Cham and his disciples taught, i 37
———— That Druius preached to his hearers in Albiō, i 34
Doctor a word of large signification, i. 253.

Dodon riuer ỳ bound to Cumberlãd and Westmerlãd, vol i page 146
Dog in a rochet vnder the name of Gardiner, iv 105
Dogs of England & their qualities, i 386
—— What serue ỳ falcon of two sorts called spaniels, i 387
—— What sort of all most cruell and tugging, i. 389
—— Of a homelie kind, i 387
—— Diuided into seuerall kinds, i 386
—— Of Scotland commended, v 104
Dolphin of France the title of the French kings eldest son, i 264
—— Of France commended, iii 92
—— Mainteined warre against the English, v 412
—— Marieth Margaret daughter to king Iames, v 424
—— Fléeceth his old mother of her treasure, and what mischéefe rose therof, iii 99.
—— Causeth solemne iusts to be proclamed at Paris, iii 603
—— He is hurt in the hand, ib
—— His secret malice, iii 606
—— Commeth before Bullen with a great power, iii 814
—— Causeth himselfe to be proclamed king of France, iii 137
—— He is tempering with the English, iii 137
—— Sentence against him for the murther of Iohn duke of Burgundie, iii 124
—— Pursued by Henrie the fift, iii 123.
—— Whie called king of Berrie, iii 128
—— Calling himselfe king of Sicill, iii 77
—— Whie the son and heire of euerie French king is so called, iv 103
—— Deceaseth, iii 84
Dolphins taken in the Thames, ii 1062
—— At London bridge, ii 816
Domitian the emperor enuieth the prosperous successe of Agricola, i 510, v 83
—— Nero emperour of Rome, i 493
Donald Bane vsurper of the crowne fled into the Iles, restored to the crowne, v 283, 284
—— Studious to mainteine his subiects in peace, conuerted to the christian beléefe, v 97
—— He dieth, v 98
Donald brother to Findocke king of Scots,
—— Dieth, v 102
Donald Balloch inuadeth Lochquhaber, v 420
—— Flieth, his head sent as a present to the king, three hundred of his complices hanged, v 420
Donald discomfited, chased, taken, dieth in prison, v 283
Donald of the Iles mainteineth robbers, v 161
—— Rebelleth, v 409.
—— Flieth, v 410
—— Submitteth himselfe, ib
—— Becommeth mad, v 416
—— Slaine by a minstrell, ib.
Donald of the Iles inuadeth Scotland, vol v page 102
—— Suddenlie setteth vpon the enimies, ib.
—— Taketh vpon him as king, and is murthered, v 102, 103
Donald king of Scots studieth to reduce his subiects to ciuilitie, promiseth to aid Fulgentius, v 96
—— Offereth to yéeld himselfe vpon certein conditions, but is not receiued, v 101
—— Deuiseth how to murther king Findocke, v 101
—— Resisteth Gormond, v 226
—— His death, ib
Donald the fourth king of Scots, of dissolute behauiour, admonished of his nobles, v 208
—— He with the noblemen are sent home againe, v 211
—— Taken with the nobilitie, v 209
—— Falleth to his old vices againe, laid in prison, v 212
—— He killeth himselfe, ib.
Donald the fift king of Scots, a good iusticer and religious, v 225
—— ¶ Sée Conspiracie
Donald prince of Ossorie a mortall enemie to Dermon Mac Morogh, vi 130
—— He putteth out Mac Moroghs sonnes eies, ib.
—— He and his countrie are pursued, ib.
—— They are ouerthrowne, vi 131
—— Submitteth himselfe, ib.
—— He attendeth Reimond at Limerike, vi. 193
Donald Obrin prince of Limerike his reuolting and rebellion, vi 188
—— His citie and himselfe besieged, ib
Donald Russe king of Desmond slaine, vi 343
Donald prince of Thomond besiegeth Limerike, vi. 193
—— He desireth a parlee, vi 194
—— He submitteth himselfe, ib
—— Is the kings baron and subiect, ib
—— Giueth his oth and hostages for the safe keeping of Limerike, ib
—— He most traitorouslie setteth the citie on fire, vi 195
Donat bishop of Dublin repaireth Christ church in Dublin, vi 240
Donat Obren murthered by his men, vi. 245.
Dondonolfe the place of Reimonds ariuall, vi 141.
Donegan Odowill taken prisoner at Limerike, vi. 216
Dongall made king of Scots, v 138.
—— His politike rule, v 193
—— A seuere punisher of malefactors, ib
—— Raiseth an armie against rebels, v 191
Dongall his displeasure with the Picts answer, v. 195
—— His good counsell, v 137
Dongard king of Scots, his acts and deeds, his vertues, v 135, 136.

Dongard slaine, vol. v page 137.
Donwald king of Scots, v 172.
—— Drowned, v 173
—— His petition for rebels reiected, v 234
—— Hee conceiueth hatred against the king, is counselled to kill him, ib
—— Committed the fact, v 235.
—— A verie dissembler, ib.
—— Taketh his flight, v 236
—— Taken prisoner, executed, v 236, 237.
Doorus writeth vnto certeine Scotish lords to mooue them to rebellion, v 100
—— His fauorers put to death, ib
Dorcester bishoprike, i 616
Dornadill king of Scots, a louer of peace and delighted in hunting, v 15.
Doue a swift riuer and for his noblenesse notable, i 167
Douer castell whense of likelihood it tooke the name, i 92.
—— Robbed by the French, ii 509
—— A conuenient and perpetuall harborough for ships, iv 845
—— The castell inuincible, ii 331
—— Deliuered to Henrie the third, ii 469.
Dowager sued vnto by the gouernor, v 553
—— She promiseth aid out of France, ib.
—— Saileth to France, v 567
—— She commeth vnto the English court, v. 569
—— She seeketh to be gouernor, v 572.
—— Made gouernor by parlement, v 574
—— Hir oration to the nobles, v 601.
—— ¶ Sée Marie & Quéene.
Dowdall shiriffe of Louth slaine, vi 260
Dowdall primat of Ardmagh, vi 59
Dowdall capteine arriueth vnto Waterford, vi 414
—— He is appointed to lie in garrison in Kilmallocke, vi 415
—— Maketh a iournie into Conilo, vi. 425
—— Attendeth the lord gouernor to Cashill, ib
—— Serueth at the fort, vi 436
—— Maketh spoill vpon the Desmonds, vi 445
—— He accompanieng capteine Zouch tooke and killed sir Iohn of Desmond, vi 444, 445
—— Entereth into Dauid Barries campe and spoileth his people, vi 447
—— He assaileth and accompanieth Fitzmoris, vi 448, 449
—— Hath the whole charge of Keirie, vi 448
—— Surpriseth the earle, vi. 451
Dowglasdale giuen in spoile vnto the men of warre, v. 440
Dowglasse Antonie taken prisoner, v. 106
—— Infortunate in battell, ib
—— Gouernor elected, v 369.
—— In armes against Edward the third, v. 370.
Dowglasse Antonie banished, vol v page 509.
—— Arrested and put in prison, v 421.
—— Inuadeth England, v 405.
—— Prisoner, v. 287
Dowglasse earle Iames disceaseth, v 398.
Douglasse Iames his valiantnesse against the Turks, v 362
—— Landeth in Spaine, slaine by the Saracens, how oft he had gotten the victorie, ib
Dowglasse conuict of treson, v 513.
Dowglasse hir birth, life, death and buriall, v 673, 674
Dowglasse William of Liddesdale prisoner, v 368
—— Ransomed, v 374.
—— Created earle of Dowglas, v 383
—— Claimeth the crowne, v 390
—— Honored for his prowesse, v 395, 396
—— Chosen admerall by the lords of Prutzen, he is slaine, v. 401, 402.
Dowglasse earle sent vnto an abbie, v 455.
—— Goeth into Italie, v 437.
—— Goeth into England without licence of the king of Scots, ib
—— Sueth for pardon, ib
—— Enuieth those that beare rule about the king, v 438
—— His great port, v 429
—— Made duke of Touraine, v 415.
—— His valiantnesse, v 396, 397.
—— Deceaseth, v 394
Dowglasse earle marrieth his brothers wife, v 440.
—— His companie shrinketh from him, v. 441
—— He withdraweth into England, ib
—— Answereth the King of Scots ouerthwartlie and is slaine, v 439
Dowglasses forfalted or atteinted at parlement, v 440
—— Of puissance and authoritie note, v. 442
—— Whie they beare the bloudie hart, v. 361
—— How they came by the earledome of Murreie, v 391
—— A name beloued of the people, v. 439.
—— They beare all the swaie and sware, v. 433
—— Of great aliance note, v 438
—— Their rising to honour, v 341.
Dowglasdale giuen in spoile vnto the men of warre, v 440
Downe a citie, vi 201
—— Spoiled, vi 312.
Downe castell yéelded, v 648
Downgarg besieged, v 225.
Downske castell besieged, v 177
Dowrie verie large demanded note, ii 215
Draffan castell yéelded, v 634
Dragon fierie séene in diuerse places, ii 829
Dragons two séene fighting in the aire, ii 374
—— Fire flieng in the aire, ii. 653.
Drake sir Francis knight ¶ Sée Uoiage.

Drake sir Francis his voiage, vol i page 398.
Drake sir Bunard knight, deceaseth, iv 868
Drake burning scene in the aire, ii 179
Drake Iohn maior of Dublin slue foure thousand Irish outlawes, vi 260
Dreame of Alured comfortable vnto him, i 671
——— Of Brightwold a moonke of Glastenburie, i 537
——— Of Dunstane, i 704
——— Of Edgina K Edwards concubine, i 682
——— Of duke Elstane interpreted by Dunstane, i 690
——— Of archbishop Laurence note, i 603
——— Whereby Rollo was warned, i 670
——— Of a knight that had long haire note, ii. 78
——— Of Richard the thirds, fortelling him of his end, iii 436
——— Of William Rufus note, ii 44
——— Of a moonke concerning William Rufus, ib
Dreames, vi 169, 171
——— Of Henrie strange and troublesome, ii 74
——— Horrible that vexed Richard the second, after the execution of the earle of Arundell, ii 842.
——— Import somewhat to befall, ii. 74
——— Prognosticat the true intent of an action, iii 381
——— Of Basilia, vi. 19, 195
——— Of Paris, vi 123
——— Of Griffith, v. 169
Dreux besieged and rendered to the Englishmen, iii 128
Drie wednesdaie, iii 578
Drifeeld sometimes a goodlie towne now a small village, i 158
Drinke vsed in England, i 284
——— More than ordinarie taken, causeth forgetfulnesse of good aduise, ii 44
——— ¶ See Beere
Drinkers great & yet no drunkards, i 71
Drodagh or Drogheda, vi 30.
Dropping well and wonderfull nature thereof i 218
Drought, ii 490
——— In the spring, ii 430.
——— At Michaelmas, ib
——— Great, ii 524, iii 520
——— Exceeding great, ii 639
——— ¶ See Summer
Drownelow sands, v 268
Drowning of a lad in a kenell, iv 325
——— Of people, cattell, &c by the breaking in of the sea, ii 380
——— Of aboue a thousand men in one place, and more in others note, ii 725
Drugs ¶ See Simples
Druides where they made their chiefe abode &c i. 430
——— Curse the Romans, i 495
——— Or Druish preests and their estimation, i. 35
Druides why so called, vol i page 34
——— Their authoritie, v. 52.
Druis the son of Sarron i 429
Druius and what points of doctrine he taught in Albion, i 34
Drumlanrig lord warden of the march, v 631
——— Writeth letters, v 533.
——— Scourged by horsemen, v 534
——— They harrie his countrie, ib
——— Pursueth the English, ib
——— Put to flight, ib
Drunkennes, vi 14
——— The ouerthrowe of right and manhood note, iii 210
——— ¶ See Quaffing
Drurie captaine his good seruise at the rebellion in Norfolke, iii 980
——— Knight his militarie seruice, his aduancement, iv 213, 244
Drurie sir William arriueth into Ireland, vi 382.
——— Is lord president of Mounster, vi 384.
——— His gouernment, ib
——— The earle of Desmond repineth at him, ib.
——— Entereth into Kerrie and executeth iustice, ib
——— The earle resisteth and complaineth of him, vi. 385
——— The earle and he are reconciled, vi 398
——— Is made lord iustice, vi 399
——— His gouernment, vi 405
——— His iournie into Mounster, vi 407
——— His painfull seruice against Iames Fitzmoris, ib.
——— Falleth sick and dieth, vi 414, 415
——— His vertues and conditions, vi. 419.
——— His seruices at Bulleine, at the seas and in Deuon, ib
——— Is dubbed and made generall of the armie for the seruice in Scotland, ib
——— Taketh Edenborough, ib
Drusken king of the Picts, v. 198
——— Hastilie inuadeth his enimies, v 200.
——— Commeth to rescue his people, v 201.
——— Perswaded vnto peace, ib
——— Imboldeneth his people, v 202.
——— Escapeth by flight, v 200
——— Slaine, v 202.
Dublin besieged, v 228.
——— An ancient citie, vi 147.
——— The name of it, vi 21
——— Builded by Auellanus, ib.
——— The situation of it, ib.
——— Inhabited by Bristolians, vi. 24.
——— The parish churches in it, ib.
——— The castle builded, vi 27
——— Besieged by Fridleie king of Denmark, vi 91
——— Set on fire, ib
——— Taken by the Danes, vi. 92
——— Besieged by Knought the Dane, ib.
——— Builded by Iuorus, vi. 94.

Dublin rebelleth against Mac Morough, vol vi pages 146, 147
——— Is taken, ib
——— Besieged by Hasculphus, vi 149.
——— It is kept, vi 155
——— Earle Strangebow yeeldeth it vnto king Henrie the second, vi 158
——— It is besieged by Oronke king of Meth, ib.
——— It is burned, vi 240.
——— Restored and beautified, ib.
——— Interdicted by the pope, vi 277 278.
——— In an vprore against the earle of Ormond, vi 276
——— The doo penance, vi 278
——— They are discomfited, vi 293.
——— Besieged by Thomas Fitzgerald, vi 295
——— The enter into league with him, vi. 297, 298
——— They break league, vi 296
——— It is besieged by Thomas Fitzgerald, vi. 296
——— Intreateth for peace, vi 297
——— Giueth his pledges, vi 298
——— They haue aid out of England, vi 299
——— Their bridge fell, they have a maior appointed to be their gouernor, vi 363
——— They haue the sword borne before the maior, ib
——— The king sendeth them his letters of thanks, vi. 299
——— They haue a mint, vi 323
——— The castell is repared, vi 403
——— They inuade Obrins countrie, vi 259
——— They inuade Scotland and Wales, vi 261
——— They discomfit Fitzgerald, vi 297
——— Their children are taken prisoners, vi 296.
Dubright bishop of Caerlon, i 572
Dubritius bishop of Landaffe his diligence in his profession, i 581
Dubtactus a capteine father to saint Briget, vi 85
Duchesse Katharine of Suffolke hated of Stephan Gardiner note, iv 104
——— Hir trouble, persecution, and voluntarie banishment, iv 104 to 110
——— Of Gloscester deceaseth, iii 9
——— Of Yorke mother to Edward the fourth, deceaseth, iii 511
——— Of Salisburie beheaded, iii 346
——— Of Bedford deceaseth, iii 176
——— Of Burgogne hir appeale, iii 123
——— ¶ See Margaret
——— Of Saxonie deliuered of a child, ii. 186, 183
——— Of Sauoie, sends for aid to king Henrie the eight against the duke of Gelders, iii 564.
——— Bestoweth new cotes on the English souldiors, iii 565.
——— Of Angolesme meet about a tretise of peace, iii. 742
Duchmen arriue in Scotland, v. 72
Duchmen comming to England holding a contrarie opinion to the Romish church, vol ii page 116.
——— Two of strange and monstrous nature, iv. 446
Dudleie chosen speaker for the commons at the parlement, iii. 531
——— ¶ Sée Empson.
Dudleie knight setteth lord admerall forth from London towards Scotland, iii 835
——— Went into France to receiue the French kings oth, his enterteinment, iii 858
——— Lord Howard impeacheth the French power, iv 101.
——— Lord Henrie slaine at the besieging of saint Quintins, iv 89
——— Bishop of Durham of honorable descent deceaseth, iii 478.
——— Robert the creation of him baron of Denbigh, and earle of Leicester, iv. 226
——— ¶ Sée Leicester
Duffe Adam an heretic burned, vi 252
——— King of Scots crowned, goeth to the western Iles, purgeth them, v 232
——— He falleth sicke, v. 233
——— His regard to haue iustice executed, ib.
——— Restored to health, v. 234
——— Rewardeth his friends, v 235
——— His seruants cut his throte, his buriall, v 235
——— His bodie taken vp out of the ground and honorablie buried, v 237
Duke in Latine Dux à ducendo, a name now of honor, i 204
——— Created of the prince, i 266
——— In England none, i 277
——— Humfreie of Glocester builded Greenwich, i 329
Duke of Summerets in king Edward the sixts time wise answers to sutors for college and church lands, i. 256
Duke of Summerset made regent of Normandie, & the duke of Yorke discharged, iii 208
——— Made capteine of Calis, iii 254
——— His valiantnesse, iii 197
——— Reuolteth from Edward the fourth, taken & beheaded, iii 280, 281.
——— Made lord protector, iii 866
——— His returne from Scotland, iii 889
——— Not desirous of slaughter, iii 882
——— With his power against Scotland, iii. 867
——— Sendeth an herald to summon a castell, iii 869
——— Answer to a Scotish herald at armes, iii 874
——— His diligence to further the fortification to Rockesburgh, iii 887
——— His statelie stile with his epistle expostulatiue sent to the Scotish nobles, &c. iii 910.

Duke of Summerset he & the earle of Warwike outwardlie freends, vol iii page 1023
—— He and others submit themselues to Edward the fourth, iii 280
—— Againe apprehended and committed to the Towre, iii 1032
—— Charged sir Peter Carew with the rebellion, iii. 953.
—— He and the earle of Deuonshire comfort queene Margaret, iii 315
—— Politike and puissant, iii 319
—— More hardie than wise, iii 319, 320
—— Striketh out the lord Wenlocks brains, iii 319.
—— His infortunatnesse, iii 191
—— Arested, iii 238
—— Set at libertie, made deputie of Calis, ib
—— Accuseth the earle of Yorke of high treason, iii 233
—— Burthened with all things that happened amisse, iii 240
—— He is slaine, ib.
—— His displacing out of his protectorships consulted on, remoueth in hast with K Edward sixt to windsore his letter to the lord priuie seale, iii 1014, 1015
—— His letters to the lords, iii 1016
—— A proclamation with articles against him, iii 1017
—— Prisoner committed to the Towre, articles obiected against him, iii 1019
—— Released and restored, iii 1020
—— Deliuered out of the Towre, iii 1023
—— Arreigned both of fellonie and treason, condemned of fellonie, people murmur at his condemnation, deliuered to be executed, his behauior at his death, iii 1032, 1033
—— His words at his death, a sudden noise & feare among the people assembled, iii 1033 1034
—— Described, iii 1036
—— Beheaded, iii 320
—— Entereth Scotland protector of England, v 547
—— He burneth a peece of Leith, v 552
—— He bridleth the Scots, v 555
—— A digression concerning him, with prophesies touching his rising and falling, v. 707
Duke Alfrike of Mercia, i 701
—— Androgeus of Troinouant, i 177
—— Asclepiodotus of Cornewall his exploits against the Romans, i 520
—— King of Britaine, ib.
Duke Berthun & Authur of Sussex, vol. i page 634
—— Blederike of Cornewall, i 599.
—— Chorthmund a murtherer, i 655.
—— Conan Meredoc of Cornewall, i 533
—— Corineus of Cornewall ¶ Sée Corineus
—— Dionethus of Cornewall, i 535
—— Eardulfe taken and wounded, i 651
—— Elsing of Norwaie, i 452
—— Elium of Demetia, i 485
—— Gorolus of Cornewall, i 571
—— Hennius of Cornewall, i 177.
—— Horgerius of Cornewall or Deuonshire, i. 695
—— Maglaunus of Albanie, i 447
—— Octauius of the Gewisses, i 533
—— Salomon of Cornewall, i. 534
—— Uortigerne of the Gewisses and Cornewall, i 552
—— ¶ Sée Uortigerne Wade a conspirator, i 655.
Duke Alexander of Albanie taketh the sea, v 448.
—— Returneth into Scotland, v 492
—— Visiteth the borders, the second person of the realme, v 488
—— His arriuall in Scotland, v 485.
—— Receiued into Edenburgh, ib
—— Blamed, v 455
—— Confirmed tutor by parlement, v. 484
—— Fleeth to Dunbar, v 455
—— Commeth into England, v 453
—— Reconciled and receiued into his countrie, ib
—— Warre denounced against him by an English herald, v 493
—— Returneth into France, v 500
—— His request and vaine brag, v 496.
—— Hee returneth into Scotland, ib.
—— Imprisoned, v 452
—— Escapeth, ib
Duke Alan of Britaine, ii 88, 89
—— Of Albanie leuieth an armie to inuade England, iii 681
Duke Albert of Holland commeth into England, iii. 85
—— An earnest mediator for peace, iii 85, 86
—— Entereth in league with Henrie the fift, ib
Duke Albert of Saxonie his policie to get the towne of Dam, he sendeth for aid to Henrie the seuenth to win Sluis, iii 497
Duke of Alanson commeth into England, iv 447
—— Departeth out of England with all the nobilitie and gentlemen attending upon him, iv 460, 461
—— Attempteth diuerse exploits unfortunatelie falleth out, iv 498
—— His ambition spreading like a canker, glad to retire notwithstanding a confident clamor he sickneth, iv 498, 499

Duke of Alanson arriueth at Flushing, vol iv page 462
———— Receiued at Midleborough, iv 463
———— Refuseth to ride on horsebacke, iv 464
———— Goeth to sée the towne of Ermwiden, iv 465
———— His ships painted with his owne colours, ib
———— He prepareth to make his entrie into Antwerpe, iv 466.
———— His roiall intertainment note, ib
———— Created duke of Brabant, the states promise their loialtie, an offer of the marquesship of the sacred empire, &c. iv. 472, 473
———— His posie, & strange habillements, the order, of his entring into Antwerpe, iv 474
———— Saileth towards Antwerpe, landeth at a village in Brabant, a theatre erected for him, kissing of his hand, his chaire of estate, obesisance done to him, iv 468, 469, 470
———— The states loialtie vnto him, his answere vnto an oration made in their behalf, his promise euen to the shedding of his bloud, he is content to sweare to articles agréed vpon, iv 470, 471
———— Keies of Antwerpe presented to him, a canopie caried ouer his head, iv 475, 476
———— Readie to take his oth of the magistrates and people, it is read in French, he casteth largesse of gold & siluer among the people, iv 484, 485
———— The manner of his disease, iv 500, 501
———— His resolutenes to die, iv 500
———— Great hope conceiued of him if he had not beene preuented with death, iv 501.
———— Falleth into an extremitie of his maladie and past recouerie, ib
———— His words vpon his death bed, iv. 501, 502
———— His departure out of this world like a lampe, whose light faileth for want of oile, iv 503
———— His death gréeuouslie lamented, ib
Duke Alphonse of Calabrie made knight of the garter, iii 503
Duke Arthur of Britaine made knight, ii 277.
———— His mistrust in his vncle king Iohn, ii 278
———— Dooth homage to K Iohn, ii 280
———— Proclameth himselfe earle of Aniou, ii 284
———— Taken prisoner, ii 285
———— His mother accuseth K Iohn for the murther of his sonne, ii 287
———— Committed to streict prison, ii. 286
Duke Arthur his death verie lamentable, vol ii page 286
Duke William of Aquitaine his feined fréendship, ii 115
Duke of Aumarle constable of England, ii 846
———— Accused, iii 5
———— His answere vnto Bagots bill, he is appealed of treason, chalengeth triall with the lord of Fitzwater, ib
Duke of Austrich while he bore king Richard no godwill, ii 235
———— Threatened the English hostages with losse of life, ii 235
———— He catcheth a fall beside his horsse, & dieth of the hurt, ib
Duke Beauford of Summerset son vnto him that was slaine, iii 243
Duke Bauier commeth to K Henrie the fift with a number of horsemen, iii 122
———— He and his troope departeth with K Henrie the fifts fauor, iii 124
Duke of Bedford against the lord Louell in armes, iii 483.
———— Regent of England, iii 88
———— Calleth a parlement, iii 129
———— He rescueth Cosnie, iii. 132.
———— Giueth the French a great ouerthrow by sea, iii 86.
———— Returneth into France, iii 156.
———— His endeuours in France where he was regent, iii 137
———— His decease· note, iii 184.
Duke of Britaine pretendeth a right to the earledome of Westmerland, iii 6.
———— Sendeth ambassadors to Henrie the fift, iii 132
———— His loue to the earle of Richmond and care of his saftie, iii 426
———— In armes against the French K iii 489, 490
———— The battells tried, he dieth, iii 490.
———— Restored to his dukedome, ii 723.
———— A freend to the Englishmen, ii. 761
———— His dissimulation, he & the French K accorded, ii 732
———— Commeth ouer into Britaine, ii 697
———— Deceaseth, ii 630
Duke of Buckingham highlie commended, iii 406.
———— Rich araie, iii 547
———— Enuied and hated of cardinall Woolsie, iii 644
———— Means to wind him out of Henrie the eights fauour, iii 645
———— Bils of complaints exhibited to him, he depriueth Keneuet of his office, ib
———— He and his companie ioine with Henrie the seauenth against Perkin Warbecke, iii. 518
———— His words to Q Elisabeth, iii 571.

Duke of Buckingham his oration to the maior, aldermen, and commons at Guildhall, vol. iii. page 390.
———— He and Glocester fall out and whie, iii. 403.
———— They mistrust one another, iii. 404.
———— Conspired against Richard the third, he is a professed enimie to him, his power of wild Welshmen (falseharted) doo faile him, a great water his undooing, his adherents & their power dispersed, iii. 416, 417, 418.
———— The principall cause whie he conceiued such inward grudge against Richard the third, iii. 409.
———— His imaginations to depriue Richard the third, iii. 410.
———— Rewards promised by proclamation for the attaching of him, betraied of his owne seruant, beheaded without arreignment or iudgement, iii. 418.
———— Conuinced with others to worke mischief, iii. 366.
———— His resolution not to medle in seeking to obteine the crowne, but by deposing Richard the third to prefer the earle of Richmond thereto, the summe of his purpose, iii. 411, 412.
———— Is sent to the duke of Yorke to know the cause of his being in armes, iii. 240.
———— Destruction deuised and practised, iii. 657.
———— He is accused and indicted of treason, iii. 658.
———— Areigned at Westminster, conuinced of hie treason, iudgement giuen vpon him, beheaded on Towre hill, the last lord high constable of England, iii. 662.
———— ¶ Sée duke of Glocester.
Duke of Burbons practises to make the Englishmen reuolt from their owne king, iii. 15.
———— Incampeth néere Rone, slaine at the assalt, iii. 716, 717.
———— Dieth at London, iii. 181.
Duke of Burgognie chiefe dooer in France, iii. 92.
———— Prepareth to besiege Calis, iii. 85.
———— Enuieth the glorie of the English, iii. 192.
———— His oth to Henrie the fift, iii. 115.
———— Prepareth an armie against Calis, iii. 187.
———— His armie of 40000 men, ib.
———— Besiegeth it, his enterprise to bar the hauen, his bastile taken, he breaketh vp his siege, & flieth, iii. 187, 188.
———— He & Charles of France at peace, and what mischiefe insued it, iii. 182.
———— Commeth to king Edward the fourth, iii. 332.
———— He departeth suddenlie to the kings discontentment, ib.
Duke of Burgognie departeth from Edward the fourth in a rage, vol. iii. page 337.
———— Commeth in hast to Edward the fourth, ib.
———— His behauiour and speech, iii. 336.
———— Sendeth ambassadors to Calis. iii. 302.
———— He inuadeth Edward the fourth, iii. 303.
———— Deceaseth, iii. 345.
Duke of Clarence lord Loinell, iii. 677.
———— Sent to aid the duke of Orleance, iii. 55.
———— Marches towards Guisnes, ib.
———— Made a rode into Aniou, ib.
———— He is betraied by Ferguse a Lombard, iii. 127.
———— He and diuerse nobles slaine, ib.
———— Before Paris with his armie, iii. 109.
———— Seeketh to make peace betweene Edward the fourth and the earle of Warwike, iii. 309.
———— Weighing the inconuience of discord, waxeth wise, & slow to aid the earle of Warwike, his dissimulation, iii. 307, 308.
———— He and the earle of Warike soiourneth at Excester to passe over the seas, they arriue on the English coasts, iii. 298, 299.
———— A conspirator against his brother Edward the fourth, he taketh the seas, iii. 294.
———— His promise to a damsell persuading him to peace, iii. 296.
———— Drowned in a but of Malmeseie, 346.
Duke of Chaterault gathereth a power, v. 646.
———— He retireth to Glasco, ib.
———— He besiegeth Glasco, ib.
———— Forfalted, v. 652.
Duke Conan of Britaine disceasseth, ii. 128.
Duke of Excester his pithie saieng, iii. 66.
———— Vncle to Henrie the fift, iii. 91.
———— Capteine of Harflue, iii. 84.
———— His ouerthrow by the French, ib.
———— With a power at Newarke, iii. 306.
———— Left for dead but recouered: note, iii. 314.
———— Deceaseth, iii. 160.
———— Found dead in the sea, iii. 330.
———— Commeth into England, disuadeth Richard the second from peace with the French King, ii. 817.
Duke of Glocesters protestation vpon his oth, ii. 784.
———— Arested, ii. 837.
———— Confessed all wherwith he was charged, he is smothered to death, ii. 837.
———— He and Richard second at priuie grudge, talke betweene them, ii. 834.

Duke of Glocester excused to K Richard by the duke of Lancaster & Yorke, he & the abbat of St Albons conspire, vol ii page 835, 836
——— Made duke of Ireland, his iournie thither vnluckilie staied, ii 821
——— His iournie into Prutzenland in great favour with the commons, ii 811.
——— A severe man, ii 764.
——— His death, the doers therein exempted from king Henrie the fourths pardon, iii 9.
——— In question, iii 29
——— His deth in part revenged, iii 9
——— Much adoo about it note, iii 5.
——— His complaint to Henrie sixt against the cardinall of Winchester, iii 199
——— Liketh well of the kings mariage with the earle of Armenaks daughter note, iii 207
——— Winneth Rockesburgh castell, iii 265.
——— His deth, and what mischiefe followed it, iii. 211.
——— He is commended. note, ib
——— Discharged of all government, the faint quarell piked against him, he is suddenlie murthered, iii 210, 211
——— Ill practises against him vnder faire countenances, iii 208
——— Spoileth Flanders, iii 189
——— Calleth a parlement, Henrie the sixt in France, iii 176
——— Articles against the bishop of Winchester, iii 147.
——— Mariage in question, he waxeth werie of his wife, iii 145
——— He and bishop of Winchester at dissention, iii. 146, 147
——— Murthereth Henrie the sixt in the Towere, iii 324
——— An enimie to peace, iii 335
——— Proclamation against the lord Hastings, iii 383
——— Marieth another mans wife, iii 137
——— His behaviour in the assemblie of lords, iii 380
——— His oration to the lords against the queene, iii 370
——— His resolution to go through with his deuilish enterprise, iii 378
——— Solicitations tending wholie to trouble and bloudshed, iii 365
——— His & Buckinghams practises, iii 366
——— Made protector, iii 370
——— ¶ Sée duke of Buckingham.
Duke Geffreie of Britaine his homage, ii. 129.
Duke Guildebald of Urbin in Italie made knight of the garter, iii 538.
Duke of Guise with a great armie commeth towards Calis, entereth the English frontiers, his police, vol iv page 90, 91.
Duke of Guise his proclamation to bring in monie, plate, &c. iv 92
——— Marched to the towne and fort of Guisnes, iv 94
——— He and monsieur Dandelot with their powers, in a rage with his soldiers, a trumpetter from him to the lord Greie, they have communication one whole houre, iv 98, 99
——— Appointed to be a principall leader and executor of forren inuasion, iv 538
Duke of Hereford appealeth the duke of Northfolke of treason, iii 844
——— Beloued of the people, honourable interteined with the French king, ib
Duke Iohn the second & Philip the second aduancers of the state, iv 486
Duke of Irelands passage stopped by the lords, his souldiors reuolt from him, he flieth from his armie, getteth him into Holland, letters found in his trunks, ii 789, 790
——— He and his associates atteinted of treason by parlement, ii 793
Duke of Lancaster and the Londoners submit their quarels to the kings order, ii 712.
——— Commeth with an armie vnto Edenburgh, v 394
——— His disloialtie, v 355
——— He & Yorke excuse the duke of Glocester to king Richard the second, ii. 835
——— High steward of England at an arreignment, ii 841.
——— He & Yorke assembleth their powers to resist Richard the seconds dealings, ii 838.
——— Returneth into England out of Gascoigne, ii 800
——— Created, ii 652
——— Debate betwixt him and the duke of Brunswike, ii 653
——— Goeth ouer sea with a navie and two of Edward the thirds sonnes with him, ii 635
——— Is sent to aid the king of Nauarre, ii 662
——— Persuadeth Edward the third to peace with the French king, ii 673
——— Maketh a iournie into France, ii. 692
——— Sent into France with an armie, fortifieth his campe, ii 691
——— Commeth to Burdeaux, ii 700
——— In danger by the Londoners note, ii 705.
——— Goeth into Spaine with an armie, ii. 768
——— He landeth at Brest, and winneth two bastides from the French, landeth at Groigne, ii 769
——— He and the king of Portingall

alied, they inuade Castile, he returneth out of Portingall into Gascoigne, vol. ii. pages 770, 771.
Duke of Lancaster reconcileth the king and the lords, ii. 800.
——— Made duke of Aquitane, ii. 809.
——— Commeth to Chester citie, the countrie submit themselues vnto him, Holt castell deliuered vnto him, ii. 856.
——— He and Glocester sent into France to treat of peace, ii. 822.
——— The grant of the duchie of Aquitane vnto him reuoked, ii. 831.
——— Calleth a parlement in Richard the seconds time, ii. 859.
——— His behauiour to the king, their méeting, his demand, & receiuing in London, ii. 853.
——— His bastards made legitimat, ii. 834.
——— Ambassador for the K. of France, ii. 814.
——— A prince of great renowne, ii. 817.
——— Saileth into Aquitane, ii. 824.
——— Solicited to expell king Richard the second, ib.
——— Solicited to take vpon him the regiment, ii. 852.
——— The duke of Britaine his great fréend, the commons denie to resist the duke, he landeth in Yorkeshire, his oth to the lords that aided him, the harts of the commons wholie bent vnto him, he marcheth vnto Bristow, ii. 852, 853.
——— Feasteth strangers, ii. 811.
——— Enuied of the rebels: note, ii. 738.
——— Not suffered to enter into the towne of Berwike, ii. 751.
——— Chargeth the erle of Northumberland with manie crimes, commeth to the parlement with a great troope of men, ii. 752.
——— Sent into France to treat of peace, ii. 764.
——— Misliking the manners of the court getteth himselfe to Killingworth castell, ii. 718.
——— He and the erle of Cambridge appointed protectors, ii. 715.
——— Saileth to Britaine with a great power, ii. 710.
——— Getteth him to his castell of Pomfret and fortifieth it, ii. 767.
——— Laieth challenge to the crowne, ii. 865.
——— He is placed in the regall throne, ib.
——— King elect, his words to the lords, ib.
——— His coronation, proclamed by the name of Henrie the fourth, ii. 864.
Duke of Lancaster inuadeth Scotland with an armie, vol. ii. page 763.
——— Appeached of treason, ib.
——— His decease, ii. 849.
——— ¶ Sée Edmund.
Duke of Leneux hath the earle Moortons lands, v. 706.
——— Banished, v. 707.
——— ¶ Sée Lennex.
Duke of Mordo and other péeres arrested, v. 418, 419.
——— He and his sonnes are beheaded, v. 419.
Duke William of Normandie, &c. arriued in Britaine to visit Edward the confessor, i. 12; ii. 624.
——— His dead carcase twelue inches longer than anie mans dwelling in ý counterie, i. 18.
——— Prepared to inuade England and conquer it, i. 759.
——— His policie to disorder his enemies, i. 762.
——— Ioifullie receiueth Harold, i. 751.
——— Sendeth an ambassage to Harold putting him in mind to remember his oth, i. 758.
——— Erecteth & buildeth fortresses for his soldiers, i. 760.
——— He landeth in Sussex, ib.
——— His politike conquest of England, ii. 1.
——— Was baselie born of the bodie of Arlet a burgesses daughter of Falois, i. 764.
——— The battell betwixt him and king Harold fought, i. 763.
——— His comming ouer into England, and returne, i. 746.
——— Pretendeth a title to the crowne of England, i. 756.
——— His enterprise fauoured of pope Alexander, i. 760.
——— Sendeth to king Harold requiring him to take his daughter to wife as he promised, i. 757.
——— Promiseth Harold his daughter in mariage, i. 752.
——— His pedigree, i. 764.
——— ¶ Sée William.
Duke of Northfolke in armes against Wiat, arriueth at Stroud, iv. 13.
——— He and the Scotish lords méete at Yorke, iv. 635.
——— He with the capteine of the gard put to their shifts, ib.
——— He and Suffolke elected into the order of S. Michaell, iii. 776.
——— Ambassador into France, iii. 815.
——— Henrie the eights lieutenant, iii. 801.
——— Cōmeth with a power against the rebels in Suffolke, iii. 709.

Duke of Northfolke & the earle of Surrie on Richard the thirds side, vol iii page 438
———— His constansie and allegiance to Richard third, he is slaine, iii. 444
———— Accused of treson, ii 844
———— Obiections against him, ii 845.
———— Committed to the Towre, atteinted, & the attaindor reuersed, iii. 861
———— Deceaseth, iii 9, 709, iv 64.
———— Inuested into the order of S Michaell, iv 230
———— Sent to the Towre, iv 235
———— Remoued from the Towre to the Charterhouse, iv 254
———— Committed to the Towre, iv 262
———— Arreigned, condemned, and iduged, iv 264
———— Beheaded, forren nations write thereof, his attire, behauiour and his speech at his execution note, iv. 267, 268, 269
Duke of Northumberlands enterprise against the ladie Marie incouraged, iii 1067.
———— His words to the lords of the councell about quéene Iane, who adhered vnto him, he setteth forward with all speed, iii 1068.
———— Writeth for more succours, iii 1087
———— His son raised out of the Towre, iv 74
———— Arrested by the earle of Arundell and comitted to the Towre with his adherents, iv 1
———— Arreigned, his request to vnderstand the opinion of the court in two points, iv 3, 4
———— His foure requests after his iudgment to die, he with others are executed at Towre hill, iv. 4
Duke of Orleance partaker with the duke of Britaine against the French king, iii. 490
———— How long prisoner in England, his ransome and release, iii 196
———— Chalenge, iii. 28
———— He beseiged Uergi in Guien, ib
———— Besiegeth townes in Gascoigne, iii 43
———— Commeth to the English armie, iii 56
———— Murthered, iii 50.
———— Philip of Burgognie surnamed the Hardie, iv 485
Duke Richard his singular dissimulation, iii 395
———— He speaketh otherwise than he meaneth, ib
———— His electiō hard to be preferred, iii 394.
———— Preferred at last by voices of confederacie, ib
———— Aduised by bishop Morton, their conference, he openeth himselfe and his secrets to the bishop, complaineth of lacke of preferment in K. Edwards daies, iii. 407, 408.
Duke Richard his title to the crowne, with the office and dignitie of a king, he is commended to the people as worthie and sufficient, vol iii. pages 393, 394
———— ¶ Sée Duke of Glocester and Richard
Duke of Richmond a martialist or warrior Henrie the eights base sonne, iii 776
———— Henrie Fitzroie Henrie the eights base sonne deceasseth, iii 798.
Duke of Saxonie in disfauour and exile, ii 183.
———— Commeth into England, his goodlie stature, ii 367
———— Pardoned and reuoked out of exile, i 186
Duke of Rothsaie and the ladie Anne de la Poole married, v 457
———— His insolent outrage, v. 404, 405
———— Committed to prison, v 405
Duke of Suffolke created, iii 212
———— Winneth the goodwill of the quéen dowager of France, iii. 611
———— They married togither, ib.
———— Entered France with an armie, iii 688
———— Breaketh vp his armie and commeth to Calis, iii 691
———— Chiualrie and valiant seruice in France, he knighteth diuerse gentlemen, iii. 689, 690
———— Pope hindred by cardinall Woolseie, iii 616
———— And others sent in France to fetch the French quéene into England, iii 611
———— Incountereth with a strong and tall Almaine, iii 606
———— He foileth the Almaine, ib
———— Deceasseth, his iust commendation, iii 849.
———— The commons exclaime against him, iii 218.
———— Committed to the Towre, his wretched deth, iii 220
———— He with others brought to the Towre, iv. 21
———— Committed to the Towre and released, iv 2.
———— Goeth downe into Leicestershire, and is a fauourer and furtherer of Wiats practises, he is kept out of Couentrie, apprehended, iv 13, 14
———— Arreigned, condemned, beheaded, iv. 24.
———— What words he spake to the people at his deth, ib
Duke of Surrie marshall of England, ii 845
Duke of Yorke lieutenant generall of England, ii. 850
———— Misliketh the court and goeth home, ii 849
———— Noted for crueltie, what maner of man he was, his end, iii. 361.

Duke of Yorke Plantagenet afterwards Richard third, vol iii page 155
———— Made regent of France, enuied of duke of Summerset, iii 185, 194, 196
———— Appointed againe to be regent of Normandie, iii 208
———— A persecuting enmie to the duke of Summerset note, iii 217
———— Assembleth an armie, his words in writing sent to the K iii 238, 239.
———— His comming against the K iustified, he is made protector of the realme, iii 242
———— Discharged of his office, iii 243.
———— Assembleth an armie, iii 251.
———— Cōmeth out of Ireland, his strange demenors, bold spéech and oration to the lords of parlement, iii 261
———— Crowned with sedge or bulrushes in derision, iii 269
———— He and his complices flie, iii. 253
———— He and others attainted, iii 256
———— Articles that he and the other earles sent to the archbishop of Canturburie and the commons, iii 257
———— Articles of peace and agréement betwéene him and Henrie the sixt, his claime to the crowne, iii 265
———— Proclamed heire apparent to the crowne, he is slaine, iii 268
———— Tempering about his title to the crowne, iii 212.
———— Reconciliation to Henrie the sixt, he accuseth the duke of Summerset of treason, iii 233
———— Set at libertie, & whie, his submission to king Henrie the sixt vnder his oth, iii 234
———— Maketh claime to the crowne, iii 229
———— Raiseth a great power to recouer it, his letter to Henrie the sixt, iii 250
———— His fauourers executed and spoiled, iii. 258
———— Séekes the destruction of the duke of Summerset, banded himselfe with Neuils, iii 237
———— Slaine in Agincourt field, iii 83.
———— Buried at Fodringhaie castell, iii 84
———— Taketh indenture sextipartite of the conspired noblemen out of his sonnes bosome note, iii 10
———— Deceaseth, iii 20
———— Accused by his sister the ladie Spenser, iii 33
———— His head set on a pole at Yorke, iii 269
———— ¶ Sée Richard the third
Dukes first created in Scotland, v 402, 692
—— Of other counteries being Scots, their catalog, v. 696
—— Of Burgogne issued out of the house of France, iv 465
Dukes none in Scotland nor England, vol v page 707
—— Their catalog, v 691
—— Of Glocester infortunate note, iii 211
—— Of Normandie were the kings of Englands eldest sonnes, ii 54
—— Of Yorkes honorable emulation, iii 501
Dukes and earles, &c created, ii 677, 767, 843, iii. 51, 67, 344, 1031.
———— Depriued of their titles, iii 7
———— Of England from the first to the last, all set downe in a collection, iv 270, 284
Dukes rebell against Oswie, i 624
Dulcitius an expert capteine in war, i. 515.
———— Appointed to put Ualentinus to death, i 516
Dunbar stronglie situated, v 619
———— Deliuered after the death of Richard the third, v 458
———— The castell in the Englishmens hands, v 456
———— Rendered to king Edward, v 329
———— Rased, v 631.
Dunbar in Angus, and Dunbar in Louthian, v 162.
Dunbar familie, v 203
Dunbreton whie so named note, v 211
———— How called before, ib
———— Ancientlie called Alcluth, &c. v. 78.
———— Burnt, v 419
———— The castell taken, v 485
———— Taken by policie, v 619
Duncane a Scot wasteth Kendall, ii 157.
Duncane king of Scotland, of a soft nature, v 265
———— Besturreth himselfe in assembling an armie, v 267
———— His small skill in warlike affaires, v 265
———— Fled to the castell of Bercha, v 267
———— His wife whose daughter, his death inforced, and buriall, v 269
Duncane the base sonne of Malcome crowned king, lacketh skill in ciuell gouernment, he is slaine, v. 284
Dundalke taken and burned by the Scots, vi 246.
Dundée and whie so named, v 403
———— Abandoned of the English, v 560.
———— Fortified by the Frenchmen, ib
———— The men craue aid of Fife, v 665
Dune a riuer where Doncaster now standeth i 566.
Dunfermling church builded, v 282
Dunkild castell, v 164
Dunkirke woone & sacked by the English, ii 758.
———— Taken and burned by the French, iv. 118
Dunmailes sonnes eies put out by king Edward, i 690.
Dunnes and Duneses whie so called, vi 2
Dunse burnt, v 583
Dunsinane castell builded, v. 274
Dunstafage builded, v 54
Dunstan, & what is reported of him, i 704.
———— His prophesies, i 703
———— His sharpe message sent to K. Ethelred, i 701

Dunstan he is restored & in estimation with Edgar, vol i page 694
——— Made bishop of Worcester, i 695.
——— In fauour with Edred, i 692
——— By working miracles he had his will when arguments failed, i 700
——— His hipocrisie, i 697
——— His vision note a vaine tale, i 690
——— He is banished, i 693
Dunwellon king of Britaine caused foure principall waies to be made in his kingdome, and, whie, i. 189
——— His laws, priuileges, & other acts, i 197
——— He is praised, i 297
Dunwich a bishoprike, i 609
Duresme citie besieged by Godfric king of Adelstans enmie, i 686
Durham from Yorkshire how diuided, i 571
——— The towne and minster builded, i 707.
——— What hauens it hath, i 182
——— The bishoprikes erection, circuit, and valuatiō, i 244
——— Abbeie spoiled, v 382
——— The bishoprike burnt by the Scots, v 355
——— The church by whome built, v 282
Durham place conuerted into a palace roiall, i 329.
Durmo, or rather Gurmo, Angelicus, why so named, i 672
Durstus chosen king of Picts besieged of the Romans, brought prisoner to London, v 119
Durstus king of Scots conspired against, v 52.
——— Besieged and slaine, v 53
——— His two sonnes slaine, v 54.
Durtie rode, v. 414
Dusdere on fire, v. 555

E.

Eadbald king of Kent, incestuous, irrelegious, and taken mad, i 602
——— Baptised becommeth a christian and buildeth a church, i 603
Eadbert K. of Northumberland becommeth a moonk, i 647
Eadhidus bishop of Lindeie, i 631.
Eadmer. ¶ Sée Archbishop.
Eadmerus of S. Albons, i. 322.
Eadulfus bishop of Litchfield adorned with a pall, i. 646.
Ealdbright K of Southsaxons slaine in battell, i 639.
Eardulfe a duke taken & wounded, i 654
Earle ¶ Sée Erle
Eartongatha a kings daughter, a professed nun, i 617
Easterlings traffike merchandise in Ireland, vi 93.
——— They build townes and cities, vi 94
——— What people they are, ib
——— ¶ Sée Danes
Easter ¶ Sée Ester
Eata bishop of Hexam, i 636.
Eaubald archbishop of Canturburie, i 656.
Eauffled, king Edwins daughter borne, vol. i. page 605
Eaufride, and Osrike kings of Northumberland slaine, i 611
Ebranke now called Yorke, i 198
Ebrank the lineal heire from the bodie of Locrine, i 197
——— First inuaded France after Brute, i 445
——— Fift ruler of Britaine, ib.
——— He had 21 wiues, 20 sonnes, 30 daughters, to be maried with Troian bloud, i 445
Ebusa ¶ See Occa
Ecberts edict to call Britaine Anglesland, i 9.
Eclipse of the sunne terrible note, i 625, 643, v. 423
——— That in the yeare when it appeared died king Ecorbert and the archbishop Deusdedit, i 625
——— Of the sunne, strange, ii 171, 598, 367, 395
——— Of the sunne and moone extraordinarie, v 75
——— Very strange, ii 223.
——— Of the moone, ii 116
——— Thirtéene daies old, ii 365
——— Of foure houres continued, ii 434
Edan K of Scots warreth Edelfred of Northumberland, i 598
Edbert ¶ See Ethelbert.
Edelfred king of Northumberland his exploits and victories, i 598, 599, v 166
——— He entereth Chester, i 599
——— Associated of the Saxon princes, méeteth Eadwan in the field, i. 601
——— Wounded in fight and put to flight, i. 599.
——— Lost one of his eies, v 167.
——— His displeasure, v 169.
——— He is slaine, v 170
Edelhere slaine by Oswie, i 620.
Edelwulfe earle of Barkshire fought at Englefield with the Danes, i. 666
Edelwulfe king of Kent chased out of his countrie, i. 657.
Edenburg castell by whome builded, i 197, 475
Edenburgh recouered to the gouernour, v 532
——— The prouost sendeth to erle of Hereford, v 537
——— Entered by force, iii. 836, v 537.
——— Burnt, v 537
——— Deliuered to the lord of Erskine, v 574.
——— Kept by the lard of Grange against the regent, v 650
——— Mils broken, v 665.
——— The castell taken by the regent and the English, v 669
——— Whie called the maiden castell, v 672.
——— The names and building thereof, ib
——— The whole towne in a tumult, v 498
——— The castell, or the castell of Maidens left of the Picts, v 205.
——— Besieged, ii 606, v 496
——— Fortified by the earle of Angus, v. 501

Edenburgh a session there instituted, vol v page 509
———— The prouost and the bailiffes thereof deposed, v 192
———— It and Striueling castels woone by the English, v 329, 330
———— ¶ See Agnedh touching the name
———— Deliuered to Edward the first, ii 517
———— Burnt by Richard the second, ii 760
———— Left desolate, ii 765
Ederus king of Scots, alias Cridiorus, i 470
———— Burneth his enimies ships, v 58
———— Deceaseth, v 59
Edgar crowned, v 285
—— His vision, ib
—— The first anointed king of Scots, ib
—— Rather reuerenced than dreaded, his death, v 286
Edgar king of Britaine sitting in a barge is rowed vpon the water by six or seuen kings, i 205
—— His nauie of one thousand six hundred, alias three thousand six hundred saile, i 339
—— His disposition, & diligent prouision for defense of his realme, i 691
—— Murthereth Ethelwold & marieth his wife, i 696
—— His wiues and children, and in what state the land was in his time, i 698
—— Rowed in the water eight kings driuing his barge, i 694
—— He preferred monks to bishoprikes, i. 695.
—— Put to seuen yeares penance for deflouring Wilfrid, i 695
—— In loue with duke of Cornewals daughter, sendeth to hir about mariage and is preuented by the messenger, ib
—— Described, i 698
—— Subdueth the Welshmen, his spoiles, his vision and death, i 697
Edgar the K of Scotlands sister wife to Henrie the first, ii 48.
Edgar Edeling why the péeres of England would not make him king, i 756
Edgar Etheling of treason, v 281.
Edgitha ¶ See Editha
Edgiua the wife or (as some saie) the concubine of king Edward hir dreame, i 682
———— Mother of K Edred, i 692
Edhrike ¶ Sée Edrike
Edilbald king of Mercia fighteth against Cuthrid, i 644
———— Put to flight, i 645
Edilred king of Mercia murdereth Kent, i 630.
———— ¶ See Ethelred
Edilwald king of Northumberland, his acts and déeds, i 647
Edilwalke king of Southsaxons licenceth Wilfrid to preach to his people, i 631
———— Expelled out of his kingdome by his subiects and slaine, i 634
Ediswald king Deira disposed to deuotion, i 622.
Editha (wife to Robert d' Oilie) superstitious & credulous note, vol i page 250
Editha the daughter of earle Goodwin maried to Edward the third, i 740
———— Put awaie by hir husband king Edward note, i 744
———— A wife and yet a virgin, i 685
———— Base daughter of Edgar made a nun, i. 696
———— Abbesse of Wilton, i 697
Edmund son to Henrie the third, ii 408
———— Shewed in parlement as K of Naples, ii 441
———— Inuested king of Sicill & Naples, ii 436
———— Created duke of Lancaster, ii 434
Edmund of Langlie borne, afterwards duke of Yorke, ii 622
Edmund the great, sonne to Harold, his exploits, ii 10
Edmund king Egelreds eldest son marieth the widow of Sigeferd ye Dane, i 719
———— His valiant exploits, ib
Edmund bishop of Shireburne slaine, i 667
Edmund fighteth in cōbat with Cnute, i 724
———— Distressed by the Danes withdraweth into Glocestershire, i 723
———— K Egelerds eldest sonne sent into England, i 717
———— Ioineth Northumberland vnto his owne estate, i 689
———— K of England by intreatie concludeth peace with Danes of Northumberland, i 689
———— His lawes, i. 598.
———— His death & the lamentable maner thereof, i 690
———— Diuerse and discordant reports of his end, i 726
———— His deth reuenged, i 727.
———— His sons banished, ib
———— They are maried, ib
Edmund king of Eastangles in armes against the Danes, he is cruellie murthered of them, i 667.
Edmund the martyr gouerned the Eastangles, i 619
Edmund why surnamed Ironside, i 721.
———— Proclamed king of England, ib
———— Offereth the combat vnto Cnute the Dane, i 721
———— He and his English discomfit Cnute and his Danes in a pitcht field, i 722
———— He sheweth himselfe to his soldiers, partlie beléeuing that he was slaine, ib
———— Traitorouslie slaine in Oxfordshire, i 726
Ednam burnt, v 581
Edoll earle of Glocester or Chester his valiantnesse against the Saxons with a stake, he taketh Hengist, i 561
Edred K of England his acts and deeds, i 691
—— Imprisoneth archbishop Wolstan, i 692
—— He dieth, ib
Edrike a Dane ruler of the Eastangles, i 677

Edrike author of K. Edmunds death, vol i page 726
——— Commandeth faire Gunthildis to be put to death, 713
——— A close furtherer of Danes doings, i 711
——— Taketh part with the Danes against Edmund, i 723
——— Put to death after he had reuealed his treacherous hart, i 728
Edrike de Streona his traitors practise against two Danish noble men, i 718
——— He with a great power flieth to ye Danes, i 719
——— Made duke or earle of Mercia, i 710.
——— His treason coulered with sicknes, i 722
Edrike king of Kent slaine in warres, i. 636.
Edrike Sylvaticus rebelleth in the absence of duke William, ii. 8
Edrington taken prisoner, v. 564
Edsinus archbishop of Canturburie, i 739.
Edward the first king of that name writeth his letters vnto the Irish lords for their seruice in Scotland, vi 242
——— Proclaimed king of England, his coronation and beginning of Regiment, ii 478, 479
——— He entereth into Wales to rescue his people against the Welsh, ii 484.
——— Goeth ouer into France, ii 482
——— His fauour and goodwill to the prince of Wales, ii 481
——— Dauid of Wales preferreth him in marriage, ib.
——— Commeth to Chester, ii 479
——— Surnamed Longshanke and why borne, ii. 386.
——— Sendeth an armie into Scotland, ii 540
——— Putteth prince Edward in prison, ii. 539.
——— Answer to pope Boniface prouing the right of Scotland to belong to him, ii 534
——— Entereth into Scotland to reuenge the death of his people, ii 537
——— Goeth with an armie into Scotland, ii 532
——— Vexeth them, ib
——— Goeth to Scotland, ii 535
——— Married to the French kings sister, ii. 532
——— His liberalitie towards his nobles, ii 531.
——— Earles Marshall and Hereford refuse to go ouer with him into Flanders, ii. 524
——— Guardians appointed ouer his sonne in his absence, passeth ouer into Flanders, ii 524
——— Taketh vpon him the crosse, ii 490
——— Passeth ouer into France, ii 489
——— Recognised for superior lord of Scotlnd note, ii 494, 495
——— Summoned to appeare at Paris, ii 501
——— Condemned in the French court, ii 502
——— His request made to Scots denied, ii 510.
Edward the first entreth into Wales, vol ii page 506
——— Shift to get monie, ii 483
——— Goeth about to purchase his peoples goodwill, ii 479
——— Renounceth the French king, his shift for monie, an excuse that he used, ii 404
——— Concludeth a league with the earle of Flanders and the earle Bar, ii 511
——— Fortifieth Berwike, ii 515
——— Summoneth and winneth Berwike, ii. 513, 514
——— Planted his siege about Edenburgh castell, ii 516
——— Passeth forth through Scotland, bringeth the marble stone from thense, the nobilitie submit themselues vnto him, the forme of their homage, his words excepting, ii 518, 519
——— Meant to haue made a full conquest of Scotland, as he had doone of Wales, ii 543.
——— The forme of fealtie that Baliol king of Scots did to him, ii 499
——— Appointeth Wardens for the realme of Scotland, beareth swaie in the election of their chancellor, the nobilitie sweare fealtie to him. note, ii 496, 497
——— Sickeneth, dieth, is buried at Westminster. his issue, his stature, & form of bodie, his Uertues and uices, ii 541
Edward created prince, ii 626
——— Setteth forward into the holie land, ii. 171
——— Traitorouslie wounded, ib
——— Getteth diuerse castels, ii 459
——— Escapeth danger, ii 465
——— He and the earle of Glocester not suffered to come within the citie of London, ii 453
——— Euill intreated in manie places, ib
——— Goeth against the Welshmen, ii. 455.
——— Receiueth the crosse, ii 473
——— Taketh monie out of the treasurie of the temple, ii 456.
——— Arriueth at Acres, in danger to be slaine by treason, ii 474
——— Hath the rule of London, he appointeth the maior and shiriffes, ib.
——— Sent to the king of Castill, ii 431.
——— He marrieth the ladie Elenor daughter to king Alfonse, ib.
——— Created prince of Wales, ib
——— His wife commeth to London, ii 435.
——— Pursueth the Londoners, ii 462
——— Imprisoned for riot, ii 539.
——— Made lord warden of the realme, ii 503.
——— Made knight, and sent into Scotland, ii 540
——— Goeth ouer into Gascoigne, ii 656
——— His proceedings in Aquitane, ii 657
——— Two bishops sent vnto him from the pope, ii 657, 658
——— His first sonne borne, ii. 680

 3 Z

Edward and duke of Aquitaine, vol ii page 570
——— Sent into France, ii 577
——— Inuadeth the French dominions, ii 662
——— His order where he came, his feats of armes, the passages stopped against him, he returneth, lodgeth in the towne of Remorentius, he is followed by the French king, ii 662, 663
——— Contented to come to a parlée, his offer, his exhortation to his soldiors when he saw he must needs fight, ii 665, 666
——— Noblemen that were with him, the number of his armie, both powers come issue, ii 666.
——— He obteineth the victorie, his méeke oration to the French king his prisoner, he returneth to Burdeaux, bringeth the French king ouer into England, ii 667, 668
——— Made lord warden of the realme, ii 583.
——— Setteth forward into Spaine, ii 681
——— He passeth into Guien, ii 677
——— Put to his shifts for default of monie, he returneth into Gascoigne, constreine to burden his subiects with a sore subsidie, ii 685, 686
——— Appealed to appéere before the French king ii 686
——— His answer, a letter published by him to appease the Gascoignes, ii. 687
——— Diseased with sicknesse, ii 689
——— Did first come the penie and small péeces round, i 367
——— Returneth out of France into England, ii 696
——— Married to the earle of Warwikes daughter, iii 295.
——— Taken in flight, he is murthered, iii 320
——— He is buried at Canturburie, his death grieuouslie taken ii 702.
Edward the second borne, ii 487
——— When he began his reigne, ii 516
——— He and the earle of Lancaster made fréends, ii 527
——— Goeth into Scotland, what he did there, his entrance, ii 550
——— Hath his nobles in no regard. note, ii. 547
——— Deposed by act of Parlement, ii 584
——— Saileth into Wales, ii 582
——— His fauor to the Welshmen, ib
——— Sought vnto to resigne his crowne, his griefe thereat, ii 584
——— Betraied into his enimies hands, brought to Killingworth castell ii 583
——— Withstood in armes by his wife, ii 577, 578
——— Sendeth for his wife and sonne home out of France, ii 577
——— Writeth to the duke of Britaine, ii 576
——— Like to be betraied, the traitors executed, ii 572, 574.
Edward the second goeth to Scotland with an armie, vol ii page 571
——— Subdueth his barons, ii 568
——— In armes against his enimies, his proclamation, ii 566
——— Passeth by a foord, commeth to Turburie, causeth hue & crie to be made, ii 567
——— Durst not but yéeld to his nobles request, ii 562.
——— He goeth to Canturburie, talketh with lord chamberleine, besiegeth the castell of Léeds, ib
——— Affection and loue to Piers Gaueston, ii 550
——— His request for his life, his displeasure for his deth, ii 551.
——— Passeth ouer to France, ii 517.
——— Dooth homage to the French king, marrieth his daughter, returneth, is receiued into London, crowned, ib
——— Goeth to Berwike, ii 557
——— Passeth into Scotland, what issue his armie had there, he escapeth danger of death, ii. 553
——— His nature and conditions, his issue, ii 587
——— Murthered, ib
——— Held a parlement at Salisburie, i 98
——— He writeth his letters vnto Ireland for aid against the Scots, vi 251
——— He sendeth thither Piers Gaueston, vi 245
——— Sendeth his letters for the apprehending of the Templers, ib
Edward the secōd king of England after much contention, i 699
——— Gouerned by good counsell, i 700
——— Shamefullie murthered by his mothers procurement, ib
——— Surnamed Martyr, i 701
Edward the third king of England by generall consent, crowned, i 739, v 357.
——— Promiseth to make duke William heire, i 747
——— Absteineth from the companie of his wife, i 740.
——— Dealtth strictlie with his mother Emma, i 740
——— In person commeth out against Goodwin and his complices, i 745.
——— His lawes instituted, i 747
——— Putteth awaie his wife Editha. note, i 741.
——— Inuadeth the Scots by land, v 375
——— Had two kings prisoners at once, and how he sat at the table with them, v 387
——— Purposeth to subdue the Scots, v 368
——— Enuieth the felicitie of the Scots, v 364.

Edward the third his purpose to destroie earle Thomas note, vol v page 361
—— In armes against the Scots, v 358.
—— Breaketh vp his campe, v 359.
—— Of whome descended, & his lawes, i 206
—— Son in law to earle Goodwine, i 12, 13
—— Surnamed the saint, i 12
—— Uisited by duke William of Normandie, ib
—— Preferreth the Normans to the greatest offices in the realme, ib
—— He had no issue, i 206
—— Deuiser of the order of the garter, i 238.
—— Got the Ile of Wight wholie into his hands, i 56.
—— First planted saffron in Walden, i 390
—— Departeth this life, his manners, and mind, i 753
—— Canonised by the name of Edward Confessor, i. 754.
—— His words vpō his death bed, ib
—— Described, i 755
Edward the third, son of Henrie the seuenth christened, iii 521
Edward the third borne, ii 552.
—— Beginneth his reigne, ii 589.
—— Passeth ouer into Calis, inuadeth France, returneth for want of vittels, the constable of France demandeth battell of him, ii 656
—— Lodgeth his armie néere Berwike, the Scots yéeld vnto him, the realme of Scotland resigned vnto him, ii 661
—— Three kings come vnto him about businesse, ii 678.
—— Advanced his sonnes to degrée of honor, ii 677.
—— Prepareth to make a iournie to France arriueth at Calis, ii 672
—— Draweth towards Paris, ii 673.
—— Returneth out of France into England, ii 675
—— His foure sons take part with the lords maiors, &c challenge at iusts, ii 671
—— Sore afflicted the Scots, ii 662
—— His honorable hart to his enimie, ii 650
—— Hath Calis surrendered vnto him. ¶ Sée Calis.
—— His pitie towards the poore note, ii 643
—— His voiage, inuasion, and victorie against the French, summarilie set down in a letter missiue, ii 640, 641
—— His words and behauiour to his son the yoong prince after his victorie against the French, ii 639.
Edward the third passeth ouer into Normandie, his arriue, landing and ordering of his souldiors, vol ii page 634
—— His enterprise and atchiuements against townes & people, his spoiles & bootes he is in danger, ii 634, 635, 636
—— Beginneth his enterprise against the enimie with prair to God, his demeanor before the battell, ii 636, 637
—— Hath towns restored to him, ii 618
—— Taketh into his hands all the profits that the cardinall, &c held within his realme, ii 631
—— Goeth ouer into Flanders, ii. 631
—— Passeth ouer into Britain, ii. 621.
—— Returneth by sea out of Britain, he is in danger of drowning, ii 626
—— Feasted by the earle of Flanders, he goeth into Zeland, arriueth at the Towre, dealeth roundlie with his officers, ii 618
—— Offended with the archbishop of Canturburie, ii 619
—— Taketh sea, setteth vpon his enimies the French, getteth his victorie, goeth to Guant, couenants betwixt him and his confederats, ii 614, 615
—— Signifieth his right to crown of France, taketh vpon him the title and armes thereof, ii 612.
—— Taketh vpon him the name of K. of France, ii 611.
—— And by what right he clamed it, ib
—— Besieged Cambrie, ii 610
—— He raseth his siege, ib
—— Hath Flanders at commandment, he saileth to Antwerpe, ii 608.
—— His Confederats, ib
—— Practiseth to alienat the Flemings harts from obedience to their earle, ii 606.
—— Entereth into Scotland with an armie, ii 602
—— Maketh spoile by fier & sword, the Scots ordeine a statute in favour of him, towns fortified by him, he studieth to gather monie to mainteine his wars, ii 604, 605
—— Aideth the king of Scots and white, ii 600
—— Passeth the sea appareled like a merchant, ii 598
—— Waxeth feeble and sicke, ii 701
—— Deceasseth, his issue, praise, proportion of bodie, and vertues, ii 706, 707
Edward the fourth borne, iii 204
—— Feasted the maior and aldermen of London, iii 349
—— He and the French king their interview the manner thereof note, iii 338
—— His shift to get monie note, iii 330.

Edward the fourth he passeth ouer into France, and sendeth a defiance to the French king, vol iii page 331.
———— Returneth into England, iii 342.
———— Without interruption passeth forward to Yorke, marcheth to the citie gates, receiued the sacrament & an oth, the Marquesse Montacute suffered him to pass by, he commeth to Northamton, iii 305, 306
———— Dispraised and fowlie spoken of by the erle of Warwike, iii 289
———— His communication with the duke of Burgognie note, iii 335, 336
———— Shamful and slanderous wordes against him, iii 338
———— His politike foresight, iii 319.
———— Commeth to Leicester, prouoketh the earle of Warwike to fight, commeth to Warwike, he and his brother the duke of Clarence reconciled vnwitting to the earle of Warwike, iii 307, 308
———— His victorie and the offering vp of his standard, iii 314
———— Lodgeth with his armie before his enimies, iii 312
———— Set forward against his enimies the nobles of England, iii 316
———— His painful march with his armie, the ordering of his battels, iii 318
———— Passeth to London, iii 309
———— The Londoners resolve to receiue him, the Towre recouered to his vse, he entereth into London, iii 310, 311
———— Arriueth on the coast of Northfolke, then at the head of Humber, landeth at Ravenspurgh, the people let him passe hearing the cause of his comming into the countrie, he passeth towards Yorke, iii 303, 304
———— Iudged a vsurper, iii 301
———— His friends take sanctuarie, iii 300.
———— Receiued verie honorablie into the citie of Excester, iii 299
———— The citizens beneuolence to him, how long he continued there, ib
———— Granted licence to transport rams & ewes into Spaine, i 371
———— Commeth to Lin, taketh ship to passe ouer sea, the number that passed ouer with him, he arriued at Alquemarle, iii 296, 297.
———— Taken prisoner and brought to Warwike castell, iii 293
———— He is deliuered out of captiuitie, commeth to London, ib.
———— His proclamation to such as were assembled vnder him, iii 277
———— His title to the crowne, iii 276
———— Proclaimed K ib
———— Notablie slandered and spoken against in the duke of Buckinghams oration, iii. 390, 391
Edward the fourth his words to his mother about marriage, vol iii page 387
———— Slandered in a sermon, iii 389.
———— His flight into Holland, iii 368
———— The cheefest deuise of his conspirators to depose him, iii 386
———— Described, his qualities, iii 360.
———— His thrée concubines, iii 384
———— His last words vttered on his death bed, iii 355
———— Deceaseth, his issue male and female, iii 358
Edward the fift his comming to London, iii 369
———— He and his brother murthered in the Towre note, iii 402, 403
Edward the sixt borne, iii 804
———— Proclamed king of England rideth through London to Westminster, crowned, iii. 865, 866
———— His letter to the citizens of London, iii 1017
———— He rideth through London, iii 1021
———— His princelie speech to doctor Ridleie after his sermon made of mercie and charitie, iii 1060
———— His message to the rebells of Cornewall and Deuonshire, iii 919
———— Founder of the hospitals in London, iii 1062
———— His victories against the Scots, iv 139.
———— His feare and mistrust of thrée marriages which fell out to be true, he falleth sicke and dieth, iii 1063, 1064
———— His praiseworthie qualities, and death reuealed, iii 1065
———— His buriall, iv 3
———— Counterfeited, and the partie executed, iv 77
Edward the elder king of England, and consecrated, i. 678.
———— Subdueth the kingdome of Eastangles, i 681
———— Seizeth into his hands the cities of London and Oxford, i. 679
———— Sendeth presents to the pope to appease his displeasure, i 683.
———— Builder and reparer of townes, i 682
———— Put the Danes still to the worst, i 680
———— His thrée wiues, his issue by them and his death, i 682
Edward the sonne of Edmund Ironside surnamed the outlaw, his death, i 719
Edward Longshanke meaneth to make some conquest of Scotland, v 323
———— Dieth, his crueltie, v 342
Edward king inuadeth Scotland, v 333
———— Commeth to Berwike, he hath homage doone to him, v 326, 327.

Edward king burdened with crueltie & tyrannie by the Scotish writers, vol v page 330
—— His great preparation to inuade the Scots, v 336
—— Maketh peace with the Danes, v 250
—— Sendeth Ambassadors into Scotland about the election of a new prince, v 215
Edward prince of Scotland deceaseth, v 283
Edward called the Blacke prince borne, ii 598.
Edward of Carnauan K of England commeth into Scotland, v 342
—— Taketh vp souldiors, v. 343
—— Out of what countries he had aid, ib
—— His promise, v 344
—— Thinketh himselfe sure of victorie, ib
—— His exhortation to his armie, v. 346
—— Entreth Scotland, put to flight, v 351
—— He is deposed, ib.
—— Sendeth a nauie into Scotland, v 352
—— Escapeth the hands of the Scots note, v 348
Edwin a right christian prince, v 170
—— Slaine, v 173
Edwin earle of Northumberland withdraweth from the battell against duke William, ii 1
—— His lands giuen to Alane earle of Britaine, ii. 11
—— Reconciled to king William, ii 15
—— He and Edgar Etheling resist duke William and his Normans, ii 9
—— He and Marcher submit themselues to duke William, ii 1.
—— Slaine of his owne soldiors, ii 16
—— ¶ Sée Marcher.
Edwin king Adelstans brother accused of conspiracie, & how punished, i 687
Edwin the sonne of king of Ella banished out of Northumberland, i 599
—— He displaceth moonks and putteth secular préests in their roomes, i 693.
—— Preuaileth against the Westsaxons, i 605
—— Useth the helpe of Pelitus a soothsaier, i 613
—— In a doubt what religion to imbrace, ib
—— His vision note, ib.
—— He with his people receiueth the christian faith, i 606
—— King of Northumberland, his regiment inlarged, and his reputation, i. 604.
Edwin the sonne of king of Ella a good commonwealth man, vol i page 609
—— His zeal in setting foorth religion, i 608
—— His two wiues and his children, ib
—— King of England his filthie lust, i 693
—— He and his two sonnes slaine in battell, i 610
—— He dieth with gréefe, i 693
Eels deuouring fishes, i 377
—— How to haue brood of them, ib
Efts both of land and water, i 384
Eganus murthereth his brother, v 194
—— Liueth in feare, ib
—— Strangled of his quéene · note, ib.
Egbert archbishop of Yorke note, i 643
—— He hath his pall from Rome, i 644
Egbert the first that began to know the necessitie of a nauie, i 339.
—— Departeth this life, i 651
Egbert king of Kent, i 625.
—— Dieth, and what is written of him, i 629
Egbert king of Northumberland, i 645
—— Expelled from his kingdome by his subiects, i 677
—— Receiued as king of the Westsaxons, i 656
—— His notable exploits & conquests, i 656, 657
—— His death, buriall, his issue, and how he diuided his kingdome among his sonnes, i 658.
Egbert one of the bloud roiall banished, i. 657
Egbright king of Northumbers & his palace where seated, i 158
Egeldred chased into Northumberland, getteth aid from the Scots, v 255
—— The battell betwixt him and Sweno, escapeth by flight, v 255, 256
Egelfrida one of the wiues of Edgars, i. 698.
Egelred is sent for home & returneth, i 717
—— K. of England & negligent in gouernment, i 703
—— Maketh himselfe strong against Danes, i. 717
—— Marieth Emma a ladie of Normandie, i. 708
—— Diuerse foretokens of euils like to befall in his time, i 703
—— Maried earle Egberts daughter, i 704
—— Determineth to giue place vnto Swaine, i 715
—— Hath no remedie against the Danes outrages, i 712
—— Passeth to Normandie, i 716
—— Discomfited by them, i 715
—— His oratiō to his soldiers, ib.

Elisabeth proclamed queene the same date that Marie died, vol iv page 137.
——— And the ladie Anne of Cléeue ride togither in a rich chariot, iv 6
——— ¶ Sée Quéene
Elisabeth wife of Henrie the seuenth hir birth, iii. 285
Elisabeth Barton hir practises discouered with hir adherents, she is attainted, becommeth a nun, iii. 789, 790, 791
——— Bishops giue credit to hir hypocriticall doings, she is executed, hir confession at hir death, iii 791
Ella the son of Histrin first king of Deira, i 584
——— King of the Southsaxōs his exploits, i 577
——— He and his thrée sons enter Britaine, i. 567, 569
——— He and Osbright king of Northumbers are slaine by the Danes, i 665
Ella the Saxō first held the kingdome of Sussex, i. 29
Ella ¶ Sée Osbert.
Ellas croft in Yorkshire why so named, i 668
Elmes great store in England, i 357
——— On the south side of Douer court notable, i 358
Elnothus archbishop of Canturburie refuseth to consecrate Harold, i 733
Elphegus bishop of Winchester, i 701, 706
Elphegus archbishop of Canturburie murthered by the Danes, i 712
Elsing ¶ Sée Duke.
Elstrida king Alureds daughter maried to Baldwin earle of Flanders, i 676
Eltham slaine by his brother, v 377
Eltham by whom builded, i 329, 330
Elutherius bishop of Rome his aduise to Lucius touching religion, i 511
Elutherius bishop of westsaxons, i. 642
Embert a notable man first husband to Ethelred, i 635
Emerits neece vnto Lucius, i 43
——— Martyred in Rhetia, i 45
Emma daughter to Richard duke of Normandie maried to K Egelred, i 708.
——— Sent for out of banishment, i 736
——— Accused of diuerse crimes purgeth hirselfe by the Ordalium law, i 740
——— The widow of Egelred maried to Cnute, i 727
——— Sendeth hir sonnes into Normandie, i 722
——— The praise of hir wisdome, i 728
——— Harolds counterfeit letter tending to the destruction of hir & hir sonnes, i 734, 735, 736
——— Banished after she had been spoiled, i. 735
Emma K Edward the thirds mother dieth, i 747
Emma the mother of duke William of Normandie, i 12
Emmanuell coledge at Cambridge founded, v. 587.
Emperor a name that no Romane should take vpon him oftener than once in anie voiage, vol i page 483
——— Commeth into England, v 493
Emperor Adulfe breaketh promise with the king of England and the earle of Flanders, ii 525
Emperor of Constantinople commeth into England, ii 414, iii 17
Emperor Ferdinand deceaseth foretelleth the vttermost date of his death, his goodlie issue male and female, iv 227 228.
Emperor Charles, preparation for receiuing of him into England, iii 641
——— Landeth in England, meeteth with Henrie the eight at Douer, laboureth to hinder the purposed interuiew betwéene Henrie the eight and the French K, saileth into Flanders, iii 646
——— Commeth to Calis to K Henrie the eight, iii 655
——— His entertemment note, ib
——— And the French king at wars, iii. 673
——— Landeth at Douer, he and Henrie the eight sweare each to other to obserue the league interchangeablie made, iii 677, 678
——— Moderation and temperance at the news of victorie, iii 699
——— And what the French kings mother offered him for the deliuerance of hir sonne, he hopeth to recouer more profit by the French king in peace than warres, iii 700, 701
——— Departeth out of England into Spaine, iii 678
——— Sendeth Henrie the eight a present, iii 693
——— His answer to the English ambassador, articles sent to them, he releaseth twelue preiudiciall articles to the French king, iii 720, 721
——— Commandeth that the French king being his prisoner, should be receiued with honour in all places where he should passe, iii 702
——— A truce betwéene him and the gouernors of France, iii 703
——— He visiteth the French king in durance, couenants of accord by him to be performed, ib
——— Commeth to hear what the English and French heralds had to saie, iii. 722, 723
——— He giueth them libertie to speake, iii 723
——— His munificence note, iii 762
——— Deceasseth and obsequie kept for him, iv 158
Emperor Maximilian & Henrie the eight meet roiallie, iii 581
——— Weareth a cross of S George as souldier to the king of England Henrie the eight, iii 583.
——— Inuested into the order of the garter, iv. 232.

Emperor Maximilian deceasseth, a description of his qualities, vol iii page 637
Emperor Sigismund commeth into England, the strange manner of receiuing him at Douer, iii 85
Emperor concludeth a peace with the French king, iii 811
——— Answereth the French kings letters, iii 731
——— Gift to Philip prince of Spaine, iv 61
——— Wonne from the king of Englands freendship, ii 620.
——— He offereth to be a meane to conclude a peace betwéene the two kings of England and France, ib
——— Hath the electing and assigning of the pope, ii 41
——— Commandeth the English herald to leaue his oration behind him in writing, his words to the French herald, he giueth him his answer in writing, iii 728, 729
——— Defied by the two kings, the one of England the other of France, iii 734
——— ¶ Sée Spanish king
Emperors. ¶ Sée Popes
Empire ¶ Sée Rome
Empson and Dudlie with their promooters, iii 531
——— Rauening woolues and caterpillers to the commonwealth, iii 536, 537
——— Attainted of treason, iii 552.
——— His words to the lords of the councell to find fauour, ib
——— Most of the lords of the councell against him, sometime recorder of Couentrie, indicted and found guiltie, condemned, iii 558, 554.
——— Committed to the Towre, iii 545
——— Beheaded, iii 561
Empson an obstinat moonke, the last moonke seen in that clothing in England till quéene Maries daies, iii 819
Emulation of the dukes of Yorke, iii 501
——— Hindereth all good seruices, vi 185
——— ¶ Sée Strife
Engins to cast stones, ii 537
Encelius opinion of the generation of gold and siluer, i 398
England called Lhoegres, i 189
——— Why called Britaine the Great, i 199.
——— Angellandt, or Angles land, i 9
——— The centre, nauill, or middest of it whereabouts, i 84
——— How manie cities and townes it hath, i 319.
——— Lesse néed of other nations than other nations of it, i 394
——— Gouerned by thrée sorts of persons, i 276.
——— Litle England or low England, i 77
——— Miles betwixt the greatest townes for trauell, how manie, i 115
——— Poore people in it of thrée sorts, i 307.
——— Laws since the first inhabitatiō thereof, i 297
England and Scotland by what riuers diuided on the east and west, vol i page 181.
——— Of the ancient and present estate of the church thereof, i 221
——— Three things growne to be verie gréeuous in it, i 318
——— It will as well yéeld wine as keepe it long, i 186
——— When there is like to be plentie and when scarcitie there, i 188
——— Of the aire, soile, wind, hils, pastures, corne, ground, &c i 183
——— Not vnfurnished of hot baths and wels i. 360
——— How the soueraigntie of it remaineth to the princes of the same, i 196
——— The tax of the whole realme, i 230
——— Gouernment thereof vpon what three kinds of laws it dependeth, i 302
——— Building and furniture of houses in it, i. 314
——— The partition wall betwéene the Picts and Scots, ib
——— Three things greatlie amended therein, i 317
——— The partition of it into shires and counties, i 257
——— The accompt of time and hir parts, i 405.
——— Of the maruels thereof, i 216
——— Punishments therein for malefactors, i 310
——— Of castels and holds in it, i 320
——— It and Wales in times past full of woods, i 355
——— Of parks and warrens therein, i 343
——— Lesse people in it than euer now, i 345
——— Four things wished to be reformed therein, i 358
——— Of the princes court and courtiers of England, i 330
——— Palaces for the prince in England, i 328
——— How manie parishes and market towns it conteineth, i 326
——— Ablemen that it can make out against the enimie, i 333
——— Of armour and munition in it, ib
——— Well furnished with guns and artillerie, ib.
——— Coines thereof in times past and now present, i 366
——— Of cattell kept for profit therein, i 369
——— It and Scotland diuided by the riuer Tweed, i 150
——— Much euill transported into it out of France, i 35
——— The number of religious houses therein at their dissolution, i 16
——— In the south parts of it are three severall toongs vsed, i 23
——— Six times subiect to reproch of conquest, i 11
——— The cause of the conquest thereof by the Normans, i 12

England sometimes called Hengistland, vol i page 588
——— Frée from troubles both on sea & land in Edward ye thirds daies, i 747
——— Danes vtterlie expelled out by decree, i. 710
——— The foure notable conquests thereof set down in an aduertisement, i 765
——— Miserable state of it vnder the Danes, i 709
——— Pestered by Danes as thick as grasshoppers, i 705
——— The more part of it conquered by Swaine, i 716.
——— Subiect to Swaine the Dane, ib.
——— How manie shires therein ye Danes wasted, i 712
——— The cause that it was so afflicted by ye Danes in king Egebrids time, i 706
——— The maiestie and glorie of it fell with the death of Edmund, i 726
——— Parted betwéene king Edmund and Cnute, i 725
——— Freshlie inuaded by Swaine, i 714
——— Contention abovt successiō to the crowne thereof, i 699
——— Iust accursed by the pope, i 683.
——— Pestered with wolues and how rid of them, i 695
——— Absolutlie in Cnutes hands, i 726.
——— State of things much altered therein by the death of Cnute, i 736.
——— State of it in K Edgars daies, i 698
——— Foure especiall destructions thereof, i 660
——— When the Danes rule and persecutiō ceased in it, i 738
——— The name of this Ile when changed made a monarchie, i 658
——— It and Scotland like to go together by the eares afresh, iii 720.
——— How manie parishes it hath: note, iii 685
——— Prouision for the defense thereof, iii. 808
——— It and Scotland made one by amitie, what able to do, iii 913.
——— Reconciled to the catholike church and what one in Rome therefore, iv 65
——— Gouerned by Normans and French kings one hundred twentie and two yeers after William Conquerors comming in, ii 202.
——— Diuided into foure parts and the gouernors. note, ii 178
——— It and France the arms quartered, ii 611.
——— How gainful to the court of Rome, ii 296
——— Become tributarie to the pope, ii 307
——— Shrewdlie vexed, subdued, and spoiled in diuerse places by the French, ii 328, 329
——— A great nauie of French ships purpose to inuade it, ii 772
——— Manie towns burnt and destroied on the coast thereof by the French & Spanish ¶ Sée Frenchmen & French king and Spaniards, ii 731, 732
——— In a lamentable case in the time of Duke William note, ii. 9.
England guided by deputies in the absence of duke William, vol ii page 9.
——— Without a king and who towards it, ii 1
——— Furnished with armor and amunition, iv. 202
——— Inuasion therof by forien forces intended: note, iv 587, 588
——— To be inuaded and diuerse plots taken by traitors and conspirators for the practise thereof, iv. 571.
——— The prosperitie thereof during the popes cursses, iv. 528
——— To be inuaded by a Scotish power, iv 568
——— In a short space brought from a trouble to peaceable estate, ii. 351.
——— Subiect to foure and twentie gouernors: note, ii 447
——— Diuided betwixt Canute and Edmund Ironside, v 266
——— Frenchmen and Scots banished from thence, v 498
——— Inuaded, & diuerse places burnt & wasted, v 355
——— The names of the kings thereof mistaken in Scotish writers, v 230
——— An armie of Frenchmen & Scots enter into it, v. 395
——— Diuided into seuen seurall kingdomes, v. 166
——— ¶ Sée Albion, Britaine, Conquest, Danes, Normans, Saxons, Britons, & Welshmen, Cumberland, Dissention, Northumberland
Englishmen noisome to their owne countrie, i 258.
——— There food and diet, i 278
——— Best on foot, i 275
——— Disguised in cutsings, i 289
——— Then in serie vnder the French and Normans, i 13
——— Their apparel, i 289
——— Brought in loue with the outlandish toies, i 395, 396
——— Of whome they learned their excessive feeding, i. 738
——— Behaue themselues like beasts, i 761
——— Their valiantness and faithfullness in fight against the Normans, i 762.
——— Ordeor embattled against duke William and his Normans, i 761
——— Preuail against the Danes, i 669
——— Whie they went into France and became moonks, i 617
——— Afflict themselues with ciuill warrs, i 655.
——— Practised in wars are commonlie victors, i 678, 679
——— Obteine grants beneficiall at the K. Cnute, i 731
——— Their good seruise vnder Cnute against the Uandals, i 729.
——— Flie to the Danes and take part against their owne king, i. 715
——— In a perplexitie, ib
——— Hardlie handled by Swaine, i 714.

Englishmen receiue the faith in Ethelberts time, vol i page 592
——— Learne vices of strangers, i 691
——— Learn to quaff of the Danes, ib
——— Discomfited by duke Williams Normans, i 762
——— Happie when Theodore was archbishop of Canturburie, i 626
——— Discomfited by the Danes, i 658
——— Sore afflicted, iii 76
——— The order of their armie and archers at Agincourt battell, iii 79
——— Giue the onset to the French, both armies ioine battell, iii 80
——— Three great victories with a short time togither, iii 102
——— Take diuers towns and castels in France, iii 106
——— Discomfited vnder the duke of Clarence, iii 127
——— A sore Conflict betweene them and the French, iii 81
——— Take castels and towns in Normandie, iii 89
——— Campe greatlie hindered for want of beasts to draw their ordinance, & the king of Nauarres gentle offer to them, iii 509
——— Their nauie and the French incounter vpon the coasts of Britain, their cruell fight the French flieth, iii 573
——— Vnrulie behauior being in souldiers seruice, iii 562
——— Marine purposing to set vpon the French in the hauen are defeated by a mischance, iii 574
——— Ouer rash hardinesse turneth them to hurt, iii 598
——— Shamfullie abused of Frenchmen and other strangers note, iii 617.
——— Plaie the coragious souldiers in France, iii 687, 688, 689
——— Besieged Hedling castell, win a great bootie from the French, iii 689
——— Negligent for not putting their vallant doings in writing, iii 812
——— Goods arrested in Burdeaux, iii 876, 837
——— Good seruice at the taking of Leith in Scotland. note, iii 835, 836
——— Burnes S. Iehans de Lucie, breake vp their campe at Biskaie, dispersed into sundrie villages vnappeasable rage among them, they returne out of Biskaie, iii 570, 771
——— Valiant seruice against the French & Scots, their horsemen discomfited, iii 802, 805
——— Go by sea & land into Scotland, iii 807
——— The order of the armie in marching forward, iii 808
——— Patient in suffering all wants of reliefe, iii 894
——— Manerlie, French vnmanerlie, iii 339
——— In a mutinie & murmuring, iv 99
——— Loose all by Henrie the sixt, that the got by Henrie the fift, ¶ Compare both stories togither, vol iii pages 164, 165
Englishmen shamfullie foiled by the French, iii 165
——— Gain eightiene standards and one banner, iii 146
——— And French at hot skirmishes note, iii 156
——— Compassion to a Frenchman an enimie, iii 211
——— Loose all in France, iii 215
——— In a mutinie committed to prison, i 215
——— Ouerthrown at Formigni, iii 216
——— And Frenchmen fight vpon a small occasion, ii 218
——— Victorie against the French their enemies, ii 230
——— Spoil Louthian, ii 153
——— God directeth their battell, fighteth for them, their valiantness, ii 630
——— Victorie at Halidon hill, ii 600
——— Derided in a rime, ii 595.
——— They and Genouese meet and fight on the seas, ii 623
——— Win the passage ouer the water of Some against the French, ii 635
——— Make forraies and rodes into the borders of France, ii 612
——— Against the Scots encouraged by the queene, ii 614
——— Obteine the victorie ii 646
——— Imbatteled before Paris, ii 673
——— Lodge with their armie before Paris, ii 694
——— Victorie against the Flemings on the sea, ii 697
——— Burn townes in France, ii 610
——— Discomfited by Constable of France, ii 699
——— The to saue their liues, a great slaughter of them, and all by the Scots, ii 535
——— Seruice against the French at Leith in Scotland, iv 189, 190
——— They giue the French the repulse, iv 191
——— A number them slaine, ib
——— Their hot skirmishes, iv 193, 194
——— They win a trench from the French, iv 195
——— Giue them the repulse, iv 196
——— Repelled by the policies of French, iv 197
——— A number slaine & hurt, ib.
——— Slaine in Scotland, ii 523
——— And Flemings vanquished by the French, i 311.
——— Assaile the French ships, ii 309
——— Spoile the Iles of Orkneie, iii 10
——— Plaie the men, they besiege Ard & Sluis, iii 35
——— Assalt Britaine in Britaine, iii 45
——— The fortune of the earle of saint Paule against them, iii 53

Englishmen die in Spaine by reason of the great heat in that countrie, vol ii page 771
——— Prouision to resist the great power of the French, ii 772
——— Subdue diuerse townes in Flanders and spoile the countrie, ii 759
——— Their armie iourne through France, ii 730
——— Driuen out of Flanders by the French K. ii 74
——— Nauie ouermatched and ouercome by the Spanish, ii 719
——— Cruellie abused under the pretence of peace by duke William, ii 16
——— Host entereth into Britaine, ii 732
——— They besiege Nauits breke vp their siege, ib
——— Atchiue an exploit against the French, ii 722
——— Sailing ouer sea scattered in a tempest, ii 725
——— Ouerthrowne by Scots, ii 716
——— Ouerthrowne by the French, ii 715
——— Cats not to be caught without mittins, ii 731.
——— Weapons before the vse of the long bow, ii 26
——— Extremelie hated and handled of duke William & his Normans, ii 12, 13
——— Miserable in the daies of Malcolme, ii 16.
——— Seruise in forren lands well liked of duke William, ii 17.
——— Kept low by duke William & his Normans, ii 22
——— Thraldome in seuere regiment of duke William, ii 1
——— Famine intreated at king William Rufus hands & whie, ii 29
——— Win townes from the French, ii 358
——— Send to Spaine against the Saracens, ii. 307
——— Distressed by the Welsh, ii 369
——— How mame vnder Henrie the third against the French K ii 397
——— Ouerthrowne by the Welsh, ii 440.
——— Distressed by the Scots, ii. 51
——— And the French incounter, ii 397
——— And Welsh at grudge, ii 480
——— Distressed by the Welsh, ii 481.
——— Taken by French, ii 507
——— Victors by sea against the French, ii 501
——— Stand in doubt of the Welsh, ii 529
——— Unquished by the Scots, ii 536
——— Reuoked from out Ireland, vi 118
——— Are made bondmen vnto the Irishrie, ib
——— Are manumised and set at libertie, ib
——— They obteine a great victorie, vi 116
——— They and Britons ioine their powers with the Picts, v 209
——— Inuade Northumberland, v 259
——— Fled into Scotland, v 279
Englishmen inuade Louthian, vol v page 210.
——— Manie of them drowned, ib
——— Slandered of the Scots, v 198
——— Thirtie thousand horssemen ouerthrowne in trenches, v 347
——— Discomfited, v 352
——— Iland of Leith, v 537.
——— The order of their armie, v 548
——— Their fleet, ib
——— Their captains taken, v 549
——— Their horssemen beaten backe, v 551.
——— They returne home, v 552
——— Horsmen ouerthrowne, v 557
——— Repelled at S Mannets, v 558
——— Put to the woorst at a skirmish neare Hadington, v 559
——— Make a rode into Scotland, v 583.
——— Put the Scots to flight at Halewell Sweire, v 585.
——— Burne the Ile of Arrane, v 586
——— Desirous to reuenge the iniuries doone vnto them, v 586
——— Inclosed in a cellar to kill K Robert Bruse, v 351
——— Put to flight by the Danes, v 256
——— Their miserie vnder the bondage of the Danes, v 256
——— Their crueltie, v 329
——— Their armie passe through Scotland from the south parts to the north, v 336
——— They and Danes fall out and fight, v. 229
——— Their harts begin to faint, put to flight, v 318
——— Chased and loose whole countries, v. 385
——— Intrapped, put to flight, taken prisoners, ib
——— Inuade the Scotish borders, slaine and drowned, v 392
——— Discomfited in Life, v 294
——— Their offer to haue Scots ioine with them in league, v 128
——— Make war vpon the Scots, and whie, v 517
——— Fetch booties out of Scotland, v 476, 435
——— Their cruell dealing towards the Scots, v 414.
——— Their policie, v 370
——— They lie in wait for the Scotish fleet incounter a fleet of Spaniards, v 124
——— Foiled and slaine by the Scots, v 436, 437.
——— Inuaded Scotland, v 435
——— Thanke God for victorie against Iames the fift, v 481
——— Inuaded Scotland, discomfited, v 499
——— ¶ Sée Britains, Britons, & Welshmen
English gentlemen mentemed by the French warres, ii 622
——— Light and toiesh behauiour in the French court, iii 635
——— Discharged of their places &

offices vnder quéene Marie the French kings wife, vol iii page 604
English gentlemen ¶ See Flanders, Flemings, French and Scots.
Englishsaxōs ¶ Sée Saxons
English lawes current throughout Ireland, vi 457
———— The noble men submit themselues to it, vi. 158
English of bloud and English of birth, vi 255
English pale how far stretcheth, vi 3
——— They repine against the cesse, vi 388
——— True to the crowne, vi 394
——— They mislike English burgesses, vi. 343.
——— In great prosperitie, Epistle
Enmie vittelled by the enmie, ii 730
Enmies domesticall verie roiallie dealt withall note, ii. 787
——— ¶ Sée Forgiuenesse.
Ensigne bearer of the Romans his valiantnesse, i 467
Enuerloch builded, v 57.
Enuernesse builded, ib
——— ¶ See Inuernesse
Enuie & spite causing murder, v 393.
—— At others honor, v 438
—— Persons indued therewith are readie to forge matters of suspicion, ii 164
—— Of the lords against the Spensers, ii 558
—— Borne for a ladie bestowed in marriage, ii. 284
—— Of quéene Elenor against Arthur, ii 274.
—— Of the Flemings, ii 109
—— At anothers prosperitie, ii 63
—— Of the erle of March at Henrie the fourths aduancement, iii 3
—— The pursuer of vertue and prowesse, ii 779
—— Issue and fruits thereof note, ii. 724
—— Against anothers honorable aduancement, ii 771
—— And spite betwéene the lords spirituall and temporall, and what mischiefe insued, ii 1.
—— How mischiefous note, iii 354, 355
—— An enimie to honor, i 570
—— To vertue and honor, i 511
—— At anothers welfare, i 610
—— At anothers aduancement, i 575
—— Of kinsmen conceiued against their vncle breaketh into murther, i 621
—— Of Fleander against Perkennus note, i 575
—— Of Penda gainst Oswald for his good procedings, i 617.
Enwulfe earle of Summerset a conspirator, i 662
Eopa a Saxon, but disguised Britaine, poisoneth Aurelius, i 566
—— ¶ See Hatred, Discord, and Spite
Epaminondas neat saieng touching the age of thirtie and thrée score, &c i 194
Epiake citie woone by the Romans, v. 75
—— Taken & burned by Uoadicea, ib.
Epistle of Eleutherus to Lucius, i 43.
Equalitie in a land how inconuenient, iii 990
——— How hurtfull and unconscionable to wish, ib
Equinocteiall ¶ See Chander and Yeare.
Equites, vol ii. page 267
Erasmus Roterodamus was in the vniuersities of England, his report of both, i 251
Erchenwin first king of East-Saxons, i. 574.
Ercombert the first of the English kings that all idols in this kingdome, i 616, 617
Erkenwijn king of Essex, i 29
Erkenwald bishop of Eastsaxons, i. 629.
Ericke a Dane king of Eastangles, put to flight, he is murthered of his subiects, i 680
Erle and aldermen by whome first appointed, ii. 258
Erle Aimer of Penbroke arrested, ii 570.
—— Alane ¶ Sée Alan.
Erle Albericke de Ueere an eloquent pleder for K. Stephan, ii 87.
———— Slaine in a seditious tumult, ii 92
Erle Arundell ¶ Sée Iusts triumphant.
Erle Auberie de Uéere of Oxenford, ii 821.
—— Of Angus commeth into England, v. 500
———— His request, v 501.
———— Feareth the sentence of forfalture, banished, v 492
———— He and the quéene his wife at mutuall hatred, v 491
———— He and others receiued into fauour, v 487
Erle Algare of Oxford, i 748
—— Adrogeus of London note, i 476
—— Of Ariane in the kings displeasure. v. 419
———— Lieutenant to Iames the fourth, v. 466.
———— Reuolteth from the gouernor, v. 487
———— He and Argus at dissention, v. 491.
———— Stealeth awaie, v 486
———— Declareth to the gouernour the minds of the lords, v 494
Erle of Atholl gouernour of the Balioll in Scotland, v 373
———— Flieth into the mounteins submitteth himselfe, v. 374.
———— Slaine, v 376.
Erle of Albemerle, ii 88, 89.
———— While supposed to bet are the towne, ii 152
Erle of Auergnes lands spoiled, i. 128.
—— Of Anjou, ii 94.
———— ¶ Sée Normandie
———— Departeth this life, ii 100
Erle of Anninaks daughter affied to Henrie the sixt, he, and his ladie, sonne, and two daughters taken, iii 203
———— An open enimie to England: note, iii. 208
———— His exploits in France: note, iii 178, 179
———— Ouerthrowne in the middest of water, ii 95.
———— Goeth to sea with fiue hundred men of armes and a thousand archers, ii 775.

Erle of Arundel his liberalitie note, vol ii. page 779
——— Saileth into Britaine with a great power, ib
——— Returneth into France, ii. 797
——— Sent to the sea with a great nauie in aid of the duke of Britaine, 796.
——— Ioineth with lords in conspiracie, ii 784
——— Professeth himselfe sorie that he goeth not with the duke of Northumberland against the ladie Marie, iii 1069
——— To be apprehended by the earle of Northumberland, ii 784
——— Apprehended, ii 837.
——— Arreigned, ii 840
——— Answer to his indictment, he is condemned, ii 841
——— Executed, ib
Erle Baldwin de Betoun first earle of the Ile of Wight, ii 38
—— Of Bullen maried king of Scots daughter, i. 345.
—— Baldwine ¶ Sée Baldwine
—— Brightnod of Essex giueth battell to the Danes, slaine, i 705.
—— Brocmale of Chester, i 598
—— Baldwin de Riuers of the Ile of Wight, i 387.
——— His oration to king Stephans armie, ii 89
Erle Belesme of Shrewesburie a factious man note, ii 54
——— Subdued and banished, ii 50.
Erle Beauchampe of Warwike protector of England, ii. 726
——— Deceaseth, iii 19
Erle Beauford of Surrey deceaseth, iii 49
—— Bigod of Northfolke a valiant chiefeteine, ii 81
——— Accorded with king Henrie the second, ii 88, 158.
Erle Bolinbrooke of Derbie afterwards king, ii 767
—— Bourchier of Essex deceaseth, iii 815.
—— Of Blois his sonne made bishop of Winchester, ii 71
—— Of Britaine assisted against the French king, he submitteth himselfe, ii 373
—— Of Buckingham sent into Britaine to aid the duke against the French king, ii 729
——— He maketh knights at his entrance into France, ii 729
——— Displeased with the duke of Britaine, returneth into England, ii 732
Erle Bullogne prepareth six hundred ships to inuade England, ii 128.
—— Of Caerleill raiseth an armie, put to death for treason, ii 571, 572
——— His iudgement and constancie at his death, ii 574
Erle of Cambridge returneth out of Portingale, ii. 756
Erle of Cambridge his sonne affianced to the king of Portingales daughter, vol ii page 756
——— He and other lords apprehended for treason, iii. 71.
——— Executed, ib
——— The effect of his indictment, iii. 71.
Erle of Chester described, ii 90.
——— His exploits being the kings lieutenant, ii 637.
——— Withstood the gathering of tenths for the pope, ii 364
——— Bare S Edwards sword before Henrie the third at his mariage, ii 379
——— His oration to the erle of Glocester, ii. 88
——— His right and title thereto, & priuileges, his foure barons vnder him note, ii 33.
——— Dieth, ib
Erle of Cornwall marrieth the countesse of Glocester, ii 369.
——— Elected emperor, ii 439
——— Stands against the K. his brother for grant of a subsidie, ii 434
——— He lendeth the king monie, ii 435
——— Elected king of Almaine, taketh his leaue of the king his brother, ii 442
——— And king of Almaine his protestation to the English ambassadors, he cometh ouer into England, receiueth an oth not to infringe the statutes of Oxford, ii 450, 451.
Erle Coell of Colchester, ii 527.
——— Father to the good empresse Helen, ii 533, 534
Erle Charles of Westmerland sore iudgements of God vpon him. note, iv 516
—— Charles of Flånders murthered and issulesse, ii 73.
—— Clinton of Lincolne ambassador into France, the maner of his interteinment, iv 266
—— Courtneie of Deuonshire the first destroier of Excester hauen, iii 929
——— Created, iv. 2
Erle Crispine of Eureux woundeth Henrie the first, and is taken prisoner, ii 65
—— Of Crawford vpon submission pardoned, deceaseth, v 410.
——— In exile, v 393
——— His pardon begged, ib
Erle of Cumberland heire apparent to the king of Scots, v 227.
—— Cochram of Mar and others hanged, v 453
Erle De Gaunt of Lincolne, ii 333
—— Dudleie of Warwike sent into Normandie with an armie, v 298
—— Dauid of Huntington, v 298
——— Entereth the citie of Acon, v 302.
——— Taken prisoner, redeemed, v. 303.
——— Deceasseth, v 308
Erle Dowglasse. ¶ See Dowglass
—— Duncan steward of Leneux beheaded, v. 419.
——— ¶ Sée Leneux
Erle of Derbies exploits in France and his taking of townes, ii. 632, 633.

Erle Goda of Deuonshire slaine, vol i page 705.
—— Godwin of Kent, i 732
—— ¶ Sée Goodwin
—— Hastings of Penbroke, as he was learning to iust wounded to death, ii 800
—— Helms ¶ Sée Helms
—— Of Henault defieth the French king, ii
—— Of Herefords euill counsell to duke William, ii 14
—————— He and Lancaster ioine, ii 565.
—————— They flée, come to Pomfret, the one slaine, the other taken, ii 568
—— Henrie of Essex dishonoured, ii 114
—— Of Hertford forraieth the middle marches of Scotland, iii 848
—— Henrie of Huntington his valientnesse, ii 85
—— Of Huntington politike and wise, iii 198
—— Herbroke of Penbroke prepareth against the erle of Warwike, iii 291
—— Of Hereford inuadeth Scotland, v 543.
—— Holland of Huntington, ii 797
—————— A great exploit doone by him against the French, iii 558
—— Of Huntleie hath lands giuen him, v 440
—— Holland of Kent in fauour with Henrie the fourth, he marrieth a daughter of a lord Millair, iii 41
—————— Sent to the sea with an armie, iii 45.
—— Hugh of Chester deceasseth, ii 152
—— Hugh of Marsh commeth ouer to Henrie the third and offereth him seruice, ii 360
—————— Worketh to induce the Normans and Poictouins to fauour king Henrie the third, ii 363
—— Hugh of Montserrat taken prisoner, ii 72
—— Hubert de Burgh created erle of Kent, and while, ii 362
—————— In Henrie the thirds displeasure, note, ii 365.
—————— Escapeth out of prison, and taketh sanctuarie, ii 375
—————— He is brought backe, restored to sanctuarie, rescued, conueied into Wales, discharged of his office of chéefe iustice, taks sanctuarie, releeued by the Londoners, apprehended, cast in prison, and banished, ii 372, 375
—— Hubert of Morenne and his daughter sold for monie, ii 144
—— Hugh of Chester in William conquerors time, i 64.
—— Hugh of Shrewesburie in William Conquerors time, ib
—— Iohn of Summerset, i 213
—— Iasper of Penbroke, iii 302
—————— Beheaded Roger Vaughan, passeth ouer into Britaine with his nepheue, iii 328
——Iohn of an ambitious nature, ii 228.
—————— No fréend to the bishop of Elie, ib.
—————— In armes to vsurpe the kingdom, ii 238
—————— Purposed to seize vpon the kingdome in his brothers absence, ii 233
—————— Submitteth himself to his brother Richard the first, and craveth pardon for his offense, ii 254
Erle Iohn pardoned of all his rebellions, vol ii page 251
—— Iohn of Chester poisoned by his wife, his foure sisters, ii 381
—— Iohn of Mortaigne licenced to returne into England, ii 210
—— Of Kent a bishop, ii 30.
—————— Dispossessed of his lands, but pardoned of life, but excluded from libertie, ii 37
—————— ¶ Sée Odo
—— Of Kent Goodwins father in law to Edward the Confessor, i 13
—— Of Kent herald sonne to Goodwin, ib
—— Of Kildare when he was first created, vi 52.
—————— Serueth honorablie at Calis, v. 256
—————— Restored to his deputiship in Ireland, iii 686.
—————— Made deputie of Ireland, iii 693.
—————— Committed to the Towre by Cardinall Wolseies means, iii 645
—————— Executed, iii 503.
—— Of Kime otherwise Angus beheaded, ii 281.
—— Leofrike of Chester, i. 223, 723.
—— Lambert ¶ Sée Lambert
—— Of Leneux in ward, v 438
—————— ¶ Sée Lennex
—— Of Lancaster vntrulie tained to be surnamed Crookebacke, iii 3
—————— Canonized for a saint, ii 609
—————— A great strife whether he should be reputed a saint or no, ii 570
—————— Arreigned, found guiltie, and beheaded, ii 568, 569.
—— Of Leicester brother to the earle of Mellent, ii 100
—————— Offered to strike the king, ii 50
—————— In armes against the French king, ii 239
—————— Put to flight by the French, his valiantnesse at a fresh assault, ii 267, 268
—————— Put to a hard shift by the Gascoignes, ii 426.
—————— Seruice in Gascoigne, ii 418
—————— Threateneth the erle of Penbroke, ii
—————— Resigned his gouernment of Gascoigne, ii 428
—————— Daunteth his enimies, ii 121
—————— His sonne raiseth an armie, winneth Winchester, his armie is discomfited, ii 466, 467
—————— His pride bringeth the barons to confusion, slaine, ib
Erle of Leicester baron Denbigh passeth ouer sea to the low countreies as the quéenes lieutenant, ii 630
—————— Arriueth at Flushing, iv 640
—————— Saileth towards Middleborough, iv 641
—————— His intertainment there, ib
—————— Honorablie feasted in christmasse time of the states, ib.

Erle of Leicester he feasteth them againe, vol iv page 642
——— Landeth at Williamstat, ib.
——— Entereth into Dort, ib
——— Commeth to Rotherdam, iv 643.
——— Entereth into Delfe, iv 643
——— Magnificent interteinment of the quéene, and the bountifull fare he kept for his attendance in progresse, iv 404
——— On the right hand of the prince Dolphin, iv 475.
——— Keepeth saint Georges feast solemnlie at Utricht, iv 658
——— Inuested with the robes of the order, ib
——— Commeth to Utricht and how receiued, iv 654
——— A placard conteining the authoritie giuen him by the states of the low countries, iv 618
——— Lodgeth in the house where the prince of Orange was slaine, iv. 643
——— Remoueth to Donhage and worthilie intertained, ib
——— Intertemed at Leyden, he rideth to Skerieling, titles of honor ascribed to him, iv. 647.
——— Commeth to Harlem and how he was receiued, iv 650
——— Goeth to Amsterdam and how interteined, iv. 651.
Erle of Leicesters onlie sonne and heire deceaseth, iv 548.
—— Of Lincolne proclamed heire apparant, iii 423
—— Sonne to Iohn de la Poole duke of Suffolke a conspirator, iii 486
——— His flight into Flanders doubted of Henrie the seuenth, he entereth Yorkshire with his power, trieth battell with the king, he is slaine, iii 486, 487.
——— Deceasseth, iv 551
——— ¶ Sée Lacies
——— Lacie of Lincolne deceaseth, his buriall, his request on his death bed, ii 550.
——— Mandeuill of Essex licenced to go into the holie land, ii 171
——— Marchar of Mercia ¶ Sée Marchar.
——— Marchell of Penbroke, his oration in the assemblie of péeres, ii 340
——— Recouereth his castelles taken by the prince of Wales, ii 354
——— Killed with a fall from his horsse, ii 395.
——— Deceaseth, his buriall, ii 349,369
Erle Mathew of Bullongne, ii 150
——— Wounded and dieth, ii 152
Erle Montacute of Salisburie a politike man and valiant, iii 160.
—— Miles of Hereford, i. 87
——— Deceaseth, ii 95.
Erle Mortimer of March his good seruise in Ireland, ii 753
—— Slaine by the wild Irish, his issue, ii 768.
Erle Mortimer last erle of March of that name deceseth without issue note, vol iii page 11.
——— Duke of Yorke, iii 269
——— The great hope of the people conceiued of him, he is elected king, he taketh vpon him the regiment, iii. 272
——— His badge note, iii 270.
Erle of Milleut, ii 88
—— Decontented with the bishops in an assemblie, ii 61, 62
—— A councellor to Henrie the first to hold the title of inuestitures of prelats, ii 54
—— Taken prisoner, ii 72
—— His sonnes praised for their learning, ii 74
Erle of Montaigne taken prisoner, ii 56.
—— Mortimer ¶ See Mortimer
Erle Montgomerie ¶ Sée Montgomerie.
—— Mowbraie. ¶ Sée Mowbraie.
—— Mulbraie ¶ Sée Mulbraie.
—— Of Mar slaine in his bed, v. 366.
—— Of Mentith poisoned, v 313
—— Of Murreie, &c elected gouernor, v 374
—— Taken prisoner, v 375
—— Sent into France, v 369.
—— Returneth out of France, v 371.
—— ¶ Sée Murreie
Erle Nonneus, i 547
—— Of Nauerre commeth into England with an armie, v 375
—— Of Northumberland made lord warden of the whole Marches, 495
—— Lieutenant of the north, v 383.
——— Charged by the duke of Lancaster with sundrie crimes, the Londoners are his friends, they are accorded, ii 752
——— Sent to apprehend the erle of Arundell, ii 784.
——— His words to the king in behalfe of the lords loialtie, ii 786
——— His message to Richard the second, ii. 856
——— Cleareth himselfe of much suspicion, iii 29.
——— Flieth, iii 38
——— Against Westmerland, he is restored, iii. 36.
——— His returne into England, ii 45
——— Slaine, ib
——— Murthered by the northern rebells, iii 492.
——— His rich arraie, iii 531.
——— Committed to prison by the cardinall Wolseies meanes, iii 645
——— Arrested Wolseie, iii. 752.
——— He and Westmerland rebell, and what ill successe it had note, iv 236, 237
——— ¶ Sée Conspiracie Erle Percie
—— Neuill of Westmerland, &c. prepareth to resist the kings enimies, his subtill policie, iii 37
——— Persuaded king Hen-

rie the fift vnto the conquest of Scotland, vol iii page 66
Erle Neuill of Salsburie his issue, iii 237
—— Oddo hath Deuonshire and Summersetshire giuen him, i 741
—— Of Ormont generall of the Scotish armie, v. 436
———— Exhorteth his people, ib
———— Victorious, v 437
———— Taken prisoner and beheaded, v 441
—— Of Ormond high treasurer of Ireland, iii 695
—— Of Oxford ¶ See erle Veere
—— Patrike of Salisburie slaine, ii 129
—— Persie of Northumberland created, iv 87
———— Warden of the whole Marches, iii 681
———— Sent to the seas, ii 779
———— Lieutenant of Calis, ii 814.
———— Conspireth with Owen Glendouer, iii 22, 23, 24, 25
———— Restored, iii 64
———— Beheaded at Yorke, iv. 320.
———— Murthered himselfe in the towre, iv 602.
———— A quest of inquirie vpon the fact, ib
———— Buried in the towre, iv 603, 604
———— The whole manner of killing himselfe, iv 604
—— Percie of Worcester leaueth the king and flieth to the duke of Lancaster, ii 855
———— Sent ouer into Gascoigne to appease the people, iii 15
—— Petwike of Perch ii. 115
—— Philip of Flaunders, ii 150
———— A meane to make peace betweene the kings of England & France, ii. 197
———— His deuotion at Thomas Beckets toome, ii. 174
———— Doth homage to the king of England, ii 179
———— His release made at Henrie the seconds request, ii 164
—— Plantagenet of Warwike sonne and heire to George duke of Clarence, committed to the towre, iii 479
—— Of Pearch slaine, ii 345
—— Of Penbroke passeth ouer into Ireland, ii 377
———— In danger of taking he is rescued, ii 375
———— Lord warden of Scotland, ii. 537
———— Diligent note, iii 147
———— Valiant manhood, iii 292
———— Discontented, waiteth for aduantage, iii 282

Erle of Penbroke conductor of the earle of Richmonds companie, vol iii page 425
———— Generall of queene Maries armie against Wiatt and his companie, they incounter, iv 19
———— Deceaseth, his epitaph, iv 338.
—— Rafe of Hereford, i 743
—— ¶ See Rafe
—— Richard of Warwike, i 56
—— Randall gouernor of Scotland, v 363
—— Richard of Glocester, v 280
—— Of Richmond causeth his men to put on armor, he setteth them in order, and appointeth chiefteins, iii 438, 439
———— His person described, his cause iust and right, a great motiue to the nobles to assist him, incouragements to his armie to plaie the men, iii 441, 442
———— His oration by Richard the third to the cheefteins of his armie, iii 439
———— Politike, iii 445
———— Preparation of ships and souldiers to the sea, disparkled by tempest, he seeth all the English bankes furnished with souldiors, iii 419
———— Sendeth to know whether they were with him or against him, arriueth in Normandie, and passeth by land into Britaine, in fauour with the French king, he lamenteth and reioiceth, the lords giue faith and promise each to other for his furtherance, he sweareth to marrie Elisabeth the daughter of Edward the fourth after possession of the crowne, diuerse of his faction apprehended and executed, iii. 419, 420, 421
———— Arriueth at Milford hauen, his power made strong by accesse of the confederats, he sendeth secret word to his mother & friends that he ment a direct passage to London, and desired their conference, he is aided of the welshmen, iii 434, 435, 436.
———— At Lichfield, remoueth his power to Tamworth, and of a strange chance that happened to him, put to a hard shift, iii. 436, 437
———— Informed of his roiall preferment, &c he maketh the duke of Britaine priuie to the matter, preparations to bring in, receiue and erect him to the kingdom, iii 415.
———— Atteinted in parlement, and all other that fled ouer sea to take his part, iii. 421.
———— Smal traine for a policie, apparelled like a page, he attendeth vpon one of his men, he is fauoured of forreine and homeborn, he goeth to the French and requireth succor to recouer the crowne, iii 425, 426
———— Diuerse Englishmen submit themselues vnto him in France, iii 428
———— Profferreth to incounter Richard the third bodie to bodie, iii 444

Erle of Richmonds deuoute behauiour after the victorie, vol iii page 443
———— Crowned by the lord Stanlie in the field by the name of Henrie the seuenth, iii 446
———— ¶ See Henrie the seuenth
—— Of Rutland generall of the English forces in Scotland, v 561
———— Put the French armie in danger of an ouerthrow, iii 985
———— Emploied in martiall affaires about Scotland, iii 1021
———— Detecteth the nobles conspiracie to Henrie the fourth, iii 10
———— Sent ouer ambassador into France, iii 18
———— His follie the cause of disclosing the noblemens conspiracie, iii 10
———— Went against the rebells in the north, iv 236
———— Being yoong cruellie murthered note, iii 269
———— ¶ Sée Manners, and Rutland
—— Raimond of Barzelon, i. 415
—— Ranulph of Chester taketh his wife the dutchesse of Britaine prisoner, ii 260
———— Laieth siege to Montsorell castel, ii 344
———— He raiseth his siege, ib
———— Retorneth from the holie land, ii 349
———— Goeth into the Holie land, ib
———— Thrice married, the partition of his lands, his exploites Deceaseth, ii 372
—— Reinold of Cornewall base sonne to king Henrie the first, departeth this life, ii 161
—— Reinold Greie of Kent, iv 264
———— Deceasseth, iv 322.
—— Richard obeieth his father Henrie, ii 189
———— Seizeth vpon his father Henrie the seconds treasure, ii 192
———— Is rebelled against, he inuaded the erle of Houlous lands, ii 191
———— Reuolteth from his father vnto the French king, ii 196
—— Richard of Chester vnder King Henrie the firsts tuition, ii 51
———— He and his wife drowned, ii 70
—— Richard of Clares submission, ii 159
—— Richard of Cornwall returneth out of Gascoigne, ii 3 1
———— Departeth from the court secretlie, ioineth himselfe with the erles of Chester and Pembroke, ib
———— King of Almaine deceaseth, his buriall & [illegible], ii 475
———— His sonne murthered, ib
—— Richard of Glocesters submission, ii 159
— Of Glocester dieth, ii 161
— Richard of Poitow king Henrie the seconds son, his victorie against the Brabanders, ii. 170
Erle Richard of Poitow his sharpe assalt of Talburgh, vol ii page 179
—— Robert of Derbie, ii 158
—— Robert of Glocester, Henrie the firsts base sonne, ii 65
———— An enimie to king Stephan, ii 83
———— Described, ii 90
———— Commeth to Glocester, ii 87
———— Father in law to Iohn king Richards brother, ii 203
———— Taken prisoner, ii 92
———— Dieth, ii 97
—— Robert of Leicester famous and valiant, ii 232.
———— Put to flight, ii 153
———— Taken prisoner, ii 250
———— Offer for his ransome, ii 251.
—— Robert Dudleie created baron and erle, iv 226.
———— Inuested into the order of Saint Michaell, iv 227
———— ¶ Sée erle of Leicester
—— Robert of Mellent rebelleth against king Henrie the first, ii 71
—— Robert of Richmond against the Frenchmen, his martiall acts, in danger to be slaine, ii 617
—— Robert de Belesme of Shrewsburie rebelleth, ii. 50
—— Robert de Uéere owner of Hidingham castell, ii 329
—— Robert passeth ouer into Normandie, ii 94.
—— Roger Fitzmiles of Hereford, ii 112
—— Siward of Northumberland, i 743
———— His exploits against the Scots, i 749.
———— Surnamed Fortis, i 223
—— Of Salisburie exchanged for the erle of Murreie, v 381
—— Of Surrie sent into the north, v 163
———— Lieutenant vnto Henrie the eight in Scotland, v 179
———— Inuadeth Scotland, v 496
———— With an armie of 40000 men, v. 498
———— Made warden generall, v 495
—— Of Sussex entereth into Scotland, v. 586
—— Of Sowtherland ¶ See Sowtherland
—— Of Sarum lord William Montacute, i 66.
—— Saier de Quincie of Winchester, ii 344
—— Seimor of Hereford lieutenant of the north goeth against the Scots, iii 831
—— Simon of Hampton, ii 85, 89
———— Dieth, ii 103
—— Simon of Huntington dieth, ii. 180
—— Simon of Leicester maried with Henrie the thirds sister, ii 381
———— Maketh his possessions into monie and goeth into the holie land, ii 384
———— Fled ouer into France, ii 386
—— Stanlie of Derbie deceaseth, his life, death, and qualities, iv 320, 321
—— Stephan of Bullougne sworne to the succession of the crowne, ii 72
———— ¶ See Stephan

Erle Strangbow marieth Dermutius his daughter, vol ii page 139
———— Confined, seeketh king Henrie the seconds fauour, and is pardoned, ib
———— He maketh surrender to king Henrie the first, ib
—— Strangbow of Stragull, ii 138
—— Summerset of Worcester sent into France, robbed vpon the sea, iv 321
—— Of Salisburie gathered a power, iii 250
———— Charged with treason, his request, he is maineprised, iii 8
———— Slaine by the Saracens, ii 119
———— Deceseth, ii 261
———— Seasicke, deceaseth, ii 358
———— Deceaseth, bruised at the iusts, ii 629.
———— Slaine, iii. 162.
—— Of Shrewsburies great diligence, policie, and true seruice against the northerne rebelles, iii 800.
———— His loialtie, what he said to them that talked lewdlie of him, prouided of all souldiors, his oth in presence of the people necessarie, iii 801
———— Generall of an armie against the Scots and French, iii 894
———— Commeth to Hadington, and of his doings against the enimie, ib
———— Inuadeth Scotland, v 493
———— Warden of the Welsh Marches, ii 71
—— Of Southampton deceaseth, iii 1024.
—— Of Suffolke in great fauour with K Richard the second note, ii 777
———— Put to his shifts and distressed iii. 528, 529
———— Greeuouslie charged by the parlement house for sundrie offenses, ii. 776
———— Fleeth ouer into Calis disguised note, i 788
———— Sudden death, ii 753
—— Of Surreie entreth Scotland, defacing castelles and towers, his valiant heart, reioicing at his hap likelie to fight hand to hand with the king of Scots, ambassadors to treat a peace betweene both nations, iii 516, 517
———— High treasuror of England, iii 514
———— Sent with a great power against the northerne rebells, iii 493
———— Valiant determination to incounter the Scots, the ordering of his armie, iii 595
———— And his sonne the lord admerall with ioined power against the Scots, iii 592
———— Their message to the king of Scots, iii 593
———— They remooue their camps to and fro as occasion mooueth, iii 595
———— High admerall his attire at the receiuing of the French kings ambassadors, vol iii page 652
Erle of Surreie his seruise against certain rebels, iii 615
———— High admerall and his companie come vnto Hampton court, iii 678.
———— Inuadeth Scotland, ii 523
———— His manner of winning Morleis in Britaine, he maketh knights, iii 678, 679
———— Sent with an armie to inuade France, commeth with his power to Calis, returneth into England, iii 681, 689
———— And Southampton sent to Calis, iii 820
———— Committed to the Tower notwithstanding his submission, iii 445.
———— Beheaded, iii 861
Erle of Sussex maketh a iournie into Scotland his valourous seruice, v 254, v 568
———— Inuadeth Scotland, iv 338.
———— Vieweth Hume Castell iv 310
———— Went against the rebelles in the north, iv 336
———— Gentle to ladie Elizabeth, iv 121
———— Visiteth madam de Parma, iv 232.
———— His iornies during his abode beyond seas, ib
———— Interteined of the emperor, ib
———— Saluted of the duke of Austria, ib.
———— Departeth from Vienna, iv 233
———— Deceaseth, iv 505.
———— His honourable funerall, ib
———— ¶ See Fitzwalter
—— Of Saint Giles accorded with Henrie the second, ii 145
———— Otherwise Tholouse, ii 115
—— Of Saint Paule reuolteth to the French, iii 197
———— Confedered with the duke of Burgogne, iii 330
———— His counsell vnto king Henrie the first, ii. 835
———— Came out of France to see a challenge performed at Couentrie, ii 847.
———— Assalted the castell of Guisnes, iii 53
———— His fortune against the Englishmen, ib
———— Landed in the Ile of Wight he maketh spoile, ii 21
———— Deceaseth, iii 178
—— Thomas of Lancastar, i 211
—— Of Tholouses lands inuaded by king Richard, ii 194
—— Talbot of Shrewsburie and his sonne manfullie slaine, iii 245
———— Sent into France with an armie, iii 576.
Erle Theobald of Champaigne his decent in armes against the French king, ii 67
———— His countrie inuaded by the French king, ib

Erle Theodorike of Flanders, vol ii page 114.
—— Tiptoft of Worcester beheaded, iii 301
—— Turketilus ¶ Sée Turketilus
—— Thomas the gouernor poisoned, v 364.
—— Of Tripolis, ii 222
—— Valeran of saint Paule put to flight, iii 35
—— Uére of Oxford created duke of Ireland, ii 774
—————— Duke of Ireland to be safely conducted to the kings presence by the shiriffe of Cheshire, ii 789
—————— He seeketh to be diuorced from his lawfull wife, ii 784
—————— His charge to his bands of men, his valiantnesse, iii. 145.
—————— Yéeldeth himselfe to king Edward the fourth, sent ouer sea, and kept prisoner twelue yeares, iii 329
—————— Made marquesse of Dublin, ii 767
—————— His corps conueied from Louraine into England and there roialie buried, iii 870.
—————— Sent ouer into Gascoigne, ii. 508
—————— His valiantnesse, ii 313
—————— Getteth out of prison and he with others go to the erle of Richmond, iii 427
—————— He leuieth a power & commeth into England, his valor and chiualrie, ib.
—————— He submitteth himselfe and yéeldeth to the king, iii 428
—————— The erle of Richmond is glad of him and his companie, ib
—————— Deceaseth in miserable necessitie note, ii 821, iii 815
—— Uoldosius of Huntington & Northumberland, ii 207
—————— A name of office among the Romans, in Latine Comes note, ii 264
—————— Created of the prince, ii 266
—— Walter of Essex saileth into Ireland, iv 323
—————— Deceaseth, iv 331
—————— The place of his birth, iv 332
—————— His praise in sundrie respects, ib
—————— Disposed to inlarge his nobilitie, ib
—————— ¶ Sée Erle of Essex.
—— Waltheof ¶ Sée Waltheof
—— Warren, ii 88
—— Warren of Surreie his words to Edward the first, ii 483
—— William of Arundell ambassador to the French king, ii 123
—————— Dieth, ii 170
—— William of Kent, William de y presse, ii 92.
—— William sonne to duke Robert erle of Flanders, ii 73
—————— Dieth of wounds, ib
—— Duke Robert of Normandies son by Sibill, ii 57
—— William named de Longspée with others go into the holie land, ii 117
—— William of Mortaigne and Bullongne, ii 113, 116.
Erle William of Mortaigne a fictious man, vol. ii. page 54.
—————————— His wilfulnesse and malcontentment, ib
Erle of Warwike made gouernor of king Henrie sixt, iii. 156
—————————— And others sent to the generall councell, iii 68
—————————— Denieth that euer he acknowledged himselfe guiltie of treason, iii 7.
—————————— Assalted, iii 249
—————————— Lord admerall & lieutenant of Calis, he scoureth the seas and taketh a rich prise, iii 250
—————————— Regent of France, iii 192
—————————— His entrance thereinto, ib
—————————— Answer to the duke of Clarence, his message, iii 309.
—————————— And Edward the fourth incounter, his manfull courage, iii 312, 313
—————————— He is slaine, iii 314.
—————————— Followeth king Edward the fourth to foile him, iii 311
—————————— And the duke of Clarance took the seas, he is kept out of Calis, landed at Diepe, iii 294, 295
—————————— The loue which the people bore vnto him, iii 296.
—————————— In a chafe because of king Edwards the fourth deliuerie, iii 293
—————————— In Couentrie prouoked to fight by king Edward the fourth, iii 306, 307
—————————— His housekeeping, instituted gouernor at the realme, his badge worne in euerie mans cap note, iii 301, 302
—————————— Discourageth king Edward the fourth and maketh him flie for feare out of England, iii 296
—————————— His standard what ensigne it bore, iii 292
—————————— The fruits of his malice, ib
—————————— Beareth a continuall grudge vnto king Edward the fourth, his persuasions to his two brethren against him, iii 288, 289, 290
—————————— Offended with king Edward the fourths marriage, iii 284
—————————— He kéepeth his gréefe secret, ib.
—————————— Sent ouer into France about King Edward the fourths Marriage, iii. 283
—————————— His courage, a trustie freende to king Edward the fourth, iii 277
—————————— The right one, order taken for the shewing of him abrode, iii 485
—————————— Had in fears and gelousie in foren regions, iii 524.
—————————— Shewed openlie in procession, iii 486
—————————— His manlie corage, iii 871.
—————————— His presence greatly incourageth the English souldiors, iii 879

Erle of Warwike his request and message to the erle of Huntleie, vol iii page 874
—— Arraigned of treason, confesseth it, submitteth himselfe is pardoned, ii 842.
—— In highest authoritie, iii 1022
—— Commended, he is slaine, iii 389.
—— Sent against the rebelles in the north, iv 236
—— Commended, iv 223.
—— Deceaseth, iii 693
—— His valiantnesse, iv 221
—— Shot through the thigh with an harquebuse, iv 221, 222
—— Noble men of France sent vnto him from the admerall about conference, iv.212.
—— Landeth at Newhauen, iv 206
—— An oth taken by him and his officers, ib
—— He and the Rheingraue talke together, iv 206
—— He is appointed to go against Norfolke rebels, iii 970
—— Commeth to Cambridge, ib.
—— He sendeth an Herald at armes offering pardon, &c iii. 977, 978
—— Counsell giuen him to abandon Norwich, gooeth forth to giue the enimies battell, iii 981, 982.
—— The rebels yeeld to him, & he sheweth them mercie, iii 983
Erle counterfeit of Warwike. ¶ Sée Sunenell
—— Of Wiltshire and others spoile Newberie, he saileth ouer seas, iii 258, 259.
—— The duke of Buckinghams brother, iii 552
—— Of Winchester besieged by his owne tenants, ii 415
—— Reproachfullie executed, ii 582
Erle of Worcester gouernor to the prince slippeth from him, iii 23
—— And others beheaded, iii. 26.
Earldome of March purchased, ii 176
—— Of Rosse, giuen vnto William Rosse, alias Lesle, v 320
—— Transferred to the Stewards, v 410
Erles of Bothwell, v 399
—— ¶ Sée Bothwell.
—— Of England how manie, i 277
—— How farmers and grasiers, i 344
—— Eight slaine in a conflict of Athelstane against certeine aliens, i. 358
—— Of Darbie commonlie said to be king of the Ile of Man, i 66
—— Of Chester the true and famous genealogie, ii 381
—— Tooke end in Iohn Scot, ib.
—— Of Leicester from the first to the last in succession, set downe in a collection, iv 630 to 639.
—— Of Richmond line that first bare their title of honor of the said castell and towne, ii 11, 12
—— Created, ii. 570, iii 107, 710, 747
Erles and dukes created, vol ii page 677.
—— And barons, iii 832
—— And lords, iii 1022
—— At a parlement, ii 605
Ermenredus his two sonnes cruellie slaine, i 629
Ermenfried bishop of Sion or Sitten a chéefe commissioner from pope Alexander, ii. 14
Erming stréet. ¶ Sée Highwaies
Ermingard vicount Beaumonts daughter married to William king of Scots, ii. 190
Erne and egle taken to be all one, i 382
Erne stone, i 402
Erning stréet one of the foure highwaies principall of Britaine and how it is extended, i 191
Erocus king of the Almans a friend to Constantine, i 530
Ersilton a prophesier or rimer, v. 321
Erth diuided into fiue parts, i 3
—— Unto what portiō thereof Britaine is referred, ib
—— Uariance among writers about the diuision of it, i 2
—— The diuisiō of it not yet perfectlie knowne, i 1
—— Diuided into thrée parts, ib
Erth woorth fiue shilling a lode thirtie yeares ago, i 397
Erth lifted vp it selfe like a huge towre, ii 177
—— Remooued in Dorsetshire, iv. 503, 504
—— And trées soonke and swallowed vp in Kent. note, iv 620
—— Strangelie moouing in the countie of Hereford, iv 258
Erthquake, ii 376, v 468.
—— In Kent, &c. iv. 430
—— Ouer all England, ii 88.
—— Generall in England, ii 19.
—— In H. the firsts time, ii 66
—— Sensible and visible, ii 75
—— That did much hurt, ii 754.
—— In the fourtéenth of duke Williams reigne, ii 23.
—— Uniuersall how frightfull and hurtfull, iv 126
—— That ouerthrew buildings, ii 413.
—— At saint Albons counted strange and while, ii 420
—— That ouerthrew houses, ii 417
—— Generall, did much hurt, ii 479
—— In diuerse places of England, iv 224
—— In sundrie places of England, and what harm was thereby doone, iv 326
—— After a thunder, ii 353.
—— With lightening and thunder, ii. 479
—— Terrible, v 304.
Erths sundrie kinds in Britaine, and which kind most common and best, i 187.
Erthus the sonne of Ethodus begot Ferguse, v 120.
Escuage demanded note, ii 368.
—— Granted, ii. 428, 452

Escuage paid, vol ii page 351
——— Gathered, twentie shillings of euerie knights fee, ii 395
——— Termed the great, ii 396
Escuinus ¶ Sée Eleanuse
Espike Walter the first that brought the order of white monkes into England, ii 44
Esquire a french word and who be such, i 273
Essex arriued into by the Danes, i 673
—— The kingdome thereof taketh end, i 659
—— A kingdome begun vnder Erkenwin, i 29
—— In time past hath wholie been forest ground, i 316
—— What havens it hath, i 182
—— It and Suffolke parted by the riuer Sture, i 177
Essexmen yeeldeth themselues to Ardelwold, i. 679
———— Beginers of a shrewd rebellion, ii 736
———— They prosecute it, ii 737
Estangles where planted in Britain, i 561
———— Their kingdome brought into decaie and subiect to diuerse, i 649
———— It ceaseth, i 667
———— Conquered by Offa, i 649.
———— Subiect vnto the Danes, i. 677
———— Kingdome & when it began first called Uffines, i 569
———— They haue Gurthun a Dane their king, i 667
———— Their kingdome subdued by king Edward, i 680
———— Their vaine hope made them venterous to their cost, i 619.
———— Wholie conuerted to the faith, i 609
Ester daie fell at the highest namelie saint Marks daie, ii 289
———— Strife about the celebrating of it, v 171
Ester feast to be uniformlie kept, i 609
———— Obseruing whereof ye the Scots will obserue their owne custome, i 627
———— About the obseruing thereof there was contention in Augustines time note, i 596
———— About the obseruation whereof the Scots varie, i 615
Esterlings ¶ Sée Riot
Estouteuille Robert taken prisoner, ii 36
Estrildis drowned by Guendoline, i 117
Estsaxons when their kingdome began, i 571
———— Will not receiue Melitus to his see in London, i 603.
———— Receiue the faith which they had renounced, i 620
———— Gouerned by a Dane, i 667
———— Notablie confirmed in the faith, i 627
———— Kingdome ceased, i 649
Etanges taken prisoner, v 561
Ethelard king of Westsaxons taketh flight out of his land, his death, i 613
Ethelbald king of Mercia of what puissance he was, i 643
———— His virtues and vices note, i 610
Ethelbald his acts and death in battell, vol i. page 610
———— ¶ Sée Ethelbright.
Ethelbert baptised, v 169
Ethelbert king of Estangles highlie commended, i. 618.
———— Builded saint Andrewes in Rochester, i. 595, 596
Ethelbert King of Kent, i 586
———— He imbraceth the gospel, i 590, 591, 592
———— Subdueth all the English Saxons, i 590
———— Taken prisoner and released in Winchcomb church, i 653
———— His lawes, death, & buriall, i 602
Ethelbert king of Northumbers his crulties, his ill life and ill death, i 631
———— ¶ Sée Alrike, and Ethelbrit.
Ethelbright & Ethelbald diuide their fathers kingdome betweene them, i 667
Ethelbrit, i 636
———— ¶ Sée Lother.
Ethelburga sister to K. Eadbald maried to K Edwin, i 601
———— Wife to king Inas, his deuise to persuade hir husband to forsake the world, i 639
———— Deliuered of a child, i 605
———— Desired in a letter from the pope to continue in the faith, ib.
———— Returneth into Kent, i 610
———— An ill woman and proud as the diuell, hir end note, i 653
———— A nun ¶ Sée Erkenwald
Ethelgina K Egelreds wife, i 704
———— She dieth, i 708.
Ethelred king of Estangles, i 615
Ethelred king of Mercia becometh a monke, i 610
Ethelred king of Westsaxons he fought with the Danes nine times in one yéere, i 664
———— ———— His death, i 667.
———— ———— ¶ Sée Edilred
Etheldred with his two sonnes Alured & Edward, v. 266
Etheldreda king Egfrides wife a virgin note, i 635
Ethelswida king Burthreds wife died in Pauia, i. 676
———— ¶ Sée Elstrida
Ethelwold bishop of Winchester, i 695
———— Put in trust to sue for king Edgar to spéede him of a wife, deceiueth the king, ib.
Ethelwulfe K of westsaxons, a subdeacon &c note, i 660
———— Marieth his butlers daughter, ib
———— Marieth the French kings daughter, i. 662.
———— His genealogie as the old Saxons draw it, i 662, 663
———— His victories against the Danes, i 661
———— His last will, how he diuideth his kingdome and dieth, i 662
Ethfine king of Scots a peaceable prince, deceaseth, v 181.

Ethodus king of Scots requireth restitution of his subiects goods, exhorteth the K of Picts to war against the Romans, vol v pages 91, 92
——— Sore wounded, & committed to the care of Surgeons, v 115
——— Confined into Denmarke, v. 117
——— Brother to Eugenius interteined in Denmarke, v 119, 120
——— Ouerthroweth the Picts, v. 114.
——— Uisiteth his countrie to sée iustice mainteined, giueth himself to hunting, murthered by a musician, v 94, 95
Ethodus the second, king of Scots couetous, slaine of his own seruants, v 98
——— ¶ Sée Eugenius
Ethus king of Scots saued by flight, v 216
——— Surnamed Lightfoot, v 217
——— Neglected oportunitie conspired against, ib
——— Arested with his fauourers, ib
Etius lieutenant of the Romans in Gallia, v. 126
——— Refused to aid the Romans, v. 130.
Euan a conspirator disquieteth the king & realme, v 213
——— Lieutenant of Dundtage, ib
——— He is executed, ib
Eueline or Gweline allied to Androgeus, i 476.
Euesham fell down by itselfe, i 113
Euers Rafe knight, inuadeth Scotland, v 540
——— Defaceth the monuments of the Dowglasses, v 541
——— Slaine, ib
——— His seruice against the Scots, ib
Euers constable of Douer castell, &c ii 821
——— Lord that now liueth, his noble ancestrie, ii 707
——— Knight his good seruice at the north, iii 803
——— His prowesse and valiant seruice, iii 836.
——— Slaine, iii 817
Euill Mae due ¶ Sée Rebellion of Lincolne
Eugenius and Ethodus the sonnes of Fincomarke, v 108
——— Conueied into the Ile of Man, v 109
Eugenius king of Scots, v 128
——— Dieth, v 135
Eugenius inuested king of Scots suspected of his predecessors death, v 158, 159
Eugenius rewarded his souldiers, v 162
——— Inuested K in armes against the Britons, v 112, 113
——— Discomfited, v 113
——— Breaketh up his campe, ib
——— Prepareth an armie to defend his countrie, ib
——— Comforteth his people, v 111
——— Slaine, v 115
Eugenius his humanitie to his people, v 159.
——— Agreeable to the Picts requests, v 160.
Eugenius a Ravisher, vol v page 164
——— Gouerneth his people with clemencie, v. 162
——— Deceaseth, v 163
Eugenius the fourth king of Scots a louer of peace and quietnesse, a sharp iusticer, v. 169, 170
Eugenius the fift K of Scots, his commandment, gathereth an armie, v 177
——— Death, v 178
Eugenius the sixt king of Scots, ib.
——— Deceaseth, ib
Eugenius the seuenth king of Scots crowned, suspected of murther, causeth his ancestors histories to be written, v 179, 180
——— Deceaseth, v. 180
Eugenius the eight inuested king of Scots, peruerted with sensual lusts, murthered, v 182 ¶ See Mordred
Eumerus a murtherer sent to kill Edwin and whie, i 605
Europe by whom first peopled, i 428
Eureux citie yéeldeth vnto the Frenchmen, ii 662
——— Taken by treason, iii 198
Eustace earle of Bullongne against William Rufus, ii 29
——— Sonne to King Stephan duke of Normandie, ii 81
——— Angrie with his father, ii 103
——— He dieth ¶ Sée monke
Eustace sir Rowland treasuror, lord chancellor and lord deputie, vi 269
——— Founder of the abbeie besides Kilcollin, ib
Eustace sir Rowland vicount Baltinglasse is against the cesse, vi 398
——— Complaineth against sir Nicholas Bagnoll, vi 399
——— His Complaints be vntrue, ib.
Ewin chosen King of Scots, v 53
Ewin the second chosen king, v 56
——— Resigneth the state his deceace, v. 57
Ewin the third king of Scots, of that name licentious, v 59, 60.
——— Pursued & forsaken of his subiects condemned to perpetuall prison, strangled, v 60.
Ewin his laws abrogated or rather altered, v 282
Exactions cause commotions, iii 210
——— Great, ii. 251
——— With shifts of extortion practised, ii. 259
——— New and strange note, ii 488, 489
——— Intollerable, ii 413
——— ¶ Sée Couetousnes, Subsidies, &c Taxes, Tenths, and Tributes.
Example euill how it preuaileth, ii 736, 737
——— Of great ones what it dooth for imitation, iii 621
Examples which be euill are soone followed, vi. 210.
Excester besieged by Danes, i 673
——— Taken by them and spoiled, i 709
——— Fortified by Brian, and besieged by king Edwin, i 613

Excester besieged of Uespasian, vol ii. page 486
——— Repared by Adelstane, i 688
——— Bishoprike when it first began, the circuit of the same, &c i 238
——— Rebelled against duke William and is subdued, ii 10
——— Preserued from fier, iii 518
——— Besieged, the loialtie of the citizens, iii 917, 918
——— Citie described, with the sundrie assaults of the same, iii 926 to 938
——— Commended for loue and loiall seruise to the king and state note, iii 997.
——— Noble and true, iii 998
——— Great practises to procure the citizens thereof to ioine the Deuonshire rebels note, iii. 948.
——— The antiquitie, foundation, and building of the cathedrall church of saint Peters in Excester, iii 901
——— ¶ Sée Clergie, Edward the fourth, and Richard the third
Exchekei when it openeth, i 306.
——— And the officers vnto the same by whome instituted, ii 13
——— Remooued from Westminster to Northampton, ii 299
——— It and the kings bench remooued vnto Shrewsburie, ii 180.
Excommunicate persons how disabled, i 332.
Excommunication for vnlawfull marriage, i 621
——— Of Uortigerne by bishop Germane, i 561
——— Denounced against the rebellious barons in king Iohns time, ii 326
——— Of Romish vserers, and the excommunicator called to his answer, ii 378
——— A dart that made both king and people to quaile, ii 586
——— Of a préest for incontinencie, ii. 418
——— And suspension threatened against the English clergie, ii 413
——— Thretened to such as assisted king Iohn, ii 313
——— Of Lewis the French kings sonne by name, ii 332
——— By name and in particular, ii. 328
——— Of king Iohn when it was to be released, ii 308.
——— Of Gmede Montfort, ii 478
——— Of duke Leopald for imprisoning of Richard the fourth, ii 255
——— Extended to the dead and buried note, ii 671.
——— Flashed and thundered out against the Wicleuists note, ii 828
——— Threatened against attempters of tumults, ii 355
——— The feare thereof constreined a contribution, ii 364
Excommunication how to be vsed, vol v page 680
——— Of pope Sixtus Quintus esteemed as nothing note, iv 597
——— Of a king, v 174
——— ¶ Sée Legats, Popes, and Préests,
Excuse of Edward to auoid an inconuenience, ii 531.
——— Of the clergie to be free from subsidies, &c. ii 520.
——— ¶ Sée Couetousnesse
Exeter Richard lord iustice of Ireland, v. 239.
——— Died, vi 210
Execution with seueritie, v 309, 310
——— Without respite, v 354, 383
——— Without iudgement vpon noblemen, iii. 292, 328
——— Of the duke of Buckingham without arreignment or iudgement, iii 418
Exham field ¶ Sée Battell
Exton knight a murtherer of king Richard the second, iii 14
——— His too late repentance and sorrow, ib.
Extortion of William Rufus made him euill spoken of among his subiects, ii 39
——— An ordinance against it, ii 449
——— ¶ Sée Oppression and Userie

F.

Fable of a fox, v 275
——— ¶ Sée Tale
Factions of Yorke and Lancaster vnpossible to be mingled without danger of discord, iii 247.
——— Of Scotland seuerallie named, v 688.
Facultie a great cause of the ruine of the cōmonwealth, i 345
——— Commodious to the prince and yet exclaimed against, i 229
Faire kept at Westminster at saint Edwards tide, ii 416.
——— Fifteen daies togither, ii 126
——— Of Lewis the French kings sonne in derision, ii 546
——— At Bristow robbed, ii 455
Faires and markets in England, i 539
——— When and where kept throughout the yeare, i 412, 413
——— Paltrie fairs and their abuses, i 411
——— One or two euerie yeare in the great market townes of England, i 343
——— And markets not to be kept on holie daies, vi. 168
Fairies. ¶ Sée Prophesie
Faith not to be kept with traitors, vi 296
Fallow déere by whome first brought into this land, i 343
Falois besieged and rendered vp to king Henrie the fift, iii 93.
——— ¶ Sée Arlet
Falshood betwixt brethren, ii 54.
Fame oftentimes exceedeth the truth, v 344.

Fame ¶ Sée Report
Familiaritie of a subject with a queene note, vol v page 418
Familie of loue, fiue of that sect stood at Paules crosse, iv 328
——— Proclamation against them note, iv 432
Famine extreme within Rone, iii 102.
——— Richard the second died therof, iii 13
——— The cause whie Rone was surrendered, ii 290.
——— Refused, and death by the sword chosen, ii 288.
——— The punishment of witchcraft, ii 302
——— Lamentable, ii 556.
——— ¶ Sée Pestilence
——— In Sussex for want of raine, i 631.
——— Warre and it signified, i 653
——— Among the Danes in Chester, ii. 673
——— ¶ Sée Hunger.
——— At hand is first séene in the horssemanger, i 283
——— Extreame and lamentable, v 380
——— ¶ Sée Derth
Farmers when could hardlie paie their rents, i 317, 318
Farrer an haberdasher of London a sore enimie to ladie Elisabeth, iv. 135.
Fast in what maner obserued in old time, i 622
—— Generall proclamed and deuoutlie obserued, iv. 647
—— Castell woone, v 552
Fastidius archbishop of London, i. 48.
Fasts and processions vsed, ii 449.
Fatall destinie upon the gouernors of Ireland, vi 325.
Fauour ¶ Sée People.
Fausta the daughter of Maximianus & wife to Constantine, i 551
Fawie towne in what kings daies it grew first famous, i 106
Fawkirke battell, v 689
Fealtie ¶ Sée Homage and Swearing
Feare the force thereof euen in nobles, v 55
—— Of outward enimies causeth quietnesse at home, v 294
—— And tumult, v 143.
—— ¶ Sée Crueltie
—— Effectuateth submission, i. 716
—— Force of feare, i 714
—— Causeth want of spéech, iii 269
—— Made king Edward the fourth forsake his kingdome, iii 296
—— What it forceth men vnto, ii. 505
—— Causeth restitution of wrongfullie deteined townes, ii 536
—— Forceth agréement note, ii 537
—— Among the people assembled at the duke of Summersets execution, iii 1034.
—— ¶ Sée Suspicion
—— Must be tempered with loue, vi 122
Feast rare and roiall, iv 465
—— At quéene Katharins coronation, iii 125.
—— Sumptuous and full of rare deuises, iv. 659
Feast ¶ Sée Banket
Feckman ¶ Sée Abbat
Fées ¶ Sée Annuities
Felix bishop of Burgognie preacheth the word to the Eastangles, vol i page 609.
Felix bishop of Dunwich a Burgundian, i 460
Fellon a word deriued from the Saxon toong, i 311.
Fellonie how punished, i 313, 314
——— In what cases the gailor doth commit it, i 310
——— Compriseth manie gréeuous crimes note, i 311
Fellons that speake not at their arreignement how punished, i 312
Felton ¶ Sée Bull seditious.
Fenella, a malicious woman & reuengefull note, v 248
Fennes in England and with what things indued, i 188
——— ¶ Sée Marishes.
Ferand William a valiant man, vi 142
Feredeth taketh from the clergie their priuileges, v 192
——— Slaine, v 196
——— He is buried, ib
Ferdinando archduke of Austrich made knight of the garter, iii 693
Fergus whie made king of the Scithians that arriued in Albanie, i 198
Fergusa a Lombard betraieth the duke of Clarence, iii 127
Ferguse is sent to aid the Goths against Rome, v 120
——— Returneth from Italie into Denmarke, ib
——— Sent vnto the Scots dispersed, prepareth himselfe to warre, v 120, 121
——— He with his ships arriued in Murreie firth, receiued ioifullie of the Picts, conueied into Argile and their inuested king, purposeth to assaile his enimies in the dawning of the daie, v 121, 122, 123
——— Married a daughter of Graham, v 123
——— Inuadeth the confins of Britaine, v. 124.
——— Disuaded to fight with the Romans, ib
——— Diuided the land in parts, v 125
——— Repareth churches, castels, &c ib
——— Exhorteth his people to valiantnesse, v 127.
——— He and Durstus slaine, ib
——— His bodie buried in the abbeie of Colmekill, v 128.
Ferguse the third king of Scots, a wicked prince, v. 183
——— Strangled by his wife, ib
Fergusus sent into Scotland, landed in Albion, made king, v 39
——— Assembleth a great power of Scots against Coilus, v 41.
——— Went into Ireland & is drowned, v. 43
Feritharis chosen K of Scots, ib
——— Inthronised, note the solemnitie, v 41
——— Suddenlie dead, ib.
Feritegus exiled, ib.

Fernihurst castell woone by the French, vol v page 562
Ferns, vi 127.
—— — Builded by Madocke bishop thereof, v 86.
——— Burned by the Irish, vi 253
Ferquard king in Ireland, v 39
Ferquhard king of Scots, v 171
———— Mainteined ciuill discord, infected with the Pelagian heresie, taken prisoner, v 171, 172.
———— His desperat end, v 172
Ferquhard the second king of Scots, first coueteous, now liberall, v 174
———— Excommunicated, ib
———— Uices whereto he was giuen, ib
———— He falleth sicke, v 175
———— Sent for his confessor, ib
———— Yéeldeth vp the ghost, ib
Ferquhard a Scot verie strong and valiant, aduanced, v 320
———— ¶ Sée Conspiracie
Ferrers lord of, misrule at a Christmas at the court, his behauiour and port, iii 1032.
Ferrers knight William taken prisoner, ii 56.
Ferrers a traitor ¶ Sée Treason
Ferrex and Portex miserablie slaine, i 197.
Ferrex the ninth ruler of Britaine, i 450.
——— Slaine, ib
Festiuall daies ¶ Sée Holidaies
Fethelmacus murthered in his bed, v 111
—— ——— ¶ Sée Angusianus
Fetherston sir William knight note, v 391
Fetherston, aliàs, Constable. ¶ Sée Counterfeit of king Edward the sixt.
Feuersham abbeie by whome founded, ii 99
Fiacre giueth himselfe to liue a solitarie life in France, v 172
—— His praier, ib.
Fidelitie of the English pale, vi 394
Fier in sundrie cities, &c i 648
Fiftéenth granted vnto king Henrie the third by the temporaltie, ii 367
———— Of the sixt penie after the rate of mens goods, ii 538
———— Of all the mooueables to be found within the realme, ii 357
———— Thrée granted, ii. 689.
———— ¶ Sée Subsidie
Fife sometimes a part of Pictland now of Scotland, v. 112
—— It with other countries in subiection to the Romans, v 77
—— Put to fire and sword, v 201
Fighte among sparrows, ii 681
Finan bishop of Northumbers, i 621
Finch knight drowned, iv 217
Fincormarke king of Scots, beginneth his reigne, v 107.
———— Raiseth his power, ioineth battell, ib
———— Deceaseth, v 108
———— His sonnes Eugenius and Ethodius, ib
Findocke king of Scots, his vertuous disposition, maketh a iorneie into the Iles, to subiect the rebells, vol v page 100, 101.
Findocke slaine, v 101
Fine for misdemeanor, iii 348
—— Of fiue thousand markes paid to King Henrie the third by the Londonors, ii 263
Fines set on prisoners for their ransoms, ii 249
—— Paid for licence to exercise turnements, ii 252
—— Set on the nobles by king Iohn, ii 288
—— Of préests that had wiues, iv 13
—— Extreme leuied vpon the clergie note, ii. 347, 348
—— Set on the maior of London and the shiriffes, ii 443
—— Set on sherriffes heads, ii 139
—— Of foure hundred pounds set vpon aldermens heads of London by king Henrie the seuenth, iii. 539.
—— Sessed vpon them that fauoured the Cornish rebels, iii 520.
—— ¶ Sée Escuage, Forfeits, and Nobilitie
Fingall the firtilist soile in Ireland, vi 3, 4.
——— Whie so called, vi 4
——— Inhabited onlie by Englishmen, ib.
——— Their language English, ib
——— Spoiled, vi 293
Finglas Allan chiefe baron tooke the castell of Dublin, vi 292.
Finmacoll the great hunter, v 151
Finnan Bishop, v 174.
Finnanus K. of Scots, v 52
Fire caused through wind, v. 322
—— Bursteth out of the earth, ii 76
—— It and the sword Gods angrie angels, iii. 915.
—— Hindred by alume, i. 397.
Firre growing in Englād, i 358
—— In times past in Lancashire, i. 359
First fruits. ¶ Sée Tenths
Firth streame of some called the Pictish and Scotish sea, i 150
—— And what riuer or streames it receiueth, ib.
Fish monstrous taken in Norffolke, iv 509
—— Of twentie yards long, &c note, iv 325.
—— Driuen to the English shore, iv 224.
—— Like vnto a man, ii 290
Fishes of the sea fight, ii. 390
——— Monstrous at Downam bridge in Suffolke, iv 231
——— In Westminster hall after the fall of an high floud, iv 345
——— Like vnto men in shape, v 216
——— Caught with nets, whose deuise in Sussex, i 631
——— Of sundrie sorts great store in the Thames, i 80, 81
——— Thrée kinds in a lake, which fishes haue but one eie, i 218
——— Fiue sorts, i 377.
——— Affeare to come with in the wind of Ospraie oile, i 382.
——— What sorts vsuallie taken vpon the English coasts, i 376

Fishes of the sea how they come into season, vol. i page 577
——— What kind preserued by prouiso of sharpe lawes, i 576
——— Without fins in Lumund lake, i 149
Fishing, a law made for it, v 450 576,
Fishmongers bound to find foure scholers at the vniuersities, &c note, iii. 5,3
——— Sore trobled by the maior of London, ii 754
——— An act against them within the citie of London, ii 755
——— The statute against them repeled and they restored to their liberties, ii 759
——— Benefited by iustice Randolph, iv 506
Fitton sir Edward president of Connagh, vi 365.
——— His gouernment, vi 366.
Fitzalan William a conspirator, ii 83
Fitzaldelme William sent into Ireland, vi 195
——— Lieutenant to the king, vi 196
——— Taketh all the cities and townes in his gouernment, ib
——— Enuieth at Reimond & Fitzstephans, ib.
——— Is greedie and couetous, vi 197
——— His hard dealing with Fitzmoris, ib
——— Taketh from Reimond his possessions, vi 198
——— His description, ib
——— Is a deepe dissembler, ib
——— He was ancestor vnto the Burks in Kent, vi 199
——— Is sent for into England, vi 204
Fitzarnulfe a Londoner procureth the citizens to reuenge their cause by rebellion, he is apprehended and executed, ii 352
Fitzbaldrike shiriffe at Yorke, ii 17
Fitzedmunds seneschall of Imokellie. ¶ See Seneschall
Fitzempresse Henrie, his returne into England, ii 99
——— Is knighted, ib
Fitzfergus Gilbert killed his brother note, ii 170
Fitzgeffreie sir Iohn lord iustice, vi 238
Fitzgefferie chamberleine vnto king Richard the first, ii 222
Fitzgirald Bartholomew seruant to the archbishop of Dublin, vi 294
——— His seruises, ib
Fitzgirald Girald of Kildare lord iustice three and thirtie yeares, vi 275
——— A dissention betwéene him and the erle of Ormond, ib
——— He appointeth a meeting at saint Patriks, vi 276
——— They are reconciled, ib
——— The description of him, ib
——— He is accused to the king, vi 277
——— Returneth from the king, lord deputie, ib
——— His policies in war, ib
——— He vanquisheth the Irishrie, ib
——— Is made knight of the garter, ib
——— He deceassed, ib
Fitzgirald Girald sonne to Girald of Kildare is lord deputie of Ireland, vol vi page 278
——— He giueth his sister in marriage to the earle of Ossorie, ib
——— He is accused and sent for into England, ib
——— Is sworne lord deputie, vi 280.
——— He is accused for diuerse disorders, ib
——— Is called before the lords of the councell, vi 281
——— The cardinall is against him, vi 280
——— He interrupteth his spéeches, vi 281
——— He is bailed, vi 283
——— He is of new accused and committed to the Towre, vi 284
——— A mandatum to execute him, ib.
——— The king countermanded, ib
——— He is deliuered out of troubles, ib.
——— He returneth home and is honourablie receiued, ib
——— He serueth vpon the Otooles, ib
——— Is made lord deputie, vi 285
——— He serueth against Ocarell and is hurt, ib
——— He is anew accused, vi 286.
——— He is committed to the Towre, vi 287
——— His aduersaries who they are, ib.
——— He died for thought, vi 304
——— His conditions and qualities, vi. 308, 309
Fitzirald Girald earle of Kildare second sonne, aged thirteene yeares saued, vi 304
——— He is conueied into France, vi 305.
——— He serueth the Dolphin, ib
——— The king his ambassadors doo require him, ib
——— He commeth to the emperors court, vi 306
——— The emperor giueth him a pension of a hundred crownes, ib
——— Cardinall Poole sendeth for him to Rome, ib
——— He is brought vp in learning, ib
——— He serueth against the Turke, vi. 307
——— He returneth rich, and serueth vnder the duke of Mantua and Florens, ib
——— He falleth into a perillous pit, and is recouered by means of a dog, ib
——— Restored to his earldome, vi 304.
——— Suspected of conspiracie, vi 440
——— Committed to ward, ib
——— Sent to the Towre, ib.
——— Died, ib
Fitzgirald Girald earle of Desmond, his warres against Ormond, vi 328.
——— they submit themselues to the queens order, vi. 332

Fitzgirald Girald he is in campe, vol vi. page 336
——— Suspected to be conioined with Onele, ib
——— He serueth against Onele, ib
——— He is committed to the castell of Dublin, and sent into England, vi 338.
——— He breaketh out of prison at Dublin, vi 373.
——— He commeth to Corke to the lord deputie, vi 381.
——— He denieth the queens officers to intermeddle within his palatine, vi 384
——— He resisteth the lord president, ib
——— He complaineth against the lord president, vi 385
——— He is falne out with the earle of Thomond, vi 388
——— Denieth to paie cesse, ib
——— He commeth to Kilkennie and is reconciled to the lord president, vi 397, 398.
——— He discouereth Iames Fitzmoris his practises, ib
——— He pretendeth to serue against him, vi 398.
——— He refuseth to doo it, vi 408
——— His chéefest men ioine with Iames Fitzmoris, vi 411
——— He commeth to the campe and is committed, vi 413
——— He humbleth himselfe and sweareth fidelitie, ib
——— His sonne is giuen in pledge, vi. 415
——— He is sent for and commeth not, ib.
——— His deepe dissembling, ib
——— He is in open rebellion, vi 417
——— He will not be persuaded to submission, vi 418
——— He is proclamed traitor, vi 424.
——— He is in danger to be taken, vi 425.
——— He lieth in an ambush, vi 426
——— He giueth an onset vpon the Englishmen, vi 426
——— His proud letters to the lord iustice, vi 428.
——— He sendeth his wife for peace, vi. 433, 434
——— Is in danger to be taken, 434
Fitzgirald Iames of Desmond putteth Irish impositions of Quinio and such like vpon Englishmen, vi 269
Fitzgirald Iames killeth Robert Talbot, vi 280
——— He is sent to London and executed, vi 303
Fitzgirald Iohn the first earle of Kildare, vi 18.
Fitzgirald of Leiship lord iustice, vi 280.
Fitzgirald sir Iohn taketh the archbishop of Dublin, 294
——— He is carried into England and executed, ib
Fitzgirald Eleanor widow to mac Artie Reogh, vi 304
Fitzgirald Eleanor is married to Odonell, vol vi page 304
——— Hir liberalitie to hir nephue Girald, vi 305
Fitzgirald Margaret espoused to the earle of Ormond, vi 278
——— Grieued with the murther of Robert Talbot, vi 280
——— She languisheth being with child, vi 275
——— She is a woman of great wisedome, vi 280
——— She adorneth hir husbands gouernment, ib.
Fitzgirald Morice lord iustice of Ireland vi 48
——— The first earle of Kildare, ib.
——— A contention betweene the lord Vessie and him, ib
——— He posteth into England, vi 50.
——— His speeches to the king, vi 51
——— He challengeth the combat of Vessie, vi 52
——— He is rewarded with the gift of Vessies lands, ib
——— His eldest sonne baron of Ophalie, ib
Fitzgirald Moris promiseth to aid Macmorogh, vi. 126.
——— He and Fitzstephans are promised to haue the gift of the towne of Wetsford, ib
——— He arriueth at Wetsford, vi 139.
——— His constancie, ib
——— He accompaneth Macmorogh to Dublin, ib.
——— He commeth to Waterford, vi 146
——— He is troubled for the distresse of Fitzstephans, vi. 151
——— His oration, ib
——— He discomfiteth Rotherike king of Conaugh, vi 154.
——— He saueth Hugh de Lacie from murthering, vi 170
——— He died, and was buried at Wetsford, vi 197
Fitzgirald Moris lord cheefe iustice of Ireland, vi 238.
——— He aideth the king against the Welshmen, ib
Fitzgirald Moris of Desmond drowned between Wales and Ireland, vi 239
Fitzgirald Marie soiorneth and keepeth hir brother Girald Fitzgirald, vi 304
Fitzgirald the archtraitor at the Glinnes, vi 435
——— A draught made vpon him, vi 449
——— His bad practises, ib
——— He is hanged, ib
Fitzgirald Oliuer partaker to the murthering of the archbishop of Dublin, vi 294
——— He is carried into England, and executed vnto death, vi 303
Fitzgriffith chéefe of Wales vnder the king, vi. 125
——— He conspireth against the king, ib.

Fitzgriffith and Fitzstephans are cousens germane, vol vi page 126
Fitzhammon Robert his tale to William Rufus, ii 44
Fitzhenries originall and aduancement, i 28
Fitziohn Eustace a conspirator, ii. 83.
——— Slaine, ii 114
Fitzleo Peter an vsurping pope, ii 75
Fitzmiles Roger ¶ See Erle
Fitzmoris his miserable end, iv 628
Fitzmoris Iames conspireth against the quéene, vi 362
——— Besiegeth Kilkennie, vi. 363.
——— He rebelleth, ib.
——— He seeketh for peace and craueth pardon, vi 370, 405, 406
——— He flieth into France, and offereth all Ireland to the French king, vi 406
——— His practises are knowne, vi 398
——— He seeketh to king Philip & to the pope, vi 406
——— He hath good interteinment, ib
——— His acquaintance with Sanders and Allen, ib
——— He is furnished with all things necessarie, ib
——— He arriueth at S. Marie weke, alias Smereweke, ib
——— The Desmonds and the countrie repare vnto him, vi 407
——— He persuadeth the Spaniards to patience, vi. 411
——— He pretendeth a pilgrimage, ib
——— He taketh a preie and is followed, ib.
——— He persuadeth the Burks to rebellion, vi 411, 412.
——— He is slaine, vi 412
——— His conditions, ib
——— His head and quarters set vpon the gates and wals of Kilmallocke, ib
Fitzmoris Girald erle of Desmond lord iustice, vi 258.
——— Slaine by Obren, ib
Fitzmoris Thomas erle of Kildare lord iustice, vi 268
Fitzosbert his vnnaturall ingratitude, and complaint to K Richard the first against the citie of London, ii 258
——— While he wore his long beard, his oration to the people, he is called before the archbishop of Canturburie, lord chéefe iustice & president of the realme, he flieth into the church of saint Marie Bow, he is attacked, his concubines, ii 259
——— Is executed, the archbishop of Canturburie euill spoken of for his death, an old whoremonger and new saint, ii 259, 260
Fitzosborne William earle of Hereford, &c gouernor of England in duke Williams absence, ii 8
Fitzroger William, prior of the Templers taken, vi. 239.
Fitzroie Oliuer sonne to king Iohn, ii. 349.
Fitzscroope Richard in armes against Edrike the rebell, vol ii page 8
Fitzsimons Robert maior of Dublin serueth against the Omores, vi 285
——— His answer to the bishop of Meth, ib
——— He vittelleth the castell of Dublin, vi 295
Fitzsimons Thomas recorder of Dublin his oration, vi 284
Fitzsimons Walter bishop of Dublin lord chancellor, vi 60
Fitzsimons Patrike put in trust with the cariage, vi 279.
——— He is accused, ib
——— The lord lieutenant chargeth the maior for him, ib
——— Fitzsimons cleareth the matter and answereth for himselfe, ib
——— The lieutenant asketh him pardon and rewardeth him, ib
Fitzstephans Robert constable of Aberteffe, vi 126
——— He arriueth in Ireland, vi 127
——— He landeth at the Banne, ib
——— He besiegeth Wexfford, vi 128
——— He is the knight bypartite, vi. 127, 128.
——— His oration to his souldiors, vi 137
——— He is besieged in the Carike, vi 151
——— He is seduced and taken by flatterie, vi 156
——— The description of him, ib
——— He is deliuered to the king, vi 160
——— He is handlockt, ib.
——— He is released, ib
——— They that betraied him are executed to death, ib
——— He and Fitzmoris are constables of Dublin, vi 165
——— The kingdome of Corke is giuen them, vi 204
——— They diuide it betwéene them, ib.
——— He is shut vp in Corke, vi. 205
——— His praises, vi 220
Fitzthomas Girald dieth, vi 242
Fitzthomas and Moris his sonne slaine, vi 239.
Fitzthomas Moris erle of Kildare is lord deputie, vi 241
Fitzthomas Moris erle of Kildare lord iustice by turnes, vi 257
——— He hath a yeerlie pension of fiue hundred pounds, ib.
——— Marrieth the earle of Ulsters daughter, vi 245.
Fitzthomas Moris erle of Desmond is lord iustice for terme of life, vi 257
——— He is put in prison, vi 253
——— He is taken prisoner, ib.
——— Is set at libertie vpon sureties, vi. 255.

Fitzthomas Moris he putteth in sueities to appeare in England, vol vi page 256
——— He died lord iustice, vi. 237
Fitzthomas Iohn lord of Ophalie giveth an ouerthrow to the Scots, vi 247
——— Is created earle of Kildare, vi. 248
——— Is taken prisoner, vi 241.
——— Is released, vi 256
Fitzwalter lord deceaseth in Spaine, ii 771
——— Appealeth the duke of Aumerle of treason, iii 5
——— He is imprisoned, iii 8.
——— Earle of Sussex, his seruise against the Scots, he is in great danger note, iii 879
Fitzwaren earle of Surrie killed Allen de la Zooche, vi 238, 239
Fitzwater Thomas Ratcliffe lord deputie, vi. 325
——— Is lord lieutenant, ib
——— His troubles with Onele, ib
Fitzwater Theobald slaine by Mac Artie of Desmond, vi 223
Fitzwaters necke broke as he was taking horssebacke, i 179
Fitzwilliams recorder of London his wisedome in a dangerous case, iii 394
Fitzwilliams Iohn slaine at Keneies by Obren, vi. 258
Fitzwilliams killeth the gunner which shot to the erle of Surreie, vi 279.
Fitzwilliams sir William lord deputie, vi 371
——— The plot of his gouernment, ib
——— His distresse and great troubles, vi 373
——— He is reuoked, vi 371.
Flamines and Archflamines in Britaine, i 39, 512
——— Eight and twentie, i 519
Flanders spoiled by the duke of Glocester, iii 189
——— Wholie at the deuotion of Edward the third, ii 608
——— Interdicted, ii. 613
——— Diuerse rodes made thereinto by the English, and great spoile doone, ii 779
——— Inuaded by the bishop of Norwich, ii 750
——— A great part drowned by an exundation, ii 58
——— ¶ See Erle of Leicester, & League
Flatterie of Ucrannius, i 493
——— Reproued actuallie by Cnute note, i 731
——— Impudent of sir Iohn Bushie to king Richard the second, ii 180
——— Used in a sermon note, iii 386
——— Notable, iii 389, 390
——— ¶ See Dissimulation
Flauius Uespasianus his valiantnesse against the Britons, i 182
——— ¶ See Uespasian.
Flauius Victor nobilissimus, i 538
Flax ought to be sowne by law in England, i 187
Fleance deflowreth the prince of Wales daughter, vol v page 272
——— Slaine note, ib
——— ¶ See Banquke
Fleetwood recorder of London, made sargent at law. ¶ See Sargents at law
Fleming bishop of Lincolne founder of Lincolne colledge in Oxford, iii 170
Fleming knight maister of the ordinance, iii 888
Fleming lord required to come to parle with the generall, iv 245
——— His dishonourable dealing, ib
——— His double dealing, iv 246
——— His letter to sir George Careie, iv 247.
Fleming lord escapeth, v 649
Fleming ladie honourable intreated, ib
Fleming Robert a woorthie yoong gentleman, v 338
——— Rewarded for his faithfull seruices, v 349
Flemings threescore thousand came to the aid of the earle of Henault, ii 615
——— Released of debts and interdiction, ii 617
——— Besiege Aire, and doo much mischeefe to the French, ii 646
——— Doo what they might to indamage the French in behalf of English, ib
——— Their harts alienated from the obedience of their erle, ii 606
——— Sweare fealtie to Edward the third, ii. 612.
——— Uanquished by the earle of Arthois, ii. 522
——— Set vpon the English men in their lodgings, ii 528
——— Banished the land, ii 510
——— Their fleete looseth the victorie to the English nauie, ii 778
——— Kill an English herald of armes, ii. 758.
——— Discomfited by the Englishmen, ii 759.
——— Sent home into Flanders, ii 159.
——— Then enuie, ii 109
——— Comming ouer into England, haue places appointed them to inhabit, ii 58
——— Motion to haue Edward the third take vpon him the title to the crowne of France, ii. 611.
——— Slaine through their owne couetousness, iv 120
Flies in Februarie the number strange, iv 326
——— Manie seene in a yeare, a prognostication naturall of a plague like to follow, iii 1002
——— Noisome and mortall, i 149
——— Of a noisome kind, i 381, 383
Flint castell built, ii 182
Flix, great death thereby in the English host, iii 74
——— By vnwoonted diet and there vpon death, iii 569
——— Gotten by excessiue eating of frutes, ii 816,
——— Causing a great death, iii 50

Flodden field, vol iii page 592.
Florin ¶ Sée coine
Florence reedified, v 190.
——— The armes thereof, ib
Flouds and high waters dooing much hurt, iv 60
——— Foretold by astronomie, but falling out false, iii 693.
——— Drowning the marishes, Essex and Kent, side, iii 731
——— That hindereth a great and bloudie conflict, iii 802
——— That did much hurt, ii 823
——— In the riuer of Thames, iv 226
——— High by means of a great thaw, iv 228.
——— High that did much hurt, iv 425
——— Thrice without ebbe betweene, iii 540
——— High that drowned Westminster hall, iv 315.
——— Great and voilent, ii 278, 609
——— That did great hurt, ii 380.
——— In the night, ii 490
——— ¶ Sée Bridges and Riuers
Floure delices three, and how they came annexed vnto the armes of England, ii 24
Flushingers trouble the English passengers, iv 330.
Folkmote at Paules, ii. 452, 451, 456
——— Ordeined by king Arthur, i 261.
Follie of a couper, iii 581
Forboise Arthur slaine, v. 662
——— Put to flight, ib
Forboise Alexander his house, ib
——— Great belied wife and his children burnt, ib
——— They receiue aid from the king, v 663
——— They follow seueral leaders, ib
——— Goeth to Aberden, ib
——— Ouerthrowne besides Aberden, ib
Forboise the master beheaded, v 513
Forboises the beginning of the nauie, v. 336.
Ford castell woone, v. 562.
Forfeits, ii 538
——— For breaking peace concluded betwixt Richard the first, and the French king, ii 257.
——— ¶ See Fines.
Forgerie of William Rufus to get monie, ii. 34
Forgetfulness of duty in yoong men aduanced to dignitie, ii 130, 131
Forgiueness of an enimie a notable example, ii 270
Fornication ridiculouslie punished, i 311
Forrest called New forest and what waste & desolation was made to make it, ii. 23.
——— Of Shirewood pleased king Richard the first verie greatlie, ii 246
——— ¶ See Frier
Forrests in England & Wales diuerse, i. 346
——— To be seuered the new from the old, ii 457
——— The perambulations of them appointed to bishops, ii 531
——— Seized into duke W hands, ii 23
——— Their gouernment diuided, ii. 187.
Forrests and ordinances for them, vol ii. page 266.
——— King Iohns commandement against the white moonks concerning them, ii 280
Forster doctor of physicke first reader of surgerie lecture in London, iv 197.
——— His faithfull and fréendlie epitaph vpon doctor Caldwell deceased, iv 535
Forswearing ¶ Sée Periurie
Fort builded at Aberladie, v. 564.
Fortescue, and the reason of the name, iii 427
Forth called the Scottish sea, v. 211
Fortresse ¶ Sée Castell
Forts how they came to be erls of Aumarle, Wight, and Deuonshire, i 56
Fortune ¶ Sée Walden.
——— Brittle, v 210.
Fosse dike clensed by bishop Atwater, i 170
Fosse one of the highwaies of Britaine, & how it is extended, i 190
Fosse streame able to beare a good vessell, i 195
——— ¶ Sée Highwaies
Foster sir Iohn, v 581
Foster Children, vi 67
Fothadus the great bishop of Scotland vndertaketh to cōclude a peace betwixt parties at deadlie variance note, v 252
Fough or pogh, vi 8.
Fouks de Brent, a man of great stomach and rashness, ii 348
——— An enimie to rest and quietnesse, ii 356
——— His foule end, ib
——— ¶ Sée Erle
Fouks de Warren vexed knight, i 27
Foules tame leave houses, and waxing wild get them to the woods, ii 23
——— Taken by sir Francis surnamed the Arragonois, iii 214.
——— Wilde forbidden to be taken, ii 299.
Fowles wild & tame in England, i. 374
——— Tame of diuerse kind, ib
——— From beyond sea, ib
——— Rauenous to be destroied by law, i 375, 381, 382
——— Vncleane, i 375
Founteins abbie famous how seated, i 160.
Founteine flowing with bloud, ii 39
Fox, his practise to deliuer certein Christians from the Turks, iv 425
Fox bishop builder of Corpus Christi colledge in Oxford his opinion, i 253.
Foxes in England, i 379
Foxleie slept more than fourteen daies and as manie nights note, iii 854
Fraie betweene the duchesse of Lancasters men and the bishop of Elies, i 241.
——— ¶ See Quarrell
——— In Canturburie betweene citizens and the erle of Bullongne, i. 742.
——— With bloudshed about a dog, v 104.
——— Among noblemen being on hunting, v 165
——— At Oxford betwixt legat Othos men and the scholers, ii 383.

Fraie betwixt the English archers and the Henuiers, vol ii page 595.
—— In saint Dunstans church in the east, iii 95
—— Neere Clerkenwell where the maior of London &c was resisted, iii 236, 237
—— In Fleetstreet betweene the street dwellers and gentlemen of courts note, iii. 216.
—— Betweene Spaniards and Englishmen about whoores, iv 74
—— On Clist Heath two miles from Excester, iii. 241
—— In London against the maior, iii 227
—— Great by night in Fleetstreet, iii 204.
—— Whereby insued murther and execution note, iii 821.
—— Betweene the Almans of king Henrie the eights campe and the Englishmen, iii 584.
—— Betweene the Englishmen and the townsmen of Sancta Maria, iii 570
—— Betweene the English and townsmen of Calis vpon a small occasion, iii 563
—— Betweene gouldsmiths and tailors of London, ii 473
—— Betwixt the monks and citizens of Norwich, ii 176
—— Betwixt the Welsh and English, ii 529
France how manie archbishopriks bishopriks & Churches it hath i 234
—— Much euill transported from thense into England, i. 35
—— By whome inuaded after Brute, i 445
—— In old time Gallia, v 61.
—— Interdicted by the popes legat, ii 277
—— At diuision in it selfe by ciuill warres, iv. 204
—— The troubles thereof touch most the Q of England, iv 205
—— Disquieted with two factions, iv 50
—— Inuaded by duke William, and what wast he made there by fire, &c ii 23
—— The ioine of the English armie through it, ii 730
—— Their whole puissance vanquished by the English archers, ii 610
—— The frontiers thereof full of men of warre, ii 613
—— And how king Edward the third took vpon him the name of king thereof, ii 611
—— And by what right he claimed it, ii 612
—— And great preparation made in England for warre against it, iii 68
—— Ciuill discord amongst the nobles thereof, iii 86
—— The oth of the thrée estates, iii 123.
—— Henrie the fift taketh vpon him to be regent there, iii 124
—— And what townes and castelles king Henrie the fift got ¶ See the historie of king Henrie the fift, iii 96 to 100
—— All lost there through ciuill discord at home, iii 228
—— The English lose all there, iii. 229
France the duchie of Britaine incorporated vnto it, vol iii page 492
—— The constable thereof a déepe dissembler, iii 332
—— His offer to king Edward the fourth, iii 337
—— All assaut in whose time, iii 126
—— It is concluded in parlement that king Henrie the eight should personallie inuade it, iii 573
—— An armie leuied to inuade it, thrée battells appointed with their seuerall lieutenants, iii. 838.
—— Afflicted by the Englishmen and their aids, iii 687
—— It is agréed among the lords of England to annoie and infest it, ii 1092
Franci or Frankeners people of Germanie, i 326
Francis knight slaine in Deuonshire rebellion, iii. 956
Francis de Ualois, &c ¶ Sée Duke of Alanson
Franke chase. i 346
—— ¶ Sée Parke
Frankeners now Frenshmen, i 551
Fratricide, i 445 450, 519 v 577
—— ¶ Sée Murther
Frea wife to Woden, i 556,
—— ¶ Sée Woden
Frederike abbat of saint Albons a rich and puissant prelat note, ii 15, 16
Frederike the emperor allied to king Henrie the third, ii 378
—— ¶ Sée Pope Alexander
Fréendship, ii 676, 677
—— Betwéene fishes by nature, i 376.
—— Intertemed by affinitie, iii 132
—— Feigned of duke William of Aquitaine, ii 115
—— Found in a forren countrie, ii 9
—— Betwéene the erle of Cornwall and the erle of Penbroke, ii 561
—— Sold for gifts and bribes note, ii 620
—— ¶ Sée Peace, and Loue
Fréemen of London, ii 207
Free schoole at Wuluerhampton, iii. 539
—— ¶ Sée Schoole
French best on horssebacke, i 275
—— Exiled out of England, i 12
—— The first footing of in Britaine since the time of Ethelbert and Sigebert, i 5
—— The miserie vnder them, i 13
—— In reporting their owne affaires not to be trusted, i 194
—— They deride our new archerie, i 333
French king taken prisoner, v 387
—— Sent to persuade the king of Scots to warre, v 472.
—— Requireth aid against England, v 471
—— Sendeth monie into Scotland, v 6[illegible]
—— Maketh warre against the duke of Normandie, ii. 100.

French king open warres proclamed against him by Q Marie, vol iv page 87.
—— His son trauelleth in vaine to take Douer, ii. 333.
—— Sendeth to the pope, commeth vnto Calis, taketh the sea, landeth in Kent, the lords doo him homage, ii 331
—— Goeth to visit Calis, iv 102
—— His sonne mainteineth his pretended title to the crowne of England, ii 330
—— Alleadgeth that king Iohn is not lawfull king of England, ii 330
—— His sonne came to fight with king Iohn, ii 316.
—— Returneth into France, ii. 310
—— Burneth his ships, ii 311
—— Inuadeth Flanders, ii 309
—— Displeased for the reconciliation of King Iohn with the pope, he meaneth to procéede in his iournie against England, ib.
—— Prepareth to inuade England, ii 305
—— Winneth diuerse things from the king of England, ii 293
—— Will not accord to peace with king Iohn, ii 288
—— Inuadeth Normandie, ii 276
—— Demands in a treatie of peace, ii 277.
—— Maketh warre against king Iohn, ii. 284.
—— Inuadeth Normandie, ii 288
—— Winneth townes from king Iohn, ii 289
—— Almost drowned pursued by king Richard the first, ii 265
—— Pursued by king Richard the first in danger of drowning, ii 256
—— Raiseth his siege from Uernuell, ii. 250
—— Inuadeth Normandie, ii 245.
—— His and earle Iohns offers to have king Richard the first kept still in prison, ii 244.
—— His euill dealing and promise breaking with king Richard the first, ii 231, 232
—— Entereth Gisors, ii 263
—— Confesseth earle Iohn to vsurpe against his Brother king Richard the first, ii 238
—— Setteth from Messina towards the holie land, ii 220.
—— Maketh an ouerture for peace he leaueth his séege, ii 161
—— Soweth sedition betweene Henrie the father and Henrie the sonne, ii. 111.
—— Commeth a madding to visit Beckets toome, ii 178.
—— Entereth the towne of Mauns and maketh spoile, ii 197
—— Hideth his head at the arriuall of Henrie the second, ii 194
—— His subiects arrested in Normandie, ii 191.
—— Troubled with a frensie, iii 18
—— Picked a quarrell against Englãd, iii 75
—— Inuested with the order of the garter, iv 560.
—— Francis the great his court and vniversitie. note, iv. 486.
—— Deceaseth an obsequie for him in Paules, the chief mourners, iv 185, 186, 325.
French king commeth to the camp before Newhauen, vol iv page 223.
—— Procureth a peace betweene duke Robert and William Rufus, ii 31.
—— His policie against the English, ii 730
—— For monie raiseth his séege and forbeareth to aid duke Robert, ii 31
—— Restoreth townes in Gascoigne to king Edward for feare, ii 536
—— With an huge armie driueth the English out of Flanders, ii 761
—— The order of seruice at his table, ii. 833.
—— Giueth his daughter to king Richard in marriage, ib
—— His priuie practises disclosed by the popes nuntio, ii 813
—— Two of his ships taken with a great prise in them, ii 777
—— Aideth the Scots against the English, ii. 765.
—— Inuadeth Flanders, ii 522
—— His vniust dealing he renounced what he had said, ii 503
—— Sendeth out a fleet against England, ii 509.
—— Deceaseth, ii 731.
—— ¶ Sée Normandie and Philip.
—— Arbitrated a matter betwixt Henrie the third and his nobles, and giueth sentence against the barons, ii 458, 459
—— Requested by the pope to make warre against England, refused so to doo, ii 411.
—— His brother named Charles made earle of Prouance, ib.
—— Inuadeth the earle of Marches lands, ii. 397.
—— To whom the earle of Britain submitteth himselfe, ii 378
—— His carriages distressed by the earls of Britain & Chester, ii 370.
—— Deceaseth, ii 354
—— His sonnes armie discomfited, and his gentlemen taken prisoners, ii 345, 346
—— Answer to Henrie the third, requiring restitution of his right, ii 351.
—— Assembleth an armie, commeth to Calis, his lords request to Edward the third he returneth into Rone, ii 646, 647
—— Licenced to depart, goeth ouer into Calis, ii 675
—— His oth of peace, hostages deliuered for him, prisoner in England foure yeares, ii. 676
—— Prisoner, and comforted by the prince, whom he thanketh for his bountie, he is brought ouer into England, ii 668.
—— He is sorowfull, he is remooued to Windsore, ii 669
—— Remooued from the castell of Hertford to Somerton, his allowance, ii. 671
—— His ransome, ii 675.
—— Followeth the prince of Wales, ii 663.
—— His presumptuous demands, ii 665.

French king commeth to giue the duke of Lancaster battell, vol ii page 662
——— Taken prisoner, ii 667
——— Departeth out of the field by constraint note, ii 639
——— His great armie and the seruice doone by them, ii 617
——— Prepareth a great nauie against Flanders, ii 611.
——— Not of sound memorie, iii 86
——— Consulteth how to deale with the Englishmen, sendeth defiance to Henrie the fift, the number of his armie, iii 77, 78
——— Deceaseth, iii 135
——— Turneth the ciuill dissention of England to his aduantage note, iii 277
——— Practiseth with a witch, iii 166.
——— Armed, fled in the night, ib.
——— Deceaseth, iii 539
——— Described both for person and qualitie, iii 503
——— Dissimulation, a motion for a treatie of peace with the English, iii 502
——— Request for aid against the duke of Britaine, iii 490
——— Feedeth Edward the fourth with faire words and promises, iii 348.
——— Large offers to Edward the fourth, iii 347
——— Buieth peace with tribut of Edward the fourth. note, iii 341
——— Nothing precise in outward shewes of honor, iii 332
——— His spéech to the English herald that gaue him defiance, iii 331.
——— Dissimulation vpon purpose and ill meaning, iii 336.
——— Promiseth the erle of Richmond assistance to recouer the crowne, iii 426
——— His benuolence vnto the erle of Richmond, iii 420
——— Francis the first comes to the crowne, his praisworthie properties, iii 611
——— His roiall ornaments at an interuiew, the description of his person, his rich araie at a iusts, iii 649, 650
——— His and his partners attire at a chalenge, iii 650
——— His furniture and diuise vpon his ornaments, iii. 653
——— Afflicted with forren power on all sides, iii 841
——— An enimie to all christian princes, his power against king Henrie the eight and the emperor, he retireth backe with his armie, iii 832, 833
——— His children deliuered when the ransome of their father was paid, iii 749, 750
——— His sitting in his roialties with his great estates about him, &c with an oration made to the assemblie, iii 732
——— His oration before an honorable assemblie at Paris wholie concerning the emperor, and sauoring of malcontentment, iii 730.
French king a writing from him directed to the emperor, vol iii page 731
——— Receiueth the order of the garter, iii. 722.
——— With the viceroie imbarked not a little glad of his libertie, not verie hastie to ratifie the accord, complaineth of the emperor to the popes ambassadors, iii 704.
——— His roialtie restreined, iii 705
——— The manner of his deliuerie out of prison, iii. 706
——— Taken prisoner, while he desired to fight in plaine field, the manner how he was vanquished and taken, iii 697
——— Led prisoner to the rocke of Pasqueton, his letter to his mother the Regent of France, iii. 699
——— Marrieth the emperor Charles his sister, iii 706
——— Led prisoner into Spaine, extremelie sicke in the castell of Madrill, iii 702, 703.
——— In durance, is visited by the emperor, his sister the ladie Alanson treateth for him, he is carefull ouer the crowne of France, a treatie touching his deliuerie, iii 703, 704
——— He and king Henrie the eight at variance note, iii 675
——— Attacheth the Englishmens goods in Burdeaux, iii 676
——— He and the Spanish begin to aspire to the empire, in hope to be emperor as well as the Spanish, builded his hope vpon the humors of the princes of Germanie, resteth vpon the fauor of the pope, iii 637, 638, 639
——— His toiesh and light behauiour abrode note, iii 635
——— Deceaseth, the variablenesse of his fortune, iii 610
——— Procureth the pope to be a meane to Henrie the eight for peace, iii 602.
——— Hath his hands full of troble, iii 568
——— Writeth to cardinall Wolseie, iii 632.
——— Prepareth an armie in aid of the Scots, iii 691
——— Purposeth to surprise Gernseie & Ierdseie, but is repelled, ashamed that any report should pass of his euill successe, perseuereth in his former martiall action, iii 1011, 1012
——— The causes that made him to breake vp his campe, iii 1012
——— Proceedeth against prince Edward in iudgment of appeale, ii 688
——— Sent to defie the king of England, the countie of Ponthieu taken by him, ii. 689
——— Prepareth a nauie, ii 691
——— Deceaseth ii 678
Frenchmen or Normans first entered into England, i 741
——————— ¶ Sée Gallies
Frenchmen their gallies compass about Scotland, v. 557.

Frenchmen they seek to make a peace between the queene and the lords, vol v page 625.
———— Depart Scotland, v 604
———— Require a crown matrimoniall, v 587
———— In miserable state in Scotland, v 563
———— They & the Scots cannot agree, v 395
———— They make a rode into England, v 562.
———— Returne home, v 566
———— Incamp at Muscelborrow, v 558.
———— Come into Scotland, v 557.
———— Why the forbare to giue an assalt, ib
———— With them of Edenborrow make a truce, v 559.
———— They giue a canuasado to Hadington, ib
———— Sent into Scotland, v. 584
———— What parts of Christendome they possessed in old time, v 188
———— Fall to the spoiling and rifling of Calis, iv. 92
———— Netled with the losse of saint Quintines, they take Newman bridge, and Rie banke, disappoint the Englishmens deuise the demand a parlee, iv 90, 91
———— Shew themselues in their kinds, ii 332
———— In king Iohns time ouerun, take spoile and subdue diuerse places of England, ii 333, 334
———— Sent ouer to aid the rebellious barons, ii 329
———— Uncommanded of the king, assalt Rouen, ii 160
———— The & Normans fight, ii 100
———— Doo much hurt in Wales, burne townes are slaine, returne home, iii 39, 40
———— Their demand of the Ile of Wight, iii 28
———— Inuade the Ile of Wight, iii 27
———— Demand a dower for quéene Isabell, iii 18
———— Their practises to make the English reuolt from their own king, iii 15.
———— Breake the law of armes, iv 221, 222
———— Spoile diuerse English ships, iv 224, 225
———— Gather cockles to their losse and vndooing, iv 190
———— Their policie in womens apparell note, iv 192.
———— Repelled by the English, iv 191.
———— Numbers slaine, ib.
———— Driuen into Leith, iv 192
———— Win a trench, ib
———— Repelled and some slaine, ib
———— Repelled by the English, iv 192.
———— Sent into Scotland to aid the queene dowager, iv 188.
———— Ships taken by the Englishmen, ii 762
———— Burne the towne of Rie, ii. 715.
———— Spoile the Ile of Wight burn Portsmouth, Dartmouth and Plimouth, ii 715
———— Their gallies chased from the English coste and vanquished, ii 731.
Frenchmen & Spaniards burne and destroie diuerse towns on the English costes. note, vol ii page 731
———— Uttel the English for feare, ii 730.
———— Spoile and burne diuerse townes in the west countrie, ii 729
———— Their admerall persuadeth the Scots to fight with the English, ii 766
———— Subtiltcie, ii 822
———— Fleet setting forward towards England is driuen backe by contrarie winds, ii 777
———— Purpose an inuasion of England with their ships, ii 772
———— Foure hundred slaine besides diuerse taken, ii 525
———— Their bloodie victorie, ii 507
———— Slaine handsmooth by the English, ii. 509
———— Rob Douer, chased to their ships, discomfited & slaine, ib.
———— Forced to retire by the English, ii. 511
———— Die thorow pestilence & other wares, ii 398
———— Their spite towards the English, ii 417
———— Taken at aduantage, ii 358.
———— Put to flight at Lincolne, ii. 345.
———— Their souldiors in a poore estate, ii 344.
———— Their pride procureth them hatred, ii 341
———— Fleet assailed and vanquished, ii 347.
———— Meant not to fight with the English, ii 700
———— Prosperous successe in Poictou, ii 698
———— Withdraw themselues into their fortresses and shire towns, ii 694
———— Take the king of Naverre, ii 681
———— And English skirmish, the French flie, & submit themselues, ii 663
———— Distressed, the ordering of their battell, ii 664
———— Seeke to saue themselues by flight, ii. 667.
———— Forsake their horses and fight on foot, ii. 650
———— Slaine the daie after the battell ii. 640.
———— Discomfited and slaine, ii 633
———— Slaine in great numbers, ii 639
———— Loose the passage ouer the water of Some, disorder amongst them, ii. 636
———— Distressed and discomfited, ii 632
———— Their armie discomfited by a few English, ii. 624
———— Set vpon the Flemings in skirmish, ii 616
———— Inuade the costes of England, ii. 609.
———— Discomfited, iii 81
———— Incountred by the earle of Huntington, iii 89
———— Repelled, iii. 905
———— Harts discouraged by the losse of Rone, iii. 107.

Frenchmen their voluntarie subjection, they yéelde diuerse castels and townes, vol iii. page 93
———— Receiued a great ouerthrow by sea by the duke of Bedford, their nauie vanquished, iii 86
———— Rob Henrie the fifts campe, iii 81.
———— The order of their armie, iii. 78
———— Six to one of the English, ib
———— Take occasion to inuade the English, iii 244
———— Soone wearie of the French gouernement, ii. 255
———— Discomfited, flie note, iii 196
———— Ouerthrown, slaine, taken prisoners and slaine, iii 178
———— Breake the peace, and take the town of S Valeran, iii 177
———— Faith and honestie not to be trusted note, iii 175
———— Recouered in Henrie the sixts time all that they had lost in Henrie the fifts daies note the course of the stories and compare them together, iii. 164, 165
———— Commit a foule murther by negligence of the watch at Montargis, iii 158
———— When inuincible, iii 492
———— Their loue, iii 340
———— Ouerthrowne to their gréefe and shame, iii 585
———— Land in Sussex, in the Ile of Wight, distressed, the number of their nauie, iii 848
———— And English haue manie skirmishes, iii 854, 855
———— Dogged nature for a matter of nothing, iii 714, 715
———— In London all arrested and put to their fines, iii 676.
———— Failing in force make supplie by policie, iii 689, 690.
———— Scoured of the English, and foiled of the Welsh, iii 679.
———— Insolent saucinesse against the English, iii 618
———— Their diuelish nature, ib
———— Foiled at iusts at their challenge and proclaming note, iii 606
———— Nauie discomfited by the English, flieth, iii 573
———— Armie approching against the power of Henrie the eight, they get the great gun called the red gun, by foolish hardinesse of the maister capteine, iii. 578, 579
———— Gallies land in Sussex, and burn certeine cotages, iii 576
———— Crueltie reported by their own writers, iii 1013.
———— Assaile Balognbergh, the number of pikes & bils broken vpon them, repelled, fifteen waggons laden with their carcases, iii 908, 909
———— They and the Scots doo resolue to besiege Hadington, iii 891
———— Remoue their campe, iii. 893.
Frenchmen dislodged from before Hadington, encamped at Muskelburgh, chased, durst not come forth of their campe, vol iii page 894
———— Of name taken prisoners, iv. 119
———— Their desperat aduenture and dastardliness, iv 97, 98
———— ¶ Sée Bullen, Englishmen, and Normans
French gentle men weare armour vnder their garments, iv 498
———— Taken prisoners and slaine, iv. 499.
Fridaie whie so named, i 556
———— Whie called the king or the worling, i 407
Fridleie king of Denmark inuadeth Ireland and by policie taketh Dublin, vi. 91.
Friei Forest seditious, his execution, iii 805
———— One of Ireland that accused the duke of Lancaster of treason, tormented & cruellie put to death note, ii. 763
———— Pateshull, ¶ Sée Pateshull, Patrike ¶ Sée Patrike
———— Randoll committed to the Towre, he is slaine by the person of the Towre, iii 106
Friers beggers, an order for them, iii 21.
—— Greie about London change their habits, iv. 528
—— Minors when they began and increased, ii 293
—— Obseruants impugne cardinall Wolseis authoritie, iii 696
—— Preachers inhabit Dunstable, ii 431.
—— Suborned to treate a peace betwixt Henrie the third and his lords, ii 403
—— Foure orders of them, a commandement against deuising new orders of them, v 321
—— Blacke, their first comming into Scotland, v. 310
—— Carmelits first cōming into Scotland, v 313.
—— Minors first cōming into Scotland, v 310.
Frieries distroied in Striueling, v. 590.
———— Suppressed, iii 792, 807.
———— ¶ Sée Abbies and Religious houses
Friswide daughter to Didanus hir chastitie note, i 649.
Frith an arme of the sea diuiding Penthland from Fiffe, i 199.
Frith martyr burned, iii 792.
Frobishers voiage for gold, in the yeare of our lord 1577, i 398
———— His first voiage for the discouerie of Eataia, iv 329
———— A rumour that he was cast awaie, iv 330.
———— His secōd voiage to Eataia, iv 343.
———— His third voiage to Eataia, iv 345
Frogs commonlie found where adders be, i 383
Fronto counted Ciceros match, i 525
Frontinus purposeth to pursue the conquest of the Silures, v 78
———— Required to ioine amitie with the Picts, ib
———— Uexed with sicknesse returneth to Rome, ib
Frost extreme, ii 99
—— Bitter and nipping, iii 691.

Frost great and long note, vol. iii pages 184, 185.
—— Of continuance, ii 19.
—— Hindering husbandrie note, ii 291
—— After a sore floud, ii 32
—— With snow on S Marks daie noisome to trees and plants, ii 412
—— With a sharp winter, iv. 321.
Frost called the greene frost, iv 228
—— Verie great and long, i 610
Frotho king of Denmarke, vi 91
Fugitiues practises to repeale pope Pius his buls, seditious and nourished in seminaries beyond seas, iv 516, 517
———— ¶ Sée Préests Seminarie.
———— Seditious labour to bring the relme into a war externall and domesticall, iv 517, 518
———— Furtherers of tresons, iv. 561.
———— ¶ Sée Parrie and Treason
Fugatius ¶ Sée Ioseph of Arimathia
Fulco a French préest his admonition to Richard the first, ii 271
Fulgentius capteine of rebels, v 96
———— Incouraged them to stick to their enterprise, ib
———— Put to flight, v 97
———— Withdraweth into Pictland, ib
Furius Camillus with his Romans ouerthroweth the Gallies, i 455, 456.
Furniture ¶ Sée Houses and Building.
Furseus a deuout person that came out of Ireland, i 619

G

Gagates, i 401.
Gaile deliuerie or great assises, i 261
Gailers in what case guiltie of fellonie, i. 309, 310.
Gaine ¶ Sée Gift
Galates married to Hercules, i. 7
Galane king of Picts, succoreth the Scots, v 139
Gald king of Scots, punished such as disturbed the peace of the state, v 74
—— Laboureth to abrogat wicked laws, ib
—— Determined to fight with the Romans, ib
—— Promiseth to ioine in league with the Picts, v 78
The fame of his puissance putteth the Romans in feare, v 79
—— Chosen generall against them, ib.
—— Setteth vpon one of his enimies in the night, ib.
—— Commeth into Dundee, consulteth how to proceed in his wars, v 81.
—— Commeth to aid the Picts, exhorteth the people to fight manfullie, ib.
—— By reson of the multitude thinketh to inclose his enimies, v 82
—— Pursueth the Romans, v 84.
—— Studieth to preserue his subiects in good quiet now after the wars ended, v 86.
—— Deceseth, ib.
Galgacus. ¶ Sée Gald
Galgagus capteine of Britains fighteth against Agricola, vol i page 508
Galles recieued their religion from the Britains, i. 35.
——What sort of them aduentured into Britaine, i 9.
Gallia now called France, i 441.
—— Inuaded by Bren and Belinc, i 454.
—— Celtica the hither parts of France, i. 479.
Galles put to flight by Brute and Corineus, i 412
—— Beaten backe by the Romans, i 455
—— Their couetousnesse preiudiciall to themselues, ib
Gallies belonging to the queens maiestie and hir seruice, i 338
—— In old time of sundrie sorts and seruice, i. 337.
—— An old inuention, i 432.
—— Rowed with ores strange to the Britons to see, i 467.
Gallio Rauenna sent in Britaine to succor the people, i 541.
———— Sent to Britaine, pursueth the Scots & Picts, causeth the wall of Abercorne to be repared, returneth into France, v 129.
Gallowaie whereof so named, v 86
———— Inuaded by the Irishmen, v 221, 222
———— Towne in great decaie, vi 381.
———— Their charter and liberties, vi 427.
Gallowglasse the best souldiour, vi 68.
———— His weapon and conditions, ib.
Gallowglasses, v. 228
Galus archbishop of Armagh, consented to the synod holden at Cashill, vi 164
—— Fed with the milk of a white cow which he carried with him, ib
Game. ¶ Sée Wrestling
Games prohibited as vnlawfull, ii 193
Gandius and Genandius the sonnes of Nemodus arriue into Ireland, vi 75
———— They possesse and diuide the same, ib
Ganteners and king Edward the firsts men at debate, ii. 527
———— Mainteine warre against the erle of Flanders, ii 768
Garbleneles inuadeth Ireland, vi 75.
Gard of the prince ¶ Sée Yeomen.
Gardens and orchards in England, i 350.
———— Of our time péerelesse, i 353
———— Ioining to houses how beautified and furnished with floures, herbs, &c i 351
———— Of the Hesperides, i. 353.
———— ¶ Sée Moorefield
Gardiner bishop of Winchester made lord chancellor, iv 2
———— An enimie to the ladie Elizabeth examined of him, iv 125, 126
———— Derided note, dog in a rocket, iv 105
———— The talk betweene the ladie Elizabeth and him, iv 134
———— Crowneth quéene Marie, iv 7.

Gardiner bishop of Winchester his tale in the star chamber against the ladie Elizabeth, vol iv page 26
——— Preacheth at Paules crosse note, iv 73
——— His practise against the ladie Elizabeth, iv 25, 26
——— His old hatred against the duchesse of Suffolke note, iv 104
——— His death visited with the sudden stroke of God, a hunter for the life of ladie Elizabeth note, iv 81
Garget a disease in cattell, i 185
Garlisch the lard, v. 631
Garnish of pewter vessell how much, i 399
Garnard the king of Picts ioifullie receiued Gildo, they assembled a councell, determined to rest all the winter & make frontier wars onlie, v. 81
——— Inuadeth Scotland, v 179
Garrisons placed in Wales by king Henrie the first, ii 64
Gascoigns refuse to receiue the king of England for their soueraigne, ii 824
———Send to Richard the first signifieng to him that they ought not to be diuided from the crowne, ii 830
——— Begin to humble themselues, ii 430
——— Complaine of their strict handling, ii 128
——— Make warre against the English subiects, they are danted, ii 423
——— They mean to complain of the erle of Leicester, their allegations disproued, ii 125
——— Cease not to make warre against the erle of Leicester, ii 126
——— Rebell and white, ii 428.
——— Pursue the Welshmen, ii 486.
——— They and other nations how they tooke the death of Richard the second, iii 15.
Gaston de Bierne noted for vnthankfulnesse, ii 414
——— Attempteth to take the citie of Baion, ii 432
——— Submitteth himselfe vnto king Henrie the third, ii 118
Gathelus giuen to will and plesure went into Egypt, his doings aduanced, seeketh other countries, repelled from Britaine landed in Portingale, v 33, 34
——— Buildeth the citie of Brachara, v 34.
——— Intituled king of Scotland, his laws, v. 34, 35
Gathelus the sonne of Nele a Grecian arriueth in Ireland, vi 76
——— His skill in languages, vi 76, 77
——— He called that land Gathelia after his own name, vi 77
Gauaro and others executed for murther his desperat end, iii 1022
Gauell kind deuised first by the Romans and why, i 303
Gaueston Péers arriueth in Ireland, vi 245
——— He hath all roialties assigned vnto him, ib
Gaueston Péers his buildings and proceedings, vol. vi page 245
Gaunt besieged by the French king, ii 309
Gawaines lonltie fighting against his owne brother in the princes quarrell, and dieng is honorablie buried by Arthur, i 576, 577
Gawen his seruice with K Arthur, v 155.
——— Slain, v 161
Geat stone, i 101
——— Of fine kinds, ib
Gebmound bishop of Rochester, i 630
Geffrie erle of Britaine, sonne to king Henrie the second, vi 210
——— Rebelleth against his father, ib.
——— He died, ib
Geffreie King Henrie the seconds fourth sonne borne, ii. 115
——— Marieth the duchesse of Britain, ii 128.
Geffreie sonne to king Henrie the second, ii 12
Geffreie bishop of Constance in armes against the erle of Camber, ii 18
Geffreie bishop. ¶ Sée Bishop
Geffreie a kings brother rebelleth, ii 112
Gegathus a noble man serued king Huglet, vi 91
Gelderland ¶ Sée Duke
Gelousie and crueltie note, ii 200.
——— Of mastifes, i 388
Geneuill lord of Meth, vi 3
——— Becommeth to be a frier and is buried at Trim, ib
Genissa the daughter of Claudius the emperour giuen in marriage to Aruiragus, i 481
——— Maketh Aruiragus and Vespasian friends, and so ended their warres, i 485
Genissa wife of Aruiragus deceaseth, v 64
Genowais stratagems to abash the English, ii 638
——— Reteined in the French kings wages, they meet the English on the seas & fight, ii 623.
Gentilitie of Ireland, vi 66
Gentlemen more trustie than the commons, more woorthie than yeomen, iii 1006
——— Restored, v. 578
——— Named in Latin Melites, i 120
——— In England of three sorts, i 263.
——— Gouernors of two sorts, i 276.
——— Of blood, i 271
——— Who to be counted, i 273
Gentlemen Itahonats, ib
Gentlemen of the second degree, i 266.
Gentlemen of the greater sort, i 263
Gentlemen rauceners of comodities, i 403.
Gentlemen shifters robbers, i 313
Gentlemen dingthrifts théeuish practises, i 335.
Gentlemens manours, i 316
——— Their diet ¶ Sée Diet
George duke of Clarence borne in Dublin, vi 267.
——— His godfathers, ib
——— Is lieutenant of Ireland, vi 268
Gerald ¶ Sée earle Gerald
Gerard de Cambill charged with felonie and treason, ii. 247.

Gerent king of Britans chased and put to flight, vol i. page 639
Germandei, i 351.
Germans cōming to serue Romans rebell against their capteins & leaders, v 80
——— A cohort of them restored the Romās side néere at point to haue had the woorst, v. 82
——— Assistants to the Romans, i 507
Germanus and Lupus bishops arriue in Britaine and preuaile against the Pleagian heresie, i 562
——— He conducteth the British armie against the Saxons, ib.
——— His miracle of a calfe, i 564.
——— He returneth into little Britaine, i. 563.
——— His death and buriall, ib
Gernseie. ¶ Sée Ierdseie.
Geta ¶ Sée Bassianus
Geuesses inhabitants of that part of Britaine which the Westsaxons afterwards held, i 553.
——— Why so named, ib
Giants and how the word is meant, i 432.
——— How long they continued in this Ile, i 434
——— Whom our chronicles meane by that name, ib.
——— Incounter Brute, i. 443.
——— One, three of whose teeth weid an hundred ounces, i. 17
——— Bones of one seventeen or eighteene cubits long, ib
——— The bodie of one found in a coffin of stone in Aldernele, i 57.
——— Ones mouth of sixteen foot widenesse, i 20
——— The bones of one whose carcasse was two and twentie foot long, i 19.
——— One of Spain that died by a fall on the Alps, i. 14
——— One found dead sitting with a staffe in his hād like the mast of a tall ship, i. 17
——— Whether anie were or inhabited Britaine, i 11
——— Sundrie exāples of proofe to confirm the opinion of them, i 17.
——— The last of the race left in the land of promise, i 16.
——— Proved by Scripture to have been in former times, i 15.
——— To what purpose God created such men of mightie stature, i 22
——— The offspring of Nimrod arriued in Ireland, vi 74.
——— They are fought with, ib
——— They preuaile vpon the sons of Nemodus, vi. 75
——— They are destroied, ib
Gigas, or Nephilim, signifieng a giant, i 15.
——— ¶ Sée Giants
Gifford William of Winchester commended, ii 48
Gifford Doctor of Physicke president of the college of physicians, iv 498
Gift of king Henrie eight vnto the citie of London, iii 861.
——— Of king Henrie the second to Hugh Lacie, ii. 141.
Gift large and bountifull refused, vol. ii. page 441.
——— Of the new yeare, ii 430
——— Of erle Edwins lands to erle Alan, note the forme, ii. 11
——— ¶ Sée Crosbie. Large refused being an vngodlie gaine, ii 426, 427.
——— Of the pope to a Scotish K v 304.
——— To king Iames the fourth, v 462
——— Of K William to K Richard, v 303
——— ¶ Sée Present
Gifts preuaile where as faire words faile, v 116
——— Giuen to king Iames by his wiues friends, v. 417.
——— Required as a lone, v 174
——— Great giuen for the fauor of Edward the fourths councellors and lords note, iii. 341.
——— They pacifie anger procure fauor, ii 819, 820.
——— And obtein lost liberties note, ii 820.
——— Of roiall magnificence bestowed by the French, iv. 560
——— A meane vsed to win the fauour of the nobilitie, ii 26, 27
——— Not respected, but the mind of the giuer note, iv. 175
——— Giuen king Henrie the eight in his pogresse into Yorkshire, iii 622.
——— ¶ Sée Bribes Presents and Rewards
Gilbert bishop of Cathnesse canonised a saint, v. 299, 300
Gilbert of Gallowaie rebelled he is vanquished, v. 299
Gilbert de Guant taken prisoner and put to his ransome, ii 11
Gilbert murthered by Liulfus, ii 20, 21
Gilbert capteine of Tunbridge castell, ii 29.
Gilbert knight his voiage to Norimbega, it hath not wished successe, he is seuered from his compane, dead, and neuer heard of, iv 391
Gilberd sir Humfreie his arriuall into Ireland, vi. 366
——— He serued in the Butlers' wars, vi 362
——— He is at the taking of Cloghgrinam, ib.
——— He hath the voward of battell at Kilkennie, vi 363
——— His noble seruice vpon the enimie, ib.
——— Is made colonell of Mounster, vi 365
——— His noble seruice there, vi 365, 366
——— He maketh the earle of Clannecar to stoope and submit himselfe, vi 366.
——— He is dubbed knight, ib
——— His descent and description, v. 367.
——— His vertues and qualities, ib
——— His death, vi 368.
Gilcombe spoileth Scotland, maketh himselfe L of Gallowaie, slaine, v 324
Gilcrist declareth what he is, v 301
——— Murthereth his wife vpon suspicion of adultrie, v 300.
——— Proclamed a traitor, ib
——— His miserable estate, deluing of clods & turfs, asketh pardon of the king in an unknown habit, v. 301.

Gilcrist recieued into the kings fauor & restored to his lands, the disposing of them after his death, vol v page 301
——— ¶ Sée Gilbert
Gildo is kept of from landing, arriueth in Taie water, is receiued, v 80, 81
Gilespie Rosse a rebel beheaded, v. 309
Gilford knight his message of thanks from king Henrie the seuenth to the Kentishmen, iii 511
——— Maister of the horse vnto king Henrie the eight, iii 586
Gilford lord Dudleie executed on the Tower hill, iv 22. ¶ Sée Sands
Gillequhalme the sonne of Donald, v 184
Gillo capteine of exiles vanquished, v. 117.
Gillomanus king of Ireland discomfited, i 565.
——— Slaine in batell, i 566.
Gillus his craftie working, v 54
——— Created king For feare goes about to murther Dothans sonnes, counterfeiteth a zeal to iustice, rebelled against, departeth secretlie to Ireland purchaseth aid, v 56
——— Taken, beheaded, v 55, 56
Gilpatrike and others spoile Scotland, v 324
Gilpins preaching effectuall in Ridsdale, Tiuidale and Lidersdale, i 154.
Gipswich now Ipswich, i 711
Gir in old Saxon speech, signifieth keepe fens and marishes, i 171
Girald William lord chancellor, vi 382
Giraldines their ancientnesse, vi 48
——— Maligned and yet aduanced, vi 238.
——— Fauourers to the house of Yorke, vi 268, 269.
Giraldines throwe and wish, vi 39
Giraldus Cambrensis attendeth king Iohn in Ireland, vi. 220
——— His descent, ib
——— Writeth the historie of Ireland, ib
——— He is verie inward with king Henrie the second, ib
Girald Fitzgirald ¶ Sée Fitzgirald
Girth king Harolds brother would not haue him fight in person against the duke, i 761
Giruij what people, i 635
Gisors beséeged by king Richard the first, ii 263.
——— Beséeged by the Englishmen, iii 110
Gita the sister of Sweine king of Denmarke escapeth into Flanders, ii 10
Githa the wife of earle Goodwin departeth England, i 744
Glames made lord chancellor, v 685.
——— Conuict of treason, v 513
Glamorgan ¶ Sée Glan Morgan
Glanduill Reginald lord chéefe Iustice of England attendeth king Iohn, vi 219
——— Gouernor of Sandwich castell, vi 174
——— No God no religion, vi 332
Glasco taken, v 597
Glasiers first brought into England, i. 627.
Glasing by whome first brought into this land, vol. i page 315.
Glasse how first found, i 316.
——— Of diuerse sorts, ib
——— How it might be made tougher, i. 400.
——— Hath been made in England before the Romans time, i 187
——— House burned, iv 329
Glasses to drink in greatlie vsed, i 280
——— Of the best sort from whense, ib.
——— In looke is made of tin, i 399
——— Of siluer common to euerie dishwasher, ib.
Glastenburie monastrie builded, i 639
Glencarne erle his double dealing, v. 553, 554
Glendouers rebellion in Wales, what he was, iii 17.
——— The occasion that mooued him to rebel, ouerthrowne, ib
——— Reputed a coniuror note, iii 20.
——— Conspired with the Persis, iii 22.
——— His daughter married vnto the erle of March, iii 21
——— He with his Welshmen full of mischeef, iii 18
——— He and his Welsh in armes against the lord Greie of Ruthen, preuailed, iii 19
——— Taketh the erle of March prisoner, iii 20
——— Wasteth the English marches, iii 29
——— Aided by the marshall Montmerancie, iii 39
——— His craftie entring the castell Abiruscwith, iii 44
——— He and fifteene hundred Welshmen taken and slaine, iii 34.
——— Endeth his life in great miserie, iii. 48.
Glocester recouered and put to fine, ii 460
——— Whie it was not assalted by quéene Margaret & hir power, iii 319
——— How called in the Romans time, i. 301.
——— It and Summersetshire by what riuer parted asunder, i 116
——— Bishoprike uerie ancient, i 246
——— Erection, circuit, & valuation of it, i 239
——— ¶ Sée Duke.
Glouernia now Glocester, i 485
Gluni ¶ Sée Duke.
Gluttonie of England in Canutus time, i 287.
Gluttons neuer satisfied, v 422
——— ¶ Sée Diet
Goche his valiant seruice, iii 140
——— Taken prisoner by the foundering of his horsse, iii 183
——— A Welshman his escape, iii 216
——— Slaine vpon London bridge, iii 225
Goda erle of Deuonshire slaine, i 505.
Goda, sister to king Edward the third, married to Baldwin earle of Flanders, i 742
Godfathers, i 622, 673
——— ¶ Sée Baptisme.
Godmanchester in old time called Gumicester,

whilome a towne of great countenance and verie ancient, vol i page 173
Godredus. ¶ Sée Olenus
Gods inferior how hatched at the first, i 38.
—— Men made such and so honored, i 39.
—— Who was properlie said in old time to haue a seat among them, i 38
Goffarius surnamed Pictus, i 441
—— Sendeth to Brute, i 442
Gogmagogs hill a strong place of incamping, i. 328
—— In wresling slaine, i 443
Gold how ingendered in the earth, i 398
—— Not wanting in England, ib
—— From the West Indies, ib.
—— Grains thereof inclosed in stones, i 396
—— Drosse in trill note, i 398
Goldwell bishop of Oxford a Iesuit, i 240.
Gonild the néece to K Swaine with hir sonnes auoid out of England, i. 740
Gonorrhea, v 239
Goodwine sands, v 283
Goodwine of Kent earle father in law to Edward the confessor, i 12
—— Accused of high treason verie slanderouslie, i. 13.
—— Defaced by the Norman writers, i 222
—— Curreth fauour with king Edward the third, and good cause whie, i 739, 740
—— Offended with king Edward the third for fauouring strangers, i 743.
—— Well fréended, i 746
—— In fauour with king Edward the third, none greater, i. 740.
—— Put to his purgation for the death of Alfred, i 737
—— He and his two sonnes rise in armes against king Edward the third, they flie, i. 744
—— They are proclamed outlawes, ib.
—— Receiued into fauour returneth home, i. 745.
—— His qualities, his wiues, his children, with the lewd life and foul end of his mother, i 748
—— Dissembling fréendship to Alfred, mischéefous, i 733, 735.
—— He and his sonnes practise pirasie vpon the English coasts, i 745
—— His seruice in Denmark, i 729
—— His authoritie in England, i 733
—— His sudden death note, i 748.
—— ¶ Sée Edmund
Goose doong beneficiall, i 375.
Gooseheard how he leadeth his géese to the féld, ib.
Gorbodian ¶ Sée Gurgustius
Gorbodug the eighteenth ruler of Britaine, i 449
Gorbonianus king of Britaine his acts & deeds, i. 459
Gordon Adam, v 662
—— Entereth Angus, v 665.
Gordon Alexander hanged, v 612
Gordon Iohn and the lord Ogiluie fight, v. 611
—— He is imprisoned, ib
Gordon Iohn he escapeth, vol v. page 611.
—— Summoned by the queene, ib
—— Accompanied with a great number, ib
—— Commanded to Struelling castle, v 612
—— He disobeyed, ib
—— Beheaded, v 613
Gordon lord maried to the kings bastard, v 472
—— Created erle of Huntleie, v 614.
Gordon erle of Southerland forfalted, v 613.
Gordons and Forboises doo fight, v 662
Goring George ¶ Sée Iusts triumphant
Gormond arriueth with a nauie in Northumberland v 225
—— Ouerthrowne by Alured, v. 226.
—— He is baptised, ib.
Gorolus duke of Cornwall slaine for his wife, i 571.
Goropius trifling about the names of places noted, i 6
Gospatrike erle of Northumberland is sent against king Malcolme of Scotland note, ii 16
—— From whome duke William taketh the erledome of Northumberland and whie, ii. 17
—— How he came to be erle of Northumberland, ii 21.
—— ¶ Sée Malcolme
Gospell the shamefull end of a contemner thereof. iii 788
—— Preached how effectually to conuert and amend mens manners, i 154
—— The successe thereof after the death of Christ, i 40
—— Had neuer frée passage in Britaine till Lucius time, i 41
—— The propagation thereof in Britaine, i 41, 42, 43
—— Augustine the monk is sent into Britaine to preach it, i 591.
Gosselme archbishop of London, i 543
Gotes great store in England and Wales, i. 372.
—— Their milke medicinable, ib
Gothlois disdainefull against Nathaliod his countriemen both Britains note, i 570.
Gothred mooueth a rebellion he is taken and beheaded, v 305
Goths make an expedition against the empire of Rome, v. 120.
—— Deuise for the destruction of their white crowes, i 375.
—— They and Uandals make lawes against learning, i 257.
Gothlanders vse wodden ancors, i 7.
Gouernement giuen by lots, v 42
Gouernor of Scotland whiles a new king was chosen, v. 55
—— Sendeth to France, v 553
—— He resigneth, v 572
—— He agreeth with the Dowager, v. 574
—— Made duke, v 579
—— ¶ Sée Duke of Albanie. Pardons, Scotland

Gouernours appointed to the kings person, vol. v page 189.
——— At dissagreement causeth ill disposed persons to wax bold in dooing mischéefe, v 419.
——— Foure vnder king Edward, v 181.
——— Of Scotland their catalog, v 678
Gowrike erle beheaded, v 421
Grace of God words misconstrued by the Scots, ii 721
Grafton Richard slandered by a Scot and defended, ii 193
——— His tale of the bons of a giant, i 18
Graham lord Montrosse made L treasuror, v 721.
——— The antiquitie of that name, ib.
Graham and his lineage, v 123
Grames authoritie in ordering the battell, ib
——— ¶ Sée Graham
Gramsdike, v 131
Granado is woone from the Turks or Saracens, iii 498
——— The state and pompe of the same, ib.
Granchester, i 459
Grandmesnill Hugh set all vpon the spoiles, ii 28.
Grandlings ¶ Sée Umbers
Grant of king Henrie the third to his Brother, ii 361
——— ¶ Sée Patents.
Granta a noble and excellent streame described, i 173
——— Now Cambridge, i 459
Grantabrishire so called of the riuer Granta, i 171
Granthom by whome builded, i. 459
——— Church in Lincolnshire out of which the people were frighted, i 353
Grasing inconuenient to the commonwealth note, iii 656, 657.
——— Superfluous how restrained by the Romans, i 359
Grasse ¶ Sée Mice, iv 434.
——— Uerie fine on Douebanke growne into a prouerb. i 167
Grasiers growen verie cunning, i 369
Grashoppers powdered in barrels & eaten, i 385.
Gratefulnesse of the ancient writers, epist.
Gratian, who and what sent from Rome to rule in Britaine, i 537
——— Intrapped by a Policie, i. 538.
——— His rough regimen causeth his own destruction, i 541
Gratian vsurpeth the gouernance of Britaine, v. 121.
——— Slaine by Maximus, v. 118.
Grauelin fortified by French for a countergarrison to Calis, ii 761
Grauesend burned by the French and Spanish, ii. 731.
Gréefe killeth an archbishop, ii 10
——— Of K Iohn turned into rage, ii. 317
——— Cause of a sore and dangerous sicknesse in king Iohn, ii 335
——— Of mind doubled the cause of K. Iohns death, ii 336.
Gréefe killed Dauid the prince of Wales, vol iii. page 411
——— Killed king Henrie the seconds heart, ii. 198
——— For losse of booties, ii 335
——— For an ouerthrowe the death of a king, iii, 329
——— The cause of death note, ii. 30, 70, 86, iii 390, 511, iv 121, v 283, 452
——— For vnkindnesse, ii 152.
——— Taken at hart the losse of life, v 408.
——— Inward bringeth death, i 69
Greeks manie trauelled into Britain in the time of Gurguntices, i 35
——— They knew Britaine by none other name for a long time than Albion, i. 9
Greene one of Richard the thirds merciles instruments to murther two innocent princes, iii 401.
Greenfield knight, sir Walter Raleighs lieutenant for the voiage of Uirginia, iv 598.
——— Singled from his companie, arriueth in Hispaniola, ib
——— His valiantness against the Spaniards, iv. 599
——— In danger of shipwrecke, ib
——— Chaseth and surpriseth a spanish ship, ib.
Greenewich by whom builded & inlarged, i. 329.
——— Repared, iii 525.
Greet outlandish, i 394.
——— ¶ Sée Whetstones.
Gregories willingnesse and desire to win the English saxons to the faith, i 591.
——— Whereby mooued to send Augustine the moonke to preach in this Iland, ib.
——— His seuenfold Letanie, i 592
——— His platforme of ecclesiasticall gouernment sent to moonke Augustine in Britaine, i 593.
——— Chosen king of Scots, v 217
——— Giuen wholie to godliness, neuer married, sober, his expedition into Fife, v. 218.
——— His saieng to his soldiors, v 219
——— Suffered the inhabitants of Northumberland to inioie their lands, v 220.
——— Wintered at Berwike, prepared an armie against the Britons his consecration, ib
——— Requireth a resignation of Cumberland & Westmorland, v. 221
——— His deuise, v 222
——— Assalted the Irish, his mercifull vse of victorie, v 222, 223.
——— His wise and godly answer, v. 224
——— Recieued into Dublin with procession, ib.
——— Kisseth the crusifix, ib.
——— Entereth the castell, ib.
——— His returne to Scotland, v 225.
——— His death, ib.
——— Buried in Colmekill, ib.
Greie lord desireth to incounter the Scots, v. 548
——— Entereth Scotland, v 600
Greie lord of Scotland taken prisoner, v 484
Greie Leonard lord deputie of Ireland, vi. 302.

Greie Leonard incountered with Thomas Fitzgirald, vol vi. page 308.
———— He holdeth a parlement, vi 308
———— He certifieth Onels rebellion, vi. 310
———— His seruice against Onele, vi. 312.
———— He is accused, ib
———— He is beheaded, vi 313.
Greie lord Arthur his arriuall to Dublin, vi 434.
———— His iournie vpon the Glinnes, vi. 435
———— He maketh a iournie into Mounster, vi 438.
———— He besiegeth the Spanish fort, vi 437.
———— He taketh it, vi 438
———— He taketh the erle of Kildare and sendeth him into England, vi 440.
———— He returneth into England, vi. 450
Greie lord committed vnto the Tower, iii 818
———— Indicted and beheaded, iii 821
Greie lord of Wilton deputie of Bullen the letter of K. Henrie the eight vnto him, iii 859, 860
———— His seruice verie honourablie accepted of the king, iii 860
———— His request vnto the duke of Summerset, iii 876
———— Receiued possession of Hume castell, iii. 886.
Greie lord Iohn duke of Suffolkes brother arreigned, condemned, pardoned, released, iv 56.
Greie lord capteine of Guisnes taketh the French at at a sleepie aduantage, commendeth his soldiors, iv 94, 95
———— The danger that he escaped sitting vpon a forme with two gentlemen, hurt by mischance, he consulted with the Englishmen, iv 96, 97.
———— His words to his soldiors being ashamed of their timorousness, agreeth with the enimie vpon articles, iv 99, 100.
Greie lord generall of the quéenes armie in Scotland, iv 189
———— His message to the Frenchmen, iv 191.
Greie Arthur hurt in the shoulder by shot, iv. 193
Greie lord of Wilton deceaseth, iv 210
Greie Henrie ¶ Sée Iusts triumphant.
Greies families aduanced, iii 281
———— A surname in Scotland, v. 418
Greiehounds, ¶ Sée Dogs
Gresham sir Thomas knight his pauing stones for the bursle, i 395
———— Suddenlie deceaseth · note, iv. 428
Gret Harrie. ¶ Sée Ship.
Gret Oneale. ¶ Sée Oneale
Greuill Fulke ¶ Sée Iusts triumphant.
Griffin ap Rees dooth much mischéefe on the marches, ii 65
Griffin K. of Wales departeth this life, vol ii page 264
Griffin of Wales breaketh his necke, ii 395.
Griffin beheaded at Tower hill, iii 775
Griffin king of Wales destroieth Hereford, i 745.
———— In armes with Algare against king Edward the third, i 719
———— He with his Welshmen are subdued, i. 742.
———— A present aid alwaies against king Edward the third, i 751.
———— His palace burned, ib
———— Renounced of all people and as a banished person, he is slaine and his head sent to Harold, i 751
Griffith nepheue vnto Moris Fitzgirald his dreame, vi 170
———— Forewarneth Hugh de Lacie, vi. 169
———— He is troubled with his dreame, vi 170.
———— He is watchfull to foresee the armes, ib
———— He pearseth through Oronke with his staffe and killeth him, ib
Grime causeth himselfe to be crowned king, his liberalitie against Malcolme, &c. of greater force than he, v. 250, 251
———— He and Malcolme reconciled, v 252.
———— His alteration from noble qualities to detestable vices . notes, v 253
———— In armes afresh against Malcolme, discomfited and miserablie ended his life, v 254
Grindstones, i 396.
Grotes and half Grotes. ¶ Sée Coines.
Ground. ¶ Sée Earth.
Groues ¶ Sée Woods
Guanor king Arthurs wife, v 161
Guannus king of the Hunnes, a mercilesse murtherer, i 538
Gudwina the wife of earle Leofrike rideth naked through couentrie towne & whie, i 750
Guenouer, and whie so named, i 580
———— Arthurs wife néere kinswoman to Cador earle of Cornewall, i 576
———— Buried with hir husband Arthur, the tresses of hir haire note, i 577.
Guendolena daughter to Corineus duke of Cornewall, i. 444.
———— Ruleth Britaine during hir sonnes minoritie, ib
———— The wife of Locrinus gouerned the kingdome of Britaine, hir crueltie, i 107.
Guenhera and the nobles of Wales made a league with Henrie the third, ii 391
Guetheline. ¶ Sée Gosseline
Guiderus king of Britaine denieth tribute to the romans, i 480
———— Traitorouslie slaine, i. 484
———— Rebelleth against the Romans, vi 61.
———— Slaine, ib.
Guido erle of Britaine his father and his three sonnes erls of Britaine, ii 12.
Guie of Warwike deceaseth, ii 554.
Guildhall inlarged, the chappell, iii. 56.

Guillomer king of Ireland aiding the Scots is repelled by Arthur, vol. i. page 576
Guilthdacus K. of Denmarke landed in Northumberland, i. 452.
Guines ¶ Sée Guisnes.
Guintoline king of Britaine, his acts and deeds, i. 457
Guisnes Henrie the eights palace roiall there described, note, iii. 646, 647, 648
——— ¶ Sée Greie lord capteine of Guisnes
Guise ¶ Sée Duke
Guise the first duke his death, 566
Gun belonging to the Turks with seuentie yoke of oxen, and two thousand men, i. 334
——Called Digeon, iii. 189
——Called the red gun ouerthrowne and recouered of the French, iii. 579
—— Shot into the court of Greenwich, iv. 85.
—— By casualtie discharged by the quéenes priuie barge, she being therein, and some hurt done: note, iv. 425.
Guns made and superscribed note, v. 470.
—— Good store and of sundrie sorts in England, their names, weight, widenesse at the mouth, and what powder will serue for shot, i. 331.
—— Of how ancient an inuention, ii. 777.
—— Gained from the French, iii. 846
—— ¶ Sée Culurings.
Gunpowder blowes vp a house and killeth fifteene persons, iii. 1059.
——— Shattereth houses in Bucklersburrie, iv. 228.
——— Strangelie set on fier, dooth much hurt, iv. 495.
Gunthilis the sister of king swaine murthered, i. 713
Guoronous gouerned Kent vnder Uortigerne, i. 556.
Guortigerne ¶ Sée Uortimer.
Gurguint king of Britaine, his acts and deeds, i. 457.
Gurguint builder of Norwich castell, iv. 376
——— His speech touching antiquitie, iv. 379.
Gurguintus builder of Cābridge castell, i. 250
Gurgustius the fourteenth ruler of Britaine, i. 449.
Gurguntus king of Spain met the Spaniards at seas, vi. 77
——— Placeth them first in Ireland, and taketh fealtie of them, ib.
Gurmo a heathenish king, vi. 90
——— He marieth Thira king Etheldreds daughter, vi. 92
——— His sonnes inuade Ireland, ib.
——— His sorrow for losse of his sonnes, ib.
——— He dieth for sorrow of them, vi. 93.
Gurmundus an archpirat, vi. 88.
——— Is sonne king of Norwaie, ib
——— He helpeth the Saxons against the Britains, ib
——— He maketh a voiage into Ireland, ib.
——— Buildeth forts and castells, ib.
Gurmundus conquereth the land, vol. vi. page 91.
——— He landeth in Wales, ib
——— He saileth into France and dieth, vi. 88
Gurmundus K. of Affrica aideth the Saxons against the Britains, i. 588
——— Spoileth Britaine in pitiful wise, ib.
——— ¶ Sée Guithun
Gurthun a principall man of the Danes is baptised, i. 671
——— King of Eastangles dieth, i. 677.
Guthlake a man of great vertue and holinesse, i. 649.
Guthmond a Danish capteine with his Danes spoile Ipswich, i. 705
Guthred king of Man, v. 318.
Guthred king of Northumberland note, i. 677.
Guthun a Dane king of Eastangles, i. 667.
Guttellus generall of the British armie, causeth fiue hundred of the enemies to be hanged, v. 138.
——— Slaine with twentie thousand Britains, v. 139
Gwinbach towne and whie it was so named, i. 179.
——— It and Radwinter, the lords whereof were at variance note, ib.
Guy of Warwike when he liued, i. 688
Gyldas words inuectiue against the British rulers and kings, i. 582, 583, 584, 585.

H.

Habren or Hasren, base daughter to Locrinus, i. 117
——— Drownded by Guendolena, ib.
Haco a Dane he arriueth into Ireland, vi. 91.
—— He is killed, ib
Hadington besieged, v. 557.
——— Uittelled, v. 565.
——— Raised and left by the English, ib
——— Siege remooued, v. 557
Hadrian the emperor first beginner of the Picts wall, i. 214.
Haie an husbandman with his two sonnes their valiantnesse note, v. 243
—— Refused costlie garments, is made one of the nobilitie, reuenues assigned him, v. 243, 244
—— His request, armes or ensigns, v. 244.
Haie at a double price, ii. 520
Hailstones which made men amazed, ii. 66.
——— Of the bignesse of hens egs, ii. 287.
——— Of sundrie strange shapes, iv. 431.
——— Great the like not séene, ii. 490
——— A mightie storme that did much hurt, ii. 432
——— That slue both men and horses note, ii. 674
——— Square and of sixteene inches about, iv. 323
——— Fashioned like mens heads, iii. 817.
Halden and Basreceg two leaders or kings of the Danes, i. 666.

Halden a Danish king inuadeth Mercia, vol. i. page 668
Hales bloud and who brought it into England, ii 475.
—— Shewed at Paules crosse, iii 807.
Hales knight will assent to the new succession of the crowne, iii 1064.
—— In trouble for religion, iv 8.
—— Greuouslie tempted, drowneth himselfe, iv 9
Halidon hill how it is seated and standeth, i 150.
Halifax law, i. 312
Halliwell bath, i. 360
Hambleton castell lost, summoned, rendered vnto the French king, the number that came forth thereof, iii. 1012, 1013.
Hamblethiew fortified by the Englishmen, iii 854.
Hamerton a capteine of 80 soldiors, vi. 299
—— Their valiantnesse, ib
—— They are all slaine, ib
—— One of them hurted Thomas Fitzgirald, ib
Hamilton sir Iames arrested, v 515.
—— Beheaded, ib
—— Hurt, v 506.
Hamilton lord marieth with the kings sister, v. 448.
—— Taketh part with the erle of Argile, v. 537.
Hamilton palace burnt, v. 647
—— The castell besieged, ib.
—— Deliuered to the English, ib.
—— Blowed vp, ib.
Hamiltons of whome descended note, v 356
—— Mingled with the kings bloud, v 357.
Hamo appareling himselfe like a Britune killeth the king thereof, i 484
—— Slaine by Aruiragus, ib.
Hamont burned ¶ Sée Heretike.
Hampton whie so called note, ib.
—— Beareth the name of Aauon or Nene a riuer, i 172
—— Court by whome builded, i 329.
Hangman hanged, iii 806.
Hanoch a citie builded sometime by Cham, i 15
Harding Stephan moonke of Shireborne, ii 44
Hardiknought ¶ Sée Hardicnute
Hardicnute proclaimed & crowned king of England, i 736.
—— His sudden death, his condition, i 737
Hardilo sands, iii 816.
Harald earle sonne of Oxonford sonne to Goodwine erle of Kent and after king of Englãd, i 13
Harald a Greeuous mall to the Britons in the time S. Edward, i. 133
Haraldston so named of Harald successor to S. Edward, ib
Harflue besieged, iii 72
—— The people desire a parlée yéelded and sacked, iii 73.
—— Besieged by the French and rescued by the English, iii 85, 86.
—— Woone by the English, iii 191.
—— Besieged, iii. 216.
Harflue yeeldeth to the French king, vol iii. page 216
Harleston knight his notable exploit note, ii. 722.
Harlots cause manie murthers, iii. 819
—— ¶ Sée Murther and Whoore
Harington sir Henrie taken prisoner, vi 396
—— Is hurted, ib
—— Deliuered, ib
—— Is made seneshall of the Obirnes, vi 496.
Harold sonne to Cormo, inuadeth Ireland, vi 92.
—— Is slaine, ib
—— His father lamenteth his death, ib.
Harold king of Man knighted, ii 412.
—— ¶ Sée Canutus
Harold father to one Kirke K. of Northumberland, i 692
Harold the base sonne of Cnute proclamed king and consecrated, i 733.
—— Degenerateth from his father Cnute, i 756.
—— Why surnamed Harefoot i 733
—— His counterfeit letter tending to the destruction of Emma and hir sonnes, i. 734
—— His bodie taken vp and throwen into the Thames, i 727.
Harold Harfager king of Norwaie is persuaded by Tostie to make conquest of England, i 758.
—— He is slaine, i 759
Harold king of England wherein note the diuerse opinions of writers, i 756
—— Hated and disdained of the popes and cardinalls, i 750
—— Battell betwixt duke William and him, i. 762
—— He and his brother Leofwin inuade the shires of Dorset and Summerset, i 745.
—— They dine with Goodwine in the Ile of Wight, ib
—— He goeth ouer into Normandie, i 751
—— He hath more hautinesse than hardinesse i 761
—— Highlie welcommed to duke William, i 752
—— He had his fathers Goodwines erledome, i 718
—— His pride, i 757, 758
—— His couetousnesse, i 759
—— He seeketh to win the peoples harts, i 756
—— He promiseth duke William to kéepe the realme of England to his vse, i 752.
—— Made generall of king Edward the thirds arme, his exploits against the Welshmen, he fortifieth the citie of Hereford, i 749
—— His answer to duke Williams ambassadors touching his oth and promise made to the duke i 757
—— He inuadeth Griffins dominions and burneth his palace, i 751
—— He is taken prisoner by the erle of Ponthieu, and set at libertie at duke Williams request, ib.

Harold king of England, his death diuerslie reported, he is described, his acts and deeds, vol i page 763
Harold passeth into Norwaie drowned in his return, v 318
Hartland called Promontorium, i. 8.
Hartlepoole towne lieng ouer into the sea in manner of a byland, i. 155
Haruest sore hindered by continuall rains, ii 364, 511.
——— Wet and raine, ii 430, 681
——— Wet a cause of death, v. 313.
——— Late, ii 419, 598
Haruie de Yuon his surrender to king Henrie the second, ii 129
——— ¶ Sée Bishop
Hasting captéene of the Danes besieged, he receiueth an oth touching baptisme euer vntrue of his word, i 673
Hastings Philip, governor of Wexford, vi 165.
Hastings his challenge to the crown of Scotland, v 325
——— The originall of the name, the manner of their armes, ii. 801
——— Their grant for exchange of lands, the record by which they executed the office of panteler, ii 803
——— The order and number of cloths laid at the kingstable, and how the Hastings had them in fee, ib.
——— Record wherebie the said office of panteler is claimed, the petition for the second word, which the erle of Arundell also claimed, the bill exhibited for the golden spurs, ii 806, 807
Hastings lord his counsell to all his acquaintance, iii 297.
——— Chamberleine maligned of the king and quéne, ii 363
——— Described, iii 382.
——— His life and deeds laid open, iii. 383.
——— Beheaded, iii, 381
Hastings lord discharged out of the Towre, iv 2
Hastings castell, ii 9
Hasculphus capteine of Dublin escapeth out of the towne, vi 117
——— He seeketh to be reuenged, vi 150
——— Hee besiegeth Dublin, ib
——— He fleeth and is taken, for his intemperat spéeches is beheaded, ib
Hatred of the English against the Normans, and contrariwise, ii 22, v. 169
——— Borne to the Iewes, ii. 210
——— Irreconcileable betwéene the dukes of Summerset and Yorke note, iii 217
——— Great betwéene the duke of Buckingham and cardinall Woolseie, iii 644
——— Against Richard the third, iii 408, 409, 410, 411, 412, 413
——— Of the erle of Glocester against king Stephan, ii 83
——— Procuring murther note, v 231.
——— Betwéene the quéene and her husband, and the cause, v 401
——— And dearth for goodwill, i. 700.
Hatfield, vol i. page 610
Hauen townes in Ireland, vi 85.
——— Of Southampton called by Ptolomie Magnus portus described, i 5
——— Of little might be made of Bride riuers mouth, placed betwixt two hilles, i 100
Hauens in Britaine that the Romans vsed in their passage to and fro, i. 5
——— ¶ Sée Ports
Haucrings dreame, vi 44
Haukestorde knight his practice to kill himselfe, iii, 299
Hawkes their seuerall names and kinds, i. 381.
Hebrides in old time subiect to Ireland, their number and situation, i 52.
Hecatompolis decaied, i 324
Hector Boetius, his fault to adorne the Scots with the honour of the Britons, i. 464
——— His error touching the Silures, Brigants and Nouants, i 493.
Hed of wax wrought by necromancie, speaketh, ii 529.
——— Or hued, in old English signification chéefe, i. 178.
Heding castell besieged by the Englishmen, iii. 680.
Hedgecote field, iii 680
——— ¶ Sée Battell.
Hedningham or Heuedingham whie so called, i 178
Heirgust chosen king of Picts, v. 111.
——— Desireth the utter destruction of Scots, v. 115
——— Killeth himselfe, v 119
Heirgust slaine ¶ Sée Maximus, v 148.
Helias the pretended earle of Mans, his bold words to William Rufus, ii 39
Helen the daughter of Coell a Britaine married to Constantius a Roman lieutenant, i. 527.
——— The religious empresse hir deuout acts and deeds, i 531
——— Hir loue to London and Colchester, hir death and buriall, i 534
Helie king of Britaine his acts and deeds, i 463
Hell kettels or the diuels kettle, three little pooles, so named, i 219
Hemecus K of Ireland, v. 36.
Hemuite, i 402
Hengist purposed at the first to make conquest of Britons, his offers misliked of British nobles, prolonged time to giue battell, v 144, 142
——— He and Horsus reteind in seruice with Uortigerne, v 139
——— ¶ Sée Yorke
——— He and his Saxons arriue in Britaine and purpose a uniuersall conquest, i 11
——— Began the first kingdome of the seuen in Kent, i 28
——— Thirsting for the whole kingdome of South he was banished, i 202
Henninus ¶ Sée Duke,
Henrie the first what kind of beasts he cherished to fight withall & and to hunt, i 380.

Henrie the first when he began his reigne, vol. ii page 47.
——— Glad to seeke his peoples fauour and whie, ii 48
——— Woone the fauour of the people from his brother Richard, ii 47.
——— His wiues concubine and children, his uertues and vices, ii 76, 77.
——— In danger of drowning, ii. 75.
——— His promises to purchase the peoples fauour, ii 47.
——— Reconciled with his brethren Robert and William, ii 31
——— Besieged by his two brethren Robert and William, ib.
——— His base sonne to whome maried, ii 63
——— Passeth ouer into Normandie and taketh diuerse cities, ii. 55.
——— Persuaded to renounce his title to the inuestiture of prelats, ii 54
——— Consulted with his nobles where to get him a wife, ii. 48
——— Hurt in battell against the French king, his valiantnesse, ii 68
——— Against the consecration of archbishop Thurstane of Yorke, ii 69
——— He and pope Calixtus come to an interuiew at Gisors, ii 68
——— Passeth ouer into Normandie to aid and assist the erle of Champaigne against the French king, ii 67.
——— Placeth garisons in Wales, ii 61
——— He, and pope Innocent méet at Chartres, ii 75
——— His sonnes and daughters drowned by shipwracke, ii. 70
——— Without issue, he marieth againe, ib.
——— Goeth ouer into Normandie and createth his sonne William duke, ii 64.
——— His passage into Normandie and neuer returneth aliue, ii. 75.
——— Departeth this life of a surfet, ii 76
Henrie the second defaced castells and holds in England, i. 327
——— Crowned king, where and by whome, iii 111
——— Offended with the bishops, ii. 119.
——— Knighted the king of Scots, ii. 130
——— Inuaded the earle of Aluergnes land, ii. 128.
——— Invadeth Wales, ii 125.
——— He and the French king have an interuiew at Corcée, ii 118.
——— His & Thomas Beckets first falling out, ii. 116, 117
——— He and the French king meet at Gisors, ii. 163
——— He and his sonnes are accorded vpon conditions, ii 162.
Henrie the second returneth out of Normandie, vol ii. page 160
——— His offer to his sonnes, ii 153
——— Knoweth not whome he mayt trust, ii. 149
——— Purgeth himself of Beckets death, ii 143
——— Seeketh to appease the quarrel betwixt his sonnes, ii 183.
——— Passeth into Normandie he and his sonnes reconciled, ii 182
——— He and the French king come to an interuiew at Vadum S remigij, ii 181
——— Riddeth all night to meet the French king at Douer, ii 103.
——— He and the French king meet at Yurie, ii 176.
——— His sonnes wife is brought to bed of a sonne ii 175
——— Against the Scots, ii 113.
——— Goeth into the north, ii 112
——— Negligent in aiding the Christians against the Saracens, ii 200.
——— Not so fauourable to the church as he might haue been, ib
——— His vices, ib
——— His sonnes and daughters, his base sonnes, the constitution of his bodie, his stature, his qualities of mind and bodie, ii. 199.
——— He and the French king at strife they talk together, ii 186.
——— His words of displeasure to his sonne erle Richard, ii. 197
——— He and the French king come to a treatie of peace, ii. 195
——— Inuadeth France and maketh waste and spoiles, ib
——— He and the French kings interuiew betwixt Trie and Gisors, ii 192.
——— Passeth into Normandie to talke with French king, ii 191.
——— His subiects arrested in France, ib
——— Nothing sorie for the death of Hugh Lacie, ii 190.
——— He and the patriarch passe ouer into France, ii. 189
——— Message to his sonne earl Richard, ib.
——— His gift to Hugh Lacie, ii 141.
——— Sorie for Thomas Beckets death, ii 137.
——— Laieth his crown on the altar, ii. 114.
——— Landeth in Ireland, and what he doeth there, ii 139
——— Becommeth seruitor to his sonne, ib
——— Made his last will, ii 131
——— His sonne crowned at seuenteene years old, ii 130
——— He and the French kings interuiew at Gisors, ii 127.
——— Whie called Sportmantell, iii. 198.

Henry the second sickeneth and dieth, vol iii page 193
——— His dead bodie laie naked a long time, ib.
——— His epitaphs, ii 201
Henrie King the second, receiueth Dermon Macmorough to his protection, vi 122
——— Proclameth libertie to all his subiects to aid him, ib
——— He taketh his oth for his allegiance, ib
——— He restreineth his licence, vi 148
——— He misliketh the erle strangebowes his successe, vi 149
——— He is sent for into England, vi 158
——— He meeteth the king and is reconciled, vi 159.
——— A composition betweene them, vi 158
——— The king arriueth into Ireland at Waterford, vi 159
——— Fitzstephens is presented vnto him, vi 158
——— He receiueth submission of all the kings, vi 160
——— He feasteth them all, vi 162
——— He commandeth a synod to be kept at Cashill, vi 163
——— He practiseth to weaken the erle, vi 165
——— His own sonnes conspire against him, ib
——— He returneth into England, vi 166
——— He appointeth gouernors ouer the land, ib
——— He arriueth into Wales, ib.
——— He is reconciled to the pope, vi 167
——— A vision appeareth vnto him, vi 168
——— A dissention betweene him and his sonnes, vi 174
——— He sendeth for his garrisons into Ireland, ib
——— His victories, ib.
——— The description of him, vi 175
——— His excellent gifts and qualities, vi 176
——— His loose life with Rosamunda, vi 178
——— He sendeth to the popes Alexander and Adrian for confirmation of his priuiledges, vi 185
——— His saieng concerning the conquest of Ireland, vi 195
——— He giueth the kingdome of Corke betweene Robert Fitzstephen, & Miles Cogan, vol vi page 204.
Henry King the second, giueth with Mounster to Philip de Bruse, ib
——— He sendeth his sonne Iohn into Ireland, vi 211
——— His answer to the patriarch of Ierusalem, vi 213.
——— His sonne Richard resisteth against him, vi 215
——— The variance betweene him and the French king, vi 214
Henrie the third borne at Winchester, ii 297.
——— The beginning of his reigne, ii. 340
——— His coronation and anointing, ii. 341.
——— The presumptuous proceedings against him, ii 454
——— Asketh counsell how to proceed in his warres against the French king, ii 402.
——— Maketh hard shift for monie, to hire soldiors to assist him, he remooueth towards Windsore, commeth to Stratford, ii 471, 472
——— Laie at Cambridge, ii 471
——— He and the lord wardens of the cinque ports reconciled, ii 469
——— The barons that rose against, their cheefe capteins, ii 456
——— Irided by his too half brethren, he incampeth at Lewes, the barons send him letters, his answer, he defieth them, the battell betweene them, ii 461, 462
——— The scholers of Oxford fight against him, ii 461
——— His potestation against the articles at Oxford, ii 458
——— Licenced to passe ouer into France, ii 455
——— Hee falleth sicke of a feuer quartane, ib
——— In his time manie gouernors ouer the land pernicious to the commonwealth, ii. 454
——— Asketh licence to pass ouer the sea, ii 452
——— Saileth into France, compoundeth all differences with the French king, ib.
——— Sore sicke and in despaire of life, ii 359.
——— His charges and wastfull expenses, ii 411
——— Passeth himselfe into Wales, ii 410
——— Lacketh monie, ii 439
——— Assaieth to get monie of the lords temperall, ii 426
——— Maketh great shift for monie to send vnto the pope, and sendeth the pope a warrant to take it vp, ii 433
——— His charges to Gascoigne, ii. 432.
——— Demandeth a subsidie, ii. 431.

Henrie the third offended with them that refused to helpe him with monie, vol ii page 431
———— His dets three hundred thousand marks, ii. 435
———— Purposeth to go himself into Gascoigne taketh the sea arriueth at Burdeaux, ii 429
———— Inuadeth Wales buildeth a castell at Gannoke, ii 410
———— Returneth out of Wales, ib
———— Flat against the pope his demands and decrees, his proclamation inhibiting monie to be sent to the pope, ii 412, 413
———— His half brethren come to see him, ii 414
———— Being in solemne procession at Paules note, ii 415
———— Disgraced by his nobles in a solemne parlement, ib.
———— His eldest sonne created duke of Aquitaine, ii 425
———— Goeth into Wales with an armie, ii 391
———— Rather hindered than helped by the countesse of Bierne, ii 397, 398
———— Spareth to set himself out of debt, ii 418
———— Driuen to sell his plate for lack of monie, ii 416
———— Procureth an inhibition to the pope, ii 418
———— His mother departeth this life, ii 413
———— Taketh vpon him the crosse, ii 418.
———— Highlie offended with the bishops, ii 426
———— Euill spoken of, ii 299
———— Passeth ouer into France against the French king, ii 396
———— His sundrie meanes of impositions to gather monie note, ib
———— His halfe brethren depart the realme, ii 416, 417.
———— They are pursued, and send to the French king for safe conduct, ii 417
———— His seuere sentence against a bribe taking iustice, iii 421
———— Goeth with an armie towards Scotland, ii 404
———— He and the king of Scots made friends, ib
———— Lieth in wait for mens goods, ii. 437
———— Fauoureth not the citie of London, ii 473
———— Put to flight
———— ¶ See London
———— Returneth into England through France, ii 432
———— Goeth ouer vnto the French king, ii. 439
———— Like to haue been destroied at Woodstocke in his bed note, ii 385
Henry the third crowned the second time and white, vol ii page 349
———— His mariage, ii 379
———— Entreth into Wales with an armie, hath but sorie successe, returneth, ii 375
———— Goeth against the Welchmen but with ill successe, ii 369
———— Gathereth monie towards his iournie into France, ii 365
———— Saileth ouer into France, he taketh diuerse townes and castells, getteth the victorie, saileth home into Britaine, his owne realme, ii 365, 366
———— Prepareth to passe ouer into France, ii 365
———— Is constreined to agree with the Welshmen, ii 363
———— In fauour with Normans and Poictouins, ib
———— His grant to his brother, ii 361
———— Glad to appoint a date of treatie for pacification betwéene him and his nobles, ib
———— And wherefore he would not admit Walter de Hamelsham archbishop of Canturburie, ii 362
———— Will in no wise bind and endanger his late fée to the church of Rome, ii 360
———— Demandeth restitution of parcels of inheritance belonging to the crowne, ii 355
———— Purchaseth a bull of the pope for his sufficiencie to gouerne, ii 351
———— Deposeth all the magistrats of the citie of London, ii 353
———— His summons to raise him an armie, the capteine of the same, ii. 345
———— He requireth restitution of his right of the French king, ii 351
———— Put in full possession of the realme, ii 348
———— Sickeneth, ii 417
———— Extreme sicke his death, buriall, issue, proportion of bodie, conditions good and bad, ii 476, 477
Henrie the fourth king of England crowned, v 403.
———— Inuadeth Scotland, v 404
Henrie the fourth duke of Lancaster, proclamed king, ii 867
Henrie Plantagenet his stile or title, the beginning of his reigne, iii. 1
———— His coronation, ib
———— His title to the crowne, iii 3
———— Meant to haue made a iournie against the infidels he is vexed with sicknesse, iii 57.
———— Of an apoplexie, his death, buriall, issue, stature, &c iii 57, 58
———— His suspicious gelousie towards his sonne prince of Wales, iii 53
———— Taketh vpon him to defend the Orleanciall faction, ib
———— The faction of Orleance sue to him for aid, iii 51.

Henrie the fourth Plantagenet articles of couenants which they offered him, the conditions which they requested of him, vol iii page 51
——— A fauourer of the clergie, iii 48
——— In danger to be taken by the French pirats, iii 39
——— His comming to Berwike, he preuaileth against the Scots, he passeth into Wales, looseth his cariages, returneth, ib
——— Wanteth monie & can get none of the lords, iii 33
——— Goeth to Yorke, iii 26
——— Charged with periurie, his answer to the messengers that brought the lords articles, he offereth pardon to his aduersaries, his manhood against them, iii 25, 26
——— His answer to the Persies libell, his speedie diligence against his enimies, he troubleth them with his sudden comming, iii 23
——— In armes against the Welshmen, he looseth his labour, iii. 20
——— His suspicion grounded vpon a guiltie conscience, his daughter maried into Germanie, ib
——— In danger to be destroied in his bed note, iii 18
——— Inuadeth Scotland, maketh great wast, iii 16, 17
——— Causeth Richard the second to be put to a violent death, iii 13.
——— Commeth to the Towre of London, the lords make towards the citie against him, he goeth foorth against them, iii 11
——— A plot laid for his destruction at a solemne iusts, iii 10
——— In his time intaileth the crowne, iii 9
——— Suspected not to be well affected towards the church before his cōming to the crowne, iii 4
——— His funerals kept at Canturburie, iii 62
Henrie the fift, his title, the beginning of his reigne, his coronation daie uerie tempestuous, he altereth his life and manners, iii 61, 62
——— His iustice in a progresse, iii. 126
——— The king of Scots in his armie, iii 121.
——— The duke of Burier cōmeth to him with a number of horssemen, he and Monsieur Bauhason, fight hand to hand, iii 122
——— The bishop of Winchester lendeth him 20000 pounds, iii 128
——— He saileth into France againe, the Scottish king serueth him, he pursueth Dolphin, iii 128
——— Returneth into England with his new wife, iii 125
——— Receiued into Paris, iii 123.
Henrie the fift taketh upon him the office of regent of France, vol iii page 124.
——— He and the French king at peace, the articles of the same, iii. 112, 113, 114
——— The effects of his oration to the French king, iii 119
——— Condescended to a treatie of peace with the French king, iii 112
——— Commeth to Trois to the French king, affieth the French king's daughter, iii 113.
——— Plaieth the porters part, iii 109
——— Accursed, his enimies deliuered into his hand, executed, his entrance into Rone, his behauior and others, a league betweene him and the duke of Britaine, remaineth at Rone sendeth his capteins abrode to subdue castells and townes, he remooueth to Uernon, iii 105, 106
——— A rare and woorthie example of equitie in him, iii 92
——— His iustice and charitie, iii 102
——— His wise answer to a presumptuous French orator, iii 104
——— Aided by the king of Portingale, iii 101
——— Towns in Normandie yeelded vnto him, iii 195
——— His exploits in France, his victories and surrenders to him, iii 93, 94, 95, 96, 97, 98, 99
——— Arriueth in Normandie, how he preuailed against his enimies, and taketh castels and townes, iii 89
——— His roiall modestie note, iii 84
——— Wise and valiant challenge, an example in him what is to be doone after victorie, iii 82
——— His valiantnesse in sleing the duke of Alanson, iii 81.
——— His campe robbed, ib
——— His policie against the French horssemen, his oration to his men, his wish and noble courage, iii 79
——— Passeth the riuer of Some with his host, the number of his armie, his iustice in warre, his answer to the French kings defiance, he rideth footh to take view of the French armie, iii 76, 77
——— His standard recouered from the French, iii 75
——— Saileth ouer to France with his host, iii 72
——— His charitable proclamation, his besieging of Harflur, iii 72
——— He taketh and sacketh it, his mercifull dealing with the French prisoners, iii 73, 74
——— His words to certeine traitors of the nobilitie, iii 70
——— Wise answer to the archbishop of Burgesse, iii 69
——— His policie in the time of a comotion, iii 63
——— His roiall port he falleth sicke, iii 132.

Henrie the fift is brought sicke to Bois de Uincennes, vol iii page 132
—— His aduice vpon his death bed, his decease, his commendation in diuerse respects, iii 752
—— Swift of foot, i 380
—— Hunted fallow deere on foot, ib
—— Taketh the prince of Scotland ouer with him into France, v 413
—— Menaceth the Scots, marieth the French kings daughter, v 412
—— Discomfited by the Welshmen, v 411.
—— Returneth into England, v 448
—— By safe conduct commeth into England, v 416.
—— Imprisoned, v 448
—— The manner of his buriall. iii 134.
Henrie the sixt borne, iii 129
—— Crowned in Paris, iii 173.
—— His coronation at Westminster, iii 167
—— The beginning of his reigne, iii 136
—— Goeth against Kentish rebels with a power, iii 221
—— The manner of his buriall, a discription of his person, his cannonization to be a saint laboured for, his qualitie, iii 624, 625
—— Sheweth himselfe to the Londoners, he is deliuered up to the hands of Edward the fourth his enimie, iii 310
—— Fetcht out of the Towre and restored to his regiment, iii 300
—— His saieng concerning Henrie of Richmond, after king Henrie the seuenth, iii 302
—— Commended by the earle of Warwike note, iii 289
—— Assembleth an armie against Edward the fourth and his adherents, iii 276.
—— His power exceeded king Edwards, iii 278
—— His part discomfited, he withdraweth to Berwike, ib
—— Maketh a solemne feast at the reconcilement of the nobles that were at strife note, created dukes and knights, iii 155
—— In person goeth with an armie into France, iii 172.
—— Returneth out of France into England, iii 176
—— His receiuing into Excester, the clergie there against him, iii 229.
—— Practises to put him beside the crowne letters interchangeable, betwixt him and the usurper, ii 229, 230, 231, 232, 233
—— In armes against the duke of Yorke, his answer to the dukes letters, iii 239
—— The armies ioine, the kings part vanquished, iii 240, 241
—— Part discomfited, he is taken, iii 260
—— Articles of peace and agreement betweene him and the duke of Yorke, iii 265
Henrie the sixt, letters kept from him of purpose, vol iii page 210
—— He to reigne in name, but not in rule, he to reuoke certeine grants agreed vpon note, iii 212
—— His power discomfited, flie, ii 270
—— Raiseth an armie against the duke of Yorke, iii 252
—— Present in habit roiall at a solemne procession in Paules, iii 249
—— Flieth, iii 281
—— He is taken and laid vp in hold, iii 282.
—— Set up againe as king, iii 389.
—— Sicke, iii 238
—— Murthered in the Towre, iii 324
—— And by whome, iii 562
Henrie the sixt crowned Henrie Beauchampe king of Wight and Iardseie, i 56
Henrie the seuenth what kind of dogs he commanded to be hanged, i 388
—— His three notable piles peerelesse within Europe, i 251
—— His birth, age descent, bringing vp, and port that he bare, and king Henrie the sixt his saieng concerning him, iii 302
—— One of the bloud of Henrie the sixt, his life and greefe to Edward the fourth, iii. 312, 313
—— His wife the ladie Elizabeth when borne, iii 285
—— Crowned by the lord Stanlie in the field, iii 446
—— Dooth some honor to Richard the third after his death, in respect of his buriall, iii 417
—— Banisheth all Flemish ware out of his dominions, iii 507
—— He and Maximilian agree to plague the Frenchmen, iii 501
—— Desireth the king of Castile to haue Edmund erle of Suffolke deliuered into his hands, iii 531
—— His progresse into Lancashire, iii. 510.
—— Wanted policie, iii 528
—— His chapels at Westminster built, iii 529
—— His policie against sir Robert Clifford, iii 508
—— He is in a quandarie, iii 509
—— Purposeth warres against France and openeth the iust cause in parlement, iii. 496
—— Sendeth espials into Flanders for a subtill policie iii 507
—— He and the queene dined at sargeants feasts kept at Elie house, iii 509
—— Request a prest of six thousand marks and goeth into the north, iii. 482, 483
—— Maketh out a power against Perkin Warbecke, iii 518

Henrie the seuenth, his gratious pardon to a great number of miserable rebels, vol. iii. page 519.
—— Couetous in his old age, iii. 531.
—— Saileth to Calis, he and the duke of Burgogne méet at saint Péeters church without the towne, iii. 525.
—— Is loth that the French king should marrie the duchesse of Britaine, iii. 495.
—— Sendeth the lord Daubnie and the lord Morleie against the French, iii. 494.
—— Borroweth a great summe of monie of the chamber of London, iii. 493.
—— Sendeth foorth his armie against the French king, iii. 492.
—— His returne, out of the north countrie, his offer to make an atonement betwixt the French king and the duke of Britaine, his loué to quéene Elizabeth, iii. 489, 490.
—— Assembleth an armie, his power soone increased, iii. 487.
—— His incounter with the conspitors he ouercometh, ib.
—— All the capteines against him slaine, he giueth thanks to God after the victorie, iii. 487, 489.
—— Commeth to London, he is crowned king, iii. 479, 480.
—— He aduanceth his fréends, redeemeth his hostages, performeth his promise touching the mariage of Edward the fourths daughter, iii. 480, 481, 482.
—— His decease, what children he had, he is described, his qualities roiall, his sepulture, executors of his last will, iii. 541, 542.
—— Roiallie buried, a description of the whole pompe: note, iii. 546.
Henrie the eight séeketh to kéepe the duke of Albanie out of Scotland, v. 491.
—— Doubteth to haue the duke of Albanie gouernor to the young king his nephew, v. 493.
—— The most prouident prince that euer reigned in England: note, i. 327.
—— His seuere executing of idle people by thousands at once, i. 314.
—— In building not inferior to Abrian or Iustunian, i. 228.
—— His answer to certeine sutors for college lands, i. 256.
—— Duke of Yorke and afterwards king, his birth, iii. 504.
—— Proclamed king, his councellors and riches, iii. 544.
—— His coronation with the pompe thereof, iii. 547, 548.
—— Good at tennise plaie, iii. 561.
—— He and the duke of Suffolke defenders at tilt against all commers, he receiueth a cap of maintenance from pope Iulie, iii. 600.
—— A notable good horsseman, iii. 612.
Henrie the eight rideth westward in progresse, vol. iii. page 612.
—— Sendeth for the quéene of Scots & her husband to his court, iii. 614.
—— Buildeth a castell at Tornaie, iii. 615.
—— Sitteth in the starchamber in iudgement, iii. 640.
—— Intituled defender of the faith, he writeth against Luther, at variance with the king of France, iii. 675.
—— His minions remooued out of the court, iii. 640.
—— Glad of the French kings deliuerie out of prison, iii. 706.
—— Procurer of his libertie, iii. 707.
—— Alledged by the French king as a president of humanitie in case of a captiuated king, iii. 708.
—— Borroweth 20000 pounds of the citie of London, iii. 678.
—— Receiueth a golden rose for a present from pope Clement, iii. 695.
—— What mooued him gratiouslie to receiue the ladie regents ambassadors of France, iii. 700.
—— Passeth ouer to Calis, an interuiew betwéene him and the French king, iii. 776.
—— His base sonne made erle and duke in one daie, iii. 710.
—— Sworne to performe the league concluded, iii. 712.
—— His articles for the reforming of religion, iii. 798.
—— His supremasie confirmed, iii. 792.
—— Proclamed K. of Ireland, iii. 823.
—— Taketh a lone of monie, iii. 826.
—— His munificence to the erle of Angus archbishop of S. Andrews his dedlie fo, iii. 831.
—— Sent a power ouer against the French king, iii. 832.
—— His message to the lord Greie by sir Thomas Palmer: note, iii. 860.
—— Passeth the seas to Bullen, iii. 839.
—— Entreth into the towne, returneth to England, iii. 841.
—— Goeth in progress into Yorkshire, gifts giuen him, iii. 822.
—— A good archer and full of actiuenesse: note, iii. 550.
—— Brake more staues at iusts than the rest and had the prise giuen him, iii. 562.
—— Runneth at tilt, diuerse pastimes wherein he was a principall actor, he runneth at the ring, iii. 554, 555, 556.
—— Forced to take armes against the Scots, iii. 827.
—— Magnificent and munificent to the French kings ambassadors, iii. 632, 633, 634.

Henrie the eight purposeth in person to passe the seas to see the French king his brother, vol iii. page 610
——— Receiueth the order of S Michaell, iii. 721.
——— He commeth to Westminster hall, and there sitteth in iudgement himself vpon the riots of ill Maie daie, his gratious and generall pardon, he and the duke of Suffolke run at iusts, iii. 624, 625
——— Riding to Portsmouth, appointeth capteins ouer his ships, iii 572
——— His nauie setteth out cōcluded in parlement that he should personallie inuade France, ib
——— Taketh the popes part against the French king, iii 566
——— He and French K their interuiewe in the vale of Andren, they two make challenge to all commers at iusts, his sumptuous furniture at the said iusts, iii 649, 650
——— He runneth against monseiur Grandeuill, the partners of his challenge, iii 651
——— His band of men with their deuise on their apparell, his interteinment of the French quéene, iii. 652, 653
——— He departeth from Guisnes to Calis, and from thense to Graueling to visit the emperor, his statlie maske, himselfe a speciall actor, iii 655
——— He returneth into England, iii 656
——— In person passeth ouer to France, iii 577
——— The order of his armie, ib
——— Incampeth at Arkes, commeth to the siege, iii 579
——— His power vnited with the emperor Maximilian his soldiors against Terwine note, iii 583, 584
——— Entreth into Terwine, the citizens are sworn vnto him, marcheth on with his armie to Fornaie, goeth to Isle to visit the yoong prince of Castile, iii 586
——— His pompe and port, iii 586, 587
——— Make certeine gentlemen knights for their good militarie seruice, iii 590
——— Falslie reported to be dead, he and his traine ignorant of the waie to his campe by means of a mist, he besiegeth Torraie, returneth to England, iii. 587, 588, 591
——— Méeteth the emperor Maximilian, his harnesse and furniture, his spéech to a Scotish herald, his answer to the Scotish kings letter, iii 581, 582
——— Intituled Christianissimo by the pope, iii 601.
——— His gift to the citie of London. note, iii 861.
——— First named supreme head, iii 766.
Henrie the eight and what there vpon followed, his voluntarie inclination to pardon the premunire of the clergie, vol iii page 766
——— His mariage in question, & how determined by diuerse vniuersities, iii 766, 767.
——— His oration in the parlement house note, iii 831
——— He and his quéen at Hauering in the Bowre, iii 640
——— Setteth forward into France, he and the emperor Charles méet at Douer castell, kéepe their whitsuntide at Canturburie, iii. 645, 646
——— Landeth at Calis lodgeth in his palace at Guisnes, ib
——— His affablenesse with his yoong courtiers made them too saucie and bold note, iii 639
——— Thankfulnes to his militarie seruitors, iii 599
——— The portion intended to be giuen with his daughter Marie in mariage, iii 636
——— His mariage by cōsent of all vniuersities iudged vnlawfull, iii. 747
——— His marriage with his brothers wife in question, iii 719
——— Is desirous to be resolued by the opinions of the lerned touching his mariage, iii 736
——— Confesseth that the sting of conscience made him mislike of the mariage, iii. 738.
——— Submitteth himselfe to the censures of the learned, mistrusteth the legats of seeking delaies, his affection to the ladie Anne Bullen, iii 738, 739
——— Marieth the ladie Anne Bullen, iii 777
——— Marieth the ladie Iane Seimor, iii 797
——— Commeth to see the ladie Anne Cleeue at Rochester, iii 811.
——— Welcometh hir to Greenwich, iii 814
——— He marieth hir, ib
——— His mariage with the ladie Anne of Cleeue iudged vnlawfull, iii 818
——— Marieth the ladie Katharine Par, iii 832
——— Maketh his last will and testament, his executors, iii 862
——— Deceaseth, described, commended, ib
Henrie the prince, his disorder of life, ii 131
——— Seeketh to seize vpon the gouernment out of his fathers hands, ii 148
——— New practises to put his father beside the crowne, ii 171
——— Falleth sicke, ii 181
——— He sendeth to his father, his repentance before his deth, his deth and buriall, ii 184 185

Henrie the prince accused to his father, vol. iii. page 53.
———— Goeth to the court with a gret train, his strange apparell, his comming to the kings presence, they woords they both vsed, his request to haue his accusors answer their wrongfull accusations, iii. 53, 54.
———— Taketh awaie the crowne before his father was dead, he is blamed of his father the king, his answer, iii. 57.
Henrie the first sonne to Henrie the eight deceaseth, iii. 61.
Henrie Beauclerke King of England, v. 235.
Henrie duke of Bauier, vi. 122.
Henrie the emperour his euill successe, vi. 124.
Henrie prince of Scotland deceaseth, v. 290.
———— His issue, ib.
Henrie inuadeth Scotland, v. 307.
Henrie Hotspur, v. 397.
———— Assaileth the Scots at Homildon, v. 405.
Henrie Fitzroie K. Henrie the eights base sonne: note, iii. 710.
Henrie the empresse hir sonne lord Henrie came into England to see his mother, ii. 95.
———— Knighted in England, ii. 99.
———— Marrieth the duchesse of Aquitain, ii. 100.
———— Returneth into England, he beseigeth Malmsburie castell and is forced to raise his seige, ii. 102.
Henrie sonne to the earle of Cornwall, and king of Almaigne murthered, ii. 475.
Henrie the emperour dead at Utrecht, ii. 72.
Henrie grace de Dieu, a gret ship otherwise called the gret Henrie, iii. 573.
Hepborne Iames his familiaritie with the Q. of Scots, mother to Iames the third, v. 448.
Hepborus their first aduancement, v. 399.
Heptarchie. ¶ Sée Britaine, & Kings seuen.
Heraclianus, is sent against Uictorine, v. 124.
———— ¶ Sée Uictorius.
Heraclius patriarch of Ierusalem, ii. 187.
———— Seeketh aid, vi. 213.
Herald at armes words from the Scotish king to Henrie the eight, and how courteouslie vsed, iii. 581. 582.
———— Of Scotland richlie rewarded of king Henrie the eight, iii. 583.
———— From the King of England and France to the emperour, the speeches and behaviors, iii. 722, 723.
———— Defiance intimated, iii. 727.
———— Killed and the déed doer executed as a traitor, iii. 832.
———— Not suffered to enter into France: note, ib.
———— Scotish his message to the duke of Summerset, iii. 874.
———— English his intimation to the Edenburghers, iii. 353, 354.
———— His office and how the French king rewarded an English herald giuing him defiance, vol. iii. page 831.
Herald of Scotland insufficient from the French king to the king of England, & his speech, iii. 338.
———— Well rewarded at Henrie the fourths hands, iii. 16.
———— At armes sent into Scotland to denounce warre, v. 498.
———— Sent to the queene of Scots, v. 598.
———— Being an Englishman his report of King Robert Bruses valiancie, v. 360, 361.
———— Slaine, ii. 758.
Herbert king of Britaine sent ambassadors to K. Gregorie, v. 221.
Herbert Francis of Dublin sent to the king, vi. 294.
———— He is dubbed knight, ib.
———— The king giueth him Eustace of Balmcolins lands, ib.
———— He returneth with comfortable letters of the kings, vi. 296.
Herbert bishop of Thetford whie depriued of his bishops staffe, ii. 35.
———— He came to it by simonie, ii. 44.
Herbert knight of gret power among the Welsh: note, iii. 434.
Herbs, Fruits &c. ¶ Sée Gardens.
Hercules passage out of Spain by the Celts to go ouer into Italie, i. 7.
———— He marieth the daughter of king Lucius, ib.
———— Whether he came into Britaine after the death of Albion, i. 8.
———— He killeth Albion and his brother Bergion, i. 7.
———— Sundrie monuments in memorie of him, i. 8.
———— His being in Britaine proued, i. 432.
———— Whie he pursued & slue his cousins Albion and Bergion, ib.
Herdulit threteneth the Scots, v. 219.
———— Assembleth his men togither, remaineth in campe, ib.
Here long how it was to be worne, ii. 52.
———— In the court redressed, ii. 72.
———— The abuse thereof, ii. 78.
Hereford. ¶ Sée Erle.
Hereford castell deliuered vnto Lewis the French king his sonne, ii. 342.
———— Bishoprikes erection circuit and valuation, i. 239.
Hereford and Monmouthshire, betweene which Monbecke riuer is the march, i. 125.
Heremit of Pomfret or Wakefield his prophesie to king Iohn: note, ii. 311.
Heremits and moonkes only allowed of in Britaine, i. 46.
Heresie to veritie as poison to the bodie, i. 609.
———— Of Pelagius spred in Britaine, i. 562.

Heresie pelagian, vol v page 131.
——— In Pictland, v 164
——— And monasticall life brought into Britaine at one time by Pelagius, 1 45
Heretikes how punished, 1 311.
——— One burned at Norwich and what opinion he held, iv 405, 507.
Hereward partaker with the English rebels against duke William, 1 16
Hericius ¶ Sée Hirke
Herlowin a noble man in Normandie husband to William conquerors mother, ii 33.
Hermon killeth his brother Hiberus, vi 78
——— He nameth the land Ireland, ib
——— He diuideth the land into fiue kingdomes, ib
Hermophrodite buried quicke note, v 445
Heries lord his lands spoiled, v 138
——— And he hanged, ib
Hertfort castell built, 1. 679
Hertfordshire men sworne vnto Richard the second, ii 750
Herue de monte Morisco arriueth into Ireland, vi 128
——— Is endowed with two cantreds of lands, vi 129
——— He was vncle and spie to the erle, vi 128
——— His oration, vi 144
——— His opinion well liked, vi 145
——— The description of him, vi 162
——— He professeth himselfe a monke of Canturburie, vi 206
Herne George his seruice vpon Onele, vi 334
——— He returneth by land to Dublin, vi. 335.
——— He passeth in great perils, ib
Hessen ¶ Sée Rhene.
Hegebald a noble man of the Westsaxons, slaine in battell, 1 699.
Hiber returneth into Spaine, and succeedeth his father, v 36
——— A conqueror, ib
Hibernia of whom so named, v 35.
Hide of land is an hundred acres, 1 711
Hide or hideland somewhere vsed in England, and somwhere not, 1. 53
——— What it is, 1 545
Highwaies foure made sometimes in Britaine by princes thereof, 1. 189
——— Incroached vpon by the erecting of tenements, 1 189
——— That are common, all seene vnto, 1 191
——— Greatlie incroched vpon within these twentie yéeres, 1 192.
Highwaies foure finished by Beline, that his father begun, 1 453
——— Priuilged, ib
——— ¶ Sée Waies, Thorowfares, and Townes.
Hisknell street ¶ Sée highwaies.
Hildelitha a nun ¶ Sée Erkenwald.
Hilliard mans salutation, and whie so named, vol v. page 312
Hildes and abbesse note, 1 623
——— Abbesse of Whitbie, she dieth, a description of certeine of hir actions, 1 632.
Hils in England great store, 1 184
——— Westward whereon in faire wether one may see the clouds gather togither in a certeine thicknesse, 1 217
——— Alps or Snowdonie hils famous as the alps beyond sea, 1 136.
Hinds haue béene milked, 1 281
Hinke the sonne of one Harold king of Northumbers, 1 191
Hirelda nephew to Cassibelane, 1 476
Histories not be made to sauour of lies, 1. 564.
——— Use of histories, the definition of a historie, Epist.
Historie writers blamed, ii 193, 194.
Hiues ¶ Sée Home
Hoddom yeelded to the regent, v 654
Hoker John, the supplier of the Irish historie, Epistola, he translateth Cambrensis, Epistola
——— He is a burgesse of the parlement, and his speeches in the same, vi 341
——— His perils for the same, vi 345
——— He giueth and writeth out the orders of the parlement, ib
——— He was agent in all sir Peter Carews causes, vi 310
Holds ¶ Sée Castells
Holie land otherwise called Palestine, ii. 207.
——— In danger ii 181
——— Whereto Richard the first goeth like a pilgrime, ii 213.
——— Aid granted to the people thereof, ii 193
——— ¶ See Ierusalem and Saracens
Holie maid of Kent ¶ Sée Elisabeth Barton
Holiburton Iames defendeth the countrie against the English, v 555.
Holie rood house, builded, v 288
Holidaies verie manie vnder the pope reduced now to seuen and twentie in England, 1 233
——— Necessarie to be remoued quite and cleane from the church, ib
Holland in Lincolnshire spoiled and made tributarie vnto the French, ii 333
Holland beyond seas commended, iv 643
Holland knight killeth the lord Stafford, ii. 766
——— Made erle of Huntington, ii 797.
Holland Robert lord iustice of Chester, vi 244
——— He receiueth a writ to apprehend the Templers, ib
Holland petit capteine to Salisburie, vi 300
——— He falleth into a pipe of feathers, ib
——— His valiant seruice, ib
Hollanders & the erle of March at warre, v 424
——— Their ships taken, v 165.
Hollocke countie his secretarie hanged, iv 654.
Homage doone to king Henrie the second by his sonnes, ii 162, 163

Homage of a thousand pounds yearelie, vol. ii. page 150.
——— Doone vnto king Henrie the third by the archbishop of Rone, ii. 417.
——— By the erle of Sauoie, ii. 412.
——— Of rebels to a forren prince intruding himselfe vpon the crowne of England, ii. 331.
——— Of K. Henrie the second vnto the French king, ii. 186.
——— Of king Iohn to the French king, ii. 279.
——— By king Edward the first vnto the French king, ii. 489.
——— Of the Scotish king, &c. vnto the kings of England, ii. 118, 164, 165, 281, 423, 439, 500, 601; iii. 139.
——— Of the Scotish lords vnto king Edward the first, with words of his accepting it: note, ii. 519.
——— Of the nobles of Scotland vnto king Edward the first set downe in expresse words: note, ii. 496.
——— ¶ Sée erle of Malcolme, Flanders, and Scots.
——— Required by summons, v. 291.
——— Of the Scotish kings for certeine erledoms: note, v. 289.
——— Doone by the king of Scots, v. 290.
——— Doone to the king of England, by the king, prelats, and nobles of Scotland, v. 298, 299.
——— To king Edward of Carnaruan, v. 342.
——— Of the barons of Scotland to king Edward, v. 330.
——— ¶ Sée Balioll.
Homilies when and where instituted to be read in churches, iii. 867.
——— Commanded to be had in churches, iii. 889.
Honie of England reputed the best, i. 384.
——— The néerer the bottom the better, ib.
Honie soit qui mal y pense, i. 272.
Honorius commended by Claudianus for deeds doone in Britaine, i. 548.
——— His drift to recouer the empire that vtterlie fell, i. 539.
Honorius archbishop of Canturburie, i. 609.
——— He dieth, i. 619.
Honors change manners: note, ii. 130; iii. 61.
Hope vain of Eastangles, ib.
——— Vaine and frustrat, ii. 334.
Hops planting growne to be a great trade in England, i. 110, 111.
——— In times past plentifull in this land, i. 350.
Hora among the Grecians what it signifieth, i. 407.
Horgerius duke of Cornwall or Deuonshire and of his faire daughter: note, i. 695.
Hornets and wasps how ingendered, i. 384.
Horne. ¶ Sée Bishop.
Horrestians inhabitants of Angus & Merne, i. 510.
Horsus. ¶ Sée Hengist.
Horsse flesh powdered and serued in at a banket, iv. 200.
Horsse stealers, i. 313.
Horsse stealers ten hanged at once in Smithfield, vol. iv. page 509.
Horsse more unfortunate than ten of Seians Colts, i. 134.
Horsses in England of sundrie sorts, i. 371.
——— Outlandish, ib.
——— ¶ Sée Inns.
Horrse coursers. ¶ Sée Ostlers, i. 370.
Horsses presented to Iames the fourth, v. 467.
——— Trapped and presented to Iames the fourth, v. 468.
——— Affrighted, v. 392.
Horsses and mares out of Hungarie into Scotland for brood, v. 424.
Horses in Ireland first out of Spaine, vi. 20, 21.
——— They are of sundrie kinds, ib.
Hose. ¶ Sée Apparell.
Hospitall of saint Leonards in Yorke whie and by whome founded, ii. 45.
Hospitals builded by archbishop Landfranke, ii. 30.
——— ¶ Sée Sawrie.
Hospitalitie of Richard the second: note, ii. 362.
——— Of a herdsman to bishop German how rewarded, i. 564.
——— Of the erle of Warwike: note, iii. 301.
——— Of the clergie bountifullie and thriftilie kept, i. 233.
——— In Dublin, vi. 23.
Hostages giuen to king Edward the second for his assurance of their loialties, vi. 247.
——— Deliuered for assurance of loialtie, i. 746.
——— Demanded by Cesar of the Britans, ib.
——— Giuen to Cesar by Anadrogeus, i. 476.
——— Required, deliuered to king Iohn, v. 304.
Hostages English threatened to lose their liues, ii. 255.
——— Executed for promise broken, iii. 158.
——— Of France had gret loue and liberalitie shewed them, ii. 678.
——— For the assurance of the French kings ransome, ii. 675.
——— Their number, ii. 676.
——— Deliuered by the Scotish lords on the kings side, iv. 244.
——— During the time of a parlee betweene enimies,
——— French for the deliuerance of Tornaie, &c. in heauinesse and sorrow courteouslie delt with and roiallie: note, iii. 635.
——— ¶ Sée Pledges.
Hounds of eight sorts, their names & games, i. 386.
——— ¶ Sée Dogs.
Houre and the originall of the worde, i. 406.
——— What portion of time, ib.
Houres vnequall or temporall, i. 405.
——— ¶ Sée Time.
Houres 24 of the daie and night, how Alured diuided for his necessarie vses, i. 675.

Houses ¶ Sée Building and Wood.
Howard sir Edmund fieshlie assaulted, vol. v. page 481
Howard knight lord admerall, iii 568
———— Goeth to Biskaie, his arriuall, ib.
———— Abused of the English soldiors, goeth to Britaine, burneth diuerse places, knighteth diuerse gentlemen, the lords of Britains request vnto him, iii 571, 572.
———— He would haue Henrie the eight present in person at the incounter and is rebuked, he cometh into the baie where as prior Iehan laie, iii 574, 575
———— Drowned, iii 575
Howard knight made lord admerall in his brothers roome, ii 576
———— Incountreth with the erles of Lenuex and Argile, iii 596
———— Atteinted of treason dieth prisoner, iii 798.
———— In the Towre, iii 805.
Howard lord gentle and fauourable to the ladie Elizabeth, iv 133
———— Priuie seale deceaseth, iv. 321.
———— ¶ Sée Erle of Surrie.
Howard Thomas arriueth lord lieutenant into Ireland, vi 278.
———— He is pledge for the erle of Kildare, vi. 283.
———— He resisteth the Mores, vi 279.
———— His good countenance to a poore souldior, ib.
———— Is sent for into England, ib
———— His commendation, ib.
Howell king of litle Britaine commeth ouer in aid of Arthur, against the Saxons, i 575
———— Besieged by Scots, i 576
Hubba saued from drowning, v. 215
Hubba a Danish capteine slaine, i 669.
———— ¶ Sée Agnerus
Hubert de Burgh assaileth the French fleet, ii. 347.
Hugh erle of Chester, his exploits against the Welshmen, ii 38.
———— Despaired of life, ii 47.
Hugh earle of Chester in the conquerors time, i 64
Hugh earle of Shrewsburie, in the conquerors time, ib
Hugh erle of Shrewsburie & Arundell his exploits, ii 38
———— Slaine by a rouer note, ib
Hugh a Norman, conspireth with the Danes, i 709
Huldorne capteine rebell executed, iii. 200.
Hull water a riuer, i 156.
———— Abounding with sturgeon and lampreie described, i 158
Humber described and what streames run there into, i 156
———— Wherevpon it was so named, i 157
Humber king of Scithia ouerthrowne in Britaine, i 117.
Humber king of Scithia, séeking to be monarch of Britaine is drowned in Humber, vol i page 157
Humber gulfe or riuer, why so named, i 441
———— A fatall place for the Britons to be vanquished in, v 161.
Hume Alexander deliuered out of prison, v. 645.
Hume lord chamberleine, v 481.
———— Submitteth himselfe, v 486
———— Denounced a rebell, ib
———— Taken, v 651.
———— He and others conuicted of treason, v. 486.
———— Arrested, committed to ward, beheaded, v 488
———— His head taken downe, v. 492
Hume castell rendered vnto the English, v 552.
———— Recouered by the Scots, v 561.
———— Besieged, yeelded vp, possessed of the English, iii 886
Hun hanged in the Lollards Towre, his death lamented, and whie, iii 608
Hundred and Wapentake, i 258
Hundreds in England, whie so called, ib
———— ¶ Sée Tithings
Hungar kept the battell, his vow, v 216.
Hungar ¶ Sée Agnerus Hubba, and Ubba
Hunger what it forced the Britons to doo, i 512
———— When people did eat horsses, iii 952
Hungerford lord executed for buggerie, iii 818
Hungus king of Picts refuseth to conclude league with the French, v 189
———— Aided with Scots inuadeth Northumberland, v 191
———— He warreth without slaughter and burning, ib
———— Repareth saint Andrews church, v 192.
———— Falleth in a consumption, v 193
Hunsdich paued, iii 532
Hunsdon lord his descent, he presenteth the order of the garter vnto the French king, iv 224, 225
———— He with others go against the rebels in the north, iv 236
———— Made lord chamberleine, iv 620
———— Maketh a rode into Scotland, v 689.
Hunting and which be the best games, i. 380
———— A pastime for ladies and gentlewomen rather than gentlemen, ib.
———— What kind vsed in old times, ib
———— That the prince of Scotland vsed it, ib.
———— Fatall of William Rufus, ii 44.
———— Préests were not vsed to it, ii 168
———— A statute made cõcerning it, ii 412
———— Lawes made for it note, v. 46, 95
Hunting roiall, ii 810
Huntington lands and Northumberland annexed to the crowne of Scotland, v 287
———— Earledome by whom and to whom giuen in dowre, ii. 18
———— Scotish, ii. 113.
———— The castell woone, ii. 158.

Huntingston earledome giuen to Dauid king of Scots, vol i page 207.
——— Forfeited and neuer restored to the crowne of Scotland, i 208
Huntleie erle giueth an ouerthrowe to the English, v 527.
——— Suspected by the queene, v 612
——— Taken prisoner, v 551
——— Entreth bond for his countriemen, ib
——— Hee conquered manie lands, v. 575
——— Sent for, v 612
——— Cometh to Cornthie in Mar, v 613
——— Fled, v 616
——— Commeth to aid the queene, v. 631.
——— Lieutenant of Scotland, v. 647.
——— He escapeth, ib
Husband men, i 275
——— Their good sticke, i 365.
——— Sometimes citizens, i 319
——— Their diet, i 282.
——— ¶ Sée Farmers.
Husband men made honourable note, v 243, 244
Husbandrie hindred by frost, ii 678, 679
——— Diminished wherbie and how remedied. note, iii 656, 657
——— In England well ammended, i. 184
——— ¶ See Frosts and Raine
Hushie Iohn, seruant to Richard, lord Birmingham, vi 247
——— Persuaded by Okeleie to leaue his master, ib
——— His valiantnesse and killing of Okeleie, ib
——— He is dubbed knight, vi 218.
——— His successours barons of Galtrim, ib.
——— Is slaine, vi 265.
Hydromel, i 286
Hypermnestra, hir loue to hir husband cõmended, i 435

I.

Iacke Cade, vi 207
——— An Irish man borne, ib.
Iacke Cads rebellion in Kent, iii 220.
——— Slaieth the Staffords, iii 224
——— Is at his witts end, disguiseth himselfe, is forsaken of his adherents, iii 224.
——— Proclamation out to take him, iii 226.
——— He is apprehended and executed, iii 227
Iacke Straw & his adherents executed, ii 747
——— His confession at the time of his death, ii 751.
——— ¶ Sée Rebellion.
Iambert ¶ Sée Lambert.
Iames prince of Scotland taken by the English, v 407
——— Stated as prisoner in England, v 408
——— His bringing up note, the gréefe of his father Robert, causing his death ib.
Iames the first ransomed, vol v page 417.
——— Marrieth the erle of Summerset his daughter, gifts giuen him, commeth to Edenburgh, ib.
——— Crowned, kéepeth an audit, v 418.
——— His solemne oth at a parlement, ib.
——— Desirous to purge his realme of vnrulie persons, v 421
——— His saieng, v. 289
——— Murthered by conspirators, v. 425, 426
Iames the second crowned king, marrieth the duke of Gelderlands daughter, v 428
——— Conueid to Sterling, ib.
——— Will rule and reigne himselfe, v. 433.
——— Warred against, v 439.
——— Would haue fled, ib
——— Writings set vp in contempt of him, v 440
——— Inuadeth England, v 444.
——— Slaine, ib
——— His buriall and lamentation of the people for him, ib
——— His conditions and issue, ib.
Iames the third king of Scots crowned, ib.
——— Marieth, v 448.
——— Raiseth an armie, v 451.
——— Giueth himselfe to keeping of women and lustfulnesse, v 458.
——— Sent an ambassage to Edward king of England, v 452
——— He prepareth an armie, ib
——— His concubine named Daisie, v. 453.
——— He is kept vnder arrest, ib.
——— Prisoner, v 454
——— Set at libertie, ib.
——— Signifieth by letters his mind, touching the articles of Dunbar, v 457
——— His answer and promise to an ambassage, v 458
——— Conspired against, ib
——— Gathereth an armie, v. 459.
——— Put to the worst, and slaine, ib.
Iames the fourth crowned, v 460
——— Repentant, wore an iron chaine, giuen to deuotion a great iusticer, lerned, ib.
——— Went on pilgrimage, v 467.
——— Protector of the faith, ib
——— In armes against the English, maketh too much hast, v 477
——— Minded to keepe his ground, v. 479.
——— His quarrell vnto the earle of Surrie, v 480
——— His practise, and tokens of ill lucke to befall him, v 480, 481.
——— Deceiued himselfe and alighted from his horsse his hardinesse marred all, v 481.
——— Commended, v 482
——— Goeth on pilgrimage, v. 470.

Iames the fourth persuadeth to peace, vol. v page 472
——— His bastard maried, ib
——— Reasoned with the counterfeit duke of Yorke, v 464
——— Requireth to talke with the bishop of Durham, purposeth to be a sutor for mariage in England, and the same compassed, v 464, 465
——— A wife sought out for him, v. 461
——— Goeth in progresse, v 462
——— Inuadeth Northumberland, v 463
——— Returneth without proffer of battell, ib
——— Maried the king of Denmarks daughter, i 76
——— Slaine, v. 431
Iames the fift crowned, and the queene appointed regent, v. 483
——— Great vnquietnesse in his minoritie, ib
——— Sutor vnto the duchesse of Longeuile, v 511.
——— He marieth Marie de Loraine, ib.
——— Hee sailleth to the Iles of Orkneie, ib
——— Assisted the pope, v 512.
——— Hee sulketh about the Iles, ib
——— He goeth the second time into France, ib
——— He is sutor for mariage, ib
——— Contracted mariage with the ladie Magdalen, ib
——— Returneth with his queene into Scotland, v 512
——— Remooued from place to place, ib
——— Deliuered to the keeping of certaine lords, v 486
Iames the sixt borne, v 618
——— His godfathers, v 619
——— Crowned, v 626.
——— His oth, v 629.
——— Displeased with erle Morton, for the lord of Iohnstone, v 712
——— His declaration of his acts confirmed in parlement, v. 713
——— His intention drawne into certeine articles, v 719
——— His spéech to the estates, concerning a league in religion with England, v 725.
——— Besieged at Sterling, v. 730
——— Sendeth to the lords of the religion, ib
——— Granteth the request of the lords, ib
——— His gard remooued, v 731.
——— In custodie of the lords of the religion, ib
Iane daughter to the earle of Summerset maried to king Iames the fift, v. 417
Iane the daughter of K Iohn maried to the erle of March, ii 316.
Iane de Ualois sister to the French king, treateth for peace, ii. 617
Iane ladie Guilford proclamed quéene, iii 1065.
Iane ladie Guilford hath the keeping of the keies of the Towre, vol iv. page 1070
——— Committed to the Towre with hir husband the lord Guilford, iv 3
——— Hir behauiour at hir execution, the words which she spake on the scaffold, iv 22.
Ianigenes were the posteritie of Noah in Italie, i 7
Iaques Arkeneld purposeth the destruction of Gerard Denise, his house beset, and he slaine, ii. 631
Iardseie an Iland of thirtie miles compasse, i 56.
Iaroman bishop, sent to the Eastsaxons to reduce them to the faith, i 627.
Icenes all placed by Leland in Norfolke and Suffolke, i 191
Iceni, v 67.
Iceni Norfolkemen, i 488.
Ida the first king of Brenicia, i 583
Ida king of Northumberland, i 27.
——— His acts, deeds and deth, i 586
Ides whie so called ¶ Sée Moneth, i 409
Idlenesse & meat of other mens charge what they doo, iii 1001
——— Auoided in the court, especially of the ladies, i 830
——— The breeder and nourisher of sensuall lusts, v 179
——— The root of all mischéefe, v 423.
Idlers not to be suffered, epistola.
Idolaters of the Saxons burned, v 149
Idolatrie erected by Sighere king of Eastsaxons, i. 627
——— How hatched at the first, i 38
Idols monstrous proportions, i 39.
——— Destroied by king Ecombert, i 616
——— Destroied by a heathenish bishop, i. 607.
Iedworth defended from assalt, v 663
Iennie a notorius known traitor & confferror with Francis Throgmorton, iv 540.
Ierdseie. ¶ Sée French king
Ierusalem taken by Saladine prince of the Saracens, ii 191
——— With more part of all other townes taken from the Christians, ii 192.
——— The king thereof doth fealtie to Richard the first, ii 221.
——— The king thereof commeth to England, ii 354
——— ¶ Sée Holieland.
——— When taken by Nabuchodonosor,
Iest of Philip the French king at duke William lieng sicke note, ii 23, 24.
——— Of Richard the first, at the castell of chateau Galliard builded, ii 269
——— Of king Iohn concerning the masse, ii 339
——— Of Edward the fourth and a widow that gaue him monie, iii 330
——— Plesent concerning the strict kéeping of ladie Elisabeth, iv. 1*0
——— Merrie at the rood of Paules, iv 63.

Iest of a cat hanged in Cheape, and of a dog clothed in a rocket, called by the name of Gardiner, vol. iv. page 105.
—— Against scripture iustlie rewarded, iv. 256.
Iesuit Goldwell, bishop of Oxford: note, i. 240.
Iesuits redie to flie, v. 731.
Iesuits and massing préests proclamed against, iv. 434.
—— Sent ouer seas and banished the realme: note well, iv. 554, 555, 556.
—— ¶ Sée Préests semenaries.
Iew ¶ Sée Inas.
Iew and of a good Iews answer to William Rufus, ii. 45, 46.
—— Striken by a christian, ii. 205.
—— Hath his teeth drawne out, ii. 301.
—— At Teukesburie, falleth into a iakes: note, ii. 453, 454.
Iewell Iohn bishop of Salisburie commended, i. 238.
—— ¶ Sée Bishop.
Iewes when they begin their weeke, i. 407.
—— They and other nations recken their moneths by the moone, ib.
—— Did eat brawne, i. 373.
—— And christians dispute, ii. 46.
—— Burnt to death, ii. 205.
—— Sute to William Rufus against Iewes, become christians: note, ii. 45.
—— Brought into this land by duke William, ii. 24.
—— At Lincolne slaine and spoiled, ii. 469.
—— Inhabiting London, slaine for treson, ii. 461.
—— Slaine at London, & whie, ii. 455.
—— Accused & executed for crucifieng of a child, ii. 437.
—— Charged on paine of hanging to paie Henrie the third, 8000 marks, ii. 435.
—— Robbed in Oxford, ii. 412.
—— Cōstreined to helpe Henrie the third with monie, ii. 419.
—— Released out of prison, ii. 438.
—— Punished by the purse for a robberie committed, ii. 387.
—— Meant to crucifie a child in spite of Christ, ii. 378.
—— Generallie imprisoned thorough out all England, hated: note, ii. 489.
—— Banished out of England, and whie, ii. 492.
—— Drowned, ib.
—— Giue Henrie the third, the third part of all their moueables, ii. 365.
—— Indicted and punished for abusing the kings coine, ii. 482.
—— Crucifie a child, ii. 96.
—— Grieuouslie taxed, tormented, and imprisoned, ii. 301.
—— And where they buried their dead, ii. 175.
—— Appointed to inroll all their debts, pledges, &c. ii. 252.
—— Excéedinglie hated and murthered: note, ii. 210, 211, 212.
—— Houses set on fier at London, ii. 205.
Iewes beaten and abused, vol. ii. page 205.
—— Meant to present king Richard with a rich gift, ib.
Igerna ¶ Sée Igwarne.
Ikenild stréet one of the foure principall highwaies of Britaine and houe extended, i. 191.
Iland discouered. ¶ Sée Sebastian.
Iland called a continent, i. 75.
Iland holie otherwise called Lindesfarne, i. 77.
Iland carried to and fro as the wind bloweth, i. 217.
—— Such as are to be séene vpon the coasts of Britaine, i. 52.
—— Such as lie in the mouth of the Thames, i. 53.
—— Such as lie vpon the west and north shore, i. 60.
—— Such as lie betwéene the Wight and the maine land, i. 54.
—— Thrée inuironed with salt streames in Maldon water, i. 78.
Ilands inuironed with the ocean waues, i. 52.
Ilands none at the first as some coniecture, i. 1.
Ile of man described, i. 65.
—— Pigmeis in Scotland, i. 72.
Ile of Rats and whie so called, i. 57.
Ile of S. Clement, and whie so called, i. 59.
Ile of Shrews, i. 70.
Iles eastward to the point of Ramshead, i. 68.
Iles moouing and remoouing by the force of the water, i. 149.
Iles in Scotland, i. 68.
Ilices aliquando in Britannia nisi intelligatur de quercu, i. 349.
Image of wax. ¶ Sée Whitches.
Images proued by a fabulous vision, i. 640.
—— Of gold and siluer, v. 192.
—— Pulled downe, v. 590.
—— Taken awaie and remooued from their places: note, iii. 816.
—— Remoued out of churches, iii. 867.
—— Throughout the realme pulled downe and defaced, iii. 889.
—— Taken downe and burned in the stréets, iv. 185.
Imanuentius slaine by Cassibelane, i. 447.
Imball king of Armorica slaine, i. 535.
Imbert slaine by Corineus, i. 442.
Imogen the wife of Brute, i. 439.
Impost of wine granted, vi. 344.
Impost. ¶ Sée Custome and Subsidie.
Imprecation: note, ii. 429.
Inas king of Westsaxons, his acts, and deeds, i. 639.
—— Selleth peace for monie, i. 637.
—— Diuideth the Westsaxon prouince into two bishopriks, i. 642.
—— How persuaded by his wife to resigne vp his crowne and become a pilgrime, i. 639.
—— Went to Rome and there died, ib.
Incest of K. Iohn, ii. 319.
Inchtuthill. ¶ Sée Tuline.

Inconueniences of euill gouernment, vol vi page 88.
Inclosures of the fields about London cast downe and ouerthrowne by archers of London, iii 599.
———— A proclamation for the laieng of them open, iii 916
Incubus, v 146
Incontinencie of Henrie the second, ii 200
Indenture sextipartite of conspired noblemen. note, iii 10
———— Tripartite touching conspiracie, iii 22.
Indians fond adorning themselues with pretious stones, i 441
Indigence, i. 432
Indulph prince of Cumberland, king of Scots prouoked to warre with England, v. 230.
———— Diligent in office, to incounter the Danes, v 231
———— Dieth of a wound with a dart, v 232
Indulgencies biennals & triennals liberallie granted, ii 734.
Ine. ¶ Sée Inas
Infection ¶ Sée Murren.
Infidelitie suspected in William Rufus, ii 16.
Ingratitude: note, iii 657.
———— Shrewdlie practised, and seuerlie punished, iii 417, 418
———— A notable example thereof, iii 173
———— Of Fitzosbert vnnaturall, ii 258
———— Striketh dead, ii 86
———— In all estates towards Richard the second, ii 869
———— For good seruice vnrewarded, and what followed, ii 36
———— Of Odo for his restitution note, ii. 27, 28
———— Of cardinall Poole to Henrie the eight that brought him vp, iv. 146
———— ¶ Sée Unthankfullnesse
Iniurie done and no reuenge sought, note, iv 56.
Iniunctions of the pope to the king, vi 167
Iniustice, ii 300.
Inkéepers what knaues and theeues they haue to their chamberleins, ostlers, tapsters, &c. i 414
Innes and thorowfares with the manner of vsage, ib.
—— None worse than in London, i 415
—— Of great capacitie and well furneshed, ib
Innocencie no barre against execution, iii 1030
Innocent hanged for the nocent, ii. 300
Inquests at assises, i 262
Inquisitions taken of diuerse matters note, ii 268.
———— Taken by a iurie of sundrie matters, ii 251.
———— Of the losses euerie bishop had and susteined, ii 312
———— Called Traill baston, ii. 538.
———— Taken of the misdemeanors of iustices, ib.
———— For abusors of the kings coine, ii 482
———— For the separating of forrests, ii 307.
———— What were the liberties in times past of K Henrie the thirds grandfather. note, vol ii page 353
———— For washers and clippers of monie, ii. 416
———— For the ualuation of benefices perteining to strangers, ii. 408.
———— For offendors abusing clergiemen strangers, ii 370.
Inskith fortified by the Englishmen, v 563
———— Assalted by the Frenchmen, ib.
———— Recouered by the French, v 564.
———— Raced, v. 631
Insurrection about the taking vp of corne, iii. 804.
———— Of Wiat, iv 11.
———— Wherein note what mischéeuous hurlie burlies doo chance in a commotion or rebellion, iv 11, 12.
———— ¶ Sée Rebellion.
Insecta animalcula, i 384
Intercalations ¶ Sée Calendar and Yeare.
Interdiction, ii 302
———— Threatened by the pope against the king & his clergie, ii 293
———— Of the land solemnie relesed, ii 316
Interteinment vnfit bréedeth malcontentment, ii. 34
———— Of the emperour Sigismund strange note, iii 85
———— ¶ Sée Fréendship and Hospitalitie
Interuiew Sée Edward the fourth and other kings of England, as French king, &c
Inuasions punished and other offenses against the kings peace, ii 538
Inuestitures of churches, thrée daies togither argued vpon, ii 57
———— Of prelates ¶ Sée Bishops and Consecrations
Inuernesse castell giuen vp, v. 612.
———— Burned, v 420
———— ¶ Sée Enuernesse.
Iohannes Cremensis a lecherous legat note, ii. 72
Iohn the king driuen into the castell of Forfaire, v. 330.
Iohn the king proclamed king of England, ii. 272, 273.
———— Made king of Ireland, ii 188
———— Married, ii 203.
———— His impatience to sée himselfe brideled by his subiects, ii 322.
———— Taketh diuerse castels, ii 326, 327
———— Aided by forren souldiors against his barons, ii 324
———— Disquieted, departeth into the Ile of Wight, ii 322.
———— Crowned king of England the second time, ii 285
———— From whome the Poictouins reuolt, ii 281
———— Commeth vpon his enimies vnlooked for, ib.

Iohn the king diuerse waies molested the white moonkes, vol. ii. page 282.
——— Diuorced from his wife Isabell the daughter of erle Robert of Glocester, ii. 280.
——— Hée and the French king come to a parlée, ii. 279.
——— Passeth ouer into Normandie, ii. 277.
——— Returneth out of Normandie, ii. 279.
——— Inuested duke of Normandie, ii. 274.
——— Commeth out of Normandie into England, ib.
——— Wanting aid against the French king commeth backe to England, ii. 288.
——— Prepareth an armie to go into France, ii. 291.
——— Goeth to the sea, returneth, chargeth certeine of his nobles with treason, ii. 292.
——— Taketh the sea, maketh war against the French king, ii. 294.
——— Repareth Angiers, ii. 295.
——— Writeth to the pope touching the archbishop of Canturburies election, ii. 296.
——— Threatened with interdiction, he and his realme put vnder the popes curse, ii. 295.
——— Passeth into Ireland, ii. 301.
——— Goeth into Wales with an armie, ii. 302.
——— Punisheth diuerse that refused to go with him into Wales, ii. 302, 303.
——— His destruction put in practise by means of the popes legat and the French king, ii. 303.
——— Deliuereth his crowne to Pendulph, and hath it againe restored, ii. 306.
——— His words of fealtie made to the pope, ii. 308.
——— What caused him to agrée with the pope, ii. 312.
——— His lords refuse to follow him into France, ib.
——— Commended to the pope for an honourable prince, ii. 314.
——— Remooueth to Angiers, ii. 317.
——— Inuadeth Britaine, ii. 316.
——— Taketh vpon him the crosse to go into the holie land, ii. 318.
——— Subscribeth to his barons notwithstanding his oth, ii. 322.
——— Commeth to his lords to talke of some pacification, ii. 321.
——— Left desolat of Fréends, ii. 320.
——— Maketh hauocke on the possessions of his aduersaries, ii. 335.
——— His noblemen reuolt from him to K. Lewes, ii. 331.
——— His children male and female, the description of his person, his fortune, his saiengs and dooings, ii. 338, 339.
——— Incestuous and couetuous: note, ii. 319.
——— The popes vassall, ii. 306, 330.
——— Assembleth a great armie against the French king, ii. 305.
Iohn the king knéeleth downe to the archbishop of Canturburie, and besought him of forgiuenesse, vol. ii. page 312.
——— His sonne named Oliuer Fitzroie, ii. 319.
——— By whose means his nephew Arthur lost his life, and whie, ii. 12.
——— Falleth sicke of an ague, his raging, ii. 335, 336.
——— His death diuerslie reported by writers, ii. 336.
——— Reported to an ill purpose, ii. 339.
——— His buriall and corpulence, ii. 336, 337.
Iohn king of England restreined all taking of wildfoule, and why, i. 375.
——— He ouerthrewe and spoiled manie parks and warrens, i. 345.
——— Benefactor to Lichfield bishoprike, i. 240.
——— Abused euen by the verie rakehels of the popish clergie, i. 266.
Iohn the kings sonne, arriueth in Ireland, vi. 211.
——— Is made lord of Ireland, ib.
——— He buildeth castells, vi. 221.
——— He maketh Ireland tributarie to the pope, vi. 237.
——— He subdueth the Welshmen, ib.
——— He is absolued, ib.
——— He dieth, vi. 238.
Iohn Ball. ¶ Sée Ball.
Iohn a Chamber a notorius northerne rebell, iii. 492.
——— Hanged like an archtraitor, iii. 493.
Iohn of Gaunt borne, ii. 612.
——— Maried, ii. 671.
——— Duke of Lancaster, ii. 677.
——— Buried and his daughter Blanch, ii. 693.
Iohn Tiler. ¶ Sée Tiler.
Iohn of Ludlow, alias Mason a sore promooter: note, i. 385.
Ione de Arc pusell de Dieu, iii. 163, 169.
——— Taken prisoner, &c.: note, iii. 170.
Iohn of Kéekes bishop of Dublin, resisteth Ioice Rowland archbishop of Ardmagh, vi. 245.
Iohn de saint Paule, bishop of Dublin, finished Christs church, vi. 240.
Iohn lord of the isles atteinted, v. 451.
——— Submitteth himselfe, ib.
Iohn Scot fasted fortie daies, v. 508.
——— ¶ Sée Scot Iohn.
Iohn archbishop of Yorke, i. 636.
Iohn the archchanter of saint Peters at Rome sent to the synod at Hatfield, and whie, i. 632.
Ioseph of Arimathia, i. 512.
——— His commeng into Britaine, i. 486.
Iohnstane lard had two houses taken by the regent, v. 635.

Iohnstane himselfe taken, vol v page 712.
Ioie immoderat the cause of death, iii. 824
Iosephus preached in England & at what time he came ouer, i. 40
Iosina crowned king, interteineth philosophers, v. 60
——— Deceaseth, v 60, 51.
Ireland sometimes called Scotland, 25
Ireland doctor sent into Scotland, v. 452
——— ¶ Sée Bruse, Edward, and Hibernia
Ireland and the Orkneies by whome first gouerned, i 432
——— When it laie wast and not inhabited, i 457
——— The peoples cursses against king Egfride preuaile, i 634
——— Civill discord there when Agricola was lieutenant of Britaine, i 506
——— Conquest thereof, pursued by Turgesus, i. 588
——— Inuaded by the Northumbers, i. 634
——— Subdued to Edgar, i 698
——— The bignes thereof, vi 1
——— The names of it, vi 1, 2
——— Inhabited by Spaniards, vi. 2.
——— By fiue brethren, vi 3.
——— By Cesara néece to Noah, vi. 73.
——— By Bergion son to Neptune, vi 74
——— By the ofspring of Iaphet, ib
——— By the Norwegians, vi 88
——— By the Grecians, vi 75
——— By the Scithians, vi. 76.
——— By Brennus and the Britains, ib
——— By the Picts, vi 78
——— Diuided into shires and prouinces, vi. 3, 78.
——— The nature of the soile, vi 9
——— The cities and townes in it, vi. 21
——— The land diuided by lots, vi 2.
——— The diuersities of spéeches, vi. 4, 5.
——— Waterish and full of floods, vi 8
——— The sweet aire, and hath no venom in it, vi. 9
——— Replenished with cattell and bées, ib
——— Did homage at Westchester to king Arthur, vi 77
——— Full of iron mines, vi. 78.
——— Ruled by one cheefe monarch ouer the whole, ib.
——— Instructed in the christian religion by saint Iames, vi 83.
——— By Paladius, ib.
——— By Patrike, ib.
——— Why it cannot be conquered, vi 224.
——— Euill gouerned, vi 225.
——— How to be reformed, vi. 14
——— Numbers of cities and townes, vi 21.
——— The nobilitie, vi 42
——— The learned men, vi. 57.
——— The reuenues of the land,
——— Is a storehouse of nature, vi 41.
——— The broken state of Ireland, vi. 7, 340
——— Diuided into seuerall estates or kingdoms, ii 138.
Ireland mostlie conquered by Henrie the second, vol ii. page 190.
——— Foure Irish kings submit themselues to Richard the second, ii 834
——— The yearlie reuenues thereof in Edward the thirds dais, ib.
——— Englishmen sent there to inhabit the Ards in Ulster, iv. 320
——— Souldiors transported thither, iv 432
——— Inuaded by the popes meanes, iv 530.
——— ¶ Sée Iohn and Soldiors
Irish sometime inhabited a parcel of Britaine, i 10.
——— A kind of Scots noted by Ierom, ib.
——— Yéeld to subscribe to receiue no Scots into their dominion, i. 11
——— Doo destroie Angleseie, ii 410.
——— Rebelling kill the English, ii 474
——— Frier appeacheth the duke of Lancaster of treason, ii. 763.
——— Miserablie tormented and put to death, ib
——— To auoid into their owne countrie by proclamation, ii 823.
——— With the lord of Kilmaine arriued at Harfleu, iii 101.
——— Their good seruice, ib
——— Wild spoile the earle of Kildars countrie, iii 749.
——— Nobilitie submit themselues to Henrie the eight in England, iii. 826.
——— Seuen hundred in warlike manner passe through London & muster before king Henrie the eight note, iii 838
——— Bowes bagpipes and darts among them,
Irish wild, Irish English, vi 247.
——— borne & Ireland borne, vi. 2.
——— borne to beare no office, vi 257
——— saints, Irish manners and dispositions, vi. 87, 69
——— The méere Irish, vi 66.
——— prophets, vi 222.
——— diets, vi 67.
——— horses, vi 21.
——— impositions, vi. 269.
——— marriages and christenings, vi 68, 69.
——— infants, vi. 67.
——— gentries, ib
——— wéeping or to weep Irish, vi 67
——— Euerie Irish marcher to dwell vpon his owne house, ib.
——— language, by whome it was first inuented, vi 6
——— The difficultie of the toong, vi 7.
——— No Irish worde for a knaue, ib
Irishmen forsake king Iohn, vi 224
——— They serue against the Scots, vi 242.
——— They inuade Scotland, ib
——— They are in open rebellion, vi 247, 253.
Irishmen fetch preies to Gallowaie, v. 396
——— They assalt the Scots in two seuerall places, ib.

Irishmen put vnto flight, vol v page 396.
——— Came in thrée battels, run awaie, v 223
——— Two gather their powers, v 222
——— Their practise, ib
——— Gentlie intreated, v 223.
——— Land in Argile, v. 94.
——— Sent upon reuenge, take a preie in Ila, & seeke peace, v 185
——— Liue by milke and by hearbes, v 185
Irish Scots speake the Irish toong, i 25
Irnirike the king of the Englishmen, v 163
Irmenrike the sonne of Oth the Saxon, i 572.
Irmenrike of Kent dies, i. 586.
Iron, i 400
Isabell daughter to the erle of Glocester maried vnto king Richards brother, ii 203.
Isabell the second wife of king Iohn & what issue she brought him, ii 280
——— Crowned, ib
Isabell Henrie the thirds mother deceaseth, ii 413.
Isabell countesse of cornwall deceaseth, ii. 390
Isabell wife to emperour Fredirik, deceaseth, ii 395
Isabell de Boubhec ¶ Sée Countesse
Isac ¶ Sée Cipriots
Isis described and what streames run thereinto, i 157
Isleie knight all his apparell not woorth four shillings,
Isoldune, where seated, ii 253
Isurium whense it taketh denomination, i 157.
Isubria ¶ Sée Scots.
Italie ¶ Sée Isulnia
Italie called the paradise of the world, i 185.
Italiance fiue successiuelie bishops of Worcester, i. 239
Ithamor bishop of Rochester consecrated archbishop of Cantuburie, i 618
Itius portus supposed to be Calis, i 465.
Iudge Morgan fell mad note, iv. 23.
——— ¶ Sée Iustice.
Iudges and other officers committed to the Towre. note, ii 618.
——— ¶ Sée Iustices.
Iudge righteous, v 258
Iudgement rash in an holie father, ii 188.
Iudgement secret of God vpon Banister & his children after the attachment of the duke of Buckingham, iii 418
Iudith, duke Williams néece, whose daughter and to whome married, and how indowed, ii 18
Iudith the daughter of Charles the bald married king Ethelwolfe,
Iudwall ¶ Sée Ludwall.
Iue. ¶ Sée Inas.
Iugants a people, i 492
Iuie cup whether it will hold wine or no, i 402
Iulius Agricola lieutenant of Britaine, i 504.
——— His good gouernment, i 505.
——— Sent into Britaine, prepareth against the Scots, v. 76
Iulius Agricola studieth to bring them to ciuilitie, vol v. page 77
——— Commeth to Sterling, ib
——— Buildeth his castell and bridge, ib
——— Corrected the calendar, i 408
——— His inuasion of Britaine note, i 505, v 58
——— His purpose to make a discouerie of Britaine, i 465
——— Appointed for to conquer Gallia, ib.
——— With two legions passeth ouer into Britaine, i 466
——— His ships lie at Calis, i 465
Iulius Cassianus at square with Suetonius, i 501.
Iulius Frontinus lieutenant of Britaine, i 502
Iulius Frontinus sent into Britaine, v. 75
Iulius Hoft, v. 59
Iupiter whie feigned to throw downe stones vpon Albion and Bergion, i. 8
Iupiters cat, vi 433
Iurmirike ¶ Sée Irmenrike.
Iurie of twelue men ancient, when instituted & how matters by them should be tried, ii 19
——— That went upon sir Nicholas Throckmorton, appéere in the starchamber, excessiuely fined, iv 64
——— Extreme dealt withall, ib
——— ¶ Sée Throckmorton knight
——— At Excester assise eleuen dead note, iv 869.
Iustice chéefe of England, giueth ouer his office & becometh a cannon, ii 178
——— An office imposed vpon prelats ¶ Sée Archbishop.
Iustice Henrie the fift note, iii. 92, 102.
——— A notable example of Edward the first vpon his sonne, ii 539.
——— Mingled with mercie, iii 541.
——— And the commendable care of Henrie the second thereof note, ii 199
——— Without regard of kindred, ii 512.
——— And followed vpon the neglect of the same, ii 21.
——— Partlie pretended, iii 400
——— Peruerted when one is hanged for another, iii. 925
——— In warre note the force thereof, iii 77.
——— Corrupted ¶ Sée Bribes
Iustice ministered without respect of persons, v. 204
——— Sharplie and speedilie executed, note, v. 421
——— Seuerlie executed against offenders, v. 365
——— Upright and tempered with mercie, v. 365, 366
——— Neglected, v. 50
Iustice against rebels, epistola
——— The nature of an Irish man, vi 369.
Iustices of peace and coram, otherwise dier and determiner, i 262.
——— Of peace when and whie instituted, ii. 13
——— Itinerants, the diuision of their circuits, ii. 168

Iustices their oth, vol ii page 169.
——— Die of infection, iv 868, 869.
——— Cheefe of England elected and others deposed, ii. 206
——— Itinerants cause inquisitions to be made in their circuits, ii 251.
——— Abuse iniustice note, ii 389
——— Keepe the term for plées at S. Sauiours, ii. 448
——— Begin to go their generall circuits, ii. 487
——— ¶ Sée Sicknesse at Excester and Oxford
——— Complained of to Edward the first, & punished note, ii 491.
——— Fined, ii 538
——— Sat neither in the Tower nor elsewhere for a whole yeare, ii 620
——— Restreined from fées briberie, and gifts &c · note, ii 633, 634
——— Iurors &c. brought to Blockham feast by the rebels, ii. 737
——— Compelled to subscribe, ii 785
Iustine ¶ Sée Guthmond
Iusts and combats betweene the Scots and Englishmen, v. 402.
——— For life and death vpon London bridge, v 402, 403
——— At Elie where P Edward began to shew proofe of his chivalrie, ii. 438.
——— At Blackleie, ii 418.
——— At Cheapside, iv 598
——— At Chalons where prince Edward behaued himselfe worthilie, ii 476
——— At Dunstable where king and queene were present, ii 623
——— At Greenwich with goodlie shews, iii 572
——— At Greenwich before the emperour Charles, iii 877
——— Where sir Francis Brian lost one of his eies, iii 711.
——— At London, the maior and aldermen challengers, ii 672
——— In the Tower of London & Greenwich, iii 246
——— Roiall in Tuthill field for the space of eight daies, ii 379
——— Deuised to be held at Oxford where Henrie the fourth should haue beene murthered, iii 10
——— Within the kings palace of Shine for the space of a moneth, iii. 500.
——— In Smithfield, ii 627, 677, 810, 811, iii. 48
——— At Westminster with the shews and triumphs there, iii 538
——— And some hurt done, iii 798
——— And much hurt doone among the people, iv 434
——— By gentlemen of name to delight nobles of France note, iv 435 to 445
——— At Windsore, ii 628
Iusts and combats against all commers, vol ii page 852
——— It and turnie appointed by the lords and by Henrie the third dissappointed, ii 409
——— Handled in a rougher manner than in these daies, ii 425
——— Whereat sir Arnold Montenisie was slaine note, ii 425
——— Prohibited by proclamation, ii 536
——— Betwixt the bastard of Burgogne and the lord Scales, iii. 285
——— With manie a proper deuised shew, iii 550, 551
——— Solemne wherein Henrie the eight was a challenger, iii 609
——— Kept for honor of his sister the French queene, iii 614, 615
——— Betweene Henrie the eight and others, iii 625, 636, 814.
——— Proclamed in sundrie nations, iii 816
——— Roiall in France note, iii 650, 651, 652.
——— At Paris the nobles go thither, decrées for the same, how long they lasted, with the maner thereof note, iii 605
——— At Tournaie for disport of the prince of Castile and the duchesse of Sauoie, iii 590
——— ¶ Sée Tilt and Turnies.
Iustus archbishop of Canturburie, i 603.
Iustus bishop of Rochester, i. 597
——— He and Melitus departe into France, i 603.
——— Both sent for againe, and the one restored to his bishoprike, ib
Iutes called Ibitti a kind of people that came into Britaine with the Saxons, i 655, 656

K

Kalendar ¶ Sée Pope Gregorie
Kaianach assaileth Sterling bridge, he is eftsoones chased, comforted by his nobles, v 77.
——— King of Picts slaine by misfortune of his own subiects, v 79
Keerkin ¶ Sée Canturburie, i 446
Karicke castle two miles from Wexsford, vi. 139
——— Builded vpon a rocke, ib
Karones a brotherhood of plaiers at cards, vi 68
Katharine daughter to the erle of Huntleie maried to Perkin the rebel, iii 511.
——— Presented to Henrie the seuenth, iii. 519
Katharine the daughter of Ferdinando sent ouer into England out of Spaine, iii 526
——— Maried to king Henrie the eight, iii 547.
——— ¶ Sée quéene Katharine and Henrie the eight
Keeper lord priuie seale, his dignitie, i 277.

Keith lord taken prisoner, vol v page 584
—— William sent vnto the queene of England, v 738
Keiths a familie aduanced for good seruice in the field, v 261.
Kelwaie Thomas ¶ Sée Iusts triumphant
Kempe Thomas a poore mans sonne, his fortunat pretermét, i 230
Kendall wasted, ii 157
Kenedie archbishop of saint Andrews v 442
—— His practise, ib
Kenedie Iames archbishop gouerned the realme of Scotland, v 447
Kenelme murthred by his mother Quédred, i 654
—— King of Mercia shamfullie murthered, i 659
Kenneth king of Scots durst not combat with king Edgar note, i 698.
Kenneth inuested king of Scots, v 198
—— Fortified the realme, v 199
—— Calleth his nobles to reuenge his fathers death, ib
—— A prettie shift of his to persuade the nobilitie, ib
—— Entreth Sterling shire, v 200
—— Getteth into Merner, v. 201
—— With horssemen disordereth the Picts armie, v 202
—— Causeth retreate to be sounded, ib
—— His oration, ib.
—— Sendeth to Camelon commanding them to yéeld, v 204
—— His extreame vow, v 206
—— A pretie craft vsed by him note, v. 204
—— His lawes and ordinances, v 206
—— Deceasseth, v. 208
Kenneth crowned king, vertuous of life, v 239.
—— His oration, v 240
—— Gathered an armie against the Danes, v 242
—— Setteth his men in arraie, exhorteth them to valiantnesse, ib
—— Worthilie commended for iustice, poisoned his cousine Malcolme, not suspected of the fact, v 215
—— Requested that the crowne might come by inheritance, v 246
—— He ministered iustice trulie, his gilty conscience, confession of his sins, repentance and pilgrimage, v 247.
—— Murthered, v 248
Kennethus Keir K of Scots dieth of the cough, v 163
Kennerike maior of Dublin a benefactor, vi 256
Kenred King of Mercia described, i 640.
Kenrie the sonne of king Cuthred slaine, i 644
Kenrike K of Westsaxons his acts and deeds, and death, i 586
Kensands a forked arme of the sea, receiuing diuerse riuers, i 146
Kent when it began to be a kingdome, & how it was extended, i 561.
Kent of whome the kings thereof descended, vol i page 583
—— Wasted, spoiled, and disquieted, i 636.
—— Uoid of a king for the space of seuen yeares, i. 637
—— The foure kings thereof in Cassebelans time, i 475
—— Noble offspring of the kings thereof decaied, i 656
—— The kingdome had two kings at once, i. 637.
—— Giuen to Hengist in reward, i 556
—— When it began to be a kingdome, i 568
—— The king taketh end, i 659
—— What hauens it hath, i 182
—— Kingdome called Gantwarland and the limits thereof, i 28
Kentigerne begotten in a rauishment, v 161.
Kentishmen plie the men against the Westsaxons, i 636
—— Uanquished in sight of the Danes, i. 707
—— Descended of the Iutes, i 556.
—— Disobeing king Edwards commandment are surprised by the enimies, i 679
—— Buie peace with monie, i 638
—— Destitute of a king, i 637
—— Doo lie in waite in woods for the comming of duke William, ii 2.
—— Cannot awaie with bondage, and determine to fight with duke William for their lawes and libertie, ib
—— The keie of England, ii 3
—— Send a message to duke William, ib
—— Had duke William at aduantage, ii. 2, 3
—— Make a hurlie burlie and commit much mischéefe, iii 300
—— Executed for rebellion, iii. 328
—— Haue thanks of Henrie the seuenth, for their good seruice, iii 511
—— Rebellion vnder Iohn Tiler. ¶ Sée Tiler.
Kenulfe K of Mercia his vertues, i 653.
—— His liberalitie towards churchmen, i 654
Kenwalch king of Westsaxons dieth, his acts and deeds, i. 629.
Kernes, v 228
Kernes and Kihernes the rakehels of Ireland, vi 68
Kerulf a capteine of Irishmen slaine, vi. 161
Ket, his rebellion, a capteine there, iii. 961 to 985.
—— He meant to haue talked with the earle of Warwike, iii 979
—— Power increaseth, iii 971
—— Apprehended, examined, iii 983.
—— Both brothers executed, iii 984
Kettell Alice accused for witchcraft, vi 251
—— Is burned at Kilkennie, vi. 252.
Keneughs tenants to sir Peter Carewe, vi. 340.
—— Submit themselues to his deuotion, vi 366.
Kilfles whie so named, v 237.

Kilkennie, whie so called, vol vi. page 34.
Kilkennie walls builded by Robert Tilbot, vi 33
—— Besieged by Iames Fitzmorice, vi. 363
Killegrew Henrie sent vnto Scotland, v 666.
Killingworth castell besieged, deliuered to Henrie the third, ii 470
—— Fortified against Henrie the third, ii 469
—— Holden against Edward the second, ii 565
Kimarus king of Britaine his sudden end, i 458.
Kimbelme king of Britaine in great fauour with Cesar, i 479, 480
Kineards conspiracie against Kinewulfe, i 650
Kine keeping profitable, i 369
King becommeth a pilgrim forsaking a crowne, i 639
—— In name but not in rule, i 552
—— A philosopher, i. 635
—— Dispossessed and restored i 447, 448.
—— Made of a herdman, i 564
—— Made of a seruant, i 677
—— Made of one bought and sold, ib.
—— Becommeth a moonke, i 641, 643.
—— The first that wore a golden crowne, i. 451.
—— Depriued, i 557
—— ¶ Sée Crowne & Uortigerne
—— Goeth secretlie to France, v 511.
—— To the west borders, v 527.
—— Receiueth the order of saint Michaell, v. 616
—— Persuaded to staie the parlement, ib.
—— He entereth into the quéenes priuie chamber, v 617
—— Persuaded by the quéene, ib
—— Goeth to Meggat land, v 619
—— As a solitarie person goeth to Striueling, murdered, ib
—— And what mischiefes insue for lack of one, v 323
—— Of Armenia ¶ Sée Armenia.
—— Of Cipriots ¶ Sée Cipriots
—— Of France ¶ See French king.
—— Of Ireland. ¶ Sée Ireland
—— Of Portingall ¶ Sée Portingall
—— Of Spaine. ¶ Sée Spaine
—— Can abide no péere in his owne realme note ii 42
—— In name but not in fame note, ii 796
—— What kind of person he is or should be, iii. 743
—— Office hard to discharge, iii 411
—— Best kind of gouernment, iii 1006.
—— Iurisdiction absolute in their owne realmes, & that the pope hath nothing then to doo, ii. 41.
—— Election and aduancement referred to the people, ii 1.
—— Oth at his coronation, ii 2
Kingdome to obteine what promises are made. ¶ Sée Promises & People.
Kingdome of Eastangles when it began, vol i page 569
—— Southsaxons when it began, i 558
Kings colledge in Cambridge founded, iii 326.
—— Of what stone it is builded, i 394
Kings Newnam baths, i 360
Kings the choosing of them not allowed, v 44.
—— ¶ Sée England, Scotland
—— Seuen in Britaine called Reguli, i 561
—— By usurpatiō and by succession, i 637
—— Eight of the English & Saxon nation at once, i 589
—— Eight row king Edgar in a barge vpon the water, i 694
—— They become monks, i 690, 645
—— Their daughters professed nuns, i 617
—— Fiue ruled this Iland all at once ¶ Sée Pentarchie
—— They gouerned Britaine before the Romans subdued it, i 478.
—— Crowned and gouerne Britaine, i 444, 445, 446, 447
—— The British kings gouernment endeth, i 637
Kingston knight is sent to fetch vp Woolseie arested of treason to Henrie the eight, talk betwixt the said sir William and him, iii 754
—— Prouost marshall, execution of marshall law note, iii 925
—— His ill iustice, iii 925, 926
—— Accused of treason, his decease, iv. 81.
Kingstone vpon Thames in times past verie famous, i 368
—— Famous by meanes of kings there crowned, i 691
Kinigils king of Westsaxons becommeth a christian, i. 616.
—— ¶ Sée Cinecistus.
Kinimacus the seuenteenth ruler of Britaine, i. 449
Kinimarus ¶ Sée Kinimacus
Kinewulfe king of Westsaxons, his victories and exploits, he is slaine of his seruants, i 654.
Kinnatill king of Scotland, v 164
—— His death, surrendereth his kingdome on his death bed, v 164, 165.
Kinter inuaded, v 539
Kircawdie causeth the prisoners not to returne at the daie appointed, v 665
Kircawdie Iames entereth Edenburgh castell, v. 669
Kirell sir Thomas, a valiant capteine, iii 645
Kisse the pax would not the K with Becket, ii 133.
—— ¶ See Reconciliation
Kisse dangerous and deadlie, i 388.
Kneuet sir Edmund knight for striking in the princes court should haue lost his hand, i 332, iii 830
Kneuet surueior depriued of his office note, iii 645
—— An instrument to bring the duke of Buckingham to destruction, iii 657

Keneuet sir Henrie knight deceaseth, vol. iii. page 858

Keneuet Edmund knight, his seruice in Norffolke rebellion, iii 969.

Knewstub ¶ Sée Sermon

Knight of the field in Cesar's time, i 479.

Knight of the garter how disgraded, i 272

———— His maner of buriall, ib

Knight red, Fowkes de warren & why so called, i 27.

Knight of the vallie, his countrie is spoiled, vi 421

———— He is a rebell, ib

Knight none borne but created, and how, i 267

Knight bipartited, vi. 129

Knighthood of Kimbeline king of Britaine giuen him by Cesar, i 480

Knighthood, iii 155

———— To be valorous gentlemen in seruice of warres, iii 571.

———— For good militarie seruice, iii 590, 679, 690

———— For seruice doone against the enemie, iii 778, 888, 898

Knights of the Bath, i 367, iii 3, 398, 780

Knights of the garter note, i 268

Knights of the round table, ib

———— When first founded

———— ¶ Sée Order of the garter

Knights of the Rhods, v 288.

———— Order of dissolued, iii 816

Knights templers apprehended, and what laid to their charge, ii 518

Knights of saint Michaels order, v. 512.

Knights fiftie dubbed, v 421.

———— Thirtie and two of one surname, v 331.

———— Three hundred of men of arms to be found, ii 265

———— Two hundred fiftie and two besides demilances taken prisoners by king John, ii 285

———— Made by Henrie the third, ii. 415.

———— According to the value of their lands, ii 428

———— To be made according to their reuenues ii 439

———— Fées, how manie in England in king Henrie the third his time, ii 452

———— Foure score made at once, ii 454

———— Made by the duke of Buckingham at his entrie into France, ii 729, 730

———— Made of capteines for good seruice in warre, iii 75

Knockfergus whie so named, vi 13

Knols knight Robert begā to build Rochester bridge, ii. 91

Knolls Francis knight sent ouer to view the state of Newhauen, iv. 218.

———— His foure sonnes in a triumphant shew, iv 112.

———— ¶ Sée Auxerre, and Iusts triumphant

Knolls sir Francis sent into Ireland, vi 333

Knolls knight sent with an armie into France, ii. 693

Knolls knight borne in Cheshire, his counsell not followed, vol ii page 695

———— The feare that the enemies had of him, ii. 696

———— His scueritie, ii 763

———— Deceaseth, remembrances of him, iii 44.

Knought ¶ Sée Cnute

Knought, sonne to Gurmo a Dane, slaine at the siege of Dublin, vi 92

L

Laabin ¶ Sée Hercules

Labienus a Romane tribune slaine, i 470

Labourers by the daie, &c the fourth degrée of people in England, i 275.

———— An act for the drawing of them in order, iii 609.

Lacie Hugh, and of King Henrie the seconds gifts vnto him, ii 141

———— Slaine in Ireland, ii 190

———— His puissance and contempt, his diligence to enlarge his possessions in Ireland, ib.

———— Sent into England, vi 212.

———— He buildeth Leighline and other forts, vi 207.

———— The description of him, vi. 203.

———— Had in suspicion, ib

———— Is sent for into England, vi 209.

———— Is made lord deputie, ib

———— He receiueth the submission of Rothorike the monark at the Shenin, vi 162

———— He is slaine, vi 212, 235

———— His buriall, vi. 235

Lacie Hugh the yoonger kéepeth the realme in quietness, ib

———— Is banished, vi 237

———— He trauelleth into France, and is disguised, ib

———— He is pardoned and is restored to his earledome, ib

———— His yéerelie reuenues, ib.

———— Dieth and is buried at Cragfergus, vi 238.

———— His daughter and heire maried to Walter de Burgh, ib

Lacie Iohn arreigned and stoned to death, vi 250.

Lacie Robert constable of Chester hangeth two for spite, ii 231

Lacie Roger a Norman, ii 28

Lacie Walter in armes against the rebels, ii 18

Lacies constables of Chester by inheritance, their estimation and credit, ii 373

———— Erls of Lincolne of whense they had their originall, ii 33.

Lacies do rebell, vi 249

———— Reuolt to the Scots, vi 250

———— Proclamed traitors, ib.

Ladies of the court enemies to idlenesse, i 330

Ladies that made great gaine by selling venison and butter, i. 344

Laignie on the riuer of Maine beséeged, iii 177

Lake ¶ Sée Waters
Lambe esquier, a good common wealths man, deceaseth, his acts and deeds full of charity note, vol iv pages 127, 128, 429
———— His epitaph, iv 430.
Lambert earle of Lens, ii 18.
Lambert Simenhill ¶ Sée Simenhill
Lambert the counterfeit sonne of George duke of Clarence, vi. 269
——— Is crowned king at Dublin, vi. 270
——— Is taken and pardoned, ib
Lambert archbishop of Canturburie, i 651
———— Depriued, i 646
———— Death, i 656.
Lamperdeuaux castell builded, ii 482
———— Taken, ii 182
Lancashire in times past hath had store of fire, i 350
Lancaster whense it tooke the name, i 145
———— Whereof ladie Wake was duchesse, i 241.
———— It hath béene to holie forrest heretofore, i 347.
———— Towne burnt, v. 355.
Lancaster and Yorke house, & the vniting of them in one intended, iii 412
———— Furthered, iii. 412, 413, 414, 416
———— Some matter concerning both worthie the reading, iii 478
Lancaster house, and how malicious Margaret the duchesse of Burgogne was therevnto, iii 504
Land, and how manie acres an hide conteineth, ii 22
Landaffe bishopikes election, circuit, & valuation, i 243
Landoise corrupted with rewards betraieth the earle of Richmond into Richard the thirds hands, iii 424, 425
——— His expectation disappointed by the priuie and vnknowne departing of the earle, iii 425
Lands let out for yearlie rent in duke Williams time, ii. 13
——— Morgaged for monie, ii 28
——— Of the church defended and recoured by archbishop Lanfranke note, ii 30, 31
Lanfranke an Italian the thrée & thirtieth archbishop of Canturburie, ii 14
———— His authoritie great among all the lords of England, ii 27
———— His counsell to William Rufus to win the nobles fauor, ii 26
———— Diligent care for the safetie of William Rufus, ii 28, 29.
———— In fauor with Pope Alexander, ii 14
———— Assisteth duke William in armes against the rebelles, ii 15.
———— Calleth a councell of the clergie, ii 19
———— Praised for holding with the moonks, ii 30
———— Enuied for his prosperities sake, ii 28
———— His death, ii. 30.
———— With a description of certeine of his qualities & diuers of his acts and déeds, vol ii. page 30
Langton burnt, v 582
Langton bishop of Lichfield beneficial to his clergie, i 240
Language British with the Gréek hath great affinitie, i 22
———— Englishmen apt to learne anie forren, i 25.
———— ¶ Sée Toong.
Languages spoken in this Ile of Britaine, i 22
Lapidaries outlandish their subtiltv, i 402
Largesse of William Rufus at his coronation note, ii 27
Lath whereof named & what it is, i 258
Laurence archbishop of Dublin intreated for and his present at the synod at Cashill, vi 163
Laurence archbishop of Canturburie laboureth to enlarge the church and augment the faith, i 600
———— Meaning to leave his sée he is otherwise warned in a dreame, i 603
Law Ordalian note, i 740.
———— Described, i 200
Law marshall a burthen intollerable, iii 1006
———— Executed, iii 102, 925, iv 211, 212.
———— ¶ Sée Soldiers
Law Salike, ii 65, 611
Law Agraria kicked against, i 308
Law ciuill and canon and their vse, i 30?
Law common and customarie, i 304
Law of parlement, i 302
Law of Halifax, i 312
Law vndooth men note, i 304.
Law for lawfull age & wardship of heires, i 205
Law of armies note, iii 128, 286
———— Violated by the French, iv 221
———— Touching heralds violated, iii 874.
Law of duke William against such as forced anie women, ii 26
Law to be quite abolished at the rebelles request, ii 740
Law against buieng and selling on the sundaie, iii 205
Lawes of king Alured note, i 674
——— Of Canutus made for his forrest, i 347
——— Of Cnute, i 674
——— Of Edward the Confessor, i 206
——— Of king Edward the third, i 747.
——— Of king Kenneth note, v 206
——— Of king Mackbeth, v 270
——— Of Martin, . 458
——— Of Mulmutius, i. 451
——— Of Mulmutius in vse to this daie, i 298
Lawes of England for a long time written in French, i 24
———— Of thrée sorts, whereupon dependeth the English gouernment, i 30?
———— How passed in parlement, i. 291, 292, 293
———— Their great numbers bréed a generall contempt of all good order, i 187.

Lawes of England in vse before the conquest, vol i pages 297, 298, 299, 300
———— Altered and abrogated, i 298.
———— Giuen in sundrie places of the land and wh , ib
———— Since the comming of the Normans, i 302
———— Since the first inhabitation thereof, i 297
———— Manie made none kept, i 358
Lawes made against learning, i 257
Lawes penall, i 302
Lawes penall of duke William note, ii 23
———— Confessed to be unequall, ii 13
———— Of S. Edward supposed to be most equall and indifferent, ii 16.
———— Of William Rufus sharpe, rigorous, and peremptorie, ii 34
———— Of king Henrie the first commanded to be vniversallie obserued, ii 313
Lawes written in the Norman toong not vnderstood of the English, note, void of conscience and equitie, ii 13
—— Of England abrogated and established, ib
———— —— Remaine in Kent onelie, ii 3
Lawes and liberties fought for, ii 2
Lawes and decrées how dangerous to be broken of them that make them, i 662
Lawes filthie, v 60
Lawdaies, i 261
———— Accustomable vsed in the arches, i 306
Lawiers of England not alwaies constant in iudgement, i 302
—— Haue all the wealth of the land note, i 304
—— Manie stooped not at small fées, ib
—— To plaid their cases in English, &c ii 678
—— Broght to Blockham feast by the rebelles, ii 737
—— Fraudulent punished, iii. 815
—— ¶ Sée Atturnies
Lecherie in Iames the third, v. 458
—— Ingendered of slouth, i 445
Lecture ¶ Sée Surgerie.
Led, i 399
—— Blacke and white, i 397.
Léeds castell besieged, ii 563
———— Yéelded, ib
Léers of our time wherof they beare a shadow, i. 258
Legat from Rome with the answer made to him, v 354, 355
—— For a collection from the pope, v 308
—— From pope Clement, his demand, v 319
—— Anselme with his authoritie from Rome, ii 67
—— Ferentino gathereth much monie in England, iii 294.
—— Gualos practises to get monie, ii 333
—— Iohn de Anagnia from Rome to procure peace betwéene kings, ii 197.
Legat Otho cardinall, and what dutie he gathered of the clergie, vol ii page 359
—— Pandulph ¶ Sée Pandulph note.
Legat from the pope about reformation, a bawdie knaue, ii 72
—— With the archbishop of Yorks pall, ii 61
—— ¶ See Archbishop note, ii 48.
—— A shift by forbearing the name, ii 414.
—— ¶ Sée Cardinall
Legats from Rome, ii 237
—— To reconcile the bishop of Elie and the archbishop of Rouen, ib
—— They practise for their owne aduantage, i 173
—— Not regarded, they excommunicate, ii 63
—— From the pope about Beckets death, ii 141
—— From the pope into England, i 651
Legion what it conteined, i 320
Legions of souldiers sent by Claudius into Ireland, i 483
Legue published by heralds, and the articles thereof, v 189
—— Betwéene France and Scotland, v. 490.
—— Concluded, v 189
—— Renewed, v 306
—— Betwéene Emdene and Scotland, v. 579, 580
—— Betwéene the Scots, Picts, and Britons, v. 145, 147.
—— Betwixt England and Flanders, ii. 608.
—— Concluded, ii 511
—— Renewed, ii 277
—— Betweene England and France, iii. 720.
—— Renewed, iii 491
—— Confirmed, iv 267, 284
—— Betwéene England and Scotland, iv 600
—— With the Scots and French to annoie the English, ii 510
—— Betwéene the emperour and king Henrie the fift, iii. 86
—— Betwéene king Henrie the eight and the emperor, iii. 831
—— Betwéene king Henrie and the duke of Britaine, iii 106
—— Betwéene king Henrie the fift and the duke of Burgogne, and how articulated, iii 119
—— With king Henrie the third and the Welsh nobilitie vpon certeine articles, ii. 391
—— Secret betwixt the pope and certeine states of Italie, iii 712
Legue of peace to breake, an euill deed, iii 583
—— ¶ Sée Peace and Truce
Legues not to be kept with traitors, vi. 296.
Leicester, i 146, 447
———— ¶ See Caerleir.
———— Woone by force, ii. 153.
———— The wals and the castell raced, ii. 170.
———— How called in the Romans time, i 321
Leigh knight. ¶ Sée Iusts triumphant.
Leighlin, vi 202

Leighlin inclosed with a wall, vol vi page 323
Leill the seuenth ruler of Britaine, i 446
Leinster the fift part of Ireland, vi 122
—— In a miserable state, vi. 328
Leir the tenth ruler of Britaine, i 446.
—— Driuen to great distresse, i 447
—— Restored to his kingdome, i 448.
Leirmouth James ambassador into England, v. 517
—— ¶ Sée Learmouth.
Leith besieged, v 594.
—— Burned, iii 837, 885, v 537.
—— Fortified, v 559, 591, 651
—— Unprouided of Uittelis, v 601.
—— More riches found there than was looked for in anie towne of Scotland, iii 835.
—— Entered by the English armie, and by them possessed and spoiled note, ib
—— Assailed on the seuenth of Maie, iv 197.
—— The great skirmishes betwéene the English and French there in quéene Elisabeths time, iv 191
—— The Frenchmen driuen into it, ib
—— A fire in it and augmented with shot of ordinance and windie wether, iv 192, 193, 195
—— Maiepoles set up therein on Maie daie, iv 195
—— Why the describing of the siege thereof is so larglie set downe, iv. 200
—— Peace concluded thereabouts, iv 200, 201
—— Burnt to the ground, iii 837
Lelands notes intricate of set purpose (as may be suspected), i 109
Leneux the earle gathered a power, v 503.
—— Goeth into Scotland, v 532
—— Confireth with quéene dowager, ib.
—— His displeasure, v 533
—— He renounceth his seruice to the French king, v 534.
—— He seizeth on the French ships, ib
—— Commeth to the gouernor, ib.
—— He fortifieth Glasgow, ib
—— He sendeth vnto the king of England, v 535
—— He goeth into England, v 538
—— He marrieth the ladie Margaret Doughasse, ib
—— He is heire to the lord of Obegnie, ib
—— Returneth into Scotland, ib
—— In danger to be betraied, v 539
—— Landeth at Dinnime, ib
—— He procureth those of the Iles to serue the king of England, v 543
—— He entereth into Scotland, v 553
—— In doubt what to do, v 554
—— Dissembleth with his dissemblers, ib
—— He with the lord Wharton inuadeth Scotland, v 555.
—— Commeth into Scotland, v 614.
—— Warden of the East Marshes, v. 615
—— Pardoned, v. 617
—— He returneth into Scotland, v 646
—— He carrieth Englishmen into Scotland, ib.
—— He commeth to Edenburgh, ib.
Leneux made regent, vol v. page 647
—— Goeth against the earle of Cassels, v 648
—— Taken in his lodging, v 652
—— Wounded, ib
—— His words before his death ib
—— His deth, v. 653
Leneux and Argile at variance, v 176
—— ¶ Sée Earle
Leneux countesse ¶ Sée Margaret
Lent how fasted, i 622
—— First ordeined to be kept in England, i 617.
Leofrike earle of Chester, i 732
—— Bare great rule in the commonwealth, ib
—— A furtherer of Edward third to the crowne, i 740
—— He dieth and was buried at Couentrie, i 750
Leofwins malicious mind against Liulfus note, ii. 20
Leogitia an Iland wherein Brute arriued, i 439
Leolin king of Southwales an aider to K Edmund, i. 690
Leolin prince of Wales summoned to come and doo his homage, ii 479
—— And the Welch rebells accurssed, ii 484
—— His wife taken from him, he beginneth to make warrs, maketh sute for peace, ii 480
—— His wife restored to him, ii 482.
—— He sueth for peace, ii. 180
—— Beginneth new warres. ii 482
—— Inuadeth Edward the firsts fréends, ii 485
—— Discomfited, ii 354
—— Inuadeth the English borders, ii. 369.
—— His courage, ib
—— Spoileth the marches of England, ii. 374.
—— Made cuckold and how he reuenged it, ii 365
—— Wasteth and spoileth all the marches betwixt Wales and Shrewesburie, ii 376
—— Deceaseth, ii 387
—— Slaine, his head presented to Edward the first, ii 486
Leopald ¶ Sée Duke of Austrich
Leoporius Agricola a Pelagian, i 562.
Lerned men of Ireland, vi 56
Lerning how effectuall, i 256
—— Lawes made against it and what followed, i 257
—— Choked by the Uandals and Goths note, i. 313.
—— In the erle of Mellents sonnes note, ii 75
Leslie their familie, v 691.
—— ¶ Sée Erldome.

Lestingo weakened by the slaughter of his brethren, vol i page 7
——— He and his issue plaie the tyrants, ib
Lether for shooes ill wrought, ii 357
Letter of Henrie the eight answering the king of Scots, v 475
——— Of Iames the fourth to the king of Portingale, v 469
——— Of the Scotish king to Henrie the eight, v 475
——— Of Robert king of Scots to his sonne prince Iames, v 407
——— Of the prior of S Andrews to the French king, v 592
——— Of the French king to the prior of S Andrews, v 591
——— Concerning the marriage of his sonne to the quéene of Scots, v 581
——— Of the nobilitie to the regent, v. 595
——— From the duke of Yorke to the earle of Salisburie, vi 267
——— From Thomas Fitzgirald to the lord Butler, vi 292
——— From the lord Butler to Thomas Fitzgirald, vi 293
——— Of king Iohn to his nobles of England, touching his victories, and taking of duke Arthur prisoner, ii 285.
——— Of the proud bishop of Elie to the shiriffe of Kent, ii 226
——— Of the pope to the clergie of England for the celebrating of a holie daie, ii 146
——— Of king Richard the first to the states of England for the deposing the bishop of Elie, ii 229
——— Of the emperor to the states of England touching his deliuerance, ii 243
——— Of Richard the first to the archbishop of Canturburie touching his deliuerance out of prison, ib
——— To the duke of Austrich, cleering Richard the first of the death of the marquesse of Montferrat, ii 250
——— Of Henrie the fourth to pope Gregorie and the cardinals, iii 46
——— Of William Northbourgh the kings confessor describing the kings voiage into France, ii 641
——— Seditious of a préest, ii 749
——— Of F W concerning the earle of Essex Walter Deuereux, iv 337
——— Of cardinall Como to Parrie for resolution to kill quéene Elisabeth, iv 573
——— Of Creitchton to sir Francis Walsingham touching Parries intended murthering of the quéene. iv 372
——— Of Boner vnto cardinall Poole, concerning persecution, iv 144
——— Of the councell to Edmund Boner as touching quéene Marie conceiued with child, iv 68
——— Of the ladie Marie touching her chalenge vnto the crowne, iii 1066
Letter of the ladie Marie with an answer of the lords, vol iii page 1066
——— Right excellent of the duke of Summerset to the Scotish nobilitie touching the marriage betwéene Edward the sixt and the quéene of Scots, iii 910, 911, 912, 913
——— Of defiance from the Scotish K to Henrie the eight, iii 581
——— Of the French K prisoner to his mother the regent of France, iii 699.
——— Of Gefferie the kings base sonne to Richard the archbishop of Canturburie, ii 180
——— Of Gardiner to Boner, touching the celebrating of pope Iulies funerals, iv 77
——— Of yoong king Henrie touching the disappointment of archbishop Richards consecration, ii 146
——— Of Henrie the second touching the pacification betwéene him and Thomas Becket, ii 133.
——— Of the popes. ¶ Sée Pope
Letters of the duke of Summerset and the lord Russell, iii 1015
——— Of Henrie the sixt to the duke of Yorke, iii 251
——— Of the duke of Yorke to Henrie the sixt, iii 230
——— Of the duke of Gelderland to Henrie the second note, ii 814, 815.
——— Concerning the prince Edwards doings and procéedings beyond sea, ii 658
——— Of Parrie to quéene Elisabeth & lords of the counsell after his voluntarie confession note, iv 571
——— Of submission and sute of one Francis Throckmorton traitor against quéene Elisabeth and the realme, iv 543, 544
——— He is executed, 548
——— Missiue taken from the quéenes ambassadors seruants, iv. 205
——— Seditious of a bishop sent into a forren realme note, ii 28
——— Treasonable, ii 733
——— Of protection from the French king to the king of England, ii. 176
Letters intercepted, ii 565
Letters patents reuoked, iii 31, 32
Leucotion like saffron, i 591
Leurouse Thomas schoolemaster to the earle of Kildare, vi 301
——— His care of the earle, i 303.
——— He is placed in the English house at Rome, i 306
Lewin a Welshman hanged, ii 517
Lewis the French king inclineth to peace with Henrie the third, ii 348
——— His sonne intituled to the kingdome of England, ib
——— Sendeth to his father for aid, ii 346
——— An armie prepared in France to succour him, ii 347
——— His faire, ib

Lewis the French king mainteined his title pretended to the crowne of England, vol. ii page 330.
——— Deceaseth, ii 360.
——— ¶ Sée French king.
Lewis le Grosse, ii 59
Lewis ¶ Sée Physcian.
Lhoegres now called England, i 195
——— And how inlarged, i 157
Libell against cardinall Woolseie, iii 716
——— Seditious against Henrie the seuenth, and the libellors executed, iii 508
——— Causing losse of life, iii 423.
——— Set on the duke of Northfolks gate forewarning him of trecherie against Richard the third, and of his owne saftie, iii 444
——— Against the quéene and realme, false, iv 253
——— Published in Italian against quéene Elisabeth, and the same answered, iv. 628, 629
——— Printed against quéene Elisabeth, iv 537.
——— Against the clergie, iii 88
——— ¶ Sée Bookes seditious
Libels against king Iames the second, v 440.
Liberalitie of king Dauid the first reproued, v. 288.
——— Of Richard the first woonderfull, ii. 219.
——— Of the earle of Arundell: note, ii 779
——— Of Edward the first to his nobles, ii. 531.
——— Of sir Thomas Sackuill to the French, iv. 259.
——— Of William Rufus, ii. 45.
——— Repented note, ii 34.
——— In a prince commended, ii 27
Libertie preferred before a kingdome, iii 388
——— Obteined by gentle language, iii 293
——— Bought with monie, ii 242, 244.
——— Obteined by great words and proud brags, ii 39
——— Desired aboue all things. note, iii. 994
——— ¶ Sée Ransome.
Liberties called, vi 255, 389
——— Of Scotland defended, v 299
——— ¶ Sée Lawes, Londoners, Priuileges, and Southworke
Lichfield, whereof it tooke the name, i 527
——— The bishop of Mercia his sée, i 627.
——— Called Mortuorum campus note, i 240
——— It and Couentrie counted but one citie, i. 319
——— The bishopriks erection, circuit, and valuation, i 240
Licence to build castels, ii 80
——— Of king Richard the first to gather riches, ii 208.
——— For the English iusts and turnie note, ii. 252.
——— Asked of Henrie the third of the commonaltie to passe ouer sea, ii. 452
——— To burie the bodies of the rebels, ii. 575
Licence and that without none should depart the realme, vol. ii page 34
Licinus chosen fellow with Maximianus in the empire, i 531
Liddesdale without the marches of England, i. 154.
Lie, and how dangerous to credit. note, iii 139, 140.
Liermouth Iames would haue rescued the cardinall, v 546
Liermouth capteine defendeth the country against the English, v 555.
Lieutenants appointed in shires when and why,
Life to saue what shifts noblemen can be content to make, ii 788
Lightening ¶ Sée Thunder
Lild Thomas bishop of Elie at contention with the king of England, i 241.
Lilingwen lake in Wales of strong nature, i. 354.
Lilla his zelous seruise cost him his life, i. 605
Limendune what it signifieth, i 96
Limerike builded by Satiricus, vi 29, 94.
——— Whie so named, vi 29, 35.
——— The king of Limerike submitteth himselfe, vi 160.
——— It was builded by the Esterlings, ib
——— It is besieged and taken, vi 188.
——— Besieged by Donald, vi. 193.
——— Recoured, ib
——— Set on fire, vi. 195
——— A kingdome, ii 174
Limoges besieged, taken by force, ii 695.
——— Rendered to king Henrie the second, ii 186
Lincolne how called in the Romans time, i 320
——— Sometime builded by Lud brother to Cassibelan, i 360
——— Written Nicholl by the Normãs, i 170.
——— In times past had two and fiftie parish churches, i 324.
——— Bishopriks erectiõ, circuit, and valuation, i 248.
——— Besieged, ii 96.
——— Taken, ii 469
——— Woone by the French, ii 333.
Lincolne castell, ii 9
Lincolne besieged by Theldrike king of Germanie and the Saxons, i. 575
Lincolne Iohn the author of the insurrection on ill Maie daie, the griefes particularised in his bill for the cities behoofe, a great enimie to strangers, prosecuteth his information of gréeuances by specialties, iii 618, 619
——— Indicted, & what laid to his charge, he is executed in Cheapside, iii 624
Lincolnshire what hauens it hath, i. 182
Lincolnshiremen in times past called Coritani, i. 169
——— Throw awaie their cotes the lighter to run awaie, iii 294.
——— In armes against Henrie the eight, iii. 793.

London under the rule of prince Edward, &c · he appointeth the maior and shiriffes, vol ii page 474
——— In charge of the bishop of Excester, ii 580
——— Bridge and the Towre there taken downe, ii. 343.
——— When much hurt was doone with winde, ii 32
——— A great part of it burnt to the ground, ii 23
——— And of the charter granted vnto the citizens by duke William, ii 25
Londoners prouident and pitifull in time of scarsitie, ii 816.
——— Pursued by prince Edward, ii 462
——— Refuse to lend the king a thousand pounds, ii 818.
——— Reuolt from the duke of Northfolke going against Wiat, iv 13
——— Take Wiats part, iv. 14
——— Receiuing of the duke of Summerset at his returne out of Scotland, iii 889
——— Keepe S. Barnabées daie holie daie, iii. 1024
——— Redinesse to assist Edward the sixt in a motion and work of charitie, iii 1061
——— They and gentlemen of courts by the ears, iii 204
——— Skirmish with Iack Cade vpon London bridge, iii 225
——— Prouidence for safegard of peace, iii 247.
——— Loiall and disclosers of treasons, ii 733
——— Are spited and enuied at, ii 721.
——— Abused of strangers whereof followed the riot of ill Maie date, iii 617 to 622
——— Enterteine and banket the king of Denmarke, iii 686.
——— Hated of cardinall Woolseie, iii 716
——— Set foorth a power into France, iii 849
——— Lend Henrie the eight 20000 pounds, iii 673
——— Glorious receiuing of Henrie the eight and the emperor Charles, iii 677
——— Stitlie and gorgious muster before Henrie the eight note, iii 809
——— Conspire to take the empresse Maud, ii 91, 99
——— Sue to king Iohn for a maior and two sherrifes, ii 248
——— Sore affraid of the Cornish rebells, iii 515
——— Resolue to receiue Edward the fourth and reuolt from Henrie the sixt, iii 310, 311
——— Grant fiue thousand markes to Edward the fourth which were seized of the fiue and twentie wards, iii. 349
——— Loiall to Edward the fourth note, iii 322
——— Riot against the Iewes at king Richard the firsts córonation, ii 205
Londoners valiantnesse, &c among them of two aldermen, vol. iii page 323
——— Present monie to king Richard the first, ii 207
——— Large priuileges and liberties, ib.
——— And the priuileges of their commonaltie by whom granted, ii 228
——— Triumphant receiuing of king Richard the first into the citie, ii 245
——— Hirdlie reported of by an Almaine lord, ib
——— Serue Richard the first in his butterie at his coronation note, ii 248.
——— Foul disorder noted and complained of to Richard the first, ii 258
——— Refused to fight against the lords, ii. 765
——— Specially affraid of the French forces, ii 773
——— In perplexity whether to take part with Richard the second or with the nobles, ii 791
——— They incline to the lords, ib.
——— Receiuing of the duke of Lancaster, ii. 865.
——— Fauorers of Wicliffes doctrine, ii 754
——— Meet the king and quéene on Blackheath. ii 834
——— Euill repaid for their unstablenesse, ii 783
——— Commend themselues to the fauor of Richard the second before the death of Edward, ii 712
——— They submit their quarrel to the erle of Lancaster to the kings order, ib
——— Friends to the erle of Northumberland, ii. 752
——— Aiders of the rebells of Kent and Essex, ii 737.
——— The lords of the land stand in doubt of them, ii 734
——— Pretilie cousened out of a thousand markes by king Henrie the third, ii 427, 428.
——— Sued vnto to make choice of two to be their king, ii 1.
——— Withstand duke William, ib
——— Appointed to kéepe the subsidie granted by the parlement, ii 717
——— Banished the citie, ii 488, 489.
——— Their magistrats deposed & new ordeined in their roome, ii 353
——— Haue frée warren granted them of king Henrie the third, and other liberties, ii. 359
——— They and the constable of the towne at variance, ii 455
——— Their outrage whetted with ill counsell, ii. 352
——— Haue frée libertie to passe toll frée through all England, ii 360
——— Paie Henrie the third 5000 marks for a fine, ib
——— Haue a grant to vse a common seale, ii 364

Londoners good deuotion towards the erle of Kent, vol ii page 371
——— Terrified with thunder, ii 373
——— Seruice at the mariage with Henrie the third, ii 379
——— Cast in prison and depriued of their liberties, ii 467
——— Sworne to be true to Henrie the third & his heirs, ii 456
——— Riot vpon the bishop of Salisburies men, ii. 818
——— Grieueouslie complained of to the king, their liberties seized vpon, a gardian appointed to gouerne them, their liberties in part confirmed in part condemned, gifts presented by them to pacifie the kings displeasure, ii 818, 819, 820
——— More gifts giuen by them to the king, their liberties ratified, ii 820
——— In great disorder, ii. 458
——— Curstlie handled, their citie committed to a gardian or custos note, ii 168.
——— Pardon by Henrie the thirds charter, ib
——— Pardoned for receiuing the erle of Glocester into their citie, ii. 472
——— Goldsmiths and tailors togither by the eares, ii 473
——— Rob the house of the lord Greie, ii. 456
——— Buie Henrie the thirds plate to his great losse, ii 416
——— They and the abbat of Westminster at strife, ii 419
——— Receiuing in of the countesse of Prouance, ii. 400
——— Paie a tallage and are grieued, ii 412
——— Fined at fiftéene hundred marks for receiuing a banished man into their citie, ii 407, 408.
——— Help Henrie the third at a pinch, ii 426.
——— Haue their liberties restored vnto them, ii 435
——— Called barons in derision, ii 428.
——— Gréedie dealing to the hurt of the commonwelth, ii 444
——— Agrée with the barons, ii 460
——— Spoiled at Croidon, ii 464.
——— In an uprore choose new officers, ii 471.
——— Glad to submit themselues to Henrie the third, put to their fine, ii 467.
——— Game of wrestling, and what tumult followed, ii. 352.
——— Take part with the quéene and her adherents, ii 580, 581, 582
——— Unrulie and giuen to sedition, note, ii 580
——— Set prisoners at libertie out of the Towre, ii 581
——— Loialtie, auouching to kéepe traitors out of their gates, ii. 580.
——— Behead a citizen and a bishop in a riot, ii 581
——— Will not permit king Edward the thirds iustices to sit within the citie, ii 620.
Londoners haue their franchises confirmed, vol ii. page 589
——— Lent Edward the third monie to be paid againe out of the subsidie monie, ii 613
——— In arms against the duke of Lancaster, ment to haue slaine him, ii 705, 706.
——— Outrage for words spoken to their bishop, ii. 705
——— Commended, iv 600
——— Foure thousand trained vp for seruice in the field, iv 599
——— Muster before quéene Elisabeth at Gréenwich, iv 184
——— Their thréefold plague, iv. 221
——— Houshold stuffe sold by a common crier or belman, iv 226.
——— Trained vp in the field, iv 265.
——— Loue and heartie goodwill towards quéene Elisabeth, iv. 550
——— Withstand duke William, ii 1.
——— Loue to quéene Elisabeth manifested on the daie of hir coronation note and obserue it well, iv. 158, 159, 160, 161.
——— Their farewell vnto hir going out at Templebar, iv. 173
——— Quéene Elisabeths last words to them by waie of promise, iv. 174
——— Victors against the Danes, i. 673
——— Uerie valiant against Swaine and his Danes, i 714.
——— Submit themselues to Swaine, i 716
——— Receiue Edmund Ironside verie ioifullie, i 721
——— Slaine by the Danes, i 706.
Londorike ¶ Sée Rrdorike
Lone of monie taken by Henrie the eight, iii 826.
Longchampe ¶ Sée Bishop of Elie.
Longland doctor misliketh of Henrie the eights mariage with his brothers wife, iii 736.
Lopoole a riuer whie so named, i. 109
——— Full of trout and éeles, ib.
Lord a title vnited to some offices, i 265
——— A title grudged at as not fit for bishops, ib
Lord Dane became a word of contempt, i 709
Lordane ¶ Sée Lurden.
Lords of Ireland giue assurance for their loialtie, vi. 247
——— They answer for their followers, vi. 381
Lords by office publike and priuat, in their dignities note, i 277.
——— In England how manie, ib.
——— Created and made, iii 821, 822
——— Conspiring against Richard the second. Sée Noblemen
——— Assemble, v 499
——— Exiled come into Scotland, v. 617.
——— They make their protestation, ib.
——— Flie into England, ib.
——— ¶ See Conspiracie and Nobles
Lords of misrule ¶ Sée Ferers
Lords and ladies put out of the court, &c. ii. 793.

Loiges sent into Scotland, vol v. page 542.
Lorison ¶ Sée Twinam
Losaunge ¶ Sée Herbert
Losecote field, iii 294
Losses recompensed, i. 631.
Loth king of the Picts, v 148
—————— Married to Aurelius Ambrose his daughter, ib
—————— Contrarie to his oth of cie-dence, &c aideth the Saxons, v 151
—————— Requireth the kingdome of Britaine, v 153
—————— Ioineth with the Saxons against Arthur, ouerthrowne, i. 575
—————— ¶ See Gouernement
Lothaire the king of Kent, i 629
——— Durst not méet Edelred in the field, i 630
——— He dieth of a wound, i. 636.
Lothian of whome so named, v 160.
Lotterie at London called the great Lotterie, iv 234.
Lou Hugh how he became erle of Chester, ii 33
——— His deth and what issue he had, ib.
Louchouse castell burnt, v 711.
Louchquhaber, the reason of the name, v 125.
Loue in mastifes, i 388
Loue put to triall note, i 447
—— Betwéene Aidan and Oswin, i. 618
—— Of Amphibalus and Alban, i. 527
—— Of Locrine lewd ill rewarded, i. 444
—— Betwéene brethren long at discord, i 454.
—— Brotherlie notablie exéplified, i 610
—— Towards enimies, &c. . purchased hatred and deth, i 621
—— Of a wife to her husband exemplified, i 649
—— Like to cost losse of life note fond Ethelwulfes dooing, i 662
—— Maketh men blind and sottish note, i 537.
—— In a woman with lust what mischiefe it bred, i. 493.
—— Vnlawfull of Algar reuenged, i 649
—— Vnlawfull of Kinewulfe note, i 650
—— Turned into no loue, i 447
—— Of ones countrie maketh a man offend against his calling, i 692.
—— That Edward the second bare Péers Gaueston, iii 549
—— ¶ Sée Péers Gaueston, and Edward the second
—— Of People to the lord Cobham note, iii 63.
—— Of Henrie the seuenth to his wife ladie Elisabeth, iii 490.
—— Of a mother naturall and kind note, iii 370 to 378.
—— Of the duke of Britaine to the earle of Richmond incorruptible, iii 424, 426
—— Unlawfull of Richard the third towards his néece, iii. 431.
—— Of naughtie men conuerted into a deadlie hate, iii 409, 410.
—— Wanton misleadeth and bréedeth discord, iii. 291, 292
—— Of the people to the erle of Warwike note, i. 303, 304.
Loue. ¶ Sée Earle of Warwike in Henrie the sixt time and Edward the fourth.
—— Of a concubine to hir paramour, vol ii page 259
—— Of king Henrie the second to the earle of Oxford and the earle of Suffolke note, ii 777
—— ¶ Sée more in Earles
—— Of the father to the children, preferment to the mother, ii. 831
—— Betwéene man and wife exemplified, ii 823
—— Of a Iewish woman made a decon, plaied the apostate, ii 352
—— Gotten by liberalitie and profit, ii. 779
—— Blind and Ungodlie, iii. 137, 138.
—— Vnlawfull, with the shamefull end thereof, iii. 792.
—— And lust with the danger and mischiefe of both, iii 64
—— Therein is losse euen of life note, ii. 70, 725.
—— Must be tempered with feare, vi. 122
Loue French, iii 340
Louell, lord Louell capteine of the conspiracie against king Henrie the seuenth, vi 270
Louell William held the castell of Carie, ii 83
——— Lord his rebellion, he escapeth, iii 483.
——— Arriueth in Flanders, continueth conspirator against Henrie the seuenth, iii 486
——— Knight, sent ouer to Calis with a power, iii 602.
Louet lord slaine, v. 543.
Louiers besieged, iii. 179.
——— And yéelded vp, iii 99
Louthian spoiled by the English, ii. 153
Low countries ¶ Sée States.
Lucie Richard lord chiefe iustice of England deceaseth, ii. 178
Lucius Antenoins lieutenant of Britaine, v. 87.
——— He is wounded, v 88.
Lucius king of Britaine deceaseth, v 96
—————— Brings true religion to a kind of good forme, i 41
—————— Sendeth for a forme of discipline to Rome, i 43
—————— The first christian king of this nation counted, i 199.
—————— Whether the church that he builded at London stood at Westminster or in Cornehill, i. 42, 43
—————— The errors of them noted of them which saie he renounced his kingdome, and became a pope, i 44
—————— Renowned in writers, i. 511.
—————— Built S. Peters at Wesminster, i 512.
Lucius king of Celts, i. 7
—————— Deliuered from an vsurper, ib.
Lud king of Britaine his acts and déeds, i. 463
Ludgate by whome builded, ib.
Ludhurdibras, the eight ruler of Britaine, i 446.
Ludlow woon by king Stephan, ii 85
Ludwall paieth a tribute of wolfeskins to Edgar, i. 695.
Lugthake king of Scots, his incontinencie and

other vile vices, murthered with a number of his men, vol v page 86
Lugtake crowned at Scone, slaine, v 278
Luidhard bishop appointed to instruct quéene Bertha note, i 590
Lumleie lord founder of surgerie lecture in London note, iv 496
Lume riuer giuing the name to Lancaster described, i 143.
Lunarie an herb and the strange effects thereof, i 220
Lupicinus is sent from Rome to relécue the Britons against Scots and Picts, i 544.
Lupus ¶ Sée Germanus.
——— ¶ Sée Lou
Lurden a terme of reproach, how it came vp, v 256
Lust and what inconueniences it bréedeth in men, i 556
—— Unlawfull, what mischéefe it bred, i 668
—— Fleshlie to satisfie occasion of deadlie villanie, i 521
—— Of Algar in séeking to ravish Friswid punished with blindnesse, i 649
—— Unlawfull of king Edwin, i 693
—— Of William Rufus, ii 30.
—— ¶ Sée Loue.
Lycisca a kind of dog, i 389
Lydius lapis, i 395
Lynceus preserued by his wife, i 435.

M.

Mac Adam Gilmore a common spoiler and burner of churches, vi 261
——— Is thereof called corthie, ib
Mac Artie Reogh married the ladie Elconor Fitzgirrald, vi 301
Mac Artie More an ancient Irish gentleman, vi. 332
——— He surrendereth his lands and taketh it anew, vi 332
——— Sweareth allegieance, ib.
——— Is made baron of Valencia and earle of Clancar, vi. 333
——— Shane Oneile scoffeth at him, ib.
——— His coming to Corke, vi 381
——— His redinesse to serue against forren power, vi 407
——— Departeth home, ib.
——— His pride and insolencie, vi 339
——— Ioineth with the Butlers, ib
——— Submitteth himselfe, vi 367
——— Inuadeth the lord Roches lands, vi 340
Mac Artie Dermon is in open rebellion, vi 205
Mac Balther burneth the castle of Kennun and the towne of Courconlie, vi 244
Mac Cartie pleieth the diuell in Desmond, vi 239
Mac Cormake Oconhor in rebellion, vi 395
Mac Coghlan capteine of the Scottish ships is taken, vi 260
Mac Coghlan killeth Omalaghlin king of Meth, vol. vi page 240
——— Discomfiteth William Burgh, ib
Mac Lughter William his countrie spoiled, vi 385
——— He is a good subiect, vi 385, 386
Mac Holan Oohalen Prince of Ossorie submitteth himselfe vnto king Henrie the second, vi 161, 162
Mac Goghganie what he got his posteritie lost, vi 265
Mac Gillmore was slaine in the church at Cragfergus, which before he had burned, vi 363.
Macbeth the vsurper of the crowne of Scotland uanquished, i. 749.
Maclogunus his wicked acts and déeds detected by Gyldas, i 596
Mac Mahon pleieth the countrie, vi 266
Mac Morice baron of Kerrie and Lexnaw, vi 54
Mac Morogh, vi 122
——— ¶ Sée Dermon.
——— Is taken prisoner, vi. 265
Maconell Iames, v 586
Macworth capteine entreth first the Spaniards fort, vi 431
Mac William the rebel taken and all his companie at Knocktow are slaine, vi 271
Madan the third ruler of Britaine deuoured of wild beasts, vi 444.
Madder a commoditie sometime in England, i. 187.
Madocke a noble man of birth, vi 86
——— He died bishop of Fernes, ib.
Magdalene the quéene dieth, v 513
Magdalen counterfeted to be K Richard the second, iii. 14.
Magi and whie so called, i. 34
Magike taught throughout all the realme, i 446
Magistrats subiect to spite and enuie, v 448
——— Authoritie great and peremtorie, iii 988
——— Are to be honoured both in spéeche and manners, iii 989, 990
Maglanus and Henrinus slaine, i. 448
Maglanus ¶ Sée Duke
Magna charta, ii 321, 527, 531.
——— Confirmed, ii 357, 538
Magnanimitie ¶ Sée Quéene Elizabeth
Magnus king of Norwaie cometh into the western Isles, v 284
——— Sendeth ambassadors to Alexander, v. 317
——— His release of the Scottish Isles, v 318
Magnus admerall of rouers his exploits, ii 38
Magus the sonne of Samothes, and what parts of the earth he gouerned, i 429
——— What learning he taught in Albion, i. 34.
Maid smiteth a maior in the face, iii 951
Maides murthered by thousands, i 536
Maidstone, esquire offereth to fight in his ladies quarrell, iii 33
Maie daie, the euill. ¶ Sée Rebellion of Lincolne.

Maiegrime roiall, vol iii pages 556, 561
Maine Iland sixtéene miles in length &c described, i 75
Maine the marquesse, v 566
Maineprise, iii 8
Mainus crowned, confirmed the league with the Picts, deuout in religion, v 45.
Maior of Yorke slaine, v 353
Maior or Maire what the word signifieth, ii 298
Maior of London sworne to be true to Henrie the third, ii 456
—— An information against him to king Henrie the third, ii 443
—— Discharged of his place for a while, ib
—— Condemned to prison and all his goods confiscat, ii. 764
—— A seuere punisher of adultrie in his time, ii 754
—— Fiue aldermen knighted, ii 747
—— His words at the rebellion of Wat Tiler, ii 741.
—— And sherriffes imprisoned at Windsore, ii 818.
—— Commended for his carefull prouision of corne from beyond the seas in the time of dearth, ii. 815.
—— His rash and unaduised answer, ii 785
—— Iustlie commended, ii 774
—— And his brethren challenge all commers at iusts, ii 671
—— Forced to take an oth, ii 581.
—— And what order he took to sée the kings peace kept, ii 561
—— Sworne, and went home in a greie cloke, iii. 539
—— He and aldermen feasted by Edward the fourth note, iii. 349
—— Accused of treason, iii 287
—— Departed from sargeants feast discontent bicause he sat not highest in the hall note, iii 283
—— His office and authoritie, ii 207
—— One for the space of twentie and one yeares, ii 298
—— And shirriffes the first that were chosen, ib
—— And bailiffes chosen out of the number of fiue and thirtie burgesses, ii 284
—— And shirriffes resisted at Clerkenwell, iii 237.
—— And welcoming home Henrie the fift out of France, iii 84
—— That first ware a rich collar of gold and whose gift, iii 834.
—— Of councell vnto Henrie the eight, ib
—— In a gown of crimson velvet, iii 781
—— And aldermen of London in black mourning come to Henrie the eight with a heauie suit of ill Maie daie, iii 624
—— Sometime an officer, iii 484
—— Feast first kept at Guildhall, iii. 528
—— ¶ Sée Contention, London and Souldiors
Maior of Bodmin in Cornewall hanged, iii 925
—— Of Excester smitten on the face by a maid, iii 951
Maior of Norwich his order of receiuing the quéene Elizabeth, vol iv pages 375, 376
—— Oration in English which he made to the quéene, iv 378
—— His gift presented vnto hir, ib
—— Purposing to make another oration to the quéene, is willed to forbeare and whie, iv 403
—— He is knighted, ib
Makbeth a valiant gentleman, v 264
—— Sent against the rebels, v 265.
—— His crueltie defamed, v. 266
—— Assaileth the campe of the Danes ouercome with drinke and sléepe, v 267
—— Made thane of Cawder, deuiseth how he might obteine the kingdome, he sleieth king Duncane, vsurpeth the crowne his liberalitie and studie to aduance iustice, v. 269
—— His lawes, v 270.
—— His counterfet zeale and equitie, his giltie conscience, his diuise to slea Banquho & his sonnes, v 271.
—— His bread, his crueltie caused through feare, v 273.
—— His confidence in wizzards, his crueltie, v 274
—— His trust in prophesies, v 276
—— He and Makduffe in armes one against another, v 277.
—— His lawes abrogated, v 278.
Makdonald proclamed king of the Isles inuadeth Lorne and Cantire, v. 185
Makdonald Rosse a notable robber notablie punished, v. 421
Macdowald offereth himselfe to be capteine of the rebels, v 265
—— He discomfiteth the kings power he slaieth himselfe, his wife and children, his head sent to the king, v 265, 266
Makduffe thane of Fife, v 274
—— His escape into England, v. 275.
—— His aduancement note, v 277
—— ¶ Sée Makbeth.
Makferlane Walter, v 539.
Makintosch Lauchlane apprehended, v 567
Makintoschs at variance with the Glenchattens, v. 504.
—— They raise sedition, v 505.
—— There wonderfull faith to their capteins, ib
Makpender earle of Merns slueth K. Duncane, v 284.
Makulzen and Makbein capteins of pirats note, v. 300
Malachias a noble man borne at Armagh, vi. 86.
—— Gouernor of Bangor, ib.
—— Bishop of Armagh, vi 86, 87
—— His stoutnesse with the soldiors, vi 86.
—— He died at Clarauell, vi 87.
Malbie sir Nicholas serueth with sir Peter Carew in the butlers warres, vi. 362.
—— His seruice at Kilkennie, ib.

Milbie sir Nicholas he is commended by the quéene, vol vi page 382.
——— He is dubbed knight, vi. 386
——— Sworne one of the priuie councell, ib
——— Made colonell of Connagh, ib
——— He serueth in Mounster vnder sir William Daurie lord iustice, vi 413
——— Is gouernor of Mounster, vi. 414
——— His seruice there, vi 315
——— He sendeth to and for the erle of Desmond, ib
——— He incountreth with sir Iohn of Desmond, vi. 416.
——— Discomfitteth him, ib
——— He writeth to the erle of Desmond for his submission, vi 418
——— Disolueth his armie, ib
——— Subscribeth to the proclamation of the erle of Desmond to be a traitor, vi 424
——— He méeteth sir William Pellam lord iustice at Limerike, vi 422
——— Presenteth him with Sanders letters, ib
Malchenus ¶ Sée Marcharus
Malchus a moonke at Winchester, vi. 87.
——— Is bishop of Lisemore, ib
Malcolme king of Scots holdeth Cumberland in homage, i 690.
——— Destroieth manie places in the north parts, ii. 16.
——— Sendeth to duke William to treat of peace, ii 17
——— Dooth homage to duke William for Scotland, ib
——— Marieth Edgar Ethelings sister, ii. 9
——— Commeth to Glocester, ii. 34
——— Did fiue times waste Northumberland note, ib
——— Enioieth the erledome of Huntington, ii 31.
——— Inuadeth England, sueth for peace, ii 32, 34
——— He and his sonne slaine, ii. 34
Malcolme the sonne of Donald the fift he is created heire apparent, v 227
——— Escapeth hurts, v. 228
——— Admitted king, v. 229.
——— Séeketh fréends against Constantine, v. 249
——— He is murthered, v 230
——— Goeth with an armie to fight with Constantine, v 249.
——— Poisoned by his cousine Kenneth, v. 245
Malcolme the sonne of K Kenneth prince of Cumberland, v 246
——— In armes against Grime for the crowne, v 251.
——— Refuseth the crowne but vpon condition he is made king, his wisedome in ordering Officers, v. 255
Malcolme sendeth ambassadors to the Danes, vol. v page 257
——— Wounded, v 258
——— His praier, v 259
——— Hasteneth forward to fight with the Danes, his oration, v 260
——— Winneth the field against the Danes, v 261.
——— His ordinances and decrées after peace obteined, v. 263
——— He waxeth auaricious, cruell to purchase riches, conspired against and murthered, v 262
Malcolme recouers the crowne, v 277
——— His manlie courage against a conspirator, v 278
——— Marrieth Margaret sister to Edgar Etheling, v 279
——— In armes against William the conquerour, v 280
——— Giueth himselfe to deuotion, v. 281.
——— Restoreth and erecteth bishop sées, ib.
——— Slaine in battell, v 282
——— A builder of churches, v 283
——— His sonnes, ib.
Malcolme the sonne of Henrie proclamed prince of Scotland, v 291, 292
——— Summoned to doo homage, v 293.
——— Beginneth his reigne, his education, ib.
——— Goeth with king Henrie into France, ib.
——— Reproоued by his nobles, goeth to Yorke, sentence against him besieged, hated of his people, v 293, 294.
——— Meaneth to gouerne in vpright iustice, not persuaded to take a wife, his death, v. 295
Malcontentment, iii 400
——— Grew to a conspiracie, iii 812
——— Of the erle of Montagne, ii 54
——— Of Parrie bicause he might not haue preferment to his liking, iv 564
——— ¶ Sée Councell, Parrie and rebellion
Malcontents against the cesse, vi 388
Malcus made and consecrated bishop of Waterford, ii 38.
Maldwin inuested king of the Scots, a louer of peace and iustice, v 176.
——— Went about to punish the authors of a commotion, ib
——— Buildeth the church of the abbie of Colmekill, ib
——— Strangled in his bed, v 177
Maldon a towne erected out of the ruins of Ithancester, i. 178.
Malefactors, i. 310
——— ¶ Sée Punishments.
Malgo made king of Britaine comlie of person but filthie of condition, i 585
Malice of mankind what mischéefe and reuenge it seeketh, i 179
——— And the nature thereof note, i 117.
——— Causeth murther, i. 520
——— Of Wilnot in burning king Egelreds ships, i 711.

Malice of duke William against the English, vol. ii page 14.
———————— ¶ Sée William
——— Of Leofin breketh into murther, ii 20.
——— Betwéene the two dukes of Burgogne and Orleance, and the chéefe cause thereof, iii 36
——— Of the erle of Cornewall to the citie of London, ii. 431
——— Betwéene king Richard the second and the duke of Glocester, ii 834.
——— Of Cardinall Poole against King Henrie the eight, iv. 89
——— Afresh betwixt Edward the fourth and the duke of Clarence, brethren, iii 316
——— Of the erle of Warwicke against Edward the fourth note, iii 288
——— Of Richard the first and the French king one against another, ii 253
——— Of the French king against Richard the first note, ii. 241
——— Betwéene dukes of Summerset & Yorke note, iii 208
——— Of the duchesse of Burgogne to the line of Lancaster, iv 504
——— ¶ Sée Margaret
——— Betwéene the duke of Summerset and the duke of Yorke, iii 185
——— Of the cardinall Wolseie mortall against the duke of Buckingham, iii 641
——— Of the Frenchmen and their dogged stomachs, iii 617, 618
——— Against Henrie, breaking out into an intent of murther and the partie executed, ii 385
——— Of the lords against the earle of Cornewall increased, ii 548
——— Betwixt great estates about matters of marriage, iii 501
——— Inconuenient vnto the malicious note, ii 27, 28
——— Cloked bursteth out, ii 436
——— Inferreth murther note, ii 836
——— Thirsteth after reuenge note, ii 521, 525
——— And the nature thereof, iv 630
——— Bursteth out into murther, ii 292
——— Whervpon arise slanders, ii 109
——— Trauelleth still to reuenge, iii 237
——— To appease a labour, dangerous, iii 217
——— In a realme, the mortall mischéefe thereof, iii 218
——— Notable dissembled note, iii 208
——— How mischéefouslie it worketh to reuenge note, iii 836, 146
——— Content with no reuenge, ii 738
——— ¶ See Enuie, Hate, and Reuenge
Millese the vice admerall of France, v 559
Millet William shirriffe of Yorke and his familie taken prisoner and put to ransome, ii 11
Malmsburie and the Uses, by whom built, i. 451
——— The abbeie founded, i 642
Malt and the making thereof, i 284
——— The best how tried, ib
Malton and of a prouerb there vsed, i. 159.
Mamertinus pallegyricall in praise of Dioclesian and Maximian in emperors note, vol i page 521
Man Ile kings and petie kings thereof, i 67
——— Taken by Robert Bruse, ii 547.
——— Spoiled, v 596.
——— ¶ Sée Ile Mona, and Harold
Man the Iland whether English or Irish, vi 9
Mandubratius in fauour with the Trinouants and for whome he sued to Cesar to be there gouernor, i 474
Manitold riuer and whie so named, i 161
Manlius slaine of his brother Mempricius, i. 445.
Manlius Ualens inuadeth the Picts, v 69
Manners Thomas knight his militarie seruice in Scotland, iv 213
———— ¶ Sée Erle and Rutland
Manners and dispositions of the Irishrie, vi 65
Manneuin Thomas baron of Scrin is taken prisoner by Oconhor of Meth, vi 264
Manslaughter how in times past and how punished, i 312
Manwood lord chéefe baron of the escheker a good common welths man note his déeds, iv 550, 551, 552
Mar erle made regent, v 661.
——— Died, v 666.
Mar for Marthea, v 125
Marble mines, i 394
——— White, store in England, ib
Marble stone wherevpon kings of Scots sat at their coronation, transferred to Westminster, ii 518
Marbodeus commendation of the English great stone and pearle, i 401
Marchades a valiant capteine, ii 268, 269, 270
——— A good seruitor in warres, i 271
Marchalks called of the Grecians pyrites note, i 362
Marcharus made erle of Northumberland, i 753
Marcher erle of Mercia flieth into Scotland, ii 9
——— Imprisoned by William Rufus, ii 27
——— Reconciled vnto king William, ii 15
——— Withdraweth from the battell against duke William, ii 1
——— Flieth into Elie for defence against duke William, ii 16
Marcus Antonius bewitched with his wife Cleopatra, vi 123
Marcus Papirius indignation and disdaine, i 435
Margadud K of South Wales, i 599
Margaret quéene of Norwaie deceaseth, v 320
Margaret Dowglasse countesse of Leneux some part of hir life, v 673
———— Hir deth, epitaph, stateliе descent, &c note, v. 674.
Margaret Dowglasse prisoner in the Tower, iii 798
———— Pardoned, released, iii 805
Margaret the wife of K. Henrie whie not crowned, ii 131
Margaret sister to earle Hugh of Chester married to John Bohune, ii 33.

Margaret and Christine, the sisters of Edgar Etheling, vol ii page 9
Margaret the daughter of king William of Scotland maried to erle Conan, ii 12
Margaret daughter to the quéene of Scots, and of the erle Angus borne, iii. 614
Margaret daughter vnto the French king affianced vnto Henrie the kings sonne of seuen yeres old, ii 116
——— Crowned quéene, ii 141
Margaret duchesse of Salisburie beheaded, iii 346
Margaret sister to Edward the fourth sent ouer to the duke of Burgogne, iii 286
Margaret countesse of Leneux sent to the Towre, iv. 229
——— Deliuered out of the Towre, iv 231
Margaret duchesse of Burgogne sister to Edward the fourth malicious to Lancaster house, iii 485
——— Hir malice against the line of Lancaster, iii 505
——— Hir new counterfet of Richard Plantagenet, iii 503.
Margaret ladie Fitzgirrald of Kildare married to the earle of Ossorie, vi. 278
——— She longeth for wine, ib.
——— Hir stoutness, ib
——— Hir wisedome and policie in gouernment, vi 280
——— Hir gréefe for the murthering of Talbot, ib.
Margraue of Baden and his wife great with child come to London, iv. 229
——— She is deliuered of a child, ib
——— The quéene giueth the name, ib
——— ¶ Sée Marquesse
Mariage of kings, and first of king Iohn after his diuorce, ii 280.
——— Of Edward the first, to the ladie Margaret sister to the French king, ii 532
——— Of Edward the second and the French king his daughter ladie Isabell, ii 547, 548
——— Of Edward the thirds sister to the duke of Gelderland, ii 603
——— Of Edward the fourth to Elizabeth being an offensiue mariage note, iii 283
——— Of Henrie the third with Elenor daughter to the earle of Prouance, ii 370.
——— Of Edward the sixt and the yoonge Scotish quéene Marie, iii 830
——— Newlie mooued, procéedeth not, iii 867
——— Written of the nobles of Scotland, iii 911.
——— Of Henrie the fift to the ladie Katharine, the French kings daughter, crowned quéene, iii 125
——— Solemnitie thereat, iii 125, 126
——— Of Henrie the sixt to the erle Armenaks daughter concluded note, iii 205, 207
——— To the ladie Margaret daughter to Reiner king of Sicill and Ierusalem, iii 207.
Mariage of Henrie the seuenth to the daughter of Edward the fourth, vol iii page 482
——— Of Henrie the eight and the duchesse of Alanson the French kings sister reported, iii 719, 720
——— With his brothers wife yet againe in question, iii 736
——— Thought vnlawfull and commeth vnto iudgement, iii 739
——— Common argument in sermons, iii 775
——— Yet againe in question, with the determination of diuers vniuersities concerning the same, iii 766 to 771
——— Debated, iii 736
——— By consent of all the vniuersities in christendome iudged vnlawfull note, iii 747, 748
——— With the ladie Anne Bullen, iii 777
——— With the ladie Anne of Cléeues concluded, iii 810
——— Solemnised, iii 814
——— Iudged vnlawfull, iii 818
——— With the ladie Katharine Par, iii 832
——— Of Richard the second to the French kings daughter, ii 833.
——— With the emperors sister, ii 753
——— And the emperor of Germanies daughter, ii 734
——— Of Richard the third vnto the ladie Anne daughter to Richard erle of Warwike, iii 379.
——— Betwixt Richard the third and the erle of Richmonds néece offensiue, iii 433
Mariage of Princes and first of Edward the first his eldest sonne and Philip daughter to the earle of Flanders, ii 511
——— Of Edward prince of Wales and the ladie Marie daughter to the erle of Henault, ii. 572
——— To the erle of Warwikes daughter, iii 295
——— Betwixt Henrie the kings sonne seuen yeares old, &c. ii. 116.
——— Of Richard, Henrie the thirds brother to the ladie Sanctia, ii 400
——— Betwixt Henrie the thirds sonne and the king of Spaines daughter, ii 439.
——— Of Edward, Henrie the thirds sonne vnto king Alfonsus daughter, ii. 441
——— Edward the thirds second sonne lord Lionell vnto the duke of Millans daughter, ii 685, 686
——— His interteinment at Surrie his receiuing into Millan, ii 685
Mariage of the kings daughter and his sonne the prince of Scotland, v. 320.
Mariage reported, v 440
——— Incestuous, v 389
Mariage of honourable men, and first of the erle of

March, and the daughter of Owen Glendouer, vol. iii. page 21.
Mariage of the lord Manchensies daughter, to William de Ualence Henrie the thirds half brother, ii. 414.
——— Of the lord William Greie with the wife of Paule Peuier, ii. 442, 423.
——— Of erle Thomas of Flanders, and Ione the widow of Ferdinando, ii. 387.
——— Of the erle Rafe of Chester vnto thrée wiues, ii. 372.
——— Betwéene the emperor Frederike and Henrie the thirds sister, ii. 378.
——— Of the erle of Cornewall and the countesse of Glocester, ii. 369.
——— Of the duke of Lancaster with a ladie of mean estate: note, ii. 831.
——— Of the duke of Lancasters daughter to the king of Portingall, ii. 770.
——— Of erle Bolingbroke of Derbie to the daughter of erle Bohune of Hereford, ii. 768.
——— Betwéene the prince of Spaine and the duke of Lancasters daughter, ii. 771, 772.
——— Of Ambrose Dudleie erle of Warwike to the erle of Bedfords eldest daughter, iv. 229.
——— Of Edmund erle of Cambridge to the ladie Constance daughter to the king of Spaine, ii. 696, 697.
——— Of Iohn of Gant duke of Richmond to the duke of Lancasters daughter, ii. 671.
——— Promised by constreint of the erle of Flanders and king Edward the thirds daughter, ii. 659.
——— Péers de Gaueston and the daughter of the erle of Glocester, ii. 457.
——— Of the lord Courtneie with king Edward the fourths daughter, iii. 529.
——— Betwixt prince Arthur and the ladie Katharine daughter to Ferdinando, not fully concluded, and whie, iii. 524.
——— ¶ Sée Katharine.
——— The solemnitie of the same, iii. 527.
——— Of the lord Courcie and the king of England king Edward the third his daughter, ii. 680.
——— Betwixt the king of Castile and the ladie Marie the king his daughter of ten yeres old, iii. 539.
——— Mooued betwixt the king of Scots and Margaret the eldest daughter of king Henrie the seuenth, iii. 521.
——— Of the erle of Kent to a daughter of lord Barnabie of Millane, iii. 46.
——— Betwixt the erle of Glocesters sonne and the daughter of the lord Guie of Angolselme, ii. 427.
——— Purposed for the erle of Richmond with Walter Herberts sister, but dissapointed, iii. 434.
——— Concluded betwixt the prince of Rothsaie and the duke of Suffolkes daughter, iii. 423.
——— Of the king of Scots, and king Edward the fourth second daughter treated vpon, iii. 349.
Mariage betwéene the king of Scots sister and the yoonge prince of Wales, vol. iii. page 279.
——— Betwéene the duke of Burgognies sonne and heire with ladie Margaret sister to king Edward the fourth, iii. 284, 285.
——— Of the duke of Clarence with the erle of Warwikes eldest daughter, iii. 290.
——— Of duke Arthurs Mother to Guie de Towre, by a dispensation, ii. 278.
——— Of the duke of Bedford with the erle of S. Paules daughter, iii. 176.
——— Of the duke of Glocester with the wife of the duke of Brabant he aliue: note, iii. 137.
——— Betwéene the erle of Richmond and king Edward the fourths daughter accorded vpon by oth, iii. 420.
——— Betwéene the duke of Bedford and the sister of the duke of Burgognie, iii. 138.
Mariage of quéenes and honorable women, and first of the countesse of Kent of hir owne choosing: note, iii. 46.
——— Of king Henrie the fourths daughter to the king of Denmarke, iii. 41.
——— Of quéene Isabell to king Richard the second, widow to duke of Orleance his son, iii. 18.
——— Of king Henrie the fourths sister vnto sir Iohn Cornwall, iii. 17.
——— Of king Henrie the fourths daughter Blanch to the duke of Bauier, iii. 20.
——— Of the countesse of Penbroke sister vnto king Henrie the third vnto Simon Montfort, iii. 384.
——— Of ladie Ione king Henrie the thirds sister vnto Alexander king of Scots, ii. 351.
——— Of quéene Isabell Henrie the thirds mother to the erle of March in France, ii. 349.
——— Of the ladie Ione de Courtenie king Richard the second his halfe sister to the erle of saint Paule, ii. 726.
——— Edward the firsts daughter to two noble men, ii. 492.
——— Of Elisabeth countesse of Holland king Edward the firsts daughter and the erle of Hereford, ii. 536.
——— Of the ladie Elen king Edward the firsts daughter, to the duke of Bar a French man, ii. 500.
——— Of Elisabeth king Edward the firsts daughter vnto the earle of Holland, ii. 520.
——— Of the countesse of Glocester with sir Rafe Monthermer, ii. 510.
——— Of Marie quéene of Scots with Henrie Stuard the eldest sonne to the erle of Leneux, iv. 228.
——— Of the countesse of Arthois married to the duke of Burgundie, ii. 688.
——— Of the countesse of Kent a widow and the prince of Wales; note, ii. 676.
——— Betwéene the ladie Iane sister vnto king Edward the third and the king of Scots, iii. 696.
——— Of an earles two daughters to two brethren, ii. 535.

Mariage of the ladie Margaret daughter to king Henrie the seuenth to Iames the fourth king of Scots, vol iii page 526
——— Of an earles daughter to an errant rascall and traitorous rebell, iii 511
——— Of the duchesse of Britaine and Charles the French king, iii 495
——— Of the ladie Margaret vnto king Charles how beneficiall vnto king Edward the fourth, iii 297.
——— Of the French ladie Bona to the duke of Millan, iii 284
——— Of quéene Marie with Philip prince of Spaine, of some liked, of most disliked note, iv. 10
——— Agréed vpon in parlement, iv 27
——— Solemnised with an abstract of the conditions of the same, iv 57, 58, 59, 60, 61.
——— Of king Iohns daughter ladie Iane vnto the earle of March, ii 516
——— Of Isabell vnto king Iohn got him enuie, ii 284
——— Of quéene Katharines mother to Henrie the sixt, with Owen Teuther, iii 190
——— Of the ladie Elisabeth vnto Edward the fourth, ib
——— Of the quéene of Scots and the Dolphin of France, iii 1014
——— Betwéene the ladie Marie Henrie the eights daughter and the king of Scots purposed, iii 690
——— Betwéene the ladie Marie eldest daughter to Henrie the eight and the Dolphin of France pretended, iii 632
——— Of quéene Katharine and Henrie the eight, iii 517
——— Of the ladie Elizabeth, now quéene, to a Spaniard solicited, iv 132
——— Mooued in the parlement and how answered by herself, iv 178
——— Sued vnto out of Denmark, iv 186
——— Of a gentlewoman in flight to a king, ii 9
Mariage forren, and first betwéene the king of France and the ladie Margaret, eldest daughter to Henrie the seuenth, iii 531
——— Betwéene the French kings daughter and Richard the second, treated of, ii 831.
——— Betwéene the Dolphin of France and Edward the fourth daughter treated vpon, iii. 348
——— Betwéene the French king and the ladie Marie sister to Henrie the eight who should haue been wife to the prince of Castile, iii. 603, 604
——— Betwéene the French kings daughter and the king of Englands son, ii 162
——— Betwéene the Dolphin and the princesse of Scots, iv 102
——— Of Lewes the French kings sonne and Blanch the néece of king Iohn, ii 279
——— Of the French king and the emperor Charles his sister, iii 706
——— Made alliance betwéene the pope and the French king, iii 631
Mariage in generall and first of one offensiue, vol ii page 381
——— Confirmed from Rome with monie, ii 384
——— Within the degrees of consanguinitie, dispensed withall by the pope, ii 671
——— Not to be forced note, ii 645
——— Malice betwéene great personages as touching the same, iii 501
——— One intended, another begun and ended note, iii 283, 284
——— A spirituall thing and how it should be made, iii 387
——— Purchased with monie, ii 144.
——— Within the seuenth degrée of consanguinitie dissolued, ii. 52
——— Broken off and reuenged, iii 228
——— Infortunate and vnprofitable to the realme of England, iii 208.
——— Betwéene children, to compose strife, and establish amitie betwéene parents, iii 1023
——— Of princes is not a matter to be trifled in, iii 867
——— Undertaken without the kings assent, made treasonable note, iii 798
——— Made vpon goodlie conditions note, i 590
——— Unlawfull punished, i 621
——— Sued for by messenger not without deceit. note, i 695
——— Granted vpon condition of becomming a christiã, i 620
——— Without dower a consent to aproue, i 417
——— Made through mistrust of enimies, i 646
——— Uoid of fleshlie pleasure, i 710
——— Unpleasurable by means of hatred, i 744, 745
——— Granted vpon religious conditions note, i. 601
——— Of a king to his butlers daughter, i 630.
——— Fatall, i. 135, 555, 648, 696, 708.
Mariages dissapointed, i 536
——— In what degrées thought tollerable, i 594.
——— Made for increase of loue and amitie, vi. 245, 363
——— Two roiall, iii 526
Marie the quéene of Scots borne, v 528
——— Seuen daies old when she began hir reigne, v 529
——— A motion made for hir to marrie king Edward the sixt, v 530
——— She is committed to the lord Leuinstone, v 529
——— Hir mariage to king Edward confirmed, v 531
——— The French king misliketh the match, ib
——— Conueid to Sterling, v 533
——— Order taken for hir custodie, ib
——— Shée goeth to Menteith, v. 551

Marie quéene of Scots, conueied into France, vol v. page 558.
——— Hir diligence, v 565
——— Shée giueth the gouernment of the realme to the quéene mother, v 574
——— Shée goeth to Inuernesse, v 577
——— Shée goeth on progresse for iustices cause, ib.
——— Hir dowre in France, v 582
——— Hir mariage to the Dolphin of France, ib
——— Shée requireth a matrimoniall crowne of Scotland to be giuen to hir husband, v. 587
——— Shée writeth out of France to the prior of saint Andrews, v. 592
——— Hir praise, ib
——— Shée goeth into Loraine, v 604
——— Causes to make hir staie in France, ib.
——— Shée commeth to Calis, v 608
——— Arriueth at Leith, ib.
——— Hir costlie iewels and household stuffe, ib
——— Shée visiteth the townes of Scotland, v 609.
——— Maketh hir progresse into the north parts, v 611.
——— Maketh a progresse to Atholl, v 614
——— Shée goeth into Fife, ib
——— Shée marieth the lord Darnelie, ib
——— Shée sendeth into France for aid, v 616
——— Shée conferreth with the king, v 617.
——— Shée commeth to Edenburgh, v 618.
——— Shée agréeth the nobilitie, ib
——— Taketh hir chamber for to be deliuered of a child, v 618.
——— Sendeth vnto the quéene of England and to the king of France, ib
——— Sendeth for the nobilitie against hir deliuerance, ib
——— Shée goeth to Allowaie, v. 619
——— Sendeth for godfathers for hir sonne, ib
——— Shée goeth into Meggatland, ib
——— Shée burieth hir husband not farre from Dauid Richio, v 620
——— Taken by force by Bothwell, ib
——— Marieth Bothwell, ib
——— He excuseth the mariage vnto the French king, v. 620
Marie quéene of Scots gathereth a power, vol v page 624
——— Shée is taken of the lords, ib.
——— Imprisoned by Lachleuine. v 625
——— Surrendereth hir title to hir sonne, v 626
——— Escapeth out of Lachleuine, v 632
——— Gathereth a power, ib
——— Discomfitted, v 633
——— Flieth into England, ib.
——— Committed to sir Rafe Sadléer, v. 721
——— Committed to sir Amies Pawlet, v 722
——— ¶ Sée Quéene of Scots
Marie Magdalens daie prosperous for the English to fight against the Scots, v 333
Marie the eldest daughter vnto Henrie the eight borne, iii 614.
——— Remooued to Fremingham castle, iii 1067
——— To Kening hall, in Norfolke, hir letters to the councell, with hir challenge vnto the crowne by right of succession iii 1065
——— With their answer, ib
——— Assembleth hir power against the duke of Northumberland, iii 1069
——— Wind and wether helpe hir, 1070
——— Proclaimed quéene by the Nobilitie for feare of afterclaps, ib
——— ¶ Sée Quéene
Marie countesse of Perch, Henrie the first his daughter drowned, ii 70
Marie Fugh Oconhor king of Offalia & his companie slaine by Iordan Cumin, vi 242
Mariners of the cinque ports at deadlie debate note, ii 525
——— Commended, ii 185.
——— Curse the arch bishop of Canturburie, and the earle of Pembroke, ii 292
——— ¶ Sée Seafaring men
Marisch the traitor executed note, ii 398
Marishes in England, i 355
——— And fenne bogs, i 359
——— ¶ Sée Fens
Mary Victoria, i 504
Marius made king of Britaine, v 72, 73
——— Doubteth rebellion of his subiects, v. 84
——— Compelleth the Romans to leaue the north parts, ib
——— Slaine, v 121
Marius king of Britaine his acts and déeds, i 503
Marius a noble Roman, vi 156
Markets and faires in England, i 339
——— Not to be kept vpon holie daies, vi 160
——— On the sundaie to be redressed, i 359
——— Abused, i 342
——— How they would be better serued than they are, ib
——— Of Horsse, i. 370.
——— ¶ See Faires.

Marle, vol i page 597.
——— White, (excellent good copesting of ground) in England, i 183
Marleswine and Gospatrike robles of Northumberland, flie into Scotland, ii 9
Marnachus thane of Buchquhane, v 261
Marquesse of Baden returneth into his owne countrie, iv 230.
——— Valiant in Chivalrie, iii 606
——— Henrie the eight and he make a challenge at iusts, iii 609
——— Entreth into Scotland and burneth diuers townes, iii 681.
——— Receiueth the emperor Charles at Graueling, iii 477
——— Forsaketh the erle of Richmond, iii 433
——— Committed to the Towre, iii 486
——— Deliuered out of the Towre, iii 490
——— Of Excester condemned, executed, iii 807.
——— Montacute sufferred Edward the fourth to passe by him, iii. 306.
——— Slaine, iii 314.
——— Of Northampton sent into Norfolke to represse the rebels, iii 971
——— Maketh shift to escape danger, iii 975
——— Of Suffolks request, iii 209
——— Chéefest in fauour with king Henrie the sixt and the quéene, iii 210
——— Created duke, iii 212
——— A name of honour next the duke, i 261
——— Created of the prince, i 266
——— In England but one, i 277.
Mart of all England commonly kept at Calis, iii 507, 508
Marteine a beast of chase, i 379
Martia Proba his laws in vse to this date, i 298.
Martia the wife of Guintoline gouerned in his sonnes roome, i 437.
Martine Sivard, a valiant capteine of the Almains assistant to the erle of Lincolne, against Henrie the seuenth a péerlesse warrior, iii 486, 487.
——— Is slaine, iii 488
Marton college in Oxford built, ii 487
Martyrdome marke the causes thereof, ii 437.
Martyrs in quéene Maries time the numbers great that were executed, iv 528
Martyrs that suffered for the gospels sake, i 44
Martyrs fit for the popes kalendar, iv 524, 525, 526.
——— ¶ Sée Christians.
Maserfield, i 617
Maske, iii 633
——— Roiall, iii 558, 567, 609
——— Both the kings of England and France, iii. 654
——— With intended mischéefe, iii 11, 12
——— Before quéene Elizabeth at hir being in Norwich, iv 379
Maske in the French court of English lords, vol iii page 603
——— Of graue and ancient courtiers and likewise of youthfull, iii. 610
——— Of lords and ladies, iii 635, 636
——— And a banket Henrie the eight in person present at the cardinalls house, iii 763
——— Stratche to solace the emperor and his companie, iii 656
Mason knight, his friendlie part towards the duchesse of Suffolke, iv 106
——— Secretarie vnto the French king, iv. 184
Masse hindered by comming in of waters into the minster of Salisburie, i 98
——— From which a bishop and his deacon could not be scared by a tempest, ii 315
——— Whereat king Iohn gaue a pretie die iest, ii 3
——— Concerning the celebrating of the same, &c note, ii 628
——— Abolished, iii 906
Massinissa confidence in dogs, i 385
Mast of oke, hogs meat and hens meat, i 357
Mastife whereof named, i 388.
——— ¶ Sée Dogs
Mathild ¶ Sée Maud
Matreuers lord, capteine of Baieux, ii. 92
Maud borne, afterward empresse, ii 50.
——— Besieged in Oxford, ii 94
——— She escapeth, i 95
——— Fleeth by night out of London, ii 92
——— Armie put to flight, ib
——— Goeth to Bristow, ii 81.
——— Followeth the victorie, she commeth to London, ii 91
——— Besieged in Arundell castell, ii 87
——— Landed in England, and what power she brought, ib
——— Married to the earle of Anjou, ii. 73
——— True to the crowne of England, ii. 72
——— Confesseth hirselfe to bée naught of hir bodie, ii 108
——— Hir decesse, ii 128
Maud daughter and heire to Robert Fitzhammon, Henrie the first his base sonne, ii 63
Maud the wife of Henrie the first a professed nun, ii. 48
Maud Henrie the first his daughter affianced to the emperor Henrie, ii 59.
Maud quéene deliuered of a daughter after hir owne name, ii 50.
Maundeuill of Barnestolle his yearlie reuenues one thousand and two hundred pounds, vi 262
Maundeuill sir Iohn is reconciled to the lord Butler, vi 216
——— Is slaine, vi 248
Maundeuill sir Thomas his good seruice at Glenfield, vi 243.
——— Dooth great enterprises vpon the Scots, vi 248
Maundeuill sir Thomas is slaine, ib.

Mauns a citie in Normandie besieged and deliuered, vol ii page 39
——— Besieged and taken, ii 274
——— Lost by treason of the citizens, recouered, iii 159
——— Yéelded to the French king, ii 197.
Mauns ¶ Sée Aruiragus.
Maunt citie in France burnt by duke William, ii 24.
Maupas the leader of a thousand thrée hundred twentie and foure men incountered with the Scots, vi 250
——— He is found dead vpon the dead bodie of Bruse his enimie, vi. 251
Maupasse ¶ Sée Uernon
Maxentius, the tyrant emperor of Rome, i 530
Maximian sent ouer to aid the king of Britaine, v 127
——— Causeth him to ioine with him against the Romans, ib
——— Pursueth the victorie, ib
——— Taketh vpon him the absolute gouernment of Britaine, with the imperiall title, v 128
——— Granteth peace to Scots, ib
Maximilian king of Romans, prisoned at Bruges by the tounes men, iii 493
——— He and Henrie the seuenth agree to plague the Frenchmen, the cause of his malice, he dealeth dishonestlie with the king of England to his great vexation breaketh promise with him, iii 501
——— Encourageth his men to plaie the men, iii 585
Maximianus slaine, i 531
Maximus the first that draue the Scots out of Britaine, i 11
Maximus successor to the empire by treason, i. 538
——— Ruler of the Britaines and Conan Meridoc at mutuall warre, i 535
——— His martiall exploits, i 536
——— Slaine by Theodosius, ib
Maximus his practise to destroie the Scots, v. 112
——— Sendeth to Heirgus king of Picts, ib
——— Sendeth an herald to Eugenius, raseth a mightie power, inuadeth the Scotish regions, v 112, 113
——— His feigned greefe, v 113
——— Approcheth towards the Scots, ib.
——— His sudden arriuall, v 114
——— Granteth peace to the Irish and séeketh by his bounteous liberalitie to win the people, v 118.
Maxwel lord inuadeth England, v. 499
——— Heareth masse, v 729
Maxwel Iohn deliuered out of prison, v. 645
Maxwel Robert base brother to the erle Moorton, v. 711
Maxwels would not be subiect to the erle of Arraine, v. 712
Mead a kind of drink made in Essex, i. 286
Meauldon now Maldon, i 679
Meaux beseiged by the Englishmen, taken by assalt, iii 129
Meaux the conditions of the surrender thereof to Henrie the fift, vol iii page 131
Medows in England great store and whie, i 185
Medulfe a Scot, founder of Malmsburie abbie, i 612
Medwaie water in Kent described, i 90
Meidhamsted now Peterborrow, and who built the monastrie there, i 629
Meilerus nephew to Fitzstephans, vi 131
——— Is ambitious, ib
——— His seruice, vi 140
——— Arriueth at Waterford, vi 184
——— The description of him, v 190, 209
——— His valiantnesse, v 193, 196
——— Hath no issue, vi 202
——— Leix is giuen vnto him for Kildare, vi. 294
Meinmouth stronglie warded, vi 299
——— Is besciged, vi 299
——— Summoned, ib
——— Betraied, ib
——— The betraiover beheaded, vi 301
Mekins burnt in Smithfield, iii 821
Melga king of Picts a cruell murtherer, i 537
Melitus bishop of London, i. 597.
——— Goeth to Rome about church matters of England, i 601
——— Whie he was faine to leaue London and get him into Kent, i 603
——— Archbishop of Canturburie, ib
——— ¶ Sée Iulius
Mempricius the fourth ruler of Britaine deuoured of wild beasts, i 445
Meliùs inquirendū a writ, i 230
Mellent ¶ Sée Erle
Melune vicount discouereth the purpose of Lewis and the English barons, his death, ii 334.
Melune besieged by king Henrie the fift, iii 121
——— Yéelded vp to Henrie the fift, iii. 122.
Men barbarous brought from the new found Iland, iii 528
Men eat men for want of uittells, vi 249
Mendmarket ¶ Sée Umfreuill
Mendoza the Spanish ambassador.
——— ¶ Sée Throckmorton Francis
Meneua now S Dauids in Wales, i 456
Mentith Iohn capteine of Dunbretton castell, v 350
Merchant of London hanged for murthering a merchant stranger at Genoa note, ii 734
Merchants of England receiued into Antwerpe with generall procession, iii 517
——— Sore hindered by a restreint, iii 507
——— Restreind out of Spaine, iv 224
——— Euillie intreated in Dutchland, iv 331
——— Susteine great losse by sea, iv 330
——— Complaine vnto quéene Elizabeth of their wrongs, ib
——— Proclamation for their free traffike as before, &c iv 339

Merchants of England robbed of the Danish pirats and haue great prises taken from them, vol ii page 530
———— Murther a strange Genoa, ii 721
———— Staied in Spaine, iii 731
Merchants strangers fauoured of king Richard the second, and their goods restored, ii 777
———— A proclamation concerning them, ii 775
———— Slaied in England, iii 535
———— Two of the stillard doo penance for heresie, iii 711
———— ¶ Sée Strangers
Merchants their dealings, i 271
———— Their attire how altered in England, i 290
———— Their couetous dealing to be redressed, i 355
———— Their diet, i 281
———— Their follie in carieng ouer sea English rams and ewes, i 371
Mercia an earldome, ii 1
Mercia kingdome when it began, 587
———— Under certeine noblemen ambitiouslie minded, i 574
———— Of whom the kings thereof descended, i 583
———— Tributarie to Rome, i 647
———— Aduanced by Offa and how, i 646
———— It and the Wels confines diuided by Offdich, i 617
———— How long continued a kingdome, i 677.
———— And when it tooke end, i 676
Mercie notable exemplified, v 228
Merheins were men of goodlie stature, v 72
Mendor and Maximus ruler of Britaine make mutuall warre, i 535
Merlin Syluestris where buried, i. 62
Merlins prophesies, vi 146, 162, 165, 199, 217, 222
Merlins birth and prophesies, i 564
———— His comparison touching Pendragon, i 570
Merton Walter bishop of Rochester and lord chancellor of England, i 237
Mesca now Bulgarie, i 544
Mesures diuerse in the markets of England ¶ Sée Markets
Mesures and weights by whome first ordeined, i 451
———— An ordinance for them, v. 422
———— Of one length vsed throughout England, ii 48
———— ¶ Sée Weights
Meta incognita ¶ Sée Frobisher
Metellan K. of Scots, v 60
———— Becometh freend to the Romans, ib
———— Departeth the world, 61
Meth in Latine Media, vi 123
Meth it is appointed for the kings diet, vol vi page 133
———— It is the fift part of Ireland, vi 2
———— It conteineth sixtéene cantreds, vi. 3
———— It is inuaded and spoiled, vi 267.
———— It is vnder Omalaghlin, vi 89
———— It is giuen vnto Hugh de Lacie, vi 235
Mettals, vi 398
Metheglin the Welshmens Nectar, i 186
Meulane a strong towne yéelded vp to the English, iii 112
Meuricus ¶ Sée Manus
Meuias Hercules ¶ Sée Iusts triumphant
Mice deuoure grass in Dansie hundred and how deuoured note, iv 431
Michaels mount how seated, a great fortification, ii 31
Middle angle people who, i 620.
———— They become christians, ib
Middleton knight proclaimed himselfe duke, ii 555.
Midsummer watch, iv. 271
———— Mainteined, iv 232
———— ¶ See Watch
Mildmaie knight founder of Emanuell college in Cambridge, iv 587
Mile end gréene whie so called, iv 316
Miles vicar of S Brides slaine and the partie executed, iii 750
Miles of saint Dauid lieutenant of Limerike, vi 191
Miles in what sense it is to be taken, vi 130
Mines, i 267
Milke castell yéelded, v 532
Milke of what beast best, v 372
Milo Cogan ¶ Sée Cogan
Millain won and rased by Richard the first, ii. 259
Miller hanged for his master, iii 925.
Milnall in Suffolke burned, iv 231.
Milstones, i 395
Mineral, i 396
Minerall stone, i 397
Minister not to be striken and how punished, i 332
Ministers called home, v 731
———— Kéepe hospitalitie, i 338
———— How weaponed when they trauell, i 335
———— Primitiue church how prouided of able ones, i 235.
———— They and deacons in the church of England, i 229
———— Unlearned how and by whome they swarmed, i 266.
———— Whie not so manie learned as otherwise should be, i 235
———— Greuouslie charged with diuers impositions, i 230, 231
———— They haue no such meanes to ease themselues of taxations as laie men, i 230
———— Shamfullie abused, i 231
———— In thredbare gowns note a practice, i 235.

Ministers learned not mainteinable by diuerse liuings in England, vol. i. page 226.
——— More fauoured than other men, iv. 215.
Minsterworth knight executed as a traitor, ii. 204.
Mints diuerse in England in old time and where kept, i. 361.
Minute what part of time, i. 405.
Miracle wherewith Adelstane was comforted, i. 688.
——— Of saint Germans, i. 564.
——— Confirms the doctrine of German, i. 563.
——— Confirming that the Scots should and ought to be subiect to the kings of England, i. 686.
——— Of Doue riuer rising exceedinglie with out apparent cause, i. 167.
Miracle, v. 169.
——— Of a Child healed, v. 305.
Miracles, v. 349.
——— Note, v. 405.
——— Wrought by praires and other means by certeine saints, i. 116.
——— Of Augustine, i. 593.
——— Of Dunstane better than his arguments, i. 700.
——— Of Oswald, i. 617.
——— Of Fitzherbert whereby he was thought to be a saint, ii. 258.
——— Whereby Robert duke of Normandie was made king of Ierusalem, ii. 49.
——— Wrought by Wolstane to his aduantage, ii. 19.
——— Séen (forsooth) in the daie of Campians execution, iv. 460.
Miracles of the holie maid of Kent, iii. 790.
Mirth that after it comith heauinesse: note, ii. 44, 70.
Miserie vpon miserie, ii. 724.
Mist thick and blind, ii. 640.
——— Made Henrie the eight and his soldiors vnable to find the waie to his campe, iii. 587.
Mistrust in murtherers one of another, iii. 1026.
——— Causeth carefull custodie, iii. 188.
——— On all sides of all states and degrées: note, ii. 299.
——— An enimie to peace: note, ii. 784.
——— Of king Henrie the third in his officers, ii. 374.
——— That the erles of Hereford and Marshall had of Edward the first, ii. 429.
——— Of the Flemings in the earle of Richmond, ii. 616, 617.
——— That the dukes of Buckingham and Glocester had in each other, iii. 405.
——— Of duke Arthers in his vncle king Iohn, ii. 278.
——— ¶ Sée Suspicion.
Mochoacan, i. 351.
Mocke of Henrie the first, against his brother Robert Curthose, ii. 76.
——— At the maior of Norwich, iv. 971.
——— ¶ Sée Derision and Iest.
Modwin, a virgin in Ireland renowned, i. 634.
Mogall admitted king studieth to redres abuses, vol. v. page 87.
——— Beloued of his fréends, ib
——— Requireth a restitution of wrongs doone by the Romans, prepareth to warres, exhorteth his men to valiantnesse, ib.
——— Through pride abuseth himselfe in sundrie kinds of vices, conspired against, flieth out of his owne house, murthered, v. 89.
Molineux constable of Chester castell, ii. 789.
——— Knight slaine: note, ii. 790.
Moll. ¶ Sée Edilwold.
Mollo brother to king Ceadwalla burnt to death, i. 636.
Molocke a preacher, v. 171.
Mona greater than Anglesei by a third, i. 65.
——— Towns, riuers, hils, hauens and manner of gouernment there, i. 66.
——— Won from the Scots by the princes of England, ib.
——— It had a king in Henrie the seconds times, i. 67.
——— Once spoiled by the Scots by whôme and when, i. 66.
——— Described by the name of Mona Cæsaris, i. 65.
Mona bishoprike named Episcoparis, Sodorch is in the Ile of Man, i. 246.
Monarch of Ireland, vi. 94.
——— His authoritie, ib.
Monarchie how safelie to be mainteined, i. 655.
——— Of Britaine how long it continued yer it became a pentarchie, i. 450.
——— ¶ Sée Ambition, Britaine England, and Kings.
Monastries how consecrated, i. 622.
——— Created in the north parts at the suit a trauell of thrée moonks, ii. 17, 18.
——— When none left in all the north parts, ii. 18.
——— Of Scotishmen in Germanie, v. 190.
——— ¶ Sée Abbies and Religious houses.
Monbarke riuer March betwéene Hereford and Monmouthshires, i. 125.
Moneth diuided into calens ides and nones, i. 408.
Moneth where of they consist and how reckned, i. 405.
Monie, and a diuise to get it for Iames the fourth, v. 466.
——— Purchaseth all things, i. 234.
——— Of copper currant in Britaine before the Romans comming hither, i. 634.
——— ¶ Sée Coine.
——— Two falles thereof, iii. 1031.
——— Henrie the sixts priuie seales for some, iii. 259.
——— Refused to be lent purchaseth disfauour and reuenge, ii. 280.
——— Larglie giuen to mainteine war against the Turks, ii. 283.
——— Carried out of the realme by a legat: note, ii. 294.

Monie sutes preferred for it, vol ii page 324
—— And what practises Gualo vsed to get it, ii 333
—— A perpetuall order of an hundred and foure pounds lent yearelie by course to certeine townes note, iv 8
—— Buieth liberties and priuileges, ii 207.
—— And what shifts king Richard the first made for it, ii 208
—— And of inquisitions to get it note, ii 266
—— Gotten with extortion to procure Richard the first his ransome, ii 241
—— To make it, offices set to sale by Richard the first, ii 217
—— Great summes gotten by Richard the first without making of recompense, ii 249
—— The practises of Richard the first to get it, ib
—— Much gotten for licences and grants of turnie, ii 252
—— The means practised to get it note, ii 251
—— Purchaseth erldoms, ii 176
—— Maketh rauiges betwéene great states, ii. 114
—— Purchaseth fauour to a murtherer, ii 170
—— What shifts Edward the fourth made for it, ii 330
—— The want thereof procureth peace iii 334
—— The desire thereof an occasion to offend against dutie and honestie, iii 417, 418
—— The means that Henrie the seuenth practised to get it, iii 532, 533.
—— Scant but vittels abundant, ii 605
—— Lent Edward the third by Londoners, ii. 613
—— Emploied vpon the common wealth, iv 506
—— Base, and fall thereof, iv 202.
—— Well imploied, iv 427
—— Gathered by Cardinalls, ii 508
—— Edward the first his shifts to get it, ii. 483
—— Forren forbidden to go as currant, ii 532.
—— Edward the first his shifts for it, ii 504
—— Purchaseth the princes fauor, ii 848, 819.
—— Of practises to get it, ii 360.
—— What cousening shifts the pope vsed to get it out of England, ii 364
—— Gathered to confirme a mariage, ii 381
—— To get it practise against practise, ii 120
—— And what indirect meanes to get it practised by the Romish clergie, ii. 390
—— What shifts Henrie the third made to send it to pope Innocent, ii 433
—— What shifts Henrie the third made to get it, ii 417
—— Procured to the procurers losse, ii 416.
—— Of the bishop of Herefords deuise to get some of the bishops, ii 434
—— More estéemed than life, ii. 436.
Monie for lands morgaged to haue it, vol. ii. page 37
—— Purchased fauour when nothing els would. note, ii 43
—— Receiued to inforce an abiuration of christianitie, ii 45
—— Giuen and taken of the French king to raise the séege, ii 31
—— The shamefull shift of William Rufus to get it, ii 34
—— Purchaseth peace, i. 636; ii 35.
—— Maketh friends, i 437
—— ¶ Sée Cardinall of Praxed, Couetousnes, Gifts, Inquisitions, Riches
Monmouth castell taken, ii 466
Monmouth and Glamorganshires, and what riuer is march betwéene them, i 128
Monsieur de la Uarenne sent out of France to aid the part of Margaret quéene of England, v 417
Monsieur de Bauiei slaine by the lord of Woodburne, v 190
Monsieur Thermes capteine of Calis, his seruice, his determination to spoile king Philips countries, sicke of the gowt, iv 116
Monsieur ¶ Sée Duke of Alanson
Monster borne, v 83
—— Of a strange forme and of no lesse strange qualities note, v 460, 461
—— Borne of a woman, iii. 1063.
—— Maried, iv 432
—— Of fourscore yeres old, iv 431
—— Of a sow that brought out a pig of strange shape, ii 63
Monsters, v. 428.
—— Bred and brought foorth in diuerse places in England, iv 204
—— Strange note, v 228
Monstreau besieged and taken, iii 120
Montacute ¶ Sée Earle
Montargis recouered by the English, iii. 171.
—— ¶ Sée Frenchmen
Montgomerie earle of Eglinton slaine, v. 745
Monument ¶ Sée Antiquities.
Monuments found at the digging of the ruines of Verolamium, i. 322.
—— ¶ Sée Antiquities
Moone in eclipse séene of king Henrie and his traine, i 178.
—— New, appéered before hir time, ii 427.
—— Worshipped, v 45
—— A strange woonder touching the same, ii. 424
—— Turned into a bloudie couler, ii 66
—— Strange sights about it, ii 177
—— Fiue séene in Yorke, ii 282
Moonke poisoneth the gouernor of Scotland, and is burned, v 264
—— Eustace what he was, ii 317.
—— Taken prisoner and beheaded, ib
—— ¶ See Malcus Samuell
—— When a woonder among the northerne people, ii. 18.

Moonke Carthusian apprehended, and an enemie vnto the pope note, vol. ii. page 389.
——— Conference with the duke of Buckingham his tresonable practises, iii 658
——— The last that was séene in moonks clothing till quéene Maries daies, iii 819
Moonks were preachers, v 171
——— Called white moonks, v 289
——— When and how they shuld inion penance, ii. 51
——— Should not be godfathers, ib
——— Should not hold nor occupie farmes, ib
——— At whose hands they should receiue parsonages, ib
——— Hindered by the comming of the friers preachers, ii. 40.
——— Presumptuous stoutnesse, ii 267
——— Displace the secular préests at Durham, ii 21
——— Life, order, and profession what it should be, ii 31
——— Supported by Lanfranke, ii 30
——— Two striuing for preferment dismissed by a third, ii 31
——— Thrée purposed to restore religion in Northumberland, ii 17
——— Cisteaux to whom the emperor was bountifull, ii 255
——— Cousened by Richard the first, ii 249
——— Of Glastenburie dispersed into diuerse religious houses, ii 22
——— Plaie the men against the abbat and his adherents, ib
——— Of Couentrie displaced, ii 223.
——— Placed in the church and the secular canons displaced, ii 264
——— Of Canturburie without knowledge of king Iohn choose a new archbishop, ii 293
——— Banished, ii 295, 296.
——— Of the Charterhouse executed, iii 798
——— Of Christs church complaine to the pope of their archbishop, iii 265
——— Called Monachi de charitate, ii 43
——— White when and by whome begunne and brought into England, ii 41
——— Not priuileged as other churches cōuentuall were, ii 299
——— Delt hardlie withall by king Iohn, ii 280.
——— Molested by king Iohn diuerse waies, ii. 282.
——— Of Norwich. ¶ Sée Friers.
Moore knight late vndershiriffe of London now of Henrie the eight his priuie councell, iii 620
——— The paines he tooke to appease all Maie daies riot, iii 421
——— Speaker for the commons, his oration and behauiour in parlement, iii 682
——— Answer the oration of Faber in the eights behalfe, iii 715
——— Lord chancellor his oration in the parlement, iii 743
——— An enimie to protestants, iii 749.
Moore deliuered vp the great seale, vol iii page 775.
——— Beheaded, a iester and scoffer at the houre of his deth, iii 793
——— In some sort commended, deuoutlie giuen, in his kind, iii. 794, 795
Moore Edward ¶ Sée Iusts triumphant
Moore fields ¶ Sée Archers
Morauians helpe to apprehend théeues and offenders, v 72
——— All slaine, ib
Morcad & Sigeferd two Danish noble men slaine, i 718
Mordacke king of Scots a louer of peace, deceaseth note, v. 181
Mordacke the kings lieutenant beareth with offenders, ib
——— Put to deth, v. 182.
Mordacke obteineth the earledome of Rosse, v 705.
Mordo ¶ Sée Duke
Mordred vsurpeth the kingdome of Britaine and resisteth Arthurs landing in Britaine, i 576, 577.
——— His sons repine at Constantines aduancement to the crowne, i 582.
——— The opinion which men conceiued of him for his wit and towardlinesse, desirous to be reuenged, v 156
——— Complaineth to king Arthur for that Constantine was created heire apparent, v 160
——— Succedeth Loth in the kingdome of Pictland, ib
——— He and Eugenius persuaded to peace, v. 161
——— Is slaine, i 577, v 162
——— ¶ Sée Gawen
Morgage of a dukedome for moneie, ii 37.
——— ¶ Sée Lands
Morgan and Cunedag at armes about the rule of this Ile, i 448
Morguison the midwaie betwéene Bullin and Calis, iii. 1022
Moriani what kind of people and where seated, i. 459
Morindus king of Britaine, his crueltie, and exploits, he is deuoured of a monster, i 458
Morini a people that now inhabit Terwine in France, i 470
Moris his deuise for conuenience of Thames water, iv 496
Moris alias Omoris vp in rebellion, vi 394.
——— They burn the Naas, vi 395.
——— They burn Leighlin, ib
Moris a runnagate préest made archbishop of Cashill. vi 339
——— Like to be killed, ib.
Morleie lord appealeth the erle of Salusburie, iii 7.
——— He is mainprised, iii 8
——— Slaine in battell against the French, iii. 494
Morleis in Britaine woon by the earle of Surrie, iii. 678

Mortaigne. ¶ See Erle Mortaigne.
Mortalitie of people verie gréeuous, vol. ii. page 272.
——— ¶ Sée Derth and Deth
Mortimer Roger, i 268
——— Lord of Meth arriueth in Ireland, vi. 245
——— Is discomfited by the Scots, vi 250
——— Is lord iustice, ib
——— He chaseth the Lacies out of Connagh, ib
——— Proclameth them traitors, ib
——— Is lord lieutenant, vi. 259.
——— Is slaine, ib.
Mortimer and Audleie banished, ii 465.
Mortimer Hugh against Henrie the second, ii 112
Mortimer king Henrie the thirds lieutenant in Wales, ii 440
——— His reuenge against the Welshmen, ii 455
Mortimer lord of Wigmore proclamed traitor, ii 580
——— In what fauour with Edward the seconds wife, ii 584
Mortimer erle of March proclamed heire apparent to the crowne, ii 768
——— He ruleth all things at his pleasure, ii 597
——— Enuieth Henrie the fourths aduancement, iii 3
——— His good seruice in Ireland, ii 753
——— Apprehended in Nottingham castell, ii 596
——— Beareth the blame of euill counsell, ii 596
——— Attainted and fiue articles objected against him, ii 599
——— Committed vnto prison in the Towre, ii 598
——— Breaketh out of the Towre: note, ii 575
——— Shamefullie executed, ii 599
Mortimers restored to the title and possessions of the earldome of March, ii 654
Mortmaine statute established, ii 482
——— Required to be repealed, i. 505
Morton doctor an old English fugitiue a stirrer vp of rebellion in the north, iv. 520
——— His secret ambassage from Rome, iv 521.
——— ¶ Sée Bishop Morton & Archbishop
Morton earle made regent, v 666.
——— Put to the worst, v 650.
——— Surrendereth his regentship, v 677
——— His examination, v 698
——— He is beheaded, v 705.
Moses capteine generall vnder Pharo, his doings not followed, he fled, called out of Madien into Egypt, not regarded, v 33
Mothelagh a Saxõ word, i. 261.
Mother killeth her sonne, vol i page 450.
——— ¶ Sée Fratricide and Murther
Mowbraie sir Philip knight valiant. note, i 343.
——— ¶ See Beaumont.
Mowbraie earle of Northumberland, ii 28
Mount Iland hauing no inhabitants, i 56
Mount of saint Michaell described by Leland, ib.
Mountacute lord William earle of Sarum selleth the Ile of Man the crowne thereof, i 66
Mountcaster now Newcastell, ii 17
Mountfort Robert combatant, ii 114
Mountgomerie Roger earle of Shrewesburie his wasting & spoiling, ii 28.
——— Reconciled to king William Rufus, ii. 29.
——— Knight passeth ouer the sea vnto the French king, his reward, iii 343
Mountioie lord made generall of Tornaie, iii. 613
——— His stratagem, iii. 842
Mountsorrell betwixt Leicester and Lughburrow, ii. 327
——— The castell besieged, ii 344.
Mudiard apprehended, v 574
——— Yéeldeth to the quéene, v 577.
Mulbraie Robert earle of Northumberland highlie commended, ii 21.
Mulmutius Dunwallon first of Britaine that were a golden crowne, i 451
——— His lawes, ib
Murmerie castell, iii 557
Municipium what it is, i 322
Munition ¶ Sée Armour.
——— For warres and of King Henrie the second his ordinance in that behalfe, ii 180
Murana a towne néere to Uenice situat on the Adriatike sea, i 280.
Murcherdach king of Ireland, ii. 36.
——— His reuerance to Henrie the first note ii 77.
Muredac. ¶ Sée Mudiard
Murkethes (an inuader) with manie more hanged, v. 59
Murreie Andrew fellow gouernor with the earle of March, v 368
——— Taken prisoner, ib.
——— Commeth out of the mountains, his wast, v 377
——— His uictories, ib.
——— Deceaseth, v 378
Murrie William departeth from the kings faction, v. 631
Murrie earle a sutor vnto the quéene, v. 614
——— Earle regent slaine, v 642.
Murreies rebell discomfitted and ouerthrowne, v. 391.
——— Destroied, ib.
Murreie land, v 73.
Murren of cattell, ii 28, 35, 124, 430, 557.
——— Uniuersall, ii 74
——— Made flesh deare, ii 555.
Murret monsieur, v. 366.

Murther wilfull how punished, vol. i. page 310.
—— Doone by the Danes vpon king Edmund verie lamentable, i 667, 690
—— Of a king by his seruant, i 649
—— Of a father reuenged on the son, i 701
—— Unnaturall procured by Alfrid vpon his son, i 700
—— Of Kinewulfe notable, i 650
—— Unnaturall of Ostrida, i 640
—— Doone by the Danes vpon a bishop, i 712
—— Upon maids, i 536.
—— Of a son by his mother, i 654
—— Most vile of two innocents, i 629
—— The consent whereto punished, i. 636.
—— Reuenged, i 444
—— Committed for pitie, i 509
—— Most villa ous note, 605
—— By poison terriblie punished, i 685.
—— Recompenced with murther, i 431, 450, 484, 519, 538, 56., 645, 651, 655, 692, 728
—— Committed in Sussex by certeine gentlemen and they executed note, iii 821
—— Of two capteines, notablie punished by iustice in the déed doers, iii 1027
—— Most shamefullie by meanes of a gentlewoman whoare being a wife note, iii 1025
—— Mercilesse vpon the yoong earle of Rutland note, iii 269
—— Most lamentable of the lord Scales, iii. 261
—— Shamefullie committed by the lord Hurton and he hanged note, iv 86
—— Intended against quéene Maries person and the offenders executed, iv 55
—— Of the marquesse of Montferrat, ii 233
—— Cruel of prince Edward and how iustlie plagued and afterwards reuenged vpon the murtherers, iii. 320
—— Of Henrie the sixt by the duke of Glocester, iii 324
—— Of the yoong princes Edward the fift & his brother in the Towre, how dispatched and how reuenged note, iii 401, 402
—— Doone vpon the prior of Shéene, iii 530.
—— An earle arreigned for the same, ib
—— Committed vpon the king of Scots, iv. 231
—— Of a man by his prentise, iv 237.
—— Mercilesse doone by a Merchant, and the offenders executed note, iv 266
—— Committed on the gaoler of Horsham, and the offender hanged in chains, iv 329.
—— Most horrible committed, by Anthonie Browne vpon George a Merchant, and the offenders executed note, iv 322.
—— It and other mischéefes by Peter Burchet and he hanged, iv 324.
—— Committed on a prentise and the offenders hanged, iv 505
—— Of an unnaturall brother committed vpon his brother naturall, iv 343
—— Committed vpon a sargent and the offended hanged vp in Cheape, iv. 426.
Murther another at Tiburne for the like offense, vol iv page 426.
—— Committed vpon a sargent and the partie hanged in Fleetstréet, iv 494
—— Of one cost manie lives, ii 405
—— Heinous of a Merchant stranger, ii 721
—— Doone vpon Richard the second, how abhorred of forren nations, iii 11.
—— Of Liultus how vnfortunatelie it fell out: note, ii 15
—— Commited at the high altar by an Italian note, ii 475
—— For the which a yeoman of the gard was hanged vp, iii 568.
—— Through couetuousnesse commited and punished, iii 792
—— Most vnnaturall note, iii 172
—— Without mercie vpon a light cause, ii 205.
—— Punished with a fine, ii 212
—— It and fellonie combined, iv. 266
—— Commited and the partie hanged on Miles end, iv 345, 346
—— Punished by the purse, ii 387
—— Most cruell commited in Westminster church, ii 720.
—— Wilful, and an act against mediation for the same, ii. 809
—— Reuenged with murther, ii 21
—— Will not be concealed note, iii 803, 804.
—— Reuenged by women note, iii 173
—— Cannot be concealed note, iii 1029
—— Not redéemable with monie note, iv 64.
—— Henrie the eight refused to leaue it but put it ouer to triall by common law, iii 640
—— Detestable, v 55
—— Most cruell, v 53
—— Of one for another v. 180.
—— Suspected and tried by the racke note, v. 181
—— Whereafter insued open warre, v 439.
—— By misfortune note, v 79
—— Most shamefull of K Duffe note, v. 235.
—— How punished, v 237.
—— Of a king doone by his own hands on himselfe, v 57.
—— ¶ Sée Conspiracie, Slaughter and Burning in the hand, Reuenge, Temptation
Murther of ones self to preuent iustice, iv 540
—— Desparate of the erle of Northumberland vpon himselfe, being prisoner in the Towre, iv. 602
—— The whole storie of the matter and order thereof, iv 603, 604.
—— Desparat of ones selfe ¶ Sée Hawkesford
Murthers commited by préests, ii 119.
Murtherer of his brother receiued into fauour, ii 170
—— Notorius ¶ Sée Backe Will Murthered note, v 103, 194.
Murtherers torne in péeces with wild horsses, v. 2,0
—— To be hanged by law, ii. 199.

Murtherers of Thomas Becket came to an euill end, vol ii page 136
Museleborrow field ¶ See Battle Leith
Muscouie a cold countrie note, iii 1063.
Musgraue rebell, iii 803
Musgraue Thomas capteine of Berwike prisoner, v 392
Musike taught by a bishop, i 690
——— ¶ Sée Singing.
Muster of horsemen before king Edward the sixt at Greenewich note, iii. 1059, 1060
——— Of pensioners before quéene Elizabeth, iv. 234.
——— Of Londoners before quéene Elizabeth at Gréenewich, iv 265, 599.
——— Verie triumphant before Henrie the eight, iii 809
——— At Gréenewich before quéene Elizabeth, iv 184
Mutinie in the English armie, iii 690, 855
——— Towards, among seruing men, iii 943
——— Of soldiors against their capteine, iv. 99
——— Betwixt the Englishmen and the townsmen of Lisbone, ii 215
——— Betwéene the English soldiors and the people of Mesina, ii 216
——— Among soldiors with outragious disorder procuring execution, iv 651
——— Sée Fraie, Riot, and Soldiors
——— In the parlement house, vi 342, 343
——— Among soldiers, i 515, v 83
——— Among the people of Louchquhaber, v 263
Muthell besieged by the English, iii 841
——— The seige thereat broken vp, iii 843.

N

Naas burned by Rorie Og, vi 395
Names of all the noble people in Ireland, vi 96, 97, 98
Nanicularc littus, vi 73
Narcissus one that might doo all with Claudius, i 186.
——— Sent to appease the soldiors at Plautius, i 181
Narne castell besieged, v. 257
——— Yelded by composition, v 258.
Natholird a man of no great ancient house, &c sent against the Saxõs at Aurelius Ambrose his death, i 570
Natholocus chosen king proclamed, v 99
———Goeth to Dunstalage to be inthronised, ib
——— Seeketh loue of his nobles by bribes, putteth such to death as he suspected, ib.
——— Murthered, v 100.
Nauar, the king whereof his gentle offer to the English, iii 569
——— His kingdome gotten to the king of Spaine, iii 570
——— King without a realme and whie, iii. 583,
Nauar hath Cherburg restored to him that was ingaged, vol ii page 823
——— Taken by the Frenchmen, ii 681, 682
——— Commeth ouer into England, his constancie suspected, ii 696
——— His roiall answer to the excommunication of pope Sixtus quintus note, iv. 597
Name roiall sent forth, iii 572
Nauie of Edgar, of 1600 alias 3600 sails, i. 339.
Nauie of England, of thrée sorts, i 337.
——— ¶ Sée Ships.
Nauigation mainteined by the Romans, i 359
——— Either neglected or not known how hurtfull, i 338
Navis how to be vnderstood, i 336
Naunts besieged by Edward the third, ii 625
——— By the Englishmen, ii 782
Nauntwich in Cheshire burnt, iv 509
Nazaleod a mightie king of the Britains, i. 486
——— He is slaine, ib
Neal baron ¶ Sée Marquesse
Nectanus king of Picts brother to another Nectanus dieth of hurts receiued in field, v 111
——— Warreth vpon the Scots, v. 110
——— Desirous of reuenge, ib.
——— Inuadeth the Scotish confines, ib
——— Refuseth all offers of peace, slaine, ib
Necromancie ¶ Sée Hed
Nele the great or Nigellus monarch of all Ireland, vi 84
Nele Donell taken prisoner, vi 267.
Nele Onele ¶ Sée Onele
Nemodus with his four sonnes arriue in Ireland, vi 75
Neninus wounded of Cesar dieth, i. 747
Nephilim ¶ Sée Giant
Neptune god of the sea and how he obteined to be so reputed, i 6
——— His thrée and thirtie sonnes, i 7
——— How he grew to be called the god of the seas, i 432
Nero his wicked life and end, vi 124
Nesse a riuer neuer frozen, and well stored with sammon, i 150
Nesta the noble ladie mother to the conqueror of all Ireland, vi 128, 209, 210
Neuill bastard Fauconbridge, iii 321
——— A maister of mischéefe, iii 322
——— Beheaded, iii 328.
Neuill knight executed for rebellion, iii 820
Neuill discouereth the intended treasons of Parrie against quéene Elizabeth, iv 562.
Newark castell built by the bishop of Lincolne, ii 86
——— Restored to the bishop of Lincolne, ii 349.
Newberrie spoiled by the earle of Wiltshire and others, iii 258
Newbolt a yeoman of the gard hanged, iii 568
Newcastell vpon tine when founded, ii 20
——— Burnt by casuall fier, ii. 416.
——— ¶ Sée Montcaster
Newes of heauinesse to Henrie the first, ii 70
——— That cast duke William into a furie, ii. 10.

Newes that made the peo a great feare, vol ii page 10
Newgate bulded, iii 56
——— Set on fire, iv 84.
——— The keeper whereof a stranger would haue murthered note, iv. 85.
Newhall in Essex called Beaulieu, iii 640.
Newhauen, the French appoint to go out of it, iv 213
——— A supplie of soldiors arriue there out of Essex, iv 206
——— And out of Deuonshire, iv 209.
——— Greatlie infected with the plague, iv 221
——— Articles of agréement touching the surrender, iv 222.
——— A new supplie of souldiers out of Norfolk, Suffolke, Wiltshire and Glocestershire, iv. 218.
——— A fresh supplie of souldiors arriue there, ib.
——— An alarum thereof, iv 206
——— Prises taken and brought thither, iv 208.
——— Proclamation forbidding resort of souldiours thither without licence, iv 218
——— The French king commeth to the campe lieng thereat, iv 228.
——— The chéefe cause while it was yéelded, ib
——— Speciall persons that died of the plague there, ib
——— Pestilence transported thense to London, ib
Newport towne of the east Saxons, i 174.
——— Besieged by Frenchmen, iii 495.
——— Sacked and burnt by the Englishmen, ii 760
Newstria lieth opposite frō Astria, that is, the east region, i 12.
Newton baths or wels medicinable, i 231
Newtons the surnames of the ladie Cobhams ancestrie, i 118
New yeares gift ¶ Sée Gift.
Nicholson alias Lambert burned, iii 807
Nichomedes king of Bithinia, i 388
Nidle riuer called Nidor in the book of statutes, i. 160
Niddesdale is so named of the riuer Nide, i. 150.
Nidred and Silebhare kings of Kent by vsurpation, i 637
Nigell ¶ Sée Neal
Night and the parts thereof, i. 406.
Nightingale parson of Crondall in Kent, his blasphemie in the pulpit punished by God note, iv. 78, 79
Nisi prius wherevpon growne to be so manie and so common, i 262
Noah, first diuided the earth among his sonnes, i 1
——— His posteritie in Italie, i. 7
——— Monarch of all the world diuided it among his sonnes, i. 428.
Noble Sée Coine
Nobilitie of England, rooted out and beggared by duke William, vol ii page 11
——— Faine to flie because of duke Williams tirannie, ii 16
——— Their liuings taken awaie by duke William, ii 8, 9
——— In armes against him and his Normans, ii 9
——— Hated of him and his people, ib
——— Forsake their natiue countrie, ib
——— In seruitude to the Romans, ii 2
——— Gréeuouslie fined by William Rufus, ii 34
Nobilitie true described, iv 338
——— Compared vnto a riuer or flood note, iv 332
Nobles created, v 410.
——— Conspire against Theseus, v 50
——— Haue the gouernment giuen them by lots, v 42
——— Slaine in battell, v 337
——— Their presumtuous demeanor, v 459
——— Diuided, v 276.
——— Sweare to stand to the king of Englands order, v 326
——— Sworne to king Edward, v 337
——— Banished into England, v 355
——— Draw their swords at a parlement and while note, v 353
——— Conspire, and are commited to ward, v. 354
——— Discontented with the kings doings, v. 232
——— They murmur and whie, v 233
——— Set witches on worke to bewitch their king, v 234
——— Go to wracke, v 227
——— Slaine and taken prisoners, v 334.
——— Slain at Dublin, v 367
——— Raise an armie against king Iames the fourth ouerthrowne, v. 160
——— Summoned, v 455
——— Through feare consent to creat Gillus king, v 55
——— Committed to custodie, v 730, 731.
——— ¶ See Dessention
Noble men of Ulster glad of Onels death, vi. 338.
——— To attend the king, vi. 241, 242
——— To attend the lord deputie, vi. 384
——— To answer for their men, vi. 381.
Noblemens diet in England, i 280.
Noblemen and king Richard the second at debate, ii 784
——— Indicted of diuerse offenses, ii 783
——— Appeale one another of treason, iii. 5.

Noblemen that conspired against King Henrie the fourth, vol iii page 9
——— They come to Circester, the bailiffe setteth vpon them in their lodgings their discomfiture and shamefull end, ii 10, 11
——— They doo yeelde themselues, iii 12
——— Beheaded for conspiracie, ib
——— Conspiracie mortlie of the Persies against Henrie the fourth, iii 22, 23, 24, 25.
——— Executed, iii 58
——— Complaine to king Henrie the third of the popes collections, ii 101
——— Reuolting from Lewis the French kings sonne, ii 313, 341.
——— Taken prisoners, ii 316
——— That rebelled in what perplexitie they were, ii. 315.
——— Their minds drawne from Lewis the French K sonne, ii 341
——— Offended at Henrie the third and not without cause, ii 374
——— That tooke part with and against Henrie the third, ii. 456, 457
——— Proclamed traitors by Henrie the third, ii 374
——— That reuolted from Henrie the third, ii 459.
——— Disgrace Henrie the third in a parlement, ii 415
——— Of rare qualities, iv 321
——— What fort and the wals of a realme, iv. 352
——— That went with the duke of Alanson ouer sea, iv 460, 461.
——— Their vantgard distressed they discomfited and executed, iii 319
——— Diuers that stood against them executed, ii 794
——— At dissention, ii 773
——— Appointed to come in warlike manner to the parlement, ii 838
——— Apprehended, imprisoned and also indicted, ii 837
——— At variance come to the parlement in armor, ii 752
——— Roughlie handled by Richard the second, ii 836 to 844
——— Against the duke of Sumerset to displace him, iii 1014, 1017
——— Consult and also practice to diuert the succession of the crowne, and how euillie it proved note iii 1066 to 1070
——— Imprisoned for eating flesh in lent, iii 832
——— At daggers drawing and bloodshed within the Towre note, iii. 381
——— Conspirators executed, iii 120
——— In armes against Edward the fourth vnder quéene Margaret the place of their incamping the ordering of their hoast, iii 318.
——— Conspire against Edward the fourth note, iii 288, 289
Noblemen at deadlie malice in Henrie the sixts time note the whole storie, called to a treatie, brought to agrée, vol iii page 247
——— Proclamed traitors, iii 252, 253
——— Their letters excusatorie to Henrie the sixt, iii 254
——— Atteinted, iii 256
——— That continued true and loiall to king Iohn, ii 344
——— Begin to mislike the match which the had made with Lewis, ii 334
——— Dealing with Richard the second as touching his deposing, ii 859
——— Sée duke of Lancaster reuolting from king Iohn to king Lewis, ii 331
——— Mistrusted and charged with treason, ii 783
——— Confer how to preuent the perils pretended against them, counsell taken how to deale against them their messengers to the king, ii 784, 785.
——— The Londoners refuse to fight against them the lords take an oth togither to prosequte their purposed enterprise, séeke the fauour of the Londoners, come before the kings presense in Westminster hall, their answer and gréefes, ii 785, 786, 787.
——— The king reprooueth their dooings cléered of treason by proclamation, ii 788
——— Tamper too far with the kings matters, and impeach his roialtie, ii 741
——— Thirtéene lords appointed to haue the gouernment vnder the king, ii 776.
——— Come to London with a great armie, ii. 789
——— Sent to the maior and citizens of London to vnderstand their meaning, ii 791
——— Enter into London, the kings words touching their procéedings, they refuse to come vnto the Towre, but after serch made they come before the kings presence, they open their gréefes to the king, ii 791, 792
——— Drowned, ii 70
——— Die, ii 186, 395, 398
——— ¶ Sée Death shipwracke
Noise ¶ Sée Sound
Nones four or six in euerie month and whie so named, i 408
Nonneus susteined the first inuasion of the Saxons into great Britaine, i 547
Norham castell besieged by the Scots rescued by the English, iii 516
——— Deliuered vp to the Scotish kings hands, iii 591, 592.
Norimbega ¶ Sée Raleigh
Normandie mortgaged to William Rufus and for what, ii 37
——— Townes therein to Henrie the fift, iii 97
——— Brought into Henrie the fift his subjection, hauing béene a long time from him deteined, iii. 111.

Normandie won by the erle of Aniou, vol. ii. page 94.
——— Inuaded by the French king, ii. 67.
——— Subdued vnto England on that daie fortie yéers past that William conqueror subdued England to Normandie, ii. 56.
——— Interdicted, ii. 237, 277.
——— By the archbishop of Normandie, ii. 262.
——— Recouered by the French king after thrée hundred and sixtéene yeares kéeping: note, ii. 290.
——— Lost the state thereof and the causes of the losse, iii. 217, 218.
——— Whie so named, i. 670.
——— Gouerned by the French king, i. 736.
Norman of passing strength ouerthrowne by a Scot, v. 320.
Normans first entring into England, i. 741.
——— Under duke William and the manner of their arraie, i. 761.
——— How they pretended a title to the crowne, i. 705.
——— Slaine by the poll, the tenth reserued, i. 733.
——— Upper lips and chéeks shauen and taken for préests, i. 760.
——— Banished the realme vpon a malicious reuenge, i. 747.
——— First comming into Britaine whence they came and of what people they consisted, i. 12.
——— Builded manie townes and villages in England, i. 324.
——— Whie deadlie enimies to the English Saxons, i. 12.
——— Preferred to the best places of authoritie in England, i. 222.
——— All saue three or four, banished out of the land by the king and their vile dealings, i. 224.
——— That came with William in the conquest of England, ii. 3.
——— Rebell, but are subdued to their smart, iii. 184.
——— Willinglie sworne English, iii. 93.
——— Affraid at Henrie the fift his ariuall, iii. 89.
——— Under duke Robert vanquished, ii. 55.
——— Inclined more to Henrie the first than to D. Robert, ii. 54, 55.
——— Their rule and the Frenches ouer England ceaseth, ii. 202.
——— Set vpon the English admerall, ii. 500.
——— Their possessions confiscated, ii. 402.
——— Whie disherited, ib.
——— Write to Henrie the third to take their part against the French, ii. 363.
——— Preferred to clergiemens roomes and liuings, ii. 14.
——— Rebell against duke William beyond the sea, and soon subdued, ii. 17.
——— Their fashion and guise taken vp of the English, ii. 8, 9.
Normans they hate the nobles euen in the time of peace, vol. ii. page 9.
——— Lieng in garrison at Yorke and their dismall daie, ii. 10, 11.
——— Pursued and slaine by the English, ii. 10.
——— Giue the Danes the discomfiture, ii. 11.
——— Haue the nobilitie and commonaltie in bondage, ii. 2.
——— Plaie the diuels in wasting and spoiling, ii. 28.
——— Slaine by the king at Worcester, ib.
——— The line touching the heires male in whome ceased, ii. 78.
——— ¶ Sée William Duke of Normandie.
Norris generall with thrée and twentie ensignes, iv. 499.
——— Taketh the sconse of Lete, iv. 635.
——— Other exploits by him doone against the enimie, ib.
Northampton besieged, ii. 320.
——— Taken by force, ii. 460.
North countries pitifullie wasted by duke William, ii. 12.
Northerne men discomfit the Welshmen, iii. 291.
——— Spoile the towne of saint Albons, their valiantnesse: note, iii. 270.
——— Rebellion and how suppressed, iii. 800, 801.
Northerne prickers plaie the men, iii. 578.
Northfolke what hauens it hath, i. 182.
Northmercia, i. 623.
Northumberland a kingdome compounded of two, i. 584.
——— Two kingdomes Deira, and Bernicia, i. 611.
——— Aduisedlie submit themselues to king Egbert, i. 658.
——— The kingdome when it was parted, i. 584.
——— Diminished by the Picts, i. 635.
——— Inuaded by two kings, i. 610.
——— Brought into a miserable state, ib.
——— Their custom to sell their néer kinsfolke at a small price, i. 591.
——— The kingdome gouerned by two Partners, i. 615.
——— Whie it remained long without anie gouernors, i. 655.
——— It had no Saxon king by title for manie yeares togither, i. 557.
——— Inhabited with Saxons, ib.
——— In subiection to the kings of Westsaxons, i. 660.
——— The kingdome thereof fatall: note, i. 655.
——— An erledome, ii. 1.
——— Rebelleth against duke William and is subdued, ii. 10.
——— Taken in possession of the Scots, ii. 91.
——— When it first began to be so called, v. 144.
——— A portion thereof restored to the Scots, v. 296.

Northumberland taketh part with king Malcolme, vol v page 230
——— Under the Englishmen, v 298
——— Allotted vnto England, v. 229
——— Inuaded, v 291
——— A kingdome other wise called Bernicia vnder Ida, i 29
——— In manner inclosed betwéene the Tweed and the Tine, i 150
——— What hauens it hath, i 182
——— ¶ Sée Analassus and Malcolme
Northumbers ouer whome duke William placeth and displaceth diuers nobles, ii 21
——— Kill Robert Cumin and his companie, ii 10
——— Inuade Ireland, i 634
——— Ouerthrowe the Picts, i 641
——— Rebell against their erle Tostie and white, i 755.
——— Yéeld to Swaine without resistance, i 714
——— In subiection to the Danes, i 677
——— Rebell and are subdued by king Edred, i 691
——— Put to the sword by king Edred, i 691, 692
——— Inuaded by Penda, i 617
——— Complained against by Corman for their neglect of religion, i 615
——— Kingdome how farre somtimes extended, i 150
Nortons ¶ Sée Rebells of the north
Norwaie the king thereof resigneth his title to the out Iles, v. 448
Norwegians inuade the land, vi 88, 90.
——— Expelled, vi 90.
——— Besiege Dublin, vi 91
——— Were first merchants, vi 93, 94.
——— They build townes, ib
——— Come to the aid of Analassus, v 231
——— Put to Flight, v 216
——— Their fleet sunk by vehement winds, v 268.
——— ¶ Sée Acho
——— Arriue in Humber, doo much mischéefe, and are discomfited, i 758.
——— Slaine by the Britaines, i 452.
Norwich taken and spoiled by the Danes, i 710
——— How ancient, iv 378
——— Besieged by the Normans, ii 18
——— Sacked, ii 470
——— Sorlie defaced with fire, iii 539
——— In commotion, their liberties seized into kings hands, iii 210.
——— Sometimes called Venta Icenorum, i 176
——— The bishopriks erection there it and valuation, i 242
Nothatus crowned king, and murthered, v 46.
Nothelmus archbishop of Canturburie, i 644
Notingham besieged by the Danes, i 666
Notingham Robert maior of Dublin taketh and imprisoneth the erle of Ulster, vi 248.
Notingham Robert spoileth saint Marie abbie, vol vi page 248
——— Taken by the erle of Derbie, ii 158
——— The castell, ii 9
——— How seated, ii 101
Nouantes inhabitants of Cumberland, i. 193
Noue account yéelded to Richard the first, ii 254
Nouiomagus, a citie in England, i 319
Nowell Henrie ¶ Sée Iusts triumphant.
Nugent baron of Delwin, a malcontentment against the cesse, vi 391
——— He with others committed to ward, vi 393
——— He is suspected to be one of the conspiracie of Desmonds rebellion, is committed to prison, he is sent into England, and then to the Towre, ib
Numbers fatall to women and men, i. 49.
Nundina dea, i 409
Nun cousin to Inas, i 639
——— Defloured and after married and afterwards restored to the nunrie, i 678
——— Alfred indued with the spirit of prophesie, i 649
——— ¶ Sée Christine
Nuns incontinencie and displaced out of their house, ii 172
——— Not to be godmothers, ii 51
——— Lecherous and murtherous life, i 640
——— Defile their bodies, i 611.
——— Concubines, i 651
——— Manie in France, that were Englishwomen, i. 617
Nunnes ¶ Sée Abbies and Religious Houses.

O

Obedience and what rigorous meanes duke William vsed to reduce the English thereto, ii 8, 9.
——— Of erle Richard to his father Henrie the second, ii 189
——— Of the church of Scotland to the church of England, ii 168
Obelisks, v 19, 261
Obren king of Thomond slaine vi 212
Obren Donat slaine by his own men, vi 215
Obren Morogh baron of Ineskellen, vi 56
——— He killeth Iohn Fitziohn, vi 258
Occa the sonne of Hengist taken and fauourablie dealt withall by Aurelius, i 565
——— He and Ebusa leaders of the Saxons, i 557.
——— He reigned in Kent foure and twentie yeares, i 572
——— He threateneth destruction to Uter · note, i. 570.
Occa returneth out of Germanie with a new power, v 154
——— Flieth by sea into Kent, v 145
——— He and Pascentius returne into Britaine, v. 150
——— Constreined to flie, v. 156
——— King slaine, v. 151.

Occasion not to be neglected, vol i page 495.
——— Not neglected, i 555
——— Taken to come to ones purpose, i 556
——— Watched and vsed, i 696, 705
——— Taken to inuade England note, ii 32
——— Taken of an inuation, ii 367
Oconher of Ophalia his victories, vi 242
Oconher K of Conagh slaine, vi 183, 217
Oconher mac Kellie slaine in Conagh, vi 217
——— ——— His victories, vi 203, 264.
Oconher Catholo slaine, vi 261
Oconher of Vlster rebelleth, vi 313
——— ——— His countrie is inuaded and burned, ib
——— He submitteth himselfe, ib
——— Giueth hostages, ib
Octauius obteineth the rule of Britaine, vi 103
——— Couetuous to inlarge his dominions, ib
——— Entreth amitie with the English king, becometh tributarie to the Romane emperor, ib
——— Vanquished, flieth into Scotland, vi 107
Octauius a British lord gouerned Britaine noblie, he dieth, i 533
Odempsie discomfitteth Oconher, vi 242.
——— Subdueth Obren, vi 245
Odo bishop of Baieux gouernor of England in duke Williams absence, ii 8
——— In armes against the erle of Cambridge, ii 18
——— Conspireth against his nephew William Rufus, ii. 28
——— Erle of Kent, ii 21, 30
——— In armes against king Williams fréends in Kent, ii 28
——— Is sent into Northumberland to reuenge Walkers death, ii 20
——— Glad to submit himselfe for lacke of vittels, ii 29
——— Lost his liuings in England and returneth into Normandie, ib
Odonell anoieth the kings subiects in Vlster, vi 238.
——— He is vanquished, ib.
——— Restored to his possessions vi 335
Odonell the great of Ireland proffessed fréendship vnto Iames the fourth, v. 473.
Oenon a citie builded sometime by Cham, i. 15.
Offa conquereth the Eastangles, i 649.
——— Maketh his realme tributarie to Rome, and dieth, i. 647
——— Alieth himselfe to other princes for feare of his enimies, i 646
——— King of Mercia his acts deeds and victories, ib
——— Called king of Eastsaxons, becommeth a monke, i 611.
Offchurch in Warwickeshire built, i 617.
Offdich or Offas dich, i 647
Offendors put in feare, v 182.
——— Thrée thousand within two yeares space put to death, v 421
——— Couer their faults with contrarie causes, iv 515
——— ¶ Sée Pardon.
Offense. ¶ Sée Punishment.
Officer of the maior of London chosen shirriffe and lord maior, vol iii page 484
——— ¶ Sée Purueior, Sargent
Officers called to accounts, and of their fraudulent dealing, ii 258
——— Go beyond their commission note, ii 241.
——— Of king Iohn oppresse the people, ii 317.
——— About Henrie the seuenth abuse the common people extremelie, iii 532, 533
——— The cause of manie mens undooing and other troubles, iii 536
——— Changed throughout the realme, iii 243
——— Chosen by sound aduise, iii 62
——— Of the king of Spaine full of tirannical lordlinesse and villanie, iv 470
——— Called to accounts, and restitution made out of hand with interests, ii 371
——— In displeasure with king Henrie for their deceit, ii 374
——— Called to account how they had spent the kings treasure, ii 377
——— Punished for negligent looking to prisoners, ii 395.
——— Appointed in an uproare, ii 471.
——— Displaced and others placed, ii 799
——— Commited to the Towre and new made in place of old discharged note, ii 618
——— Complained of to king Edward the third and punished, ii 399
——— Created, v 669.
——— Changed, v 575
——— Of king Edward Chased out of Scotland, v 335.
——— ¶ Sée Exchecker and Iustices
Offices peculiar to the kings house, i 277
——— Concerning the realme, ib
——— In the prince of Englands court furnished with books, i 331
——— Set to sale for monie, iv 247
——— Clamed at the coronation of Henrie the fourth, iii 1
Oile in vessels that neerest the top is best, i 384.
——— Odoriferous found in a stone, i 296
Oilie Robert builder of Oxford castell, i 250.
Oisters where continuallie eaten, i. 373
Oke for what vse it is to be reserued, i 357
——— Growing in England what sort is the softest and to what vse it was put in times past, i 357
——— As fine as wainscot, ib.
Oke barke bought vp by the faddam to tan lether withall, ib
Oke of saint Augustine, i 596
Okes whose roots are verie hard stone, i 218
Okensile in Leinster, vi 183.
Olauus and Godredus diuide the kingdome of the Iles betwéene them, v 318
Oldcastell knight accused of heresie, scapeth out of the Towre, iii. 62.
——— Shifteth from place to place he is laid in wait to be taken, iii 91
——— Taken and wounded, executed, iii. 91.

Oliuer a Scot in seruice with the Saracens to their losse and hindrance, vol v. page 302.
Omalaghlin king of Meth, vi 89
——— In credit with Turgesius, ib
——— His politiks to beguile Turgesius, vi. 90.
——— His persuasions to his countrimen, ib
——— His daughter maried to Ororike, vi 121
——— He is slaine, vi 210
Omores rebell, vi 372
Oneile the great of Ireland made knight, iii 560
Onele was chased in battell, vi 210
——— He is slaine and 352 men with him, vi 239.
——— He paieth tribute, vi 238
Onele Con beareth the sword before the earle of Kildare, vi 280
——— Maketh insurrection against the erle of Ossorie, vi 238
——— He inuadeth the English pale, vi. 310.
——— The first erle of Tiron, vi 329.
——— He had two sonnes, ib
——— His first sonne baron of Dungannon, ib
——— Onele and all the north vnquiet, vi. 325.
——— He is taken prisoner, ib
Onele Shane by blood and murther preuaileth, vi. 329.
——— The proudest man, vi 329, 331, 401.
——— The causes of his rebellion, vi 329
——— He vsurpeth the name of Onele, ib
——— He breaketh into rebellion, ib
——— He praieth the lord deputie to be his godcept, vi 329, 330
——— His obiections against his elder brother, vi 330
——— He promiseth to be quiet, ib.
——— He is pursued by the erle of Essex, vi 331.
——— Is become a tyrant ib.
——— He is a drunkard, ib.
——— He is buried in the ground to recouer his drunkenesse, ib
——— His force and gard, ib
——— He trameth vp his pesants in warres, ib.
——— He taunteth at the earle of Clancar, vi 333
——— He besiegeth Dundalke, ib
——— He is discomfitted, ib
——— His cowardlienesse, vi 335.
——— His fréends forsake him, vi 337.
——— His countrie is preied, ib.
——— He is distressed, ib
——— He is slaine, vi 238
——— His head set vpon the castell of Dublin, ib
Onele would speake no English, vi. 6
Onetus a Danish capteine slaine, v. 257
Onichellinus ¶ Sée Richellinus
Onoran one of the Macmurghes and his companie, were set vpon and discomfited, and carried awaie prisoners, vi 265.
Opportunitie, ¶ Sée Occasion
Oppression punished, vol, ii page 443
——— Of the poore commonaltie where to it grew ¶ Sée Curses, Empson, Extortion, Officers
Oracle that Brute consulted withall, i 439
Orange prince commeth into England, iv 74.
——— Taketh order for the interteinment of the duke of Alanson, iv 462.
Oration of Donald of Ossorie, vi 193
——— Of Rodorike king of Picts, vi 78
——— Of Omalaghlin, vi 90
——— Of Rodorike Oconher, vi 134.
——— Of Macmorough, vi 136
——— Of Reimond, vi 137, 138
——— Of Herime, vi 144
——— Of Moris Fitsgirrald, vi 151
——— Of Worshe lord Chancellor, vi 281.
——— Of Fitzgirrald erle of Kildare, vi. 281, 282.
——— To his sonne, vi 286
——— Of Thomas Fitzgirrald, vi 289, 292
——— Of Weston lord chancellor, vi 341.
——— Of Stanihurst, ib
——— Of sir Henrie Sidneie, vi 342.
——— Of Colman in the hearing of king Achaius, note, v 186.
——— Of Albian a noble man, v 187
——— Of king Dauid to his nobles at the death of his sonne, v 290
——— Of the Scotish ambassadors to the French king, to excuse the marriage of Bothwell, v 620
——— Of an ambassador to Acho king of Norwaie, v 314
——— Of Leslie against the erle of Murrie, v. 606, 607
——— Of the Q Dowager at hir deth to the nobilitie, v 601
——— Of Kenneth king of Scots, v. 201, 202.
——— Of Thomas Randolph sent into Scotland, v 642
——— Of the erle Baldwine to king Stephans armie, ii 89, 90
——— Of the French king to a great assemblie, he sitting in his roialties, iii 732
——— Of the duke of Yorke made vnto the lords of parlement, iii 262
——— Of prince Edward, the French king taken prisoner, ii 268
——— Of the archbishop of Canturburie after the deposing of Richard the second, ii 865, 866
——— Of the bishop of Lincolne lord chancellor to the lords of the parlement house, ii 787.
——— Of erle Marshall of Pembroke in the assemblie of péeres, ii 341
——— Of quéene Elizabeth which she made to the parlement house, iv 588.
——— Of the deputies of the states of the low countries vnto quéene Elizabeth note, iv 616.
——— In Latine and English of a Dutch minister to quéene Elizabeth being in Norwich, iv. 391, 392.

Oration of quéene Elizabeth to the vniversitie in Latine, vol iv. pages 225, 226
——— Of quéene Elizabeth in the parlement house by waie of answer touching a motion of marriage, iv 178, 179.
——— Of Henrie the fift to the king of France, iii. 119, 120.
——— Of the duke of Buckinghame to the maior of London, aldermen, and commoners in the Guildhall, iii 390
——— Of Henrie the seuenth to his armie, iii. 441
——— Of king Edward the fourth lieng on his deth bed note, iii 355, 363
——— Of a French herald to Edward the fourth vttered with boldnesse of face and libertie of toong, iii 333
——— Of the French king to an English herald giuing him defiance, iii 331
——— Of Faber summarlie set downe, iii 715.
——— Of Empson to find fauor, iii 532
——— Of Henrie the eight in the parlement house, iii 851.
——— Of the French king before an honorable assemblie, and sauouring of displeasure, iii 729
——— Of sir Thomas Moore in the parlement house, iii 743
——— Of two heralds to the emperor Charles, iii 723.
——— Of sir Thomas Moore in the parlement, iii. 682
——— Of Tunstall made to the parlement, ib
——— Of the archbishop of Canturburie in the parlement summarlie touched, ii 567.
——— Of Perkin Warbecke the counterfet vnto the king of Scots, iii. 511.
——— Of cardinall Poole in the parlement house, iv 65
——— Of quéene Marie in Guildhall to the Londoners, iv 16, 17.
——— As touching the restitution of abbie lands, iv 75, 76.
——— Of archbishop Hubert of Canturburie vnto the lords at the crowning of king Iohn, ii 275
——— Of the bishop of Durham to his souldiors, ii 81
——— Of the erle of Chester to the erle of Glocester, ii 88
——— In Latine & English of Stephan Limbert schoolmaster in Norwich to quéene Elizabeth at hir being there, iv 391, 395
——— The same highlie commended by the quéene, iv. 396, 397
Orator proud and presumtuous, iii. 104
Oratorie to praie in erected by bishop Cead, i 628.
——— Built by Ioseph of Aremathea, i 639.
Orban the Dane a good enginer, maker of the Turks guns, .. 331
Orchades which inhabited and which not, i 75
——— The description of them that belong to the crowne of Scotland, i 73.
Orchades they and other Ilands when perfectlie vnited to the crowne of Scotland, vol i page 75
——— Their number and situation, i 52
——— First inhabited by the Scithians, i 17
——— Orchards and gardens in England, i 351
——— Furnished with all kinds of fruits, i. 352
——— ¶ See Gardés
Ordalian law brought in by the Saxons, i 209, 210, 211
Order of the garter by whom first deuised, i 238
——— The institution and ceremonies thereof, i. 207, 268, 269.
——— Degrées of reproach inhibiting from the same, i 271.
——— ¶ Sée Knight.
Order of the golden fleece and saint Michaell i 272
Order of the round table, i 268
——— ¶ Sée Knights.
——— Of the round table the feast kept, ii. 184.
——— Of the garter founded note and the cause thereof, ii 628
Order of a parlement, vi 345
Orders that are good and prouided by law, whie so easilie broken, i 187
Ordinance ¶ See Guns.
Ordinances ¶ Sée Clergie Exofficio.
Ordouices mistaken by the Scots, v. 71
——— Old inhabitants of Shropshire, Cheshire, and Lancashire, i. 489
——— In manner destroied, i 501
Orgin an accuser &c. slaine within lists. note, v 284
Organs brought to Scotland, v 122
Orkneie whie called Pictland, v 47, 48.
Orkneie Iles and Shetland ingaged, v 450
Orkneie ¶ Sée Englishmen
Orleance besieged, and a bulwark there taken, iii 160
——— The siege broken vp, iii 165
Orwell hauen, alias Urewell whie so called, i 177,
Osbert put to flight, v 209
——— His prouision by water taken, ib
——— He and Ella kings of Northumberland, ib.
——— He and Ella slaine, v 217
Osbert of Barnewell runneth at tilt with a spirit, i 216, 217
Osborne with a name out of Denmarke arriueth in England, and whie, ii 10
——— He is proffered great kindnesse of duke William to depart out of the north countries, ii 12
Osbright king of Northumbers deposed and Ella placed, i 665
Osmond bishop of Salisburie made the seruice after Salisburie vse, ii 26
Osneie abbie when founded. note, iii 1058.
Osneie ¶ Sée Abbie
Ospraies where they breed, i 382
Osred king of Northumberland expelled, i 654
——— His filthie life and death in battell, i. 641
Osrike king of Northumberland, i 636

Osrike his counsell to reuenge the death of Kinnewulfe, vol i page 650
——— He renounceth his kingdome and becommeth a monke, i. 641
Osrike an infidell, v 173
Ossestrie towne in Wales burnt in thrée yeares, ii 231
Ossorie is ouerrun, vi 131
Ossories there be two, vi 132
Ostemen, vi 183
Ostlers knauerie ¶ See Inns
Ostorius Scapula sent into Britaine, v 67
——— Incourageth his Romans to fight, v 68.
——— His exploits in Britaine, i 487
——— Giueth the Britaines a sore ouerthrowe, i. 489, 190
——— The Britains chéerfullnesse against his Romans, i. 189
——— His triumph for victories against Caratake, i 191
——— He dieth, ib.
Ostrida the wife of king Ethelred, cruellie slaine, i 640
Osulph king of Northumberland slaine by treason, i. 647
Osulte stranglie slaine by a théefe, ii 21.
Oswald a noble man ordeined king of Northumbers expelled, i 651.
——— Raiseth warre against Ethelred, i 612.
——— King of Northumbers his valiantnes against Cadwallo, i 671
——— The true storie concerning him, i 614.
——— His zeal to aduance religion, i 616
——— He breaketh his siluer plate to the poore, ib
——— An interpreter to the preacher, i. 615
——— Cruellie slaine by Penda, i 617.
——— Canonised a saint, ib.
Oswald archbishop of Yorke, i 697
Oswald bishop of Winchester, i 695
Oswie king of Northumberland, i. 622
——— His vow that he made if he might haue the victorie, ib
——— He sickeneth and dieth, i 628
Oswin ¶ Sée Oswie.
Oswis the grandfather of Lestrigo, i 7
——— Slaine by the sonnes of Neptune and white, ib
Oth of king Edward the confessor, i 232
——— Of king Iames the first at a parlement, v 118
——— Of knights in Norwaie to reuenge the death of their fréends, v 265
——— ¶ Sée Fealtie & Ooth
——— For the confirmation of peace betwéene the two kings of England and France doone by more, iii 293
——— Of obseruing the league interchangablie made and taken of Henrie the eight and the emperour Charles, iii 678
——— Most wicked and disloiall of noblemen, against their king, iii 293
——— Fulfilled by the lord Granuill, iii 137
——— Of fealtie to prince Edward, ii 239
Oth not to infringe the statutes of Oxford, vol ii. page 451
——— Corporall receiued vpon the holie mysteries and sword, of Thomas Becket, ii. 523
——— Of fealtie to Edward the third taken of the Flemings, ii 612.
——— Concerning the peace betwéene the king of England and France taken solemnlie in parlement of the states note, ii 677
——— Solemne of the second king of England to sée peace performed, ii 676
——— Of the nobles to be true to prince Richard after his fathers decease, ii 701
——— Of rebels ministred vnto all passengers, ii 736
——— Of the commons of Herttordshire to Richard the second, ii 750
——— Of the gentlemen of Norfolke forced by the rebels, ii 745
——— Of the duke of Lancaster & Hereford combattant touching the iustnesse of his quarrell, ii 847.
——— Taken of the two kings of England and France for the assurance of both their faithfull meanings, ii 833
——— Of Richard the second to performe the noblemens orders, ii 796
——— Of the lords handled against their king, ii. 786
——— Receiued of Leolin prince of Wales to Edward the first, ii 481
——— Of Edward the first in his anger to one of his nobles note, ii 521
——— Of the French king to aid the sonne against the father, ii 150
——— Forced vpon the lord maior of London, ii. 582
——— Of Edward the second at his coronation, hée said hée would not vnsweare, ii 561
——— Nothing regarded of Edward the second, ii. 552
——— Exacted of Henrie the third by his nobles, ii. 416
——— Of Henrie the third at a parlement, with an imprecation note, ii 429
——— Of Thomas Becket whereof he repented him. note, ii 118
——— Of a cardinall not to preiudice the realme, ii. 414
——— Giuen to the erle of Glocester by Henrie the third on his deathbed, ii 476
——— Of the maior aldermen, and comonaltie of London sworne to Henrie the third, ii 456
——— Nothing regarded of the French king, ii 354.
——— Of Lewes vrged vpon him by Henrie the third, ib
——— Of the traitor Parrie in a tresonable action, iv 569
——— Interchangable of the duke of Alanson and the people, iv 584.
——— Of the duke of Alanson read openlie to the people, ib
——— Of K. Richard the first at his coronation, ii, 201

Oth receiued of the erle of Warwike and other officers at Newhauen, vol iv. page 206
—— Taken of the bishops and barons for their loiallie, ii 2
—— Of duke William at his coronation, ib
—— Of duke William solemnlie taken and cruellie broken, ii 16
—— Of William Rufus by saint Lukes face, ii 16
—— Of the thrée estates of France, iii 123
—— Of the duke of Burgogne with others to Henrie the fift, iii 111
—— It and submission of the duke of Yorke to Henrie the sixt, iii 231
—— Of the duke of Norfolke kept with the losse of his life, iii 442
—— Corporall of the erle of Richmond to marrie Edward the fourths daughter, iii 420
—— Of the French king at an interuiew, iii 340
—— Taken of the nobilitie in Henrie the firsts time for their fealtie, ii 65
—— Taken of the lords touching the succession of the crowne, ii 72
—— Of Lewes the sonne of the French king when he laboured to get the crowne of England, ii 33
—— Of pope Innocent vsed vpon a complaint, ii 324
—— Of allegiance to be true to king Iohn aboue all other persons, ii 318
—— Of diuerse erles and barons of France to K Iohn to assist him, ii 277
—— Of K Iohn when his nobles were vp in armes against him, ii 320
—— Of the erle of Poictou Richard the first his nephew, ii 260
—— Of allegiance receiued of the people to Richard the first in his abscence, ii 230
—— Of allegiance to K. Richard the first at a counsell, ii 208.
—— Of Londoners to be true to K Richard the first and his heires, ii 228
—— Of the king of Cypres to Richard the first, and broken. note, ii 221
—— Of king Richard the first the king of France and their barons, ii 216
—— Of iustices of itinerants, ii 169
—— Taken about a place of méeting. note, ii 194
—— A dispensation for the same, ii 112
—— Of purgation taken solemnlie, ii 113
—— Ouer all the realme to obserue the kings peace, ii 256
—— Of fealtie Saluo semper ordine suo, ii 146
—— Of allegiance newlie taken, ii 299
—— Taken and broken for preferment note, ii 72
—— Touching an act of establishing the crowne, taken of euerie person of lawfull age, iii 792
—— It and the sacrament taken but not ment to be obserued, iii 305
—— Cruellie made and cruellie kept note, iii 381.
—— Of allegiance broken and notablie punished, by God: note, iii. 269
Oth added to a promise and the same performed, vol i page 23
—— Taken to be true to the king and his heires, ib
—— Of a noble man by his honor. note, iv 340
—— Upon the euangelists to stand to the iudgement of the holie church, ii 148
—— For restitution of heritages, rights, liberties, &c. ib
—— Inforced, absolued, ii 340
—— Made broken and punished, ii 717.
—— With protestation in a case of innocencie note, ii 784
—— Of allegiance confirmed by writing, ii 850
—— Constreined is no oth, i 757
—— Taken for purgation in a case of Murther, i 737
Oth the sonne of Occa the saxon, i 572
Oths that the dukes of Brabant were accustomed to take, iv. 172.
—— Corporall receiued for performance of agréement, iv 50
—— Of obedience willinglie taken to K. Iohn, ii. 273
—— Outragious order a disciplne for them, ii. 193
—— ¶ See Periurie, Promises and Uow
Otho the emperor commeth ouer into England, ii 295
—— ¶ Sée Odo
Otuell an erles sonne, tutor to K. Henrie the firsts children, ii 33
Ouze riuer described, i 157
—— Called the third Isis and his fall into the sea, i 172
—— ¶ Sée Trent.
Outlawes ¶ Sée Brudeus, Conrane
Owen Glendouer ¶ Sée Glendouer.
Owen prince of Wales, slaine, ii 66
Owles deuoure mice note, a wonder, ii 434
Oxen of England not to be matched in all Europe, i. 369
Oxford forsaken of the scholers, ii 200
—— Verie forward in preferring quéene Maries religion, iv 27
—— Quéene Elizabeths progresse thither, iv. 230
—— The strange sicknesse there at the assise, whereof iudges died, iv 343.
—— Their manner of interteining Albertus de Lasco, iv 508
—— The ministers of the vniuersitie summoned to the parlement about the conclusion of a peace, &c ii. 441.
—— The scholers thereof fight against Henrie the third, ii 461
—— ¶ Sée Debate, Fraie, Statutes, Treason, & Variance
—— How to be thought and estéemed the elder vniuersitie, i 256
—— Fiftie miles from London, i. 250.
—— The longitude and latitude thereof, ib

Oxford erection of colleges therein the ouerthrowe of halles, vol i page 255.
——— Colleges there with their founders names, ib
——— The bishoprikes, erection, circuit and situation, i 210
——— Burned by the Danes, i 711.
——— The vniuersitie when founded and erected, i 675
——— ¶ Sée Castells and Vniuersities
Oxfordshire assalted, v 67
Oxfordshiremen resist the Romans and are slaine, i 487.

P

Packington strangle murthered, iii 203
Padstow a corrupted worde for Adlestone, i 111.
Paganels. ¶ Sée Painell
Pagents and shews sumtuous and sightlie, iii 633
——— At quéene Anne coronation, iii 779
——— Vpon the sudden at a Candlemas tide, iii 641
——— At the coronation of Henrie the eight, iii 550, 551
——— Of neat deuise, iii 609
——— Of quéene Maries coronation, iii 6
——— In London at the comming of Philip and Marie through the citie, iv 62
——— Of pleasing inuention, iii 560, 561
——— Of the receiuing of quéene Elizabeth into Norwich, iv 378 to 380
——— In Antwerpe at the receiuing of the duke of Alanson, iv 465 to 468
——— Of triumph at the coronation of quéene Elizabeth, iv 158 to 171
——— At a triumphant iusts holden at Westminster, iv 535 to 545
——— At Christmas, iii 558, 567, 574, 617.
——— On a Maie daie, iii 561, 562
——— ¶ Sée Sights
Paget, lord ¶ See Throckmorton Francis, and erle Persie of Northumberland
Painell kept the castell of Ludlow, ii 89
Painters brought into England, i 627
Palace of Henrie the eight at Gyisnes described note, iii 446, 447
——— Of the prince, and of striking within it, how punished, i 332
——— Called the bishops palace by Paules by whome builded, i 468
Palaces belonging to the prince of this land, i 328
Paladour mount now Shaftsburie, i 446.
Palatine of Siradie ¶ Sée Albertus de Lasco
Palestine ¶ Sée Holie Land
Pall of an archbishop, i 594.
—— What it is, vi 42
Palladius accounted the apostle of the Scots, i 48.
——— Instructeth Scots in the faith, i. 562
——— Sent into Scotland, v 134.
——— Their apostle, ib
Palladius archdeacon of Rome arriueth in Ireland, vi 83
Palladius appointed to preach, vol vi page 83.
——— He trauelleth into Scotland, ib.
Palmer knight beheaded, his words at his death, iv 5
——— ¶ Sée Pilgrime
Palme sundaie field ¶ Sée Butted
Palsgraue of Rhene, his traine come to receiue Henrie the eight, iii. 587
——— He and others come ouer into England, iii 810
Pandulph the popes legat, a practiser of much mischéefe against king Iohn, ii 302, 306
——— Made bishop of Norwich, ii 349
Pandrasus prepareth an armie to suppresse the Troian offspring, he is taken prisoner, i 438, 439
Pangs of gelousie, vi. 32
Pannonia now Hungarie, i 479
Pant and what spring méeteth or ioineth with it, i. 185
Papist did eat brawne in Lent, i 373
Papists dedicated their cities to Bolulph and Giles, i 39
——— Their crueltie against the Martyrs in quéene Maries time, iv 523.
——— Their obiections that préests executed are but scholers and vnarmed, iv 530
——— They call the protestants heretikes and enimies to the crosse of Christ euen as Ahab called Elias the disturber of Israell, himselfe being the onely disturber, iv 71, 72
——— Their praiers and of what little effect they be, iv 70
——— Animated by rebellion, iii 1008
——— By rebellion haue an ill opinion of Gods holie truth, iii 1009.
——— Such as were neuer charged with capitoll crimes, iii 518 519.
Paraphrase of Erasmus commanded to be had in churches, iii 889
Pardon offered to conspirators and traitors, iii. 252
——— Upon mistrust refused, ib
——— Offered to rebels, ii 739
——— At a parlement, ii 678
——— Of six yeares and one hundred daies preached, ii 415
——— To Appletrée hauing the alter about his necke, iv 425
——— With exceptions at quéene Maries coronation, iv 7
——— Generall to all rebels conditionallie published, iii. 1013, 1014.
——— To the liuing, pitie on the dead, iii. 320
——— Generall proclamed, iii 801
——— No offense excepted, iii 185
——— By proclamation dispersed the Kentish rebels, iii 226
——— At a pinch for treason, iii 211.
——— Upon submission, ii. 234.
——— For prisoners at a womans sute obteined, ii 618.
——— ¶ Sée Forgiuenesse and Parlement.

Pardon none to offendors for the space of seuen yeares, vol v. p ge 458
——— Generall to rebels note, v. 413, 460.
——— Granted by the gouernors are uoid, v. 420.
Pardoners two set on the pillorie, ii 500
Parishes how manie in euerie shire of England, i 326.
——— ¶ Sée England
Paris where Henrie the sixt was crowned, iii 176.
——— Henrie the fift receiued in there, iii. 123.
——— Edward the third draweth néere it with his power, the Englishmen lie before it, the suburbs burned, ii. 673, 674
——— For multitude it passeth Antwerpe, iv 468
——— The duke of Bedfords entrance thereinto, and executing certeine conspirators, iv. 138, 139
——— The treason of the inhabitants, iii. 166
——— Yéelded to the French king, ib.
——— ¶ Sée Uniuersitie
Paris garden. ¶ Sée Slaughter
Paris Christopher betraieth Marmouth, vi. 299
——— His promised reward, is paid, vi. 300
——— Beheaded, vi 301
Parkes and Warrens in England, i 343
——— How commonly inclosed, ib.
——— More in England, than in all Europe, i 345
——— None left in England at the comming of the Normans, ib
——— Tillage and making diminished by them, i 344
Parkekéepers ordinarie fée, ib.
Parker Nicholas valiantlie defendeth himselfe, vi 430
Parker Iohn lieutenant to capteine Furse slaine in the Glinnes, vi. 435
Parker afterwards archbishop of Canturburie, preached to the rebels at Norfolke, iii 967
——— They threaten him, he conueieth himselfe from among them, iii 968
——— ¶ See Archbishops of Canturburie
Parkin Warbecke raised vp to be a king, vi. 270.
——— ¶ Sée Perkin.
Parlement at Dublin, vi. 254, 260, 265, 282, 285, 341.
——— At Kilkennie, vi 255, 258.
——— At Galidale, vi. 250.
——— Orders, vi. 341.
——— At Trim, vi 265
——— Summoned, v. 651
——— Holden, v. 578, 604, 616.
——— At saint Andrews, v. 723
——— At Edenburgh, v 581, 586, 587, 667, 742, 743, 603, 631, 650.
——— At Striueling, v. 614.
——— Held at Berwike, i. 210.
——— At Chester, i. 125
——— At Salisburie by Edward ye Second, i. 98
——— Number of the congregats therein, i. 302.
Parlement holden at Blackfriars, vol iii page 682
——— At Cambridge, ii 797
——— At Couentrie, iii 256
——— Made frustrate, iii 268
——— At Glocester, ii 721
——— In Ireland, ii 524
——— At Lambeth, ii 372
——— At Leicester, ii 116
——— At London, ii 433, 431, 451.
——— Adiourned, ii 71, 93, 133, 414, 412, 415, 426, 128, 473, 158, 349, 181, 531, 5 2
——— At Marleburrow, ii 473
——— At Merton in Surrie, ii 380
——— At Northampton, ii 168, 218, 547, 696, 734.
——— At Nottingham, ii 217
——— At Oxford, ii 174, 289, 360
——— At Rone by the duke of Bedford, iii 168
——— At saint Edmunsburie, ii. 211, 519
——— At Salisburie, ii 763
——— At Shrewsburie, ii 487.
——— At Westminster, ii 357, 359, 364, 371, 379, 396, 403, 452, 467, 470, 479, 480
——— King Richard the second being in Ireland, ii 427
——— Crownes of England and France intailed to Henrie the sixt, iv 301
——— With an atteindor and a pardon generall, iii. 480
——— Where Elizabeth and her lords did ride, iv 550.
——— At Winchester, ii 448, 467, 821.
——— At Windsore, ii 178
——— At Yorke, ii 327, 570.
——— Called by the duke of Bedford Henrie the fift being in France, iii 129
——— It and Richard the second at dissention, ii. 775
——— Call, Richard the second being prisoner in the Towre, ii 859.
——— Called by the duke of Glocester, Henrie the sixt being in France, iii. 176
——— Dissolued quéene Elizabeth making an oration to the whole house, iv 588.
——— Wherein church liuings are restored, iv 80.
——— Whereat Philip and Marie are present, iv. 64
——— Of white bands, ii 561
——— Parlementum insanum, ii 146.
——— Iniurious and offensiue, ii. 813
——— Determination concerning the intaling of the crowne, iii 265
——— Of seuen wéeks continuance, iii 21
——— Called the laiemens parlement, iii 30
——— Long, iii 49.
——— That wrought wonders, ii 793.
——— Of thrée estates of the realme, iii. 513.
——— Wherevnto noble men are appointed to come in warlike manner, ii 838.

Parlement summoned and new lawes for the common wealth enacted, vol iii page 183.
——— Called the great parlement, ii 839
——— Called mercilesse, and of a head that spake then, ii 829
——— The lords sit in the house in their armour, ii 752
——— Held on that time fiftie yeares that Edward the third was borne, ii. 678
——— For the order of knighthood, ii. 498
——— Proroged, ii 445
——— And the king of Scots came there, ii 168
——— Adiourned from place to place, iii 218
——— At diuision note, iii 744, 746
——— Great and solemn, ii 441.
——— Called the mad parlement, ii 445
——— The first vse thereof in Henrie the first his time, ii 65, 66
——— The authoritie thereof, iii 923
——— The causes and conditions thereof note, ii 775
——— The authoritie of both houses granted to certeine persons, ii 813
——— ¶ Sée Burgesse, Councell, Priuilege
——— Of the thrée estates, v 458.
——— Called the black parlement, v 351
——— Court, the orders, officers, and authoritie of the same, i 291
——— Law, i 302
Parlements after what order held in Scotland, v 720
——— Nicknamed, v 721
——— Running parlement, ib
Parricide ¶ Sée Murther, i 738
Parrie sueth for licence to trauell beyond the sea, iv 566
—— Iustifieth himselfe in religion before the inquisitor of Millan, ib
—— Resolueth in the plot of his trecherous deuise, iv 567
—— With what enimies vnto God he linketh himselfe, ib
—— He voweth to vndertake the killing of the quéene, ib
—— And resolued himselfe so to doo, iv 567, 568
—— Committed vnto the custodie and examination of sir Francis Walsingham, iv 562
—— Denieth with protestations whatsoeuer was demanded of him, iv 563
—— Examined before certeine lords of the councell, ib
—— Commited to the Towre, iv 563
—— His discontentment because he might not haue preferment to his owne liking, iv 564.
—— Confesseth himselfe giltie of all things conteined in his inditement, iv 575
—— His confession of treasons openlie read by his owne assent, iv 576
—— Iudgement giuen against him, ib.
Parrie he chargeth the lords of the councell with vntruth, vol iv. page 577
—— Reprooued, ib
—— His exclamation of outrage and vnpatientnesse, iv 578
—— Abuseth the assemblie with termes and words vncooth, ib
—— The forme of iudgment pronounced against him, iv 579
—— Desparat, iv 569
—— How long his practise was in handling ere it was detected, ib
—— His oth in that ill matter, ib
—— He chargeth Neuill with gréeuous spéeches of cursed disloialtie, ib
—— What mooued him to attempt the murthering of the queene, iv 564.
—— He counted it a déed meritorious, ib
—— His pestilent humour of malice against hir, iv. 565
—— How his traitorous practise should haue béene doone, ib
—— His resolutenesse to doo it, ib
—— His voluntarie confession in the hearing of certeine lords, iv 566
—— Certeine obseruations out of his words and writings note, iv 583, 584, 585
—— A dilemma proouing that hée died a periured traitor, iv 586
—— An epigram of fit deuise for so vile a wretch, iv 586, 587
—— Rageth at the iustice barre without all reuerence, iv 579
—— Euen at his execution he séeketh to cléere himselfe, iv 580
—— A description of him by linage and his life verie lewd note, iv 580, 581.
—— His letters to quéene Elizabeth and to the lords of the councell, after his voluntarie confession, iv 570
—— His treasons practised against quéene Elizabeth at full declared, iv 561
—— Described, reconciled to the pope, ib
—— His malice growth to an extremitie of mischéefe against queene Elizabeth, iv 562
—— Saith and vnsaith to shift of the heuie charge of his treasons, iv 572
—— Conuicted, iv 573
—— Arreigned, iv 574, 575
Parsonages with a decrée touching the same, ii 51
Pasalpine in Scotland and whie so named, i 203
Pascentius Uortigerns youngest sonne his exploits, i 566
——— His practise of treason against Aurelius, ib
Pascentius ¶ Sée Occa.
Pase doctor described, iii 671
—— His oration in praise of peace, iii. 633.
—— Falleth out of his wits, iii 737.
Paslee taken, v 648.
——— Besieged by the regent, ib.
——— Surrendered to the regent, ib

Pasport giuen to Anselme to depart the land, vol. ii. page 45.
——— ¶ Sée Safe Conduct
Pasture best in what part of England and Wales, i 184
——— It differeth according to the soile, i. 183, 181.
Paten ¶ Sée Bishop Wainfléet
Patents resumed into Richard the firsts hand by act of parlement, ii 249
Pateshull a frier Augustine and a Wickleuist, forsaketh his profession, preacheth openlie against his order, publisheth a libell against his brotherhood, his fauourers, ii 780, 781
Patience of the English in suffering all wants of releefe, iii 894
Patillocke called Le perie roy de Gascoigne,
Patriarch Heraclius commeth to king Henrie the second for aid, vi 23.
——— Intreated the king to go into the holie land, ib
——— He threateneth the king for denieng, ib.
——— Of Ierusalem commeth into England, ii 187
Patrike his life, vi 84
——— Where he was borne, vi 83
——— His purgatorie, vi 36
——— Made an archbishop, vi 85
——— He baptized Ruanus, vi 74, 75
——— He conuerteth all Ireland to christianitie, vi 86, 212
Patrike an augustine frier, seditious and an enimie vnto Lancaster house, iii 323
Patrike Dunbar vanquished théeues, made erle of March, his armes, v 278.
Patrons directed well to bestow benifices in the vacancies, i 234
——— ¶ Sée Benefices and Ministers
Pauia beséeged and how the battell was tried, iii 696, 697
Pauia in Lumbardie, i. 676
——— ¶ Sée Paris
Pauier a contemner of the gospell, and his shamfull end note, iii 738
Paule abbat of S Albons commended, ii 30.
Paule preached vnto the Britains, i. 487.
Paules presence in Britaine, i 40
Paules church first a temple by whom builded, i 463
——— By whom builded doubtfull, i 595, 597
——— In London dedicate, ii 389, 390.
——— The gates blew open with a tempest, iv 229
——— Church stéeple finished, ii 352
——— It laie at anchor, iii 866.
——— Upon the weather cocke whereof stood a Duchman holding a streamer, &c iv 6.
——— It is burnt by lightening note, iii 206
——— Meanes made to repaire it, iv 202
——— Ten thousand pounds insufficient to repare it as it was at first, iv 203
Paulet William lord treasuror deceaseth, his ancient and honorable seruice, blessed in his children, vol. iv page 263
Pauline bishop of Rochester, i 611
——— Diligent in his office, i 604.
——— His preaching and baptising preuaileth much, i 608
——— He prospereth in the dischaige of his function, i 609
——— He flieth into Kent, i 610
Pauline archbishop of Yorke, i 609
——— He receiueth the pall, ib
——— He deceaseth, i 617, 618
Peace concluded vpon conditions betwéene king Edmund Ironside, and Cnute, i 724, 725
——— Concluded to make open warre for treason, i. 722
——— Purchased with monie, i. 637, 638, 704, 705, 710.
——— Mainteined within the prince of Englands court note, i 331.
——— Betwéene England and France, iv. 224.
——— Concluded, iii 503
——— Difficulties about the practise thereof, the French counsell accord for it, the contents of the capitulation for it, iii 607, 608
——— Proclaimed, iii 711
——— Concluded and proclamed, iii. 856.
——— Mooued, iii 502
——— Commissioners sent ouer to Calis about the same, while the English prefer it before war, a conclusion thereof betwéene both nations, iii 502, 503
——— Treated of at Towres, iii 206.
——— Treated but not concluded, iii 106
——— Conditionallie concluded note, iii 1022, 1023
——— With a mariage, ii 279
——— After werie wars, ii 254, 822.
——— In memorie whereof, the chapell of our ladie of peace was builded note, ii 832, 833
——— Perpetuall treated, ii 813
——— Treated but not obteined, ii 621
——— Treated by the ladie Iane de Ualois, ii. 617.
——— And articles drawne, ii. 670
——— Commissioners appointed to treat thereabouts, ii 700
——— Concluded for one whole yeare, ii 651
——— Conditionall at the moderation of the quéene of England, ii 577
——— Treted by a cardinall, ii 508
——— Decided by the pope, ii 537
——— Treated vpon by two duchesses note, iii. 712, 743
——— Betwéene the French king and the emperor, treated but not concluded, iv 79
——— Procured betwéene the king of Spaine and France at the sute of the duchesse of Loraine, iv. 120
——— Broken by the French king, ii 689
——— Hard to be made betwixt Henrie the second and the French king, ii 197

Peace concluded betwéene Henrie the second and the French king with much adoo, vol. ii. page 198
—— Treated betwéene Henrie the eight and the French king by a legat from Rome, iii 694
—— Betwéene Edward the fourth and the French king the same articulated, iii 334
—— Said to be made by the Holie Ghost note, iii 311
—— Betwixt Henrie the sixt and the French king solemnlie treated at Paris, iii 182.
—— Betwéene Henrie the fift and the French king and the articles of the said peace, iii 112, 113
—— Betwéene king Iohn and the French king after war, ii 278
—— Said to be mooued by the popes Nuncios, ii. 288
—— Betwéene Richard the first and the French king, ii 209
—— Betwéene Edward the third and the French king after manie bloodie skirmishes and vpon what articles, ii 674
—— Betwéene William Rufus and his brother Robert for monie, ii 35.
—— Treated and proclaimed after long troubles betwéene Henrie the third and his barons note, ii 463, 464
—— Painfullie procured by the countesse of Wales betwéene the king and the duke of Lancaster, ii 765
—— Betwéene Robert and Henrie the first Brethren, ii 50
—— Of brethren namlie Edward the fourth and the duke of Clarence, iii 308
—— Betwéene king Henrie the second and his sonne, ii 153
—— Betwéene the king of England and Scotland, ii 81.
—— With king Iohn compounded for by the king of Scots, iii 176
—— Betwixt Edward the first and Leolin prince of Wales vpon articles, ii 480, 481
—— Betwéene the king of England and the Scots with the charters of the same, ii 165
—— Sought by king Iohn but withstood of the French king, ii 289
—— Betwéene the king of France and the king of Spaine solemnlie celebrated, iii 636.
—— Betwéene Lewis and Henrie the third after sharpe wars, ii 318
—— Of quéenes by them procured note, ii 303
—— Betwéene the king of France and the duke of Britaine with the articles thereof, ii 733
—— Betwéene king Stephan and Henrie Fitzempresse after their long warrs, ii 105
—— Betwéene the two factions of Burgogne and Orleance, iii 51
—— Sought for of Soldan Saladin to Richard the first and concluded, ii 234
—— Betwéene Charles of France and the duke of Burgogne, iii 183
Peace and what mischéefe came thereof, vol iii. pages 183, 184
—— Betwéene the emperor Charles and the French K iii 704
—— Henrie the eight and the prince of Orange, included in the same, whie it set all Christendome in a wondering, iii 705, 706
—— Treated vpon betwéene the emperor Charles and the French K iii 672
—— Betwixt the king of Spaine and France treated of, iv. 183
—— The articles thereof, ib
—— Betwéene France and Scotland proclamed, iv. 199
—— Articles of the same peace to the end thereof, with the commendation of the same, iv 201
—— The praise and benefits thereof, iv 1010
—— A treatise thereof before an encounter, ii 17
—— Granted vpon mutuall conditions, ib
—— Made a pretense to execute inward malice, ii 16
—— Concluded to one partie dishonourable, ii 31.
—— Sought but not wrought, ii 391
—— Contemned, and reuenged, pursued, ii 352.
—— Concluded after much trouble, ii 472
—— And what a foule end an enimie thereto had, ii 356, 357.
—— Hindred by hard demands, ii 702, 703
—— Solemnlie made and rechleslie broken, ii 689
—— Wrought by the grace of the Holie ghost. note, ii 674
—— Dishonourable, ii 596
—— Hindred with stoutnesse, ii 604.
—— Offensiue, ii 732
—— Sought for but not admitted · note, ii 846.
—— Sought but not obteined note, ii 55
—— Persuaded nothing preuailed, ii. 253
—— Disaduantagable, ii 279
—— Displeasant, ib
—— After sharpe wars and victorie note, iii 118
—— Sought for the supplanting of ciuill discord, iii 265
—— Procured by want of monie, iii 334
—— Begun betwéene two an occasion thereof betwéene manie, iii 308.
—— Sought after much malice and bloodshed, betwéene persons of great honour, iii 307
—— Called the womens peace, iii 743
—— Treated vpon at Cambrie executed note, iii. 719
—— Concluded vpon articles, ii 165
—— After great troubles vpon conditions note, ii. 162
—— Broken of set purpose note, ii 193.
—— Intreated, v 565.
—— Concluded, v 511, 566, 714, 575.
—— Betweene England and Scotland, v 465, 580.
—— Articles thereof, v 608
—— At Nottingham, v. 455.

Peace concluded for thrée yeares, vol. v pages 466, 511.
—— Concluded betwixt the Danes and Scots, v 268
—— Betwéene king Iohn and king William of Scotland, v. 304
—— Concluded betwixt the lords of the religion and the quéene, v 590, 591
—— Betwéene England and France, v 464
—— Concluded for want of power to manteine battell, v 262.
—— Exhorted vnto after warrs, v 12.
—— ¶ Sée Parlement.
Peada. ¶ Sée Penda and Wenda
Peda king of Middleangles married, baptised, i 620
—— His opinion and saieng of Lipgospellers, ib
Pedegrées wherein the Britons are diligent and readie, i 23.
Pedlers French whereof compact, i 309.
—— ¶ Sée Beggers and Rouges
Péers Alice is banished the realme note, ii 717.
Péers Gaueston earle of Cornwall, ii 547
—— Edward the seconds lewd compa-mion, ib.
—— Married, ib
—— Accursed, ii. 549.
—— Hated of the noblemen and whie, ii 548.
—— Banished the realme, ii 549
—— The king his fauour towards him, ib
—— Made deputie of the land, placed in Banburgh castell, banished into Flanders, ii. 549, 550, 551
—— His sawcie abusing of the nobles they assalt and take him, he is brought vnto Warwike and beheaded, the king displeased at his death, ii. 551, 552
—— ¶ Sée Gaueston
Péet signifieth a magician, vi 85.
Pelagian heresie. ¶ See Heresie, i 134
Pelagian errors greatlie preuailed in Britaine, i 561
—— To be suppressed, i 609
Pelagius where borne, his heresie, i 562.
—— Brought heresie and monasticall life into Britaine at one time, i 46.
—— Attempted to be suppressed, i 48
Pellam sir William is dubbed knight, vi 415
—— Is chosen lord iustice, vi. 421.
—— He dubbed sir William Girald and sir Thomas Perot, knights, ib
—— He maketh a iournie to Mounster, vi 421, 422
—— He sendeth for the erle of Desmond, vi. 422
—— He sendeth the erle of Ormond vnto him, vi 423
—— He proclamed the erle traitor, vi 421.
—— He commeth to Limerike and then to Gallowaie, and his honourablie receiued, he maketh a second iournie then to Mounster, vol. vi pages 427, 428.
Pellam sir William is verie honourablie receiued at Waterford, vi 429
—— He sendeth the chancellor of Limerike to ward, and the bishop he commandeth to his owne house, vi 429
—— He besiegeth and taketh the castell of Caregfoile, vi 430
—— He taketh Asketten castell, vi 431
—— He createth sir William Burcke baron of Connell, vi 432
—— He deliuereth the sword to the lord Greie, vi 436
Penance of Paules crosse · note, iii. 789, 803
—— Of Anabaptists, iii 326, 807
—— Of a most horrible offender, iv. 889
—— Of fiue persons of the familie of loue, iv. 328.
—— At Paules crosse by a spirit in a wall, without Aldersgate, iv 56
—— Of two wenches counterfeiting themselues to be possessed with the diuell, iv 325
—— Of bishop Herbert, ii 41
—— That the regents and rulers of Oxford did at cardinall Otho his cursse, ii 383
—— Inioined vnto the burgesses of Oxford note, ii 314
—— Of the ladie Cobham for hir intended treason against Henrie the sixt, iii 208
—— Of doctor Barnes and two merchants of the Stilliard for heresie, iii 711.
—— That a wrongfull iustice did, ii 491
—— With penaltie for murther note, iii. 95
—— Ridiculous note, ii 828
—— That Edgar did for deflouring Wilfrid, i 696
—— Uoluntarie that Robert duke of Normandie vndertooke, i. 764
Pembroke coniuror ¶ Sée Sorcerer
Pence and small coines when square, and by whom made round, i 367
—— ¶ See Coines and Monie.
Penda king of Mercie, i 610, v 175
—— His crueltie, i 610
—— His regiment, his acts and déeds, i 612
—— He enuieth Oswalds well doing, i 617.
—— Slaine by Oswie, i 620
Pendleton doctor preaching at Paules crosse hath a gun shot at him, iv 56
Peninus Posthumus killeth himselfe, i 401.
Penke doctor lost his life in his sermon, &c · note, iii 386
Pensioners muster before the quéene Elizabeth, iv 234
Pentarchie of Britaine, i. 530
—— ¶ Sée Britaine and Kings
Peoples fauour fixed when it is once gotten note, ii 258, 259.
—— In Henrie the eight glad to seek and whie, ii. 47.

Peoples fauour great vnto the duke of Summerset, vol iii page 1035
———— Sought by faire words, ii 29
———— Their furious reuenge for the deth of one whome the loued note, ii 20, 21
———— What promises to purchase it, ii. 13, 14
———— In England of four sorts, i 263.
———— Lesse neuer than now, i 345
———— Their decaie by diuerse causes, i 314
———— Their decaie the destruction of a kingdome, i 341
Perdex his prophesies, i 449
Perers Alice Edward the third his concubine note, ii 703
———— Banished the realme, ii 717
Peredus ¶ See Urgenius
Perhennis all in all vnder the emperor Comōdus, i 514
Perie made of peares, i 286
Periurie how punished, i 311
———— Neuer left vnpunished, i. 761.
———— ¶ See Oth and Promise
———— How punished, ii 79, iii 305
———— By God, iv 329
———— Laid to William Rufus charge by his brother Robert, ii 35
———— Said to Henrie the fourths charge, iii 26.
———— ¶ Sée Baftuling
Perkin Warbecke was a long time taken for the yoonger of the two princes whom Richard the third murthered, iii 100
———— The counterfet duke of Yorke his redie wit to learn all that made for his preferment, vnto honour, he arriueth in Ireland, saileth into France all aflant, returneth vnto the ladie Margaret his first founder, named by hir the white rose of England, iii 501, 505.
———— Counterfeteth the duke of Yorke verie cunninglie his true linage his conspiring fautors, iii 506, 507.
———— Sir William Stanlie his fauourer, iii 529
———— He attempteth to land in Kent his men discomfited, his capteins taken and executed, he reculeth into Flanders, iii 510, 511
———— Saileth into Ireland and is in sundrie opinions, hee marieth the erle of Huntlies daughter, saith that hée is Edward the fourth his lawfull sonne telleth the Scotish king how he was preserued and kept aliue, calleth the ladie Margaret his aunt, craueth aid of the Scotish K toward the recouerie of the crowne of England from Henrie the seuenth, iii 511, 512
———— His counterfet compassion, iii 513
———— Hée is faine to pack out of Scotland his three counsellors, hee assaileth Excester, iii 517, 518
———— Hée taketh sanctuarie, his wife presented to Henrie the seuenth, all his partakers in their shirts and with halters about their necks appéere before Henrie the seuenth, hée is assalted in sanctuarie, submitteth himselfe vnto the K and is strictlie seene vnto, vol iii page 519
Perkin Warbecke escapeth from his kéepers, his confession as it was written with his owne hands and read openlie vpon a scaffold by the standard in Chepe, iii 521, 522
———— Hee corrupteth his kéepers, hée is executed at Tiburne, iii. 523, 524.
Perle mother in an Ile of Scotland, i. 70
Perles in England, i 402.
———— Whie called orient, i 403
———— Whether they be good that are found in muskels or no, i 402.
Peror sir Thomas knight ¶ See Iusts triumphant.
Perot sir Iohn lord president of Mounster, vi. 308
———— His state and conditions, ib
———— Iames Fitmoris rebelleth at his gouernment, vi. 369
———— His gouernment, ib
———— His seruice against him, ib
———— The peace of the countrie, ib.
———— His assistance, ib
———— Hée reformeth Irish maners, ib
———— Admerall of the quéenes ships, vi 415.
———— He is lord deputie he subdueth the Scots he maketh the land all shire ground, ib.
Perot sir Thomas is dubbed knight, vi. 415.
Persecution. ¶ Sée Christians
———— In England ceaseth, and the protestants returne out of exile, iv 179
———— ¶ Sée Martyrs, Religion, Priéests, Seminarie
Persie lord sent against the Scots, ii. 523.
———— Put to flight by the king of Scots, ii. 512
———— ¶ See Conspiracie and Erle
Persie erle of Northumberland, v 292
———— ¶ Sée Henrie Hotspur
Persies Rafe and Henrie prisoners, v 395
Persies with others conspire against Henrie the fourth, v 406
———— Their name and generation, v. 285
Persiuall ¶ See Maior and Officer.
Pertinax sent as lieutenant to Britaine driueth backe the Scots and Picts, chosen emperor, v. 94
———— Lieutenant of Britaine, i 515
Pestilence the first comming of it into Scotland, v 522.
———— The second that was heard of in Scotland, v 385
———— The third time in Scotland, v 392
———— And dearth great, v 176.
———— In the English pale, vi 374
———— In Calis, iii 552
———— Foloweth famine, iii 1001.
———— In manie places especiallie in London, iii 521
———— In diuerse parts of that realme, iii 343.

Pestilence that deuoureth wonderfull multitudes. note, vol iii page 346
——— Not in London, iv 235
——— Among the souldiors at Newhauen, iv. 221
——— The cause that Newhauen fell into the hands of the French, iv 223
——— Transported from thense to London, ib
——— And what a consumption of people it wrought in the citie and subburbs this was called the great plague, iv 224
——— Like to haue increased, iv 325
——— In Germanie whereof thrée hundred thousand died, iv 225
Peterburgh spoiled, ii 595
Peterburrow, i 629
——— ¶ Sée Meidhamsted
——— Bishoprikes erection circuit and valuation, i 248
Peterpence first granted in England, i 204.
——— First paid to Rome, i 639
——— Paid to Rome in Offas time, i 617
——— Their grant confirmed by Ethelwulfe, i. 662
——— Forbidden to be anie more gathered in England, ii 68
Peter Landoise ¶ Sée Landoise
Peter William knight deceaseth, his charitie, iv 267
Petifoggers Sée Lawiers and Promooters.
Petilus Cerealis a Romane capteine sent into Britaine, v 74
——— His men slaine and he returneth, v 71
——— Dieth, v 76
Petitions thrée that quéene Philip made to hir husband on hir death bed note, ii 692.
——— ¶ Sée Demands and Requests
Peto cardinall became a begging frier note, iv 527
Petreolum, i 307.
Petronius Tirpilianus an idle lieutenant, i 502.
Petus Cerealis his hard escape, i 599
Pewter how mixed, compounded, and made, i 399
——— The garnish, ib
Pewterers verie cunning, ib
——— Beyond sea not so cunning as here, ib
Philip of Worcester sent for Lacie, vi 212
——— His gouernment, ib.
Philip his preparation to come into England, the English ambassadors méet him at saint Iames of Compostella his arriuall in Southampton, receiued of the nobilitie, interteined of the quéene Marie, maried vnto hir, what nobles where attendant on him, the conditions of their mariage, iv 56, 57
——— Installed at Windsor, hée and shée go through London to Westminster, ii 62
——— Passeth ouer into Flanders to encounter the French king, iv 80, 87.
——— His returne into England, iv 86
Philip the hardie, and whie so surnamed, ii 688.
Philip of Austrich afterwards king of Castile, or Spaine, landeth in west parts of England, vol iii page 533
——— His honourable interteinment, his vow unuiolable kept his death and description, iii 534
Philip the French king bribed to procure peace betwéene William Rufus and Robert, ii 35
——— Setteth Robert the sonne against his father, William duke of Normandie, ii 19
——— His iest at duke William lieng sicke, ii 23.
——— His deth, ii. 59, 354
Philip king Richard the firsts base sonne, slue the vicount of Limoges, ii 278
Philip quéene of England ¶ Sée Quéene.
Philosopher made a king, i 635
Philosophers through shipwracke arriue in Scotland, v 51.
Philpot a woorthie citizen of London and Alderman, ii 718, 719
——— Discloseth treasons, ii 733
Physician Lewes sheweth to quéene Elizabeth the whole conceit and deuise of vniting the house of Lancaster and Yorke in one, iii 419
Physicians and surgeans a law for them, v 50.
——— Counsell neglected dangerous to the death, ii 76
——— Partition of the daie and night, i 406
——— Of our time thankesworthie, i 352
Picts longer planted in Britaine than the Scots, and whie so called, i 10
——— Called Redshanks and Pictons, and when they were settled in Britaine, ib
——— Whether these be they of whom Cesar speaketh to staine their faces, i 11
——— When they came out of Sarmatia and arriued in Britaine, ib
——— From whense the came and arriued in Britaine, i. 10
——— Their crueltie in slaieng the English, i 29.
——— The first beginner and finisher of their wall, i 197
——— They sweare to the king of Britaine neuer to erect anie king peculiar to their owne nation, i 199
——— And Scots ioine their power and enter into their enemies lands, v. 87
——— Ouerthrowne by the Romans, v. 74.
——— Vanquished, v 200
——— Sue for peace, ib
——— Desire aid of the Scots against the Romans, v 87
——— Their cruell dealing, v 116
——— Punished for their vntruth, v 121.
——— ¶ Sée Victorie
——— Become tributarie, put to base seruices, commanded to dwell beyond the water of Forth diuided from the Britons by a wall, v 158, 189.
——— Are forbidden to creat a king, v 119
——— Offended with Maximus, v 116.

Picts their king vanquished, vol v page 140.
—— Stand in feare of the king of Britaine, v. 137
—— Their king refuseth to be in league with the Romans, v 76.
—— Burne the citie of Tuline, v 80
—— Send for aid to king Gald, v 78.
—— Brought to agréement among themselues, v 79
—— Mooue war against the Romans ouerthrow their forragers, v 69
—— Ioine with Scots and Britains against the Romans, v 92
—— Send to the Scots for aid, v 70
—— Choose Federeth to be their king, v. 194
—— Their hope deceiued, v 212
—— Went into Denmarke and Norwaie, ib
—— Miserablie slaine without regard of person, their whole nation destroied, v 205
—— Remaining after a great slaughter dispersed, v. 206
—— Giue God thanke for victorie, v 198
—— Fall at variance among themselues, ib
—— Purpose to be reuenged on the Britons by open warre, v. 160.
—— Begin the battell rashlie, v 197.
—— Exiled, require aid of the Englishmen, v 209
—— Came into Scotland out of Germanie, v. 37.
—— Came first to Orkeneie, v. 37, 38
—— Make strong holds, require women of the Scots, good husbandmen, become enimies vnto the Scots, v 38
—— Admonished by their wiues to peace mooued to pitie, v 40
—— ¶ Sée Constancie and Policie
—— Arriue in Ireland, vi. 78
—— They marie with the Irish, ib
—— Inhabit in part of Britain, vi. 80
—— The amitie betwéene them and the Scots, vi 81
—— They fall out and are reconciled, ib
—— They be rooted out, vi 82.
—— Whie so called, i. 441
—— Diuided into two nations, i. 545.
—— In no Romane writer mentioned before Mamentinus time, i 526.
—— Inuaded this land and of what nation descended, i 503
—— The next after the Romans (of strangers) that inuaded this land, ib
—— Cut off one part of the limits of the kingdome of Northumberland, i 635
—— They and Scots recouer a part of their countrie long possessed of the English, i. 635
—— Whie they had the south parts of Scotland giuen them, i 519
—— Allied with the Saxons, i 575.
—— Ouerthrowne by the Northumbers, i. 641
—— ¶ Sée Scots
Pictland or Pightland, i 442
—— Parted vnto diuerse men, v. 203.
Pictland ¶ Sée Orkneie.
Pigmeies Ile in Scotland, vol. i. page 72
Piemont prince commeth into England, iv. 74.
Piers Exton ¶ Sée Exton.
Pietie is necessarie in a gouernment, vi. 143
Pike a deuouring fish, i 376
—— As he ageth he receiueth diverse names, ib.
Pilgrime his scrip and staffe, ii 213
—— With letters of conspiracie in a staffe, note, v. 354
Pilgrimage of Robert duke of Normandie that he voluntarilie tooke to Ierusalem, i 764
—— Of king Inas to Rome, i 639
—— Of Sweine the sonne of the erle Goodwine, i 746
Pinnesses, i 432
—— ¶ Sée Gallies
Pipes of lead vnder the ground to conueie water, and when the casting of them was inuented, iii. 804.
—— ¶ Sée Water
Pirat ¶ See Crab
—— Barton ¶ Sée Barton Campbell
Pirats how punished, i 315.
—— Put to death on the whéele, v 301
—— On the west taken and executed, iv 322.
—— Hanged at Wapping, iv 323, 345, 506.
—— Had like to haue taken Henrie the fourth, iii 43, 44.
—— Followed so that they durst not peep out, iii. 50
—— To the number of twentie and two condemned and iudged to die, iv 329.
Pitie procured murther, i. 510.
—— Of Adelstan vpon certeine kings that stood to his mercie, i. 686
—— Of Henrie the second to the poore note, ii. 199
—— Of Henrie the seuenth on a companie of haltered rebels, iii 519.
—— Of Henrie the sixt notable, iii 325
—— Of king Henrie the fift. note, iii 92.
—— Of Hubert de Burgh towards duke Arthur of Britaine in prison, ii 386
—— Of Edward the third towards the poore notable, ii 642, 643
—— Of a queene of England vnto six burgesses of Calis note, ii 648
—— Of capteine Randall notable, iv. 228.
—— Foolish in bearing with pardoning offenders: note, iii. 1000
—— Of one the casting awaie of another, ii. 70.
—— On the dead, pardon to the liuing, iii 320.
—— Procureth perill, ii. 425.
—— ¶ Sée Charitie
Placidus lieutenant of Britaine, his exploits séeketh to haue peace, v. 124.
—— Dieth, v. 126.
Plague called the great plague asswaged in London, iv. 329.
—— Thréefold to the poore citizens, iv. 224.
—— A naturall prognostication thereof, iii. 1002.
—— Great in Essex, ii. 823.

Plague in diuerse places in England great, vol iii. page 554
——— Sée Pestilence
Plaie publike and conference there to further the rebellion in Norfolke, but note the issue, iii 963.
——— Of a tragedie in Oxford with misfortune, iv 230
Plaies and enterludes forbidden for a time, iv 184.
Planets superior coniunctions, ii 829
Planetius sent forth with an armie against Caratake, setteth vpon the Scotish campe, v 65, 66
——— Left a gouernour, prepareth to meet the Scots, falleth sicke, dieth, v 66, 67.
Plantagenet the true erle of Warwike a verie innocent, he is executed note, iii 524
——— Knight deceased in the towre, the cause of his trouble, iii 823, 824.
——— The last of the right line and name, iii. 820
——— In whome that name rested, iii. 343
——— A counterfet of the ladie Margarets imagining, iii 503
——— ¶ Sée Arthur and Earle.
Pledges that duke William led ouer with him into Normandie, ii. 8.
——— Scotish appointed to passe into England, iv 190
——— Sent into England, v. 596
——— Executed, v. 556.
——— No sufficient warrant of freedome from danger, i 721
——— Giuen vpon securities, i 751.
——— English cruellie handled, i 717.
——— ¶ Sée Hostages
Plimond archbishop of Canturburie, i 675.
——— President of the English prouinciall councell, i. 683
Plentie accompanied with manie outragious sinnes note, i 554.
——— And scarsitie when their is like to be in England, i. 188.
——— Recompensed with penurie, i 392.
——— And aboundance note, ii 490.
——— Of vittels and scarsitie of monie, iv 86.
——— ¶ Sée Vittels
Plesure which bringing gréefe is to be forborne. note, i. 674
——— Of the flesh to losse of life, i 650
——— Déerlie bought, i 168, 696.
——— Granted bringeth preferment, i. 696.
——— ¶ Sée Lust
Plimouth standeth betwéen two rockes, i. 104.
——— Burnt, ii 602.
Plumbum cinereum, i 400
Pocks whereof manie died, ii 681.
Poer Ranulfe slaine, ii 183.
Poer Dominik sent to Charles the emperor for aid, vi 303, 304
——— Presented him with hawkes and horsses, vi 304
——— He hath the kings pardon, ib.
——— He hath the emperors pension, ib
Poer Arnold accused of heresie, vol vi page 252.
——— He died, vi 253
——— Was senechall of Kilkennie, vi 252
——— He killed the lord Bonneuill, vi 245
Poer Eustace vicount Baltinglasse complaineth against the cesse, vi 398
——— His letter to the erle of Ormond, ib
——— Complaineth against sir Nicholas Bagnoll, vi. 399
——— His cōplaints found vntrue, ib
——— He was baron of Kilcolen, vi 54
——— Hideth in the Glinnes, vi 434
——— Is werie of life, vi. 455
——— He died miserablie, vi 456
Poer baron of Coraghmore, vi 56.
Poer William senechall of Waterford, vi. 308
Poer Roger his seruice in Ulster, vi 200.
——— His race and progenie, ib
——— Gouernor at Leighlin and in Ossorie, vi 200, 208.
——— Slaine in Ossorie, vi 219.
Poer Robert senechall of Waterford and Wexford, vi 204, 207
Poets were at the first chronographers, Epistola.
Poictiers battell when it was, ii 667.
Poictouins reuolt from king Iohn, ii 284
——— Send king Henrie the third word of their redinesse to reuolt from the French king, ii 357.
——— Suspected to haue poisoned the English lords, ii 448.
——— Discomfited, ii 376.
——— Put to flight by Corineus, ii 442
Poinings knight lieutenant of Furnaie, iii 590.
——— Discharged of keeping it, iii. 613.
——— A valiant capteine sent into Flanders, iii. 497
——— Sent into Ireland with an armie, his valiantnesse and successe, iii. 570.
——— His decease, iii 849
Poison and what sharpe punishment was executed vpon one that poisoned her husband, i. 685.
——— Giuen but preuented, v. 455.
——— To the gouernor practised, v 364
——— Of Malcome brought into suspicion, v 245.
——— ¶ Sée Uter.
Poisoning how punished, i 311
——— A woman burnt for it at Tunbridge, iv. 330
——— And also at Maidstone, iv. 262.
——— Punished with boiling to death in hot water, iii. 773.
——— Practised and the parties punished with standing in the pillorie, iv 323
——— For the which a wench was burnt in Smithfield, iv. 600.
——— An execution for the same, ii. 448, 449.

Poisoning bewraied by the sweating of pretious stones, vol ii page 336.
——— Of erle Scot of Chester with his wife, ii 351
——— Of the erle of Deuonshire, iii 248
——— In Italie practised note, iii, 537.
Polander. ¶ Sée Albertus de Lasco
Policie whereby Compeigne was surrendered to the English, iii 140
——— Of the Parisiens to outreach the duke of Bedford, iii 155.
——— Of the French in taking Pont de Larch, iii 214
——— In buing peace of the English, iii 311
——— Of Edward the fourth against his enimies, iii 312
——— Ungratious and tending to the slaughter of princelie innocents, iii 409
——— Of the earle of Richmond in getting the sun at the back of his souldiors, iii. 443
——— To auoid danger, iii 245.
——— Of Henrie the seuenth against sir Robert Clifford, iii 506
——— In sending foorth especialls into Flanders, iii 507.
——— To preuent an intended mischéefe note, iii 19
——— Of duke Albert of Saxonie to get the towne of Dam, iii 497
——— Of the English archers against their enimies shot, iii. 494
——— Of Henrie the seuenth to match suspected persons especially if they fled, iii 571
——— In surprising the towne of Pont Meulan, iii 181
——— For a bridge, iii 191.
——— Of sir Francis the Arragonois, iii 197
——— Of Henrie the fift at the time of a comotion, iii 63.
——— Oftentimes passeth force, iii 249
——— Of Henrie the fift against the French horse men, iii 98, 99
——— For redie bridges, iii. 112
——— Of a préest fauouring conspirators, iii 12
——— Of the erle of Westmerland, iii 36, 37.
——— Of the English against the Flemish, ii 778.
——— Of the French king against the English, ii. 723, 730.
——— Dastardlie of the French king, to make Edward the third raise his siege from Calis, ii 643
———Of the Scots discomfitting the English, ii 558.
——— Of a capteine against the Welshmen, ii 408.
——— Of the English, ii 509
——— Of the duke of Guise against the English, iv 91
——— Of the French to make bridges, iv 97
——— To restreine the people at Summersets execution, iii 1032
——— Of a yeoman of the gard a rebel whereby he got pardon, iii 625.
Policie of Scattergood a gunner to deceiue the French, vol iv page 199
——— Of Frenchmen disguised in womens apparell, iv 192.
——— Of the French to giue the English a repulse, iv 194
——— Of duke William making a part of England waste, ii 18
——— ¶ Sée Dissimulation, Stratagem
——— Of throwing of stones in warrs at the crime, i 7
——— Policie, v 380, 221
——— Wonderfull, v 167.
——— Subtill, v. 387
——— To affright horsses, v 392
——— Of king Edward to win Berwike, v 529
——— Of the English to vanquish the Scots, v. 428
——— Of the Picts to escape danger, v. 144
——— Of the Scots, v 142
——— To relieue in the time of dearth, v 322.
Policie of Aulafe discouered note, i. 687
——— Of Alured to know the state of the Danes his enimies campe, i 671
——— Of duke William to disorder the Englishmens armie, i 702
——— Of Girmundus to take Cirencester, i. 588.
——— Of Hengist, i 551, 556
Polycletus great port offensiue, i 502
Polymnestor Milesius a swift runner, i 380.
Pomfret castle rendered to Edward the second, ii. 568
Pomona a Iland called a continent, i 75.
Pomonia now Kirkwale, v 61
Pontium, the name of Reading in times past, i 79.
Pontoise surprised by the Englishmen, iii 109
——— Recouered by them, iii 193.
——— Besieged by the French king but valiantlie deffended, iii 194
——— Gotten by the French, iii 195
Pont Meulan surprised by entrance of a common priuie, iii. 181
Poole cardinall ¶ Sée Cardinall Poole and Pope
——— Sendeth to Rome for Girald Fitzgirald, vi 306.
——— He carefullie bringeth him vp, ib
——— Giueth him a yéerlie pension, ib.
——— Increaseth his pension, vi 307.
Poore pittied, v 292
——— Cared for, v 288
——— Of three degrees which to be cherished and which to be punished, iii 1061
Poore people increase in England how it is procured, i 325
——— ——— And in what places, iii 1061, 1062
——— Prouision for them, i 307.
——— Of thrée sorts, ib
——— Their necessitie reléeued by Gods prouidence, iv 70
———¶ Sée Beggers.

Poor people prouided for in time of scarsitie, vol ii page 658
Pope writeth verie vehementlie to the king of England, i 242
—— His going out of England in time of blindnesse note, i 245.
—— His generall corection of the calendar, i 110
—— When he first cursed England, i 683
—— Alexander a fauourer of duke Williams conquest of England, i 760.
—— Urbanus, i 623
—— And king Iohn at dissention, v 303
—— Hath a thousand marks sent him out of Scotland, v 319
—— Sent to intreat for peace, v. 455
—— His present to king William of Scotland note, v 305
—— Sendeth a rose and a scepter to the king of Scotland, v 162
—— His buls published, v 485.
—— His ambassadors not regarded, v. 371.
—— His authoritie abolished, v 631.
—— Destroieth the templers, vi 243
Pope Adrian, ii 673
—— An Englishman borne, ii 113
—— His election to the popedome wondered, and whie, he commeth to Rome, iii 674
—— His creation corruption of the cardinals, in his election corupted with manie vices, iii 468
—— His pride note, ii 118
—— His grant to make Iohn king of Ireland, ii 174
—— Maketh profit of his great pardon or heuenly grace, iii 525
—— Letters for the reliefe of the holie land, ii 181
—— Fatherlie words to archbishop Landfranke, ii 14
—— Depriued bishops and restoreth them, ib
—— Heareth the contention for the primasie betwéene the archbishops, ib
—— Sent commissioners into England, ib.
—— He and the emperor Frederik at debate, ii. 129
—— His answer to Beckets complaint, iii 124, 125
—— His priuiledges, vi 185, 186
—— He keepeth a synod at Dublin, vi 203
—— He maketh peace, vi. 199
Pope Alexander his priuiledges to Ireland, vi 185
—— He demandeth tenths and peterpence, vi 186
Pope Boniface prohibiteth Edward the first further to vex the Scots, ii 533
Pope Calixtus held a councell at Reimes, and consecrated the archbishop of Canturburie with his owne hands, ii. 68.
Pope Calixtus a sutor for archbishop Thurstane, vol ii page 68
—— His curse against both archbishops of Canturburie and Yorke, ii 71
Pope Celestine as fréend to archbishop Geffrie of Yorke, ii 226
—— Maketh an archbishop of Canturburie legat of all England, ii 256
—— Inuested Patrike archbishop of Ardmach, vi 83
—— He sendeth Palladius into Scotland, ib
Pope Clements reformation in England, ii 543
—— And what summes of monie are had of the archbishop of Yorke note, ii 542
—— Procureth a peace for one yeare betwixt the two kings of England and France, ii. 651
—— Sent two cardinals to accord the two kings of England and France, ii 647.
—— Letters in fauor of the bishop of Elie and how he defended his chaplems, ii 229
—— Sendeth Henrie the eight a golden rose, iii 695
—— Pretended a title to the realme of Sicil, ii. 216
—— Requireth Henrie the eight personally to appear at a generall councell, iii 778.
—— Taken prisoner by the emperors armie, iv 526
—— Deceseth, more vnfortunat than fortunat, iii 788
—— His death preiudiciall, iii 228.
Pope Eugenie sendeth a legat to treat of peace betwéene the two kings of England and France, iii 173
Pope Gelasius the second his death, ii 67
Pope Gregorie sendeth the bishop of Rauenna to treat a peace betwéene England and France, ii 700
—— Messengers sent to him about reseruation of offices, ii 700
—— Denied to be true pope note, ii. 389
—— Sendeth cardinall Otho into England, ii. 782
—— His means to moue the people to a jorneie against the Saracens, ii 362
—— His plaine song whereabouts was great strife, ii 22
—— His bul against the hearing of a maried préests masses, ii 19
—— Deposed by king Henrie the seuenth, iv 525
—— His faculties granted to parsons and Campian for England, iv 522
—— Parries letters to him, and whereto the tended, iv 517
—— A lewd sermon, and full of papisticall adulation, made at his funerals, iv 591 to 595.
—— Deceaseth

Pope Honorius, his legat a bawdie knaue sent into England about reformation, vol ii page 72
———— His legat to king Henrie the third, ii. 359.
———— Mainteiner of king Iohns cause, ii 334, 335.
Pope Hildbrand the first that made warre against the emperor, iv 525
Pope Innocent summoned a generall counsell, ii 408
———— His request for maintenance of the warres against the Turks, ii 283
———— Offereth to king Henrie the third the kingdome of Sicill, ii 482
———— And hath England tributarie, ii. 306
———— Would not confirme archbishop Reignolds of Canturburies election and whie, ii 292, 293
———— His answer to the English ambassadors, ii 324
———— His licence to king Richard the first to gather riches, ii 208.
————Commandeth that the church at Lambeth should be raced, ii 267.
———— His councell held at Cléremont, ii. 75
———— He findeth fauor at king Henrie the first his hands and is thankfull, ib
———— Sendeth cardinals about a treatie of peace, ii 669
———— Aided with monie by king Henrie the third against the emperor, ii 388
———— Deceaseth, ii 334, 473
Pope Iulies election a description of his qualities, and how he came to the popedome, iii 566.
———— Sendeth king Henrie the eight a cup of maintenance, &c Compared to Anteus his purposes and death, a malcontentment, iii 600
————Intituled king Henriethe eight Christianisimo, his daughters request, a description of his properties, iii 601, 602
———— Gaue cardinall Pooles authoritie, apostolike, iv. 67
———— Dieth a porkish pope, his monstrous blasphemie against God about a pecocke, iv 77.
Pope Leo the tenth his creatione, iii 602, 603
———— His coronation, a poore prisoner on the same date tweluemonth of his election and inthronization, iii 603
———— He soliciteth all the princes of Christendome against the Turke, iii 628.
———— Receiueth two elephants for a present · note, iii 613
———— His craftie feare, iii 627
———— His decease supposed by poison, the manner and order of his death, iii 673, 674.
Pope Martine legateth the bishop of Winchester and vnlegateth him againe, iii 166, 167
Pope Othobone named Adrian the fift, ii 473
Pope Paschall his bulles vnto Anselme of Canturburie. ii 46.
Pope Paschall grieued because his authoritie is not regarded in England, vol ii page 63
———— Courteouslie receiueth the English ambassadors, ii 53.
———— Authorised Anselme to order things to his owne liking, ii 54.
———— His stout words to bishop Haslewast touching the inuestiture of churches, ii 53
———— Hath the determining of the strife about bishops inuesting and consecrating, ib.
———— Writeth most courteouslie to king Henrie the first in Anselmes behalfe, ii 53, 54.
———— Sicke at Beneuento, dieth, ii 67.
Pope Paule a roman borne created, iii 789
Pope Pius an ambassage to him out of England, certein notes concerning him, iii. 537.
———— His bull against quéene Elizabeth, the effect thereof, iv 576
———— The practices of traitors to execute it, ib.
———— Harts confession of the interpretation thereof, iv 528
———— His bul seditious hanged on the bishop of Londons gate, iv 252
———— A treasonable action, iv 529.
Pope Sixtus Quintus successor to Gregorie the thirtéenth excommunacateth princes, and his by them defied, iv 597
Popa Urban in mislike with William Rufus, and whie note, ii 41
———— His legat for the crowning of erle Iohn king of Ireland, ii 191
———— Whie he could not redresse the English inormities, i 30
———— Calleth a councell at Cléeremont and whie, ii 37
———— Giueth faculties to a frier Carmelite, ii 780
———— His beneficiall pardons to such as would fight against Clement antipope, note, ii. 755, 756
———— Sendeth to Richard the second for aid against an antipope, ii 721.
Pope Wirbeth aduanced by the emperor against pope Urban, ii 41.
Pope his fauour vnto Thomas Stukelie, vi. 398
—— He giueth him titles of honour, ib.
Pope sendeth aid with Iames Fitzmoris, vi. 406.
—— Appointeth doctor Sanders to be his legat, ib.
—— The fruits of his religion he sendeth foren aid into Ireland, ib.
—— His banner is displaied, vi 416
—— Dispenseth with murther, vi 410
—— His wicked practise, vi 460
—— Sendeth a frier minor into England to restore Henrie the thirds half brethren to their possessions, ii 452
—— His nuncio commanded to auoid the realme, and sent awaie, ii 409
—— Allowed eleuen thousand marke among them of the spiritualtie, ii 414
—— Out of fauour with the lords temporall of England, ii 364.

Pope sendeth his legat to pacifie Henrie the third and his nobles, vol. ii page 468
—— Complaineth to Henrie the third and blameth him, and commandeth offenders to be cursed, ii. 370
—— Requireth mainteinance for his warres against the emperor, ii 304
—— His demands out of spirituall liuings in England, ii 359
—— Lacketh monie to mainteine his estate: note, ib
—— His chapleine inhibite to leuie monie, ii. 543
—— Exhorteth king Edward the first to make warre against France, ii 536.
—— His decrée of peace betwixt the kings of England and France, ii 532
—— His request for the releasing of Iohn Balioll, ib.
—— Intermeddleth in princes matters, ii 511,512.
—— Desirous of peace betwéene the kings of England and France note, ii 605
—— His pretended right to be iudge for the title of the realme of Scotland answered. note, ii. 534
—— His letters and the deliuerers of them hanged, ii 671
—— Sendeth to bishops to the prince of Wales, ii 657, 658
—— Interdicteth Flanders, ii 613, 614.
—— Taketh vpon him to bestow and deale in benefices at his pleasures note, ii 626, 627
—— Sendeth a bull for the apprehension of Wicliffe note, ii 717
—— Two at diuisions for the dignitie of S. Peters chaire, ii 829.
—— Sendeth his nuncio to Richard the second. note whie, ii. 813
—— A disputation betwixt diuines of Oxford and Cambridge for their obedience to him, iii 46.
—— Beareth out the monks against the king and the archbishop of Canturburie, ii 269
—— Offended at king Richard the firsts imprisonment, ii 240
—— Into what a lamentable case he brought K Iohn and his nobles, ii 322.
—— His messengers to persuade the K of England, and the French king to peace, ii. 253
—— Sendeth to take awaie the interdiction vpon conditions, ii 313
—— He and king Iohn reconciled, ii 303.
—— His decree and inhibition contemned, ii. 324
—— Threateneth interdiction against king Iohn and his clergie, ii 297.
—— Dismisseth two archbishops at strife and electeth a third, ii 29
—— His dispensation for a mariage· note, ii 278.
—— Giueth sentence with the monkes of Canturburie against the bishops, ii 294
—— Interdicteth France and Normandie, ii 277.
—— Sendeth his nuncio to France, ii. 288.
Pope dispenseth for an oth of allegiance broken by the duke of Yorke, vol iii page 269.
—— Sendeth Lionell bishop of Concordia to the French king, iii 496.
—— Poisoned with the wine which his owne sonne had sent to poison another, iii 538.
—— He and the state of Italie abandoned of all hope compoundeth with the imperiall a hard article and to be maruelled how he might brooke it, the castell whereof he was prisoner infected with the plague, iii 712, 713
—— He and the emperors agent at accord, heauie paiment for him to discharge, the manner of his going out of prison, iii 728
—— He by the instigation of cardinall Poole intended mischéefe against England, iii. 808, 809.
—— His supremasie denied in sermons, iii 792
—— Causeth Henrie the eight and the realme· note, iii 790
—— His authoritie banished out of England by proclamation, iii 751.
—— He with certeine cardinals flie to the castell of S Angelo, iii 717, 718
—— His legats scrape and rake monie togither for him. note, ii 390
—— Hath Henrie the second in a seruile subiection note, ii 142
—— His forces vanquished in Ireland, iv 580.
—— The cause of rebellions in England and of treasons. note, iv 529
—— His cursses no hindrance of Englands prosperitie, iv 528
—— Not to be suffered to make rebellions in England, iv. 527.
—— Kings of Christendome neuer suffer him to abridge their titles or rights though they suffer him to haue rule ouer the people, ib
—— And that kings of France, Spaine, and England haue béene against him note, ib.
—— Haue cruellie persecuted emperors, iv 525
—— His title to vniuersall bishop is a preamble of antichrist, iv 526
—— His authoritie not warranted by Christ or his two apostles Peter and Paule, iv 524.
—— His bull and the mainteiners thereof onelie condemned of treason, iv 520
—— Supremasie, no person for the onlie maintenance thereof charged with capitall crime, ib
—— Sendeth aid to the erle of Desmond his banner erected note, iv 423
—— His bull, a full proofe that the mainteiners thereof are directlie guiltie of treason, note the words of the bull, &c iv 520, 521
—— His dutie what it is not and what it should be, ii. 11.
—— His decrée for confirmation and benediction, ii 442.
—— Mens deuotion to him waxeth cold, ii. 438.
—— He is liberall of another mans pursse, ii. 433
—— Offereth the kingdome of Sicil to earle of Cornwall, ii 127.

Pope complained of to Henrie the third the king writeth vnto him, vol ii pages 401, 402
—— A collect to be said for him, another for his election, a woman imprisoned for not praieng for him, iv 78
—— An enimie to peace except he might haue his owne will, ii 391
—— Sendeth for monie to mainteine his warres against the emperor, ii 403.
—— His letters intercepted and staied, ii 408
—— He & French king allied, iii 631
—— His decrée that all spirituall men dieng intestat, their goods should remaine vnto him, ii 412.
—— Requireth the French king to make warre against England, the French king refuseth so to do, ii, 411
—— Sendeth for the third part of one yeares profit of euerie beneficed mans residue, ii 413
—— Maketh uoid the election of archbishop Neuil, ii. 369
—— Sueth to Henrie the third for licence to soiorne at Burdeux, ii 420
—— His presence more like to impaire than amend things, ib.
—— His bull read at Paules crosse, ii 234
—— His grant authorising the bishop of Lincolne to institute vicars churches impropriat, ii 425
—— Hath six thousand markes giuen him for a moderation note, ii 421
—— Consecrateth William Raleigh bishop of Winchester, ii 400
—— He and king Iohn at strife and white, ii 295, 296
—— Two die in one yeare, ii. 395.
—— Sueth vnto Henrie the third for his good will in benefices to bestow on his fréends, ii 412
—— ¶ Sée Antipope, Cardinals, Legats, Mariage, Rome
Poplar growing in England and serue turners to make dishes, i 358
Porchester woon by the Romans, i 484
———— How called in the Romans time, i 321
Porpass neuer but once heard to be found in Auon, i. 115.
Porphyrie stone, i 402
Portex ¶ Sée Ferrex
Portl the Saxon arriuall in Britaine, i 573.
Portesmouth while so named, ib
Ports noted by seafaring men, for their benefits vpon the coasts of England, i 181
Portlands commended to be good slingers of stones, i 56
Portingall prince commeth to London, iii 111
Portingall king sended aid to Henrie the fift, iii 101
———— Aided with an armie out of England against the king of Castile, ii 735
———— He with duke of Lancaster inuade Castile, ii 770, 771
———— Sendeth six gallies to king Richard the seconds aid, ii 767.
———— Deceaseth an obseque for him, iv 83
Portgréeues and the reason of the name, vol ii. page 207
Posie of the duke of Alanson, iv 474
—— Interpreted, iv 480.
Posts set betwéene England and Ireland, vi. 321, 322
Potato root venereous, i 281.
Pouertie prefered i. 236
Prafutagus king of Britaine ¶ Sée Aruiragus.
Praier and inuocation to God before a battell enterprised, ii 637.
———— Of quéene Elizabeth as she went to hir coronation, iv. 176
———— Superstitious of the Scots in a time of mortalitie among the English, ii 727
———— Of Fiacre, v 172
———— Of king Malcolme, v 259.
———— Of Voadicia before hir incounter with the Romans, i 498
———— For victorie before the battell begun, i 611
Praiers and what effect they haue, i 649
———— Of S Came effectuall to worke miracles, i. 116
———— Public made for deliuerance from the Danes, v 263
———— Used by housholders in the suspicious & troublesome times of duke William, ii 9
———— For quéene Marie being with child that she may be safelie deliuered, iv. 71
———— ¶ See Collects, Papists, and Saints
Preacher at Paules crosse hath a dagger thrown at him, defended by the gard, iv. 3, 4
———— Hath a gun shot at him, iv 56
———— Popish blasphemie in the pulpit and how seuerlie punished by God, iv 78
Preachers, v 171.
Preaching dispised, v. 249
———— Of pardon at the shew of a relike, ii 415
———— To moue christians to make a iorneie against the Saracens, ii 362
———— Of a cardinall, ii 543
———— Of the archbishop of Canturburie at the deposing of Edward the second, ii 481
———— Of Cementarius incensing K Iohn to crueltie, ii 300
———— Good wanting was the cause of rebellion in Deuonshire, iii 939
———— ¶ See Recantation and Sermon.
Preaching and such as are called to it should haue the knowledge of toongs, i 615
———— Of what sort preuaileth and is most effectuall, i 611, 615
Prebends giuen to vicors, i 697, 698
———— Superfluous additamets to former excesse, i 235.
Prebendaries made monkes, vi 236
Préest excommunicat for incontenencie, ii 418
—— Committed a shameful murther, iii 300.
—— Killeth a frier being prisoner, iii. 106.
—— Executed for treason, iii 610.

Préest hanged for fauouring the rebels, vol iii page 802
—— Murthered and the murtherer hanged in chains, iii 750.
—— A valiant soldior, iii 881
—— Seditious. ¶ Sée Simon
Préest Wighart well séene in the scriptures, i 625
—— That serued in Claudius temple spoilers and robbers, i 495
—— Go to warre with euill spéed, i 598
—— Went with Peda to teach and baptise the Middleangels, i 620
—— In battell with their Allelicies note, i. 422
—— Not to come to the alter barelegged, and whie, i 651.
—— Four all brethren, i 622
—— Secular had wiues in monastries, i 699.
—— Put in the roome of moonks, i 698
—— Little regarded and moonks estéemed note, i. 697.
—— Receiued into monastries and moonks remoued, i 696
Préests popish beholden to their good fréends the Gothes, i 375.
—— What honour was doone to them of old time in Rome, i. 36.
—— Apparrelled in colours like peacocks with spreaded tales, i 233
—— To be tried before secular iudges, v 192
—— Liuings prouided for them, v 45.
—— Which should onelie attend their vocation, v 213
—— That were hunters an act against them, ii. 168.
—— Their concubines forbidden christian buriall, ii 352
—— Religious men hardie souldiors, ii 759.
—— Their sonnes not to succéed in their fathers benefices, ii. 51
—— Mariage forbidden, and whie, ib
—— Prohibited to marie and to keepe women, ii 63
—— Sequestered from their wiues, ii 58
—— Maried in what respect to be excommunicated, ii 51
—— Should not haunt alehouses and of their app well, ib.
—— To weare crownes, ib.
—— All in Normandie excommunicated, and whie, ii. 63
—— Unchast how punished, ii 74
—— Of Rome taken in bed with a whore note, ii 72.
—— Fauoured by the establishment of a statute, ii. 93
—— To be arrested, offending in forrests, ii 266.
Préests popish hated of king Iohn note, vol. ii. page 297
—— Of old in Britaine as archbishops are now, i 39
Préests of the Druides in what estimation, i. 36
Préests seminarie, as Campian Sherwin Kerbie Rishton and others of high treason note well, iv. 447
—— Condemned, iv 455
—— Behauiour at their execution, iv 459
—— Of a miracle (forsooth) on the daie of their death ¶ Sée more of them, iv 512, 533 to 621
—— Banished and how courteouslie vsed by their owne reporte, iv 620, 621
—— Executed at Tiburne, iv 660, 891.
—— Died for treason and not for religion, iv. 520
—— Not to be compared to the martyrs that died in Q Maries time, in number, iv 523
—— Their practises to exercise the popes bull, nursseries erected for them, their secret comming to the realme, to induce the people to obeie the said bull, iv 516, 517
—— Shert and Iohnson arraigned and condemned, with their behauiour and speeches at their death, iv 488, 489
—— Of Kerbie, Filbie, Cateham and Richardson, iv 491 to 494
—— ¶ Sée Iesuits, Scholers, and Treson
Preferment without looking or séeking obteined, ii 31.
Premunire statute begun, ii 701
—— Whereof followed losse of goods, iii 816
—— A cause of malcontentment. note, iii 771.
—— ¶ Sée Wolseie
Pren ¶ Sée Ethelbert, i 653
Prendergast Moris arriueth into Ireland at the Banne, vi 128
—— Borne in Wales, ib
Prendergast William slaine, vi 216
Prentise hanged in London for killing his maister, iv 237
—— Killed and the offendors hanged. ¶ Sée Riot.
Prerogatiue of a king, vi 380.
—— Of king Edgar testified, i 694.
Present that earle Goodwine gaue Hardicnute to win his fauour, i 737
—— Of Cambridge vniuersitie to quéene Elizabeth, iv. 404
—— Of a Dutch minister to queene Elizabeth at Norwich, iv 292, 293
—— Of white kine and a bull offered to king Iohn, ii 301.
—— Sent by Rhengraue to the earle of Warwike, iv 209
—— That the emperor Charles sent to Henrie the eight note, iii. 693.

Present ¶ Sée Gift
——— Of horsses and hounds, vol ii page 104
——— ¶ Sée Horsses
Presents sent to king Adelstan from diuerse kings note, i 688
——— Rich & sumtuous sent to Henrie the third, ii 435
Prest monie, demanded of the citie of London for quéene Maries behoofe, iv. 5
——— Of twentie thousand pounds to quéene Marie out of London, iv 103
Presumption of the archbishop of Yorke, ii. 169.
——— Of Anselme, ii 40
——— And of Ranulfe bishop of Chichester, ii 43.
——— Of Cardinall Otho, ii 386, 387.
——— Of an oration in French to Henrie the fift note, iii 104.
——— Of a cardinall, ii. 314.
——— Punished in posteritie, ii 70.
——— ¶ Sée Pride.
——— Presumption, v 453.
——— Hath a fall, i 446.
Pretious stones, i 401
——— How to be tried, i. 400
Priapus and of the honor that the Saxonish women did him, i 47
Prices of things while become excessiue, i 342.
——— ¶ Sée Mariners
Pride of Cnute turned into humilitie, i 731
——— Of Henrie crowned and serued of his father, ii 130, 131
——— Of prelats misliked by Edward the first, ii 541.
——— Of the erle of Leicesters sons bringeth the barons to confusion, ii 466
——— Of the French procureth them hatred, ii. 341
——— Of the duke of Orleance, iii 28
——— Of Hugh Creshingham, ii 525
——— Of Pandulph the popes legat notable, ii 306
——— Of great ruffes reproued and reformed in a seruing man, iv 433
——— Hath a fall, ii 255.
——— Note, ii 228.
——— ¶ Sée Ambition, Contention, Presumption, Wolseie, ii 321.
Primasie ¶ Sée Archbishops.
Prime ¶ Sée Calendar and Yeare
Prince a title properlie belonging to the kings eldest sonne, i 261
Prince of Wales alwaies the kings eldest sonne, iv. 103
Princes palaces, i 328.
Printer executed for seditious books, iv 511.
Printing first inuented, v 144, iii 250
Prior of S Andrews ¶ Sée Letter.
Prior Iehan bringeth aid to the French king, iii. 573
——— Lieth in Blanke sable baie with his power he loseth one of his best foists, a consultation about the assailing of him the admerall roweth into the baie where he lieth, vol. iii pages 574, 575
Prior Iehan landeth in Sussex with the French gallies he is driuen to his gallies, iii 576
——— Arriueth on the borders of Sussex, Burneth the towne of Brighthelmstone, with other mischeefes, he is shot into the eie with an arrow, iii 602
Priors executed for treason, iii 793.
——— ¶ Sée Abbats.
Priories suppressed, iii 810
Prise rich taken by the earle of Warwike, iii 250
——— Of wines to the quantitie of two hundred tun, iv 206
——— More, iv 208.
——— Of foure hundred tun of Gascoigne and French wines, iv 233
Prises taken by Frenchmen of about fiftie thousand crownes value, iv. 211.
——— Of French goods taken by the Westerne ships, iii 846
——— ¶ Sée Gréenefield
——— Of Englishmen fourtéene taken, v 472
Prisoner ¶ Sée Captiuitie
——— Shifting to escape breaketh his necke, ii. 395
——— Escapeth and the sherriffe of London is punished, ii 435.
——— Rescued by an officer and the rescuers punished note, ii 449
——— Carefullie séene vnto note, ii 645.
——— Faithfull a notable example, ii. 724.
——— Coienes made of siluer, ii 221.
——— That should haue béene hanged his good seruice, iii 494
——— Brake from the sessions house note, iii. 736
Prisoners French mercifullie vsed note, iii 74
——— Pittifullie slaine, iii 81, 82
——— Taken in warres and slaine, iii 178
——— Discharged, iv 2
——— Slaine by French as they were taken, iii. 165.
——— Of the Marshallseie brake out, iii. 532
——— Sold in open markets note, iii 581
——— Scotish of name taken by the English, iii. 883.
——— Deliuered out of the Tower, iv 74.
——— Released, ii 163
——— Set at libertie by duke William before his death, ii 24
——— Released in an vproare, ii 471
——— Arrained for not comming to the church, iv 447
——— Proclamations for the lawfull taking of them in warre, iv 214
——— Set at libertie at William Rufus coronation, ii 27.
——— Taken diuerse nobles & gentlemen of France, ii 345, 346.
——— Beheaded, ii 230.

Prophesie suppressed, vol i page 228
Prophesie, v 175
——— Of saint Colme, v 169
——— Of Kinmatill, v 164
——— Of a tempest, v 341.
——— Of a witch, v 427
——— Of thrée women supposed to be faries, v 268
——— Of death naturall, fell out true in proofe, iv 228.
——— Of a cardinall, ii 665
——— Of Ball a seditious préest, ii 719
——— Of the reuolting of the subiects from their prince, ii 315
——— Of the decaie of the Persies stocke, ii. 45
——— Of an hermit of Wakefield to king Iohn, ii 311,
——— Of Henrie the fift touching Henrie the sixt his sonne, iii 179
——— Of winning France, iii 66
——— Betokening the translation of the crowne, iii 241, 242
——— Concerning the duke of Clarence his name beginning with a G, iii 346
——— The memorie whereof appalled Richard the thirds spirits note, iii 421
——— Of a monke vnto the duke of Buckingham false, iii 658, 679
——— Touching Calis, iv. 102
——— Fulfilled, ii 486, iii 502, 806
——— Uaine note, iii 22, 23
Prophesies of astronomers false in euent note iv 549
——— Diuelish fantasies, iii 346
——— Deceiptfull to the Norfolke rebels note, iv 981
——— ¶ Sée Dreames, Signs, & Tokens
——— To be doubtfull frō what spirit they procéed, i 14
Prophesies, v 38, vi 146, 162, 173, 217, 222, 291
——— Moue men to vnlawfull attempts, v 269
——— Of the dukes of England and Scotland, v. 707
——— Trusted, v. 276
Prophet false serued right, ii 754.
Propheter of Ireland, vi 222
Prosperitie changeth conditions, v 90
——— Persecuted with malice, ii 28
——— Unstable, ii 706, 707
——— Of king Henrie enuied, ii 63
Protection ¶ Sée Letters, Pasport and Safe conduct, ii 176
Protectors of England from the first to the last collected, iii 1036 to 1060
——— Of Scotland their catalog, v. 678
Prouerbe a bushell of rie and another of malt worth six pence, i 159
——— No musca quidem, i 288
——— No better secce on Doue banke, ii. 167.
Prouerbe of plentie and scarsitie like to be in England when the sand, &c. vol ii, page 128
——— Yoong seruing men old beggers, i 175
——— The Britaines neither valiant in war nor faithfull in peace, i 484
——— Seians horsse cast his rider, i 655
——— In trust his trecherie proued true, i 435
——— Man purposeth but God disposeth, verefied, ii 57, iii 610, v 317
——— Ill will neuer said well, verefied, iii 210, 211, 302, 389
——— Isclus piscator sapit applied, ii 196
——— Profered seruice stinkes verefied, ii 464; iii 610
——— Hast makes waste verefied, ii 70, 217
——— He falleth into the fire that flieth from the smoke verefied, ii 395.
——— When I lend, I am a fréend, when I aske I am a foe verefied, ii 537
——— It is good sléeping in a whole skin, verefied, ib.
——— Necessitie hath no law, verefied, ii 73
——— Soone hot soone cold, verefied, ii 761
——— One mischéefe asketh another, verefied, ii 764.
——— Wit or cunning dearlie bought, verefied, ii 766
——— One soweth but another reapeth, verefied, ii 61.
——— Pitch and paie, verefied, iii 41
——— Looke yer you leap practised note, iii 18
——— Set a beggar on horseback and he will ride full gallop, verefied, ii. 332, 333
——— He is an ill cooke cannot licke his owne fingers, verefied, ii 333
——— He makes a rod for his owne taile, verefied, ii 334, 794
——— Plaine fashion is best practise, iii 332.
——— Marriage for pleasure repented by leasure proued true, iii 383
——— Marriage goeth by destinie, verefied, ib
——— The lambe betaken to the wolfe toképe, iii 370
——— To giue rostmeat and beat with the spit, verefied, iii. 367.
——— Crooked of bodie crooked of qualitie, iii. 369
——— One ill turne requireth another, verefied, iii. 511.
——— After mirth commeth mone, iii 561.
——— He that gapeth after other mens goods loseth his owne, verefied, iii 581
——— What the eie vieweth the hart rueth, verefied, iii 837
——— Too much familiaritie bréeds contempt, verefied, iii 639
——— Delaie bréedeth danger verefied, iii 1069
——— To come a daie after the faire, verefied, iv 93.

Prouerbe truth purchaseth hate, verefied, vol ii page 570.
——— In trust is treason, verefied, iii 415
——— Faire words make fooles faine, ii 249, 301
Prouinces onelie two now in England, i 221
Prouision for ships and armour, and what order for mainteining the name, i 711
Prouost ¶ Sée Edenburgh.
Psalter by whome distributed into psalmes and appointed to be read amongst the prebendaries, i 244
Puffins a kind of foules described, i 77.
Pulpit in S Paules churchyard ¶ Sée Sermon.
——— At Paules crosse all beraied and beastlie, iv 180
Punishment for sinnes make a quiet commonwealth, vi 383
——— Seuere vpon Welshmen, ii 125
——— Of Thomas Louell for counterfeting letters note, iv 886.
——— Ridiculous for a great offense note, ii 540
——— Upon the sonne for the fathers offense, i 706
Punishments according to the offense, ii 199.
——— In England for malefactors, i 310
——— For such as smite within the limits of the princes court prohibited, i 332
——— In England what greatest, i. 310
Pursseuant of Henrie the third had his hard cut off, ii 461.
Pursuants sent into France, v. 472
Purueior of king Iohn resisted, and the resistors punished. note, ii 296, 297
Purueiors pester most places of England note, i 341.
——— Punished, ii 633
——— Proclamed against, ii 448
——— A statute against them, ii. 678.
——— Set in the pillorie note, iv 179
Putta a good musician made bishop of Rochester, i. 626
——— Teacheth song and musike, i 630
——— Bishop of Rochester is faine to flée, ib
Pyramides of stone of the Romans placing, &c. i. 191.
Pyrites found in euerie veine of mettal in great plentie note, i 342
Pyrrhus his thrée sonnes fréends to Brute, i 438

Q

Quaffing excessiue reformed by king Edgar, i 694
Qualities of the mind according to the qualities of the bodie, i 194
Quarell ¶ Sée Fraie
——— Upon a light cause procureth slaughter, i. 455
——— Upon a light occasion, i 762.
Quarell upon words whereof insued wounds and slaughter, vol i page 476
——— ¶ See Wounds & Fraie
——— Betwixt the bishops and monks of Canturburie about the archbishops election, ii 293
——— That the French king picked against England, iii 16
——— Faint picked against the duke of Glocester, iii 211
——— Upon a small cause, ii 218
——— Prosecuted vnto great mischéefe note, ii 524, 525
——— Ended with murther, iii 106
——— ¶ See Debate, Fraie, Mutinie, Riot, & Warres
——— In the daies of Edward the confessor and what mischéefe grew therevpon, i. 12.
——— Of moonks Augustine cost 2100 monks liues, i 62
Quarries what they be and their sundrie sorts, i 394
——— Of stone enow in England note, ib
——— In Scotland of sundrie kinds, i 184
Quaterage kept by the Scots for defense of their liberties, v 581
Quéene of England desirous to speake with the quéene of Scots, v 611
——— Disswadeth the mariage of the lord Darnelie with the Scotish quéene, v. 614
——— Sendeth to the quéene of Scots, v 616.
——— Hir answer to the quéene of Scots, v 618.
Quéene Adelicia second wife to Henrie the first descended of the duke of Loraine, barren, ii. 70
Quéene Algitha sent to Chester and whose sister she was, ii 1
Queene Annabell deceaseth, v 404
Quéene Annes coronation proclamed & the same celebrated with great pompe, iii. 778 to 785
——— With child, iii 778
——— Brought to bed of quéene Elizabeth, iii. 786.
——— Committed to the Towre, hir imprisonment at the Towre gate, she is arraigned hir words at hir death, iii 796, 797.
Quéene Anne wife to king Richard the third and daughter to Richard earle of Warwike, iii 399.
Quéene Anne wife to king Richard the second, deceaseth, ii 823
Quéene Berengaria crowned the wife of Richard the first, ii 222
Quéene Dowager fled with hir sonnes into Ireland, v. 159
Quéene Elenor Richard the firsts mother returneth home into England, ii 220
Quéene Elenor king Iohns mother an enimie to hir nephew Arthur, ii. 274.
——— Brought a bed of a daughter, ii 118

Quéene Elenor sendeth for spéedie succor to king Iohn, vol ii page 281
———— Studieth to mainteine the strife betwixt his sonnes, i 149
———— Committed to close prison, ii 159
———— Set at libertie after long imprisonment, ii 203
———— Deceaseth, ii 290
Quéene Elenor the wife of Henrie the third, ii. 379
———— Passeth into Normandie, ii 271
———— Forsaketh the world and becommeth a nun, ii 489
———— Deceaseth, hir praise, ii 492
———— Hir buriall, ii 497
Quéene Elisabeth hir continuall care for Ireland, vi 327
———— Crowned and anointed quéene, iii 490
———— Deliuered of hir first sonne, iii 492
———— Forward and readie to further the vniting of the two houses of Lancaster and Yorke, iii 414.
———— Taketh sanctuarie, iii. 368
———— Hir desolate estate, ib
Queene Elisabeth late wife to Edward the fourth, iii 190
———— Adiudged to forfet all hir lands for promise breaking, iii 485
———— She liueth a miserable and wretched life she erecteth a college in Cambridge, iii 485 486
———— Inconstant, she allureth hir sonne the marquesse Dorsset from out of France, iii 429
———— The cardinall thought the fittest man to deale with for the surrendering of hir sonne, reasons wherit was thought méet to fetch him out of sanctuarie, the duke of Buckinghams words vnto hir, iii 370 371
———— Hir answer to the persuaders, she is loth to part with hir sonne,
———— Hir mistrust of the lord protector she falleth to a resolution touching hir sonnes deliuerie, iii 371, 375, 376, 377
Quéene Elisabeth Greie wife to Edward the fourth, iii 281
———— Hir father and brother beheaded note, iii 292
———— Deliuered of a prince, the same christened like a poore mans child, iii 300
Quéene Elisabeth surnamed the good, deceaseth, iii 5 0
Quéene Elisabeth of Castile dieth without issue male, iii 533
Quéene Elisabeth second daughter to Henrie the eight, borne and christened the statelie order thereof, iii 786
———— Proclaimed quéene the beginning of hir reigne, hir remoue from Hatfield the goodlie state of this land vnder her reigne, iv 156
Quéene Elisabeth hir remoue to the Towre, to Summerset house, vol iv. page 156
———— Hir praier as she went to be crowned, iv 176
———— Crowned, ib
———— Desirous to know the meaning of the representations of the pageants, iv 161, 162
———— Listened to a childs oration, iv. 164
———— Hir promise with thanks to the citie of London, iv. 165
———— Remooueth from Westminster to the Towre by water, from thense to Westminster through London, salute them that salute hir, pageants and shews of reioising, iv. 158, 159
———— Hir words vnto the lord maior of London, iv. 167
———— She receiueth Verbum Dei, kisseth it and laieth in her lap, iv 168
———— She thinketh vpon the cities charge, how willing she was to heare a childs speach, iv 170.
———— The cities farewell vnto hir going out at Temple barre, iv 173
———— Hir last words to the citie by waie of promise, iv 174
———— Notes of hir mercie, iv 175
———— Hir humilitie in receiuing verie trifles thankfullie, ib
———— Not forgetfull to glorifie God who glorified hir, iv 175, 176
———— A motion made to hir in the parlement house touching marriage, with hir answer thereto and promise, iv 178, 179.
———— Determineth to aid the Scots suing for aid, iv 189
———— Sued vnto out of Denmark about marriage, iv 187
———— Furnished hir land with armour and amunition, iv. 202.
———— Grieued with the losse of Paules stéeple, hir beneuolence towards the repairing thereof, ib.
———— And what cause mooued hir to send a power into France, iv 205.
———— Hir progresse to & through Cambridge, hir oration to the vniuersitie, iv 225
———— To Oxford she maketh an oration to the vniuersitie, iv 230
———— Hir owne words importing how deerlie she loued hir people, iv 253
———— Hir manifold vertues, ib
———— Goeth to the Bursse being finished nameth it the Roiall exchange, iv 258
———— Hir destruction deuised to be practised ¶ Sée Priests seminarie and note it well, hir answer to the maior of Norwich, his oration, iv 378, 379
———— Incouraging words vnto Stephan Lambeth redie to make an oration vnto hir, iv. 394

Quéene Elisabeth highlie commendeth it, vol. iv. page 397.
——— Hir behauiour after hir welcomming, iv. 400.
——— Hir words at hir parting with water in her eies, iv. 403.
——— The progresse into Suffolke and Norfolke, with the whole manner of the sumptuous sights, and whatsoeuer else was deuised for plesure and delight, iv. 375, 376, 377.
——— In danger of gunshot, being in the priuie barge, iv. 425.
——— The place of hir abode during the time of her tarriance in Norwich, iv. 265.
——— Accompanieth the duke of Alanson to Canturburie, iv. 461.
——— An intention to murther and the partie executed, iv. 510.
——— She giueth to the defense of the low countries and whie so mooued to do, iv. 621 to 630.
——— Shamfullie slandered by hir enimies and the same answered: note, iv. 623.
——— Hir oration to the parlement house: note, iv. 588.
——— Hir magnanimitie knowing Parries auowed treasons and yet concealing it, iv. 578.
——— Parries treasonable practises to kill hir and vndoo the whole realme: note well, iv. 560, 567.
——— Hir magnanimitie in suffering a known and swoarne traitor against hir to haue accesse vnto and talke with hir, iv. 562.
——— Conspired against and hir depunation sought by traitors: note, iv. 536 to 547.
——— ¶ Sée Elisabeth and Badington.
Quéene Iane of Scots deliuered of two sonnes at one birth, v. 421.
——— Deceaseth, v. 311.
Quéene Iane proclamed with sound of trumpet quéene of England, iii. 1065.
——— ¶ Sée Iane.
Quéene Ione late wife to king Henrie the fourth arested by the duke of Bedford and commited, iii. 106.
Quéene Isabell the wife of king Edward the second, ii. 547.
Quéene Isabell second wife of king Iohn, ii 280.
Quéene Isabell wife vnto king Richard the second, transported into France, iii. 18.
——— And conueied to Paris hir second marriage, ib.
Quéene Isabell maried vnto Hugh Brune erle of March, ii. 349.
Quéene Katharine, hir coronation, the wife of king Henrie the fift, iii. 123.
——— Solemnitie, iii. 129.
——— Saileth into France, iii. 130.
Quéene Katharines coronation traine and sumptuousnesse, iii. 534.
Quéene Katharine deliuered of hir first sonne named Henrie, vol. iii. page 558.
——— Chooseth lawiers in hir behalfe to iustifie hir mariage, hir lamentable spéech in presence of the court, she auoucheth the coniunction good, she departeth out of the court, is called againe, iii. 737, 738, 739.
——— Procureth a cursse against king Henrie the eight and his realme from the pope, iii. 790.
——— Hir words vpon the motion of diuorce standing stiffe in the lawfulnesse of hir mariage, iii. 773.
——— Accuseth cardinall Woolseie hath communication with the cardinall in hir priuie chamber, refuseth to make sudden answer to a diuorce, iii. 739.
——— Is diuorced from king Henrie the eight, iii. 778.
——— Princesse dowager, iii. 777.
——— Deceaseth, iii. 795, 796,
Quéene Katharine hir paramours detected of incontinent liuing, iii. 822.
——— She is atteinted by parlement sent to the Towre and beheaded, iii. 823.
Quéene Margaret dieth for gréefe, v. 283.
——— Hir bones translated, v. 313.
Quéene Margaret the wife of Henrie the sonne of Henrie second, ii. 141.
——— Brought a bed, ii. 175.
Quéene Margaret wife to Edward the first deliuered of Thomas Burtherton hir first sonne, ii. 539.
Quéene Margaret Henrie the sixt his wife lieth at Couentrie, she is a better capteine than hir husband the king, iii. 260.
——— Described, she taketh vpon hir the gouernment, and dischargeth the duke of Glocester, iii. 210.
——— With hir sonne goeth into Wales, iii. 279.
——— She returneth out of France, iii. 288.
——— Fortunat in hir two battels: note, iii. 271.
——— Sendeth to the maior of London for vittells some sent by the maior and staied by the commons shée returneth northward, iii. 271.
——— Hir flight, she is robbed, iii. 261.
——— Commeth to Ambois to sée the erle of Warwike, iii. 295.
——— She with hir sonne prince Edward land with a power out of France, iii 315.
——— She is comforted by the nobles of England, ib.
——— The feare which she had for hir sonne, ib.
——— Taken prisoner, iii. 320.
Quéene Marie commeth vnto London, iii. 1071.
——— Proclamed quéene, iii. 1070.
——— Hir coronation pompe and traine,

Quéene Maries mariage, diuers diuerslie affected thereabout and what they did, vol iv page 61
———— A report that she was with child, iv 68
———— And what curious order is taken for the yoong prince yet vnborne note, iv 69, 70
———— Talke betwéene hir and hir sister the ladie Elisabeth note, iv 134
———— Hir stout courage and kind of manhood, iv 20
———— Hir death conspired and the parties executed, iv 55
———— She and cardinall Poole resisted the pope, iv 527.
———— Hir oration in Guildhall to the Londoners, iv 16
———— Is compared of the papists to quéene Iudith, iv 72
———— Hir motion touching the restitution of abbie lands, iv 76
———— Great preparation and triumph for hir being in childbed, iv 82.
———— What became of hir child no man can tell. note, ib
———— Proclameth open wars against the French king, the capteins of hir forces, iv 87.
———— With what indignation she tooke the losse of Calis, iv 117.
———— Pensife for the losse thereof sickeneth and dieth, iv 121
———— Had neuer good successe in anie thing she went about, iv 138
———— How long and when she prospered hir promise to the gospellers broken, iv 138, 139
———— Hir ill luck in the losse of Calis, iv. 139
———— Hir finall end and death, iv 140
———— Hir ill lucke in hir childbirth, iv 139.
———— With hir husband, ib
———— The time of her reigne, iv 140
———— Hir death, the manner thereof, thought to be for the losse of Calis, more bloud spilt in hir reigne than in anie kings daies before, how vnprosperous it was vnto hir and hir realme in all respects, iv 137, 138
———— Buried and the manner thereof, iv 158
Quéene Marie king Henrie the eights sister crowned quéene of France note with what pompe, iii 605
———— Dowager of France. ¶ Sée duke of Suffolke
Quéene Marie Dowager of Scotland deceaseth, iv. 198
Quéene Maud deceaseth, v. 289.
Quéene Maud deliuered of a sonne called William, ii 52
———— Departeth this life, ii. 66.
Quéene Maud wife to king Stephan sueth for the release of hir husband to the emperor, vol ii. page 91
Quéene mother maried, v. 486.
———— In armes, v 502
———— Deceaseth, v 418.
———— Gouernor of the realme, iii 69
———— ¶ Sée Marie
Quéene Philip wife to king Edward the third, ii 598
———— Deliuered of Iohn of Gaunt hir fourth sonne, ii 612
———— Brought a bed of Edmund Langleie afterwards duke of Yorke, ii 622.
———— Deceaseth hir thrée petitions of the king, hir praise, ii 692.
Quéene a name withdrawne from the Westsaxon kings wiues, i 653
Quéene of England with hir sonne goeth vnto Henault, ii 579
———— They both arriue in Suffolke, she is assisted by the prelats hir proclamation, ii 580
———— She followeth the king to Oxford, the bishop of Hereford maketh an oration to hir armie, she goeth to Glocester and Bristow, the lords cleaue to hir, ii 582, 583.
———— In danger of drowning, ii 457.
———— Deliuered of a daughter, ii 338, 430, 621, 648
———— Deliuered of Edmund, ii 408.
———— Hir request and letters withstood by a subiect note, ii. 645
———— Hir liberalitie towards king Henrie the third, ii 430
———— Out of fauour with Edward the second hir husband, ii 570.
———— Sent ouer into France to talke with hir brother, ii. 577
Quéene of Denmarke was the daughter of king Henrie the fourth, iii 40.
———— She is sent ouer to hir husband, iii. 41.
Quéene of Scots, and the earle of Angus hir husband come into England, iii 614
———— She commeth vnto the English court, how interteined, ib
———— Returneth to Scotland, iii 621
———— Conueied into France, and maried vnto the Dolphin, iii 1014
Quéene of Scots doubted of hir owne people note, v 189.
———— Taketh the gouernment into hir owne hands, v 500
———— Hir faction ouercome, v 664
Quéene of Scots ¶ Sée Marie
Quéene Dowager of Scotland dooth what she can to procure warre against England, iv 103.
———— ¶ Sée Agatha, Francis, Throckmorton, Margaret, Maud

Quéene a murtherer, hir confession, note, vol. v. page 183.
——— Giueth her owne sentence and executeth hirselfe: note, ib.
Quéene slaine in the sted of her husband, v. 180.
Quéenes their meeting appointed betwéene them, v. 611.
Quéenes of France and Hungarie, iv. 158.
Quéenes thrée in the English court at once, iii. 614.
Quéenes college in Cambridge founded by the ladie Elisabeth, wife to king Edward the fourth, iii. 486.
Quendred king Offa his wife wise but malicious, i. 649.
——— Her ambitious and enuious mind at hir brothers aduācement, i. 659.
——— Murthered his sonne Henelme, 654.
Questions cōcerning gouernment, vi. 255.
——— In law demanded of the iustices: note, ii. 782, 783.
Quick silver, i. 397.
——— It and sulphur father and mother to all mettals, i. 398.
——— The nature of it, i. 369.
Quinburga the daughter of Cearlus king of Mercia, i. 608.
Quintus Atrius ouersēer of the Roman navie, i.472.
Quintus Laherius Durus a tribune slaine, i. 473.

R.

Raalegh Walter is the first that entred into the Spaniards fort, vi. 438.
——— Complaineth for the too much bearing with the traitors, vi. 449.
——— His conflict with the Senechall, vi. 441.
——— Is commissioner of Mounster, vi.442.
——— His seruice vpon David Barrie, vi.441.
——— He taketh the lord Roch, vi. 444.
——— His seruice at Rekell, vi. 437.
——— His pedigrée, Epistola. His care for the commonwealth, ib.
——— The blasoning of his armes, Epistola.
Racke. ¶ Sée Suspicion.
Radegund a maid droue cowes to the pound, which hurt her cowes while she went to masse, i. 116.
Radington knight lord warden of London, ii. 819.
Radwaiter, the lord whereof at variance with the lord Gwinbach: note, i. 179.
Rafe earle of Cambridge or Norfolke marieth earle Rogers sister, ii. 18.
——— His wife beseiged in Norwich, ib.
Rafe the kings collector or proctor, his extortions of pollings of the people, ii. 40.
Rafe bishop of Durham commited to the Towre and whie, ii. 48.
——— Brake out of prison, and his persuasions to duke Robert, ii. 49.
Rafe Wilford. ¶ Sée Wilford.
Raier founder of S. Bartholomews by Smithfield, vol. ii. page 52.
Raine in Sussex, none for thrée yeares space, i. 631.
——— Whereof grew a dearth, ii. 99, 490.
——— And death, ii. 693.
——— That did hurt haruest, ii. 554.
——— That hindered séed time, ii. 609.
——— Hindreth corne from ripening, ii. 598.
——— Continuall for a long time: note, ii. 414.
——— From midsummer to Christmasse, ii. 649.
——— That did hurt vnto houses, trees, corne and other things, ii. 417.
——— Of great continuance and no lesse abundance, ii. 380.
——— For the space of foure moneths togither, ii. 386.
——— Causing a verie wet season, iii. 715.
——— Glutting and continuall in the spring, ii. 282.
——— Excessive. ¶ Sée Floods.
Raine of bloud, i. 459. ii. 174, 479. iii. 250.
Raine artificiall of rosewater, and haile of sugar confects, ii. 508.
——— ¶ Sée Flouds.
Raleigh esquire in danger of the Deuonshire rebels, iii. 942.
Raleigh knight his voiage for the discouerie of that land that lieth betwéene Norimbega and Floride, iv. 534.
——— His preparation for a second voiage, ib.
——— He saileth as far as Cape de Uerde and arriueth in safetie at Plymouth, ib.
——— His changeable voiage to Uerginia, iv. 598.
——— An English colonie established there, iv. 599.
——— His resolution vpon another voiage for the supplie of those that were left there, ib.
Ralph Fitzstephans sonne, vi. 170.
Ramseie Alexander so renowned, that euerie nobleman was glad to haue his sonne serue vnder him, v. 381.
——— Imprisoned, ib.
Ramhounds, i. 349.
Ramielius ambassador out of Denmarke honorablie interteined both in court and elsewhere: note, iv. 894.
——— Randall a pitifull capteine, iv. 223.
Randolph iustice. ¶ Sée Charitie.
Randolph Thomas ambassador, i. 642.
——— Sent ambassador into Scotland, i. 705.
Randolph capteine and colonell arriueth in Ireland, vi. 334.
——— He prepareth to fight with the Onele, ib.
——— He is slaine, ib.
——— His monument, vi. 240.
Randon castell destroied, vi. 239.
——— Burned, vi. 246.
Ransome gentle and tolerable, v. 225.
——— Of king Iames, v. 417.
——— Of a bishop out of the Danes hands, i. 679.
——— Of Richard the first out of the emperors hands, ii. 210.

Ransome amounted to the summe of an hundred and fiftie thousand markes, vol ii page 242
——— Three thousand markes thereof giuen to the white monkes and wine, ii 255
——— Of Robert erle of Leicester, ii 251
——— Of the king of Scots Dauid, ii 670
——— For the monke Eustace would not be receiued, ii 347
——— Of Q Margaret, iii 313
——— Of the French king paid and his children deliuered, iii 749
——— Of the French king, ii 675
——— Of a lord by exchange, iii 175.
——— Sought for gaine, ii 11
——— For townes, ii 334
Ranulfe bishop of Chichester onlie held with Anselme against the king note, ii 43
Ranulfe de Mechines how he came to be erle of Chester, ii 33
Rape a Raperdo, i 259
Rape oile made somtimes in England, i 187
Rashnesse of Adelstane discomendable, i 687
Rasins chéefe generall of the Danes in England, v 219
Ratcliffe knight a favourer and coadiutor of Richard the third, iii 385
Ratcliffe Thomas. ¶ Sée Iusts triumphant and earle of Essex
Rat Iland and whie so named, i 60.
Rauen and Uulture of some thought to be all one, i 382
Rauishment, i 164
——— Reuenged, i 138.
——— Of anie woman how punished in duke Williams time, ii 26
Rauishments inforced by the Romans, i. 500.
——— ¶ Sée Fleance and Lust
Reading William bishop of Chichester a famous man, i 237
Reading name of *few* that is to ouerflowe, i 79.
——— In times past Porstilunand and why, ib
Rebellions cannot properlie be but by subiects, i 199.
——— First atempted in Ireland, vi. 94.
——— Of Kildare, vi 283
——— In the whole land, vi 329
——— Of Onele, ib
——— Of the Butlers, vi 362
——— Of Iames Fitsmoris, vi. 369.
——— Of Omore, vi 372
——— In Conagh, vi 372, 373.
——— Of the Oconhors, vi 273
——— Of Clanicard, vi 381, 382
——— Of Rorie Og, vi 394
——— Of Iames of Desmond, vi 412
——— Of the earle of Desmond, vi 415
——— In Cornwall, v. 463
——— In England of Jacke Straw, v 393
——— In Kent, v. 113
——— In Wales, v 411
——— In Gallowaie, v 280
——— And Murreie, ib.
——— Of commons that beheaded their king, v. 73
——— Moued by Donald of the Iles, v. 409
Rebellion of Gothred sorted to an euill end, vol v page 305
——— Mooued by the Murreis, v 291
——— Practised note, vi 33
——— In what euill an end it sorteth note, v 436
——— With ill successe, v 299
——— ¶ Sée Commotion, Treason
——— Preuented and punished, i 546
——— Of subiects, i 677
——— Actuall of people against their prince, i 640
——— Of the Britains against their lords and gouernors, i 512
——— Of the middle part of England against king Edwin, i 693
——— Of Northumbers against Tostie their earle, i 753
——— Of certeine dukes against Oswie, i 624
——— Of Henrie the sonne against his father to put him from the crowne, ii 171
——— Of nobles against erle Richard, ii 194
——— Of Welshmen, ii 114
——— Of Richard against his father Henrie the second note, ii 161
——— Of Geffreie, ii. 148
——— Of the Welshmen against king Iohn and the successe thereof, ii 304
——— Of lords bandred against king Iohn . note, ii. 319
——— Of the lords against king Iohn notwithstanding the popes decree, ii 324
——— Of the erle of Shrewsburie Robert de Belesme, ii 50
——— In Yorkshire and what euent it had, iii 290.
——— In the north pacified, iii 321
——— In Northfolke furthered at a publike plaie, iii 963
——— In Deuonshire, and capteines names, their number, their hope in others failed, their end note well, iii 917 vnto 960
——— Afresh in Suffolke and Essex, and the principals executed, iii 1023
——— Of Iacke Cade in Kent verie mischéeuous note, iii 220 to 224
——— And what end it had, iii 226
——— In Ireland, iii 215
——— Of Owen Glendouer in Wales, iii 17.
——— In the north for a tax or subsidie granted by parlement, iii 493
——— In Flanders, ib
——— In Cornewall for the paiement of a subsidie, iii 513.
——— Of the lord Louell and the end thereof, iii 483
——— Of Iohn Lincolne the cause of ill Maie daie note, iii 618 to 624.
——— In the north proceeded from the pope, iv 529
——— In Suffolke by the gréeuousnesse of a subsidie, pouertie and necessitie complaints thereof, it is suppressed and the offenders punished, iii 709.
——— Now in Norfolke intended and bewraied

by one of the conspiracie before it burst out, vol. ii. page 755.
Rebellion in the north notable, iii. 800.
——— The same suppressed, ib.
——— Of the Lincolnshiremen, iii. 798.
——— In Westmerland and the capteines executed, iii. 803.
——— Practised in Yorkeshire and the offendors executed, iii. 820.
——— Of the erle of Aubemarle, ii. 349.
——— Of the Gascoignes and the cause thereof, ii. 428.
——— Of the Welshmen and what caused it: note, ii. 439.
——— Of the erles of Northumberland and Westmerland, iv. 235.
——— And what euill end it had: note, iv. 237.
——— Of Normans against duke William soone suppressed, ii. 17.
——— Of two earles against duke William punished: note, ii. 18.
——— Of the sonne against the father procured by the French king: note, ii. 19.
——— Of Edrike Siluaticus in the absence of duke William, ii. 8.
——— Of lords with there adherents executed, ii. 568, 569.
——— Of the Welshmen chastised, ii. 490.
——— Of Dauid, ii. 484.
——— He persueth his enterprise, ii. 484.
——— Condemned, executed, ii. 487.
——— Of the Irish against erle Mortimer, ii. 768.
——— In Scotland by means of one William Wallase, ii. 522, 523.
——— In England, iv. 515.
——— In diuerse parts of England by reason of a great subsidie and other oppressions, ii. 735, 736 vnto 745.
——— Note the whole storie of Henrie the second, ii. 161, 162.
——— What it procureth vnto Rebels; note the words of vicount Mehune, ii. 334.
——— The hurts which it dooth: note in the storie of king Iohn, ii. 328 to 333.
——— The benefit thereof in one respect, iii. 1004.
——— What inconueniences flow from it, iii. 1007.
——— Bringeth the bréeders of it to a shamefull end, iii. 507.
——— ¶ Sée Perkin Warbecke.
——— The fauourors thereof executed: note, iii. 800.
——— That it is all princes duties to repell the practises therof, iv. 518.
——— Attempted but euill successe, ii. 15.
——— What a mischéeuous reuenge it wrought vpon the innocent, ii. 8.
——— The reward thereof: note, ii. 486, iii. 44.
——— Note in Robert Bruse, ii. 540.
Rebellion orders taken to preuent it, vol. ii. page 743.
——— ¶ Sée Action, Commotion, Excester, Glendouer, Insurrection, Ket, Neuill bastard, Normans, Northumberland, Rebels, Riot, Sedition, Wiat.
Rebellion against gouernors, vi. 74, 141.
Rebells. ¶ Sée Gilespie.
Rebels would giue awaie the crowne from their soueraigne to a stranger, ii. 328.
——— Excommunicated by name, ib.
——— How rewarded, iii. 328.
——— There bones buried by a licence obteined, ii. 573.
——— Of Essex vp afresh scattered and slaine, ii. 747.
——— Executed in euerie lordship, ii. 748.
——— Of saint Albons and Suffolke their outragious behauiour, ii. 743.
——— Of Kent vp againe, ii. 747.
——— Of Northfolke and their outrages, ii. 745, 746.
——— In Kent and Essex, ii. 735, 736.
——— They minister an oth to all passengers, they kill lawiers and iustices, &c.: an huge number of them, their capteins and ringleaders, they send to Richard the second to come and speake with them, they spoile Southwarke and set prisoners at large, aided by the Londoners, they pretend a reformation, ii. 736, 737, 738.
——— They burn the Sauoie, their strange deling, their iustice, they put lords to death, make a pastime to kill them, respect no place, but spoile all, the K. offereth them their pardons, ii. 738, 739.
——— They would haue all laws abolished, the king persuadeth them to be quiet, ii. 740, 741.
——— Quite discouraged, throw down their weapons, ii. 741.
——— Seuerlie executed and punished by duke William, ii. 10.
——— Of the north executed at Tiburne, iv. 253.
——— In Ireland their strange and miserable end, iv. 528.
——— Most dangerouslie couer their faults, iv. 515.
——— Of the north Hall and Wilkinson executed at Tiburne, iv. 321.
——— Executed at Durham, iv. 327.
——— At Yorke, ib.
——— Disherited by parlement: note, iv. 467.
——— Against their prince in a perplexitie, ii. 343.
——— Notablie pardoned, and too well rewarded, iii. 801.
——— Of Suffolke, pardoned after their appearance in the starchamber, iii. 710.
——— How miserablie and yet mercifullie pardoned, iii. 519.
——— Fauorers fined, iii. 520.
——— Of Deuonshire their articles sent to Ed-

ward the sixt, with and answer therevnto, vol iii page 918
Rebels executed note, iii 804
——— ¶ Sée Conspiracie, Fugitiues, Noblemen, Sandwich and Traitors
——— Cruell, v 291
——— Seuerlie punished note, v 303, 304
——— Persued by the king, apprehended and executed, v 234
——— Kill a sargent at armes, v 263
——— Sharplie punished, v 364
——— In armes against Iames the third & kill him, v 459
Recantation of certeine anabaptists at Paules crosse, iv 327.
——— Of Cranmer how detested of him at his death, iv 84
——— ¶ Sée Barnes and Crome, Smith and Sermon
Reconciliation signified by kissing of the pax, ii 133.
Reding where the Danes got the victorie, i 666
——— Discomfited, i. 667
Redshanks the wild or rough footed Scots, i 25
——— Mixed with Scots and Picts, vi 82
Redwald king of Eastangles interteineth Edwine in exile, i 599
——— Baptised he would serue God and the diuell, i 608
Rees king of Wales slaine in battell, ii 31
Rees ap Meridoc accused and executed, ii 497
Reformation ought to be no priuat mans but the princes action, iii 1004
Regiment ¶ Sée Monarchie
Regents of Scotland the catalog, v 678
Regicides, v. 159.
Register for christening and burieng, &c in euerie church to be kept, iii 806
Reguli of Britaine seuen, ii 561.
Raimond le Grosse arriueth into Ireland, vi. 141.
——— He is assailed by the men of Waterford, vi 141, 142
——— He preuaileth against the men of Corke, vi 182
——— He is assailed by Mac Artie prince of Desmond and discomfiteth him, ib
——— He passeth ouer into Wales vpon the death of his father William Fitzgirald, ib
——— He returneth and marieth Basilia the earles daughter, v 184
——— He winneth Meth, ib.
——— Haruie conspireth against him, vi. 185.
——— He beseigeth and taketh Limerike, vi. 193, 194
——— His orations, and his description, vi 189, 191
——— His coldnesse in religion, vi 161
——— He is accused by Heruie to the king, ib
——— The king sendeth for him, vi 192
——— He rescueth Limerike, vi. 194.
Raimond le Grosse he parteth with the kings of Connagh and Thomond, vol vi page 191
——— He restoreth Mac Artie of Desmond against his sonne, ib
——— The kings submit themselues vnto him, ib
——— He méeteth Fitzaldelme at Wexford, vi 196
——— His destruction practised, vi 197, 198
——— His lands taken from him, vi. 198
Reingraue returneth into France, v 561
Religion reformed, vi. 382
——— Scotish approued, v 51
——— Disputed, v. 590, 591
——— Certeine burnt therefore, v 515.
——— Established, v 608.
——— That the posteritie of Cham brought ouer into Britaine, i 37, 38, 39
——— Ancient vsed in Albion, i 33
——— When it fell in decaie after it was first vsed in Albion, i 37
——— From whense Brute did learn his, i 39
——— Of the Druides and their chéefe schoole held in Britaine, i 35
——— Houses therof in England their reuenues & number at their dissolution, i 46
——— Corruptors of it, i 34.
——— And christian faith that king Edmund would not renounce to the losse of his life note, i 667
——— Zelouslie aduanced by king Oswald, i 616.
——— Receiued of the Middleangles, i 620
——— And of the Eastsaxons, ib
——— Greatlie decaied in Britaine, i 561
——— Restored by Mortimer after the vanquishing of the Saxons, i 560
——— In Britaine in Octauius time, i 534
——— Embraced for commodities sake, i 631
——— Embraced of the Eastsaxons with zeale to die for it, i 637
——— Greatlie decaied, i 589.
——— Not to be lingered or dallied withall, i. 605, 606, 607
——— A cloke to rob and spoile, i 495
——— Reuolting from it punished by God, i 611
——— Aduanced by king Edred, i. 692
——— Decaied againe among the Britaines, i 581
——— The professors of it hated of the Eastsaxons, i. 602, 603
——— Heathenish nothing worth note, iv 607, 608
——— Altered, iii 5, 6, 8.
——— Trouble and persecution for it, iv 75
——— Professors thereof persecuted, iv 84.
——— It goeth not by age, but by truth, iv 105.
——— Aduanced note, iii 889
——— Beareth the blame and is counted the cause of rebellion note, iii 1008.
——— Reformed in Edward the sixts daies, iii 867.

Religion a booke touching the reformation thereof published, vol. iii. page 798.
——— Laid open to great danger, ii. 442.
——— A conference thereabouts with the clergie on both sides, iv. 180, 181
——— Restored into the English toong, iv. 158.
——— Commissioners sent abrode to establish it, iv. 185.
——— None charged with capitall crimes being of a contrarie religion, and professing to withstand forren forces, iv. 518, 519.
——— Of Rome established by act of parlement: note, iii. 17.
——— ¶ Sée Monkes, Treason.
Religious houses giuen to Henrie the eight in parlement, iii. 889.
——— Giuen to Henrie the eight, iii. 796.
——— Uisited, iii. 795.
——— Henrie the eights promise for the well disposing of them, iii. 852.
——— Suppressed, iv. 185.
——— ¶ Sée Abbeies.
——— Ouerthrowen in Edinburgh, v. 590.
——— In Ireland, vi. 85.
Reliks. ¶ Sée Becket, Christ, Hales.
Remes besieged, ii. 672.
——— The citizens thereof saue their corne fields from destroieing by sending vittells to the English host, ii. 730.
Remelie. ¶ Sée Bishop.
Remelius. ¶ Sée Ramelius.
Remigius bishop of Dorchester depriued of his crosier and ring, ii. 14.
Remission of sins granted to as manie as would fight against Clement the antipape: note, ii. 756, 757.
Rent for a mans owne lands by the yeare paied, ii. 13.
Rents inhansed, i. 318.
Repentance too late, i. 687; ii. 54, 334; iii. 14.
——— Of Alfred for murthering hir stepsonne, i. 700.
——— Of Elfer too late, i. 701.
——— Of yoong king Henrie before his death, his superstitious deuotion, his death & buriall, ii. 185.
——— Of rash aduancement: note, ii. 130.
——— Of an act past, ii. 221.
——— Of a déed doone not foreséeing losses to insue, ii. 295.
——— Of William Rufus in his sicknesse: note, ii. 33.
——— Of duke William for his crueltie against the English, ii. 24.
——— Despised of a desperat malefactor at his death, iii. 1022.
Report that Richard ment to yéeld vp Calis to the French kings hands, ii. 791.
——— False of Henrie the eights death, iii. 587.
——— Of great disquietnesse, iii. 799.
——— How hurtfull and troublesome, ii. 81; iii. 924.
——— In the starchamber against ladie Elizabeth, iv. 26.
Report. ¶ Sée Fame.
Request of Haie: note, vol. v. page 914.
——— Granted vpon necessarie constraint, ii. [illegible]
——— Of the commons denieng a subsidie, ii. 70[illegible]
Reseruation and prouisions apostolike, ii. 626.
Resignation by compultion recompensed, iv. 89.
Restitution of townes to king Edward the third, ii. 618.
Restitutus bishop of London, i. 534.
Reuenge with slaughter of manie for killing some few, ii. 651.
——— Sought with euill successe, i. 489.
——— That God himselfe tooke for wrong doone, i. 720.
——— Of an old grudge, i. 730.
——— Sought of iniuries receiued, i. 496.
——— Without mercie, i. 499, 500.
——— Long thought vpon, i. 127.
——— Of the Scots and Picts vpon Uortigerne and the Britaines, i. 554.
——— Iustlie taken by God against prophane men, i. 603.
——— With sore outrage, i. 636.
——— Upon the dead for iniuries receiued, i. 737.
——— Upon a light occasion, i. 742.
——— Of an old wrong, i. 747.
——— Of murther by murther: note, i. 645, 655.
——— Of the Londoners, ii. 581.
——— Of the people for the death of one whome they fauoured, ii. 21.
——— Against the dead bodie of duke William for iniurie past, ii. 25.
——— Of the duke of Austrich vpon king Richard the first, ii. 231.
——— Of king Iohn vpon the white monks, ii. 280.
——— Of Richard the first a bastard for the death of his father being a king: note, ii. 278.
——— Sought by the French king for the death of duke Arthur, ii. 289.
——— Of sir Robert de Twing, ii. 370, 371.
——— Of the lord Mortimer against the Welshmen, ii. 455.
——— Of Edward the first vpon the Scots, ii. 537.
——— Of duke William for the losse of his subiects, ii. 17.
——— Of a bishop in a riotous manner, ii. 427.
——— Of Henrie the third vpon the bishop of Elie, ii. 426.
——— Of wrongs and iniuries multiplied, ii. 293.
——— Of iniuries, ii. 236, 237.
——— Counselled and pursued: note, ii. 352.
——— Of an old grudge, ii. 362.
——— Interchangeable, ii. 353.
——— For cuckoldrie, ii. 365.
——— For wast, ii. 443.
——— Noblie taken: note, ii. 783, 784.
——— Upon reuenge, ii. 764.
——— With murther, ii. 766.
——— Neglected where it might haue béene executed: note, ii. 787.
——— Of murther with murther, ii. 631.

Reuenge taken as occasion serued, vol ii. page 584
——— Sought for murthering a bishop, ii 20.
——— Of almightie God vpon lasciuious and disordered liues note, ii 726
——— ¶ Sée Enuie, Malice, & Murther
——— Of remembered grudge, iv 3
——— A notable example to forbere it note, iv 58
——— Of an old grudge, iii 228
——— Upon reuenge note, iii 617, 619
Reuda gaineth the countrie of Riddesdale, vi 81
——— He is slaine, ib.
Reutha king of Scots, v. 49
——— Resigneth the state roiall to his cousine Thereus, v 50.
Reuther king of Scots slaine, i 199
——— Crowned king, conspired against, fled, pursued, pardoned of life, v 47
——— Escapeth danger passeth into Ireland is sent for, his death, v 48, 49
Reutherdale whie so named, v. 49.
Rewards moue men to anie attempt, i. 651
——— How they preuaile and worke with a wicked mind, iii. 424
——— Verie large offered to the duke of Britaine to betraie the earle of Richmond into Richard the third his hands, iii 423, 424
——— Corrupt a kéeper of a prisoner, ii 263
——— ¶ Sée Bribes, Gifts, Monie.
Rhée or Rée a Saxon word for a water course, i 79
——— A word in vse in Essex for a riuer, ib
——— A common name of all waters that run from their head, i 163.
Rhene riuer swalloweth bastards and casteth vp yᵉ right begotten, i 80
——— And Hessen now called Hachrug, &c. note, v 80
Rhodes taken by Soliman Ottoman the Turke, iii 683
——— Rendered vp vnto him, ib.
Rice ap Thomas swereth fealtie and seruice to the earle of Richmond, iii 435.
——— ¶ Sée Rées.
——— ¶ Sée Griffin
Rich lord saileth into England, iv 323
Richard the first crowned king of England, ii. 202.
——— In armes against the French king, ii 253
——— His bastard sonne Philips reuenge note, ii 278.
——— His practises to get monie, ii 249
——— Marieth the ladie Berengaria, ii 222.
——— His letters to the states of England for the deposing of the bishop of Elie, ii 229
——— Like to haue béene deliuered vnto the French kings hands, ii 242
——— He and the French king in armes, they talke togither, the emperour disuadeth Richard from peace, the war is renewed betwixt them, they talke togither againe, a peace conditionally concluded, vol ii pages 256, 257.
Richard the first offended with the bishop of Elie lord chancellor, ii 252
——— He transporteth ouer into France, ii 250
——— Crowned king anew, ii. 248
——— His grant of allowance to the king of Scots, when he came ouer into England, ib.
——— His commandement not obeied, ii 213
——— Winneth Nottingham castell, ii. 216
——— Released out of captiuitie, ii 244.
——— Returneth into England, his triumphant receiuing into London, ii 245
——— Raiseth his siege from Gisors, ii 263
——— He and the erle of Tholouse agréed, ii 262.
——— His lands wasted by certeine Gascoignes, ii 237
——— Setteth things to sale for his going to the holie land, ii 208
——— His thrée daughters and how he bestowed them in mariage, ii 271
——— Charged by the emperor with iniuries doone to the Sicilians, ii 239
——— His wisdome in making his answer, ii 240
——— Cléered of the murthering of the marquesse of Montferrat. note, ii. 236
——— Is deliuered to the emperor, he is commited close prisoner, ii 237
——— And the cause of displeasure betwixt him and the duke of Austrich, ii. 235
——— The confession of his lewd life in a chapell, ii 219
——— Uanquisheth the Cipriots and chaseth them out of their campe, ii 221
——— His nauie setteth foorth towards the holie land, ii 213.
——— Returneth home out of the holie land, ii 234
——— Slandered for the death of the marquesse Montferrat, ib.
——— He commeth to Uienna, ib.
——— Submitteth himselfe to the duke of Austrich, ii 235.
——— Discomfiteth the Saracens néere to port Iaph, ii 233.
——— Fell sick at Cephas and recouereth, ii. 234.
——— His talke with king Tancred, ii. 219
——— His expenses out of reason & measure, ib
——— What were the causes of grudge betwéene him and the French king, ii 218
——— He and the king of France receiued a solemne oth, ii 216.

Richard the first his demands for the dowrie of his sister wife to king William, vol. ii. page 215.
——— Arriueth at Messina, ib.
——— Blameth the court of Rome for couetousnes, ib.
——— Setteth forward to the holie land his fléet staied by contrarie winds, ii. 213.
——— Taketh a castell and hangeth the owner, ii. 212, 213.
——— Passeth ouer into Normandie, ii. 209.
——— Desirous of monie and of his shifts, ii. 208.
——— Findeth his fathers treasure, the order of his coronation, ii. 204.
——— He and the king of France determine to go into the holie land, ii. 203.
——— Besiegeth Chalus, he is wounded, despaireth of his life, ordeineth his testament, ii. 269, 270.
——— His bequests and legacies, his death, his stature and shape of bodie, his disposition of mind the vices that were in him, ii. 270, 271.
Richard the second king of England arriueth in Ireland, ii. 259.
——— Returneth and passeth the second time and arriueth to Waterford, ib.
——— He commeth to Dublin, ib.
——— He imprisoneth the duke of Glocester and the duke of Lancasters sonne at Trim, ib.
——— He returneth home by Wales and is deposed, ib.
——— The second borne, ii. 681.
——— Counterfeited: note, iii. 41.
——— Created prince of Wales, ii. 704.
——— Prince of Chester, ii. 843.
——— Beginneth his reigne, the Londoners commend themselues to his fauour before the death of king Edward, ii. 711, 712.
——— The solemne manner of his coronation: note, ii. 713.
——— Maried, the solemnitie thereat, ii. 833.
——— His euill gouernement, ii. 844.
——— The emperor agréeth with him for his ransome, ii. 240.
——— Lands assigned to him, ib.
——— Order taken for leuieng of monie for his ransome, ii. 241.
——— Leaueth Conwaie castell and betaketh himselfe to his enimies, ii. 856.
——— His cognisance or badge, ii. 857.
——— The parlement house at dissention he absenteth himselfe for the space of fortie daies: note, ii. 744.
——— Loued erle de Uéere of Oxford excéedinglie, ii. 776, 777.
——— ¶ Sée Earle Uéere.
——— His inordinat affection towards the duke of Ireland, and the earle of Suffolke, ii. 777.
Richard the second Reteineth souldiors on all sides against the lords, vol. ii. pages 783, 784.
——— his manner of gréeting and speaking to the lords that were banded against him, ii. 787.
——— A report that he meant to yéeld vp Calis vnto the French kings hands, ii. 791.
——— Kéepeth his christmasse in the Towre of London, ib.
——— Brought to his wits end, ii. 792
——— His inconstancie, he is compelled to the nobles request, ib.
——— Ruled not but was ruled, ii. 796.
——— His question to his lords in the councell chamber, taking vpon him the gouernment of all things, he displaceth diuers officers, ii. 798, 799.
——— Kept open house hold in the bishop of London his palace, ii. 811.
——— Passeth ouer into Ireland with a m gh ie armie, ii. 824.
——— Knighteth the foure Irish kings and others, ii. 824, 825.
——— Openeth his gréeuances in the parlement, ii. 839.
——— Saileth ouer into Ireland with a great armie, ii. 851.
——— Letteth the realme to farme, ii. 850.
——— A gard of Cheshire men about him, ii. 838.
——— Roiallie receiued into London and his fauour recouered with gifts, ii. 819.
——— Taketh the death of quéene Anne his wife gréeuouslie, ii. 823.
——— Goeth ouer to Calis, the interuiew betwéene him and the French king, both their oths, ii. 832, 833.
——— Expenses at the interuiew betwéene him & the French king, ii. 833.
——— He and the duke of Glocesters priuie grudge, ii. 834.
——— Conspireth the death of the duke of Glocester, ii. 837.
——— He and the dukes of Lancaster and Yorke reconciled, ii. 839.
——— He beareth saint Edwards armes, ii. 843.
——— Greatlie vexed in his sléepe after the execution of the earle of Arundell, ii. 842.
——— Procureth the popes bul against reakers of his statutes, ii. 844.
——— His doome betwixt the dukes of Lancaster and Norfolke, ii. 847.
——— Affianced and maried to the emperors sister, ii. 753.
——— Sumptuous in his apparell, he is conunited to the Towre, ii. 859.
——— Articles obiected against him, whereby he was counted woorthie to be deposed, ib.

Richard the second he is persuaded to resign the crowne to the duke, vol ii page 861
———— A copie of the said voluntarie renunciation, ii 862
———— His resignation is confirmed, ib
———— The publication of the same, ib
———— Returneth out of Ireland, and landeth in Wales, ii 851
———— He despaireth of his saftie stealeth awaie from his armie and taketh the castell of Flint, ii 855
———— He and his quéene in progresse, ii 617
———— Appointed to be kept in perpetuall prison, iii 7
———— He and his nobles at dissention, ii. 784
———— Goeth with an armie against the Scots, ii 765
———— Burneth Edenburgh castell, ib
———— Returneth out of Ireland, his dealing against the Wickleuists and their fauourers, ii 825
———— Remooueth to S Albans to sée execution doone vpon the rebels, ii 748.
———— Calleth in his letters of infranchising granted vnto the bondmen, ib
———— Calleth in all such letters of manumission as the abbat of S Albans had granted vnto his bondmen, ii 750
———— He and the duke of Lancaster accorded, ii 765.
———— Maketh an agréement betwéene the duke of Lancaster and the earle of Northumberland, ii 752
———— Depriued, he deliuered to king Henrie the fourth all the goods that he hath, his death, personage, fortune, ii 868
———— His noble housekéeping, and excess of apparell, the state of the relme in his time, ib
———— The commons request against him, iii 8
———— His desprat manhood in prison he is murthered, he is brought to the Towre, he is buried at Langlie, forren princes abhor to hear of the shamfull murthering of him, how the Gascoignes tooke his deathe, iii 14, 15
———— The sundrie reports of his death, iii 13
———— Reported to be aliue againe, iii 19, 21, 29, 43
———— And what harm it bred, iii 29.
Richard the third described the manner of his natiuitie, his qualities, iii. 362
———— Dispraised, iii 406
———— Beginneth his vsurped reigne, iii 397
———— He createth seuentéene knights of the Bath, what péeres and estates were attendant on him at his coronation, the solemne ceremonies vsed thereat, his wife quéene Anne and her traine, vol iii pages 398, 399
Richard the third practiseth the murthering of his nephues, iii 401
———— Proclameth promises of rewards for the apprehending of the duke of Buckingham, sendeth fourth a nauie to scowre the sea ouer against Britaine, iii 418
———— Commeth to Excester and is receiued with presents, iii 421
———— Attemoteth the duke of Britaine to deliuer the earle of Richmond into his hands, iii 424
———— His deuise to infringe and defeat the earle of Richmonds purpose, his lewd practise to beguile him, iii 129
———— Casteth his loue on his néece, purposing to marie hir, iii 431
———— What noblemen he most mistrusted whie he gaue licence to all in Hames castell to depart in saftie with bag and baggage, ib
———— His offenses and euill qualities summarilie touched, a notorious tyrant, iii 42
———— Contemneth the earle of Richmond and his power, sendeth to his fréends for chosen men, the ordering of his armie, iii 436, 437.
———— His forged complaint against his wife to be rid of hir, iii 430
———— His purpose in the case of coniuration against him, his drift in deposing his armie, he preuaileth, iii 416
———— Calleth home his ships of warre from the narrow seas his pretended mariage offensiue to the erle of Richmond, iii 432, 433
———— The principals of his power fall from him, his dream foretels him of his end, bringeth all his men into a plaine, his oration to the chieftens of his armie, iii 436, 439.
———— His vaine confidence and bootlesse courage, iii 440
———— His armie discomfitted, fléeth, what persons of name were slaine on his side, he himselfe taken and how he might haue escaped, iii 444, 445
———— The shamfull carriage of his bodie to Leicester his badge and cognisance euerie where defaced, the description of his person and certeine of his behauiours, iii 746, 717
———— Honour doone him after his deth by the earle of Richmond his enimie, iii 447.
———— Would not deliuer the castell of Dunbar ouerthrowne by the earle of Richmond, v 157
Richard de la wich bishop of Chichester note, i. 403.
Richard earle of Warwicke, i 56
Richard king of England inuadeth Scotland, v 395.
———— Deposed iudged to perpetuall prison, escapeth, deceaseth, v 403
Richard de lancts victorie, v 457
Richard the second sonne of K Iohn, ii 299
Richard the base sonne of king Iohn beheaded, monke Eustace, ii 347.

Richard Henrie the second his sonne affianced to earle Raimonds daughter, vol. ii. page 115.
———— Prepareth to resist his father, ii. 161.
———— Despaireth of good successe, ib.
———— Submitteth himselfe to his father, ib.
Richard king Henrie the third his brother maried, ii. 400.
———— ¶ Sée Archbishop of Canturburie.
Richard Strangbow arriueth into Ireland,
———— ¶ Sée Strangbow.
Richard duke of Yorke, his letter to the earle of Salisburie, vi. 267.
Richard archbishop of Dublin vpon a vision yéeldeth vp his bishoprike, vi. 243.
Richborugh. ¶ Sée Sandwich.
Richelinus. ¶ Sée Cinegiseus.
Riches, and what means king Richard the first had to gather them, ii. 208.
—— Of London great, what then of all England, ii. 245.
—— They and inheritance, from whome to whome, and to what end giuen, iii. 990.
—— The right waie therevnto, iii. 991.
—— Of Henrie the eight, iii. 544.
—— ¶ Sée Monie.
Richmond built and whie so named, ii. 525.
—— On fire, ii. 533.
—— By whome builded, i. 329.
Richmonshire redéemed from spoile with a summe of monie, v. 355.
—— And Westmerland in some places bounded by the riuer Swaie, i. 159.
Richmont castell néere Gilhingham when built, ii. 11, 12.
Ricsag king of Northumbers dieth, i. 677.
Ricula sister to Ethelbert, i. 597.
Ridlie doctor persuadeth the people in a sermon at Paules crosse in the title of quéene Iane, iii. 1070.
—— He an Latimer examined for their doctrine, iv. 80.
—— Whie he was more rigorouslie handled than the residue of the bishops, iv. 3.
—— His sermon of mercie and charitie before Edward the sixt how effectuall, iii. 1060.
Riddesdale where it lieth, i. 154.
Rie burnt by the Frenchmen, ii. 715.
— The ships thereof win a good prise, ii. 754.
Right mainteined by might, i. 197.
— Administreth hope of good successe, v. 127.
Rijc in the old Scithian toong dooth signifie a region or kingdome, i. 12.
Ripe signifieth the banke of euerie brooke, i. 503.
Riot. ¶ Sée Scotland.
Riot at king Richard the first his coronation, ii. 205.
— By the Suffolke men: note, ii. 590, 591, 592.
Riot of the people against the Iewes: note vol. ii. pages 210, 211.
— Of the Kentishmen: note, iii. 300.
— In the citie of London betwéene strangers of diuers nations and the Londoners, iii. 243.
— Made on the Easterlings by the Londoners, iii. 508.
— Of prince Edward punished by imprisonment, ii. 539.
— Of the Londoners vpon the bishop of Salisburie his men, ii. 818.
— Betwixt the earle of Warwike and the tenants of the abbat of Euesham, ii. 704.
— At Calis vpon the cutting of a purse, iii. 688.
— Committed vnder pretense of wrestling, ii. 352.
— Toward in west Smithfield and the principals punished, iv. 446.
— Brought within the compasse of treason by a statute, iii. 622.
— ¶ Sée Fraie, Rebellion.
Riotousnes the mother of sicknesses, v. 176.
Rithwall king of Wales partaker with a rebell, ii. 8.
Riuer what finest for water in all Scotland, i. 150.
—One by Chester that changeth its chanell euerie month, i. 217.
Riuers that ebbed and flowed became shallow, ii. 64.
—— Ouerflowing and drowning the land, ii. 34.
—— ¶ Sée Thames.
—— In Angleseie and their courses, i. 139.
—— Great plentie in England, i. 184.
—— That fall into the Thames, i. 81.
—— The lesse mingle their names with the greater, i. 157.
—— That fall into the sea betwéene the Thames and the Seuern mouth, i. 91.
—— In Denbighshire and Flintshire, i. 138.
—— In Deuonshire, i. 111.
—— Upon the coasts of Northfolke, i. 174.
—— That fall and ioine with the sea betwéene Humber & the Thames, i. 168.
—— That fall into the sea in cõpasse betwéene the Sauerne & Humber, i. 123.
—— That discharge themselues into the Sauerne, i. 117.
—— Lieng upon the coasts of Southwales, i. 123.
—— In Summersetshire, i. 101.
—— To be found vpon the Scotish shore, i. 149.
—— Of strange qualities as others write, i. 80.
—— Two called the two swords, i. 132.
—— Thrée called thrée sisters, i. 117.
—— Of forren parts endued with strange properties, i. 354.
Riuers lord and others beheaded, iii. 368, 385.
Riuers Richard. ¶ Sée Mellent.
Robbers punished, v. 221.
Robbers. ¶ Sée Théeues.
Robberies doone in England oft by whome and in what manner, i. 313.
Robert archbishop of Canturburie, i. 741.
—— Banished, i. 747.

Robert duke of Normandie, father to duke William, diuerse acts of his, as well wanton as serious, vol. i. page 764.
——— Whie he was not king of Ierusalem, v. 285.
Robert a Norman archbishop of Canturburie, i. 12.
——— An ambitious préest and contentious, i. 222.
——— ¶ Sée Archbishop.
Robert the sonne of William conqueror, v. 288.
Robert generall of the Normans slaine by the Northumbers, and whie, ii. 10.
Robert rebelleth against his father duke William and how it came to passe, ii. 19.
——— Duke of Normandie, soliciteth to come into England to claime the crowne, ii. 49.
——— Arriueth at Portsmouth, his mild nature, ii. 50.
——— Commeth into England to visit his brother Henrie the first, ii. 54.
——— Proclamed after the decease of his father, ii. 27.
——— Arriueth at Southampton, ii. 29.
——— How he might haue recouered England from his brother, ib.
——— Returneth out of the holie land, and laboureth to recouer England from Henrie the first, ii. 49.
——— Engageth a part of his dukedome for monie, and whie, ii. 28.
——— His valiantnesse in fight, ii. 55.
——— Maketh earnest sute to his brother Henrie for peace, ib.
——— Prisoner in Cardiff castell and there dieth, ii. 56.
——— More credulous than suspicious, ii. 50.
——— In disfauour with the English nobilitie and commons, ii. 47.
——— Chosen K. of Ierusalem by reson of a miracle, ii. 49.
——— Morgageth his duchie of Normandie to his brother William Rufus, ii. 37.
——— It was he whome the nobles would haue had for king being the eldest brother, ii. 27.
——— Returneth into Normandie displesed with his brother William Rufus, ii. 32.
——— At discord afresh with his brother William, ii. 35.
——— His deuise and desire to bereaue William Rufus his brother of the kingdome of England, ii. 27.
——— To whome married, and his issue, ii. 57.
——— Taken prisoner, ii. 56.
——— Described, and his lamentable end, ib.
Robert earle of Northumberland refuseth to come to king William Rufus, vol. ii. page 36.
——— Taketh santuarie, ib.
——— Inuironeth king Malcolme, ii. 34.
——— Prisoner in Winsore castell, and the cause of his conspiracie, ii. 36.
Robert the base sonne of Henrie the first maried, & made earle of Glocester, ii. 63.
——— ¶ Sée Earle.
Robert the onelie sonne and heire of Robert the earle of Leicester deceaseth, iv. 448.
Robin Hood and little Iohn his companion, v. 313.
——— Outlawes, vi. 26.
Robin Hoods baie, i. 156.
Roch knight sent to the Fléet: note, iii. 846.
Roch lord of Poole castell his yéerlie reuenues 10000, vi. 262.
Roch lord had in suspicion of disloialtie, vi. 443.
——— He is taken in his castell by capteine Raleigh and carried to Corke, ib.
——— He acquitteth himselfe, vi. 444.
——— The good seruice of his sonnes, ib.
Rochester besieged, ii. 467.
——— The castell fortified and by whome, ii. 23.
——— Besieged by K. Rufus, ii. 29.
——— Besieged & yéelded to king Iohn, ii. 325.
——— Restored to the archbishop of Canturburie, ii. 322.
——— The bridge when builded & by whome, iv. 552.
——— How it began to decaie, means to kéepe it repared by act of parlement, ib.
——— Called Durobreuum, i. 365.
——— How called in the Romans time, i. 321.
——— The bishoprike when & by whome erected, and the circuit of the same, i. 236.
——— A preparitiue to an higher place, ib.
——— The bridge by whome begun and finished, i. 94.
——— Besieged by Danes, i. 672.
——— Saint Andrews church there by whome builded, i. 597.
——— The church defaced by Edilred, i. 630.
——— The sée void, i. 611.
——— Bishop Ithamar consecrateth archbishops of Canturburie, i. 620.
Rochford lord condemned and beheaded with others, iii. 797.
Rockesburgh, and the situation thereof, in what sort to bée fortified, iii. 887.
——— The same burned by the Scots, ii. 719.
Rocke called the Horsse more infortunate than ten of Seians colts, i. 134.
Rocks called the Check stones, i. 102.
——— Called the cow and calfe verie cruell, i. 134.

Rocks dangerous Keng on a row vpon the west end of Southwales, called the bishops and clerks, vol. i. page 134.
——— Taken for Iles, i. 58.
Rodorike king of Ulster vanquished, ii. 172.
Rodorike a Scithian, king of the Picts arriueth into Ireland, vi. 78.
——— His oration to the king, ib.
——— Is sent into Scotland and slaine, vi. 79.
Roger a bishop builder of Uies castell, i. 238.
Roger earle of Hereford conspireth against duke William, ii. 18.
Roges how punished, i. 312.
——— Full of mischéefe, i. 330.
——— Egyptian, i. 309.
——— Burnt through the eare, iv. 265.
——— Punished, iv. 241.
——— ¶ Sée Uagabonds.
Roiall Exchange. ¶ Sée Bursse.
Roiston set on fier, iii. 40.
Rollo a Dane with a fresh power entreth into England, i. 670.
——— The first duke of Normandie and how he came to it, i. 764.
Rome sacked, iv. 526; v. 120.
——— Builded, i. 449.
——— The empire diuided betwéene two, i. 528, 530.
——— Taken by Bren and Belin, i. 454.
——— And Babylon a sinke of mischéefe saith the popes owne factor: note, i. 230.
——— Blamed by Richard the first for couetuousnesse, ii. 214.
——— What gaines it had out of England, ii. 396.
——— Henrie the third would in no wise bind and endanger his la..e fée to it, ii. 357.
——— Besieged, iii. 717.
——— Taken and sacked, ib.
——— Compositions with the souldiors to saue certeine places vnspoiled, iii. 719.
——— The spoile verie rich, ib.
——— Besieged by the duke of Alua and king Philips armie, iii. 527.
Rome Scot. ¶ Sée Peterpence.
Romacus séeks means to destroie his cousins, receiued for their king, gouerneth tyranicallie, apprehended and put to death, v. 109.
Romans colonies in what places of this land, i. 365.
——— What coines they had, of what mettall and what stamps, i. 364.
——— Made looking glasses of English tin, i. 399.
——— Secure authoritie in this land apparent, i. 364.
——— Wore lõg haire before they receiued barbers into their citie, i. 173.
——— Coine found in Godmanchester, ib.
——— Cõtemptuouslie call their fooles, bards, i. 37.
——— Diuide all Britaine into fiue prouinces, i. 30.
Romans what hauens in Britaine they vsed for their passage and repassage to & fro, vol. i. page 5.
——— Armie consisted of manie sorts of people, i. 10.
——— Subdue Britaine to their dominion, i. 9.
——— Brought in the Latine toong into Britaine, i. 23.
——— In what places of Britaine they planted their legions, i. 10.
——— Wofull guests to Britaine and whie, ib.
——— Their senate follo..ed the trade of merchandise, i. 344.
——— Decrée for the restraint of superfluous grasing, i. 359.
——— Brought fallow déere first into this land, i. 343.
——— Prescribe limits to euerie mans tenure, i. 325.
——— Coine found in the covrse of the Pictish wall, i. 215.
——— Deuiseth Gauell kind first & whie, i. 303.
——— Brought in the gelding of cocks, i. 375.
——— Placed certeine pyramids of stones, i. 191.
——— Somtimes inhabited Cambridge, i. 156.
——— Soiourned at Chester, i. 125.
——— Their ancient calendar, i. 408.
——— Whereof so named, i. 518.
——— Land in Britaine without resistance, i. 471.
——— Whie the warred against Britaine, i. 465.
——— Utterlie subdue the Britons but not without much bloodshed and slaughter, i. 473.
——— Take Carataks wife and daughter prisoners, i. 490.
——— Plaie the diuels in Britaine vnder Ostorius Scapula, i. 486.
——— Proud and ambitions, i. 492.
——— In despaire withdrawe into the capitoll, i. 455.
——— Incountering with the Gallies, ouerthrowne, ib.
——— Discouer Britaine, i. 465.
——— Pursue the Britons and put them to flight, i. 469.
——— Outragious rauishers and deflourers of woman kind, i. 500.
——— Receiue a great ouerthrowe in Britaine, and put to their hard shifts in Domitians daies, i. 493.
——— Put to their shifts by the Britaines, i. 466.
——— Get to land and vnable to follow the Britains farre, i. 467.
——— Refuse for euerie light occasion to come ouer and aid the Britains, i. 541.
——— Knew not Britaine but by report, i. 465.
——— Natiues why placed in townes subdued, i. 488.
——— Their ensigne an eagle, i. 467.
——— They reléeue the Britans against the Scots and Picts, repining to be alwaies their aidors, i. 541.
——— Cursed of the Druides, i. 494.

Romans opinion touching the partile conquest of Britaine by them, vol i page 183
——— Manifold oppressions moueth the Britans to rebellion, i 494 495
——— In all their martiall affaires were fortunat, i 547
——— Go to the pot appased by thousands vnder Seuerus his conduct, i 518
——— Heauie armour their great hinderance, i 472
——— Terrified at the strange noise of belles vsed in the British armie, i 478
——— Villanous and vnnaturall crueltie, i 495
——— By thousands slaine of the Britains, i 500.
——— Folloing too forwardlie the chase receiue damage, v 113.
——— Preuaile against the Scots, v 114
——— Withdraw into Cantire, v 81
——— Thorough policie vanquish the Scots, v 66
——— Passe through Calidon and ouer the riuer Amond, v 80
——— Their ships for want of pilots lost in Pictland frith, v 81.
——— Withdrawe to their campe and the Scots to the mounteins, v 82
——— In pursuing vnaduisedlie distressed, v 83.
——— Their fléet saileth round about the north part of Albion, ib
——— Determined againe to fight with the Scots, fiercelie assalt them put to flight require a communication, submit themselues is vanquished, depart out of Gallowaie, giue vp all their holds and fortresses, v 85.
——— Discomfited, v 84
——— Withdrawe to Iulme, send vnto Marius king of Britaine for aid, v 83, 84
——— Giue batteil to the Britons, fortune fauoureth them, v. 63, 65
——— The people of Gallowaie doo submit themselues vnto them, v 66
——— Trained foorth into ambushes and sore distressed, v 69.
——— Slaine, v 72
——— Put to flight and ouerthrowne, ib.
——— Thrée score and ten thousand slaine, ib.
——— Ouerthrowe the Scots and Picts, ib
——— Put to flight, v. 88
——— Inuade Scotish borders, v 87
——— Their campe assailed in the night by Uoadicia, v 75
——— Uanquished, v 69.
——— Slaine, v 106
——— Flée and slaine, v 107.
——— ¶ Sée Scots, Picts, Triumphs, and Britains.
Romanus bishop of Rochester drowned as he went to Rome, i. 611.
Romeneie a march betwéene Monmouth & Glamourganshire, i 128
Romeneie marsh in old time called Romana or Romanorum insula, i 5
Romero Iulianus distressed, v. 565.
Rone besieged by Henrie the fift, vol iii page 100.
——— Inuironed with enimies and succourlesse, the number within the towne, extreme famine within it, iii 102
——— They within the towne demand parlie, a truce for eight daies, articles concerning the yéelding vp thereof iii 103, 104, 105
——— King Henrie the fift his entrance thereinto, iii 105
——— A conspiracie of the Frenchmen against the Englishmen, iii 107
——— The castell like to be taken by treason of the capteine, iii 178.
——— Yéelded vnto the French king, iii 216
Ronix a Saxonish ladie and daughter to Hengist arriueth in Britaine, i. 555
——— Taketh Uortigerne with the bait of hir Beautie, i 556
——— Poisoneth Uortimer his sonne in law, i 558, 559
Rood of grace shewed at Paules crosse, iii 805.
Rood of Paules erected note, iv. 63
Rood speaketh, i 700
Rookesbie shirriffe of Yorkeshire, his hardie courage to fight, iii 805.
Roots ¶ Sée Gardens
Rorie Og submitteth himselfe, vi 375
——— Rebelleth, vi 394
——— Burneth the Naas and Leighlin, vi. 395.
——— Is driuen to run awaie, ib
——— He traitorouslie taketh capteine Harrington prisoner, vi 396
——— A draught is made vpon him, ib
——— He burneth Catherlough, vi 397.
——— He laieth a bait for the lord of upper Ossorie, ib
——— He is slaine, ib
Ros lord reuolteth vnto the Scots, his brother continueth faithfull vnto the king of England, ii. 513
Ros a noble man of France accused, ii 433
Rosamond the faire concubine to Henrie the second where buried, ii 339
——— Hir cofer hir death and epitaph, ii 200.
Roscoman castle destroied, vi 239
——— New réedified, ib
——— Taken by the Irishie, ib
Rose that bare a triple number of leaues to thrée score and vpō one butten, i 353.
Rosse castell taken, v 602.
Rosse towne a hauen towne in Leinster, vi 30.
——— Inclosed with a wall, ib
——— Interdicted by the pope, vi 32.
——— Decaied and impouerished, vi 33
——— A long controuersie betwéene them and the citie of Waterford for liberties, vi. 379
Rot in sheepe and cattell whense it commeth, i. 372.
Rother riuer separated Sussex frō Kent, i 92.
Rothorike Oconhir monarch of Ireland, vi 139.
——— Summoneth a parlement, ib.

Rothorike Oconhir declameth against Dermon Macmorough, vol. vi page 133.
——— Inuadeth Leinster, ib
——— His oration, vi. 134
——— Sueth for peace, ib.
——— Is sworne to be true, vi 139
——— Braketh with Macmorough, vi 147.
——— He beheadeth Dermonds sonne, ib
——— Besiegeth Dublin, vi 150
——— Submitteth himselfe, vi 161
——— Sweareth allegiance, ib
Rothsaie a transporter of the Scots, v 37
Rouks a pirat and a rebell, vi. 295
——— Besiegeth Dublin, ib.
——— He scowreth the seas and taketh an English barke, vi 299
——— He is hanged, vi 302
Rouen besieged by the king of France, ii 159
——— Through famine surrendred vnto the king of France, ii. 290
Round table ¶ Sée Windsor castell.
Round Ile and why so called, ii 69.
Rouers ¶ Sée Pirats
Rous knight a valiant capteine, ii 721, 722.
Routs ¶ See Brabanders
Rowland in fauour with the king of England made lord of Galloway e, v 325
——— Constable of Scotland, ib
Roxburgh in old times called Marken, v 289, 290
——— The castell taken and broken down, v 416
Rurnus baptised by saint Patrike, vi 74, 75
——— He liued 2011 yeres, vi. 74.
Rufus William, his promises to purchase the peoples fauour, ii 13
——— ¶ Sée William Rufus.
Rugemont castell note, iii 522
Ruin of the ecclesiasticall state, vi. 262.
Rule parted betwéene two or more ¶ Sée Ambition, Brennus, Ferrex, and Morgan
Rulers gouern Britaine, i 444, 445, 446, 447, 448, 449, 450
——— Sundrie in a land wekeneth it, ii 139
Rumours false spread to worke an alteration, ii. 329.
——— ¶ Sée Report
——— Catcheth fethers, vi 16.
Runners on foote verie swift, i 381
Running at the quintine, ii. 428, iii 556.
——— At tilt, iii. 554.
Ruptary, ii 171
——— ¶ Sée Brabanders
Russell sir Francis knight slaine, his epitaph, v. 728
Russell knight his sober and discréet vsage in seruice commended, iii 688
Russell lord deliuerer of the citie of Excester, note, iii 952, 953
——— Distrusteth himselfe and is vpon departing out of Deuonshire, he marcheth against the rebels towards Excester, iii 953, 954, 955.
Russell lord L. priuie seale his letters to the L protector, vol iii. page 1015
——— He sueth for peace betwéene the lords, iii 1016
Rutland earle lord Edward ambassador into Scotland note, iv 895
Rutland castell built, ii 482
——— Besieged, ii 484
——— Taken, ii 480
Rutheranus one of the posteritie of Nimrod, vi 75
Ruthurgus arriueth in Ireland, vi 74
——— His poole, ib
Ruthwen lord repenteth, v 618.
——— Commeth to Hawike, v 664
Ruthwen William commeth with a power to Driburge, ib
Rutland earle goeth into Scotland, v. 744.
——— ¶ Sée Earle
Rutters, ii 171.
——— Deride our new archerie, i 333
Rutupium. ¶ Sée Richborough and Sandwich

S

Sabboth a superstitious and hurtfull obseruation thereof, ii 453, 454
Saberts reigned ouer the Eastsaxons, and receiueth the faith, i 597
Saberts the most lewd sonnes deseruedlie slaine togither, i 603
Sabinus his valiantnesse against the Britans, i 482
Sacribell king of Scots séeketh to destroie such as were in fauor with his predecessors, conspired against, strangled by his owne seruants, v 95.
Sacrament, of baptisme how the rebels would haue it ministred, iii 918
Sacraments forbidden to bée vsed, of the clergie, ii 130
——— Contemned and how the offendor punished, ii 352
Sacrifices by whome to be made, i 423.
——— Of prisoners, i 491
Sacrilege and no sacrilege, ii 37
——— Seuerlie punished, iii 318
Sikuill knight ambassador to the French king, iv 238
——— His interteinment verie honourable, ib
——— The first place of his ordinance his liberalitie, iv 239.
——— His returne into England, iv 214
——— ¶ Sée Buckehurst
Safe conduct sued for of the king of Armenia, ii. 777
——— Granted vnto soldiors, ii. 35
——— And the force thereof, ii 737
——— Preuaileth not, ii 119
——— ¶ Sée Licence, Protection, & Cardinall Uiuiano
Sadler sir Rafe knight, treasuror of the English armie, iii 668.

Sadler sir Rafe his seruice against the Scots commended, vol iii page 882
———— Sent to Scotland, v 530.
Sagundus one of the posteritie of Nimrod, vi 75
Saie lord treasuror beheaded at the standard in Cheape, iii 225
Saint Albans martyrdome found written in an old booke, i 521.
Saint Anderie of Elie ¶ Sée Egelredi
Saint Andrews quondam, called saint Reule, v 208
———— His crosse, v 192.
———— The Scotishmens pittione, ib
———— The castell besieged by the French, v 547
———— ———— Yéelded, ib
Saint Albons destroied, ii 348
Saint Albones taken vp and put into a rich shrine, ii 646
S Albones when most of all it excelled, i. 322
———— How called in the Romans time, i 320.
———— Sometimes Werlamcester, i 190
———— ¶ See Verolamium
Saint Anthonies ¶ See Church
S Andrews in Scotland standeth vpon the mouth of the lake Londors, i 150
S Assaphs bishopikes circuit erection and valuation, i. 244
Saint Bartholomewes by Smithfield when builded, ii 52
———— The hospitall builded in part, ii 56
Saint Clements Danes without Temple barre, i. 737
Saint Colme endued with the spirit of secret knowledge deceaseth, v 168
———— His prophesie of Eugenius, v 169, 170
———— He commeth ouer forth of Ireland into Scotland, v 163
———— Returneth into Ireland, v 164.
Saint Cuthberts banner, v 285.
———— Appéered to K Alured, i 671
———— His shrine priuiledged, i 678
S Cuthberts foules, i. 77.
S Dauids bishopriks erection circuits and valuation, i 243
S Dauids lands, i 134
Saint Ellutus bell, i 697
Saint Germaine preacheth to the campe, v 131
———— Leadeth their fore ward, beareth the kings standard, ib
Saint Iames somtimes a nunnerie by whome builded, i 329
Saint Iohns towne besieged, v 367.
———— Fortified, v 368.
———— Woone, ib
———— ¶ Sée Picts.
Saint Marie Queries made a parish church, iii. 815
Saint Marie ouer Rhée, i 79.
S Magnus hole, i 74
S Néeds. ¶ Sée Newton.
Saint Osmonds time commended and extolled by the papists, vol i page 238
Saint Patrikes staffe full of vertue, i 116
Saint Patrike ¶ Sée Patrike
Saint Patriks church in Dublin, vi 44
Saint Paule archbishop of Dublin, vi 256
Saint Philline, v 315
Saint Quintins besieged and taken by the English, iv 89
Saint Thomas hospitall erected, iii 1061
Saint Reule commeth into Fife, v 112
———— ¶ Sée Saint Andrews
Saint Uincents bath, i. 360
Saints and praieng to them misliked by William Rufus note ii 16
—— Of Ireland, vi 83
Sabrina a wood compounded of Aber and Ina, &c i 117
Sacrifices of mankind to Idols and yet thought most acceptable, i. 39
Saffron in England described and the dressing thereof, i 390
———— Not commonlie planted here till Richard the seconds time, i 391
———— English rekoned among spices, i 390
———— How commonlie priced, i 391
———— That more deceit is vsed in no trade more and how to perceiue it, i 392
———— Hot in the second, and drie in the first degrée, i 393
———— When great plentie and whē scarsitie, i. 392
———— The vertues thereof, i 393.
———— When the comoditie of it was first brought into this Iland, ib
———— *Where the greatest mart is for it, i 394*
Saladine causeth the christian prisoners to be beheaded, ii 230.
———— ¶ Sée Ierusalem, Saracens, Turks
Salassians inhabitants about Italie and Switserland, i. 479.
Salike ¶ Sée Law
Salisburie the old how it fell into vtter decaie, i. 97, 98
———— The new when begun and hindred by waters, i 98.
———— The bishoprike by whome erected and of the circuit and iurisdiction of the same, i. 238.
———— Made a citie, ii 350
———— Besieged by the Danes, i 722
———— ¶ Sée Salisburie, and Ambrie.
Salisburie the traitor ¶ Sée Babington.
Salisburie plaine where the Saxons and Britons met, i 560
Salisburie capteine arriueth into Ireland with 200 archers, vi 299
———— His seruice at the siege of Mainmouth, vi 300
Salt called Baie salt déer, iv. 326.
—— Made in England, i 404.
Salt Springs thrée in the towne of Wich, i 403
Salt Artificiall of sundrie sortes note, ib.
Salsa parrilla, i 351.

Salomon king of Britaine Armorike, vol. i. page 613
Salute ¶ Sée Come
Salutation of an Hillandman, v 312
Samaritans manner of seruing God, i. 608.
Sammons where in season when out of season else where, i 123
——— When to be taken, 376.
——— Of the greatest size in what riuers of Scotland to be found, i 150
——— Taken in the Thames, i 80
Samothei the name of Britaine a long while called, i 6, 428
Samotheans subdued by Albion, i 432
Samothes brought a part of the lineage of Iaphet into Britaine, i 9
——— One of the sonnes of Iaphet, i 6
——— The religion that he published in Albion, i 33.
——— What part of the world he had for his portion, i 428
Samson ¶ Sée Bishop
Samuell monke of S Albons made bishop of Dublin, ii. 36
Sanctuarie and of such as flie for succour therevnto note, ii 57
——— No safe harbour for rebels, iii 519.
——— Nor for traitors note, iii 483, 484
——— ¶ Sée Robert of Northumberland and Westminster ii 36
Sanctuaries, v 136
——— Their vse and abuse note, iii 372
——— Restreined, ii. 529.
Sanders murthered ¶ Sée Murther
Sanders doctor a mainteiner of the popes bull, iv. 510
——— His miserable end, iv 529.
Sands a whip unto the Frenchmen, iii 679
Sands doctor his trouble persecution and voluntarie banishment iv 110 to 116
Sandwich kept by rebels, they sue for pardon, iii. 328
——— Spoiled by the French, iii 244
——— Or Richborough, i 515
——— Where Uespasian durst not arriue, i 486
Sandford Iohn archbishop of Dublin, v 240
——— Is lord iustice, ib
Saracens lose the citie of Acon, v. 312
——— Discomfitted by Richard the first, ii 232
——— Uanquish the christians and kill the earle of Salisburie with others, ii 416.
——— Called Arsacides their generation and dealing with prince Edward, ii 471
——— Against whome went diuerse nobles of England, ii 389.
——— Make sore warre vpon the christians in Spaine and are vanquished, ii 367
——— Had the whole land in possession, ii 354.
——— Besiege the citie of Damieta, ii 349.
——— Win the same from the christians, ii 353
——— A iorneie against them, ii. 810.
Saracens out of whose hand the whole land was to be recouered, vol ii page 37
——— Win lands from the christians, ii. 187.
——— Traitorouslie kill the marquesse of Montferrat, ii 233.
——— Yéeld Acres into the christians hands, ii 230
——— Make warre against the Portingals, ii 214.
——— ¶ See Christians, Granado
Sargent murthered and the offendor hanged in Cheapside, iv 426
——— Slaine and the murtherer hanged in Fleetstreet, iv 491
——— ¶ Sée Officer
Sargents at law their fest kept at Elie house whereat Henrie the seuenth and his quéene were present, iii 509, 510
——— In the archbishop of Canturburies palace whereat were present Henrie the seuenth and his nobles, ii 531
——— At Greies inne, iv 231.
——— At the new temple, ii 432.
Sarisburie so named of Saxon, i 319.
Saron the sonne of Magus, i 429
Saronides doo neuer saue fire without a philosopher, i. 129.
Saronides and whereof they were so called, i 34
Satisfaction for sinnes, i 701.
——— That Henrie the second sware to make for the death of Becket, ii 143
Saturdaie after noone to be kept holie, v 304.
Saturne and Iupiter. ¶ Sée Planets.
Sauage sir Robert fortified his house and castell, vi 256
——— His sonnes answer, ib
——— His liberalitie to his soldiors, v. 257.
Sauage knight slaine at the siege of Bullongue, iii 502
Sauage the traitor. ¶ Sée Babington
Sauerne described and what waters discharge them selues thereinto, i 117
——— Whense it tooke its name, ib
——— Wherein comparable to the Thames and wherein inferiour, ib
Sauerie de Mauleon and the erle of Salisburie at discord, ii 335, 355
——— He reuolteth to the French king, ii 356
——— An assistant of king Iohn against his rebels, iii 324 to 328
——— Sore hurt and wounded, ii. 329
Sauoie burnt vp by the Rebels, ii 438
——— The hospitall, iii 540.
Sawtrie a préest burned for religion, iii 18
Saxon the sonne of Magus and what teaching he had in Albion, i. 34.
Saxons described, i 586
——— Traitorous, i 560
——— They and the Picts renew their league, i. 562.

Saxons sue for licence to Uortimer to depart home into Germanie, vol i page 559
——— Came swarming like bées into Britaine, ib
——— Remouing Britans out of their seats still gained ground of them, i 588
——— First inuasion into great Britaine note, i 547
——— Plagued by Arthur of Britaine, i 574
——— Foure notable battells giuen them by the Britaines to their ouerthrowe, i 558.
——— Slaughtered at Badon hill, i 571
——— Appointed to plague the Britains from time to time for their fowle sinnes, i 556
——— Pursue the Britaines without ceassing, i 585
——— Erect an heptarchie or seuen kingdoms, ib.
——— What parts of Britaine they had in their hands in Uortigens time, i 563.
——— The first fight betwixt in this Iland, i 586
——— Ouerthrowne, besieging Bath, i. 576, 577
——— Arriue and dwell in Northumberland, i 557
——— Well enterteined of Uortigerne, i 554
——— Well nigh wasted by Uortimers warres, i. 558
——— Ioine with the Scots and Picts against the Britaines, i 559
——— Rouers, pirats and more cruell than all other enimies, i 549, 550
——— Waged to aid the Britaines against the Picts and Scots, i 554
——— Slaine and not one left to carrie newes to their owne contrie out of Britaine, i 547
——— Came thick and thréefold into Britaine, i. 556, 557
——— Make miserable destruction in this land, i. 557
——— Notablie discomfitted by the Britans conducted by two holie bishops note, i. 562
——— Called English what they were, i. 555
——— English subdued by Ethelbert, i 590
——— The bloud or race of them ceasseth to reigne in England, i 763
——— ¶ See Eastangles, Southsaxons, and Westsaxons.
——— Encounter with the Scots, v 145
——— Uanquished expelled out of Kent flie out of Britaine, v 83, 84
——— English breakers of promise, v 144
——— Resisted by the Scots and Picts note, v. 152
——— Miraculouslie discomfitted, v. 151
——— Chaced made their race towards Yorke, v. 154
——— In hope of good successe, begin the warres against the Scots with bloud, v 140
——— Receiued vpon their submission, v 156.
——— Discomfit and discomfitted, v 157
——— Their hatred towards the British priests, v. 169
——— Conuerted by bishop Colman, v. 175.
——— Put to flight, v. 155
Saxons uanquished and diuerse idolaters of them burned, vol. v page 149
——— Uanquished by the Britons become their tributaries, v 155
——— In danger of an ouerthrow, v 143
——— First inhabited in Linsete against the Scots and Picts, v. 142
——— A new power cometh ouer into Britaine, ib
———Their women praised and the Britaines noted of cowardise, v 140
——— Returne into England and driue the Britaines into Wales, v 162.
——— ¶ See Peare
——— Diuided this land into families, i 257
——— Builded manie townes and villages in England, i 324
——— What nation came with them into Britaine, i 9
——— Left no idol vnhonoured no not filthie Priapus, i 47
——— Conuerted from paganisme by Augustine ye monke, i 47
——— Became first acquainted with Britaine, i 11.
——— Under Hengists armie in Britaine, ib
——— What name they gaue the wéeke daies, i 407
——— The Normans whie deadlie enimies to the English Saxons, i 12.
——— Their kings vsed to be crowned at kings town vpon Thames, i 368
Scald brother a théefe, ib.
——— His caue, ib
——— His swiftnesse, ib
——— His théeuerie and his death, ib
Scales lord his chiualrie note, iii 285
——— Slaine most cruellie, iii 264
Scahot a blacksmith ¶ See Workmanship
Scarsitie of prouision thereagainst for the poores behoofe, ii 816
——— ¶ Sée Dearth.
Scattergood ¶ Sée Policie
Schisme betwéene two popes for the dignitie of saint Peters chaire, ii 829.
——— In the church and wherevpon, ii. 41
Scolds how punished, i 312
Schoole of S Anthonies in the citie of London, iii. 510
——— At Tunbridge, iii 1024
——— At Draiton in Shropshire, iii 1021
——— At Bristow and Reading iv 8.
——— At Holt in Norfolke founded, iv 83
——— At Sandwich erected, iv 551
——— At Sutton Ualens in Kent, iv 427
——— Founded by archbishop Parker, iv 327, 328
——— In Bedford founded by William Harper, ii 203
——— Of the merchant tailors erected, iv 202.
——— At Ratcliffe builded, iii 807
——— At Walthamstow builded, iii 599, 600

Schoole erected at Cambridge by king Sigebert, vol i page 460
——— In the primitiue church vnder the bishops iurisdiction, i 235
Scholars disputations, iv 80
——— Tried for traitors by six questions. note, iv 521
——— ¶ See Oxford
Schoolemaisters to teach scholars to construe their lessons in English, ii 578
Scithians arriue in Albania made thēselues Scots, i. 198
——— First inhabited the Orchades, i 73.
——— Diuerse into Ireland, vi. 78.
——— A seditious people, ib.
——— ¶ Sée Picts
Scone abbie repared, v. 287
——— The abbie burnt, v 590
Scorpion, i 384
Scorpions two found in Scotland, v 470
Scorie Edward builder of the new crosse in the market place of Chichester, i 237
Scorch Villen archbishop of Dublin, vi 238
——— Whie so named, ib
Scotia the first name of Ireland, vi. 2.
——— Named also Gathela, ib
——— It is inuaded by the citizens of Dublin, vi. 260
——— Inuaded by the Irish people, vi. 146
Scota daughter to Pharo, v 32, 33
Scots Iohn an Englishman, he taught king Alured, killed of his owne scholars, v. 225.
Scot sir Thomas, knight of Kent, a good politian, excéedinglie beloued of the people, iv 853, 856, 866
Scot Thomas, v 663
Scot ¶ Sée Erle of Chester.
Scot Adam of Tushlaw named king of théeues, v. 508
Scotland had sometimes two kingdomes beside that of the Orchades, i 28
——— Stored with plentie of quarries of sundrie sorts, i 184.
——— Iles in it, i 69
——— Hunting that their princes vsed, i 380
——— Not so fruitfull as Wales, i 183
——— The soueraigntie of it all belongeth of right to the kings of England, i 196
——— A parcell of ground besides the new palace of Westminster whie so called, i 205
——— All the holds thereof taken by Constantine king of Britaine into his owne possession, i 201
——— How it first tooke that denomination, i. 198
——— Deliuered vp of the king by his letters patent, i 213
——— When the Orchades and other Ilands were vnited to the crowne thereof, i 76
——— All the land inhabited with Britons, i 199
Scotland giuen to gormandising and bellichéere, vol. i page 276.
——— Under the dominion of the kings of Britaine, i 200
——— Conuerted to the faith of Christ, i. 48
——— The first attempt of the bishop of Rome to bring it vnder his obedience, ib
——— Thrée seuerall toongs spoken in it, i. 25
——— The whole realme discomfited, v 210
——— Subiect to diuerse gouernors, v 98
——— The bounds of the kingdome, v 208.
——— When it tooke it name, v 33.
——— Inuaded, v 493, 455, 496
——— Instructed in crafts and occupations, v. 46
——— Parted into portions, v 42
——— Riot and superfluous chéere brought thither, v 281
——— The armes thereof, v 190
——— Was frée of the pestilence and plague, v 176
——— Without a king and gouernor, v. 322.
——— Interdicted, v 307
——— In great disquietnesse during the minoritie of Iames the fift, v 483
——— Organs brought thither, v 422
——— Use of baked meats when it began, ib
——— Manifoldlie plagued note, v. 424.
——— Gouerned by two rulers, v. 365.
——— In peace and quietnesse, v. 467.
——— ¶ Sée Horses and Mares
——— Men of occupation brought thither to instruct the Scots therein, v 423
——— Inuaded both by sea and land, v 373
——— The north parts sore disquieted by two clans, v. 402.
——— Inuaded by king Richard, v 395.
——— The line of the kings thereof, v 271.
——— A new act for the succession of the crowne, v. 247
——— Entred into by the kings of Denmarke and Norwaie, v 231
——— Inuaded by the Danes, v 257
——— Ruled by seuen gouernors, v 446
——— Twelue gouernors elected to rule it, v. 330
——— King Edward his officers chased from thense, v 335
——— Six gouernors chosen to haue the rule thereof, v 323
——— At ciuill warres, v 241
——— More indamaged by domesticall théeues than by forren enimies, v 296.
——— ¶ Sée Bishops, Crowne, Gilpatrike, Liberties, Nobles, Swene, Warres
——— Henrie the fift is counselled to the conquest of it, iii. 66
——— Inuaded by the lord Ros and Dacres, iii. 680
——— Sore spoiled by the erle of Surrie and his power, iii 686.

Scotland inuaded and diuerse townes burned by the English, vol iii page 681
———— Itand Englnd at wars, the causes of the same, iii 826
———— And what townes villages &c and the English armie burned and spoiled, iii 837
———— The middle marches forued, iii 848, 849
———— The countrie inuaded by the earle of Hereford, iii 849.
———— An English armie goeth against it, their number arriueth in Ireland, iii. 855.
———— An harbour for rebels and malecontents note the whole storie of duke William and page, iii. 17.
———— Trouble their, Frenchmen sent thither the lords thereot that were confedered against the French, iv 188, 189
———— The earle of Sussex maketh a iournie thereinto wasted by fire and sword, iv. 235.
———— Inuaded by the earle of Sussex, iv 238.
———— Wasted by fire and sword, iv 239 to 250
———— Woone fiue times by one king of England, iii 911
———— Diuerse places therein burned, besieged and otherwaies dealt withall by the English, iii 885
———— Inuaded on the west side, iii 889
———— Places gained there by the English, iii. 890
———— An English power both by sea and land sent thither, cheifteins of the armie, iii. 867
———— The borderers of England make a rode thereinto, ii 764
———— Inuaded, ii 763
———— ¶ Sée Duke of Lancaster Inuaded by the earle of Warwike, ii 606
———— Countries subdued therein by the English, ii 644
———— Resigned into the hands of king Edward the third, ii 661
———— When it had great want of men, ii. 355
———— Wasted by king Adelstane, i 686
———— Controuersie there, about the crowne thereof, ii. 493, 494.
———— The kings fealtie set downe in forme, ii 499.
———— And his homage, ii 500.
———— Edward the first appointed wardens for the same, ii 496.
———— That the right and title thereof belonged to Edward the first, note, ii 534
———— The lord Segraue sent with an armie thither, ii 536
———— ¶ See Britaine, Church, Henrie the fourth
Scots, their king inuadeth Northumberland, ii 150, 151.
—— His thought at the view of the English armie, the order of his host, French capteins among them, the Scots are put to the woorst in the right wing, the left wing discomfitted, vol iii. page 597
Scots the kings magnanimitie, he fighteth himselfe verie valiantlie, the stoutnesse of his stomach, he is slaine, his bodie found hauing diuerse wounds, iii 598
—— Serueth king Henrie the fift, iii. 128.
—— In Henrie the fift his armie, iii 121
—— His letter of defiance to king Henrie the eight, ii 592
—— Commeth to the English parlement, ii 168
—— He with others deliuered out of prison, ii. 163
—— Dooth homage to Henrie the second, ii. 126.
—— Knighted by king Henrie the second, ii 130
—— Slaine by his owne subiects, iii 495.
—— Inuadeth England with a great armie in Perkins behalfe, iii 513
—— Desireth the ladie Margaret eldest daughter of Henrie the seuenth to wife, iii. 521.
—— Dooth homage to Henrie the sixt, iii. 139
—— Fled from his siege at Rockesboreugh, iii 189
—— Iames is murthered note, iii 101
—— Besiegeth Rockesborough and is slaine, iii 265
—— Taken prisoner, ii 158
—— Inuadeth Northumberland, ii 152
—— Presented vnto the king of England, ii 159
—— Inuadeth England, ii 157
—— Deliuereth vp castels, ii 163
—— Dooth homage to the king of England, i. 164, 165, 515
—— Knight of the garter, iii 795
—— Murthered, iv 231
—— Proclameth open warres against England, iii. 16
—— Inuadeth England the lords assemble a power to fight against him, the quéene present in person, ii 644
—— He is taken prisoner, ib.
—— Resigneth the realme of Scotland into the hands of Edward the third, ii 661.
—— Ransomed and set at libertie, ii. 670
—— Sueth for peace vnto king Edward the first and submitteth himselfe, ii 518.
—— Would serue two masters, ii 513.
—— Concludeth a league with the king of France, ii 510
—— Renounceth his homage vnto the king of England, ii 423
—— Kept christmasse with the king of England at Yorke, ii 365.
—— Commeth vnto London, ii 356
—— Warden of the English marches, ii 396
—— His allegiance to K. Henrie the third, testified by a charter, ii 404.
—— Inuadeth England, ii 403.
—— Commeth into England, ii. 439

Scots aided against the English by the French they inuade the frontiers of England, they spoile Cumberland, assault Carleill, vol. ii. pages 765, 766.
—— Burn Warke castell, ii. 762.
—— Spoile the north parts in the time of dearth, ii. 734.
—— Inuade the English borders, spoile whole countries, and carrie awaie great booties, ii. 733.
—— Their nobilitie at dissention, their prince staied in Scotland, iii. 40.
—— Inuade England, ii. 595.
—— Disloiall to king Edward the third, he assalteth them, they submit themselues, ii. 602, 603.
—— Their stoutnesse hindereth the conclusion of peace, a statute ordeined by them in fauor of king Edward the third, ii. 604, 605.
—— Fight with axes, ii. 644.
—— Sore afflicted by king Edward the third, ii. 661, 662.
—— Enter into England and doo much hurt, compounded withall for moneie, ii. 555.
—— Discomfit the lord Beaumont, ib.
—— Accurssed and interdicted, ib.
—— Inuade the English borders, ii. 515.
—— Their crueltie, the castell of Dunbar rendered to them put to flight and slaine, ii. 513, 516.
—— They raise their seige from Carleill, ii. 518.
—— Disloiall in dealing, ii. 510.
—— Their nobles vnto king Edward the first set downe in expresse words, ii. 496.
—— Their vnfaithfull dealing, in armes, ii. 523.
—— At discord, they sue for peace discomfited, ii. 523, 424.
—— Promise breakers, they assaile the English discomfit them, enter into Berwike, inuade Northumberland, spoile the countrie returne home, discomfited and slaine, ii. 525, 526, 527.
—— Beséege Rockesborough, ii. 528.
—— Summoned vnto the parlement at Yorke, ii. 529.
—— The order of their battells their horssemen flie, their archers slaine, ii. 530.
—— The slaughter of them, ib.
—— Uexed by king Edward the first, forbidden so to doo by pope Boniface, ii. 532.
—— Flie from king Edward the firsts power, hide themselues, fall to submission, ii. 532.
—— In armes vnder Bruse discomfited, ii. 540, 541.
—— Plagued for their beastlie crueltie, v. 116.
—— They and Picts pursue the Britons, v. 141.
—— Assembled against the Romans, v. 127.
—— Inuade the Britons, v. 129.
—— Their carters furious rage, v. 115.
—— Their king dooth fealtie to the king of England for Scotland, v. 298.
—— Slaine by the Romans, v. 114.
—— Their battell ouerthrowne, v. 115.
—— Indamage the Picts, v. 113.
—— Repaire into Ireland, v. 117.
Scots ioine with the Irish, both encounter the Picts, and are ouerthrowne, vol. v. page 117.
—— All not of one mind, v. 74.
—— Agrée to fight with the Romans, ib.
—— Discomfited, v. 75.
—— Durst not fight with the Romans, submit themselues, v. 74.
—— Deceiued with a counterfet troope of horssemen, fled, v. 198.
—— Honourablie receiued of Carolus the French king, v. 189.
—— Raise the wall of Abercorne, v. 131.
—— They and Picts put in feare of the Saxons valiancie, v. 152.
—— Put to flight, ib.
—— Liue in quiet, v. 206.
—— They and Danes ioine battell, v. 215.
—— Their immoderate ioie for victorie maketh them fall out, ib.
—— Consult to elect them a new king, v. 43.
—— Giuen to hunting and hawking, v. 38.
—— Séeke new seats, v. 35.
—— Arriue in Ireland, ib.
—— When they receiued the christian faith, v. 99.
—— How they came to be so called, v. 33.
—— Slanderouslie writ against the English: note, v. 497.
—— They and French retire ouer the water, they burne Glendale enter into England, v. 498, 499.
—— Banished out of England, v. 498.
—— A great disorder in their campe, v. 209.
—— Suddenlie inuaded, ib.
—— Twentie thousand slaine, ib.
—— That went with Lewis the king of France into Aegypt, v. 311.
—— They and Picts inuade the Britains, v. 41.
—— Reuenge iniuries doone vnto them, v. 39.
—— Send for aid into Ireland, ib.
—— Slaine, v. 551.
—— Assure themselues vnto the English, v. 552.
—— They deliuer pledges, v. 555.
—— Assured and yet reuolt, v. 556.
—— Put to flight, ib.
—— Their crueltie, v. 562.
—— They gain by spoile, ib.
—— They inuade England, v. 580.
—— Resisted by the earle of Westmerland, ib.
—— Brake vp their armie, v. 581.
—— Discomfited by the erle of Northumberland, ib.
—— They assaile the English at Swinton, v. 583.
—— Their horssemen flie, v. 584.
—— Footmen slaine, ib.
—— Put to flight at Gordón, ib.
—— Repell their enimies at Bonuill, v. 594.
—— Denie their furtherance to the writing of the annals of Scotland, v. 673.
—— Put to flight besides Brege, ib.
—— Obteine victories in the low countries, v. 687, 709.
—— Inhabit the Ile of Rothsaie, and the maine land of Scotland, make laws and ordinances, liue in peace, v. 37.

Scots discomfited and discomfit, vol v pages 110, 111
—— Their first anointed king, v 285
—— Their ancient sparnesse of diet, v 281.
—— Rob the Pictish borders discomfited, v 104.
—— The line of their kings, v 271
—— They and Picts fight for a greiehound, v 104
—— Determined to warre onelie with incursions, v 196
—— They and Danes one afraid of another, v 259
—— Made sober and able to abide hardnesse their vnquiet nature, v 213
—— Shoot arrows and darts as thick as haile, they are put to flight, v 216
—— Egerlie inuade their enimies, v 219
—— Peace concluded with them, and lands surrendered vnto them, v 220.
—— Ouerthrowe the Britons, ib
—— Their policie to haue taken Yorke, v 221.
—— Their spiced cups for the Danes, v 267.
—— Grant to aid the Britons against the Romans, v 58
—— Ouerthrowne deuoure one another, v 48.
—— Prosperous successe, v 129.
—— They and Picts kill the Romans, v 71
—— Their vsage to burne dead bodies, v 67.
—— Their contribution for a iornie into the holie land, v. 321
—— Shew themselues too malicious in most things which they writ in defamation of K Edward, v. 323
—— Ill used at the French kings hands, v 490
—— Reuiled of their owne people, v 482
—— Inuade the borders of England raise their siege, v. 463
—— Inuade England, v. 135
—— A great slaughter of them, v 366.
—— An armie of them sent into France, v. 412
—— Certeine noble families of Italie and Isubria sprung from them, v. 451.
—— Put to flight slaine and taken prisoners, v. 370.
—— Their writers slander Edward the third verie maliciouslie, v 364.
—— Set vpon the Romans, v 83
—— Giue the Romans notable discomfitures, v. 83, 84
—— Assalt the Romans at aduantage, v 84.
—— They and Picts breake vp their campe, v 83
—— Determined to giue battell to the Romans, v. 81
—— Disaduantaged by reson of their vnfit weapons, v. 82.
—— Slea the Romans in certeine garrisons, v 78.
—— Assemble, ib.
—— Summoned by the Irish, v. 79.
—— Their negligence, v 366.
—— Forced downe a hill, discomfited and slaine, v 405
—— Releeued at point to be ouercome, v. 398
—— Wild, called Caterans, v 102.
Scots their manner to carrie a horne about their necks and whie, vol v page 400.
—— To the number of thirtie thousand inuade England, v. 395
—— Inuade Northumberland, v 394.
—— Redie to help the French and hinder the English, v 382
—— Preparation against them both by sea and land, v 394
—— Discomfited at Falkirke, v 339
—— Euer false to the English, v 227
—— They and the Danes confedered, ib.
—— Ouerthrowne, ib
—— Keepe off the Danes from landing, v 260.
—— Their request to their king for licence to fight, v. 262
—— They win the name of victorie rather than victorie itselfe, ib
—— Though feare are astonished, v. 257
—— Disorderlie rush out to battell and put to flight by the Danes, v 258
—— Discomfited by the English, v 528.
—— Go in procession for raine, v 229
—— Staied from running awaie note, v. 243.
—— Enter further into England than they were accustomed, v 352
—— Inuade England, v 353
—— Whie they vsed saint Andrewes crosse in warfare, v 192
—— Receiue peace, v. 211.
—— Their writers burthen king Edward of England with tyrannie, v 330
—— That were learned command to be resident in Oxford, v 337
—— Slaine to the number of foure thousand, v. 343.
—— Write maliciouslie of king Edward and whie, v. 326
—— Slaine like dogs, v 329
—— Deceiued and intrapped, ib
—— Withdraw to their holds, v 336
—— With king Richard in the holie land, v 302.
—— Restored to their countries, v 122.
—— When they got certeine seats in the Ile of Britaine, ib
—— Make rodes into England, v. 289.
—— Hated of the Picts to the death note, v. 115
—— They and Picts would agree vpon no reasonable conditions of peace, prepare against the Picts, their manner of entring into the lands of the Britaines, v 132
—— Foure thousand slaine, v 139
—— Renew the warre against the Romans, v 93.
—— They are set vpon spoile and wast, ib
—— Made prouisions of vittels aforehand, v 222.
—— ¶ See Bruse, Crueltie, Heirgust, Religion, Romans, Seruilitie, Spaniards, Sweno.
—— Whie so often ouercome of the English, v. 192.

Scots alwaies desirous to shake off the English subiection, haue often made odious attempts so to doo, but in vaine, vol i page 196
—— Enter in league with Charles king of France, and what effect followed, i 205
—— Newlie arriue in Albania, and crowne a second Fergus king, i 195
—— Their king feined himselfe a minstrell and harped before him note dissimulation, i 204
—— Slender shift alledging that their kings homage to the kings of England was for the earldome of Huntington, i 207
—— Driuen out of all the bounds of Britaine by Coell, i 199
—— Their dream that a stone now at Westminster was the same wheron Iacob slept when he fled in Mesopotamia, i 210
—— Thréescore thousand slaine at Fawkirke, i 211
—— Destitute of anie heire to the crowne from Alexander their last king, i 209
—— Palladius accounted their apostle, i. 18
—— Called Scots because they are an obscure nation in the sight of the world, i 10
—— Wild called the Redshanks, or roughfooted Scots & why so called, i 25
—— Mixed of the Scithian and Spanish blood, i 10
—— When they arriued in Britaine out of Ireland, ib
—— They came stealing into Britaine and are no long continuers, i 10
—— Neuer made cōquest in England, i. 11
—— Great crakers, braggers and liers in their histories, ib
—— Properlie the Redshanks and Irish, i 10.
—— First driuen out of England by Maximus, i 11.
—— Dwelt some time in the Ile of Man, i 65
—— Greatlie giuen to withcraft and vnto sorcerie, i 66
—— Vsed to feed on the buttocks of boies and womens paps, i 10
—— ¶ Sée Irish and Picts
—— Had no habitations in Britaine in the time of Honorius the emperour, i 513
—— They and the Picts trouble this Ile, i 541
—— Plague the Britains extremlie, i 511
—— Not once named in Romane writers till about Constantius time note, i 193
—— First comming out of Spaine into Ireland, i 550
—— First comming out of Scithia, ib
—— Descended of Scithians as some thinke, i 503.
—— Inhabited Ireland, ib.
—— Forced to submit themselues to Arthur, i. 575, 576
—— Instructed in the faith, ib
—— Their king hath Cumberland giuen him and holdeth it by homage, i 690
—— Varie about the kéeping of Easter, i 615
—— Receiue an oth to be true to king Edred, i 691.
Scots subdued, and their king forced to deliuer his sonne as hostage to king Adelstan, vol i page 686
—— Vanquished by the Saxons, i. 555
—— Afflicted by the Saxons, i 557.
—— Inuade the Britains in Uortigerns time, i. 554
—— Made the third nation that inhabited Britaine, i 550
—— Hampered for comming into Britaine to giue battell, i 598
—— ¶ Sée Picts
—— Under Bruse inuade and spoile Ireland, vi 246
—— Refuse to be of the Britanes race, vi 237.
—— Liue in friendship with Picts, vi 80
—— They fall out, vi 81
—— They are expelled out of England by the Picts, vi 82.
—— They make title to Ireland, ib
—— Their king landeth at Caerfergus, vi 218
—— They are slaine, ib
—— They are vanquished, vi 151
—— They disguise with Onele and kill him, vi 237.
Scotish king ¶ Sée King, v 190
Scotsgilmore, v 100
Scripture abused. note, iv 250
Scroope lord by king Richard the thirds commission kept a session against diuerse indicted of high treason, iii 421
Scroope William the kings vicechamberlaine bought the Ile of Man and the crowne thereof, i 66.
Scroope lord ambassador in Scotland, v 423
———— Ended the controuersie betwixt Moorton and Iohnstone, v 712
Scroope lord deputie to Thomas of Lancaster, vi 260.
———— Exclamed for his extortion, ib
———— His wife procureth his amendment, ib
———— He inuadeth vpon Macmorough, ib
———— He returneth into England, vi 261
Sea decreaseth, ii 64
—— Ouerflowne and doing much hurt by breaking into the land, ii 601, iii 32
—— With huge tides that did much hurt, ii 380
—— Séemeth to burne note, ii. 419, 420
—— Riseth higher than the naturall course gaue, ii. 422
—— Ceased from ebbing and flowing thrée moneths, ii 113
—— Riseth with verie high tides, ii 435
—— Extraordinarie, ii 351
Seafaring men and of certeine orders to be obserued amongst them, ii 213.
Seas tempestuous about the Orchades, and whie, i. 71
Sebastian Cabato his voiage, iii 1063.
———— His discouerie of an Iland of rich commodities, iii. 520
———— Bringeth strange men from the new found Ilands, iii 528
Sebbi king of Eastsaxons a profest monke, i 630.

Sebert king of the Eastsaxons conuerted to the faith and baptised, vol i page 602.
Secrets disclosed, iii 4
——— Not to be discouered note, ii 517.
——— Of princes disclosed by a craftie knaue, iii. 568
Seculum ¶ Sée Acuum.
Sedition, i 644.
——— ¶ Sée Discord and Warres
——— To what issue it commeth, iii. 523
——— Sowers thereof taken conuicted and executed, iii 517
——— Condemned by ancient lawes made two hundred yéeres ago, ib
——— Some condemned and yet spared from execution, and whie, ib
——— The mischéefe springing from the same, iii 1010
——— Punished by imprisonment, and confiscation, ii 761.
——— Sowen by a seditious préest and counterfet earle of Warwike, iii 484
——— How gréeuous vnto a commonwealth, discoursed by sir Iohn Cheeke knight, iii 988, to 1010
——— Note well it is woorth the reading ¶ Sée Books Counsell and Letters.
Segburga quéene of the Westsaxons hir gouernment, i 629
——— Wife of Excombeit, i 617.
Seginus duke of the Allobrogs, i 452
Seians horsse, i. 655
Seimors descent supposed to be from Edulph de Samo a noble man of Britaine, i 202
Segraue lord in armes against the Scots, taken wounded and rescued, ii 536
Selbie sir Walter knight beheaded by the Scots, v. 383
Sele common granted vnto the Londoners, ii 359.
——— Roiall old made void, and a new confirmed, ii 360
——— Newlie made, ii. 478.
——— And the old with all things called therewith annulled, ii 252
Selfe will cause rebellion, vi 383
Selred king of Eastsaxons, i 641
——— Slaine, i 649
Selim prince of Turkes his ambition and tyrannie against his father and affines, he ouerthroweth the Sophie of Persia, iii 628.
——— Deceaseth and Soliman dooth succéed, iii 631
——— ¶ Sée Saracens.
Selling and buieng of men like oxen and kine, ii 52
Semiramis ouercometh Staurobates to his losse, i 7
Semple lord taken, v 647
Semor knight sent vnto the Tower, atteinted and beheaded, iii 906
Sempringham William deceaseth, ii 196.
Sencler Oliuer goeth with the king, v 527
——— Enuied of the lords, v. 528.
Sencler bishop of S Andrews goeth into France, vol v page 614
Seneca ¶ Sée Guenera
Seneshall of Imokellie Fitzedmunds entred into Youghall, vi 425.
——— A principall with Iames Fitzmoris, vi 365
——— His castell of Balie martyr beseiged and taken, ib
——— He stealeth secretlie awaie by night, ib
——— He lieth in wait for capteine Ralegh, vi 441
——— His cowardlienes, ib
——— He is challenged to the fight and refuseth, ib
——— He praieth vpon Lisemore, vi 442.
——— He and the lord Barrie at variance, vi 445
——— A spoill made on him by capteine Dowdall, vi 445
Sens besieged and taken, iii 120
Sentleger sir Anthonie sent into England, vi 308
——— His gouernement there and reuocation, v 323
——— Is sent back lord deputie the second time, vi 324, 325
——— Is lord deputie the third time, vi 325
——— Is lord deputie the fourth time, vi. 313
——— He sendeth an armie to Bullein, vi 315
——— He sendeth aid to the lord Leneux, ib
——— A quarrell betwéene him and the earle of Ormond, vi 317
——— They are both sent for into England, ib
——— They are reconciled, ib
——— He returneth lord deputie, vi 320
Sentleger Warham made prouost marshall of Ireland, vi 421
——— Is one of the priuie counsell, vi 456
Sentlone knight sent into the Towre, iv. 123
Septimus Seuerus, v. 95
Sequestration of benifices. note a shift to get monie, ii 333
Serle maior of London in a roit, not estéemed nor regarded, ii 352
Serle one of king Richard the second his chamber, noiseth abrode that king Richard is aliue he is apprehended examined for the duke of Glocesters death, drawne through euerie good towne, executed at London, iii 29, 30
Sermon of George Closse at Paules crosse offensiue, for the which he was inioined submission. note, iv. 889
——— Of Stephan Gardiner note, iv. 73
——— Of frier Pateshall, ii. 780.

Sermon of Ball a seditious priest vnto certeine rebels, vol ii page 749
——— Of the bishop of Rochester at king Richard the second his coronation, ii 715
——— Full of slander against king Edward the fourth note, iii 389
——— That turned the preacher to shame and losse of life, iii 390.
——— Undiscreet and seditious, iii 619.
——— Inuectiue against bishop Gardiner, and the preacher asketh forgiuenesse, iii 815
——— In Paules church, for victorie against the Turkes, iv 262.
——— The assemblie thereat, ib
——— Made by Iohn Knewstubs, at Utrecht in the low countries in a statelie assemblie, iv 238
——— Of doctor Ridleie before king Edward the sixt what effects it wrought touching charitie, &c. note, iii 1060
——— That procured rigorous handling to the preacher note, iv 2, 3
——— At Paules crosse where the people were persuaded vnto the title of quéene Iane, iii 1070
——— At the Spittle without Bishopsgate, and house of the maior and aldermen by whome built, iii 345
——— Full of papisticall adulation made at pope Gregorie the thirteenth his buriall, iv 591 to 596
——— ¶ Sée Oration, Preacher, Shaw, Submission
——— At Paules crosse and the pulpit when first ordeined and builded, i. 236.
Sermons ordinarie in cathedrall churches, i 227
——— Perpetuallie founded at Norwich, iv 238
——— At Paules crosse none for the space of a quarter of a yeare note, iv 180
——— Made to and for the marriage of king Henrie the eight with quéene Katharine, iii 775
——— That brought the preacher vnto losse of credit honestie and life note, iii 386
Serpents none venomous in Ireland, vi 9.
——— They die being brought thither, ib.
——— They are killed with the water and earth of that land, vi 10, 11
——— Whie there be none there, vi. 10.
Serred ¶ Sée Seward.
Seruant constant and trustie, ii 857
——— Trustie and loial vnto the ladie Elizabeth, iv 136
——— Murthering his maister is hanged, iv 237.
——— Accuseth his maister and commeth vnto an ill end himselfe note, iii 210
——— Betraieth his maister for reward note, iii 117, 418
——— ¶ Sée Banister
Seruants wages rated by statute note, i 652.
——— Louing their maisters, i. 650.
Seruice old remembered, ii 350
——— Good in war vnrewarded bréedeth conspiracie note, 36
——— Well thought of and sought for by yoong gentlemen, v 381
Seruice in the vulgar toong offensiue to the popes, vol v page 232
Seruingman reprooued and reformed note, i 433, 431
——— Noted, i 275
——— Shifters and robbers, i 329
Seruilitie most impudent intruded, &c note, v 134
Seruitude none in England before duke Williams comming in, ii 1
——— Spurned at verie sore, ii 2.
——— Forsaking of natiue countrie preferred before it, ii 9
——— Under the Normans signified vnto the world by outward testimonie, ii 8
Sessions quarterlie, and petie sessions, i 262, 263.
——— ¶ Sée Sicknesse
——— To be kept yearlie, v 165.
Sessment refused to be paid as it was leuied and how punished, iii 846
Sesseford the lard slaine, v. 502
Seton in Deuonshire full of aliens at the conquest of England, &c note, i 101
Seton Alexander capteine of Berwike, v 369.
——— His wiues manlie stomach, ib
——— His sonnes executed, ib
——— Slaine, ib
Seuerus setteth footh towards his enmies, commeth vnto Yorke incountred by his enmies, v 97.
——— Wintereth at Yorke, ib
——— Sickneth, ib
——— Dieth, ib
Seuerus arriueth in Britaine and would be surnamed Britannicus, i 517
——— Reigneth as king, i 515
——— His seuere and cruell comandment, i 518
——— Séeketh the destruction of Albinus, i 515.
——— Slaine by Fulgentius, i. 514.
——— His death, i 518.
——— And manner of funerall after the Romane fashion, i 519
Seuerus coronel of the footmen putteth the Saxons in feare, i. 547.
Seuerus by birth a Romane, but in bloud a Briton, i 300.
——— Finisher of the Picts wall, i 211.
Sewfred ¶ Sée Sighere
Sexbotte bishop of Mercies, i 629.
Sforce duke of Milan by vsurpation, iii 478.
Shaftesburie how called in the Romans time, i. 231.
——— Called mount Paladour, i 416
Shandois lord his false report in the starchamber against ladie Elisabeth, iv 26
——— Deceaseth, iv 322
Shane Onele of Ireland discomfited by the English power, iv 230
——— Mangled and hackt in péeces, iv 231.
Shaw maior of London a proud man and a fauourer of king Richard the third, iii 385, 386.
Shaw doctor his sermon that lost him his honestie and his life note, iii. 386.

Shaw doctor commended by the duke of Buckingham, vol iii page 392
———— He was taught his lesson yer he came into the pulpit, iii 389
Shéene the kings manour burnt, iii 525
Shéepe of England passe all other, i 371.
—— Without horns, ib
—— Wild often hunted but seldom or neuer eaten, i 72
—— As big as our fallow déere, i 71
Shepherd called the holie shepheird, iii 174
Shefféeld lord is lamentablie slaine in the Norfolke rebellion, iii 974
———— Laid to the rebels charge, iii 996
Shellie how he was affectioned to Throckmortons treason, iv 542
—— An actor in the conspiracie of the earle of Northumberland, iv 609
Shenin riuer, vi 162
Shews of disport with Robin Hood, &c before king Henrie the eight, iii 611
—— Of estate on the twelfe night, ii. 613.
—— At iusts at Gréenewich, iii 572
—— Of delight wherein great personages were actors, iii 554, 555
—— Triumphant of proper deuise at the receiuing of the erle of Leicester into the low countries, note well, iv 641 to 652
—— ¶ Sée Pagents, and Sights.
Shift ¶ Sée Police
Shilling currant of Siluer when and by whome first coined, i 367
Ship called great Henrie, i 337
—— Roiall called Henrie grace de Dieu, iii 573
—— The Marie rose drowned through negligence note, iii 848
—— The Barke Agar recouered from the French, iii. 854
—— The Regent burnt, iii 573
—— The Greihound cast awaie, iv 217
—— The great Henrie burnt, iv. 5
Ship séene in the aire, ii 430
Ships well diuided how far they will passe in a wéeke, i 339
—— Of fiue hundred tun, i. 338
—— Old of what burthen, and how ours & theirs differ, i 337
—— Belonging to the quéenes maiestie and her seruice, ib.
—— The northerlie regiōs naile not theirs with iron and whie, i 6
—— The manner of dressing them in old time, ib
—— Wrought of wickers somtimes vsed in Britaine, i 7
—— Made of canes, ib.
—— When first made and prouided in this Iland, i. 338
—— Made of wicker and couered with buffle hides, ib
—— Of Cnute passing for pompe, i 718
—— English spoiled by the French, iv. 204, 205.
Ships of quéene Elisabeth sent foorth vnto the narrow seas, vol. iv. page 233
—— Scowre the narrow seas, iv 321.
—— Their seruice in Ireland, iv. 433
—— Thrée of name wone from the Scots, iii 885
—— Set on fire by the English, iii 905
—— Two of the French kings taken with a prise in them, ii 777, iii 27
—— Of Rie win a good prise, ii 754
—— Of a strange mold and forme driuen on the coasts of England, ii 431
Ships and castels séene in the aire, iv 430
—— ¶ Sée French and Flemish, Thames.
Shipwracke, ii 626, iii 95, v 56, 375, 450
———— Wherein two hundred persons were drowned, ii 725, iv 217
———— Lamentable, ii. 70
———— ¶ Sée noblemen.
Shires fortie in England, i 259
—— By whome first made out, i 257.
—— Some lieng in old parcels, i 260
—— Diuided into lathes, i 258
—— In time of néed haue their leiutenants, i 261
—— The number of their market townes and parishes, i 326
—— Such as send knights and burgesses to the parlement, i 294
—— Thirtéene in Wales, i 259.
—— And shares all one, i 257
—— Or counties in Ireland, vi 3
Shireburne bishoprike diuided into thrée, i 239.
Shirewood forest. ¶ Sée Forest
Shiriffes authoritie and office and the reason of the name, i 261
———— Their turne, i 262
———— Of Shires when instituted, ii 13
———— Of all shires when sent for to the court, ii 783
———— Orders deuise for their appearance and bringing of accounts, ii 439
———— Of London put awaie their officers, iii. 834
———— ¶ Sée London.
Sholts a kind of dogs out of Iseland, i 389.
Shooes long piked forbidden, iii 285
Shoomaker called the cock of Westminster, his gifts to the hospitals, iii. 1063
Shooting in the long bow when it first came into England, ii 26
———— A Decrée for the same to be vsed, v. 450.
Shooters hill and the length of the same, i. 184
Shores wife king Edward the fourth his concubine note, iii 386
———— More sued vnto than all the lords in England, iii 392
———— Spoiled of all that she had, put to open penance, described, iii 384.
Shordich knight his words to the pope and the popes to him, ii 627.

Shrewsburie towne partlie burnt, vol ii page 376
Shrewes Ile in Scotland, i 70
Shrimps in Midwaie as much esteemed as the Westerne smelts, i 90
Sicilius king of Britaine, i 158
——— ¶ See Sisilius
Sibert king of Eastangles christened, i 618, 619
Sicill king of Britaine warreth against the Scots, i 199
——— He and his brother at ciuill discord, ib
Sicknesse called stoope gallant, v 470
——— ¶ See Diet, and Riotousnesse
Sicknesse extreame amongst people in all places, ii 23
——— Strange at Oxford assises whereof iudges &c died note, iv 313
——— Strange in Excester, at a sessions there held like that of Oxford note, iv 868
Sider made of apples, i 286
Sidneie sir Henrie treasuror at warres vi 325
——— Is lord iustice four times, ib
——— Lord deputie, ib
——— And knight of the garter, vi 325, 401
——— Lord president of Wales, vi 326
——— Is honourablie receiued into Ireland, vi 327
——— Taketh his oth, ib.
——— His eloquent oration then, ib
——— Is godcept to Oneile, vi 330
——— His iourneie into Ulster, vi 335
——— He passeth into England, vi 339
——— His comming to the court, ib
——— Returneth into Ireland, vi 340
——— Summoneth a parlement, vi 341.
——— His answer to the speakers oration, vi 342
——— He dubbeth sir Humphrie Gilbert knight, vi 366
——— Returneth into England and is honourablie receiued, vi 371
——— Is lord deputie the third time, vi 371
——— He maketh a iourneie into Ulster, and the same wholie commeth to submission, vi 371, 375
——— He maketh an hosting through the whole land, vi 375
——— He is present at the funeral of sir Peter Carew, vi 378
——— The earle of Essex his letters and garter sent to him, vi 388
——— The malcontents of the English pale repine against the cesse, vi 388, 402
——— He deliuereth the sword to sir William Drurie, vi 399
——— His saiengs at the entring into his ship, ib
——— His parentage and education, vi 400
Sidneie sir Henrie is dubbed knight, vol vi page 400
——— His ambassadors and gouernment, his religion, ib.
——— He tameth Oneile, placeth presidents reformeth the courts, and causeth the statutes to be imprinted and ordereth places for the records, vi 403, 404
——— He repaireth the castle of Dublin he reduceeth the Irish countries into shires, he repaireth sundrie decaied townes, he buildeth the bridge of Athelon, and increaseth the reuenues, vi 403
——— His noble vertues, vi 402, 403.
——— His death and buriall, vi 405.
——— He renewed Strangbows monument, vi 240.
——— He erecteth capteine Randolphs acheiuement, ib
——— Sent ambassador into France, iv 204.
——— The historie of his life and death, iv 869
Sidneie sir Philip knight dead of a wound, right honorablie reported of beyond and on this side the seas note, iv 879
Sidneie ladie, the said knights mother deceaseth, hir godlie end, ib
Sidroc a Danish earle slaine in fight, i 666
Sigbert ¶ See Sigibert
Sigebert ¶ See Sabert and Sibert.
Sigeferd ¶ See Morcad
Sighere gouernor of a part of the Eastsaxons with Sebbi, i 630
——— Confirmed notablie in the faith, i 627
——— King of Eastsaxons renounceeth the faith and imbraceth idolatrie, ib
Sighard ¶ See Sewfred
Sighes strange import an alteration of the state, i. 756.
——— Strange in the aire, i 653
——— In the aire fearfull and strange ii 433, 677, 829, iv 313, 430, 431
——— Of fierie impressions in the aire, iv 228, 326, 329, 363, 364
——— Out of the earth, ii 379, 380
——— ¶ See Moone, Pageants, Shews, and Wonders
Sigibert king of Eastangles loueth learning, buildeth schooles, resigneth his kingdome & becommeth a moonke, he is slaine, i 619
Sigibert king of Westsaxons cruell at home but a coward abrode, i 645
Sigibert the second receiueth the faith, i. 621
——— Murthered by two of his owne kinsmen, ib.
Signes of ill lucke, i 648
——— ¶ See Tokens
Silcester how called in the Romans time, i 320
Sill in Ilands then number and difference in greatnesse, i 59
Siluer mines found in Deuonshire, ii 545
——— Not wanting in England, i 398.

Siluer mines how produced and engendred, vol i page 398
Siluer quicke its nature, vi 396.
Silken Thomas, vi 292
Silures inhabited in the South Wales or néere vnto vnto the Welsh marches, i 488
——— Whie so wetted and eger against the Romans i 491
——— Mistaken for Scotishmen, v. 76
Simnell the counterfiet earle of Warwike, iii 484.
——— He is honorablie receiued into Ireland, iii 485
——— Proclamed king of England, iii 486
——— He with all his adherents landeth in England, iii 487
———He is taken, pardoned, and in place of homelie seruice vnder Henrie the seuenth, iii 488
Simon a fraudulent and seditious préest, iii 484
Simon Zelotes ¶ Sée Ioseph of Arimathia.
Simonie wherein note Anselmes opinion, ii 40
——— A practise in William Rufus his time, ib
——— A thousand pounds for a bishoprike, ib
——— Greatlie abhorred by an archbishop of Canturburie note, ii 368
——— ¶ Sée Abbasies and Bishoprikes
——— Practised to obteine a bishoprike, i 231.
Simples thrée hũdred in a little garden of little aboue thrée hundred foot of ground, i. 353.
——— ¶ Sée Gardens.
Simplicitie abused, iii. 1026
——— Of king Constantius abused by Uortigerne, i 552
Singing brought into churches, i 626
Sinne cause of all ouerthrows, vi 222
——— Being neuer so great, want no excuse, vi 214.
Sinnes abominable of the Britains the cause of their scourging by the Saxons, i 536.
Siricus, archbishop of Canturburie, i 705,
Sisallius the fiftéenth ruler of Britaine, i 449
Sisters thrée being thrée riuers, i 117
Sisters seuen being seuen springs in a hill, i 113
Sithrike king of Northumberland, i 678.
Sitomagus a citie in England, i. 319
Siwald earle of Northumberland, v. 269, 276
——— Dieth note, i 750.
Siward duke of Northumberland, ii 8
Six articles sued for to be renewed, iii 919
——— ¶ Sée Statute
Skeuington sir William lord deputie, vi 284
——— He is verie honourablie receiued, ib
——— His answer to the recorders oration, ib.
——— He recordeth the sword, vi 285.
——— His falling out with the earle of Kildare, ib
——— He passeth into England and returneth lord deputie the second time, vi. 285, 299.
Skeuington sir William besiegeth the castle of Mainouth, vol vi. page 299
——— His rewarding of Péeis the traitour, his death, vi 302.
Skie the greatest Ile about Scotland, i 71.
¶ Sée Ile & Ilãds
Skinks valourous seruice against the Spaniards, iv. 653
——— Taketh the towne of Wulk, iv 650
——— Where he burned it, ib.
——— Knighted, iv. 659
——— His good seruice against the enimie, ib
Skipton castell by whome founded and finished, i. 56
Skipwith Richard ¶ Sée Iusts Triumphant
Skirmish at Kilka, vi 45.
——— At Halidon hill, v 535
Skirmishes about Edenburgh, v 661.
Skringeour a surname note, v 287
Slander that went of king Richard for the death of the marquesse of Montferrat, ii 235
——— Against king Edward the fourth confirmed note, iii 392
——— ¶ Sée Sermon.
——— Preuented, i 943
Slanders deuised by malicious heads against quéene Elisabeth. ¶ Sée Books, Seditious Libell and Quéene Elisabeth
Slate of sundrie colours, i 395
Slaues none in England, i 275.
Slaughter of fiue or six people by the fall of a wall, iv 620
——— Of eight persons by the fall of a scaffold at Paris garden, iv 504
Sléepe of fourtéene daies and as manie nights, iii. 854
Slouth engendereth lechrie, i 445.
Sloworme described, i 383
Smith Thomas esquier and customer, a good commonweatlh man: note, iv. 852.
Smith doctor his recantation, iii 867
Smith embroderer ¶ Sée Charitie.
Smithfield sometimes a common laistall and place of execution, ii 52
——— And to that vse euer since oftentimes applied ¶ Sée Arden and Horssestealers
Smithfield in the east giuen by Canutus to certeine knights, i 186
Snake described, i 383
Snow great in April, iv 346
——— In Maie, ii 500
——— And frost verie great, i. 648.
——— Of aboue foure months continuance, i 741.
Snowdone hills verie famous, i 136
Soda salt, i 396
Sodomitrie punished in clergimen and laiemen, ii 52
Sodomie commited, i 445
Soldan king of Soria and Egypt his state, by whose election they were chosen, two of them slaine, and all Soria and Egypt subdued, iii 629
Soldan inuadeth the christians, v. 321.

Soldior valiant aduanced for seruice ¶ Sée Hide
Soldiors rewarded, vol v page 162
——— ¶ Sée Britons Burnll, Keith, Spoile
——— Torren inue to aid king Iohn against his barons, ii 321
——— Set altogither vpon the spoile, ii 333.
——— Of certaine ordinances deuised by them to be obserued, ii 217
——— English inriched, iii 495.
——— Trained vp in iournaies, ii 251
——— Make a fraie against the lord maior of London, iii 227
——— Commended with words and rewarded with spoiles, iii 91
——— English haue new cotes bestowed vpon them by the duchesse of Sauoie, iii 565
——— Their vnrulie and drunken behauiour noted, iii 562, 563
——— Their misbehauiour against the L. admerall, iii 571
——— Of Tornaie, reward of Henrie the eight, iii 636
——— Euill vnder a good capteine, iii 801
——— Slaie their capteine, ii 16
——— Their wages borne by the lords and péeres of the realme, ii 23
——— How well affected William Rufus was to to them, ii 45.
——— Prest and released for ten shillings or twentie shillings a man note, ii 35
——— Their outrage, a proclamation to restreine it, iv 208
——— Good orders proclamed to be kept amongst them, ib
——— Hanged for reuolting, iv 214, 215
——— Executed for drawing vpon their capteine, iv 218.
——— Transported into Ireland to vanquish Shane Oneile, iv 230, 231.
——— Yoong trained vp in the field at the citie of Londons charge, iv 265
——— Transported into Ireland, iv 432
——— Sent ouer sea to aid the low countries, iv 620
——— To what shifts they fall after decamping, iii 1002
——— Reteined on all sides by king Richard the second against the lords, ii 783, 784.
——— Hardie of préests and religious men, ii 759
——— A great abuse in the choice of them, ii 778.
——— Called the crossed soldiors, ii 757
——— Incouraged by hope of gaine, ii 759
——— Out of wages by means of peace doo much hurt in France, ii 677.
——— Defrauded of their wages and the partie executed as a traitor, ii 704.
——— Of the French in a poore estate note, ii 344
——— Do much hurt, they spoile Westminster, they are sacked and are throwne into the Thames, ii. 172
Soldiors then paie a thing preferred before race of men, vol ii page 390
——— ¶ Sée Aduentures, Law, Marshall, Mutinie.
——— Of Aulus Plautius, disordered, i 481
——— Of Briton valourous, i 540
——— Péerlesse, i 538
——— Like not laws to keepe them in order, i 515
——— Against their capteine, i 502
——— Are of thrée degrées, vi 129, 130.
——— Kept in decipline, vi 371
Soliman Ottoman beseigeth and taketh Rhodes, iii 683
——— It is véelded vp vnto him, his contempt of christian religion, iii 683, 684
——— Successor after Selims decease, iii 631
Solitarinesse ¶ Sée Fiacre
Soluathius an impotent man, admitted king of Scotland, v 184
——— Deceaseth, ib.
Somerleid thane of Argile goeth about to make himselfe king, v. 292
——— His crueltie and flight into Ireland, v. 293
——— Returned into Scotland vanquished hanged, v 295
——— Rebelleth, his humble submission, v. 311
Sonchus somewhat like our saffron, i 392
Sonne stood still for the space of a daie, i 265.
Sooch ¶ Sée Zooch
Sophia of Persia ¶ Sée Selim
Sorcerie and inchantment ¶ Sée Coniuror, Elenor Cobham.
Sound most strange and wonderfull heard, ii 390.
Southmercia, i 623
Southāpton hauē described, i. 90.
——— Burned, ii 610
Southwell knight his words touching quéene Maries child yet vnborne, iv 69.
Southwell the archbishop of Yorke his manor, ii. 60
Southwarke in the iurisdiction of an alderman, iii. 1024.
——— Liberties purchased for it, ib.
Southsaxons kingdome what number of families it conteined, i 631.
——— It ceaseth, i 639
——— ¶ Sée Sussex.
Sow a kind of engine so called, v 378
Sowtherland Iohn heire apparent to the crowne his deth, v 388
Spaine a deadlie bane vnto the English soldiors, ii. 771
——— The king thereof his armie vnder the conduct of the duke of Alua and the kingdome of Nauarre ioined vnto his, iii 570.
——— His claime to the empire, iii 638
——— He is chosen gouernor, iii 639
——— Philip of his proclamation against English merchants, iv. 224

Stanclie knight a fauoured of Perkin Warbecke, coniectures of his alienated mind from Henrie the seuenth, vol. iii page 509
——— He is beheaded, ib
——— He and his archers breake the Scots arraie, iii 597
Stanelie lord his deuise to auoid suspicion of king Richard the third and to saue his owne life, iii 135
——— He and others meet embrace and consult, iii 137
——— Setteth the crowne on the earl of Richmond his head, his bold answer to king Richard, his purseuants, iii 446
——— His faithfulnesse, iii 293.
Sanesmore, i 501.
Stanlie sir Edward knight his valiantnes against the Scots, v 481
Stanlie sir William he lieth at Adar, vi 420
——— His good seruice, ib
Stanlie sir Thomas his good seruice, vi 267
Stanihurst speaker of the parlement, vi 311
——— His oration, ib
——— His request, vi 312
Stanton Richard gaoler of Newgate, vi 297.
——— A good sailor and his seruice, ib
Staple of woolles remoued to Calis, ii 678.
——— Out of Flanders into England, ii 653
Staples bishop of Meth landeth at Dublin, vi. 284
——— His question of the Dublians, vi. 285.
——— He was fullie answered, ib
Starre honoring how hatched at the first, i 38
——— In the constellation of Cassiopeia, iii 320.
——— Bright appéering in the skie, v 466
Starrs falling after a strange manner, ii 386
——— Séene at the verie time of an eclipse, ii 75
——— ¶ Sée Blasing Starre
Starch ¶ Sée Wheat.
States of the low countries, then deputies annuall in London, their message vnto quéene Elisabeth, iv 616, 617, 618
——— Their sute granted: note, iv 620 to 630
——— Sworne vnto the quéene of England, and what authoritie the gaue the earle of Leicester by placard, iv. 647, 648, 649
——— ¶ Sée Quéene Elisabeth, Duke of Alanson and Earle of Leicester
Statute of the six articles with the extreame proceedings therein, iii 808
——— Spoken against to the losse of life, iii 820
——— Repealed, iii 869
——— Described, iii 922.
——— Ex officio remued, iv 74
——— Of premunire begun, ii 701
——— Of Mortmaine, ii 182
Statutes of Wesminster ordeined, ii 179.
——— Established, ii 492
——— Of Glocester, ii 482
——— Called Additamenta, ii 488
——— Of quo warranto, ii 483
——— Of Eltham, iii 711
——— Of Oxford note, ii 452
——— Protested against by Henrie the third, ii 458.
Statutes penall not executed, vol 5. page 357
——— Repealed, ii 467
——— Of Kilkennie confirmed, vi 263
——— They are imprinted, vi. 102
——— ¶ Sée Lawes, Apparell
Staues ¶ Sée Weapons
Staurobates, his ships of canes wherein he fought against Semiramis, i 7
Stéele, i 400
Stéeples in France how manie, i. 234
Stephan king of England licenced his barons to build castels, but with repentance, i 237
——— Ill dealt withall of his clergie, i 225
Stephan when and by whome he was crowned king, ii 79.
——— His valiantnes, ii 91
——— Ordering of his armie redie to giue battell, ii 88.
——— Besiegeth Wallingford, ib.
——— Winneth Lincolne, ib
——— His power put to flight, ii 90, 91.
——— Taken prisoner and led vnto Mawd the empresse, ii 91
——— He and the earl of Glocester deliuered vp by exchange, ii 93
——— Entreth Lincolne with a crowne vpon his head, ii 97
——— With an armie runneth to Yorke, ii 99
——— Encampeth néere his enimies the Scots, ii 80.
——— Agréeth with the earle of Aniou, ii 82
——— Inuadeth Scotland, ib
——— Maketh haste to rescue the north parts, ib
——— Burnt the south part of Scotland, ib.
——— Hée and Henrie the fourth meet at Dunstable about a peace, they come to Canturburie, ii. 109.
——— His promise to purchase the peoples fauour, ii 13.
——— Doubted whome to trust, ii 87.
——— Raiseth his séege, ib
——— Beginneth to incline his mind vnto peace, ii 101
——— Falleth sicke, ii 81.
——— Departeth this life, ii 110
——— A discription of his person qualities and actions, ib
Stephan earle of Britaine, ii 12
——— ¶ Sée Erle
Stephan Gardiner his oration to the councell touching quéene Marie hir mariage, he commendeth the Spanish king, iv 10
——— ¶ Sée Bishop Gardiner
Stephan the king an vsurper, v 289.
——— His repentance, ib
——— Passeth into Roxburgh, returneth into Kent, v 290
Stephan de long Espe lord iustice, vi 239
——— He killeth Oneile, ib
——— He dieth, ib
Sepmothers loue, v. 63
Sterbrie a place where an armie hath lien, i 366.
Sterling castle bulded, v 77.

Sterling castle besieged, vol. v. page 730.
Steward Henrie created erle of Methwen, v 507
——— Lord Dernelie commeth into Scotland, v 614.
——— Made earle of Rosse, ib
——— Made duke of Albania, ib.
——— Proclaimed king, ib
——— Buchanans verses of him, v 706
Steward Iames surnamed the black knight banished, v 434.
Steward Iames made erle of Murreie, v. 611
——— Created earle of Arrane, v 705
——— His marriage, v 731
Steward Iohn admitted to the crowne, v. 401
——— Prisoner, put to death, v 432
Steward Mordo gouernor of Scotland, repugnant vices in him, v 414.
Steward Robert created earle of Leneux, v 687.
——— Made earle of Mar, v 692
Steward Robert disinherited of the crowne, v 388
——— Ordeined againe heire apparent, ib
——— Crowned king, v 390
Steward Walter put in prison, v 419
Steward erle of Atholl sent into the north parts, v 376.
Steward lord of Obegneie made erle of Leneux, v 692.
Stewards their descent, v 265.
——— First comming to the crowne of Scotland, v. 300
——— Kings of Scotland neuer of full age when they come to the crowne, v 630
Stiermarke. See Ualeria
Stigand archbishop of Canturburie by intrusion, i. 747
——— Made but a iest at K Edwards propheticall speeches, i. 751
——— Canturburie hated and whie duke William refused to be crowned at his hands, ii 2
——— His stout message vnto duke William, ii 3.
——— Flieth into Scotland, ii. 13
——— His martiall mind vnpatient of seruitude, ii 2
——— Capteine of an armie of Kentishmen, ib
——— Depriued for three speciall causes, ii 14
——— Kept in perpetuall prison and there ended his life, ib
Stilico the sonne in law to Honorius, his acts and deeds in Britaine, i 549
Stinke noisome after a thunder note, ii. 353
——— Filthie after a tempest, ii 365
——— Most horrible in Winchecomb church, ii 32
——— Of Henrie the first his dead bodie odious, ii 76
Stockfish is light loding saie the Hollanders or Hulmen, i 393
Stoke battell ¶ See Battell.
Stone that had verie sweet sauouring oile in it, vol. i page 396
——— Regall of Scotland, now in Westminster abbeie and called Iacobs stone, i 210.
——— Huge at Pemberin Gulthene parish, i 218.
——— Specular vsed before glasse was known, i. 316
——— Ueric great how moueable and how vnmoueable, i 219
——— Pretious how to be tried, i 402
——— Vsed and dedicated in times past to building of churches, i 394
——— ¶ Sée Quarries
Stones vpon Salisburie plaine to be wondered at, i. 217
——— Found vpon certein hils in Glocestershire note, i 102.
——— Throwne a defense against the enimie, i 7
——— Found in the heads of certeine fishes, i 102
——— Pretious, i 401
——— Taken out of oisters, toads, muskels, &c. i 402
——— With verie strange things found in them, i 396.
——— Including graines of gold, ib
——— Fashioned like cockles and mightie oisters, i 218
——— Of sundrie sorts, and not of common kinds where dailie found, i. 362
Stonie hil in Scotia, and whie so named, v. 310.
Stoniheng on Salisburie plaine whie so called, i. 565.
——— Called Chorea gigantum, i 571
Stoope gallant, v 170
Storie doctor impudent and sawsie his words in the parlement house, iv 177
——— An enimie vnto ladie Elizabeth, iv 136
——— Executed for treason, his education and birth, a persecutor and exquisite tormentor of Gods seruants, apprehended, conueied himselfe ouer seas, continuing their a persecutor, a commissioner to search for English bookes, intended the ouerthrowe of England, searched the English ships, apprehended by a wile, conueied into England indicted arreigned executed as a traitor note, &c iv 259, 260
Storke, i 141
Stradiotes, iii 585
——— Described and encountred of the English horssemen, iii 582
Strange and wonderfull things in Ireland, vi 37
Strange le Thomas placed in castle Balirogh, vi 38?
——— He is besieged and his good seruice, ib
——— He is knighted and of the counsell, vi 436
Strangers sufered to vse our priuileges and commodities in England, &c which we may not doo in their countries, i 194.
——— Teach Englishmen diuerse vile vices, i 694.

Strangers suspected of the Britons for their multitudes, vol i page 557
——— Ought not to quarrell in forien countries, i 743
——— Resort to king Stephan, ii 80.
——— Courtouslie prouided for by king Henries intertéinment, ii 58
——— Outface Englishmen against all honestie and conscience, iii 615
——— Iniuriouslie abused of certeine yoonkers note, iii 620
——— Appointed to depart the realme, ii. 111.
——— Greatlie grudged at for procuring licences to sell woad, iii 713
——— Ouer sawcie lewd and knauish in dealing with Englishmen, iii 620
——— Skirmish with the rebels of Norwich, iii 972
——— Went against the Deuonshire rebels, iii 919
——— Resisted by king Richard the secõd and so dooth the duke of Lancaster, ii 811
——— Sent for by king Henrie the third to serue him in his wars, ii 374
——— A great complaint exhibited for that they got the best benefices, ii 626
——— In fauour with king Richard the third, alwaies odious vnto the homeborne, ii 374
——— Valuation of their benefices taken, ii 408
——— The value of spirituall liuings in their hands, ii 427
——— Kéepe the castell of Windsor, ii 408
——— Merchants a new order for them, sent to the towne, i 189
——— ¶ Sée Proclamation
Strangbowe earle of Chepstone, vi 125
——— Promeseth aid to Mac Morough, and to Marie his daughter, ib
——— Is sent for into Ireland, vi 140.
——— He with the good leaue of the king arriueth into Waterford, vi 141, 145
——— He moueth Iua the daughter and heire to Mac Morough, vi 146
——— He marcheth to Dublin and taketh it, vi 147
——— The king proclameth against him, vi 148
——— He sendeth Reimond to the king with his submission, vi. 149
——— The description of him, vi 157.
——— He returneth into England, vi 158
——— He hath peace with the king, ib
——— He dieth, vi 183
——— His sepulchre is in Dublin, vi 240.
Stratagem of the lord Montioie, iii 816.
——— ¶ Sée Policie
Stratagems at Ardath and Lestoile, vi 147.
Stratford bridge vpon Auon builded, iii 505
Streame that fall into the sea betwéene the Thames and the mouth of Seuerne, i 91
Streame ¶ Sée Riuers.
Strenwold a valiant man slaine, vol i. page 705
Strife for the leading of a vantgard, v 339
——— Betwixt Mowbraie and Beaumont, v 371.
——— Godlie and commendable, v 281.
——— ¶ Sée Contention
——— About a dog, vi 81
——— Among the English subiects on the other side the sea, ii 273
——— It and emulation in sumptuous apparelling of seruants, ii 262
——— Betwixt the two archbishops, ii 246
——— Betwixt the laitie and the spiritualitie, iii 30
——— Betwixt the Londoners and the abbat of Westminster, ii 410
——— Betwixt king Henrie the third and his barons, ii 376
——— Betwéene the archbishop of Canturburie and the bishop of Winchester, ii 427
——— One ended, all ended note, iii 145
——— ¶ See Quarrell and Uariance
Striueling burned, v 439
——— ¶ Sée Sterling
Stues suppressed, iii. 854.
Stukelie a defamed person and faithless beast note, iv 516.
Stukelie Thomas in great fauor with the pope, vi. 398.
——— Suspected to come to Ireland, ib
——— Great preparation against him, ib
——— His titles of honor giuen by the pope, ib
Sturbridge faire the most famous mart in England, i 174
Sture riuer whereof Sturbridge faire had his name, i 174
——— Parteth Essex from Suffolke, i 177
——— By Ptolomie called Edomania, ib
——— With his six heads described, i 98
——— With what kind of fishes it aboundeth, i 99
Sturgeon great plentie in Medwaie riuer in times past, i. 90
——— Taken in Rochester water and giuen to the quéene, i 115
Sturton baronie whense it taketh the name, i 98
——— What the lord giueth in his armes, ib
Sturton lord commiteth a shamfull murther, hée is hanged, iv 86
Subdeacons admission not without professions of chastitie, ii 51
Subiéction most vile and vnseeming a king note, ii. 113
——— Forren how abhorred of a valorous mind, note, ii 332
——— Of Yorke vnto the archbish of Canturburie,
——— ¶ See Archbishop
——— Makes kings know themselues, i. 460.

Subiection of Britaine to the Romans when it was, vol i page 477
Subiects bridle their king to their great impatience, ii. 322
Submission of the Londoners to Henrie the third, ii 467
——— Of Dauid of Wales to Henrie the third, conteined in articles, ii. 393.
——— Of the duke of Yorke to king Henrie the sixt vnder his oth, iii 234
——— Of king Iohn to the pope testified in a charter, iii. 307
——— Purchaseth peace and pardon, ii 350
——— By constreint, ii 290, 322
——— Of George Closse Preacher ¶ Sée Sermon.
——— Of gentlemen, v. 281
Subsidie demanded and denied, ii 372, 433
——— To king Henrie the third by his brother the earle of Cornewall, ii 134.
——— Of the richer sort, ii 407
——— Causeth a commotion and insurrection in the realme note, ii 735
——— Granted by the parlement appointed to be kept of two citizens of London, ii 717
——— For the staie of parlements, ii 126
——— Grieeuous causing manie a bitter curse and much mischéefe, ii 734
——— To be paid by the great men and fat backs but the poore to go frée, ii 722
——— Granted, and appointed to be spent according to the diseretion of the nobilitie, ii 774.
——— Of surcharge, iii. 27, 28.
——— Pardoned, iv. 5
——— Of the laitie, iv 81.
——— Uerie sore and intolerable laid vpon his subiects by William Rufus, ii 37
——— Called the great note, iii 513, 514
——— To be paid by anticipation, iii 693.
——— Granted to be paid in thrée yeares note, iii 832
——— Raised by king Henrie the first to bestowe with his daughters, ii 61
——— Granted of euerie knights fée and clergie, ii 289
——— The collectors thereof complaine to the earle of Northumberland, that they cannot get it note, iii 492
——— Raised of wools, ii 501
——— Called chimmage, ii. 687.
——— Of fuage for the space of fiue yeares, ii 686
——— Dissuaded, ii. 687.
——— Of wooll, ii 609
——— Of tunnage and poundage, iii 144
——— Of three shillings for euerie plowland, ii 279.
——— Of the thirtieth part of all moueable goods granted vpon condition, ii 380.
——— Of the fortieth part of euerie mans goods towards the discharge of the kings debt, ii 372
——— Of two shillings of euerie plowland, ii. 379.
Subsidie of the ninth part the peoples goods granted to king Edward the first, vol. ii page 527
——— Of the eight part of the peoples goods granted, ii 519
——— Of the twentieth part of euerie mans goods ii 182
——— Of four pense and fiue pense out of euerie marke, ii 570
——— Of the one half of wools through the realme, ii 607
——— Of fiftie thousand pounds demand of the clergie, ii 696
——— Of fiftie shillings of euerie sacke of wool transportable ouer the sea, ii 657
——— Of four pence of euerie person aboue fortie years of age, ii 703
——— Of six and twentie shillings eight pense of euerie sacke of wooll &c ii 678.
——— For euerie last of lether fortie shillings, ii 613
——— Of a new kind granted by the clergie, iii. 40
——— Of the moietie of a tenth and a fiteenth, ii 762
——— Of twentie shillings of euerie knights fee, iii 27.
——— Of six shillings in the pound, iv 257
——— Of moueables and vnmoueables granted, iv. 184
——— Of six shillings in the pound granted of the spiritualtie, iii 762
——— Of the sixt parts of euerie mans goods demanded and what cursing and rebellion followed, iii 709
——— Of two shillings of euerie plowland, ii. 247
——— Of fiue shillings of euerie hide land, ii. 265.
——— Called the great subsidie about the grant thereof there was hard hold, iii 685
——— An enimie to them was bishop Hugh of Lincolne, ii 231
——— Of sundrie sorts repeated, ii 396.
——— Greater imposed vpō the clergie than the laietie, i 230.
——— ¶ Sée Contribution, Custome, Fiftéenth, and Rebellion
Subtiltie of Uortigerne to conceale his treason, i 552
Succession ¶ See Crowne
Succession to the crowne consulted vpon to be diuerted note, iii. 1064.
Sudburie hill, iii 317.
Suebhard ¶ Sée Nidred.
Suetonius lieutenant of Britaine inuadeth Anglesea, i 494.
——— Encourageth his bands against Uoadocia and his Britains, i 501.
——— Supplied with fresh forces setteth vpon the Britains, i 500.
——— Thinking vpon safetie withdraweth himselfe and his forces, i 499

Suetonius by hart grudge thrust at to lose his dignitie, vol i page 501
——— Inuadeth Anglesey, v 71
Suffolke what hauens it hath, i 182
Suffolke men the first that resorted to the ladie Marie against the duke of Northumberland, iii 1069
Sundbelme king of Estsaxons christened, i 622.
Sullomaca ¶ Sée Barnet
Sulphur, i 397
——— It and quicksiluer father and mother to all metals, i 398.
Summer drie extreme, ii 577
——— For the space of foure moneths, ii 380
——— From March untill Julie, ii 653.
——— Wet with manie floods, ii 378
——— Dear, ii 653
Summerset ¶ Sée Herald and Duke.
Summerset place, i 329
——— ¶ Sée Duke
Summersetshire and Glocestershire parted asunder by Swinford riuer, i 116.
——— Cold baths there, i 360.
Summeruile ¶ Sée Traitor
Sun appeareth like bloud, ii 570, 571.
——— Counterfeit séene, ii 580
——— Eclipsed excedinglie, i 643.
——— Lost his light in the dayes of Athelstane, i. 101.
Suns two appeared, ii 272
——— Thrée séene at once, iii 535
——— Four beside the accustomed, ii 374
Sundaie profaned, i 359.
——— By paltrie faires, i 411
——— And how punished by God. note, iv 504
——— Buieng and selling a law against it, iii 205
Superintendents and ministers how to be elected, v 605.
Superstition of some foolish countrie folks when their cattel die of the garget, i. 185.
——— ¶ Sée Religion
Supremacy of Henrie the eight and the parties executed, iii 792, 815, 819, 831
——— ¶ See Pope, Traitor
Sure the riuer, vi 161
Surfetting the cause of strange diseases, v. 51
——— ¶ Sée Riot
Surgerie lecture founded in London and how to be exercised note, iv 197, 499
——— An excellent institution and for common benefit note, iv 531
Surrender made to a use, v 304, 305
Suspension of the archbishop of Yorke by the archbishop of Canturburie, ii 60, 61.
——— Of Ranulfe bishop of Chichester note, ii 43
——— Pronounced by a legat in a synod holden at Paules, ii 468
Suspicion in a prince how mischiefous, iii 407
——— Sometimes good and aduantagable, iii 1075
——— Cause of apprehension and execution note, ii 448, 449
Suspicion of Henrie the eight grounded vpon a guiltie conscience note, vol iii. page 20
——— That he had in his son prince Henrie, iii. 53
——— Sometimes necessarie, i 560
——— Caused by great power, v 142
——— For murther and the parties racked, v. 183
——— ¶ Sée Enuie and Mistrust
Sussex separated from Kent by the riuer of Rother, i 92
——— A kingdome vnder Ella the Saxon, i 29
——— What hauens it hath, i 182
——— And Essex receiue the christian faith, v. 169
Sussex of Southsex with the beginning of the Southsexons kingdoms, i 567
——— Embraces the faith, i 631
——— Afflicted with famine for lack of raine, ib
——— ¶ See Erle, Southsex, and Southsaxons
Sutherie whie so called, i 79.
Sutors what shifts they made to be heard, iii 545
Swaine arriuing at Sandwich spoileth all the countrie neer the sea side, i 710
——— Reputed full king of England, handleth the people hardlie, i 716.
——— Conquereth the greater part of England, ib.
——— King of Denmarke taketh Norwaie, and spoileth it, i 710
——— Prepareth a fresh armie to inuade England, i 711
——— Erle Goodwins son, banished, his lewd life, i 741.
——— He rebelleth against his father Goodwin, his miserable end going on pilgrimage, i 746
——— His end and death, ib.
Swale riuer the bound in some place betwéene Richmondshire and Westmorland, i, 159
Swanecombe in Kent where the Kentishmen met against duke William, ii 2
Swand ¶ Sée Martine
Swearing of fealtie first begun, v 53
Sweine king of Denmarke married erle Goodwins widow, ii. 10
——— Reported to intend an inuasion of England, ii 23
——— Sendeth his sonnes into England for recouerie of his right, ii 10.
Sweting sicknesse, iii 536
——— The manner thereof, iii 482
——— The remedie therefore, ib
——— Speedie and deadlie, iii 626.
——— Whereof died both mariners and others, iii 735
——— And remedie against it, iii 736.
Sweno king of Denmarke landed in England, conuerted to the christian faith, v. 255
——— His cruel imagination, vnder what conditions he licenced the English to liue in their owne countrie, v 256.

Sweno king of Denmarke prepareth to inuade the Scots, vol. v page 257
—— Prepareth a third time to inuade Scotland, v 262
—— Landeth in Fife, v 266
—— His crueltie, v. 267.
—— His commandement to spare fier and wood, ib
—— Vanquisheth the Scots, ib
—— Beseigeth king Duncane, ib.
—— He with ten others escapeth, ib
Swifts a noisome vermin, i 381
Swimming a practice vsed among the Britons, i 505
Swine in England and how diuerslie their flesh is vsed, i 372.
Swineford riuer, parted Summerset and Glocestershires asunder, i 116
Swithed ¶ Sée Swithred
Swithred king of Eastsaxons expelled, i 619
Swithune bishop of Winchester of king Egberts councell, i 661
Swords two, being two riuers so named, i 102
Synod prouinciall to reforme wants in the church, i 683
—— Holden for the approouing of images, i 640.
—— Held in Augustines time, i 596
—— Held in Hatfield, i 632
—— Held at Herford, i 628
—— Held in Mercia and what was there doone, i 651
—— Called by the archbishop of Canturburie, ii 112
—— Held by Anselme present thereat Henrie the fourth with erls and barons, ii 58
—— At Dunstable, ii 314
—— At Lambeth, ii 481.
—— At London, ii 19, 100, 164, 387.
—— At Northampton, ii 468
—— At Oxford, ii 351.
—— At Reading, ii 183
—— Of bishops held at Westminster, ii 51.
—— At Winchester and what was there decreed, ii. 14
—— At Windsor about the archbishops primacie, ii 15.
—— At Yorke by the archbishop of Canturburie, ii. 256.
—— ¶ See Assemblie and Councell.
Syria Phenices, i. 316.

T.

Tabaco, i 351.
Taberd made of English pearle, i 401
Tacwine archbishop of Canturburie, i 642, 644.
Taffe a citie of countenance, indued with the see cathedrall of a bishop, i 127
—— A swift riuer and violent in Glamorganshire described, ib
Tagus a riuer yéeldeth clots of gold, i 8
Tailors their malapertnesse at the election of an alderman iii 204.
Tailors and the goldsmiths of London togither by the ears, vol ii page 473
—— They had six kings of England brethren of their companie, iii 530
Talbot well learned, vi 65
Talbot knight with his six score archers, iii. 494.
Talbot lord saileth into France, iii 178.
—— A valiant capteine, iii 158
—— Ransomed by exchange, iii 174
—— Created erle of Shrewesburie, iii. 204.
—— ¶ Sée Erle
Talbot Iohn lord Furniual lord deputie, vi 264.
Talbot Richard giuen for an hostage to the rebells, vi 298
Talbot Robert walketh in the suburbs of Kilkennie towne, vi 264.
Talbot Robert (of Belgard) hatefull to the Girandines, is slaine, vi 280
Talbot Thomas is slaine, vi. 259
Talbot William defendeth Hereford in Wales, ii. 83
Tale of a Welshman that slept betwixt two swords with a knife at his hart, i 132.
—— Of quéene Gunnors grave, v 162
—— Of spirits, v 116, 117
Tale tellers, vi 68
Tallage of an eight thousand marks leuied vpon the Iews, ii 135
Tame lord of Tame his gentle hart to the ladie Elisabeth, iv 129
Tame riuer and the course thereof, i 16
—— Diuideth Chestershire & Lancastershire, i 112
Tanners buie oke by the faddam yearelie in Maie, i 357
Tanister his diuision of the daie and the night, i. 606.
Tantallon castell besieged, v 507.
Tapsters ¶ Sée Innes
Taragh hill, vi 39
Tarantula or Neapolitan spider, i 384.
Tartas besieged, iii 197
Taw the finest riuer for water that is in all Scotland, v 150
Tax or tribute leuied on the cōmons by duke William, ii 13
—— Leuied throughout the relme, ii 249
—— Of fiue shillings of euerie plough land, ii. 269
—— Leuied of the thirteenth part of euerie mans goods, ii. 295
—— Leuied of an hundred thousand pounds, ii. 302
Tax yearelie to be leuied, v. 578.
—— Not granted, v 579
—— ¶ Sée Benefices and Tenths
Taxes and subsidies raised in duke Williams time, ii 8
—— Gréeuous of D William vpon the English, ii 13.
—— ¶ Sée Lone, Subsidie, and Toll.

Teemen toll, or Theme toll ¶ Sée Subsidie
Teeth, men borne with fewer than in times past, vol ii page 651
Temse a noble riuer, where the beuer is onelie found, i 131
Tempest great, v 141
——— Prophesied, v 321
——— On sea, i 460
——— Wherein Cesar lost 40 ships, i 472
Tempests that did much hurt, ii 353, 810, 823, iii 793
——— Grislie and hideous, ii 287
——— The like neuer séene procuring peace, ii. 674
——— That made great waste, ii 677
——— That stroke manie high buildings, ii 435
——— Wonderfull, ii 283
——— Most terrible with a stinke, ii 32
——— Of wind and raine verie hideous, ii. 102
——— That did exceeding much hurt note, ii. 439
——— Verie sore, & that lasted sixtéene houres, ii 413
——— Boisterous vpon the seas, iv 93
——— That scattered Richard the first his ships sailing into the Holie land, ii 220, 725
——— Generall, ii 726
——— By sea and land doing harme in most shires of England iv 254, 255, 256, 257
——— Great on Easter daie in the morning, ii. 487
——— Sore of lightening and thunder, &c ii. 78, 141, 399
——— Of raine and thunder with an eclipse note, ii 638
——— Few the like note, ii 422
——— Verie wonderfull note, iv 103.
——— That did much hurt, iv 185
——— In December, ii 450
——— At Chelmesford, iv 229.
——— Great in Leicester towne note, iv 210.
——— Strange at London, ii. 365
——— By lightening and thunder, with sore hurt doore, iv 221
——— In Northfolke strange, vehement and hurtfull note, iv. 495
——— In Richmondshire, iv 343.
——— In Suffolke that did much hurt. note, iv 344
——— ¶ See Wind
Temple gatehouse newlie builded, iii 757
Templers, lands belonging to them, ii 375
——— Three knights of this order in the French kings displeasure, ii 117
——— ¶ See Knights
Temptation great with large offers, iii 424
——— Preuaileth euen to violent death note, iv 9
——— ¶ Sée Murther
Tennincius assisted Cassibelane against Cesar, i 470
Tenancius ¶ Sée Germantus
Tenants rebell against their landlord, the erle of Winchester note, vol ii page 115
Tench is the pikes leach or surgeon note, i 376.
Tenet Ile a refuge for Saxons, i 558
Tenths first deuised by the pope and after taken vp by prescription of the king, i. 230
——— Two granted to the king of England towards the recouerie of Burdeaux, i 229
——— Yearelie paid to the prince in times past not annuall but voluntarie, i 229
——— Of the bishopriks in Englãd to what summes they yearelie amounted, i 245
——— Leuied for Henrie the seconds behoofe, ii. 193
——— Thrée granted, ii 689.
——— Of spirituall mens liuings for the space of thrée yeares, ii 693
——— For three years space granted of the clergie vnto Henrie the third, ii 428.
——— Granted vnto king Henrie by the cleargie, ii. 367
——— Of the spiritualtie granted to the pope, ii. 364
——— Of all the moueables in England, Wales and Ireland, required by the pope, ib
——— Of ecclesiasticall liuings granted to Edward the second by the pope, ii 558.
——— Demanded of the cleargie by Henrie the third, ii 426
——— To the pope withstood by the earle of Chester, ii 364
——— They and first frutes restored to the crowne, iv 177
——— Giuen to the cleargie, v 192.
——— Demanded, vi 242
——— ¶ Sée Subsidie
Terme kept at Hertford castell, iv 224, 496
——— Begun at Oxford and adiorned to Westminster, iii 626
——— Adiourned, iv 325
——— Adiorned because of the plague, iv 235
Termes foure yearelie kept by whome instituted, ii 18
——— Quarterlie kept through out the yeare, i. 303
——— A rule to know the beginning and ending of them with their returnes, i 305
——— Then times no hinderance vnto iustice, ib
——— When they begin at the ciuil law courts, i 306
Terronan woone by force by the English, ii 642.
Terwin besieged, iii 576
——— By the English, Henrie the eight being present, iii 583.
——— Sore beaten with the English ordinance, iii 580
——— Yéelded vp to Henrie the eight, the citizens sworne vnto him, it is burnt and spoiled, iii 586.
Testament new translated into English, iii 749
——— ¶ Sée Gospell
Teukesburie field, iii 319

Teuther with others taken and beheaded, vol. iii page 270
——— ¶ Sée Mariage
Thamar an Englishman bishop of Rochester, i. 618.
Thamar parteth Deuonshire from Cornwall, i. 104.
Thames ebbeth and floweth twise daie and night, & at what houres, i 81
——— Whether it came by S Albons or no in times past, i. 323.
——— The cause why it ouerfloweth hir banks neere to London, i. 81
——— Whense it hath its head or beginning, i 79
——— The length of it with the commodities of the same, i 80
——— Such riuers as fall into the same described, i 78
——— Choked with sands and shelues, i. 81
——— The number of botes and watermen kept and mainteined vpon it, i 82.
——— With what fishes it aboundeth, i 80.
——— Carps lately brought into it, i. 81.
——— The course thereof, i. 82
——— Passable by foord in one place in Cesars time, i. 70
——— Rose with an high tide, ii. 380
——— Swolne with high spring tides, &c. note, ii 44
——— So high that Westminster hall was on a floud, iv. 345.
——— Ouerfloweth and dooth much hurt, ii. 473.
——— Drowneth all the countrie for the space of six miles about Lambeth, ii 399
——— Passable from London bridge to the Tower, it was so shallow, ii 64.
——— The water thereof conueied ouer saint Magnus steeple, iv 496.
——— ¶ See Tides.
Thames frozen ouer, iv 228
——————— Exceedinglie note, ii 99, 455, 473
——————— And not passable, iii 808
——————— Ships and vessels could not come vp the riuer, iii 181.
Thanes changed into erles, v 277
Thankfulnes for old seruice, ii 350.
——————— Of H the eight to his good militarie seruitors, iii 599
——————— Of queene Elisabeth vnto hir subjects, &c note, iv 904
Tharan king of Picts is slain, v 65
Theater erected for the duke of Alanson to stand vpon and shew himselfe to the people, iv 469
Thebe (and hir thrée sonnes) conspire the death of hir husband, i 389
Thebes giuen vnto Gathelus, v, 33
Théefe that robbed pilgrims taken and hanged, ii. 212.
——— ¶ Sée Murtherer, Osulfe
——— Murthered king Edmund, i 690
——— Nor robber but died in king Edgars time, i. 695.
Théefe that vsed to kill yoong persons and to eat them, executed note, vol. v. page 145.
——— Burnt to death, v 509
Théeves how to be apprehended by law, i 314
——— Saued by their booke how punished, i. 313
——— Bandeled and vanquished, v 278
——— Laws deuised against them, v. 301.
——— Their crueltie v 286
——— Punished note, v 363
——— Notable notablie executed note, v 421.
——— And robbers verie few or none in England in duke Williams time note, ii 25
——————— An ordinance against them, ii 428
——————— Notable, and their whole nest broken, ii 417.
——————— Appointed to be hanged, ii. 77.
——————— They and murtherers saued by their books and committed to the bishops custodie, iii 531
——————— Sacrilegious seuerelie executed, iii 948
Theft how punished, i 312
——— Restrained by laws note, i 675.
——— Punished, i 451:
Thelargus king of Picts an aged man desirous of peace, v 101
Theobald ¶ Sée Erle
Theobaldus the brother of Edelferd slaine, i. 598
Theodora married to Constantius, i. 528
Theodore made archbishop of Canturburie vpon conditions, i 626
——— Calleth and holdeth a synod at Herford, i 628
——— His acts and déeds after his instalment, i. 626
——— Worthilie praised, ib.
——— Reconcileth two kings being at warres, i. 631
——— Holdeth a synod at Hatfield, i 632
——— His articles proponed in the synod, i. 628.
——— Eightie and eight yeares old, i 637
Theodosius changeth the name of Britaine into Valentia, and whie, i. 9
——————— His acts and deeds in Britaine, i 515, 516.
——————— Preuenteth a conspiracy against him and punisheth the offenders, i 516.
——————— His praise, ib
Theomantius K of Britaine giueth tribut to the Romans, i 179
Thereus king of Scots fled to the Britons, v 50
Thermes monsieur succéedeth Dessée, v 561
——— ¶ Sée Monsieur
Thetford, a bishops see remoued to Norwich, ii. 44
Thin knight sir Iohn his watche house, . 80.
Thira daughter to king Ethelwod married to Gurmo, ii. 92.

Thyra hir issue, vol vi page 92.
— — Hir policie, ib
—— Hir lamentation and moorning, vi 93
Thistle benet, i 351
Tholouse besieged, v 293
Thomas archbishop of Yorke, while depriued ii 11
—— A canon of Baieux, the fiue and twentieth archbishop of Yorke, ib
—— Depriued of his crosier and ring, ib
Thomas bishop of the Eastangles after Felix, i 619
Thomas of Lancaster arriueth into Ireland, vi 260
—— Is lord deputie, ib
—— Putteth the earle of Kildare vnder arrest, vi 263
—— Is hurt and wounded, ib
—— Returneth into England, ib
Thongcastell, v 142
Thorneburie Walter lord chancellor, vi 216
—— Elected bishop of Dublin, ib
—— Drowned, ib
Thorowfares ascribed to Antoninus, i 118
—— And Innes, i 414.
—— ¶ Sée Townes
Threatening procureth submission note, ii 36.
Threshers masking note, ii 370
Throckmorton Francis esquire, some great secrets betwéene the Scotish quéene and him, iv 513
—— What moued him to denie his confessions at his arreignement, ib
—— His letter of submission to quéene Elisabeth, ib.
—— With a declaration of all his practises treasonable against hir, iv 514
—— Surprised and put to a narrow shift, iv 511
—— What mind he carried towards quéene Elisabeth, iv 512.
—— Hir treasons communicable to the erle of Northumberland, iv 606.
—— Arreigned and condemned of high treason, the whole declaration thereof, with the manner of proceeding against him, iv 536
Throckmorton Iohn of Norwich a conspirator, executed as a traitor, iv 255
—— ¶ Sée Traitors
Throckmorton sir Nicholas knight arriueth at Newhauen, iv 212
—— Arreigned of high treason, the whole manner thereof, with his purgations note, iv 31.
—— Eight of his iurie appeare in the star chamber, hard iudgement against them, iv 64
—— Extreamelie dealt withall, ib
—— Fine of his iurie released, iv 74
—— Sent into Scotland, v. 614
Throng, certeine thrust to death on London bridge, vol ii. page 884
—— ¶ Sée Blackwell, Iusts, and Paris Garden.
Thule of some taken to be Ireland, of other some Scotland, i 518
Thunder in winter, ii 78, 430.
—— With lightening in December, ii 380, iv 224
—— At Christmas, and on Christmas daie, ii 380, 120.
—— Verie terrible and fearefull note, ii. 198
—— That made men amazed, ii 66
—— For the space of fiftéene daies togither, ii 373, 108.
—— With an earthquake, ii 376
—— Generall and hurtfull, ii 353
—— With wonder, ii 490.
—— Terrible and mortall, v 283.
—— ¶ Sée Tempest and Wind
Thunnir chéefe ruler of the land vnder Egbert, i 629
—— A vile murtherer, ib
Thuringers a people in Saxonie, i 556
Thurstan abbat of Glastenburie, and the moonks of that house at strife, and whie, a lewd man note, ii 22
—— Deposed, returneth into Normandie, ib
—— Buieth his place againe for fiue hundred pounds, ib
—— Refuseth to obeie king Henrie the seconds pleasure, ii 65
Tiberio an Italian, his valiantnesse, iii. 812
Tiburne, called the elmes in Edward the thirds time, ii 599
Tichborne and his fellow traitors ¶ Sée Babington
Tida bishop of Northumbers, i. 625.
Tides two in one houre, iv 925.
—— ¶ Sée Flouds, Raine, Sea, and Thames
Tigers bastard in Scotlãd, i 72
Tiler beginner of the rebellion in Dertford in Kent note, ii. 735
—— His proceedings, ii 737
—— A verie craftie fellow, his proud sawcinesse, he is thrust through and slaine, ii 741
Tillage and mankind diminished by parkes, i 311
—— ¶ Sée Husbandmen
Tilneie ¶ Sée Tichborne
Tilt roiall, with deuises thereat, ii. 600.
—— ¶ Sée Iusts
Timber turned to stones and iron, vi 40.
—— ¶ Sée Wood
Time and hir parts how accounted in England, i 405
Tin, i 399
—— And lead to be found in six of the Orchades, i 75
—— Looking glasses, i 399
Tindall burned, his painfulnes in writing and translating, iii 196
—— ¶ Sée Testament new.

Tine north notablie stored with sammon, &c: described, vol i page 152
—— South described, i 153
Tirell Hugh serueth against the Scots, vi 249
—— Is put to ransome, ib
Tirrell knight described, iii 401.
—— He receiueth the keies of the Tower, purposeth to destroie the two princes, dispatcheth the action, sheweth the whole maner thereof to Richard the third, the murther confessed, he is beheaded for treason, ib
Tirrell sir Walter killeth William Rufus with an arrow in hunting, by chance note, ii 44
Tith of wines in Kent, i 186
Tithes paid with great scrupulositie, i 76
—— None to be giuen but to the church, ii. 51.
—— ¶ See Tenths and Clergie
Tithing preposterous, nine slaine, and the tenth reserued, i 738.
—— Of the people of Canturburie by the Danes preposterous, i 725
Tithing man in Latine Decurio, i. 259
Tithings, & who diuided countries into tithings, and what it meaneth, i 674.
—— ¶ See Hundreds
Tithwales in Scotland, i 73
Tiuidale where it lieth, i 154
Todes commonlie found where adders be, i 383
Togodumnus a British by the Romans vanquished, i 483.
Tokens foreshewing Wolseis ruine and fall, iii 752
—— Of victorie note, iii 270
—— Of things falling out in euent, iii 534
—— Of imminent misfortune to the lord Hastings, iii 381
—— Prodigious note, iii 264
—— ¶ Sée Sights, Signs, Warning, and Woonders
Tolls of the hound note, iii 775.
—— ¶ Sée Tax
Tongue castell taken by the English, iii 89
Toong British called Camberaec, i 23
—— Could neuer by anie attempts be extinguished, ib
—— Corrupted by Latine and Saxon, ib
Toong the French brought into England & in great practise, i 24
—— When it ceased to be spoken in England generallie, ib.
Toong Cornish hath some affinitie with the Armorican, i 25
—— Helpers of our English to be restored and perfected, i 24.
—— When the English began to recouer and grow in more estimation than before, ib
—— The Latine brought into Britaine by the Romans, ib
—— The Saxon brought into England whereof some relikes remaine vnabolished, ib
—— In the south parts of England are thrée seuerall toongs used, i 25
Tornacc. ¶ Sée Theomantius.
Torments extreme, vol. ii page 763.
Tornaie furnished with a strong power of men, besieged, the great number of people at the siege thereof, iii 616
—— Besieged by the emperor Charles his forces, deliuered to him, iii 675
—— Summoned by Garter king of armes, the prouosts words to the distressed townesmen, it is besieged, iii 587
—— On all sides besieged, and the prouost with eleuen more submit themselues, and yeeld vp the citie to Henrie the eight, iii 588.
—— Articles of agreement betwixt the kings of England and France for the deliuerie thereof to the French, &c note, iii 632
—— The maner how it was deliuered to the French king, iii 635.
—— A castell builded there by Henrie the eight, iii 615.
Tostie earle of Northumbers his crueltie, i 753.
—— Disquieteth his brother Harold, spoiling his countries, he is repelled, i 758.
—— His cruell dealing procureth a rebellion, i 753
—— Slaine, i 759.
Totnesse, where Vespasian arriued, i 466.
Touchstone, i. 395
Tours whether built by Brute or no, i 442
Towne, or hold, & what so called of the Britains, i 474.
Townes and cities in England, how manie, i 319
—— What called thorowfares, i 414
—— Of greatest trauell, i 415
—— More in old time than now, i 324
—— How manie market townes in euerie shire, i. 326
—— Decaied by changing of one waie, i 97
—— Erected and repaired by Elfleda note, i. 681
—— By king Edward, i. 682
—— In England burnt by the Frenchmen, ii. 715
—— In old time how fortified, ii 759
—— In France taken by the earle of Derbie, ii. 632
—— ¶ Sée Cities
Towre of London, sometimes a kings palace, i 329
—— Built by Belne, and first called Belines towre, i 456
—— New walled about by William Rufus, ii 39
—— Besieged, ii 92.
—— Deliuered to the earle of March, iii 261
—— Yéelded vp to Lewis the French kings sonne, ii 332
—— At the Londoners commandement, ii. 581.
Towre on London bridge taken downe, iv 343.
—— New builded, iv 344.

Traherne slaine, vol i. page 533.
Traherus inuadeth Westmerland, v 107
——— Resisted by Fincomarke, ib.
——— Returneth into Britaine, vanquisheth Octauius, v 108.
——— By conspiracie murthered, ib.
Traile baston, ii 536
——— ¶ Sée Inquisition.
Traitor Summeruile his miserable and desperat death, iv 528
——— Carter executed at Tiborne, iv 511
——— Elks for counterfeiting the quéenes signet manuell, iv. 697.
——— Maine executed for denieng the Q supremasie, iv 311
——— Nelson and Sherwood executed for denieng the quéenes supremasie, iv 345
——— Paine executed at Tiborne, iv 488
——— Thomas Woodhouse préest executed, iv. 323
Traitors, Barneie, Mather, and Rolfe executed, iv 264
——— Fen, Haddocke, Munden, Nutter, and Somerfoord, executed at Tiborne, iv 533
———Arden and Sommeruile executed for treason, iv 510.
——— Slade and Bodie executed, iv 509
——— Babington, Ballard, to the number of fouretéene, their wonderfull conspiracie and shape execution note, iv. 898
——— To the crowne proclamed, ii 248
——— King Henries nobles, ii 374.
——— Care not for their liues, so they may atchiue the end of their treasons note, ii 383.
——— Manie though they haue no armor nor weapon note, iv 530
——— Their rebels, and fugitiues practises to execute pope Pius bulles against quéene Elisabeth, iv 515
——— Forren continue sending of persons to mooue sedition in the realme, iv 517
——— Fiue, all of one linage executed, iii 803
——— They & rebels what ignominious ends they came to, iii 515
——— Put to flight and proclamed, iii 253.
——— Atteinted, executed, iii 266.
——— Their heads remooued from the tower on London bridge, & set on the gate at the bridge foot, iv 313
——— For a time may escape, but at length come to the gallows, ii 386
——— Executed, wherein note the ancient kind of punishment, ii 398
——— Executed for denieng the quéenes supremasie, iv 416
——— A declaration of quéene Elisabeths commissioners their fauorable dealing for their examining, iv 512 to 535
——— Executed in Lincolnshire and Yorkshire, iii 189
——— That murthered king Iames the first, most terrible executed note, v. 427.
Traitors an article for them, vol. v page 456.
——— ¶ See Préests seminarie, Fugitiues, Babington, Felton, and Storie
Traitors scholasticall note, iv. 530
——— Six questions to trie them from scholers, iv. 531.
Trauellers ¶ Sée Innes
Trauelling commended and discommended as necessarie and vnnecessarie, iv 907
Trauers sir Iohn capteine of the armie, vi 315
Treason practised by Alfred to kéepe Adelstane from the crowne, i. 684.
——— Of Almaricus in betraieng Canturburie to the Danes, i 712
——— Of Andragatius in killing of Gratian the emperour, i 538
——— Most villanous of Edrike in a fought battell, i 722
——— Notablie coloured, i 710.
——— Procuring K Edmunds death, punished with death, i 726
——— Of Fumerus, i 605
——— Of Harold by a counterfet letter, i. 734, 735
——— Of Hengist to kill the Britains vnarmed, i. 560
——— Against Ostrida, i 640
——— Of Pascentius practised by a counterfet monke vpon Aurelius, i 566.
——— Of a Pict in killing king Constantine, i. 552
——— Of the Picts against Bassianus, i 519
——— Of the Scots and Picts killing their king, i. 552.
——— Of Vortigerne to atteine the kingdome: note, ib
——— Of archbishop Wolstane, i 642
——— Of cousins, i 641
——— Persuaded by a wife to hir husband, and practised, i 619
——— In trust note, i. 490.
——— Coloured with counterfet sicknesse, i. 710.
——— Bringeth an euill end note, i 730
——— Punished with sudden deth, i 684
——— Against king Henrie the fourth to haue destroied him in his bed note, iii 18
——— Against Edward the second the traitor executed note, ii 572, 573, 574
———Against Henrie the third by a clerke of Oxford, ii 385
——— Of Thomas Becket, ii. 118
——— Of noble men iustlie punished, iii 11.
——— Of a Saracen against prince Edward, ii 474
——— Said to the duke of Aumerle, and how he challenged triall, iii 7
——— Of sir Thomas Turberuile, & he executed, ii. 509
——— Of a messenger disclosing the secrets of Edward the firsts letters, ii 16.
——— Of Foulks de Brent how punished, ii. 359

Treason of certeine Iewes, and how reuenged, vol ii page 161
——— Notable of Francis Throckmorton, set downe in full discourse with the maner of procéeding against him note, iv 536 to 548
——— Notorious of Parrie to haue murthered quéene Elisabeth set downe at large note, iv. 561 to 587
——— Of erle Persie of Northumberland summarilie set downe note, and vnto what foule end he came, iv 602 to 616
——— Of the duke of Buckingham ¶ Sée Duke.
——— Of nobles for the which they were apprehended, and executed, iii. 70
——— Of erle Iohn moued in the parlement, and iudgement denounced against him, ii 247
——— Laid vnto the archbishop of Canturburies charge by the speaker in parlement, ii 839
——— Laid to the duke of Northfolke by the duke of Hereford, ii. 844.
——— Laid to the duke of Lancaster, he cleared, and the accuser extremelie tormented, ii 763
——— In great men, and they executed note, iii 807.
——— Practised against the erle of Richmond, but preuented, iii. 421
——— Of the citizens that lost Mans, iii. 159.
——— Laid to the bishop of Winchester, with his answers, iii. 147, 148
——— Wherewith the dukes of Yorke and Summerset mutuallie charge each other, iii 233
——— Against the duke of Clarence, he is slaine, iii. 127.
——— Laid to the nobles charge by king Iohn, ii 292.
——— Laid to ones charge, and pledges sent to and fro to follow the sute, ii. 247.
——— Of two sorts punished with death note, iv 264
——— Purposed at a maske against Henrie the fourth his person, iii 11
——— In letters written by sir Ralfe Ferrers to certeine French lords, arrested, released, ii. 428
——— For misgouerning the king and realme, and the parties executed, ii 853.
——— Tried by a combat note, ii 726, 727.
——— Suspected among the nobles, and inquisition for the same, ii. 783
——— Intended and preuented, ii 508
——— Will euer come to light by one meane or other, ii 572
——— It and not religion the cause of the popes fauorers execution, proued note, iv. 529 to 533
——— The fauorers thereof punished, iii 816.
——— Punished in honorable personages of both sex, iii 316
——— To defraud souldiors of their wages, ii. 704
——— Punished by death, though disclosed, ii. 18.
Treason and execution, vol. iii pages 805, 818
——— Of two persons two waies note, ii 539; iii 775.
——— Vpon clergie men, iii 19
——— Most seuerelie punished, iv 920
——— Of conspirators to haue slaine king Alexander, v 286
——— Tried by combat note, v 281
——— Of the thane of Cawder for the which he is condemned, v 269
——— Of Vortigerne, v 138
——— Pretended, v 111
——— Against king Bruse of Scotland, & what issue it had, v 350
——— Seuerelie executed vpon a woman, v. 70
——— ¶ Sée Charters, Conspiracie, Elenor Cobham, Euan, Eureux, Noble men, Paris, Parrie, Préests seminarie, Rebellion, Rone castell, Scotish king Iames, Serlo, Traitors, Trust, and Woolseie.
Treason of Alfrike in fleeing to the Danes, i 706.
——— Punished in his son Algar, ib.
Treason of Androgeus in aiding Cesar against Cassibelane, i 476
——— What insued vpon it to the author, i 476
Treason in the nobilitie, i 708.
——— How punished and tried, i. 311.
Trebellius lieutenant of Britaine, giuen to couetousnesse, hated of the Britons, fighteth against his enimies, forsaken of his owne men, chased out of the field, writeth for aid to Rome, v 93
——— Certifieth the emperour of the state of Britaine, v 96
Trées in England of what sorts, i 358
——— Supposed to haue béene in the ground since Noahs floud, i 359
——— ¶ Sée Orchards
Treport suburbs set on fire by the English, iii 687
Trenchuile lord William, a man of great power, ii 115.
Trent riuer described, i 162
——— Where duke William pitched his tent against the Danes, ii. 11
——— Hoised out of the chanell with a tempest, iv. 103
——— Dried vp for the space of a mile, ii 63
——— ¶ Sée Chanell
Tresham knight made lord of saint Iohns of Ierusalem, iv 90
Tresham William ¶ Sée Iusts triumphant
Tresilian, chiefe iustice descried by his owne man & executed at Tiborne, ii 794
Trespasses ¶ Sée Punishments
Tresure great of Richard king of Almaine, ii 430
——— Of Richard the first where it laie, and deliuered to king Iohn, ii 272
——— Of Henrie the second found at Salisburie, ii 204
——— ¶ See Officers.

Tresuror lord of England his dignitie, vol. i. page 277.
———— Sitteth aboue the lord maior at the sargents feast, iii. 283.
Tresurors of England from the first to the last set downe in a collection, iv. 285 to 320.
———— ¶ Sée Cicill.
Tribute of Augustin out of Britaine of what things raised, i. 157.
—— Of woolfes skins, i. 373, 695.
—— Paid to England out of Wales, i. 751.
—— Of thrée thousand pounds paid to the Romans, i. 476.
—— Paid by the Britans to the Romans, i. 475.
—— Paid by the Danes to the king of Britaine, i. 457.
—— Denied to the Romans and what warres insued, i. 480.
—— Of gold, siluer, neat, hawks, and hounds paid to Adelstan, i. 688.
—— Of ox hides, ii. 166.
—— Of twelue pense for euerie horsse or yoke of oxen, ii. 170.
—— Of thrée thousand marks by yeare released, ii. 54.
—— Leuied throughout all England, and how: note, ii. 21.
—— Denied vnto the pope with oths and protestations, ii. 408.
—— To be paid vnto the pope moued for the maintenance of his estate, ii. 359.
—— Of the French king to king Edward for peace and amitie: note, iii. 341.
—— For Tholouse, ii. 145.
—— Released, v. 373.
—— ¶ Sée Exactions, Subsidies, Taxes, Tenths, and Toll.
Tribute exacted by the Danes of the English, i. 713.
———— Paid to the Danes that lie at Gréenewich, i. 718.
———— By them inhansed, i. 708.
———— Raised by king Hardicnute, i. 737.
Tripton sir Hugh serueth against the Scots, vi. 230.
Triuet knight slaine with a fall from his horsse, ii. 797.
Triumph. ¶ Sée Victorie.
Triumphs of the Romans excelled all other shews, iv. 466.
———— ¶ Sée Pagents.
Triulse a noble seruitor in the French affaires, iii. 636.
Troians accompanie Brute, i. 441.
Troinouant now London, i. 463.
———— Where, when, & by whome builded, i. 443.
Trolop forsaketh the rebellious lords, his estimation, iii. 253.
Truce betwixt England and France, vol. ii. pages 398, 762.
———— For fiue yeares, ii. 399.
———— Treated, ii 797.
———— For thrée yeares, ii. 370.
———— Generall, ii. 342.
———— For thrée years expired, ii. 378.
———— For fortie daies, iii. 711.
———— For a moneth, ii. 525.
———— For eightéene moneths, iii. 206.
———— For six yeares, iii. 175.
———— For two yeares, ii. 317, 648, 654, 669.
———— For thrée yeares, with the conditions of the same, ii. 625.
———— For a yeare at the mediation of a woman, ii. 617.
———— For a yeare, ii 161, 701.
———— Conditionall for two yeares, ii. 294.
———— For foure yeares, ii. 823.
———— For fiftie daies, ii. 268, 277.
———— For fiue yeares, ii. 268.
———— For thirtie yeares, ii. 232.
Truce for thrée yeares betwixt six kings, ii. 798.
—— Betwixt the emperor Charles and the gouernors of France, iii. 703.
—— Betwixt Henrie the fift and the duke of Burgogne, iii. 87.
—— Betwixt Henrie the fift and the dutchesse of Burgogne, iii. 189.
—— Betwixt Henrie the fift and the duke of Britaine, iii. 93.
—— Betwixt Henrie the eight and sundrie forren princes, iii. 622.
—— Betwixt the English and the Britons for six daies, iii. 572.
—— Prolonged for a yeare, ii. 817.
—— Tripartite, iii. 113.
—— Taken for a moneth, ii. 116.
—— The benefits insuing from the same, iii. 735.
—— ¶ Sée League and Peace.
Truce betwéene England and Scotland, ii. 751; iii. 681; v. 485, 487.
———— At request of the French king, ii. 536, 603.
———— With a treatie of aliance, iii. 423.
———— For nine yeares, ii. 632.

Truce betwéene England and Scotland for seuen yeares, vol. iii. page 489.
——— After much mischiefe and trouble, ii. 574.
——— For certeine yeares, v. 464.
——— For one yeare, v. 500.
——— For thrée moneths, v. 290.
——— For fouretéene yeares, v. 388.
——— For thrée yeares, v. 363, 437.
——— For fiftéene yeares, iii. 385; v. 447.
——— Renewed, v. 501.
——— ¶ Sée League and Peace.
Trumbils with others taken by king Iames the fourth, v. 470.
Trust treasonable, i. 560, 618. note, i. 646, 654, 659, 700, 706.
——— in treson: note, iii. 417, 418.
——— ¶ Sée Treason.
Truth purchaseth hatred, iii. 6.
——— Told with reproofe purchaseth disfauour, i. 693.
Tuidale recouered out of the Englishmens hands, v. 379.
Tuline citie now called Inchtuthill, v. 80.
Tunstall doctor, maister of the rolles, iii. 633.
——— Made bishop of Durham, iii. 742.
——— Baselie borne: note, i. 219.
——— Made bishop of London, iii. 675.
——— His oration and sermon in the parlement house, iii. 682.
——— Described and commended, his armes, the offices he bare, iv. 186.
——— Buildings by him founded, iv. 187.
——— Depriued of his bishoprike, ib.
——— Restored, ib.
——— His death, ib.
——— He and Budeus compared, iv. 188.
Turgesius, vi. 88.
——— Pursueth the conquest of Ireland, i. 588.
——— Vanquisheth Edlumding, ib.
——— Abideth manie troubles, vi. 89.
——— Buildeth fortresses and castles, ib.
——— Mastereth the Irish kings, ib.
——— Demandeth Omalaghitus daughter to wife, ib.
——— Is killed, vi. 90.
Turinus the nephue of Brute slaine, i. 442.
Turke is mortallie hated of the pope, iii. 630.
——— His victorie against the Soldane, his ambition hath no bounds, iii. 629.
Turkes great gunnes made by one Orban a Dane, i. 334.
——— When they begin their wéeke, i. 407.
——— Warred against by the earle of Flanders and others, ii. 283.
Turkes at the siege of Vienna how manie slaine, vol. iii. page 749.
——— Ouerthrowne and vanquished by the christians, principall men slaine, iv. 262.
——— ¶ Sée Dowglasse Iames, Ottoman, Rhodes, Saracens, Soliman.
Turkes or Indish peacocks gelded, i. 375.
Turketell Mireneheued whie he deserued an euerlasting reproch, i. 711.
Turketillus a Danish erle subdued, i. 630.
——— Guider of the Danish armie against the Normans, ii. 12.
Turkillus a Dane ruler in Northfolke & Suffolke, i. 713.
——— Reteined in seruice with Egeldred, i. 718.
——— Discloseth the secrets of this land to K. Swaine, i. 713.
——— His drift (being sworne to Egeldred) to aduance Cnute, i. 717, 718.
Turnements. ¶ Sée Charter, and Turnies.
Turner doctor of physicke his saieng, i. 253.
——— His opinion of the hot baths, i. 362.
Turne spits a kind of dogs, i. 389.
Turnham Stephan committed to prison, ii. 202.
Turnies, wherein earle Marshall of Penbroke was hurt and died, ii. 395.
——— Exercised for the training vp of souldiors, ii. 252.
——— At Blie betwixt the southerne and northerne men, ii. 383.
——— ¶ Sée Iusts.
Turonium. ¶ Sée Tours.
Twang castell, v. 142.
Twéede riuer the bound betwéene England and Scotland described, i. 150.
——— A troublesome and dangerous streame, iii. 888.
Twelue men in euerie hundred, i. 259.
——— ¶ Sée Inquest.
Twilight, i. 406.
——— ¶ Sée Night.
Twinam Lorison his historie: note, v. 565.
Tyrannie importable, v. 73.
——— Of Lestrigo and the sons of Neptune, i. 7.
——— Of duke William against the English: note, ii. 12, 13, 25.
——— Of Richard the second, ii. 337.
——— ¶ Sée Crueltie and William duke of Normandie.
Tyrant & a king distinguished, i. 589.
——— ¶ Sée Richard the third, or Duke of Glocester.
Tyrants estate vnquiet: note, iii. 403.

V.

Vagabonds their seuerall disorders and degrées, i. 309.
——— How punishable by law, ib.

Vagabonds an ordinance for them, vol v page 363
———— Compelled to learne an occupation, v. 232
———— Iudged to die note, v 241
———— And roges by proclamation to auoid the citie of London, iv 64.
———— Increased by rebellions, iv 1002
———— ¶ Sée Roges
Valdois profession, their examination, protestation, striued to death, ii. 116
———— ¶ Sée Dutchmen
Valdred doctor of the Picts, v 169
Valens Iouinus master of the horsses, i 517
Valentia one of the names of Britaine, i 9
———— A part of Britaine, i 546
Valentians, now Romans, i 548
Valentinus banished into Britaine, his wicked practises, i 546
———— Rescueth & succoreth the distressed Britains, i 492
———— Put in danger by Maximus, i 538
———— Slaine, i 563
Valeria adioining to Pannonia, i. 546
———— Now Stiermarke, ib.
Valiantnesse and manhood, iii 45
———— Of king Stephan, ii 91
———— Of Edoll with a hedgestake, i 561
———— Of a Romane ensignebearer, i. 467
———— Of Siward euen at his death, i 719.
Vallies in England that are famous, i 188.
———— ¶ Sée Dales
Valuasores a name appliable to all degrées of honours, i 267
Vandals where incamped at ye entering into this Iland, i 216
Vandosme taken by king Henrie, ii 155
Vannes in Armorica, now Britaine in France, i. 465
———— Besieged by king Edward the third, ii. 624
Variance betwéene the lord chamberleine and the ladie Elisabeths seruants, iv 127
———— Betwéene one Iohn Courtneie and Philip Duffeld, iii 950
———— Betwixt the lords and the Spensers, and whie, ii 558, 559, 560
———— Betwixt the students of Oxford, ii 450.
———— Betwixt the earle of Penbroke and others, ii 145
———— Betwéene the duke of Lancaster and the earle of Arundell, ii 823
———— Betwéene the lord Latimer, and two esquires, and to what a bloudie issue it grew, ii. 720
———— Betwixt the bishop of Durham and earle Patrike, ii 278
———— Betwéene sir Iohn Hollands seruants, and the lord Richard Stafford, ii 706
———— Verie roallie debated note, ii 787.
———— Betwixt the scholers of Oxford, ii. 798.
Variance betwixt the Londoners and the constable of the Towre, vol ii page 455
———— Betwixt Henrie the third and the earle of Penbroke, ii 386.
———— Betwéene the kings of England and France, iii 677
———— Betwéene the lord Paine Tiptost and Rice ap Meriduc, ii 189
———— Betwéene the bishop of Elie and the ladie Wake, ii 671
———— Betwéene them of Lennox and Argile, v 176.
———— Betwéene king Robert and the earle of March, v 403
———— Betwéene the Butlers and the Burghs, vi 252
———— Betwéene the earle of Ormond and the earle of Kildare, vi 275
———— Betwéene the earle of Ormond and the earle of Desmond, vi 332
———— Betwéene Vessie and Kildare, vi 241
———— About a dog, vi. 81
———— ¶ Sée Archbishop, Contention, Debate, Discord and Strife
Vaudemont besieged, iii 171.
Vbba and Hungar two Danish capteins and cruell of nature, i. 665
Véere Henrie constable of Gisors, ii 191
Véere brother to the earle of Oxford, slaine, iii 497.
———— ¶ Sée Erle Veere of Oxford
Vellocatus a squire marrieth quéene Cartimanda, hir husband Venutius being reiected, i 492
Venedocia now Northwales i 470
Vengeance ¶ Sée Reuenge
Venison in Englãd neither bought nor sold · note, i. 344.
———— ¶ Sée Hunting and Parks
Venlow besieged by the English, iii 564.
Venusius the husband of Cartimandia, he reuolteth, v 70.
———— A skilfull British capteine, reiected of his wife, his acts and déeds, i 492
Verannius lieutenant of Britaine, dieth, v 71.
———— His purpose against Britaine preuented by death, i 495
Verdon Milo a valiant capteine, vi 250
Verdon Robert maketh a riot, vi 245.
———— Submitteth himselfe, ib
Verdon Theobald is besieged in the castell of Athlon,
Verdon lord Verdon marieth Margaret daughter to Lacie, vi 338
Verlamcester, i 321.
Vermilion, i 397.
Vermine ¶ Sée Beasts venemous and Flies
Vernon sir Warren born at Shipbrooke, ii 33.
Vernueill besieged and obteined by the French, ii. 151
———— Gotten from the English by crediting a lie, iii 141
Verolamium now S Albons, i 190
———— Whether the Thames came by it or no in times past, i 323.

Verolamium a towne of great fame in the daies of Voadicia, vol i page 499
——— ¶ See S. Albons.
Vertex the crowne of the head, and why so called, i. 18
Vespasian sent by Claudius into Britaine & where he arriued, i 586.
——— Commeth into Britaine, assaileth the Britons in their campe, v. 64
——— Appeaseth the rebels, returneth to Rome, v 66
——— He is dead, i 510.
Vessell exchanged now in England, i 317.
Vessie William lord iustice, vi 240
——— His variance with the earle of Kildare, vi 241
——— The combat demanded betwéene them, ib
——— He refuseth it, ib.
——— Flieth into France, ib
Vffa a Saxon & his dominion in Britaine, i 569
Vfford lord iustice arriueth into Ireland, vi 255.
——— Maried the countesse of Ulster, ib
——— A heauie friend to the earle of Desmond, ib
——— Great reioising at his death, vi 256.
Vgh growing in England, i 358
Vice ¶ See Welth
Vices following delicat fare, v 422
——— Repugnant in one man, v. 414.
Vicount a name of dignitie next to the earle, i. 264
——— Is created of the prince, i 266.
Vicounts in Englād two, i. 277
Victius Volanus lieutenant of Britaine, i 502
Victorie wauering and inconstant, i 558
——— Abused with excessiue crueltie, i 500
——— Of the Britains against the legion of Manlius Valens, i 492
——— Of Marius against the Picts ingrauen vpon a stone in place where it was gotten, i 503
——— Of Ostorius against Caratake note, i 491
——— Of Oswies vow if he might obteine it against the enimie, i 623
——— Notable against the Saxons, by the conduct of a British armie vnder two bishops, i 562
——— Abused by Swaine, i 716
——— Of the English against the French at the battell of Agincourt, their reioising note, iii 82
——— Against the Turks by the Christians note, iv 262
——— Of king Iohn against his rebels, ii 325
——— Of the English at the battell of Sluise, ii 614.
——— Bloudie gotten by the Frenchmen, ii 507
——— Against the Irish and others in Ireland, iv 433
——— Good of them of Calis against the French king, ii 767
Victorie of the English nauie against the Flemish fléet, vol. ii page 778
——— Of the English against Scots signified with a great shout, iii 883
——— Against rebels, and what is to be doone after the same, iii 935
——— Of the English against the French note, iii. 908
——— What is to be doone after the obteinment thereof, iii 145
——— Consisteth not in multitude but in manlinesse, iii 443
——— Rich and honourable against the French, ii. 547
——— What is to be doone after getting thereof, iii 699
——— Obteined, and God praised note, i' 266.
——— Without bloudshed, ii 56.
——— Vsed with rigor feared note, ii 288
——— To whome the same is to be ascribed note, ii 639
——— What is to be doone after the obteinment thereof, iii 489
——— The Spanish manner of thanksgiuing after the getting thereof, iii 499
——— Generall processions after it, iii 144
——— Thrée within a short time falling to the English, iii 102
——— Of Edward the sixt against the Scots, iv 139.
——— Doubtfull, v 410
——— Assured before the battell fought, v 344.
——— In name not in déed gotten by the Scots, v 262
——— Modestlie vsed, v. 116.
——— Vsed with mercie, v 223
——— Vsed with gentlenesse, v 154
——— With triumphant ioy, v 167
——— With crueltie, v 205.
——— ¶ Sée Battell, Crueltie, and Warre.
Victories ascribed to Arthur, v 159
——— ¶ See Procession.
Victorine his answer to Ethodius request, v 91.
——— Sendeth letters to Rome, is sent for to returne, v 92
——— Prepareth an armie against the Scots, séeketh to persuade the Picts from talking with the Scots, incampeth néere Camelon with 30000 men, v 122.
——— Inuadeth Gallowaie, accused vnto Honorius, taketh vpon him the name & authoritie of emperor in Britaine, v 124
——— Deliuered vnto Heraclianus his hands, ib.
Vies, i 151
——— Castell the strongest hold in England in Henrie the first time, i 238
——— ¶ Sée Malmesburie
Vigenius and Peredurus reigne iointlie as kings, i. 461
Vikillus gouernour of Northfolke killeth a great manie of the Danes, i. 710

Villages more in England in old time than now, vol i page 324.
——— The cause of their increase, i. 320
Villegaignon departed from Leith, v. 557.
Vincentius Clemens the popes factor in England, i 230
Vintiesme (a kind of collection) gotten in Ireland for the pope, ii 390.
Viper. ¶ See Adder
Virgine & yet a wife, i 635
——— Of Friswide hir withstanding of prince Algar, i 649
——— Of Ireland called Modwen renowned, i 663
Virginia an English colonie ¶ Sée Raleigh.
Virginitie of the daughter saued by the losse of the maid note, i 696.
Vision note, v 199
——— Of Edgar, v. 285
——— Of Dunstane, telling him of king Edreds death, i, 691
——— Of K. Edgar a litle before his death, i. 697
——— Appearing to Edwin, i 605
——— Of Egwin bishop of Worcester, i 640
——— Of Augustine the moonke ¶ See Dreame
——— Of Richard archbishop of Canturburie, ii. 187.
——— Of a Iew become a Christian, ii 45.
——— Strange appearing to Henrie the second, ii 142
——— Of diuerse likenesses, ii 629.
——— ¶ Sée Dreames.
Visions of admonition are to be estéemed, ii. 142.
——— ¶ See Wonders.
Vitalianus pope, i 626
Vita ¶ Sée Iutes
Vittels plentie sold good cheape, iii. 508
——— ¶ Sée Death
Vlpius Marcellus lieutenant in Britaine verie watchfull note, i 514
Vlster in Ireland a kingdome, ii 172.
——— The fift part of Ireland, vi. 2, 78.
——— Conquered by Curcie, vi 199.
——— Giuen to Hugh Lacie, vi 237
——— Spoiled by Scots, vi 249
——— The townes in the same, vi 35.
Vlysses in Britaine, i. 436.
Vmber a fish onlie in the riuer Wie, i 123
Vmfreuill knight, his exploits in Scotland, iii 49
——— Surnamed Mendmarket note, iii. 50.
Vndershiriffes office and charge, i 261.
Vngust king of Picts, i 643.
Vniuersitie of saint Andrewes when first begun note, v 410.
——— In Arthurs time, i 320
——— In Chester verie famous, i. 126
——— College in Oxford, when founded, ii. 21
——— At Dublin, vi 251.
——— Of Glascow founded, v 442.
——— In London, i. 254.
Vniuersitie of Paris and Pauia, vol v page 191.
——— ¶ See Cambridge & Oxford, and Priuileges.
Vniuersities in England sometimes manie, i 249
——— Now in England thrée at this date, ib.
——— Of Cambridge and Oxford by diuerse abuses out of order, i 251.
——— How seated and their prouision, i 250
——— Their orders, schooles, colleges, i. 251.
——— Exercises, studies, degrées, & dignities, i. 252
——— When builded, vncerteine, i 249.
——— Their lands laid wait for and gaped at: note, i 256.
——— Eleuen in France, i 234
Vnkindnesse of Leirs daughters to their father, i. 447
Vnthankefulnesse to God punished, i. 611.
——— Punished, i 392
——— Noted in earle Stephan, ii 72.
——— Of Gaston de Bierne, ii 414.
Voada quéene desireth aid of hir brother Corbreid, she killeth hirselfe, v 71, 72
——— Assembled an armie against the Romans, v. 72
——— Imprisoned, v 62.
——— Released, conueied into Wales, ib
Voadicia the wife of Aruiragus beaten of the Romane souldiers, i 495.
——— Described, with the pithie spéech that she made to the Britains against the Romans, i 496, 497, 498
——— Hir daughters cruellie abused at the Romans hands, i 500
——— Chosen of the Britans to be their capteine against the Romans, i 496.
——— Reneweth wars with the Romans, v 75.
——— Hir death doubtfull, i 501.
——— Slaine, v. 75
Voiage venturous of sir Hugh Willoughbie, to the losse of his owne and his peoples liues, iii. 1063
——— Of sir Francis Drake, atchiued with extraordinarie honor and successe. note, iv 905
——— ¶ Sée Frobisher, Gilbert, Gréenfield, Raleigh, Sebastian
Vortigerne his ambition to reigne & rule, i 552.
——— Chosen K. of Britaine, i 553.
——— A meane that Constantius the moonke was made king, i 552
——— His treason, v 138
——— Doubting the hatred of his people would haue fled out of his realme, v. 139.
——— Counselled to send for aid into Germanie, ib
——— Dooth honor to Hengist, v 141
——— Sent for the Saxons into Britaine, i 11.
——— Deposed by his subiects, v. 144
——— Depriued of roialtie by his people, i 557.
——— Welcommeth the Saxons in Britaine, i, 554.

Vortigerne much giuen to sensuall lust, vol i. page 556
——— Forsaketh his wife to marrie Ronix a Saxonish damsell, Hengists daughter, i 556; v. 144.
——— Taken prisoner by Hengist & how released, i 561
——— Put in feare of his vsurped estate, i 554.
——— Restored to his kingdome, i. 560.
——— Busie in building a castell, i
——— Incestuous and lewd of life, i 561.
——— Burned to deth within a castell, ib, v. 146.
——— His vale, i 137.
Vortimer generall of the Britons, v 142
——— Succéedeth Vortigerne as king of Britaine, i 557.
——— Chosen to gouerne the Britons, v. 144
——— He is made king, i 558.
——— Restored religion after he had vanquished the Saxons, i. 560.
——— Imbattelled against the Saxons, ib.
——— Noble victories against Saxons, i 559.
——— Vseth the victorie modestlie, v 146
——— Poisoned by his mother in law Ronix, i. 558, 559
Vortiporus king of Britains, his exploits, & Gyldas exclamations against him, i 584
Vow of chastitie inuiolablie kept, i 635
——— Of Ceadwalla if he might get and conquer the Ile of Wight, i. 634
——— Of Ethelwulfe whereof the pope absolued him, i 660
——— That Osure made, if he might haue victorie, performed, i. 623.
——— Inuiolablie kept· note, iii 534
——— Professed of a nun broken, ii. 48.
——— Of chastitie broken note, ii 384
——— Of king Henrie the first whereof the pope offereth to discharge him, ii. 68.
——— Of the Scots noisome to themselues· note, iii. 882.
——— Kept and performed, v 303
——— Of Hungus and his soldiors, v 216.
——— Of king Malcome if he might obteine victorie, v. 281.
——— ¶ Sée Kenneth
Vow of Parrie the traitor to murther quéene Elizabeth, iv 5[illegible]7
——— And of other traitors to the same end note, iv. 955.
Vowes absolued, ii 145
——— ¶ Sée Oth and Promise
Vratislaus duke of Bohemia durst not erect seruice in the vulgar toong without the popes consent, i. 232
Vre mouth, there is a pit whose bottome is not soundable, i 177.
Vre riuer described, i. 157.
Vres and alkes i 281.
Vrswike, king Henrie the seauenths chapleine ambassadour into France, iii. 490.
Vsipites what kind of people, vol. v. page 80.
Vsuers goods seized, ii. 252
——— Came from Rome into England vnder the name of merchants· note, ii 384
——— Called *Caursini* note, ib
——— Excommunicated, but to no purpose, ii. 378
——— Accused and committed to prison, ii 422
Vsurie for the lone of monie forbidden note, iii. 1024.
——— A trade brought into England by the Iewes note, i 318
——— Of the Iewes the cause of hating & killing them note, ii. 211
——— By the Romans inforced vpon the Britons, i 195
Vsurpation note the whole storie of Richard the the third, and Edward the fift hath no good end ¶ Sée Bruse, ii 540, 541, 542, 543, 544.
——— Commeth to an euill end, ii 457.
——— ¶ Sée Makbeth, Somerleid, and Stephan.
Vter why surnamed Pendragon, i 570.
——— Made K. of Britaine, ib
——— Encountereth Pascentius and his aids and killeth them, i 566.
——— Falleth in loue with ladie Igwarne another mans wife, i 571
——— Goeth into Ireland, and incountreth Gallomanus, i 565
——— Begat Arthur the Great, v 150
——— Poisoned, v 153.
——— His decease, i 571.
——— ¶ Sée Aurelius Ambrose
Vtred deliuered pledges vnto Cnute [illegible] tto th notwithstanding, i 719 720
Vulfhere king of Mercia his acts and déeds, i. 621.
——— A great furtherer of religion, he dieth, i. 627, 628
Vulfrea son of Edwin, i 611
Vulture ¶ Sée Rauen.

W.

Wad a commoditie sometime in England, i 187.
Wade a duke conspirator of Ethelberts death, i. 655.
Waggons for warre when vsed in England, i. 336.
Waie high and of townes decaied by changing of them, i 97.
——— ¶ Sée High waies.
Wainescot equalled by some English oke, i 357.
Wainfleet. ¶ Sée Paten
Wake, ladie and duchesse of Lancaster against bishop Lild note, i 241.
Walbrooke in London whie so called, i. 509.
Walden in Essex whereof so named, i 316
——— Sometimes called Waldenburgh when first planted with saffron, i 390
Walden his variable fortune note, iii. 11.

Waldes in the Celtike toong signifieth forests, &c. vol i page 316
Waldhere bishop of London, i 630
Wales a word derived of the Saxons, i 195.
——— Not so fruitful as England, i 185
——— So called of the German word Walsh, i 117
——— Full of fens and bogs, i 359
——— Diuided into three kingdomes, i 26
——— Destroid and harried by the Englishmen, i. 751
——— Inuaded by king William Rufus, and wasted, ii 36
——— Subdued by duke William, ii 19
——— Diuided into shires, ii 186.
——— The marches thereof sore impouerished, ii. 444
——— Inuaded by the Dublins, vi 261
Walkeher bishop of Durham had the whole rule of Northumberland, ii 21
——— A furtherer of monasteries to be erected, ii 17
——— Slaine by the Northumbers, and whie note, ii 20
Walkhelme bishop of Winchester, ii. 14
Wall Roger his words of the duke of Summerset, v 707
Wallace William beginneth to wax famous, v 331.
——— Winneth castels, &c ib
——— His policie to relieue the people time of derth, v. 332
——— Inuadeth Northumberland, ib.
——— His answer to the king of Englands message, ib
——— Entred England with an armie of 30000 men, ib
——— He is enuied, ib
——— Raiseth a power to resist the king of England, v 333
——— Conference between him and Bruse, ib.
——— Refuseth the offers of king Edward, v 336
——— Eschewetl. to agree with the Englishmen, v 337
——— Is taken, brought to London and put to death · note, v 349
Walles that in times past were limits to England and Scotland, i 214
Wallop sir Henrie knight, tresuror at armes, commeth to Asketten castle, vi 431
——— His companie left in garrison at Asketten, ib
——— Is made one of the lord iustices, vi 450
——— His good gouernement, ib
——— A combat fought before him, vi 455
——— He yeeldeth vp the swoord to sir Iohn Perot, vi 450
——— He is one of the councell, ib
——— He lace at Limerike, vi 426
Wallop sir Iohn ambassador in France, vol vi page 305
——— he requireth to haue Fitzgirald, and is denied, ib.
——— Aduertiseth the king, vi 306
——— His martiall act in Normandie, iii. 602
Wallus brooke ¶ Sée Walbrooke
Walon lord came to serue Henrie the eight, iii. 579
Walsh vsed of the Saxons as we vse the word strange, i 195
Walsh Robert seruant to the earle of Kildare, vi 305.
——— Accompanieth the yoong earle into France, ib
——— Returneth into England, v 306
Walteof sonne to Siward, ii 8.
——— Valiant, reconciled into the kings fauor, ii 11
——— Earle of Northumberland, Northampton and Huntington, ii 8
——— Maried duke Williams néece, and his issue, ib
——— He and Gospatrike depriued, ii 17
——— Beheaded as a rebell though he disclosed the same note, ii 18
——— Described, and where he was buried, ib
Walter bishop of Hereford submitteth himselfe to duke William, ii 1
Walter, knight ¶ Sée Mildmaie, and Ralegh
Walter the son of Fleance high steward of Scotland, v 280
Wandleburne hils and whie so called, i 216.
Wandles in times past called Windles, i 328
Wanthop archbishop of Armacham, v 571
Wapentake a word compounded, and how, i 258
——— ¶ Sée Hundred
Warbecke ¶ Sée Perkin Warbecke
Ward Richard ¶ Sée Iusts triumphant.
Wards. ¶ Sée London.
Warens ¶ Sée Parkes, i 343.
Warfare in waggons when vsed in this land, i 336
Warham doctor of lawes, the sum of his speach to the archduke of Burgognie, iii 506.
Warke castell besieged, v 580
——— Assalted, v 498.
——— Woone, i 449
——— Burned by the Scots, ii 762
Warlwast William taketh from Anselme all that he had note, ii 43
Warne riuer runneth almost nine miles from the head within the land, i 151.
Warners or whapels a kind of dogs, i 389.
Warning of amendment of life, ii 74.
——— Reiected both by woonders and dreames, and iested at, ii 44
——— Neglected cause of inconuenience note ii 142
——— Of a French préest giuen to Richard the first note, ii 271
——— Of a yoong babe to his mother note, v 212.
——— Of some great mischance, v 480
——— ¶ Sée Visions
Warre is to be begun with praier example, i 611.
——— And famine signified, i 653
——— Betweene two brethren, kings sonnes, ii 183.

Warre in Normandie betwixt king Rufus and his brother Robert, vol i page 35
——— Of barons against king Iohn note, ii 327.
——— Proclamed against England by the king of Scots, iii 16
——— Prepared against France, iii 567
——— Betwixt England and France, ii 600
——— Proclaimed betwixt England and France, ii 605.
——— Prosecuted with egernesse, ii 607, 608
——— Upon a light occasion, ii 66
——— Renewed, ii 595
——— Betwéene diuerse nations in one yéere ended, iv 200
——— Ciuill and the miserie of England then, ii. 101
——— Maketh no difference of time note, iv 192
——— Certeine ordinances deuised for that time, ii 216
——— The frutes thereof, iii 181
——— Forren better than sedition at home, iii 1010.
——— Open not so ill as ciuill, the occasion of manie great inconueniences, iii 391
——— Without slaughter and burning, v 191
——— Continuall in Scotland what calamitie it caused, v 377
——— Ciuill and what mischéefes insue, v 251.
——— The frutes thereof, v 252.
——— ¶ Sée Armie, Battell, Beneuolence, Commotion, France, Frenchmen, Monie, Munition, Scots, Subsidie, and Victorie
Warre ciuill turneth to the enimies aduantage i 199.
——— How God disappointeth as abhorring it, and louing peace, i 167.
Warren ¶ Sée Erle.
Wars ciuill fiftie yeares in Britaine, i 450.
——— Among the Britains, i 588
——— Decaied the force of the Britains, i 542
——— Betwéene the British kings, i 589
——— Betwixt K Cuthred and one of his earls, i. 644
——— In Edriks time, i 636
——— Betweene Ethelard and Oswald, i 642
——— Betwéne Madred and Constantine for succession to the crowne, i 582
——— Among the Englishmen, i 655
——— Betwéene the kings of Northumberland, i 618
——— By a womans meanes, i 492
——— Ceased betwéene the Britains and Romans by quéene Genissas meanes, i 486
——— Betwéene Lacie and Marshall, vi 238.
Warwike how called in the Romãs time, and how manie parish churches it had, i 320
——— Castell taken and rased, ii 461
Warwikeshire wasted by the Danes, i. 719.
Waspes ¶ Sée Hornets
Wassall what it signifies, i 556.
Waste ¶ Sée Northcountrie
Wat Tiler. ¶ Sée Tiler.
Watch appointed to be kept by night in cities and burrowes, vol i page 428
——— It and ward from foure till six, and from six till foure, ii 561
——— The mischiefe that groweth by the negligence of them, iii 158
——— In sléepe what aduantage to the enimie, ii. 562
——— Found sleeping iustlie serued, iii 580
——— At Midsummer discontinued, iii 1021.
——— ¶ Sée Midsummer.
Watches ¶ Sée Night
Watchword of treason *Nempt your sexes*, i 560.
Water what best to brue béere withall, i 286
——— The greatest fresh in England, i. 146
——— Conueied from out the Thames by pipes into seuerall houses, iv 496
——— ¶ Sée Tidès and Thames.
Waterford citie builded by Sitaracus, vi 29
——— Alwaies faithfull to the crowne of England, ib.
——— The conquest of it by Richard Strangbow, vi 145.
——— The description of it, vi 378
——— Their variance with the earle of Kildare, vi 379
——— Their riuer and the commoditie of the same, ib
——— Their priuileges, ib
——— An admonition unto them, vi 380.
——— Their honorable receiuing of the lord deputie, vi 378
——— They stand vpon terms with the lord deputie, vi 365.
Waterhouse sir Edward knight one of the quéenes priuie councell, vi 456.
——— Subscribeth to the proclamation against the earle of Desmond, vi 424
Waterquake, ii 753, 754, iv 426
Waters executed for Treason, ii 539.
——— ¶ Sée Traitors.
Waters of a strange nature in Ireland, vi 39.
——— Came into yͤ minster of Salisburie at high masse time, i 98
——— ¶ See Riuers
Waters in England of what sorts, natures, and qualities, i 354
——— None hurtfull, ib
——— Of speciall vertues to help the wounded and diseased, i 360, 361.
Watling stéeet (rightly named Guthelme stréet, and which) one of the highwaies of Britaine, and how it is extẽded, i 190
——— By whom builded, i 189.
——— ¶ Sée Highwaies.
Wednesdaie, iii. 578
——— Why so named, i 556.
——— ¶ Sée Daie.
Wéeke and of how manie daies it consisteth note, i 407
——— Named after the English, Saxonish, and Scotish manner, i 411.

Weights and measures, vol ii. page 264
——— Reformed after one standard, ii 362
——— ¶ Sée Measures
Weiland lord chéefe iustice of the kings bench, his storie, ii. 191
Well in Gnaresborow forrest conuerting wood, &c. into hard stone, i 218.
—— That ebbeth and floweth as the sea dooth, i 220
—— ¶ Sée Founteine.
Wellowin where great slaughter of Danes did begin, i 703.
Wels in sundrie places of diuerse strange qualities, i. 218, 219
—— Two whose water participating of one soile differ in qualitie, i 219.
—— Thrée néere Couentrie of strange and effectuall vertue, i. 360
Wels & Baths hot, ib
——— ¶ Sée Baths, Riuers, Springs and Waters
Welsh Iohn maketh a draught vpon the earle of Desmond, vi 451.
——— His deuise to passe ouer the riuer, ib.
Welshmans tale that slept betwéene two swords and a knife at his hart, i 132
Welshmen call Angleseie the mother of their countrie, i 63.
——— They let in the Saxons, and whie, i. 11.
——— The errours of some noted, which will have them come from the French, &c i 6
——— Contentious to go to law, i 301.
——— What shift they make for plastering, i. 315
——— Obteined victorie against the Englishmen, i 719
——— Being in armes, were alwaies subdued, i. 742
——— Whense they tooke their name, i. 637
——— Preuent a slander, i. 743.
——— Their kings in the daies of Edgar, i 694
——— Ioine with the Danes & are vanquished, i 658.
——— Rebell against Edgar and are subdued, i. 697
——— Good seruice against the Romans, i. 470
——— Are the verie Britons in déed, i 574.
——— Agrée to paie their accustomed tribut to England, i. 731
——— Ouerthrowne in battell, i. 614
——— Vnder their kings, waste Hereford, ii 8
——— Cruellie handled in their ouerthrow, ii. 38
——— Inuaded by William Rufus, flie into the woods, ib
——— Vanquished at Brecknocke by William Rufus, ii 34
——— Inuade England, ii 35.
Welshmen dare not fight in open field, but worke all vpon aduantage, vol ii page 36.
——— Preuaile greatlie against the English, ii. ii 374
——— Besieged the castell of Montgomerie, ii. 363
——— They are discomfited, ib.
——— Put to flight, ii 369
——— Sent ouer to the aid of the earle of Britaine, ii 378
——— Warre against the lord Mortimers tenants, ii 455
——— Subiect to the English laws, ii 422
——— Take castels, ii. 565
——— Wastfull without remorse, ii 603
——— Appointed to Iaques Arteueld for a gard against Gerard Denise, ii 361
——— Molest the English subiects, iii. 27.
——— Rebell by the setting on of Owen Glendouer, iii. 17
——— Waste Cheshire, ii. 96
——— Vp in armes, they use for peace to Henrie the first, ii. 71.
——— Fickle and by what means allured to Henrie the firsts side, ii 50.
——— Moue rebellion, discomfited, and punished, ii 304
——— Not well delt withall, ii 164
——— Their good seruice against the French, ii. 195.
——— Staie the shriffe of Glocestershire, ii 183.
——— Their good seruice, ii 161.
——— Make war on the English marches, seuerelie punished, ii 125
——— Vanquished and slaine, ii 267
——— Win Cardigan, ii 125
——— Rebell, inuaded and subdued, ii 114
——— Their valiancie against the French, iii. 679.
——— Make a riot at Calis, iii 688
——— Discomfited by the Northerne men, iii. 291
——— Slaine, iii 292
——— Inuade the English marches, ii 64
——— Slaine and discomfited by Henrie the first, on all hands note, ib
——— Subdued, ii 351.
——— Flie, ii 166
——— Submit themselues, ii 114.
——— Drowned within an ambush note, ii 108
——— Rebelling against the Romans brought to their former obedience, v 92.
——— Subdued by Henrie the fift, v. 411.
Welshwomens villanie against the English dead corpses, iii 20
——— Their beastlie and barbarous crueltie vpon the dead carcases of the English, iii. 34.
——— ¶ Sée Fraie, and Lewin.
Welth superfluous occasion of vice, v. 135

Wentworth lord deputie of Calis sendeth to the French to demand parlée, vol iv page 91.
—— Taken prisoner, iv 92
—— Arreigned and acquited, iv 184
Weapons of what kinds vsed and worne in England, i 335
—— ¶ Sée Armour
Were riuer described, whose mouth is eight miles from Durham, i 155
Weicfredus bishop of Worcester, i. 675.
Weremouth moonke, and whie so called, i 154
Wermans ¶ Sée Thuringers.
Werlamchester, now saint Albons, i 327
Wesell in Cleueland a free towne note, iv 107.
West doctor ambassador into Scotland, v. 472
Westburie vnder the plaine neuer without a théef or twaine, i 115
Westmaria, now Westmerland, i 504
Westmerland of whome first named, ib
—— Why so named, v 73
—— Assigned to the Scotishmen, i 108
—— It and Cumberland recouered, v 228
—— It and Kendall by the Scots and Picts spoiled, v 93
Westmerland and Richmonshire how bounded, i 159
—— By certeine stones in yᵉ edge of Stanes moore, i 191
Westminster spoiled by souldiors, ii 472
—— A new house made within the palace for the arreignment of the lords, ii 839
—— The palace of the king burned, iii 571
—— The new church there begun, ii 349
Wesminster church built, i 512
—— By whom builded, vncerteine, i 595.
—— Inlarged and repared, ii 409.
—— The new worke there begun, ii 488
—— Of a cruell murther there committed, ii 720
—— The sanctuarie confirmed by parlement, ii 722
Wesminster hall founded note, ii 39
—— Ouerflowne with waters note, iv 80.
—— Full of water and not to be gotten into but on horssebacke, ii 399
—— Where botes might haue beene rowed up and downe, ii 380
Weston doctor the duke of Suffolks ghostlie father, iv 24
—— Against the ladie Elisabeth, the lord maiors iudgement of him, iv 26.
—— Resigneth the deanrie of Westminster by compulsion, and is recompensed, iv 89
Weston Robert arriued into Ireland as lord chancellor, vi. 336
—— His vprightnesse, ib.
—— His oration to the parlement, vi. 341
—— Is made lord iustice, vi. 339
Weston Robert His death, vol vi page 373
—— His vertues and conditions, ib
—— His exhortation to the councell, iv 373.
Westsaxons conuerted vnto the faith, i 616.
—— Their conquest or victories, i 657
—— Their kings and of whom descended, i 583
—— They would not let their wiues be called quéenes, i 653
—— Haue the whole monarchie of the land, i 638
—— Their progenie ceased in Edward the third, i 755
——Their kingdome vnder whome it began, i 569, 573
—— Subiect to two, i 600, 633
—— Kent and Essex annexed to that kingdome, i 639
Wether intemperat by coniuring as was thought, iii 20
—— ¶ Sée Tempest
Wexford men by craft do take Fitzstephans, vi 155
—— They present Fitzstephans to the king, vi 160
—— Make warres against Brian mac Kahir, vi 372
—— They are vanquished, ib
Wexford towne, vi 33.
—— It is wonne by mac Morough and by Fitstephans, vi 127
—— The chéefest towne in Leinster, ib
—— Is giuen to Fitzstephans and Morice Fitzgerald, vi 129
—— It is left to the gouernement of Fitzaldelme, vi 166
—— The marriage betwéene Reimond and Basilic is celebrated there, vi 183
—— Fitzgirald died and was buried there, vi 197
Whales tithed in Scotland, i 73
Wharton Henrie, v 555
Wharton lord Thomas deceaseth, iii 285
Wheat of summer, and wheat of winter, i. 284
——And other corn scarse, with politike orders to redresse it for the poore peoples reléefe note, iv 944
Whetstones, i 395.
—— ¶ Sée Quarries and Stones
White Henrie made a broile in Dublin, vi 285.
—— He is pardoned, ib
White Iohn his good seruice in the rebellion against Fitzgirald, vi 292
—— Is dubbed knight, ib
White bishop of Lincolne his comming to be bishop of Winchester note, i 231
Whitemeates licenced to be eaten in Lent, and noblemen punished for breaking the law, iv 332
Whitegift Iohn ¶ Sée Archbishop
Whitehall, when and by whom erected, i 329
Whiteherne (in Latine *Candida casa*) whie so called, i 246
—— A place of sanctuarie, v 291

Whitcherne ¶ Sée *Candida casa*
Whittington college erected, vol iii. page 56
Whoore the cause of a notorious and shamefull murther note, iii 1024
——— ¶ Sée Concubine, Shores wife, Spaniards, iv 74
Whooredome how punished in Canutus daies, i 312
——— Reproued and the reprouer taken in the déed dooing, ii 72
——— Strangelie punished by the iust iudgement of God, iv 504
——— It and murther go together, iii 792, 819
Whoorlepooles taken in the Thames, iii 775
Wiat knight his insurrection, his proclamation at Maidstone, he commeth to Rochester, méeteth with his adherents, causeth much trouble, iv 10, 11.
——— Soliciteth certeine gentlemen to adhere vnto him, an herald of armes sent vnto him, the lord warden desirous to be tempering against him, iv. 11, 12
——— A proclamation that none should keepe in his house anie of his faction, he is sent to the Tower, hardlie delt withall at the lieutenants hands, the furniture of his bodie, iv. 20, 21.
——— Marcheth with his power and executeth feats of armes against the aduerse parts, preuaileth against the lord Cobham, iv. 14
——— His requests, iv 15
——— Marcheth to Detford Strand, suffereth his prisoners to go abrode vpon their word, commeth to Southworke, his desperat attempt, he and his complices fall to consultation, at his wits end, vi 17, 18
——— He marcheth to Kingstone, commeth vnto the parke corner, and skirmisheth with the quéenes power, marcheth along the wall of S Iames toward London, submitteth himselfe to the quéene, iv 18 to 20
——— Arreigned, the effect of his indictment, he answereth not directlie to the question guiltie or vnguiltie, his exhortation to loialtie, altereth his mind touching the mariage, his answers to diuerse speaking at his arreignment, iv 28, 29.
——— His confession and execution, iv 30.
Wich how it is situated, i. 403.
Wichstred king of Kent dieth leauing issue thrée sons, i 642
Wicliffe a secular préest his conclusions, the chéefest articles that he preached, ii 705
——— He and his fellowes mainteined by certeine lords, ib
——— His doctrine, ii 734, 753
——— Fauoured of the Londoners, ii 751
——— Mainteined by the learned, sentence pronounced against his books, iii 47.
——— Lnill spoken of, and his followers reproched, ii 717
Wicliuists increase, ii 800, 832
——— Popes letter to Richard the second against them, ii 832
Wicliuists bewraid by some of their owne sect, vol. iii page 21.
——— Wrote against the clergie, ii. 825
——— They are complained of, they increase, the lords séeke that they might be surprised, ib
——— Richard the seconds commission against them and their sectaries, ii 826
——— Excommunicated note, ii 828
——— ¶ Sée Piteshull.
Widow without Aldgate murthered, iii 172.
——— ¶ Sée Beneuolence and Iest
Widowes prouided for and releeued by the charitie of Dauid Smith note, iv. 543.
Wie riuer, ii 8
——— Described, i 165
Wife and yet a virgin, i 635, 685
——— Forsaken note, i 556
——— Not to be forsaken without cause note danger, i. 654
——— Faithlesse and adulterous exemplified, i. 492
——— Louing to hir husband, i 435, 649.
——— Loued with dotage, i 557
——— Of Berne a noble man rauished, bred much mischiefe, i 668
——— Put awaie and taken againe, ii 75
——— Robbed by hir husband and he hanged note, iv. 893
Wighart a préest well séene in the scriptures, i. 625
——— Dieth of the pestilence, ib.
Wight Ile conquered by Ceadwalla, i 634.
——— Subdued to the Romans, i. 486.
——— Conquered by Vulfhere, i 624
——— Receiueth the faith, i 634
——— Wholie gotten into the hands of Edward the third, i. 56.
——— Called in Latine *Vectis*, i 54
——— The names of the parsonages and vicarages in the same, i 55
——— First conuerted to the faith though the last that harkened to the word, ib,
——— Rebelleth, v 66
Wightam towne in Essex built, i 679.
Wiland or Welland riuer described, i 171.
Wilfcketell ¶ Sée Vikillus
Wilford sir Iames knight taken prisoner, iii 906, v 561
Wilford the counterfet earle of Warwike, he is executed, iii 523.
Wilfrid the second archbishop of Cantuburie, i. 641
Wilfrid archbishop of Yorke, i 626
——— How far his iurisdiction extended, i 627
Wilfrid bishop of Northumbers, i 625.
Wilfrid a yoong damsell defloured by king Edgar, i 696
Wilfride by licence of king Edelwalke preacheth the gospel to them of Sussex, i 631
——— Taught the Southsaxons to catch fishes with nets, ib

Wilfride what part of the Ile of Wight king Ceadwalla gaue him, vol i page 634.
—— First conuerted the Ile of Wight to the faith, i 55
—— Deposed for disobedience, i 629.
—— Banished, i 630
—— A long time in exile now restored, i 636.
—— A bréefe rehearsall of him, i. 641
Wilfulnesse in opinion of Thomas Becket, ii. 132
Willes two in a monster & both contrarie, v 228
William conqueror, duke of Normandie, when he began his reigne, ii 1.
—— So named, not by cōquest but by challenge, i. 205.
—— Constituted heire testamentarie to Edward confessor, ib
—— Crownd king on Christmas daie, ii 2
—— Sworne at his coronation, with the sum of his oth, ib
—— Whie he refused to be crowned at archbishop Stigands hands, ib.
—— Tooke an oth and hostages of the nobles and lords of England, ii 1
—— His conditions and qualities, ii 24.
—— His deuise to disburthen himselfe of souldiours wages, ii. 23.
—— What he beareth to his armes, ii. 24
—— His descent, ii. 1
—— Vanquisheth the English power, and wasteth certeine countries, ib
—— Seizeth vpon the Englishmens lands, and renteth them out by the yeare, ii. 13.
—— His couetous dealing and exactions note, ii. 14
—— Maketh a lamentable waste of the north countries, ii 12.
—— Hateth the Englishmen more than euer he did before, ib.
—— Subdueth certeine rebels that fled to Elie for defense, ii. 16.
—— Glad to deale with the Danes by promises and faire proffers, ii 12
—— Present at a synod, wherein note his malice against the English, ii 14
—— Saileth ouer sea, and besiegeth Doll castle in Britaine, ii. 19.
—— Pitcheth his tents and fighteth against the Danes, and putteth them to flight, ii 11.
—— In a perplexitie and glad to créepe in fauour with the English note, ii 16
—— His oth and promise, with his crueltie and abusing of peace, ib
—— Threteneth king Malcolme, v 280.
—— He proclamed open warres, ib.
—— Goeth with an huge armie against Malcolme king of Scots, and whie, ii 17.
William conqueror his iustice in restoring the right heire, vol ii page 17
—— Taketh awaie from the English their armor, ii 9.
—— Subdueth the rebels of Excester, ii 10
—— Subdueth Wales, ii 19
—— Goeth ouer into Normandie, leauing guides ouer England, ii 8
—— Forced to yéeld to the Kentishmens request, ii 3
—— Hateth the English nobilitie euen in the time of peace, ii 9.
—— His thrée sonnes, their names and places of their birth, ib
—— His foure sonnes, and what he bequeathed to them, ii 25.
—— His fiue daughters, ib
—— Returneth into England and waxeth vigorous against the English, ii 8
—— In possession of London and his promised courtesie, ii 1
—— What strangers came in with him at the conquest, their names, ii 3.
—— His charter granted to the citie of London, ii 25.
—— He is politike, painefull, and tyrannicall against the English, ii 9
—— Ouerthrowne and wounded in battell by his son Robert, ii. 19
—— Falleth sicke in Normandie note, ii 23
—— In despaire of his life by the Kentishmen, ii. 3.
—— Departeth this life, in what yeare of his age, ii 24.
—— His sepulchre opened, his statue and epitaph, ii 26.
William bishop of Durham the kings household chapleine in armes against the king, ii 28.
—— Founder of vniuersitie colledge in Oxford, ii 21
—— Besieged at Durham, forced to yéeld and exiled, ii 29
—— Restored, and dieth for sorrow, and whie, ii 30
William bishop of London banished, i 747
William the poore bishop of Rochester, i 630
William duke of Normandie aideth Edward the third going to take sea into England, i 739
—— ¶ Sée Duke.
William earle of Ew renounceth Robert, and becommeth king William Rufus man, ii 36.
William lieutenant of Tuscane, v 190
—— Maketh Christ his heire, ib
William surnamed the Lion crowned king of Scotland, required to doo homage, his request, goeth ouer with K Henrie into France, v. 296
—— His zeal of iustice, he receiueth a péece of Northumberland, with his

right sued to the residue, he inuadeth Northumberland, vol v pages 296, 297
William surnamed the Lion yéeldeth himselfe prisoner, conueied into Normandie, v 298
———— Ransomed, v 299
———— His gift vnto king Richard, v 303
———— Did homage to king Iohn, v 304
———— Surrendereth to king Iohn the lands of Cumberland, &c ib
———— Deceaseth, v 305
William Rufus when he began his reigne, ii 26
———— Crowned king, and of his munificence, ii 27
———— What means he vsed for to purchase the noble mens fauour, ib
———— Giuen to sensuall lust and couetousnesse, ii. 30
———— In armes against the Normans, ii 28
———— Inuadeth Wales but to little effect, ii 38
———— Goeth ouer into Normandie, ii 39
———— A bitter enimie to the popes of Rome, ii 41.
———— Renounceth archbishop Anselme for his subiect, ii 42
———— Farmeth archbishopriks, bishopriks, and abbeies, ii. 43.
———— Passeth into Normandie, and whie, ii 31
———— Against his brother Robert, ii 35
———— Depriueth bishops, ib
———— His great courtesie to the English to win their fauours, ii 29
———— In armes against the Welshmen, but with little successe, ii 36
———— In armes against the Scots, v 282
———— Suspected of infidelitie, ii 46
———— Falleth sicke at Glocester, ii. 33
———— Where buried, his conditions, proportion and no issue, ii 45
William king of Scotland allied to the earles of Britaine, ii. 12
William the sonne of Henrie the first, made duke of Normandie, ii 64
———— Drowned, and how he might haue escaped, ii 70
Willoughbie capteine honourablie buried, iv 648.
Willoughbie sir Hugh knight, v 565
———— Found frozen to death in his ship note, iii 1063
Willoughbie lord ambassador into Denmarke, his oration in Latine to the king, inuesteth the king into the order of the garter, returneth and arriueth in England, iv 495
Wilnot a Sussex gentleman an enimie to king Egelred, i 711.
Wilton hauing sometime twelue parish churches, how it grew to be but a poore village, i. 97.
Wilton spoiled by the Danes, vol i page 710.
Winander riuer maketh the greatest meere or fresh water in England, i 116
Winchester called Caergwent, ib
———— How called in the Romans time, i 320
———— Bishoprike when first erected, by whom, and the circuit thereof, i 238
———— Destroied by the Danes, i 611
———— The church where the bishops sée of all that prouince was then placed, by whō builded, i 629
———— An erls sonne bishop there, ii 71.
———— ¶ Sée Bishop
Winciga a kind of strange people late at Fulham, i. 672
Wind sold to mariners vnder certeine knots of thred, &c i 66
———— Vehement and strong issuing out of the hilles called the Peake a wonder, i 217
———— Blustering that ouerthrew cities, i 652
———— Monstrous and big, and dooing much harme, ii 295
———— Full of annoiance, ii. 423, iii 751, iv 425, 926
———— That troubled the skie, ii 390
———— Extreme & terrible, ii 419
———— Big and boisterous that blew open Paules gates, iv 229
———— Tempestuous out of the south, iv 326.
———— That ouerthrew houses, ii 380, 598.
———— In diuerse places of England note, ii 32.
———— Continuing six or seuen daies, ii 677
———— For thrée moneths space hindering the spring, ii 432
———— Prognosticating trouble, iii 654.
————Vpon the seas, iv 233
———— ¶ Sée Fire
Windleburie, i 328
Windsore builded by king Arthur or Aruiragus, &c. i 329
———— Castell repaired, ii 671
———— And of the chamber there built called the round table, ii 627
Windsore lord Windsore the first lieutenant in Ireland, vi 258
———— He kept a parlement in which a subsidie was granted, ib
———— ¶ Sée Iusts triumphant
Wine wanting in England, and whereto the fault is to be imputed, i 186
———— Sometime grew in England, ib
———— No where more spent than in England, i. 281
———— Whether it will be kept in an iuie cup or no, i 402
———— Naturall and artificiall, i 282
———— Sometimes tithed in Kent, i 186
———— The best called Theologicum note, i 281
———— Forbidden moonks and at last granted, ii. 618
———— Prised at a rate, iv 278.

Wine sold for thirtéene shillings & foure pense the tun, vol ii page 779
—— Sold by weight, v 423
—— ¶ Sée Ale and Measure
Wingfield Iaques master of the ordinance is verie carefull for the safetie of his nephues, vi 135
——— He is sent to the Spaniards fort, vi 439
——— The capteine submitteth himselfe vnto him, ib
——— He presented him to the lord deputie, ib
Wini bishop admitted by king Chenwald & expelled againe, i 618
Winnebert a traitorous murtherer of his lord and master, i 649
Winter sharpe following a drie summer, v 233
——— With great frost, iv. 321
——— An enimie to warlike enterprises, ii. 11.
——— Extreame note, ii 64
——— More than ordinarie, ii 282
——— Neuer the like, ii 287
——— That killed all kind of small foules, iii 41
——— With a death, iii 711.
——— Long, v 217.
Winter sir William knight, and vice admerall, saileth towards Scotland, iv 189
——— Arriueth in Ireland at the Ventrie, vi 427.
——— He distrusting no harme returneth into England, ib
——— He returneth, and by water besiegeth the fort at Smereweke, vi 437
——— The notable good seruice of him & his mariners at that siege, vi 438
——— He gaue protection to the Irish rebels, vi 427
Wipets field in Kent and when fought, i 558
Wire a créeke where ships lie oft at rode, i 147
Wiscart George burnt, v 545
Wisdome of Richard the first in making his answer, ii 210
Witch hanged at Feuersham wherein note the indirect course of iustice, iv 891
—— Of one that allured the Dolphin of France to take vpon him the title of K. of France, iii 166.
Witchcraft and sorcerie much vsed in the Ile of Man, i 66
——— How punished, i 312.
——— Punished with famine, ii 352
Witches consulted withall, and what happened by giuing credit to their words, v 100
——— In Fores inquirie made for them found out, their practise against king Duffe, examined confesse and are burnt, v 233
——— Burnt, &c v 452.
——— ¶ Sée Prophesie.
Witham riuer and what riuers fall into the same, i. 170.
Withred king of Kent after seuen yeares vacancie, vol i page 637
Wiuer riuer watereth all the west parts of England, i 111
Wiues twentie and one had Fbranke, i 445
Woden an ancient prince of the Saxon kings pedegrée, i 555, 556
——— His thrée sonnes, & what kings of Britaine descended of them, i 583
Woldosius earle of Northumberland and Huntington, v 257.
Wolfes wife a notable harlot, her shamefull end, iii 792
Wolfhere archbishop of Northumbers, i 677
Wollen cloth at two shillings the brode yard, iii 528
Wolseie described, iii. 599
——— Made bishop of Durham, he demandeth a great subsidie, his obstinat answer to the motion of the commons, iii 684, 685
——— Taketh it in scorne to be called brother by the archbishop, iii 631
——— Reproued by Henrie the eight, dissolueth the archbishop of Canturburie, his conuocation, iii 685, 686
——— His princelie port at a banket & other recreations note, iii 633
——— He will haue euerie man sworne what he is worth, iii 680
——— He hateth the duke of Buckingham, causeth the earle of Kildare to be committed to ward, iii 644, 645
——— Deuiseth the destruction of the duke of Buckingham, iii 657
——— Imboldeneth Kneuet against him, iii. 658
——— Accuseth him to Henrie the eight, ib
——— What forren chroniclers report of him, iii. 701.
——— Altereth the state of Henrie the eight his household, iii 711
——— Erecteth two new colleges, he excuseth himselfe touching the strict commission for the tax, iii 708 to 710
——— His authoritie impugned, iii 696
——— Offended at a plaie, & punisheth the author and actors of the same, iii 714
——— Goeth ambassador into France, his pompe, the manner of his receiuing by the French king, iii 720
——— His commissions to take vp monie by anticipation, iii 693
——— His ambitious humor, the ordering of the two kings of England and France, their interview committed to him, iii 641
——— His great pompe, put in great trust by the kings of England and France, iii 649
——— His liberalitie by vertue (forsooth) of his spirituall power, iii 676
——— His crueltie, iii 715.
——— His excessiue pride, iii 627, 631
——— A Caueat giuen by a libell sett up in Lon-

don, he cannot abide the citizens, vol iii page 716
Woolseie his pompe when he receiued the emperor Charles at Douer, his pride at high masse, iii 677, 678
——— Returneth out of France, iii 721
——— Is sent ouer to Calis, the emperor receiueth him, carrieth the great seale with him, and there sealeth writs and patents, iii 672
——— Maketh meanes to be elected pope, iii 674
——— Singeth masse before the two kings of England and France, iii 654.
——— Archbishop of Yorke cardinall, chancellor of England, his cardinalls hat receiued by Kentish gentlemen with great solemnitie, iustice executed by him vpon offendors, he erecteth new courts by Henrie the eights commission, iii. 610, 612, 613, 615
——— He taketh vpon him to determine causes, diuerse péeres offended at him, he hindereth the duke of Suffolks hope, an enimie to peace, iii. 615, 616
——— His aduise to the maior of London at Ill Maie daies riot, iii 620.
——— Suspected to be against Henrie the eight his marriage with quéene Katharine his brothers wife, iii 736.
——— Articles exhibited against him, iii 717.
——— At his manor of Cawood keepeth a good house, was to be arrested of treason, prognostications of his fall, arrested, taketh the action in good part, iii 751, 752
——— Desireth to sée the commission of the arrest, committed to the custodie of certeine gentlemen, sickneth sitting at the table, falleth into a flux that cost him his life, iii 753, 754.
——— In displeasure with Henrie the eight, articles exhibited against him, sued in a premunire, loth to part from the great seale, but yet discharged, calleth all his officers to accounts, goeth to Ashur and hath his plentie turned into penurie, condemned in a premunire, iii 740, 741.
———Licenced to repaire into Yorkeshire, his college lands seized vpon to the behoof of Henrie the eight, iii 748, 749
——— Remooued to Richmond, prepareth for his iourneie in the north, iii 750.
——— Auoucheth that he cannot liue, ascribeth his fall to the iust iudgement of God, the complet historie of his behavior, life, and death, iii 755 to 765
Wolstan archbishop of Yorke, i 683
——— Imprisoned by king Edred, i. 692.
Wolstan bishop of Worcester and others resist the erle of Hereford rebelling, ii 18.
——— Refuseth a place of safeguard against the Normans, ii 28
——— Like to haue been deposed for his insufficiencie of learning, ii 19
——— His miracle whereby he kept his bishoprike, ib
Wolstan bishop of Worcester submitteth himselfe to duke William, vol ii. page 1.
——— Dieth, ii 46.
Wolverhampton, and how to be rightlie called note, ii 539
Woman not without a mischiefous practise, i 558
——— Wicked counsell, i 649.
——— Good counsell, i 599.
——— Persuasion worketh much, i 693
——— Deuise to make hir husband forsake the world i 639.
——— Gouernment ouer the Westsaxons, i 629
——— Commended, i. 458.
——— Wisdome praiseworthie, i 728
——— Request preuaileth in a great matter with a great personage, ii 54.
——— Pitifull note, ii 648
——— Hanged, drawne, and quartered, iii 804.
——— Ones request denied occasion of much broile, ii. 563
——— One treateth for peace, and preuaileth betwéene two kings note, ii 617
——— One brought to bed of a monster note, iv. 432
——— One of fourescore yeres old brought to bed of a monster, iv. 431
——— One brought to bed of foure children at one burthen, iv 329
——— Abused with a spirit, v 146
——— Of vnnatural crueltie, v 445
——— Of a stout stomach, being a quéene, v. 446.
——— Hir manlie stomach note, v 369
——— Of manlike force and stature, v. 375
——— Manlie. ¶ See Blacke Agnes
Women of England excessiue and vaine, i 290
——— In a strange maner of habit and attire, i 491.
——— Beare rule in Britaine, i 444, 418
——— Restreined of their great and supreme titles, i 653.
——— They as well as men admitted to publike gouernment among the Britains, i. 496.
——— Their rule disdained, i 493
——— Their dissimulation, ii 578
——— Will hardlie be of one mind, ii 274
——— Their boldnes in ecclesiastical matters note, ii 829.
——— That to be severe against them is dishonorable note, ii 540
——— Causes of mischéefe note, iii. 95
——— Counterfeiting themselues one our Ladie the other Marie Magdalen, ii. 351.
——— Their malice what mischéefe it breweth note, iii 210, 211
——— Reuenge a murther doone upon one, iii 173
——— Hard to be reconciled, ii. 648.

Women of England their peace, vol iv. page 120.
——— As redie to the battell as men, v 88
——— A combrance to the Picts, v. 202.
——— Desirous of high estate, v. 269
——— They and children are kept harmelesse, v. 223
——— Set vpon mischiefe ¶ Sée Counsell and Fenella.
——— Waile their friends, v. 82.
——— Placed in order of battell, v. 68
——— Come with the quéene in armour, v 72
Women with child taught a lesson of continence by Elfleda, i 674
——— To be baptised and purified note, i 594
——— What parents should doo when they haue a child brought into the world, i 605
Wood knighted. ¶ Sée Maior of Norwich
Wood decaied by burning of bricke, i 394.
—— Consumed in Wales by melting of lead, i. 399
—— Exceedinglie wasted with making of pots, glasses, &c i 400
—— Sold in some countries of England by the pound, i 359.
—— Whie in some places of England it cannot grow, i. 356
—— What kinds were occupied vsuallie in building in times past, ib
—— What will follow of the decaie thereof, if not looked vnto, i 358.
—— One acre of ground of fortie, wished for the supplie of it, i 359.
—— Much destroied by making of salt, i 401
Woodhurne lord indicted, v 490.
Woods euerie where decaied and by what means, i. 179.
——— In Englãd great store in times past, i. 355.
——— Of béech & hazel, i 358
——— Decaied in the West Indies and how, i 356
——— Cut downe in Angleseie by Suetonius, &c. i. 494.
Woodstocke manour by whome builded, i 329, ii 77
Wooduile lord aideth the duke of Britaine without Henrie the seauenths consent, iii 491.
——— Slaine, iii 492
Woold what it signifieth, i 347
Wooll of English shéepe excellent, and how emploied, i. 371
——— Sold dog chepe by the stone, ii 816.
——— Sessed at a certeine price, and what for the transporting out of the realme, ii 626.
——— Transporting ouer sea, an act against it, ii. 606
Wool what K Edward the third might spend a date there by which was transported, vol ii page 657
——— Granted in subsidie by the merchants, ii 753
——— ¶ Sée Subsidie, Staple.
Woolues become dogs, and dogs woolues, i 389.
——— Destroied in England and how, i 378
Wonder of crosses that fell from heauen signifieng affliction, i 653
——— Of a Dutchman standing on Pauls wethercocke note, iv 6
——— Of peason without tilth growing vpon hard stone and pible, iv 79.
——— Of a man preserued from drowning, iv 256
——— Of a lad drowned in a kennell, iv 325
——— Of a child speaking strange speeches, iv 433.
——— Of mice deuouring grasse, iv 434
——— Of the ground swallowed vp, iv. 620.
——— Of bare trées, ii 850
——— Of a fish like a man note, ii 290.
——— Of fighting fishes, ii. 198
——— Of Rosamunds cofer, ii. 200
——— Of a dead carcase, iii 1030.
——— To be noted in a dead corps that laie long in the ground, iii 510
——— Of a young babe giuing warning to his mother, v 212.
——— Strange of a voice, v 247.
——— Of adders, v 303
Wonders or maruels of England, i. 216.
——— Of dogs, i 386.
——— Of mastifes, i. 388.
——— Found in stones, i 396
——— Strange séene import an alteration of the state, i. 756.
——— And propheticall, i 495.
——— Strange estéemed to be warnings note, ii. 44.
——— Strange in heauen and earth, ii 35.
——— In the air or element, ii 245.
——— Great, and whereof they were tokens, ii 353
——— What they betoken, ii 272
——— In the sunne, moone, and the earth, ii. 177
——— In dansing note, v 322
——— And strange sights, v 68, 83, 264, 321, 428
——— Maruellous and vncouth, v 134, 162, 212
——— Rare and notorious, v 216.
——— And visions, v 178, 199.
——— Terrible, v 117.
——— Most dreadfull, v. 219
——— And prodigious chances, v 480
——— Séene in the aire, v 205, 300, 306, 509
——— Appearing to the Scottish armie, v. 74.
——— Import a meaning, v. 229.
——— Interpreted, v 205, 212.

Wonders of Ireland, vol ii page 36
——— Strange note, i 63, 64, 66, 75, 111, 174, 177, 287, 353, 363, 373, 374, 390, 413, 424, 435, 479, 676, 755, 820, ii 244, 554, 535, v 237, 268, 283 390
——— ¶ See Irish, Miracle and Monsters.
Worcester how called in the Romās time, i 321
——— In old time called Cair Brangon, or Cair Frāgon, i 120
——— The bishopriks erection, circuit, and valuatio, i 289
——— Assalted, ii 100.
——— Assalted by the Normans, with the valiantnesse of the people, ii 28
——— Besieged and taken, ii 460
——— The citie burnt by casualtie, ii 64
Words of a Spaniard that taught quéene Elisabeth wit, i 333
——— Fine make fooles faine to their smart, i. 646
——— Not lightlie to be trusted, i 645
——— Bréed displeasure, i 698
——— Ill taken and bréed hatred note, i 91
——— Bréed wounds and slaughter, i 470
——— The price of life note, i 687
——— Malicious and foolish of a French lord note, iii 495
——— Of Henrie the second that cost Becket his life, ii 134
——— Of displeasure uttered by the father to his sonne, ii 197
——— Stout of a prelat to a péere, ii 784
——— Of a graue gentleman spoken on his death bed, doo good, ii 341
——— Whet Henrie the third vnto warre, ii 361.
——— Fair ouercome, ii 54
——— Make fooles faine, ii 249, 331
——— Preuaile not, ii 191
——— With fraud note, ii 192
——— Smooth how mightilie they preuaile euen in the enimie, iii 295
——— Faire with ill meaning note, ii 235.
——— Procure wounds and death, iii 821
——— Procure wounds and bloodshed, ii 766.
——— Procure wounds and slaughter note, ii 22
——— Shamefull and slanderous against Edward the fourth, iii 538
——— Obscure and doubtfull to be opened, ii 823
——— Vndecent to the lord chancellor punished in the speaker, iii 1059
——— Gentle appeased strife, iii 690
——— That kindled heat and indignation to reuenge, ii 298.
——— Of wrath kindle displeasure and warre, ii 51
——— Faire and gentle with like behauiour how forceable, iii 16
——— Misconstrued by the Scots note, ii 721
——— Multiplied kindle displeasure, ii 835.
——— Roiall and well beséeming a king to rebellious lords note, ii. 787
Words wiselie uttered, appease the wrath of a king, vol ii page 784
——— Opprobrious procure ill will note, ii 721.
——— Of reproch how mischéefous in issue note, iii 705
——— Great with little manhood, ii 39
——— Of disdaine bréeding mischéefe note, iii 243
——— Punished with standing on the pillorie, and losse of both the eares, iii 1065
——— Mixed with dreadfull allegation preuaile much note, ii 249
——— ¶ See Gifts, Oth and Promises
Workemanship verie cunning of comprising much matter in a little roome, iv 330
——— Of a locke and a keie weighing but one wheat corne, iv 406
Works good of duke William before his death, ii 25
——— Of king Henrie the first to win the peoples fauour, ii 18.
World diuided into thrée parts, i 1
——— ¶ Sée Earth.
Worship to creatures not permitted to be doone without the bishops authoritie, ii 52
Wotton ambassador into Scotlands of an ancient familie note, iv 600
Wrecks by sea pardoned by K Richard the first, through all his dominions, ii 218
Wrestling an ancient exercise, i 443
——— At the hospitall of S James, betwixt the Londoners and all commers, ii 352
——— At Clerkenwell, a great fraie there, iii. 237
——— Betwéene a Norman and a Scot, v 320
Wright Nicholas his good seruice to his master capteine Raleigh, vi 442
Wriotheslie lord ¶ Sée Erle of Southampton
Writers of Scotland their catalog, v 715
——— ¶ Sée Scots and Scotland.
Writing of much matter within a penie compasse, iv 330

Y.

Yard ¶ Sée Mesure
Yarmouth ¶ Sée Cerdicshore
Yeare counted after the course of the sunne, i 410
——— Beginning thereof different among diuerse people, ib.
——— Cynike ib
——— The beginning thereof not vniforme and certeine, ib
——— Of Iubile, iii 525
——— Of wonders, 1588 note, iv. 510, 511
——— More talked of then feared, iv 511
Yeomen in our law called *Homines legales* note, i. 275
——— How intituled and named, i 216
Yeomen of the gard, their institution or first bringing in, iii 482

Yeomen of the gard shift of one to saue himselfe from hanging, vol iii page 625
——— One hanged, iii. 563
——— Two hanged for robbing, iii 820
——— Defend the preacher at Pauls crosse, iv 3, 4
Yorke called Caerbranke and by whom builded and named, i 445.
—— Somtimes called Victrix, and why, i 365
—— Placed in Scotland by Leonitius, i. 320
—— Called Vrewije, and whie, i 147
—— How called in the Romans time, i 320
—— Yéelded to Octauius, v 108
—— Besieged by Arthur, i 575
—— In possession of Hengist, v 144
—— Burnt by the Danes, i 665
—— The chiefe citie of the kingdome of Northumberland, i 29
—— The archbishopricke curtailed, & whie, i 244
—— Bishopriks vnder the said sée foure, i 227
—— Besieged by duke William, ii 11
—— Burned by the Normans & whie, ii 10
—— The people in a perplexitie by the means of two aduerse parties, ib
—— The castell, ii 9.
—— The shire subdued to Lewes the French kings son, ii 333.
—— Besieged, v 154.
—— ¶ Sée Scots
Yorke place infeoffed to Henrie the eight, iii 765
Yorkshire what hauens it hath, i 182
——— ¶ Sée Commotion
Yorkeshiremen rebell and the authors punished by Ostorius Scapula, i 488
Yorkeswold wasted by the Scots, vol v page 356
Youghall towne taken and spoiled, vi 425
——— The maior hanged before his owne doore, vi 426
——— It is forsaken and the people called home, ib
Youth trained vp in hardnesse, v 213
——— Should eate but one meale a daie, ib
Ypres William warlike, ii. 74, 88
——— A Fleming earle of Kent, departeth the realme, ii 112
Ypresse besieged, ii 759
——— The siege broken up, ii 760

Z

Zeale of Edwin in preferring religion, i 608
—— Of Oswald to aduance the same, i 616.
Zouch aduertiseth sir William Pelham lord iustice of the lord Greie his arriuall, vi. 134
——— He serueth vpon the Spaniards at Smerewcke, vi. 438
——— He is gouernor at Kerrie and Desmond, vi 539
——— A sicknesse fell in his campe at Dingham, vi 444
——— He is gouernor of Mounster, vi 445
——— He killeth sir Iohn of Desmond, vi 446
——— He serueth noblie vpon Barrie, and receiueth him to protection, vi 447
——— He maketh a iourneie vpon Fitzmoris of Lexna, and preieth his countrie, vi 448
——— He receiueth a new supplie of souldiers, ib
——— He returneth into England, vi 450

FINIS PROPOSITI LAUS CHRISTO NESCIA FINIS.

Printed by T Davison, White-friars

CPSIA information can be obtained
at www.ICGtesting.com
Printed in the USA
BVHW070526020721
610987BV00015B/665

9 781175 690739